C++ Primer
Fifth Edition

C++ *Primer*
Fifth Edition

Stanley B. Lippman
Josée Lajoie
Barbara E. Moo

♦♦Addison-Wesley

Upper Saddle River, NJ • Boston • Indianapolis • San Francisco
New York • Toronto • Montreal • London • Munich • Paris • Madrid
Capetown • Sidney • Tokyo • Singapore • Mexico City

Many of the designations used by manufacturers and sellers to distinguish their products are claimed as trademarks. Where those designations appear in this book, and the publisher was aware of a trademark claim, the designations have been printed with initial capital letters or in all capitals.

The authors and publisher have taken care in the preparation of this book, but make no expressed or implied warranty of any kind and assume no responsibility for errors or omissions. No liability is assumed for incidental or consequential damages in connection with or arising out of the use of the information or programs contained herein.

The publisher offers excellent discounts on this book when ordered in quantity for bulk purchases or special sales, which may include electronic versions and/or custom covers and content particular to your business, training goals, marketing focus, and branding interests. For more information, please contact:

U. S. Corporate and Government Sales
(800) 382-3419
corpsales@pearsontechgroup.com

For sales outside the U. S., please contact:

International Sales
international@pearsoned.com

Visit us on the Web: informit.com/aw

Library of Congress Cataloging-in-Publication Data

Lippman, Stanley B.
  C++ primer / Stanley B. Lippman, Josée Lajoie, Barbara E. Moo. – 5th ed.
    p.   cm.
  Includes index.
  ISBN 0-321-71411-3 (pbk. : alk. paper)   1. C++ (Computer program language) I. Lajoie, Josée. II. Moo, Barbara E. III. Title.

QA76.73.C153L57697 2013
005.13′3–dc23   2012020184

ISBN-13: 978-0-321-71411-4
ISBN-10:   0-321-71411-3
Text printed in the United States on recycled paper at Courier in Westford, Massachusetts.

First printing, August 2012

To Beth,
who makes this,
and all things,
possible.

———

To Daniel and Anna,
who contain
virtually
all possibilities.
—SBL

To Mark and Mom,
for their
unconditional love and support.
—JL

To Andy,
who taught me
to program
and so much more.
—BEM

Contents

Part III   Tools for Class Authors   493

Part IV Advanced Topics   715

New Features in C++11

Preface

Countless programmers have learned C++ from previous editions of *C++ Primer*. During that time, C++ has matured greatly: Its focus, and that of its programming community, has widened from looking mostly at *machine* efficiency to devoting more attention to *programmer* efficiency.

In 2011, the C++ standards committee issued a major revision to the ISO C++ standard. This revised standard is latest step in C++'s evolution and continues the emphasis on programmer efficiency. The primary goals of the new standard are to

- Make the language more uniform and easier to teach and to learn
- Make the standard libraries easier, safer, and more efficient to use
- Make it easier to write efficient abstractions and libraries

In this edition, we have completely revised the *C++ Primer* to use the latest standard. You can get an idea of how extensively the new standard has affected C++ by reviewing the New Features Table of Contents, which lists the sections that cover new material and appears on page xxi.

Some additions in the new standard, such as `auto` for type inference, are pervasive. These facilities make the code in this edition easier to read and to understand. Programs (and programmers!) can ignore type details, which makes it easier to concentrate on what the program is intended to do. Other new features, such as smart pointers and move-enabled containers, let us write more sophisticated classes without having to contend with the intricacies of resource management. As a result, we can start to teach how to write your own classes much earlier in the book than we did in the Fourth Edition. We—and you—no longer have to worry about many of the details that stood in our way under the previous standard.

We've marked those parts of the text that cover features defined by the new standard, with a marginal icon. We hope that readers who are already familiar with the core of C++ will find these alerts useful in deciding where to focus their attention. We also expect that these icons will help explain error messages from compilers that might not yet support every new feature. Although nearly all of the examples in this book have been compiled under the current release of the GNU compiler, we realize some readers will not yet have access to completely updated compilers. Even though numerous capabilities have been added by the latest standard, the core language remains unchanged and forms the bulk of the material that we cover. Readers can use these icons to note which capabilities may not yet be available in their compiler.

Why Read This Book?

Modern C++ can be thought of as comprising three parts:

- The low-level language, much of which is inherited from C

- More advanced language features that allow us to define our own types and to organize large-scale programs and systems

- The standard library, which uses these advanced features to provide useful data structures and algorithms

Most texts present C++ in the order in which it evolved. They teach the C subset of C++ first, and present the more abstract features of C++ as advanced topics at the end of the book. There are two problems with this approach: Readers can get bogged down in the details inherent in low-level programming and give up in frustration. Those who do press on learn bad habits that they must unlearn later.

We take the opposite approach: Right from the start, we use the features that let programmers ignore the details inherent in low-level programming. For example, we introduce and use the library `string` and `vector` types along with the built-in arithmetic and array types. Programs that use these library types are easier to write, easier to understand, and much less error-prone.

Too often, the library is taught as an "advanced" topic. Instead of using the library, many books use low-level programming techniques based on pointers to character arrays and dynamic memory management. Getting programs that use these low-level techniques to work correctly is much harder than writing the corresponding C++ code using the library.

Throughout *C++ Primer*, we emphasize good style: We want to help you, the reader, develop good habits immediately and avoid needing to unlearn bad habits as you gain more sophisticated knowledge. We highlight particularly tricky matters and warn about common misconceptions and pitfalls.

We also explain the rationale behind the rules—explaining the why not just the what. We believe that by understanding why things work as they do, readers can more quickly cement their grasp of the language.

Although you do not need to know C in order to understand this book, we assume you know enough about programming to write, compile, and run a program in at least one modern block-structured language. In particular, we assume you have used variables, written and called functions, and used a compiler.

Changes to the Fifth Edition

New to this edition of *C++ Primer* are icons in the margins to help guide the reader. C++ is a large language that offers capabilities tailored to particular kinds of programming problems. Some of these capabilities are of great import for large project teams but might not be necessary for smaller efforts. As a result, not every programmer needs to know every detail of every feature. We've added these marginal icons to help the reader know which parts can be learned later and which topics are more essential.

 We've marked sections that cover the fundamentals of the language with an image of a person studying a book. The topics covered in sections marked this way form the core part of the language. Everyone should read and understand these sections.

We've also indicated those sections that cover advanced or special-purpose topics. These sections can be skipped or skimmed on a first reading. We've marked such sections with a stack of books to indicate that you can safely put down the book at that point. It is probably a good idea to skim such sections so you know that the capability exists. However, there is no reason to spend time studying these topics until you actually need to use the feature in your own programs.

To help readers guide their attention further, we've noted particularly tricky concepts with a magnifying-glass icon. We hope that readers will take the time to understand thoroughly the material presented in the sections so marked. In at least some of these sections, the import of the topic may not be readily apparent; but we think you'll find that these sections cover topics that turn out to be essential to understanding the language.

Another aid to reading this book, is our extensive use of cross-references. We hope these references will make it easier for readers to dip into the middle of the book, yet easily jump back to the earlier material on which later examples rely.

What remains unchanged is that C++ *Primer* is a clear, correct, and thorough tutorial guide to C++. We teach the language by presenting a series of increasingly sophisticated examples, which explain language features and show how to make the best use of C++.

Structure of This Book

We start by covering the basics of the language and the library together in Parts I and II. These parts cover enough material to let you, the reader, write significant programs. Most C++ programmers need to know essentially everything covered in this portion of the book.

In addition to teaching the basics of C++, the material in Parts I and II serves another important purpose: By using the abstract facilities defined by the library, you will become more comfortable with using high-level programming techniques. The library facilities are themselves abstract data types that are usually written in C++. The library can be defined using the same class-construction features that are available to any C++ programmer. Our experience in teaching C++ is that by first using well-designed abstract types, readers find it easier to understand how to build their own types.

Only after a thorough grounding in using the library—and writing the kinds of abstract programs that the library allows—do we move on to those C++ features that will enable you to write your own abstractions. Parts III and IV focus on writing abstractions in the form of classes. Part III covers the fundamentals; Part IV covers more specialized facilities.

In Part III, we cover issues of copy control, along with other techniques to make classes that are as easy to use as the built-in types. Classes are the foundation for object-oriented and generic programming, which we also cover in Part III. C++ *Primer* concludes with Part IV, which covers features that are of most use in structuring large, complicated systems. We also summarize the library algorithms in Appendix A.

Aids to the Reader

Each chapter concludes with a summary, followed by a glossary of defined terms, which together recap the chapter's most important points. Readers should use these sections as a personal checklist: If you do not understand a term, restudy the corresponding part of the chapter.

We've also incorporated a number of other learning aids in the body of the text:

- Important terms are indicated in **bold**; important terms that we assume are already familiar to the reader are indicated in ***bold italics***. Each term appears in the chapter's Defined Terms section.

- Throughout the book, we highlight parts of the text to call attention to important aspects of the language, warn about common pitfalls, suggest good programming practices, and provide general usage tips.

- To make it easier to follow the relationships among features and concepts, we provide extensive forward and backward cross-references.

- We provide sidebar discussions on important concepts and for topics that new C++ programmers often find most difficult.

- Learning any programming language requires writing programs. To that end, the Primer provides extensive examples throughout the text. Source code for the extended examples is available on the Web at the following URL:

```
http://www.informit.com/title/032174113
```

A Note about Compilers

As of this writing (July, 2012), compiler vendors are hard at work updating their compilers to match the latest ISO standard. The compiler we use most frequently is the GNU compiler, version 4.7.0. There are only a few features used in this book that this compiler does not yet implement: inheriting constructors, reference qualifiers for member functions, and the regular-expression library.

Acknowledgments

In preparing this edition we are very grateful for the help of several current and former members of the standardization committee: Dave Abrahams, Andy Koenig, Stephan T. Lavavej, Jason Merrill, John Spicer, and Herb Sutter. They provided invaluable assistance to us in understanding some of the more subtle parts of the new standard. We'd also like to thank the many folks who worked on updating the GNU compiler making the standard a reality.

As in previous editions of *C++ Primer*, we'd like to extend our thanks to Bjarne Stroustrup for his tireless work on C++ and for his friendship to the authors during most of that time. We'd also like to thank Alex Stepanov for his original insights that led to the containers and algorithms at the core of the standard library. Finally, our thanks go to all the C++ Standards committee members for their hard work in clarifying, refining, and improving C++ over many years.

We extend our deep-felt thanks to our reviewers, whose helpful comments led us to make improvements great and small throughout the book: Marshall Clow, Jon Kalb, Nevin Liber, Dr. C. L. Tondo, Daveed Vandevoorde, and Steve Vinoski.

This book was typeset using LaTeX and the many packages that accompany the LaTeX distribution. Our well-justified thanks go to the members of the LaTeX community, who have made available such powerful typesetting tools.

Finally, we thank the fine folks at Addison-Wesley who have shepherded this edition through the publishing process: Peter Gordon, our editor, who provided the impetus for us to revise *C++ Primer* once again; Kim Boedigheimer, who keeps us all on schedule; Barbara Wood, who found lots of editing errors for us during the copy-edit phase, and Elizabeth Ryan, who was again a delight to work with as she guided us through the design and production process.

CHAPTER 1

GETTING STARTED

CONTENTS

This chapter introduces most of the basic elements of C++: types, variables, expressions, statements, and functions. Along the way, we'll briefly explain how to compile and execute a program.

After having read this chapter and worked through the exercises, you should be able to write, compile, and execute simple programs. Later chapters will assume that you can use the features introduced in this chapter, and will explain these features in more detail.

The way to learn a new programming language is to write programs. In this chapter, we'll write a program to solve a simple problem for a bookstore.

Our store keeps a file of transactions, each of which records the sale of one or more copies of a single book. Each transaction contains three data elements:

```
0-201-70353-X 4 24.99
```

The first element is an ISBN (International Standard Book Number, a unique book identifier), the second is the number of copies sold, and the last is the price at which each of these copies was sold. From time to time, the bookstore owner reads this file and for each book computes the number of copies sold, the total revenue from that book, and the average sales price.

To be able to write this program, we need to cover a few basic C++ features. In addition, we'll need to know how to compile and execute a program.

Although we haven't yet designed our program, it's easy to see that it must

- Define variables

- Do input and output

- Use a data structure to hold the data

- Test whether two records have the same ISBN

- Contain a loop that will process every record in the transaction file

We'll start by reviewing how to solve these subproblems in C++ and then write our bookstore program.

1.1 Writing a Simple C++ Program

Every C++ program contains one or more *functions*, one of which must be named **main**. The operating system runs a C++ program by calling main. Here is a simple version of main that does nothing but return a value to the operating system:

```
int main()
{
    return 0;
}
```

A function definition has four elements: a *return type*, a *function name*, a (possibly empty) *parameter list* enclosed in parentheses, and a *function body*. Although main is special in some ways, we define main the same way we define any other function.

In this example, main has an empty list of parameters (shown by the () with nothing inside). § 6.2.5 (p. 218) will discuss the other parameter types that we can define for main.

The main function is required to have a return type of int, which is a type that represents integers. The int type is a **built-in type**, which means that it is one of the types the language defines.

The final part of a function definition, the function body, is a *block of statements* starting with an open **curly brace** and ending with a close curly:

```
{
    return 0;
}
```

The only statement in this block is a `return`, which is a statement that terminates a function. As is the case here, a `return` can also send a value back to the function's caller. When a `return` statement includes a value, the value returned must have a type that is compatible with the return type of the function. In this case, the return type of `main` is `int` and the return value is `0`, which is an `int`.

 Note the semicolon at the end of the `return` statement. Semicolons mark the end of most statements in C++. They are easy to overlook but, when forgotten, can lead to mysterious compiler error messages.

On most systems, the value returned from `main` is a status indicator. A return value of `0` indicates success. A nonzero return has a meaning that is defined by the system. Ordinarily a nonzero return indicates what kind of error occurred.

KEY CONCEPT: TYPES

Types are one of the most fundamental concepts in programming and a concept that we will come back to over and over in this Primer. A type defines both the contents of a data element and the operations that are possible on those data.

The data our programs manipulate are stored in variables and every variable has a type. When the type of a variable named `v` is `T`, we often say that "`v` has type `T`" or, interchangeably, that "`v` is a `T`."

1.1.1 Compiling and Executing Our Program

Having written the program, we need to compile it. How you compile a program depends on your operating system and compiler. For details on how your particular compiler works, check the reference manual or ask a knowledgeable colleague.

Many PC-based compilers are run from an integrated development environment (IDE) that bundles the compiler with build and analysis tools. These environments can be a great asset in developing large programs but require a fair bit of time to learn how to use effectively. Learning how to use such environments is well beyond the scope of this book.

Most compilers, including those that come with an IDE, provide a command-line interface. Unless you already know the IDE, you may find it easier to start with the command-line interface. Doing so will let you concentrate on learning C++ first. Moreover, once you understand the language, the IDE is likely to be easier to learn.

Program Source File Naming Convention

Whether you use a command-line interface or an IDE, most compilers expect program source code to be stored in one or more files. Program files are normally referred to as a *source files*. On most systems, the name of a source file ends with a suffix, which is a period followed by one or more characters. The suffix tells the system that the file is a C++ program. Different compilers use different suffix conventions; the most common include `.cc`, `.cxx`, `.cpp`, `.cp`, and `.C`.

Running the Compiler from the Command Line

If we are using a command-line interface, we will typically compile a program in a console window (such as a shell window on a UNIX system or a Command Prompt window on Windows). Assuming that our `main` program is in a file named `prog1.cc`, we might compile it by using a command such as

```
$ CC prog1.cc
```

where `CC` names the compiler and `$` is the system prompt. The compiler generates an executable file. On a Windows system, that executable file is named `prog1.exe`. UNIX compilers tend to put their executables in files named `a.out`.

To run an executable on Windows, we supply the executable file name and can omit the `.exe` file extension:

```
$ prog1
```

On some systems you must specify the file's location explicitly, even if the file is in the current directory or folder. In such cases, we would write

```
$ .\prog1
```

The "`.`" followed by a backslash indicates that the file is in the current directory.

To run an executable on UNIX, we use the full file name, including the file extension:

```
$ a.out
```

If we need to specify the file's location, we'd use a "`.`" followed by a forward slash to indicate that our executable is in the current directory:

```
$ ./a.out
```

The value returned from `main` is accessed in a system-dependent manner. On both UNIX and Windows systems, after executing the program, you must issue an appropriate `echo` command.

On UNIX systems, we obtain the status by writing

```
$ echo $?
```

To see the status on a Windows system, we write

```
$ echo %ERRORLEVEL%
```

RUNNING THE GNU OR MICROSOFT COMPILERS

The command used to run the C++ compiler varies across compilers and operating systems. The most common compilers are the GNU compiler and the Microsoft Visual Studio compilers. By default, the command to run the GNU compiler is g++:

```
$ g++ -o prog1 prog1.cc
```

Here $ is the system prompt. The -o prog1 is an argument to the compiler and names the file in which to put the executable file. This command generates an executable file named prog1 or prog1.exe, depending on the operating system. On UNIX, executable files have no suffix; on Windows, the suffix is .exe. If the -o prog1 is omitted, the compiler generates an executable named a.out on UNIX systems and a.exe on Windows. (Note: Depending on the release of the GNU compiler you are using, you may need to specify -std=c++0x to turn on C++ 11 support.)

The command to run the Microsoft Visual Studio 2010 compiler is cl:

```
C:\Users\me\Programs> cl /EHsc prog1.cpp
```

Here C:\Users\me\Programs> is the system prompt and \Users\me\Programs is the name of the current directory (aka the current folder). The cl command invokes the compiler, and /EHsc is the compiler option that turns on standard exception handling. The Microsoft compiler automatically generates an executable with a name that corresponds to the first source file name. The executable has the suffix .exe and the same name as the source file name. In this case, the executable is named prog1.exe.

Compilers usually include options to generate warnings about problematic constructs. It is usually a good idea to use these options. Our preference is to use -Wall with the GNU compiler, and to use /W4 with the Microsoft compilers.

For further information consult your compiler's user's guide.

EXERCISES SECTION 1.1.1

Exercise 1.1: Review the documentation for your compiler and determine what file naming convention it uses. Compile and run the main program from page 2.

Exercise 1.2: Change the program to return -1. A return value of -1 is often treated as an indicator that the program failed. Recompile and rerun your program to see how your system treats a failure indicator from main.

1.2 A First Look at Input/Output

The C++ language does not define any statements to do input or output (IO). Instead, C++ includes an extensive **standard library** that provides IO (and many other facilities). For many purposes, including the examples in this book, one needs to know only a few basic concepts and operations from the IO library.

Most of the examples in this book use the **iostream** library. Fundamental to the iostream library are two types named **istream** and **ostream**, which represent input and output streams, respectively. A stream is a sequence of characters read from or written to an IO device. The term *stream* is intended to suggest that the characters are generated, or consumed, sequentially over time.

Standard Input and Output Objects

The library defines four IO objects. To handle input, we use an object of type
istream named **cin** (pronounced *see-in*). This object is also referred to as the
standard input. For output, we use an ostream object named **cout** (pronounced
see-out). This object is also known as the **standard output**. The library also defines
two other ostream objects, named **cerr** and **clog** (pronounced *see-err* and *see-log*, respectively). We typically use cerr, referred to as the **standard error**, for
warning and error messages and clog for general information about the execution
of the program.

Ordinarily, the system associates each of these objects with the window in
which the program is executed. So, when we read from cin, data are read from
the window in which the program is executing, and when we write to cout, cerr,
or clog, the output is written to the same window.

A Program That Uses the IO Library

In our bookstore problem, we'll have several records that we'll want to combine
into a single total. As a simpler, related problem, let's look first at how we might
add two numbers. Using the IO library, we can extend our main program to
prompt the user to give us two numbers and then print their sum:

```
#include <iostream>
int main()
{
    std::cout << "Enter two numbers:" << std::endl;
    int v1 = 0, v2 = 0;
    std::cin >> v1 >> v2;
    std::cout << "The sum of " << v1 << " and " << v2
              << " is " << v1 + v2 << std::endl;
    return 0;
}
```

This program starts by printing

Enter two numbers:

on the user's screen and then waits for input from the user. If the user enters

3 7

followed by a newline, then the program produces the following output:

The sum of 3 and 7 is 10

The first line of our program

```
#include <iostream>
```

tells the compiler that we want to use the iostream library. The name inside
angle brackets (iostream in this case) refers to a **header**. Every program that
uses a library facility must include its associated header. The #include directive

must be written on a single line—the name of the header and the #include must appear on the same line. In general, #include directives must appear outside any function. Typically, we put all the #include directives for a program at the beginning of the source file.

Writing to a Stream

The first statement in the body of main executes an **expression**. In C++ an expression yields a result and is composed of one or more operands and (usually) an operator. The expressions in this statement use the output operator (the **« operator**) to print a message on the standard output:

```
std::cout << "Enter two numbers:" << std::endl;
```

The << operator takes two operands: The left-hand operand must be an ostream object; the right-hand operand is a value to print. The operator writes the given value on the given ostream. The result of the output operator is its left-hand operand. That is, the result is the ostream on which we wrote the given value.

Our output statement uses the << operator twice. Because the operator returns its left-hand operand, the result of the first operator becomes the left-hand operand of the second. As a result, we can chain together output requests. Thus, our expression is equivalent to

```
(std::cout << "Enter two numbers:") << std::endl;
```

Each operator in the chain has the same object as its left-hand operand, in this case std::cout. Alternatively, we can generate the same output using two statements:

```
std::cout << "Enter two numbers:";
std::cout << std::endl;
```

The first output operator prints a message to the user. That message is a **string literal**, which is a sequence of characters enclosed in double quotation marks. The text between the quotation marks is printed to the standard output.

The second operator prints endl, which is a special value called a **manipulator**. Writing endl has the effect of ending the current line and flushing the *buffer* associated with that device. Flushing the buffer ensures that all the output the program has generated so far is actually written to the output stream, rather than sitting in memory waiting to be written.

WARNING

Programmers often add print statements during debugging. Such statements should *always* flush the stream. Otherwise, if the program crashes, output may be left in the buffer, leading to incorrect inferences about where the program crashed.

Using Names from the Standard Library

Careful readers will note that this program uses std::cout and std::endl rather than just cout and endl. The prefix std:: indicates that the names cout and endl are defined inside the **namespace** named **std**. Namespaces allow us to avoid inadvertent collisions between the names we define and uses of those same names inside a library. All the names defined by the standard library are in the `std` namespace.

One side effect of the library's use of a namespace is that when we use a name from the library, we must say explicitly that we want to use the name from the `std` namespace. Writing `std::cout` uses the scope operator (the `::` **operator**) to say that we want to use the name `cout` that is defined in the namespace `std`. § 3.1 (p. 82) will show a simpler way to access names from the library.

Reading from a Stream

Having asked the user for input, we next want to read that input. We start by defining two *variables* named `v1` and `v2` to hold the input:

```
int v1 = 0, v2 = 0;
```

We define these variables as type `int`, which is a built-in type representing integers. We also *initialize* them to `0`. When we initialize a variable, we give it the indicated value at the same time as the variable is created.

The next statement

```
std::cin >> v1 >> v2;
```

reads the input. The input operator (the **»** **operator**) behaves analogously to the output operator. It takes an `istream` as its left-hand operand and an object as its right-hand operand. It reads data from the given `istream` and stores what was read in the given object. Like the output operator, the input operator returns its left-hand operand as its result. Hence, this expression is equivalent to

```
(std::cin >> v1) >> v2;
```

Because the operator returns its left-hand operand, we can combine a sequence of input requests into a single statement. Our input operation reads two values from `std::cin`, storing the first in `v1` and the second in `v2`. In other words, our input operation executes as

```
std::cin >> v1;
std::cin >> v2;
```

Completing the Program

What remains is to print our result:

```
std::cout << "The sum of " << v1 << " and " << v2
          << " is " << v1 + v2 << std::endl;
```

This statement, although longer than the one that prompted the user for input, is conceptually similar. It prints each of its operands on the standard output. What is interesting in this example is that the operands are not all the same kinds of values. Some operands are string literals, such as `"The sum of "`. Others are `int` values, such as `v1`, `v2`, and the result of evaluating the arithmetic expression `v1 + v2`. The library defines versions of the input and output operators that handle operands of each of these differing types.

Exercise 1.3: Write a program to print `Hello, World` on the standard output.

Exercise 1.4: Our program used the addition operator, `+`, to add two numbers. Write a program that uses the multiplication operator, `*`, to print the product instead.

Exercise 1.5: We wrote the output in one large statement. Rewrite the program to use a separate statement to print each operand.

Exercise 1.6: Explain whether the following program fragment is legal.

```
std::cout << "The sum of " << v1;
          << " and " << v2;
          << " is " << v1 + v2 << std::endl;
```

If the program is legal, what does it do? If the program is not legal, why not? How would you fix it?

1.3   A Word about Comments

Before our programs get much more complicated, we should see how C++ handles *comments*. Comments help the human readers of our programs. They are typically used to summarize an algorithm, identify the purpose of a variable, or clarify an otherwise obscure segment of code. The compiler ignores comments, so they have no effect on the program's behavior or performance.

Although the compiler ignores comments, readers of our code do not. Programmers tend to believe comments even when other parts of the system documentation are out of date. An incorrect comment is worse than no comment at all because it may mislead the reader. When you change your code, be sure to update the comments, too!

Kinds of Comments in C++

There are two kinds of comments in C++: single-line and paired. A single-line comment starts with a double slash (`//`) and ends with a newline. Everything to the right of the slashes on the current line is ignored by the compiler. A comment of this kind can contain any text, including additional double slashes.

The other kind of comment uses two delimiters (`/*` and `*/`) that are inherited from C. Such comments begin with a `/*` and end with the next `*/`. These comments can include anything that is not a `*/`, including newlines. The compiler treats everything that falls between the `/*` and `*/` as part of the comment.

A comment pair can be placed anywhere a tab, space, or newline is permitted. Comment pairs can span multiple lines of a program but are not required to do so. When a comment pair does span multiple lines, it is often a good idea to indicate visually that the inner lines are part of a multiline comment. Our style is to begin each line in the comment with an asterisk, thus indicating that the entire range is part of a multiline comment.

Programs typically contain a mixture of both comment forms. Comment pairs generally are used for multiline explanations, whereas double-slash comments tend to be used for half-line and single-line remarks:

```cpp
#include <iostream>
/*
 * Simple main function:
 * Read two numbers and write their sum
 */
int main()
{
    // prompt user to enter two numbers
    std::cout << "Enter two numbers:" << std::endl;
    int v1 = 0, v2 = 0;     // variables to hold the input we read
    std::cin >> v1 >> v2; // read input
    std::cout << "The sum of " << v1 << " and " << v2
              << " is " << v1 + v2 << std::endl;
    return 0;
}
```

 In this book, we italicize comments to make them stand out from the normal program text. In actual programs, whether comment text is distinguished from the text used for program code depends on the sophistication of the programming environment you are using.

Comment Pairs Do Not Nest

A comment that begins with /* ends with the next */. As a result, one comment pair cannot appear inside another. The compiler error messages that result from this kind of mistake can be mysterious and confusing. As an example, compile the following program on your system:

```cpp
/*
 * comment pairs /*   */ cannot nest.
 * "cannot nest" is considered source code,
 * as is the rest of the program
 */
int main()
{
    return 0;
}
```

We often need to comment out a block of code during debugging. Because that code might contain nested comment pairs, the best way to comment a block of code is to insert single-line comments at the beginning of each line in the section we want to ignore:

```cpp
// /*
// * everything inside a single-line comment is ignored
// * including nested comment pairs
//   */
```

Exercise 1.7: Compile a program that has incorrectly nested comments.

Exercise 1.8: Indicate which, if any, of the following output statements are legal:

```
std::cout << "/*";
std::cout << "*/";
std::cout << /* "*/" */;
std::cout << /*  "*/" /*  "/*"  */;
```

After you've predicted what will happen, test your answers by compiling a program with each of these statements. Correct any errors you encounter.

1.4   Flow of Control

Statements normally execute sequentially: The first statement in a block is executed first, followed by the second, and so on. Of course, few programs—including the one to solve our bookstore problem—can be written using only sequential execution. Instead, programming languages provide various flow-of-control statements that allow for more complicated execution paths.

1.4.1   The `while` Statement

A **`while` statement** repeatedly executes a section of code so long as a given condition is true. We can use a `while` to write a program to sum the numbers from 1 through 10 inclusive as follows:

```
#include <iostream>
int main()
{
    int sum = 0, val = 1;
    // keep executing the while as long as val is less than or equal to 10
    while (val <= 10) {
        sum += val;   // assigns sum + val to sum
        ++val;        // add 1 to val
    }
    std::cout << "Sum of 1 to 10 inclusive is "
              << sum << std::endl;
    return 0;
}
```

When we compile and execute this program, it prints

```
Sum of 1 to 10 inclusive is 55
```

As before, we start by including the `iostream` header and defining `main`. Inside `main` we define two `int` variables: `sum`, which will hold our summation, and `val`, which will represent each of the values from 1 through 10. We give `sum` an initial value of `0` and start `val` off with the value `1`.

The new part of this program is the `while` statement. A `while` has the form

```
while (condition)
    statement
```

A `while` executes by (alternately) testing the *condition* and executing the associated *statement* until the *condition* is false. A **condition** is an expression that yields a result that is either true or false. So long as *condition* is true, *statement* is executed. After executing *statement*, *condition* is tested again. If *condition* is again true, then *statement* is again executed. The `while` continues, alternately testing the *condition* and executing *statement* until the *condition* is false.

In this program, the `while` statement is

```
//  keep executing the while as long as val is less than or equal to 10
while (val <= 10) {
    sum += val;   //  assigns sum + val to sum
    ++val;        //  add 1 to val
}
```

The condition uses the less-than-or-equal operator (the **<= operator**) to compare the current value of `val` and `10`.   As long as `val` is less than or equal to 10, the condition is true. If the condition is true, we execute the body of the `while`. In this case, that body is a block with two statements:

```
{
    sum += val;   //  assigns sum + val to sum
    ++val;        //  add 1 to val
}
```

A block is a sequence of zero or more statements enclosed by curly braces. A block is a statement and may be used wherever a statement is required. The first statement in this block uses the compound assignment operator (the **+= operator**). This operator adds its right-hand operand to its left-hand operand and stores the result in the left-hand operand. It has essentially the same effect as writing an addition and an **assignment**:

```
sum = sum + val;   //  assign sum + val to sum
```

Thus, the first statement in the block adds the value of `val` to the current value of `sum` and stores the result back into `sum`.

The next statement

```
++val;        //  add 1 to val
```

uses the prefix increment operator (the **++ operator**). The increment operator adds 1 to its operand. Writing `++val` is the same as writing `val = val + 1`.

After executing the `while` body, the loop evaluates the condition again. If the (now incremented) value of `val` is still less than or equal to 10, then the body of the `while` is executed again. The loop continues, testing the condition and executing the body, until `val` is no longer less than or equal to 10.

Once `val` is greater than 10, the program falls out of the `while` loop and continues execution with the statement following the `while`. In this case, that statement prints our output, followed by the `return`, which completes our `main` program.

Exercise 1.9:   Write a program that uses a `while` to sum the numbers from 50 to 100.

Exercise 1.10:   In addition to the `++` operator that adds 1 to its operand, there is a decrement operator (`--`) that subtracts 1. Use the decrement operator to write a `while` that prints the numbers from ten down to zero.

Exercise 1.11:   Write a program that prompts the user for two integers. Print each number in the range specified by those two integers.

1.4.2   The `for` Statement

In our `while` loop we used the variable `val` to control how many times we executed the loop. We tested the value of `val` in the condition and incremented `val` in the `while` body.

This pattern—using a variable in a condition and incrementing that variable in the body—happens so often that the language defines a second statement, the **`for` statement**, that abbreviates code that follows this pattern. We can rewrite this program using a `for` loop to sum the numbers from 1 through 10 as follows:

```
#include <iostream>
int main()
{
    int sum = 0;
    // sum values from 1 through 10 inclusive
    for (int val = 1; val <= 10; ++val)
        sum += val;   // equivalent to sum = sum + val
    std::cout << "Sum of 1 to 10 inclusive is "
              << sum << std::endl;
    return 0;
}
```

As before, we define `sum` and initialize it to zero. In this version, we define `val` as part of the `for` statement itself:

```
for (int val = 1; val <= 10; ++val)
    sum += val;
```

Each `for` statement has two parts: a header and a body. The header controls how often the body is executed. The header itself consists of three parts: an *init-statement*, a *condition*, and an *expression*. In this case, the *init-statement*

```
int val = 1;
```

defines an `int` object named `val` and gives it an initial value of 1. The variable `val` exists only inside the `for`; it is not possible to use `val` after this loop terminates. The *init-statement* is executed only once, on entry to the `for`. The *condition*

```
val <= 10
```

compares the current value in `val` to `10`. The *condition* is tested each time through the loop. As long as `val` is less than or equal to `10`, we execute the `for` body. The *expression* is executed after the `for` body. Here, the *expression*

```
++val
```

uses the prefix increment operator, which adds `1` to the value of `val`. After executing the *expression*, the `for` retests the *condition*. If the new value of `val` is still less than or equal to `10`, then the `for` loop body is executed again. After executing the body, `val` is incremented again. The loop continues until the *condition* fails.

In this loop, the `for` body performs the summation

```
sum += val;   // equivalent to sum = sum + val
```

To recap, the overall execution flow of this `for` is:

1. Create `val` and initialize it to `1`.

2. Test whether `val` is less than or equal to `10`. If the test succeeds, execute the `for` body. If the test fails, exit the loop and continue execution with the first statement following the `for` body.

3. Increment `val`.

4. Repeat the test in step 2, continuing with the remaining steps as long as the condition is true.

EXERCISES SECTION 1.4.2

Exercise 1.12: What does the following `for` loop do? What is the final value of `sum`?
```
int sum = 0;
for (int i = -100; i <= 100; ++i)
    sum += i;
```

Exercise 1.13: Rewrite the exercises from § 1.4.1 (p. 13) using `for` loops.

Exercise 1.14: Compare and contrast the loops that used a `for` with those using a `while`. Are there advantages or disadvantages to using either form?

Exercise 1.15: Write programs that contain the common errors discussed in the box on page 16. Familiarize yourself with the messages the compiler generates.

1.4.3 Reading an Unknown Number of Inputs

In the preceding sections, we wrote programs that summed the numbers from 1 through 10. A logical extension of this program would be to ask the user to input a set of numbers to sum. In this case, we won't know how many numbers to add. Instead, we'll keep reading numbers until there are no more numbers to read:

```
#include <iostream>
int main()
{
    int sum = 0, value = 0;
    // read until end-of-file, calculating a running total of all values read
    while (std::cin >> value)
        sum += value; // equivalent to sum = sum + value
    std::cout << "Sum is: " << sum << std::endl;
    return 0;
}
```

If we give this program the input

```
3 4 5 6
```

then our output will be

```
Sum is: 18
```

The first line inside `main` defines two `int` variables, named `sum` and `value`, which we initialize to `0`. We'll use `value` to hold each number as we read it from the input. We read the data inside the condition of the `while`:

```
while (std::cin >> value)
```

Evaluating the `while` condition executes the expression

```
std::cin >> value
```

That expression reads the next number from the standard input and stores that number in `value`. The input operator (§ 1.2, p. 8) returns its left operand, which in this case is `std::cin`. This condition, therefore, tests `std::cin`.

When we use an `istream` as a condition, the effect is to test the state of the stream. If the stream is valid—that is, if the stream hasn't encountered an error—then the test succeeds. An `istream` becomes invalid when we hit *end-of-file* or encounter an invalid input, such as reading a value that is not an integer. An `istream` that is in an invalid state will cause the condition to yield false.

Thus, our `while` executes until we encounter end-of-file (or an input error). The `while` body uses the compound assignment operator to add the current value to the evolving `sum`. Once the condition fails, the `while` ends. We fall through and execute the next statement, which prints the `sum` followed by `endl`.

ENTERING AN END-OF-FILE FROM THE KEYBOARD

When we enter input to a program from the keyboard, different operating systems use different conventions to allow us to indicate end-of-file. On Windows systems we enter an end-of-file by typing a control-z—hold down the Ctrl key and press z—followed by hitting either the Enter or Return key. On UNIX systems, including on Mac OS X machines, end-of-file is usually control-d.

COMPILATION REVISITED

Part of the compiler's job is to look for errors in the program text. A compiler cannot detect whether a program does what its author intends, but it can detect errors in the *form* of the program. The following are the most common kinds of errors a compiler will detect.

Syntax errors: The programmer has made a grammatical error in the C++ language. The following program illustrates common syntax errors; each comment describes the error on the following line:

```
// error: missing ) in parameter list for main
int main ( {
    // error: used colon, not a semicolon, after endl
    std::cout << "Read each file." << std::endl:
    // error: missing quotes around string literal
    std::cout << Update master. << std::endl;
    // error: second output operator is missing
    std::cout << "Write new master." std::endl;
    // error: missing ; on return statement
    return 0
}
```

Type errors: Each item of data in C++ has an associated type. The value 10, for example, has a type of int (or, more colloquially, "is an int"). The word "hello", including the double quotation marks, is a string literal. One example of a type error is passing a string literal to a function that expects an int argument.

Declaration errors: Every name used in a C++ program must be declared before it is used. Failure to declare a name usually results in an error message. The two most common declaration errors are forgetting to use std:: for a name from the library and misspelling the name of an identifier:

```
#include <iostream>
int main()
{
    int v1 = 0, v2 = 0;
    std::cin >> v >> v2;  // error: uses "v" not "v1"
    // error: cout not defined; should be std::cout
    cout << v1 + v2 << std::endl;
    return 0;
}
```

Error messages usually contain a line number and a brief description of what the compiler believes we have done wrong. It is a good practice to correct errors in the sequence they are reported. Often a single error can have a cascading effect and cause a compiler to report more errors than actually are present. It is also a good idea to recompile the code after each fix—or after making at most a small number of obvious fixes. This cycle is known as *edit-compile-debug*.

1.4.4　The if Statement

Like most languages, C++ provides an **if statement** that supports conditional execution. We can use an if to write a program to count how many consecutive times each distinct value appears in the input:

```cpp
#include <iostream>
int main()
{
    // currVal is the number we're counting; we'll read new values into val
    int currVal = 0, val = 0;
    // read first number and ensure that we have data to process
    if (std::cin >> currVal) {
        int cnt = 1;    // store the count for the current value we're processing
        while (std::cin >> val) { // read the remaining numbers
            if (val == currVal)    // if the values are the same
                ++cnt;             // add 1 to cnt
            else { // otherwise, print the count for the previous value
                std::cout << currVal << " occurs "
                          << cnt << " times" << std::endl;
                currVal = val;    // remember the new value
                cnt = 1;          // reset the counter
            }
        }   // while loop ends here
        // remember to print the count for the last value in the file
        std::cout << currVal << " occurs "
                  << cnt << " times" << std::endl;
    } // outermost if statement ends here
    return 0;
}
```

If we give this program the following input:

```
42 42 42 42 42 55 55 62 100 100 100
```

then the output should be

```
42 occurs 5 times
55 occurs 2 times
62 occurs 1 times
100 occurs 3 times
```

Much of the code in this program should be familiar from our earlier programs. We start by defining val and currVal: currVal will keep track of which number we are counting; val will hold each number as we read it from the input. What's new are the two if statements. The first if

```
if (std::cin >> currVal) {
    // ...
} // outermost if statement ends here
```

ensures that the input is not empty. Like a `while`, an `if` evaluates a condition. The
condition in the first `if` reads a value into `currVal`. If the read succeeds, then the
condition is true and we execute the block that starts with the open curly following the condition. That block ends with the close curly just before the `return`
statement.

Once we know there are numbers to count, we define `cnt`, which will count
how often each distinct number occurs. We use a `while` loop similar to the one in
the previous section to (repeatedly) read numbers from the standard input.

The body of the `while` is a block that contains the second `if` statement:

```
if (val == currVal)    // if the values are the same
    ++cnt;             // add 1 to cnt
else { // otherwise, print the count for the previous value
    std::cout << currVal << " occurs "
              << cnt << " times" << std::endl;
    currVal = val;     // remember the new value
    cnt = 1;           // reset the counter
}
```

The condition in this `if` uses the equality operator (the **== operator**) to test whether
`val` is equal to `currVal`. If so, we execute the statement that immediately follows the condition. That statement increments `cnt`, indicating that we have seen
`currVal` once more.

If the condition is false—that is, if `val` is not equal to `currVal`—then we execute the statement following the `else`. This statement is a block consisting of
an output statement and two assignments. The output statement prints the count
for the value we just finished processing. The assignments reset `cnt` to `1` and
`currVal` to `val`, which is the number we just read.

WARNING C++ uses = for assignment and == for equality. Both operators can appear inside a condition. It is a common mistake to write = when you
mean == inside a condition.

EXERCISES SECTION 1.4.4

Exercise 1.17: What happens in the program presented in this section if the input values are all equal? What if there are no duplicated values?

Exercise 1.18: Compile and run the program from this section giving it only equal
values as input. Run it again giving it values in which no number is repeated.

Exercise 1.19: Revise the program you wrote for the exercises in § 1.4.1 (p. 13) that
printed a range of numbers so that it handles input in which the first number is smaller
than the second.

> KEY CONCEPT: INDENTATION AND FORMATTING OF C++ PROGRAMS
>
> C++ programs are largely free-format, meaning that where we put curly braces, indentation, comments, and newlines usually has no effect on what our programs mean. For example, the curly brace that denotes the beginning of the body of `main` could be on the same line as `main`; positioned as we have done, at the beginning of the next line; or placed anywhere else we'd like. The only requirement is that the open curly must be the first nonblank, noncomment character following `main`'s parameter list.
>
> Although we are largely free to format programs as we wish, the choices we make affect the readability of our programs. We could, for example, have written `main` on a single long line. Such a definition, although legal, would be hard to read.
>
> Endless debates occur as to the right way to format C or C++ programs. Our belief is that there is no single correct style but that there is value in consistency. Most programmers indent subsidiary parts of their programs, as we've done with the statements inside `main` and the bodies of our loops. We tend to put the curly braces that delimit functions on their own lines. We also indent compound IO expressions so that the operators line up. Other indentation conventions will become clear as our programs become more sophisticated.
>
> The important thing to keep in mind is that other ways to format programs are possible. When you choose a formatting style, think about how it affects readability and comprehension. Once you've chosen a style, use it consistently.

1.5 Introducing Classes

The only remaining feature we need to understand before solving our bookstore problem is how to define a *data structure* to represent our transaction data. In C++ we define our own data structures by defining a **class**. A class defines a type along with a collection of operations that are related to that type. The class mechanism is one of the most important features in C++. In fact, a primary focus of the design of C++ is to make it possible to define **class types** that behave as naturally as the built-in types.

In this section, we'll describe a simple class that we can use in writing our bookstore program. We'll implement this class in later chapters as we learn more about types, expressions, statements, and functions.

To use a class we need to know three things:

- What is its name?

- Where is it defined?

- What operations does it support?

For our bookstore problem, we'll assume that the class is named `Sales_item` and that it is already defined in a header named `Sales_item.h`.

As we've seen, to use a library facility, we must include the associated header. Similarly, we use headers to access classes defined for our own applications. Conventionally, header file names are derived from the name of a class defined in that header. Header files that we write usually have a suffix of `.h`, but some programmers use `.H`, `.hpp`, or `.hxx`. The standard library headers typically have no suffix at all. Compilers usually don't care about the form of header file names, but IDEs sometimes do.

1.5.1   The `Sales_item` Class

The purpose of the `Sales_item` class is to represent the total revenue, number of copies sold, and average sales price for a book. How these data are stored or computed is not our concern. To use a class, we need not care about how it is implemented. Instead, what we need to know is what operations objects of that type can perform.

Every class defines a type. The type name is the same as the name of the class. Hence, our `Sales_item` class defines a type named `Sales_item`. As with the built-in types, we can define a variable of a class type. When we write

```
Sales_item item;
```

we are saying that `item` is an object of type `Sales_item`. We often contract the phrase "an object of type `Sales_item`" to "a `Sales_item` object" or even more simply to "a `Sales_item`."

In addition to being able to define variables of type `Sales_item`, we can:

- Call a function named `isbn` to fetch the ISBN from a `Sales_item` object.

- Use the input (`>>`) and output (`<<`) operators to read and write objects of type `Sales_item`.

- Use the assignment operator (`=`) to assign one `Sales_item` object to another.

- Use the addition operator (`+`) to add two `Sales_item` objects. The two objects must refer to the same ISBN. The result is a new `Sales_item` object whose ISBN is that of its operands and whose number sold and revenue are the sum of the corresponding values in its operands.

- Use the compound assignment operator (`+=`) to add one `Sales_item` object into another.

KEY CONCEPT: CLASSES DEFINE BEHAVIOR

The important thing to keep in mind when you read these programs is that the author of the `Sales_item` class defines *all* the actions that can be performed by objects of this class. That is, the `Sales_item` class defines what happens when a `Sales_item` object is created and what happens when the assignment, addition, or the input and output operators are applied to `Sales_items`.

In general, the class author determines all the operations that can be used on objects of the class type. For now, the only operations we know we can perform on `Sales_item` objects are the ones listed in this section.

Reading and Writing `Sales_items`

Now that we know what operations we can use with `Sales_item` objects, we can write programs that use the class. For example, the following program reads data from the standard input into a `Sales_item` object and writes that `Sales_item` back onto the standard output:

```cpp
#include <iostream>
#include "Sales_item.h"
int main()
{
    Sales_item book;
    //  read ISBN, number of copies sold, and sales price
    std::cin >> book;
    //  write ISBN, number of copies sold, total revenue, and average price
    std::cout << book << std::endl;
    return 0;
}
```

If the input to this program is

```
0-201-70353-X 4 24.99
```

then the output will be

```
0-201-70353-X 4 99.96 24.99
```

Our input says that we sold four copies of the book at $24.99 each, and the output indicates that the total sold was four, the total revenue was $99.96, and the average price per book was $24.99.

This program starts with two `#include` directives, one of which uses a new form. Headers from the standard library are enclosed in angle brackets (< >). Those that are not part of the library are enclosed in double quotes (" ").

Inside `main` we define an object, named `book`, that we'll use to hold the data that we read from the standard input. The next statement reads into that object, and the third statement prints it to the standard output followed by printing `endl`.

Adding `Sales_items`

A more interesting example adds two `Sales_item` objects:

```cpp
#include <iostream>
#include "Sales_item.h"
int main()
{
    Sales_item item1, item2;
    std::cin >> item1 >> item2;     // read a pair of transactions
    std::cout << item1 + item2 << std::endl; // print their sum
    return 0;
}
```

If we give this program the following input

```
0-201-78345-X 3 20.00
0-201-78345-X 2 25.00
```

our output is

```
0-201-78345-X 5 110 22
```

This program starts by including the `Sales_item` and `iostream` headers. Next we define two `Sales_item` objects to hold the transactions. We read data into these objects from the standard input. The output expression does the addition and prints the result.

It's worth noting how similar this program looks to the one on page 6: We read two inputs and write their sum. What makes this similarity noteworthy is that instead of reading and printing the sum of two integers, we're reading and printing the sum of two `Sales_item` objects. Moreover, the whole idea of "sum" is different. In the case of `int`s we are generating a conventional sum—the result of adding two numeric values. In the case of `Sales_item` objects we use a conceptually new meaning for sum—the result of adding the components of two `Sales_item` objects.

USING FILE REDIRECTION

It can be tedious to repeatedly type these transactions as input to the programs you are testing. Most operating systems support file redirection, which lets us associate a named file with the standard input and the standard output:

```
$ addItems <infile >outfile
```

Assuming $ is the system prompt and our addition program has been compiled into an executable file named `addItems.exe` (or `addItems` on UNIX systems), this command will read transactions from a file named `infile` and write its output to a file named `outfile` in the current directory.

EXERCISES SECTION 1.5.1

Exercise 1.20: `http://www.informit.com/title/032174113` contains a copy of `Sales_item.h` in the Chapter 1 code directory. Copy that file to your working directory. Use it to write a program that reads a set of book sales transactions, writing each transaction to the standard output.

Exercise 1.21: Write a program that reads two `Sales_item` objects that have the same ISBN and produces their sum.

Exercise 1.22: Write a program that reads several transactions for the same ISBN. Write the sum of all the transactions that were read.

1.5.2   A First Look at Member Functions

Our program that adds two `Sales_items` should check whether the objects have the same ISBN. We'll do so as follows:

```
#include <iostream>
#include "Sales_item.h"
int main()
{
    Sales_item item1, item2;
    std::cin >> item1 >> item2;
    // first check that item1 and item2 represent the same book
    if (item1.isbn() == item2.isbn()) {
        std::cout << item1 + item2 << std::endl;
        return 0;     // indicate success
    } else {
        std::cerr << "Data must refer to same ISBN"
                    << std::endl;
        return -1;  // indicate failure
    }
}
```

The difference between this program and the previous version is the `if` and its associated `else` branch. Even without understanding the `if` condition, we know what this program does. If the condition succeeds, then we write the same output as before and return `0`, indicating success. If the condition fails, we execute the block following the `else`, which prints a message and returns an error indicator.

What Is a Member Function?

The `if` condition

```
item1.isbn() == item2.isbn()
```

calls a **member function** named `isbn`. A member function is a function that is defined as part of a class. Member functions are sometimes referred to as **methods**.

Ordinarily, we call a member function on behalf of an object. For example, the first part of the left-hand operand of the equality expression

```
item1.isbn
```

uses the dot operator (the **"." operator**) to say that we want "the `isbn` member of the object named `item1`." The dot operator applies only to objects of class type. The left-hand operand must be an object of class type, and the right-hand operand must name a member of that type. The result of the dot operator is the member named by the right-hand operand.

When we use the dot operator to access a member function, we usually do so to call that function. We call a function using the call operator (the **() operator**). The call operator is a pair of parentheses that enclose a (possibly empty) list of *arguments*. The `isbn` member function does not take an argument. Thus,

```
item1.isbn()
```

calls the isbn function that is a member of the object named item1. This function returns the ISBN stored in item1.

The right-hand operand of the equality operator executes in the same way—it returns the ISBN stored in item2. If the ISBNs are the same, the condition is true; otherwise it is false.

EXERCISES SECTION 1.5.2

Exercise 1.23: Write a program that reads several transactions and counts how many transactions occur for each ISBN.

Exercise 1.24: Test the previous program by giving multiple transactions representing multiple ISBNs. The records for each ISBN should be grouped together.

1.6 The Bookstore Program

We are now ready to solve our original bookstore problem. We need to read a file of sales transactions and produce a report that shows, for each book, the total number of copies sold, the total revenue, and the average sales price. We'll assume that all the transactions for each ISBN are grouped together in the input.

Our program will combine the data for each ISBN in a variable named total. We'll use a second variable named trans to hold each transaction we read. If trans and total refer to the same ISBN, we'll update total. Otherwise we'll print total and reset it using the transaction we just read:

```cpp
#include <iostream>
#include "Sales_item.h"
int main()
{
    Sales_item total; //  variable to hold data for the next transaction
    //  read the first transaction and ensure that there are data to process
    if (std::cin >> total) {
        Sales_item trans; //  variable to hold the running sum
        //  read and process the remaining transactions
        while (std::cin >> trans) {
            //  if we're still processing the same book
            if (total.isbn() == trans.isbn())
                total += trans; //  update the running total
            else {
                //  print results for the previous book
                std::cout << total << std::endl;
                total = trans;  //  total now refers to the next book
            }
        }
        std::cout << total << std::endl; //  print the last transaction
    } else {
```

```
          //   no input! warn the user
          std::cerr << "No data?!" << std::endl;
          return -1;   //   indicate failure
     }
     return 0;
}
```

This program is the most complicated one we've seen so far, but it uses only facilities that we have already seen.

As usual, we begin by including the headers that we use, iostream from the library and our own Sales_item.h. Inside main we define an object named total, which we'll use to sum the data for a given ISBN. We start by reading the first transaction into total and testing whether the read was successful. If the read fails, then there are no records and we fall through to the outermost else branch, which tells the user that there was no input.

Assuming we have successfully read a record, we execute the block following the outermost if. That block starts by defining the object named trans, which will hold our transactions as we read them. The while statement will read all the remaining records. As in our earlier programs, the while condition reads a value from the standard input. In this case, we read a Sales_item object into trans. As long as the read succeeds, we execute the body of the while.

The body of the while is a single if statement. The if checks whether the ISBNs are equal. If so, we use the compound assignment operator to add trans to total. If the ISBNs are not equal, we print the value stored in total and reset total by assigning trans to it. After executing the if, we return to the condition in the while, reading the next transaction, and so on until we run out of records.

When the while terminates, total contains the data for the last ISBN in the file. We write the data for the last ISBN in the last statement of the block that concludes the outermost if statement.

EXERCISES SECTION 1.6

Exercise 1.25: Using the Sales_item.h header from the Web site, compile and execute the bookstore program presented in this section.

CHAPTER SUMMARY

This chapter introduced enough of C++ to let you compile and execute simple C++ programs. We saw how to define a `main` function, which is the function that the operating system calls to execute our program. We also saw how to define variables, how to do input and output, and how to write `if`, `for`, and `while` statements. The chapter closed by introducing the most fundamental facility in C++: the class. In this chapter, we saw how to create and use objects of a class that someone else has defined. Later chapters will show how to define our own classes.

DEFINED TERMS

argument Value passed to a function.

assignment Obliterates an object's current value and replaces that value by a new one.

block Sequence of zero or more statements enclosed in curly braces.

buffer A region of storage used to hold data. IO facilities often store input (or output) in a buffer and read or write the buffer independently from actions in the program. Output buffers can be explicitly flushed to force the buffer to be written. By default, reading `cin` flushes `cout`; `cout` is also flushed when the program ends normally.

built-in type Type, such as `int`, defined by the language.

cerr `ostream` object tied to the standard error, which often writes to the same device as the standard output. By default, writes to `cerr` are not buffered. Usually used for error messages or other output that is not part of the normal logic of the program.

character string literal Another term for string literal.

cin `istream` object used to read from the standard input.

class Facility for defining our own data structures together with associated operations. The class is one of the most fundamental features in C++. Library types, such as `istream` and `ostream`, are classes.

class type A type defined by a class. The name of the type is the class name.

clog `ostream` object tied to the standard error. By default, writes to `clog` are buffered. Usually used to report information about program execution to a log file.

comments Program text that is ignored by the compiler. C++ has two kinds of comments: single-line and paired. Single-line comments start with a `//`. Everything from the `//` to the end of the line is a comment. Paired comments begin with a `/*` and include all text up to the next `*/`.

condition An expression that is evaluated as true or false. A value of zero is false; any other value yields true.

cout `ostream` object used to write to the standard output. Ordinarily used to write the output of a program.

curly brace Curly braces delimit blocks. An open curly (`{`) starts a block; a close curly (`}`) ends one.

data structure A logical grouping of data and operations on that data.

edit-compile-debug The process of getting a program to execute properly.

end-of-file System-specific marker that indicates that there is no more input in a file.

expression The smallest unit of computation. An expression consists of one or more operands and usually one or more operators. Expressions are evaluated to produce a result. For example, assuming i and j are ints, then i + j is an expression and yields the sum of the two int values.

for statement Iteration statement that provides iterative execution. Often used to repeat a calculation a fixed number of times.

function Named unit of computation.

function body Block that defines the actions performed by a function.

function name Name by which a function is known and can be called.

header Mechanism whereby the definitions of a class or other names are made available to multiple programs. A program uses a header through a #include directive.

if statement Conditional execution based on the value of a specified condition. If the condition is true, the if body is executed. If not, the else body is executed if there is one.

initialize Give an object a value at the same time that it is created.

iostream Header that provides the library types for stream-oriented input and output.

istream Library type providing stream-oriented input.

library type Type, such as istream, defined by the standard library.

main Function called by the operating system to execute a C++ program. Each program must have one and only one function named main.

manipulator Object, such as std::endl, that when read or written "manipulates" the stream itself.

member function Operation defined by a class. Member functions ordinarily are called to operate on a specific object.

method Synonym for member function.

namespace Mechanism for putting names defined by a library into a single place. Namespaces help avoid inadvertent name clashes. The names defined by the C++ library are in the namespace std.

ostream Library type providing stream-oriented output.

parameter list Part of the definition of a function. Possibly empty list that specifies what arguments can be used to call the function.

return type Type of the value returned by a function.

source file Term used to describe a file that contains a C++ program.

standard error Output stream used for error reporting. Ordinarily, the standard output and the standard error are tied to the window in which the program is executed.

standard input Input stream usually associated with the window in which the program executes.

standard library Collection of types and functions that every C++ compiler must support. The library provides the types that support IO. C++ programmers tend to talk about "the library," meaning the entire standard library. They also tend to refer to particular parts of the library by referring to a library type, such as the "iostream library," meaning the part of the standard library that defines the IO classes.

standard output Output stream usually associated with the window in which the program executes.

statement A part of a program that specifies an action to take place when the program is executed. An expression followed by a semicolon is a statement; other kinds of statements include blocks and `if`, `for`, and `while` statements, all of which contain other statements within themselves.

std Name of the namespace used by the standard library. `std::cout` indicates that we're using the name `cout` defined in the `std` namespace.

string literal Sequence of zero or more characters enclosed in double quotes (`"a string literal"`).

uninitialized variable Variable that is not given an initial value. Variables of class type for which no initial value is specified are initialized as specified by the class definition. Variables of built-in type defined inside a function are uninitialized unless explicitly initialized. It is an error to try to use the value of an uninitialized variable. *Uninitialized variables are a rich source of bugs.*

variable A named object.

while statement Iteration statement that provides iterative execution so long as a specified condition is true. The body is executed zero or more times, depending on the truth value of the condition.

( ) operator Call operator. A pair of parentheses "`( )`" following a function name. The operator causes a function to be invoked. Arguments to the function may be passed inside the parentheses.

++ operator Increment operator. Adds 1 to the operand; `++i` is equivalent to `i = i + 1`.

+= operator Compound assignment operator that adds the right-hand operand to the left and stores the result in the left-hand operand; `a += b` is equivalent to `a = a + b`.

. operator Dot operator. Left-hand operand must be an object of class type and the right-hand operand must be the name of a member of that object. The operator yields the named member of the given object.

:: operator Scope operator. Among other uses, the scope operator is used to access names in a namespace. For example,

`std::cout` denotes the name `cout` from the namespace `std`.

= operator Assigns the value of the right-hand operand to the object denoted by the left-hand operand.

-- operator Decrement operator. Subtracts 1 from the operand; `--i` is equivalent to `i = i - 1`.

<< operator Output operator. Writes the right-hand operand to the output stream indicated by the left-hand operand: `cout << "hi"` writes `hi` to the standard output. Output operations can be chained together: `cout << "hi" << "bye"` writes `hibye`.

>> operator Input operator. Reads from the input stream specified by the left-hand operand into the right-hand operand: `cin >> i` reads the next value on the standard input into `i`. Input operations can be chained together: `cin >> i >> j` reads first into `i` and then into `j`.

#include Directive that makes code in a header available to a program.

== operator The equality operator. Tests whether the left-hand operand is equal to the right-hand operand.

!= operator The inequality operator. Tests whether the left-hand operand is not equal to the right-hand operand.

<= operator The less-than-or-equal operator. Tests whether the left-hand operand is less than or equal to the right-hand operand.

< operator The less-than operator. Tests whether the left-hand operand is less than the right-hand operand.

>= operator Greater-than-or-equal operator. Tests whether the left-hand operand is greater than or equal to the right-hand operand.

> operator Greater-than operator. Tests whether the left-hand operand is greater than the right-hand operand.

PART I

THE BASICS

CONTENTS

Every widely used programming language provides a common set of features, which differ in detail from one language to another. Understanding the details of how a language provides these features is the first step toward understanding the language. Among the most fundamental of these common features are

- Built-in types such as integers, characters, and so forth

- Variables, which let us give names to the objects we use

- Expressions and statements to manipulate values of these types

- Control structures, such as `if` or `while`, that allow us to conditionally or repeatedly execute a set of actions

- Functions that let us define callable units of computation

Most programming languages supplement these basic features in two ways: They let programmers extend the language by defining their own types, and they provide library routines that define useful functions and types not otherwise built into the language.

In C++, as in most programming languages, the type of an object determines what operations can be performed on it. Whether a particular expression is legal depends on the type of the objects in that expression. Some languages, such as Smalltalk and Python, check types at run time. In contrast, C++ is a statically typed language; type checking is done at compile time. As a consequence, the compiler must know the type of every name used in the program.

C++ provides a set of built-in types, operators to manipulate those types, and a small set of statements for program flow control. These elements form an alphabet from which we can write large, complicated, real-world systems. At this basic level, C++ is a simple language. Its expressive power arises from its support for mechanisms that allow the programmer to define new data structures. Using these facilities, programmers can shape the language to their own purposes without the language designers having to anticipate the programmers' needs.

Perhaps the most important feature in C++ is the class, which lets programmers define their own types. In C++ such types are sometimes called "class types" to distinguish them from the types that are built into the language. Some languages let programmers define types that specify only what data make up the type. Others, like C++, allow programmers to define types that include operations as well as data. A major design goal of C++ is to let programmers define their own types that are as easy to use as the built-in types. The Standard C++ library uses these features to implement a rich library of class types and associated functions.

The first step in mastering C++—learning the basics of the language and library—is the topic of Part I. Chapter 2 covers the built-in types and looks briefly at the mechanisms for defining our own new types. Chapter 3 introduces two of the most fundamental library types: `string` and `vector`. That chapter also covers arrays, which are a lower-level data structure built into C++ and many other languages. Chapters 4 through 6 cover expressions, statements, and functions. This part concludes in Chapter 7, which describes the basics of building our own class types. As we'll see, defining our own types brings together all that we've learned before, because writing a class entails using the facilities covered in Part I.

CHAPTER 2

VARIABLES AND BASIC TYPES

CONTENTS

Types are fundamental to any program: They tell us what our data mean and what operations we can perform on those data.

C++ has extensive support for types. The language defines several primitive types (characters, integers, floating-point numbers, etc.) and provides mechanisms that let us define our own data types. The library uses these mechanisms to define more complicated types such as variable-length character strings, vectors, and so on. This chapter covers the built-in types and begins our coverage of how C++ supports more complicated types.

Types determine the meaning of the data and operations in our programs. The meaning of even as simple a statement as

```
i = i + j;
```

depends on the types of i and j. If i and j are integers, this statement has the ordinary, arithmetic meaning of +. However, if i and j are Sales_item objects (§ 1.5.1, p. 20), this statement adds the components of these two objects.

2.1 Primitive Built-in Types

C++ defines a set of primitive types that include the **arithmetic types** and a special type named **void**. The arithmetic types represent characters, integers, boolean values, and floating-point numbers. The void type has no associated values and can be used in only a few circumstances, most commonly as the return type for functions that do not return a value.

2.1.1 Arithmetic Types

The arithmetic types are divided into two categories: **integral types** (which include character and boolean types) and floating-point types.

The size of—that is, the number of bits in—the arithmetic types varies across machines. The standard guarantees minimum sizes as listed in Table 2.1. However, compilers are allowed to use larger sizes for these types. Because the number of bits varies, the largest (or smallest) value that a type can represent also varies.

Table 2.1: C++: Arithmetic Types		
Type	**Meaning**	**Minimum Size**
bool	boolean	NA
char	character	8 bits
wchar_t	wide character	16 bits
char16_t	Unicode character	16 bits
char32_t	Unicode character	32 bits
short	short integer	16 bits
int	integer	16 bits
long	long integer	32 bits
long long	long integer	64 bits
float	single-precision floating-point	6 significant digits
double	double-precision floating-point	10 significant digits
long double	extended-precision floating-point	10 significant digits

The bool type represents the truth values true and false.

There are several character types, most of which exist to support internationalization. The basic character type is char. A char is guaranteed to be big enough to hold numeric values corresponding to the characters in the machine's basic character set. That is, a char is the same size as a single machine byte.

The remaining character types—wchar_t, char16_t, and char32_t—are used for extended character sets. The wchar_t type is guaranteed to be large enough to hold any character in the machine's largest extended character set. The types char16_t and char32_t are intended for Unicode characters. (Unicode is a standard for representing characters used in essentially any natural language.)

The remaining integral types represent integer values of (potentially) different sizes. The language guarantees that an int will be at least as large as short, a long at least as large as an int, and long long at least as large as long. The type long long was introduced by the new standard.

C++
11

MACHINE-LEVEL REPRESENTATION OF THE BUILT-IN TYPES

Computers store data as a sequence of bits, each holding a 0 or 1, such as

00011011011100010110010000111011 ...

Most computers deal with memory as chunks of bits of sizes that are powers of 2. The smallest chunk of addressable memory is referred to as a "byte." The basic unit of storage, usually a small number of bytes, is referred to as a "word." In C++ a byte has at least as many bits as are needed to hold a character in the machine's basic character set. On most machines a byte contains 8 bits and a word is either 32 or 64 bits, that is, 4 or 8 bytes.

Most computers associate a number (called an "address") with each byte in memory. On a machine with 8-bit bytes and 32-bit words, we might view a word of memory as follows

736424	0	0	1	1	1	0	1	1
736425	0	0	0	1	1	0	1	1
736426	0	1	1	1	0	0	0	1
736427	0	1	1	0	0	1	0	0

Here, the byte's address is on the left, with the 8 bits of the byte following the address.

We can use an address to refer to any of several variously sized collections of bits starting at that address. It is possible to speak of the word at address 736424 or the byte at address 736427. To give meaning to memory at a given address, we must know the type of the value stored there. The type determines how many bits are used and how to interpret those bits.

If the object at location 736424 has type float and if floats on this machine are stored in 32 bits, then we know that the object at that address spans the entire word. The value of that float depends on the details of how the machine stores floating-point numbers. Alternatively, if the object at location 736424 is an unsigned char on a machine using the ISO-Latin-1 character set, then the byte at that address represents a semicolon.

The floating-point types represent single-, double-, and extended-precision values. The standard specifies a minimum number of significant digits. Most compilers provide more precision than the specified minimum. Typically, floats are represented in one word (32 bits), doubles in two words (64 bits), and long doubles in either three or four words (96 or 128 bits). The float and double types typically yield about 7 and 16 significant digits, respectively. The type long double is often used as a way to accommodate special-purpose floating-point hardware; its precision is more likely to vary from one implementation to another.

Signed and Unsigned Types

Except for `bool` and the extended character types, the integral types may be **signed** or **unsigned**. A signed type represents negative or positive numbers (including zero); an unsigned type represents only values greater than or equal to zero.

The types `int`, `short`, `long`, and `long long` are all signed. We obtain the corresponding unsigned type by adding `unsigned` to the type, such as `unsigned long`. The type `unsigned int` may be abbreviated as `unsigned`.

Unlike the other integer types, there are three distinct basic character types: `char`, `signed char`, and `unsigned char`. In particular, `char` is not the same type as `signed char`. Although there are three character types, there are only two representations: signed and unsigned. The (plain) `char` type uses one of these representations. Which of the other two character representations is equivalent to `char` depends on the compiler.

In an unsigned type, all the bits represent the value. For example, an 8-bit `unsigned char` can hold the values from 0 through 255 inclusive.

The standard does not define how signed types are represented, but does specify that the range should be evenly divided between positive and negative values. Hence, an 8-bit `signed char` is guaranteed to be able to hold values from –127 through 127; most modern machines use representations that allow values from –128 through 127.

ADVICE: DECIDING WHICH TYPE TO USE

C++, like C, is designed to let programs get close to the hardware when necessary. The arithmetic types are defined to cater to the peculiarities of various kinds of hardware. Accordingly, the number of arithmetic types in C++ can be bewildering. Most programmers can (and should) ignore these complexities by restricting the types they use. A few rules of thumb can be useful in deciding which type to use:

- Use an unsigned type when you know that the values cannot be negative.

- Use `int` for integer arithmetic. `short` is usually too small and, in practice, `long` often has the same size as `int`. If your data values are larger than the minimum guaranteed size of an `int`, then use `long long`.

- Do not use plain `char` or `bool` in arithmetic expressions. Use them *only* to hold characters or truth values. Computations using `char` are especially problematic because `char` is `signed` on some machines and `unsigned` on others. If you need a tiny integer, explicitly specify either `signed char` or `unsigned char`.

- Use `double` for floating-point computations; `float` usually does not have enough precision, and the cost of double-precision calculations versus single-precision is negligible. In fact, on some machines, double-precision operations are faster than single. The precision offered by `long double` usually is unnecessary and often entails considerable run-time cost.

Exercise 2.1: What are the differences between int, long, long long, and short? Between an unsigned and a signed type? Between a float and a double?

Exercise 2.2: To calculate a mortgage payment, what types would you use for the rate, principal, and payment? Explain why you selected each type.

2.1.2 Type Conversions

The type of an object defines the data that an object might contain and what operations that object can perform. Among the operations that many types support is the ability to **convert** objects of the given type to other, related types.

Type conversions happen automatically when we use an object of one type where an object of another type is expected. We'll have more to say about conversions in § 4.11 (p. 159), but for now it is useful to understand what happens when we assign a value of one type to an object of another type.

When we assign one arithmetic type to another:

```
bool b = 42;            //  b is true
int i = b;              //  i has value 1
i = 3.14;               //  i has value 3
double pi = i;          //  pi has value 3.0
unsigned char c = -1;   //  assuming 8-bit chars, c has value 255
signed char c2 = 256;   //  assuming 8-bit chars, the value of c2 is undefined
```

what happens depends on the range of the values that the types permit:

- When we assign one of the nonbool arithmetic types to a bool object, the result is false if the value is 0 and true otherwise.

- When we assign a bool to one of the other arithmetic types, the resulting value is 1 if the bool is true and 0 if the bool is false.

- When we assign a floating-point value to an object of integral type, the value is truncated. The value that is stored is the part before the decimal point.

- When we assign an integral value to an object of floating-point type, the fractional part is zero. Precision may be lost if the integer has more bits than the floating-point object can accommodate.

- If we assign an out-of-range value to an object of unsigned type, the result is the remainder of the value modulo the number of values the target type can hold. For example, an 8-bit unsigned char can hold values from 0 through 255, inclusive. If we assign a value outside this range, the compiler assigns the remainder of that value modulo 256. Therefore, assigning –1 to an 8-bit unsigned char gives that object the value 255.

- If we assign an out-of-range value to an object of signed type, the result is **undefined**. The program might appear to work, it might crash, or it might produce garbage values.

> **ADVICE: AVOID UNDEFINED AND IMPLEMENTATION-DEFINED BEHAVIOR**
>
> Undefined behavior results from errors that the compiler is not required (and some-times is not able) to detect. Even if the code compiles, a program that executes an undefined expression is in error.
>
> Unfortunately, programs that contain undefined behavior can appear to execute correctly in some circumstances and/or on some compilers. There is no guarantee that the same program, compiled under a different compiler or even a subsequent release of the same compiler, will continue to run correctly. Nor is there any guarantee that what works with one set of inputs will work with another.
>
> Similarly, programs usually should avoid implementation-defined behavior, such as assuming that the size of an `int` is a fixed and known value. Such programs are said to be *nonportable*. When the program is moved to another machine, code that relied on implementation-defined behavior may fail. Tracking down these sorts of problems in previously working programs is, mildly put, unpleasant.

The compiler applies these same type conversions when we use a value of one arithmetic type where a value of another arithmetic type is expected. For example, when we use a nonbool value as a condition (§ 1.4.1, p. 12), the arithmetic value is converted to `bool` in the same way that it would be converted if we had assigned that arithmetic value to a `bool` variable:

```
int i = 42;
if (i) // condition will evaluate as true
    i = 0;
```

If the value is `0`, then the condition is `false`; all other (nonzero) values yield `true`.

By the same token, when we use a `bool` in an arithmetic expression, its value always converts to either `0` or `1`. As a result, using a `bool` in an arithmetic expression is almost surely incorrect.

Expressions Involving Unsigned Types

Although we are unlikely to intentionally assign a negative value to an object of unsigned type, we can (all too easily) write code that does so implicitly. For example, if we use both `unsigned` and `int` values in an arithmetic expression, the `int` value ordinarily is converted to `unsigned`. Converting an `int` to `unsigned` executes the same way as if we assigned the `int` to an `unsigned`:

```
unsigned u = 10;
int i = -42;
std::cout << i + i << std::endl;   // prints -84
std::cout << u + i << std::endl;   // if 32-bit ints, prints 4294967264
```

In the first expression, we add two (negative) `int` values and obtain the expected result. In the second expression, the `int` value `-42` is converted to `unsigned` before the addition is done. Converting a negative number to `unsigned` behaves exactly as if we had attempted to assign that negative value to an `unsigned` object. The value "wraps around" as described above.

Regardless of whether one or both operands are unsigned, if we subtract a value from an unsigned, we must be sure that the result cannot be negative:

```
unsigned u1 = 42, u2 = 10;
std::cout << u1 - u2 << std::endl; //  ok: result is 32
std::cout << u2 - u1 << std::endl; //  ok: but the result will wrap around
```

The fact that an unsigned cannot be less than zero also affects how we write loops.
For example, in the exercises to § 1.4.1 (p. 13), you were to write a loop that used
the decrement operator to print the numbers from 10 down to 0. The loop you
wrote probably looked something like

```
for (int i = 10; i >= 0; --i)
    std::cout << i << std::endl;
```

We might think we could rewrite this loop using an unsigned. After all, we don't
plan to print negative numbers. However, this simple change in type means that
our loop will never terminate:

```
//  WRONG: u can never be less than 0; the condition will always succeed
for (unsigned u = 10; u >= 0; --u)
    std::cout << u << std::endl;
```

Consider what happens when u is 0. On that iteration, we'll print 0 and then
execute the expression in the for loop. That expression, --u, subtracts 1 from u.
That result, -1, won't fit in an unsigned value. As with any other out-of-range
value, -1 will be transformed to an unsigned value. Assuming 32-bit ints, the
result of --u, when u is 0, is 4294967295.

One way to write this loop is to use a while instead of a for. Using a while
lets us decrement before (rather than after) printing our value:

```
unsigned u = 11;  //  start the loop one past the first element we want to print
while (u > 0) {
    --u;          //  decrement first, so that the last iteration will print 0
    std::cout << u << std::endl;
}
```

This loop starts by decrementing the value of the loop control variable. On the last
iteration, u will be 1 on entry to the loop. We'll decrement that value, meaning
that we'll print 0 on this iteration. When we next test u in the while condition, its
value will be 0 and the loop will exit. Because we start by decrementing u, we have
to initialize u to a value one greater than the first value we want to print. Hence,
we initialize u to 11, so that the first value printed is 10.

CAUTION: DON'T MIX SIGNED AND UNSIGNED TYPES

Expressions that mix signed and unsigned values can yield surprising results when
the signed value is negative. It is essential to remember that signed values are automatically converted to unsigned. For example, in an expression like a * b, if a is -1
and b is 1, then if both a and b are ints, the value is, as expected -1. However, if a is
int and b is an unsigned, then the value of this expression depends on how many
bits an int has on the particular machine. On our machine, this expression yields
4294967295.

Exercise 2.3: What output will the following code produce?

```
unsigned u = 10, u2 = 42;
std::cout << u2 - u << std::endl;
std::cout << u - u2 << std::endl;
int i = 10, i2 = 42;
std::cout << i2 - i << std::endl;
std::cout << i - i2 << std::endl;
std::cout << i - u << std::endl;
std::cout << u - i << std::endl;
```

Exercise 2.4: Write a program to check whether your predictions were correct. If not, study this section until you understand what the problem is.

2.1.3 Literals

A value, such as 42, is known as a **literal** because its value self-evident. Every literal has a type. The form and value of a literal determine its type.

Integer and Floating-Point Literals

We can write an integer literal using decimal, octal, or hexadecimal notation. Integer literals that begin with 0 (zero) are interpreted as octal. Those that begin with either 0x or 0X are interpreted as hexadecimal. For example, we can write the value 20 in any of the following three ways:

```
20 /* decimal */   024 /* octal */   0x14 /* hexadecimal */
```

The type of an integer literal depends on its value and notation. By default, decimal literals are signed whereas octal and hexadecimal literals can be either signed or unsigned types. A decimal literal has the smallest type of int, long, or long long (i.e., the first type in this list) in which the literal's value fits. Octal and hexadecimal literals have the smallest type of int, unsigned int, long, unsigned long, long long, or unsigned long long in which the literal's value fits. It is an error to use a literal that is too large to fit in the largest related type. There are no literals of type short. We'll see in Table 2.2 (p. 40) that we can override these defaults by using a suffix.

Although integer literals may be stored in signed types, technically speaking, the value of a decimal literal is never a negative number. If we write what appears to be a negative decimal literal, for example, -42, the minus sign is *not* part of the literal. The minus sign is an operator that negates the value of its (literal) operand.

Floating-point literals include either a decimal point or an exponent specified using scientific notation. Using scientific notation, the exponent is indicated by either E or e:

```
3.14159   3.14159E0   0.   0e0   .001
```

By default, floating-point literals have type `double`. We can override the default using a suffix from Table 2.2 (overleaf).

Character and Character String Literals

A character enclosed within single quotes is a literal of type `char`. Zero or more characters enclosed in double quotation marks is a string literal:

```
'a'   // character literal
"Hello World!"   // string literal
```

The type of a string literal is *array* of constant `char`s, a type we'll discuss in § 3.5.4 (p. 122). The compiler appends a null character (`'\0'`) to every string literal. Thus, the actual size of a string literal is one more than its apparent size. For example, the literal `'A'` represents the single character A, whereas the string literal `"A"` represents an array of two characters, the letter A and the null character.

Two string literals that appear adjacent to one another and that are separated only by spaces, tabs, or newlines are concatenated into a single literal. We use this form of literal when we need to write a literal that would otherwise be too large to fit comfortably on a single line:

```
// multiline string literal
std::cout << "a really, really long string literal "
             "that spans two lines" << std::endl;
```

Escape Sequences

Some characters, such as backspace or control characters, have no visible image. Such characters are **nonprintable**. Other characters (single and double quotation marks, question mark, and backslash) have special meaning in the language. Our programs cannot use any of these characters directly. Instead, we use an **escape sequence** to represent such characters. An escape sequence begins with a backslash. The language defines several escape sequences:

newline	`\n`	horizontal tab	`\t`	alert (bell)	`\a`
vertical tab	`\v`	backspace	`\b`	double quote	`\"`
backslash	`\\`	question mark	`\?`	single quote	`\'`
carriage return	`\r`	formfeed	`\f`		

We use an escape sequence as if it were a single character:

```
std::cout << '\n';          // prints a newline
std::cout << "\tHi!\n";     // prints a tab followd by "Hi!" and a newline
```

We can also write a generalized escape sequence, which is `\x` followed by one or more hexadecimal digits or a `\` followed by one, two, or three octal digits. The value represents the numerical value of the character. Some examples (assuming the Latin-1 character set):

```
\7  (bell)      \12  (newline)     \40  (blank)
\0  (null)      \115 ('M')         \x4d ('M')
```

As with an escape sequence defined by the language, we use these escape sequences as we would any other character:

```
std::cout << "Hi \x4dO\115!\n";  // prints Hi MOM! followed by a newline
std::cout << '\115' << '\n';       // prints M followed by a newline
```

Note that if a \ is followed by more than three octal digits, only the first three are associated with the \. For example, "\1234" represents two characters: the character represented by the octal value 123 and the character 4. In contrast, \x uses up all the hex digits following it; "\x1234" represents a single, 16-bit character composed from the bits corresponding to these four hexadecimal digits. Because most machines have 8-bit chars, such values are unlikely to be useful. Ordinarily, hexadecimal characters with more than 8 bits are used with extended characters sets using one of the prefixes from Table 2.2.

Specifying the Type of a Literal

We can override the default type of an integer, floating- point, or character literal by supplying a suffix or prefix as listed in Table 2.2.

```
L'a'       // wide character literal, type is wchar_t
u8"hi!"    // utf-8 string literal (utf-8 encodes a Unicode character in 8 bits)
42ULL      // unsigned integer literal, type is unsigned long long
1E-3F      // single-precision floating-point literal, type is float
3.14159L   // extended-precision floating-point literal, type is long double
```

> **Best Practices** When you write a long literal, use the uppercase L; the lowercase letter l is too easily mistaken for the digit 1.

Table 2.2: Specifying the Type of a Literal

Character and Character String Literals		
Prefix	**Meaning**	**Type**
u	Unicode 16 character	char16_t
U	Unicode 32 character	char32_t
L	wide character	wchar_t
u8	utf-8 (string literals only)	char

Integer Literals		Floating-Point Literals	
Suffix	**Minimum Type**	**Suffix**	**Type**
u or U	unsigned	f or F	float
l or L	long	l or L	long double
ll or LL	long long		

We can independently specify the signedness and size of an integral literal. If the suffix contains a U, then the literal has an unsigned type, so a decimal, octal, or hexadecimal literal with a U suffix has the smallest type of unsigned int, unsigned long, or unsigned long long in which the literal's value fits. If the suffix contains an L, then the literal's type will be at least long; if the suffix contains LL, then the literal's type will be either long long or unsigned long long.

We can combine U with either L or LL. For example, a literal with a suffix of UL will be either unsigned long or unsigned long long, depending on whether its value fits in unsigned long.

Boolean and Pointer Literals

The words true and false are literals of type bool:

```
bool test = false;
```

The word nullptr is a pointer literal. We'll have more to say about pointers and nullptr in § 2.3.2 (p. 52).

EXERCISES SECTION 2.1.3

Exercise 2.5: Determine the type of each of the following literals. Explain the differences among the literals in each of the four examples:

   (a) 'a', L'a', "a", L"a"
   (b) 10, 10u, 10L, 10uL, 012, 0xC
   (c) 3.14, 3.14f, 3.14L
   (d) 10, 10u, 10., 10e-2

Exercise 2.6: What, if any, are the differences between the following definitions:

```
int month = 9, day = 7;
int month = 09, day = 07;
```

Exercise 2.7: What values do these literals represent? What type does each have?

   (a) "Who goes with F\145rgus?\012"
   (b) 3.14e1L   (c) 1024f   (d) 3.14L

Exercise 2.8: Using escape sequences, write a program to print 2M followed by a newline. Modify the program to print 2, then a tab, then an M, followed by a newline.

2.2   Variables

A *variable* provides us with named storage that our programs can manipulate. Each variable in C++ has a type. The type determines the size and layout of the variable's memory, the range of values that can be stored within that memory, and the set of operations that can be applied to the variable. C++ programmers tend to refer to variables as "variables" or "objects" interchangeably.

2.2.1   Variable Definitions

A simple variable definition consists of a **type specifier**, followed by a list of one or more variable names separated by commas, and ends with a semicolon. Each name in the list has the type defined by the type specifier. A definition may (optionally) provide an initial value for one or more of the names it defines:

```
int sum = 0, value,  // sum, value, and units_sold have type int
    units_sold = 0;  // sum and units_sold have initial value 0
Sales_item item;      // item has type Sales_item (see § 1.5.1 (p. 20))
// string is a library type, representing a variable-length sequence of characters
std::string book("0-201-78345-X");  // book initialized from string literal
```

The definition of book uses the std::string library type. Like iostream (§ 1.2, p. 7), string is defined in namespace std. We'll have more to say about the string type in Chapter 3. For now, what's useful to know is that a string is a type that represents a variable-length sequence of characters. The string library gives us several ways to initialize string objects. One of these ways is as a copy of a string literal (§ 2.1.3, p. 39). Thus, book is initialized to hold the characters 0-201-78345-X.

TERMINOLOGY: WHAT IS AN OBJECT?

C++ programmers tend to be cavalier in their use of the term *object*. Most generally, an object is a region of memory that can contain data and has a type.

Some use the term *object* only to refer to variables or values of class types. Others distinguish between named and unnamed objects, using the term *variable* to refer to named objects. Still others distinguish between objects and values, using the term *object* for data that can be changed by the program and the term *value* for data that are read-only.

In this book, we'll follow the more general usage that an object is a region of memory that has a type. We will freely use the term *object* regardless of whether the object has built-in or class type, is named or unnamed, or can be read or written.

Initializers

An object that is **initialized** gets the specified value at the moment it is created. The values used to initialize a variable can be arbitrarily complicated expressions. When a definition defines two or more variables, the name of each object becomes visible immediately. Thus, it is possible to initialize a variable to the value of one defined earlier in the same definition.

```
// ok: price is defined and initialized before it is used to initialize discount
double price = 109.99, discount = price * 0.16;
// ok: call applyDiscount and use the return value to initialize salePrice
double salePrice = applyDiscount(price, discount);
```

Initialization in C++ is a surprisingly complicated topic and one we will return to again and again. Many programmers are confused by the use of the = symbol to initialize a variable. It is tempting to think of initialization as a form of assignment, but initialization and assignment are different operations in C++. This concept is particularly confusing because in many languages the distinction is irrelevant and can be ignored. Moreover, even in C++ the distinction often doesn't matter. Nonetheless, it is a crucial concept and one we will reiterate throughout the text.

 WARNING   Initialization is not assignment. Initialization happens when a variable is given a value when it is created. Assignment obliterates an object's current value and replaces that value with a new one.

List Initialization

One way in which initialization is a complicated topic is that the language defines several different forms of initialization. For example, we can use any of the following four different ways to define an int variable named units_sold and initialize it to 0:

```
int units_sold = 0;
int units_sold = {0};
int units_sold{0};
int units_sold(0);
```

The generalized use of curly braces for initialization was introduced as part of the new standard. This form of initialization previously had been allowed only in more restricted ways. For reasons we'll learn about in § 3.3.1 (p. 98), this form of initialization is referred to as **list initialization**. Braced lists of initializers can now be used whenever we initialize an object and in some cases when we assign a new value to an object.

When used with variables of built-in type, this form of initialization has one important property: The compiler will not let us list initialize variables of built-in type if the initializer might lead to the loss of information:

```
long double ld = 3.1415926536;
int a{ld}, b = {ld}; // error: narrowing conversion required
int c(ld), d = ld;   // ok: but value will be truncated
```

The compiler rejects the initializations of a and b because using a long double to initialize an int is likely to lose data. At a minimum, the fractional part of ld will be truncated. In addition, the integer part in ld might be too large to fit in an int.

As presented here, the distinction might seem trivial—after all, we'd be unlikely to directly initialize an int from a long double. However, as we'll see in Chapter 16, such initializations might happen unintentionally. We'll say more about these forms of initialization in § 3.2.1 (p. 84) and § 3.3.1 (p. 98).

Default Initialization

When we define a variable without an initializer, the variable is **default initialized**. Such variables are given the "default" value. What that default value is depends on the type of the variable and may also depend on where the variable is defined.

The value of an object of built-in type that is not explicitly initialized depends on where it is defined. Variables defined outside any function body are initialized to zero. With one exception, which we cover in § 6.1.1 (p. 205), variables of built-in type defined inside a function are **uninitialized**. The value of an uninitialized variable of built-in type is undefined (§ 2.1.2, p. 36). It is an error to copy or otherwise try to access the value of a variable whose value is undefined.

Each class controls how we initialize objects of that class type. In particular, it is up to the class whether we can define objects of that type without an initializer. If we can, the class determines what value the resulting object will have.

Most classes let us define objects without explicit initializers. Such classes supply an appropriate default value for us. For example, as we've just seen, the library `string` class says that if we do not supply an initializer, then the resulting `string` is the empty string:

```
std::string empty;    // empty implicitly initialized to the empty string
Sales_item item;      // default-initialized Sales_item object
```

Some classes require that every object be explicitly initialized. The compiler will complain if we try to create an object of such a class with no initializer.

Uninitialized objects of built-in type defined inside a function body have undefined value. Objects of class type that we do not explicitly initialize have a value that is defined by the class.

EXERCISES SECTION 2.2.1

Exercise 2.9: Explain the following definitions. For those that are illegal, explain what's wrong and how to correct it.

    (a) `std::cin >> int input_value;`   (b) `int i = { 3.14 };`
    (c) `double salary = wage = 9999.99;`   (d) `int i = 3.14;`

Exercise 2.10: What are the initial values, if any, of each of the following variables?

```
std::string global_str;
int global_int;
int main()
{
    int local_int;
    std::string local_str;
}
```

 ## 2.2.2 Variable Declarations and Definitions

To allow programs to be written in logical parts, C++ supports what is commonly known as *separate compilation*. Separate compilation lets us split our programs into several files, each of which can be compiled independently.

When we separate a program into multiple files, we need a way to share code across those files. For example, code defined in one file may need to use a variable defined in another file. As a concrete example, consider `std::cout` and

---

CAUTION: UNINITIALIZED VARIABLES CAUSE RUN-TIME PROBLEMS

An uninitialized variable has an indeterminate value. Trying to use the value of an uninitialized variable is an error that is often hard to debug. Moreover, the compiler is not required to detect such errors, although most will warn about at least some uses of uninitialized variables.

What happens when we use an uninitialized variable is undefined. Sometimes, we're lucky and our program crashes as soon as we access the object. Once we track down the location of the crash, it is usually easy to see that the variable was not properly initialized. Other times, the program completes but produces erroneous results. Even worse, the results may appear correct on one run of our program but fail on a subsequent run. Moreover, adding code to the program in an unrelated location can cause what we thought was a correct program to start producing incorrect results.

 We recommend initializing every object of built-in type. It is not always necessary, but it is easier and safer to provide an initializer until you can be certain it is safe to omit the initializer.

`std::cin`. These are objects defined somewhere in the standard library, yet our programs can use these objects.

To support separate compilation, C++ distinguishes between declarations and definitions. A **declaration** makes a name known to the program. A file that wants to use a name defined elsewhere includes a declaration for that name. A **definition** creates the associated entity.

A variable declaration specifies the type and name of a variable. A variable definition is a declaration. In addition to specifying the name and type, a definition also allocates storage and may provide the variable with an initial value.

To obtain a declaration that is not also a definition, we add the `extern` keyword and may not provide an explicit initializer:

```
extern int i;    // declares but does not define i
int j;           // declares and defines j
```

Any declaration that includes an explicit initializer is a definition. We can provide an initializer on a variable defined as `extern`, but doing so overrides the `extern`. An `extern` that has an initializer is a definition:

```
extern double pi = 3.1416; // definition
```

It is an error to provide an initializer on an `extern` inside a function.

> Note Variables must be defined exactly once but can be declared many times.

The distinction between a declaration and a definition may seem obscure at this point but is actually important. To use a variable in more than one file requires declarations that are separate from the variable's definition. To use the same variable in multiple files, we must define that variable in one—and only one—file. Other files that use that variable must declare—but not define—that variable.

We'll have more to say about how C++ supports separate compilation in § 2.6.3 (p. 76) and § 6.1.3 (p. 207).

We'll have more to say about how C++ supports separate compilation in § 2.6.3 (p. 76) and § 6.1.3 (p. 207).

EXERCISES SECTION 2.2.2

Exercise 2.11: Explain whether each of the following is a declaration or a definition:

    (a) `extern int ix = 1024;`
    (b) `int iy;`
    (c) `extern int iz;`

KEY CONCEPT: STATIC TYPING

C++ is a *statically typed* language, which means that types are checked at compile time. The process by which types are checked is referred to as *type checking*.

As we've seen, the type of an object constrains the operations that the object can perform. In C++, the compiler checks whether the operations we write are supported by the types we use. If we try to do things that the type does not support, the compiler generates an error message and does not produce an executable file.

As our programs get more complicated, we'll see that static type checking can help find bugs. However, a consequence of static checking is that the type of every entity we use must be known to the compiler. As one example, we must declare the type of a variable before we can use that variable.

2.2.3 Identifiers

Identifiers in C++ can be composed of letters, digits, and the underscore character. The language imposes no limit on name length. Identifiers must begin with either a letter or an underscore. Identifiers are case-sensitive; upper- and lowercase letters are distinct:

```
//  defines four different int variables
int somename, someName, SomeName, SOMENAME;
```

The language reserves a set of names, listed in Tables 2.3 and Table 2.4, for its own use. These names may not be used as identifiers.

The standard also reserves a set of names for use in the standard library. The identifiers we define in our own programs may not contain two consecutive underscores, nor can an identifier begin with an underscore followed immediately by an uppercase letter. In addition, identifiers defined outside a function may not begin with an underscore.

Conventions for Variable Names

There are a number of generally accepted conventions for naming variables. Following these conventions can improve the readability of a program.

- An identifier should give some indication of its meaning.

- Variable names normally are lowercase—index, not Index or INDEX.

- Like Sales_item, classes we define usually begin with an uppercase letter.

- Identifiers with multiple words should visually distinguish each word, for example, student_loan or studentLoan, not studentloan.

Best Practices Naming conventions are most useful when followed consistently.

Table 2.3: C++ Keywords				
alignas	continue	friend	register	true
alignof	decltype	goto	reinterpret_cast	try
asm	default	if	return	typedef
auto	delete	inline	short	typeid
bool	do	int	signed	typename
break	double	long	sizeof	union
case	dynamic_cast	mutable	static	unsigned
catch	else	namespace	static_assert	using
char	enum	new	static_cast	virtual
char16_t	explicit	noexcept	struct	void
char32_t	export	nullptr	switch	volatile
class	extern	operator	template	wchar_t
const	false	private	this	while
constexpr	float	protected	thread_local	
const_cast	for	public	throw	

Table 2.4: C++ Alternative Operator Names					
and	bitand	compl	not_eq	or_eq	xor_eq
and_eq	bitor	not	or	xor	

EXERCISES SECTION 2.2.3

Exercise 2.12: Which, if any, of the following names are invalid?

(a) `int double = 3.14;`   (b) `int _;`
(c) `int catch-22;`   (d) `int 1_or_2 = 1;`
(e) `double Double = 3.14;`

2.2.4 Scope of a Name

At any particular point in a program, each name that is in use refers to a specific entity—a variable, function, type, and so on. However, a given name can be reused to refer to different entities at different points in the program.

A **scope** is a part of the program in which a name has a particular meaning. Most scopes in C++ are delimited by curly braces.

The same name can refer to different entities in different scopes. Names are visible from the point where they are declared until the end of the scope in which the declaration appears.

As an example, consider the program from § 1.4.2 (p. 13):

```
#include <iostream>
int main()
{
    int sum = 0;
    // sum values from 1 through 10 inclusive
    for (int val = 1; val <= 10; ++val)
        sum += val;  // equivalent to sum = sum + val
    std::cout << "Sum of 1 to 10 inclusive is "
              << sum << std::endl;
    return 0;
}
```

This program defines three names—main, sum, and val—and uses the namespace name std, along with two names from that namespace—cout and endl.

The name main is defined outside any curly braces. The name main—like most names defined outside a function—has **global scope**. Once declared, names at the global scope are accessible throughout the program. The name sum is defined within the scope of the block that is the body of the main function. It is accessible from its point of declaration throughout the rest of the main function but not outside of it. The variable sum has **block scope**. The name val is defined in the scope of the for statement. It can be used in that statement but not elsewhere in main.

> **ADVICE: DEFINE VARIABLES WHERE YOU FIRST USE THEM**
>
> It is usually a good idea to define an object near the point at which the object is first used. Doing so improves readability by making it easy to find the definition of the variable. More importantly, it is often easier to give the variable a useful initial value when the variable is defined close to where it is first used.

Nested Scopes

Scopes can contain other scopes. The contained (or nested) scope is referred to as an **inner scope**, the containing scope is the **outer scope**.

Once a name has been declared in a scope, that name can be used by scopes nested inside that scope. Names declared in the outer scope can also be redefined in an inner scope:

```
#include <iostream>
// Program for illustration purposes only: It is bad style for a function
// to use a global variable and also define a local variable with the same name
int reused = 42;  // reused has global scope
int main()
{
    int unique = 0; // unique has block scope
    // output #1: uses global reused; prints 42 0
    std::cout << reused << " " << unique << std::endl;
    int reused = 0; // new, local object named reused hides global reused
    // output #2: uses local reused; prints 0 0
    std::cout << reused << " " <<  unique << std::endl;
    // output #3: explicitly requests the global reused; prints 42 0
    std::cout << ::reused << " " <<  unique << std::endl;
    return 0;
}
```

Output #1 appears before the local definition of reused. Therefore, this output statement uses the name reused that is defined in the global scope. This statement prints 42 0. Output #2 occurs after the local definition of reused. The local reused is now **in scope**. Thus, this second output statement uses the local object named reused rather than the global one and prints 0 0. Output #3 uses the scope operator (§ 1.2, p. 8) to override the default scoping rules. The global scope has no name. Hence, when the scope operator has an empty left-hand side, it is a request to fetch the name on the right-hand side from the global scope. Thus, this expression uses the global reused and prints 42 0.

It is almost always a bad idea to define a local variable with the same name as a global variable that the function uses or might use.

Exercise 2.13: What is the value of j in the following program?

```
int i = 42;
int main()
{
    int i = 100;
    int j = i;
}
```

Exercise 2.14: Is the following program legal? If so, what values are printed?

```
int i = 100, sum = 0;
for (int i = 0; i != 10; ++i)
    sum += i;
std::cout << i << " " << sum << std::endl;
```

2.3 Compound Types

A **compound type** is a type that is defined in terms of another type. C++ has several compound types, two of which—references and pointers—we'll cover in this chapter.

Defining variables of compound type is more complicated than the declarations we've seen so far. In § 2.2 (p. 41) we said that simple declarations consist of a type followed by a list of variable names. More generally, a declaration is a **base type** followed by a list of **declarators**. Each declarator names a variable and gives the variable a type that is related to the base type.

The declarations we have seen so far have declarators that are nothing more than variable names. The type of such variables is the base type of the declaration. More complicated declarators specify variables with compound types that are built from the base type of the declaration.

2.3.1 References

> *Note* The new standard introduced a new kind of reference: an "rvalue reference," which we'll cover in § 13.6.1 (p. 532). These references are primarily intended for use inside classes. Technically speaking, when we use the term *reference*, we mean "lvalue reference."

A **reference** defines an alternative name for an object. A reference type "refers to" another type. We define a reference type by writing a declarator of the form &d, where d is the name being declared:

```
int ival = 1024;
int &refVal = ival;   //  refVal refers to (is another name for) ival
int &refVal2;         //  error: a reference must be initialized
```

Ordinarily, when we initialize a variable, the value of the initializer is copied into the object we are creating. When we define a reference, instead of copying the initializer's value, we **bind** the reference to its initializer. Once initialized, a reference remains bound to its initial object. There is no way to rebind a reference to refer to a different object. Because there is no way to rebind a reference, references *must* be initialized.

A Reference Is an Alias

> *Note* A reference is not an object. Instead, a reference is *just another name for an already existing object*.

After a reference has been defined, *all* operations on that reference are actually operations on the object to which the reference is bound:

```
refVal = 2;        //  assigns 2 to the object to which refVal refers, i.e., to ival
int ii = refVal;   //  same as ii = ival
```

When we assign to a reference, we are assigning to the object to which the reference is bound. When we fetch the value of a reference, we are really fetching the value of the object to which the reference is bound. Similarly, when we use a reference as an initializer, we are really using the object to which the reference is bound:

```
//  ok: refVal3 is bound to the object to which refVal is bound, i.e., to ival
int &refVal3 = refVal;
//  initializes i from the value in the object to which refVal is bound
int i = refVal;   //  ok: initializes i to the same value as ival
```

Because references are not objects, we may not define a reference to a reference.

Reference Definitions

We can define multiple references in a single definition. Each identifier that is a reference must be preceded by the & symbol:

```
int i = 1024, i2 = 2048;   //  i and i2 are both ints
int &r = i, r2 = i2;       //  r is a reference bound to i; r2 is an int
int i3 = 1024, &ri = i3;   //  i3 is an int; ri is a reference bound to i3
int &r3 = i3, &r4 = i2;    //  both r3 and r4 are references
```

With two exceptions that we'll cover in § 2.4.1 (p. 61) and § 15.2.3 (p. 601), the type of a reference and the object to which the reference refers must match exactly. Moreover, for reasons we'll explore in § 2.4.1, a reference may be bound only to an object, not to a literal or to the result of a more general expression:

```
int &refVal4 = 10;     //  error: initializer must be an object
double dval = 3.14;
int &refVal5 = dval; //  error: initializer must be an int object
```

EXERCISES SECTION 2.3.1

Exercise 2.15: Which of the following definitions, if any, are invalid? Why?

    (a) `int ival = 1.01;`   (b) `int &rval1 = 1.01;`
    (c) `int &rval2 = ival;`   (d) `int &rval3;`

Exercise 2.16: Which, if any, of the following assignments are invalid? If they are valid, explain what they do.

```
int i = 0, &r1 = i; double d = 0, &r2 = d;
```
    (a) `r2 = 3.14159;`   (b) `r2 = r1;`
    (c) `i = r2;`   (d) `r1 = d;`

Exercise 2.17: What does the following code print?

```
int i, &ri = i;
i = 5; ri = 10;
std::cout << i << " " << ri << std::endl;
```

2.3.2 Pointers

A **pointer** is a compound type that "points to" another type. Like references, pointers are used for indirect access to other objects. Unlike a reference, a pointer is an
object in its own right. Pointers can be assigned and copied; a single pointer can
point to several different objects over its lifetime. Unlike a reference, a pointer
need not be initialized at the time it is defined. Like other built-in types, pointers
defined at block scope have undefined value if they are not initialized.

> ⚠ **WARNING** Pointers are often hard to understand. Debugging problems due to
> pointer errors bedevil even experienced programmers.

We define a pointer type by writing a declarator of the form *d, where d is the
name being defined. The * must be repeated for each pointer variable:

```
int *ip1, *ip2;  // both ip1 and ip2 are pointers to int
double dp, *dp2; // dp2 is a pointer to double; dp is a double
```

Taking the Address of an Object

A pointer holds the address of another object. We get the address of an object by
usin the address-of operator (the **& operator**):

```
int ival = 42;
int *p = &ival; // p holds the address of ival; p is a pointer to ival
```

The second statement defines p as a pointer to int and initializes p to point to
the int object named ival. Because references are not objects, they don't have
addresses. Hence, we may not define a pointer to a reference.

With two exceptions, which we cover in § 2.4.2 (p. 62) and § 15.2.3 (p. 601), the
types of the pointer and the object to which it points must match:

```
double dval;
double *pd = &dval;  // ok: initializer is the address of a double
double *pd2 = pd;    // ok: initializer is a pointer to double

int *pi = pd;  // error: types of pi and pd differ
pi = &dval;    // error: assigning the address of a double to a pointer to int
```

The types must match because the type of the pointer is used to infer the type of
the object to which the pointer points. If a pointer addressed an object of another
type, operations performed on the underlying object would fail.

Pointer Value

The value (i.e., the address) stored in a pointer can be in one of four states:

1. It can point to an object.

2. It can point to the location just immediately past the end of an object.

3. It can be a null pointer, indicating that it is not bound to any object.

4. It can be invalid; values other than the preceding three are invalid.

It is an error to copy or otherwise try to access the value of an invalid pointer. As when we use an uninitialized variable, this error is one that the compiler is unlikely to detect. The result of accessing an invalid pointer is undefined. Therefore, we must always know whether a given pointer is valid.

Although pointers in cases 2 and 3 are valid, there are limits on what we can do with such pointers. Because these pointers do not point to any object, we may not use them to access the (supposed) object to which the pointer points. If we do attempt to access an object through such pointers, the behavior is undefined.

Using a Pointer to Access an Object

When a pointer points to an object, we can use the dereference operator (the ***** **operator**) to access that object:

```
int ival = 42;
int *p = &ival; // p holds the address of ival; p is a pointer to ival
cout << *p;     // * yields the object to which p points; prints 42
```

Dereferencing a pointer yields the object to which the pointer points. We can assign to that object by assigning to the result of the dereference:

```
*p = 0;         // * yields the object; we assign a new value to ival through p
cout << *p; // prints 0
```

When we assign to *p, we are assigning to the object to which p points.

> *Note* We may dereference only a valid pointer that points to an object.

KEY CONCEPT: SOME SYMBOLS HAVE MULTIPLE MEANINGS

Some symbols, such as & and *, are used as both an operator in an expression and as part of a declaration. The context in which a symbol is used determines what the symbol means:

```
int i = 42;
int &r = i;     // & follows a type and is part of a declaration; r is a reference
int *p;         // * follows a type and is part of a declaration; p is a pointer
p = &i;         // & is used in an expression as the address-of operator
*p = i;         // * is used in an expression as the dereference operator
int &r2 = *p;   // & is part of the declaration; * is the dereference operator
```

In declarations, & and * are used to form compound types. In expressions, these same symbols are used to denote an operator. Because the same symbol is used with very different meanings, it can be helpful to ignore appearances and think of them as if they were different symbols.

Null Pointers

A **null pointer** does not point to any object. Code can check whether a pointer is null before attempting to use it. There are several ways to obtain a null pointer:

```
int *p1 = nullptr;  // equivalent to int *p1 = 0;
int *p2 = 0;        // directly initializes p2 from the literal constant 0
// must #include cstdlib
int *p3 = NULL;     // equivalent to int *p3 = 0;
```

The most direct approach is to initialize the pointer using the literal **nullptr**, which was introduced by the new standard. nullptr is a literal that has a special type that can be converted (§ 2.1.2, p. 35) to any other pointer type. Alternatively, we can initialize a pointer to the literal 0, as we do in the definition of p2.

Older programs sometimes use a **preprocessor variable** named NULL, which the cstdlib header defines as 0.

We'll describe the preprocessor in a bit more detail in § 2.6.3 (p. 77). What's useful to know now is that the preprocessor is a program that runs before the compiler. Preprocessor variables are managed by the preprocessor, and are not part of the std namespace. As a result, we refer to them directly without the std:: prefix.

When we use a preprocessor variable, the preprocessor automatically replaces the variable by its value. Hence, initializing a pointer to NULL is equivalent to initializing it to 0. Modern C++ programs generally should avoid using NULL and use nullptr instead.

It is illegal to assign an int variable to a pointer, even if the variable's value happens to be 0.

```
int zero = 0;
pi = zero;          // error: cannot assign an int to a pointer
```

ADVICE: INITIALIZE ALL POINTERS

Uninitialized pointers are a common source of run-time errors.

As with any other uninitialized variable, what happens when we use an uninitialized pointer is undefined. Using an uninitialized pointer almost always results in a run-time crash. However, debugging the resulting crashes can be surprisingly hard.

Under most compilers, when we use an uninitialized pointer, the bits in the memory in which the pointer resides are used as an address. Using an uninitialized pointer is a request to access a supposed object at that supposed location. There is no way to distinguish a valid address from an invalid one formed from the bits that happen to be in the memory in which the pointer was allocated.

Our recommendation to initialize all variables is particularly important for pointers. If possible, define a pointer only after the object to which it should point has been defined. If there is no object to bind to a pointer, then initialize the pointer to nullptr or zero. That way, the program can detect that the pointer does not point to an object.

Assignment and Pointers

Both pointers and references give indirect access to other objects. However, there are important differences in how they do so. The most important is that a reference is not an object. Once we have defined a reference, there is no way to make that reference refer to a different object. When we use a reference, we always get the object to which the reference was initially bound.

There is no such identity between a pointer and the address that it holds. As with any other (nonreference) variable, when we assign to a pointer, we give the pointer itself a new value. Assignment makes the pointer point to a different object:

```
int i = 42;
int *pi = 0;      //  pi is initialized but addresses no object
int *pi2 = &i;    //  pi2 initialized to hold the address of i
int *pi3;         //  if pi3 is defined inside a block, pi3 is uninitialized

pi3 = pi2;        //  pi3 and pi2 address the same object, e.g., i
pi2 = 0;          //  pi2 now addresses no object
```

It can be hard to keep straight whether an assignment changes the pointer or the object to which the pointer points. The important thing to keep in mind is that assignment changes its left-hand operand. When we write

```
pi = &ival; // value in pi is changed; pi now points to ival
```

we assign a new value to pi, which changes the address that pi holds. On the other hand, when we write

```
*pi = 0;     // value in ival is changed; pi is unchanged
```

then *pi (i.e., the value to which pi points) is changed.

Other Pointer Operations

So long as the pointer has a valid value, we can use a pointer in a condition. Just as when we use an arithmetic value in a condition (§ 2.1.2, p. 35), if the pointer is 0, then the condition is false:

```
int ival = 1024;
int *pi = 0;          //  pi is a valid, null pointer
int *pi2 = &ival;     //  pi2 is a valid pointer that holds the address of ival
if (pi)   //  pi has value 0, so condition evaluates as false
    //  ...
if (pi2) //  pi2 points to ival, so it is not 0; the condition evaluates as true
    //  ...
```

Any nonzero pointer evaluates as true

Given two valid pointers of the same type, we can compare them using the equality (==) or inequality (!=) operators. The result of these operators has type bool. Two pointers are equal if they hold the same address and unequal otherwise. Two pointers hold the same address (i.e., are equal) if they are both null, if they address the same object, or if they are both pointers one past the same object. Note that it is possible for a pointer to an object and a pointer one past the end of a different object to hold the same address. Such pointers will compare equal.

Because these operations use the value of the pointer, a pointer used in a condition or in a comparsion must be a valid pointer. Using an invalid pointer as a condition or in a comparison is undefined.

§ 3.5.3 (p. 117) will cover additional pointer operations.

void* Pointers

The type **void*** is a special pointer type that can hold the address of any object. Like any other pointer, a void* pointer holds an address, but the type of the object at that address is unknown:

```
double obj = 3.14, *pd = &obj;
// ok: void* can hold the address value of any data pointer type
void *pv = &obj;   // obj can be an object of any type
pv = pd;           // pv can hold a pointer to any type
```

There are only a limited number of things we can do with a void* pointer: We can compare it to another pointer, we can pass it to or return it from a function, and we can assign it to another void* pointer. We cannot use a void* to operate on the object it addresses—we don't know that object's type, and the type determines what operations we can perform on the object.

Generally, we use a void* pointer to deal with memory as memory, rather than using the pointer to access the object stored in that memory. We'll cover using void* pointers in this way in § 19.1.1 (p. 821). § 4.11.3 (p. 163) will show how we can retrieve the address stored in a void* pointer.

EXERCISES SECTION 2.3.2

Exercise 2.18: Write code to change the value of a pointer. Write code to change the value to which the pointer points.

Exercise 2.19: Explain the key differences between pointers and references.

Exercise 2.20: What does the following program do?

```
int i = 42;
int *p1 = &i;
*p1 = *p1 * *p1;
```

Exercise 2.21: Explain each of the following definitions. Indicate whether any are illegal and, if so, why.

```
int i = 0;
(a) double* dp = &i;   (b) int *ip = i;   (c) int *p = &i;
```

Exercise 2.22: Assuming p is a pointer to int, explain the following code:

```
if (p) // ...
if (*p) // ...
```

Exercise 2.23: Given a pointer p, can you determine whether p points to a valid object? If so, how? If not, why not?

Exercise 2.24: Why is the initialization of p legal but that of lp illegal?

```
int i = 42;    void *p = &i;    long *lp = &i;
```

2.3.3   Understanding Compound Type Declarations

As we've seen, a variable definition consists of a base type and a list of declarators. Each declarator can relate its variable to the base type differently from the other declarators in the same definition. Thus, a single definition might define variables of different types:

```
//  i is an int; p is a pointer to int; r is a reference to int
int i = 1024, *p = &i, &r = i;
```

 WARNING Many programmers are confused by the interaction between the base type and the type modification that may be part of a declarator.

Defining Multiple Variables

It is a common misconception to think that the type modifier (* or &) applies to all the variables defined in a single statement. Part of the problem arises because we can put whitespace between the type modifier and the name being declared:

```
int* p;    // legal but might be misleading
```

We say that this definition might be misleading because it suggests that int* is the type of each variable declared in that statement. Despite appearances, the base type of this declaration is int, not int*. The * modifies the type of p. It says nothing about any other objects that might be declared in the same statement:

```
int* p1, p2; // p1 is a pointer to int; p2 is an int
```

There are two common styles used to define multiple variables with pointer or reference type. The first places the type modifier adjacent to the identifier:

```
int *p1, *p2; // both p1 and p2 are pointers to int
```

This style emphasizes that the variable has the indicated compound type.

The second places the type modifier with the type but defines only one variable per statement:

```
int* p1;        // p1 is a pointer to int
int* p2;        // p2 is a pointer to int
```

This style emphasizes that the declaration defines a compound type.

Tip There is no single right way to define pointers or references. The important thing is to choose a style and use it consistently.

In this book we use the first style and place the * (or the &) with the variable name.

Pointers to Pointers

In general, there are no limits to how many type modifiers can be applied to a declarator. When there is more than one modifier, they combine in ways that are logical but not always obvious. As one example, consider a pointer. A pointer is an object in memory, so like any object it has an address. Therefore, we can store the address of a pointer in another pointer.

We indicate each pointer level by its own *. That is, we write ** for a pointer to a pointer, *** for a pointer to a pointer to a pointer, and so on:

```
int ival = 1024;
int *pi = &ival;      //  pi points to an int
int **ppi = &pi;      //  ppi points to a pointer to an int
```

Here pi is a pointer to an int and ppi is a pointer to a pointer to an int. We might represent these objects as

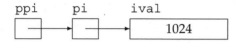

Just as dereferencing a pointer to an int yields an int, dereferencing a pointer to a pointer yields a pointer. To access the underlying object, we must dereference the original pointer twice:

```
cout << "The value of ival\n"
     << "direct value: " << ival << "\n"
     << "indirect value: " << *pi << "\n"
     << "doubly indirect value: " << **ppi
     << endl;
```

This program prints the value of ival three different ways: first, directly; then, through the pointer to int in pi; and finally, by dereferencing ppi twice to get to the underlying value in ival.

References to Pointers

A reference is not an object. Hence, we may not have a pointer to a reference. However, because a pointer is an object, we can define a reference to a pointer:

```
int i = 42;
int *p;        //  p is a pointer to int
int *&r = p;   //  r is a reference to the pointer p

r = &i; //  r refers to a pointer; assigning &i to r makes p point to i
*r = 0; //  dereferencing r yields i, the object to which p points; changes i to 0
```

The easiest way to understand the type of r is to read the definition right to left. The symbol closest to the name of the variable (in this case the & in &r) is the one that has the most immediate effect on the variable's type. Thus, we know that r is a reference. The rest of the declarator determines the type to which r refers. The next symbol, * in this case, says that the type r refers to is a pointer type. Finally, the base type of the declaration says that r is a reference to a pointer to an int.

> It can be easier to understand complicated pointer or reference declarations if you read them from right to left.

EXERCISES SECTION 2.3.3

Exercise 2.25: Determine the types and values of each of the following variables.

    (a) `int* ip, &r = ip;`   (b) `int i, *ip = 0;`   (c) `int* ip, ip2;`

2.4 const Qualifier

Sometimes we want to define a variable whose value we know cannot be changed. For example, we might want to use a variable to refer to the size of a buffer size. Using a variable makes it easy for us to change the size of the buffer if we decided the original size wasn't what we needed. On the other hand, we'd also like to prevent code from inadvertently giving a new value to the variable we use to represent the buffer size. We can make a variable unchangeable by defining the variable's type as **const**:

```
const int bufSize = 512;      // input buffer size
```

defines `bufSize` as a constant. Any attempt to assign to `bufSize` is an error:

```
bufSize = 512; //  error: attempt to write to const object
```

Because we can't change the value of a `const` object after we create it, it must be initialized. As usual, the initializer may be an arbitrarily complicated expression:

```
const int i = get_size();  //  ok: initialized at run time
const int j = 42;          //  ok: initialized at compile time
const int k;               //  error: k is uninitialized const
```

Initialization and const

As we have observed many times, the type of an object defines the operations that can be performed by that object. A `const` type can use most but not all of the same operations as its nonconst version. The one restriction is that we may use only those operations that cannot change an object. So, for example, we can use a `const int` in arithmetic expressions in exactly the same way as a plain, nonconst `int`. A `const int` converts to `bool` the same way as a plain `int`, and so on.

Among the operations that don't change the value of an object is initialization—when we use an object to initialize another object, it doesn't matter whether either or both of the objects are `const`s:

```
int i = 42;
const int ci = i;  //  ok: the value in i is copied into ci
int j = ci;        //  ok: the value in ci is copied into j
```

Although `ci` is a `const int`, the value in `ci` is an `int`. The constness of `ci` matters only for operations that might change `ci`. When we copy `ci` to initialize `j`, we don't care that `ci` is a `const`. Copying an object doesn't change that object. Once the copy is made, the new object has no further access to the original object.

By Default, `const` Objects Are Local to a File

When a `const` object is initialized from a compile-time constant, such as in our definition of `bufSize`:

```
const int bufSize = 512;      //  input buffer size
```

the compiler will usually replace uses of the variable with its corresponding value during compilation. That is, the compiler will generate code using the value `512` in the places that our code uses `bufSize`.

To substitute the value for the variable, the compiler has to see the variable's initializer. When we split a program into multiple files, every file that uses the `const` must have access to its initializer. In order to see the initializer, the variable must be defined in every file that wants to use the variable's value (§ 2.2.2, p. 45). To support this usage, yet avoid multiple definitions of the same variable, `const` variables are defined as local to the file. When we define a `const` with the same name in multiple files, it is as if we had written definitions for separate variables in each file.

Sometimes we have a `const` variable that we want to share across multiple files but whose initializer is not a constant expression. In this case, we don't want the compiler to generate a separate variable in each file. Instead, we want the `const` object to behave like other (nonconst) variables. We want to define the `const` in one file, and declare it in the other files that use that object.

To define a single instance of a `const` variable, we use the keyword `extern` on both its definition and declaration(s):

```
//  file_1.cc defines and initializes a const that is accessible to other files
extern const int bufSize = fcn();
//  file_1.h
extern const int bufSize; //  same bufSize as defined in file_1.cc
```

In this program, `file_1.cc` defines and initializes `bufSize`. Because this declaration includes an initializer, it is (as usual) a definition. However, because `bufSize` is `const`, we must specify `extern` in order for `bufSize` to be used in other files.

The declaration in `file_1.h` is also `extern`. In this case, the `extern` signifies that `bufSize` is not local to this file and that its definition will occur elsewhere.

> *Note* To share a `const` object among multiple files, you must define the variable as `extern`.

EXERCISES SECTION 2.4

Exercise 2.26: Which of the following are legal? For those that are illegal, explain why.

(a) `const int buf;`	(b) `int cnt = 0;`
(c) `const int sz = cnt;`	(d) `++cnt; ++sz;`

2.4.1 References to const

As with any other object, we can bind a reference to an object of a const type. To do so we use a **reference to const**, which is a reference that refers to a const type. Unlike an ordinary reference, a reference to const cannot be used to change the object to which the reference is bound:

```
const int ci = 1024;
const int &r1 =  ci;   // ok: both reference and underlying object are const
r1 = 42;               // error: r1 is a reference to const
int &r2 = ci;          // error: nonconst reference to a const object
```

Because we cannot assign directly to ci, we also should not be able to use a reference to change ci. Therefore, the initialization of r2 is an error. If this initialization were legal, we could use r2 to change the value of its underlying object.

TERMINOLOGY: const REFERENCE IS A REFERENCE TO const

C++ programmers tend to abbreviate the phrase "reference to const" as "const reference." This abbreviation makes sense—if you remember that it is an abbreviation.

Technically speaking, there are no const references. A reference is not an object, so we cannot make a reference itself const. Indeed, because there is no way to make a reference refer to a different object, in some sense all references are const. Whether a reference refers to a const or nonconst type affects what we can do with that reference, not whether we can alter the binding of the reference itself.

Initialization and References to const

In § 2.3.1 (p. 51) we noted that there are two exceptions to the rule that the type of a reference must match the type of the object to which it refers. The first exception is that we can initialize a reference to const from any expression that can be converted (§ 2.1.2, p. 35) to the type of the reference. In particular, we can bind a reference to const to a nonconst object, a literal, or a more general expression:

```
int i = 42;
const int &r1 = i;      // we can bind a const int& to a plain int object
const int &r2 = 42;     // ok: r1 is a reference to const
const int &r3 = r1 * 2; // ok: r3 is a reference to const
int &r4 = r * 2;        // error: r4 is a plain, nonconst reference
```

The easiest way to understand this difference in initialization rules is to consider what happens when we bind a reference to an object of a different type:

```
double dval = 3.14;
const int &ri = dval;
```

Here ri refers to an int. Operations on ri will be integer operations, but dval is a floating-point number, not an integer. To ensure that the object to which ri is bound is an int, the compiler transforms this code into something like

```
const int temp = dval;    // create a temporary const int from the double
const int &ri = temp;     // bind ri to that temporary
```

In this case, `ri` is bound to a **temporary** object. A temporary object is an unnamed object created by the compiler when it needs a place to store a result from evaluating an expression. C++ programmers often use the word temporary as an abbreviation for temporary object.

Now consider what could happen if this initialization were allowed but `ri` was not `const`. If `ri` weren't `const`, we could assign to `ri`. Doing so would change the object to which `ri` is bound. That object is a temporary, not `dval`. The programmer who made `ri` refer to `dval` would probably expect that assigning to `ri` would change `dval`. After all, why assign to `ri` unless the intent is to change the object to which `ri` is bound? Because binding a reference to a temporary is almost surely *not* what the programmer intended, the language makes it illegal.

A Reference to `const` May Refer to an Object That Is Not `const`

It is important to realize that a reference to `const` restricts only what we can do through that reference. Binding a reference to `const` to an object says nothing about whether the underlying object itself is `const`. Because the underlying object might be nonconst, it might be changed by other means:

```
int i = 42;
int &r1 = i;              // r1 bound to i
const int &r2 = i;        // r2 also bound to i; but cannot be used to change i
r1 = 0;                   // r1 is not const; i is now 0
r2 = 0;                   // error: r2 is a reference to const
```

Binding `r2` to the (nonconst) `int` `i` is legal. However, we cannot use `r2` to change `i`. Even so, the value in `i` still might change. We can change `i` by assigning to it directly, or by assigning to another reference bound to `i`, such as `r1`.

 ## 2.4.2 Pointers and `const`

As with references, we can define pointers that point to either `const` or nonconst types. Like a reference to `const`, a **pointer to `const`** (§ 2.4.1, p. 61) may not be used to change the object to which the pointer points. We may store the address of a `const` object only in a pointer to `const`:

```
const double pi = 3.14;   // pi is const; its value may not be changed
double *ptr = &pi;        // error: ptr is a plain pointer
const double *cptr = &pi; // ok: cptr may point to a double that is const
*cptr = 42;               // error: cannot assign to *cptr
```

In § 2.3.2 (p. 52) we noted that there are two exceptions to the rule that the types of a pointer and the object to which it points must match. The first exception is that we can use a pointer to `const` to point to a nonconst object:

```
double dval = 3.14;       // dval is a double; its value can be changed
cptr = &dval;             // ok: but can't change dval through cptr
```

Like a reference to const, a pointer to const says nothing about whether the object to which the pointer points is const. Defining a pointer as a pointer to const affects only what we can do with the pointer. It is important to remember that there is no guarantee that an object pointed to by a pointer to const won't change.

 It may be helpful to think of pointers and references to const as pointers or references "that *think* they point or refer to const."

const Pointers

Unlike references, pointers are objects. Hence, as with any other object type, we can have a pointer that is itself const. Like any other const object, a **const pointer** must be initialized, and once initialized, its value (i.e., the address that it holds) may not be changed. We indicate that the pointer is const by putting the const after the *. This placement indicates that it is the pointer, not the pointed-to type, that is const:

```
int errNumb = 0;
int *const curErr = &errNumb;   // curErr will always point to errNumb
const double pi = 3.14159;
const double *const pip = &pi; // pip is a const pointer to a const object
```

As we saw in § 2.3.3 (p. 58), the easiest way to understand these declarations is to read them from right to left. In this case, the symbol closest to curErr is const, which means that curErr itself will be a const object. The type of that object is formed from the rest of the declarator. The next symbol in the declarator is *, which means that curErr is a const pointer. Finally, the base type of the declaration completes the type of curErr, which is a const pointer to an object of type int. Similarly, pip is a const pointer to an object of type const double.

The fact that a pointer is itself const says nothing about whether we can use the pointer to change the underlying object. Whether we can change that object depends entirely on the type to which the pointer points. For example, pip is a const pointer to const. Neither the value of the object addressed by pip nor the address stored in pip can be changed. On the other hand, curErr addresses a plain, nonconst int. We can use curErr to change the value of errNumb:

```
*pip = 2.72;      // error: pip is a pointer to const
// if the object to which curErr points (i.e., errNumb) is nonzero
if (*curErr) {
    errorHandler();
    *curErr = 0; // ok: reset the value of the object to which curErr is bound
}
```

2.4.3 Top-Level const

As we've seen, a pointer is an object that can point to a different object. As a result, we can talk independently about whether a pointer is const and whether

---

EXERCISES SECTION 2.4.2

Exercise 2.27: Which of the following initializations are legal? Explain why.

(a) `int i = -1, &r = 0;`   (b) `int *const p2 = &i2;`
(c) `const int i = -1, &r = 0;` (d) `const int *const p3 = &i2;`
(e) `const int *p1 = &i2;`   (f) `const int &const r2;`
(g) `const int i2 = i, &r = i;`

Exercise 2.28: Explain the following definitions. Identify any that are illegal.

(a) `int i, *const cp;`   (b) `int *p1, *const p2;`
(c) `const int ic, &r = ic;`   (d) `const int *const p3;`
(e) `const int *p;`

Exercise 2.29: Uing the variables in the previous exercise, which of the following assignments are legal? Explain why.

(a) `i = ic;`   (b) `p1 = p3;`
(c) `p1 = &ic;`   (d) `p3 = &ic;`
(e) `p2 = p1;`   (f) `ic = *p3;`

---

the objects to which it can point are `const`. We use the term **top-level `const`** to indicate that the pointer itself is a `const`. When a pointer can point to a `const` object, we refer to that `const` as a **low-level `const`**.

More generally, top-level `const` indicates that an object itself is `const`. Top-level `const` can appear in any object type, i.e., one of the built-in arithmetic types, a class type, or a pointer type. Low-level `const` appears in the base type of compound types such as pointers or references. Note that pointer types, unlike most other types, can have both top-level and low-level `const` independently:

```
int i = 0;
int *const p1 = &i;    // we can't change the value of p1; const is top-level
const int ci = 42;     // we cannot change ci; const is top-level
const int *p2 = &ci;   // we can change p2; const is low-level
const int *const p3 = p2; // right-most const is top-level, left-most is not
const int &r = ci;     // const in reference types is always low-level
```

The distinction between top-level and low-level matters when we copy an object. When we copy an object, top-level `const`s are ignored:

```
i = ci;   // ok: copying the value of ci; top-level const in ci is ignored
p2 = p3;  // ok: pointed-to type matches; top-level const in p3 is ignored
```

Copying an object doesn't change the copied object. As a result, it is immaterial whether the object copied from or copied into is `const`.

On the other hand, low-level `const` is never ignored. When we copy an object, both objects must have the same low-level `const` qualification or there must be a conversion between the types of the two objects. In general, we can convert a nonconst to `const` but not the other way round:

```
int *p = p3;   // error: p3 has a low-level const but p doesn't
p2 = p3;       // ok: p2 has the same low-level const qualification as p3
p2 = &i;       // ok: we can convert int* to const int*
int &r = ci;   // error: can't bind an ordinary int& to a const int object
const int &r2 = i;  // ok: can bind const int& to plain int
```

p3 has both a top-level and low-level const. When we copy p3, we can ignore its top-level const but not the fact that it points to a const type. Hence, we cannot use p3 to initialize p, which points to a plain (nonconst) int. On the other hand, we can assign p3 to p2. Both pointers have the same (low-level const) type. The fact that p3 is a const pointer (i.e., that it has a top-level const) doesn't matter.

EXERCISES SECTION 2.4.3

Exercise 2.30: For each of the following declarations indicate whether the object being declared has top-level or low-level const.

```
const int v2 = 0;     int v1 = v2;
int *p1 = &v1, &r1 = v1;
const int *p2 = &v2, *const p3 = &i, &r2 = v2;
```

Exercise 2.31: Given the declarations in the previous exercise determine whether the following assignments are legal. Explain how the top-level or low-level const applies in each case.

```
r1 = v2;
p1 = p2;     p2 = p1;
p1 = p3;     p2 = p3;
```

2.4.4 constexpr and Constant Expressions

A **constant expression** is an expression whose value cannot change and that can be evaluated at compile time. A literal is a constant expression. A const object that is initialized from a constant expression is also a constant expression. As we'll see, there are several contexts in the language that require constant expressions.

Whether a given object (or expression) is a constant expression depends on the types and the initializers. For example:

```
const int max_files = 20;     // max_files is a constant expression
const int limit = max_files + 1; // limit is a constant expression
int staff_size = 27;          // staff_size is not a constant expression
const int sz = get_size();    // sz is not a constant expression
```

Although staff_size is initialized from a literal, it is not a constant expression because it is a plain int, not a const int. On the other hand, even though sz is a const, the value of its initializer is not known until run time. Hence, sz is not a constant expression.

`constexpr` Variables

In a large system, it can be difficult to determine (for certain) that an initializer is a constant expression. We might define a `const` variable with an initializer that we think is a constant expression. However, when we use that variable in a context that requires a constant expression we may discover that the initializer was not a constant expression. In general, the definition of an object and its use in such a context can be widely separated.

 Under the new standard, we can ask the compiler to verify that a variable is a constant expression by declaring the variable in a **constexpr** declaration. Variables declared as `constexpr` are implicitly `const` and must be initialized by constant expressions:

```
constexpr int mf = 20;        //  20 is a constant expression
constexpr int limit = mf + 1; //  mf + 1 is a constant expression
constexpr int sz = size();    //  ok only if size is a constexpr function
```

Although we cannot use an ordinary function as an initializer for a `constexpr` variable, we'll see in § 6.5.2 (p. 239) that the new standard lets us define certain functions as `constexpr`. Such functions must be simple enough that the compiler can evaluate them at compile time. We can use `constexpr` functions in the initializer of a `constexpr` variable.

> **Best Practices** Generally, it is a good idea to use `constexpr` for variables that you intend to use as constant expressions.

Literal Types

Because a constant expression is one that can be evaluated at compile time, there are limits on the types that we can use in a `constexpr` declaration. The types we can use in a `constexpr` are known as "literal types" because they are simple enough to have literal values.

Of the types we have used so far, the arithmetic, reference, and pointer types are literal types. Our `Sales_item` class and the library IO and `string` types are not literal types. Hence, we cannot define variables of these types as `constexprs`. We'll see other kinds of literal types in § 7.5.6 (p. 299) and § 19.3 (p. 832).

Although we can define both pointers and reference as `constexprs`, the objects we use to initialize them are strictly limited. We can initialize a `constexpr` pointer from the `nullptr` literal or the literal (i.e., constant expression) `0`. We can also point to (or bind to) an object that remains at a fixed address.

For reasons we'll cover in § 6.1.1 (p. 204), variables defined inside a function ordinarily are not stored at a fixed address. Hence, we cannot use a `constexpr` pointer to point to such variables. On the other hand, the address of an object defined outside of any function is a constant expression, and so may be used to initialize a `constexpr` pointer. We'll see in § 6.1.1 (p. 205), that functions may define variables that exist across calls to that function. Like an object defined outside any function, these special local objects also have fixed addresses. Therefore, a `constexpr` reference may be bound to, and a `constexpr` pointer may address, such variables.

Pointers and `constexpr`

It is important to understand that when we define a pointer in a `constexpr` declaration, the `constexpr` specifier applies to the pointer, not the type to which the pointer points:

```
const int *p = nullptr;     // p is a pointer to a const int
constexpr int *q = nullptr; // q is a const pointer to int
```

Despite appearances, the types of p and q are quite different; p is a pointer to const, whereas q is a constant pointer. The difference is a consequence of the fact that `constexpr` imposes a top-level `const` (§ 2.4.3, p. 63) on the objects it defines.

Like any other constant pointer, a `constexpr` pointer may point to a `const` or a nonconst type:

```
constexpr int *np = nullptr; // np is a constant pointer to int that is null
int j = 0;
constexpr int i = 42;    // type of i is const int
//  i and j must be defined outside any function
constexpr const int *p = &i; // p is a constant pointer to the const int i
constexpr int *p1 = &j;      // p1 is a constant pointer to the int j
```

Exercise 2.32: Is the following code legal or not? If not, how might you make it legal?

```
int null = 0, *p = null;
```

2.5 Dealing with Types

As our programs get more complicated, we'll see that the types we use also get more complicated. Complications in using types arise in two different ways. Some types are hard to "spell." That is, they have forms that are tedious and error-prone to write. Moreover, the form of a complicated type can obscure its purpose or meaning. The other source of complication is that sometimes it is hard to determine the exact type we need. Doing so can require us to look back into the context of the program.

2.5.1 Type Aliases

A **type alias** is a name that is a synonym for another type. Type aliases let us simplify complicated type definitions, making those types easier to use. Type aliases also let us emphasize the purpose for which a type is used.

We can define a type alias in one of two ways. Traditionally, we use a **typedef**:

```
typedef double wages;     // wages is a synonym for double
typedef wages base, *p;   // base is a synonym for double, p for double*
```

The keyword `typedef` may appear as part of the base type of a declaration (§ 2.3, p. 50). Declarations that include `typedef` define type aliases rather than variables. As in any other declaration, the declarators can include type modifiers that define compound types built from the base type of the definition.

The new standard introduced a second way to define a type alias, via an **alias declaration**:

```
using SI = Sales_item;   // SI is a synonym for Sales_item
```

An alias declaration starts with the keyword `using` followed by the alias name and an `=`. The alias declaration defines the name on the left-hand side of the `=` as an alias for the type that appears on the right-hand side.

A type alias is a type name and can appear wherever a type name can appear:

```
wages hourly, weekly;    // same as double hourly, weekly;
SI item;                 // same as Sales_item item
```

Pointers, `const`, and Type Aliases

Declarations that use type aliases that represent compound types and `const` can yield surprising results. For example, the following declarations use the type `pstring`, which is an alias for the the type `char*`:

```
typedef char *pstring;
const pstring cstr = 0; // cstr is a constant pointer to char
const pstring *ps;      // ps is a pointer to a constant pointer to char
```

The base type in these declarations is `const pstring`. As usual, a `const` that appears in the base type modifies the given type. The type of `pstring` is "pointer to `char`." So, `const pstring` is a constant pointer to `char`—not a pointer to `const char`.

It can be tempting, albeit incorrect, to interpret a declaration that uses a type alias by conceptually replacing the alias with its corresponding type:

```
const char *cstr = 0;  // wrong interpretation of const pstring cstr
```

However, this interpretation is wrong. When we use `pstring` in a declaration, the base type of the declaration is a pointer type. When we rewrite the declaration using `char*`, the base type is `char` and the `*` is part of the declarator. In this case, `const char` is the base type. This rewrite declares `cstr` as a pointer to `const char` rather than as a `const` pointer to `char`.

2.5.2 The `auto` Type Specifier

It is not uncommon to want to store the value of an expression in a variable. To declare the variable, we have to know the type of that expression. When we write a program, it can be surprisingly difficult—and sometimes even impossible—to determine the type of an expression. Under the new standard, we can let the compiler figure out the type for us by using the **auto** type specifier. Unlike type specifiers, such as `double`, that name a specific type, `auto` tells the compiler to deduce the type from the initializer. By implication, a variable that uses `auto` as its type specifier must have an initializer:

```
//  the type of item is deduced from the type of the result of adding val1 and val2
auto item = val1 + val2;  //  item initialized to the result of val1 + val2
```

Here the compiler will deduce the type of `item` from the type returned by applying `+` to `val1` and `val2`. If `val1` and `val2` are `Sales_item` objects (§ 1.5, p. 19), `item` will have type `Sales_item`. If those variables are type `double`, then `item` has type `double`, and so on.

As with any other type specifier, we can define multiple variables using `auto`. Because a declaration can involve only a single base type, the initializers for all the variables in the declaration must have types that are consistent with each other:

```
auto i = 0, *p = &i;      //  ok: i is int and p is a pointer to int
auto sz = 0, pi = 3.14;   //  error: inconsistent types for sz and pi
```

Compound Types, `const`, and `auto`

The type that the compiler infers for `auto` is not always exactly the same as the initializer's type. Instead, the compiler adjusts the type to conform to normal initialization rules.

First, as we've seen, when we use a reference, we are really using the object to which the reference refers. In particular, when we use a reference as an initializer, the initializer is the corresponding object. The compiler uses that object's type for `auto`'s type deduction:

```
int i = 0, &r = i;
auto a = r;   //  a is an int (r is an alias for i, which has type int)
```

Second, `auto` ordinarily ignores top-level `const`s (§ 2.4.3, p. 63). As usual in initializations, low-level `const`s, such as when an initializer is a pointer to `const`, are kept:

```
const int ci = i, &cr = ci;
auto b = ci;  //  b is an int (top-level const in ci is dropped)
auto c = cr;  //  c is an int (cr is an alias for ci whose const is top-level)
auto d = &i;  //  d is an int * (& of an int object is int *)
auto e = &ci; //  e is const int * (& of a const object is low-level const)
```

If we want the deduced type to have a top-level `const`, we must say so explicitly:

```
const auto f = ci;   //  deduced type of ci is int; f has type const int
```

We can also specify that we want a reference to the `auto`-deduced type. Normal initialization rules still apply:

```
auto &g = ci;          //  g is a const int& that is bound to ci
auto &h = 42;          //  error: we can't bind a plain reference to a literal
const auto &j = 42;  //  ok: we can bind a const reference to a literal
```

When we ask for a reference to an auto-deduced type, top-level consts in the initializer are not ignored. As usual, consts are not top-level when we bind a reference to an initializer.

When we define several variables in the same statement, it is important to remember that a reference or pointer is part of a particular declarator and not part of the base type for the declaration. As usual, the initializers must provide consistent auto-deduced types:

```
auto k = ci, &l = i;     // k is int; l is int&
auto &m = ci, *p = &ci; // m is a const int&; p is a pointer to const int
// error: type deduced from i is int; type deduced from &ci is const int
auto &n = i, *p2 = &ci;
```

EXERCISES SECTION 2.5.2

Exercise 2.33: Using the variable definitions from this section, determine what happens in each of these assignments:

```
a = 42;    b = 42;    c = 42;
d = 42;    e = 42;    g = 42;
```

Exercise 2.34: Write a program containing the variables and assignments from the previous exercise. Print the variables before and after the assignments to check whether your predictions in the previous exercise were correct. If not, study the examples until you can convince yourself you know what led you to the wrong conclusion.

Exercise 2.35: Determine the types deduced in each of the following definitions. Once you've figured out the types, write a program to see whether you were correct.

```
const int i = 42;
auto j = i; const auto &k = i; auto *p = &i;
const auto j2 = i, &k2 = i;
```

2.5.3 The decltype Type Specifier

Sometimes we want to define a variable with a type that the compiler deduces from an expression but do not want to use that expression to initialize the variable. For such cases, the new standard introduced a second type specifier, **decltype**, which returns the type of its operand. The compiler analyzes the expression to determine its type but does not evaluate the expression:

```
decltype(f()) sum = x; // sum has whatever type f returns
```

Here, the compiler does not call f, but it uses the type that such a call would return as the type for sum. That is, the compiler gives sum the same type as the type that would be returned if we were to call f.

The way decltype handles top-level const and references differs subtly from the way auto does. When the expression to which we apply decltype is a variable, `decltype` returns the type of that variable, including top-level `const` and references:

```
const int ci = 0, &cj = ci;
decltype(ci) x = 0;  // x has type const int
decltype(cj) y = x;  // y has type const int& and is bound to x
decltype(cj) z;      // error: z is a reference and must be initialized
```

Because `cj` is a reference, `decltype(cj)` is a reference type. Like any other reference, z must be initialized.

It is worth noting that `decltype` is the *only* context in which a variable defined as a reference is not treated as a synonym for the object to which it refers.

`decltype` and References

When we apply `decltype` to an expression that is not a variable, we get the type that that expression yields. As we'll see in § 4.1.1 (p. 135), some expressions will cause `decltype` to yield a reference type. Generally speaking, `decltype` returns a reference type for expressions that yield objects that can stand on the left-hand side of the assignment:

```
// decltype of an expression can be a reference type
int i = 42, *p = &i, &r = i;
decltype(r + 0) b;   // ok: addition yields an int; b is an (uninitialized) int
decltype(*p) c;      // error: c is int& and must be initialized
```

Here r is a reference, so `decltype(r)` is a reference type. If we want the type to which r refers, we can use r in an expression, such as r + 0, which is an expression that yields a value that has a nonreference type.

On the other hand, the dereference operator is an example of an expression for which `decltype` returns a reference. As we've seen, when we dereference a pointer, we get the object to which the pointer points. Moreover, we can assign to that object. Thus, the type deduced by `decltype(*p)` is `int&`, not plain `int`.

Another important difference between `decltype` and `auto` is that the deduction done by `decltype` *depends on the form of its given expression*. What can be confusing is that enclosing the name of a variable in parentheses affects the type returned by `decltype`. When we apply `decltype` to a variable without any parentheses, we get the type of that variable. If we wrap the variable's name in one or more sets of parentheses, the compiler will evaluate the operand as an expression. A variable is an expression that can be the left-hand side of an assignment. As a result, `decltype` on such an expression yields a reference:

```
// decltype of a parenthesized variable is always a reference
decltype((i)) d;     // error: d is int& and must be initialized
decltype(i) e;       // ok: e is an (uninitialized) int
```

WARNING

Remember that `decltype((`*variable*`))` (note, double parentheses) is always a reference type, but `decltype(`*variable*`)` is a reference type only if *variable* is a reference.

EXERCISES SECTION 2.5.3

Exercise 2.36: In the following code, determine the type of each variable and the value each variable has when the code finishes:

```
int a = 3, b = 4;
decltype(a) c = a;
decltype((b)) d = a;
++c;
++d;
```

Exercise 2.37: Assignment is an example of an expression that yields a reference type. The type is a reference to the type of the left-hand operand. That is, if i is an int, then the type of the expression i = x is int&. Using that knowledge, determine the type and value of each variable in this code:

```
int a = 3, b = 4;
decltype(a) c = a;
decltype(a = b) d = a;
```

Exercise 2.38: Describe the differences in type deduction between decltype and auto. Give an example of an expression where auto and decltype will deduce the same type and an example where they will deduce differing types.

2.6 Defining Our Own Data Structures

At the most basic level, a data structure is a way to group together related data elements and a strategy for using those data. As one example, our Sales_item class groups an ISBN, a count of how many copies of that book had been sold, and the revenue associated with those sales. It also provides a set of operations such as the isbn function and the >>, <<, +, and += operators.

In C++ we define our own data types by defining a class. The library types string, istream, and ostream are all defined as classes, as is the Sales_item type we used in Chapter 1. C++ support for classes is extensive—in fact, Parts III and IV are largely devoted to describing class-related features. Even though the Sales_item class is pretty simple, we won't be able to fully define that class until we learn how to write our own operators in Chapter 14.

2.6.1 Defining the Sales_data Type

Although we can't yet write our Sales_item class, we can write a more concrete class that groups the same data elements. Our strategy for using this class is that users will be able to access the data elements directly and must implement needed operations for themselves.

Because our data structure does not support any operations, we'll name our version Sales_data to distinguish it from Sales_item. We'll define our class as follows:

```
struct Sales_data {
    std::string bookNo;
    unsigned units_sold = 0;
    double revenue = 0.0;
};
```

Our class begins with the keyword **struct**, followed by the name of the class and
a (possibly empty) class body. The class body is surrounded by curly braces and
forms a new scope (§ 2.2.4, p. 48). The names defined inside the class must be
unique within the class but can reuse names defined outside the class.

The close curly that ends the class body must be followed by a semicolon. The
semicolon is needed because we can define variables after the class body:

```
struct Sales_data { /* ... */ } accum, trans, *salesptr;
// equivalent, but better way to define these objects
struct Sales_data { /* ... */ };
Sales_data accum, trans, *salesptr;
```

The semicolon marks the end of the (usually empty) list of declarators. Ordinarily,
it is a bad idea to define an object as part of a class definition. Doing so obscures
the code by combining the definitions of two different entities—the class and a
variable—in a single statement.

 It is a common mistake among new programmers to forget the semicolon
at the end of a class definition.

Class Data Members

The class body defines the **members** of the class. Our class has only **data members**. The data members of a class define the contents of the objects of that class
type. Each object has its own copy of the class data members. Modifying the data
members of one object does not change the data in any other Sales_data object.

We define data members the same way that we define normal variables: We
specify a base type followed by a list of one or more declarators. Our class has
three data members: a member of type string named bookNo, an unsigned
member named units_sold, and a member of type double named revenue.
Each Sales_data object will have these three data members.

Under the new standard, we can supply an **in-class initializer** for a data mem- `C++ 11`
ber. When we create objects, the in-class initializers will be used to initialize the
data members. Members without an initializer are default initialized (§ 2.2.1, p. 43).
Thus, when we define Sales_data objects, units_sold and revenue will be
initialized to 0, and bookNo will be initialized to the empty string.

In-class initializers are restricted as to the form (§ 2.2.1, p. 43) we can use: They
must either be enclosed inside curly braces or follow an = sign. We may not specify
an in-class initializer inside parentheses.

In § 7.2 (p. 268), we'll see that C++ has a second keyword, class, that can be
used to define our own data structures. We'll explain in that section why we use
struct here. Until we cover additional class-related features in Chapter 7, you
should use struct to define your own data structures.

EXERCISES SECTION 2.6.1

Exercise 2.39: Compile the following program to see what happens when you forget the semicolon after a class definition. Remember the message for future reference.

```
struct Foo { /* empty */ } // Note: no semicolon
int main()
{
    return 0;
}
```

Exercise 2.40: Write your own version of the `Sales_data` class.

2.6.2   Using the `Sales_data` Class

Unlike the `Sales_item` class, our `Sales_data` class does not provide any operations. Users of `Sales_data` have to write whatever operations they need. As an example, we'll write a version of the program from § 1.5.2 (p. 23) that printed the sum of two transactions. The input to our program will be transactions such as

```
0-201-78345-X 3 20.00
0-201-78345-X 2 25.00
```

Each transaction holds an ISBN, the count of how many books were sold, and the price at which each book was sold.

Adding Two `Sales_data` Objects

Because `Sales_data` provides no operations, we will have to write our own code to do the input, output, and addition operations. We'll assume that our `Sales_data` class is defined inside `Sales_data.h`. We'll see how to define this header in § 2.6.3 (p. 76).

Because this program will be longer than any we've written so far, we'll explain it in separate parts. Overall, our program will have the following structure:

```
#include <iostream>
#include <string>
#include "Sales_data.h"

int main()
{
    Sales_data data1, data2;
    //  code to read into data1 and data2
    //  code to check whether data1 and data2 have the same ISBN
    //       and if so print the sum of data1 and data2
}
```

As in our original program, we begin by including the headers we'll need and define variables to hold the input. Note that unlike the `Sales_item` version, our new program includes the `string` header. We need that header because our code will have to manage the `bookNo` member, which has type `string`.

Reading Data into a `Sales_data` Object

Although we won't describe the library `string` type in detail until Chapters 3 and 10, we need to know only a little bit about `string`s in order to define and use our ISBN member. The `string` type holds a sequence of characters. Its operations include the `>>`, `<<`, and `==` operators to read, write, and compare `string`s, respectively. With this knowledge we can write the code to read the first transaction:

```
double price = 0;   // price per book, used to calculate total revenue
// read the first transactions: ISBN, number of books sold, price per book
std::cin >> data1.bookNo >> data1.units_sold >> price;
// calculate total revenue from price and units_sold
data1.revenue = data1.units_sold * price;
```

Our transactions contain the price at which each book was sold but our data structure stores the total revenue. We'll read the transaction data into a `double` named `price`, from which we'll calculate the `revenue` member. The input statement

```
std::cin >> data1.bookNo >> data1.units_sold >> price;
```

uses the dot operator (§ 1.5.2, p. 23) to read into the `bookNo` and `units_sold` members of the object named `data1`.

The last statement assigns the product of `data1.units_sold` and `price` into the `revenue` member of `data1`.

Our program will next repeat the same code to read data into `data2`:

```
// read the second transaction
std::cin >> data2.bookNo >> data2.units_sold >> price;
data2.revenue = data2.units_sold * price;
```

Printing the Sum of Two `Sales_data` Objects

Our other task is to check that the transactions are for the same ISBN. If so, we'll print their sum, otherwise, we'll print an error message:

```
if (data1.bookNo == data2.bookNo) {
    unsigned totalCnt = data1.units_sold + data2.units_sold;
    double totalRevenue = data1.revenue + data2.revenue;
    // print: ISBN, total sold, total revenue, average price per book
    std::cout << data1.bookNo << " " << totalCnt
              << " " << totalRevenue << " ";
    if (totalCnt != 0)
        std::cout << totalRevenue/totalCnt << std::endl;
    else
        std::cout  << "(no sales)" << std::endl;
    return 0;   // indicate success
} else {  // transactions weren't for the same ISBN
    std::cerr << "Data must refer to the same ISBN"
              << std::endl;
    return -1; // indicate failure
}
```

In the first `if` we compare the `bookNo` members of `data1` and `data2`. If those members are the same ISBN, we execute the code inside the curly braces. That code adds the components of our two variables. Because we'll need to print the average price, we start by computing the total of `units_sold` and `revenue` and store those in `totalCnt` and `totalRevenue`, respectively. We print those values. Next we check that there were books sold and, if so, print the computed average price per book. If there were no sales, we print a message noting that fact.

EXERCISES SECTION 2.6.2

Exercise 2.41:   Use your `Sales_data` class to rewrite the exercises in § 1.5.1 (p. 22), § 1.5.2 (p. 24), and § 1.6 (p. 25). For now, you should define your `Sales_data` class in the same file as your `main` function.

2.6.3   Writing Our Own Header Files

Although as we'll see in § 19.7 (p. 852), we can define a class inside a function, such classes have limited functionality. As a result, classes ordinarily are not defined inside functions. When we define a class outside of a function, there may be only one definition of that class in any given source file. In addition, if we use a class in several different files, the class' definition must be the same in each file.

In order to ensure that the class definition is the same in each file, classes are usually defined in header files. Typically, classes are stored in headers whose name derives from the name of the class. For example, the `string` library type is defined in the `string` header. Similarly, as we've already seen, we will define our `Sales_data` class in a header file named `Sales_data.h`.

Headers (usually) contain entities (such as class definitions and `const` and `constexpr` variables (§ 2.4, p. 60)) that can be defined only once in any given file. However, headers often need to use facilities from other headers. For example, because our `Sales_data` class has a `string` member, `Sales_data.h` must `#include` the `string` header. As we've seen, programs that use `Sales_data` also need to include the `string` header in order to use the `bookNo` member. As a result, programs that use `Sales_data` will include the `string` header twice: once directly and once as a side effect of including `Sales_data.h`. Because a header might be included more than once, we need to write our headers in a way that is safe even if the header is included multiple times.

Whenever a header is updated, the source files that use that header must be recompiled to get the new or changed declarations.

A Brief Introduction to the Preprocessor

The most common technique for making it safe to include a header multiple times relies on the **preprocessor**. The preprocessor—which C++ inherits from C—is a program that runs before the compiler and changes the source text of our programs. Our programs already rely on one preprocessor facility, #include. When the preprocessor sees a #include, it replaces the #include with the contents of the specified header.

C++ programs also use the preprocessor to define **header guards**. Header guards rely on preprocessor variables (§ 2.3.2, p. 53). Preprocessor variables have one of two possible states: defined or not defined. The **#define** directive takes a name and defines that name as a preprocessor variable. There are two other directives that test whether a given preprocessor variable has or has not been defined: **#ifdef** is true if the variable has been defined, and **#ifndef** is true if the variable has *not* been defined. If the test is true, then everything following the #ifdef or #ifndef is processed up to the matching **#endif**.

We can use these facilities to guard against multiple inclusion as follows:

```
#ifndef SALES_DATA_H
#define SALES_DATA_H

#include <string>
struct Sales_data {
    std::string bookNo;
    unsigned units_sold = 0;
    double revenue = 0.0;
};
#endif
```

The first time Sales_data.h is included, the #ifndef test will succeed. The preprocessor will process the lines following #ifndef up to the #endif. As a result, the preprocessor variable SALES_DATA_H will be defined and the contents of Sales_data.h will be copied into our program. If we include Sales_data.h later on in the same file, the #ifndef directive will be false. The lines between it and the #endif directive will be ignored.

WARNING

Preprocessor variable names do not respect C++ scoping rules.

Preprocessor variables, including names of header guards, must be unique throughout the program. Typically we ensure uniqueness by basing the guard's name on the name of a class in the header. To avoid name clashes with other entities in our programs, preprocessor variables usually are written in all uppercase.

Best Practices

Headers should have guards, even if they aren't (yet) included by another header. Header guards are trivial to write, and by habitually defining them you don't need to decide whether they are needed.

EXERCISES SECTION 2.6.3

Exercise 2.42: Write your own version of the Sales_data.h header and use it to rewrite the exercise from § 2.6.2 (p. 76).

CHAPTER SUMMARY

Types are fundamental to all programming in C++.

Each type defines the storage requirements and the operations that may be performed on objects of that type. The language provides a set of fundamental built-in types such as `int` and `char`, which are closely tied to their representation on the machine's hardware. Types can be nonconst or `const`; a `const` object must be initialized and, once initialized, its value may not be changed. In addition, we can define compound types, such as pointers or references. A compound type is one that is defined in terms of another type.

The language lets us define our own types by defining classes. The library uses the class facility to provide a set of higher-level abstractions such as the IO and `string` types.

DEFINED TERMS

address Number by which a byte in memory can be found.

alias declaration Defines a synonym for another type: using *name* = *type* declares *name* as a synonym for the type *type*.

arithmetic types Built-in types representing boolean values, characters, integers, and floating-point numbers.

array Data structure that holds a collection of unnamed objects that are accessed by an index. Section 3.5 covers arrays in detail.

auto Type specifier that deduces the type of a variable from its initializer.

base type type specifier, possibly qualified by `const`, that precedes the declarators in a declaration. The base type provides the common type on which the declarators in a declaration can build.

bind Associating a name with a given entity so that uses of the name are uses of the underlying entity. For example, a reference is a name that is bound to an object.

byte Smallest addressable unit of memory. On most machines a byte is 8 bits.

class member Part of a class.

compound type A type that is defined in terms of another type.

const Type qualifier used to define objects that may not be changed. `const` objects must be initialized, because there is no way to give them a value after they are defined.

const pointer Pointer that is `const`.

const reference Colloquial synonym for reference to `const`.

constant expression Expression that can be evaluated at compile time.

constexpr Variable that represents a constant expression. § 6.5.2 (p. 239) covers `constexpr` functions.

conversion Process whereby a value of one type is transformed into a value of another type. The language defines conversions among the built-in types.

data member Data elements that constitute an object. Every object of a given class has its own copies of the class' data members. Data members may be initialized when declared inside the class.

declaration Asserts the existence of a variable, function, or type defined elsewhere. Names may not be used until they are defined or declared.

declarator The part of a declaration that includes the name being defined and an optional type modifier.

decltype Type specifier that deduces the type of a variable or an expression.

default initialization How objects are initialized when no explicit initializer is given. How class type objects are initialized is controlled by the class. Objects of built-in type defined at global scope are initialized to 0; those defined at local scope are uninitialized and have undefined values.

definition Allocates storage for a variable of a specified type and optionally initializes the variable. Names may not be used until they are defined or declared.

escape sequence Alternative mechanism for representing characters, particularly for those without printable representations. An escape sequence is a backslash followed by a character, three or fewer octal digits, or an x followed by a hexadecimal number.

global scope The scope that is outside all other scopes.

header guard Preprocessor variable used to prevent a header from being included more than once in a single file.

identifier Sequence of characters that make up a name. Identifiers are case-sensitive.

in-class initializer Initializer provided as part of the declaration of a class data member. In-class initializers must follow an = symbol or be enclosed inside curly braces.

in scope Name that is visible from the current scope.

initialized A variable given an initial value when it is defined. Variables usually should be initialized.

inner scope Scope that is nested inside another scope.

integral types See arithmetic type.

list initialization Form of initialization that uses curly braces to enclose one or more initializers.

literal A value such as a number, a character, or a string of characters. The value cannot be changed. Literal characters are enclosed in single quotes, literal strings in double quotes.

local scope Colloquial synonym for block scope.

low-level const A const that is not top-level. Such consts are integral to the type and are never ignored.

member Part of a class.

nonprintable character A character with no visible representation, such as a control character, a backspace, newline, and so on.

null pointer Pointer whose value is 0. A null pointer is valid but does not point to any object.

nullptr Literal constant that denotes the null pointer.

object A region of memory that has a type. A variable is an object that has a name.

outer scope Scope that encloses another scope.

pointer An object that can hold the address of an object, the address one past the end of an object, or zero.

pointer to const Pointer that can hold the address of a const object. A pointer to const may not be used to change the value of the object to which it points.

preprocessor Program that runs as part of compilation of a C++ program.

preprocessor variable Variable managed by the preprocessor. The preprocessor replaces each preprocessor variable by its value before our program is compiled.

reference An alias for another object.

reference to const A reference that may not change the value of the object to which it refers. A reference to const may be bound to a const object, a nonconst object, or the result of an expression.

scope The portion of a program in which names have meaning. C++ has several levels of scope:

> **global**—names defined outside any other scope
>
> **class**—names defined inside a class
>
> **namespace**—names defined inside a namespace
>
> **block**—names defined inside a block

Scopes nest. Once a name is declared, it is accessible until the end of the scope in which it was declared.

separate compilation Ability to split a program into multiple separate source files.

signed Integer type that holds negative or positive values, including zero.

string Library type representing variable-length sequences of characters.

struct Keyword used to define a class.

temporary Unnamed object created by the compiler while evaluating an expression. A temporary exists until the end of the largest expression that encloses the expression for which it was created.

top-level const The const that specifies that an object may not be changed.

type alias A name that is a synonym for another type. Defined through either a typedef or an alias declaration.

type checking Term used to describe the process by which the compiler verifies that the way objects of a given type are used is consistent with the definition of that type.

type specifier The name of a type.

typedef Defines an alias for another type. When typedef appears in the base type of a declaration, the names defined in the declaration are type names.

undefined Usage for which the language does not specify a meaning. Knowingly or unknowingly relying on undefined behavior is a great source of hard-to-track runtime errors, security problems, and portability problems.

uninitialized Variable defined without an initial value. In general, trying to access the value of an uninitialized variable results in undefined behavior.

unsigned Integer type that holds only values greater than or equal to zero.

variable A named object or reference. In C++, variables must be declared before they are used.

void* Pointer type that can point to any nonconst type. Such pointers may not be dereferenced.

void type Special-purpose type that has no operations and no value. It is not possible to define a variable of type void.

word The natural unit of integer computation on a given machine. Usually a word is large enough to hold an address. On a 32-bit machine a word is typically 4 bytes.

& operator Address-of operator. Yields the address of the object to which it is applied.

* operator Dereference operator. Dereferencing a pointer returns the object to which the pointer points. Assigning to the result of a dereference assigns a new value to the underlying object.

#define Preprocessor directive that defines a preprocessor variable.

#endif Preprocessor directive that ends an #ifdef or #ifndef region.

#ifdef Preprocessor directive that determines whether a given variable is defined.

#ifndef Preprocessor directive that determines whether a given variable is not defined.

C H A P T E R **3**
STRINGS, VECTORS, AND
ARRAYS

<u>CONTENTS</u>

In addition to the built-in types covered in Chapter 2, C++ defines a rich library of abstract data types. Among the most important library types are string, which supports variable-length character strings, and vector, which defines variable-size collections. Associated with string and vector are companion types known as iterators, which are used to access the characters in a string or the elements in a vector.

The string and vector types defined by the library are abstractions of the more primitive built-in array type. This chapter covers arrays and introduces the library vector and string types.

The built-in types that we covered in Chapter 2 are defined directly by the C++ language. These types represent facilities present in most computer hardware, such as numbers or characters. The standard library defines a number of additional types of a higher-level nature that computer hardware usually does not implement directly.

In this chapter, we'll introduce two of the most important library types: `string` and `vector`. A `string` is a variable-length sequence of characters. A `vector` holds a variable-length sequence of objects of a given type. We'll also cover the built-in array type. Like other built-in types, arrays represent facilities of the hardware. As a result, arrays are less convenient to use than the library `string` and `vector` types.

Before beginning our exploration of the library types, we'll look at a mechanism for simplifying access to the names defined in the library.

3.1 Namespace `using` Declarations

Up to now, our programs have explicitly indicated that each library name we use is in the `std` namespace. For example, to read from the standard input, we write `std::cin`. These names use the scope operator (`::`) (§ 1.2, p. 8), which says that the compiler should look in the scope of the left-hand operand for the name of the right-hand operand. Thus, `std::cin` says that we want to use the name `cin` from the namespace `std`.

Referring to library names with this notation can be cumbersome. Fortunately, there are easier ways to use namespace members. The safest way is a **using declaration**. § 18.2.2 (p. 793) covers another way to use names from a namespace.

A `using` declaration lets us use a name from a namespace without qualifying the name with a `namespace_name::` prefix. A `using` declaration has the form

```
using namespace::name;
```

Once the `using` declaration has been made, we can access *name* directly:

```
#include <iostream>
// using declaration; when we use the name cin, we get the one from the namespace std
using std::cin;
int main()
{
    int i;
    cin >> i;        // ok: cin is a synonym for std::cin
    cout << i;       // error: no using declaration; we must use the full name
    std::cout << i;  // ok: explicitly use cout from namepsace std
    return 0;
}
```

A Separate `using` Declaration Is Required for Each Name

Each `using` declaration introduces a single namespace member. This behavior lets us be specific about which names we're using. As an example, we'll rewrite the program from § 1.2 (p. 6) with `using` declarations for the library names it uses:

```
#include <iostream>
//  using declarations for names from the standard library
using std::cin;
using std::cout; using std::endl;
int main()
{
    cout << "Enter two numbers:" << endl;
    int v1, v2;
    cin >> v1 >> v2;
    cout << "The sum of " << v1 << " and " << v2
         << " is " << v1 + v2 << endl;
    return 0;
}
```

The using declarations for cin, cout, and endl mean that we can use those names without the std:: prefix. Recall that C++ programs are free-form, so we can put each using declaration on its own line or combine several onto a single line. The important part is that there must be a using declaration for each name we use, and each declaration must end in a semicolon.

Headers Should Not Include using Declarations

Code inside headers (§ 2.6.3, p. 76) ordinarily should not use using declarations. The reason is that the contents of a header are copied into the including program's text. If a header has a using declaration, then every program that includes that header gets that same using declaration. As a result, a program that didn't intend to use the specified library name might encounter unexpected name conflicts.

A Note to the Reader

From this point on, our examples will assume that using declarations have been made for the names we use from the standard library. Thus, we will refer to cin, not std::cin, in the text and in code examples.

Moreover, to keep the code examples short, we won't show the using declarations, nor will we show the necessary #include directives. Table A.1 (p. 866) in Appendix A lists the names and corresponding headers for standard library names we use in this Primer.

WARNING Readers should be aware that they must add appropriate #include and using declarations to our examples before compiling them.

EXERCISES SECTION 3.1

Exercise 3.1: Rewrite the exercises from § 1.4.1 (p. 13) and § 2.6.2 (p. 76) with appropriate using declarations.

3.2 Library `string` Type

A **string** is a variable-length sequence of characters. To use the `string` type, we must include the `string` header. Because it is part of the library, `string` is defined in the `std` namespace. Our examples assume the following code:

```
#include <string>
using std::string;
```

This section describes the most common `string` operations; § 9.5 (p. 360) will cover additional operations.

> **Note**   In addition to specifying the operations that the library types provide, the standard also imposes efficiency requirements on implementors. As a result, library types are efficient enough for general use.

3.2.1 Defining and Initializing `strings`

Each class defines how objects of its type can be initialized. A class may define many different ways to initialize objects of its type. Each way must be distinguished from the others either by the number of initializers that we supply, or by the types of those initializers. Table 3.1 lists the most common ways to initialize `strings`. Some examples:

```
string s1;             // default initialization; s1 is the empty string
string s2 = s1;        // s2 is a copy of s1
string s3 = "hiya";    // s3 is a copy of the string literal
string s4(10, 'c');    // s4 is cccccccccc
```

We can default initialize a `string` (§ 2.2.1, p. 44), which creates an empty `string`; that is, a `string` with no characters. When we supply a string literal (§ 2.1.3, p. 39), the characters from that literal—up to but not including the null character at the end of the literal—are copied into the newly created `string`. When we supply a count and a character, the `string` contains that many copies of the given character.

Direct and Copy Forms of Initialization

In § 2.2.1 (p. 43) we saw that C++ has several different forms of initialization. Using `strings`, we can start to understand how these forms differ from one another. When we initialize a variable using `=`, we are asking the compiler to **copy initialize** the object by copying the initializer on the right-hand side into the object being created. Otherwise, when we omit the `=`, we use **direct initialization**.

When we have a single initializer, we can use either the direct or copy form of initialization. When we initialize a variable from more than one value, such as in the initialization of `s4` above, we must use the direct form of initialization:

```
string s5 = "hiya";    // copy initialization
string s6("hiya");     // direct initialization
string s7(10, 'c');    // direct initialization; s7 is cccccccccc
```

When we want to use several values, we can indirectly use the copy form of initialization by explicitly creating a (temporary) object to copy:

```
string s8 = string(10, 'c'); // copy initialization; s8 is cccccccccc
```

The initializer of s8—string(10, 'c')—creates a string of the given size and character value and then copies that value into s8. It is as if we had written

```
string temp(10, 'c'); // temp is cccccccccc
string s8 = temp;      // copy temp into s8
```

Although the code used to initialize s8 is legal, it is less readable and offers no compensating advantage over the way we initialized s7.

Table 3.1: Ways to Initialize a string	
string s1	Default initialization; s1 is the empty string.
string s2(s1)	s2 is a copy of s1.
string s2 = s1	Equivalent to s2(s1), s2 is a copy of s1.
string s3("value")	s3 is a copy of the string literal, not including the null.
string s3 = "value"	Equivalent to s3("value"), s3 is a copy of the string literal.
string s4(n, 'c')	Initialize s4 with n copies of the character 'c'.

3.2.2 Operations on strings

Along with defining how objects are created and initialized, a class also defines the operations that objects of the class type can perform. A class can define operations that are called by name, such as the isbn function of our Sales_item class (§ 1.5.2, p. 23). A class also can define what various operator symbols, such as << or +, mean when applied to objects of the class' type. Table 3.2 (overleaf) lists the most common string operations.

Reading and Writing strings

As we saw in Chapter 1, we use the iostream library to read and write values of built-in types such as int, double, and so on. We use the same IO operators to read and write strings:

```
// Note: #include and using declarations must be added to compile this code
int main()
{
    string s;            // empty string
    cin >> s;            // read a whitespace-separated string into s
    cout << s << endl;   // write s to the output
    return 0;
}
```

Table 3.2: `string` Operations	
`os << s`	Writes s onto output stream os. Returns os.
`is >> s`	Reads whitespace-separated string from is into s. Returns is.
`getline(is, s)`	Reads a line of input from is into s. Returns is.
`s.empty()`	Returns true if s is empty; otherwise returns false.
`s.size()`	Returns the number of characters in s.
`s[n]`	Returns a reference to the char at position n in s; positions start at 0.
`s1 + s2`	Returns a string that is the concatenation of s1 and s2.
`s1 = s2`	Replaces characters in s1 with a copy of s2.
`s1 == s2` `s1 != s2`	The strings s1 and s2 are equal if they contain the same characters. Equality is case-sensitive.
`<, <=, >, >=`	Comparisons are case-sensitive and use dictionary ordering.

This program begins by defining an empty `string` named s. The next line reads the standard input, storing what is read in s. The `string` input operator reads and discards any leading whitespace (e.g., spaces, newlines, tabs). It then reads characters until the next whitespace character is encountered.

So, if the input to this program is   **Hello World!**   (note leading and trailing spaces), then the output will be **Hello** with no extra spaces.

Like the input and output operations on the built-in types, the `string` operators return their left-hand operand as their result. Thus, we can chain together multiple reads or writes:

```
string s1, s2;
cin >> s1 >> s2; // read first input into s1, second into s2
cout << s1 << s2 << endl; // write both strings
```

If we give this version of the program the same input,   **Hello World!**   , our output would be "**HelloWorld!**"

Reading an Unknown Number of `strings`

In § 1.4.3 (p. 14) we wrote a program that read an unknown number of int values. We can write a similar program that reads `strings` instead:

```
int main()
{
    string word;
    while (cin >> word)      // read until end-of-file
        cout << word << endl; // write each word followed by a new line
    return 0;
}
```

In this program, we read into a `string`, not an `int`. Otherwise, the `while` condition executes similarly to the one in our previous program. The condition tests the stream after the read completes. If the stream is valid—it hasn't hit end-of-file or encountered an invalid input—then the body of the while is executed. The body prints the value we read on the standard output. Once we hit end-of-file (or invalid input), we fall out of the while.

Using getline to Read an Entire Line

Sometimes we do not want to ignore the whitespace in our input. In such cases, we can use the **getline** function instead of the >> operator. The getline function takes an input stream and a string. This function reads the given stream up to and including the first newline and stores what it read—*not including* the newline—in its string argument. After getline sees a newline, even if it is the first character in the input, it stops reading and returns. If the first character in the input is a newline, then the resulting string is the empty string.

Like the input operator, getline returns its istream argument. As a result, we can use getline as a condition just as we can use the input operator as a condition (§ 1.4.3, p. 14). For example, we can rewrite the previous program that wrote one word per line to write a line at a time instead:

```
int main()
{
    string line;
    //  read input a line at a time until end-of-file
    while (getline(cin, line))
        cout << line << endl;
    return 0;
}
```

Because line does not contain a newline, we must write our own. As usual, we use endl to end the current line and flush the buffer.

> The newline that causes getline to return is discarded; the newline is *not* stored in the string.

The string empty and size Operations

The **empty** function does what one would expect: It returns a bool (§ 2.1, p. 32) indicating whether the string is empty. Like the isbn member of Sales_item (§ 1.5.2, p. 23), empty is a member function of string. To call this function, we use the dot operator to specify the object on which we want to run the empty function.

We can revise the previous program to only print lines that are not empty:

```
//  read input a line at a time and discard blank lines
while (getline(cin, line))
    if (!line.empty())
        cout << line << endl;
```

The condition uses the logical NOT operator (the **! operator**). This operator returns the inverse of the bool value of its operand. In this case, the condition is true if str is not empty.

The **size** member returns the length of a `string` (i.e., the number of characters in it). We can use `size` to print only lines longer than 80 characters:

```
string line;
//   read input a line at a time and print lines that are longer than 80 characters
while (getline(cin, line))
    if (line.size() > 80)
        cout << line << endl;
```

The `string::size_type` Type

It might be logical to expect that `size` returns an `int` or, thinking back to § 2.1.1 (p. 34), an `unsigned`. Instead, `size` returns a `string::size_type` value. This type requires a bit of explanation.

The `string` class—and most other library types—defines several companion types. These companion types make it possible to use the library types in a machine-independent manner. The type **size_type** is one of these companion types. To use the `size_type` defined by `string`, we use the scope operator to say that the name `size_type` is defined in the `string` class.

Although we don't know the precise type of `string::size_type`, we do know that it is an unsigned type (§ 2.1.1, p. 32) big enough to hold the size of any `string`. Any variable used to store the result from the `string size` operation should be of type `string::size_type`.

Admittedly, it can be tedious to type `string::size_type`. Under the new standard, we can ask the compiler to provide the appropriate type by using `auto` or `decltype` (§ 2.5.2, p. 68):

```
auto len = line.size(); // len has type string::size_type
```

Because `size` returns an unsigned type, it is essential to remember that expressions that mix signed and unsigned data can have surprising results (§ 2.1.2, p. 36). For example, if n is an `int` that holds a negative value, then `s.size() < n` will almost surely evaluate as `true`. It yields `true` because the negative value in n will convert to a large unsigned value.

> You can avoid problems due to conversion between `unsigned` and `int` by not using `int`s in expressions that use `size()`.

Comparing `strings`

The `string` class defines several operators that compare `strings`. These operators work by comparing the characters of the `strings`. The comparisons are case-sensitive—upper- and lowercase versions of a letter are different characters.

The equality operators (`==` and `!=`) test whether two `strings` are equal or unequal, respectively. Two `strings` are equal if they are the same length and contain the same characters. The relational operators `<`, `<=`, `>`, `>=` test whether one `string` is less than, less than or equal to, greater than, or greater than or equal to another. These operators use the same strategy as a (case-sensitive) dictionary:

1. If two strings have different lengths and if every character in the shorter string is equal to the corresponding character of the longer string, then the shorter string is less than the longer one.

2. If any characters at corresponding positions in the two strings differ, then the result of the string comparison is the result of comparing the first character at which the strings differ.

As an example, consider the following strings:

```
string str = "Hello";
string phrase = "Hello World";
string slang  = "Hiya";
```

Using rule 1, we see that str is less than phrase. By applying rule 2, we see that slang is greater than both str and phrase.

Assignment for strings

In general, the library types strive to make it as easy to use a library type as it is to use a built-in type. To this end, most of the library types support assignment. In the case of strings, we can assign one string object to another:

```
string st1(10, 'c'), st2; //  st1 is cccccccccc; st2 is an empty string
st1 = st2; //  assignment: replace contents of st1 with a copy of st2
           //  both st1 and st2 are now the empty string
```

Adding Two strings

Adding two strings yields a new string that is the concatenation of the left-hand followed by the right-hand operand. That is, when we use the plus operator (+) on strings, the result is a new string whose characters are a copy of those in the left-hand operand followed by those from the right-hand operand. The compound assignment operator (+=) (§ 1.4.1, p. 12) appends the right-hand operand to the left-hand string:

```
string s1  = "hello, ", s2 = "world\n";
string s3 = s1 + s2;    //  s3 is hello, world\n
s1 += s2;    //  equivalent to s1 = s1 + s2
```

Adding Literals and strings

As we saw in § 2.1.2 (p. 35), we can use one type where another type is expected if there is a conversion from the given type to the expected type. The string library lets us convert both character literals and character string literals (§ 2.1.3, p. 39) to strings. Because we can use these literals where a string is expected, we can rewrite the previous program as follows:

```
string s1 = "hello", s2 = "world";   //  no punctuation in s1 or s2
string s3 = s1 + ", " + s2 + '\n';
```

When we mix strings and string or character literals, at least one operand to each + operator must be of string type:

```
string s4 = s1 + ", ";            // ok: adding a string and a literal
string s5 = "hello" + ", ";       // error: no string operand
string s6 = s1 + ", " + "world";  // ok: each + has a string operand
string s7 = "hello" + ", " + s2;  // error: can't add string literals
```

The initializations of s4 and s5 involve only a single operation each, so it is easy to see whether the initialization is legal. The initialization of s6 may appear surprising, but it works in much the same way as when we chain together input or output expressions (§ 1.2, p. 7). This initialization groups as

```
string s6 = (s1 + ", ") + "world";
```

The subexpression s1 + ", " returns a string, which forms the left-hand operand of the second + operator. It is as if we had written

```
string tmp = s1 + ", ";  // ok: + has a string operand
s6 = tmp + "world";      // ok: + has a string operand
```

On the other hand, the initialization of s7 is illegal, which we can see if we parenthesize the expression:

```
string s7 = ("hello" + ", ") + s2;  // error: can't add string literals
```

Now it should be easy to see that the first subexpression adds two string literals. There is no way to do so, and so the statement is in error.

 WARNING For historical reasons, and for compatibility with C, string literals are *not* standard library strings. It is important to remember that these types differ when you use string literals and library strings.

EXERCISES SECTION 3.2.2

Exercise 3.2: Write a program to read the standard input a line at a time. Modify your program to read a word at a time.

Exercise 3.3: Explain how whitespace characters are handled in the string input operator and in the getline function.

Exercise 3.4: Write a program to read two strings and report whether the strings are equal. If not, report which of the two is larger. Now, change the program to report whether the strings have the same length, and if not, report which is longer.

Exercise 3.5: Write a program to read strings from the standard input, concatenating what is read into one large string. Print the concatenated string. Next, change the program to separate adjacent input strings by a space.

 ## 3.2.3 Dealing with the Characters in a string

Often we need to deal with the individual characters in a string. We might want to check to see whether a string contains any whitespace, or to change the characters to lowercase, or to see whether a given character is present, and so on.

One part of this kind of processing involves how we gain access to the characters themselves. Sometimes we need to process every character. Other times we need to process only a specific character, or we can stop processing once some condition is met. It turns out that the best way to deal with these cases involves different language and library facilities.

The other part of processing characters is knowing and/or changing the characteristics of a character. This part of the job is handled by a set of library functions, described in Table 3.3 (overleaf). These functions are defined in the `cctype` header.

ADVICE: USE THE C++ VERSIONS OF C LIBRARY HEADERS

In addition to facilities defined specifically for C++, the C++ library incorporates the C library. Headers in C have names of the form *name*`.h`. The C++ versions of these headers are named c*name*—they remove the `.h` suffix and precede the *name* with the letter `c`. The `c` indicates that the header is part of the C library.

Hence, `cctype` has the same contents as `ctype.h`, but in a form that is appropriate for C++ programs. In particular, the names defined in the c*name* headers are defined inside the `std` namespace, whereas those defined in the `.h` versions are not.

Ordinarily, C++ programs should use the c*name* versions of headers and not the *name*`.h` versions. That way names from the standard library are consistently found in the `std` namespace. Using the `.h` headers puts the burden on the programmer to remember which library names are inherited from C and which are unique to C++.

Processing Every Character? Use Range-Based `for`

If we want to do something to every character in a `string`, by far the best approach is to use a statement introduced by the new standard: the **range `for`** statement. This statement iterates through the elements in a given sequence and performs some operation on each value in that sequence. The syntactic form is

```
for (declaration : expression)
    statement
```

where *expression* is an object of a type that represents a sequence, and *declaration* defines the variable that we'll use to access the underlying elements in the sequence. On each iteration, the variable in *declaration* is initialized from the value of the next element in *expression*.

A `string` represents a sequence of characters, so we can use a `string` as the *expression* in a range `for`. As a simple example, we can use a range `for` to print each character from a `string` on its own line of output:

```
string str("some string");
// print the characters in str one character to a line
for (auto c : str)         // for every char in str
    cout << c << endl;     // print the current character followed by a newline
```

The `for` loop associates the variable `c` with `str`. We define the loop control variable the same way we do any other variable. In this case, we use `auto` (§ 2.5.2,

p. 68) to let the compiler determine the type of c, which in this case will be char. On each iteration, the next character in str will be copied into c. Thus, we can read this loop as saying, "For every character c in the string str," do something. The "something" in this case is to print the character followed by a newline.

As a somewhat more complicated example, we'll use a range for and the ispunct function to count the number of punctuation characters in a string:

```
string s("Hello World!!!");
// punct_cnt has the same type that s.size returns; see § 2.5.3 (p. 70)
decltype(s.size()) punct_cnt = 0;
// count the number of punctuation characters in s
for (auto c : s)            // for every char in s
    if (ispunct(c))         // if the character is punctuation
        ++punct_cnt;        // increment the punctuation counter
cout << punct_cnt
     << " punctuation characters in " << s << endl;
```

The output of this program is

3 punctuation characters in Hello World!!!

Here we use decltype (§ 2.5.3, p. 70) to declare our counter, punct_cnt. Its type is the type returned by calling s.size, which is string::size_type. We use a range for to process each character in the string. This time we check whether each character is punctuation. If so, we use the increment operator (§ 1.4.1, p. 12) to add 1 to the counter. When the range for completes, we print the result.

Table 3.3: cctype Functions	
isalnum(c)	true if c is a letter or a digit.
isalpha(c)	true if c is a letter.
iscntrl(c)	true if c is a control character.
isdigit(c)	true if c is a digit.
isgraph(c)	true if c is not a space but is printable.
islower(c)	true if c is a lowercase letter.
isprint(c)	true if c is a printable character (i.e., a space or a character that has a visible representation).
ispunct(c)	true if c is a punctuation character (i.e., a character that is not a control character, a digit, a letter, or a printable whitespace).
isspace(c)	true if c is whitespace (i.e., a space, tab, vertical tab, return, newline, or formfeed).
isupper(c)	true if c is an uppercase letter.
isxdigit(c)	true if c is a hexadecimal digit.
tolower(c)	If c is an uppercase letter, returns its lowercase equivalent; otherwise returns c unchanged.
toupper(c)	If c is a lowercase letter, returns its uppercase equivalent; otherwise returns c unchanged.

Using a Range `for` to Change the Characters in a `string`

If we want to change the value of the characters in a `string`, we must define the loop variable as a reference type (§ 2.3.1, p. 50). Remember that a reference is just another name for a given object. When we use a reference as our control variable, that variable is bound to each element in the sequence in turn. Using the reference, we can change the character to which the reference is bound.

Suppose that instead of counting punctuation, we wanted to convert a `string` to all uppercase letters. To do so we can use the library `toupper` function, which takes a character and returns the uppercase version of that character. To convert the whole `string` we need to call `toupper` on each character and put the result back in that character:

```
string s("Hello World!!!");
// convert s to uppercase
for (auto &c : s)     // for every char in s (note: c is a reference)
    c = toupper(c); // c is a reference, so the assignment changes the char in s
cout << s << endl;
```

The output of this code is

```
HELLO WORLD!!!
```

On each iteration, `c` refers to the next character in `s`. When we assign to `c`, we are changing the underlying character in `s`. So, when we execute

```
c = toupper(c); // c is a reference, so the assignment changes the char in s
```

we're changing the value of the character to which `c` is bound. When this loop completes, all the characters in `str` will be uppercase.

Processing Only Some Characters?

A range `for` works well when we need to process every character. However, sometimes we need to access only a single character or to access characters until some condition is reached. For example, we might want to capitalize only the first character or only the first word in a `string`.

There are two ways to access individual characters in a `string`: We can use a subscript or an iterator. We'll have more to say about iterators in § 3.4 (p. 106) and in Chapter 9.

The subscript operator (the **[] operator**) takes a `string::size_type` (§ 3.2.2, p. 88) value that denotes the position of the character we want to access. The operator returns a reference to the character at the given position.

Subscripts for `strings` start at zero; if `s` is a `string` with at least two characters, then `s[0]` is the first character, `s[1]` is the second, and the last character is in `s[s.size() - 1]`.

The values we use to subscript a `string` must be >= 0 and < `size()`. **The result of using an index outside this range is undefined. By implication, subscripting an empty `string` is undefined.**

The value in the subscript is referred to as "a subscript" or "an **index**." The index we supply can be any expression that yields an integral value. However, if our index has a signed type, its value will be converted to the unsigned type that `string::size_type` represents (§ 2.1.2, p. 36).

The following example uses the subscript operator to print the first character in a `string`:

```
if (!s.empty())              // make sure there's a character to print
    cout << s[0] << endl;    // print the first character in s
```

Before accessing the character, we check that s is not empty. Any time we use a subscript, we must ensure that there is a value at the given location. If s is empty, then s[0] is undefined.

So long as the `string` is not `const` (§ 2.4, p. 59), we can assign a new value to the character that the subscript operator returns. For example, we can capitalize the first letter as follows:

```
string s("some string");
if (!s.empty())              // make sure there's a character in s[0]
    s[0] = toupper(s[0]);    // assign a new value to the first character in s
```

The output of this program is

```
Some string
```

Using a Subscript for Iteration

As a another example, we'll change the first word in s to all uppercase:

```
// process characters in s until we run out of characters or we hit a whitespace
for (decltype(s.size()) index = 0;
     index != s.size() && !isspace(s[index]); ++index)
        s[index] = toupper(s[index]); // capitalize the current character
```

This program generates

```
SOME string
```

Our `for` loop (§ 1.4.2, p. 13) uses `index` to subscript s. We use `decltype` to give `index` the appropriate type. We initialize `index` to 0 so that the first iteration will start on the first character in s. On each iteration we increment `index` to look at the next character in s. In the body of the loop we capitalize the current letter.

The new part in this loop is the condition in the `for`. That condition uses the logical AND operator (the **&& operator**). This operator yields `true` if both operands are `true` and `false` otherwise. The important part about this operator is that we are guaranteed that it evaluates its right-hand operand *only* if the left-hand operand is `true`. In this case, we are guaranteed that we will not subscript s unless we know that `index` is in range. That is, s[index] is executed only if `index` is not equal to s.size(). Because `index` is never incremented beyond the value of s.size(), we know that `index` will always be less than s.size().

Using a Subscript for Random Access

In the previous example we advanced our subscript one position at a time to capitalize each character in sequence. We can also calculate an subscript and directly fetch the indicated character. There is no need to access characters in sequence.

As an example, let's assume we have a number between 0 and 15 and we want to generate the hexadecimal representation of that number. We can do so using a `string` that is initialized to hold the 16 hexadecimal "digits":

```
const string hexdigits = "0123456789ABCDEF";   // possible hex digits
cout << "Enter a series of numbers between 0 and 15"
     << " separated by spaces.  Hit ENTER when finished: "
     << endl;
string result;            // will hold the resulting hexify'd string
string::size_type n;   // hold numbers from the input
while (cin >> n)
    if (n < hexdigits.size())     // ignore invalid input
        result += hexdigits[n];   // fetch the indicated hex digit
cout << "Your hex number is: " << result << endl;
```

If we give this program the input

```
12 0 5 15 8 15
```

the output will be

```
Your hex number is: C05F8F
```

We start by initializing `hexdigits` to hold the hexadecimal digits 0 through F. We make that `string const` (§ 2.4, p. 59) because we do not want these values to change. Inside the loop we use the input value n to subscript `hexdigits`. The value of `hexdigits[n]` is the `char` that appears at position n in `hexdigits`. For example, if n is 15, then the result is F; if it's 12, the result is C; and so on. We append that digit to `result`, which we print once we have read all the input.

Whenever we use a subscript, we should think about how we know that it is in range. In this program, our subscript, n, is a `string::size_type`, which as we know is an unsigned type. As a result, we know that n is guaranteed to be greater than or equal to 0. Before we use n to subscript `hexdigits`, we verify that it is less than the `size` of `hexdigits`.

Exercise 3.6: Use a range `for` to change all the characters in a `string` to X.

Exercise 3.7: What would happen if you define the loop control variable in the previous exercise as type `char`? Predict the results and then change your program to use a `char` to see if you were right.

Exercise 3.8: Rewrite the program in the first exercise, first using a `while` and again using a traditional `for` loop. Which of the three approaches do you prefer and why?

Exercise 3.9: What does the following program do? Is it valid? If not, why not?

```
string s;
cout << s[0] << endl;
```

Exercise 3.10: Write a program that reads a string of characters including punctuation and writes what was read but with the punctuation removed.

Exercise 3.11: Is the following range `for` legal? If so, what is the type of c?

```
const string s = "Keep out!";
for (auto &c : s) { /* ... */ }
```

3.3 Library `vector` Type

A **vector** is a collection of objects, all of which have the same type. Every object in the collection has an associated index, which gives access to that object. A `vector` is often referred to as a **container** because it "contains" other objects. We'll have much more to say about containers in Part II.

To use a `vector`, we must include the appropriate header. In our examples, we also assume that an appropriate `using` declaration is made:

```
#include <vector>
using std::vector;
```

A `vector` is a **class template**. C++ has both class and function templates. Writing a template requires a fairly deep understanding of C++. Indeed, we won't see how to create our own templates until Chapter 16! Fortunately, we can use templates without knowing how to write them.

Templates are not themselves functions or classes. Instead, they can be thought of as instructions to the compiler for generating classes or functions. The process that the compiler uses to create classes or functions from templates is called **instantiation**. When we use a template, we specify what kind of class or function we want the compiler to instantiate.

For a class template, we specify which class to instantiate by supplying additional information, the nature of which depends on the template. How we specify the information is always the same: We supply it inside a pair of angle brackets following the template's name.

In the case of `vector`, the additional information we supply is the type of the objects the `vector` will hold:

```
vector<int> ivec;              //  ivec holds objects of type int
vector<Sales_item> Sales_vec;  //  holds Sales_items
vector<vector<string>> file;   //  vector whose elements are vectors
```

In this example, the compiler generates three distinct types from the vector template: vector<int>, vector<Sales_item>, and vector<vector<string>>.

> vector is a template, not a type. Types generated from vector must include the element type, for example, vector<int>.

We can define vectors to hold objects of most any type. Because references are not objects (§ 2.3.1, p. 50), we cannot have a vector of references. However, we can have vectors of most other (nonreference) built-in types and most class types. In particular, we can have vectors whose elements are themselves vectors.

It is worth noting that earlier versions of C++ used a slightly different syntax C++ 11 to define a vector whose elements are themselves vectors (or another template type). In the past, we had to supply a space between the closing angle bracket of the outer vector and its element type—vector<vector<int> > rather than vector<vector<int>>.

WARNING

> Some compilers may require the old-style declarations for a vector of vectors, for example, vector<vector<int> >.

3.3.1 Defining and Initializing vectors

As with any class type, the vector template controls how we define and initialize vectors. Table 3.4 (p. 99) lists the most common ways to define vectors.

We can default initialize a vector (§ 2.2.1, p. 44), which creates an empty vector of the specified type:

```
vector<string> svec;  //  default initialization; svec has no elements
```

It might seem that an empty vector would be of little use. However, as we'll see shortly, we can (efficiently) add elements to a vector at run time. Indeed, the most common way of using vectors is to define an initially empty vector to which elements are added as their values become known at run time.

We can also supply initial value(s) for the element(s) when we define a vector. For example, we can copy elements from another vector. When we copy a vector, each element in the new vector is a copy of the corresponding element in the original vector. The two vectors must be the same type:

```
vector<int> ivec;             //  initially empty
//  give ivec some values
vector<int> ivec2(ivec);      //  copy elements of ivec into ivec2
vector<int> ivec3 = ivec;     //  copy elements of ivec into ivec3
vector<string> svec(ivec2);   //  error: svec holds strings, not ints
```

List Initializing a `vector`

Another way to provide element values, is that under the new standard, we can list initialize (§ 2.2.1, p. 43) a `vector` from a list of zero or more initial element values enclosed in curly braces:

```
vector<string> articles = {"a", "an", "the"};
```

The resulting `vector` has three elements; the first holds the `string "a"`, the second holds `"an"`, and the last is `"the"`.

As we've seen, C++ provides several forms of initialization (§ 2.2.1, p. 43). In many, but not all, cases we can use these forms of initialization interchangably. So far, we have seen two examples where the form of initialization matters: when we use the copy initialization form (i.e., when we use =) (§ 3.2.1, p. 84), we can supply only a single initializer; and when we supply an in-class initializer (§ 2.6.1, p. 73), we must either use copy initialization or use curly braces. A third restriction is that we can supply a list of element values only by using list initialization in which the initializers are enclosed in curly braces. We cannot supply a list of initializers using parentheses:

```
vector<string> v1{"a", "an", "the"};    //  list initialization
vector<string> v2("a", "an", "the");    //  error
```

Creating a Specified Number of Elements

We can also initialize a `vector` from a count and an element value. The count determines how many elements the `vector` will have; the value provides the initial value for each of those elements:

```
vector<int> ivec(10, -1);        //  ten int elements, each initialized to -1
vector<string> svec(10, "hi!");  //  ten strings; each element is "hi!"
```

Value Initialization

We can usually omit the value and supply only a size. In this case the library creates a **value-initialized** element initializer for us. This library-generated value is used to initialize each element in the container. The value of the element initializer depends on the type of the elements stored in the `vector`.

If the `vector` holds elements of a built-in type, such as `int`, then the element initializer has a value of 0. If the elements are of a class type, such as `string`, then the element initializer is itself default initialized:

```
vector<int> ivec(10);        //  ten elements, each initialized to 0
vector<string> svec(10);     //  ten elements, each an empty string
```

There are two restrictions on this form of initialization: The first restriction is that some classes require that we always supply an explicit initializer (§ 2.2.1, p. 44). If our `vector` holds objects of a type that we cannot default initialize, then we must supply an initial element value; it is not possible to create `vectors` of such types by supplying only a size.

The second restriction is that when we supply an element count without also supplying an initial value, we must use the direct form of initialization:

```
vector<int> vi = 10;      // error: must use direct initialization to supply a size
```

Here we are using 10 to instruct `vector` how to create the `vector`—we want a `vector` with ten value-initialized elements. We are not "copying" 10 into the `vector`. Hence, we cannot use the copy form of initialization. We'll see more about how this restriction works in § 7.5.4 (p. 296).

Table 3.4: Ways to Initialize a vector	
`vector<T> v1`	`vector` that holds objects of type `T`. Default initialization; `v1` is empty.
`vector<T> v2(v1)`	`v2` has a copy of each element in `v1`.
`vector<T> v2 = v1`	Equivalent to `v2(v1)`, `v2` is a copy of the elements in `v1`.
`vector<T> v3(n, val)`	`v3` has n elements with value `val`.
`vector<T> v4(n)`	`v4` has n copies of a value-initialized object.
`vector<T> v5{a,b,c...}`	`v5` has as many elements as there are initializers; elements are initialized by corresponding initializers.
`vector<T> v5 = {a,b,c...}`	Equivalent to `v5{a,b,c...}`.

List Initializer or Element Count?

In a few cases, what initialization means depends upon whether we use curly braces or parentheses to pass the initializer(s). For example, when we initialize a `vector<int>` from a single `int` value, that value might represent the `vector`'s size or it might be an element value. Similarly, if we supply exactly two `int` values, those values could be a size and an initial value, or they could be values for a two-element `vector`. We specify which meaning we intend by whether we use curly braces or parentheses:

```
vector<int> v1(10);     // v1 has ten elements with value 0
vector<int> v2{10};     // v2 has one element with value 10
vector<int> v3(10, 1);  // v3 has ten elements with value 1
vector<int> v4{10, 1};  // v4 has two elements with values 10 and 1
```

When we use parentheses, we are saying that the values we supply are to be used to *construct* the object. Thus, `v1` and `v3` use their initializers to determine the `vector`'s size, and its size and element values, respectively.

When we use curly braces, {...}, we're saying that, if possible, we want to *list initialize* the object. That is, if there is a way to use the values inside the curly braces as a list of element initializers, the class will do so. Only if it is not possible to list initialize the object will the other ways to initialize the object be considered. The values we supply when we initialize `v2` and `v4` can be used as element values. These objects are list initialized; the resulting `vector`s have one and two elements, respectively.

On the other hand, if we use braces and there is no way to use the initializers to list initialize the object, then those values will be used to construct the object. For example, to list initialize a `vector` of `strings`, we must supply values that can be used as `strings`. In this case, there is no confusion about whether to list initialize the elements or construct a `vector` of the given size:

```
vector<string> v5{"hi"};    //  list initialization: v5 has one element
vector<string> v6("hi");    //  error: can't construct a vector from a string literal
vector<string> v7{10};      //  v7 has ten default-initialized elements
vector<string> v8{10, "hi"}; //  v8 has ten elements with value "hi"
```

Although we used braces on all but one of these definitions, only v5 is list initialized. In order to list initialize the `vector`, the values inside braces must match the element type. We cannot use an `int` to initialize a `string`, so the initializers for v7 and v8 can't be element initializers. If list initialization isn't possible, the compiler looks for other ways to initialize the object from the given values.

EXERCISES SECTION 3.3.1

Exercise 3.12: Which, if any, of the following `vector` definitions are in error? For those that are legal, explain what the definition does. For those that are not legal, explain why they are illegal.

    (a) `vector<vector<int>> ivec;`
    (b) `vector<string> svec = ivec;`
    (c) `vector<string> svec(10, "null");`

Exercise 3.13: How many elements are there in each of the following `vectors`? What are the values of the elements?

    (a) `vector<int> v1;`   (b) `vector<int> v2(10);`
    (c) `vector<int> v3(10, 42);` (d) `vector<int> v4{10};`
    (e) `vector<int> v5{10, 42};` (f) `vector<string> v6{10};`
    (g) `vector<string> v7{10, "hi"};`

 ## 3.3.2 Adding Elements to a `vector`

Directly initializing the elements of a `vector` is feasible only if we have a small number of known initial values, if we want to make a copy of another `vector`, or if we want to initialize all the elements to the same value. More commonly, when we create a `vector`, we don't know how many elements we'll need, or we don't know the value of those elements. Even if we do know all the values, if we have a large number of different initial element values, it can be cumbersome to specify them when we create the `vector`.

As one example, if we need a `vector` with values from 0 to 9, we can easily use list initialization. What if we wanted elements from 0 to 99 or 0 to 999? List initialization would be too unwieldy. In such cases, it is better to create an empty `vector` and use a `vector` member named **push_back** to add elements at run time. The push_back operation takes a value and "pushes" that value as a new last element onto the "back" of the `vector`. For example:

```
vector<int> v2;            // empty vector
for (int i = 0; i != 100; ++i)
    v2.push_back(i);       // append sequential integers to v2
// at end of loop v2 has 100 elements, values 0 ... 99
```

Even though we know we ultimately will have 100 elements, we define v2 as empty. Each iteration adds the next sequential integer as a new element in v2.

We use the same approach when we want to create a vector where we don't know until run time how many elements the vector should have. For example, we might read the input, storing the values we read in the vector:

```
// read words from the standard input and store them as elements in a vector
string word;
vector<string> text;       // empty vector
while (cin >> word) {
    text.push_back(word);  // append word to text
}
```

Again, we start with an initially empty vector. This time, we read and store an unknown number of values in text.

KEY CONCEPT: VECTORS GROW EFFICIENTLY

The standard requires that vector implementations can efficiently add elements at run time. Because vectors grow efficiently, it is often unnecessary—and can result in poorer performance—to define a vector of a specific size. The exception to this rule is if *all* the elements actually need the same value. If differing element values are needed, it is usually more efficient to define an empty vector and add elements as the values we need become known at run time. Moreover, as we'll see in § 9.4 (p. 355), vector offers capabilities to allow us to further enhance run-time performance when we add elements.

Starting with an empty vector and adding elements at run time is distinctly different from how we use built-in arrays in C and in most other languages. In particular, if you are accustomed to using C or Java, you might expect that it would be best to define the vector at its expected size. In fact, the contrary is usually the case.

Programming Implications of Adding Elements to a vector

The fact that we can easily and efficiently add elements to a vector greatly simplifies many programming tasks. However, this simplicity imposes a new obligation on our programs: We must ensure that any loops we write are correct even if the loop changes the size of the vector.

Other implications that follow from the dynamic nature of vectors will become clearer as we learn more about using them. However, there is one implication that is worth noting already: For reasons we'll explore in § 5.4.3 (p. 188), we cannot use a range for if the body of the loop adds elements to the vector.

 The body of a range for must not change the size of the sequence over which it is iterating.

3.3.3 Other vector Operations

In addition to push_back, vector provides only a few other operations, most of which are similar to the corresponding operations on strings. Table 3.5 lists the most important ones.

We access the elements of a vector the same way that we access the characters in a string: through their position in the vector. For example, we can use a range for (§ 3.2.3, p. 91) to process all the elements in a vector:

```
vector<int> v{1,2,3,4,5,6,7,8,9};
for (auto &i : v)        //  for each element in v (note: i is a reference)
    i *= i;              //  square the element value
for (auto i : v)         //  for each element in v
    cout << i << " ";    //  print the element
cout << endl;
```

In the first loop, we define our control variable, i, as a reference so that we can use i to assign new values to the elements in v. We let auto deduce the type of i. This loop uses a new form of the compound assignment operator (§ 1.4.1, p. 12). As we've seen, += adds the right-hand operand to the left and stores the result in the left-hand operand. The *= operator behaves similarly, except that it multiplies the left- and right-hand operands, storing the result in the left-hand one. The second range for prints each element.

The empty and size members behave as do the corresponding string members (§ 3.2.2, p. 87): empty returns a bool indicating whether the vector has any elements, and size returns the number of elements in the vector. The size member returns a value of the size_type defined by the corresponding vector type.

> To use size_type, we must name the type in which it is defined. A vector type *always* includes its element type (§ 3.3, p. 97):
>
> ```
> vector<int>::size_type // ok
> vector::size_type      // error
> ```

The equality and relational operators have the same behavior as the corresponding string operations (§ 3.2.2, p. 88). Two vectors are equal if they have the same number of elements and if the corresponding elements all have the same value. The relational operators apply a dictionary ordering: If the vectors have differing sizes, but the elements that are in common are equal, then the vector with fewer elements is less than the one with more elements. If the elements have differing values, then the relationship between the vectors is determined by the relationship between the first elements that differ.

We can compare two vectors only if we can compare the elements in those vectors. Some class types, such as string, define the meaning of the equality and relational operators. Others, such as our Sales_item class, do not. The only operations Sales_item supports are those listed in § 1.5.1 (p. 20). Those operations did not include the equality or relational operators. As a result, we cannot compare two vector<Sales_item> objects.

Table 3.5: vector Operations	
v.empty()	Returns true if v is empty; otherwise returns false.
v.size()	Returns the number of elements in v.
v.push_back(t)	Adds an element with value t to end of v.
v[n]	Returns a reference to the element at position n in v.
v1 = v2	Replaces the elements in v1 with a copy of the elements in v2.
v1 = {a,b,c...}	Replaces the elements in v1 with a copy of the elements in the comma-separated list.
v1 == v2	v1 and v2 are equal if they have the same number of elements and each
v1 != v2	element in v1 is equal to the corresponding element in v2.
<, <=, >, >=	Have their normal meanings using dictionary ordering.

Computing a vector Index

We can fetch a given element using the subscript operator (§ 3.2.3, p. 93). As with strings, subscripts for vector start at 0; the type of a subscript is the corresponding size_type; and—assuming the vector is nonconst—we can write to the element returned by the subscript operator. In addition, as we did in § 3.2.3 (p. 95), we can compute an index and directly fetch the element at that position.

As an example, let's assume that we have a collection of grades that range from 0 through 100. We'd like to count how many grades fall into various clusters of 10. Between zero and 100 there are 101 possible grades. These grades can be represented by 11 clusters: 10 clusters of 10 grades each plus one cluster for the perfect score of 100. The first cluster will count grades of 0 through 9, the second will count grades from 10 through 19, and so on. The final cluster counts how many scores of 100 were achieved.

Clustering the grades this way, if our input is

    42 65 95 100 39 67 95 76 88 76 83 92 76 93

then the output should be

    0 0 0 1 1 0 2 3 2 4 1

which indicates that there were no grades below 30, one grade in the 30s, one in the 40s, none in the 50s, two in the 60s, three in the 70s, two in the 80s, four in the 90s, and one grade of 100.

We'll use a `vector` with 11 elements to hold the counters for each cluster. We can determine the cluster index for a given grade by dividing that grade by 10. When we divide two integers, we get an integer in which the fractional part is truncated. For example, $42/10$ is 4, $65/10$ is 6 and $100/10$ is 10. Once we've computed the cluster index, we can use it to subscript our `vector` and fetch the counter we want to increment:

```
//  count the number of grades by clusters of ten: 0--9, 10--19, ... 90--99, 100
vector<unsigned> scores(11, 0);  // 11 buckets, all initially 0
unsigned grade;
while (cin >> grade) {            //  read the grades
    if (grade <= 100)            //  handle only valid grades
        ++scores[grade/10];      //  increment the counter for the current cluster
}
```

We start by defining a `vector` to hold the cluster counts. In this case, we do want each element to have the same value, so we allocate all 11 elements, each of which is initialized to 0. The `while` condition reads the grades. Inside the loop, we check that the grade we read has a valid value (i.e., that it is less than or equal to 100). Assuming the grade is valid, we increment the appropriate counter for `grade`.

The statement that does the increment is a good example of the kind of terse code characteristic of C++ programs. This expression

```
++scores[grade/10];  //  increment the counter for the current cluster
```

is equivalent to

```
auto ind = grade/10;  // get the bucket index
scores[ind] = scores[ind] + 1;  //  increment the count
```

We compute the bucket index by dividing `grade` by 10 and use the result of the division to index `scores`. Subscripting `scores` fetches the appropriate counter for this grade. We increment the value of that element to indicate the occurrence of a score in the given range.

As we've seen, when we use a subscript, we should think about how we know that the indices are in range (§ 3.2.3, p. 95). In this program, we verify that the input is a valid grade in the range between 0 and 100. Thus, we know that the indices we can compute are between 0 and 10. These indices are between 0 and `scores.size() - 1`.

Subscripting Does Not Add Elements

Programmers new to C++ sometimes think that subscripting a `vector` adds elements; it does not. The following code intends to add ten elements to `ivec`:

```
vector<int> ivec;    // empty vector
for (decltype(ivec.size()) ix = 0; ix != 10; ++ix)
    ivec[ix] = ix;   // disaster: ivec has no elements
```

However, it is in error: `ivec` is an empty `vector`; there are no elements to subscript! As we've seen, the right way to write this loop is to use `push_back`:

```
for (decltype(ivec.size()) ix = 0; ix != 10; ++ix)
    ivec.push_back(ix);   //  ok: adds a new element with value ix
```

The subscript operator on vector (and string) fetches an existing element; it does *not* add an element.

CAUTION: SUBSCRIPT ONLY ELEMENTS THAT ARE KNOWN TO EXIST!

It is crucially important to understand that we may use the subscript operator (the [] operator) to fetch only elements that actually exist. For example,

```
vector<int> ivec;        //  empty vector
cout << ivec[0];         //  error: ivec has no elements!

vector<int> ivec2(10);   //  vector with ten elements
cout << ivec2[10];       //  error: ivec2 has elements 0 ... 9
```

It is an error to subscript an element that doesn't exist, but it is an error that the compiler is unlikely to detect. Instead, the value we get at run time is undefined.

Attempting to subscript elements that do not exist is, unfortunately, an extremely common and pernicious programming error. So-called *buffer overflow* errors are the result of subscripting elements that don't exist. Such bugs are the most common cause of security problems in PC and other applications.

A good way to ensure that subscripts are in range is to avoid subscripting altogether by using a range for whenever possible.

EXERCISES SECTION 3.3.3

Exercise 3.16: Write a program to print the size and contents of the vectors from exercise 3.13. Check whether your answers to that exercise were correct. If not, restudy § 3.3.1 (p. 97) until you understand why you were wrong.

Exercise 3.17: Read a sequence of words from cin and store the values a vector. After you've read all the words, process the vector and change each word to uppercase. Print the transformed elements, eight words to a line.

Exercise 3.18: Is the following program legal? If not, how might you fix it?

```
vector<int> ivec;
ivec[0] = 42;
```

Exercise 3.19: List three ways to define a vector and give it ten elements, each with the value 42. Indicate whether there is a preferred way to do so and why.

Exercise 3.20: Read a set of integers into a vector. Print the sum of each pair of adjacent elements. Change your program so that it prints the sum of the first and last elements, followed by the sum of the second and second-to-last, and so on.

3.4 Introducing Iterators

Although we can use subscripts to access the characters of a string or the elements in a vector, there is a more general mechanism—known as **iterators**—that we can use for the same purpose. As we'll see in Part II, in addition to vector, the library defines several other kinds of containers. All of the library containers have iterators, but only a few of them support the subscript operator. Technically speaking, a string is not a container type, but string supports many of the container operations. As we've seen string, like vector has a subscript operator. Like vectors, strings also have iterators.

Like pointers (§ 2.3.2, p. 52), iterators give us indirect access to an object. In the case of an iterator, that object is an element in a container or a character in a string. We can use an iterator to fetch an element and iterators have operations to move from one element to another. As with pointers, an iterator may be valid or invalid. A valid iterator either denotes an element or denotes a position one past the last element in a container. All other iterator values are invalid.

3.4.1 Using Iterators

Unlike pointers, we do not use the address-of operator to obtain an iterator. Instead, types that have iterators have members that return iterators. In particular, these types have members named **begin** and **end**. The begin member returns an iterator that denotes the first element (or first character), if there is one:

```
//  the compiler determines the type of b and e; see § 2.5.2 (p. 68)
//  b denotes the first element and e denotes one past the last element in v
auto b = v.begin(), e = v.end(); //  b and e have the same type
```

The iterator returned by end is an iterator positioned "one past the end" of the associated container (or string). This iterator denotes a nonexistent element "off the end" of the container. It is used as a marker indicating when we have processed all the elements. The iterator returned by end is often referred to as the **off-the-end iterator** or abbreviated as "the end iterator." If the container is empty, begin returns the same iterator as the one returned by end.

If the container is empty, the iterators returned by begin and end are equal—they are both off-the-end iterators.

In general, we do not know (or care about) the precise type that an iterator has. In this example, we used auto to define b and e (§ 2.5.2, p. 68). As a result, these variables have whatever type is returned by the begin and end members, respectively. We'll have more to say about those types on page 108.

Iterator Operations

Iterators support only a few operations, which are listed in Table 3.6. We can compare two valid iterators using == or !=. Iterators are equal if they denote the same element or if they are both off-the-end iterators for the same container. Otherwise, they are unequal.

As with pointers, we can dereference an iterator to obtain the element denoted by an iterator. Also, like pointers, we may dereference only a valid iterator that denotes an element (§ 2.3.2, p. 53). Dereferencing an invalid iterator or an off-the-end iterator has undefined behavior.

As an example, we'll rewrite the program from § 3.2.3 (p. 94) that capitalized the first character of a `string` using an iterator instead of a subscript:

```
string s("some string");
if (s.begin() != s.end()) { //  make sure s is not empty
    auto it = s.begin();    //  it denotes the first character in s
    *it = toupper(*it);     //  make that character uppercase
}
```

As in our original program, we first check that s isn't empty. In this case, we do so by comparing the iterators returned by `begin` and `end`. Those iterators are equal if the `string` is empty. If they are unequl, there is at least one character in s.

Inside the `if` body, we obtain an iterator to the first character by assigning the iterator returned by `begin` to `it`. We dereference that iterator to pass that character to `toupper`. We also dereference `it` on the left-hand side of the assignment in order to assign the character returned from `toupper` to the first character in s. As in our original program, the output of this loop will be:

Some string

Table 3.6: Standard Container Iterator Operations	
`*iter`	Returns a reference to the element denoted by the iterator `iter`.
`iter->mem`	Dereferences `iter` and fetches the member named `mem` from the underlying element. Equivalent to `(*iter).mem`.
`++iter`	Increments `iter` to refer to the next element in the container.
`--iter`	Decrements `iter` to refer to the previous element in the container.
`iter1 == iter2` `iter1 != iter2`	Compares two iterators for equality (inequality). Two iterators are equal if they denote the same element or if they are the off-the-end iterator for the same container.

Moving Iterators from One Element to Another

Iterators use the increment (++) operator (§ 1.4.1, p. 12) to move from one element to the next. Incrementing an iterator is a logically similar operation to incrementing an integer. In the case of integers, the effect is to "add 1" to the integer's value. In the case of iterators, the effect is to "advance the iterator by one position."

Because the iterator returned from end does not denote an element, it may not be incremented or dereferenced.

Using the increment operator, we can rewrite our program that changed the case of the first word in a `string` to use iterators instead:

```
//  process characters in s until we run out of characters or we hit a whitespace
for (auto it = s.begin(); it != s.end() && !isspace(*it); ++it)
    *it = toupper(*it);  // capitalize the current character
```

This loop, like the one in § 3.2.3 (p. 94), iterates through the characters in s, stopping when we encounter a whitespace character. However, this loop accesses these characters using an iterator, not a subscript.

The loop starts by initializing it from s.begin, meaning that it denotes the first character (if any) in s. The condition checks whether it has reached the end of s. If not, the condition next dereferences it to pass the current character to isspace to see whether we're done. At the end of each iteration, we execute ++it to advance the iterator to access the next character in s.

The body of this loop, is the same as the last statement in the previous if. We dereference it to pass the current character to toupper and assign the resulting uppercase letter back into the character denoted by it.

KEY CONCEPT: GENERIC PROGRAMMING

Programmers coming to C++ from C or Java might be surprised that we used != rather than < in our for loops such as the one above and in the one on page 94. C++ programmers use != as a matter of habit. They do so for the same reason that they use iterators rather than subscripts: This coding style applies equally well to various kinds of containers provided by the library.

As we've seen, only a few library types, vector and string being among them, have the subscript operator. Similarly, all of the library containers have iterators that define the == and != operators. Most of those iterators do not have the < operator. By routinely using iterators and !=, we don't have to worry about the precise type of container we're processing.

Iterator Types

Just as we do not know the precise type of a vector's or string's size_type member (§ 3.2.2, p. 88), so too, we generally do not know—and do not need to know—the precise type of an iterator. Instead, as with size_type, the library types that have iterators define types named iterator and const_iterator that represent actual iterator types:

```
vector<int>::iterator it;        // it can read and write vector<int> elements
string::iterator it2;            // it2 can read and write characters in a string
vector<int>::const_iterator it3; // it3 can read but not write elements
string::const_iterator it4;      // it4 can read but not write characters
```

A const_iterator behaves like a const pointer (§ 2.4.2, p. 62). Like a const pointer, a const_iterator may read but not write the element it denotes; an object of type iterator can both read and write. If a vector or string is const, we may use only its const_iterator type. With a nonconst vector or string, we can use either iterator or const_iterator.

> ### TERMINOLOGY: ITERATORS AND ITERATOR TYPES
>
> The term iterator is used to refer to three different entities. We might mean the *concept* of an iterator, or we might refer to the iterator *type* defined by a container, or we might refer to an *object* as an iterator.
>
> What's important to understand is that there is a collection of types that are related conceptually. A type is an iterator if it supports a common set of actions. Those actions let us access an element in a container and let us move from one element to another.
>
> Each container class defines a type named iterator; that iterator type supports the actions of an (conceptual) iterator.

The begin and end Operations

The type returned by begin and end depends on whether the object on which they operator is const. If the object is const, then begin and end return a const_iterator; if the object is not const, they return iterator:

```
vector<int> v;
const vector<int> cv;
auto it1 = v.begin();  // it1 has type vector<int>::iterator
auto it2 = cv.begin(); // it2 has type vector<int>::const_iterator
```

Often this default behavior is not what we want. For reasons we'll explain in § 6.2.3 (p. 213), it is usually best to use a const type (such as const_iterator) when we need to read but do not need to write to an object. To let us ask specifically for the const_iterator type, the new standard introduced two new functions named cbegin and cend:

```
auto it3 = v.cbegin(); // it3 has type vector<int>::const_iterator
```

As do the begin and end members, these members return iterators to the first and one past the last element in the container. However, regardless of whether the vector (or string) is const, they return a const_iterator.

Combining Dereference and Member Access

When we dereference an iterator, we get the object that the iterator denotes. If that object has a class type, we may want to access a member of that object. For example, we might have a vector of strings and we might need to know whether a given element is empty. Assuming it is an iterator into this vector, we can check whether the string that it denotes is empty as follows:

```
(*it).empty()
```

For reasons we'll cover in § 4.1.2 (p. 136), the parentheses in (*it).empty() are necessary. The parentheses say to apply the dereference operator to it and to apply the dot operator (§ 1.5.2, p. 23) to the result of dereferencing it. Without parentheses, the dot operator would apply to it, not to the resulting object:

```
(*it).empty() // dereferences it and calls the member empty on the resulting object
*it.empty()   // error: attempts to fetch the member named empty from it
              //        but it is an iterator and has no member named empty
```

The second expression is interpreted as a request to fetch the `empty` member from the object named `it`. However, `it` is an iterator and has no member named `empty`. Hence, the second expression is in error.

To simplify expressions such as this one, the language defines the arrow operator (the **-> operator**). The arrow operator combines dereference and member access into a single operation. That is, `it->mem` is a synonym for `(*it).mem`.

For example, assume we have a `vector<string>` named `text` that holds the data from a text file. Each element in the `vector` is either a sentence or an empty `string` representing a paragraph break. If we want to print the contents of the first paragraph from `text`, we'd write a loop that iterates through `text` until we encounter an element that is empty:

```
//  print each line in text up to the first blank line
for (auto it = text.cbegin();
     it != text.cend() && !it->empty(); ++it)
    cout << *it << endl;
```

We start by initializing `it` to denote the first element in `text`. The loop continues until either we process every element in `text` or we find an element that is empty. So long as there are elements and we haven't seen an empty element, we print the current element. It is worth noting that because the loop reads but does not write to the elements in `text`, we use `cbegin` and `cend` to control the iteration.

Some `vector` Operations Invalidate Iterators

In § 3.3.2 (p. 101) we noted that there are implications of the fact that `vector`s can grow dynamically. We also noted that one such implication is that we cannot add elements to a `vector` inside a range `for` loop. Another implication is that any operation, such as `push_back`, that changes the size of a `vector` potentially invalidates all iterators into that `vector`. We'll explore how iterators become invalid in more detail in § 9.3.6 (p. 353).

WARNING   For now, it is important to realize that loops that use iterators should not add elements to the container to which the iterators refer.

EXERCISES SECTION 3.4.1

Exercise 3.21: Redo the first exercise from § 3.3.3 (p. 105) using iterators.

Exercise 3.22: Revise the loop that printed the first paragraph in `text` to instead change the elements in `text` that correspond to the first paragraph to all uppercase. After you've updated `text`, print its contents.

Exercise 3.23: Write a program to create a `vector` with ten `int` elements. Using an iterator, assign each element a value that is twice its current value. Test your program by printing the `vector`.

3.4.2 Iterator Arithmetic

Incrementing an iterator moves the iterator one element at a time. All the library containers have iterators that support increment. Similarly, we can use == and != to compare two valid iterators (§ 3.4, p. 106) into any of the library container types.

Iterators for string and vector support additional operations that can move an iterator multiple elements at a time. They also support all the relational operators. These operations, which are often referred to as **iterator arithmetic**, are described in Table 3.7.

Table 3.7: Operations Supported by vector and string Iterators	
`iter + n` `iter - n`	Adding (subtracting) an integral value n to (from) an iterator yields an iterator that many elements forward (backward) within the container. The resulting iterator must denote elements in, or one past the end of, the same container.
`iter1 += n` `iter1 -= n`	Compound-assignment for iterator addition and subtraction. Assigns to iter1 the value of adding n to, or subtracting n from, iter1.
`iter1 - iter2`	Subtracting two iterators yields the number that when added to the right-hand iterator yields the left-hand iterator. The iterators must denote elements in, or one past the end of, the same container.
`>, >=, <, <=`	Relational operators on iterators. One iterator is less than another if it refers to an element that appears in the container before the one referred to by the other iterator. The iterators must denote elements in, or one past the end of, the same container.

Arithmetic Operations on Iterators

We can add (or subtract) an integral value and an iterator. Doing so returns an iterator positioned forward (or backward) that many elements. When we add or subtract an integral value and an iterator, the result must denote an element in the same vector (or string) or denote one past the end of the associated vector (or string). As an example, we can compute an iterator to the element nearest the middle of a vector:

```
// compute an iterator to the element closest to the midpoint of vi
auto mid = vi.begin() + vi.size() / 2;
```

If vi has 20 elements, then vi.size()/2 is 10. In this case, we'd set mid equal to vi.begin() + 10. Remembering that subscripts start at 0, this element is the same as vi[10], the element ten past the first.

In addition to comparing two iterators for equality, we can compare vector and string iterators using the relational operators (<, <=, >, >=). The iterators must be valid and must denote elements in (or one past the end of) the same vector or string. For example, assuming it is an iterator into the same vector as mid, we can check whether it denotes an element before or after mid as follows:

```
if (it < mid)
    // process elements in the first half of vi
```

We can also subtract two iterators so long as they refer to elements in, or one off the end of, the same `vector` or `string`. The result is the distance between the iterators. By distance we mean the amount by which we'd have to change one iterator to get the other. The result type is a signed integral type named **difference_type**. Both `vector` and `string` define `difference_type`. This type is signed, because subtraction might have a negative result.

Using Iterator Arithmetic

A classic algorithm that uses iterator arithmetic is binary search. A binary search looks for a particular value in a sorted sequence. It operates by looking at the element closest to the middle of the sequence. If that element is the one we want, we're done. Otherwise, if that element is smaller than the one we want, we continue our search by looking only at elements after the rejected one. If the middle element is larger than the one we want, we continue by looking only in the first half. We compute a new middle element in the reduced range and continue looking until we either find the element or run out of elements.

We can do a binary search using iterators as follows:

```
//  text must be sorted
//  beg and end will denote the range we're searching
auto beg = text.begin(), end = text.end();
auto mid = text.begin() + (end - beg)/2; //  original midpoint
//  while there are still elements to look at and we haven't yet found sought
while (mid != end && *mid != sought) {
    if (sought < *mid)         //  is the element we want in the first half?
        end = mid;             //  if so, adjust the range to ignore the second half
    else                       //  the element we want is in the second half
        beg = mid + 1;         //  start looking with the element just after mid
    mid = beg + (end - beg)/2; //  new midpoint
}
```

We start by defining three iterators: `beg` will be the first element in the range, `end` one past the last element, and `mid` the element closest to the middle. We initialize these iterators to denote the entire range in a `vector<string>` named `text`.

Our loop first checks that the range is not empty. If `mid` is equal to the current value of `end`, then we've run out of elements to search. In this case, the condition fails and we exit the `while`. Otherwise, `mid` refers to an element and we check whether `mid` denotes the one we want. If so, we're done and we exit the loop.

If we still have elements to process, the code inside the `while` adjusts the range by moving `end` or `beg`. If the element denoted by `mid` is greater than `sought`, we know that if `sought` is in `text`, it will appear before the element denoted by `mid`. Therefore, we can ignore elements after `mid`, which we do by assigning `mid` to `end`. If `*mid` is smaller than `sought`, the element must be in the range of elements after the one denoted by `mid`. In this case, we adjust the range by making `beg` denote the element just after `mid`. We already know that `mid` is not the one we want, so we can eliminate it from the range.

At the end of the `while`, `mid` will be equal to `end` or it will denote the element for which we are looking. If `mid` equals `end`, then the element was not in `text`.

Exercise 3.24: Redo the last exercise from § 3.3.3 (p. 105) using iterators.

Exercise 3.25: Rewrite the grade clustering program from § 3.3.3 (p. 104) using iterators instead of subscripts.

Exercise 3.26: In the binary search program on page 112, why did we write mid = beg + (end - beg) / 2; instead of mid = (beg + end) /2;?

3.5 Arrays

An array is a data structure that is similar to the library vector type (§ 3.3, p. 96) but offers a different trade-off between performance and flexibility. Like a vector, an array is a container of unnamed objects of a single type that we access by position. Unlike a vector, arrays have fixed size; we cannot add elements to an array. Because arrays have fixed size, they sometimes offer better run-time performance for specialized applications. However, that run-time advantage comes at the cost of lost flexibility.

 If you don't know exactly how many elements you need, use a vector.

3.5.1 Defining and Initializing Built-in Arrays

Arrays are a compound type (§ 2.3, p. 50). An array declarator has the form a [d], where a is the name being defined and d is the dimension of the array. The dimension specifies the number of elements and must be greater than zero. The number of elements in an array is part of the array's type. As a result, the dimension must be known at compile time, which means that the dimension must be a constant expression (§ 2.4.4, p. 65):

```
unsigned cnt = 42;            //  not a constant expression
constexpr unsigned sz = 42;   //  constant expression
                              //  constexpr see § 2.4.4 (p. 66)
int arr[10];                  //  array of ten ints
int *parr[sz];                //  array of 42 pointers to int
string bad[cnt];              //  error: cnt is not a constant expression
string strs[get_size()];      //  ok if get_size is constexpr, error otherwise
```

By default, the elements in an array are default initialized (§ 2.2.1, p. 43).

 As with variables of built-in type, a default-initialized array of built-in type that is defined inside a function will have undefined values.

When we define an array, we must specify a type for the array. We cannot use auto to deduce the type from a list of initializers. As with vector, arrays hold objects. Thus, there are no arrays of references.

Explicitly Initializing Array Elements

We can list initialize (§ 3.3.1, p. 98) the elements in an array. When we do so, we can omit the dimension. If we omit the dimension, the compiler infers it from the number of initializers. If we specify a dimension, the number of initializers must not exceed the specified size. If the dimension is greater than the number of initializers, the initializers are used for the first elements and any remaining elements are value initialized (§ 3.3.1, p. 98):

```
const unsigned sz = 3;
int ia1[sz] = {0,1,2};    // array of three ints with values 0, 1, 2
int a2[] = {0, 1, 2};     // an array of dimension 3
int a3[5] = {0, 1, 2};    // equivalent to a3[] = {0, 1, 2, 0, 0}
string a4[3] = {"hi", "bye"}; // same as a4[] = {"hi", "bye", ""}
int a5[2] = {0,1,2};      // error: too many initializers
```

Character Arrays Are Special

Character arrays have an additional form of initialization: We can initialize such arrays from a string literal (§ 2.1.3, p. 39). When we use this form of initialization, it is important to remember that string literals end with a null character. That null character is copied into the array along with the characters in the literal:

```
char a1[] = {'C', '+', '+'};        // list initialization, no null
char a2[] = {'C', '+', '+', '\0'};  // list initialization, explicit null
char a3[] = "C++";                  // null terminator added automatically
const char a4[6] = "Daniel";        // error: no space for the null!
```

The dimension of a1 is 3; the dimensions of a2 and a3 are both 4. The definition of a4 is in error. Although the literal contains only six explicit characters, the array size must be at least seven—six to hold the literal and one for the null.

No Copy or Assignment

We cannot initialize an array as a copy of another array, nor is it legal to assign one array to another:

```
int a[] = {0, 1, 2}; // array of three ints
int a2[] = a;        // error: cannot initialize one array with another
a2 = a;              // error: cannot assign one array to another
```

WARNING

> Some compilers allow array assignment as a **compiler extension**. It is usually a good idea to avoid using nonstandard features. Programs that use such features, will not work with a different compiler.

Understanding Complicated Array Declarations

Like vectors, arrays can hold objects of most any type. For example, we can have an array of pointers. Because an array is an object, we can define both pointers and references to arrays. Defining arrays that hold pointers is fairly straightforward, defining a pointer or reference to an array is a bit more complicated:

```
int *ptrs[10];              //  ptrs is an array of ten pointers to int
int &refs[10] = /* ? */;   //  error: no arrays of references
int (*Parray)[10] = &arr;  //  Parray points to an array of ten ints
int (&arrRef)[10] = arr;   //  arrRef refers to an array of ten ints
```

By default, type modifiers bind right to left. Reading the definition of `ptrs` from right to left (§ 2.3.3, p. 58) is easy: We see that we're defining an array of size 10, named `ptrs`, that holds pointers to `int`.

Reading the definition of `Parray` from right to left isn't as helpful. Because the array dimension follows the name being declared, it can be easier to read array declarations from the inside out rather than from right to left. Reading from the inside out makes it much easier to understand the type of `Parray`. We start by observing that the parentheses around `*Parray` mean that `Parray` is a pointer. Looking right, we see that `Parray` points to an array of size 10. Looking left, we see that the elements in that array are `int`s. Thus, `Parray` is a pointer to an array of ten `int`s. Similarly, `(&arrRef)` says that `arrRef` is a reference. The type to which it refers is an array of size 10. That array holds elements of type `int`.

Of course, there are no limits on how many type modifiers can be used:

```
int *(&arry)[10] = ptrs; //  arry is a reference to an array of ten pointers
```

Reading this declaration from the inside out, we see that `arry` is a reference. Looking right, we see that the object to which `arry` refers is an array of size 10. Looking left, we see that the element type is pointer to `int`. Thus, `arry` is a reference to an array of ten pointers.

It can be easier to understand array declarations by starting with the array's name and reading them from the inside out.

EXERCISES SECTION 3.5.1

Exercise 3.27: Assuming `txt_size` is a function that takes no arguments and returns an `int` value, which of the following definitions are illegal? Explain why.

```
unsigned buf_size = 1024;
(a) int ia[buf_size];       (b) int ia[4 * 7 - 14];
(c) int ia[txt_size()];     (d) char st[11] = "fundamental";
```

Exercise 3.28: What are the values in the following arrays?

```
string sa[10];
int ia[10];
int main() {
    string sa2[10];
    int    ia2[10];
}
```

Exercise 3.29: List some of the drawbacks of using an array instead of a `vector`.

3.5.2 Accessing the Elements of an Array

As with the library `vector` and `string` types, we can use a range `for` or the subscript operator to access elements of an array. As usual, the indices start at 0. For an array of ten elements, the indices are 0 through 9, not 1 through 10.

When we use a variable to subscript an array, we normally should define that variable to have type **size_t**. `size_t` is a machine-specific unsigned type that is guaranteed to be large enough to hold the size of any object in memory. The `size_t` type is defined in the `cstddef` header, which is the C++ version of the `stddef.h` header from the C library.

With the exception that arrays are fixed size, we use arrays in ways that are similar to how we use `vectors`. For example, we can reimplement our grading program from § 3.3.3 (p. 104) to use an array to hold the cluster counters:

```
// count the number of grades by clusters of ten: 0--9, 10--19, . . . 90--99, 100
unsigned scores[11] = {};   // 11 buckets, all value initialized to 0
unsigned grade;
while (cin >> grade) {
    if (grade <= 100)
        ++scores[grade/10]; // increment the counter for the current cluster
}
```

The only obvious difference between this program and the one on page 104 is the declaration of `scores`. In this program `scores` is an array of 11 `unsigned` elements. The not so obvious difference is that the subscript operator in this program is the one that is defined as part of the language. This operator can be used on operands of array type. The subscript operator used in the program on page 104 was defined by the library `vector` template and applies to operands of type `vector`.

As in the case of `string` or `vector`, it is best to use a range `for` when we want to traverse the entire array. For example, we can print the resulting `scores` as follows:

```
for (auto i : scores)      // for each counter in scores
    cout << i << " ";      // print the value of that counter
cout << endl;
```

Because the dimension is part of each array type, the system knows how many elements are in `scores`. Using a range `for` means that we don't have to manage the traversal ourselves.

Checking Subscript Values

As with `string` and `vector`, it is up to the programmer to ensure that the subscript value is in range—that is, that the index value is equal to or greater than zero and less than the size of the array. Nothing stops a program from stepping across an array boundary except careful attention to detail and thorough testing of the code. It is possible for programs to compile and execute yet still be fatally wrong.

WARNING The most common source of security problems are buffer overflow bugs. Such bugs occur when a program fails to check a subscript and mistakenly uses memory outside the range of an array or similar data structure.

Exercise 3.30: Identify the indexing errors in the following code:

```
constexpr size_t array_size = 10;
int ia[array_size];
for (size_t ix = 1; ix <= array_size; ++ix)
        ia[ix] = ix;
```

Exercise 3.31: Write a program to define an array of ten `ints`. Give each element the same value as its position in the array.

Exercise 3.32: Copy the array you defined in the previous exercise into another array. Rewrite your program to use `vectors`.

Exercise 3.33: What would happen if we did not initialize the `scores` array in the program on page 116?

3.5.3 Pointers and Arrays

In C++ pointers and arrays are closely intertwined. In particular, as we'll see, when we use an array, the compiler ordinarily converts the array to a pointer.

Normally, we obtain a pointer to an object by using the address-of operator (§ 2.3.2, p. 52). Generally speaking, the address-of operator may be applied to any object. The elements in an array are objects. When we subscript an array, the result is the object at that location in the array. As with any other object, we can obtain a pointer to an array element by taking the address of that element:

```
string nums[] = {"one", "two", "three"};  // array of strings
string *p = &nums[0];     // p points to the first element in nums
```

However, arrays have a special property—in most places when we use an array, the compiler automatically substitutes a pointer to the first element:

```
string *p2 = nums;        // equivalent to p2 = &nums[0]
```

 In most expressions, when we use an object of array type, we are really using a pointer to the first element in that array.

There are various implications of the fact that operations on arrays are often really operations on pointers. One such implication is that when we use an array as an initializer for a variable defined using `auto` (§ 2.5.2, p. 68), the deduced type is a pointer, not an array:

```
int ia[] = {0,1,2,3,4,5,6,7,8,9}; // ia is an array of ten ints
auto ia2(ia); // ia2 is an int * that points to the first element in ia
ia2 = 42;        // error: ia2 is a pointer, and we can't assign an int to a pointer
```

Although `ia` is an array of ten `ints`, when we use `ia` as an initializer, the compiler treats that initialization as if we had written

```
auto ia2(&ia[0]);   // now it's clear that ia2 has type int*
```

It is worth noting that this conversion does not happen when we use `decltype`
(§ 2.5.3, p. 70). The type returned by `decltype(ia)` is array of ten `int`s:

```
//   ia3 is an array of ten ints
decltype(ia) ia3 = {0,1,2,3,4,5,6,7,8,9};
ia3 = p;      // error: can't assign an int* to an array
ia3[4] = i;  // ok: assigns the value of i to an element in ia3
```

Pointers Are Iterators

Pointers that address elements in an array have additional operations beyond
those we described in § 2.3.2 (p. 52). In particular, pointers to array elements support the same operations as iterators on `vectors` or `strings` (§ 3.4, p. 106). For
example, we can use the increment operator to move from one element in an array
to the next:

```
int arr[] = {0,1,2,3,4,5,6,7,8,9};
int *p = arr; //  p points to the first element in arr
++p;          //  p points to arr[1]
```

Just as we can use iterators to traverse the elements in a `vector`, we can use
pointers to traverse the elements in an array. Of course, to do so, we need to obtain
pointers to the first and one past the last element. As we've just seen, we can obtain
a pointer to the first element by using the array itself or by taking the address-of
the first element. We can obtain an off-the-end pointer by using another special
property of arrays. We can take the address of the nonexistent element one past
the last element of an array:

```
int *e = &arr[10]; //  pointer just past the last element in arr
```

Here we used the subscript operator to index a nonexisting element; `arr` has ten
elements, so the last element in `arr` is at index position 9. The only thing we can
do with this element is take its address, which we do to initialize e. Like an off-the-
end iterator (§ 3.4.1, p. 106), an off-the-end pointer does not point to an element.
As a result, we may not dereference or increment an off-the-end pointer.

Using these pointers we can write a loop to print the elements in `arr` as follows:

```
for (int *b = arr; b != e; ++b)
    cout << *b << endl; //  print the elements in arr
```

The Library begin and end Functions

Although we can compute an off-the-end pointer, doing so is error-prone. To make
it easier and safer to use pointers, the new library includes two functions, named
`begin` and `end`. These functions act like the similarly named container members
(§ 3.4.1, p. 106). However, arrays are not class types, so these functions are not
member functions. Instead, they take an argument that is an array:

```
int ia[] = {0,1,2,3,4,5,6,7,8,9}; //  ia is an array of ten ints
int *beg = begin(ia); //  pointer to the first element in ia
int *last = end(ia);  //  pointer one past the last element in ia
```

begin returns a pointer to the first, and end returns a pointer one past the last element in the given array: These functions are defined in the iterator header.

Using begin and end, it is easy to write a loop to process the elements in an array. For example, assuming arr is an array that holds int values, we might find the first negative value in arr as follows:

```
// pbeg points to the first and pend points just past the last element in arr
int *pbeg = begin(arr),   *pend = end(arr);
// find the first negative element, stopping if we've seen all the elements
while (pbeg != pend && *pbeg >= 0)
    ++pbeg;
```

We start by defining two int pointers named pbeg and pend. We position pbeg to denote the first element and pend to point one past the last element in arr. The while condition uses pend to know whether it is safe to dereference pbeg. If pbeg does point at an element, we dereference and check whether the underlying element is negative. If so, the condition fails and we exit the loop. If not, we increment the pointer to look at the next element.

> A pointer "one past" the end of a built-in array behaves the same way as the iterator returned by the end operation of a vector. In particular, we may not dereference or increment an off-the-end pointer.

Pointer Arithmetic

Pointers that address array elements can use all the iterator operations listed in Table 3.6 (p. 107) and Table 3.7 (p. 111). These operations—dereference, increment, comparisons, addition of an integral value, subtraction of two pointers—have the same meaning when applied to pointers that point at elements in a built-in array as they do when applied to iterators.

When we add (or subtract) an integral value to (or from) a pointer, the result is a new pointer. That new pointer points to the element the given number ahead of (or behind) the original pointer:

```
constexpr size_t sz = 5;
int arr[sz] = {1,2,3,4,5};
int *ip = arr;        // equivalent to int *ip = &arr[0]
int *ip2 = ip + 4; // ip2 points to arr[4], the last element in arr
```

The result of adding 4 to ip is a pointer that points to the element four elements further on in the array from the one to which ip currently points.

The result of adding an integral value to a pointer must be a pointer to an element in the same array, or a pointer just past the end of the array:

```
// ok: arr is converted to a pointer to its first element; p points one past the end of arr
int *p = arr + sz; // use caution -- do not dereference!
int *p2 = arr + 10; // error: arr has only 5 elements; p2 has undefined value
```

When we add sz to arr, the compiler converts arr to a pointer to the first element in arr. When we add sz to that pointer, we get a pointer that points sz positions (i.e., 5 positions) past the first one. That is, it points one past the last element in arr. Computing a pointer more than one past the last element is an error, although the compiler is unlikely to detect such errors.

As with iterators, subtracting two pointers gives us the distance between those pointers. The pointers must point to elements in the same array:

```
auto n = end(arr) - begin(arr); // n is 5, the number of elements in arr
```

The result of subtracting two pointers is a library type named **ptrdiff_t**. Like size_t, the ptrdiff_t type is a machine-specific type and is defined in the cstddef header. Because subtraction might yield a negative distance, ptrdiff_t is a signed integral type.

We can use the relational operators to compare pointers that point to elements of an array, or one past the last element in that array. For example, we can traverse the elements in arr as follows:

```
int *b = arr, *e = arr + sz;
while (b < e) {
    // use *b
    ++b;
}
```

We cannot use the relational operators on pointers to two unrelated objects:

```
int i = 0, sz = 42;
int *p = &i, *e = &sz;
// undefined: p and e are unrelated; comparison is meaningless!
while (p < e)
```

Although the utility may be obscure at this point, it is worth noting that pointer arithmetic is also valid for null pointers (§ 2.3.2, p. 53) and for pointers that point to an object that is not an array. In the latter case, the pointers must point to the same object, or one past that object. If p is a null pointer, we can add or subtract an integral constant expression (§ 2.4.4, p. 65) whose value is 0 to p. We can also subtract two null pointers from one another, in which case the result is 0.

Interaction between Dereference and Pointer Arithmetic

The result of adding an integral value to a pointer is itself a pointer. Assuming the resulting pointer points to an element, we can dereference the resulting pointer:

```
int ia[] = {0,2,4,6,8}; // array with 5 elements of type int
int last = *(ia + 4);   // ok: initializes last to 8, the value of ia[4]
```

The expression *(ia + 4) calculates the address four elements past ia and dereferences the resulting pointer. This expression is equivalent to writing ia[4].

Recall that in § 3.4.1 (p. 109) we noted that parentheses are required in expressions that contain dereference and dot operators. Similarly, the parentheses around this pointer addition are essential. Writing

```
last = *ia + 4;    // ok: last = 4, equivalent to ia[0] + 4
```

means dereference ia and add 4 to the dereferenced value. We'll cover the reasons for this behavior in § 4.1.2 (p. 136).

Subscripts and Pointers

As we've seen, in most places when we use the name of an array, we are really using a pointer to the first element in that array. One place where the compiler does this transformation is when we subscript an array. Given

```
int ia[] = {0,2,4,6,8};   // array with 5 elements of type int
```

if we write ia[0], that is an expression that uses the name of an array. When we subscript an array, we are really subscripting a pointer to an element in that array:

```
int i = ia[2];   //   ia is converted to a pointer to the first element in ia
                 //   ia[2] fetches the element to which (ia + 2) points
int *p = ia;     //   p points to the first element in ia
i = *(p + 2);    //   equivalent to i = ia[2]
```

We can use the subscript operator on any pointer, as long as that pointer points to an element (or one past the last element) in an array:

```
int *p = &ia[2];   //   p points to the element indexed by 2
int j = p[1];      //   p[1] is equivalent to *(p + 1),
                   //   p[1] is the same element as ia[3]
int k = p[-2];     //   p[-2] is the same element as ia[0]
```

This last example points out an important difference between arrays and library types such as vector and string that have subscript operators. The library types force the index used with a subscript to be an unsigned value. The built-in subscript operator does not. The index used with the built-in subscript operator can be a negative value. Of course, the resulting address must point to an element in (or one past the end of) the array to which the original pointer points.

 Unlike subscripts for vector and string, the index of the built-in subscript operator is not an unsigned type.

WARNING

EXERCISES SECTION 3.5.3

Exercise 3.34: Given that p1 and p2 point to elements in the same array, what does the following code do? Are there values of p1 or p2 that make this code illegal?

```
p1 += p2 - p1;
```

Exercise 3.35: Using pointers, write a program to set the elements in an array to zero.

Exercise 3.36: Write a program to compare two arrays for equality. Write a similar program to compare two vectors.

3.5.4   C-Style Character Strings

 Although C++ supports C-style strings, they should not be used by C++ programs. C-style strings are a surprisingly rich source of bugs and are **WARNING** the root cause of many security problems. They're also harder to use!

Character string literals are an instance of a more general construct that C++ inherits from C: **C-style character strings**. C-style strings are not a type. Instead, they are a convention for how to represent and use character strings. Strings that follow this convention are stored in character arrays and are **null terminated**. By null-terminated we mean that the last character in the string is followed by a null character (`'\0'`). Ordinarily we use pointers to manipulate these strings.

C Library String Functions

The Standard C library provides a set of functions, listed in Table 3.8, that operate on C-style strings. These functions are defined in the `cstring` header, which is the C++ version of the C header `string.h`.

 The functions in Table 3.8 do not verify their string parameters.
WARNING

The pointer(s) passed to these routines must point to null-terminated array(s):

```
char ca[] = {'C', '+', '+'};   // not null terminated
cout << strlen(ca) << endl;    // disaster: ca isn't null terminated
```

In this case, `ca` is an array of `char` but is not null terminated. The result is undefined. The most likely effect of this call is that `strlen` will keep looking through the memory that follows `ca` until it encounters a null character.

Table 3.8: C-Style Character String Functions	
`strlen(p)`	Returns the length of p, *not counting the null.*
`strcmp(p1, p2)`	Compares p1 and p2 for equality. Returns 0 if p1 == p2, a positive value if p1 > p2, a negative value if p1 < p2.
`strcat(p1, p2)`	Appends p2 to p1. Returns p1.
`strcpy(p1, p2)`	Copies p2 into p1. Returns p1.

Comparing Strings

Comparing two C-style strings is done quite differently from how we compare library `string`s. When we compare two library `string`s, we use the normal relational or equality operators:

```
string s1 = "A string example";
string s2 = "A different string";
if (s1 < s2)  // false: s2 is less than s1
```

Using these operators on similarly defined C-style strings compares the pointer values, not the strings themselves:

```
const char ca1[] = "A string example";
const char ca2[] = "A different string";
if (ca1 < ca2)   // undefined: compares two unrelated addresses
```

Remember that when we use an array, we are really using a pointer to the first element in the array (§ 3.5.3, p. 117). Hence, this condition actually compares two const char* values. Those pointers do not address the same object, so the comparison is undefined.

To compare the strings, rather than the pointer values, we can call strcmp. That function returns 0 if the strings are equal, or a positive or negative value, depending on whether the first string is larger or smaller than the second:

```
if (strcmp(ca1, ca2) < 0)  // same effect as string comparison s1 < s2
```

Caller Is Responsible for Size of a Destination String

Concatenating or copying C-style strings is also very different from the same operations on library strings. For example, if we wanted to concatenate the two strings s1 and s2 defined above, we can do so directly:

```
//  initialize largeStr as a concatenation of s1, a space, and s2
string largeStr = s1 + " " + s2;
```

Doing the same with our two arrays, ca1 and ca2, would be an error. The expression ca1 + ca2 tries to add two pointers, which is illegal and meaningless.

Instead we can use strcat and strcpy. However, to use these functions, we must pass an array to hold the resulting string. The array we pass *must* be large enough to hold the generated string, including the null character at the end. The code we show here, although a common usage pattern, is fraught with potential for serious error:

```
//  disastrous if we miscalculated the size of largeStr
strcpy(largeStr, ca1);       //  copies ca1 into largeStr
strcat(largeStr, " ");       //  adds a space at the end of largeStr
strcat(largeStr, ca2);       //  concatenates ca2 onto largeStr
```

The problem is that we can easily miscalculate the size needed for largeStr. Moreover, any time we change the values we want to store in largeStr, we have to remember to double-check that we calculated its size correctly. Unfortunately, programs similar to this code are widely distributed. Programs with such code are error-prone and often lead to serious security leaks.

> For most applications, in addition to being safer, it is also more efficient to use library strings rather than C-style strings.

3.5.5 Interfacing to Older Code

Many C++ programs predate the standard library and do not use the `string` and `vector` types. Moreover, many C++ programs interface to programs written in C or other languages that cannot use the C++ library. Hence, programs written in modern C++ may have to interface to code that uses arrays and/or C-style character strings. The C++ library offers facilities to make the interface easier to manage.

Mixing Library `string`s and C-Style Strings

In § 3.2.1 (p. 84) we saw that we can initialize a `string` from a string literal:

```
string s("Hello World");  // s holds Hello World
```

More generally, we can use a null-terminated character array anywhere that we can use a string literal:

- We can use a null-terminated character array to initialize or assign a `string`.
- We can use a null-terminated character array as one operand (but not both operands) to the `string` addition operator or as the right-hand operand in the `string` compound assignment (+=) operator.

The reverse functionality is not provided: There is no direct way to use a library `string` when a C-style string is required. For example, there is no way to initialize a character pointer from a `string`. There is, however, a `string` member function named `c_str` that we can often use to accomplish what we want:

```
char *str = s; // error: can't initialize a char* from a string
const char *str = s.c_str(); // ok
```

The name `c_str` indicates that the function returns a C-style character string. That is, it returns a pointer to the beginning of a null-terminated character array that holds the same data as the characters in the `string`. The type of the pointer is `const char*`, which prevents us from changing the contents of the array.

The array returned by `c_str` is not guaranteed to be valid indefinitely. Any subsequent use of s that might change the value of s can invalidate this array.

WARNING If a program needs continuing access to the contents of the array returned by `str()`, the program must copy the array returned by `c_str`.

Using an Array to Initialize a `vector`

In § 3.5.1 (p. 114) we noted that we cannot initialize a built-in array from another array. Nor can we initialize an array from a `vector`. However, we can use an array to initialize a `vector`. To do so, we specify the address of the first element and one past the last element that we wish to copy:

```
int int_arr[] = {0, 1, 2, 3, 4, 5};
// ivec has six elements; each is a copy of the corresponding element in int_arr
vector<int> ivec(begin(int_arr), end(int_arr));
```

The two pointers used to construct `ivec` mark the range of values to use to initialize the elements in `ivec`. The second pointer points one past the last element to be copied. In this case, we used the library `begin` and `end` functions (§ 3.5.3, p. 118) to pass pointers to the first and one past the last elements in `int_arr`. As a result, `ivec` will have six elements each of which will have the same value as the corresponding element in `int_arr`.

The specified range can be a subset of the array:

```
// copies three elements: int_arr[1], int_arr[2], int_arr[3]
vector<int> subVec(int_arr + 1, int_arr + 4);
```

This initialization creates `subVec` with three elements. The values of these elements are copies of the values in `int_arr[1]` through `int_arr[3]`.

ADVICE: USE LIBRARY TYPES INSTEAD OF ARRAYS

Pointers and arrays are surprisingly error-prone. Part of the problem is conceptual: Pointers are used for low-level manipulations and it is easy to make bookkeeping mistakes. Other problems arise because of the syntax, particularly the declaration syntax used with pointers.

Modern C++ programs should use `vectors` and iterators instead of built-in arrays and pointers, and use `strings` rather than C-style array-based character strings.

3.6 Multidimensional Arrays

Strictly speaking, there are no multidimensional arrays in C++. What are commonly referred to as multidimensional arrays are actually arrays of arrays. It can

Exercise 3.41: Write a program to initialize a `vector` from an array of `int`s.

Exercise 3.42: Write a program to copy a `vector` of `int`s into an array of `int`s.

be helpful to keep this fact in mind when you use what appears to be a multidimensional array.

We define an array whose elements are arrays by providing two dimensions: the dimension of the array itself and the dimension of its elements:

```
int ia[3][4];  // array of size 3; each element is an array of ints of size 4
// array of size 10; each element is a 20-element array whose elements are arrays of 30 ints
int arr[10][20][30] = {0}; // initialize all elements to 0
```

As we saw in § 3.5.1 (p. 115), we can more easily understand these definitions by reading them from the inside out. We start with the name we're defining (`ia`) and see that `ia` is an array of size 3. Continuing to look to the right, we see that the elements of `ia` also have a dimension. Thus, the elements in `ia` are themselves arrays of size 4. Looking left, we see that the type of those elements is `int`. So, `ia` is an array of size 3, each of whose elements is an array of four `int`s.

We read the definition for `arr` in the same way. First we see that `arr` is an array of size 10. The elements of that array are themselves arrays of size 20. Each of those arrays has 30 elements that are of type `int`. There is no limit on how many subscripts are used. That is, we can have an array whose elements are arrays of elements that are arrays, and so on.

In a two-dimensional array, the first dimension is usually referred to as the row and the second as the column.

Initializing the Elements of a Multidimensional Array

As with any array, we can initialize the elements of a multidimensional array by providing a bracketed list of initializers. Multidimensional arrays may be initialized by specifying bracketed values for each row:

```
int ia[3][4] = {       // three elements; each element is an array of size 4
    {0, 1, 2, 3},      // initializers for the row indexed by 0
    {4, 5, 6, 7},      // initializers for the row indexed by 1
    {8, 9, 10, 11}     // initializers for the row indexed by 2
};
```

The nested braces are optional. The following initialization is equivalent, although considerably less clear:

```
// equivalent initialization without the optional nested braces for each row
int ia[3][4] = {0,1,2,3,4,5,6,7,8,9,10,11};
```

As is the case for single-dimension arrays, elements may be left out of the initializer list. We can initialize only the first element of each row as follows:

```
//  explicitly initialize only element 0 in each row
int ia[3][4] = {{ 0 }, { 4 }, { 8 }};
```

The remaining elements are value initialized in the same way as ordinary, single-dimension arrays (§ 3.5.1, p. 114). If the nested braces were omitted, the results would be very different. This code

```
//  explicitly initialize row 0; the remaining elements are value initialized
int ix[3][4] = {0, 3, 6, 9};
```

initializes the elements of the first row. The remaining elements are initialized to 0.

Subscripting a Multidimensional Array

As with any array, we can use a subscript to access the elements of a multidimensional array. To do so, we use a separate subscript for each dimension.

If an expression provides as many subscripts as there are dimensions, we get an element with the specified type. If we supply fewer subscripts than there are dimensions, then the result is the inner-array element at the specified index:

```
//  assigns the first element of arr to the last element in the last row of ia
ia[2][3] = arr[0][0][0];
int (&row)[4] = ia[1]; //  binds row to the second four-element array in ia
```

In the first example we supply indices for all the dimensions for both arrays. On the left-hand side, `ia[2]` returns the last row in `ia`. It does not fetch an element from that array but returns the array itself. We subscript that array, fetching element `[3]`, which is the last element in that array.

Similarly, the right-hand operand has three dimensions. We first fetch the array at index 0 from the outermost array. The result of that operation is a (multidimensional) array of size 20. We take the first element from that 20-element array, yielding an array of size 30. We then fetch the first element from that array.

In the second example, we define `row` as a reference to an array of four `int`s. We bind that reference to the second row in `ia`.

As another example, it is common to use a pair of nested `for` loops to process the elements in a multidimensional array:

```
constexpr size_t rowCnt = 3, colCnt = 4;
int ia[rowCnt][colCnt];      //  12 uninitialized elements
//  for each row
for (size_t i = 0; i != rowCnt; ++i) {
    //  for each column within the row
    for (size_t j = 0; j != colCnt; ++j) {
        //  assign the element's positional index as its value
        ia[i][j] = i * colCnt + j;
    }
}
```

The outer `for` loops through each of the array elements in `ia`. The inner `for` loops through the elements of those interior arrays. In this case, we set the value of each element as its index in the overall array.

Using a Range `for` with Multidimensional Arrays

Under the new standard we can simplify the previous loop by using a range `for`:

```
size_t cnt = 0;
for (auto &row : ia)            // for every element in the outer array
    for (auto &col : row) {     // for every element in the inner array
        col = cnt;              // give this element the next value
        ++cnt;                  // increment cnt
    }
```

This loop gives the elements of `ia` the same values as the previous loop, but this time we let the system manage the indices for us. We want to change the value of the elements, so we declare our control variables, `row` and `col`, as references (§ 3.2.3, p. 93). The first `for` iterates through the elements in `ia`. Those elements are arrays of size 4. Thus, the type of `row` is a reference to an array of four `int`s. The second `for` iterates through one of those 4-element arrays. Hence, `col` is `int&`. On each iteration we assign the value of `cnt` to the next element in `ia` and increment `cnt`.

In the previous example, we used references as our loop control variables because we wanted to change the elements in the array. However, there is a deeper reason for using references. As an example, consider the following loop:

```
for (const auto &row : ia)    // for every element in the outer array
    for (auto col : row)      // for every element in the inner array
        cout << col << endl;
```

This loop does not write to the elements, yet we still define the control variable of the outer loop as a reference. We do so in order to avoid the normal array to pointer conversion (§ 3.5.3, p. 117). Had we neglected the reference and written these loops as:

```
for (auto row : ia)
    for (auto col : row)
```

our program would not compile. As before, the first `for` iterates through `ia`, whose elements are arrays of size 4. Because `row` is not a reference, when the compiler initializes `row` it will convert each array element (like any other object of array type) to a pointer to that array's first element. As a result, in this loop the type of `row` is `int*`. The inner `for` loop is illegal. Despite our intentions, that loop attempts to iterate over an `int*`.

> **Note**
> To use a multidimensional array in a range `for`, the loop control variable for all but the innermost array must be references.

Pointers and Multidimensional Arrays

As with any array, when we use the name of a multidimensional array, it is automatically converted to a pointer to the first element in the array.

> When you define a pointer to a multidimensional array, remember that
> a multidimensional array is really an array of arrays.

Because a multidimensional array is really an array of arrays, the pointer type
to which the array converts is a pointer to the first inner array:

```
int ia[3][4];        // array of size 3; each element is an array of ints of size 4
int (*p)[4] = ia;  // p points to an array of four ints
p = &ia[2];          // p now points to the last element in ia
```

Applying the strategy from § 3.5.1 (p. 115), we start by noting that (*p) says p is
a pointer. Looking right, we see that the object to which p points has a dimension
of size 4, and looking left that the element type is int. Hence, p is a pointer to an
array of four ints.

> The parentheses in this declaration are essential:
>
> ```
> int *ip[4];      // array of pointers to int
> int (*ip)[4];    // pointer to an array of four ints
> ```

With the advent of the new standard, we can often avoid having to write the
type of a pointer into an array by using auto or decltype (§ 2.5.2, p. 68):

```
// print the value of each element in ia, with each inner array on its own line
// p points to an array of four ints
for (auto p = ia; p != ia + 3; ++p) {
    // q points to the first element of an array of four ints; that is, q points to an int
    for (auto q = *p; q != *p + 4; ++q)
        cout << *q << ' ';
    cout << endl;
}
```

The outer for loop starts by initializing p to point to the first array in ia. That
loop continues until we've processed all three rows in ia. The increment, ++p, has
the effect of moving p to point to the next row (i.e., the next element) in ia.

The inner for loop prints the values of the inner arrays. It starts by making q
point to the first element in the array to which p points. The result of *p is an array
of four ints. As usual, when we use an array, it is converted automatically to a
pointer to its first element. The inner for loop runs until we've processed every
element in the inner array. To obtain a pointer just off the end of the inner array,
we again dereference p to get a pointer to the first element in that array. We then
add 4 to that pointer to process the four elements in each inner array.

Of course, we can even more easily write this loop using the library begin and
end functions (§ 3.5.3, p. 118):

```
// p points to the first array in ia
for (auto p = begin(ia); p != end(ia); ++p) {
    // q points to the first element in an inner array
    for (auto q = begin(*p); q != end(*p); ++q)
        cout << *q << ' ';    // prints the int value to which q points
    cout << endl;
}
```

Here we let the library determine the end pointer, and we use `auto` to avoid having to write the type returned from `begin`. In the outer loop, that type is a pointer to an array of four `int`s. In the inner loop, that type is a pointer to `int`.

Type Aliases Simplify Pointers to Multidimensional Arrays

A type alias (§ 2.5.1, p. 67) can make it easier to read, write, and understand pointers to multidimensional arrays. For example:

```
using int_array = int[4]; // new style type alias declaration; see § 2.5.1 (p. 68)
typedef int int_array[4]; // equivalent typedef declaration; § 2.5.1 (p. 67)
// print the value of each element in ia, with each inner array on its own line
for (int_array *p = ia; p != ia + 3; ++p) {
    for (int *q = *p; q != *p + 4; ++q)
        cout << *q << ' ';
    cout << endl;
}
```

Here we start by defining `int_array` as a name for the type "array of four `int`s." We use that type name to define our loop control variable in the outer `for` loop.

EXERCISES SECTION 3.6

Exercise 3.43: Write three different versions of a program to print the elements of `ia`. One version should use a range `for` to manage the iteration, the other two should use an ordinary `for` loop in one case using subscripts and in the other using pointers. In all three programs write all the types directly. That is, do not use a type alias, `auto`, or `decltype` to simplify the code.

Exercise 3.44: Rewrite the programs from the previous exercises using a type alias for the type of the loop control variables.

Exercise 3.45: Rewrite the programs again, this time using `auto`.

CHAPTER SUMMARY

Among the most important library types are vector and string. A string is a variable-length sequence of characters, and a vector is a container of objects of a single type.

Iterators allow indirect access to objects stored in a container. Iterators are used to access and navigate between the elements in strings and vectors.

Arrays and pointers to array elements provide low-level analogs to the vector and string libraries. In general, the library classes should be used in preference to low-level array and pointer alternatives built into the language.

DEFINED TERMS

begin Member of string and vector that returns an iterator to the first element. Also, free-standing library function that takes an array and returns a pointer to the first element in the array.

buffer overflow Serious programming bug that results when we use an index that is out-of-range for a container, such as a string, vector, or an array.

C-style strings Null-terminated character array. String literals are C-style strings. C-style strings are inherently error-prone.

class template A blueprint from which specific clas types can be created. To use a class template, we must specify additional information. For example, to define a vector, we specify the element type: vector<int> holds ints.

compiler extension Feature that is added to the language by a particular compiler. Programs that rely on compiler extensions cannot be moved easily to other compilers.

container A type whose objects hold a collection of objects of a given type. vector is a container type.

copy initialization Form of initialization that uses an =. The newly created object is a copy of the given initializer.

difference_type A signed integral type defined by vector and string that can hold the distance between any two iterators.

direct initialization Form of initialization that does not include an =.

empty Member of string and vector. Returns bool, which is true if size is zero, false otherwise.

end Member of string and vector that returns an off-the-end iterator. Also, free-standing library function that takes an array and returns a pointer one past the last element in the array.

getline Function defined in the string header that takes an istream and a string. The function reads the stream up to the next newline, storing what it read into the string, and returns the istream. The newline is read and discarded.

index Value used in the subscript operator to denote the element to retrieve from a string, vector, or array.

instantiation Compiler process that generates a specific template class or function.

iterator A type used to access and navigate among the elements of a container.

iterator arithmetic Operations on vector or string iterators: Adding or subtracting an integral value and an iterator yields an iterator that many elements ahead of or behind the original iterator. Subtracting one iterator from another yields the distance between them. Iterators must refer to elements in, or off-the-end of the same container.

null-terminated string String whose last character is followed by the null character (`'\0'`).

off-the-end iterator The iterator returned by end that refers to a nonexistent element one past the end of a container.

pointer arithmetic The arithmetic operations that can be applied to pointers. Pointers to arrays support the same operations as iterator arithmetic.

ptrdiff_t Machine-dependent signed integral type defined in the `cstddef` header that is large enough to hold the difference between two pointers into the largest possible array.

push_back Member of `vector`. Appends elements to the back of a `vector`.

range for Control statement that iterates through a specified collection of values.

size Member of `string` and `vector`. Returns the number of characters or elements, respectively. Returns a value of the `size_type` for the type.

size_t Machine-dependent unsigned integral type defined in the `cstddef` header that is large enough to hold the size of the largest possible array.

size_type Name of types defined by the `string` and `vector` classes that are capable of containing the size of any `string` or `vector`, respectively. Library classes that define `size_type` define it as an `unsigned` type.

string Library type that represents a sequence of characters.

using declarations Make a name from a namespace accessible directly.

```
using namespace::name;
```

makes *name* accessible without the *namespace*:: prefix.

value initialization Initialization in which built-in types are initialized to zero and class types are initialized by the class's default constructor. Objects of a class type can be value initialized only if the class has a default constructor. Used to initialize a container's elements when a size, but not an element initializer, is specified. Elements are initialized as a copy of this compiler-generated value.

vector Library type that holds a collection of elements of a specified type.

++ operator The iterator types and pointers define the increment operator to "add one" by moving the iterator to refer to the next element.

[ ] operator Subscript operator. `obj[i]` yields the element at position `i` from the container object `obj`. Indices count from zero—the first element is element 0 and the last is the element indexed by `obj.size() - 1`. Subscript returns an object. If `p` is a pointer and `n` an integer, `p[n]` is a synonym for `*(p+n)`.

-> operator Arrow operator. Combines the operations of dereference and dot operators: `a->b` is a synonym for `(*a).b`.

<< operator The `string` library type defines an output operator. The `string` operator prints the characters in a `string`.

>> operator The `string` library type defines an input operator. The `string` operator reads whitespace-delimited chunks of characters, storing what is read into the right-hand (`string`) operand.

! operator Logical NOT operator. Returns the inverse of the `bool` value of its operand. Result is `true` if operand is `false` and vice versa.

&& operator Logical AND operator. Result is `true` if both operands are `true`. The right-hand operand is evaluated *only* if the left-hand operand is `true`.

|| operator Logical OR operator. Yields `true` if either operand is `true`. The right-hand operand is evaluated *only* if the left-hand operand is `false`.

C H A P T E R 4

E X P R E S S I O N S

CONTENTS

C++ provides a rich set of operators and defines what these operators
do when applied to operands of built-in type. It also allows us to define the meaning of most of the operators when applied to operands
of class types. This chapter focuses on the operators as defined in the
language and applied to operands of built-in type. We will also look
at some of the operators defined by the library. Chapter 14 will show
how we can define operators for our own types.

An expression is composed of one or more **operands** and yields a **result** when it is evaluated. The simplest form of an **expression** is a single literal or variable. The result of such an expression is the value of the variable or literal. More complicated expressions are formed from an **operator** and one or more operands.

4.1 Fundamentals

There are a few fundamental concepts that affect how expressions are evaluated. We start by briefly discussing the concepts that apply to most (if not all) expressions. Subsequent sections will cover these topics in more detail.

4.1.1 Basic Concepts

There are both *unary operators* and *binary operators*. Unary operators, such as address-of (&) and dereference (*), act on one operand. Binary operators, such as equality (==) and multiplication (*), act on two operands. There is also one ternary operator that takes three operands, and one operator, function call, that takes an unlimited number of operands.

Some symbols, such as *, are used as both a unary (dereference) and a binary (multiplication) operator. The context in which a symbol is used determines whether the symbol represents a unary or binary operator. The uses of such symbols are independent; it can be helpful to think of them as two different symbols.

Grouping Operators and Operands

Understanding expressions with multiple operators requires understanding the *precedence* and *associativity* of the operators and may depend on the *order of evaluation* of the operands. For example, the result of the following expression depends on how the operands are grouped to the operators:

```
5 + 10 * 20/2;
```

The operands to the * operator could be 10 and 20, or 10 and 20/2, or 15 and 20, or 15 and 20/2. Understanding such expressions is the topic of the next section.

Operand Conversions

As part of evaluating an expression, operands are often converted from one type to another. For example, the binary operators usually expect operands with the same type. These operators can be used on operands with differing types so long as the operands can be converted (§ 2.1.2, p. 35) to a common type.

Although the rules are somewhat complicated, for the most part conversions happen in unsurprising ways. For example, we can convert an integer to floating-point, and vice versa, but we cannot convert a pointer type to floating-point. What may be a bit surprising is that small integral type operands (e.g., bool, char, short, etc.) are generally **promoted** to a larger integral type, typically int. We'll look in detail at conversions in § 4.11 (p. 159).

Overloaded Operators

The language defines what the operators mean when applied to built-in and compound types. We can also define what most operators mean when applied to class types. Because such definitions give an alternative meaning to an existing operator symbol, we refer to them as **overloaded operators**. The IO library >> and << operators and the operators we used with `strings`, `vectors`, and iterators are all overloaded operators.

When we use an overloaded operator, the meaning of the operator—including the type of its operand(s) and the result—depend on how the operator is defined. However, the number of operands and the precedence and the associativity of the operator cannot be changed.

Lvalues and Rvalues

Every expression in C++ is either an **rvalue** (pronounced "are-value") or an **lvalue** (pronounced "ell-value"). These names are inherited from C and originally had a simple mnemonic purpose: lvalues could stand on the left-hand side of an assignment whereas rvalues could not.

In C++, the distinction is less simple. In C++, an lvalue expression yields an object or a function. However, some lvalues, such as `const` objects, may not be the left-hand operand of an assignment. Moreover, some expressions yield objects but return them as rvalues, not lvalues. Roughly speaking, when we use an object as an rvalue, we use the object's value (its contents). When we use an object as an lvalue, we use the object's identity (its location in memory).

Operators differ as to whether they require lvalue or rvalue operands and as to whether they return lvalues or rvalues. The important point is that (with one exception that we'll cover in § 13.6 (p. 531)) we can use an lvalue when an rvalue is required, but we cannot use an rvalue when an lvalue (i.e., a location) is required. When we use an lvalue in place of an rvalue, the object's contents (its value) are used. We have already used several operators that involve lvalues.

- Assignment requires a (nonconst) lvalue as its left-hand operand and yields its left-hand operand as an lvalue.

- The address-of operator (§ 2.3.2, p. 52) requires an lvalue operand and returns a pointer to its operand as an rvalue.

- The built-in dereference and subscript operators (§ 2.3.2, p. 53, and § 3.5.2, p. 116) and the iterator dereference and `string` and `vector` subscript operators (§ 3.4.1, p. 106, § 3.2.3, p. 93, and § 3.3.3, p. 102) all yield lvalues.

- The built-in and iterator increment and decrement operators (§ 1.4.1, p. 12, and § 3.4.1, p. 107) require lvalue operands and the prefix versions (which are the ones we have used so far) also yield lvalues.

As we present the operators, we will note whether an operand must be an lvalue and whether the operator returns an lvalue.

Lvalues and rvalues also differ when used with `decltype` (§ 2.5.3, p. 70). When we apply `decltype` to an expression (other than a variable), the result is a reference type if the expression yields an lvalue. As an example, assume p is an int*. Because dereference yields an lvalue, decltype(*p) is int&. On the other hand, because the address-of operator yields an rvalue, decltype(&p) is int**, that is, a pointer to a pointer to type int.

4.1.2 Precedence and Associativity

An expression with two or more operators is a **compound expression**. Evaluating a compound expression involves grouping the operands to the operators. Precedence and associativity determine how the operands are grouped. That is, they determine which parts of the expression are the operands for each of the operators in the expression. Programmers can override these rules by parenthesizing compound expressions to force a particular grouping.

In general, the value of an expression depends on how the subexpressions are grouped. Operands of operators with higher precedence group more tightly than operands of operators at lower precedence. Associativity determines how to group operands with the same precedence. For example, multiplication and division have the same precedence as each other, but they have higher precedence than addition. Therefore, operands to multiplication and division group before operands to addition and subtraction. The arithmetic operators are left associative, which means operators at the same precdence group left to right:

- Because of precedence, the expression 3+4*5 is 23, not 35.

- Because of associativity, the expression 20-15-3 is 2, not 8.

As a more complicated example, a left-to-right evaluation of the following expression yields 20:

```
6 + 3 * 4 / 2 + 2
```

Other imaginable results include 9, 14, and 36. In C++, the result is 14, because this expression is equivalent to

```
// parentheses in this expression match default precedence and associativity
((6 + ((3 * 4) / 2)) + 2)
```

Parentheses Override Precedence and Associativity

We can override the normal grouping with parentheses. Parenthesized expressions are evaluated by treating each parenthesized subexpression as a unit and otherwise applying the normal precedence rules. For example, we can parenthesize the expression above to force the result to be any of the four possible values:

```
// parentheses result in alternative groupings
cout << (6 + 3) * (4 / 2 + 2) << endl;      // prints 36
cout << ((6 + 3) * 4) / 2 + 2 << endl;      // prints 20
cout << 6 + 3 * 4 / (2 + 2) << endl;        // prints 9
```

When Precedence and Associativity Matter

We have already seen examples where precedence affects the correctness of our programs. For example, consider the discussion in § 3.5.3 (p. 120) about dereference and pointer arithmetic:

```
int ia[] = {0,2,4,6,8}; // array with five elements of type int
int last = *(ia + 4);    // initializes last to 8, the value of ia[4]
last = *ia + 4;          // last = 4, equivalent to ia[0] + 4
```

If we want to access the element at the location ia + 4, then the parentheses around the addition are essential. Without parentheses, *ia is grouped first and 4 is added to the value in *ia.

The most common case that we've seen in which associativity matters is in input and output expressions. As we'll see in § 4.8 (p. 155), the operators used for IO are left associative. This associativity means we can combine several IO operations in a single expression:

```
cin >> v1 >> v2;  // read into v1 and then into v2
```

Table 4.12 (p. 166) lists all the operators organized into segments separated by double lines. Operators in each segment have the same precedence, and have higher precedence than operators in subsequent segments. For example, the prefix increment and dereference operators share the same precedence, which is higher than that of the arithmetic operators. The table includes a page reference to each operator's description. We have seen some of these operators already and will cover most of the rest in this chapter. However, there are a few operators that we will not cover until later.

EXERCISES SECTION 4.1.2

Exercise 4.1: What is the value returned by 5 + 10 * 20/2?

Exercise 4.2: Using Table 4.12 (p. 166), parenthesize the following expressions to indicate the order in which the operands are grouped:

    (a)   * vec.begin()   (b)   * vec.begin() + 1

4.1.3 Order of Evaluation

Precedence specifies how the operands are grouped. It says nothing about the order in which the operands are evaluated. In most cases, the order is largely unspecified. In the following expression

```
int i = f1() * f2();
```

we know that f1 and f2 must be called before the multiplication can be done. After all, it is their results that are multiplied. However, we have no way of knowing whether f1 will be called before f2 or vice versa.

For operators that do not specify evaluation order, it is an error for an expression to *refer to and change* the same object. Expressions that do so have undefined behavior (§ 2.1.2, p. 36). As a simple example, the << operator makes no guarantees about when or how its operands are evaluated. As a result, the following output expression is undefined:

```
int i = 0;
cout << i << " " << ++i << endl;   // undefined
```

Because this program is undefined, we cannot draw any conclusions about how it might behave. The compiler might evaluate ++i before evaluating i, in which case the output will be 1 1. Or the compiler might evaluate i first, in which case the output will be 0 1. *Or the compiler might do something else entirely.* Because this expression has undefined behavior, the program is in error, regardless of what code the compiler generates.

There are four operators that do guarantee the order in which operands are evaluated. We saw in § 3.2.3 (p. 94) that the logical AND (&&) operator guarantees that its left-hand operand is evaluated first. Moreover, we are also guaranteed that the right-hand operand is evaluated only if the left-hand operand is true. The only other operators that guarantee the order in which operands are evaluated are the logical OR (||) operator (§ 4.3, p. 141), the conditional (? :) operator (§ 4.7, p. 151), and the comma (,) operator (§ 4.10, p. 157).

Order of Evaluation, Precedence, and Associativity

Order of operand evaluation is independent of precedence and associativity. In an expression such as f() + g() * h() + j():

- Precedence guarantees that the results of g() and h() are multiplied.

- Associativity guarantees that the result of f() is added to the product of g() and h() and that the result of that addition is added to the value of j().

- There are no guarantees as to the order in which these functions are called.

If f, g, h, and j are independent functions that do not affect the state of the same objects or perform IO, then the order in which the functions are called is irrelevant. If any of these functions do affect the same object, then the expression is in error and has undefined behavior.

EXERCISES SECTION 4.1.3

Exercise 4.3: Order of evaluation for most of the binary operators is left undefined to give the compiler opportunities for optimization. This strategy presents a trade-off between efficient code generation and potential pitfalls in the use of the language by the programmer. Do you consider that an acceptable trade-off? Why or why not?

ADVICE: MANAGING COMPOUND EXPRESSIONS

When you write compound expressions, two rules of thumb can be helpful:

1. When in doubt, parenthesize expressions to force the grouping that the logic of your program requires.

2. If you change the value of an operand, don't use that operand elsewhere in the same expresion.

An important exception to the second rule occurs when the subexpression that changes the operand is itself the operand of another subexpression. For example, in *++iter, the increment changes the value of iter. The (now changed) value of iter is the operand to the dereference operator. In this (and similar) expressions, order of evaluation isn't an issue. The increment (i.e., the subexpression that changes the operand) must be evaluated before the dereference can be evaluated. Such usage poses no problems and is quite common.

4.2 Arithmetic Operators

Table 4.1: Arithmetic Operators (Left Associative)		
Operator	Function	Use
+	unary plus	+ expr
-	unary minus	- expr
*	multiplication	expr * expr
/	division	expr / expr
%	remainder	expr % expr
+	addition	expr + expr
-	subtraction	expr - expr

Table 4.1 (and the operator tables in subsequent sections) groups the operators by their precedence. The unary arithmetic operators have higher precedence than the multiplication and division operators, which in turn have higher precedence than the binary addition and subtraction operators. Operators of higher precedence group more tightly than do operators with lower precedence. These operators are all left associative, meaning that they group left to right when the precedence levels are the same.

Unless noted otherwise, the arithmetic operators may be applied to any of the arithmetic types (§ 2.1.1, p. 32) or to any type that can be converted to an arithmetic type. The operands and results of these operators are rvalues. As described in § 4.11 (p. 159), operands of small integral types are promoted to a larger integral type, and all operands may be converted to a common type as part of evaluating these operators.

The unary plus operator and the addition and subtraction operators may also be applied to pointers. § 3.5.3 (p. 119) covered the use of binary + and - with pointer operands. When applied to a pointer or arithmetic value, unary plus returns a (possibly promoted) copy of the value of its operand.

The unary minus operator returns the result of negating a (possibly promoted) copy of the value of its operand:

```
int i = 1024;
int k = -i; // i is -1024
bool b = true;
bool b2 = -b; // b2 is true!
```

In § 2.1.1 (p. 34) we noted that bool values should not be used for computation. The result of -b is a good example of what we had in mind.

For most operators, operands of type bool are promoted to int. In this case, the value of b is true, which promotes to the int value 1 (§ 2.1.2, p. 35). That (promoted) value is negated, yielding -1. The value -1 is converted back to bool and used to initialize b2. This initializer is a nonzero value, which when converted to bool is true. Thus, the value of b2 is true!

CAUTION: OVERFLOW AND OTHER ARITHMETIC EXCEPTIONS

Some arithmetic expressions yield undefined results. Some of these undefined expressions are due to the nature of mathematics—for example, division by zero. Others are undefined due to the nature of computers—for example, due to overflow. Overflow happens when a value is computed that is outside the range of values that the type can represent.

Consider a machine on which shorts are 16 bits. In that case, the maximum short is 32767. On such a machine, the following compound assignment overflows:

```
short short_value = 32767; // max value if shorts are 16 bits

short_value += 1; // this calculation overflows
cout << "short_value: " << short_value << endl;
```

The assignment to short_value is undefined. Representing a signed value of 32768 requires 17 bits, but only 16 are available. On many systems, there is *no* compile-time or run-time warning when an overflow occurs. As with any undefined behavior, what happens is unpredictable. On our system the program completes and writes

```
short_value: -32768
```

The value "wrapped around": The sign bit, which had been 0, was set to 1, resulting in a negative value. On another system, the result might be different, or the program might behave differently, including crashing entirely.

When applied to objects of arithmetic types, the arithmetic operators, +, -, *, and /, have their obvious meanings: addition, subtraction, multiplication, and division. Division between integers returns an integer. If the quotient contains a fractional part, it is truncated toward zero:

```
int ival1 = 21/6; // ival1 is 3; result is truncated; remainder is discarded
int ival2 = 21/7; // ival2 is 3; no remainder; result is an integral value
```

The % operator, known as the "remainder" or the "modulus" operator, computes the remainder that results from dividing the left-hand operand by the right-hand operand. The operands to % must have integral type:

```
int ival = 42;
double dval = 3.14;

ival % 12;     //  ok: result is 6
ival % dval;   //  error: floating-point operand
```

In a division, a nonzero quotient is positive if the operands have the same sign and negative otherwise. Earlier versions of the language permitted a negative quotient to be rounded up or down; the new standard requires the quotient to be rounded toward zero (i.e., truncated).

The modulus operator is defined so that if m and n are integers and n is nonzero, then (m/n)*n + m%n is equal to m. By implication, if m%n is nonzero, it has the same sign as m. Earlier versions of the language permitted m%n to have the same sign as n on implementations in which negative m/n was rounded away from zero, but such implementations are now prohibited. Moreover, except for the obscure case where -m overflows, (-m)/n and m/(-n) are always equal to -(m/n), m%(-n) is equal to m%n, and (-m)%n is equal to -(m%n). More concretely:

```
21 %  6;    /*  result is 3  */        21 /  6;    /*  result is 3  */
21 %  7;    /*  result is 0  */        21 /  7;    /*  result is 3  */
-21 % -8;   /*  result is -5 */        -21 / -8;   /*  result is 2  */
21 % -5;    /*  result is 1  */        21 / -5;    /*  result is -4 */
```

EXERCISES SECTION 4.2

Exercise 4.4: Parenthesize the following expression to show how it is evaluated. Test your answer by compiling the expression (without parentheses) and printing its result.

```
12 / 3 * 4 + 5 * 15 + 24 % 4 / 2
```

Exercise 4.5: Determine the result of the following expressions.

(a) -30 * 3 + 21 / 5   (b) -30 + 3 * 21 / 5
(c) 30 / 3 * 21 % 5   (d) -30 / 3 * 21 % 4

Exercise 4.6: Write an expression to determine whether an int value is even or odd.

Exercise 4.7: What does overflow mean? Show three expressions that will overflow.

4.3 Logical and Relational Operators

The relational operators take operands of arithmetic or pointer type; the logical operators take operands of any type that can be converted to bool. These operators all return values of type bool. Arithmetic and pointer operand(s) with a value of zero are false; all other values are true. The operands to these operators are rvalues and the result is an rvalue.

		Table 4.2: Logical and Relational Operators	
Associativity	**Operator**	**Function**	**Use**
Right	!	logical NOT	`!expr`
Left	<	less than	`expr < expr`
Left	<=	less than or equal	`expr <= expr`
Left	>	greater than	`expr > expr`
Left	>=	greater than or equal	`expr >= expr`
Left	==	equality	`expr == expr`
Left	!=	inequality	`expr != expr`
Left	&&	logical AND	`expr && expr`
Left	||	logical OR	`expr || expr`

Logical AND and OR Operators

The overall result of the logical AND operator is `true` if and only if both its operands evaluate to `true`. The logical OR (`||`) operator evaluates as `true` if either of its operands evaluates as `true`.

The logical AND and OR operators always evaluate their left operand before the right. Moreover, the right operand is evaluated *if and only if* the left operand does not determine the result. This strategy is known as **short-circuit evaluation**:

- The right side of an `&&` is evaluated if and only if the left side is `true`.

- The right side of an `||` is evaluated if and only if the left side is `false`.

Several of the programs in Chapter 3 used the logical AND operator. Those programs used the left-hand operand to test whether it was safe to evaluate the right-hand operand. For example, the `for` condition on page 94:

```
index != s.size() && !isspace(s[index])
```

first checks that `index` has not reached the end of its associated `string`. We're guaranteed that the right operand won't be evaluated unless `index` is in range.

As an example that uses the logical OR, imagine we have some text in a `vector` of `strings`. We want to print the `strings`, adding a newline after each empty `string` or after a `string` that ends with a period. We'll use a range-based `for` loop (§ 3.2.3, p. 91) to process each element:

```cpp
// note s as a reference to const; the elements aren't copied and can't be changed
for (const auto &s : text) { // for each element in text
    cout << s;          // print the current element
    // blank lines and those that end with a period get a newline
    if (s.empty() || s[s.size() - 1] == '.')
        cout << endl;
    else
        cout << " ";   // otherwise just separate with a space
}
```

After we print the current element, we check to see if we need to print a newline. The condition in the `if` first checks whether `s` is an empty `string`. If so, we need to print a newline regardless of the value of the right-hand operand. Only if the `string` is not empty do we evaluate the second expression, which checks whether the `string` ends with a period. In this expression, we rely on short-circuit evaluation of `||` to ensure that we subscript `s` only if `s` is not empty.

It is worth noting that we declared `s` as a reference to `const` (§ 2.5.2, p. 69). The elements in `text` are `string`s, and might be large. By making `s` a reference, we avoid copying the elements. Because we don't need to write to the elements, we made `s` a reference to `const`.

Logical NOT Operator

The logical NOT operator (`!`) returns the inverse of the truth value of its operand. We first used this operator in § 3.2.2 (p. 87). As another example, assuming `vec` is a `vector` of `int`s, we might use the logical NOT operator to see whether `vec` has elements by negating the value returned by `empty`:

```
// print the first element in vec if there is one
if (!vec.empty())
    cout << vec[0];
```

The subexpression

```
!vec.empty()
```

evaluates as `true` if the call to `empty` returns `false`.

The Relational Operators

The relational operators (`<`, `<=`, `>`, `<=`) have their ordinary meanings and return `bool` values. These operators are left associative.

Because the relational operators return `bool`s, the result of chaining these operators together is likely to be surprising:

```
// oops! this condition compares k to the bool result of i < j
if (i < j < k) // true if k is greater than 1!
```

This condition groups `i` and `j` to the first `<` operator. The `bool` result of that expression is the left-hand operand of the second less-than operator. That is, `k` is compared to the `true`/`false` result of the first comparison! To accomplish the test we intended, we can rewrite the expression as follows:

```
// ok: condition is true if i is smaller than j and j is smaller than k
if (i < j && j < k) { /* ... */ }
```

Equality Tests and the bool Literals

If we want to test the truth value of an arithmetic or pointer object, the most direct way is to use the value as a condition:

```
if (val)  { /* ... */ } // true if val is any nonzero value
if (!val) { /* ... */ } // true if val is zero
```

In both conditions, the compiler converts `val` to `bool`. The first condition succeeds so long as `val` is nonzero; the second succeeds if `val` is zero.

We might think we could rewrite a test of this kind as

```
if (val == true)  { /* ... */ } // true only if val is equal to 1!
```

There are two problems with this approach. First, it is longer and less direct than the previous code (although admittedly when first learning C++ this kind of abbreviation can be perplexing). Much more importantly, when `val` is not a `bool`, this comparison does not work as expected.

If `val` is not a `bool`, then `true` is converted to the type of `val` before the `==` operator is applied. That is, when `val` is not a `bool`, it is as if we had written

```
if (val == 1) { /* ... */ }
```

As we've seen, when a `bool` is converted to another arithmetic type, `false` converts to 0 and `true` converts to 1 (§ 2.1.2, p. 35). If we really cared whether `val` was the specific value 1, we should write the condition to test that case directly.

 It is usually a bad idea to use the boolean literals `true` and `false` as
WARNING operands in a comparison. These literals should be used only to compare
to an object of type `bool`.

EXERCISES SECTION 4.3

Exercise 4.8: Explain when operands are evaluated in the logical AND, logical OR, and equality operators.

Exercise 4.9: Explain the behavior of the condition in the following `if`:

```
const char *cp = "Hello World";
if (cp && *cp)
```

Exercise 4.10: Write the condition for a `while` loop that would read `int`s from the standard input and stop when the value read is equal to `42`.

Exercise 4.11: Write an expression that tests four values, a, b, c, and d, and ensures that a is greater than b, which is greater than c, which is greater than d.

Exercise 4.12: Assuming i, j, and k are all `int`s, explain what i `!=` j `<` k means.

4.4 Assignment Operators

The left-hand operand of an assignment operator must be a modifiable lvalue. For example, given

```
int i = 0, j = 0, k = 0; // initializations, not assignment
const int ci = i;        // initialization, not assignment
```

Each of these assignments is illegal:

```
1024 = k;          //  error: literals are rvalues
i + j = k;         //  error: arithmetic expressions are rvalues
ci = k;            //  error: ci is a const (nonmodifiable) lvalue
```

The result of an assignment is its left-hand operand, which is an lvalue. The type of the result is the type of the left-hand operand. If the types of the left and right operands differ, the right-hand operand is converted to the type of the left:

```
k = 0;             //  result: type int, value 0
k = 3.14159;       //  result: type int, value 3
```

Under the new standard, we can use a braced initializer list (§ 2.2.1, p. 43) on the right-hand side: `[C++ 11]`

```
k = {3.14};                      //  error: narrowing conversion

vector<int> vi;                  //  initially empty
vi = {0,1,2,3,4,5,6,7,8,9};      //  vi now has ten elements, values 0 through 9
```

If the left-hand operand is of a built-in type, the initializer list may contain at most one value, and that value must not require a narrowing conversion (§ 2.2.1, p. 43).

For class types, what happens depends on the details of the class. In the case of `vector`, the `vector` template defines its own version of an assignment operator that can take an initializer list. This operator replaces the elements of the left-hand side with the elements in the list on the right-hand side.

Regardless of the type of the left-hand operand, the initializer list may be empty. In this case, the compiler generates a value-initialized (§ 3.3.1, p. 98) temporary and assigns that value to the left-hand operand.

Assignment Is Right Associative

Unlike the other binary operators, assignment is right associative:

```
int ival, jval;
ival = jval = 0; // ok: each assigned 0
```

Because assignment is right associative, the right-most assignment, `jval = 0`, is the right-hand operand of the left-most assignment operator. Because assignment returns its left-hand operand, the result of the right-most assignment (i.e., `jval`) is assigned to `ival`.

Each object in a multiple assignment must have the same type as its right-hand neighbor or a type to which that neighbor can be converted (§ 4.11, p. 159):

```
int ival, *pval; //  ival is an int; pval is a pointer to int
ival = pval = 0; //  error: cannot assign the value of a pointer to an int
string s1, s2;
s1 = s2 = "OK";  //  string literal "OK" converted to string
```

The first assignment is illegal because `ival` and `pval` have different types and there is no conversion from the type of `pval` (`int*`) to the type of `ival` (`int`). It is illegal even though zero is a value that can be assigned to either object.

On the other hand, the second assignment is fine. The string literal is converted to `string`, and that `string` is assigned to `s2`. The result of that assignment is `s2`, which has the same type as `s1`.

Assignment Has Low Precedence

Assignments often occur in conditions. Because assignment has relatively low precedence, we usually must parenthesize the assignment for the condition to work properly. To see why assignment in a condition is useful, consider the following loop. We want to call a function until it returns a desired value—say, 42:

```
// a verbose and therefore more error-prone way to write this loop
int i = get_value();   // get the first value
while (i != 42) {
    // do something ...
    i = get_value();   // get remaining values
}
```

Here we start by calling `get_value` followed by a loop whose condition uses the value returned from that call. The last statement in this loop makes another call to `get_value`, and the loop repeats. We can write this code more directly as

```
int i;
// a better way to write our loop---what the condition does is now clearer
while ((i = get_value()) != 42) {
    // do something ...
}
```

The condition now more clearly expresses our intent: We want to continue until `get_value` returns 42. The condition executes by assigning the result returned by `get_value` to `i` and then comparing the result of that assignment with 42.

Without the parentheses, the operands to `!=` would be the value returned from `get_value` and 42. The `true` or `false` result of that test would be assigned to `i`—clearly not what we intended!

 Because assignment has lower precedence than the relational operators, parentheses are usually needed around assignments in conditions.

Beware of Confusing Equality and Assignment Operators

The fact that we can use assignment in a condition can have surprising effects:

```
if (i = j)
```

The condition in this `if` assigns the value of `j` to `i` and then tests the result of the assignment. If `j` is nonzero, the condition will be `true`. The author of this code almost surely intended to test whether `i` and `j` have the same value:

```
if (i == j)
```

Bugs of this sort are notoriously difficult to find. Some, but not all, compilers are kind enough to warn about code such as this example.

Compound Assignment Operators

We often apply an operator to an object and then assign the result to that same object. As an example, consider the sum program from § 1.4.2 (p. 13):

```
int sum = 0;
//  sum values from 1 through 10 inclusive
for (int val = 1; val <= 10; ++val)
    sum += val;   //  equivalent to sum = sum + val
```

This kind of operation is common not just for addition but for the other arithmetic operators and the bitwise operators, which we cover in § 4.8 (p. 152). There are compound assignments for each of these operators:

```
+=     -=    *=    /=    %=      //  arithmetic operators
<<=    >>=   &=    ^=    |=      //  bitwise operators; see § 4.8 (p. 152)
```

Each compound operator is essentially equivalent to

```
a = a op b;
```

with the exception that, when we use the compound assignment, the left-hand operand is evaluated only once. If we use an ordinary assignment, that operand is evaluated twice: once in the expression on the right-hand side and again as the operand on the left hand. In many, perhaps most, contexts this difference is immaterial aside from possible performance consequences.

EXERCISES SECTION 4.4

Exercise 4.13: What are the values of i and d after each assignment?
```
int i;    double d;
(a) d = i = 3.5;      (b) i = d = 3.5;
```

Exercise 4.14: Explain what happens in each of the if tests:
```
if (42 = i)    // ...
if (i = 42)    // ...
```

Exercise 4.15: The following assignment is illegal. Why? How would you correct it?
```
double dval; int ival; int *pi;
dval = ival = pi = 0;
```

Exercise 4.16: Although the following are legal, they probably do not behave as the programmer expects. Why? Rewrite the expressions as you think they should be.
```
(a) if (p = getPtr() != 0)      (b) if (i = 1024)
```

4.5   Increment and Decrement Operators

The increment (++) and decrement (- -) operators provide a convenient notational shorthand for adding or subtracting 1 from an object. This notation rises above mere convenience when we use these operators with iterators, because many iterators do not support arithmetic.

There are two forms of these operators: prefix and postfix. So far, we have used only the prefix form. This form increments (or decrements) its operand and yields the *changed* object as its result. The postfix operators increment (or decrement) the operand but yield a copy of the original, *unchanged* value as its result:

```
int i = 0, j;
j = ++i; //   j = 1, i = 1: prefix yields the incremented value
j = i++; //   j = 1, i = 2: postfix yields the unincremented value
```

These operators require lvalue operands. The prefix operators return the object itself as an lvalue. The postfix operators return a copy of the object's original value as an rvalue.

ADVICE: USE POSTFIX OPERATORS ONLY WHEN NECESSARY

Readers from a C background might be surprised that we use the prefix increment in the programs we've written. The reason is simple: The prefix version avoids unnecessary work. It increments the value and returns the incremented version. The postfix operator must store the original value so that it can return the unincremented value as its result. If we don't need the unincremented value, there's no need for the extra work done by the postfix operator.

For ints and pointers, the compiler can optimize away this extra work. For more complicated iterator types, this extra work potentially might be more costly. By habitually using the prefix versions, we do not have to worry about whether the performance difference matters. Moreover—and perhaps more importantly—we can express the intent of our programs more directly.

Combining Dereference and Increment in a Single Expression

The postfix versions of ++ and - - are used when we want to use the current value of a variable and increment it in a single compound expression.

As one example, we can use postfix increment to write a loop to print the values in a vector up to but not including the first negative value:

```
auto pbeg = v.begin();
//   print elements up to the first negative value
while (pbeg != v.end() && *beg >= 0)
      cout << *pbeg++ << endl; // print the current value and advance pbeg
```

The expression *pbeg++ is usually confusing to programmers new to both C++ and C. However, because this usage pattern is so common, C++ programmers must understand such expressions.

The precedence of postfix increment is higher than that of the dereference operator, so *pbeg++ is equivalent to *(pbeg++). The subexpression pbeg++ increments pbeg and yields a copy of the previous value of pbeg as its result. Accordingly, the operand of * is the unincremented value of pbeg. Thus, the statement prints the element to which pbeg originally pointed and increments pbeg.

This usage relies on the fact that postfix increment returns a copy of its original, unincremented operand. If it returned the incremented value, we'd dereference the incremented value, with disastrous results. We'd skip the first element. Worse, if the sequence had no negative values, we would attempt to dereference one too many elements.

ADVICE: BREVITY CAN BE A VIRTUE

Expressions such as *pbeg++ can be bewildering—at first. However, it is a useful and widely used idiom. Once the notation is familiar, writing

```
cout << *iter++ << endl;
```

is easier and less error-prone than the more verbose equivalent

```
cout << *iter << endl;
++iter;
```

It is worthwhile to study examples of such code until their meanings are immediately clear. Most C++ programs use succinct expressions rather than more verbose equivalents. Therefore, C++ programmers must be comfortable with such usages. Moreover, once these expressions are familiar, you will find them less error-prone.

Remember That Operands Can Be Evaluated in Any Order

Most operators give no guarantee as to the order in which operands will be evaluated (§ 4.1.3, p. 137). This lack of guaranteed order often doesn't matter. The cases where it does matter are when one subexpression changes the value of an operand that is used in another subexpression. Because the increment and decrement operators change their operands, it is easy to misuse these operators in compound expressions.

To illustrate the problem, we'll rewrite the loop from § 3.4.1 (p. 108) that capitalizes the first word in the input. That example used a for loop:

```
for (auto it = s.begin(); it != s.end() && !isspace(*it); ++it)
    *it = toupper(*it); // capitalize the current character
```

which allowed us to separate the statement that dereferenced beg from the one that incremented it. Replacing the for with a seemingly equivalent while

```
// the behavior of the following loop is undefined!
while (beg != s.end() && !isspace(*beg))
    *beg = toupper(*beg++);   // error: this assignment is undefined
```

results in undefined behavior. The problem is that in the revised version, both the left- and right-hand operands to = use beg *and* the right-hand operand changes beg. The assignment is therefore undefined. The compiler might evaluate this expression as either

```
*beg = toupper(*beg);        // execution if left-hand side is evaluated first
*(beg + 1) = toupper(*beg);  // execution if right-hand side is evaluated first
```

or it might evaluate it in yet some other way.

Exercise 4.17: Explain the difference between prefix and postfix increment.

Exercise 4.18: What would happen if the `while` loop on page 148 that prints the elements from a `vector` used the prefix increment operator?

Exercise 4.19: Given that `ptr` points to an `int`, that `vec` is a `vector<int>`, and that `ival` is an `int`, explain the behavior of each of these expressions. Which, if any, are likely to be incorrect? Why? How might each be corrected?

    (a) `ptr != 0 && *ptr++`   (b) `ival++ && ival`
    (c) `vec[ival++] <= vec[ival]`

4.6 The Member Access Operators

The dot (§ 1.5.2, p. 23) and arrow (§ 3.4.1, p. 110) operators provide for member access. The dot operator fetches a member from an object of class type; arrow is defined so that *ptr->mem* is a synonym for (*ptr).*mem*:

```
string s1 = "a string", *p = &s1;
auto n = s1.size();  // run the size member of the string s1
n = (*p).size();     // run size on the object to which p points
n = p->size();       // equivalent to (*p).size()
```

Because dereference has a lower precedence than dot, we must parenthesize the dereference subexpression. If we omit the parentheses, this code means something quite different:

```
// run the size member of p, then dereference the result!
*p.size();      // error: p is a pointer and has no member named size
```

This expression attempts to fetch the `size` member of the object p. However, p is a pointer, which has no members; this code will not compile.

The arrow operator requires a pointer operand and yields an lvalue. The dot operator yields an lvalue if the object from which the member is fetched is an lvalue; otherwise the result is an rvalue.

Exercise 4.20: Assuming that `iter` is a `vector<string>::iterator`, indicate which, if any, of the following expressions are legal. Explain the behavior of the legal expressions and why those that aren't legal are in error.

    (a) `*iter++;`   (b) `(*iter)++;` (c) `*iter.empty()`
    (d) `iter->empty();` (e) `++*iter;`   (f) `iter++->empty();`

4.7 The Conditional Operator

The conditional operator (the **? : operator**) lets us embed simple if-else logic inside an expression. The conditional operator has the following form:

```
cond ? expr1 : expr2;
```

where *cond* is an expression that is used as a condition and *expr1* and *expr2* are expressions of the same type (or types that can be converted to a common type). This operator executes by evaluating *cond*. If the condition is true, then *expr1* is evaluated; otherwise, *expr2* is evaluated. As one example, we can use a conditional operator to determine whether a grade is pass or fail:

```
string finalgrade = (grade < 60) ? "fail" : "pass";
```

The condition checks whether grade is less than 60. If so, the result of the expression is "fail"; otherwise the result is "pass". Like the logical AND and logical OR (&& and ||) operators, the conditional operator guarantees that only one of *expr1* or *expr2* is evaluated.

That result of the conditional operator is an lvalue if both expressions are lvalues or if they convert to a common lvalue type. Otherwise the result is an rvalue.

Nesting Conditional Operations

We can nest one conditional operator inside another. That is, the conditional operator can be used as the *cond* or as one or both of the *exprs* of another conditional expression. As an example, we'll use a pair of nested conditionals to perform a three-way test to indicate whether a grade is a high pass, an ordinary pass, or fail:

```
finalgrade = (grade > 90) ? "high pass"
                          : (grade < 60) ? "fail" : "pass";
```

The first condition checks whether the grade is above 90. If so, the expression after the ? is evaluated, which yields "high pass". If the condition fails, the : branch is executed, which is itself another conditional expression. This conditional asks whether the grade is less than 60. If so, the ? branch is evaluated and yields "fail". If not, the : branch returns "pass".

The conditional operator is right associative, meaning (as usual) that the operands group right to left. Associativity accounts for the fact that the right-hand conditional—the one that compares grade to 60—forms the : branch of the left-hand conditional expression.

> ⚠ **WARNING** Nested conditionals quickly become unreadable. It's a good idea to nest no more than two or three.

Using a Conditional Operator in an Output Expression

The conditional operator has fairly low precedence. When we embed a conditional expression in a larger expression, we usually must parenthesize the conditional subexpression. For example, we often use the conditional operator to print one or another value, depending on the result of a condition. An incompletely parenthe-sized conditional operator in an output expression can have surprising results:

```
cout << ((grade < 60) ?  "fail" : "pass"); //  prints pass or fail
cout << (grade < 60) ?  "fail" : "pass";   //  prints 1 or 0!
cout << grade < 60 ?  "fail" : "pass"; //  error: compares cout to 60
```

The second expression uses the comparison between grade and 60 as the operand to the << operator. The value 1 or 0 is printed, depending on whether grade < 60 is true or false. The << operator returns cout, which is tested as the condition for the conditional operator. That is, the second expression is equivalent to

```
cout << (grade < 60);    //  prints 1 or 0
cout ?  "fail" : "pass"; //  test cout and then yield one of the two literals
                         //  depending on whether cout is true or false
```

The last expression is an error because it is equivalent to

```
cout << grade;     //  less-than has lower precedence than shift, so print grade first
cout < 60 ? "fail" : "pass"; //  then compare cout to 60!
```

EXERCISES SECTION 4.7

Exercise 4.21: Write a program to use a conditional operator to find the elements in a vector<int> that have odd value and double the value of each such element.

Exercise 4.22: Extend the program that assigned high pass, pass, and fail grades to also assign low pass for grades between 60 and 75 inclusive. Write two versions: One version that uses only conditional operators; the other should use one or more if statements. Which version do you think is easier to understand and why?

Exercise 4.23: The following expression fails to compile due to operator precedence. Using Table 4.12 (p. 166), explain why it fails. How would you fix it?

```
string s = "word";
string pl = s + s[s.size() - 1] == 's' ? "" : "s" ;
```

Exercise 4.24: Our program that distinguished between high pass, pass, and fail de-pended on the fact that the conditional operator is right associative. Describe how that operator would be evaluated if the operator were left associative.

4.8 The Bitwise Operators

The bitwise operators take operands of integral type that they use as a collection of bits. These operators let us test and set individual bits. As we'll see in § 17.2 (p. 723), we can also use these operators on a library type named bitset that represents a flexibly sized collection of bits.

As usual, if an operand is a "small integer," its value is first promoted (§ 4.11.1, p. 160) to a larger integral type. The operand(s) can be either signed or unsigned.

Table 4.3: Bitwise Operators (Left Associative)		
Operator	**Function**	**Use**
~	bitwise NOT	`~expr`
<<	left shift	`expr1 << expr2`
>>	right shift	`expr1 >> expr2`
&	bitwise AND	`expr1 & expr2`
^	bitwise XOR	`expr1 ^ expr2`
|	bitwise OR	`expr1 | expr2`

If the operand is signed and its value is negative, then the way that the "sign bit" is handled in a number of the bitwise operations is machine dependent. Moreover, doing a left shift that changes the value of the sign bit is undefined.

WARNING Because there are no guarantees for how the sign bit is handled, we strongly recommend using `unsigned` types with the bitwise operators.

Bitwise Shift Operators

We have already used the overloaded versions of the `>>` and `<<` operators that the IO library defines to do input and output. The built-in meaning of these operators is that they perform a bitwise shift on their operands. They yield a value that is a copy of the (possibly promoted) left-hand operand with the bits shifted as directed by the right-hand operand. The right-hand operand must not be negative and must be a value that is strictly less than the number of bits in the result. Otherwise, the operation is undefined. The bits are shifted left (`<<`) or right (`>>`). Bits that are shifted off the end are discarded:

> *These illustrations have the low-order bit on the right*
> *These examples assume* `char` *has 8 bits, and* `int` *has 32*
>
>   // 0233 is an octal literal (§ 2.1.3, p. 38)
>   unsigned char bits = 0233;   `1 0 0 1 1 0 1 1`

`bits << 8` // *bits promoted to* `int` *and then shifted left by 8 bits*

`0 0 0 0 0 0 0 0 | 0 0 0 0 0 0 0 0 | 1 0 0 1 1 0 1 1 | 0 0 0 0 0 0 0 0`

`bits << 31` // *left shift 31 bits, left-most bits discarded*

`1 0 0 0 0 0 0 0 | 0 0 0 0 0 0 0 0 | 0 0 0 0 0 0 0 0 | 0 0 0 0 0 0 0 0`

`bits >> 3` // *right shift 3 bits, 3 right-most bits discarded*

`0 0 0 0 0 0 0 0 | 0 0 0 0 0 0 0 0 | 0 0 0 0 0 0 0 0 | 0 0 0 1 0 0 1 1`

The left-shift operator (the **<< operator**) inserts 0-valued bits on the right. The behavior of the right-shift operator (the **>> operator**) depends on the type of the left-hand operand: If that operand is `unsigned`, then the operator inserts 0-valued bits on the left; if it is a signed type, the result is implementation defined—either copies of the sign bit or 0-valued bits are inserted on the left.

Bitwise NOT Operator

The bitwise NOT operator (the **~operator**) generates a new value with the bits of its operand inverted. Each 1 bit is set to 0; each 0 bit is set to 1:

```
unsigned char bits = 0227;    1 0 0 1 0 1 1 1
```

~bits

```
1 1 1 1 1 1 1 1 | 1 1 1 1 1 1 1 1 | 1 1 1 1 1 1 1 1 | 0 1 1 0 1 0 0 0
```

Here, our `char` operand is first promoted to `int`. Promoting a `char` to `int` leaves the value unchanged but adds 0 bits to the high order positions. Thus, promoting `bits` to `int` adds 24 high order bits, all of which are 0-valued. The bits in the promoted value are inverted.

Bitwise AND, OR, and XOR Operators

The AND (&), OR (|), and XOR (^) operators generate new values with the bit pattern composed from its two operands:

```
unsigned char b1 = 0145;      0 1 1 0 0 1 0 1

unsigned char b2 = 0257;      1 0 1 0 1 1 1 1

    b1 & b2   24 high-order bits all 0 | 0 0 1 0 0 1 0 1

    b1 | b2   24 high-order bits all 0 | 1 1 1 0 1 1 1 1

    b1 ^ b2   24 high-order bits all 0 | 1 1 0 0 1 0 1 0
```

For each bit position in the result of the bitwise AND operator (the **& operator**) the bit is 1 if both operands contain 1; otherwise, the result is 0. For the OR (inclusive or) operator (the **| operator**), the bit is 1 if either or both operands contain 1; otherwise, the result is 0. For the XOR (exclusive or) operator (the **^ operator**), the bit is 1 if either but not both operands contain 1; otherwise, the result is 0.

WARNING It is a common error to confuse the bitwise and logical operators (§ 4.3, p. 141). For example to confuse the bitwise & with the logical &&, the bitwise | with the logical ||, and the bitwise ~and the logical !).

Using Bitwise Operators

As an example of using the bitwise operators let's assume a teacher has 30 students in a class. Each week the class is given a pass/fail quiz. We'll track the results of each quiz using one bit per student to represent the pass or fail grade on a given test. We might represent each quiz in an `unsigned` integral value:

```
unsigned long quiz1 = 0;   // we'll use this value as a collection of bits
```

We define `quiz1` as an `unsigned long`. Thus, `quiz1` will have at least 32 bits on any machine. We explicitly initialize `quiz1` to ensure that the bits start out with well-defined values.

The teacher must be able to set and test individual bits. For example, we'd like to be able to set the bit corresponding to student number 27 to indicate that this student passed the quiz. We can indicate that student number 27 passed by creating a value that has only bit 27 turned on. If we then bitwise OR that value with `quiz1`, all the bits except bit 27 will remain unchanged.

For the purpose of this example, we will count the bits of `quiz1` by assigning 0 to the low-order bit, 1 to the next bit, and so on.

We can obtain a value indicating that student 27 passed by using the left-shift operator and an `unsigned long` integer literal 1 (§ 2.1.3, p. 38):

```
1UL << 27    // generate a value with only bit number 27 set
```

`1UL` has a 1 in the low-order bit and (at least) 31 zero bits. We specified `unsigned long` because `int`s are only guaranteed to have 16 bits, and we need at least 17. This expression shifts the 1 bit left 27 positions inserting 0 bits behind it.

Next we OR this value with `quiz1`. Because we want to update the value of `quiz1`, we use a compound assignment (§ 4.4, p. 147):

```
quiz1 |= 1UL << 27;    // indicate student number 27 passed
```

The `|=` operator executes analogously to how `+=` does. It is equivalent to

```
quiz1 = quiz1 | 1UL << 27;    // equivalent to quiz1 |= 1UL << 27;
```

Imagine that the teacher reexamined the quiz and discovered that student 27 actually had failed the test. The teacher must now turn off bit 27. This time we need an integer that has bit 27 turned off and all the other bits turned on. We'll bitwise AND this value with `quiz1` to turn off just that bit:

```
quiz1 &= ~(1UL << 27);    // student number 27 failed
```

We obtain a value with all but bit 27 turned on by inverting our previous value. That value had 0 bits in all but bit 27, which was a 1. Applying the bitwise NOT to that value will turn off bit 27 and turn on all the others. When we bitwise AND this value with `quiz1`, all except bit 27 will remain unchanged.

Finally, we might want to know how the student at position 27 fared:

```
bool status = quiz1 & (1UL << 27);    // how did student number 27 do?
```

Here we AND a value that has bit 27 turned on with `quiz1`. The result is nonzero (i.e., true) if bit 27 of `quiz1` is also on; otherwise, it evaluates to zero.

Shift Operators (aka IO Operators) Are Left Associative

Although many programmers never use the bitwise operators directly, most programmers do use overloaded versions of these operators for IO. An overloaded operator has the same precedence and associativity as the built-in version of that operator. Therefore, programmers need to understand the precedence and associativity of the shift operators even if they never use them with their built-in meaning.

Because the shift operators are left associative, the expression

```
cout << "hi" << " there" << endl;
```

executes as

```
( (cout << "hi") << " there" ) << endl;
```

In this statement, the operand `"hi"` is grouped with the first `<<` symbol. Its result is grouped with the second, and then that result is grouped with the third.

The shift operators have midlevel precedence: lower than the arithmetic operators but higher than the relational, assignment, and conditional operators. These relative precedence levels mean we usually have to use parentheses to force the correct grouping of operators with lower precedence.

```
cout << 42 + 10;     //  ok: + has higher precedence, so the sum is printed
cout << (10 < 42);   //  ok: parentheses force intended grouping; prints 1
cout << 10 < 42;     //  error: attempt to compare cout to 42!
```

The last `cout` is interpreted as

```
(cout << 10) < 42;
```

which says to "write `10` onto `cout` and then compare the result of that operation (i.e., `cout`) to `42`."

EXERCISES SECTION 4.8

Exercise 4.25: What is the value of `~'q' << 6` on a machine with 32-bit `int`s and 8 bit `char`s, that uses Latin-1 character set in which `'q'` has the bit pattern `01110001`?

Exercise 4.26: In our grading example in this section, what would happen if we used `unsigned int` as the type for `quiz1`?

Exercise 4.27: What is the result of each of these expressions?

```
unsigned long ul1 = 3, ul2 = 7;
(a)   ul1 & ul2           (b)   ul1 | ul2
(c)   ul1 && ul2          (d)   ul1 || ul2
```

4.9 The `sizeof` Operator

The **`sizeof`** operator returns the size, in bytes, of an expression or a type name. The operator is right associative. The result of `sizeof` is a constant expression (§ 2.4.4, p. 65) of type `size_t` (§ 3.5.2, p. 116). The operator takes one of two forms:

```
sizeof (type)
sizeof expr
```

In the second form, `sizeof` returns the size of the type returned by the given expression. The `sizeof` operator is unusual in that it does not evaluate its operand:

```
Sales_data data, *p;
sizeof(Sales_data); // size required to hold an object of type Sales_data
sizeof data; // size of data's type, i.e., sizeof(Sales_data)
sizeof p;      // size of a pointer
sizeof *p;     // size of the type to which p points, i.e., sizeof(Sales_data)
sizeof data.revenue; // size of the type of Sales_data's revenue member
sizeof Sales_data::revenue; // alternative way to get the size of revenue
```

The most interesting of these examples is `sizeof *p`. First, because `sizeof` is right associative and has the same precedence as `*`, this expression groups right to left. That is, it is equivalent to `sizeof (*p)`. Second, because `sizeof` does not evaluate its operand, it doesn't matter that `p` is an invalid (i.e., uninitialized) pointer (§ 2.3.2, p. 52). Dereferencing an invalid pointer as the operand to `sizeof` is safe because the pointer is not actually used. `sizeof` doesn't need dereference the pointer to know what type it will return.

Under the new standard, we can use the scope operator to ask for the size of a member of a class type. Ordinarily we can only access the members of a class through an object of that type. We don't need to supply an object, because `sizeof` does not need to fetch the member to know its size.

The result of applying `sizeof` depends in part on the type involved:

- `sizeof` char or an expression of type char is guaranteed to be 1.

- `sizeof` a reference type returns the size of an object of the referenced type.

- `sizeof` a pointer returns the size needed hold a pointer.

- `sizeof` a dereferenced pointer returns the size of an object of the type to which the pointer points; the pointer need not be valid.

- `sizeof` an array is the size of the entire array. It is equivalent to taking the `sizeof` the element type times the number of elements in the array. Note that `sizeof` does not convert the array to a pointer.

- `sizeof` a string or a vector returns only the size of the fixed part of these types; it does not return the size used by the object's elements.

Because `sizeof` returns the size of the entire array, we can determine the number of elements in an array by dividing the array size by the element size:

```
// sizeof(ia)/sizeof(*ia) returns the number of elements in ia
constexpr size_t sz = sizeof(ia)/sizeof(*ia);
int arr2[sz];    // ok sizeof returns a constant expression § 2.4.4 (p. 65)
```

Because `sizeof` returns a constant expression, we can use the result of a `sizeof` expression to specify the dimension of an array.

4.10 Comma Operator

The **comma operator** takes two operands, which it evaluates from left to right. Like the logical AND and logical OR and the conditional operator, the comma operator guarantees the order in which its operands are evaluated.

Exercise 4.28: Write a program to print the size of each of the built-in types.

Exercise 4.29: Predict the output of the following code and explain your reasoning. Now run the program. Is the output what you expected? If not, figure out why.

```
int x[10];   int *p = x;
cout << sizeof(x)/sizeof(*x) << endl;
cout << sizeof(p)/sizeof(*p) << endl;
```

Exercise 4.30: Using Table 4.12 (p. 166), parenthesize the following expressions to match the default evaluation:

(a) `sizeof x + y`   (b) `sizeof p->mem[i]`
(c) `sizeof a < b`   (d) `sizeof f()`

The left-hand expression is evaluated and its result is discarded. The result of a comma expression is the value of its right-hand expression. The result is an lvalue if the right-hand operand is an lvalue.

One common use for the comma operator is in a `for` loop:

```
vector<int>::size_type cnt = ivec.size();
//   assign values from size ... 1 to the elements in ivec
for(vector<int>::size_type ix = 0;
                ix != ivec.size(); ++ix, --cnt)
    ivec[ix] = cnt;
```

This loop increments `ix` and decrements `cnt` in the expression in the `for` header. Both `ix` and `cnt` are changed on each trip through the loop. As long as the test of `ix` succeeds, we reset the next element to the current value of `cnt`.

Exercise 4.31: The program in this section used the prefix increment and decrement operators. Explain why we used prefix and not postfix. What changes would have to be made to use the postfix versions? Rewrite the program using postfix operators.

Exercise 4.32: Explain the following loop.

```
constexpr int size = 5;
int ia[size] = {1,2,3,4,5};
for (int *ptr = ia, ix = 0;
     ix != size && ptr != ia+size;
     ++ix, ++ptr)   { /* ... */ }
```

Exercise 4.33: Using Table 4.12 (p. 166) explain what the following expression does:

```
someValue ? ++x, ++y : --x, --y
```

4.11   Type Conversions

In C++ some types are related to each other. When two types are related, we can use an object or value of one type where an operand of the related type is expected. Two types are related if there is a **conversion** between them.

As an example, consider the following expression, which initializes ival to 6:

```
int ival = 3.541 + 3; // the compiler might warn about loss of precision
```

The operands of the addition are values of two different types: 3.541 has type double, and 3 is an int. Rather than attempt to add values of the two different types, C++ defines a set of conversions to transform the operands to a common type. These conversions are carried out automatically without programmer intervention—and sometimes without programmer knowledge. For that reason, they are referred to as **implicit conversions**.

The implicit conversions among the arithmetic types are defined to preserve precision, if possible. Most often, if an expression has both integral and floating-point operands, the integer is converted to floating-point. In this case, 3 is converted to double, floating-point addition is done, and the result is a double.

The initialization happens next. In an initialization, the type of the object we are initializing dominates. The initializer is converted to the object's type. In this case, the double result of the addition is converted to int and used to initialize ival. Converting a double to an int truncates the double's value, discarding the decimal portion. In this expression, the value 6 is assigned to ival.

When Implicit Conversions Occur

The compiler automatically converts operands in the following circumstances:

* In most expressions, values of integral types smaller than int are first promoted to an appropriate larger integral type.

* In conditions, nonbool expressions are converted to bool.

* In initializations, the initializer is converted to the type of the variable; in assignments, the right-hand operand is converted to the type of the left-hand.

* In arithmetic and relational expressions with operands of mixed types, the types are converted to a common type.

* As we'll see in Chapter 6, conversions also happen during function calls.

4.11.1   The Arithmetic Conversions

The **arithmetic conversions**, which we introduced in § 2.1.2 (p. 35), convert one arithmetic type to another. The rules define a hierarchy of type conversions in which operands to an operator are converted to the widest type. For example, if one operand is of type long double, then the other operand is converted to type long double regardless of what the second type is. More generally, in expressions that mix floating-point and integral values, the integral value is converted to an appropriate floating-point type.

Integral Promotions

The **integral promotions** convert the small integral types to a larger integral type. The types bool, char, signed char, unsigned char, short, and unsigned short are promoted to int if all possible values of that type fit in an int. Otherwise, the value is promoted to unsigned int. As we've seen many times, a bool that is false promotes to 0 and true to 1.

The larger char types (wchar_t, char16_t, and char32_t) are promoted to the smallest type of int, unsigned int, long, unsigned long, long long, or unsigned long long in which all possible values of that character type fit.

Operands of Unsigned Type

If the operands of an operator have differing types, those operands are ordinarily converted to a common type. If any operand is an unsigned type, the type to which the operands are converted depends on the relative sizes of the integral types on the machine.

As usual, integral promotions happen first. If the resulting type(s) match, no further conversion is needed. If both (possibly promoted) operands have the same signedness, then the operand with the smaller type is converted to the larger type.

When the signedness differs and the type of the unsigned operand is the same as or larger than that of the signed operand, the signed operand is converted to unsigned. For example, given an unsigned int and an int, the int is converted to unsigned int. It is worth noting that if the int has a negative value, the result will be converted as described in § 2.1.2 (p. 35), with the same results.

The remaining case is when the signed operand has a larger type than the unsigned operand. In this case, the result is machine dependent. If all values in the unsigned type fit in the larger type, then the unsigned operand is converted to the signed type. If the values don't fit, then the signed operand is converted to the unsigned type. For example, if the operands are long and unsigned int, and int and long have the same size, the long will be converted to unsigned int. If the long type has more bits, then the unsigned int will be converted to long.

Understanding the Arithmetic Conversions

One way to understand the arithmetic conversions is to study lots of examples:

```
bool      flag;        char            cval;
short     sval;        unsigned short  usval;
int       ival;        unsigned int    uival;
long      lval;        unsigned long   ulval;
float     fval;        double          dval;

3.14159L + 'a'; // 'a' promoted to int, then that int converted to long double
dval + ival;    // ival converted to double
dval + fval;    // fval converted to double
ival = dval;    // dval converted (by truncation) to int
flag = dval;    // if dval is 0, then flag is false, otherwise true
cval + fval;    // cval promoted to int, then that int converted to float
sval + cval;    // sval and cval promoted to int
```

```
cval + lval;     // cval converted to long
ival + ulval;    // ival converted to unsigned long
usval + ival;    // promotion depends on the size of unsigned short and int
uival + lval;    // conversion depends on the size of unsigned int and long
```

In the first addition, the character constant lowercase 'a' has type char, which is a numeric value (§ 2.1.1, p. 32). What that value is depends on the machine's character set. On our machine, 'a' has the numeric value 97. When we add 'a' to a long double, the char value is promoted to int, and then that int value is converted to a long double. The converted value is added to the literal. The other interesting cases are the last two expressions involving unsigned values. The type of the result in these expressions is machine dependent.

EXERCISES SECTION 4.11.1

Exercise 4.34: Given the variable definitions in this section, explain what conversions take place in the following expressions:

    (a) if (fval) (b) dval = fval + ival; (c) dval + ival * cval;

Remember that you may need to consider the associativity of the operators.

Exercise 4.35: Given the following definitions,

```
char cval;      int ival;     unsigned int ui;
float fval;     double dval;
```

identify the implicit type conversions, if any, taking place:

    (a) cval = 'a' + 3;   (b) fval = ui - ival * 1.0;
    (c) dval = ui * fval;   (d) cval = ival + fval + dval;

4.11.2 Other Implicit Conversions

In addition to the arithmetic conversions, there are several additional kinds of implicit conversions. These include:

Array to Pointer Conversions: In most expressions, when we use an array, the array is automatically converted to a pointer to the first element in that array:

```
int ia[10];     // array of ten ints
int* ip = ia;   // convert ia to a pointer to the first element
```

This conversion is not performed when an array is used with decltype or as the operand of the address-of (&), sizeof, or typeid (which we'll cover in § 19.2.2 (p. 826)) operators. The conversion is also omitted when we initialize a reference to an array (§ 3.5.1, p. 114). As we'll see in § 6.7 (p. 247), a similar pointer conversion happens when we use a function type in an expression.

Pointer Conversions: There are several other pointer conversions: A constant integral value of 0 and the literal nullptr can be converted to any pointer type; a pointer to any nonconst type can be converted to void*, and a pointer to any type can be converted to a `const void*`. We'll see in § 15.2.2 (p. 597) that there is an additional pointer conversion that applies to types related by inheritance.

Conversions to `bool`: There is an automatic conversion from arithmetic or pointer types to `bool`. If the pointer or arithmetic value is zero, the conversion yields `false`; any other value yields `true`:

```
char *cp = get_string();
if (cp) /* ... */      // true if the pointer cp is not zero
while (*cp) /* ... */ // true if *cp is not the null character
```

Conversion to `const`: We can convert a pointer to a nonconst type to a pointer to the corresponding `const` type, and similarly for references. That is, if `T` is a type, we can convert a pointer or a reference to `T` into a pointer or reference to `const T`, respectively (§ 2.4.1, p. 61, and § 2.4.2, p. 62):

```
int i;
const int &j = i;   // convert a nonconst to a reference to const int
const int *p = &i;  // convert address of a nonconst to the address of a const
int &r = j, *q = p; // error: conversion from const to nonconst not allowed
```

The reverse conversion—removing a low-level `const`—does not exist.

Conversions Defined by Class Types: Class types can define conversions that the compiler will apply automatically. The compiler will apply only one class-type conversion at a time. In § 7.5.4 (p. 295) we'll see an example of when multiple conversions might be required, and will be rejected.

Our programs have already used class-type conversions: We use a class-type conversion when we use a C-style character string where a library `string` is expected (§ 3.5.5, p. 124) and when we read from an `istream` in a condition:

```
string s, t = "a value";  // character string literal converted to type string
while (cin >> s)          // while condition converts cin to bool
```

The condition (`cin >> s`) reads `cin` and yields `cin` as its result. Conditions expect a value of type `bool`, but this condition tests a value of type `istream`. The IO library defines a conversion from `istream` to `bool`. That conversion is used (automatically) to convert `cin` to `bool`. The resulting `bool` value depends on the state of the stream. If the last read succeeded, then the conversion yields `true`. If the last attempt failed, then the conversion to `bool` yields `false`.

4.11.3 Explicit Conversions

Sometimes we want to explicitly force an object to be converted to a different type. For example, we might want to use floating-point division in the following code:

```
int i, j;
double slope = i/j;
```

To do so, we'd need a way to explicitly convert `i` and/or `j` to `double`. We use a **cast** to request an explicit conversion.

WARNING Although necessary at times, casts are inherently dangerous constructs.

Named Casts

A named cast has the following form:

> *cast-name<type>* (*expression*) ;

where *type* is the target type of the conversion, and *expression* is the value to be cast. If *type* is a reference, then the result is an lvalue. The *cast-name* may be one of `static_cast`, `dynamic_cast`, `const_cast`, and `reinterpret_cast`. We'll cover dynamic_cast, which supports the run-time type identification, in § 19.2 (p. 825). The *cast-name* determines what kind of conversion is performed.

static_cast

Any well-defined type conversion, other than those involving low-level const, can be requested using a `static_cast`. For example, we can force our expression to use floating-point division by casting one of the operands to `double`:

```
// cast used to force floating-point division
double slope = static_cast<double>(j) / i;
```

A `static_cast` is often useful when a larger arithmetic type is assigned to a smaller type. The cast informs both the reader of the program and the compiler that we are aware of and are not concerned about the potential loss of precision. Compilers often generate a warning for assignments of a larger arithmetic type to a smaller type. When we do an explicit cast, the warning message is turned off.

A `static_cast` is also useful to perform a conversion that the compiler will not generate automatically. For example, we can use a `static_cast` to retrieve a pointer value that was stored in a `void*` pointer (§ 2.3.2, p. 56):

```
void* p = &d;    // ok: address of any nonconst object can be stored in a void*
// ok: converts void* back to the original pointer type
double *dp = static_cast<double*>(p);
```

When we store a pointer in a `void*` and then use a `static_cast` to cast the pointer back to its original type, we are guaranteed that the pointer value is preserved. That is, the result of the cast will be equal to the original address value. However, we must be certain that the type to which we cast the pointer is the actual type of that pointer; if the types do not match, the result is undefined.

const_cast

A `const_cast` changes only a low-level (§ 2.4.3, p. 63) const in its operand:

```
const char *pc;
char *p = const_cast<char*>(pc); // ok: but writing through p is undefined
```

Conventionally we say that a cast that converts a const object to a nonconst type "casts away the const." Once we have cast away the const of an object, the compiler will no longer prevent us from writing to that object. If the object was originally not a const, using a cast to obtain write access is legal. However, using a `const_cast` in order to write to a const object is undefined.

Only a const_cast may be used to change the constness of an expression. Trying to change whether an expression is const with any of the other forms of named cast is a compile-time error. Similarly, we cannot use a const_cast to change the type of an expression:

```
const char *cp;
// error: static_cast can't cast away const
char *q = static_cast<char*>(cp);

static_cast<string>(cp);   // ok: converts string literal to string
const_cast<string>(cp);    // error: const_cast only changes constness
```

A const_cast is most useful in the context of overloaded functions, which we'll describe in § 6.4 (p. 232).

reinterpret_cast

A reinterpret_cast generally performs a low-level reinterpretation of the bit pattern of its operands. As an example, given the following cast

```
int *ip;
char *pc = reinterpret_cast<char*>(ip);
```

we must never forget that the actual object addressed by pc is an int, not a character. Any use of pc that assumes it's an ordinary character pointer is likely to fail at run time. For example:

```
string str(pc);
```

is likely to result in bizarre run-time behavior.

The use of pc to initialize str is a good example of why reinterpret_cast is dangerous. The problem is that types are changed, yet there are no warnings or errors from the compiler. When we initialized pc with the address of an int, there is no error or warning from the compiler because we explicitly said the conversion was okay. Any subsequent use of pc will assume that the value it holds is a char*. The compiler has no way of knowing that it actually holds a pointer to an int. Thus, the initialization of str with pc is absolutely correct—albeit in this case meaningless or worse! Tracking down the cause of this sort of problem can prove extremely difficult, especially if the cast of ip to pc occurs in a file separate from the one in which pc is used to initialize a string.

A reinterpret_cast is inherently machine dependent. Safely using reinterpret_cast requires completely understanding the types involved as well as the details of how the compiler implements the cast.

Old-Style Casts

In early versions of C++, an explicit cast took one of the following two forms:

```
type (expr);   // function-style cast notation
(type) expr;   // C-language-style cast notation
```

ADVICE: AVOID CASTS

Casts interfere with normal type checking (§ 2.2.2, p. 46). As a result, we strongly recommend that programmers avoid casts. This advice is particularly applicable to `reinterpret_casts`. Such casts are always hazardous. A `const_cast` can be useful in the context of overloaded functions, which we'll cover in § 6.4 (p. 232). Other uses of `const_cast` often indicate a design flaw. The other casts, `static_cast` and `dynamic_cast`, should be needed infrequently. Every time you write a cast, you should think hard about whether you can achieve the same result in a different way. If the cast is unavoidable, errors can be mitigated by limiting the scope in which the cast value is used and by documenting all assumptions about the types involved.

Depending on the types involved, an old-style cast has the same behavior as a `const_cast`, a `static_cast`, or a `reinterpret_cast`. When we use an old-style cast where a `static_cast` or a `const_cast` would be legal, the old-style cast does the same conversion as the respective named cast. If neither cast is legal, then an old-style cast performs a `reinterpret_cast`. For example:

```
char *pc = (char*) ip;   // ip is a pointer to int
```

has the same effect as using a `reinterpret_cast`.

 Old-style casts are less visible than are named casts. Because they are **WARNING** easily overlooked, it is more difficult to track down a rogue cast.

EXERCISES SECTION 4.11.3

Exercise 4.36: Assuming `i` is an `int` and `d` is a `double` write the expression `i *= d` so that it does integral, rather than floating-point, multiplication.

Exercise 4.37: Rewrite each of the following old-style casts to use a named cast:

```
int i;  double d;  const string *ps;  char *pc;  void *pv;
(a) pv = (void*)ps;    (b) i = int(*pc);
(c) pv = &d;           (d) pc = (char*) pv;
```

Exercise 4.38: Explain the following expression:

```
double slope = static_cast<double>(j/i);
```

4.12   Operator Precedence Table

Associativity and Operator		Function	Use	See Page
L	::	global scope	::name	286
L	::	class scope	class::name	88
L	::	namespace scope	namespace::name	82
L	.	member selectors	object.member	23
L	->	member selectors	pointer->member	110
L	[]	subscript	expr [expr]	116
L	()	function call	name (expr_list)	23
L	()	type construction	type (expr_list)	164
R	++	postfix increment	lvalue++	147
R	--	postfix decrement	lvalue--	147
R	typeid	type ID	typeid(type)	826
R	typeid	run-time type ID	typeid(expr)	826
R	explicit cast	type conversion	*cast_name*<type>(expr)	162
R	++	prefix increment	++lvalue	147
R	--	prefix decrement	--lvalue	147
R	~	bitwise NOT	~expr	152
R	!	logical NOT	!expr	141
R	-	unary minus	-expr	140
R	+	unary plus	+expr	140
R	*	dereference	*expr	53
R	&	address-of	&lvalue	52
R	()	type conversion	(type) expr	164
R	sizeof	size of object	sizeof expr	156
R	sizeof	size of type	sizeof(type)	156
R	sizeof...	size of parameter pack	sizeof...(name)	700
R	new	allocate object	new type	458
R	new[]	allocate array	new type[size]	458
R	delete	deallocate object	delete expr	460
R	delete[]	deallocate array	delete[] expr	460
R	noexcept	can expr throw	noexcept (expr)	780
L	->*	ptr to member select	ptr->*ptr_to_member	837
L	.*	ptr to member select	obj.*ptr_to_member	837
L	*	multiply	expr * expr	139
L	/	divide	expr / expr	139
L	%	modulo (remainder)	expr % expr	139
L	+	add	expr + expr	139
L	-	subtract	expr - expr	139
L	<<	bitwise shift left	expr << expr	152
L	>>	bitwise shift right	expr >> expr	152
L	<	less than	expr < expr	141
L	<=	less than or equal	expr <= expr	141
L	>	greater than	expr > expr	141

Continued on next page

Table 4.4: Operator Precedence
(continued)

Associativity and Operator		Function	Use	See Page
L	>=	greater than or equal	expr >= expr	141
L	==	equality	expr == expr	141
L	!=	inequality	expr != expr	141
L	&	bitwise AND	expr & expr	152
L	^	bitwise XOR	expr ^ expr	152
L	|	bitwise OR	expr | expr	152
L	&&	logical AND	expr && expr	141
L	||	logical OR	expr || expr	141
R	?:	conditional	expr ? expr : expr	151
R	=	assignment	lvalue = expr	144
R	*=, /=, %=,	compound assign	lvalue += expr, etc.	144
R	+=, -=,			144
R	<<=, >>=,			144
R	&=, |=, ^=			144
R	throw	throw exception	throw expr	193
L	,	comma	expr , expr	157

CHAPTER SUMMARY

C++ provides a rich set of operators and defines their meaning when applied to values of the built-in types. Additionally, the language supports operator overloading, which allows us to define the meaning of the operators for class types. We'll see in Chapter 14 how to define operators for our own types.

To understand expressions involving more than one operator it is necessary to understand precedence, associativity, and order of operand evaluation. Each operator has a precedence level and associativity. Precedence determines how operators are grouped in a compound expression. Associativity determines how operators at the same precedence level are grouped.

Most operators do not specify the order in which operands are evaluated: The compiler is free to evaluate either the left- or right-hand operand first. Often, the order of operand evaluation has no impact on the result of the expression. However, if both operands refer to the same object and one of the operands *changes* that object, then the program has a serious bug—and a bug that may be hard to find.

Finally, operands are often converted automatically from their initial type to another related type. For example, small integral types are promoted to a larger integral type in every expression. Conversions exist for both built-in and class types. Conversions can also be done explicitly through a cast.

DEFINED TERMS

arithmetic conversion A conversion from one arithmetic type to another. In the context of the binary arithmetic operators, arithmetic conversions usually attempt to preserve precision by converting a smaller type to a larger type (e.g., integral types are converted to floating point).

associativity Determines how operators with the same precedence are grouped. Operators can be either right associative (operators are grouped from right to left) or left associative (operators are grouped from left to right).

binary operators Operators that take two operands.

cast An explicit conversion.

compound expression An expression involving more than one operator.

const_cast A cast that converts a low-level const object to the corresponding nonconst type or vice versa.

conversion Process whereby a value of one type is transformed into a value of another type. The language defines conversions among the built-in types. Conversions to and from class types are also possible.

dynamic_cast Used in combination with inheritance and run-time type identification. See § 19.2 (p. 825).

expression The lowest level of computation in a C++ program. Expressions generally apply an operator to one or more operands. Each expression yields a result. Expressions can be used as operands, so we can write compound expressions requiring the evaluation of multiple operators.

implicit conversion A conversion that is automatically generated by the compiler. Given an expression that needs a particular type but has an operand of a differing type, the compiler will automatically convert the operand to the desired type if an appropriate conversion exists.

integral promotions conversions that take a smaller integral type to its most closely related larger integral type. Operands of small integral types (e.g., short, char, etc.) are always promoted, even in contexts where such conversions might not seem to be required.

lvalue An expression that yields an object or function. A nonconst lvalue that denotes an object may be the left-hand operand of assignment.

operands Values on which an expression operates. Each operator has one or more operands associated with it.

operator Symbol that determines what action an expression performs. The language defines a set of operators and what those operators mean when applied to values of built-in type. The language also defines the precedence and associativity of each operator and specifies how many operands each operator takes. Operators may be overloaded and applied to values of class type.

order of evaluation Order, if any, in which the operands to an operator are evaluated. In most cases, the compiler is free to evaluate operands in any order. However, the operands are always evaluated before the operator itself is evaluated. Only the &&, ||, ?:, and comma operators specify the order in which their operands are evaluated.

overloaded operator Version of an operator that is defined for use with a class type. We'll see in Chapter 14 how to define overloaded versions of operators.

precedence Defines the order in which different operators in a compound expression are grouped. Operators with higher precedence are grouped more tightly than operators with lower precedence.

promoted See integral promotions.

reinterpret_cast Interprets the contents of the operand as a different type. Inherently machine dependent and dangerous.

result Value or object obtained by evaluating an expression.

rvalue Expression that yields a value but not the associated location, if any, of that value.

short-circuit evaluation Term used to describe how the logical AND and logical OR operators execute. If the first operand to these operators is sufficient to determine the overall result, evaluation stops. We are guaranteed that the second operand is not evaluated.

sizeof Operator that returns the size, in bytes, to store an object of a given type name or of the type of a given expression.

static_cast An explicit request for a well-defined type conversion. Often used to override an implicit conversion that the compiler would otherwise perform.

unary operators Operators that take a single operand.

, operator Comma operator. Binary operator that is evaluated left to right. The result of a comma expression is the value of the right-hand operand. The result is an lvalue if and only if that operand is an lvalue.

?: operator Conditional operator. Provides an if-then-else expression of the form

```
cond ? expr1 : expr2;
```

If the condition *cond* is true, then *expr1* is evaluated. Otherwise, *expr2* is evaluated. The type *expr1* and *expr2* must be the same type or be convertible to a common type. Only one of *expr1* or *expr2* is evaluated.

&& operator Logical AND operator. Result is true if both operands are true. The right-hand operand is evaluated *only* if the left-hand operand is true.

& operator Bitwise AND operator. Generates a new integral value in which each bit position is 1 if both operands have a 1 in that position; otherwise the bit is 0.

^ **operator** Bitwise exclusive or operator. Generates a new integral value in which each bit position is 1 if either but not both operands contain a 1 in that bit position; otherwise, the bit is 0.

|| **operator** Logical OR operator. Yields `true` if either operand is `true`. The right-hand operand is evaluated *only* if the left-hand operand is `false`.

| **operator** Bitwise OR operator. Generates a new integral value in which each bit position is 1 if either operand has a 1 in that position; otherwise the bit is 0.

++ **operator** The increment operator. The increment operator has two forms, prefix and postfix. Prefix increment yields an lvalue. It adds 1 to the operand and returns the changed value of the operand. Postfix increment yields an rvalue. It adds 1 to the operand and returns a copy of the original, unchanged value of the operand. Note: Iterators have ++ even if they do not have the + operator.

-- **operator** The decrement operator has two forms, prefix and postfix. Prefix decrement yields an lvalue. It subtracts 1 from the operand and returns the changed value of the operand. Postfix decrement yields an rvalue. It subtracts 1 from the operand and returns a copy of the original, unchanged value of the operand. Note: Iterators have -- even if they do not have the -.

<< **operator** The left-shift operator. Shifts bits in a (possibly promoted) copy of the value of the left-hand operand to the left. Shifts as many bits as indicated by the right-hand operand. The right-hand operand must be zero or positive and strictly less than the number of bits in the result. Left-hand operand should be `unsigned`; if the left-hand operand is `signed`, it is undefined if a shift causes a different bit to shift into the sign bit.

>> **operator** The right-shift operator. Like the left-shift operator except that bits are shifted to the right. If the left-hand operand is `signed`, it is implementation defined whether bits shifted into the result are 0 or a copy of the sign bit.

~ **operator** Bitwise NOT operator. Generates a new integral value in which each bit is an inverted copy of the corresponding bit in the (possibly promoted) operand.

! **operator** Logical NOT operator. Returns the inverse of the `bool` value of its operand. Result is `true` if operand is `false` and vice versa.

CHAPTER 5

STATEMENTS

Like most languages, C++ provides statements for conditional execution, loops that repeatedly execute the same body of code, and jump statements that interrupt the flow of control. This chapter looks in detail at the statements supported by C++.

Statements are executed sequentially. Except for the simplest programs, sequential execution is inadequate. Therefore, C++ also defines a set of *flow-of-control* statements that allow more complicated execution paths.

5.1   Simple Statements

Most statements in C++ end with a semicolon. An expression, such as `ival + 5`, becomes an **expression statement** when it is followed by a semicolon. Expression statements cause the expression to be evaluated and its result discarded:

```
ival + 5;        // rather useless expression statement
cout << ival;    // useful expression statement
```

The first statement is pretty useless: The addition is done but the result is not used. More commonly, an expression statement contains an expression that has a side effect—such as assigning a new value to a variable, or printing a result—when it is evaluated.

Null Statements

The simplest statement is the empty statement, also known as a **null statement**. A null statement is a single semicolon:

```
;    // null statement
```

A null statement is useful where the language requires a statement but the program's logic does not. Such usage is most common when a loop's work can be done within its condition. For example, we might want to read an input stream, ignoring everything we read until we encounter a particular value:

```
// read until we hit end-of-file or find an input equal to sought
while (cin >> s && s != sought)
    ;  // null statement
```

This condition reads a value from the standard input and implicitly tests `cin` to see whether the read was successful. Assuming the read succeeded, the second part of the condition tests whether the value we read is equal to the value in `sought`. If we found the value we want, the `while` loop is exited. Otherwise, the condition is evaluated again, which reads another value from `cin`.

Null statements should be commented. That way anyone reading the code can see that the statement was omitted intentionally.

Beware of Missing or Extraneous Semicolons

Because a null statement is a statement, it is legal anywhere a statement is expected. For this reason, semicolons that might appear illegal are often nothing more than null statements. The following fragment contains two statements—the expression statement and the null statement:

```
ival = v1 + v2;; // ok: second semicolon is a superfluous null statement
```

Although an unnecessary null statement is often harmless, an extra semicolon following the condition in a `while` or `if` can drastically alter the programmer's intent. For example, the following code will loop indefinitely:

```
// disaster: extra semicolon: loop body is this null statement
while (iter != svec.end()) ; // the while body is the empty statement
    ++iter;        // increment is not part of the loop
```

Contrary to the indentation, the increment is not part of the loop. The loop body is the null statement formed by the semicolon that follows the condition.

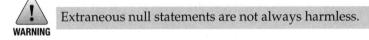 Extraneous null statements are not always harmless.

WARNING

Compound Statements (Blocks)

A **compound statement**, usually referred to as a **block**, is a (possibly empty) sequence of statements and declarations surrounded by a pair of curly braces. A block is a scope (§ 2.2.4, p. 48). Names introduced inside a block are accessible only in that block and in blocks nested inside that block. Names are visible from where they are defined until the end of the (immediately) enclosing block.

Compound statements are used when the language requires a single statement but the logic of our program needs more than one. For example, the body of a `while` or `for` loop must be a single statement, yet we often need to execute more than one statement in the body of a loop. We do so by enclosing the statements in curly braces, thus turning the sequence of statements into a block.

As one example, recall the `while` loop in the program in § 1.4.1 (p. 11):

```
while (val <= 10) {
    sum += val;  // assigns sum + val to sum
    ++val;       // add 1 to val
}
```

The logic of our program needed two statements but a `while` loop may contain only one statement. By enclosing these statements in curly braces, we made them into a single (compound) statement.

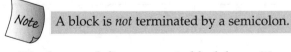 A block is *not* terminated by a semicolon.

Note

We also can define an empty block by writing a pair of curlies with no statements. An empty block is equivalent to a null statement:

```
while (cin >> s && s != sought)
    { } // empty block
```

5.2 Statement Scope

We can define variables inside the control structure of the `if`, `switch`, `while`, and `for` statements. Variables defined in the control structure are visible only within that statement and are out of scope after the statement ends:

```
while (int i = get_num()) //  i is created and initialized on each iteration
    cout << i << endl;
i = 0;   //  error: i is not accessible outside the loop
```

If we need access to the control variable, then that variable must be defined outside the statement:

```
//  find the first negative element
auto beg = v.begin();
while (beg != v.end() && *beg >= 0)
    ++beg;
if (beg == v.end())
    //  we know that all elements in v are greater than or equal to zero
```

The value of an object defined in a control structure is used by that structure. Therefore, such variables must be initialized.

5.3 Conditional Statements

C++ provides two statements that allow for conditional execution. The `if` statement determines the flow of control based on a condition. The `switch` statement evaluates an integral expression and chooses one of several execution paths based on the expression's value.

5.3.1 The `if` Statement

An **`if` statement** conditionally executes another statement based on whether a specified condition is true. There are two forms of the `if`: one with an `else` branch and one without. The syntactic form of the simple `if` is

```
if (condition)
    statement
```

An **`if else` statement** has the form

```
if (condition)
        statement
else
        statement2
```

In both versions, *condition* must be enclosed in parentheses. *condition* can be an expression or an initialized variable declaration (§ 5.2, p. 174). The expression or variable must have a type that is convertible (§ 4.11, p. 159) to `bool`. As usual, either or both *statement* and *statement2* can be a block.

If *condition* is `true`, then *statement* is executed. After *statement* completes, execution continues with the statement following the `if`.

If *condition* is `false`, *statement* is skipped. In a simple `if`, execution continues with the statement following the `if`. In an `if else`, *statement2* is executed.

Using an `if else` Statement

To illustrate an `if` statement, we'll calculate a letter grade from a numeric grade. We'll assume that the numeric grades range from zero to 100 inclusive. A grade of 100 gets an "A++," grades below 60 get an "F," and the others range in clumps of ten: grades from 60 to 69 inclusive get a "D," 70 to 79 a "C," and so on. We'll use a `vector` to hold the possible letter grades:

```
vector<string> scores = {"F", "D", "C", "B", "A", "A++"};
```

To solve this problem, we can use an `if else` statement to execute different actions for failing and passing grades:

```
//  if grade is less than 60 it's an F, otherwise compute a subscript
string lettergrade;
if (grade < 60)
    lettergrade = scores[0];
else
    lettergrade = scores[(grade - 50)/10];
```

Depending on the value of `grade`, we execute the statement after the `if` or the one after the `else`. In the `else`, we compute a subscript from a grade by reducing the grade to account for the larger range of failing grades. Then we use integer division (§ 4.2, p. 141), which truncates the remainder, to calculate the appropriate `scores` index.

Nested `if` Statements

To make our program more interesting, we'll add a plus or minus to passing grades. We'll give a plus to grades ending in 8 or 9, and a minus to those ending in 0, 1, or 2:

```
if (grade % 10 > 7)
    lettergrade += '+';      //  grades ending in 8 or 9 get a +
else if (grade % 10 < 3)
    lettergrade += '-';      //  those ending in 0, 1, or 2 get a -
```

Here we use the modulus operator (§ 4.2, p. 141) to get the remainder and decide based on the remainder whether to add plus or minus.

We next will incorporate the code that adds a plus or minus to the code that fetches the letter grade from scores:

```
//  if failing grade, no need to check for a plus or minus
if (grade < 60)
    lettergrade = scores[0];
else {
    lettergrade = scores[(grade - 50)/10];   //  fetch the letter grade
    if (grade != 100)   //  add plus or minus only if not already an A++
        if (grade % 10 > 7)
            lettergrade += '+';      //  grades ending in 8 or 9 get a +
        else if (grade % 10 < 3)
            lettergrade += '-';      //  grades ending in 0, 1, or 2 get a -
}
```

Note that we use a block to enclose the two statements that follow the first `else`. If the `grade` is `60` or more, we have two actions that we need to do: Fetch the letter grade from `scores`, and conditionally set the plus or minus.

Watch Your Braces

It is a common mistake to forget the curly braces when multiple statements must be executed as a block. In the following example, contrary to the indentation, the code to add a plus or minus happens unconditionally:

```
if (grade < 60)
    lettergrade = scores[0];
else   //  WRONG: missing curly
    lettergrade = scores[(grade - 50)/10];
    //  despite appearances, without the curly brace, this code is always executed
    //  failing grades will incorrectly get a - or a +
    if (grade != 100)
        if (grade % 10 > 7)
            lettergrade += '+';      //  grades ending in 8 or 9 get a +
        else if (grade % 10 < 3)
            lettergrade += '-';      //  grades ending in 0, 1, or 2 get a -
```

Uncovering this error may be very difficult because the program looks correct.

To avoid such problems, some coding styles recommend always using braces after an `if` or an `else` (and also around the bodies of `while` and `for` statements).

Doing so avoids any possible confusion. It also means that the braces are already in place if later modifications of the code require adding statements.

Best Practices Many editors and development environments have tools to automatically indent source code to match its structure. It is a good idea to use such tools if they are available.

Dangling `else`

When we nest an `if` inside another `if`, it is possible that there will be more `if` branches than `else` branches. Indeed, our grading program has four `if`s and two `else`s. The question arises: How do we know to which `if` a given `else` belongs?

This problem, usually referred to as a **dangling `else`**, is common to many programming languages that have both `if` and `if else` statements. Different languages solve this problem in different ways. In C++ the ambiguity is resolved by specifying that each `else` is matched with the closest preceding unmatched `if`.

Programmers sometimes get into trouble when they write code that contains more `if` than `else` branches. To illustrate the problem, we'll rewrite the innermost `if else` that adds a plus or minus using a different set of conditions:

```
//  WRONG: execution does NOT match indentation; the else goes with the inner if
if (grade % 10 >= 3)
    if (grade % 10 > 7)
        lettergrade += '+';   //  grades ending in 8 or 9 get a +
else
    lettergrade += '-'; //  grades ending in 3, 4, 5, 6 will get a minus!
```

The indentation in our code indicates that we intend the `else` to go with the outer `if`—we intend for the `else` branch to be executed when the `grade` ends in a digit less than 3. However, despite our intentions, and contrary to the indentation, the `else` branch is part of the inner `if`. This code adds a `'-'` to grades ending in 3 to 7 inclusive! Properly indented to match the actual execution, what we wrote is:

```
//  indentation matches the execution path, not the programmer's intent
if (grade % 10 >= 3)
    if (grade % 10 > 7)
        lettergrade += '+';   //  grades ending in 8 or 9 get a +
    else
        lettergrade += '-';   //  grades ending in 3, 4, 5, 6 will get a minus!
```

Controlling the Execution Path with Braces

We can make the `else` part of the outer `if` by enclosing the inner `if` in a block:

```
//  add a plus for grades that end in 8 or 9 and a minus for those ending in 0, 1, or 2
if (grade % 10 >= 3) {
    if (grade % 10 > 7)
        lettergrade += '+';   //  grades ending in 8 or 9 get a +
} else                        //  curlies force the else to go with the outer if
    lettergrade += '-'; //  grades ending in 0, 1, or 2 will get a minus
```

Statements do not span block boundaries, so the inner `if` ends at the close curly before the `else`. The `else` cannot be part of the inner `if`. Now, the nearest un-matched `if` is the outer `if`, which is what we intended all along.

EXERCISES SECTION 5.3.1

Exercise 5.5: Using an `if–else` statement, write your own version of the program to generate the letter grade from a numeric grade.

Exercise 5.6: Rewrite your grading program to use the conditional operator (§ 4.7, p. 151) in place of the `if–else` statement.

Exercise 5.7: Correct the errors in each of the following code fragments:

```
(a) if (ival1 != ival2)
        ival1 = ival2
    else ival1 = ival2 = 0;
(b) if (ival < minval)
        minval = ival;
        occurs = 1;
(c) if (int ival = get_value())
        cout << "ival = " << ival << endl;
    if (!ival)
        cout << "ival = 0\n";
(d) if (ival = 0)
        ival = get_value();
```

Exercise 5.8: What is a "dangling `else`"? How are `else` clauses resolved in C++?

5.3.2 The `switch` Statement

A **switch statement** provides a convenient way of selecting among a (possibly large) number of fixed alternatives. As one example, suppose that we want to count how often each of the five vowels appears in some segment of text. Our program logic is as follows:

- Read every character in the input.
- Compare each character to the set of vowels.
- If the character matches one of the vowels, add 1 to that vowel's count.
- Display the results.

For example, when we run the program on the text of this chapter, the output is

```
Number of vowel a:   3195
Number of vowel e:   6230
Number of vowel i:   3102
Number of vowel o:   3289
Number of vowel u:   1033
```

We can solve our problem most directly using a `switch` statement:

```
// initialize counters for each vowel
unsigned aCnt = 0, eCnt = 0, iCnt = 0, oCnt = 0, uCnt = 0;
char ch;
while (cin >> ch) {
    // if ch is a vowel, increment the appropriate counter
    switch (ch) {
        case 'a':
            ++aCnt;
            break;
        case 'e':
            ++eCnt;
            break;
        case 'i':
            ++iCnt;
            break;
        case 'o':
            ++oCnt;
            break;
        case 'u':
            ++uCnt;
            break;
    }
}
// print results
cout << "Number of vowel a: \t" << aCnt << '\n'
     << "Number of vowel e: \t" << eCnt << '\n'
     << "Number of vowel i: \t" << iCnt << '\n'
     << "Number of vowel o: \t" << oCnt << '\n'
     << "Number of vowel u: \t" << uCnt << endl;
```

A `switch` statement executes by evaluating the parenthesized expression that follows the keyword `switch`. That expression may be an initialized variable declaration (§ 5.2, p. 174). The expression is converted to integral type. The result of the expression is compared with the value associated with each `case`.

If the expression matches the value of a `case` label, execution begins with the first statement following that label. Execution continues normally from that statement through the end of the `switch` or until a `break` statement.

We'll look at `break` statements in detail in § 5.5.1 (p. 190), but, briefly, a `break` interrupts the current control flow. In this case, the `break` transfers control out of the `switch`. In this program, the `switch` is the only statement in the body of a `while`. Breaking out of this `switch` returns control to the enclosing `while`. Because there are no other statements in that `while`, execution continues at the condition in the `while`.

If no match is found, execution falls through to the first statement following the `switch`. As we already know, in this example, exiting the `switch` returns control to the condition in the `while`.

The `case` keyword and its associated value together are known as the **case label**. case labels must be integral constant expressions (§ 2.4.4, p. 65):

```
char ch = getVal();
int ival = 42;
switch(ch) {
    case 3.14: //  error: noninteger as case label
    case ival: //  error: nonconstant as case label
    //  ...
```

It is an error for any two case labels to have the same value. There is also a special-case label, default, which we cover on page 181.

Control Flow within a switch

It is important to understand that execution flows across case labels. After a case label is matched, execution starts at that label and continues across all the remaining cases or until the program explicitly interrupts it. To avoid executing code for subsequent cases, we must explicitly tell the compiler to stop execution. Under most conditions, the last statement before the next case label is break.

However, there are situations where the default switch behavior is exactly what is needed. Each case label can have only a single value, but sometimes we have two or more values that share a common set of actions. In such instances, we omit a break statement, allowing the program to *fall through* multiple case labels.

For example, we might want to count only the total number of vowels:

```
unsigned vowelCnt = 0;
//  ...
switch (ch)
{
    //  any occurrence of a, e, i, o, or u increments vowelCnt
    case 'a':
    case 'e':
    case 'i':
    case 'o':
    case 'u':
        ++vowelCnt;
        break;
}
```

Here we stacked several case labels together with no intervening break. The same code will be executed whenever ch is a vowel.

Because C++ programs are free-form, case labels need not appear on a new line. We can emphasize that the cases represent a range of values by listing them all on a single line:

```
switch (ch)
{
    //  alternative legal syntax
    case 'a': case 'e': case 'i': case 'o': case 'u':
        ++vowelCnt;
        break;
}
```

Best Practices Omitting a `break` at the end of a `case` happens rarely. If you do omit a `break`, include a comment explaining the logic.

Forgetting a `break` Is a Common Source of Bugs

It is a common misconception to think that only the statements associated with the matched `case` label are executed. For example, here is an *incorrect* implementation of our vowel-counting `switch` statement:

```
//  warning: deliberately incorrect!
switch (ch) {
    case 'a':
        ++aCnt;    //  oops: should have a break statement
    case 'e':
        ++eCnt;    //  oops: should have a break statement
    case 'i':
        ++iCnt;    //  oops: should have a break statement
    case 'o':
        ++oCnt;    //  oops: should have a break statement
    case 'u':
        ++uCnt;
}
```

To understand what happens, assume that the value of `ch` is `'e'`. Execution jumps to the code following the `case 'e'` label, which increments `eCnt`. Execution *continues* across the `case` labels, incrementing `iCnt`, `oCnt`, and `uCnt` as well.

Best Practices Although it is not necessary to include a `break` after the last label of a `switch`, the safest course is to provide one. That way, if an additional `case` is added later, the `break` is already in place.

The `default` Label

The statements following the **default label** are executed when no `case` label matches the value of the `switch` expression. For example, we might add a counter to track how many nonvowels we read. We'll increment this counter, which we'll name `otherCnt`, in the `default` case:

```
//  if ch is a vowel, increment the appropriate counter
switch (ch) {
    case 'a': case 'e': case 'i': case 'o': case 'u':
        ++vowelCnt;
        break;
    default:
        ++otherCnt;
        break;
    }
}
```

In this version, if ch is not a vowel, execution will start at the default label and we'll increment otherCnt.

Best Practices

> It can be useful to define a default label even if there is no work for the default case. Defining an empty default section indicates to subsequent readers that the case was considered.

A label may not stand alone; it must precede a statement or another case label. If a switch ends with a default case that has no work to do, then the default label must be followed by a null statement or an empty block.

Variable Definitions inside the Body of a `switch`

As we've seen, execution in a switch can jump across case labels. When execution jumps to a particular case, any code that occurred inside the switch before that label is ignored. The fact that code is bypassed raises an interesting question: What happens if the code that is skipped includes a variable definition?

The answer is that it is illegal to jump from a place where a variable with an initializer is out of scope to a place where that variable is in scope:

```
case true:
    // this switch statement is illegal because these initializations might be bypassed
    string file_name; // error: control bypasses an implicitly initialized variable
    int ival = 0;     // error: control bypasses an explicitly initialized variable
    int jval;         // ok: because jval is not initialized
    break;
case false:
    // ok: jval is in scope but is uninitialized
    jval = next_num(); // ok: assign a value to jval
    if (file_name.empty()) // file_name is in scope but wasn't initialized
        // ...
```

If this code were legal, then any time control jumped to the false case, it would bypass the initialization of file_name and ival. Those variables would be in scope. Code following false could use those variables. However, these variables would not have been initialized. As a result, the language does not allow us to jump over an initialization if the initialized variable is in scope at the point to which control transfers.

If we need to define and initialize a variable for a particular case, we can do so by defining the variable inside a block, thereby ensuring that the variable is out of scope at the point of any subsequent label.

```
case true:
    {
        // ok: declaration statement within a statement block
        string file_name = get_file_name();
        // ...
    }
    break;
case false:
        if (file_name.empty()) // error: file_name is not in scope
```

EXERCISES SECTION 5.3.2

Exercise 5.9: Write a program using a series of `if` statements to count the number of vowels in text read from `cin`.

Exercise 5.10: There is one problem with our vowel-counting program as we've implemented it: It doesn't count capital letters as vowels. Write a program that counts both lower- and uppercase letters as the appropriate vowel—that is, your program should count both `'a'` and `'A'` as part of `aCnt`, and so forth.

Exercise 5.11: Modify our vowel-counting program so that it also counts the number of blank spaces, tabs, and newlines read.

Exercise 5.12: Modify our vowel-counting program so that it counts the number of occurrences of the following two-character sequences: `ff`, `fl`, and `fi`.

Exercise 5.13: Each of the programs in the highlighted text on page 184 contains a common programming error. Identify and correct each error.

5.4 Iterative Statements

Iterative statements, commonly called loops, provide for repeated execution until a condition is true. The `while` and `for` statements test the condition before executing the body. The `do while` executes the body and then tests its condition.

5.4.1 The `while` Statement

A **while statement** repeatedly executes a target statement as long as a condition is true. Its syntactic form is

```
while (condition)
        statement
```

In a `while`, *statement* (which is often a block) is executed as long as *condition* evaluates as `true`. *condition* may not be empty. If the first evaluation of *condition* yields `false`, *statement* is not executed.

The condition can be an expression or an initialized variable declaration (§ 5.2, p. 174). Ordinarily, the condition itself or the loop body must do something to change the value of the expression. Otherwise, the loop might never terminate.

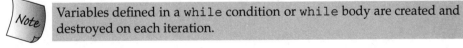

> Variables defined in a `while` condition or `while` body are created and destroyed on each iteration.

Using a `while` Loop

A `while` loop is generally used when we want to iterate indefinitely, such as when we read input. A `while` is also useful when we want access to the value of the loop control variable after the loop finishes. For example:

CODE FOR EXERCISE 5.13

```
(a) unsigned aCnt = 0, eCnt = 0, iouCnt = 0;
    char ch = next_text();
    switch (ch) {
        case 'a': aCnt++;
        case 'e': eCnt++;
        default: iouCnt++;
    }

(b) unsigned index = some_value();
    switch (index) {
        case 1:
            int ix = get_value();
            ivec[ ix ] = index;
            break;
        default:
            ix = ivec.size()-1;
            ivec[ ix ] = index;
    }

(c) unsigned evenCnt = 0, oddCnt = 0;
    int digit = get_num() % 10;
    switch (digit) {
        case 1, 3, 5, 7, 9:
            oddcnt++;
            break;
        case 2, 4, 6, 8, 10:
            evencnt++;
            break;
    }

(d) unsigned ival=512, jval=1024, kval=4096;
    unsigned bufsize;
    unsigned swt = get_bufCnt();
    switch(swt) {
        case ival:
            bufsize = ival * sizeof(int);
            break;
        case jval:
            bufsize = jval * sizeof(int);
            break;
        case kval:
            bufsize = kval * sizeof(int);
            break;
    }
```

```
vector<int> v;
int i;
//   read until end-of-file or other input failure
while (cin >> i)
    v.push_back(i);
//   find the first negative element
auto beg = v.begin();
while (beg != v.end() && *beg >= 0)
    ++beg;
if (beg == v.end())
    //   we know that all elements in v are greater than or equal to zero
```

The first loop reads data from the standard input. We have no idea how many times this loop will execute. The condition fails when `cin` reads invalid data, encounters some other input failure, or hits end-of-file. The second loop continues until we find a negative value. When the loop terminates, `beg` is either equal to `v.end()`, or it denotes an element in `v` whose value is less than zero. We can use the state of `beg` outside the `while` to determine further processing.

EXERCISES SECTION 5.4.1

Exercise 5.14: Write a program to read `strings` from standard input looking for duplicated words. The program should find places in the input where one word is followed immediately by itself. Keep track of the largest number of times a single repetition occurs and which word is repeated. Print the maximum number of duplicates, or else print a message saying that no word was repeated. For example, if the input is

```
how now now now brown cow cow
```

the output should indicate that the word now occurred three times.

5.4.2 Traditional `for` Statement

The syntactic form of the **`for` statement** is:

    for (*init-statement condition*; *expression*)
        statement

The `for` and the part inside the parentheses is often referred to as the `for` header.

init-statement must be a declaration statement, an expression statement, or a null statement. Each of these statements ends with a semicolon, so the syntactic form can also be thought of as

    for (*initializer*; *condition*; *expression*)
        statement

In general, *init-statement* is used to initialize or assign a starting value that is modified over the course of the loop. *condition* serves as the loop control. As long as *condition* evaluates as `true`, *statement* is executed. If the first evaluation of *condition* yields `false`, *statement* is not executed. *expression* usually modifies the variable(s) initialized in *init-statement* and tested in *condition*. *expression* is evaluated after each iteration of the loop. As usual, *statement* can be either a single or a compound statement.

Execution Flow in a Traditional `for` Loop

Given the following `for` loop from § 3.2.3 (p. 94):

```
// process characters in s until we run out of characters or we hit a whitespace
for (decltype(s.size()) index = 0;
        index != s.size() && !isspace(s[index]); ++index)
            s[index] = toupper(s[index]); // capitalize the current character
```

the order of evaluation is as follows:

1. *init-statement* is executed once at the start of the loop. In this example, `index` is defined and initialized to zero.

2. Next, *condition* is evaluated. If `index` is not equal to `s.size()` and the character at `s[index]` is not whitespace, the `for` body is executed. Otherwise, the loop terminates. If the condition is `false` on the first iteration, then the `for` body is not executed at all.

3. If the condition is `true`, the `for` body executes. In this case, the `for` body makes the character at `s[index]` uppercase.

4. Finally, *expression* is evaluated. In this example, `index` is incremented by 1.

These four steps represent the first iteration of the `for` loop. Step 1 is executed only once on entry to the loop. Steps 2, 3, and 4 are repeated until the condition evaluates as `false`—that is, when we encounter a whitespace character in `s`, or `index` is greater than `s.size()`.

It is worth remembering that the visibility of any object defined within the `for` header is limited to the body of the `for` loop. Thus, in this example, `index` is inaccessible after the `for` completes.

Multiple Definitions in the `for` Header

As in any other declaration, *init-statement* can define several objects. However, *init-statement* may be only a single declaration statement. Therefore, all the variables must have the same base type (§ 2.3, p. 50). As one example, we might write a loop to duplicate the elements of a `vector` on the end as follows:

```
// remember the size of v and stop when we get to the original last element
for (decltype(v.size()) i = 0, sz = v.size(); i != sz; ++i)
    v.push_back(v[i]);
```

In this loop we define both the index, `i`, and the loop control, `sz`, in *init-statement*.

Omitting Parts of the `for` Header

A `for` header can omit any (or all) of *init-statement*, *condition*, or *expression*.

We can use a null statement for *init-statement* when an initialization is unnecessary. For example, we might rewrite the loop that looked for the first negative number in a `vector` so that it uses a `for`:

```
auto beg = v.begin();
for ( /* null */; beg != v.end() && *beg >= 0; ++beg)
    ; // no work to do
```

Note that the semicolon is necessary to indicate the absence of *init-statement*—more precisely, the semicolon represents a null *init-statement*. In this loop, the `for` body is also empty because all the work of the loop is done inside the `for` condition and expression. The condition decides when it's time to stop looking and the expression increments the iterator.

Omitting *condition* is equivalent to writing `true` as the condition. Because the condition always evaluates as `true`, the `for` body must contain a statement that exits the loop. Otherwise the loop will execute indefinitely:

```
for (int i = 0; /* no condition */ ; ++i) {
    // process i; code inside the loop must stop the iteration!
}
```

We can also omit *expression* from the `for` header. In such loops, either the condition or the body must do something to advance the iteration. As an example, we'll rewrite the `while` loop that read input into a `vector` of `int`s:

```
vector<int> v;
for (int i; cin >> i; /* no expression */ )
    v.push_back(i);
```

In this loop there is no need for an expression because the condition changes the value of `i`. The condition tests the input stream so that the loop ends when we've read all the input or encounter an input error.

5.4.3 Range `for` Statement

The new standard introduced a simpler `for` statement that can be used to iterate through the elements of a container or other sequence. The syntactic form of the **range `for` statement** is:

C++
11

```
for (declaration : expression)
    statement
```

expression must represent a sequence, such as a braced initializer list (§ 3.3.1, p. 98), an array (§ 3.5, p. 113), or an object of a type such as `vector` or `string` that has `begin` and `end` members that return iterators (§ 3.4, p. 106).

declaration defines a variable. It must be possible to convert each element of the sequence to the variable's type (§ 4.11, p. 159). The easiest way to ensure that the

EXERCISES SECTION 5.4.2

Exercise 5.15: Explain each of the following loops. Correct any problems you detect.

```
(a) for (int ix = 0; ix != sz; ++ix)   { /* ... */ }
    if (ix != sz)
        // ...
(b) int ix;
    for (ix != sz; ++ix) { /* ... */ }
(c) for (int ix = 0; ix != sz; ++ix, ++ sz)   { /* ... */ }
```

Exercise 5.16: The `while` loop is particularly good at executing while some condition holds; for example, when we need to read values until end-of-file. The `for` loop is generally thought of as a step loop: An index steps through a range of values in a collection. Write an idiomatic use of each loop and then rewrite each using the other loop construct. If you could use only one loop, which would you choose? Why?

Exercise 5.17: Given two `vector`s of `int`s, write a program to determine whether one `vector` is a prefix of the other. For `vector`s of unequal length, compare the number of elements of the smaller `vector`. For example, given the `vector`s containing 0, 1, 1, and 2 and 0, 1, 1, 2, 3, 5, 8, respectively your program should return `true`.

types match is to use the `auto` type specifier (§ 2.5.2, p. 68). That way the compiler will deduce the type for us. If we want to write to the elements in the sequence, the loop variable must be a reference type.

On each iteration, the control variable is defined and initialized by the next value in the sequence, after which *statement* is executed. As usual, *statement* can be a single statement or a block. Execution ends once all the elements have been processed.

We have already seen several such loops, but for completeness, here is one that doubles the value of each element in a `vector`:

```
vector<int> v = {0,1,2,3,4,5,6,7,8,9};
// range variable must be a reference so we can write to the elements
for (auto &r : v)       // for each element in v
    r *= 2;             // double the value of each element in v
```

The `for` header declares the loop control variable, `r`, and associates it with `v`. We use `auto` to let the compiler infer the correct type for `r`. Because we want to change the value of the elements in `v`, we declare `r` as a reference. When we assign to `r` inside the loop, that assignment changes the element to which `r` is bound.

A range `for` is defined in terms of the equivalent traditional `for`:

```
for (auto beg = v.begin(), end = v.end(); beg != end; ++beg) {
    auto &r = *beg;  // r must be a reference so we can change the element
    r *= 2;          // double the value of each element in v
}
```

Now that we know how a range `for` works, we can understand why we said in § 3.3.2 (p. 101) that we cannot use a range `for` to add elements to a `vector` (or other container). In a range `for`, the value of `end()` is cached. If we add elements to (or remove them from) the sequence, the value of `end` might be invalidated (§ 3.4.1, p. 110). We'll have more to say about these matters in § 9.3.6 (p. 353).

5.4.4 The `do while` Statement

A **`do while` statement** is like a `while` but the condition is tested after the statement body completes. Regardless of the value of the condition, we execute the loop at least once. The syntactic form is as follows:

```
do
        statement
while (condition);
```

 A do while ends with a semicolon after the parenthesized condition.

In a `do`, *statement* is executed before *condition* is evaluated. *condition* cannot be empty. If *condition* evaluates as `false`, then the loop terminates; otherwise, the loop is repeated. Variables used in *condition* must be defined outside the body of the `do while` statement.

We can write a program that (indefinitely) does sums using a `do while`:

```
// repeatedly ask the user for a pair of numbers to sum
string rsp;   // used in the condition; can't be defined inside the do
do {
    cout << "please enter two values: ";
    int val1 = 0, val2 = 0;
    cin  >> val1 >> val2;
    cout << "The sum of " << val1 << " and " << val2
         << " = " << val1 + val2 << "\n\n"
         << "More? Enter yes or no: ";
    cin  >> rsp;
} while (!rsp.empty() && rsp[0] != 'n');
```

The loop starts by prompting the user for two numbers. It then prints their sum and asks whether the user wishes to do another sum. The condition checks that the user gave a response. If not, or if the input starts with an `n`, the loop is exited. Otherwise the loop is repeated.

Because the condition is not evaluated until after the statement or block is executed, the `do while` loop does not allow variable definitions inside the condition:

```
do {
    // ...
    mumble(foo);
} while (int foo = get_foo()); // error: declaration in a do condition
```

If we could define variables in the condition, then any use of the variable would happen *before* the variable was defined!

Exercise 5.18: Explain each of the following loops. Correct any problems you detect.

(a) do
```
        int v1, v2;
        cout << "Please enter two numbers to sum:" ;
        if (cin >> v1 >> v2)
            cout << "Sum is: " << v1 + v2 << endl;
    while (cin);
```
(b) do {
```
        // ...
    } while (int ival = get_response());
```
(c) do {
```
        int ival = get_response();
    } while (ival);
```

Exercise 5.19: Write a program that uses a `do while` loop to repetitively request two `strings` from the user and report which `string` is less than the other.

5.5   Jump Statements

Jump statements interrupt the flow of execution. C++ offers four jumps: `break`, `continue`, and `goto`, which we cover in this chapter, and the `return` statement, which we'll describe in § 6.3 (p. 222).

5.5.1   The `break` Statement

A **break statement** terminates the nearest enclosing `while`, `do while`, `for`, or `switch` statement. Execution resumes at the statement immediately following the terminated statement.

A `break` can appear only within an iteration statement or `switch` statement (including inside statements or blocks nested inside such loops). A `break` affects only the nearest enclosing loop or `switch`:

```
string buf;
while (cin >> buf && !buf.empty()) {
    switch(buf[0]) {
    case '-':
        // process up to the first blank
        for (auto it = buf.begin()+1; it != buf.end(); ++it) {
            if (*it == ' ')
                break; // #1, leaves the for loop
            // ...
        }
        // break #1 transfers control here
        // remaining '-' processing:
        break; // #2, leaves the switch statement
```

```
        case '+':
            // ...
    } // end switch
    // end of switch: break #2 transfers control here
} // end while
```

The break labeled #1 terminates the for loop that follows the hyphen case label. It does not terminate the enclosing switch statement and in fact does not even terminate the processing for the current case. Processing continues with the first statement following the for, which might be additional code to handle a hyphen or the break that completes that section.

The break labeled #2 terminates the switch but does not terminate the enclosing while loop. Processing continues after that break by executing the condition in the while.

EXERCISES SECTION 5.5.1

Exercise 5.20: Write a program to read a sequence of strings from the standard input until either the same word occurs twice in succession or all the words have been read. Use a while loop to read the text one word at a time. Use the break statement to terminate the loop if a word occurs twice in succession. Print the word if it occurs twice in succession, or else print a message saying that no word was repeated.

5.5.2 The continue Statement

A **continue statement** terminates the current iteration of the nearest enclosing loop and immediately begins the next iteration. A continue can appear only inside a for, while, or do while loop, including inside statements or blocks nested inside such loops. Like the break statement, a continue inside a nested loop affects only the nearest enclosing loop. Unlike a break, a continue may appear inside a switch only if that switch is embedded inside an iterative statement.

A continue interrupts the current iteration; execution stays inside the loop. In the case of a while or a do while, execution continues by evaluating the condition. In a traditional for loop, execution continues at the *expression* inside the for header. In a range for, execution continues by initializing the control variable from the next element in the sequence.

For example, the following loop reads the standard input one word at a time. Only words that begin with an underscore will be processed. For any other value, we terminate the current iteration and get the next input:

```
string buf;
while (cin >> buf && !buf.empty()) {
    if (buf[0] != '_')
        continue; // get another input
    // still here? the input starts with an underscore; process buf ...
}
```

5.5.3   The goto Statement

 A **goto statement** provides an unconditional jump from the goto to a another statement in the same function.

> **Best Practices**
> Programs should not use gotos. gotos make programs hard to understand and hard to modify.

The syntactic form of a goto statement is

```
goto label;
```

where *label* is an identifier that identifies a statement. A **labeled statement** is any statement that is preceded by an identifier followed by a colon:

```
end: return;     // labeled statement; may be the target of a goto
```

Label identifiers are independent of names used for variables and other identifiers. Hence, a label may have the same identifier as another entity in the program without interfering with the other uses of that identifier. The goto and the labeled statement to which it transfers control must be in the same function.

As with a switch statement, a goto cannot transfer control from a point where an initialized variable is out of scope to a point where that variable is in scope:

```
        // ...
        goto end;
        int ix = 10; // error: goto bypasses an initialized variable definition
end:
        // error: code here could use ix but the goto bypassed its declaration
        ix = 42;
```

A jump backward over an already executed definition is okay. Jumping back to a point before a variable is defined destroys the variable and constructs it again:

```
    // backward jump over an initialized variable definition is okay
    begin:
        int sz = get_size();
        if (sz <= 0) {
                goto begin;
        }
```

Here sz is destroyed when the goto executes. It is defined and initialized anew when control passes back through its definition after the jump back to begin.

Exercise 5.22: The last example in this section that jumped back to begin could be better written using a loop. Rewrite the code to eliminate the goto.

5.6 try Blocks and Exception Handling

Exceptions are run-time anomalies—such as losing a database connection or encountering unexpected input—that exist outside the normal functioning of a program. Dealing with anomalous behavior can be one of the most difficult parts of designing any system.

Exception handling is generally used when one part of a program detects a problem that it cannot resolve and the problem is such that the detecting part of the program cannot continue. In such cases, the detecting part needs a way to signal that something happened and that it cannot continue. Moreover, the detecting part needs a way to signal the problem without knowing what part of the program will deal with the exceptional condition. Having signaled what happened, the detecting part stops processing.

A program that contains code that might raise an exception (usually) has another part to handle whatever happened. For example, if the problem is invalid input, the handling part might ask the user to provide correct input. If the database was lost, the handling part might alert an operator.

Exception handling supports this cooperation between the detecting and handling parts of a program. In C++, exception handling involves

- **throw expressions**, which the detecting part uses to indicate that it encountered something it can't handle. We say that a throw **raises** an exception.

- **try blocks**, which the handling part uses to deal with an exception. A try block starts with the keyword try and ends with one or more **catch clauses**. Exceptions thrown from code executed inside a try block are usually handled by one of the catch clauses. Because they "handle" the exception, catch clauses are also known as **exception handlers**.

- A set of **exception classes** that are used to pass information about what happened between a throw and an associated catch.

In the remainder of this section, we'll introduce these three components of exception handling. We'll also have more to say about exceptions in § 18.1 (p. 772).

5.6.1 A throw Expression

The detecting part of a program uses a throw expression to raise an exception. A throw consists of the keyword throw followed by an expression. The type of the expression determines what kind of exception is thrown. A throw expression is usually followed by a semicolon, making it into an expression statement.

As a simple example, recall the program in § 1.5.2 (p. 23) that added two objects of type `Sales_item`. That program checked whether the records it read referred to the same book. If not, it printed a message and exited.

```
Sales_item item1, item2;
cin >> item1 >> item2;
// first check that item1 and item2 represent the same book
if (item1.isbn() == item2.isbn()) {
    cout << item1 + item2 << endl;
    return 0;     // indicate success
} else {
    cerr << "Data must refer to same ISBN"
              << endl;
    return -1;   // indicate failure
}
```

In a more realistic program, the part that adds the objects might be separated from the part that manages the interaction with a user. In this case, we might rewrite the test to throw an exception rather than returning an error indicator:

```
// first check that the data are for the same item
if (item1.isbn() != item2.isbn())
    throw runtime_error("Data must refer to same ISBN");
// if we're still here, the ISBNs are the same
cout << item1 + item2 << endl;
```

In this code, if the ISBNs differ, we throw an expression that is an object of type `runtime_error`. Throwing an exception terminates the current function and transfers control to a handler that will know how to handle this error.

The type `runtime_error` is one of the standard library exception types and is defined in the `stdexcept` header. We'll have more to say about these types in § 5.6.3 (p. 197). We must initialize a `runtime_error` by giving it a `string` or a C-style character string (§ 3.5.4, p. 122). That string provides additional information about the problem.

5.6.2   The `try` Block

The general form of a `try` block is

```
try {
    program-statements
} catch (exception-declaration) {
    handler-statements
} catch (exception-declaration) {
    handler-statements
} // ...
```

A `try` block begins with the keyword `try` followed by a block, which, as usual, is a sequence of statements enclosed in curly braces.

Following the `try` block is a list of one or more `catch` clauses. A `catch` consists of three parts: the keyword `catch`, the declaration of a (possibly unnamed) object within parentheses (referred to as an **exception declaration**), and a block. When a `catch` is selected to handle an exception, the associated block is executed. Once the `catch` finishes, execution continues with the statement immediately following the last `catch` clause of the `try` block.

The *program-statements* inside the `try` constitute the normal logic of the program. Like any other blocks, they can contain any C++ statement, including declarations. As with any block, variables declared inside a `try` block are inaccessible outside the block—in particular, they are not accessible to the `catch` clauses.

Writing a Handler

In the preceding example, we used a `throw` to avoid adding two `Sales_items` that represented different books. We imagined that the part of the program that added two `Sales_items` was separate from the part that communicated with the user. The part that interacts with the user might contain code something like the following to handle the exception that was thrown:

```
while (cin >> item1 >> item2) {
    try {
        //  execute code that will add the two Sales_items
        //  if the addition fails, the code throws a runtime_error exception
    } catch (runtime_error err) {
        //  remind the user that the ISBNs must match and prompt for another pair
        cout << err.what()
             << "\nTry Again?  Enter y or n" << endl;
        char c;
        cin >> c;
        if (!cin || c == 'n')
            break;          //  break out of the while loop
    }
}
```

The ordinary logic of the program that manages the interaction with the user appears inside the `try` block. This part of the program is wrapped inside a `try` because it might throw an exception of type `runtime_error`.

This `try` block has a single `catch` clause, which handles exceptions of type `runtime_error`. The statements in the block following the `catch` are executed if code inside the `try` block throws a `runtime_error`. Our `catch` handles the error by printing a message and asking the user to indicate whether to continue. If the user enters 'n', then the `break` is executed and we exit the `while`. Otherwise, execution falls through to the closing brace of the `while`, which transfers control back to the `while` condition for the next iteration.

The prompt to the user prints the return from `err.what()`. We know that `err` has type `runtime_error`, so we can infer that `what` is a member function (§ 1.5.2, p. 23) of the `runtime_error` class. Each of the library exception classes defines a member function named `what`. These functions take no arguments and return a C-style character string (i.e., a `const char*`). The `what` member of runtime_error returns a copy of the string used to initialize the particular object. If the code described in the previous section threw an exception, then this catch would print

```
Data must refer to same ISBN
Try Again?  Enter y or n
```

Functions Are Exited during the Search for a Handler

In complicated systems, the execution path of a program may pass through multiple try blocks before encountering code that throws an exception. For example, a try block might call a function that contains a try, which calls another function with its own try, and so on.

The search for a handler reverses the call chain. When an exception is thrown, the function that threw the exception is searched first. If no matching catch is found, that function terminates. The function that called the one that threw is searched next. If no handler is found, that function also exits. That function's caller is searched next, and so on back up the execution path until a catch of an appropriate type is found.

If no appropriate catch is found, execution is transferred to a library function named **terminate**. The behavior of that function is system dependent but is guaranteed to stop further execution of the program.

Exceptions that occur in programs that do not define any try blocks are handled in the same manner: After all, if there are no try blocks, there can be no handlers. If a program has no try blocks and an exception occurs, then terminate is called and the program is exited.

CAUTION: WRITING EXCEPTION SAFE CODE IS *Hard*

It is important to realize that exceptions interrupt the normal flow of a program. At the point where the exception occurs, some of the computations that the caller requested may have been done, while others remain undone. In general, bypassing part of the program might mean that an object is left in an invalid or incomplete state, or that a resource is not freed, and so on. Programs that properly "clean up" during exception handling are said to be *exception safe*. Writing exception safe code is surprisingly hard, and (largely) beyond the scope of this language Primer.

Some programs use exceptions simply to terminate the program when an exceptional condition occurs. Such programs generally don't worry about exception safety.

Programs that do handle exceptions and continue processing generally must be constantly aware of whether an exception might occur and what the program must do to ensure that objects are valid, that resources don't leak, and that the program is restored to an appropriate state.

We will occasionally point out particularly common techniques used to promote exception safety. However, readers whose programs require robust exception handling should be aware that the techniques we cover are insufficient by themselves to achieve exception safety.

5.6.3 Standard Exceptions

The C++ library defines several classes that it uses to report problems encountered in the functions in the standard library. These exception classes are also intended to be used in the programs we write. These classes are defined in four headers:

- The `exception` header defines the most general kind of exception class named `exception`. It communicates only that an exception occurred but provides no additional information.

- The `stdexcept` header defines several general-purpose exception classes, which are listed in Table 5.1.

- The `new` header defines the `bad_alloc` exception type, which we cover in § 12.1.2 (p. 458).

- The `type_info` header defines the `bad_cast` exception type, which we cover in § 19.2 (p. 825).

Table 5.1: Standard Exception Classes Defined in `<stdexcept>`	
`exception`	The most general kind of problem.
`runtime_error`	Problem that can be detected only at run time.
`range_error`	Run-time error: result generated outside the range of values that are meaningful.
`overflow_error`	Run-time error: computation that overflowed.
`underflow_error`	Run-time error: computation that underflowed.
`logic_error`	Error in the logic of the program.
`domain_error`	Logic error: argument for which no result exists.
`invalid_argument`	Logic error: inappropriate argument.
`length_error`	Logic error: attempt to create an object larger than the maximum size for that type.
`out_of_range`	Logic error: used a value outside the valid range.

The library exception classes have only a few operations. We can create, copy, and assign objects of any of the exception types.

We can only default initialize (§ 2.2.1, p. 43) `exception`, `bad_alloc`, and `bad_cast` objects; it is not possible to provide an initializer for objects of these exception types.

The other exception types have the opposite behavior: We can initialize those objects from either a `string` or a C-style string, but we *cannot* default initialize them. When we create objects of any of these other exception types, we must supply an initializer. That initializer is used to provide additional information about the error that occurred.

The exception types define only a single operation named `what`. That function takes no arguments and returns a `const char*` that points to a C-style character string (§ 3.5.4, p. 122). The purpose of this C-style character string is to provide some sort of textual description of the exception thrown.

The contents of the C-style string that what returns depends on the type of the exception object. For the types that take a string initializer, the what function returns that string. For the other types, the value of the string that what returns varies by compiler.

EXERCISES SECTION 5.6.3

Exercise 5.23: Write a program that reads two integers from the standard input and prints the result of dividing the first number by the second.

Exercise 5.24: Revise your program to throw an exception if the second number is zero. Test your program with a zero input to see what happens on your system if you don't catch an exception.

Exercise 5.25: Revise your program from the previous exercise to use a try block to catch the exception. The catch clause should print a message to the user and ask them to supply a new number and repeat the code inside the try.

CHAPTER SUMMARY

C++ provides a limited number of statements. Most of these affect the flow of control within a program:

- `while`, `for`, and `do while` statements, which provide iterative execution.

- `if` and `switch`, which provide conditional execution.

- `continue`, which stops the current iteration of a loop.

- `break`, which exits a loop or `switch` statement.

- `goto`, which transfers control to a labeled statement.

- `try` and `catch`, which define a `try` block enclosing a sequence of statements that might throw an exception. The `catch` clause(s) are intended to handle the exception(s) that the enclosed code might throw.

- `throw` expression statements, which exit a block of code, transferring control to an associated `catch` clause.

- `return`, which stops execution of a function. (We'll cover `return` statements in Chapter 6.)

In addition, there are expression statements and declaration statements. An expression statement causes the subject expression to be evaluated. Declarations and definitions of variables were described in Chapter 2.

DEFINED TERMS

block Sequence of zero or more statements enclosed in curly braces. A block is a statement, so it can appear anywhere a statement is expected.

break statement Terminates the nearest enclosing loop or `switch` statement. Execution transfers to the first statement following the terminated loop or `switch`.

case label Constant expression (§ 2.4.4, p. 65) that follows the keyword `case` in a `switch` statement. No two `case` labels in the same `switch` statement may have the same value.

catch clause The `catch` keyword, an exception declaration in parentheses, and a block of statements. The code inside a `catch` clause does whatever is necessary to handle an exception of the type defined in its exception declaration.

compound statement Synonym for block.

continue statement Terminates the current iteration of the nearest enclosing loop. Execution transfers to the loop condition in a `while` or `do`, to the next iteration in a range `for`, or to the expression in the header of a traditional `for` loop.

dangling else Colloquial term used to refer to the problem of how to process nested `if` statements in which there are more `if`s than `else`s. In C++, an `else` is always paired with the closest preceding unmatched `if`. Note that curly braces can be used to effectively hide an inner `if` so that the programmer can control which `if` a given `else` should match.

default label `case` label that matches any otherwise unmatched value computed in the `switch` expression.

do while statement Like a `while`, except that the condition is tested at the end of the loop, not the beginning. The statement inside the `do` is executed at least once.

exception classes Set of classes defined by the standard library to be used to represent errors. Table 5.1 (p. 197) lists the general-purpose exception classes.

exception declaration The declaration in a `catch` clause. This declaration specifies the type of exceptions the `catch` can handle.

exception handler Code that deals with an exception raised in another part of the program. Synonym for `catch` clause.

exception safe Term used to describe programs that behave correctly when exceptions are thrown.

expression statement An expression followed by a semicolon. An expression statement causes the expression to be evaluated.

flow of control Execution path through a program.

for statement Iteration statement that provides iterative execution. Ordinarily used to step through a container or to repeat a calculation a given number of times.

goto statement Statement that causes an unconditional transfer of control to a specified labeled statement elsewhere in the same function. `goto`s obfuscate the flow of control within a program and should be avoided.

if else statement Conditional execution of code following the `if` or the `else`, depending on the truth value of the condition.

if statement Conditional execution based on the value of the specified condition. If the condition is `true`, then the `if` body is executed. If not, control flows to the statement following the `if`.

labeled statement Statement preceded by a label. A label is an identifier followed by a colon. Label identifiers are independent of other uses of the same identifier.

null statement An empty statement. Indicated by a single semicolon.

raise Often used as a synonym for throw. C++ programmers speak of "throwing" or "raising" an exception interchangeably.

range for statement Statement that iterates through a sequence.

switch statement A conditional statement that starts by evaluating the expression that follows the `switch` keyword. Control passes to the labeled statement with a `case` label that matches the value of the expression. If there is no matching label, execution either continues at the `default` label, if there is one, or falls out of the `switch` if there is no `default` label.

terminate Library function that is called if an exception is not caught. `terminate` aborts the program.

throw expression Expression that interrupts the current execution path. Each `throw` throws an object and transfers control to the nearest enclosing `catch` clause that can handle the type of exception that is thrown.

try block Block enclosed by the keyword `try` and one or more `catch` clauses. If the code inside a `try` block raises an exception and one of the `catch` clauses matches the type of the exception, then the exception is handled by that `catch`. Otherwise, the exception is handled by an enclosing `try` block or the program terminates.

while statement Iteration statement that executes its target statement as long as a specified condition is `true`. The statement is executed zero or more times, depending on the truth value of the condition.

C H A P T E R 6

FUNCTIONS

This chapter describes how to define and declare functions. We'll cover how arguments are passed to and values returned from functions. In C++, functions can be overloaded, which means that we can use the same name for several different functions. We'll cover both how to overload functions and how the compiler selects the matching version for a particular call from several overloaded functions. The chapter closes by describing pointers to functions.

A function is a block of code with a name. We execute the code by calling the function. A function may take zero or more arguments and (usually) yields a result. Functions can be overloaded, meaning that the same name may refer to several different functions.

6.1 Function Basics

A *function* definition typically consists of a *return type*, a name, a list of zero or more *parameters*, and a body. The parameters are specified in a comma-separated list enclosed in parentheses. The actions that the function performs are specified in a statement block (§ 5.1, p. 173), referred to as the *function body*.

We execute a function through the **call operator**, which is a pair of parentheses. The call operator takes an expression that is a function or points to a function. Inside the parentheses is a comma-separated list of *arguments*. The arguments are used to initialize the function's parameters. The type of a call expression is the return type of the function.

Writing a Function

As an example, we'll write a function to determine the factorial of a given number. The factorial of a number n is the product of the numbers from 1 through n. The factorial of 5, for example, is 120.

```
1 * 2 * 3 * 4 * 5 = 120
```

We might define this function as follows:

```
// factorial of val is val * (val - 1) * (val - 2) ... * ((val - (val - 1)) * 1)
int fact(int val)
{
    int ret = 1; // local variable to hold the result as we calculate it
    while (val > 1)
        ret *= val--;   // assign ret * val to ret and decrement val
    return ret;         // return the result
}
```

Our function is named `fact`. It takes one `int` parameter and returns an `int` value. Inside the `while` loop, we compute the factorial using the postfix decrement operator (§ 4.5, p. 147) to reduce the value of `val` by 1 on each iteration. The `return` statement ends execution of `fact` and returns the value of `ret`.

Calling a Function

To call `fact`, we must supply an `int` value. The result of the call is also an `int`:

```
int main()
{
    int j = fact(5);    // j equals 120, i.e., the result of fact(5)
    cout << "5! is " << j << endl;
    return 0;
}
```

A function call does two things: It initializes the function's parameters from the corresponding arguments, and it transfers control to that function. Execution of the *calling* function is suspended and execution of the *called* function begins.

Execution of a function begins with the (implicit) definition and initialization of its parameters. Thus, when we call `fact`, the first thing that happens is that an `int` variable named `val` is created. This variable is initialized by the argument in the call to `fact`, which in this case is 5.

Execution of a function ends when a `return` statement is encountered. Like a function call, the `return` statement does two things: It returns the value (if any) in the `return`, and it transfers control out of the *called* function back to the *calling* function. The value returned by the function is used to initialize the result of the call expression. Execution continues with whatever remains of the expression in which the call appeared. Thus, our call to `fact` is equivalent to the following:

```
int val = 5;      //  initialize val from the literal 5
int ret = 1;      //  code from the body of fact
while (val > 1)
    ret *= val--;
int j = ret;      //  initialize j as a copy of ret
```

Parameters and Arguments

Arguments are the initializers for a function's parameters. The first argument initializes the first parameter, the second argument initializes the second parameter, and so on. Although we know which argument initializes which parameter, we have no guarantees about the order in which arguments are evaluated (§ 4.1.3, p. 137). The compiler is free to evaluate the arguments in whatever order it prefers.

The type of each argument must match the corresponding parameter in the same way that the type of any initializer must match the type of the object it initializes. We must pass exactly the same number of arguments as the function has parameters. Because every call is guaranteed to pass as many arguments as the function has parameters, parameters are always initialized.

Because `fact` has a single parameter of type `int`, every time we call it we must supply a single argument that can be converted (§ 4.11, p. 159) to `int`:

```
fact("hello");     //  error: wrong argument type
fact();            //  error: too few arguments
fact(42, 10, 0);   //  error: too many arguments
fact(3.14);        //  ok: argument is converted to int
```

The first call fails because there is no conversion from `const char*` to `int`. The second and third calls pass the wrong number of arguments. The `fact` function must be called with one argument; it is an error to call it with any other number. The last call is legal because there is a conversion from `double` to `int`. In this call, the argument is implicitly converted to `int` (through truncation). After the conversion, this call is equivalent to

```
fact(3);
```

Function Parameter List

A function's parameter list can be empty but cannot be omitted. Typically we define a function with no parameters by writing an empty parameter list. For compatibility with C, we also can use the keyword void to indicate that there are no parameters:

```
void f1(){ /* ... */ }      // implicit void parameter list
void f2(void){ /* ... */ } // explicit void parameter list
```

A parameter list typically consists of a comma-separated list of parameters, each of which looks like a declaration with a single declarator. Even when the types of two parameters are the same, the type must be repeated:

```
int f3(int v1, v2) { /* ... */ }      // error
int f4(int v1, int v2) { /* ... */ } // ok
```

No two parameters can have the same name. Moreover, local variables at the outermost scope of the function may not use the same name as any parameter.

Parameter names are optional. However, there is no way to use an unnamed parameter. Therefore, parameters ordinarily have names. Occasionally a function has a parameter that is not used. Such parameters are often left unnamed, to indicate that they aren't used. Leaving a parameter unnamed doesn't change the number of arguments that a call must supply. A call must supply an argument for every parameter, even if that parameter isn't used.

Function Return Type

Most types can be used as the return type of a function. In particular, the return type can be void, which means that the function does not return a value. However, the return type may not be an array type (§ 3.5, p. 113) or a function type. However, a function may return a pointer to an array or a function. We'll see how to define functions that return pointers (or references) to arrays in § 6.3.3 (p. 228) and how to return pointers to functions in § 6.7 (p. 247).

6.1.1 Local Objects

In C++, names have scope (§ 2.2.4, p. 48), and objects have **lifetimes**. It is important to understand both of these concepts.

- The scope of a name is *the part of the program's text* in which that name is visible.

- The lifetime of an object is *the time during the program's execution* that the object exists.

As we've seen, the body of a function is a statement block. As usual, the block forms a new scope in which we can define variables. Parameters and variables defined inside a function body are referred to as **local variables**. They are "local" to that function and **hide** declarations of the same name made in an outer scope.

Exercise 6.1: What is the difference between a parameter and an argument?

Exercise 6.2: Indicate which of the following functions are in error and why. Suggest how you might correct the problems.

```
(a) int f() {
        string s;
        // ...
        return s;
    }
(b) f2(int i) { /* ... */ }
(c) int calc(int v1, int v1) /* ... */ }
(d) double square(double x) return x * x;
```

Exercise 6.3: Write and test your own version of fact.

Exercise 6.4: Write a function that interacts with the user, asking for a number and generating the factorial of that number. Call this function from main.

Exercise 6.5: Write a function to return the absolute value of its argument.

Objects defined outside any function exist throughout the program's execution. Such objects are created when the program starts and are not destroyed until the program ends. The lifetime of a local variable depends on how it is defined.

Automatic Objects

The objects that correspond to ordinary local variables are created when the function's control path passes through the variable's definition. They are destroyed when control passes through the end of the block in which the variable is defined. Objects that exist only while a block is executing are known as **automatic objects**. After execution exits a block, the values of the automatic objects created in that block are undefined.

Parameters are automatic objects. Storage for the parameters is allocated when the function begins. Parameters are defined in the scope of the function body. Hence they are destroyed when the function terminates.

Automatic objects corresponding to the function's parameters are initialized by the arguments passed to the function. Automatic objects corresponding to local variables are initialized if their definition contains an initializer. Otherwise, they are default initialized (§ 2.2.1, p. 43), which means that uninitialized local variables of built-in type have undefined values.

Local static Objects

It can be useful to have a local variable whose lifetime continues across calls to the function. We obtain such objects by defining a local variable as static. Each **local static object** is initialized before the *first* time execution passes through the object's definition. Local `statics` are not destroyed when a function ends; they are destroyed when the program terminates.

As a trivial example, here is a function that counts how many times it is called:

```
size_t count_calls()
{
    static size_t ctr = 0;   // value will persist across calls
    return ++ctr;
}
int main()
{
    for (size_t i = 0; i != 10; ++i)
        cout << count_calls() << endl;
    return 0;
}
```

This program will print the numbers from 1 through 10 inclusive.

Before control flows through the definition of `ctr` for the first time, `ctr` is created and given an initial value of `0`. Each call increments `ctr` and returns its new value. Whenever `count_calls` is executed, the variable `ctr` already exists and has whatever value was in that variable the last time the function exited. Thus, on the second invocation, the value of `ctr` is `1`, on the third it is `2`, and so on.

If a local `static` has no explicit initializer, it is value initialized (§ 3.3.1, p. 98), meaning that local `statics` of built-in type are initialized to zero.

> **EXERCISES SECTION 6.1.1**
>
> **Exercise 6.6:** Explain the differences between a parameter, a local variable, and a local `static` variable. Give an example of a function in which each might be useful.
>
> **Exercise 6.7:** Write a function that returns 0 when it is first called and then generates numbers in sequence each time it is called again.

6.1.2 Function Declarations

Like any other name, the name of a function must be declared before we can use it. As with variables (§ 2.2.2, p. 45), a function may be defined only once but may be declared multiple times. With one exception that we'll cover in § 15.3 (p. 603), we can declare a function that is not defined so long as we never use that function.

A function declaration is just like a function definition except that a declaration has no function body. In a declaration, a semicolon replaces the function body.

Because a function declaration has no body, there is no need for parameter names. Hence, parameter names are often omitted in a declaration. Although parameter names are not required, they can be used to help users of the function understand what the function does:

```
// parameter names chosen to indicate that the iterators denote a range of values to print
void print(vector<int>::const_iterator beg,
           vector<int>::const_iterator end);
```

These three elements—the return type, function name, and parameter types—describe the function's interface. They specify all the information we need to call the function. Function declarations are also known as the **function prototype**.

Function Declarations Go in Header Files

Recall that variables are declared in header files (§ 2.6.3, p. 76) and defined in source files. For the same reasons, functions should be declared in header files and defined in source files.

It may be tempting—and would be legal—to put a function declaration directly in each source file that uses the function. However, doing so is tedious and error-prone. When we use header files for our function declarations, we can ensure that all the declarations for a given function agree. Moreover, if the interface to the function changes, only one declaration has to be changed.

The source file that defines a function should include the header that contains that function's declaration. That way the compiler will verify that the definition and declaration are consistent.

 Best Practices The header that *declares* a function should be included in the source file that *defines* that function.

EXERCISES SECTION 6.1.2

Exercise 6.8: Write a header file named Chapter6.h that contains declarations for the functions you wrote for the exercises in § 6.1 (p. 205).

6.1.3 Separate Compilation

As our programs get more complicated, we'll want to store the various parts of the program in separate files. For example, we might store the functions we wrote for the exercises in § 6.1 (p. 205) in one file and store code that uses these functions in other source files. To allow programs to be written in logical parts, C++ supports what is commonly known as *separate compilation*. Separate compilation lets us split our programs into several files, each of which can be compiled independently.

Compiling and Linking Multiple Source Files

As an example, assume that the definition of our fact function is in a file named fact.cc and its declaration is in a header file named Chapter6.h. Our fact.cc file, like any file that uses these functions, will include the Chapter6.h header. We'll store a main function that calls fact in a second file named factMain.cc.

To produce an *executable file*, we must tell the compiler where to find all of the code we use. We might compile these files as follows:

```
$ CC factMain.cc fact.cc   # generates factMain.exe or a.out
$ CC factMain.cc fact.cc -o main # generates main or main.exe
```

Here CC is the name of our compiler, $ is our system prompt, and # begins a command-line comment. We can now run the executable file, which will run our main function.

If we have changed only one of our source files, we'd like to recompile only the file that actually changed. Most compilers provide a way to separately compile each file. This process usually yields a file with the .obj (Windows) or .o (UNIX) file extension, indicating that the file contains *object code*.

The compiler lets us *link* object files together to form an executable. On the system we use, we would separately compile our program as follows:

```
$ CC -c factMain.cc     # generates factMain.o
$ CC -c fact.cc         # generates fact.o
$ CC factMain.o fact.o  # generates factMain.exe or a.out
$ CC factMain.o fact.o -o main # generates main or main.exe
```

You'll need to check with your compiler's user's guide to understand how to compile and execute programs made up of multiple source files.

EXERCISES SECTION 6.1.3

Exercise 6.9: Write your own versions of the fact.cc and factMain.cc files. These files should include your Chapter6.h from the exercises in the previous section. Use these files to understand how your compiler supports separate compilation.

 ## 6.2 Argument Passing

As we've seen, each time we call a function, its parameters are created and initialized by the arguments passed in the call.

 Parameter initialization works the same way as variable initialization.

As with any other variable, the type of a parameter determines the interaction between the parameter and its argument. If the parameter is a reference (§ 2.3.1, p. 50), then the parameter is bound to its argument. Otherwise, the argument's value is copied.

When a parameter is a reference, we say that its corresponding argument is **"passed by reference"** or that the function is **"called by reference."** As with any other reference, a reference parameter is an alias for the object to which it is bound; that is, the parameter is an alias for its corresponding argument.

When the argument value is copied, the parameter and argument are independent objects. We say such arguments are **"passed by value"** or alternatively that the function is **"called by value."**

6.2.1 Passing Arguments by Value

When we initialize a nonreference type variable, the value of the initializer is copied. Changes made to the variable have no effect on the initializer:

```
int n = 0;          //  ordinary variable of type int
int i = n;          //  i is a copy of the value in n
i = 42;             //  value in i is changed; n is unchanged
```

Passing an argument by value works exactly the same way; nothing the function does to the parameter can affect the argument. For example, inside `fact` (§ 6.1, p. 202) the parameter `val` is decremented:

```
ret *= val--;   //  decrements the value of val
```

Although `fact` changes the value of `val`, that change has no effect on the argument passed to `fact`. Calling `fact(i)` does not change the value of `i`.

Pointer Parameters

Pointers (§ 2.3.2, p. 52) behave like any other nonreference type. When we copy a pointer, the value of the pointer is copied. After the copy, the two pointers are distinct. However, a pointer also gives us indirect access to the object to which that pointer points. We can change the value of that object by assigning through the pointer (§ 2.3.2, p. 55):

```
int n = 0, i = 42;
int *p = &n, *q = &i; //  p points to n; q points to i
*p = 42;              //  value in n is changed; p is unchanged
p = q;                //  p now points to i; values in i and n are unchanged
```

The same behavior applies to pointer parameters:

```
//  function that takes a pointer and sets the pointed-to value to zero
void reset(int *ip)
{
    *ip = 0;   //  changes the value of the object to which ip points
    ip = 0;    //  changes only the local copy of ip; the argument is unchanged
}
```

After a call to `reset`, the object to which the argument points will be 0, but the pointer argument itself is unchanged:

```
int i = 42;
reset(&i);                          //  changes i but not the address of i
cout << "i = "  << i << endl; //  prints i = 0
```

Best Practices | Programmers accustomed to programming in C often use pointer parameters to access objects outside a function. In C++, programmers generally use reference parameters instead.

EXERCISES SECTION 6.2.1

Exercise 6.10: Using pointers, write a function to swap the values of two ints. Test the function by calling it and printing the swapped values.

6.2.2 Passing Arguments by Reference

Recall that operations on a reference are actually operations on the object to which the reference refers (§ 2.3.1, p. 50):

```
int n = 0, i = 42;
int &r = n;           //  r is bound to n (i.e., r is another name for n)
r = 42;               //  n is now 42
r = i;                //  n now has the same value as i
i = r;                //  i has the same value as n
```

Reference parameters exploit this behavior. They are often used to allow a function to change the value of one or more of its arguments.

As one example, we can rewrite our `reset` program from the previous section to take a reference instead of a pointer:

```
//  function that takes a reference to an int and sets the given object to zero
void reset(int &i)    //  i is just another name for the object passed to reset
{
    i = 0;    //  changes the value of the object to which i refers
}
```

As with any other reference, a reference parameter is bound directly to the object from which it is initialized. When we call this version of `reset`, `i` will be bound to whatever int object we pass. As with any reference, changes made to `i` are made to the object to which `i` refers. In this case, that object is the argument to `reset`.

When we call this version of `reset`, we pass an object directly; there is no need to pass its address:

```
int j = 42;
reset(j);    //  j is passed by reference; the value in j is changed
cout << "j = " << j  << endl;  //  prints j = 0
```

In this call, the parameter `i` is just another name for `j`. Any use of `i` inside `reset` is a use of `j`.

Using References to Avoid Copies

It can be inefficient to copy objects of large class types or large containers. More-over, some class types (including the IO types) cannot be copied. Functions must use reference parameters to operate on objects of a type that cannot be copied.

As an example, we'll write a function to compare the length of two `strings`. Because `strings` can be long, we'd like to avoid copying them, so we'll make our parameters references. Because comparing two `strings` does not involve chang-ing the `strings`, we'll make the parameters references to `const` (§ 2.4.1, p. 61):

```
// compare the length of two strings
bool isShorter(const string &s1, const string &s2)
{
    return s1.size() < s2.size();
}
```

As we'll see in § 6.2.3 (p. 213), functions should use references to `const` for refer-ence parameters they do not need to change.

Best
Practices

Reference parameters that are not changed inside a function should be references to `const`.

Using Reference Parameters to Return Additional Information

A function can return only a single value. However, sometimes a function has more than one value to return. Reference parameters let us effectively return mul-tiple results. As an example, we'll define a function named `find_char` that will return the position of the first occurrence of a given character in a `string`. We'd also like the function to return a count of how many times that character occurs.

How can we define a function that returns a position and an occurrence count? We could define a new type that contains the position and the count. An easier solution is to pass an additional reference argument to hold the occurrence count:

```
//   returns the index of the first occurrence of c in s
//   the reference parameter occurs counts how often c occurs
string::size_type find_char(const string &s, char c,
                            string::size_type &occurs)
{
    auto ret = s.size();      //   position of the first occurrence, if any
    occurs = 0;               //   set the occurrence count parameter
    for (decltype(ret) i = 0; i != s.size(); ++i) {
        if (s[i] == c) {
            if (ret == s.size())
                ret = i;      //   remember the first occurrence of c
            ++occurs;         //   increment the occurrence count
        }
    }
    return ret;               //   count is returned implicitly in occurs
}
```

When we call find_char, we have to pass three arguments: a string in which to look, the character to look for, and a size_type (§ 3.2.2, p. 88) object to hold the occurrence count. Assuming s is a string, and ctr is a size_type object, we can call find_char as follows:

```
auto index = find_char(s, 'o', ctr);
```

After the call, the value of ctr will be the number of times o occurs, and index will refer to the first occurrence if there is one. Otherwise, index will be equal to s.size() and ctr will be zero.

6.2.3 const Parameters and Arguments

When we use parameters that are const, it is important to remember the discussion of top-level const from § 2.4.3 (p. 63). As we saw in that section, a top-level const is one that applies to the object itself:

```
const int ci = 42;      // we cannot change ci; const is top-level
int i = ci;             // ok: when we copy ci, its top-level const is ignored
int * const p = &i;     // const is top-level; we can't assign to p
*p = 0;                 // ok: changes through p are allowed; i is now 0
```

Just as in any other initialization, when we copy an argument to initialize a parameter, top-level consts are ignored. As a result, top-level const on parameters are ignored. We can pass either a const or a nonconst object to a parameter that has a top-level const:

```
void fcn(const int i) { /* fcn can read but not write to i */ }
```

We can call fcn passing it either a const int or a plain int. The fact that top-level consts are ignored on a parameter has one possibly surprising implication:

```
void fcn(const int i) { /* fcn can read but not write to i */ }
void fcn(int i) { /* ... */ }   // error: redefines fcn(int)
```

In C++, we can define several different functions that have the same name. However, we can do so only if their parameter lists are sufficiently different. Because top-level `const`s are ignored, we can pass exactly the same types to either version of `fcn`. The second version of `fcn` is an error. Despite appearances, its parameter list doesn't differ from the list in the first version of `fcn`.

Pointer or Reference Parameters and `const`

Because parameters are initialized in the same way that variables are initialized, it can be helpful to remember the general initialization rules. We can initialize an object with a low-level `const` from a nonconst object but not vice versa, and a plain reference must be initialized from an object of the same type.

```
int i = 42;
const int *cp = &i;  // ok: but cp can't change i (§ 2.4.2 (p. 62))
const int &r = i;    // ok: but r can't change i (§ 2.4.1 (p. 61))
const int &r2 = 42;  // ok: (§ 2.4.1 (p. 61))
int *p = cp;   // error: types of p and cp don't match (§ 2.4.2 (p. 62))
int &r3 = r;   // error: types of r3 and r don't match (§ 2.4.1 (p. 61))
int &r4 = 42;  // error: can't initialize a plain reference from a literal (§ 2.3.1 (p. 50))
```

Exactly the same initialization rules apply to parameter passing:

```
int i = 0;
const int ci = i;
string::size_type ctr = 0;
reset(&i);     // calls the version of reset that has an int* parameter
reset(&ci);    // error: can't initialize an int* from a pointer to a const int object
reset(i);      // calls the version of reset that has an int& parameter
reset(ci);     // error: can't bind a plain reference to the const object ci
reset(42);     // error: can't bind a plain reference to a literal
reset(ctr);    // error: types don't match; ctr has an unsigned type
// ok: find_char's first parameter is a reference to const
find_char("Hello World!", 'o', ctr);
```

We can call the reference version of `reset` (§ 6.2.2, p. 210) only on `int` objects. We cannot pass a literal, an expression that evaluates to an `int`, an object that requires conversion, or a `const int` object. Similarly, we may pass only an `int*` to the pointer version of `reset` (§ 6.2.1, p. 209). On the other hand, we can pass a string literal as the first argument to `find_char` (§ 6.2.2, p. 211). That function's reference parameter is a reference to `const`, and we can initialize references to `const` from literals.

Use Reference to `const` When Possible

It is a somewhat common mistake to define parameters that a function does not change as (plain) references. Doing so gives the function's caller the misleading impression that the function might change its argument's value. Moreover, using a reference instead of a reference to const unduly limits the type of arguments that can be used with the function. As we've just seen, we cannot pass a const object, or a literal, or an object that requires conversion to a plain reference parameter.

The effect of this mistake can be surprisingly pervasive. As an example, consider our find_char function from § 6.2.2 (p. 211). That function (correctly) made its string parameter a reference to const. Had we defined that parameter as a plain string&:

```
// bad design: the first parameter should be a const string&
string::size_type find_char(string &s, char c,
                            string::size_type &occurs);
```

we could call find_char only on a string object. A call such as

```
find_char("Hello World", 'o', ctr);
```

would fail at compile time.

More subtly, we could not use this version of find_char from other functions that (correctly) define their parameters as references to const. For example, we might want to use find_char inside a function that determines whether a string represents a sentence:

```
bool is_sentence(const string &s)
{
    // if there's a single period at the end of s, then s is a sentence
    string::size_type ctr = 0;
    return find_char(s, '.', ctr) == s.size() - 1 && ctr == 1;
}
```

If find_char took a plain string&, then this call to find_char would be a compile-time error. The problem is that s is a reference to a const string, but find_char was (incorrectly) defined to take a plain reference.

It might be tempting to try to fix this problem by changing the type of the parameter in is_sentence. But that fix only propagates the error—callers of is_sentence could pass only nonconst strings.

The right way to fix this problem is to fix the parameter in find_char. If it's not possible to change find_char, then define a local string copy of s inside is_sentence and pass that string to find_char.

6.2.4 Array Parameters

Arrays have two special properties that affect how we define and use functions that operate on arrays: We cannot copy an array (§ 3.5.1, p. 114), and when we use an array it is (usually) converted to a pointer (§ 3.5.3, p. 117). Because we cannot copy an array, we cannot pass an array by value. Because arrays are converted to pointers, when we pass an array to a function, we are actually passing a pointer to the array's first element.

Even though we cannot pass an array by value, we can write a parameter that looks like an array:

EXERCISES SECTION 6.2.3

Exercise 6.16: The following function, although legal, is less useful than it might be. Identify and correct the limitation on this function:

```
bool is_empty(string& s) { return s.empty(); }
```

Exercise 6.17: Write a function to determine whether a `string` contains any capital letters. Write a function to change a `string` to all lowercase. Do the parameters you used in these functions have the same type? If so, why? If not, why not?

Exercise 6.18: Write declarations for each of the following functions. When you write these declarations, use the name of the function to indicate what the function does.

(a) A function named `compare` that returns a `bool` and has two parameters that are references to a class named `matrix`.

(b) A function named `change_val` that returns a `vector<int>` iterator and takes two parameters: One is an `int` and the other is an iterator for a `vector<int>`.

Exercise 6.19: Given the following declarations, determine which calls are legal and which are illegal. For those that are illegal, explain why.

```
double calc(double);
int count(const string &, char);
int sum(vector<int>::iterator, vector<int>::iterator, int);
vector<int> vec(10);
(a) calc(23.4, 55.1);    (b) count("abcda", 'a');
(c) calc(66);            (d) sum(vec.begin(), vec.end(), 3.8);
```

Exercise 6.20: When should reference parameters be references to const? What happens if we make a parameter a plain reference when it could be a reference to const?

```
//  despite appearances, these three declarations of print are equivalent
//  each function has a single parameter of type const int *
void print(const int*);
void print(const int[]);      //  shows the intent that the function takes an array
void print(const int[10]);    //  dimension for documentation purposes (at best)
```

Regardless of appearances, these declarations are equivalent: Each declares a function with a single parameter of type const int *. When the compiler checks a call to print, it checks only that the argument has type const int *:

```
int i = 0, j[2] = {0, 1};
print(&i);  // ok: &i is int *
print(j);   // ok: j is converted to an int * that points to j[0]
```

If we pass an array to print, that argument is automatically converted to a pointer to the first element in the array; the size of the array is irrelevant.

> ⚠️ **WARNING** As with any code that uses arrays, functions that take array parameters must ensure that all uses of the array stay within the array bounds.

Because arrays are passed as pointers, functions ordinarily don't know the size of the array they are given. They must rely on additional information provided by the caller. There are three common techniques used to manage pointer parameters.

Using a Marker to Specify the Extent of an Array

The first approach to managing array arguments requires the array itself to contain an end marker. C-style character strings (§ 3.5.4, p. 122) are an example of this approach. C-style strings are stored in character arrays in which the last character of the string is followed by a null character. Functions that deal with C-style strings stop processing the array when they see a null character:

```
void print(const char *cp)
{
    if (cp)             //  if cp is not a null pointer
        while (*cp)     //  so long as the character it points to is not a null character
            cout << *cp++;  //  print the character and advance the pointer
}
```

This convention works well for data where there is an obvious end-marker value (like the null character) that does not appear in ordinary data. It works less well with data, such as `ints`, where every value in the range is a legitimate value.

Using the Standard Library Conventions

A second technique used to manage array arguments is to pass pointers to the first and one past the last element in the array. This approach is inspired by techniques used in the standard library. We'll learn more about this style of programming in Part II. Using this approach, we'll print the elements in an array as follows:

```
void print(const int *beg, const int *end)
{
    //  print every element starting at beg up to but not including end
    while (beg != end)
        cout << *beg++ << endl;  //  print the current element
                                 //  and advance the pointer
}
```

The `while` uses the dereference and postfix increment operators (§ 4.5, p. 148) to print the current element and advance `beg` one element at a time through the array. The loop stops when `beg` is equal to `end`.

To call this function, we pass two pointers—one to the first element we want to print and one just past the last element:

```
int j[2] = {0, 1};
//  j is converted to a pointer to the first element in j
//  the second argument is a pointer to one past the end of j
print(begin(j), end(j));  //  begin and end functions, see § 3.5.3 (p. 118)
```

This function is safe, as long as the caller correctly calculates the pointers. Here we let the library `begin` and `end` functions (§ 3.5.3, p. 118) provide those pointers.

Explicitly Passing a Size Parameter

A third approach for array arguments, which is common in C programs and older C++ programs, is to define a second parameter that indicates the size of the array. Using this approach, we'll rewrite `print` as follows:

```
// const int ia[] is equivalent to const int* ia
// size is passed explicitly and used to control access to elements of ia
void print(const int ia[], size_t size)
{
    for (size_t i = 0; i != size; ++i) {
        cout << ia[i] << endl;
    }
}
```

This version uses the `size` parameter to determine how many elements there are to print. When we call `print`, we must pass this additional parameter:

```
int j[] = { 0, 1 };  // int array of size 2
print(j, end(j) - begin(j));
```

The function executes safely as long as the size passed is no greater than the actual size of the array.

Array Parameters and `const`

Note that all three versions of our `print` function defined their array parameters as pointers to `const`. The discussion in § 6.2.3 (p. 213) applies equally to pointers as to references. When a function does not need write access to the array elements, the array parameter should be a pointer to `const` (§ 2.4.2, p. 62). A parameter should be a plain pointer to a `nonconst` type only if the function needs to change element values.

Array Reference Parameters

Just as we can define a variable that is a reference to an array (§ 3.5.1, p. 114), we can define a parameter that is a reference to an array. As usual, the reference parameter is bound to the corresponding argument, which in this case is an array:

```
// ok: parameter is a reference to an array; the dimension is part of the type
void print(int (&arr)[10])
{
    for (auto elem : arr)
        cout << elem << endl;
}
```

> **Note**
>
> The parentheses around `&arr` are necessary (§ 3.5.1, p. 114):
>
> ```
> f(int &arr[10])     // error: declares arr as an array of references
> f(int (&arr)[10])   // ok: arr is a reference to an array of ten ints
> ```

Because the size of an array is part of its type, it is safe to rely on the dimension in the body of the function. However, the fact that the size is part of the type limits the usefulness of this version of print. We may call this function only for an array of exactly ten ints:

```
int i = 0, j[2] = {0, 1};
int k[10] = {0,1,2,3,4,5,6,7,8,9};
print(&i);    // error: argument is not an array of ten ints
print(j);     // error: argument is not an array of ten ints
print(k);     // ok: argument is an array of ten ints
```

We'll see in § 16.1.1 (p. 654) how we might write this function in a way that would allow us to pass a reference parameter to an array of any size.

Passing a Multidimensional Array

Recall that there are no multidimensional arrays in C++ (§ 3.6, p. 125). Instead, what appears to be a multidimensional array is an array of arrays.

As with any array, a multidimensional array is passed as a pointer to its first element (§ 3.6, p. 128). Because we are dealing with an array of arrays, that element is an array, so the pointer is a pointer to an array. The size of the second (and any subsequent) dimension is part of the element type and must be specified:

```
// matrix points to the first element in an array whose elements are arrays of ten ints
void print(int (*matrix)[10], int rowSize) { /* ... */ }
```

declares matrix as a pointer to an array of ten ints.

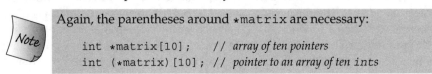

> Again, the parentheses around *matrix are necessary:
>
> ```
> int *matrix[10];    // array of ten pointers
> int (*matrix)[10];  // pointer to an array of ten ints
> ```

We can also define our function using array syntax. As usual, the compiler ignores the first dimension, so it is best not to include it:

```
// equivalent definition
void print(int matrix[][10], int rowSize) { /* ... */ }
```

declares matrix to be what looks like a two-dimensional array. In fact, the parameter is a pointer to an array of ten ints.

6.2.5 main: Handling Command-Line Options

It turns out that main is a good example of how C++ programs pass arrays to functions. Up to now, we have defined main with an empty parameter list:

```
int main() { ... }
```

However, we sometimes need to pass arguments to main. The most common use of arguments to main is to let the user specify a set of options to guide the operation of the program. For example, assuming our main program is in an executable file named prog, we might pass options to the program as follows:

EXERCISES SECTION 6.2.4

Exercise 6.21: Write a function that takes an `int` and a pointer to an `int` and returns the larger of the `int` value or the value to which the pointer points. What type should you use for the pointer?

Exercise 6.22: Write a function to swap two `int` pointers.

Exercise 6.23: Write your own versions of each of the `print` functions presented in this section. Call each of these functions to print `i` and `j` defined as follows:

```
int i = 0, j[2] = {0, 1};
```

Exercise 6.24: Explain the behavior of the following function. If there are problems in the code, explain what they are and how you might fix them.

```
void print(const int ia[10])
{
    for (size_t i = 0; i != 10; ++i)
        cout << ia[i] << endl;
}
```

```
prog -d -o ofile data0
```

Such command-line options are passed to `main` in two (optional) parameters:

```
int main(int argc, char *argv[]) { ... }
```

The second parameter, `argv`, is an array of pointers to C-style character strings. The first parameter, `argc`, passes the number of strings in that array. Because the second parameter is an array, we might alternatively define `main` as

```
int main(int argc, char **argv) { ... }
```

indicating that `argv` points to a `char*`.

When arguments are passed to `main`, the first element in `argv` points either to the name of the program or to the empty string. Subsequent elements pass the arguments provided on the command line. The element just past the last pointer is guaranteed to be 0.

Given the previous command line, `argc` would be 5, and `argv` would hold the following C-style character strings:

```
argv[0] = "prog";    // or argv[0] might point to an empty string
argv[1] = "-d";
argv[2] = "-o";
argv[3] = "ofile";
argv[4] = "data0";
argv[5] = 0;
```

WARNING When you use the arguments in `argv`, remember that the optional arguments begin in `argv[1]`; `argv[0]` contains the program's name, not user input.

Exercise 6.25: Write a `main` function that takes two arguments. Concatenate the supplied arguments and print the resulting `string`.

Exercise 6.26: Write a program that accepts the options presented in this section. Print the values of the arguments passed to `main`.

6.2.6 Functions with Varying Parameters

Sometimes we do not know in advance how many arguments we need to pass to a function. For example, we might want to write a routine to print error messages generated from our program. We'd like to use a single function to print these error messages in order to handle them in a uniform way. However, different calls to our error-printing function might pass different arguments, corresponding to different kinds of error messages.

The new standard provides two primary ways to write a function that takes a varying number of arguments: If all the arguments have the same type, we can pass a library type named `initializer_list`. If the argument types vary, we can write a special kind of function, known as a variadic template, which we'll cover in § 16.4 (p. 699).

C++ also has a special parameter type, ellipsis, that can be used to pass a varying number of arguments. We'll look briefly at ellipsis parameters in this section. However, it is worth noting that this facility ordinarily should be used only in programs that need to interface to C functions.

`initializer_list` Parameters

We can write a function that takes an unknown number of arguments of a single type by using an **`initializer_list`** parameter. An `initializer_list` is a library type that represents an array (§ 3.5, p. 113) of values of the specified type. This type is defined in the `initializer_list` header. The operations that `initializer_list` provides are listed in Table 6.1.

Table 6.1: Operations on `initializer_lists`	
`initializer_list<T> lst;`	
	Default initialization; an empty list of elements of type `T`.
`initializer_list<T> lst{a,b,c...};`	
	`lst` has as many elements as there are initializers; elements are copies of the corresponding initializers. Elements in the list are `const`.
`lst2(lst)`	Copying or assigning an `initializer_list` does not copy the elements
`lst2 = lst`	in the list. After the copy, the original and the copy share the elements.
`lst.size()`	Number of elements in the list.
`lst.begin()`	Returns a pointer to the first and one past the last element in `lst`.
`lst.end()`	

Like a vector, initializer_list is a template type (§ 3.3, p. 96). When we define an initializer_list, we must specify the type of the elements that the list will contain:

```
initializer_list<string> ls; // initializer_list of strings
initializer_list<int> li;    // initializer_list of ints
```

Unlike vector, the elements in an initializer_list are always const values; there is no way to change the value of an element in an initializer_list.

We can write our function to produce error messages from a varying number of arguments as follows:

```
void error_msg(initializer_list<string> il)
{
    for (auto beg = il.begin(); beg != il.end(); ++beg)
        cout << *beg << " " ;
    cout << endl;
}
```

The begin and end operations on initializer_list objects are analogous to the corresponding vector members (§ 3.4.1, p. 106). The begin() member gives us a pointer to the first element in the list, and end() is an off-the-end pointer one past the last element. Our function initializes beg to denote the first element and iterates through each element in the initializer_list. In the body of the loop we dereference beg in order to access the current element and print its value.

When we pass a sequence of values to an initializer_list parameter, we must enclose the sequence in curly braces:

```
// expected, actual are strings
if (expected != actual)
    error_msg({"functionX", expected, actual});
else
    error_msg({"functionX", "okay"});
```

Here we're calling the same function, error_msg, passing three values in the first call and two values in the second.

A function with an initializer_list parameter can have other parameters as well. For example, our debugging system might have a class, named ErrCode, that represents various kinds of errors. We can revise our program to take an ErrCode in addition to an initializer_list as follows:

```
void error_msg(ErrCode e, initializer_list<string> il)
{
    cout << e.msg() << ": ";
    for (const auto &elem : il)
        cout << elem << " " ;
    cout << endl;
}
```

Because initializer_list has begin and end members, we can use a range for (§ 5.4.3, p. 187) to process the elements. This program, like our previous version, iterates an element at a time through the braced list of values passed to the il parameter.

To call this version, we need to revise our calls to pass an `ErrCode` argument:

```
if (expected != actual)
    error_msg(ErrCode(42), {"functionX", expected, actual});
else
    error_msg(ErrCode(0), {"functionX", "okay"});
```

Ellipsis Parameters

Ellipsis parameters are in C++ to allow programs to interface to C code that uses a C library facility named `varargs`. Generally an ellipsis parameter should not be used for other purposes. Your C compiler documentation will describe how to use `varargs`.

> Ellipsis parameters should be used only for types that are common to both C and C++. In particular, objects of most class types are not copied properly when passed to an ellipsis parameter.

WARNING

An ellipsis parameter may appear only as the last element in a parameter list and may take either of two forms:

```
void foo(parm_list, ...);
void foo(...);
```

The first form specifies the type(s) for some of `foo`'s parameters. Arguments that correspond to the specified parameters are type checked as usual. No type checking is done for the arguments that correspond to the ellipsis parameter. In this first form, the comma following the parameter declarations is optional.

EXERCISES SECTION 6.2.6

Exercise 6.27: Write a function that takes an `initializer_list<int>` and produces the sum of the elements in the list.

Exercise 6.28: In the second version of `error_msg` that has an `ErrCode` parameter, what is the type of `elem` in the `for` loop?

Exercise 6.29: When you use an `initializer_list` in a range `for` would you ever use a reference as the loop control variable? If so, why? If not, why not?

6.3 Return Types and the `return` Statement

A `return` statement terminates the function that is currently executing and returns control to the point from which the function was called. There are two forms of `return` statements:

```
return;
return expression;
```

6.3.1 Functions with No Return Value

A `return` with no value may be used only in a function that has a return type of `void`. Functions that return `void` are not required to contain a `return`. In a void function, an implicit `return` takes place after the function's last statement.

Typically, `void` functions use a `return` to exit the function at an intermediate point. This use of `return` is analogous to the use of a `break` statement (§ 5.5.1, p. 190) to exit a loop. For example, we can write a `swap` function that does no work if the values are identical:

```cpp
void swap(int &v1, int &v2)
{
    // if the values are already the same, no need to swap, just return
    if (v1 == v2)
        return;
    // if we're here, there's work to do
    int tmp = v2;
    v2 = v1;
    v1 = tmp;
    // no explicit return necessary
}
```

This function first checks if the values are equal and, if so, exits the function. If the values are unequal, the function swaps them. An implicit return occurs after the last assignment statement.

A function with a `void` return type may use the second form of the `return` statement only to return the result of calling another function that returns `void`. Returning any other expression from a `void` function is a compile-time error.

6.3.2 Functions That Return a Value

The second form of the `return` statement provides the function's result. Every return in a function with a return type other than `void` must return a value. The value returned must have the same type as the function return type, or it must have a type that can be implicitly converted (§ 4.11, p. 159) to that type.

Although C++ cannot guarantee the correctness of a result, it can guarantee that every `return` includes a result of the appropriate type. Although it cannot do so in all cases, the compiler attempts to ensure that functions that return a value are exited only through a valid `return` statement. For example:

```cpp
// incorrect return values, this code will not compile
bool str_subrange(const string &str1, const string &str2)
{
    // same sizes: return normal equality test
    if (str1.size() == str2.size())
        return str1 == str2;    // ok: == returns bool
    // find the size of the smaller string; conditional operator, see § 4.7 (p. 151)
    auto size = (str1.size() < str2.size())
                    ? str1.size() : str2.size();
```

```
    //  look at each element up to the size of the smaller string
    for (decltype(size) i = 0; i != size; ++i) {
        if (str1[i] != str2[i])
            return;  //  error #1: no return value; compiler should detect this error
    }
    //  error #2: control might flow off the end of the function without a return
    //  the compiler might not detect this error
}
```

The return from within the for loop is an error because it fails to return a value. The compiler should detect this error.

The second error occurs because the function fails to provide a return after the loop. If we call this function with one string that is a subset of the other, execution would fall out of the for. There should be a return to handle this case. The compiler may or may not detect this error. If it does not detect the error, what happens at run time is undefined.

Failing to provide a return after a loop that contains a return is an error. However, many compilers will not detect such errors.

How Values Are Returned

Values are returned in exactly the same way as variables and parameters are initialized: The return value is used to initialize a temporary at the call site, and that temporary is the result of the function call.

It is important to keep in mind the initialization rules in functions that return local variables. As an example, we might write a function that, given a counter, a word, and an ending, gives us back the plural version of the word if the counter is greater than 1:

```
//  return the plural version of word if ctr is greater than 1
string make_plural(size_t ctr, const string &word,
                                const string &ending)
{
    return (ctr > 1) ? word + ending : word;
}
```

The return type of this function is string, which means the return value is copied to the call site. This function returns a copy of word, or it returns an unnamed temporary string that results from adding word and ending.

As with any other reference, when a function returns a reference, that reference is just another name for the object to which it refers. As an example, consider a function that returns a reference to the shorter of its two string parameters:

```
//  return a reference to the shorter of two strings
const string &shorterString(const string &s1, const string &s2)
{
    return s1.size() <= s2.size() ? s1 : s2;
}
```

The parameters and return type are references to const string. The strings are not copied when the function is called or when the result is returned.

Never Return a Reference or Pointer to a Local Object

When a function completes, its storage is freed (§ 6.1.1, p. 204). After a function terminates, references to local objects refer to memory that is no longer valid:

```
//   disaster: this function returns a reference to a local object
const string &manip()
{
    string ret;
    //   transform ret in some way
    if (!ret.empty())
        return ret;         //   WRONG: returning a reference to a local object!
    else
        return "Empty"; //   WRONG: "Empty" is a local temporary string
}
```

Both of these return statements return an undefined value—what happens if we try to use the value returned from manip is undefined. In the first return, it should be obvious that the function returns a reference to a local object. In the second case, the string literal is converted to a local temporary string object. That object, like the string named s, is local to manip. The storage in which the temporary resides is freed when the function ends. Both returns refer to memory that is no longer available.

 One good way to ensure that the return is safe is to ask: To what *preexisting* object is the reference referring?

For the same reasons that it is wrong to return a reference to a local object, it is also wrong to return a pointer to a local object. Once the function completes, the local objects are freed. The pointer would point to a nonexistent object.

Functions That Return Class Types and the Call Operator

Like any operator the call operator has associativity and precedence (§ 4.1.2, p. 136). The call operator has the same precedence as the dot and arrow operators (§ 4.6, p. 150). Like those operators, the call operator is left associative. As a result, if a function returns a pointer, reference or object of class type, we can use the result of a call to call a member of the resulting object.

For example, we can determine the size of the shorter string as follows:

```
//   call the size member of the string returned by shorterString
auto sz = shorterString(s1, s2).size();
```

Because these operators are left associative, the result of shorterString is the left-hand operand of the dot operator. That operator fetches the size member of that string. That member is the left-hand operand of the second call operator.

Reference Returns Are Lvalues

Whether a function call is an lvalue (§ 4.1.1, p. 135) depends on the return type of the function. Calls to functions that return references are lvalues; other return types yield rvalues. A call to a function that returns a reference can be used in the same ways as any other lvalue. In particular, we can assign to the result of a function that returns a reference to nonconst:

```
char &get_val(string &str, string::size_type ix)
{
    return str[ix]; // get_val assumes the given index is valid
}
int main()
{
    string s("a value");
    cout << s << endl;    // prints a value
    get_val(s, 0) = 'A';  // changes s[0] to A
    cout << s << endl;    // prints A value
    return 0;
}
```

It may be surprising to see a function call on the left-hand side of an assignment. However, nothing special is involved. The return value is a reference, so the call is an lvalue. Like any other lvalue, it may appear as the left-hand operand of the assignment operator.

If the return type is a reference to const, then (as usual) we may not assign to the result of the call:

```
shorterString("hi", "bye") = "X"; // error: return value is const
```

List Initializing the Return Value

Under the new standard, functions can return a braced list of values. As in any other return, the list is used to initialize the temporary that represents the function's return. If the list is empty, that temporary is value initialized (§ 3.3.1, p. 98). Otherwise, the value of the return depends on the function's return type.

As an example, recall the error_msg function from § 6.2.6 (p. 220). That function took a varying number of string arguments and printed an error message composed from the given strings. Rather than calling error_msg, in this function we'll return a vector that holds the error-message strings:

```
vector<string> process()
{
    // ...
    // expected and actual are strings
    if (expected.empty())
        return {};  // return an empty vector
    else if (expected == actual)
        return {"functionX", "okay"}; // return list-initialized vector
    else
        return {"functionX", expected, actual};
}
```

In the first return statement, we return an empty list. In this case, the `vector` that `process` returns will be empty. Otherwise, we return a `vector` initialized with two or three elements depending on whether `expected` and `actual` are equal.

In a function that returns a built-in type, a braced list may contain at most one value, and that value must not require a narrowing conversion (§ 2.2.1, p. 43). If the function returns a class type, then the class itself defines how the intiailizers are used (§ 3.3.1, p. 99).

Return from `main`

There is one exception to the rule that a function with a return type other than `void` must return a value: The `main` function is allowed to terminate without a return. If control reaches the end of `main` and there is no return, then the compiler implicitly inserts a return of 0.

As we saw in § 1.1 (p. 2), the value returned from `main` is treated as a status indicator. A zero return indicates success; most other values indicate failure. A nonzero value has a machine-dependent meaning. To make return values machine independent, the `cstdlib` header defines two preprocessor variables (§ 2.3.2, p. 54) that we can use to indicate success or failure:

```
int main()
{
    if (some_failure)
        return EXIT_FAILURE;   // defined in cstdlib
    else
        return EXIT_SUCCESS;   // defined in cstdlib
}
```

Because these are preprocessor variables, we must not precede them with `std::`, nor may we mention them in `using` declarations.

Recursion

A function that calls itself, either directly or indirectly, is a *recursive function*. As an example, we can rewrite our factorial function to use recursion:

```
// calculate val!, which is 1 * 2 * 3 ... * val
int factorial(int val)
{
    if (val > 1)
        return factorial(val-1) * val;
    return 1;
}
```

In this implementation, we recursively call `factorial` to compute the factorial of the numbers counting down from the original value in `val`. Once we have reduced `val` to 1, we stop the recursion by returning 1.

There must always be a path through a recursive function that does not involve a recursive call; otherwise, the function will recurse "forever," meaning that the function will continue to call itself until the program stack is exhausted. Such functions are sometimes described as containing a **recursion loop**. In the case of `factorial`, the stopping condition occurs when `val` is 1.

The following table traces the execution of `factorial` when passed the value 5.

Trace of `factorial(5)`

Call	Returns	Value
`factorial(5)`	`factorial(4) * 5`	120
`factorial(4)`	`factorial(3) * 4`	24
`factorial(3)`	`factorial(2) * 3`	6
`factorial(2)`	`factorial(1) * 2`	2
`factorial(1)`	1	1

> **Note** The `main` function may *not* call itself.

EXERCISES SECTION 6.3.2

Exercise 6.30: Compile the version of `str_subrange` as presented on page 223 to see what your compiler does with the indicated errors.

Exercise 6.31: When is it valid to return a reference? A reference to `const`?

Exercise 6.32: Indicate whether the following function is legal. If so, explain what it does; if not, correct any errors and then explain it.

```
int &get(int *arry, int index) { return arry[index]; }
int main() {
    int ia[10];
    for (int i = 0; i != 10; ++i)
        get(ia, i) = i;
}
```

Exercise 6.33: Write a recursive function to print the contents of a `vector`.

Exercise 6.34: What would happen if the stopping condition in `factorial` were

```
if (val != 0)
```

Exercise 6.35: In the call to `fact`, why did we pass `val - 1` rather than `val--`?

6.3.3 Returning a Pointer to an Array

Because we cannot copy an array, a function cannot return an array. However, a function can return a pointer or a reference to an array (§ 3.5.1, p. 114). Unfortunately, the syntax used to define functions that return pointers or references to arrays can be intimidating. Fortunately, there are ways to simplify such declarations. The most straightforward way is to use a type alias (§ 2.5.1, p. 67):

```
typedef int arrT[10];  // arrT is a synonym for the type array of ten ints
using arrtT = int[10]; // equivalent declaration of arrT; see § 2.5.1 (p. 68)
arrT* func(int i);     // func returns a pointer to an array of five ints
```

Here `arrT` is a synonym for an array of ten `int`s. Because we cannot return an array, we define the return type as a pointer to this type. Thus, `func` is a function that takes a single `int` argument and returns a pointer to an array of ten `int`s.

Declaring a Function That Returns a Pointer to an Array

To declare `func` without using a type alias, we must remember that the dimension of an array follows the name being defined:

```
int arr[10];             // arr is an array of ten ints
int *p1[10];             // p1 is an array of ten pointers
int (*p2)[10] = &arr;    // p2 points to an array of ten ints
```

As with these declarations, if we want to define a function that returns a pointer to an array, the dimension must follow the function's name. However, a function includes a parameter list, which also follows the name. The parameter list precedes the dimension. Hence, the form of a function that returns a pointer to an array is:

> *Type* (**function* (*parameter_list*)) [*dimension*]

As in any other array declaration, *Type* is the type of the elements and *dimension* is the size of the array. The parentheses around (**function* (*parameter_list*)) are necessary for the same reason that they were required when we defined p2. Without them, we would be defining a function that returns an array of pointers.

As a concrete example, the following declares `func` without using a type alias:

```
int (*func(int i))[10];
```

To understand this declaration, it can be helpful to think about it as follows:

- `func(int)` says that we can call `func` with an `int` argument.

- `(*func(int))` says we can dereference the result of that call.

- `(*func(int))[10]` says that dereferencing the result of a call to `func` yields an array of size ten.

- `int (*func(int))[10]` says the element type in that array is `int`.

Using a Trailing Return Type

Under the new standard, another way to simplify the declaration of `func` is by using a **trailing return type**. Trailing returns can be defined for any function, but are most useful for functions with complicated return types, such as pointers (or references) to arrays. A trailing return type follows the parameter list and is preceded by `->`. To signal that the return follows the parameter list, we use `auto` where the return type ordinarily appears:

```
//  fcn takes an int argument and returns a pointer to an array of ten ints
auto func(int i) -> int(*)[10];
```

Because the return type comes after the parameter list, it is easier to see that `func` returns a pointer and that that pointer points to an array of ten `int`s.

Using `decltype`

As another alternative, if we know the array(s) to which our function can return a pointer, we can use `decltype` to declare the return type. For example, the following function returns a pointer to one of two arrays, depending on the value of its parameter:

```
int odd[] = {1,3,5,7,9};
int even[] = {0,2,4,6,8};
//  returns a pointer to an array of five int elements
decltype(odd) *arrPtr(int i)
{
    return (i % 2) ? &odd : &even; //  returns a pointer to the array
}
```

The return type for `arrPtr` uses `decltype` to say that the function returns a pointer to whatever type `odd` has. That object is an array, so `arrPtr` returns a pointer to an array of five `int`s. The only tricky part is that we must remember that `decltype` does not automatically convert an array to its corresponding pointer type. The type returned by `decltype` is an array type, to which we must add a `*` to indicate that `arrPtr` returns a pointer.

EXERCISES SECTION 6.3.3

Exercise 6.36: Write the declaration for a function that returns a reference to an array of ten `strings`, without using either a trailing return, `decltype`, or a type alias.

Exercise 6.37: Write three additional declarations for the function in the previous exercise. One should use a type alias, one should use a trailing return, and the third should use `decltype`. Which form do you prefer and why?

Exercise 6.38: Revise the `arrPtr` function on to return a reference to the array.

 ## 6.4 Overloaded Functions

Functions that have the same name but different parameter lists and that appear in the same scope are **overloaded**. For example, in § 6.2.4 (p. 214) we defined several functions named `print`:

```
void print(const char *cp);
void print(const int *beg, const int *end);
void print(const int ia[], size_t size);
```

These functions perform the same general action but apply to different parameter types. When we call these functions, the compiler can deduce which function we want based on the argument type we pass:

```
int j[2] = {0,1};
print("Hello World");        // calls print(const char*)
print(j, end(j) - begin(j)); // calls print(const int*, size_t)
print(begin(j), end(j));     // calls print(const int*, const int*)
```

Function overloading eliminates the need to invent—and remember—names that exist only to help the compiler figure out which function to call.

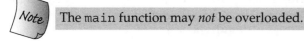 The main function may *not* be overloaded.

Defining Overloaded Functions

Consider a database application with several functions to find a record based on name, phone number, account number, and so on. Function overloading lets us define a collection of functions, each named `lookup`, that differ in terms of how they do the search. We can call `lookup` passing a value of any of several types:

```
Record lookup(const Account&);   // find by Account
Record lookup(const Phone&);     // find by Phone
Record lookup(const Name&);      // find by Name

Account acct;
Phone phone;
Record r1 = lookup(acct);   // call version that takes an Account
Record r2 = lookup(phone);  // call version that takes a Phone
```

Here, all three functions share the same name, yet they are three distinct functions. The compiler uses the argument type(s) to figure out which function to call.

Overloaded functions must differ in the number or the type(s) of their parameters. Each of the functions above takes a single parameter, but the parameters have different types.

It is an error for two functions to differ only in terms of their return types. If the parameter lists of two functions match but the return types differ, then the second declaration is an error:

```
Record lookup(const Account&);
bool lookup(const Account&);   // error: only the return type is different
```

Determining Whether Two Parameter Types Differ

Two parameter lists can be identical, even if they don't look the same:

```
// each pair declares the same function
Record lookup(const Account &acct);
Record lookup(const Account&); // parameter names are ignored

typedef Phone Telno;
Record lookup(const Phone&);
Record lookup(const Telno&); // Telno and Phone are the same type
```

In the first pair, the first declaration names its parameter. Parameter names are only a documentation aid. They do not change the parameter list.

In the second pair, it looks like the types are different, but `Telno` is not a new type; it is a synonym for `Phone`. A type alias (§ 2.5.1, p. 67) provides an alternative name for an existing type; it does not create a new type. Therefore, two parameters that differ only in that one uses an alias and the other uses the type to which the alias corresponds are not different.

Overloading and `const` Parameters

As we saw in § 6.2.3 (p. 212), top-level `const` (§ 2.4.3, p. 63) has no effect on the objects that can be passed to the function. A parameter that has a top-level `const` is indistinguishable from one without a top-level `const`:

```
Record lookup(Phone);
Record lookup(const Phone);   // redeclares Record lookup(Phone)

Record lookup(Phone*);
Record lookup(Phone* const);  // redeclares Record lookup(Phone*)
```

In these declarations, the second declaration declares the same function as the first.

On the other hand, we can overload based on whether the parameter is a reference (or pointer) to the `const` or nonconst version of a given type; such `const`s are low-level:

```
//  functions taking const and nonconst references or pointers have different parameters
//  declarations for four independent, overloaded functions
Record lookup(Account&);        //  function that takes a reference to Account
Record lookup(const Account&);  //  new function that takes a const reference

Record lookup(Account*);        //  new function, takes a pointer to Account
Record lookup(const Account*);  //  new function, takes a pointer to const
```

In these cases, the compiler can use the const`ness` of the argument to distinguish which function to call. Because there is no conversion (§ 4.11.2, p. 162) *from* `const`, we can pass a `const` object (or a pointer to `const`) only to the version with a `const` parameter. Because there is a conversion *to* `const`, we can call either function on a nonconst object or a pointer to nonconst. However, as we'll see in § 6.6.1 (p. 246), the compiler will prefer the nonconst versions when we pass a nonconst object or pointer to nonconst.

`const_cast` and Overloading

In § 4.11.3 (p. 163) we noted that `const_cast`s are most useful in the context of overloaded functions. As one example, recall our `shorterString` function from § 6.3.2 (p. 224):

```
//  return a reference to the shorter of two strings
const string &shorterString(const string &s1, const string &s2)
{
    return s1.size() <= s2.size() ? s1 : s2;
}
```

ADVICE: WHEN NOT TO OVERLOAD A FUNCTION NAME

Although overloading lets us avoid having to invent (and remember) names for common operations, we should only overload operations that actually do similar things. There are some cases where providing different function names adds information that makes the program easier to understand. Consider a set of functions that move the cursor on a Screen.

```
Screen& moveHome();
Screen& moveAbs(int, int);
Screen& moveRel(int, int, string direction);
```

It might at first seem better to overload this set of functions under the name move:

```
Screen& move();
Screen& move(int, int);
Screen& move(int, int, string direction);
```

However, by overloading these functions, we've lost information that was inherent in the function names. Although cursor movement is a general operation shared by all these functions, the specific nature of that movement is unique to each of these functions. moveHome, for example, represents a special instance of cursor movement. Whether to overload these functions depends on which of these two calls is easier to understand:

```
// which is easier to understand?
myScreen.moveHome(); // we think this one!
myScreen.move();
```

This function takes and returns references to const string. We can call the function on a pair of nonconst string arguments, but we'll get a reference to a const string as the result. We might want to have a version of shorterString that, when given nonconst arguments, would yield a plain reference. We can write this version of our function using a const_cast:

```
string &shorterString(string &s1, string &s2)
{
    auto &r = shorterString(const_cast<const string&>(s1),
                            const_cast<const string&>(s2));
    return const_cast<string&>(r);
}
```

This version calls the const version of shorterString by casting its arguments to references to const. That function returns a reference to a const string, which we know is bound to one of our original, nonconst arguments. Therefore, we know it is safe to cast that string back to a plain string& in the return.

Calling an Overloaded Function

Once we have defined a set of overloaded functions, we need to be able to call them with appropriate arguments. **Function matching** (also known as **overload resolution**) is the process by which a particular function call is associated with a specific function from a set of overloaded functions. The compiler determines which function to call by comparing the arguments in the call with the parameters offered by each function in the overload set.

In many—probably most—cases, it is straightforward for a programmer to determine whether a particular call is legal and, if so, which function will be called. Often the functions in the overload set differ in terms of the number of arguments, or the types of the arguments are unrelated. In such cases, it is easy to determine which function is called. Determining which function is called when the overloaded functions have the same number of parameters and those parameters are related by conversions (§ 4.11, p. 159) can be less obvious. We'll look at how the compiler resolves calls involving conversions in § 6.6 (p. 242).

For now, what's important to realize is that for any given call to an overloaded function, there are three possible outcomes:

- The compiler finds exactly one function that is a **best match** for the actual arguments and generates code to call that function.

- There is no function with parameters that match the arguments in the call, in which case the compiler issues an error message that there was **no match**.

- There is more than one function that matches and none of the matches is clearly best. This case is also an error; it is an **ambiguous call**.

EXERCISES SECTION 6.4

Exercise 6.39: Explain the effect of the second declaration in each one of the following sets of declarations. Indicate which, if any, are illegal.

```
(a) int calc(int, int);
    int calc(const int, const int);
(b) int get();
    double get();
(c) int *reset(int *);
    double *reset(double *);
```

 ## 6.4.1 Overloading and Scope

> **⚠ WARNING** Ordinarily, it is a bad idea to declare a function locally. However, to explain how scope interacts with overloading, we will violate this practice and use local function declarations.

Programmers new to C++ are often confused about the interaction between scope and overloading. However, overloading has no special properties with respect to scope: As usual, if we declare a name in an inner scope, that name *hides* uses of that name declared in an outer scope. Names do not overload across scopes:

```
string read();
void print(const string &);
void print(double);     // overloads the print function
void fooBar(int ival)
{
    bool read = false; // new scope: hides the outer declaration of read
    string s = read(); // error: read is a bool variable, not a function
    // bad practice: usually it's a bad idea to declare functions at local scope
    void print(int);   // new scope: hides previous instances of print
    print("Value: "); // error: print(const string &) is hidden
    print(ival);       // ok: print(int) is visible
    print(3.14);       // ok: calls print(int); print(double) is hidden
}
```

Most readers will not be surprised that the call to `read` is in error. When the compiler processes the call to `read`, it finds the local definition of `read`. That name is a `bool` variable, and we cannot call a `bool`. Hence, the call is illegal.

Exactly the same process is used to resolve the calls to `print`. The declaration of `print(int)` in `fooBar` hides the earlier declarations of `print`. It is as if there is only one `print` function available: the one that takes a single `int` parameter.

When we call `print`, the compiler first looks for a declaration of that name. It finds the local declaration for `print` that takes an `int`. Once a name is found, the compiler ignores uses of that name in any outer scope. Instead, the compiler assumes that the declaration it found is the one for the name we are using. What remains is to see if the use of the name is valid.

> **Note** In C++, name lookup happens before type checking.

The first call passes a string literal, but the only declaration for `print` that is in scope has a parameter that is an `int`. A string literal cannot be converted to an `int`, so this call is an error. The `print(const string&)` function, which would have matched this call, is hidden and is not considered.

When we call `print` passing a `double`, the process is repeated. The compiler finds the local definition of `print(int)`. The `double` argument can be converted to an `int`, so the call is legal.

Had we declared `print(int)` in the same scope as the other `print` functions, then it would be another overloaded version of `print`. In that case, these calls would be resolved differently, because the compiler will see all three functions:

```
void print(const string &);
void print(double); // overloads the print function
void print(int);    // another overloaded instance
void fooBar2(int ival)
{
    print("Value: "); // calls print(const string &)
    print(ival);       // calls print(int)
    print(3.14);       // calls print(double)
}
```

6.5 Features for Specialized Uses

In this section we'll cover three function-related features that are useful in many, but not all, programs: default arguments, inline and `constexpr` functions, and some facilities that are often used during debugging.

6.5.1 Default Arguments

Some functions have parameters that are given a particular value in most, but not all, calls. In such cases, we can declare that common value as a **default argument** for the function. Functions with default arguments can be called with or without that argument.

For example, we might use a `string` to represent the contents of a window. By default, we might want the window to have a particular height, width, and background character. However, we might also want to allow users to pass values other than the defaults. To accommodate both default and specified values we would declare our function to define the window as follows:

```
typedef string::size_type sz;   // typedef see § 2.5.1 (p. 67)
string screen(sz ht = 24, sz wid = 80, char backgrnd = ' ');
```

Here we've provided a default for each parameter. A default argument is specified as an initializer for a parameter in the parameter list. We may define defaults for one or more parameters. However, if a parameter has a default argument, all the parameters that follow it must also have default arguments.

Calling Functions with Default Arguments

If we want to use the default argument, we omit that argument when we call the function. Because `screen` provides defaults for all of its parameters, we can call `screen` with zero, one, two, or three arguments:

```
string window;
window = screen();  // equivalent to screen(24,80,' ')
window = screen(66);// equivalent to screen(66,80,' ')
window = screen(66, 256);      // screen(66,256,' ')
window = screen(66, 256, '#'); // screen(66,256,'#')
```

Arguments in the call are resolved by position. The default arguments are used for the trailing (right-most) arguments of a call. For example, to override the default for background, we must also supply arguments for `height` and `width`:

```
window = screen(, , '?'); // error: can omit only trailing arguments
window = screen('?');     // calls screen('?',80,' ')
```

Note that the second call, which passes a single character value, is legal. Although legal, it is unlikely to be what was intended. The call is legal because `'?'` is a `char`, and a `char` can be converted (§ 4.11.1, p. 160) to the type of the left-most parameter. That parameter is `string::size_type`, which is an unsigned integral type. In this call, the `char` argument is implicitly converted to `string::size_type`, and is passed as the argument to `height`. On our machine, `'?'` has the hexadecimal value `0x3F`, which is decimal `63`. Thus, this call passes `63` to the `height` parameter.

Part of the work of designing a function with default arguments is ordering the parameters so that those least likely to use a default value appear first and those most likely to use a default appear last.

Default Argument Declarations

Although it is normal practice to declare a function once inside a header, it is legal to redeclare a function multiple times. However, each parameter can have its default specified only once in a given scope. Thus, any subsequent declaration can add a default only for a parameter that has not previously had a default specified. As usual, defaults can be specified only if all parameters to the right already have defaults. For example, given

```
//  no default for the height or width parameters
string screen(sz, sz, char = ' ');
```

we cannot change an already declared default value:

```
string screen(sz, sz, char = '*'); //  error: redeclaration
```

but we can add a default argument as follows:

```
string screen(sz = 24, sz = 80, char);   //  ok: adds default arguments
```

Best Practices Default arguments ordinarily should be specified with the function declaration in an appropriate header.

Default Argument Initializers

Local variables may not be used as a default argument. Excepting that restriction, a default argument can be any expression that has a type that is convertible to the type of the parameter:

```
//  the declarations of wd, def, and ht must appear outside a function
sz wd = 80;
char def = ' ';
sz ht();
string screen(sz = ht(), sz = wd, char = def);
string window = screen(); //  calls screen(ht(), 80, ' ')
```

Names used as default arguments are resolved in the scope of the function declaration. The value that those names represent is evaluated at the time of the call:

```
void f2()
{
    def = '*';    //  changes the value of a default argument
    sz wd = 100;  //  hides the outer definition of wd but does not change the default
    window = screen(); //  calls screen(ht(), 80, '*')
}
```

Inside f2, we changed the value of def. The call to screen passes this updated value. Our function also declared a local variable that hides the outer wd. However, the local named wd is unrelated to the default argument passed to screen.

6.5.2 Inline and `constexpr` Functions

In § 6.3.2 (p. 224) we wrote a small function that returned a reference to the shorter of its two string parameters. The benefits of defining a function for such a small operation include the following:

- It is easier to read and understand a call to shorterString than it would be to read and understand the equivalent conditional expression.

- Using a function ensures uniform behavior. Each test is guaranteed to be done the same way.

- If we need to change the computation, it is easier to change the function than to find and change every occurrence of the equivalent expression.

- The function can be reused rather than rewritten for other applications.

There is, however, one potential drawback to making shorterString a function: Calling a function is apt to be slower than evaluating the equivalent expression. On most machines, a function call does a lot of work: Registers are saved before the call and restored after the return; arguments may be copied; and the program branches to a new location.

`inline` Functions Avoid Function Call Overhead

A function specified as **inline** (usually) is expanded "in line" at each call. If shorterString were defined as inline, then this call

```
cout << shorterString(s1, s2) << endl;
```

(probably) would be expanded during compilation into something like

```
cout << (s1.size() < s2.size() ? s1 : s2) << endl;
```

The run-time overhead of making `shorterString` a function is thus removed.

We can define `shorterString` as an inline function by putting the keyword `inline` before the function's return type:

```
// inline version: find the shorter of two strings
inline const string &
shorterString(const string &s1, const string &s2)
{
        return s1.size() <= s2.size() ? s1 : s2;
}
```

 The `inline` specification is only a *request* to the compiler. The compiler may choose to ignore this request.

In general, the `inline` mechanism is meant to optimize small, straight-line functions that are called frequently. Many compilers will not inline a recursive function. A 75-line function will almost surely not be expanded inline.

`constexpr` Functions

A **`constexpr` function** is a function that can be used in a constant expression (§ 2.4.4, p. 65). A `constexpr` function is defined like any other function but must meet certain restrictions: The `return` type and the type of each parameter in a must be a literal type (§ 2.4.4, p. 66), and the function body must contain exactly one `return` statement:

```
constexpr int new_sz() { return 42; }
constexpr int foo = new_sz();   // ok: foo is a constant expression
```

Here we defined `new_sz` as a `constexpr` that takes no arguments. The compiler can verify—at compile time—that a call to `new_sz` returns a constant expression, so we can use `new_sz` to initialize our `constexpr` variable, `foo`.

When it can do so, the compiler will replace a call to a `constexpr` function with its resulting value. In order to be able to expand the function immediately, `constexpr` functions are implicitly `inline`.

A `constexpr` function body may contain other statements so long as those statements generate no actions at run time. For example, a `constexpr` function may contain null statements, type aliases (§ 2.5.1, p. 67), and `using` declarations.

A `constexpr` function is permitted to return a value that is not a constant:

```
// scale(arg) is a constant expression if arg is a constant expression
constexpr size_t scale(size_t cnt) { return new_sz() * cnt; }
```

The `scale` function will return a constant expression if its argument is a constant expression but not otherwise:

```
int arr[scale(2)];    // ok: scale(2) is a constant expression
int i = 2;            // i is not a constant expression
int a2[scale(i)];     // error: scale(i) is not a constant expression
```

When we pass a constant expression—such as the literal 2—then the return is a constant expression. In this case, the compiler will replace the call to scale with the resulting value.

If we call scale with an expression that is not a constant expression—such as on the int object i—then the return is not a constant expression. If we use scale in a context that requires a constant expression, the compiler checks that the result is a constant expression. If it is not, the compiler will produce an error message.

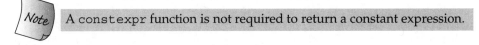

A constexpr function is not required to return a constant expression.

Put inline and constexpr Functions in Header Files

Unlike other functions, inline and constexpr functions may be defined multiple times in the program. After all, the compiler needs the definition, not just the declaration, in order to expand the code. However, all of the definitions of a given inline or constexpr must match exactly. As a result, inline and constexpr functions normally are defined in headers.

EXERCISES SECTION 6.5.2

Exercise 6.43: Which one of the following declarations and definitions would you put in a header? In a source file? Explain why.

```
(a) inline bool eq(const BigInt&, const BigInt&) {...}
(b) void putValues(int *arr, int size);
```

Exercise 6.44: Rewrite the isShorter function from § 6.2.2 (p. 211) to be inline.

Exercise 6.45: Review the programs you've written for the earlier exercises and decide whether they should be defined as inline. If so, do so. If not, explain why they should not be inline.

Exercise 6.46: Would it be possible to define isShorter as a constexpr? If so, do so. If not, explain why not.

6.5.3 Aids for Debugging

C++ programmers sometimes use a technique similar to header guards (§ 2.6.3, p. 77) to conditionally execute debugging code. The idea is that the program will contain debugging code that is executed only while the program is being developed. When the application is completed and ready to ship, the debugging code is turned off. This approach uses two preprocessor facilities: assert and NDEBUG.

The `assert` Preprocessor Macro

`assert` is a **preprocessor macro**. A preprocessor macro is a preprocessor variable that acts somewhat like an inline function. The `assert` macro takes a single expression, which it uses as a condition:

```
assert(expr);
```

evaluates *expr* and if the expression is false (i.e., zero), then `assert` writes a message and terminates the program. If the expression is true (i.e., is nonzero), then `assert` does nothing.

The `assert` macro is defined in the `cassert` header. As we've seen, preprocessor names are managed by the preprocessor not the compiler (§ 2.3.2, p. 54). As a result, we use preprocessor names directly and do not provide a `using` declaration for them. That is, we refer to `assert`, not `std::assert`, and provide no `using` declaration for `assert`.

As with preprocessor variables, macro names must be unique within the program. Programs that include the `cassert` header may not define a variable, function, or other entity named `assert`. In practice, it is a good idea to avoid using the name `assert` for our own purposes even if we don't include `cassert`. Many headers include the `cassert` header, which means that even if you don't directly include that file, your programs are likely to have it included anyway.

The `assert` macro is often used to check for conditions that "cannot happen." For example, a program that does some manipulation of input text might know that all words it is given are always longer than a threshold. That program might contain a statement such as

```
assert(word.size() > threshold);
```

The `NDEBUG` Preprocessor Variable

The behavior of `assert` depends on the status of a preprocessor variable named `NDEBUG`. If `NDEBUG` is defined, `assert` does nothing. By default, `NDEBUG` is *not* defined, so, by default, `assert` performs a run-time check.

We can "turn off" debugging by providing a `#define` to define `NDEBUG`. Alternatively, most compilers provide a command-line option that lets us define preprocessor variables:

```
$ CC -D NDEBUG main.C  # use /D with the Microsoft compiler
```

has the same effect as writing `#define NDEBUG` at the beginning of `main.C`.

If `NDEBUG` is defined, we avoid the potential run-time overhead involved in checking various conditions. Of course, there is also no run-time check. Therefore, `assert` should be used only to verify things that truly should not be possible. It can be useful as an aid in getting a program debugged but should not be used to substitute for run-time logic checks or error checking that the program should do.

In addition to using `assert`, we can write our own conditional debugging code using `NDEBUG`. If `NDEBUG` is *not* defined, the code between the `#ifndef` and the `#endif` is executed. If `NDEBUG` *is* defined, that code is ignored:

```
void print(const int ia[], size_t size)
{
#ifndef NDEBUG
// __func__ is a local static defined by the compiler that holds the function's name
cerr << __func__ << ": array size is " << size << endl;
#endif
// ...
```

Here we use a variable named __func__ to print the name of the function we are debugging. The compiler defines __func__ in every function. It is a local static array of const char that holds the name of the function.

In addition to __func__, which the C++ compiler defines, the preprocessor defines four other names that can be useful in debugging:

__FILE__ string literal containing the name of the file

__LINE__ integer literal containing the current line number

__TIME__ string literal containing the time the file was compiled

__DATE__ string literal containing the date the file was compiled

We might use these constants to report additional information in error messages:

```
if (word.size() < threshold)
    cerr << "Error: " << __FILE__
         << " : in function " << __func__
         << " at line " << __LINE__ << endl
         << "         Compiled on " << __DATE__
         << " at " << __TIME__ << endl
         << "         Word read was \"" << word
         << "\": Length too short" << endl;
```

If we give this program a string that is shorter than the threshold, then the following error message will be generated:

```
Error: wdebug.cc : in function main at line 27
        Compiled on Jul 11 2012 at 20:50:03
        Word read was "foo": Length too short
```

6.6 Function Matching

In many (if not most) cases, it is easy to figure out which overloaded function matches a given call. However, it is not so simple when the overloaded functions have the same number of parameters and when one or more of the parameters have types that are related by conversions. As an example, consider the following set of functions and function call:

```
void f();
void f(int);
void f(int, int);
void f(double, double = 3.14);
f(5.6);  // calls void f(double, double)
```

Exercise 6.47: Revise the program you wrote in the exercises in § 6.3.2 (p. 228) that used recursion to print the contents of a vector to conditionally print information about its execution. For example, you might print the size of the vector on each call. Compile and run the program with debugging turned on and again with it turned off.

Exercise 6.48: Explain what this loop does and whether it is a good use of assert:

```
string s;
while (cin >> s && s != sought) { }  // empty body
assert(cin);
```

Determining the Candidate and Viable Functions

The first step of function matching identifies the set of overloaded functions considered for the call. The functions in this set are the **candidate functions**. A candidate function is a function with the same name as the called function and for which a declaration is visible at the point of the call. In this example, there are four candidate functions named f.

The second step selects from the set of candidate functions those functions that can be called with the arguments in the given call. The selected functions are the **viable functions**. To be viable, a function must have the same number of parameters as there are arguments in the call, and the type of each argument must match—or be convertible to—the type of its corresponding parameter.

We can eliminate two of our candidate functions based on the number of arguments. The function that has no parameters and the one that has two int parameters are not viable for this call. Our call has only one argument, and these functions have zero and two parameters, respectively.

The function that takes a single int and the function that takes two doubles might be viable. Either of these functions can be called with a single argument. The function taking two doubles has a default argument, which means it can be called with a single argument.

When a function has default arguments (§ 6.5.1, p. 236), a call may appear to have fewer arguments than it actually does.

Having used the number of arguments to winnow the candidate functions, we next look at whether the argument types match those of the parameters. As with any call, an argument might match its parameter either because the types match exactly or because there is a conversion from the argument type to the type of the parameter. In this example, both of our remaining functions are viable:

- f(int) is viable because a conversion exists that can convert the argument of type double to the parameter of type int.

- f(double, double) is viable because a default argument is provided for the function's second parameter and its first parameter is of type double, which exactly matches the type of the parameter.

If there are no viable functions, the compiler will complain that there is no matching function.

Finding the Best Match, If Any

The third step of function matching determines which viable function provides the best match for the call. This process looks at each argument in the call and selects the viable function (or functions) for which the corresponding parameter best matches the argument. We'll explain the details of "best" in the next section, but the idea is that the closer the types of the argument and parameter are to each other, the better the match.

In our case, there is only one (explicit) argument in the call. That argument has type double. To call f(int), the argument would have to be converted from double to int. The other viable function, f(double, double), is an exact match for this argument. An exact match is better than a match that requires a conversion. Therefore, the compiler will resolve the call f(5.6) as a call to the function that has two double parameters. The compiler will add the default argument for the second, missing argument.

Function Matching with Multiple Parameters

Function matching is more complicated if there are two or more arguments. Given the same functions named f, let's analyze the following call:

```
f(42, 2.56);
```

The set of viable functions is selected in the same way as when there is only one parameter. The compiler selects those functions that have the required number of parameters and for which the argument types match the parameter types. In this case, the viable functions are f(int, int) and f(double, double). The compiler then determines, argument by argument, which function is (or functions are) the best match. There is an overall best match if there is one and only one function for which

- The match for each argument is no worse than the match required by any other viable function

- There is at least one argument for which the match is better than the match provided by any other viable function

If after looking at each argument there is no single function that is preferable, then the call is in error. The compiler will complain that the call is ambiguous.

In this call, when we look only at the first argument, we find that the function f(int, int) is an exact match. To match the second function, the int argument 42 must be converted to double. A match through a built-in conversion is "less good" than one that is exact. Considering only the first argument, f(int, int) is a better match than f(double, double).

When we look at the second argument, f(double, double) is an exact match to the argument 2.56. Calling f(int, int) would require that 2.56 be converted from double to int. When we consider only the second parameter, the function f(double, double) is a better match.

The compiler will reject this call because it is ambiguous: Each viable function is a better match than the other on one of the arguments to the call. It might be tempting to force a match by explicitly casting (§ 4.11.3, p. 162) one of our arguments. However, in well-designed systems, argument casts should not be necessary.

 Casts should not be needed to call an overloaded function. The need for a cast suggests that the parameter sets are designed poorly.

EXERCISES SECTION 6.6

Exercise 6.49: What is a candidate function? What is a viable function?

Exercise 6.50: Given the declarations for f from page 242, list the viable functions, if any for each of the following calls. Indicate which function is the best match, or if the call is illegal whether there is no match or why the call is ambiguous.

    (a) f(2.56, 42)   (b) f(42)   (c) f(42, 0)   (d) f(2.56, 3.14)

Exercise 6.51: Write all four versions of f. Each function should print a distinguishing message. Check your answers for the previous exercise. If your answers were incorrect, study this section until you understand why your answers were wrong.

6.6.1 Argument Type Conversions

In order to determine the best match, the compiler ranks the conversions that could be used to convert each argument to the type of its corresponding parameter. Conversions are ranked as follows:

1. An exact match. An exact match happens when:

   - The argument and parameter types are identical.
   - The argument is converted from an array or function type to the corresponding pointer type. (§ 6.7 (p. 247) covers function pointers.)
   - A top-level const is added to or discarded from the argument.

2. Match through a const conversion (§ 4.11.2, p. 162).

3. Match through a promotion (§ 4.11.1, p. 160).

4. Match through an arithmetic (§ 4.11.1, p. 159) or pointer conversion (§ 4.11.2, p. 161).

5. Match through a class-type conversion. (§ 14.9 (p. 579) covers these conversions.)

Matches Requiring Promotion or Arithmetic Conversion

> **WARNING**
> Promotions and conversions among the built-in types can yield surprising results in the context of function matching. Fortunately, well-designed systems rarely include functions with parameters as closely related as those in the following examples.

In order to analyze a call, it is important to remember that the small integral types always promote to `int` or to a larger integral type. Given two functions, one of which takes an `int` and the other a `short`, the `short` version will be called only on values of type `short`. Even though the smaller integral values might appear to be a closer match, those values are promoted to `int`, whereas calling the `short` version would require a conversion:

```
void ff(int);
void ff(short);
ff('a');    // char promotes to int; calls f(int)
```

All the arithmetic conversions are treated as equivalent to each other. The conversion from `int` to `unsigned int`, for example, does not take precedence over the conversion from `int` to `double`. As a concrete example, consider

```
void manip(long);
void manip(float);
manip(3.14);  // error: ambiguous call
```

The literal 3.14 is a `double`. That type can be converted to either `long` or `float`. Because there are two possible arithmetic conversions, the call is ambiguous.

Function Matching and `const` Arguments

When we call an overloaded function that differs on whether a reference or pointer parameter refers or points to `const`, the compiler uses the `const`ness of the argument to decide which function to call:

```
Record lookup(Account&);        // function that takes a reference to Account
Record lookup(const Account&);  // new function that takes a const reference
const Account a;
Account b;
lookup(a);    // calls lookup(const Account&)
lookup(b);    // calls lookup(Account&)
```

In the first call, we pass the `const` object a. We cannot bind a plain reference to a `const` object. In this case the only viable function is the version that takes a reference to `const`. Moreover, that call is an exact match to the argument a.

In the second call, we pass the nonconst object b. For this call, both functions are viable. We can use b to initialize a reference to either `const` or nonconst type. However, initializing a reference to `const` from a nonconst object requires a conversion. The version that takes a nonconst parameter is an exact match for b. Hence, the nonconst version is preferred.

Pointer parameters work in a similar way. If two functions differ only as to whether a pointer parameter points to `const` or nonconst, the compiler can distinguish which function to call based on the `constness` of the argument: If the argument is a pointer to `const`, the call will match the function that takes a `const *`; otherwise, if the argument is a pointer to nonconst, the function taking a plain pointer is called.

EXERCISES SECTION 6.6.1

Exercise 6.52: Given the following declarations,

```
void manip(int, int);
double dobj;
```

what is the rank (§ 6.6.1, p. 245) of each conversion in the following calls?

(a) `manip('a', 'z');`   (b) `manip(55.4, dobj);`

Exercise 6.53: Explain the effect of the second declaration in each one of the following sets of declarations. Indicate which, if any, are illegal.

(a) `int calc(int&, int&);`
    `int calc(const int&, const int&);`
(b) `int calc(char*, char*);`
    `int calc(const char*, const char*);`
(c) `int calc(char*, char*);`
    `int calc(char* const, char* const);`

6.7 Pointers to Functions

A function pointer is just that—a pointer that denotes a function rather than an object. Like any other pointer, a function pointer points to a particular type. A function's type is determined by its return type and the types of its parameters. The function's name is not part of its type. For example:

```
// compares lengths of two strings
bool lengthCompare(const string &, const string &);
```

has type `bool(const string&, const string&)`. To declare a pointer that can point at this function, we declare a pointer in place of the function name:

```
// pf points to a function returning bool that takes two const string references
bool (*pf)(const string &, const string &);   // uninitialized
```

Starting from the name we are declaring, we see that `pf` is preceded by a `*`, so `pf` is a pointer. To the right is a parameter list, which means that `pf` points to a function. Looking left, we find that the type the function returns is `bool`. Thus, `pf` points to a function that has two `const string&` parameters and returns `bool`.

> **Note**
>
> The parentheses around *pf are necessary. If we omit the parentheses, then we declare pf as a function that returns a pointer to bool:
>
> ```
> //   declares a function named pf that returns a bool *
> bool *pf(const string &, const string &);
> ```

Using Function Pointers

When we use the name of a function as a value, the function is automatically converted to a pointer. For example, we can assign the address of lengthCompare to pf as follows:

```
pf = lengthCompare;    // pf now points to the function named lengthCompare
pf = &lengthCompare;   // equivalent assignment: address-of operator is optional
```

Moreover, we can use a pointer to a function to call the function to which the pointer points. We can do so directly—there is no need to dereference the pointer:

```
bool b1 = pf("hello", "goodbye");      // calls lengthCompare
bool b2 = (*pf)("hello", "goodbye");   // equivalent call
bool b3 = lengthCompare("hello", "goodbye");   // equivalent call
```

There is no conversion between pointers to one function type and pointers to another function type. However, as usual, we can assign nullptr (§ 2.3.2, p. 53) or a zero-valued integer constant expression to a function pointer to indicate that the pointer does not point to any function:

```
string::size_type sumLength(const string&, const string&);
bool cstringCompare(const char*, const char*);
pf = 0;                // ok: pf points to no function
pf = sumLength;        // error: return type differs
pf = cstringCompare;   // error: parameter types differ
pf = lengthCompare;    // ok: function and pointer types match exactly
```

Pointers to Overloaded Functions

As usual, when we use an overloaded function, the context must make it clear which version is being used. When we declare a pointer to an overloaded function

```
void ff(int*);
void ff(unsigned int);
void (*pf1)(unsigned int) = ff;   // pf1 points to ff(unsigned)
```

the compiler uses the type of the pointer to determine which overloaded function to use. The type of the pointer must match one of the overloaded functions exactly:

```
void (*pf2)(int) = ff;      // error: no ff with a matching parameter list
double (*pf3)(int*) = ff;   // error: return type of ff and pf3 don't match
```

Function Pointer Parameters

Just as with arrays (§ 6.2.4, p. 214), we cannot define parameters of function type but can have a parameter that is a pointer to function. As with arrays, we can write a parameter that looks like a function type, but it will be treated as a pointer:

```
// third parameter is a function type and is automatically treated as a pointer to function
void useBigger(const string &s1, const string &s2,
               bool pf(const string &, const string &));
// equivalent declaration: explicitly define the parameter as a pointer to function
void useBigger(const string &s1, const string &s2,
               bool (*pf)(const string &, const string &));
```

When we pass a function as an argument, we can do so directly. It will be automatically converted to a pointer:

```
// automatically converts the function lengthCompare to a pointer to function
useBigger(s1, s2, lengthCompare);
```

As we've just seen in the declaration of useBigger, writing function pointer types quickly gets tedious. Type aliases (§ 2.5.1, p. 67), along with decltype (§ 2.5.3, p. 70), let us simplify code that uses function pointers:

```
// Func and Func2 have function type
typedef bool Func(const string&, const string&);
typedef decltype(lengthCompare) Func2; // equivalent type
// FuncP and FuncP2 have pointer to function type
typedef bool(*FuncP)(const string&, const string&);
typedef decltype(lengthCompare) *FuncP2;  // equivalent type
```

Here we've used typedef to define our types. Both Func and Func2 are function types, whereas FuncP and FuncP2 are pointer types. It is important to note that decltype returns the function type; the automatic conversion to pointer is not done. Because decltype returns a function type, if we want a pointer we must add the * ourselves. We can redeclare useBigger using any of these types:

```
// equivalent declarations of useBigger using type aliases
void useBigger(const string&, const string&, Func);
void useBigger(const string&, const string&, FuncP2);
```

Both declarations declare the same function. In the first case, the compiler will automatically convert the function type represented by Func to a pointer.

Returning a Pointer to Function

As with arrays (§ 6.3.3, p. 228), we can't return a function type but can return a pointer to a function type. Similarly, we must write the return type as a pointer type; the compiler will not automatically treat a function return type as the corresponding pointer type. Also as with array returns, by far the easiest way to declare a function that returns a pointer to function is by using a type alias:

```
using F = int(int*, int);      // F is a function type, not a pointer
using PF = int(*)(int*, int);  // PF is a pointer type
```

Here we used type alias declarations (§ 2.5.1, p. 68) to define F as a function type and PF as a pointer to function type. The thing to keep in mind is that, unlike what happens to parameters that have function type, the return type is not automatically converted to a pointer type. We must explicitly specify that the return type is a pointer type:

```
PF f1(int);     //  ok: PF is a pointer to function; f1 returns a pointer to function
F f1(int);      //  error: F is a function type; f1 can't return a function
F *f1(int);     //  ok: explicitly specify that the return type is a pointer to function
```

Of course, we can also declare f1 directly, which we'd do as

```
int (*f1(int))(int*, int);
```

Reading this declaration from the inside out, we see that f1 has a parameter list, so f1 is a function. f1 is preceded by a * so f1 returns a pointer. The type of that pointer itself has a parameter list, so the pointer points to a function. That function returns an int.

For completeness, it's worth noting that we can simplify declarations of functions that return pointers to function by using a trailing return (§ 6.3.3, p. 229):

```
auto f1(int) -> int (*)(int*, int);
```

Using `auto` or `decltype` for Function Pointer Types

If we know which function(s) we want to return, we can use decltype to simplify writing a function pointer return type. For example, assume we have two functions, both of which return a string::size_type and have two const string& parameters. We can write a third function that takes a string parameter and returns a pointer to one of these two functions as follows:

```
string::size_type sumLength(const string&, const string&);
string::size_type largerLength(const string&, const string&);
//  depending on the value of its string parameter,
//  getFcn returns a pointer to sumLength or to largerLength
decltype(sumLength) *getFcn(const string &);
```

The only tricky part in declaring getFcn is to remember that when we apply decltype to a function, it returns a function type, not a pointer to function type. We must add a * to indicate that we are returning a pointer, not a function.

EXERCISES SECTION 6.7

Exercise 6.54: Write a declaration for a function that takes two int parameters and returns an int, and declare a vector whose elements have this function pointer type.

Exercise 6.55: Write four functions that add, subtract, multiply, and divide two int values. Store pointers to these values in your vector from the previous exercise.

Exercise 6.56: Call each element in the vector and print their result.

CHAPTER SUMMARY

Functions are named units of computation and are essential to structuring even modest programs. Every function has a return type, a name, a (possibly empty) list of parameters, and a function body. The function body is a block that is executed when the function is called. When a function is called, the arguments passed to the function must be compatible with the types of the corresponding parameters.

In C++, functions may be overloaded: The same name may be used to define different functions as long as the number or types of the parameters in the functions differ. The compiler automatically figures out which function to call based on the arguments in a call. The process of selecting the right function from a set of overloaded functions is referred to as function matching.

DEFINED TERMS

ambiguous call Compile-time error that results during function matching when two or more functions provide an equally good match for a call.

arguments Values supplied in a function call that are used to initialize the function's parameters.

assert Preprocessor macro that takes a single expression, which it uses as a condition. When the preprocessor variable NDEBUG is not defined, assert evaluates the condition and, if the condition is false, writes a message and terminates the program.

automatic objects Objects that exist only during the execution of a function. They are created when control passes through their definition and are destroyed at the end of the block in which they are defined.

best match Function selected from a set of overloaded functions for a call. If a best match exists, the selected function is a better match than all the other viable candidates for at least one argument in the call and is no worse on the rest of the arguments.

call by reference See pass by reference.

call by value See pass by value.

candidate functions Set of functions that are considered when resolving a function call. The candidate functions are all the functions with the name used in the call for which a declaration is in scope at the time of the call.

constexpr Function that may return a constant expression. A constexpr function is implicitly inline.

default argument Value specified to be used when an argument is omitted in a call to the function.

executable file File, which the operating system executes, that contains code corresponding to our program.

function Callable unit of computation.

function body Block that defines the actions of a function.

function matching Compiler process by which a call to an overloaded function is resolved. Arguments used in the call are compared to the parameter list of each overloaded function.

function prototype Function declaration, consisting of the name, return type, and parameter types of a function. To call a function, its prototype must have been declared before the point of call.

hidden names Names declared inside a scope hide previously declared entities with the same names declared outside that scope.

initializer_list Library class that represents a comma-separated list of objects of a single type enclosed inside curly braces.

inline function Request to the compiler to expand a function at the point of call, if possible. Inline functions avoid the normal function-calling overhead.

link Compilation step in which multiple object files are put together to form an executable program.

local static objects Local objects whose value persists across calls to the function. Local `static` objects that are created and initialized before control reaches their use and are destroyed when the program ends.

local variables Variables defined inside a block.

no match Compile-time error that results during function matching when there is no function with parameters that match the arguments in a given call.

object code Format into which the compiler transforms our source code.

object file File holding object code generated by the compiler from a given source file. An executable file is generated from one or more object files after the files are linked together.

object lifetime Every object has an associated lifetime. Nonstatic objects that are defined inside a block exist from when their definition is encountered until the end of the block in which they are defined. Global objects are created during program startup. Local `static` objects are created before the first time execution passes through the object's definition. Global objects and local `static` objects are destroyed when the `main` function ends.

overload resolution See function matching.

overloaded function Function that has the same name as at least one other function. Overloaded functions must differ in the number or type of their parameters.

parameters Local variables declared inside the function parameter list. Parameters are initialized by the arguments provided in each function call.

pass by reference Description of how arguments are passed to parameters of reference type. Reference parameters work the same way as any other use of references; the parameter is bound to its corresponding argument.

pass by value How arguments are passed to parameters of a nonreference type. A nonreference parameter is a copy of the value of its corresponding argument.

preprocessor macro Preprocessor facility that behaves like an inline function. Aside from `assert`, modern C++ programs make very little use of preprocessor macros.

recursion loop Description of a recursive function that omits a stopping condition and which calls itself until exhausting the program stack.

recursive function Function that calls itself directly or indirectly.

return type Part of a function declaration that specifies the type of the value that the function returns.

separate compilation Ability to split a program into multiple separate source files.

trailing return type Return type specified after the parameter list.

viable functions Subset of the candidate functions that could match a given call. Viable functions have the same number of parameters as arguments to the call, and each argument type can be converted to the corresponding parameter type.

() operator Call operator. Executes a function. The name of a function or a function pointer precedes the parentheses, which enclose a (possibly empty) comma-separated list of arguments.

CHAPTER 7

CLASSES

In C++ we use classes to define our own data types. By defining types that mirror concepts in the problems we are trying to solve, we can make our programs easier to write, debug, and modify.

This chapter continues the coverage of classes begun in Chapter 2. Here we will focus on the importance of data abstraction, which lets us separate the implementation of an object from the operations that that object can perform. In Chapter 13 we'll learn how to control what happens when objects are copied, moved, assigned, or destroyed. In Chapter 14 we'll learn how to define our own operators.

The fundamental ideas behind **classes** are **data abstraction** and **encapsulation**. Data abstraction is a programming (and design) technique that relies on the separation of **interface** and **implementation**. The interface of a class consists of the operations that users of the class can execute. The implementation includes the class' data members, the bodies of the functions that constitute the interface, and any functions needed to define the class that are not intended for general use.

Encapsulation enforces the separation of a class' interface and implementation. A class that is encapsulated hides its implementation—users of the class can use the interface but have no access to the implementation.

A class that uses data abstraction and encapsulation defines an **abstract data type**. In an abstract data type, the class designer worries about how the class is implemented. Programmers who use the class need not know how the type works. They can instead think *abstractly* about what the type does.

7.1　Defining Abstract Data Types

The Sales_item class that we used in Chapter 1 is an abstract data type. We use a Sales_item object by using its interface (i.e., the operations described in § 1.5.1 (p. 20)). We have no access to the data members stored in a Sales_item object. Indeed, we don't even know what data members that class has.

Our Sales_data class (§ 2.6.1, p. 72) is not an abstract data type. It lets users of the class access its data members and forces users to write their own operations. To make Sales_data an abstract type, we need to define operations for users of Sales_data to use. Once Sales_data defines its own operations, we can encapsulate (that is, hide) its data members.

7.1.1　Designing the Sales_data Class

Ultimately, we want Sales_data to support the same set of operations as the Sales_item class. The Sales_item class had one **member function** (§ 1.5.2, p. 23), named isbn, and supported the +, =, +=, <<, and >> operators.

We'll learn how to define our own operators in Chapter 14. For now, we'll define ordinary (named) functions for these operations. For reasons that we will explain in § 14.1 (p. 555), the functions that do addition and IO will not be members of Sales_data. Instead, we'll define those functions as ordinary functions. The function that handles compound assignment will be a member, and for reasons we'll explain in § 7.1.5 (p. 267), our class doesn't need to define assignment.

Thus, the interface to Sales_data consists of the following operations:

- An isbn member function to return the object's ISBN

- A combine member function to add one Sales_data object into another

- A function named add to add two Sales_data objects

- A read function to read data from an istream into a Sales_data object

- A print function to print the value of a Sales_data object on an ostream

KEY CONCEPT: DIFFERENT KINDS OF PROGRAMMING ROLES

Programmers tend to think about the people who will run their applications as *users*. Similarly a class designer designs and implements a class for *users* of that class. In this case, the user is a programmer, not the ultimate user of the application.

When we refer to a *user*, the context makes it clear which kind of user is meant. If we speak of *user code* or the *user* of the `Sales_data` class, we mean a programmer who is using a class. If we speak of the *user* of the bookstore application, we mean the manager of the store who is running the application.

 C++ programmers tend to speak of *users* interchangeably as users of the application or users of a class.

In simple applications, the user of a class and the designer of the class might be one and the same person. Even in such cases, it is useful to keep the roles distinct. When we design the interface of a class, we should think about how easy it will be to use the class. When we use the class, we shouldn't think about how the class works.

Authors of successful applications do a good job of understanding and implementing the needs of the application's users. Similarly, good class designers pay close attention to the needs of the programmers who will use the class. A well-designed class has an interface that is intuitive and easy to use and has an implementation that is efficient enough for its intended use.

Using the Revised `Sales_data` Class

Before we think about how to implement our class, let's look at how we can use our interface functions. As one example, we can use these functions to write a version of the bookstore program from § 1.6 (p. 24) that works with `Sales_data` objects rather than `Sales_items`:

```
Sales_data total;              // variable to hold the running sum
if (read(cin, total))  {  //  read the first transaction
    Sales_data trans;          //  variable to hold data for the next transaction
    while(read(cin, trans)) {          //  read the remaining transactions
        if (total.isbn() == trans.isbn())    //  check the isbns
            total.combine(trans);  //  update the running total
        else {
            print(cout, total) << endl;  //  print the results
            total = trans;                 //  process the next book
        }
    }
    print(cout, total) << endl;                 //  print the last transaction
} else {                                        //  there was no input
    cerr << "No data?!" << endl;                //  notify the user
}
```

We start by defining a `Sales_data` object to hold the running total. Inside the `if` condition, we call `read` to read the first transaction into `total`. This condition works like other loops we've written that used the `>>` operator. Like the `>>` operator, our `read` function will return its stream parameter, which the condition checks (§ 4.11.2, p. 162). If the read fails, we fall through to the else to print an error message.

If there are data to read, we define trans, which we'll use to hold each transaction. The condition in the while also checks the stream returned by read. So long as the input operations in read succeed, the condition succeeds and we have another transaction to process.

Inside the while, we call the isbn members of total and trans to fetch their respective ISBNs. If total and trans refer to the same book, we call combine to add the components of trans into the running total in total. If trans represents a new book, we call print to print the total for the previous book. Because print returns a reference to its stream parameter, we can use the result of print as the left-hand operand of the <<. We do so to print a newline following the output generated by print. We next assign trans to total, thus setting up to process the records for the next book in the file.

After we have exhausted the input, we have to remember to print the data for the last transaction, which we do in the call to print following the while loop.

EXERCISES SECTION 7.1.1

Exercise 7.1: Write a version of the transaction-processing program from § 1.6 (p. 24) using the Sales_data class you defined for the exercises in § 2.6.1 (p. 72).

 ## 7.1.2 Defining the Revised Sales_data Class

Our revised class will have the same data members as the version we defined in § 2.6.1 (p. 72): bookNo, a string representing the ISBN; units_sold, an unsigned that says how many copies of the book were sold; and revenue, a double representing the total revenue for those sales.

As we've seen, our class will also have two member functions, combine and isbn. In addition, we'll give Sales_data another member function to return the average price at which the books were sold. This function, which we'll name avg_price, isn't intended for general use. It will be part of the implementation, not part of the interface.

We define (§ 6.1, p. 202) and declare (§ 6.1.2, p. 206) member functions similarly to ordinary functions. Member functions *must* be declared inside the class. Member functions *may* be defined inside the class itself or outside the class body. Non-member functions that are part of the interface, such as add, read, and print, are declared and defined outside the class.

With this knowledge, we're ready to write our revised version of Sales_data:

```
struct Sales_data {
    // new members: operations on Sales_data objects
    std::string isbn() const { return bookNo; }
    Sales_data& combine(const Sales_data&);
    double avg_price() const;
```

```
    //  data members are unchanged from § 2.6.1 (p. 72)
    std::string bookNo;
    unsigned units_sold = 0;
    double revenue = 0.0;
};
//  nonmember Sales_data interface functions
Sales_data add(const Sales_data&, const Sales_data&);
std::ostream &print(std::ostream&, const Sales_data&);
std::istream &read(std::istream&, Sales_data&);
```

 Functions defined in the class are implicitly `inline` (§ 6.5.2, p. 238).

Defining Member Functions

Although every member must be declared inside its class, we can define a member function's body either inside or outside of the class body. In `Sales_data`, `isbn` is defined inside the class; `combine` and `avg_price` will be defined elsewhere.

We'll start by explaining the `isbn` function, which returns a `string` and has an empty parameter list:

```
    std::string isbn() const { return bookNo; }
```

As with any function, the body of a member function is a block. In this case, the block contains a single `return` statement that returns the `bookNo` data member of a `Sales_data` object. The interesting thing about this function is how it gets the object from which to fetch the `bookNo` member.

Introducing `this`

Let's look again at a call to the `isbn` member function:

```
    total.isbn()
```

Here we use the dot operator (§ 4.6, p. 150) to fetch the `isbn` member of the object named `total`, which we then call.

With one exception that we'll cover in § 7.6 (p. 300), when we call a member function we do so on behalf of an object. When `isbn` refers to members of `Sales_data` (e.g., `bookNo`), it is referring implicitly to the members of the object on which the function was called. In this call, when `isbn` returns `bookNo`, it is implicitly returning `total.bookNo`.

Member functions access the object on which they were called through an extra, implicit parameter named **this**. When we call a member function, `this` is initialized with the address of the object on which the function was invoked. For example, when we call

```
    total.isbn()
```

the compiler passes the address of `total` to the implicit `this` parameter in `isbn`. It is as if the compiler rewrites this call as

```
// pseudo-code illustration of how a call to a member function is translated
Sales_data::isbn(&total)
```

which calls the isbn member of Sales_data passing the address of total.

Inside a member function, we can refer directly to the members of the object on which the function was called. We do not have to use a member access operator to use the members of the object to which this points. Any direct use of a member of the class is assumed to be an implicit reference through this. That is, when isbn uses bookNo, it is implicitly using the member to which this points. It is as if we had written this->bookNo.

The this parameter is defined for us implicitly. Indeed, it is illegal for us to define a parameter or variable named this. Inside the body of a member function, we can use this. It would be legal, although unnecessary, to define isbn as

```
std::string isbn() const { return this->bookNo; }
```

Because this is intended to always refer to "this" object, this is a const pointer (§ 2.4.2, p. 62). We cannot change the address that this holds.

Introducing const Member Functions

The other important part about the isbn function is the keyword const that follows the parameter list. The purpose of that const is to modify the type of the implicit this pointer.

By default, the type of this is a const pointer to the nonconst version of the class type. For example, by default, the type of this in a Sales_data member function is Sales_data *const. Although this is implicit, it follows the normal initialization rules, which means that (by default) we cannot bind this to a const object (§ 2.4.2, p. 62). This fact, in turn, means that we cannot call an ordinary member function on a const object.

If isbn were an ordinary function and if this were an ordinary pointer parameter, we would declare this as const Sales_data *const. After all, the body of isbn doesn't change the object to which this points, so our function would be more flexible if this were a pointer to const (§ 6.2.3, p. 213).

However, this is implicit and does not appear in the parameter list. There is no place to indicate that this should be a pointer to const. The language resolves this problem by letting us put const after the parameter list of a member function. A const following the parameter list indicates that this is a pointer to const. Member functions that use const in this way are **const member functions**.

We can think of the body of isbn as if it were written as

```
// pseudo-code illustration of how the implicit this pointer is used
// this code is illegal: we may not explicitly define the this pointer ourselves
// note that this is a pointer to const because isbn is a const member
std::string Sales_data::isbn(const Sales_data *const this)
{ return this->isbn; }
```

The fact that this is a pointer to const means that const member functions cannot change the object on which they are called. Thus, isbn may read but not write to the data members of the objects on which it is called.

Objects that are const, and references or pointers to const objects, may call only const member functions.

Class Scope and Member Functions

Recall that a class is itself a scope (§ 2.6.1, p. 72). The definitions of the member functions of a class are nested inside the scope of the class itself. Hence, isbn's use of the name bookNo is resolved as the data member defined inside Sales_data.

It is worth noting that isbn can use bookNo even though bookNo is defined *after* isbn. As we'll see in § 7.4.1 (p. 283), the compiler processes classes in two steps—the member declarations are compiled first, after which the member function bodies, if any, are processed. Thus, member function bodies may use other members of their class regardless of where in the class those members appear.

Defining a Member Function outside the Class

As with any other function, when we define a member function outside the class body, the member's definition must match its declaration. That is, the return type, parameter list, and name must match the declaration in the class body. If the member was declared as a const member function, then the definition must also specify const after the parameter list. The name of a member defined outside the class must include the name of the class of which it is a member:

```
double Sales_data::avg_price() const {
    if (units_sold)
        return revenue/units_sold;
    else
        return 0;
}
```

The function name, Sales_data::avg_price, uses the scope operator (§ 1.2, p. 8) to say that we are defining the function named avg_price that is declared in the scope of the Sales_data class. Once the compiler sees the function name, the rest of the code is interpreted as being inside the scope of the class. Thus, when avg_price refers to revenue and units_sold, it is implicitly referring to the members of Sales_data.

Defining a Function to Return "This" Object

The combine function is intended to act like the compound assignment operator, +=. The object on which this function is called represents the left-hand operand of the assignment. The right-hand operand is passed as an explicit argument:

```
Sales_data& Sales_data::combine(const Sales_data &rhs)
{
    units_sold += rhs.units_sold; // add the members of rhs into
    revenue += rhs.revenue;       // the members of "this" object
    return *this; // return the object on which the function was called
}
```

When our transaction-processing program calls

```
total.combine(trans);  // update the running total
```

the address of `total` is bound to the implicit `this` parameter and `rhs` is bound to `trans`. Thus, when `combine` executes

```
units_sold += rhs.units_sold; // add the members of rhs into
```

the effect is to add `total.units_sold` and `trans.units_sold`, storing the result back into `total.units_sold`.

The interesting part about this function is its return type and the `return` statement. Ordinarily, when we define a function that operates like a built-in operator, our function should mimic the behavior of that operator. The built-in assignment operators return their left-hand operand as an lvalue (§ 4.4, p. 144). To return an lvalue, our `combine` function must return a reference (§ 6.3.2, p. 226). Because the left-hand operand is a `Sales_data` object, the return type is `Sales_data&`.

As we've seen, we do not need to use the implicit `this` pointer to access the members of the object on which a member function is executing. However, we do need to use `this` to access the object as a whole:

```
return *this; // return the object on which the function was called
```

Here the `return` statement dereferences `this` to obtain the object on which the function is executing. That is, for the call above, we return a reference to `total`.

EXERCISES SECTION 7.1.2

Exercise 7.2: Add the `combine` and `isbn` members to the `Sales_data` class you wrote for the exercises in § 2.6.2 (p. 76).

Exercise 7.3: Revise your transaction-processing program from § 7.1.1 (p. 256) to use these members.

Exercise 7.4: Write a class named `Person` that represents the name and address of a person. Use a `string` to hold each of these elements. Subsequent exercises will incrementally add features to this class.

Exercise 7.5: Provide operations in your `Person` class to return the name and address. Should these functions be `const`? Explain your choice.

 ## 7.1.3 Defining Nonmember Class-Related Functions

Class authors often define auxiliary functions, such as our `add`, `read`, and `print` functions. Although such functions define operations that are conceptually part of the interface of the class, they are not part of the class itself.

We define nonmember functions as we would any other function. As with any other function, we normally separate the declaration of the function from its definition (§ 6.1.2, p. 206). Functions that are conceptually part of a class, but not defined inside the class, are typically declared (but not defined) in the same header as the class itself. That way users need to include only one file to use any part of the interface.

 Ordinarily, nonmember functions that are part of the interface of a class should be declared in the same header as the class itself.

Defining the `read` and `print` Functions

The `read` and `print` functions do the same job as the code in § 2.6.2 (p. 75) and not surprisingly, the bodies of our functions look a lot like the code presented there:

```
//   input transactions contain ISBN, number of copies sold, and sales price
istream &read(istream &is, Sales_data &item)
{
    double price = 0;
    is >> item.bookNo >> item.units_sold >> price;
    item.revenue = price * item.units_sold;
    return is;
}
ostream &print(ostream &os, const Sales_data &item)
{
    os << item.isbn() << " " << item.units_sold << " "
       << item.revenue << " " << item.avg_price();
    return os;
}
```

The `read` function reads data from the given stream into the given object. The `print` function prints the contents of the given object on the given stream.

However, there are two points worth noting about these functions. First, both `read` and `write` take a reference to their respective IO class types. The IO classes are types that cannot be copied, so we may only pass them by reference (§ 6.2.2, p. 210). Moreover, reading or writing to a stream changes that stream, so both functions take ordinary references, not references to `const`.

The second thing to note is that `print` does not print a newline. Ordinarily, functions that do output should do minimal formatting. That way user code can decide whether the newline is needed.

Defining the `add` Function

The `add` function takes two `Sales_data` objects and returns a new `Sales_data` representing their sum:

```
Sales_data add(const Sales_data &lhs, const Sales_data &rhs)
{
    Sales_data sum = lhs;    //  copy data members from lhs into sum
    sum.combine(rhs);        //  add data members from rhs into sum
    return sum;
}
```

In the body of the function we define a new `Sales_data` object named `sum` to hold the sum of our two transactions. We initialize `sum` as a copy of `lhs`. By default, copying a class object copies that object's members. After the copy, the `bookNo`, `units_sold`, and `revenue` members of `sum` will have the same values as those in `lhs`. Next we call `combine` to add the `units_sold` and `revenue` members of `rhs` into `sum`. When we're done, we return a copy of `sum`.

EXERCISES SECTION 7.1.3

Exercise 7.6: Define your own versions of the add, read, and `print` functions.

Exercise 7.7: Rewrite the transaction-processing program you wrote for the exercises in § 7.1.2 (p. 260) to use these new functions.

Exercise 7.8: Why does read define its `Sales_data` parameter as a plain reference and `print` define its parameter as a reference to `const`?

Exercise 7.9: Add operations to read and print `Person` objects to the code you wrote for the exercises in § 7.1.2 (p. 260).

Exercise 7.10: What does the condition in the following `if` statement do?

```
if (read(read(cin, data1), data2))
```

 ## 7.1.4 Constructors

Each class defines how objects of its type can be initialized. Classes control object initialization by defining one or more special member functions known as **constructors**. The job of a constructor is to initialize the data members of a class object. A constructor is run whenever an object of a class type is created.

In this section, we'll introduce the basics of how to define a constructor. Constructors are a surprisingly complex topic. Indeed, we'll have more to say about constructors in § 7.5 (p. 288), § 15.7 (p. 622), and § 18.1.3 (p. 777), and in Chapter 13.

Constructors have the same name as the class. Unlike other functions, constructors have no return type. Like other functions, constructors have a (possibly empty) parameter list and a (possibly empty) function body. A class can have multiple constructors. Like any other overloaded function (§ 6.4, p. 230), the constructors must differ from each other in the number or types of their parameters.

Unlike other member functions, constructors may not be declared as `const` (§ 7.1.2, p. 258). When we create a `const` object of a class type, the object does not assume its "constness" until after the constructor completes the object's initialization. Thus, constructors can write to `const` objects during their construction.

The Synthesized Default Constructor

Our `Sales_data` class does not define any constructors, yet the programs we've written that use `Sales_data` objects compile and run correctly. As an example, the program on page 255 defined two objects:

```
Sales_data total;      //  variable to hold the running sum
Sales_data trans;      //  variable to hold data for the next transaction
```

The question naturally arises: How are `total` and `trans` initialized?

We did not supply an initializer for these objects, so we know that they are default initialized (§ 2.2.1, p. 43). Classes control default initialization by defining a special constructor, known as the **default constructor**. The default constructor is one that takes no arguments.

As we'll, see the default constructor is special in various ways, one of which is that if our class does not *explicitly* define any constructors, the compiler will *implicitly* define the default constructor for us

The compiler-generated constructor is known as the **synthesized default constructor**. For most classes, this synthesized constructor initializes each data member of the class as follows:

- If there is an in-class initializer (§ 2.6.1, p. 73), use it to initialize the member.

- Otherwise, default-initialize (§ 2.2.1, p. 43) the member.

Because `Sales_data` provides initializers for `units_sold` and `revenue`, the synthesized default constructor uses those values to initialize those members. It default initializes `bookNo` to the empty string.

Some Classes Cannot Rely on the Synthesized Default Constructor

Only fairly simple classes—such as the current definition of `Sales_data`—can rely on the synthesized default constructor. The most common reason that a class must define its own default constructor is that the compiler generates the default for us *only if we do not define any other constructors for the class*. If we define any constructors, the class will not have a default constructor unless we define that constructor ourselves. The basis for this rule is that if a class requires control to initialize an object in one case, then the class is likely to require control in all cases.

 The compiler generates a default constructor automatically only if a class declares *no* constructors.

A second reason to define the default constructor is that for some classes, the synthesized default constructor does the wrong thing. Remember that objects of built-in or compound type (such as arrays and pointers) that are defined inside a block have undefined value when they are default initialized (§ 2.2.1, p. 43). The same rule applies to members of built-in type that are default initialized. Therefore, classes that have members of built-in or compound type should ordinarily either initialize those members inside the class or define their own version of the default constructor. Otherwise, users could create objects with members that have undefined value.

 WARNING Classes that have members of built-in or compound type usually should rely on the synthesized default constructor *only* if all such members have in-class initializers.

A third reason that some classes must define their own default constructor is that sometimes the compiler is unable to synthesize one. For example, if a class has a member that has a class type, and that class doesn't have a default constructor, then the compiler can't initialize that member. For such classes, we must define our own version of the default constructor. Otherwise, the class will not have a usable default constructor. We'll see in § 13.1.6 (p. 508) additional circumstances that prevent the compiler from generating an appropriate default constructor.

Defining the `Sales_data` Constructors

For our `Sales_data` class we'll define four constructors with the following parameters:

- An `istream&` from which to read a transaction.

- A `const string&` representing an ISBN, an `unsigned` representing the count of how many books were sold, and a `double` representing the price at which the books sold.

- A `const string&` representing an ISBN. This constructor will use default values for the other members.

- An empty parameter list (i.e., the default constructor) which as we've just seen we must define because we have defined other constructors.

Adding these members to our class, we now have

```
struct Sales_data {
    // constructors added
    Sales_data() = default;
    Sales_data(const std::string &s): bookNo(s) { }
    Sales_data(const std::string &s, unsigned n, double p):
                bookNo(s), units_sold(n), revenue(p*n) { }
    Sales_data(std::istream &);
    // other members as before
    std::string isbn() const { return bookNo; }
    Sales_data& combine(const Sales_data&);
    double avg_price() const;
    std::string bookNo;
    unsigned units_sold = 0;
    double revenue = 0.0;
};
```

What = `default` Means

We'll start by explaining the default constructor:

```
Sales_data() = default;
```

First, note that this constructor defines the default constructor because it takes no arguments. We are defining this constructor *only* because we want to provide other constructors as well as the default constructor. We want this constructor to do exactly the same work as the synthesized version we had been using.

Under the new standard, if we want the default behavior, we can ask the compiler to generate the constructor for us by writing `= default` after the parameter list. The `= default` can appear with the declaration inside the class body or on the definition outside the class body. Like any other function, if the `= default` appears inside the class body, the default constructor will be inlined; if it appears on the definition outside the class, the member will not be inlined by default.

WARNING The default constructor works for `Sales_data` only because we provide initializers for the data members with built-in type. If your compiler does not support in-class initializers, your default constructor should use the constructor initializer list (described immediately following) to initialize every member of the class.

Constructor Initializer List

Next we'll look at the other two constructors that were defined inside the class:

```
Sales_data(const std::string &s): bookNo(s) { }
Sales_data(const std::string &s, unsigned n, double p):
        bookNo(s), units_sold(n), revenue(p*n) { }
```

The new parts in these definitions are the colon and the code between it and the curly braces that define the (empty) function bodies. This new part is a **constructor initializer list**, which specifies initial values for one or more data members of the object being created. The constructor initializer is a list of member names, each of which is followed by that member's initial value in parentheses (or inside curly braces). Multiple member initializations are separated by commas.

The constructor that has three parameters uses its first two parameters to initialize the `bookNo` and `units_sold` members. The initializer for `revenue` is calculated by multiplying the number of books sold by the price per book.

The constructor that has a single `string` parameter uses that `string` to initialize `bookNo` but does not explicitly initialize the `units_sold` and `revenue` members. When a member is omitted from the constructor initializer list, it is implicitly initialized using the same process as is used by the synthesized default constructor. In this case, those members are initialized by the in-class initializers. Thus, the constructor that takes a `string` is equivalent to

```
//  has the same behavior as the original constructor defined above
Sales_data(const std::string &s):
        bookNo(s), units_sold(0), revenue(0){ }
```

It is usually best for a constructor to use an in-class initializer if one exists and gives the member the correct value. On the other hand, if your compiler does not yet support in-class initializers, then every constructor should explicitly initialize every member of built-in type.

Best Practices Constructors should not override in-class initializers except to use a different initial value. If you can't use in-class initializers, each constructor should explicitly initialize every member of built-in type.

It is worth noting that both constructors have empty function bodies. The only work these constructors need to do is give the data members their values. If there is no further work, then the function body is empty.

Defining a Constructor outside the Class Body

Unlike our other constructors, the constructor that takes an `istream` does have work to do. Inside its function body, this constructor calls `read` to give the data members new values:

```
Sales_data::Sales_data(std::istream &is)
{
    read(is, *this); //  read will read a transaction from is into this object
}
```

Constructors have no return type, so this definition starts with the name of the function we are defining. As with any other member function, when we define a constructor outside of the class body, we must specify the class of which the constructor is a member. Thus, `Sales_data::Sales_data` says that we're defining the `Sales_data` member named `Sales_data`. This member is a constructor because it has the same name as its class.

In this constructor there is no constructor initializer list, although technically speaking, it would be more correct to say that the constructor initializer list is empty. Even though the constructor initializer list is empty, the members of this object are still initialized before the constructor body is executed.

Members that do not appear in the constructor initializer list are initialized by the corresponding in-class initializer (if there is one) or are default initialized. For `Sales_data` that means that when the function body starts executing, `bookNo` will be the empty `string`, and `units_sold` and `revenue` will both be 0.

To understand the call to `read`, remember that `read`'s second parameter is a reference to a `Sales_data` object. In § 7.1.2 (p. 259), we noted that we use `this` to access the object as a whole, rather than a member of the object. In this case, we use `*this` to pass "this" object as an argument to the `read` function.

EXERCISES SECTION 7.1.4

Exercise 7.11: Add constructors to your `Sales_data` class and write a program to use each of the constructors.

Exercise 7.12: Move the definition of the `Sales_data` constructor that takes an `istream` into the body of the `Sales_data` class.

Exercise 7.13: Rewrite the program from page 255 to use the `istream` constructor.

Exercise 7.14: Write a version of the default constructor that explicitly initializes the members to the values we have provided as in-class initializers.

Exercise 7.15: Add appropriate constructors to your `Person` class.

7.1.5   Copy, Assignment, and Destruction

In addition to defining how objects of the class type are initialized, classes also control what happens when we copy, assign, or destroy objects of the class type. Objects are copied in several contexts, such as when we initialize a variable or when we pass or return an object by value (§ 6.2.1, p. 209, and § 6.3.2, p. 224). Objects are assigned when we use the assignment operator (§ 4.4, p. 144). Objects are destroyed when they cease to exist, such as when a local object is destroyed on exit from the block in which it was created (§ 6.1.1, p. 204). Objects stored in a vector (or an array) are destroyed when that vector (or array) is destroyed.

If we do not define these operations, the compiler will synthesize them for us. Ordinarily, the versions that the compiler generates for us execute by copying, assigning, or destroying each member of the object. For example, in our bookstore program in § 7.1.1 (p. 255), when the compiler executes this assignment

```
total = trans;                    // process the next book
```

it executes as if we had written

```
// default assignment for Sales_data is equivalent to:
total.bookNo = trans.bookNo;
total.units_sold = trans.units_sold;
total.revenue = trans.revenue;
```

We'll show how we can define our own versions of these operations in Chapter 13.

Some Classes Cannot Rely on the Synthesized Versions

Although the compiler will synthesize the copy, assignment, and destruction operations for us, it is important to understand that for some classes the default versions do not behave appropriately. In particular, the synthesized versions are unlikely to work correctly for classes that allocate resources that reside outside the class objects themselves. As one example, in Chapter 12 we'll see how C++ programs allocate and manage dynamic memory. As we'll see in § 13.1.4 (p. 504), classes that manage dynamic memory, generally cannot rely on the synthesized versions of these operations.

However, it is worth noting that many classes that need dynamic memory can (and generally should) use a vector or a string to manage the necessary storage. Classes that use vectors and strings avoid the complexities involved in allocating and deallocating memory.

Moreover, the synthesized versions for copy, assignment, and destruction work correctly for classes that have vector or string members. When we copy or assign an object that has a vector member, the vector class takes care of copying or assigning the elements in that member. When the object is destroyed, the vector member is destroyed, which in turn destroys the elements in the vector. Similarly for strings.

> **WARNING** Until you know how to define the operations covered in Chapter 13, the resources your classes allocate should be stored directly as data members of the class.

7.2 Access Control and Encapsulation

At this point, we have defined an interface for our class; but nothing forces users to use that interface. Our class is not yet encapsulated—users can reach inside a Sales_data object and meddle with its implementation. In C++ we use **access specifiers** to enforce encapsulation:

- Members defined after a **public** specifier are accessible to all parts of the program. The public members define the interface to the class.

- Members defined after a **private** specifier are accessible to the member functions of the class but are not accessible to code that uses the class. The private sections encapsulate (i.e., hide) the implementation.

Redefining Sales_data once again, we now have

```
class Sales_data {
public:                     // access specifier added
    Sales_data() = default;
    Sales_data(const std::string &s, unsigned n, double p):
              bookNo(s), units_sold(n), revenue(p*n) { }
    Sales_data(const std::string &s): bookNo(s) { }
    Sales_data(std::istream&);
    std::string isbn() const { return bookNo; }
    Sales_data &combine(const Sales_data&);
private:                    // access specifier added
    double avg_price() const
        { return units_sold ? revenue/units_sold : 0; }
    std::string bookNo;
    unsigned units_sold = 0;
    double revenue = 0.0;
};
```

The constructors and member functions that are part of the interface (e.g., isbn and combine) follow the public specifier; the data members and the functions that are part of the implementation follow the private specifier.

A class may contain zero or more access specifiers, and there are no restrictions on how often an access specifier may appear. Each access specifier specifies the access level of the succeeding members. The specified access level remains in effect until the next access specifier or the end of the class body.

Using the class or struct Keyword

We also made another, more subtle, change: We used the **class keyword** rather than **struct** to open the class definition. This change is strictly stylistic; we can define a class type using either keyword. The only difference between struct and class is the default access level.

A class may define members before the first access specifier. Access to such members depends on how the class is defined. If we use the struct keyword, the members defined before the first access specifier are public; if we use class, then the members are private.

As a matter of programming style, when we define a class intending for all of its members to be public, we use struct. If we intend to have private members, then we use class.

 The *only* difference between using class and using struct to define a class is the default access level.

EXERCISES SECTION 7.2

Exercise 7.16: What, if any, are the constraints on where and how often an access specifier may appear inside a class definition? What kinds of members should be defined after a public specifier? What kinds should be private?

Exercise 7.17: What, if any, are the differences between using class or struct?

Exercise 7.18: What is encapsulation? Why is it useful?

Exercise 7.19: Indicate which members of your Person class you would declare as public and which you would declare as private. Explain your choice.

7.2.1 Friends

Now that the data members of Sales_data are private, our read, print, and add functions will no longer compile. The problem is that although these functions are part of the Sales_data interface, they are not members of the class.

A class can allow another class or function to access its nonpublic members by making that class or function a **friend**. A class makes a function its friend by including a declaration for that function preceded by the keyword friend:

```
class Sales_data {
// friend declarations for nonmember Sales_data operations added
friend Sales_data add(const Sales_data&, const Sales_data&);
friend std::istream &read(std::istream&, Sales_data&);
friend std::ostream &print(std::ostream&, const Sales_data&);
// other members and access specifiers as before
public:
    Sales_data() = default;
    Sales_data(const std::string &s, unsigned n, double p):
                bookNo(s), units_sold(n), revenue(p*n) { }
    Sales_data(const std::string &s): bookNo(s) { }
    Sales_data(std::istream&);
    std::string isbn() const { return bookNo; }
    Sales_data &combine(const Sales_data&);
private:
    std::string bookNo;
    unsigned units_sold = 0;
    double revenue = 0.0;
};
```

```
//  declarations for nonmember parts of the Sales_data interface
Sales_data add(const Sales_data&, const Sales_data&);
std::istream &read(std::istream&, Sales_data&);
std::ostream &print(std::ostream&, const Sales_data&);
```

Friend declarations may appear only inside a class definition; they may appear anywhere in the class. Friends are not members of the class and are not affected by the access control of the section in which they are declared. We'll have more to say about friendship in § 7.3.4 (p. 279).

> Ordinarily it is a good idea to group friend declarations together at the beginning or end of the class definition.

KEY CONCEPT: BENEFITS OF ENCAPSULATION

Encapsulation provides two important advantages:

- User code cannot inadvertently corrupt the state of an encapsulated object.
- The implementation of an encapsulated class can change over time without requiring changes in user-level code.

By defining data members as `private`, the class author is free to make changes in the data. If the implementation changes, only the class code needs to be examined to see what effect the change may have. User code needs to change only when the interface changes. If the data are `public`, then any code that used the old data members might be broken. It would be necessary to locate and rewrite any code that relied on the old representation before the program could be used again.

Another advantage of making data members `private` is that the data are protected from mistakes that users might introduce. If there is a bug that corrupts an object's state, the places to look for the bug are localized: Only code that is part of the implementation could be responsible for the error. The search for the mistake is limited, greatly easing the problems of maintenance and program correctness.

> **Note** Although user code need not change when a class definition changes, the source files that use a class must be recompiled any time the class changes.

Declarations for Friends

A friend declaration only specifies access. It is not a general declaration of the function. If we want users of the class to be able to call a friend function, then we must also declare the function separately from the friend declaration.

To make a friend visible to users of the class, we usually declare each friend (outside the class) in the same header as the class itself. Thus, our `Sales_data` header should provide separate declarations (aside from the friend declarations inside the class body) for `read`, `print`, and `add`.

> **Note** Many compilers do not enforce the rule that friend functions must be declared *outside* the class before they can be used.

Some compilers allow calls to a `friend` function when there is no ordinary declaration for that function. Even if your compiler allows such calls, it is a good idea to provide separate declarations for `friend`s. That way you won't have to change your code if you use a compiler that enforces this rule.

EXERCISES SECTION 7.2.1

Exercise 7.20: When are friends useful? Discuss the pros and cons of using friends.

Exercise 7.21: Update your `Sales_data` class to hide its implementation. The programs you've written to use `Sales_data` operations should still continue to work. Recompile those programs with your new class definition to verify that they still work.

Exercise 7.22: Update your `Person` class to hide its implementation.

7.3 Additional Class Features

The `Sales_data` class is pretty simple, yet it allowed us to explore quite a bit of the language support for classes. In this section, we'll cover some additional class-related features that `Sales_data` doesn't need to use. These features include type members, in-class initializers for members of class type, `mutable` data members, `inline` member functions, returning `*this` from a member function, more about how we define and use class types, and class friendship.

7.3.1 Class Members Revisited

To explore several of these additional features, we'll define a pair of cooperating classes named `Screen` and `Window_mgr`.

Defining a Type Member

A `Screen` represents a window on a display. Each `Screen` has a `string` member that holds the `Screen`'s contents, and three `string::size_type` members that represent the position of the cursor, and the height and width of the screen.

In addition to defining data and function members, a class can define its own local names for types. Type names defined by a class are subject to the same access controls as any other member and may be either `public` or `private`:

```cpp
class Screen {
public:
    typedef std::string::size_type pos;
private:
    pos cursor = 0;
    pos height = 0, width = 0;
    std::string contents;
};
```

We defined pos in the public part of Screen because we want users to use that name. Users of Screen shouldn't know that Screen uses a string to hold its data. By defining pos as a public member, we can hide this detail of how Screen is implemented.

There are two points to note about the declaration of pos. First, although we used a typedef (§ 2.5.1, p. 67), we can equivalently use a type alias (§ 2.5.1, p. 68):

```
class Screen {
public:
    //  alternative way to declare a type member using a type alias
    using pos = std::string::size_type;
    //  other members as before
};
```

The second point is that, for reasons we'll explain in § 7.4.1 (p. 284), unlike ordinary members, members that define types must appear before they are used. As a result, type members usually appear at the beginning of the class.

Member Functions of class Screen

To make our class more useful, we'll add a constructor that will let users define the size and contents of the screen, along with members to move the cursor and to get the character at a given location:

```
class Screen {
public:
    typedef std::string::size_type pos;
    Screen() = default;   //  needed because Screen has another constructor
    //  cursor initialized to 0 by its in-class initializer
    Screen(pos ht, pos wd, char c): height(ht), width(wd),
                                    contents(ht * wd, c) { }
    char get() const               //  get the character at the cursor
        { return contents[cursor]; }        //  implicitly inline
    inline char get(pos ht, pos wd) const; //  explicitly inline
    Screen &move(pos r, pos c);       //  can be made inline later
private:
    pos cursor = 0;
    pos height = 0, width = 0;
    std::string contents;
};
```

Because we have provided a constructor, the compiler will not automatically generate a default constructor for us. If our class is to have a default constructor, we must say so explicitly. In this case, we use = default to ask the compiler to synthesize the default constructor's definition for us (§ 7.1.4, p. 264).

It's also worth noting that our second constructor (that takes three arguments) implicitly uses the in-class initializer for the cursor member (§ 7.1.4, p. 266). If our class did not have an in-class initializer for cursor, we would have explicitly initialized cursor along with the other members.

Making Members `inline`

Classes often have small functions that can benefit from being inlined. As we've seen, member functions defined inside the class are automatically `inline` (§ 6.5.2, p. 238). Thus, `Screen`'s constructors and the version of `get` that returns the character denoted by the cursor are `inline` by default.

We can explicitly declare a member function as `inline` as part of its declaration inside the class body. Alternatively, we can specify `inline` on the function definition that appears outside the class body:

```
inline                      //  we can specify inline on the definition
Screen &Screen::move(pos r, pos c)
{
    pos row = r * width; //  compute the row location
    cursor = row + c;    //  move cursor to the column within that row
    return *this;        //  return this object as an lvalue
}

char Screen::get(pos r, pos c) const //  declared as inline in the class
{
    pos row = r * width;        //  compute row location
    return contents[row + c]; //  return character at the given column
}
```

Although we are not required to do so, it is legal to specify `inline` on both the declaration and the definition. However, specifying `inline` only on the definition outside the class can make the class easier to read.

> For the same reasons that we define `inline` functions in headers (§ 6.5.2, p. 240), `inline` member functions should be defined in the same header as the corresponding class definition.

Overloading Member Functions

As with nonmember functions, member functions may be overloaded (§ 6.4, p. 230) so long as the functions differ by the number and/or types of parameters. The same function-matching (§ 6.4, p. 233) process is used for calls to member functions as for nonmember functions.

For example, our `Screen` class defined two versions of `get`. One version returns the character currently denoted by the cursor; the other returns the character at a given position specified by its row and column. The compiler uses the number of arguments to determine which version to run:

```
Screen myscreen;
char ch = myscreen.get();// calls Screen::get()
ch = myscreen.get(0,0);  //  calls Screen::get(pos, pos)
```

`mutable` Data Members

It sometimes (but not very often) happens that a class has a data member that we want to be able to modify, even inside a `const` member function. We indicate such members by including the `mutable` keyword in their declaration.

A **mutable data member** is never const, even when it is a member of a const object. Accordingly, a const member function may change a mutable member. As an example, we'll give Screen a mutable member named access_ctr, which we'll use to track how often each Screen member function is called:

```
class Screen {
public:
    void some_member() const;
private:
    mutable size_t access_ctr; //  may change even in a const object
    //  other members as before
};
void Screen::some_member() const
{
    ++access_ctr;       //  keep a count of the calls to any member function
    //  whatever other work this member needs to do
}
```

Despite the fact that some_member is a const member function, it can change the value of access_ctr. That member is a mutable member, so any member function, including const functions, can change its value.

Initializers for Data Members of Class Type

In addition to defining the Screen class, we'll define a window manager class that represents a collection of Screens on a given display. This class will have a vector of Screens in which each element represents a particular Screen. By default, we'd like our Window_mgr class to start up with a single, default-initialized Screen. Under the new standard, the best way to specify this default value is as an in-class initializer (§ 2.6.1, p. 73):

```
class Window_mgr {
private:
    //  Screens this Window_mgr is tracking
    //  by default, a Window_mgr has one standard sized blank Screen
    std::vector<Screen> screens{Screen(24, 80, ' ')};
};
```

When we initialize a member of class type, we are supplying arguments to a constructor of that member's type. In this case, we list initialize our vector member (§ 3.3.1, p. 98) with a single element initializer. That initializer contains a Screen value that is passed to the vector<Screen> constructor to create a one-element vector. That value is created by the Screen constructor that takes two size parameters and a character to create a blank screen of the given size.

As we've seen, in-class initializers must use either the = form of initialization (which we used when we initialized the the data members of Screen) or the direct form of initialization using curly braces (as we do for screens).

Note When we provide an in-class initializer, we must do so following an = sign or inside braces.

EXERCISES SECTION 7.3.1

Exercise 7.23: Write your own version of the `Screen` class.

Exercise 7.24: Give your `Screen` class three constructors: a default constructor; a constructor that takes values for height and width and initializes the contents to hold the given number of blanks; and a constructor that takes values for height, width, and a character to use as the contents of the screen.

Exercise 7.25: Can `Screen` safely rely on the default versions of copy and assignment? If so, why? If not, why not?

Exercise 7.26: Define `Sales_data::avg_price` as an `inline` function.

7.3.2 Functions That Return `*this`

Next we'll add functions to set the character at the cursor or at a given location:

```
class Screen {
public:
    Screen &set(char);
    Screen &set(pos, pos, char);
    //  other members as before
};
inline Screen &Screen::set(char c)
{
    contents[cursor] = c;   // set the new value at the current cursor location
    return *this;           //  return this object as an lvalue
}
inline Screen &Screen::set(pos r, pos col, char ch)
{
    contents[r*width + col] = ch;   //  set specified location to given value
    return *this;                   //  return this object as an lvalue
}
```

Like the `move` operation, our `set` members return a reference to the object on which they are called (§ 7.1.2, p. 259). Functions that return a reference are lvalues (§ 6.3.2, p. 226), which means that they return the object itself, not a copy of the object. If we concatenate a sequence of these actions into a single expression:

```
//  move the cursor to a given position, and set that character
myScreen.move(4,0).set('#');
```

these operations will execute on the same object. In this expression, we first `move` the `cursor` inside `myScreen` and then `set` a character in `myScreen`'s `contents` member. That is, this statement is equivalent to

```
myScreen.move(4,0);
myScreen.set('#');
```

Had we defined `move` and `set` to return `Screen`, rather than `Screen&`, this statement would execute quite differently. In this case it would be equivalent to:

```
// if move returns Screen not Screen&
Screen temp = myScreen.move(4,0);   // the return value would be copied
temp.set('#'); // the contents inside myScreen would be unchanged
```

If move had a nonreference return type, then the return value of move would be a copy of *this (§ 6.3.2, p. 224). The call to set would change the temporary copy, not myScreen.

Returning *this from a const Member Function

Next, we'll add an operation, which we'll name display, to print the contents of the Screen. We'd like to be able to include this operation in a sequence of set and move operations. Therefore, like set and move, our display function will return a reference to the object on which it executes.

Logically, displaying a Screen doesn't change the object, so we should make display a const member. If display is a const member, then this is a pointer to const and *this is a const object. Hence, the return type of display must be const Sales_data&. However, if display returns a reference to const, we won't be able to embed display into a series of actions:

```
Screen myScreen;
// if display returns a const reference, the call to set is an error
myScreen.display(cout).set('*');
```

Even though myScreen is a nonconst object, the call to set won't compile. The problem is that the const version of display returns a reference to const and we cannot call set on a const object.

> A const member function that returns *this as a reference should have a return type that is a reference to const.

Overloading Based on const

We can overload a member function based on whether it is const for the same reasons that we can overload a function based on whether a pointer parameter points to const (§ 6.4, p. 232). The nonconst version will not be viable for const objects; we can only call const member functions on a const object. We can call either version on a nonconst object, but the nonconst version will be a better match.

In this example, we'll define a private member named do_display to do the actual work of printing the Screen. Each of the display operations will call this function and then return the object on which it is executing:

```
class Screen {
public:
    // display overloaded on whether the object is const or not
    Screen &display(std::ostream &os)
                    { do_display(os); return *this; }
    const Screen &display(std::ostream &os) const
                    { do_display(os); return *this; }
```

```
private:
    // function to do the work of displaying a Screen
    void do_display(std::ostream &os) const {os << contents;}
    // other members as before
};
```

As in any other context, when one member calls another the this pointer is passed implicitly. Thus, when display calls do_display, its own this pointer is implicitly passed to do_display. When the nonconst version of display calls do_display, its this pointer is implicitly converted from a pointer to nonconst to a pointer to const (§ 4.11.2, p. 162).

When do_display completes, the display functions each return the object on which they execute by dereferencing this. In the nonconst version, this points to a nonconst object, so that version of display returns an ordinary (nonconst) reference; the const member returns a reference to const.

When we call display on an object, whether that object is const determines which version of display is called:

```
Screen myScreen(5,3);
const Screen blank(5, 3);
myScreen.set('#').display(cout);    // calls nonconst version
blank.display(cout);                // calls const version
```

ADVICE: USE PRIVATE UTILITY FUNCTIONS FOR COMMON CODE

Some readers might be surprised that we bothered to define a separate do_display operation. After all, the calls to do_display aren't much simpler than the action done inside do_display. Why bother? We do so for several reasons:

- A general desire to avoid writing the same code in more than one place.

- We expect that the display operation will become more complicated as our class evolves. As the actions involved become more complicated, it makes more obvious sense to write those actions in one place, not two.

- It is likely that we might want to add debugging information to do_display during development that would be eliminated in the final product version of the code. It will be easier to do so if only one definition of do_display needs to be changed to add or remove the debugging code.

- There needn't be any overhead involved in this extra function call. We defined do_display inside the class body, so it is implicitly inline. Thus, there likely be no run-time overhead associating with calling do_display.

In practice, well-designed C++ programs tend to have lots of small functions such as do_display that are called to do the "real" work of some other set of functions.

7.3.3 Class Types

Every class defines a unique type. Two different classes define two different types even if they define the same members. For example:

```
struct First {
    int memi;
    int getMem();
};
struct Second {
    int memi;
    int getMem();
};
First obj1;
Second obj2 = obj1; //  error: obj1 and obj2 have different types
```

Even if two classes have exactly the same member list, they are different types. The members of each class are distinct from the members of any other class (or any other scope).

We can refer to a class type directly, by using the class name as a type name. Alternatively, we can use the class name following the keyword `class` or `struct`:

```
Sales_data item1;        // default-initialized object of type Sales_data
class Sales_data item1; // equivalent declaration
```

Both methods of referring to a class type are equivalent. The second method is inherited from C and is also valid in C++.

Class Declarations

Just as we can declare a function apart from its definition (§ 6.1.2, p. 206), we can also declare a class without defining it:

```
class Screen; // declaration of the Screen class
```

This declaration, sometimes referred to as a **forward declaration**, introduces the name Screen into the program and indicates that Screen refers to a class type. After a declaration and before a definition is seen, the type Screen is an **incomplete type**—it's known that Screen is a class type but not known what members that type contains.

We can use an incomplete type in only limited ways: We can define pointers or references to such types, and we can declare (but not define) functions that use an incomplete type as a parameter or return type.

A class must be defined—not just declared—before we can write code that creates objects of that type. Otherwise, the compiler does not know how much storage such objects need. Similarly, the class must be defined before a reference or pointer is used to access a member of the type. After all, if the class has not been defined, the compiler can't know what members the class has.

With one exception that we'll describe in § 7.6 (p. 300), data members can be specified to be of a class type only if the class has been defined. The type must be complete because the compiler needs to know how much storage the data member requires. Because a class is not defined until its class body is complete, a class cannot have data members of its own type. However, a class is considered declared (but not yet defined) as soon as its class name has been seen. Therefore, a class can have data members that are pointers or references to its own type:

```
class Link_screen {
    Screen window;
    Link_screen *next;
    Link_screen *prev;
};
```

EXERCISES SECTION 7.3.3

Exercise 7.31: Define a pair of classes X and Y, in which X has a pointer to Y, and Y has an object of type X.

7.3.4 Friendship Revisited

Our Sales_data class defined three ordinary nonmember functions as friends (§ 7.2.1, p. 269). A class can also make another class its friend or it can declare specific member functions of another (previously defined) class as friends. In addition, a friend function can be defined inside the class body. Such functions are implicitly inline.

Friendship between Classes

As an example of class friendship, our Window_mgr class (§ 7.3.1, p. 274) will have members that will need access to the internal data of the Screen objects it manages. For example, let's assume that we want to add a member, named clear to `Window_mgr` that will reset the contents of a particular `Screen` to all blanks. To do this job, `clear` needs to access the `private` data members of `Screen`. To allow this access, `Screen` can designate `Window_mgr` as its friend:

```
class Screen {
    // Window_mgr members can access the private parts of class Screen
    friend class Window_mgr;
    // ... rest of the Screen class
};
```

The member functions of a friend class can access all the members, including the nonpublic members, of the class granting friendship. Now that `Window_mgr` is a friend of `Screen`, we can write the `clear` member of `Window_mgr` as follows:

```
class Window_mgr {
public:
    // location ID for each screen on the window
    using ScreenIndex = std::vector<Screen>::size_type;
    // reset the Screen at the given position to all blanks
    void clear(ScreenIndex);
private:
    std::vector<Screen> screens{Screen(24, 80, ' ')};
};
void Window_mgr::clear(ScreenIndex i)
{
    // s is a reference to the Screen we want to clear
    Screen &s = screens[i];
    // reset the contents of that Screen to all blanks
    s.contents = string(s.height * s.width, ' ');
}
```

We start by defining `s` as a reference to the `Screen` at position `i` in the `screens` vector. We then use the `height` and `width` members of that `Screen` to compute a new `string` that has the appropriate number of blank characters. We assign that string of blanks to the `contents` member.

If `clear` were not a friend of `Screen`, this code would not compile. The `clear` function would not be allowed to use the `height` `width`, or `contents` members of `Screen`. Because `Screen` grants friendship to `Window_mgr`, all the members of `Screen` are accessible to the functions in `Window_mgr`.

It is important to understand that friendship is not transitive. That is, if class `Window_mgr` has its own friends, those friends have no special access to `Screen`.

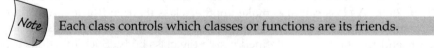
Each class controls which classes or functions are its friends.

Making A Member Function a Friend

Rather than making the entire `Window_mgr` class a friend, `Screen` can instead specify that only the `clear` member is allowed access. When we declare a member function to be a friend, we must specify the class of which that function is a member:

```
class Screen {
    //  Window_mgr::clear must have been declared before class Screen
    friend void Window_mgr::clear(ScreenIndex);
    //  ... rest of the Screen class
};
```

Making a member function a friend requires careful structuring of our programs to accommodate interdependencies among the declarations and definitions. In this example, we must order our program as follows:

- First, define the Window_mgr class, which declares, but cannot define, clear. Screen must be declared before clear can use the members of Screen.

- Next, define class Screen, including a friend declaration for clear.

- Finally, define clear, which can now refer to the members in Screen.

Overloaded Functions and Friendship

Although overloaded functions share a common name, they are still different functions. Therefore, a class must declare as a friend each function in a set of overloaded functions that it wishes to make a friend:

```
//  overloaded storeOn functions
extern std::ostream& storeOn(std::ostream &, Screen &);
extern BitMap& storeOn(BitMap &, Screen &);
class Screen {
    //  ostream version of storeOn may access the private parts of Screen objects
    friend std::ostream& storeOn(std::ostream &, Screen &);
    //  ...
};
```

Class Screen makes the version of storeOn that takes an ostream& its friend. The version that takes a BitMap& has no special access to Screen.

Friend Declarations and Scope

Classes and nonmember functions need not have been declared before they are used in a friend declaration. When a name first appears in a friend declaration, that name is implicitly *assumed* to be part of the surrounding scope. However, the friend itself is not actually declared in that scope (§ 7.2.1, p. 270).

Even if we define the function inside the class, we must still provide a declaration outside of the class itself to make that function visible. A declaration must exist even if we only call the friend from members of the friendship granting class:

```
struct X {
    friend void f() { /* friend function can be defined in the class body */ }
    X() { f(); } // error: no declaration for f
    void g();
    void h();
};
void X::g() { return f(); } // error: f hasn't been declared
```

```
void f();                        //  declares the function defined inside X
void X::h() { return f(); } //  ok: declaration for f is now in scope
```

It is important to understand that a friend declaration affects access but is not a declaration in an ordinary sense.

 Remember, some compilers do not enforce the lookup rules for friends (§ 7.2.1, p. 270).

7.4 Class Scope

Every class defines its own new scope. Outside the class scope, ordinary data and function members may be accessed only through an object, a reference, or a pointer using a member access operator (§ 4.6, p. 150). We access type members from the class using the scope operator . In either case, the name that follows the operator must be a member of the associated class.

```
Screen::pos ht = 24, wd = 80; //  use the pos type defined by Screen
Screen scr(ht, wd, ' ');
Screen *p = &scr;
char c = scr.get(); //  fetches the get member from the object scr
c = p->get();       //  fetches the get member from the object to which p points
```

Scope and Members Defined outside the Class

The fact that a class is a scope explains why we must provide the class name as well as the function name when we define a member function outside its class (§ 7.1.2, p. 259). Outside of the class, the names of the members are hidden.

Once the class name is seen, the remainder of the definition—including the parameter list and the function body—is in the scope of the class. As a result, we can refer to other class members without qualification.

For example, recall the `clear` member of class `Window_mgr` (§ 7.3.4, p. 280). That function's parameter uses a type that is defined by `Window_mgr`:

```
void Window_mgr::clear(ScreenIndex i)
{
    Screen &s = screens[i];
    s.contents = string(s.height * s.width, ' ');
}
```

Because the compiler sees the parameter list after noting that we are in the scope of class `WindowMgr`, there is no need to specify that we want the `ScreenIndex` that is defined by WindowMgr. For the same reason, the use of screens in the function body refers to name declared inside class Window_mgr.

On the other hand, the return type of a function normally appears before the function's name. When a member function is defined outside the class body, any name used in the return type is outside the class scope. As a result, the return type must specify the class of which it is a member. For example, we might give Window_mgr a function, named addScreen, to add another screen to the display. This member will return a ScreenIndex value that the user can subsequently use to locate this Screen:

```
class Window_mgr {
public:
    //   add a Screen to the window and returns its index
    ScreenIndex addScreen(const Screen&);
    //   other members as before
};
//   return type is seen before we're in the scope of Window_mgr
Window_mgr::ScreenIndex
Window_mgr::addScreen(const Screen &s)
{
    screens.push_back(s);
    return screens.size() - 1;
}
```

Because the return type appears before the name of the class is seen, it appears outside the scope of class Window_mgr. To use ScreenIndex for the return type, we must specify the class in which that type is defined.

EXERCISES SECTION 7.4

Exercise 7.33: What would happen if we gave Screen a size member defined as follows? Fix any problems you identify.

```
pos Screen::size() const
{
    return height * width;
}
```

7.4.1 Name Lookup and Class Scope

In the programs we've written so far, **name lookup** (the process of finding which declarations match the use of a name) has been relatively straightforward:

- First, look for a declaration of the name in the block in which the name was used. Only names declared before the use are considered.

- If the name isn't found, look in the enclosing scope(s).

- If no declaration is found, then the program is in error.

The way names are resolved inside member functions defined inside the class may seem to behave differently than these lookup rules. However, in this case, appearances are deceiving. Class definitions are processed in two phases:

- First, the member declarations are compiled.

- Function bodies are compiled only after the entire class has been seen.

 Member function definitions are processed *after* the compiler processes all of the declarations in the class.

Classes are processed in this two-phase way to make it easier to organize class code. Because member function bodies are not processed until the entire class is seen, they can use any name defined inside the class. If function definitions were processed at the same time as the member declarations, then we would have to order the member functions so that they referred only to names already seen.

Name Lookup for Class Member Declarations

This two-step process applies only to names used in the body of a member function. Names used in declarations, including names used for the return type and types in the parameter list, must be seen before they are used. If a member declaration uses a name that has not yet been seen inside the class, the compiler will look for that name in the scope(s) in which the class is defined. For example:

```
typedef double Money;
string bal;
class Account {
public:
    Money balance() { return bal; }
private:
    Money bal;
    // ...
};
```

When the compiler sees the declaration of the `balance` function, it will look for a declaration of `Money` in the `Account` class. The compiler considers only declarations inside `Account` that appear before the use of `Money`. Because no matching member is found, the compiler then looks for a declaration in the enclosing scope(s). In this example, the compiler will find the `typedef` of `Money`. That type will be used for the return type of the function `balance` and as the type for the data member `bal`. On the other hand, the function body of `balance` is processed only after the entire class is seen. Thus, the `return` inside that function returns the member named `bal`, not the `string` from the outer scope.

Type Names Are Special

Ordinarily, an inner scope can redefine a name from an outer scope even if that name has already been used in the inner scope. However, in a class, if a member uses a name from an outer scope and that name is a type, then the class may not subsequently redefine that name:

```
typedef double Money;
class Account {
public:
    Money balance() { return bal; }   // uses Money from the outer scope
private:
    typedef double Money; // error: cannot redefine Money
    Money bal;
    // ...
};
```

It is worth noting that even though the definition of Money inside Account uses the same type as the definition in the outer scope, this code is still in error.

Although it is an error to redefine a type name, compilers are not required to diagnose this error. Some compilers will quietly accept such code, even though the program is in error.

 Definitions of type names usually should appear at the beginning of a class. That way any member that uses that type will be seen after the type name has already been defined.

Normal Block-Scope Name Lookup inside Member Definitions

A name used in the body of a member function is resolved as follows:

- First, look for a declaration of the name inside the member function. As usual, only declarations in the function body that precede the use of the name are considered.

- If the declaration is not found inside the member function, look for a declaration inside the class. All the members of the class are considered.

- If a declaration for the name is not found in the class, look for a declaration that is in scope before the member function definition.

Ordinarily, it is a bad idea to use the name of another member as the name for a parameter in a member function. However, in order to show how names are resolved, we'll violate that normal practice in our dummy_fcn function:

```
//  note: this code is for illustration purposes only and reflects bad practice
//  it is generally a bad idea to use the same name for a parameter and a member
int height;     // defines a name subsequently used inside Screen
class Screen {
public:
    typedef std::string::size_type pos;
    void dummy_fcn(pos height) {
        cursor = width * height; // which height? the parameter
    }
```

```
private:
    pos cursor = 0;
    pos height = 0, width = 0;
};
```

When the compiler processes the multiplication expression inside dummy_fcn, it first looks for the names used in that expression in the scope of that function. A function's parameters are in the function's scope. Thus, the name height, used in the body of dummy_fcn, refers to this parameter declaration.

In this case, the height parameter hides the member named height. If we wanted to override the normal lookup rules, we can do so:

```
// bad practice: names local to member functions shouldn't hide member names
void Screen::dummy_fcn(pos height) {
    cursor = width * this->height;    // member height
    // alternative way to indicate the member
    cursor = width * Screen::height; // member height
}
```

Even though the class member is hidden, it is still possible to use that member by qualifying the member's name with the name of its class or by using the this pointer explicitly.

A much better way to ensure that we get the member named height would be to give the parameter a different name:

```
// good practice: don't use a member name for a parameter or other local variable
void Screen::dummy_fcn(pos ht) {
    cursor = width * height;  // member height
}
```

In this case, when the compiler looks for the name height, it won't be found inside dummy_fcn. The compiler next looks at all the declarations in Screen. Even though the declaration of height appears after its use inside dummy_fcn, the compiler resolves this use to the data member named height.

After Class Scope, Look in the Surrounding Scope

If the compiler doesn't find the name in function or class scope, it looks for the name in the surrounding scope. In our example, the name height is defined in the outer scope before the definition of Screen. However, the object in the outer scope is hidden by our member named height. If we want the name from the outer scope, we can ask for it explicitly using the scope operator:

```
// bad practice: don't hide names that are needed from surrounding scopes
void Screen::dummy_fcn(pos height) {
    cursor = width * ::height;// which height? the global one
}
```

Even though the outer object is hidden, it is still possible to access that object by using the scope operator.

Names Are Resolved Where They Appear within a File

When a member is defined outside its class, the third step of name lookup includes names declared in the scope of the member definition as well as those that appear in the scope of the class definition. For example:

```
int height;    // defines a name subsequently used inside Screen
class Screen {
public:
    typedef std::string::size_type pos;
    void setHeight(pos);
    pos height = 0;   // hides the declaration of height in the outer scope
};
Screen::pos verify(Screen::pos);
void Screen::setHeight(pos var) {
    // var: refers to the parameter
    // height: refers to the class member
    // verify: refers to the global function
    height = verify(var);
}
```

Notice that the declaration of the global function `verify` is not visible before the definition of the class `Screen`. However, the third step of name lookup includes the scope in which the member definition appears. In this example, the declaration for `verify` appears before `setHeight` is defined and may, therefore, be used.

EXERCISES SECTION 7.4.1

Exercise 7.34: What would happen if we put the `typedef` of `pos` in the `Screen` class on page 285 as the last line in the class?

Exercise 7.35: Explain the following code, indicating which definition of `Type` or `initVal` is used for each use of those names. Say how you would fix any errors.

```
typedef string Type;
Type initVal();
class Exercise {
public:
    typedef double Type;
    Type setVal(Type);
    Type initVal();
private:
    int val;
};
Type Exercise::setVal(Type parm) {
    val = parm + initVal();
    return val;
}
```

7.5 Constructors Revisited

Constructors are a crucial part of any C++ class. We covered the basics of constructors in § 7.1.4 (p. 262). In this section we'll cover some additional capabilities of constructors, and deepen our coverage of the material introduced earlier.

7.5.1 Constructor Initializer List

When we define variables, we typically initialize them immediately rather than defining them and then assigning to them:

```
string foo = "Hello World!";  //  define and initialize
string bar;                   //  default initialized to the empty string
bar = "Hello World!";         //  assign a new value to bar
```

Exactly the same distinction between initialization and assignment applies to the data members of objects. If we do not explicitly initialize a member in the constructor initializer list, that member is default initialized before the constructor body starts executing. For example:

```
//  legal but sloppier way to write the Sales_data constructor: no constructor initializers
Sales_data::Sales_data(const string &s,
                       unsigned cnt, double price)
{
    bookNo = s;
    units_sold = cnt;
    revenue = cnt * price;
}
```

This version and our original definition on page 264 have the same effect: When the constructor finishes, the data members will hold the same values. The difference is that the original version *initializes* its data members, whereas this version *assigns* values to the data members. How significant this distinction is depends on the type of the data member.

Constructor Initializers Are Sometimes Required

We can often, *but not always*, ignore the distinction between whether a member is initialized or assigned. Members that are const or references must be initialized. Similarly, members that are of a class type that does not define a default constructor also must be initialized. For example:

```
class ConstRef {
public:
    ConstRef(int ii);
private:
    int i;
    const int ci;
    int &ri;
};
```

Like any other `const` object or reference, the members `ci` and `ri` must be initialized. As a result, omitting a constructor initializer for these members is an error:

```
//  error: ci and ri must be initialized
ConstRef::ConstRef(int ii)
{                    //  assignments:
    i = ii;   //  ok
    ci = ii;  //  error: cannot assign to a const
    ri = i;   //  error: ri was never initialized
}
```

By the time the body of the constructor begins executing, initialization is complete. Our only chance to initialize `const` or reference data members is in the constructor initializer. The correct way to write this constructor is

```
//  ok: explicitly initialize reference and const members
ConstRef::ConstRef(int ii): i(ii), ci(ii), ri(i) {  }
```

We *must* use the constructor initializer list to provide values for members that are `const`, reference, or of a class type that does not have a default constructor.

ADVICE: USE CONSTRUCTOR INITIALIZERS

In many classes, the distinction between initialization and assignment is strictly a matter of low-level efficiency: A data member is initialized and then assigned when it could have been initialized directly.

More important than the efficiency issue is the fact that some data members must be initialized. By routinely using constructor initializers, you can avoid being surprised by compile-time errors when you have a class with a member that requires a constructor initializer.

Order of Member Initialization

Not surprisingly, each member may be named only once in the constructor initializer. After all, what might it mean to give a member two initial values?

What may be more surprising is that the constructor initializer list specifies only the values used to initialize the members, not the order in which those initializations are performed.

Members are initialized in the order in which they appear in the class definition: The first member is initialized first, then the next, and so on. The order in which initializers appear in the constructor initializer list does not change the order of initialization.

The order of initialization often doesn't matter. However, if one member is initialized in terms of another, then the order in which members are initialized is crucially important.

As an example, consider the following class:

```
class X {
    int i;
    int j;
public:
    // undefined: i is initialized before j
    X(int val): j(val), i(j) { }
};
```

In this case, the constructor initializer makes it *appear* as if j is initialized with val and then j is used to initialize i. However, i is initialized first. The effect of this initializer is to initialize i with the undefined value of j!

Some compilers are kind enough to generate a warning if the data members are listed in the constructor initializer in a different order from the order in which the members are declared.

 It is a good idea to write constructor initializers in the same order as the members are declared. Moreover, when possible, avoid using members to initialize other members.

If possible, it is a good idea write member initializers to use the constructor's parameters rather than another data member from the same object. That way we don't even have to think about the order of member initialization. For example, it would be better to write the constructor for X as

```
    X(int val): i(val), j(val) { }
```

In this version, the order in which i and j are initialized doesn't matter.

Default Arguments and Constructors

The actions of the Sales_data default constructor are similar to those of the constructor that takes a single string argument. The only difference is that the constructor that takes a string argument uses that argument to initialize bookNo. The default constructor (implicitly) uses the string default constructor to initialize bookNo. We can rewrite these constructors as a single constructor with a default argument (§ 6.5.1, p. 236):

```
class Sales_data {
public:
    // defines the default constructor as well as one that takes a string argument
    Sales_data(std::string s = ""): bookNo(s) { }
    // remaining constructors unchanged
    Sales_data(std::string s, unsigned cnt, double rev):
          bookNo(s), units_sold(cnt), revenue(rev*cnt) { }
    Sales_data(std::istream &is) { read(is, *this); }
    // remaining members as before
};
```

This version of our class provides the same interface as our original on page 264. Both versions create the same object when given no arguments or when given a single string argument. Because we can call this constructor with no arguments, this constructor defines a default constructor for our class.

Note A constructor that supplies default arguments for all its parameters also defines the default constructor.

It is worth noting that we probably should not use default arguments with the `Sales_data` constructor that takes three arguments. If a user supplies a nonzero count for the number of books sold, we want to ensure that the user also supplies the price at which those books were sold.

EXERCISES SECTION 7.5.1

Exercise 7.36: The following initializer is in error. Identify and fix the problem.

```
struct X {
    X (int i, int j): base(i), rem(base % j) { }
    int rem, base;
};
```

Exercise 7.37: Using the version of `Sales_data` from this section, determine which constructor is used to initialize each of the following variables and list the values of the data members in each object:

```
Sales_data first_item(cin);

int main() {
    Sales_data next;
    Sales_data last("9-999-99999-9");
}
```

Exercise 7.38: We might want to supply `cin` as a default argument to the constructor that takes an `istream&`. Write the constructor declaration that uses `cin` as a default argument.

Exercise 7.39: Would it be legal for both the constructor that takes a `string` and the one that takes an `istream&` to have default arguments? If not, why not?

Exercise 7.40: Choose one of the following abstractions (or an abstraction of your own choosing). Determine what data are needed in the class. Provide an appropriate set of constructors. Explain your decisions.

(a) `Book`   (b) `Date`   (c) `Employee`
(d) `Vehicle`   (e) `Object`   (f) `Tree`

7.5.2 Delegating Constructors

The new standard extends the use of constructor initializers to let us define so-called **delegating constructors**. A delegating constructor uses another constructor from its own class to perform its initialization. It is said to "delegate" some (or all) of its work to this other constructor.

Like any other constructor, a delegating constructor has a member initializer list and a function body. In a delegating constructor, the member initializer list has a single entry that is the name of the class itself. Like other member initializers, the name of the class is followed by a parenthesized list of arguments. The argument list must match another constructor in the class.

As an example, we'll rewrite the `Sales_data` class to use delegating constructors as follows:

```
class Sales_data {
public:
    // nondelegating constructor initializes members from corresponding arguments
    Sales_data(std::string s, unsigned cnt, double price):
            bookNo(s), units_sold(cnt), revenue(cnt*price) { }
    // remaining constructors all delegate to another constructor
    Sales_data(): Sales_data("", 0, 0) {}
    Sales_data(std::string s): Sales_data(s, 0,0) {}
    Sales_data(std::istream &is): Sales_data()
                                        { read(is, *this); }
    // other members as before
};
```

In this version of `Sales_data`, all but one of the constructors delegate their work. The first constructor takes three arguments, uses those arguments to initialize the data members, and does no further work. In this version of the class, we define the default constructor to use the three-argument constructor to do its initialization. It too has no additional work, as indicated by the empty constructor body. The constructor that takes a `string` also delegates to the three-argument version.

The constructor that takes an `istream&` also delegates. It delegates to the default constructor, which in turn delegates to the three-argument constructor. Once those constructors complete their work, the body of the `istream&` constructor is run. Its constructor body calls `read` to read the given `istream`.

When a constructor delegates to another constructor, the constructor initializer list and function body of the delegated-to constructor are both executed. In `Sales_data`, the function bodies of the delegated-to constructors happen to be empty. Had the function bodies contained code, that code would be run before control returned to the function body of the delegating constructor.

EXERCISES SECTION 7.5.2

Exercise 7.41: Rewrite your own version of the `Sales_data` class to use delegating constructors. Add a statement to the body of each of the constructors that prints a message whenever it is executed. Write declarations to construct a `Sales_data` object in every way possible. Study the output until you are certain you understand the order of execution among delegating constructors.

Exercise 7.42: For the class you wrote for exercise 7.40 in § 7.5.1 (p. 291), decide whether any of the constructors might use delegation. If so, write the delegating constructor(s) for your class. If not, look at the list of abstractions and choose one that you think would use a delegating constructor. Write the class definition for that abstraction.

7.5.3 The Role of the Default Constructor

The default constructor is used automatically whenever an object is default or value initialized. Default initialization happens

- When we define nonstatic variables (§ 2.2.1, p. 43) or arrays (§ 3.5.1, p. 114) at block scope without initializers

- When a class that itself has members of class type uses the synthesized default constructor (§ 7.1.4, p. 262)

- When members of class type are not explicitly initialized in a constructor initializer list (§ 7.1.4, p. 265)

Value initialization happens

- During array initialization when we provide fewer initializers than the size of the array (§ 3.5.1, p. 114)

- When we define a local static object without an initializer (§ 6.1.1, p. 205)

- When we explicitly request value initialization by writing án expressions of the form T() where T is the name of a type (The vector constructor that takes a single argument to specify the vector's size (§ 3.3.1, p. 98) uses an argument of this kind to value initialize its element initializer.)

Classes must have a default constructor in order to be used in these contexts. Most of these contexts should be fairly obvious.

What may be less obvious is the impact on classes that have data members that do not have a default constructor:

```
class NoDefault {
public:
    NoDefault(const std::string&);
    //  additional members follow, but no other constructors
};
struct A {   //  my_mem is public by default; see § 7.2 (p. 268)
    NoDefault my_mem;
};
A a;          //  error: cannot synthesize a constructor for A
struct B {
    B() {}  //  error: no initializer for b_member
    NoDefault b_member;
};
```

Best Practices In practice, it is almost always right to provide a default constructor if other constructors are being defined.

Using the Default Constructor

The following declaration of obj compiles without complaint. However, when we try to use obj

```
Sales_data obj();    // ok: but defines a function, not an object
if (obj.isbn() == Primer_5th_ed.isbn())   // error: obj is a function
```

the compiler complains that we cannot apply member access notation to a function. The problem is that, although we intended to declare a default-initialized object, obj actually declares a function taking no parameters and returning an object of type Sales_data.

The correct way to define an object that uses the default constructor for initialization is to leave off the trailing, empty parentheses:

```
//  ok: obj is a default-initialized object
Sales_data obj;
```

WARNING

It is a common mistake among programmers new to C++ to try to declare an object initialized with the default constructor as follows:

```
Sales_data obj();  //  oops! declares a function, not an object
Sales_data obj2;   //  ok: obj2 is an object, not a function
```

EXERCISES SECTION 7.5.3

Exercise 7.43: Assume we have a class named NoDefault that has a constructor that takes an int, but has no default constructor. Define a class C that has a member of type NoDefault. Define the default constructor for C.

Exercise 7.44: Is the following declaration legal? If not, why not?

```
vector<NoDefault> vec(10);
```

Exercise 7.45: What if we defined the vector in the previous execercise to hold objects of type C?

Exercise 7.46: Which, if any, of the following statements are untrue? Why?

(a) A class must provide at least one constructor.
(b) A default constructor is a constructor with an empty parameter list.
(c) If there are no meaningful default values for a class, the class should not provide a default constructor.
(d) If a class does not define a default constructor, the compiler generates one that initializes each data member to the default value of its associated type.

 ## 7.5.4 Implicit Class-Type Conversions

As we saw in § 4.11 (p. 159), the language defines several automatic conversions among the built-in types. We also noted that classes can define implicit conversions as well. Every constructor that can be called with a single argument defines an implicit conversion *to* a class type. Such constructors are sometimes referred to as

converting constructors. We'll see in § 14.9 (p. 579) how to define conversions *from* a class type to another type.

 A constructor that can be called with a single argument defines an implicit conversion from the constructor's parameter type to the class type.

The `Sales_data` constructors that take a `string` and that take an `istream` both define implicit conversions from those types to `Sales_data`. That is, we can use a `string` or an `istream` where an object of type `Sales_data` is expected:

```
string null_book = "9-999-99999-9";
// constructs a temporary Sales_data object
// with units_sold and revenue equal to 0 and bookNo equal to null_book
item.combine(null_book);
```

Here we call the `Sales_data` combine member function with a `string` argument. This call is perfectly legal; the compiler automatically creates a `Sales_data` object from the given `string`. That newly generated (temporary) `Sales_data` is passed to `combine`. Because `combine`'s parameter is a reference to `const`, we can pass a temporary to that parameter.

Only One Class-Type Conversion Is Allowed

In § 4.11.2 (p. 162) we noted that the compiler will automatically apply only one class-type conversion. For example, the following code is in error because it implicitly uses two conversions:

```
// error: requires two user-defined conversions:
//        (1) convert "9-999-99999-9" to string
//        (2) convert that (temporary) string to Sales_data
item.combine("9-999-99999-9");
```

If we wanted to make this call, we can do so by explicitly converting the character string to either a `string` or a `Sales_data` object:

```
// ok: explicit conversion to string, implicit conversion to Sales_data
item.combine(string("9-999-99999-9"));
// ok: implicit conversion to string, explicit conversion to Sales_data
item.combine(Sales_data("9-999-99999-9"));
```

Class-Type Conversions Are Not Always Useful

Whether the conversion of a `string` to `Sales_data` is desired depends on how we think our users will use the conversion. In this case, it might be okay. The `string` in `null_book` probably represents a nonexistent ISBN.

More problematic is the conversion from `istream` to `Sales_data`:

```
// uses the istream constructor to build an object to pass to combine
item.combine(cin);
```

This code implicitly converts `cin` to `Sales_data`. This conversion executes the `Sales_data` constructor that takes an `istream`. That constructor creates a (temporary) `Sales_data` object by reading the standard input. That object is then passed to `combine`.

This `Sales_data` object is a temporary (§ 2.4.1, p. 62). We have no access to it once `combine` finishes. Effectively, we have constructed an object that is discarded after we add its value into `item`.

Suppressing Implicit Conversions Defined by Constructors

We can prevent the use of a constructor in a context that requires an implicit conversion by declaring the constructor as **explicit**:

```
class Sales_data {
public:
    Sales_data() = default;
    Sales_data(const std::string &s, unsigned n, double p):
                bookNo(s), units_sold(n), revenue(p*n) { }
    explicit Sales_data(const std::string &s): bookNo(s) { }
    explicit Sales_data(std::istream&);
    // remaining members as before
};
```

Now, neither constructor can be used to implicitly create a `Sales_data` object. Neither of our previous uses will compile:

```
item.combine(null_book);  // error: string constructor is explicit
item.combine(cin);        // error: istream constructor is explicit
```

The `explicit` keyword is meaningful only on constructors that can be called with a single argument. Constructors that require more arguments are not used to perform an implicit conversion, so there is no need to designate such constructors as `explicit`. The `explicit` keyword is used only on the constructor declaration inside the class. It is not repeated on a definition made outside the class body:

```
// error: explicit allowed only on a constructor declaration in a class header
explicit Sales_data::Sales_data(istream& is)
{
    read(is, *this);
}
```

`explicit` Constructors Can Be Used Only for Direct Initialization

One context in which implicit conversions happen is when we use the copy form of initialization (with an =) (§ 3.2.1, p. 84). We cannot use an `explicit` constructor with this form of initialization; we must use direct initialization:

```
Sales_data item1(null_book);   // ok: direct initialization
// error: cannot use the copy form of initialization with an explicit constructor
Sales_data item2 = null_book;
```

When a constructor is declared `explicit`, it can be used only with the direct form of initialization (§ 3.2.1, p. 84). Moroever, the compiler will *not* use this constructor in an automatic conversion.

Explicitly Using Constructors for Conversions

Although the compiler will not use an `explicit` constructor for an implicit conversion, we can use such constructors explicitly to force a conversion:

```
// ok: the argument is an explicitly constructed Sales_data object
item.combine(Sales_data(null_book));
// ok: static_cast can use an explicit constructor
item.combine(static_cast<Sales_data>(cin));
```

In the first call, we use the `Sales_data` constructor directly. This call constructs a temporary `Sales_data` object using the `Sales_data` constructor that takes a `string`. In the second call, we use a `static_cast` (§ 4.11.3, p. 163) to perform an explicit, rather than an implicit, conversion. In this call, the `static_cast` uses the `istream` constructor to construct a temporary `Sales_data` object.

Library Classes with `explicit` Constructors

Some of the library classes that we've used have single-parameter constructors:

- The `string` constructor that takes a single parameter of type `const char*` (§ 3.2.1, p. 84) is not `explicit`.

- The `vector` constructor that takes a size (§ 3.3.1, p. 98) is `explicit`.

EXERCISES SECTION 7.5.4

Exercise 7.47: Explain whether the `Sales_data` constructor that takes a `string` should be `explicit`. What are the benefits of making the constructor `explicit`? What are the drawbacks?

Exercise 7.48: Assuming the `Sales_data` constructors are not `explicit`, what operations happen during the following definitions

```
string null_isbn("9-999-99999-9");
Sales_data item1(null_isbn);
Sales_data item2("9-999-99999-9");
```

What happens if the `Sales_data` constructors are `explicit`?

Exercise 7.49: For each of the three following declarations of `combine`, explain what happens if we call `i.combine(s)`, where `i` is a `Sales_data` and `s` is a `string`:

```
(a) Sales_data &combine(Sales_data);
(b) Sales_data &combine(Sales_data&);
(c) Sales_data &combine(const Sales_data&) const;
```

Exercise 7.50: Determine whether any of your `Person` class constructors should be `explicit`.

Exercise 7.51: Why do you think `vector` defines its single-argument constructor as `explicit`, but `string` does not?

7.5.5 Aggregate Classes

An **aggregate class** gives users direct access to its members and has special initialization syntax. A class is an aggregate if

- All of its data members are `public`

- It does not define any constructors

- It has no in-class initializers (§ 2.6.1, p. 73)

- It has no base classes or `virtual` functions, which are class-related features that we'll cover in Chapter 15

For example, the following class is an aggregate:

```
struct Data {
    int ival;
    string s;
};
```

We can initialize the data members of an aggregate class by providing a braced list of member initializers:

```
// val1.ival = 0; val1.s = string("Anna")
Data val1 = { 0, "Anna" };
```

The initializers must appear in declaration order of the data members. That is, the initializer for the first member is first, for the second is next, and so on. The following, for example, is an error:

```
// error: can't use "Anna" to initialize ival, or 1024 to initialize s
Data val2 = { "Anna" , 1024 };
```

As with initialization of array elements (§ 3.5.1, p. 114), if the list of initializers has fewer elements than the class has members, the trailing members are value initialized (§ 3.5.1, p. 114). The list of initializers must not contain more elements than the class has members.

It is worth noting that there are three significant drawbacks to explicitly initializing the members of an object of class type:

- It requires that all the data members of the class be `public`.

- It puts the burden on the user of the class (rather than on the class author) to correctly initialize every member of every object. Such initialization is tedious and error-prone because it is easy to forget an initializer or to supply an inappropriate initializer.

- If a member is added or removed, all initializations have to be updated.

Exercise 7.52: Using our first version of Sales_data from § 2.6.1 (p. 72), explain the following initialization. Identify and fix any problems.

```
Sales_data item = {"978-0590353403", 25, 15.99};
```

7.5.6 Literal Classes

In § 6.5.2 (p. 239) we noted that the parameters and return type of a constexpr function must be literal types. In addition to the arithmetic types, references, and pointers, certain classes are also literal types. Unlike other classes, classes that are literal types may have function members that are constexpr. Such members must meet all the requirements of a constexpr function. These member functions are implicitly const (§ 7.1.2, p. 258).

An aggregate class (§ 7.5.5, p. 298) whose data members are all of literal type is a literal class. A nonaggregate class, that meets the following restrictions, is also a literal class:

- The data members all must have literal type.

- The class must have at least one constexpr constructor.

- If a data member has an in-class initializer, the initializer for a member of built-in type must be a constant expression (§ 2.4.4, p. 65), or if the member has class type, the initializer must use the member's own constexpr constructor.

- The class must use default definition for its destructor, which is the member that destroys objects of the class type (§ 7.1.5, p. 267).

constexpr Constructors

Although constructors can't be const (§ 7.1.4, p. 262), constructors in a literal class can be constexpr (§ 6.5.2, p. 239) functions. Indeed, a literal class must provide at least one constexpr constructor.

A constexpr constructor can be declared as = default (§ 7.1.4, p. 264) (or as a deleted function, which we cover in § 13.1.6 (p. 507)). Otherwise, a constexpr constructor must meet the requirements of a constructor—meaning it can have no return statement—and of a constexpr function—meaning the only executable statement it can have is a return statement (§ 6.5.2, p. 239). As a result, the body of a constexpr constructor is typically empty. We define a constexpr constructor by preceding its declaration with the keyword constexpr:

```
class Debug {
public:
    constexpr Debug(bool b = true): hw(b), io(b), other(b) { }
    constexpr Debug(bool h, bool i, bool o):
                           hw(h), io(i), other(o) { }
```

```
    constexpr bool any() { return hw || io || other; }
    void set_io(bool b) { io = b; }
    void set_hw(bool b) { hw = b; }
    void set_other(bool b) { hw = b; }
private:
    bool hw;      //  hardware errors other than IO errors
    bool io;      //  IO errors
    bool other;   //  other errors
};
```

A constexpr constructor must initialize every data member. The initializers must either use a constexpr constructor or be a constant expression.

A constexpr constructor is used to generate objects that are constexpr and for parameters or return types in constexpr functions:

```
constexpr Debug io_sub(false, true, false);   //  debugging IO
if (io_sub.any())   //  equivalent to if (true)
    cerr << "print appropriate error messages" << endl;

constexpr Debug prod(false); //  no debugging during production
if (prod.any())     //  equivalent to if (false)
    cerr << "print an error message" << endl;
```

EXERCISES SECTION 7.5.6

Exercise 7.53: Define your own version of Debug.

Exercise 7.54: Should the members of Debug that begin with set_ be declared as constexpr? If not, why not?

Exercise 7.55: Is the Data class from § 7.5.5 (p. 298) a literal class? If not, why not? If so, explain why it is literal.

7.6 static Class Members

Classes sometimes need members that are associated with the class, rather than with individual objects of the class type. For example, a bank account class might need a data member to represent the current prime interest rate. In this case, we'd want to associate the rate with the class, not with each individual object. From an efficiency standpoint, there'd be no reason for each object to store the rate. Much more importantly, if the rate changes, we'd want each object to use the new value.

Declaring static Members

We say a member is associated with the class by adding the keyword static to its declaration. Like any other member, static members can be public or private. The type of a static data member can be const, reference, array, class type, and so forth.

As an example, we'll define a class to represent an account record at a bank:

```
class Account {
public:
    void calculate() { amount += amount * interestRate; }
    static double rate() { return interestRate; }
    static void rate(double);
private:
    std::string owner;
    double amount;
    static double interestRate;
    static double initRate();
};
```

The static members of a class exist outside any object. Objects do not contain data associated with static data members. Thus, each Account object will contain two data members—owner and amount. There is only one interestRate object that will be shared by all the Account objects.

Similarly, static member functions are not bound to any object; they do not have a this pointer. As a result, static member functions may not be declared as const, and we may not refer to this in the body of a static member. This restriction applies both to explicit uses of this and to implicit uses of this by calling a nonstatic member.

Using a Class static Member

We can access a static member directly through the scope operator:

```
double r;
r = Account::rate(); // access a static member using the scope operator
```

Even though static members are not part of the objects of its class, we can use an object, reference, or pointer of the class type to access a static member:

```
Account ac1;
Account *ac2 = &ac1;
// equivalent ways to call the static member rate function
r = ac1.rate();      // through an Account object or reference
r = ac2->rate();     // through a pointer to an Account object
```

Member functions can use static members directly, without the scope operator:

```
class Account {
public:
    void calculate() { amount += amount * interestRate; }
private:
    static double interestRate;
    // remaining members as before
};
```

Defining `static` Members

As with any other member function, we can define a `static` member function inside or outside of the class body. When we define a `static` member outside the class, we do not repeat the `static` keyword. The keyword appears only with the declaration inside the class body:

```
void Account::rate(double newRate)
{
    interestRate = newRate;
}
```

As with any class member, when we refer to a class `static` member outside the class body, we must specify the class in which the member is defined. The `static` keyword, however, is used *only* on the declaration inside the class body.

Because `static` data members are not part of individual objects of the class type, they are not defined when we create objects of the class. As a result, they are not initialized by the class' constructors. Moreover, in general, we may not initialize a `static` member inside the class. Instead, we must define and initialize each `static` data member outside the class body. Like any other object, a `static` data member may be defined only once.

Like global objects (§ 6.1.1, p. 204), `static` data members are defined outside any function. Hence, once they are defined, they continue to exist until the program completes.

We define a `static` data member similarly to how we define class member functions outside the class. We name the object's type, followed by the name of the class, the scope operator, and the member's own name:

```
//  define and initialize a static class member
double Account::interestRate = initRate();
```

This statement defines the object named `interestRate` that is a `static` member of class `Account` and has type `double`. Once the class name is seen, the remainder of the definition is in the scope of the class. As a result, we can use `initRate` without qualification as the initializer for `rate`. Note also that even though `initRate` is `private`, we can use this function to initialize `interestRate`. The definition of `interestRate`, like any other member definition, has access to the `private` members of the class.

The best way to ensure that the object is defined exactly once is to put the definition of `static` data members in the same file that contains the definitions of the class noninline member functions.

In-Class Initialization of `static` Data Members

Ordinarily, class `static` members may not be initialized in the class body. However, we can provide in-class initializers for `static` members that have `const` integral type and must do so for `static` members that are `constexprs` of literal type (§ 7.5.6, p. 299). The initializers must be constant expressions. Such members are themselves constant expressions; they can be used where a constant expression is required. For example, we can use an initialized static data member to specify the dimension of an array member:

```
class Account {
public:
    static double rate() { return interestRate; }
    static void rate(double);
private:
    static constexpr int period = 30;// period is a constant expression
    double daily_tbl[period];
};
```

If the member is used only in contexts where the compiler can substitute the member's value, then an initialized const or constexpr static need not be separately defined. However, if we use the member in a context in which the value cannot be substituted, then there must be a definition for that member.

For example, if the only use we make of period is to define the dimension of daily_tbl, there is no need to define period outside of Account. However, if we omit the definition, it is possible that even seemingly trivial changes to the program might cause the program to fail to compile because of the missing definition. For example, if we pass Account::period to a function that takes a const int&, then period must be defined.

If an initializer is provided inside the class, the member's definition must not specify an initial value:

```
// definition of a static member with no initializer
constexpr int Account::period; // initializer provided in the class definition
```

Best Practices

Even if a const static data member is initialized in the class body, that member ordinarily should be defined outside the class definition.

static Members Can Be Used in Ways Ordinary Members Can't

As we've seen, static members exist independently of any other object. As a result, they can be used in ways that would be illegal for nonstatic data members. As one example, a static data member can have incomplete type (§ 7.3.3, p. 278). In particular, a static data member can have the same type as the class type of which it is a member. A nonstatic data member is restricted to being declared as a pointer or a reference to an object of its class:

```
class Bar {
public:
    // ...
private:
    static Bar mem1; // ok: static member can have incomplete type
    Bar *mem2;       // ok: pointer member can have incomplete type
    Bar mem3;        // error: data members must have complete type
};
```

Another difference between `static` and ordinary members is that we can use a `static` member as a default argument (§ 6.5.1, p. 236):

```
class Screen {
public:
    //  bkground refers to the static member
    //  declared later in the class definition
    Screen& clear(char = bkground);
private:
    static const char bkground;
};
```

A nonstatic data member may not be used as a default argument because its value is part of the object of which it is a member. Using a nonstatic data member as a default argument provides no object from which to obtain the member's value and so is an error.

EXERCISES SECTION 7.6

Exercise 7.56: What is a `static` class member? What are the advantages of `static` members? How do they differ from ordinary members?

Exercise 7.57: Write your own version of the `Account` class.

Exercise 7.58: Which, if any, of the following `static` data member declarations and definitions are errors? Explain why.

```
//  example.h
class Example {
public:
    static double rate = 6.5;
    static const int vecSize = 20;
    static vector<double> vec(vecSize);
};
//  example.C
#include "example.h"
double Example::rate;
vector<double> Example::vec;
```

CHAPTER SUMMARY

Classes are the most fundamental feature in C++. Classes let us define new types for our applications, making our programs shorter and easier to modify.

Data abstraction—the ability to define both data and function members—and encapsulation—the ability to protect class members from general access—are fundamental to classes. We encapsulate a class by defining its implementation members as `private`. Classes may grant access to their nonpublic member by designating another class or function as a friend.

Classes may define constructors, which are special member functions that control how objects are initialized. Constructors may be overloaded. Constructors should use a constructor initializer list to initialize all the data members.

Classes may also define `mutable` or `static` members. A `mutable` member is a data member that is never `const`; its value may be changed inside a `const` member function. A `static` member can be either function or data; `static` members exist independently of the objects of the class type.

DEFINED TERMS

abstract data type Data structure that encapsulates (hides) its implementation.

access specifier Keywords `public` and `private`. Used to define whether members are accessible to users of the class or only to friends and members of the class. Specifiers may appear multiple times within a class. Each specifier sets the access of the following members up to the next specifier.

aggregate class Class with only `public` data members that has no in-class initializers or constructors. Members of an aggregate can be initialized by a brace-enclosed list of initializers.

class C++ mechanism for defining our own abstract data types. Classes may have data, function, or type members. A class defines a new type and a new scope.

class declaration The keyword `class` (or `struct`) followed by the class name followed by a semicolon. If a class is declared but not defined, it is an incomplete type.

class keyword Keyword used to define a class; by default members are `private`.

class scope Each class defines a scope. Class scopes are more complicated than

other scopes—member functions defined within the class body may use names that appear even after the definition.

const member function A member function that may not change an object's ordinary (i.e., neither `static` nor `mutable`) data members. The `this` pointer in a `const` member is a pointer to `const`. A member function may be overloaded based on whether the function is `const`.

constructor A special member function used to initialize objects. Each constructor should give each data member a well-defined initial value.

constructor initializer list Specifies initial values of the data members of a class. The members are initialized to the values specified in the initializer list before the body of the constructor executes. Class members that are not initialized in the initializer list are default initialized.

converting constructor A nonexplicit constructor that can be called with a single argument. Such constructors implicitly convert from the argument's type to the class type.

data abstraction Programming technique that focuses on the interface to a type. Data abstraction lets programmers ignore the details of how a type is represented and think instead about the operations that the type can perform. Data abstraction is fundamental to both object-oriented and generic programming.

default constructor Constructor that is used if no initializer is supplied.

delegating constructor Constructor with a constructor-initializer list that has one entry that designates another constructor of the same class to do the initialization.

encapsulation Separation of implementation from interface; encapsulation hides the implementation details of a type. In C++, encapsulation is enforced by putting the implementation in the `private` part of a class.

explicit constructor Constructor that can be called with a single argument but cannot be used in an implicit conversion. A constructor is made explicit by prepending the keyword `explicit` to its declaration.

forward declaration Declaration of an as yet undefined name. Most often used to refer to the declaration of a class that appears prior to the definition of that class. See incomplete type.

friend Mechanism by which a class grants access to its `nonpublic` members. Friends have the same access rights as members. Both classes and functions may be named as friends.

implementation The (usually `private`) members of a class that define the data and any operations that are not intended for use by code that uses the type.

incomplete type Type that is declared but not defined. It is not possible to use an incomplete type to define a variable or class member. It is legal to define references or pointers to incomplete types.

interface The (`public`) operations supported by a type. Ordinarily, the interface does not include data members.

member function Class member that is a function. Ordinary member functions are bound to an object of the class type through the implicit `this` pointer. `static` member functions are not bound to an object and have no `this` pointer. Member functions may be overloaded; when they are, the implicit `this` pointer participates in the function matching.

mutable data member Data member that is never `const`, even when it is a member of a `const` object. A `mutable` member can be changed inside a `const` function.

name lookup Process by which the use of a name is matched to its declaration.

private members Members defined after a `private` access specifier; accessible only to the friends and other class members. Data members and utility functions used by the class that are not part of the type's interface are usually declared `private`.

public members Members defined after a `public` access specifier; accessible to any user of the class. Ordinarily, only the functions that define the interface to the class should be defined in the `public` sections.

struct keyword Keyword used to define a class; by default members are `public`.

synthesized default constructor The default constructor created (synthesized) by the compiler for classes that do not explicitly define any constructors. This constructor initializes the data members from their in-class initializers, if present; otherwise it default initializes the data members.

this pointer Implicit value passed as an extra argument to every `nonstatic` member function. The `this` pointer points to the object on which the function is invoked.

= default Syntax used after the parameter list of the declaration of the default constructor inside a class to signal to the compiler that it should generate the constructor, even if the class has other constructors.

PART II

THE C++ LIBRARY

CONTENTS

With each revision of the C++ language, the library has also grown. Indeed, more than two-thirds of the text of the new standard is devoted to the library. Although we cannot cover every library facility in depth, there are core facilities that the library defines that every C++ programmer should be comfortable using. We cover these core facilities in this part.

We'll start by covering the basic IO library facilities in Chapter 8. Beyond using the library to read and write streams associated with the console window, the library defines types that let us read and write named files and do in-memory IO to strings.

Central to the library are a number of container classes and a family of generic algorithms that let us write programs that are succinct and efficient. The library worries about bookkeeping details—in particular, taking care of memory management—so that our programs can worry about the actual problems we need to solve.

In Chapter 3 we introduced the vector container type. We'll learn more about vector in Chapter 9, which will cover the other sequential container types as well. We'll also cover more operations provided by the string type. We can think of a string as a special kind of container that contains only characters. The string type supports many, but not all, of the container operations.

Chapter 10 introduces the generic algorithms. The algorithms typically operate on a range of elements in a sequential container or other sequence. The algorithms library offers efficient implementations of various classical algorithms, such as sorting and searching, and other common tasks as well. For example, there is a `copy` algorithm, which copies elements from one sequence to another; `find`, which looks for a given element; and so on. The algorithms are generic in two ways: They can be applied to different kinds of sequences, and those sequences may contain elements of most types.

The library also provides several associative containers, which are the topic of Chapter 11. Elements in an associative container are accessed by key. The associative containers share many operations with the sequential containers and also define operations that are specific to the associative containers.

This part concludes with Chapter 12, which looks at language and library facilities for managing dynamic memory. This chapter covers one of the most important new library classes, which are standardized versions of smart pointers. By using smart pointers, we can make code that uses dynamic memory much more robust. This chapter closes with an extended example that uses library facilities introduced throughout Part II.

C H A P T E R 8

THE IO LIBRARY

The C++ language does not deal directly with input and output. Instead, IO is handled by a family of types defined in the standard library. These types support IO to and from devices such as files and console windows. Additional types allow in-memory IO to and from `strings`.

The IO library defines operations to read and write values of the built-in types. In addition, classes, such as `string`, typically define similar IO operations to work on objects of their class type as well.

This chapter introduces the fundamentals of the IO library. Later chapters will cover additional capabilities: Chapter 14 will look at how we can write our own input and output operators, and Chapter 17 will cover how to control formatting and how to perform random access on files.

Our programs have already used many IO library facilities. Indeed, we introduced most of these facilities in § 1.2 (p. 5):

- `istream` (input stream) type, which provides input operations

- `ostream` (output stream) type, which provides output operations

- `cin`, an `istream` object that reads the standard input

- `cout`, an `ostream` object that writes to the standard output

- `cerr`, an `ostream` object, typically used for program error messages, that writes to the standard error

- The `>>` operator, which is used to read input from an `istream` object

- The `<<` operator, which is used to write output to an `ostream` object

- The `getline` function (§ 3.2.2, p. 87), which reads a line of input from a given `istream` into a given `string`

8.1 The IO Classes

The IO types and objects that we've used so far manipulate `char` data. By default these objects are connected to the user's console window. Of course, real programs cannot be limited to doing IO solely to or from a console window. Programs often need to read or write named files. Moreover, it can be convenient to use IO operations to process the characters in a `string`. Applications also may have to read and write languages that require wide-character support.

To support these different kinds of IO processing, the library defines a collection of IO types in addition to the `istream` and `ostream` types that we have already used. These types, which are listed in Table 8.1, are defined in three separate headers: `iostream` defines the basic types used to read from and write to a stream, `fstream` defines the types used to read and write named files, and `sstream` defines the types used to read and write in-memory `string`s.

Table 8.1: IO Library Types and Headers	
Header	**Type**
`iostream`	`istream`, `wistream` reads from a stream
	`ostream`, `wostream` writes to a stream
	`iostream`, `wiostream` reads and writes a stream
`fstream`	`ifstream`, `wifstream` reads from a file
	`ofstream`, `wofstream` writes to a file
	`fstream`, `wfstream` reads and writes a file
`sstream`	`istringstream`, `wistringstream` reads from a `string`
	`ostringstream`, `wostringstream` writes to a `string`
	`stringstream`, `wstringstream` reads and writes a `string`

To support languages that use wide characters, the library defines a set of types and objects that manipulate `wchar_t` data (§ 2.1.1, p. 32). The names of the wide-character versions begin with a w. For example, `wcin`, `wcout`, and `wcerr` are the wide-character objects that correspond to `cin`, `cout`, and `cerr`, respectively. The wide-character types and objects are defined in the same header as the plain `char` types. For example, the `fstream` header defines both the `ifstream` and `wifstream` types.

Relationships among the IO Types

Conceptually, neither the kind of device nor the character size affects the IO operations we want to perform. For example, we'd like to use `>>` to read data regardless of whether we're reading a console window, a disk file, or a `string`. Similarly, we'd like to use that operator regardless of whether the characters we read fit in a `char` or require a `wchar_t`.

The library lets us ignore the differences among these different kinds of streams by using **inheritance**. As with templates (§ 3.3, p. 96), we can use classes related by inheritance without understanding the details of how inheritance works. We'll cover how C++ supports inheritance in Chapter 15 and in § 18.3 (p. 802).

Briefly, inheritance lets us say that a particular class inherits from another class. Ordinarily, we can use an object of an inherited class as if it were an object of the same type as the class from which it inherits.

The types `ifstream` and `istringstream` inherit from `istream`. Thus, we can use objects of type `ifstream` or `istringstream` as if they were `istream` objects. We can use objects of these types in the same ways as we have used `cin`. For example, we can call `getline` on an `ifstream` or `istringstream` object, and we can use the `>>` to read data from an `ifstream` or `istringstream`. Similarly, the types `ofstream` and `ostringstream` inherit from `ostream`. Therefore, we can use objects of these types in the same ways that we have used `cout`.

Everything that we cover in the remainder of this section applies equally to plain streams, file streams, and `string` streams and to the `char` or wide-character stream versions.

8.1.1 No Copy or Assign for IO Objects

As we saw in § 7.1.3 (p. 261), we cannot copy or assign objects of the IO types:

```
ofstream out1, out2;
out1 = out2;                    // error: cannot assign stream objects
ofstream print(ofstream);  // error: can't initialize the ofstream parameter
out2 = print(out2);        // error: cannot copy stream objects
```

Because we can't copy the IO types, we cannot have a parameter or return type that is one of the stream types (§ 6.2.1, p. 209). Functions that do IO typically pass and return the stream through references. Reading or writing an IO object changes its state, so the reference must not be `const`.

8.1.2 Condition States

Inherent in doing IO is the fact that errors can occur. Some errors are recoverable; others occur deep within the system and are beyond the scope of a program to correct. The IO classes define functions and flags, listed in Table 8.2, that let us access and manipulate the **condition state** of a stream.

As an example of an IO error, consider the following code:

```
int ival;
cin >> ival;
```

If we enter Boo on the standard input, the read will fail. The input operator expected to read an int but got the character B instead. As a result, cin will be put in an error state. Similarly, cin will be in an error state if we enter an end-of-file.

Once an error has occurred, subsequent IO operations on that stream will fail. We can read from or write to a stream only when it is in a non-error state. Because a stream might be in an error state, code ordinarily should check whether a stream is okay before attempting to use it. The easiest way to determine the state of a stream object is to use that object as a condition:

```
while (cin >> word)
        // ok: read operation successful . . .
```

The while condition checks the state of the stream returned from the >> expression. If that input operation succeeds, the state remains valid and the condition will succeed.

Interrogating the State of a Stream

Using a stream as a condition tells us only whether the stream is valid. It does not tell us what happened. Sometimes we also need to know why the stream is invalid. For example, what we do after hitting end-of-file is likely to differ from what we'd do if we encounter an error on the IO device.

The IO library defines a machine-dependent integral type named iostate that it uses to convey information about the state of a stream. This type is used as a collection of bits, in the same way that we used the quiz1 variable in § 4.8 (p. 154). The IO classes define four constexpr values (§ 2.4.4, p. 65) of type iostate that represent particular bit patterns. These values are used to indicate particular kinds of IO conditions. They can be used with the bitwise operators (§ 4.8, p. 152) to test or set multiple flags in one operation.

The badbit indicates a system-level failure, such as an unrecoverable read or write error. It is usually not possible to use a stream once badbit has been set. The failbit is set after a recoverable error, such as reading a character when numeric data was expected. It is often possible to correct such problems and continue using the stream. Reaching end-of-file sets both eofbit and failbit. The goodbit, which is guaranteed to have the value 0, indicates no failures on the stream. If any of badbit, failbit, or eofbit are set, then a condition that evaluates that stream will fail.

The library also defines a set of functions to interrogate the state of these flags. The good operation returns true if none of the error bits is set. The bad, fail,

Table 8.2: IO Library Condition State	
strm::iostate	*strm* is one of the IO types listed in Table 8.1 (p. 310). iostate is a machine-dependent integral type that represents the condition state of a stream.
strm::badbit	*strm*::iostate value used to indicate that a stream is corrupted.
strm::failbit	*strm*::iostate value used to indicate that an IO operation failed.
strm::eofbit	*strm*::iostate value used to indicate that a stream hit end-of-file.
strm::goodbit	*strm*::iostate value used to indicate that a stream is not in an error state. This value is guaranteed to be zero.
s.eof()	true if eofbit in the stream s is set.
s.fail()	true if failbit or badbit in the stream s is set.
s.bad()	true if badbit in the stream s is set.
s.good()	true if the stream s is in a valid state.
s.clear()	Reset all condition values in the stream s to valid state. Returns void.
s.clear(flags)	Reset the condition of s to flags. Type of flags is *strm*::iostate. Returns void.
s.setstate(flags)	Adds specified condition(s) to s. Type of flags is *strm*::iostate. Returns void.
s.rdstate()	Returns current condition of s as a *strm*::iostate value.

and eof operations return true when the corresponding bit is on. In addition, fail returns true if bad is set. By implication, the right way to determine the overall state of a stream is to use either good or fail. Indeed, the code that is executed when we use a stream as a condition is equivalent to calling !fail(). The eof and bad operations reveal only whether those specific errors have occurred.

Managing the Condition State

The rdstate member returns an iostate value that corresponds to the current state of the stream. The setstate operation turns on the given condition bit(s) to indicate that a problem occurred. The clear member is overloaded (§ 6.4, p. 230): One version takes no arguments and a second version takes a single argument of type iostate.

The version of clear that takes no arguments turns off all the failure bits. After clear(), a call to good returns true. We might use these members as follows:

```
// remember the current state of cin
auto old_state = cin.rdstate();   // remember the current state of cin
cin.clear();                       // make cin valid
process_input(cin);                // use cin
cin.setstate(old_state);           // now reset cin to its old state
```

The version of clear that takes an argument expects an iostate value that represents the new state of the stream. To turn off a single condition, we use the rdstate member and the bitwise operators to produce the desired new state.

For example, the following turns off `failbit` and `badbit` but leaves `eofbit` untouched:

```
//  turns off failbit and badbit but all other bits unchanged
cin.clear(cin.rdstate() & ~cin.failbit & ~cin.badbit);
```

EXERCISES SECTION 8.1.2

Exercise 8.1: Write a function that takes and returns an `istream&`. The function should read the stream until it hits end-of-file. The function should print what it reads to the standard output. Reset the stream so that it is valid before returning the stream.

Exercise 8.2: Test your function by calling it, passing `cin` as an argument.

Exercise 8.3: What causes the following `while` to terminate?

```
while (cin >> i) /* ...   */
```

8.1.3   Managing the Output Buffer

Each output stream manages a buffer, which it uses to hold the data that the program reads and writes. For example, when the following code is executed

```
os << "please enter a value: ";
```

the literal string might be printed immediately, or the operating system might store the data in a buffer to be printed later. Using a buffer allows the operating system to combine several output operations from our program into a single system-level write. Because writing to a device can be time-consuming, letting the operating system combine several output operations into a single write can provide an important performance boost.

There are several conditions that cause the buffer to be flushed—that is, to be written—to the actual output device or file:

- The program completes normally. All output buffers are flushed as part of the `return` from `main`.

- At some indeterminate time, the buffer can become full, in which case it will be flushed before writing the next value.

- We can flush the buffer explicitly using a manipulator such as `endl` (§ 1.2, p. 7).

- We can use the `unitbuf` manipulator to set the stream's internal state to empty the buffer after each output operation. By default, `unitbuf` is set for `cerr`, so that writes to `cerr` are flushed immediately.

- An output stream might be tied to another stream. In this case, the buffer of the tied stream is flushed whenever the tied stream is read or written. By default, `cin` and `cerr` are both tied to `cout`. Hence, reading `cin` or writing to `cerr` flushes the buffer in `cout`.

Flushing the Output Buffer

Our programs have already used the `endl` manipulator, which ends the current line and flushes the buffer. There are two other similar manipulators: `flush` and `ends`. `flush` flushes the stream but adds no characters to the output; `ends` inserts a null character into the buffer and then flushes it:

```
cout << "hi!" << endl;   // writes hi and a newline, then flushes the buffer
cout << "hi!" << flush;  // writes hi, then flushes the buffer; adds no data
cout << "hi!" << ends;   // writes hi and a null, then flushes the buffer
```

The `unitbuf` Manipulator

If we want to flush after every output, we can use the `unitbuf` manipulator. This manipulator tells the stream to do a `flush` after every subsequent write. The `nounitbuf` manipulator restores the stream to use normal, system-managed buffer flushing:

```
cout << unitbuf;         // all writes will be flushed immediately
// any output is flushed immediately, no buffering
cout << nounitbuf;       // returns to normal buffering
```

> **CAUTION: BUFFERS ARE NOT FLUSHED IF THE PROGRAM CRASHES**
>
> Output buffers are *not* flushed if the program terminates abnormally. When a program crashes, it is likely that data the program wrote may be sitting in an output buffer waiting to be printed.
>
> When you debug a program that has crashed, it is essential to make sure that any output you *think* should have been written was actually flushed. Countless hours of programmer time have been wasted tracking through code that appeared not to have executed when in fact the buffer had not been flushed and the output was pending when the program crashed.

Tying Input and Output Streams Together

When an input stream is tied to an output stream, any attempt to read the input stream will first flush the buffer associated with the output stream. The library ties `cout` to `cin`, so the statement

```
cin >> ival;
```

causes the buffer associated with `cout` to be flushed.

> Interactive systems usually should tie their input stream to their output stream. Doing so means that all output, which might include prompts to the user, will be written before attempting to read the input.

There are two overloaded (§ 6.4, p. 230) versions of `tie`: One version takes no argument and returns a pointer to the output stream, if any, to which this object is currently tied. The function returns the null pointer if the stream is not tied.

The second version of `tie` takes a pointer to an `ostream` and ties itself to that `ostream`. That is, `x.tie(&o)` ties the stream x to the output stream o.

We can tie either an `istream` or an `ostream` object to another `ostream`:

```
cin.tie(&cout);      // illustration only: the library ties cin and cout for us
// old_tie points to the stream (if any) currently tied to cin
ostream *old_tie = cin.tie(nullptr); // cin is no longer tied
// ties cin and cerr; not a good idea because cin should be tied to cout
cin.tie(&cerr);      // reading cin flushes cerr, not cout
cin.tie(old_tie);    // reestablish normal tie between cin and cout
```

To tie a given stream to a new output stream, we pass `tie` a pointer to the new stream. To untie the stream completely, we pass a null pointer. Each stream can be tied to at most one stream at a time. However, multiple streams can tie themselves to the same `ostream`.

8.2 File Input and Output

The `fstream` header defines three types to support file IO: **ifstream** to read from a given file, **ofstream** to write to a given file, and **fstream**, which reads and writes a given file. In § 17.5.3 (p. 763) we'll describe how to use the same file for both input and output.

These types provide the same operations as those we have previously used on the objects `cin` and `cout`. In particular, we can use the IO operators (`<<` and `>>`) to read and write files, we can use `getline` (§ 3.2.2, p. 87) to read an `ifstream`, and the material covered in § 8.1 (p. 310) applies to these types.

In addition to the behavior that they inherit from the `iostream` types, the types defined in `fstream` add members to manage the file associated with the stream. These operations, listed in Table 8.3, can be called on objects of `fstream`, `ifstream`, or `ofstream` but not on the other IO types.

Table 8.3: `fstream`-Specific Operations	
fstream `fstrm;`	Creates an unbound file stream. *fstream* is one of the types defined in the `fstream` header.
fstream `fstrm(s);`	Creates an *fstream* and opens the file named s. s can have type `string` or can be a pointer to a C-style character string (§ 3.5.4, p. 122). These constructors are `explicit` (§ 7.5.4, p. 296). The default file mode depends on the type of *fstream*.
fstream `fstrm(s, mode);`	Like the previous constructor, but opens s in the given mode.
`fstrm.open(s)` `fstrm.open(s, mode)`	Opens the file named by the s and binds that file to `fstrm`. s can be a `string` or a pointer to a C-style character string. The default file mode depends on the type of *fstream*. Returns `void`.
`fstrm.close()`	Closes the file to which `fstrm` is bound. Returns `void`.
`fstrm.is_open()`	Returns a `bool` indicating whether the file associated with `fstrm` was successfully opened and has not been closed.

8.2.1 Using File Stream Objects

When we want to read or write a file, we define a file stream object and associate that object with the file. Each file stream class defines a member function named `open` that does whatever system-specific operations are required to locate the given file and open it for reading or writing as appropriate.

When we create a file stream, we can (optionally) provide a file name. When we supply a file name, `open` is called automatically:

```
ifstream in(ifile); // construct an ifstream and open the given file
ofstream out;       // output file stream that is not associated with any file
```

This code defines `in` as an input stream that is initialized to read from the file named by the `string` argument `ifile`. It defines `out` as an output stream that is not yet associated with a file. With the new standard, file names can be either library `strings` or C-style character arrays (§ 3.5.4, p. 122). Previous versions of the library allowed only C-style character arrays.

Using an `fstream` in Place of an `iostream&`

As we noted in § 8.1 (p. 311), we can use an object of an inherited type in places where an object of the original type is expected. This fact means that functions that are written to take a reference (or pointer) to one of the `iostream` types can be called on behalf of the corresponding `fstream` (or `sstream`) type. That is, if we have a function that takes an `ostream&`, we can call that function passing it an `ofstream` object, and similarly for `istream&` and `ifstream`.

For example, we can use the `read` and `print` functions from § 7.1.3 (p. 261) to read from and write to named files. In this example, we'll assume that the names of the input and output files are passed as arguments to `main` (§ 6.2.5, p. 218):

```
ifstream input(argv[1]);    // open the file of sales transactions
ofstream output(argv[2]);   // open the output file
Sales_data total;           // variable to hold the running sum
if (read(input, total)) {   // read the first transaction
    Sales_data trans;       // variable to hold data for the next transaction
    while(read(input, trans)) {    // read the remaining transactions
        if (total.isbn() == trans.isbn()) // check isbns
            total.combine(trans);  // update the running total
        else {
            print(output, total) << endl; // print the results
            total = trans;         // process the next book
        }
    }
    print(output, total) << endl;  // print the last transaction
} else                             // there was no input
    cerr << "No data?!" << endl;
```

Aside from using named files, this code is nearly identical to the version of the addition program on page 255. The important part is the calls to `read` and to `print`. We can pass our `fstream` objects to these functions even though the parameters to those functions are defined as `istream&` and `ostream&`, respectively.

The `open` and `close` Members

When we define an empty file stream object, we can subsequently associate that object with a file by calling `open`:

```
ifstream in(ifile);  // construct an ifstream and open the given file
ofstream out;        // output file stream that is not associated with any file
out.open(ifile + ".copy");  // open the specified file
```

If a call to `open` fails, `failbit` is set (§ 8.1.2, p. 312). Because a call to `open` might fail, it is usually a good idea to verify that the `open` succeeded:

```
if (out)       // check that the open succeeded
    //  the open succeeded, so we can use the file
```

This condition is similar to those we've used on `cin`. If the `open` fails, this condition will fail and we will not attempt to use `in`.

Once a file stream has been opened, it remains associated with the specified file. Indeed, calling `open` on a file stream that is already open will fail and set `failbit`. Subsequent attempts to use that file stream will fail. To associate a file stream with a different file, we must first close the existing file. Once the file is closed, we can open a new one:

```
in.close();          // close the file
in.open(ifile + "2");  // open another file
```

If the `open` succeeds, then `open` sets the stream's state so that `good()` is `true`.

Automatic Construction and Destruction

Consider a program whose `main` function takes a list of files it should process (§ 6.2.5, p. 218). Such a program might have a loop like the following:

```
//  for each file passed to the program
for (auto p = argv + 1; p != argv + argc; ++p) {
    ifstream input(*p);    // create input and open the file
    if (input) {           // if the file is ok, "process" this file
        process(input);
    } else
        cerr << "couldn't open: " + string(*p);
} //  input goes out of scope and is destroyed on each iteration
```

Each iteration constructs a new `ifstream` object named `input` and opens it to read the given file. As usual, we check that the `open` succeeded. If so, we pass that file to a function that will read and process the input. If not, we print an error message and continue.

Because `input` is local to the `while`, it is created and destroyed on each iteration (§ 5.4.1, p. 183). When an `fstream` object goes out of scope, the file it is bound to is automatically closed. On the next iteration, `input` is created anew.

Note When an `fstream` object is destroyed, `close` is called automatically.

Exercise 8.4: Write a function to open a file for input and read its contents into a `vector` of `strings`, storing each line as a separate element in the `vector`.

Exercise 8.5: Rewrite the previous program to store each word in a separate element.

Exercise 8.6: Rewrite the bookstore program from § 7.1.1 (p. 256) to read its transactions from a file. Pass the name of the file as an argument to `main` (§ 6.2.5, p. 218).

8.2.2 File Modes

Each stream has an associated **file mode** that represents how the file may be used. Table 8.4 lists the file modes and their meanings.

Table 8.4: File Modes	
`in`	Open for input
`out`	Open for output
`app`	Seek to the end before every write
`ate`	Seek to the end immediately after the open
`trunc`	Truncate the file
`binary`	Do IO operations in binary mode

We can supply a file mode whenever we open a file—either when we call `open` or when we indirectly open the file when we initialize a stream from a file name. The modes that we can specify have the following restrictions:

- `out` may be set only for an `ofstream` or `fstream` object.
- `in` may be set only for an `ifstream` or `fstream` object.
- `trunc` may be set only when `out` is also specified.
- `app` mode may be specified so long as `trunc` is not. If `app` is specified, the file is always opened in output mode, even if `out` was not explicitly specified.
- By default, a file opened in `out` mode is truncated even if we do not specify `trunc`. To preserve the contents of a file opened with `out`, either we must also specify `app`, in which case we can write only at the end of the file, or we must also specify `in`, in which case the file is open for both input and output (§ 17.5.3 (p. 763) will cover using the same file for input and output).
- The `ate` and `binary` modes may be specified on any file stream object type and in combination with any other file modes.

Each file stream type defines a default file mode that is used whenever we do not otherwise specify a mode. Files associated with an `ifstream` are opened in `in` mode; files associated with an `ofstream` are opened in `out` mode; and files associated with an `fstream` are opened with both `in` and `out` modes.

Opening a File in out Mode Discards Existing Data

By default, when we open an ofstream, the contents of the file are discarded. The only way to prevent an ostream from emptying the given file is to specify app:

```
//  file1 is truncated in each of these cases
ofstream out("file1");      //  out and trunc are implicit
ofstream out2("file1", ofstream::out);      //  trunc is implicit
ofstream out3("file1", ofstream::out | ofstream::trunc);
//  to preserve the file's contents, we must explicitly specify app mode
ofstream app("file2", ofstream::app);      //  out is implicit
ofstream app2("file2", ofstream::out | ofstream::app);
```

 The only way to preserve the existing data in a file opened by an ofstream is to specify app or in mode explicitly.

File Mode Is Determined Each Time open Is Called

The file mode of a given stream may change each time a file is opened.

```
ofstream out;      //  no file mode is set
out.open("scratchpad"); //  mode implicitly out and trunc
out.close();      //  close out so we can use it for a different file
out.open("precious", ofstream::app);   //  mode is out and app
out.close();
```

The first call to open does not specify an output mode explicitly; this file is implicitly opened in out mode. As usual, out implies trunc. Therefore, the file named scratchpad in the current directory will be truncated. When we open the file named precious, we ask for append mode. Any data in the file remains, and all writes are done at the end of the file.

 Any time open is called, the file mode is set, either explicitly or implicitly. Whenever a mode is not specified, the default value is used.

EXERCISES SECTION 8.2.2

Exercise 8.7: Revise the bookstore program from the previous section to write its output to a file. Pass the name of that file as a second argument to main.

Exercise 8.8: Revise the program from the previous exercise to append its output to its given file. Run the program on the same output file at least twice to ensure that the data are preserved.

8.3 **string** Streams

The sstream header defines three types to support in-memory IO; these types read from or write to a string as if the string were an IO stream.

The **istringstream** type reads a string, **ostringstream** writes a string, and **stringstream** reads and writes the string. Like the fstream types, the types defined in sstream inherit from the types we have used from the iostream header. In addition to the operations they inherit, the types defined in sstream add members to manage the string associated with the stream. These operations are listed in Table 8.5. They may be called on stringstream objects but not on the other IO types.

Note that although fstream and sstream share the interface to iostream, they have no other interrelationship. In particular, we cannot use open and close on a stringstream, nor can we use str on an fstream.

Table 8.5: **stringstream**-Specific Operations	
sstream strm;	strm is an unbound stringstream. *sstream* is one of the types defined in the sstream header.
sstream strm(s);	strm is an *sstream* that holds a copy of the string s. This constructor is explicit (§ 7.5.4, p. 296).
strm.str()	Returns a copy of the string that strm holds.
strm.str(s)	Copies the string s into strm. Returns void.

8.3.1 Using an **istringstream**

An istringstream is often used when we have some work to do on an entire line, and other work to do with individual words within a line.

As one example, assume we have a file that lists people and their associated phone numbers. Some people have only one number, but others have several—a home phone, work phone, cell number, and so on. Our input file might look like the following:

```
morgan 2015552368 8625550123
drew 9735550130
lee 6095550132 2015550175 8005550000
```

Each record in this file starts with a name, which is followed by one or more phone numbers. We'll start by defining a simple class to represent our input data:

```
// members are public by default; see § 7.2 (p. 268)
struct PersonInfo {
    string name;
    vector<string> phones;
};
```

Objects of type PersonInfo will have one member that represents the person's name and a vector holding a varying number of associated phone numbers.

Our program will read the data file and build up a `vector` of `PersonInfo`. Each element in the `vector` will correspond to one record in the file. We'll process the input in a loop that reads a record and then extracts the name and phone numbers for each person:

```
string line, word;   // will hold a line and word from input, respectively
vector<PersonInfo> people;   // will hold all the records from the input
// read the input a line at a time until cin hits end-of-file (or another error)
while (getline(cin, line)) {
    PersonInfo info;        // create an object to hold this record's data
    istringstream record(line); // bind record to the line we just read
    record >> info.name;   // read the name
    while (record >> word)       // read the phone numbers
        info.phones.push_back(word);   // and store them
    people.push_back(info); // append this record to people
}
```

Here we use `getline` to read an entire record from the standard input. If the call to `getline` succeeds, then `line` holds a record from the input file. Inside the `while` we define a local `PersonInfo` object to hold data from the current record.

Next we bind an `istringstream` to the line that we just read. We can now use the input operator on that `istringstream` to read each element in the current record. We first read the name followed by a `while` loop that will read the phone numbers for that person.

The inner `while` ends when we've read all the data in `line`. This loop works analogously to others we've written to read `cin`. The difference is that this loop reads data from a `string` rather than from the standard input. When the `string` has been completely read, "end-of-file" is signaled and the next input operation on `record` will fail.

We end the outer `while` loop by appending the `PersonInfo` we just processed to the `vector`. The outer `while` continues until we hit end-of-file on `cin`.

EXERCISES SECTION 8.3.1

Exercise 8.9: Use the function you wrote for the first exercise in § 8.1.2 (p. 314) to print the contents of an `istringstream` object.

Exercise 8.10: Write a program to store each line from a file in a `vector<string>`. Now use an `istringstream` to read each element from the `vector` a word at a time.

Exercise 8.11: The program in this section defined its `istringstream` object inside the outer `while` loop. What changes would you need to make if `record` were defined outside that loop? Rewrite the program, moving the definition of `record` outside the `while`, and see whether you thought of all the changes that are needed.

Exercise 8.12: Why didn't we use in-class initializers in `PersonInfo`?

8.3.2 Using `ostringstreams`

An `ostringstream` is useful when we need to build up our output a little at a time but do not want to print the output until later. For example, we might want to validate and reformat the phone numbers we read in the previous example. If all the numbers are valid, we want to print a new file containing the reformatted numbers. If a person has any invalid numbers, we won't put them in the new file. Instead, we'll write an error message containing the person's name and a list of their invalid numbers.

Because we don't want to include any data for a person with an invalid number, we can't produce the output until we've seen and validated all their numbers. We can, however, "write" the output to an in-memory `ostringstream`:

```
for (const auto &entry : people) {     // for each entry in people
    ostringstream formatted, badNums; // objects created on each loop
    for (const auto &nums : entry.phones) {  // for each number
        if (!valid(nums)) {
            badNums << " " << nums;   // string in badNums
        } else
            // "writes" to formatted's string
            formatted << " " << format(nums);
    }
    if (badNums.str().empty())        // there were no bad numbers
        os << entry.name << " "       // print the name
            << formatted.str() << endl; // and reformatted numbers
    else                              // otherwise, print the name and bad numbers
        cerr << "input error: " << entry.name
            << " invalid number(s) " << badNums.str() << endl;
}
```

In this program, we've assumed two functions, `valid` and `format`, that validate and reformat phone numbers, respectively. The interesting part of the program is the use of the string streams `formatted` and `badNums`. We use the normal output operator (`<<`) to write to these objects. But, these "writes" are really `string` manipulations. They add characters to the `strings` inside `formatted` and `badNums`, respectively.

EXERCISES SECTION 8.3.2

Exercise 8.13: Rewrite the phone number program from this section to read from a named file rather than from `cin`.

Exercise 8.14: Why did we declare `entry` and `nums` as `const auto &`?

CHAPTER SUMMARY

C++ uses library classes to handle stream-oriented input and output:

- The `iostream` classes handle IO to console
- The `fstream` classes handle IO to named files
- The `stringstream` classes do IO to in-memory `strings`

The `fstream` and `stringstream` classes are related by inheritance to the `iostream` classes. The input classes inherit from `istream` and the output classes from `ostream`. Thus, operations that can be performed on an `istream` object can also be performed on either an `ifstream` or an `istringstream`. Similarly for the output classes, which inherit from `ostream`.

Each IO object maintains a set of condition states that indicate whether IO can be done through this object. If an error is encountered—such as hitting end-of-file on an input stream—then the object's state will be such that no further input can be done until the error is rectified. The library provides a set of functions to set and test these states.

DEFINED TERMS

condition state Flags and associated functions usable by any of the stream classes that indicate whether a given stream is usable.

file mode Flags defined by the `fstream` classes that are specified when opening a file and control how a file can be used.

file stream Stream object that reads or writes a named file. In addition to the normal `iostream` operations, file streams also define `open` and `close` members. The `open` member takes a `string` or a C-style character string that names the file to open and an optional open mode argument. The `close` member closes the file to which the stream is attached. It must be called before another file can be opened.

fstream File stream that reads and writes to the same file. By default `fstream`s are opened with `in` and `out` mode set.

ifstream File stream that reads an input file. By default `ifstream`s are opened with `in` mode set.

inheritance Programming feature that lets a type inherit the interface of another type. The `ifstream` and `istringstream` classes inherit from `istream` and the `ofstream` and `ostringstream` classes inherit from `ostream`. Chapter 15 covers inheritance.

istringstream String stream that reads a given `string`.

ofstream File stream that writes to an output file. By default, `ofstream`s are opened with `out` mode set.

ostringstream String stream that writes to a given `string`.

string stream Stream object that reads or writes a `string`. In addition to the normal `iostream` operations, string streams define an overloaded member named `str`. Calling `str` with no arguments returns the `string` to which the string stream is attached. Calling it with a `string` attaches the string stream to a copy of that `string`.

stringstream String stream that reads and writes to a given `string`.

CHAPTER 9

SEQUENTIAL CONTAINERS

CONTENTS

This chapter expands on the material from Chapter 3 and completes our discussion of the standard-library sequential containers. The order of the elements in a sequential container corresponds to the positions in which the elements are added to the container. The library also defines several associative containers, which hold elements whose position depends on a key associated with each element. We'll cover operations specific to the associative containers in Chapter 11.

The container classes share a common interface, which each of the containers extends in its own way. This common interface makes the library easier to learn; what we learn about one kind of container applies to another. Each kind of container offers a different set of performance and functionality trade-offs.

A container holds a collection of objects of a specified type. The **sequential containers** let the programmer control the order in which the elements are stored and accessed. That order does not depend on the values of the elements. Instead, the order corresponds to the position at which elements are put into the container. By contrast, the ordered and unordered associative containers, which we cover in Chapter 11, store their elements based on the value of a key.

The library also provides three container adaptors, each of which adapts a container type by defining a different interface to the container's operations. We cover the adaptors at the end of this chapter.

> *Note* This chapter builds on the material covered in § 3.2, § 3.3, and § 3.4. We assume that the reader is familiar with the material covered there.

9.1 Overview of the Sequential Containers

The sequential containers, which are listed in Table 9.1, all provide fast sequential access to their elements. However, these containers offer different performance trade-offs relative to

- The costs to add or delete elements to the container

- The costs to perform nonsequential access to elements of the container

Table 9.1: Sequential Container Types	
vector	Flexible-size array. Supports fast random access. Inserting or deleting elements other than at the back may be slow.
deque	Double-ended queue. Supports fast random access. Fast insert/delete at front or back.
list	Doubly linked list. Supports only bidirectional sequential access. Fast insert/delete at any point in the list.
forward_list	Singly linked list. Supports only sequential access in one direction. Fast insert/delete at any point in the list.
array	Fixed-size array. Supports fast random access. Cannot add or remove elements.
string	A specialized container, similar to vector, that contains characters. Fast random access. Fast insert/delete at the back.

With the exception of array, which is a fixed-size container, the containers provide efficient, flexible memory management. We can add and remove elements, growing and shrinking the size of the container. The strategies that the containers use for storing their elements have inherent, and sometimes significant, impact on the efficiency of these operations. In some cases, these strategies also affect whether a particular container supplies a particular operation.

For example, string and vector hold their elements in contiguous memory. Because elements are contiguous, it is fast to compute the address of an element from its index. However, adding or removing elements in the middle of one of these containers takes time: All the elements after the one inserted or removed have to be moved to maintain contiguity. Moreover, adding an element can sometimes require that additional storage be allocated. In that case, every element must be moved into the new storage.

The `list` and `forward_list` containers are designed to make it fast to add or remove an element anywhere in the container. In exchange, these types do not support random access to elements: We can access an element only by iterating through the container. Moreover, the memory overhead for these containers is often substantial, when compared to `vector`, `deque`, and `array`.

A `deque` is a more complicated data structure. Like `string` and `vector`, `deque` supports fast random access. As with `string` and `vector`, adding or removing elements in the middle of a `deque` is a (potentially) expensive operation. However, adding or removing elements at either end of the `deque` is a fast operation, comparable to adding an element to a `list` or `forward_list`.

The `forward_list` and `array` types were added by the new standard. An `array` is a safer, easier-to-use alternative to built-in arrays. Like built-in arrays, library `array`s have fixed size. As a result, `array` does not support operations to add and remove elements or to resize the container. A `forward_list` is intended to be comparable to the best handwritten, singly linked list. Consequently, `forward_list` does not have the `size` operation because storing or computing its size would entail overhead compared to a handwritten list. For the other containers, `size` is guaranteed to be a fast, constant-time operation.

For reasons we'll explain in § 13.6 (p. 531), the new library containers are dramatically faster than in previous releases. The library containers almost certainly perform as well as (and usually better than) even the most carefully crafted alternatives. Modern C++ programs should use the library containers rather than more primitive structures like arrays.

Deciding Which Sequential Container to Use

Ordinarily, it is best to use `vector` unless there is a good reason to prefer another container.

There are a few rules of thumb that apply to selecting which container to use:

- Unless you have a reason to use another container, use a `vector`.

- If your program has lots of small elements and space overhead matters, don't use `list` or `forward_list`.

- If the program requires random access to elements, use a `vector` or a `deque`.

- If the program needs to insert or delete elements in the middle of the container, use a `list` or `forward_list`.

- If the program needs to insert or delete elements at the front and the back, but not in the middle, use a `deque`.

- If the program needs to insert elements in the middle of the container only while reading input, and subsequently needs random access to the elements:

    - First, decide whether you actually need to add elements in the middle of a container. It is often easier to append to a vector and then call the library sort function (which we shall cover in § 10.2.3 (p. 384)) to reorder the container when you're done with input.

    - If you must insert into the middle, consider using a list for the input phase. Once the input is complete, copy the list into a vector.

What if the program needs random access *and* needs to insert and delete elements in the middle of the container? This decision will depend on the relative cost of accessing the elements in a list or forward_list versus the cost of inserting or deleting elements in a vector or deque. In general, the predominant operation of the application (whether it does more access or more insertion or deletion) will determine the choice of container type. In such cases, performance testing the application using both containers will probably be necessary.

> **Best Practices**
>
> If you're not sure which container to use, write your code so that it uses only operations common to both vectors and lists: Use iterators, not subscripts, and avoid random access to elements. That way it will be easy to use either a vector or a list as necessary.

EXERCISES SECTION 9.1

Exercise 9.1: Which is the most appropriate—a vector, a deque, or a list—for the following program tasks? Explain the rationale for your choice. If there is no reason to prefer one or another container, explain why not.

(a) Read a fixed number of words, inserting them in the container alphabetically as they are entered. We'll see in the next chapter that associative containers are better suited to this problem.

(b) Read an unknown number of words. Always insert new words at the back. Remove the next value from the front.

(c) Read an unknown number of integers from a file. Sort the numbers and then print them to standard output.

 ## 9.2 Container Library Overview

The operations on the container types form a kind of hierarchy:

- Some operations (Table 9.2 (p. 330)) are provided by all container types.

- Other operations are specific to the sequential (Table 9.3 (p. 335)), the associative (Table 11.7 (p. 438)), or the unordered (Table 11.8 (p. 445)) containers.

- Still others are common to only a smaller subset of the containers.

In this section, we'll cover aspects common to all of the containers. The remainder of this chapter will then focus solely on sequential containers; we'll cover operations specific to the associative containers in Chapter 11.

In general, each container is defined in a header file with the same name as the type. That is, deque is in the deque header, list in the list header, and so on. The containers are class templates (§ 3.3, p. 96). As with vectors, we must supply additional information to generate a particular container type. For most, but not all, of the containers, the information we must supply is the element type:

```
list<Sales_data>    // list that holds Sales_data objects
deque<double>       // deque that holds doubles
```

Constraints on Types That a Container Can Hold

Almost any type can be used as the element type of a sequential container. In particular, we can define a container whose element type is itself another container. We define such containers exactly as we do any other container type: We specify the element type (which in this case is a container type) inside angle brackets:

```
vector<vector<string>> lines;      // vector of vectors
```

Here lines is a vector whose elements are vectors of strings.

 Older compilers may require a space between the angle brackets, for example, vector<vector<string> >.

Although we can store almost any type in a container, some container operations impose requirements of their own on the element type. We can define a container for a type that does not support an operation-specific requirement, but we can use an operation only if the element type meets that operation's requirements.

As an example, the sequential container constructor that takes a size argument (§ 3.3.1, p. 98) uses the element type's default constructor. Some classes do not have a default constructor. We can define a container that holds objects of such types, but we cannot construct such containers using only an element count:

```
// assume noDefault is a type without a default constructor
vector<noDefault> v1(10, init); // ok: element initializer supplied
vector<noDefault> v2(10);       // error: must supply an element initializer
```

As we describe the container operations, we'll note the additional constraints, if any, that each container operation places on the element type.

Table 9.2: Container Operations	
Type Aliases	
`iterator`	Type of the iterator for this container type
`const_iterator`	Iterator type that can read but not change its elements
`size_type`	Unsigned integral type big enough to hold the size of the largest possible container of this container type
`difference_type`	Signed integral type big enough to hold the distance between two iterators
`value_type`	Element type
`reference`	Element's lvalue type; synonym for `value_type&`
`const_reference`	Element's `const` lvalue type (i.e., `const value_type&`)
Construction	
`C c;`	Default constructor, empty container (`array`; see p. 336)
`C c1(c2);`	Construct `c1` as a copy of `c2`
`C c(b, e);`	Copy elements from the range denoted by iterators b and e; **(not valid for `array`)**
`C c{a,b,c...};`	List initialize c
Assignment and `swap`	
`c1 = c2`	Replace elements in `c1` with those in `c2`
`c1 = {a,b,c...}`	Replace elements in `c1` with those in the list **(not valid for `array`)**
`a.swap(b)`	Swap elements in a with those in b
`swap(a, b)`	Equivalent to `a.swap(b)`
Size	
`c.size()`	Number of elements in c **(not valid for `forward_list`)**
`c.max_size()`	Maximum number of elements c can hold
`c.empty()`	`false` if c has any elements, `true` otherwise
Add/Remove Elements (*not valid for `array`*)	
Note: the interface to these operations varies by container type	
`c.insert`(*args*)	Copy element(s) as specified by *args* into c
`c.emplace`(*inits*)	Use *inits* to construct an element in c
`c.erase`(*args*)	Remove element(s) specified by *args*
`c.clear()`	Remove all elements from c; returns `void`
Equality and Relational Operators	
`==, !=`	Equality valid for all container types
`<, <=, >, >=`	Relationals **(not valid for unordered associative containers)**
Obtain Iterators	
`c.begin(), c.end()`	Return iterator to the first, one past the last element in c
`c.cbegin(), c.cend()`	Return `const_iterator`
Additional Members of Reversible Containers (not valid for `forward_list`)	
`reverse_iterator`	Iterator that addresses elements in reverse order
`const_reverse_iterator`	Reverse iterator that cannot write the elements
`c.rbegin(), c.rend()`	Return iterator to the last, one past the first element in c
`c.crbegin(), c.crend()`	Return `const_reverse_iterator`

9.2.1 Iterators

As with the containers, iterators have a common interface: If an iterator provides an operation, then the operation is supported in the same way for each iterator that supplies that operation. For example, all the iterators on the standard container types let us access an element from a container, and they all do so by providing the dereference operator. Similarly, the iterators for the library containers all define the increment operator to move from one element to the next.

With one exception, the container iterators support all the operations listed in Table 3.6 (p. 107). The exception is that the `forward_list` iterators do not support the decrement (`--`) operator. The iterator arithmetic operations listed in Table 3.7 (p. 111) apply only to iterators for `string`, `vector`, `deque`, and `array`. We cannot use these operations on iterators for any of the other container types.

Iterator Ranges

> The concept of an iterator range is fundamental to the standard library.

An **iterator range** is denoted by a pair of iterators each of which refers to an element, or to *one past the last element*, in the same container. These two iterators, often referred to as `begin` and `end`—or (somewhat misleadingly) as `first` and `last`—mark a range of elements from the container.

The name `last`, although commonly used, is a bit misleading, because the second iterator never refers to the last element of the range. Instead, it refers to a point one past the last element. The elements in the range include the element denoted by `first` and every element from `first` up to but not including `last`.

This element range is called a **left-inclusive interval**. The standard mathematical notation for such a range is

> [`begin`, `end`)

indicating that the range begins with `begin` and ends with, but does not include, `end`. The iterators `begin` and `end` must refer to the same container. The iterator `end` may be equal to `begin` but must not refer to an element before the one denoted by `begin`.

REQUIREMENTS ON ITERATORS FORMING AN ITERATOR RANGE

Two iterators, `begin` and `end`, form an iterator range, if

- They refer to elements of, or one past the end of, the same container, and

- It is possible to reach `end` by repeatedly incrementing `begin`. In other words, `end` must not precede `begin`.

⚠ **WARNING** The compiler cannot enforce these requirements. It is up to us to ensure that our programs follow these conventions.

Programming Implications of Using Left-Inclusive Ranges

The library uses left-inclusive ranges because such ranges have three convenient properties. Assuming `begin` and `end` denote a valid iterator range, then

- If `begin` equals `end`, the range is empty

- If `begin` is not equal to `end`, there is at least one element in the range, and `begin` refers to the first element in that range

- We can increment `begin` some number of times until `begin == end`

These properties mean that we can safely write loops such as the following to process a range of elements:

```
while (begin != end) {
    *begin = val;      //  ok: range isn't empty so begin denotes an element
    ++begin;           //  advance the iterator to get the next element
}
```

Given that `begin` and `end` form a valid iterator range, we know that if `begin == end`, then the range is empty. In this case, we exit the loop. If the range is nonempty, we know that `begin` refers to an element in this nonempty range. Therefore, inside the body of the `while`, we know that it is safe to dereference `begin` because `begin` must refer to an element. Finally, because the loop body increments `begin`, we also know the loop will eventually terminate.

> ### EXERCISES SECTION 9.2.1
>
> **Exercise 9.3:** What are the constraints on the iterators that form iterator ranges?
>
> **Exercise 9.4:** Write a function that takes a pair of iterators to a `vector<int>` and an `int` value. Look for that value in the range and return a `bool` indicating whether it was found.
>
> **Exercise 9.5:** Rewrite the previous program to return an iterator to the requested element. Note that the program must handle the case where the element is not found.
>
> **Exercise 9.6:** What is wrong with the following program? How might you correct it?
> ```
> list<int> lst1;
> list<int>::iterator iter1 = lst1.begin(),
>                     iter2 = lst1.end();
> while (iter1 < iter2) /*   ...   */
> ```

9.2.2 Container Type Members

Each container defines several types, shown in Table 9.2 (p. 330). We have already used three of these container-defined types: `size_type` (§ 3.2.2, p. 88), `iterator`, and `const_iterator` (§ 3.4.1, p. 108).

In addition to the iterator types we've already used, most containers provide reverse iterators. Briefly, a reverse iterator is an iterator that goes backward through a container and inverts the meaning of the iterator operations. For example, saying ++ on a reverse iterator yields the previous element. We'll have more to say about reverse iterators in § 10.4.3 (p. 407).

The remaining type aliases let us use the type of the elements stored in a container without knowing what that type is. If we need the element type, we refer to the container's value_type. If we need a reference to that type, we use reference or const_reference. These element-related type aliases are most useful in generic programs, which we'll cover in Chapter 16.

To use one of these types, we must name the class of which they are a member:

```
// iter is the iterator type defined by list<string>
list<string>::iterator iter;
// count is the difference_type type defined by vector<int>
vector<int>::difference_type count;
```

These declarations use the scope operator (§ 1.2, p. 8) to say that we want the iterator member of the list<string> class and the difference_type defined by vector<int>, respectively.

9.2.3 begin and end Members

The begin and end operations (§ 3.4.1, p. 106) yield iterators that refer to the first and one past the last element in the container. These iterators are most often used to form an iterator range that encompasses all the elements in the container.

As shown in Table 9.2 (p. 330), there are several versions of begin and end: The versions with an r return reverse iterators (which we cover in § 10.4.3 (p. 407)). Those that start with a c return the const version of the related iterator:

```
list<string> a = {"Milton", "Shakespeare", "Austen"};
auto it1 = a.begin();   // list<string>::iterator
auto it2 = a.rbegin();  // list<string>::reverse_iterator
auto it3 = a.cbegin();  // list<string>::const_iterator
auto it4 = a.crbegin(); // list<string>::const_reverse_iterator
```

The functions that do not begin with a c are overloaded. That is, there are actually two members named begin. One is a const member (§ 7.1.2, p. 258) that returns the container's const_iterator type. The other is nonconst and returns the container's iterator type. Similarly for rbegin, end, and rend. When we

call one of these members on a nonconst object, we get the version that returns
`iterator`. We get a `const` version of the iterators *only* when we call these functions on a `const` object. As with pointers and references to `const`, we can convert
a plain `iterator` to the corresponding `const_iterator`, but not vice versa.

The c versions were introduced by the new standard to support using `auto`
with `begin` and `end` functions (§ 2.5.2, p. 68). In the past, we had no choice but to
say which type of iterator we want:

```
// type is explicitly specified
list<string>::iterator it5 = a.begin();
list<string>::const_iterator it6 = a.begin();
// iterator or const_iterator depending on a's type of a
auto it7 = a.begin();   // const_iterator only if a is const
auto it8 = a.cbegin();  // it8 is const_iterator
```

When we use `auto` with `begin` or `end`, the iterator type we get depends on the
container type. How we intend to use the iterator is irrelevant. The c versions let
us get a `const_iterator` regardless of the type of the container.

> **Best Practices**   When write access is not needed, use `cbegin` and `cend`.

EXERCISES SECTION 9.2.3

Exercise 9.9: What is the difference between the `begin` and `cbegin` functions?

Exercise 9.10: What are the types of the following four objects?
```
vector<int> v1;
const vector<int> v2;
auto it1 = v1.begin(), it2 = v2.begin();
auto it3 = v1.cbegin(), it4 = v2.cbegin();
```

9.2.4 Defining and Initializing a Container

Every container type defines a default constructor (§ 7.1.4, p. 263). With the exception of `array`, the default constructor creates an empty container of the specified
type. Again excepting `array`, the other constructors take arguments that specify
the size of the container and initial values for the elements.

Initializing a Container as a Copy of Another Container

There are two ways to create a new container as a copy of another one: We can
directly copy the container, or (excepting `array`) we can copy a range of elements
denoted by a pair of iterators.

To create a container as a copy of another container, the container and element
types must match. When we pass iterators, there is no requirement that the container types be identical. Moreover, the element types in the new and original

Table 9.3: Defining and Initializing Containers

`C c;`	Default constructor. If `C` is `array`, then the elements in `c` are default-initialized; otherwise `c` is empty.
`C c1(c2)` `C c1 = c2`	`c1` is a copy of `c2`. `c1` and `c2` must have the same type (i.e., they must be the same container type and hold the same element type; for `array` must also have the same size).
`C c{a,b,c...}` `C c = {a,b,c...}`	`c` is a copy of the elements in the initializer list. Type of elements in the list must be compatible with the element type of `C`. For `array`, the list must have same number or fewer elements than the size of the `array`, any missing elements are value-initialized (§ 3.3.1, p. 98).
`C c(b, e)`	`c` is a copy of the elements in the range denoted by iterators `b` and `e`. Type of the elements must be compatible with the element type of `C`. **(Not valid for `array`.)**

Constructors that take a size are valid for sequential containers (not including `array`) only

`C seq(n)`	`seq` has n value-initialized elements; this constructor is `explicit` (§ 7.5.4, p. 296). **(Not valid for `string`.)**
`C seq(n,t)`	`seq` has n elements with value `t`.

containers can differ as long as it is possible to convert (§ 4.11, p. 159) the elements we're copying to the element type of the container we are initializing:

```
// each container has three elements, initialized from the given initializers
list<string> authors = {"Milton", "Shakespeare", "Austen"};
vector<const char*> articles = {"a", "an", "the"};

list<string> list2(authors);       // ok: types match
deque<string> authList(authors);   // error: container types don't match
vector<string> words(articles);    // error: element types must match
// ok: converts const char* elements to string
forward_list<string> words(articles.begin(), articles.end());
```

 When we initialize a container as a copy of another container, the container type and element type of both containers must be identical.

The constructor that takes two iterators uses them to denote a range of elements that we want to copy. As usual, the iterators mark the first and one past the last element to be copied. The new container has the same size as the number of elements in the range. Each element in the new container is initialized by the value of the corresponding element in the range.

Because the iterators denote a range, we can use this constructor to copy a subsequence of a container. For example, assuming `it` is an iterator denoting an element in `authors`, we can write

```
// copies up to but not including the element denoted by it
deque<string> authList(authors.begin(), it);
```

List Initialization

C++
11 Under the new standard, we can list initialize (§ 3.3.1, p. 98) a container:

```
// each container has three elements, initialized from the given initializers
list<string> authors = {"Milton", "Shakespeare", "Austen"};
vector<const char*> articles = {"a", "an", "the"};
```

When we do so, we explicitly specify values for each element in the container. For types other than `array`, the initializer list also implicitly specifies the size of the container: The container will have as many elements as there are initializers.

Sequential Container Size-Related Constructors

In addition to the constructors that sequential containers have in common with associative containers, we can also initialize the sequential containers (other than `array`) from a size and an (optional) element initializer. If we do not supply an element initializer, the library creates a value-initialized one for us § 3.3.1 (p. 98):

```
vector<int> ivec(10, -1);     // ten int elements, each initialized to -1
list<string> svec(10, "hi!"); // ten strings; each element is "hi!"
forward_list<int> ivec(10);   // ten elements, each initialized to 0
deque<string> svec(10);       // ten elements, each an empty string
```

We can use the constructor that takes a size argument if the element type is a built-in type or a class type that has a default constructor (§ 9.2, p. 329). If the element type does not have a default constructor, then we must specify an explicit element initializer along with the size.

The constructors that take a size are valid *only* for sequential containers; they are not supported for the associative containers.

Library `arrays` Have Fixed Size

Just as the size of a built-in array is part of its type, the size of a library `array` is part of its type. When we define an `array`, in addition to specifying the element type, we also specify the container size:

```
array<int, 42>     // type is: array that holds 42 ints
array<string, 10>  // type is: array that holds 10 strings
```

To use an `array` type we must specify both the element type and the size:

```
array<int, 10>::size_type i;  // array type includes element type and size
array<int>::size_type j;      // error: array<int> is not a type
```

Because the size is part of the `array`'s type, `array` does not support the normal container constructors. Those constructors, implicitly or explicitly, determine the size of the container. It would be redundant (at best) and error-prone to allow users to pass a size argument to an `array` constructor.

The fixed-size nature of `arrays` also affects the behavior of the constructors that `array` does define. Unlike the other containers, a default-constructed `array` is not empty: It has as many elements as its size. These elements are default initialized (§ 2.2.1, p. 43) just as are elements in a built-in array (§ 3.5.1, p. 114). If we list initialize the array, the number of the initializers must be equal to or less than the size of the array. If there are fewer initializers than the size of the array, the initializers are used for the first elements and any remaining elements are value initialized (§ 3.3.1, p. 98). In both cases, if the element type is a class type, the class must have a default constructor in order to permit value initialization:

```
array<int, 10> ia1;   // ten default-initialized ints
array<int, 10> ia2 = {0,1,2,3,4,5,6,7,8,9};   // list initialization
array<int, 10> ia3 = {42};   // ia3[0] is 42, remaining elements are 0
```

It is worth noting that although we cannot copy or assign objects of built-in array types (§ 3.5.1, p. 114), there is no such restriction on array:

```
int digs[10] = {0,1,2,3,4,5,6,7,8,9};
int cpy[10] = digs;   // error: no copy or assignment for built-in arrays
array<int, 10> digits = {0,1,2,3,4,5,6,7,8,9};
array<int, 10> copy = digits;   // ok: so long as array types match
```

As with any container, the initializer must have the same type as the container we are creating. For arrays, the element type and the size must be the same, because the size of an array is part of its type.

EXERCISES SECTION 9.2.4

Exercise 9.11: Show an example of each of the six ways to create and initialize a vector. Explain what values each vector contains.

Exercise 9.12: Explain the differences between the constructor that takes a container to copy and the constructor that takes two iterators.

Exercise 9.13: How would you initialize a vector<double> from a list<int>? From a vector<int>? Write code to check your answers.

9.2.5 Assignment and swap

The assignment-related operators, listed in Table 9.4 (overleaf) act on the entire container. The assignment operator replaces the entire range of elements in the left-hand container with copies of the elements from the right-hand operand:

```
c1 = c2;       // replace the contents of c1 with a copy of the elements in c2
c1 = {a,b,c};  // after the assignment c1 has size 3
```

After the first assignment, the left- and right-hand containers are equal. If the containers had been of unequal size, after the assignment both containers would have the size of the right-hand operand. After the second assignment, the size of c1 is 3, which is the number of values provided in the braced list.

Unlike built-in arrays, the library `array` type does allow assignment. The left- and right-hand operands must have the same type:

```
array<int, 10> a1 = {0,1,2,3,4,5,6,7,8,9};
array<int, 10> a2 = {0}; // elements all have value 0
a1 = a2;   // replaces elements in a1
a2 = {0}; // error: cannot assign to an array from a braced list
```

Because the size of the right-hand operand might differ from the size of the left-hand operand, the `array` type does not support `assign` and it does not allow assignment from a braced list of values.

Table 9.4: Container Assignment Operations	
`c1 = c2`	Replace the elements in `c1` with copies of the elements in `c2`. `c1` and `c2` must be the same type.
`c = {a,b,c...}`	Replace the elements in `c1` with copies of the elements in the initializer list. **(Not valid for `array`.)**
`swap(c1, c2)` `c1.swap(c2)`	Exchanges elements in `c1` with those in `c2`. `c1` and `c2` must be the same type. `swap` is usually *much* faster than copying elements from `c2` to `c1`.
`assign` operations not valid for associative containers or `array`	
`seq.assign(b,e)`	Replaces elements in `seq` with those in the range denoted by iterators `b` and `e`. The iterators `b` and `e` must not refer to elements in `seq`.
`seq.assign(il)`	Replaces the elements in `seq` with those in the initializer list `il`.
`seq.assign(n,t)`	Replaces the elements in `seq` with `n` elements with value `t`.

⚠️ **WARNING** Assignment related operations invalidate iterators, references, and pointers into the left-hand container. Aside from `string` they remain valid after a `swap`, and (excepting `array`s) the containers to which they refer are swapped.

Using `assign` (Sequential Containers Only)

The assignment operator requires that the left-hand and right-hand operands have the same type. It copies all the elements from the right-hand operand into the left-hand operand. The sequential containers (except `array`) also define a member named `assign` that lets us assign from a different but compatible type, or assign from a subsequence of a container. The `assign` operation replaces all the elements in the left-hand container with (copies of) the elements specified by its arguments. For example, we can use `assign` to assign a range of `char*` values from a `vector` into a `list` of `string`:

```
list<string> names;
vector<const char*> oldstyle;
names = oldstyle;   // error: container types don't match
// ok: can convert from const char* to string
names.assign(oldstyle.cbegin(), oldstyle.cend());
```

The call to assign replaces the elements in names with copies of the elements in the range denoted by the iterators. The arguments to assign determine how many elements and what values the container will have.

 WARNING Because the existing elements are replaced, the iterators passed to assign must not refer to the container on which assign is called.

A second version of assign takes an integral value and an element value. It replaces the elements in the container with the specified number of elements, each of which has the specified element value:

```
// equivalent to slist1.clear();
// followed by slist1.insert(slist1.begin(), 10, "Hiya!");
list<string> slist1(1);        // one element, which is the empty string
slist1.assign(10, "Hiya!");  // ten elements; each one is Hiya!
```

Using swap

The swap operation exchanges the contents of two containers of the same type. After the call to swap, the elements in the two containers are interchanged:

```
vector<string> svec1(10);   // vector with ten elements
vector<string> svec2(24);   // vector with 24 elements
swap(svec1, svec2);
```

After the swap, svec1 contains 24 string elements and svec2 contains ten. With the exception of arrays, swapping two containers is guaranteed to be fast—the elements themselves are not swapped; internal data structures are swapped.

Note Excepting array, swap does not copy, delete, or insert any elements and is guaranteed to run in constant time.

The fact that elements are not moved means that, with the exception of string, iterators, references, and pointers into the containers are not invalidated. They refer to the same elements as they did before the swap. However, after the swap, those elements are in a different container. For example, had iter denoted the string at position svec1[3] before the swap, it will denote the element at position svec2[3] after the swap. Differently from the containers, a call to swap on a string may invalidate iterators, references and pointers.

Unlike how swap behaves for the other containers, swapping two arrays does exchange the elements. As a result, swapping two arrays requires time proportional to the number of elements in the array.

After the swap, pointers, references, and iterators remain bound to the same element they denoted before the swap. Of course, the value of that element has been swapped with the corresponding element in the other array.

In the new library, the containers offer both a member and nonmember version C++ 11 of swap. Earlier versions of the library defined only the member version of swap. The nonmember swap is of most importance in generic programs. As a matter of habit, it is best to use the nonmember version of swap.

EXERCISES SECTION 9.2.5

Exercise 9.14: Write a program to assign the elements from a `list` of `char*` pointers to C-style character strings to a `vector` of `strings`.

9.2.6 Container Size Operations

With one exception, the container types have three size-related operations. The `size` member (§ 3.2.2, p. 87) returns the number of elements in the container; `empty` returns a `bool` that is `true` if `size` is zero and `false` otherwise; and `max_size` returns a number that is greater than or equal to the number of elements a container of that type can contain. For reasons we'll explain in the next section, `forward_list` provides `max_size` and `empty`, but not `size`.

9.2.7 Relational Operators

Every container type supports the equality operators (`==` and `!=`); all the containers except the unordered associative containers also support the relational operators (`>`, `>=`, `<`, `<=`). The right- and left-hand operands must be the same kind of container and must hold elements of the same type. That is, we can compare a `vector<int>` only with another `vector<int>`. We cannot compare a `vector<int>` with a `list<int>` or a `vector<double>`.

Comparing two containers performs a pairwise comparison of the elements. These operators work similarly to the `string` relationals (§ 3.2.2, p. 88):

- If both containers are the same size and all the elements are equal, then the two containers are equal; otherwise, they are unequal.

- If the containers have different sizes but every element of the smaller one is equal to the corresponding element of the larger one, then the smaller one is less than the other.

- If neither container is an initial subsequence of the other, then the comparison depends on comparing the first unequal elements.

The following examples illustrate how these operators work:

```
vector<int> v1 = { 1, 3, 5, 7, 9, 12 };
vector<int> v2 = { 1, 3, 9 };
vector<int> v3 = { 1, 3, 5, 7 };
vector<int> v4 = { 1, 3, 5, 7, 9, 12 };
v1 < v2   // true; v1 and v2 differ at element [2]: v1[2] is less than v2[2]
v1 < v3   // false; all elements are equal, but v3 has fewer of them;
v1 == v4  // true; each element is equal and v1 and v4 have the same size()
v1 == v2  // false; v2 has fewer elements than v1
```

Relational Operators Use Their Element's Relational Operator

> **Note:** We can use a relational operator to compare two containers only if the appropriate comparison operator is defined for the element type.

The container equality operators use the element's == operator, and the relational operators use the element's < operator. If the element type doesn't support the required operator, then we cannot use the corresponding operations on containers holding that type. For example, the `Sales_data` type that we defined in Chapter 7 does not define either the == or the < operation. Therefore, we cannot compare two containers that hold `Sales_data` elements:

```
vector<Sales_data> storeA, storeB;
if (storeA < storeB) // error: Sales_data has no less-than operator
```

EXERCISES SECTION 9.2.7

Exercise 9.15: Write a program to determine whether two vector<int>s are equal.

Exercise 9.16: Repeat the previous program, but compare elements in a list<int> to a vector<int>.

Exercise 9.17: Assuming c1 and c2 are containers, what (if any) constraints does the following usage place on the types of c1 and c2?

```
if (c1 < c2)
```

9.3 Sequential Container Operations

The sequential and associative containers differ in how they organize their elements. These differences affect how elements are stored, accessed, added, and removed. The previous section covered operations common to all containers (those listed in Table 9.2 (p. 330)). We'll cover the operations specific to the sequential containers in the remainder of this chapter.

9.3.1 Adding Elements to a Sequential Container

Excepting `array`, all of the library containers provide flexible memory management. We can add or remove elements dynamically changing the size of the container at run time. Table 9.5 (p. 343) lists the operations that add elements to a (nonarray) sequential container.

When we use these operations, we must remember that the containers use different strategies for allocating elements and that these strategies affect performance. Adding elements anywhere but at the end of a `vector` or `string`, or anywhere but the beginning or end of a `deque`, requires elements to be moved.

Moreover, adding elements to a vector or a string may cause the entire object to be reallocated. Reallocating an object requires allocating new memory and moving elements from the old space to the new.

Using push_back

In § 3.3.2 (p. 100) we saw that push_back appends an element to the back of a vector. Aside from array and forward_list, every sequential container (including the string type) supports push_back.

As an example, the following loop reads one string at a time into word:

```
// read from standard input, putting each word onto the end of container
string word;
while (cin >> word)
    container.push_back(word);
```

The call to push_back creates a new element at the end of container, increasing the size of container by 1. The value of that element is a copy of word. The type of container can be any of list, vector, or deque.

Because string is just a container of characters, we can use push_back to add characters to the end of the string:

```
void pluralize(size_t cnt, string &word)
{
    if (cnt > 1)
        word.push_back('s');   // same as word += 's'
}
```

KEY CONCEPT: CONTAINER ELEMENTS ARE COPIES

When we use an object to initialize a container, or insert an object into a container, a copy of that object's value is placed in the container, not the object itself. Just as when we pass an object to a nonreference parameter (§ 6.2.1, p. 209), there is no relationship between the element in the container and the object from which that value originated. Subsequent changes to the element in the container have no effect on the original object, and vice versa.

Using push_front

In addition to push_back, the list, forward_list, and deque containers support an analogous operation named push_front. This operation inserts a new element at the front of the container:

```
list<int> ilist;
// add elements to the start of ilist
for (size_t ix = 0; ix != 4; ++ix)
    ilist.push_front(ix);
```

This loop adds the elements 0, 1, 2, 3 to the beginning of ilist. Each element is inserted at the *new beginning* of the list. That is, when we insert 1, it goes in front of 0, and 2 in front of 1, and so forth. Thus, the elements added in a loop such as this one wind up in reverse order. After executing this loop, ilist holds the sequence 3, 2, 1, 0.

Note that deque, which like vector offers fast random access to its elements, provides the push_front member even though vector does not. A deque guarantees constant-time insert and delete of elements at the beginning and end of the container. As with vector, inserting elements other than at the front or back of a deque is a potentially expensive operation.

Table 9.5: Operations That Add Elements to a Sequential Container

These operations change the size of the container; they are not supported by array.
forward_list has special versions of insert and emplace; see § 9.3.4 (p. 350).
push_back and emplace_back not valid for forward_list.
push_front and emplace_front not valid for vector or string.

c.push_back(t) c.emplace_back(*args*)	Creates an element with value t or constructed from *args* at the end of c. Returns void.
c.push_front(t) c.emplace_front(*args*)	Creates an element with value t or constructed from *args* on the front of c. Returns void.
c.insert(p,t) c.emplace(p, *args*)	Creates an element with value t or constructed from *args* before the element denoted by iterator p. Returns an iterator referring to the element that was added.
c.insert(p,n,t)	Inserts n elements with value t before the element denoted by iterator p. Returns an iterator to the first element inserted; if n is zero, returns p.
c.insert(p,b,e)	Inserts the elements from the range denoted by iterators b and e before the element denoted by iterator p. b and e may not refer to elements in c. Returns an iterator to the first element inserted; if the range is empty, returns p.
c.insert(p,il)	il is a braced list of element values. Inserts the given values before the element denoted by the iterator p. Returns an iterator to the first inserted element; if the list is empty returns p.

⚠ **WARNING**   Adding elements to a vector, string, or deque potentially invalidates all existing iterators, references, and pointers into the container.

Adding Elements at a Specified Point in the Container

The push_back and push_front operations provide convenient ways to insert a single element at the end or beginning of a sequential container. More generally, the insert members let us insert zero or more elements at any point in the container. The insert members are supported for vector, deque, list, and string. forward_list provides specialized versions of these members that we'll cover in § 9.3.4 (p. 350).

Each of the insert functions takes an iterator as its first argument. The iterator indicates where in the container to put the element(s). It can refer to any position in the container, including one past the end of the container. Because the iterator might refer to a nonexistent element off the end of the container, and because it is useful to have a way to insert elements at the beginning of a container, element(s) are inserted *before* the position denoted by the iterator. For example, this statement

```
slist.insert(iter, "Hello!"); // insert "Hello!" just before iter
```

inserts a `string` with value `"Hello"` just before the element denoted by `iter`.

Even though some containers do not have a `push_front` operation, there is no similar constraint on `insert`. We can `insert` elements at the beginning of a container without worrying about whether the container has `push_front`:

```
vector<string> svec;
list<string> slist;

// equivalent to calling slist.push_front("Hello!");
slist.insert(slist.begin(), "Hello!");

// no push_front on vector but we can insert before begin()
// warning: inserting anywhere but at the end of a vector might be slow
svec.insert(svec.begin(), "Hello!");
```

 It is legal to insert anywhere in a `vector`, `deque`, or `string`. However, doing so can be an expensive operation.

Inserting a Range of Elements

The arguments to `insert` that appear after the initial iterator argument are analogous to the container constructors that take the same parameters. The version that takes an element count and a value adds the specified number of identical elements before the given position:

```
svec.insert(svec.end(), 10, "Anna");
```

This code inserts ten elements at the end of `svec` and initializes each of those elements to the `string` `"Anna"`.

The versions of `insert` that take a pair of iterators or an initializer list insert the elements from the given range before the given position:

```
vector<string> v = {"quasi", "simba", "frollo", "scar"};
// insert the last two elements of v at the beginning of slist
slist.insert(slist.begin(), v.end() - 2, v.end());
slist.insert(slist.end(), {"these", "words", "will",
                           "go", "at", "the", "end"});
// run-time error: iterators denoting the range to copy from
// must not refer to the same container as the one we are changing
slist.insert(slist.begin(), slist.begin(), slist.end());
```

When we pass a pair of iterators, those iterators may not refer to the same container as the one to which we are adding elements.

Under the new standard, the versions of `insert` that take a count or a range return an iterator to the first element that was inserted. (In prior versions of the library, these operations returned `void`.) If the range is empty, no elements are inserted, and the operation returns its first parameter.

Using the Return from `insert`

We can use the value returned by `insert` to repeatedly insert elements at a specified position in the container:

```
list<string> lst;
auto iter = lst.begin();
while (cin >> word)
    iter = lst.insert(iter, word);  // same as calling push_front
```

 It is important to understand how this loop operates—in particular, to understand why the loop is equivalent to calling `push_front`.

Before the loop, we initialize `iter` to `lst.begin()`. The first call to `insert` takes the `string` we just read and puts it in front of the element denoted by `iter`. The value returned by `insert` is an iterator referring to this new element. We assign that iterator to `iter` and repeat the `while`, reading another word. As long as there are words to insert, each trip through the `while` inserts a new element ahead of `iter` and reassigns to `iter` the location of the newly inserted element. That element is the (new) first element. Thus, each iteration inserts an element ahead of the first element in the `list`.

Using the Emplace Operations

The new standard introduced three new members—`emplace_front`, `emplace`, and `emplace_back`—that construct rather than copy elements. These operations correspond to the `push_front`, `insert`, and `push_back` operations in that they let us put an element at the front of the container, in front of a given position, or at the back of the container, respectively.

When we call a push or insert member, we pass objects of the element type and those objects are copied into the container. When we call an emplace member, we pass arguments to a constructor for the element type. The emplace members use those arguments to construct an element directly in space managed by the container. For example, assuming `c` holds `Sales_data` (§ 7.1.4, p. 264) elements:

```
// construct a Sales_data object at the end of c
// uses the three-argument Sales_data constructor
c.emplace_back("978-0590353403", 25, 15.99);
// error: there is no version of push_back that takes three arguments
c.push_back("978-0590353403", 25, 15.99);
// ok: we create a temporary Sales_data object to pass to push_back
c.push_back(Sales_data("978-0590353403", 25, 15.99));
```

The call to `emplace_back` and the second call to `push_back` both create new `Sales_data` objects. In the call to `emplace_back`, that object is created directly in space managed by the container. The call to `push_back` creates a local temporary object that is pushed onto the container.

The arguments to an emplace function vary depending on the element type. The arguments must match a constructor for the element type:

```
// iter refers to an element in c, which holds Sales_data elements
c.emplace_back(); // uses the Sales_data default constructor
c.emplace(iter, "999-999999999"); // uses Sales_data(string)
// uses the Sales_data constructor that takes an ISBN, a count, and a price
c.emplace_front("978-0590353403", 25, 15.99);
```

> The *emplace* functions construct elements in the container. The arguments to these functions must match a constructor for the element type.

EXERCISES SECTION 9.3.1

Exercise 9.18: Write a program to read a sequence of `strings` from the standard input into a deque. Use iterators to write a loop to print the elements in the deque.

Exercise 9.19: Rewrite the program from the previous exercise to use a `list`. List the changes you needed to make.

Exercise 9.20: Write a program to copy elements from a `list<int>` into two deques. The even-valued elements should go into one deque and the odd ones into the other.

Exercise 9.21: Explain how the loop from page 345 that used the return from `insert` to add elements to a `list` would work if we inserted into a `vector` instead.

Exercise 9.22: Assuming `iv` is a `vector` of ints, what is wrong with the following program? How might you correct the problem(s)?

```
vector<int>::iterator iter = iv.begin(),
                      mid = iv.begin() + iv.size()/2;
while (iter != mid)
    if (*iter == some_val)
        iv.insert(iter, 2 * some_val);
```

 ## 9.3.2 Accessing Elements

Table 9.6 lists the operations we can use to access elements in a sequential container. The access operations are undefined if the container has no elements.

Each sequential container, including `array`, has a `front` member, and all except `forward_list` also have a `back` member. These operations return a reference to the first and last element, respectively:

```
// check that there are elements before dereferencing an iterator or calling front or back
if (!c.empty()) {
    // val and val2 are copies of the value of the first element in c
    auto val = *c.begin(), val2 = c.front();
    // val3 and val4 are copies of the of the last element in c
    auto last = c.end();
    auto val3 = *(--last);  // can't decrement forward_list iterators
    auto val4 = c.back();   // not supported by forward_list
}
```

This program obtains references to the first and last elements in c in two different ways. The direct approach is to call front or back. Indirectly, we can obtain a reference to the same element by dereferencing the iterator returned by begin or decrementing and then dereferencing the iterator returned by end.

Two things are noteworthy in this program: The end iterator refers to the (nonexistent) element one past the end of the container. To fetch the last element we must first decrement that iterator. The other important point is that before calling front or back (or dereferencing the iterators from begin or end), we check that c isn't empty. If the container were empty, the operations inside the if would be undefined.

Table 9.6: Operations to Access Elements in a Sequential Container
at and subscript operator valid only for string, vector, deque, and array.   **back not valid for forward_list.**

c.back()	Returns a reference to the last element in c. Undefined if c is empty.
c.front()	Returns a reference to the first element in c. Undefined if c is empty.
c[n]	Returns a reference to the element indexed by the unsigned integral value n. Undefined if n >= c.size().
c.at(n)	Returns a reference to the element indexed by n. If the index is out of range, throws an out_of_range exception.

> ⚠ **WARNING** Calling front or back on an empty container, like using a subscript that is out of range, is a serious programming error.

The Access Members Return References

The members that access elements in a container (i.e., front, back, subscript, and at) return references. If the container is a const object, the return is a reference to const. If the container is not const, the return is an ordinary reference that we can use to change the value of the fetched element:

```
if (!c.empty()) {
    c.front() = 42;        // assigns 42 to the first element in c
    auto &v = c.back();    // get a reference to the last element
    v = 1024;              // changes the element in c
    auto v2 = c.back();    // v2 is not a reference; it's a copy of c.back()
    v2 = 0;                // no change to the element in c
}
```

As usual, if we use auto to store the return from one of these functions and we want to use that variable to change the element, we must remember to define our variable as a reference type.

Subscripting and Safe Random Access

The containers that provide fast random access (string, vector, deque, and array) also provide the subscript operator (§ 3.3.3, p. 102). As we've seen, the subscript operator takes an index and returns a reference to the element at that position in the container. The index must be "in range," (i.e., greater than or equal to 0 and less than the size of the container). It is up to the program to ensure that the index is valid; the subscript operator does not check whether the index is in range. Using an out-of-range value for an index is a serious programming error, but one that the compiler will not detect.

If we want to ensure that our index is valid, we can use the `at` member instead. The `at` member acts like the subscript operator, but if the index is invalid, `at` throws an `out_of_range` exception (§ 5.6, p. 193):

```
vector<string> svec;   // empty vector
cout << svec[0];       // run-time error: there are no elements in svec!
cout << svec.at(0);    // throws an out_of_range exception
```

Exercise 9.23: In the first program in this section on page 346, what would the values of `val`, `val2`, `val3`, and `val4` be if `c.size()` is 1?

Exercise 9.24: Write a program that fetches the first element in a `vector` using `at`, the subscript operator, `front`, and `begin`. Test your program on an empty `vector`.

9.3.3 Erasing Elements

Just as there are several ways to add elements to a (nonarray) container there are also several ways to remove elements. These members are listed in Table 9.7.

The members that remove elements do not check their argument(s). The programmer must ensure that element(s) exist before removing them.

The `pop_front` and `pop_back` Members

The `pop_front` and `pop_back` functions remove the first and last elements, respectively. Just as there is no `push_front` for `vector` and `string`, there is also no `pop_front` for those types. Similarly, `forward_list` does not have `pop_back`. Like the element access members, we may not use a pop operation on an empty container.

These operations return `void`. If you need the value you are about to pop, you must store that value before doing the pop:

```
while (!ilist.empty()) {
    process(ilist.front());  // do something with the current top of ilist
    ilist.pop_front();       // done; remove the first element
}
```

Table 9.7: `erase` Operations on Sequential Containers	
These operations change the size of the container and so are not supported by `array`. `forward_list` has a special version of `erase`; see § 9.3.4 (p. 350). `pop_back` not valid for `forward_list`; `pop_front` not valid for `vector` and `string`.	
`c.pop_back()`	Removes last element in c. Undefined if c is empty. Returns `void`.
`c.pop_front()`	Removes first element in c. Undefined if c is empty. Returns `void`.
`c.erase(p)`	Removes the element denoted by the iterator p and returns an iterator to the element after the one deleted or the off-the-end iterator if p denotes the last element. Undefined if p is the off-the-end iterator.
`c.erase(b,e)`	Removes the range of elements denoted by the iterators b and e. Returns an iterator to the element after the last one that was deleted, or an off-the-end iterator if e is itself an off-the-end iterator.
`c.clear()`	Removes all the elements in c. Returns `void`.

> ⚠️ **WARNING** Removing elements anywhere but the beginning or end of a deque invalidates all iterators, references, and pointers. Iterators, references, and pointers to elements after the erasure point in a `vector` or `string` are invalidated.

Removing an Element from within the Container

The `erase` members remove element(s) at a specified point in the container. We can delete a single element denoted by an iterator or a range of elements marked by a pair of iterators. Both forms of `erase` return an iterator referring to the location *after* the (last) element that was removed. That is, if j is the element following i, then `erase(i)` will return an iterator referring to j.

As an example, the following loop erases the odd elements in a `list`:

```
list<int> lst = {0,1,2,3,4,5,6,7,8,9};
auto it = lst.begin();
while (it != lst.end())
    if (*it % 2)                // if the element is odd
        it = lst.erase(it);    // erase this element
    else
        ++it;
```

On each iteration, we check whether the current element is odd. If so, we `erase` that element, setting `it` to denote the element after the one we erased. If `*it` is even, we increment `it` so we'll look at the next element on the next iteration.

Removing Multiple Elements

The iterator-pair version of `erase` lets us delete a range of elements:

```
// delete the range of elements between two iterators
// returns an iterator to the element just after the last removed element
elem1 = slist.erase(elem1, elem2); // after the call elem1 == elem2
```

The iterator `elem1` refers to the first element we want to erase, and `elem2` refers to one past the last element we want to remove.

To delete all the elements in a container, we can either call `clear` or pass the iterators from `begin` and `end` to `erase`:

```
slist.clear();  // delete all the elements within the container
slist.erase(slist.begin(), slist.end());  // equivalent
```

EXERCISES SECTION 9.3.3

Exercise 9.25: In the program on page 349 that erased a range of elements, what happens if `elem1` and `elem2` are equal? What if `elem2` or both `elem1` and `elem2` are the off-the-end iterator?

Exercise 9.26: Using the following definition of `ia`, copy `ia` into a `vector` and into a `list`. Use the single-iterator form of `erase` to remove the elements with odd values from your `list` and the even values from your `vector`.

```
int ia[] = { 0, 1, 1, 2, 3, 5, 8, 13, 21, 55, 89 };
```

9.3.4 Specialized `forward_list` Operations

To understand why `forward_list` has special versions of the operations to add and remove elements, consider what must happen when we remove an element from a singly linked list. As illustrated in Figure 9.1, removing an element changes the links in the sequence. In this case, removing *elem*$_3$ changes *elem*$_2$; *elem*$_2$ had pointed to *elem*$_3$, but after we remove *elem*$_3$, *elem*$_2$ points to *elem*$_4$.

Figure 9.1: `forward_list` Specialized Operations

Removing *elem*$_3$ changes the value of *elem*$_2$

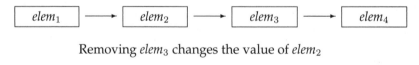

When we add or remove an element, the element before the one we added or removed has a different successor. To add or remove an element, we need access to its predecessor in order to update that element's links. However, `forward_list` is a singly linked list. In a singly linked list there is no easy way to get to an element's predecessor. For this reason, the operations to add or remove elements in a `forward_list` operate by changing the element *after* the given element. That way, we always have access to the elements that are affected by the change.

Because these operations behave differently from the operations on the other containers, `forward_list` does not define `insert`, `emplace`, or `erase`. Instead it defines members (listed in Table 9.8) named `insert_after`, `emplace_after`, and `erase_after`. For example, in our illustration, to remove *elem₃*, we'd call `erase_after` on an iterator that denoted *elem₂*. To support these operations, `forward_list` also defines `before_begin`, which returns an **off-the-beginning** iterator. This iterator lets us add or remove elements "after" the nonexistent element before the first one in the list.

Table 9.8: Operations to Insert or Remove Elements in a `forward_list`	
`lst.before_begin()` `lst.cbefore_begin()`	Iterator denoting the nonexistent element just before the beginning of the list. This iterator may not be dereferenced. `cbefore_begin()` returns a `const_iterator`.

`lst.insert_after(p,t)`
`lst.insert_after(p,n,t)`
`lst.insert_after(p,b,e)`
`lst.insert_after(p,il)`
	Inserts element(s) *after* the one denoted by iterator p. t is an object, n is a count, b and e are iterators denoting a range (b and e must not refer to `lst`), and il is a braced list. Returns an iterator to the *last* inserted element. If the range is empty, returns p. Undefined if p is the off-the-end iterator.

`emplace_after(p, args)`	Uses *args* to construct an element after the one denoted by iterator p. Returns an iterator to the new element. Undefined if p is the off-the-end iterator.
`lst.erase_after(p)` `lst.erase_after(b,e)`	Removes the element *after* the one denoted by iterator p or the range of elements from the one *after* the iterator b up to but not including the one denoted by e. Returns an iterator to the element after the one deleted, or the off-the-end iterator if there is no such element. Undefined if p denotes the last element in `lst` or is the off-the-end iterator.

When we add or remove elements in a `forward_list`, we have to keep track of two iterators—one to the element we're checking and one to that element's predecessor. As an example, we'll rewrite the loop from page 349 that removed the odd-valued elements from a `list` to use a `forward_list`:

```
forward_list<int> flst = {0,1,2,3,4,5,6,7,8,9};
auto prev = flst.before_begin();  // denotes element "off the start" of flst
auto curr = flst.begin();         // denotes the first element in flst
while (curr != flst.end()) {      // while there are still elements to process
    if (*curr % 2)                    // if the element is odd
        curr = flst.erase_after(prev); // erase it and move curr
    else {
        prev = curr;              // move the iterators to denote the next
        ++curr;                   // element and one before the next element
    }
}
```

Here, `curr` denotes the element we're checking, and `prev` denotes the element before `curr`. We call `begin` to initialize `curr`, so that the first iteration checks whether the first element is even or odd. We initialize `prev` from `before_begin`, which returns an iterator to the nonexistent element just before `curr`.

When we find an odd element, we pass `prev` to `erase_after`. This call erases the element after the one denoted by `prev`; that is, it erases the element denoted by `curr`. We reset `curr` to the return from `erase_after`, which makes `curr` denote the next element in the sequence and we leave `prev` unchanged; `prev` still denotes the element before the (new) value of `curr`. If the element denoted by `curr` is not odd, then we have to move both iterators, which we do in the `else`.

EXERCISES SECTION 9.3.4

Exercise 9.27: Write a program to find and remove the odd-valued elements in a `forward_list<int>`.

Exercise 9.28: Write a function that takes a `forward_list<string>` and two additional `string` arguments. The function should find the first `string` and insert the second immediately following the first. If the first `string` is not found, then insert the second `string` at the end of the list.

9.3.5 Resizing a Container

With the usual exception of `arrays`, we can use `resize`, described in Table 9.9, to make a container larger or smaller. If the current size is greater than the requested size, elements are deleted from the back of the container; if the current size is less than the new size, elements are added to the back of the container:

```
list<int> ilist(10, 42); // ten ints: each has value 42
ilist.resize(15);        // adds five elements of value 0 to the back of ilist
ilist.resize(25, -1);    // adds ten elements of value -1 to the back of ilist
ilist.resize(5);         // erases 20 elements from the back of ilist
```

The `resize` operation takes an optional element-value argument that it uses to initialize any elements that are added to the container. If this argument is absent, added elements are value initialized (§ 3.3.1, p. 98). If the container holds elements of a class type and `resize` adds elements, we must supply an initializer or the element type must have a default constructor.

Table 9.9: Sequential Container Size Operations
`resize` not valid for array.
`c.resize(n)` Resize c so that it has n elements. If n < c.size(), the excess elements are discarded. If new elements must be added, they are value initialized.
`c.resize(n,t)` Resize c to have n elements. Any elements added have value t.

> ⚠ **WARNING**
> If `resize` shrinks the container, then iterators, references, and pointers to the deleted elements are invalidated; `resize` on a `vector`, `string`, or `deque` potentially invalidates all iterators, pointers, and references.

Exercise 9.29: Given that vec holds 25 elements, what does vec.resize(100) do? What if we next wrote vec.resize(10)?

Exercise 9.30: What, if any, restrictions does using the version of resize that takes a single argument place on the element type?

9.3.6 Container Operations May Invalidate Iterators

Operations that add or remove elements from a container can invalidate pointers, references, or iterators to container elements. An invalidated pointer, reference, or iterator is one that no longer denotes an element. Using an invalidated pointer, reference, or iterator is a serious programming error that is likely to lead to the same kinds of problems as using an uninitialized pointer (§ 2.3.2, p. 54).

After an operation that adds elements to a container

- Iterators, pointers, and references to a vector or string are invalid if the container was reallocated. If no reallocation happens, indirect references to elements before the insertion remain valid; those to elements after the insertion are invalid.

- Iterators, pointers, and references to a deque are invalid if we add elements anywhere but at the front or back. If we add at the front or back, iterators are invalidated, but references and pointers to existing elements are not.

- Iterators, pointers, and references (including the off-the-end and the before-the-beginning iterators) to a list or forward_list remain valid,

It should not be surprising that when we remove elements from a container, iterators, pointers, and references to the removed elements are invalidated. After all, those elements have been destroyed. After we remove an element,

- All other iterators, references, or pointers (including the off-the-end and the before-the-beginning iterators) to a list or forward_list remain valid.

- All other iterators, references, or pointers to a deque are invalidated if the removed elements are anywhere but the front or back. If we remove elements at the back of the deque, the off-the-end iterator is invalidated but other iterators, references, and pointers are unaffected; they are also unaffected if we remove from the front.

- All other iterators, references, or pointers to a vector or string remain valid for elements before the removal point. Note: The off-the-end iterator is always invalidated when we remove elements.

 WARNING It is a serious run-time error to use an iterator, pointer, or reference that has been invalidated.

ADVICE: MANAGING ITERATORS

ADVICE: MANAGING ITERATORS

When you use an iterator (or a reference or pointer to a container element), it is a good idea to minimize the part of the program during which an iterator must stay valid.

   Because code that adds or removes elements to a container can invalidate iterators, you need to ensure that the iterator is repositioned, as appropriate, after each operation that changes the container. This advice is especially important for `vector`, `string`, and `deque`.

Writing Loops That Change a Container

Loops that add or remove elements of a `vector`, `string`, or `deque` must cater to the fact that iterators, references, or pointers might be invalidated. The program must ensure that the iterator, reference, or pointer is refreshed on each trip through the loop. Refreshing an iterator is easy if the loop calls `insert` or `erase`. Those operations return iterators, which we can use to reset the iterator:

```
// silly loop to remove even-valued elements and insert a duplicate of odd-valued elements
vector<int> vi = {0,1,2,3,4,5,6,7,8,9};
auto iter = vi.begin();  // call begin, not cbegin because we're changing vi
while (iter != vi.end()) {
    if (*iter % 2) {
        iter = vi.insert(iter, *iter);  // duplicate the current element
        iter += 2;  // advance past this element and the one inserted before it
    } else
        iter = vi.erase(iter);           // remove even elements
        // don't advance the iterator; iter denotes the element after the one we erased
}
```

This program removes the even-valued elements and duplicates each odd-valued one. We refresh the iterator after both the `insert` and the `erase` because either operation can invalidate the iterator.

   After the call to `erase`, there is no need to increment the iterator, because the iterator returned from `erase` denotes the next element in the sequence. After the call to `insert`, we increment the iterator twice. Remember, `insert` inserts *before* the position it is given and returns an iterator to the inserted element. Thus, after calling `insert`, `iter` denotes the (newly added) element in front of the one we are processing. We add two to skip over the element we added and the one we just processed. Doing so positions the iterator on the next, unprocessed element.

Avoid Storing the Iterator Returned from `end`

When we add or remove elements in a `vector` or `string`, or add elements or remove any but the first element in a `deque`, the iterator returned by `end` is *always* invalidated. Thus, loops that add or remove elements should always call `end` rather than use a stored copy. Partly for this reason, C++ standard libraries are usually implemented so that calling `end()` is a very fast operation.

   As an example, consider a loop that processes each element and adds a new element following the original. We want the loop to ignore the added elements, and to process only the original elements. After each insertion, we'll position the iterator to denote the next original element. If we attempt to "optimize" the loop, by storing the iterator returned by end(), we'll have a disaster:

```
// disaster: the behavior of this loop is undefined
auto begin = v.begin(),
     end = v.end(); // bad idea, saving the value of the end iterator
while (begin != end) {
    // do some processing
    // insert the new value and reassign begin, which otherwise would be invalid
    ++begin;    // advance begin because we want to insert after this element
    begin = v.insert(begin, 42);    // insert the new value
    ++begin;    // advance begin past the element we just added
}
```

The behavior of this code is undefined. On many implementations, we'll get an infinite loop. The problem is that we stored the value returned by the end operation in a local variable named end. In the body of the loop, we added an element. Adding an element invalidates the iterator stored in end. That iterator neither refers to an element in v nor any longer refers to one past the last element in v.

> Don't cache the iterator returned from end() in loops that insert or delete elements in a deque, string, or vector.

Rather than storing the end() iterator, we must recompute it after each insertion:

```
// safer: recalculate end on each trip whenever the loop adds/erases elements
while (begin != v.end()) {
    // do some processing
    ++begin;    // advance begin because we want to insert after this element
    begin = v.insert(begin, 42);    // insert the new value
    ++begin;    // advance begin past the element we just added
}
```

9.4 How a vector Grows

To support fast random access, vector elements are stored contiguously—each element is adjacent to the previous element. Ordinarily, we should not care about how a library type is implemented; all we should care about is how to use it. However, in the case of vectors and strings, part of the implementation leaks into its interface.

Given that elements are contiguous, and that the size of the container is flexible, consider what must happen when we add an element to a vector or a string: If there is no room for the new element, the container can't just add an element somewhere else in memory—the elements must be contiguous. Instead, the container must allocate new memory to hold the existing elements plus the new one, move the elements from the old location into the new space, add the new element, and deallocate the old memory. If vector did this memory allocation and deallocation each time we added an element, performance would be unacceptably slow.

EXERCISES SECTION 9.3.6

Exercise 9.31: The program on page 354 to remove even-valued elements and duplicate odd ones will not work on a `list` or `forward_list`. Why? Revise the program so that it works on these types as well.

Exercise 9.32: In the program onpage 354 would it be legal to write the call to `insert` as follows? If not, why not?

```
iter = vi.insert(iter, *iter++);
```

Exercise 9.33: In the final example in this section what would happen if we did not assign the result of `insert` to `begin`? Write a program that omits this assignment to see if your expectation was correct.

Exercise 9.34: Assuming `vi` is a container of `int`s that includes even and odd values, predict the behavior of the following loop. After you've analyzed this loop, write a program to test whether your expectations were correct.

```
iter = vi.begin();
while (iter != vi.end())
    if (*iter % 2)
        iter = vi.insert(iter, *iter);
    ++iter;
```

To avoid these costs, library implementors use allocation strategies that reduce the number of times the container is reallocated. When they have to get new memory, `vector` and `string` implementations typically allocate capacity beyond what is immediately needed. The container holds this storage in reserve and uses it to allocate new elements as they are added. Thus, there is no need to reallocate the container for each new element.

This allocation strategy is dramatically more efficient than reallocating the container each time an element is added. In fact, its performance is good enough that in practice a `vector` usually grows more efficiently than a `list` or a `deque`, even though the `vector` has to move all of its elements each time it reallocates memory.

Members to Manage Capacity

The `vector` and `string` types provide members, described in Table 9.10, that let us interact with the memory-allocation part of the implementation. The `capacity` operation tells us how many elements the container can hold before it must allocate more space. The `reserve` operation lets us tell the container how many elements it should be prepared to hold.

> *Note* reserve does not change the number of elements in the container; it affects only how much memory the `vector` preallocates.

A call to `reserve` changes the capacity of the `vector` only if the requested space exceeds the current capacity. If the requested size is greater than the current capacity, `reserve` allocates at least as much as (and may allocate more than) the requested amount.

If the requested size is less than or equal to the existing capacity, `reserve` does nothing. In particular, calling `reserve` with a size smaller than `capacity` does not cause the container to give back memory. Thus, after calling `reserve`, the `capacity` will be greater than or equal to the argument passed to `reserve`.

As a result, a call to `reserve` will never reduce the amount of space that the container uses. Similarly, the `resize` members (§ 9.3.5, p. 352) change only the number of elements in the container, not its capacity. We cannot use `resize` to reduce the memory a container holds in reserve.

Under the new library, we can call `shrink_to_fit` to ask a deque, vector, or `string` to return unneeded memory. This function indicates that we no longer need any excess capacity. However, the implementation is free to ignore this request. There is no guarantee that a call to `shrink_to_fit` will return memory.

Table 9.10: Container Size Management	
`shrink_to_fit` valid only for `vector`, `string`, and `deque`. `capacity` and `reserve` valid only for `vector` and `string`.	
`c.shrink_to_fit()`	Request to reduce `capacity()` to equal `size()`.
`c.capacity()`	Number of elements c can have before reallocation is necessary.
`c.reserve(n)`	Allocate space for at least n elements.

`capacity` and `size`

It is important to understand the difference between `capacity` and `size`. The `size` of a container is the number of elements it already holds; its `capacity` is how many elements it can hold before more space must be allocated.

The following code illustrates the interaction between `size` and `capacity`:

```
vector<int> ivec;
//  size should be zero; capacity is implementation defined
cout << "ivec: size: " << ivec.size()
     << " capacity: "  << ivec.capacity() << endl;
//  give ivec 24 elements
for (vector<int>::size_type ix = 0; ix != 24; ++ix)
    ivec.push_back(ix);

//  size should be 24; capacity will be >= 24 and is implementation defined
cout << "ivec: size: " << ivec.size()
     << " capacity: "  << ivec.capacity() << endl;
```

When run on our system, this code produces the following output:

```
ivec: size: 0 capacity: 0
ivec: size: 24 capacity: 32
```

We know that the `size` of an empty `vector` is zero, and evidently our library also sets the `capacity` of an empty `vector` to zero. When we add elements to the `vector`, we know that the `size` is the same as the number of elements we've added. The `capacity` must be at least as large as `size` but can be larger. The details of how much excess capacity is allocated vary by implementations of the library. Under this implementation, adding 24 elements one at a time results in a `capacity` of 32.

Visually we can think of the current state of `ivec` as

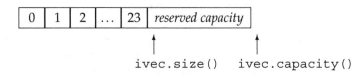

We can now `reserve` some additional space:

```
ivec.reserve(50);  //  sets capacity to at least 50; might be more
//  size should be 24; capacity will be >= 50 and is implementation defined
cout << "ivec: size: " << ivec.size()
     << " capacity: "  << ivec.capacity() << endl;
```

Here, the output indicates that the call to `reserve` allocated exactly as much space as we requested:

ivec: size: 24 capacity: 50

We might next use up that reserved capacity as follows:

```
//  add elements to use up the excess capacity
while (ivec.size() != ivec.capacity())
    ivec.push_back(0);
//  capacity should be unchanged and size and capacity are now equal
cout << "ivec: size: " << ivec.size()
     << " capacity: "  << ivec.capacity() << endl;
```

The output indicates that at this point we've used up the reserved capacity, and `size` and `capacity` are equal:

ivec: size: 50 capacity: 50

Because we used only reserved capacity, there is no need for the `vector` to do any allocation. In fact, as long as no operation exceeds the `vector`'s capacity, the `vector` must not reallocate its elements.

If we now add another element, the `vector` will have to reallocate itself:

```
ivec.push_back(42);  //  add one more element
//  size should be 51; capacity will be >= 51 and is implementation defined
cout << "ivec: size: " << ivec.size()
     << " capacity: "  << ivec.capacity() << endl;
```

The output from this portion of the program

```
ivec: size: 51 capacity: 100
```

indicates that this `vector` implementation appears to follow a strategy of doubling the current capacity each time it has to allocate new storage.

We can call `shrink_to_fit` to ask that memory beyond what is needed for the current size be returned to the system:

```
ivec.shrink_to_fit();   // ask for the memory to be returned
// size should be unchanged; capacity is implementation defined
cout << "ivec: size: " << ivec.size()
     << " capacity: "  << ivec.capacity() << endl;
```

Calling `shrink_to_fit` is only a request; there is no guarantee that the library will return the memory.

Each `vector` implementation can choose its own allocation strategy. However, it must not allocate new memory until it is forced to do so.

A `vector` may be reallocated only when the user performs an insert operation when the `size` equals `capacity` or by a call to `resize` or `reserve` with a value that exceeds the current `capacity`. How much memory is allocated beyond the specified amount is up to the implementation.

Every implementation is required to follow a strategy that ensures that it is efficient to use `push_back` to add elements to a `vector`. Technically speaking, the execution time of creating an *n*-element `vector` by calling push_back *n* times on an initially empty `vector` must never be more than a constant multiple of *n*.

EXERCISES SECTION 9.4

Exercise 9.35: Explain the difference between a `vector`'s capacity and its `size`.

Exercise 9.36: Can a container have a `capacity` less than its `size`?

Exercise 9.37: Why don't `list` or `array` have a `capacity` member?

Exercise 9.38: Write a program to explore how `vector`s grow in the library you use.

Exercise 9.39: Explain what the following program fragment does:

```
vector<string> svec;
svec.reserve(1024);
string word;
while (cin >> word)
        svec.push_back(word);
svec.resize(svec.size()+svec.size()/2);
```

Exercise 9.40: If the program in the previous exercise reads 256 words, what is its likely `capacity` after it is `resize`d? What if it reads 512? 1,000? 1,048?

9.5 Additional `string` Operations

The `string` type provides a number of additional operations beyond those common to the sequential containers. For the most part, these additional operations either support the close interaction between the `string` class and C-style character arrays, or they add versions that let us use indices in place of iterators.

The `string` library defines a great number of functions. Fortunately, these functions use repeated patterns. Given the number of functions supported, this section can be mind-numbing on first reading; so readers might want to skim it. Once you know what kinds of operations are available, you can return for the details when you need to use a particular operation.

9.5.1 Other Ways to Construct `strings`

In addition to the constructors we covered in § 3.2.1 (p. 84) and to the constructors that `string` shares with the other sequential containers (Tables 9.3 (p. 335)) the `string` type supports three more constructors that are described in Table 9.11.

Table 9.11: Additional Ways to Construct `strings`	
n, `len2` and `pos2` are all unsigned values	
`string s(cp, n);`	s is a copy of the first n characters in the array to which cp points. That array must have at least n characters.
`string s(s2, pos2);`	s is a copy of the characters in the `string` s2 starting at the index pos2. Undefined if `pos2 > s2.size()`.
`string s(s2, pos2, len2);`	s is a copy of `len2` characters from s2 starting at the index pos2. Undefined if `pos2 > s2.size()`. Regardless of the value of `len2`, copies at most `s2.size() - pos2` characters.

The constructors that take a `string` or a `const char*` take additional (optional) arguments that let us specify how many characters to copy. When we pass a `string`, we can also specify the index of where to start the copy:

```
const char *cp = "Hello World!!!";  // null-terminated array
char noNull[] = {'H', 'i'};         // not null terminated
string s1(cp);     // copy up to the null in cp; s1 == "Hello World!!!"
string s2(noNull,2); // copy two characters from no_null; s2 == "Hi"
string s3(noNull);    // undefined: noNull not null terminated
string s4(cp + 6, 5);// copy 5 characters starting at cp[6]; s4 == "World"
string s5(s1, 6, 5); // copy 5 characters starting at s1[6]; s5 == "World"
string s6(s1, 6);    // copy from s1[6] to end of s1; s6 == "World!!!"
string s7(s1,6,20);  // ok, copies only to end of s1; s7 == "World!!!"
string s8(s1, 16);   // throws an out_of_range exception
```

Ordinarily when we create a `string` from a `const char*`, the array to which the pointer points must be null terminated; characters are copied up to the null. If we also pass a count, the array does not have to be null terminated. If we do not pass a count and there is no null, or if the given count is greater than the size of the array, the operation is undefined.

When we copy from a `string`, we can supply an optional starting position and a count. The starting position must be less than or equal to the size of the given `string`. If the position is greater than the size, then the constructor throws an `out_of_range` exception (§ 5.6, p. 193). When we pass a count, that many characters are copied, starting from the given position. Regardless of how many characters we ask for, the library copies up to the size of the `string`, but not more.

The `substr` Operation

The `substr` operation (described in Table 9.12) returns a `string` that is a copy of part or all of the original `string`. We can pass `substr` an optional starting position and count:

```
string s("hello world");
string s2 = s.substr(0, 5);   // s2 = hello
string s3 = s.substr(6);      // s3 = world
string s4 = s.substr(6, 11);  // s3 = world
string s5 = s.substr(12);     // throws an out_of_range exception
```

The `substr` function throws an `out_of_range` exception (§ 5.6, p. 193) if the position exceeds the size of the `string`. If the position plus the count is greater than the size, the count is adjusted to copy only up to the end of the `string`.

Table 9.12: Substring Operation
`s.substr(pos, n)`   Return a `string` containing n characters from s starting at pos. pos defaults to 0. n defaults to a value that causes the library to copy all the characters in s starting from pos.

EXERCISES SECTION 9.5.1

Exercise 9.41: Write a program that initializes a `string` from a `vector<char>`.

Exercise 9.42: Given that you want to read a character at a time into a `string`, and you know that you need to read at least 100 characters, how might you improve the performance of your program?

9.5.2 Other Ways to Change a `string`

The `string` type supports the sequential container assignment operators and the `assign`, `insert`, and `erase` operations (§ 9.2.5, p. 337, § 9.3.1, p. 342, and § 9.3.3, p. 348). It also defines additional versions of `insert` and `erase`.

In addition to the versions of insert and erase that take iterators, string provides versions that take an index. The index indicates the starting element to erase or the position before which to insert the given values:

```
s.insert(s.size(), 5, '!'); // insert five exclamation points at the end of s
s.erase(s.size() - 5, 5);   // erase the last five characters from s
```

The string library also provides versions of insert and assign that take C-style character arrays. For example, we can use a null-terminated character array as the value to insert or assign into a string:

```
const char *cp = "Stately, plump Buck";
s.assign(cp, 7);              // s == "Stately"
s.insert(s.size(), cp + 7); // s == "Stately, plump Buck"
```

Here we first replace the contents of s by calling assign. The characters we assign into s are the seven characters starting with the one pointed to by cp. The number of characters we request must be less than or equal to the number of characters (excluding the null terminator) in the array to which cp points.

When we call insert on s, we say that we want to insert the characters before the (nonexistent) element at s[size()]. In this case, we copy characters starting seven characters past cp up to the terminating null.

We can also specify the characters to insert or assign as coming from another string or substring thereof:

```
string s = "some string", s2 = "some other string";
s.insert(0, s2); // insert a copy of s2 before position 0 in s
// insert s2.size() characters from s2 starting at s2[0] before s[0]
s.insert(0, s2, 0, s2.size());
```

The append and replace Functions

The string class defines two additional members, append and replace, that can change the contents of a string. Table 9.13 summarizes these functions. The append operation is a shorthand way of inserting at the end:

```
string s("C++ Primer"), s2 = s; // initialize s and s2 to "C++ Primer"
s.insert(s.size(), " 4th Ed."); // s == "C++ Primer 4th Ed."
s2.append(" 4th Ed."); // equivalent: appends " 4th Ed." to s2; s == s2
```

The replace operations are a shorthand way of calling erase and insert:

```
// equivalent way to replace "4th" by "5th"
s.erase(11, 3);              // s == "C++ Primer Ed."
s.insert(11, "5th");        // s == "C++ Primer 5th Ed."
// starting at position 11, erase three characters and then insert "5th"
s2.replace(11, 3, "5th"); // equivalent: s == s2
```

In the call to replace, the text we inserted happens to be the same size as the text we removed. We can insert a larger or smaller string:

```
s.replace(11, 3, "Fifth");      // s == "C++ Primer Fifth Ed."
```

In this call we remove three characters but insert five in their place.

Table 9.13: Operations to Modify strings	
s.insert(*pos*, *args*)	Insert characters specified by *args* before *pos*. *pos* can be an index or an iterator. Versions taking an index return a reference to s; those taking an iterator return an iterator denoting the first inserted character.
s.erase(pos, len)	Remove len characters starting at position pos. If len is omitted, removes characters from pos to the end of the s. Returns a reference to s.
s.assign(*args*)	Replace characters in s according to *args*. Returns a reference to s.
s.append(*args*)	Append *args* to s. Returns a reference to s.
s.replace(*range*, *args*)	Remove *range* of characters from s and replace them with the characters formed by *args*. *range* is either an index and a length or a pair of iterators into s. Returns a reference to s.

**args can be one of the following; append and assign can use all forms
str must be distinct from s and the iterators b and e may not refer to s**

str	The string str.
str, pos, len	Up to len characters from str starting at pos.
cp, len	Up to len characters from the character array pointed to by cp.
cp	Null-terminated array pointed to by pointer cp.
n, c	n copies of character c.
b, e	Characters in the range formed by iterators b and e.
initializer list	Comma-separated list of characters enclosed in braces.

args for replace and insert depend on how *range* or *pos* is specified.

replace (pos,len,*args*)	replace (b,e,*args*)	insert (pos,*args*)	insert (iter,*args*)	*args* can be
yes	yes	yes	no	str
yes	no	yes	no	str, pos, len
yes	yes	yes	no	cp, len
yes	yes	no	no	cp
yes	yes	yes	yes	n, c
no	yes	no	yes	b2, e2
no	yes	no	yes	*initializer list*

The Many Overloaded Ways to Change a string

The append, assign, insert, and replace functions listed Table 9.13 have several overloaded versions. The arguments to these functions vary as to how we specify what characters to add and what part of the string to change. Fortunately, these functions share a common interface.

The assign and append functions have no need to specify what part of the string is changed: assign always replaces the entire contents of the string and append always adds to the end of the string.

The replace functions provide two ways to specify the range of characters to remove. We can specify that range by a position and a length, or with an iterator range. The insert functions give us two ways to specify the insertion point: with either an index or an iterator. In each case, the new element(s) are inserted in front of the given index or iterator.

There are several ways to specify the characters to add to the string. The new characters can be taken from another string, from a character pointer, from a brace-enclosed list of characters, or as a character and a count. When the characters come from a string or a character pointer, we can pass additional arguments to control whether we copy some or all of the characters from the argument.

Not every function supports every version of these arguments. For example, there is no version of insert that takes an index and an initializer list. Similarly, if we want to specify the insertion point using an iterator, then we cannot pass a character pointer as the source for the new characters.

EXERCISES SECTION 9.5.2

Exercise 9.43: Write a function that takes three strings, s, oldVal, and newVal. Using iterators, and the insert and erase functions replace all instances of oldVal that appear in s by newVal. Test your function by using it to replace common abbreviations, such as "tho" by "though" and "thru" by "through".

Exercise 9.44: Rewrite the previous function using an index and replace.

Exercise 9.45: Write a funtion that takes a string representing a name and two other strings representing a prefix, such as "Mr." or "Ms." and a suffix, such as "Jr." or "III". Using iterators and the insert and append functions, generate and return a new string with the suffix and prefix added to the given name.

Exercise 9.46: Rewrite the previous exercise using a position and length to manage the strings. This time use only the insert function.

9.5.3 string Search Operations

The string class provides six different search functions, each of which has four overloaded versions. Table 9.14 describes the search members and their arguments. Each of these search operations returns a string::size_type value that is the index of where the match occurred. If there is no match, the function returns a static member (§ 7.6, p. 300) named string::npos. The library defines npos as a const string::size_type initialized with the value -1. Because npos is an unsigned type, this initializer means npos is equal to the largest possible size any string could have (§ 2.1.2, p. 35).

> **⚠ WARNING** The string search functions return string::size_type, which is an unsigned type. As a result, it is a bad idea to use an int, or other signed type, to hold the return from these functions (§ 2.1.2, p. 36).

The find function does the simplest search. It looks for its argument and returns the index of the first match that is found, or npos if there is no match:

```
string name("AnnaBelle");
auto pos1 = name.find("Anna"); // pos1 == 0
```

returns 0, the index at which the substring "Anna" is found in "AnnaBelle".

Searching (and other string operations) are case sensitive. When we look for a value in the string, case matters:

```
string lowercase("annabelle");
pos1 = lowercase.find("Anna");   // pos1 == npos
```

This code will set pos1 to npos because Anna does not match anna.

A slightly more complicated problem requires finding a match to any character in the search string. For example, the following locates the first digit within name:

```
string numbers("0123456789"), name("r2d2");
//  returns 1, i.e., the index of the first digit in name
auto pos = name.find_first_of(numbers);
```

Instead of looking for a match, we might call find_first_not_of to find the first position that is *not* in the search argument. For example, to find the first non-numeric character of a string, we can write

```
string dept("03714p3");
//  returns 5, which is the index to the character 'p'
auto pos = dept.find_first_not_of(numbers);
```

Table 9.14: string Search Operations	
Search operations return the index of the desired character or npos if not found	
s.find(*args*)	Find the first occurrence of *args* in s.
s.rfind(*args*)	Find the last occurrence of *args* in s.
s.find_first_of(*args*)	Find the first occurrence of any character from *args* in s.
s.find_last_of(*args*)	Find the last occurrence of any character from *args* in s.
s.find_first_not_of(*args*)	Find the first character in s that is not in *args*.
s.find_last_not_of(*args*)	Find the last character in s that is not in *args*.
args **must be one of**	
c, pos	Look for the character c starting at position pos in s. pos defaults to 0.
s2, pos	Look for the string s2 starting at position pos in s. pos defaults to 0.
cp, pos	Look for the C-style null-terminated string pointed to by the pointer cp. Start looking at position pos in s. pos defaults to 0.
cp, pos, n	Look for the first n characters in the array pointed to by the pointer cp. Start looking at position pos in s. No default for pos or n.

Specifying Where to Start the Search

We can pass an optional starting position to the find operations. This optional argument indicates the position from which to start the search. By default, that position is set to zero. One common programming pattern uses this optional argument to loop through a string finding all occurrences:

```
string::size_type pos = 0;
// each iteration finds the next number in name
while ((pos = name.find_first_of(numbers, pos))
                != string::npos) {
    cout << "found number at index: " << pos
         << " element is " << name[pos] << endl;
    ++pos; // move to the next character
}
```

The condition in the while resets pos to the index of the first number encountered, starting from the current value of pos. So long as find_first_of returns a valid index, we print the current result and increment pos.

Had we neglected to increment pos, the loop would never terminate. To see why, consider what would happen if we didn't do the increment. On the second trip through the loop we start looking at the character indexed by pos. That character would be a number, so find_first_of would (repeatedly) returns pos!

Searching Backward

The find operations we've used so far execute left to right. The library provides analogous operations that search from right to left. The rfind member searches for the last—that is, right-most—occurrence of the indicated substring:

```
string river("Mississippi");
auto first_pos = river.find("is");   // returns 1
auto last_pos = river.rfind("is");   // returns 4
```

find returns an index of 1, indicating the start of the first "is", while rfind returns an index of 4, indicating the start of the last occurrence of "is".

Similarly, the find_last functions behave like the find_first functions, except that they return the *last* match rather than the first:

- find_last_of searches for the last character that matches any element of the search string.

- find_last_not_of searches for the last character that does not match any element of the search string.

Each of these operations takes an optional second argument indicating the position within the string to begin searching.

9.5.4 The compare Functions

In addition to the relational operators (§ 3.2.2, p. 88), the string library provides a set of compare functions that are similar to the C library strcmp function (§ 3.5.4, p. 122). Like strcmp, s.compare returns zero or a positive or negative value depending on whether s is equal to, greater than, or less than the string formed from the given arguments.

Exercise 9.47: Write a program that finds each numeric character and then each alphabetic character in the string "ab2c3d7R4E6". Write two versions of the program. The first should use find_first_of, and the second find_first_not_of.

Exercise 9.48: Given the definitions of name and numbers on page 365, what does numbers.find(name) return?

Exercise 9.49: A letter has an ascender if, as with d or f, part of the letter extends above the middle of the line. A letter has a descender if, as with p or g, part of the letter extends below the line. Write a program that reads a file containing words and reports the longest word that contains neither ascenders nor descenders.

As shown in Table 9.15, there are six versions of compare. The arguments vary based on whether we are comparing two strings or a string and a character array. In both cases, we might compare the entire string or a portion thereof.

Table 9.15: Possible Arguments to s.compare	
s2	Compare s to s2.
pos1, n1, s2	Compares n1 characters starting at pos1 from s to s2.
pos1, n1, s2, pos2, n2	Compares n1 characters starting at pos1 from s to the n2 characters starting at pos2 in s2.
cp	Compares s to the null-terminated array pointed to by cp.
pos1, n1, cp	Compares n1 characters starting at pos1 from s to cp.
pos1, n1, cp, n2	Compares n1 characters starting at pos1 from s to n2 characters starting from the pointer cp.

9.5.5 Numeric Conversions

Strings often contain characters that represent numbers. For example, we represent the numeric value 15 as a string with two characters, the character '1' followed by the character '5'. In general, the character representation of a number differs from its numeric value. The numeric value 15 stored in a 16-bit short has the bit pattern 0000000000001111, whereas the character string "15" represented as two Latin-1 chars has the bit pattern 0011000100110101. The first byte represents the character '1' which has the octal value 061, and the second byte represents '5', which in Latin-1 is octal 065.

The new standard introduced several functions that convert between numeric data and library strings:

```
int i = 42;
string s = to_string(i);    // converts the int i to its character representation
double d = stod(s);         // converts the string s to floating-point
```

Table 9.16: Conversions between strings and Numbers	
.to_string(val);	Overloaded functions returning the string representation of val. val can be any arithmetic type (§ 2.1.1, p. 32). There are versions of to_string for each floating-point type and integral type that is int or larger. Small integral types are promoted (§ 4.11.1, p. 160) as usual.
stoi(s, p, b) stol(s, p, b) stoul(s, p, b) stoll(s, p, b) stoull(s, p, b)	Return the initial substring of s that has numeric content as an int, long, unsigned long, long long, unsigned long long, respectively. b indicates the numeric base to use for the conversion; b defaults to 10. p is a pointer to a size_t in which to put the index of the first nonnumeric character in s; p defaults to 0, in which case the function does not store the index.
stof(s, p) stod(s, p) stold(s, p)	Return the initial numeric substring in s as a float, double, or long double, respectively. p has the same behavior as described for the integer conversions.

Here we call to_string to convert 42 to its corresponding string representation and then call stod to convert that string to floating-point.

The first non-whitespace character in the string we convert to numeric value must be a character that can appear in a number:

```
string s2 = "pi = 3.14";
// convert the first substring in s that starts with a digit, d = 3.14
d = stod(s2.substr(s2.find_first_of("+-.0123456789")));
```

In this call to stod, we call find_first_of (§ 9.5.3, p. 364) to get the position of the first character in s that could be part of a number. We pass the substring of s starting at that position to stod. The stod function reads the string it is given until it finds a character that cannot be part of a number. It then converts the character representation of the number it found into the corresponding double-precision floating-point value.

The first non-whitespace character in the string must be a sign (+ or -) or a digit. The string can begin with 0x or 0X to indicate hexadecimal. For the functions that convert to floating-point the string may also start with a decimal point (.) and may contain an e or E to designate the exponent. For the functions that convert to integral type, depending on the base, the string can contain alphabetic characters corresponding to numbers beyond the digit 9.

> **Note**
> If the string can't be converted to a number, These functions throw an invalid_argument exception (§ 5.6, p. 193). If the conversion generates a value that can't be represented, they throw out_of_range.

9.6 Container Adaptors

In addition to the sequential containers, the library defines three sequential container adaptors: stack, queue, and priority_queue. An **adaptor** is a general concept in the library. There are container, iterator, and function adaptors. Essentially, an adaptor is a mechanism for making one thing act like another. A container adaptor takes an existing container type and makes it act like a different type. For example, the stack adaptor takes a sequential container (other than array or forward_list) and makes it operate as if it were a stack. Table 9.17 lists the operations and types that are common to all the container adaptors.

Table 9.17: Operations and Types Common to the Container Adaptors	
size_type	Type large enough to hold the size of the largest object of this type.
value_type	Element type.
container_type	Type of the underlying container on which the adaptor is implemented.
A a;	Create a new empty adaptor named a.
A a(c);	Create a new adaptor named a with a copy of the container c.
relational operators	Each adaptor supports all the relational operators: ==, !=, <, <=, >, >=. These operators return the result of comparing the underlying containers.
a.empty()	false if a has any elements, true otherwise.
a.size()	Number of elements in a.
swap(a, b) a.swap(b)	Swaps the contents of a and b; a and b must have the same type, including the type of the container on which they are implemented.

Defining an Adaptor

Each adaptor defines two constructors: the default constructor that creates an empty object, and a constructor that takes a container and initializes the adaptor by copying the given container. For example, assuming that deq is a deque<int>, we can use deq to initialize a new stack as follows:

```
stack<int> stk(deq);  // copies elements from deq into stk
```

By default both stack and queue are implemented in terms of deque, and a priority_queue is implemented on a vector. We can override the default container type by naming a sequential container as a second type argument when we create the adaptor:

```
// empty stack implemented on top of vector
stack<string, vector<string>> str_stk;
// str_stk2 is implemented on top of vector and initially holds a copy of svec
stack<string, vector<string>> str_stk2(svec);
```

There are constraints on which containers can be used for a given adaptor. All of the adaptors require the ability to add and remove elements. As a result, they cannot be built on an `array`. Similarly, we cannot use `forward_list`, because all of the adaptors require operations that add, remove, or access the last element in the container. A `stack` requires only push_back, pop_back, and back operations, so we can use any of the remaining container types for a `stack`. The queue adaptor requires back, push_back, front, and push_front, so it can be built on a `list` or deque but not on a `vector`. A `priority_queue` requires random access in addition to the front, push_back, and pop_back operations; it can be built on a `vector` or a deque but not on a `list`.

Stack Adaptor

The `stack` type is defined in the `stack` header. The operations provided by a `stack` are listed in Table 9.18. The following program illustrates the use of `stack`:

```
stack<int> intStack;   // empty stack
// fill up the stack
for (size_t ix = 0; ix != 10; ++ix)
    intStack.push(ix);    // intStack holds 0 ... 9 inclusive
while (!intStack.empty()) {    // while there are still values in intStack
    int value = intStack.top();
    // code that uses value
    intStack.pop();  // pop the top element, and repeat
}
```

The declaration

```
stack<int> intStack;   // empty stack
```

defines `intStack` to be an empty `stack` that holds integer elements. The `for` loop adds ten elements, initializing each to the next integer in sequence starting from zero. The `while` loop iterates through the entire `stack`, examining the `top` value and popping it from the `stack` until the `stack` is empty.

Table 9.18: Stack Operations in Addition to Those in Table 9.17	
Uses deque by default; can be implemented on a `list` or `vector` as well.	
s.pop()	Removes, but does not return, the top element from the `stack`.
s.push(item)	Creates a new top element on the `stack` by copying or moving item, or
s.emplace(*args*)	by constructing the element from *args*.
s.top()	Returns, but does not remove, the top element on the `stack`.

Each container adaptor defines its own operations in terms of operations provided by the underlying container type. We can use only the adaptor operations and cannot use the operations of the underlying container type. For example,

```
intStack.push(ix);    // intStack holds 0...9 inclusive
```

calls push_back on the deque object on which intStack is based. Although stack is implemented by using a deque, we have no direct access to the deque operations. We cannot call push_back on a stack; instead, we must use the stack operation named push.

The Queue Adaptors

The queue and priority_queue adaptors are defined in the queue header. Table 9.19 lists the operations supported by these types.

Table 9.19: queue, priority_queue Operations in Addition to Table 9.17	
By default queue uses deque and priority_queue uses vector; queue can use a list or vector as well, priority_queue can use a deque.	
q.pop()	Removes, but does not return, the front element or highest-priority element from the queue or priority_queue, respectively.
q.front() q.back()	Returns, but does not remove, the front or back element of q. **Valid only for queue**
q.top()	Returns, but does not remove, the highest-priority element. **Valid only for priority_queue.**
q.push(item) q.emplace(args)	Create an element with value item or constructed from args at the end of the queue or in its appropriate position in priority_queue.

The library queue uses a first-in, first-out (FIFO) storage and retrieval policy. Objects entering the queue are placed in the back and objects leaving the queue are removed from the front. A restaurant that seats people in the order in which they arrive is an example of a FIFO queue.

A priority_queue lets us establish a priority among the elements held in the queue. Newly added elements are placed ahead of all the elements with a lower priority. A restaurant that seats people according to their reservation time, regardless of when they arrive, is an example of a priority queue. By default, the library uses the < operator on the element type to determine relative priorities. We'll learn how to override this default in § 11.2.2 (p. 425).

EXERCISES SECTION 9.6

Exercise 9.52: Use a stack to process parenthesized expressions. When you see an open parenthesis, note that it was seen. When you see a close parenthesis after an open parenthesis, pop elements down to and including the open parenthesis off the stack. push a value onto the stack to indicate that a parenthesized expression was replaced.

CHAPTER SUMMARY

The library containers are template types that holds objects of a given type. In a sequential container, elements are ordered and accessed by position. The sequential containers share a common, standardized interface: If two sequential containers offer a particular operation, then the operation has the same interface and meaning for both containers.

All the containers (except `array`) provide efficient dynamic memory management. We may add elements to the container without worrying about where to store the elements. The container itself manages its storage. Both `vector` and `string` provide more detailed control over memory management through their `reserve` and `capacity` members.

For the most part, the containers define surprisingly few operations. Containers define constructors, operations to add or remove elements, operations to determine the size of the container, and operations to return iterators to particular elements. Other useful operations, such as sorting or searching, are defined not by the container types but by the standard algorithms, which we shall cover in Chapter 10.

When we use container operations that add or remove elements, it is essential to remember that these operations can invalidate iterators, pointers, or references to elements in the container. Many operations that invalidate an iterator, such as `insert` or `erase`, return a new iterator that allows the programmer to maintain a position within the container. Loops that use container operations that change the size of a container should be particularly careful in their use of iterators, pointers, and references.

DEFINED TERMS

adaptor Library type, function, or iterator that, given a type, function, or iterator, makes it act like another. There are three sequential container adaptors: `stack`, `queue`, and `priority_queue`. Each adaptor defines a new interface on top of an underlying sequential container type.

array Fixed-size sequential container. To define an `array`, we must give the size in addition to specifying the element type. Elements in an `array` can be accessed by their positional index. Supports fast random access to elements.

begin Container operation that returns an iterator referring to the first element in the container, if there is one, or the off-the-end iterator if the container is empty. Whether the returned iterator is `const` depends on the type of the container.

cbegin Container operation that returns a `const_iterator` referring to the first element in the container, if there is one, or the off-the-end iterator if the container is empty.

cend Container operation that returns a `const_iterator` referring to the (nonexistent) element one past the end of the container.

container Type that holds a collection of objects of a given type. Each library container type is a template type. To define a container, we must specify the type of the elements stored in the container. With the exception of `array`, the library containers are variable-size.

deque Sequential container. Elements in a `deque` can be accessed by their positional index. Supports fast random access to elements. Like a `vector` in all respects except that it supports fast insertion and deletion at the front of the container as well as at the back and does not relocate elements as a result of insertions or deletions at either end.

end Container operation that returns an iterator referring to the (nonexistent) element one past the end of the container. Whether the returned iterator is `const` depends on the type of the container.

forward_list Sequential container that represents a singly linked list. Elements in a `forward_list` may be accessed only sequentially; starting from a given element, we can get to another element only by traversing each element between them. Iterators on `forward_list` do not support decrement (`--`). Supports fast insertion (or deletion) anywhere in the `forward_list`. Unlike other containers, insertions and deletions occur *after* a given iterator position. As a consequence, `forward_list` has a "before-the-beginning" iterator to go along with the usual off-the-end iterator. Iterators remain valid when new elements are added. When an element is removed, only the iterators to that element are invalidated.

iterator range Range of elements denoted by a pair of iterators. The first iterator denotes the first element in the sequence, and the second iterator denotes one past the last element. If the range is empty, then the iterators are equal (and vice versa—if the iterators are unequal, they denote a nonempty range). If the range is not empty, then it must be possible to reach the second iterator by repeatedly incrementing the first iterator. By incrementing the iterator, each element in the sequence can be processed.

left-inclusive interval A range of values that includes its first element but not its last. Typically denoted as `[i, j)`, meaning the sequence starting at and including i up to but excluding j.

list Sequential container representing a doubly linked list. Elements in a `list` may be accessed only sequentially; starting from a given element, we can get to another element only by traversing each element between them. Iterators on `list` support both increment (`++`) and decrement (`--`). Supports fast insertion (or deletion) anywhere in the `list`. Iterators remain valid when new elements are added. When an element is removed, only the iterators to that element are invalidated.

off-the-beginning iterator Iterator denoting the (nonexistent) element just before the beginning of a `forward_list`. Returned from the `forward_list` member `before_begin`. Like the `end()` iterator, it may not be dereferenced.

off-the-end iterator Iterator that denotes one past the last element in the range. Commonly referred to as the "end iterator".

priority_queue Adaptor for the sequential containers that yields a queue in which elements are inserted, not at the end but according to a specified priority level. By default, priority is determined by using the less-than operator for the element type.

queue Adaptor for the sequential containers that yields a type that lets us add elements to the back and remove elements from the front.

sequential container Type that holds an ordered collection of objects of a single type. Elements in a sequential container are accessed by position.

stack Adaptor for the sequential containers that yields a type that lets us add and remove elements from one end only.

vector Sequential container. Elements in a `vector` can be accessed by their positional index. Supports fast random access to elements. We can efficiently add or remove `vector` elements only at the back. Adding elements to a `vector` might cause it to be reallocated, invalidating all iterators into the `vector`. Adding (or removing) an element in the middle of a `vector` invalidates all iterators to elements after the insertion (or deletion) point.

CHAPTER 10

GENERIC ALGORITHMS

CONTENTS

The library containers define a surprisingly small set of operations. Rather than adding lots of functionality to each container, the library provides a set of algorithms, most of which are independent of any particular container type. These algorithms are *generic*: They operate on different types of containers and on elements of various types.

The generic algorithms, and a more detailed look at iterators, form the subject matter of this chapter.

The sequential containers define few operations: For the most part, we can add and remove elements, access the first or last element, determine whether a container is empty, and obtain iterators to the first or one past the last element.

We can imagine many other useful operations one might want to do: We might want to find a particular element, replace or remove a particular value, reorder the container elements, and so on.

Rather than define each of these operations as members of each container type, the standard library defines a set of **generic algorithms**: "algorithms" because they implement common classical algorithms such as sorting and searching, and "generic" because they operate on elements of differing type and across multiple container types—not only library types such as `vector` or `list`, but also the built-in array type—and, as we shall see, over other kinds of sequences as well.

10.1 Overview

Most of the algorithms are defined in the `algorithm` header. The library also defines a set of generic numeric algorithms that are defined in the `numeric` header.

In general, the algorithms do not work directly on a container. Instead, they operate by traversing a range of elements bounded by two iterators (§ 9.2.1, p. 331). Typically, as the algorithm traverses the range, it does something with each element. For example, suppose we have a `vector` of `ints` and we want to know if that `vector` holds a particular value. The easiest way to answer this question is to call the library `find` algorithm:

```
int val = 42; // value we'll look for
// result will denote the element we want if it's in vec, or vec.cend() if not
auto result = find(vec.cbegin(), vec.cend(), val);
// report the result
cout << "The value " << val
     << (result == vec.cend()
            ? " is not present" : " is present") << endl;
```

The first two arguments to `find` are iterators denoting a range of elements, and the third argument is a value. `find` compares each element in the given range to the given value. It returns an iterator to the first element that is equal to that value. If there is no match, `find` returns its second iterator to indicate failure. Thus, we can determine whether the element was found by comparing the return value with the second iterator argument. We do this test in the output statement, which uses the conditional operator (§ 4.7, p. 151) to report whether the value was found.

Because `find` operates in terms of iterators, we can use the same `find` function to look for values in any type of container. For example, we can use `find` to look for a value in a `list` of `strings`:

```
string val = "a value";   // value we'll look for
// this call to find looks through string elements in a list
auto result = find(lst.cbegin(), lst.cend(), val);
```

Similarly, because pointers act like iterators on built-in arrays, we can use `find` to look in an array:

```
int ia[] = {27, 210, 12, 47, 109, 83};
int val = 83;
int* result = find(begin(ia), end(ia), val);
```

Here we use the library `begin` and `end` functions (§ 3.5.3, p. 118) to pass a pointer to the first and one past the last elements in `ia`.

We can also look in a subrange of the sequence by passing iterators (or pointers) to the first and one past the last element of that subrange. For example, this call looks for a match in the elements `ia[1]`, `ia[2]`, and `ia[3]`:

```
// search the elements starting from ia[1] up to but not including ia[4]
auto result = find(ia + 1, ia + 4, val);
```

How the Algorithms Work

To see how the algorithms can be used on varying types of containers, let's look a bit more closely at `find`. Its job is to find a particular element in an unsorted sequence of elements. Conceptually, we can list the steps `find` must take:

1. It accesses the first element in the sequence.

2. It compares that element to the value we want.

3. If this element matches the one we want, `find` returns a value that identifies this element.

4. Otherwise, `find` advances to the next element and repeats steps 2 and 3.

5. `find` must stop when it has reached the end of the sequence.

6. If `find` gets to the end of the sequence, it needs to return a value indicating that the element was not found. This value and the one returned from step 3 must have compatible types.

None of these operations depends on the type of the container that holds the elements. So long as there is an iterator that can be used to access the elements, `find` doesn't depend in any way on the container type (or even whether the elements are stored in a container).

Iterators Make the Algorithms Container Independent, . . .

All but the second step in the `find` function can be handled by iterator operations: The iterator dereference operator gives access to an element's value; if a matching element is found, `find` can return an iterator to that element; the iterator increment operator moves to the next element; the "off-the-end" iterator will indicate when `find` has reached the end of its given sequence; and `find` can return the off-the-end iterator (§ 9.2.1, p. 331) to indicate that the given value wasn't found.

. . . But Algorithms Do Depend on Element-Type Operations

Although iterators make the algorithms container independent, most of the algorithms use one (or more) operation(s) on the element type. For example, step 2, uses the element type's `==` operator to compare each element to the given value.

Other algorithms require that the element type have the < operator. However, as we'll see, most algorithms provide a way for us to supply our own operation to use in place of the default operator.

EXERCISES SECTION 10.1

Exercise 10.1: The algorithm header defines a function named count that, like find, takes a pair of iterators and a value. count returns a count of how often that value appears. Read a sequence of ints into a vector and print the count of how many elements have a given value.

Exercise 10.2: Repeat the previous program, but read values into a list of strings.

KEY CONCEPT: ALGORITHMS NEVER EXECUTE CONTAINER OPERATIONS

The generic algorithms do not themselves execute container operations. They operate solely in terms of iterators and iterator operations. The fact that the algorithms operate in terms of iterators and not container operations has a perhaps surprising but essential implication: Algorithms never change the size of the underlying container. Algorithms may change the values of the elements stored in the container, and they may move elements around within the container. They do not, however, ever add or remove elements directly.

As we'll see in § 10.4.1 (p. 401), there is a special class of iterator, the inserters, that do more than traverse the sequence to which they are bound. When we assign to these iterators, they execute insert operations on the underlying container. When an algorithm operates on one of these iterators, the *iterator* may have the effect of adding elements to the container. The *algorithm* itself, however, never does so.

10.2 A First Look at the Algorithms

The library provides more than 100 algorithms. Fortunately, like the containers, the algorithms have a consistent architecture. Understanding this architecture makes learning and using the algorithms easier than memorizing all 100+ of them. In this chapter, we'll illustrate how to use the algorithms, and describe the unifying principles that characterize them. Appendix A lists all the algorithms classified by how they operate.

With only a few exceptions, the algorithms operate over a range of elements. We'll refer to this range as the "input range." The algorithms that take an input range always use their first two parameters to denote that range. These parameters are iterators denoting the first and one past the last elements to process.

Although most algorithms are similar in that they operate over an input range, they differ in how they use the elements in that range. The most basic way to understand the algorithms is to know whether they read elements, write elements, or rearrange the order of the elements.

10.2.1 Read-Only Algorithms

A number of the algorithms read, but never write to, the elements in their input range. The find function is one such algorithm, as is the count function we used in the exercises for § 10.1 (p. 378).

Another read-only algorithm is accumulate, which is defined in the numeric header. The accumulate function takes three arguments. The first two specify a range of elements to sum. The third is an initial value for the sum. Assuming vec is a sequence of integers, the following

```
// sum the elements in vec starting the summation with the value 0
int sum = accumulate(vec.cbegin(), vec.cend(), 0);
```

sets sum equal to the sum of the elements in vec, using 0 as the starting point for the summation.

> **Note** The type of the third argument to accumulate determines which addition operator is used and is the type that accumulate returns.

Algorithms and Element Types

The fact that accumulate uses its third argument as the starting point for the summation has an important implication: It must be possible to add the element type to the type of the sum. That is, the elements in the sequence must match or be convertible to the type of the third argument. In this example, the elements in vec might be ints, or they might be double, or long long, or any other type that can be added to an int.

As another example, because string has a + operator, we can concatenate the elements of a vector of strings by calling accumulate:

```
string sum = accumulate(v.cbegin(), v.cend(), string(""));
```

This call concatenates each element in v onto a string that starts out as the empty string. Note that we explicitly create a string as the third parameter. Passing the empty string as a string literal would be a compile-time error:

```
// error: no + on const char*
string sum = accumulate(v.cbegin(), v.cend(), "");
```

Had we passed a string literal, the type of the object used to hold the sum would be const char*. That type determines which + operator is used. Because there is no + operator for type const char*, this call will not compile.

> **Best Practices** Ordinarily it is best to use cbegin() and cend() (§ 9.2.3, p. 334) with algorithms that read, but do not write, the elements. However, if you plan to use the iterator returned by the algorithm to change an element's value, then you need to pass begin() and end().

Algorithms That Operate on Two Sequences

Another read-only algorithm is `equal`, which lets us determine whether two sequences hold the same values. It compares each element from the first sequence to the corresponding element in the second. It returns `true` if the corresponding elements are equal, `false` otherwise. The algorithm takes three iterators: The first two (as usual) denote the range of elements in the first sequence; the third denotes the first element in the second sequence:

```
// roster2 should have at least as many elements as roster1
equal(roster1.cbegin(), roster1.cend(), roster2.cbegin());
```

Because `equal` operates in terms of iterators, we can call `equal` to compare elements in containers of different types. Moreover, the element types also need not be the same so long as we can use `==` to compare the element types. For example, `roster1` could be a `vector<string>` and `roster2` a `list<const char*>`.

However, `equal` makes one critically important assumption: It assumes that the second sequence is at least as big as the first. This algorithm potentially looks at every element in the first sequence. It assumes that there is a corresponding element for each of those elements in the second sequence.

> **WARNING** Algorithms that take a single iterator denoting a second sequence *assume* that the second sequence is at least as large at the first.

EXERCISES SECTION 10.2.1

Exercise 10.3: Use `accumulate` to sum the elements in a `vector<int>`.

Exercise 10.4: Assuming `v` is a `vector<double>`, what, if anything, is wrong with calling `accumulate(v.cbegin(), v.cend(), 0)`?

Exercise 10.5: In the call to `equal` on rosters, what would happen if both rosters held C-style strings, rather than library `string`s?

10.2.2 Algorithms That Write Container Elements

Some algorithms assign new values to the elements in a sequence. When we use an algorithm that assigns to elements, we must take care to ensure that the sequence into which the algorithm writes is at least as large as the number of elements we ask the algorithm to write. Remember, algorithms do not perform container operations, so they have no way themselves to change the size of a container.

Some algorithms write to elements in the input range itself. These algorithms are not inherently dangerous because they write only as many elements as are in the specified range.

As one example, the `fill` algorithm takes a pair of iterators that denote a range and a third argument that is a value. `fill` assigns the given value to each element in the input sequence:

```
fill(vec.begin(), vec.end(), 0);   //  reset each element to 0
//  set a subsequence of the container to 10
fill(vec.begin(), vec.begin() + vec.size()/2, 10);
```

Because `fill` writes to its given input sequence, so long as we pass a valid input sequence, the writes will be safe.

Algorithms Do Not Check Write Operations

Some algorithms take an iterator that denotes a separate destination. These algorithms assign new values to the elements of a sequence starting at the element denoted by the destination iterator. For example, the `fill_n` function takes a single iterator, a count, and a value. It assigns the given value to the specified number of elements starting at the element denoted to by the iterator. We might use `fill_n` to assign a new value to the elements in a `vector`:

```
vector<int> vec;   //  empty vector
//  use vec giving it various values
fill_n(vec.begin(), vec.size(), 0); //  reset all the elements of vec to 0
```

The `fill_n` function assumes that it is safe to write the specified number of elements. That is, for a call of the form

```
fill_n(dest, n, val)
```

`fill_n` assumes that `dest` refers to an element and that there are at least n elements in the sequence starting from `dest`.

It is a fairly common beginner mistake to call `fill_n` (or similar algorithms that write to elements) on a container that has no elements:

```
vector<int> vec;  // empty vector
//  disaster: attempts to write to ten (nonexistent) elements in vec
fill_n(vec.begin(), 10, 0);
```

This call to `fill_n` is a disaster. We specified that ten elements should be written, but there are no such elements—`vec` is empty. The result is undefined.

> Algorithms that write to a destination iterator *assume* the destination is large enough to hold the number of elements being written.

Introducing `back_inserter`

One way to ensure that an algorithm has enough elements to hold the output is to use an **insert iterator**. An insert iterator is an iterator that *adds* elements to a container. Ordinarily, when we assign to a container element through an iterator, we assign to the element that iterator denotes. When we assign through an insert iterator, a new element equal to the right-hand value is added to the container.

We'll have more to say about insert iterators in § 10.4.1 (p. 401). However, in order to illustrate how to use algorithms that write to a container, we will use **back_inserter**, which is a function defined in the `iterator` header.

`back_inserter` takes a reference to a container and returns an insert iterator bound to that container. When we assign through that iterator, the assignment calls `push_back` to add an element with the given value to the container:

```
vector<int> vec; // empty vector
auto it = back_inserter(vec); // assigning through it adds elements to vec
*it = 42;            // vec now has one element with value 42
```

We frequently use `back_inserter` to create an iterator to use as the destination of an algorithm. For example:

```
vector<int> vec; // empty vector
// ok: back_inserter creates an insert iterator that adds elements to vec
fill_n(back_inserter(vec), 10, 0);  // appends ten elements to vec
```

On each iteration, `fill_n` assigns to an element in the given sequence. Because we passed an iterator returned by `back_inserter`, each assignment will call `push_back` on `vec`. As a result, this call to `fill_n` adds ten elements to the end of `vec`, each of which has the value `0`.

Copy Algorithms

The `copy` algorithm is another example of an algorithm that writes to the elements of an output sequence denoted by a destination iterator. This algorithm takes three iterators. The first two denote an input range; the third denotes the beginning of the destination sequence. This algorithm copies elements from its input range into elements in the destination. It is essential that the destination passed to `copy` be at least as large as the input range.

As one example, we can use copy to copy one built-in array to another:

```
int a1[] = {0,1,2,3,4,5,6,7,8,9};
int a2[sizeof(a1)/sizeof(*a1)];  // a2 has the same size as a1
// ret points just past the last element copied into a2
auto ret = copy(begin(a1), end(a1), a2);  // copy a1 into a2
```

Here we define an array named a2 and use sizeof to ensure that a2 has as many elements as the array a1 (§ 4.9, p. 157). We then call copy to copy a1 into a2. After the call to copy, the elements in both arrays have the same values.

The value returned by copy is the (incremented) value of its destination iterator. That is, ret will point just past the last element copied into a2.

Several algorithms provide so-called "copying" versions. These algorithms compute new element values, but instead of putting them back into their input sequence, the algorithms create a new sequence to contain the results.

For example, the replace algorithm reads a sequence and replaces every instance of a given value with another value. This algorithm takes four parameters: two iterators denoting the input range, and two values. It replaces each element that is equal to the first value with the second:

```
// replace any element with the value 0 with 42
replace(ilst.begin(), ilst.end(), 0, 42);
```

This call replaces all instances of 0 by 42. If we want to leave the original sequence unchanged, we can call replace_copy. That algorithm takes a third iterator argument denoting a destination in which to write the adjusted sequence:

```
// use back_inserter to grow destination as needed
replace_copy(ilst.cbegin(), ilst.cend(),
             back_inserter(ivec), 0, 42);
```

After this call, ilst is unchanged, and ivec contains a copy of ilst with the exception that every element in ilst with the value 0 has the value 42 in ivec.

10.2.3 Algorithms That Reorder Container Elements

Some algorithms rearrange the order of elements within a container. An obvious example of such an algorithm is sort. A call to sort arranges the elements in the input range into sorted order using the element type's < operator.

As an example, suppose we want to analyze the words used in a set of children's stories. We'll assume that we have a vector that holds the text of several stories. We'd like to reduce this vector so that each word appears only once, regardless of how many times that word appears in any of the given stories.

For purposes of illustration, we'll use the following simple story as our input:

the quick red fox jumps over the slow red turtle

Given this input, our program should produce the following vector:

fox	jumps	over	quick	red	slow	the	turtle

Eliminating Duplicates

To eliminate the duplicated words, we will first sort the `vector` so that duplicated words appear adjacent to each other. Once the `vector` is sorted, we can use another library algorithm, named `unique`, to reorder the `vector` so that the unique elements appear in the first part of the `vector`. Because algorithms cannot do container operations, we'll use the `erase` member of `vector` to actually remove the elements:

```
void elimDups(vector<string> &words)
{
    // sort words alphabetically so we can find the duplicates
    sort(words.begin(), words.end());
    // unique reorders the input range so that each word appears once in the
    // front portion of the range and returns an iterator one past the unique range
    auto end_unique = unique(words.begin(), words.end());
    // erase uses a vector operation to remove the nonunique elements
    words.erase(end_unique, words.end());
}
```

The `sort` algorithm takes two iterators denoting the range of elements to sort. In this call, we sort the entire `vector`. After the call to `sort`, `words` is ordered as

fox	jumps	over	quick	red	red	slow	the	the	turtle

Note that the words `red` and `the` appear twice.

Using `unique`

Once `words` is sorted, we want to keep only one copy of each word. The `unique` algorithm rearranges the input range to "eliminate" adjacent duplicated entries, and returns an iterator that denotes the end of the range of the unique values. After the call to `unique`, the `vector` holds

| fox | jumps | over | quick | red | slow | the | turtle | ??? | ??? |

> end_unique
> *(one past the last unique element)*

The size of `words` is unchanged; it still has ten elements. The order of those elements is changed—the adjacent duplicates have been "removed." We put remove in quotes because `unique` doesn't remove any elements. Instead, it overwrites adjacent duplicates so that the unique elements appear at the front of the sequence. The iterator returned by `unique` denotes one past the last unique element. The elements beyond that point still exist, but we don't know what values they have.

> **Note** The library algorithms operate on iterators, not containers. Therefore, an algorithm cannot (directly) add or remove elements.

Using Container Operations to Remove Elements

To actually remove the unused elements, we must use a container operation, which we do in the call to `erase` (§ 9.3.3, p. 349). We erase the range of elements from the one to which `end_unique` refers through the end of `words`. After this call, `words` contains the eight unique words from the input.

It is worth noting that this call to `erase` would be safe even if `words` has no duplicated words. In that case, `unique` would return `words.end()`. Both arguments to `erase` would have the same value: `words.end()`. The fact that the iterators are equal would mean that the range passed to `erase` would be empty. Erasing an empty range has no effect, so our program is correct even if the input has no duplicates.

EXERCISES SECTION 10.2.3

Exercise 10.9: Implement your own version of `elimDups`. Test your program by printing the `vector` after you read the input, after the call to `unique`, and after the call to `erase`.

Exercise 10.10: Why do you think the algorithms don't change the size of containers?

10.3 Customizing Operations

Many of the algorithms compare elements in the input sequence. By default, such algorithms use either the element type's `<` or `==` operator. The library also defines versions of these algorithms that let us supply our own operation to use in place of the default operator.

For example, the `sort` algorithm uses the element type's < operator. However, we might want to sort a sequence into a different order from that defined by <, or our sequence might have elements of a type (such as `Sales_data`) that does not have a < operator. In both cases, we need to override the default behavior of `sort`.

10.3.1 Passing a Function to an Algorithm

As one example, assume that we want to print the `vector` after we call `elimDups` (§ 10.2.3, p. 384). However, we'll also assume that we want to see the words ordered by their size, and then alphabetically within each size. To reorder the `vector` by length, we'll use a second, overloaded version of `sort`. This version of `sort` takes a third argument that is a **predicate**.

Predicates

A predicate is an expression that can be called and that returns a value that can be used as a condition. The predicates used by library algorithms are either **unary predicates** (meaning they have a single parameter) or **binary predicates** (meaning they have two parameters). The algorithms that take predicates call the given predicate on the elements in the input range. As a result, it must be possible to convert the element type to the parameter type of the predicate.

The version of `sort` that takes a binary predicate uses the given predicate in place of < to compare elements. The predicates that we supply to `sort` must meet the requirements that we'll describe in § 11.2.2 (p. 425). For now, what we need to know is that the operation must define a consistent order for all possible elements in the input sequence. Our `isShorter` function from § 6.2.2 (p. 211) is an example of a function that meets these requirements, so we can pass `isShorter` to `sort`. Doing so will reorder the elements by size:

```
//  comparison function to be used to sort by word length
bool isShorter(const string &s1, const string &s2)
{
    return s1.size() < s2.size();
}
//  sort on word length, shortest to longest
sort(words.begin(), words.end(), isShorter);
```

If `words` contains the same data as in § 10.2.3 (p. 384), this call would reorder `words` so that all the words of length 3 appear before words of length 4, which in turn are followed by words of length 5, and so on.

Sorting Algorithms

When we sort `words` by size, we also want to maintain alphabetic order among the elements that have the same length. To keep the words of the same length in alphabetical order we can use the `stable_sort` algorithm. A stable sort maintains the original order among equal elements.

Ordinarily, we don't care about the relative order of equal elements in a sorted sequence. After all, they're equal. However, in this case, we have defined "equal" to mean "have the same length." Elements that have the same length still differ from one another when we view their contents. By calling `stable_sort`, we can maintain alphabetical order among those elements that have the same length:

```
elimDups(words);  // put words in alphabetical order and remove duplicates
// resort by length, maintaining alphabetical order among words of the same length
stable_sort(words.begin(), words.end(), isShorter);
for (const auto &s : words)   // no need to copy the strings
    cout << s << " ";  // print each element separated by a space
cout << endl;
```

Assuming `words` was in alphabetical order before this call, after the call, `words` will be sorted by element size, and the words of each length remain in alphabetical order. If we run this code on our original `vector`, the output will be

fox red the over slow jumps quick turtle

EXERCISES SECTION 10.3.1

Exercise 10.11: Write a program that uses `stable_sort` and `isShorter` to sort a `vector` passed to your version of `elimDups`. Print the `vector` to verify that your program is correct.

Exercise 10.12: Write a function named `compareIsbn` that compares the `isbn()` members of two `Sales_data` objects. Use that function to `sort` a `vector` that holds `Sales_data` objects.

Exercise 10.13: The library defines an algorithm named `partition` that takes a predicate and partitions the container so that values for which the predicate is `true` appear in the first part and those for which the predicate is `false` appear in the second part. The algorithm returns an iterator just past the last element for which the predicate returned `true`. Write a function that takes a `string` and returns a `bool` indicating whether the `string` has five characters or more. Use that function to partition `words`. Print the elements that have five or more characters.

10.3.2 Lambda Expressions

The predicates we pass to an algorithm must have exactly one or two parameters, depending on whether the algorithm takes a unary or binary predicate, respectively. However, sometimes we want to do processing that requires more arguments than the algorithm's predicate allows. For example, the solution you wrote for the last exercise in the previous section had to hard-wire the size 5 into the predicate used to partition the sequence. It would be move useful to be able to partition a sequence without having to write a separate predicate for every possible size.

As a related example, we'll revise our program from § 10.3.1 (p. 387) to report how many words are of a given size or greater. We'll also change the output so that it prints only the words of the given length or greater.

A sketch of this function, which we'll name `biggies`, is as follows:

```
void biggies(vector<string> &words,
             vector<string>::size_type sz)
{
    elimDups(words); // put words in alphabetical order and remove duplicates
    // resort by length, maintaining alphabetical order among words of the same length
    stable_sort(words.begin(), words.end(), isShorter);
    // get an iterator to the first element whose size() is >= sz
    // compute the number of elements with size >= sz
    // print words of the given size or longer, each one followed by a space
}
```

Our new problem is to find the first element in the vector that has the given size. Once we know that element, we can use its position to compute how many elements have that size or greater.

We can use the library find_if algorithm to find an element that has a particular size. Like find (§ 10.1, p. 376), the find_if algorithm takes a pair of iterators denoting a range. Unlike find, the third argument to find_if is a predicate. The find_if algorithm calls the given predicate on each element in the input range. It returns the first element for which the predicate returns a nonzero value, or its end iterator if no such element is found.

It would be easy to write a function that takes a string and a size and returns a bool indicating whether the size of a given string is greater than the given size. However, find_if takes a unary predicate—any function we pass to find_if must have exactly one parameter that can be called with an element from the input sequence. There is no way to pass a second argument representing the size. To solve this part of our problem we'll need to use some additional language facilities.

Introducing Lambdas

We can pass any kind of **callable object** to an algorithm. An object or expression is callable if we can apply the call operator (§ 1.5.2, p. 23) to it. That is, if e is a callable expression, we can write e(args) where args is a comma-separated list of zero or more arguments.

The only callables we've used so far are functions and function pointers (§ 6.7, p. 247). There are two other kinds of callables: classes that overload the function-call operator, which we'll cover in § 14.8 (p. 571), and **lambda expressions**.

C++
11

A lambda expression represents a callable unit of code. It can be thought of as an unnamed, inline function. Like any function, a lambda has a return type, a parameter list, and a function body. Unlike a function, lambdas may be defined inside a function. A lamba expression has the form

> [*capture list*] (*parameter list*) -> *return type* { *function body* }

where *capture list* is an (often empty) list of local variables defined in the enclosing function; *return type*, *parameter list*, and *function body* are the same as in any ordinary function. However, unlike ordinary functions, a lambda must use a trailing return (§ 6.3.3, p. 229) to specify its return type.

We can omit either or both of the parameter list and return type but must always include the capture list and function body:

```
auto f = [] { return 42; };
```

Here, we've defined f as a callable object that takes no arguments and returns 42. We call a lambda the same way we call a function by using the call operator:

```
cout << f() << endl;   // prints 42
```

Omitting the parentheses and the parameter list in a lambda is equivalent to specifying an empty parameter list. Hence, when we call f, the argument list is empty. If we omit the return type, the lambda has an inferred return type that depends on the code in the function body. If the function body is just a return statement, the return type is inferred from the type of the expression that is returned. Otherwise, the return type is void.

 Lambdas with function bodies that contain anything other than a single return statement that do not specify a return type return void.

Passing Arguments to a Lambda

As with an ordinary function call, the arguments in a call to a lambda are used to initialize the lambda's parameters. As usual, the argument and parameter types must match. Unlike ordinary functions, a lambda may not have default arguments (§ 6.5.1, p. 236). Therefore, a call to a lambda always has as many arguments as the lambda has parameters. Once the parameters are initialized, the function body executes.

As an example of a lambda that takes arguments, we can write a lambda that behaves like our isShorter function:

```
[] (const string &a, const string &b)
  { return a.size() < b.size();}
```

The empty capture list indicates that this lambda will not use any local variables from the surrounding function. The lambda's parameters, like the parameters to isShorter, are references to const string. Again like isShorter, the lambda's function body compares its parameters' size()s and returns a bool that depends on the relative sizes of the given arguments.

We can rewrite our call to stable_sort to use this lambda as follows:

```
// sort words by size, but maintain alphabetical order for words of the same size
stable_sort(words.begin(), words.end(),
            [] (const string &a, const string &b)
              { return a.size() < b.size();});
```

When stable_sort needs to compare two elements, it will call the given lambda expression.

Using the Capture List

We're now ready to solve our original problem, which is to write a callable expression that we can pass to find_if. We want an expression that will compare the length of each string in the input sequence with the value of the sz parameter in the biggies function.

Although a lambda may appear inside a function, it can use variables local to that function *only* if it specifies which variables it intends to use. A lambda specifies the variables it will use by including those local variables in its capture list. The capture list directs the lambda to include information needed to access those variables within the lambda itself.

In this case, our lambda will capture sz and will have a single string parameter. The body of our lambda will compare the given string's size with the captured value of sz:

```
[sz] (const string &a)
    { return a.size() >= sz; };
```

Inside the [] that begins a lambda we can provide a comma-separated list of names defined in the surrounding function.

Because this lambda captures sz, the body of the lambda may use sz. The lambda does not capture words, and so has no access to that variable. Had we given our lambda an empty capture list, our code would not compile:

```
// error: sz not captured
[] (const string &a)
    { return a.size() >= sz; };
```

A lambda may use a variable local to its surrounding function *only* if the lambda captures that variable in its capture list.

Calling find_if

Using this lambda, we can find the first element whose size is at least as big as sz:

```
// get an iterator to the first element whose size() is >= sz
auto wc = find_if(words.begin(), words.end(),
            [sz] (const string &a)
                { return a.size() >= sz; });
```

The call to find_if returns an iterator to the first element that is at least as long as the given sz, or a copy of words.end() if no such element exists.

We can use the iterator returned from find_if to compute how many elements appear between that iterator and the end of words (§ 3.4.2, p. 111):

```
// compute the number of elements with size >= sz
auto count = words.end() - wc;
cout << count << " " << make_plural(count, "word", "s")
        << " of length " << sz << " or longer" << endl;
```

Our output statement calls make_plural (§ 6.3.2, p. 224) to print word or words, depending on whether that size is equal to 1.

The `for_each` Algorithm

The last part of our problem is to print the elements in `words` that have length `sz` or greater. To do so, we'll use the `for_each` algorithm. This algorithm takes a callable object and calls that object on each element in the input range:

```
//  print words of the given size or longer, each one followed by a space
for_each(wc, words.end(),
        [](const string &s){cout << s << " ";});
cout << endl;
```

The capture list in this lambda is empty, yet the body uses two names: its own parameter, named s, and `cout`.

The capture list is empty, because we use the capture list only for (nonstatic) variables defined in the surrounding function. A lambda can use names that are defined outside the function in which the lambda appears. In this case, `cout` is not a name defined locally in `biggies`; that name is defined in the `iostream` header. So long as the `iostream` header is included in the scope in which `biggies` appears, our lambda can use `cout`.

> The capture list is used for local `nonstatic` variables only; lambdas can use local `statics` and variables declared outside the function directly.

Putting It All Together

Now that we've looked at the program in detail, here is the program as a whole:

```
void biggies(vector<string> &words,
            vector<string>::size_type sz)
{
    elimDups(words);  //  put words in alphabetical order and remove duplicates
    //  sort words by size, but maintain alphabetical order for words of the same size
    stable_sort(words.begin(), words.end(),
                [](const string &a, const string &b)
                    { return a.size() < b.size();});
    //  get an iterator to the first element whose size() is >= sz
    auto wc = find_if(words.begin(), words.end(),
                [sz](const string &a)
                    { return a.size() >= sz; });
    //  compute the number of elements with size >= sz
    auto count = words.end() - wc;
    cout << count << " " << make_plural(count, "word", "s")
        << " of length " << sz << " or longer" << endl;
    //  print words of the given size or longer, each one followed by a space
    for_each(wc, words.end(),
            [](const string &s){cout << s << " ";});
    cout << endl;
}
```

10.3.3 Lambda Captures and Returns

When we define a lambda, the compiler generates a new (unnamed) class type that corresponds to that lambda. We'll see how these classes are generated in § 14.8.1 (p. 572). For now, what's useful to understand is that when we pass a lambda to a function, we are defining both a new type and an object of that type: The argument is an unnamed object of this compiler-generated class type. Similarly, when we use `auto` to define a variable initialized by a lambda, we are defining an object of the type generated from that lambda.

By default, the class generated from a lambda contains a data member corresponding to the variables captured by the lambda. Like the data members of any class, the data members of a lambda are initialized when a lambda object is created.

Capture by Value

Similar to parameter passing, we can capture variables by value or by reference. Table 10.1 (p. 395) covers the various ways we can form a capture list. So far, our lambdas have captured variables by value. As with a parameter passed by value, it must be possible to copy such variables. Unlike parameters, the value of a captured variable is copied when the lambda is created, not when it is called:

```
void fcn1()
{
    size_t v1 = 42;  // local variable
    // copies v1 into the callable object named f
    auto f = [v1] { return v1; };
    v1 = 0;
    auto j = f(); // j is 42; f stored a copy of v1 when we created it
}
```

Because the value is copied when the lambda is created, subsequent changes to a captured variable have no effect on the corresponding value inside the lambda.

Capture by Reference

We can also define lambdas that capture variables by reference. For example:

```
void fcn2()
{
    size_t v1 = 42;  // local variable
    // the object f2 contains a reference to v1
    auto f2 = [&v1] { return v1; };
    v1 = 0;
    auto j = f2();  // j is 0; f2 refers to v1; it doesn't store it
}
```

The `&` before `v1` indicates that `v1` should be captured as a reference. A variable captured by reference acts like any other reference. When we use the variable inside the lambda body, we are using the object to which that reference is bound. In this case, when the lambda returns `v1`, it returns the value of the object to which `v1` refers.

Reference captures have the same problems and restrictions as reference returns (§ 6.3.2, p. 225). If we capture a variable by reference, we must be *certain* that the referenced object exists at the time the lambda is executed. The variables captured by a lambda are local variables. These variables cease to exist once the function completes. If it is possible for a lambda to be executed after the function finishes, the local variables to which the capture refers no longer exist.

Reference captures are sometimes necessary. For example, we might want our `biggies` function to take a reference to an `ostream` on which to write and a character to use as the separator:

```
void biggies(vector<string> &words,
             vector<string>::size_type sz,
             ostream &os = cout, char c = ' ')
{
    // code to reorder words as before
    // statement to print count revised to print to os
    for_each(words.begin(), words.end(),
             [&os, c](const string &s) { os << s << c; });
}
```

We cannot copy `ostream` objects (§ 8.1.1, p. 311); the only way to capture `os` is by reference (or through a pointer to `os`).

When we pass a lambda to a function, as in this call to `for_each`, the lambda executes immediately. Capturing `os` by reference is fine, because the variables in `biggies` exist while `for_each` is running.

We can also return a lambda from a function. The function might directly return a callable object or the function might return an object of a class that has a callable object as a data member. If the function returns a lambda, then—for the same reasons that a function must not return a reference to a local variable—that lambda must not contain reference captures.

⚠ **WARNING**   When we capture a variable by reference, we must ensure that the variable exists at the time that the lambda executes.

Implicit Captures

Rather than explicitly listing the variables we want to use from the enclosing function, we can let the compiler infer which variables we use from the code in the lambda's body. To direct the compiler to infer the capture list, we use an & or = in the capture list. The & tells the compiler to capture by reference, and the = says the values are captured by value. For example, we can rewrite the lambda that we passed to find_if as

```
//  sz implicitly captured by value
wc = find_if(words.begin(), words.end(),
             [=] (const string &s)
                { return s.size() >= sz; });
```

If we want to capture some variables by value and others by reference, we can mix implicit and explicit captures:

```
void biggies(vector<string> &words,
             vector<string>::size_type sz,
             ostream &os = cout, char c = ' ')
{
    //  other processing as before
    //  os implicitly captured by reference; c explicitly captured by value
    for_each(words.begin(), words.end(),
             [&, c](const string &s) { os << s << c; });
    //  os explicitly captured by reference; c implicitly captured by value
    for_each(words.begin(), words.end(),
             [=, &os](const string &s) { os << s << c; });
}
```

When we mix implicit and explicit captures, the first item in the capture list must be an & or =. That symbol sets the default capture mode as by reference or by value, respectively.

When we mix implicit and explicit captures, the explicitly captured variables must use the alternate form. That is, if the implicit capture is by reference (using &), then the explicitly named variables must be captured by value; hence their names may not be preceded by an &. Alternatively, if the implicit capture is by value (using =), then the explicitly named variables must be preceded by an & to indicate that they are to be captured by reference.

Table 10.1: Lambda Capture List	
[]	Empty capture list. The lambda may not use variables from the enclosing function. A lamba may use local variables only if it captures them.
[*names*]	*names* is a comma-separated list of names local to the enclosing function. By default, variables in the capture list are copied. A name preceded by & is captured by reference.
[&]	Implicit by reference capture list. Entities from the enclosing function used in the lambda body are used by reference.
[=]	Implicit by value capture list. Entities from the enclosing function used in the lambda body are copied into the lambda body.
[&, *identifier_list*]	*identifier_list* is a comma-separated list of zero or more variables from the enclosing function. These variables are captured by value; any implicitly captured variables are captured by reference. The names in *identifier_list* must not be preceded by an &.
[=, *reference_list*]	Variables included in the *reference_list* are captured by reference; any implicitly captured variables are captured by value. The names in *reference_list* may not include this and must be preceded by an &.

Mutable Lambdas

By default, a lambda may not change the value of a variable that it copies by value. If we want to be able to change the value of a captured variable, we must follow the parameter list with the keyword `mutable`. Lambdas that are mutable may not omit the parameter list:

```
void fcn3()
{
    size_t v1 = 42;  // local variable
    // f can change the value of the variables it captures
    auto f = [v1] () mutable { return ++v1; };
    v1 = 0;
    auto j = f();  // j is 43
}
```

Whether a variable captured by reference can be changed (as usual) depends only on whether that reference refers to a `const` or nonconst type:

```
void fcn4()
{
    size_t v1 = 42;   // local variable
    // v1 is a reference to a nonconst variable
    // we can change that variable through the reference inside f2
    auto f2 = [&v1] { return ++v1; };
    v1 = 0;
    auto j = f2(); // j is 1
}
```

Specifying the Lambda Return Type

The lambdas we've written so far contain only a single `return` statement. As a
result, we haven't had to specify the return type. By default, if a lambda body
contains any statements other than a `return`, that lambda is assumed to return
`void`. Like other functions that return `void`, lambdas inferred to return `void`
may not return a value.

As a simple example, we might use the library `transform` algorithm and a
lambda to replace each negative value in a sequence with its absolute value:

```
transform(vi.begin(), vi.end(), vi.begin(),
          [](int i) { return i < 0 ? -i : i; });
```

The `transform` function takes three iterators and a callable. The first two iterators
denote an input sequence and the third is a destination. The algorithm calls the
given callable on each element in the input sequence and writes the result to the
destination. As in this call, the destination iterator can be the same as the iterator
denoting the start of the input. When the input iterator and the destination iterator
are the same, `transform` replaces each element in the input range with the result
of calling the callable on that element.

In this call, we passed a lambda that returns the absolute value of its parameter.
The lambda body is a single `return` statement that returns the result of a conditional expression. We need not specify the return type, because that type can be
inferred from the type of the conditional operator.

However, if we write the seemingly equivalent program using an `if` statement,
our code won't compile:

```
// error: cannot deduce the return type for the lambda
transform(vi.begin(), vi.end(), vi.begin(),
          [](int i) { if (i < 0) return -i; else return i; });
```

This version of our lambda infers the return type as `void` but we returned a value.

When we need to define a return type for a lambda, we must use a trailing
return type (§ 6.3.3, p. 229):

```
transform(vi.begin(), vi.end(), vi.begin(),
          [](int i) -> int
          { if (i < 0) return -i; else return i; });
```

In this case, the fourth argument to `transform` is a lambda with an empty capture
list, which takes a single parameter of type `int` and returns a value of type `int`. Its
function body is an `if` statement that returns the absolute value of its parameter.

10.3.4 Binding Arguments

Lambda expressions are most useful for simple operations that we do not need to use in more than one or two places. If we need to do the same operation in many places, we should usually define a function rather than writing the same lambda expression multiple times. Similarly, if an operation requires many statements, it is ordinarily better to use a function.

It is usually straightforward to use a function in place of a lambda that has an empty capture list. As we've seen, we can use either a lambda or our `isShorter` function to order the `vector` on word length. Similarly, it would be easy to replace the lambda that printed the contents of our `vector` by writing a function that takes a `string` and prints the given `string` to the standard output.

However, it is not so easy to write a function to replace a lambda that captures local variables. For example, the lambda that we used in the call to `find_if` compared a `string` with a given size. We can easily write a function to do the same work:

```
bool check_size(const string &s, string::size_type sz)
{
    return s.size() >= sz;
}
```

However, we can't use this function as an argument to `find_if`. As we've seen, `find_if` takes a unary predicate, so the callable passed to `find_if` must take a single argument. The lambda that `biggies` passed to `find_if` used its capture list to store `sz`. In order to use `check_size` in place of that lambda, we have to figure out how to pass an argument to the `sz` parameter.

The Library `bind` Function

We can solve the problem of passing a size argument to `check_size` by using a new library function named **bind**, which is defined in the `functional` header. The `bind` function can be thought of as a general-purpose function adaptor (§ 9.6, p. 368). It takes a callable object and generates a new callable that "adapts" the parameter list of the original object.

The general form of a call to bind is:

```
auto newCallable = bind(callable, arg_list);
```

where *newCallable* is itself a callable object and *arg_list* is a comma-separated list of arguments that correspond to the parameters of the given *callable*. That is, when we call *newCallable*, *newCallable* calls *callable*, passing the arguments in *arg_list*.

The arguments in *arg_list* may include names of the form _*n*, where *n* is an integer. These arguments are "placeholders" representing the parameters of *newCallable*. They stand "in place of" the arguments that will be passed to *newCallable*. The number *n* is the position of the parameter in the generated callable: _1 is the first parameter in *newCallable*, _2 is the second, and so forth.

Binding the `sz` Parameter of `check_size`

As a simple example, we'll use bind to generate an object that calls check_size with a fixed value for its size parameter as follows:

```
//  check6 is a callable object that takes one argument of type string
//  and calls check_size on its given string and the value 6
auto check6 = bind(check_size, _1, 6);
```

This call to bind has only one placeholder, which means that check6 takes a single argument. The placeholder appears first in *arg_list*, which means that the parameter in check6 corresponds to the first parameter of check_size. That parameter is a const string&, which means that the parameter in check6 is also a const string&. Thus, a call to check6 must pass an argument of type string, which check6 will pass as the first argument to check_size.

The second argument in *arg_list* (i.e., the third argument to bind) is the value 6. That value is bound to the second parameter of check_size. Whenever we call check6, it will pass 6 as the second argument to check_size:

```
string s = "hello";
bool b1 = check6(s);   //  check6(s) calls check_size(s, 6)
```

Using bind, we can replace our original lambda-based call to find_if

```
auto wc = find_if(words.begin(), words.end(),
             [sz](const string &a)
```

with a version that uses check_size:

```
auto wc = find_if(words.begin(), words.end(),
             bind(check_size, _1, sz));
```

This call to bind generates a callable object that binds the second argument of check_size to the value of sz. When find_if calls this object on the strings in words those calls will in turn call check_size passing the given string and sz. So, find_if (effectively) will call check_size on each string in the input range and compare the size of that string to sz.

Using `placeholders` Names

The _n names are defined in a namespace named `placeholders`. That namespace is itself defined inside the `std` namespace (§ 3.1, p. 82). To use these names, we must supply the names of both namespaces. As with our other examples, our calls to `bind` assume the existence of appropriate `using` declarations. For example, the `using` declaration for _1 is

```
using std::placeholders::_1;
```

This declaration says we're using the name _1, which is defined in the namespace `placeholders`, which is itself defined inside namespace `std`.

We must provide a separate `using` declaration for each placeholder name that we use. Writing such declarations can be tedious and error-prone. Rather than separately declaring each placeholder, we can use a different form of `using` that we will cover in more detail in § 18.2.2 (p. 793). This form:

```
using namespace namespace_name;
```

says that we want to make all the names from *namespace_name* accessible to our program. For example:

```
using namespace std::placeholders;
```

makes all the names defined by `placeholders` usable. Like the `bind` function, the `placeholders` namespace is defined in the `functional` header.

Arguments to `bind`

As we've seen, we can use `bind` to fix the value of a parameter. More generally, we can use `bind` to bind or rearrange the parameters in the given callable. For example, assuming `f` is a callable object that has five parameters, the following call to `bind`:

```
// g is a callable object that takes two arguments
auto g = bind(f, a, b, _2, c, _1);
```

generates a new callable that takes two arguments, represented by the placeholders _2 and _1. The new callable will pass its own arguments as the third and fifth arguments to `f`. The first, second, and fourth arguments to `f` are bound to the given values, a, b, and c, respectively.

The arguments to `g` are bound positionally to the placeholders. That is, the first argument to `g` is bound to _1, and the second argument is bound to _2. Thus, when we call `g`, the first argument to `g` will be passed as the last argument to `f`; the second argument to `g` will be passed as `g`'s third argument. In effect, this call to `bind` maps

```
g(_1, _2)
```

to

```
f(a, b, _2, c, _1)
```

That is, calling `g` calls `f` using `g`'s arguments for the placeholders along with the bound arguments, a, b, and c. For example, calling `g(X, Y)` calls

```
f(a, b, Y, c, X)
```

Using to `bind` to Reorder Parameters

As a more concrete example of using `bind` to reorder arguments, we can use `bind` to invert the meaning of `isShorter` by writing

```
//   sort on word length, shortest to longest
sort(words.begin(), words.end(), isShorter);
//   sort on word length, longest to shortest
sort(words.begin(), words.end(), bind(isShorter, _2, _1));
```

In the first call, when `sort` needs to compare two elements, A and B, it will call `isShorter(A, B)`. In the second call to `sort`, the arguments to `isShorter` are swapped. In this case, when `sort` compares elements, it will be as if `sort` called `isShorter(B, A)`.

Binding Reference Parameters

By default, the arguments to `bind` that are not placeholders are copied into the callable object that `bind` returns. However, as with lambdas, sometimes we have arguments that we want to bind but that we want to pass by reference or we might want to bind an argument that has a type that we cannot copy.

For example, to replace the lambda that captured an `ostream` by reference:

```
//   os is a local variable referring to an output stream
//   c is a local variable of type char
for_each(words.begin(), words.end(),
         [&os, c](const string &s) { os << s << c; });
```

We can easily write a function to do the same job:

```
ostream &print(ostream &os, const string &s, char c)
{
    return os << s << c;
}
```

However, we can't use `bind` directly to replace the capture of `os`:

```
//   error: cannot copy os
for_each(words.begin(), words.end(), bind(print, os, _1, ' '));
```

because `bind` copies its arguments and we cannot copy an `ostream`. If we want to pass an object to `bind` without copying it, we must use the library **ref** function:

```
for_each(words.begin(), words.end(),
         bind(print, ref(os), _1, ' '));
```

The `ref` function returns an object that contains the given reference and that is itself copyable. There is also a **cref** function that generates a class that holds a reference to `const`. Like `bind`, the `ref` and `cref` functions are defined in the `functional` header.

BACKWARD COMPATIBILITY: BINDING ARGUMENTS

Older versions of C++ provided a much more limited, yet more complicated, set of facilities to bind arguments to functions. The library defined two functions named bind1st and bind2nd. Like bind, these functions take a function and generate a new callable object that calls the given function with one of its parameters bound to a given value. However, these functions can bind only the first or second parameter, respectively. Because they are of much more limited utility, they have been *deprecated* in the new standard. A deprecated feature is one that may not be supported in future releases. Modern C++ programs should use bind.

EXERCISES SECTION 10.3.4

Exercise 10.22: Rewrite the program to count words of size 6 or less using functions in place of the lambdas.

Exercise 10.23: How many arguments does bind take?

Exercise 10.24: Use bind and check_size to find the first element in a vector of ints that has a value greater than the length of a specified string value.

Exercise 10.25: In the exercises for § 10.3.2 (p. 392) you wrote a version of biggies that uses partition. Rewrite that function to use check_size and bind.

10.4 Revisiting Iterators

In addition to the iterators that are defined for each of the containers, the library defines several additional kinds of iterators in the iterator header. These iterators include

- **Insert iterators**: These iterators are bound to a container and can be used to insert elements into the container.

- **Stream iterators**: These iterators are bound to input or output streams and can be used to iterate through the associated IO stream.

- **Reverse iterators**: These iterators move backward, rather than forward. The library containers, other than forward_list, have reverse iterators.

- **Move iterators**: These special-purpose iterators move rather than copy their elements. We'll cover move iterators in § 13.6.2 (p. 543).

10.4.1 Insert Iterators

An inserter is an iterator adaptor (§ 9.6, p. 368) that takes a container and yields an iterator that adds elements to the specified container. When we assign a value through an insert iterator, the iterator calls a container operation to add an element at a specified position in the given container. The operations these iterators support are listed in Table 10.2 (overleaf).

There are three kinds of inserters. Each differs from the others as to where elements are inserted:

- `back_inserter` (§ 10.2.2, p. 382) creates an iterator that uses `push_back`.

- **`front_inserter`** creates an iterator that uses `push_front`.

- **`inserter`** creates an iterator that uses `insert`. This function takes a second argument, which must be an iterator into the given container. Elements are inserted ahead of the element denoted by the given iterator.

> We can use `front_inserter` *only* if the container has `push_front`. Similarly, we can use `back_inserter` *only* if it has `push_back`.

Table 10.2: Insert Iterator Operations	
`it = t`	Inserts the value `t` at the current position denoted by `it`. Depending on the kind of insert iterator, and assuming `c` is the container to which `it` is bound, calls `c.push_back(t)`, `c.push_front(t)`, or `c.insert(t, p)`, where `p` is the iterator position given to `inserter`.
`*it, ++it, it++`	These operations exist but do nothing to `it`. Each operator returns `it`.

It is important to understand that when we call `inserter(c, iter)`, we get an iterator that, when used successively, inserts elements ahead of the element originally denoted by `iter`. That is, if `it` is an iterator generated by `inserter`, then an assignment such as

```
*it = val;
```

behaves as

```
it = c.insert(it, val); // it points to the newly added element
++it; // increment it so that it denotes the same element as before
```

The iterator generated by `front_inserter` behaves quite differently from the one created by `inserter`. When we use `front_inserter`, elements are always inserted ahead of the then first element in the container. Even if the position we pass to `inserter` initially denotes the first element, as soon as we insert an element in front of that element, that element is no longer the one at the beginning of the container:

```
list<int> lst = {1,2,3,4};
list<int> lst2, lst3;        // empty lists
// after copy completes, lst2 contains 4 3 2 1
copy(lst.cbegin(), lst.cend(), front_inserter(lst2));
// after copy completes, lst3 contains 1 2 3 4
copy(lst.cbegin(), lst.cend(), inserter(lst3, lst3.begin()));
```

When we call `front_inserter(c)`, we get an insert iterator that successively calls `push_front`. As each element is inserted, it becomes the new first element in c. Therefore, `front_inserter` yields an iterator that reverses the order of the sequence that it inserts; `inserter` and `back_inserter` don't.

Exercise 10.26: Explain the differences among the three kinds of insert iterators.

Exercise 10.27: In addition to `unique` (§ 10.2.3, p. 384), the library defines function named `unique_copy` that takes a third iterator denoting a destination into which to copy the unique elements. Write a program that uses `unique_copy` to copy the unique elements from a `vector` into an initially empty `list`.

Exercise 10.28: Copy a `vector` that holds the values from 1 to 9 inclusive, into three other containers. Use an `inserter`, a `back_inserter`, and a `front_inserter`, respectivly to add elements to these containers. Predict how the output sequence varies by the kind of inserter and verify your predictions by running your programs.

10.4.2 `iostream` Iterators

Even though the `iostream` types are not containers, there are iterators that can be used with objects of the IO types (§ 8.1, p. 310). An **`istream_iterator`** (Table 10.3 (overleaf)) reads an input stream, and an **`ostream_iterator`** (Table 10.4 (p. 405)) writes an output stream. These iterators treat their corresponding stream as a sequence of elements of a specified type. Using a stream iterator, we can use the generic algorithms to read data from or write data to stream objects.

Operations on `istream_iterators`

When we create a stream iterator, we must specify the type of objects that the iterator will read or write. An `istream_iterator` uses `>>` to read a stream. Therefore, the type that an `istream_iterator` reads must have an input operator defined. When we create an `istream_iterator`, we can bind it to a stream. Alternatively, we can default initialize the iterator, which creates an iterator that we can use as the off-the-end value.

```
istream_iterator<int> int_it(cin);    // reads ints from cin
istream_iterator<int> int_eof;        // end iterator value
ifstream in("afile");
istream_iterator<string> str_it(in);  // reads strings from "afile"
```

As an example, we can use an `istream_iterator` to read the standard input into a `vector`:

```
istream_iterator<int> in_iter(cin);   // read ints from cin
istream_iterator<int> eof;            // istream "end" iterator
while (in_iter != eof)   // while there's valid input to read
    // postfix increment reads the stream and returns the old value of the iterator
    // we dereference that iterator to get the previous value read from the stream
    vec.push_back(*in_iter++);
```

This loop reads `ints` from `cin`, storing what was read in `vec`. On each iteration, the loop checks whether `in_iter` is the same as `eof`. That iterator was defined as the empty `istream_iterator`, which is used as the end iterator. An iterator bound to a stream is equal to the end iterator once its associated stream hits end-of-file or encounters an IO error.

The hardest part of this program is the argument to `push_back`, which uses the dereference and postfix increment operators. This expression works just like others we've written that combined dereference with postfix increment (§ 4.5, p. 148). The postfix increment advances the stream by reading the next value but returns the *old* value of the iterator. That old value contains the previous value read from the stream. We dereference that iterator to obtain that value.

What is more useful is that we can rewrite this program as

```
istream_iterator<int> in_iter(cin), eof;  // read ints from cin
vector<int> vec(in_iter, eof);   // construct vec from an iterator range
```

Here we construct `vec` from a pair of iterators that denote a range of elements. Those iterators are `istream_iterators`, which means that the range is obtained by reading the associated stream. This constructor reads `cin` until it hits end-of-file or encounters an input that is not an `int`. The elements that are read are used to construct `vec`.

Table 10.3: `istream_iterator` Operations	
`istream_iterator<T> in(is);`	`in` reads values of type T from input stream `is`.
`istream_iterator<T> end;`	Off-the-end iterator for an `istream_iterator` that reads values of type T.
`in1 == in2` `in1 != in2`	`in1` and `in2` must read the same type. They are equal if they are both the end value or are bound to the same input stream.
`*in`	Returns the value read from the stream.
`in->mem`	Synonym for `(*in).mem`.
`++in, in++`	Reads the next value from the input stream using the `>>` operator for the element type. As usual, the prefix version returns a reference to the incremented iterator. The postfix version returns the old value.

Using Stream Iterators with the Algorithms

Because algorithms operate in terms of iterator operations, and the stream iterators support at least some iterator operations, we can use stream iterators with at least some of the algorithms. We'll see in § 10.5.1 (p. 410) how to tell which algorithms can be used with the stream iterators. As one example, we can call `accumulate` with a pair of `istream_iterators`:

```
istream_iterator<int> in(cin), eof;
cout << accumulate(in, eof, 0) << endl;
```

This call will generate the sum of values read from the standard input. If the input to this program is

```
23 109 45 89 6 34 12 90 34 23 56 23 8 89 23
```

then the output will be 664.

`istream_iterators` Are Permitted to Use Lazy Evaluation

When we bind an `istream_iterator` to a stream, we are not guaranteed that it will read the stream immediately. The implementation is permitted to delay reading the stream until we use the iterator. We are guaranteed that before we dereference the iterator for the first time, the stream will have been read. For most programs, whether the read is immediate or delayed makes no difference. However, if we create an `istream_iterator` that we destroy without using or if we are synchronizing reads to the same stream from two different objects, then we might care a great deal when the read happens.

Operations on `ostream_iterators`

An `ostream_iterator` can be defined for any type that has an output operator (the `<<` operator). When we create an `ostream_iterator`, we may (optionally) provide a second argument that specifies a character string to print following each element. That string must be a C-style character string (i.e., a string literal or a pointer to a null-terminated array). We must bind an `ostream_iterator` to a specific stream. There is no empty or off-the-end `ostream_iterator`.

Table 10.4: `ostream` Iterator Operations	
`ostream_iterator<T> out(os);`	`out` writes values of type `T` to output stream `os`.
`ostream_iterator<T> out(os, d);`	`out` writes values of type `T` followed by `d` to output stream `os`. `d` points to a null-terminated character array.
`out = val`	Writes `val` to the `ostream` to which `out` is bound using the `<<` operator. `val` must have a type that is compatible with the type that `out` can write.
`*out, ++out, out++`	These operations exist but do nothing to `out`. Each operator returns `out`.

We can use an `ostream_iterator` to write a sequence of values:

```
ostream_iterator<int> out_iter(cout, " ");
for (auto e : vec)
    *out_iter++ = e;  // the assignment writes this element to cout
cout << endl;
```

This program writes each element from `vec` onto `cout` following each element with a space. Each time we assign a value to `out_iter`, the write is committed.

It is worth noting that we can omit the dereference and the increment when we assign to `out_iter`. That is, we can write this loop equivalently as

```
for (auto e : vec)
    out_iter = e;  // the assignment writes this element to cout
cout << endl;
```

The `*` and `++` operators do nothing on an `ostream_iterator`, so omitting them has no effect on our program. However, we prefer to write the loop as first presented. That loop uses the iterator consistently with how we use other iterator types. We can easily change this loop to execute on another iterator type. Moreover, the behavior of this loop will be clearer to readers of our code.

Rather than writing the loop ourselves, we can more easily print the elements in vec by calling copy:

```
copy(vec.begin(), vec.end(), out_iter);
cout << endl;
```

Using Stream Iterators with Class Types

We can create an istream_iterator for any type that has an input operator (>>). Similarly, we can define an ostream_iterator so long as the type has an output operator (<<). Because Sales_item has both input and output operators, we can use IO iterators to rewrite the bookstore program from § 1.6 (p. 24):

```
istream_iterator<Sales_item> item_iter(cin), eof;
ostream_iterator<Sales_item> out_iter(cout, "\n");
//  store the first transaction in sum and read the next record
Sales_item sum = *item_iter++;
while (item_iter != eof) {
    //  if the current transaction (which is stored in item_iter) has the same ISBN
    if (item_iter->isbn() == sum.isbn())
        sum += *item_iter++; //  add it to sum and read the next transaction
    else {
        out_iter = sum;       //  write the current sum
        sum = *item_iter++;   //  read the next transaction
    }
}
out_iter = sum;    //  remember to print the last set of records
```

This program uses item_iter to read Sales_item transactions from cin. It uses out_iter to write the resulting sums to cout, following each output with a newline. Having defined our iterators, we use item_iter to initialize sum with the value of the first transaction:

```
//  store the first transaction in sum and read the next record
Sales_item sum = *item_iter++;
```

Here, we dereference the result of the postfix increment on item_iter. This expression reads the next transaction, and initializes sum from the value previously stored in item_iter.

The while loop executes until we hit end-of-file on cin. Inside the while, we check whether sum and the record we just read refer to the same book. If so, we add the most recently read Sales_item into sum. If the ISBNs differ, we assign sum to out_iter, which prints the current value of sum followed by a newline. Having printed the sum for the previous book, we assign sum a copy of the most recently read transaction and increment the iterator, which reads the next transaction. The loop continues until an error or end-of-file is encountered. Before exiting, we remember to print the values associated with the last book in the input.

Exercise 10.29: Write a program using stream iterators to read a text file into a `vector` of `strings`.

Exercise 10.30: Use stream iterators, `sort`, and `copy` to read a sequence of integers from the standard input, sort them, and then write them back to the standard output.

Exercise 10.31: Update the program from the previous exercise so that it prints only the unique elements. Your program should use `unqiue_copy` (§ 10.4.1, p. 403).

Exercise 10.32: Rewrite the bookstore problem from § 1.6 (p. 24) using a `vector` to hold the transactions and various algorithms to do the processing. Use `sort` with your `compareIsbn` function from § 10.3.1 (p. 387) to arrange the transactions in order, and then use `find` and `accumulate` to do the sum.

Exercise 10.33: Write a program that takes the names of an input file and two output files. The input file should hold integers. Using an `istream_iterator` read the input file. Using `ostream_iterators`, write the odd numbers into the first output file. Each value should be followed by a space. Write the even numbers into the second file. Each of these values should be placed on a separate line.

10.4.3 Reverse Iterators

A reverse iterator is an iterator that traverses a container backward, from the last element toward the first. A reverse iterator inverts the meaning of increment (and decrement). Incrementing (`++it`) a reverse iterator moves the iterator to the previous element; derementing (`--it`) moves the iterator to the next element.

The containers, aside from `forward_list`, all have reverse iterators. We obtain a reverse iterator by calling the `rbegin`, `rend`, `crbegin`, and `crend` members. These members return reverse iterators to the last element in the container and one "past" (i.e., one before) the beginning of the container. As with ordinary iterators, there are both `const` and `nonconst` reverse iterators.

Figure 10.1 illustrates the relationship between these four iterators on a hypothetical `vector` named `vec`.

Figure 10.1: Comparing begin/cend and rbegin/crend Iterators

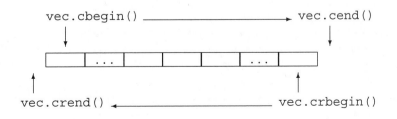

As an example, the following loop prints the elements of `vec` in reverse order:

```
vector<int> vec = {0,1,2,3,4,5,6,7,8,9};
// reverse iterator of vector from back to front
for (auto r_iter = vec.crbegin();  // binds r_iter to the last element
          r_iter != vec.crend();   // crend refers 1 before 1st element
          ++r_iter)                 // decrements the iterator one element
     cout << *r_iter << endl;       // prints 9, 8, 7, ... 0
```

Although it may seem confusing to have the meaning of the increment and decrement operators reversed, doing so lets us use the algorithms transparently to process a container forward or backward. For example, we can sort our vector in descending order by passing sort a pair of reverse iterators:

```
sort(vec.begin(), vec.end()); // sorts vec in "normal" order
// sorts in reverse: puts the smallest element at the end of vec
sort(vec.rbegin(), vec.rend());
```

Reverse Iterators Require Decrement Operators

Not surprisingly, we can define a reverse iterator only from an iterator that supports -- as well as ++. After all, the purpose of a reverse iterator is to move the iterator backward through the sequence. Aside from forward_list, the iterators on the standard containers all support decrement as well as increment. However, the stream iterators do not, because it is not possible to move backward through a stream. Therefore, it is not possible to create a reverse iterator from a forward_list or a stream iterator.

Relationship between Reverse Iterators and Other Iterators

Suppose we have a string named line that contains a comma-separated list of words, and we want to print the first word in line. Using find, this task is easy:

```
// find the first element in a comma-separated list
auto comma = find(line.cbegin(), line.cend(), ',');
cout << string(line.cbegin(), comma) << endl;
```

If there is a comma in line, then comma refers to that comma; otherwise it is line.cend(). When we print the string from line.cbegin() to comma, we print characters up to the comma, or the entire string if there is no comma.

If we wanted the last word, we can use reverse iterators instead:

```
// find the last element in a comma-separated list
auto rcomma = find(line.crbegin(), line.crend(), ',');
```

Because we pass crbegin() and crend(), this call starts with the last character in line and searches backward. When find completes, if there is a comma, then rcomma refers to the last comma in the line—that is, it refers to the first comma found in the backward search. If there is no comma, then rcomma is line.crend().

The interesting part comes when we try to print the word we found. The seemingly obvious way

```
// WRONG: will generate the word in reverse order
cout << string(line.crbegin(), rcomma) << endl;
```

generates bogus output. For example, had our input been

```
FIRST,MIDDLE,LAST
```

then this statement would print TSAL!

Figure 10.2 illustrates the problem: We are using reverse iterators, which process the string backward. Therefore, our output statement prints from crbegin backward through line. Instead, we want to print from rcomma forward to the end of line. However, we can't use rcomma directly. That iterator is a reverse iterator, which means that it goes backward toward the beginning of the string. What we need to do is transform rcomma back into an ordinary iterator that will go forward through line. We can do so by calling the reverse_iterator's base member, which gives us its corresponding ordinary iterator:

```
//  ok: get a forward iterator and read to the end of line
cout << string(rcomma.base(), line.cend()) << endl;
```

Given the same preceding input, this statement prints LAST as expected.

Figure 10.2: Relationship between Reverse and Ordinary Iterators

The objects shown in Figure 10.2 illustrate the relationship between ordinary and reverse iterators. For example, rcomma and rcomma.base() refer to different elements, as do line.crbegin() and line.cend(). These differences are needed to ensure that the *range* of elements, whether processed forward or backward, is the same.

Technically speaking, the relationship between normal and reverse iterators accommodates the properties of a left-inclusive range (§ 9.2.1, p. 331). The point is that [line.crbegin(), rcomma) and [rcomma.base(), line.cend()) refer to the same elements in line. In order for that to happen, rcomma and rcomma.base() must yield adjacent positions, rather than the same position, as must crbegin() and cend().

The fact that reverse iterators are intended to represent ranges and that these ranges are asymmetric has an important consequence: When we initialize or assign a reverse iterator from a plain iterator, the resulting iterator does not refer to the same element as the original.

10.5   Structure of Generic Algorithms

The most fundamental property of any algorithm is the list of operations it requires from its iterator(s). Some algorithms, such as `find`, require only the ability to access an element through the iterator, to increment the iterator, and to compare two iterators for equality. Others, such as `sort`, require the ability to read, write, and randomly access elements. The iterator operations required by the algorithms are grouped into five **iterator categories** listed in Table 10.5. Each algorithm specifies what kind of iterator must be supplied for each of its iterator parameters.

A second way is to classify the algorithms (as we did in the beginning of this chapter) is by whether they read, write, or reorder the elements in the sequence. Appendix A covers all the algorithms according to this classification.

The algorithms also share a set of parameter-passing conventions and a set of naming conventions, which we shall cover after looking at iterator categories.

Table 10.5: Iterator Categories	
Input iterator	Read, but not write; single-pass, increment only
Output iterator	Write, but not read; single-pass, increment only
Forward iterator	Read and write; multi-pass, increment only
Bidirectional iterator	Read and write; multi-pass, increment and decrement
Random-access iterator	Read and write; multi-pass, full iterator arithmetic

10.5.1   The Five Iterator Categories

Like the containers, iterators define a common set of operations. Some operations are provided by all iterators; other operations are supported by only specific kinds of iterators. For example, `ostream_iterators` have only increment, dereference, and assignment. Iterators on `vector`, `strings`, and `deques` support these operations and the decrement, relational, and arithmetic operators.

Iterators are categorized by the operations they provide and the categories form a sort of hierarchy. With the exception of output iterators, an iterator of a higher category provides all the operations of the iterators of a lower categories.

The standard specifies the minimum category for each iterator parameter of the generic and numeric algorithms. For example, `find`—which implements a one-pass, read-only traversal over a sequence—minimally requires an input iterator. The `replace` function requires a pair of iterators that are at least forward iterators. Similarly, `replace_copy` requires forward iterators for its first two iterators. Its third iterator, which represents a destination, must be at least an output iterator, and so on. For each parameter, the iterator must be at least as powerful as the stipulated minimum. Passing an iterator of a lesser power is an error.

 WARNING Many compilers will not complain when we pass the wrong category of iterator to an algorithm.

The Iterator Categories

Input iterators: can read elements in a sequence. An input iterator must provide

- Equality and inequality operators (`==`, `!=`) to compare two iterators
- Prefix and postfix increment (`++`) to advance the iterator
- Dereference operator (`*`) to read an element; dereference may appear only on the right-hand side of an assignment
- The arrow operator (`->`) as a synonym for (`*it`).`member`—that is, dereference the iterator and fetch a member from the underlying object

Input iterators may be used only sequentially. We are guaranteed that `*it++` is valid, but incrementing an input iterator may invalidate all other iterators into the stream. As a result, there is no guarantee that we can save the state of an input iterator and examine an element through that saved iterator. Input iterators, therefore, may be used only for single-pass algorithms. The `find` and `accumulate` algorithms require input iterators; `istream_iterators` are input iterators.

Output iterators: can be thought of as having complementary functionality to input iterators; they write rather than read elements. Output iterators must provide

- Prefix and postfix increment (`++`) to advance the iterator
- Dereference (`*`), which may appear only as the left-hand side of an assignment (Assigning to a dereferenced output iterator writes to the underlying element.)

We may assign to a given value of an output iterator only once. Like input iterators, output iterators may be used only for single-pass algorithms. Iterators used as a destination are typically output iterators. For example, the third parameter to `copy` is an output iterator. The `ostream_iterator` type is an output iterator.

Forward iterators: can read and write a given sequence. They move in only one direction through the sequence. Forward iterators support all the operations of both input iterators and output iterators. Moreover, they can read or write the same element multiple times. Therefore, we can use the saved state of a forward iterator. Hence, algorithms that use forward iterators may make multiple passes through the sequence. The `replace` algorithm requires a forward iterator; iterators on `forward_list` are forward iterators.

Bidirectional iterators: can read and write a sequence forward or backward. In addition to supporting all the operations of a forward iterator, a bidirectional iterator also supports the prefix and postfix decrement (`--`) operators. The `reverse` algorithm requires bidirectional iterators, and aside from `forward_list`, the library containers supply iterators that meet the requirements for a bidirectional iterator.

Random-access iterators: provide constant-time access to any position in the sequence. These iterators support all the functionality of bidirectional iterators. In addition, random-access iterators support the operations from Table 3.7 (p. 111):

- The relational operators (`<`, `<=`, `>`, and `>=`) to compare the relative positions of two iterators.

- Addition and subtraction operators (`+`, `+=`, `-`, and `-=`) on an iterator and an integral value. The result is the iterator advanced (or retreated) the integral number of elements within the sequence.

- The subtraction operator (`-`) when applied to two iterators, which yields the distance between two iterators.

- The subscript operator (`iter[n]`) as a synonym for `*(iter + n)`.

The `sort` algorithms require random-access iterators. Iterators for `array`, `deque`, `string`, and `vector` are random-access iterators, as are pointers when used to access elements of a built-in array.

EXERCISES SECTION 10.5.1

Exercise 10.38: List the five iterator categories and the operations that each supports.

Exercise 10.39: What kind of iterator does a `list` have? What about a `vector`?

Exercise 10.40: What kinds of iterators do you think `copy` requires? What about `reverse` or `unique`?

10.5.2 Algorithm Parameter Patterns

Superimposed on any other classification of the algorithms is a set of parameter conventions. Understanding these parameter conventions can aid in learning new algorithms—by knowing what the parameters mean, you can concentrate on understanding the operation the algorithm performs. Most of the algorithms have one of the following four forms:

```
alg(beg, end, other args);
alg(beg, end, dest, other args);
alg(beg, end, beg2, other args);
alg(beg, end, beg2, end2, other args);
```

where *alg* is the name of the algorithm, and `beg` and `end` denote the input range on which the algorithm operates. Although nearly all algorithms take an input range, the presence of the other parameters depends on the work being performed. The common ones listed here—dest, beg2, and end2—are all iterators. When used, these iterators fill similar roles. In addition to these iterator parameters, some algorithms take additional, noniterator parameters that are algorithm specific.

Algorithms with a Single Destination Iterator

A dest parameter is an iterator that denotes a destination in which the algorithm can write its output. Algorithms *assume* that it is safe to write as many elements as needed.

 Algorithms that write to an output iterator assume the destination is large enough to hold the output.

If dest is an iterator that refers directly to a container, then the algorithm writes its output to existing elements within the container. More commonly, dest is bound to an insert iterator (§ 10.4.1, p. 401) or an ostream_iterator (§ 10.4.2, p. 403). An insert iterator adds new elements to the container, thereby ensuring that there is enough space. An ostream_iterator writes to an output stream, again presenting no problem regardless of how many elements are written.

Algorithms with a Second Input Sequence

Algorithms that take either beg2 alone or beg2 and end2 use those iterators to denote a second input range. These algorithms typically use the elements from the second range in combination with the input range to perform a computation.

When an algorithm takes both beg2 and end2, these iterators denote a second range. Such algorithms take two completely specified ranges: the input range denoted by [beg, end), and a second input range denoted by [beg2, end2).

Algorithms that take only beg2 (and not end2) treat beg2 as the first element in a second input range. The end of this range is not specified. Instead, these algorithms *assume* that the range starting at beg2 is at least as large as the one denoted by beg, end.

 Algorithms that take beg2 alone *assume* that the sequence beginning at beg2 is as large as the range denoted by beg and end.

10.5.3 Algorithm Naming Conventions

Separate from the parameter conventions, the algorithms also conform to a set of naming and overload conventions. These conventions deal with how we supply an operation to use in place of the default < or == operator and with whether the algorithm writes to its input sequence or to a separate destination.

Some Algorithms Use Overloading to Pass a Predicate

Algorithms that take a predicate to use in place of the < or == operator, and that do not take other arguments, typically are overloaded. One version of the function uses the element type's operator to compare elements; the second takes an extra parameter that is a predicate to use in place of < or ==:

```
unique(beg, end);          // uses the == operator to compare the elements
unique(beg, end, comp);  // uses comp to compare the elements
```

Both calls reorder the given sequence by removing adjacent duplicated elements. The first uses the element type's == operator to check for duplicates; the second calls comp to decide whether two elements are equal. Because the two versions of the function differ as to the number of arguments, there is no possible ambiguity (§ 6.4, p. 233) as to which function is being called.

Algorithms with _if Versions

Algorithms that take an element value typically have a second named (not overloaded) version that takes a predicate (§ 10.3.1, p. 386) in place of the value. The algorithms that take a predicate have the suffix _if appended:

```
find(beg, end, val);       // find the first instance of val in the input range
find_if(beg, end, pred);  // find the first instance for which pred is true
```

These algorithms both find the first instance of a specific element in the input range. The find algorithm looks for a specific value; the find_if algorithm looks for a value for which pred returns a nonzero value.

These algorithms provide a named version rather than an overloaded one because both versions of the algorithm take the same number of arguments. Overloading ambiguities would therefore be possible, albeit rare. To avoid any possible ambiguities, the library provides separate named versions for these algorithms.

Distinguishing Versions That Copy from Those That Do Not

By default, algorithms that rearrange elements write the rearranged elements back into the given input range. These algorithms provide a second version that writes to a specified output destination. As we've seen, algorithms that write to a destination append _copy to their names (§ 10.2.2, p. 383):

```
reverse(beg, end);                  // reverse the elements in the input range
reverse_copy(beg, end, dest); // copy elements in reverse order into dest
```

Some algorithms provide both _copy and _if versions. These versions take a destination iterator and a predicate:

```
// removes the odd elements from v1
remove_if(v1.begin(), v1.end(),
                      [](int i) { return i % 2; });
// copies only the even elements from v1 into v2; v1 is unchanged
remove_copy_if(v1.begin(), v1.end(), back_inserter(v2),
              [](int i) { return i % 2; });
```

Both calls use a lambda (§ 10.3.2, p. 388) to determine whether an element is odd. In the first case, we remove the odd elements from the input sequence itself. In the second, we copy the non-odd (aka even) elements from the input range into v2.

EXERCISES SECTION 10.5.3

Exercise 10.41: Based only on the algorithm and argument names, describe the operation that the each of the following library algorithms performs:

```
replace(beg, end, old_val, new_val);
replace_if(beg, end, pred, new_val);
replace_copy(beg, end, dest, old_val, new_val);
replace_copy_if(beg, end, dest, pred, new_val);
```

10.6 Container-Specific Algorithms

Unlike the other containers, `list` and `forward_list` define several algorithms as members. In particular, the list types define their own versions of `sort`, `merge`, `remove`, `reverse`, and `unique`. The generic version of `sort` requires random-access iterators. As a result, `sort` cannot be used with `list` and `forward_list` because these types offer bidirectional and forward iterators, respectively.

The generic versions of the other algorithms that the list types define can be used with lists, but at a cost in performance. These algorithms swap elements in the input sequence. A list can "swap" its elements by changing the links among its elements rather than swapping the values of those elements. As a result, the list-specific versions of these algorithms can achieve much better performance than the corresponding generic versions.

These `list`-specific operations are described in Table 10.6. Generic algorithms not listed in the table that take appropriate iterators execute equally efficiently on `list`s and `forward_list`ss as on other containers.

Best Practices

> The list member versions should be used in preference to the generic algorithms for `list`s and `forward_list`s.

Table 10.6: Algorithms That are Members of `list` and `forward_list`	
These operations return `void`.	
`lst.merge(lst2)` `lst.merge(lst2, comp)`	Merges elements from `lst2` onto `lst`. Both `lst` and `lst2` must be sorted. Elements are removed from `lst2`. After the merge, `lst2` is empty. The first version uses the `<` operator; the second version uses the given comparison operation.
`lst.remove(val)` `lst.remove_if(pred)`	Calls `erase` to remove each element that is `==` to the given value or for which the given unary predicate succeeds.
`lst.reverse()`	Reverses the order of the elements in `lst`.
`lst.sort()` `lst.sort(comp)`	Sorts the elements of `lst` using `<` or the given comparison operation.
`lst.unique()` `lst.unique(pred)`	Calls `erase` to remove consecutive copies of the same value. The first version uses `==`; the second uses the given binary predicate.

The `splice` Members

The list types also define a `splice` algorithm, which is described in Table 10.7. This algorithm is particular to list data structures. Hence a generic version of this algorithm is not needed.

Table 10.7: Arguments to the `list` and `forward_list` splice Members	
`lst.splice(`*args*`)` or `flst.splice_after(`*args*`)`	
`(p, lst2)`	`p` is an iterator to an element in `lst` or an iterator just before an element in `flst`. Moves all the element(s) from `lst2` into `lst` just before `p` or into `flst` just after `p`. Removes the element(s) from `lst2`. `lst2` must have the same type as `lst` or `flst` and may not be the same list.
`(p, lst2, p2)`	`p2` is a valid iterator into `lst2`. Moves the element denoted by `p2` into `lst` or moves the element just after `p2` into `flst`. `lst2` can be the same list as `lst` or `flst`.
`(p, lst2, b, e)`	`b` and `e` must denote a valid range in `lst2`. Moves the elements in the given range from `lst2`. `lst2` and `lst` (or `flst`) can be the same list but `p` must not denote an element in the given range.

The List-Specific Operations Do Change the Containers

Most of the list-specific algorithms are similar—but not identical—to their generic counterparts. However, a crucially important difference between the list-specific and the generic versions is that the list versions change the underlying container. For example, the list version of `remove` removes the indicated elements. The list version of `unique` removes the second and subsequent duplicate elements.

Similarly, `merge` and `splice` are destructive on their arguments. For example, the generic version of `merge` writes the merged sequence to a given destination iterator; the two input sequences are unchanged. The list `merge` function destroys the given list—elements are removed from the argument list as they are merged into the object on which `merge` was called. After a `merge`, the elements from both lists continue to exist, but they are all elements of the same list.

EXERCISES SECTION 10.6

Exercise 10.42: Reimplement the program that eliminated duplicate words that we wrote in § 10.2.3 (p. 383) to use a `list` instead of a `vector`.

CHAPTER SUMMARY

The standard library defines about 100 type-independent algorithms that operate on sequences. Sequences can be elements in a library container type, a built-in array, or generated (for example) by reading or writing to a stream. Algorithms achieve their type independence by operating in terms of iterators. Most algorithms take as their first two arguments a pair of iterators denoting a range of elements. Additional iterator arguments might include an output iterator denoting a destination, or another iterator or iterator pair denoting a second input sequence.

Iterators are categorized into one of five categories depending on the operations they support. The iterator categories are input, output, forward, bidirectional, and random access. An iterator belongs to a particular category if it supports the operations required for that iterator category.

Just as iterators are categorized by their operations, iterator parameters to the algorithms are categorized by the iterator operations they require. Algorithms that only read their sequences require only input iterator operations. Those that write to a destination iterator require only the actions of an output iterator, and so on.

Algorithms *never* directly change the size of the sequences on which they operate. They may copy elements from one position to another but cannot directly add or remove elements.

Although algorithms cannot add elements to a sequence, an insert iterator may do so. An insert iterator is bound to a container. When we assign a value of the container's element type to an insert iterator, the iterator adds the given element to the container.

The `forward_list` and `list` containers define their own versions of some of the generic algorithms. Unlike the generic algorithms, these list-specific versions modify the given lists.

DEFINED TERMS

back_inserter Iterator adaptor that takes a reference to a container and generates an insert iterator that uses `push_back` to add elements to the specified container.

bidirectional iterator Same operations as forward iterators plus the ability to use `--` to move backward through the sequence.

binary predicate Predicate that has two parameters.

bind Library function that binds one or more arguments to a callable expression. `bind` is defined in the `functional` header.

callable object Object that can appear as the left-hand operand of the call operator. Pointers to functions, lambdas, and objects of a class that defines an overloaded function call operator are all callable objects.

capture list Portion of a lambda expression that specifies which variables from the surrounding context the lambda expression may access.

cref Library function that returns a copyable object that holds a reference to a `const` object of a type that cannot be copied.

forward iterator Iterator that can read and write elements but is not required to support `--`.

front_inserter Iterator adaptor that, given a container, generates an insert iterator that uses `push_front` to add elements to the beginning of that container.

generic algorithms Type-independent algorithms.

input iterator Iterator that can read, but not write, elements of a sequence.

insert iterator Iterator adaptor that generates an iterator that uses a container operation to add elements to a given container.

inserter Iterator adaptor that takes an iterator and a reference to a container and generates an insert iterator that uses `insert` to add elements just ahead of the element referred to by the given iterator.

istream_iterator Stream iterator that reads an input stream.

iterator categories Conceptual organization of iterators based on the operations that an iterator supports. Iterator categories form a hierarchy, in which the more powerful categories offer the same operations as the lesser categories. The algorithms use iterator categories to specify what operations the iterator arguments must support. As long as the iterator provides at least that level of operation, it can be used. For example, some algorithms require only input iterators. Such algorithms can be called on any iterator other than one that meets only the output iterator requirements. Algorithms that require random-access iterators can be used only on iterators that support random-access operations.

lambda expression Callable unit of code. A lambda is somewhat like an unnamed, inline function. A lambda starts with a capture list, which allows the lambda to access variables in the enclosing function. Like a function, it has a (possibly empty) parameter list, a return type, and a function body. A lambda can omit the return type. If the function body is a single `return` statement, the return type is inferred from the type of the object that is returned. Otherwise, an omitted return type defaults to `void`.

move iterator Iterator adaptor that generates an iterator that moves elements instead of copying them. Move iterators are covered in Chapter 13.

ostream_iterator Iterator that writes to an output stream.

output iterator Iterator that can write, but not necessarily read, elements.

predicate Function that returns a type that can be converted to `bool`. Often used by the generic algorithms to test elements. Predicates used by the library are either unary (taking one argument) or binary (taking two).

random-access iterator Same operations as bidirectional iterators plus the relational operators to compare iterator values, and the subscript operator and arithmetic operations on iterators, thus supporting random access to elements.

ref Library function that generates a copyable object from a reference to an object of a type that cannot be copied.

reverse iterator Iterator that moves backward through a sequence. These iterators exchange the meaning of ++ and --.

stream iterator Iterator that can be bound to a stream.

unary predicate Predicate that has one parameter.

C H A P T E R   **11**

A S S O C I A T I V E   C O N T A I N E R S

Associative and sequential containers differ from one another in a fundamental way: Elements in an associative container are stored and retrieved by a key. In contrast, elements in a sequential container are stored and accessed sequentially by their position in the container.

Although the associative containers share much of the behavior of the sequential containers, they differ from the sequential containers in ways that reflect the use of keys.

Associative containers support efficient lookup and retrieval by a key. The two primary **associative-container** types are `map` and `set`. The elements in a map are key–value pairs: The key serves as an index into the `map`, and the value represents the data associated with that index. A `set` element contains only a key; a `set` supports efficient queries as to whether a given key is present. We might use a `set` to hold words that we want to ignore during some kind of text processing. A dictionary would be a good use for a `map`: The word would be the key, and its definition would be the value.

The library provides eight associative containers, listed in Table 11.1. These eight differ along three dimensions: Each container is (1) a `set` or a `map`, (2) requires unique keys or allows multiple keys, and (3) stores the elements in order or not. The containers that allow multiple keys include the word `multi`; those that do not keep their keys ordered start with the word `unordered`. Hence an `unordered_multi_set` is a set that allows multiple keys whose elements are not stored in order, whereas a `set` has unique keys that are stored in order. The unordered containers use a hash function to organize their elements. We'll have more to say about the hash function in § 11.4 (p. 444).

The `map` and **multimap** types are defined in the `map` header; the `set` and **multiset** types are in the `set` header; and the unordered containers are in the `unordered_map` and `unordered_set` headers.

Table 11.1: Associative Container Types	
Elements Ordered by Key	
`map`	Associative array; holds key–value pairs
`set`	Container in which the key is the value
`multimap`	map in which a key can appear multiple times
`multiset`	set in which a key can appear multiple times
Unordered Collections	
`unordered_map`	map organized by a hash function
`unordered_set`	set organized by a hash function
`unordered_multimap`	Hashed map; keys can appear multiple times
`unordered_multiset`	Hashed set; keys can appear multiple times

11.1 Using an Associative Container

Although most programmers are familiar with data structures such as `vectors` and `lists`, many have never used an associative data structure. Before we look at the details of how the library supports these types, it will be helpful to start with examples of how we can use these containers.

A `map` is a collection of key–value pairs. For example, each pair might contain a person's name as a key and a phone number as its value. We speak of such a data structure as "mapping names to phone numbers." The `map` type is often referred to as an **associative array**. An associative array is like a "normal" array except that its subscripts don't have to be integers. Values in a `map` are found by a key rather than by their position. Given a map of names to phone numbers, we'd use a person's name as a subscript to fetch that person's phone number.

In contrast, a set is simply a collection of keys. A set is most useful when we simply want to know whether a value is present. For example, a business might define a set named bad_checks to hold the names of individuals who have written bad checks. Before accepting a check, that business would query bad_checks to see whether the customer's name was present.

Using a map

A classic example that relies on associative arrays is a word-counting program:

```
//   count the number of times each word occurs in the input
map<string, size_t> word_count; // empty map from string to size_t
string word;
while (cin >> word)
        ++word_count[word];      // fetch and increment the counter for word
for (const auto &w : word_count) // for each element in the map
    //   print the results
    cout <<  w.first << " occurs " << w.second
          << ((w.second > 1) ? " times" : " time") << endl;
```

This program reads its input and reports how often each word appears.

Like the sequential containers, the associative containers are templates (§ 3.3, p. 96). To define a map, we must specify both the key and value types. In this program, the map stores elements in which the keys are strings and the values are size_ts (§ 3.5.2, p. 116). When we subscript word_count, we use a string as the subscript, and we get back the size_t counter associated with that string.

The while loop reads the standard input one word at a time. It uses each word to subscript word_count. If word is not already in the map, the subscript operator creates a new element whose key is word and whose value is 0. Regardless of whether the element had to be created, we increment the value.

Once we've read all the input, the range for (§ 3.2.3, p. 91) iterates through the map, printing each word and the corresponding counter. When we fetch an element from a map, we get an object of type pair, which we'll describe in § 11.2.3 (p. 426). Briefly, a pair is a template type that holds two (public) data elements named first and second. The pairs used by map have a first member that is the key and a second member that is the corresponding value. Thus, the effect of the output statement is to print each word and its associated counter.

If we ran this program on the text of the first paragraph in this section, our output would be

```
Although occurs 1 time
Before occurs 1 time
an occurs 1 time
and occurs 1 time
...
```

Using a set

A logical extension to our program is to ignore common words like "the," "and," "or," and so on. We'll use a set to hold the words we want to ignore and count only those words that are not in this set:

```
// count the number of times each word occurs in the input
map<string, size_t> word_count; // empty map from string to size_t
set<string> exclude = {"The", "But", "And", "Or", "An", "A",
                       "the", "but", "and", "or", "an", "a"};
string word;
while (cin >> word)
    // count only words that are not in exclude
    if (exclude.find(word) == exclude.end())
        ++word_count[word];     // fetch and increment the counter for word
```

Like the other containers, set is a template. To define a set, we specify the type of its elements, which in this case are strings. As with the sequential containers, we can list initialize (§ 9.2.4, p. 336) the elements of an associative container. Our exclude set holds the 12 words we want to ignore.

The important difference between this program and the previous program is that before counting each word, we check whether the word is in the exclusion set. We do this check in the if:

```
// count only words that are not in exclude
if (exclude.find(word) == exclude.end())
```

The call to find returns an iterator. If the given key is in the set, the iterator refers to that key. If the element is not found, find returns the off-the-end iterator. In this version, we update the counter for word only if word is not in exclude.

If we run this version on the same input as before, our output would be

```
Although occurs 1 time
Before occurs 1 time
are occurs 1 time
as occurs 1 time
. . .
```

EXERCISES SECTION 11.1

Exercise 11.1: Describe the differences between a map and a vector.

Exercise 11.2: Give an example of when each of list, vector, deque, map, and set might be most useful.

Exercise 11.3: Write your own version of the word-counting program.

Exercise 11.4: Extend your program to ignore case and punctuation. For example, "example." "example," and "Example" should all increment the same counter.

11.2 Overview of the Associative Containers

Associative containers (both ordered and unordered) support the general container operations covered in § 9.2 (p. 328) and listed in Table 9.2 (p. 330). The associative containers do *not* support the sequential-container position-specific operations, such as push_front or back. Because the elements are stored based on their keys, these operations would be meaningless for the associative containers. Moreover, the associative containers do not support the constructors or insert operations that take an element value and a count.

In addition to the operations they share with the sequential containers, the associative containers provide some operations (Table 11.7 (p. 438)) and type aliases (Table 11.3 (p. 429)) that the sequential containers do not. In addition, the unordered containers provide operations for tuning their hash performance, which we'll cover in § 11.4 (p. 444).

The associative container iterators are bidirectional (§ 10.5.1, p. 410).

11.2.1 Defining an Associative Container

As we've just seen, when we define a map, we must indicate both the key and value type; when we define a set, we specify only a key type, because there is no value type. Each of the associative containers defines a default constructor, which creates an empty container of the specified type. We can also initialize an associative container as a copy of another container of the same type or from a range of values, so long as those values can be converted to the type of the container. Under the new standard, we can also list initialize the elements:

```
map<string, size_t> word_count;  // empty
// list initialization
set<string> exclude = {"the", "but", "and", "or", "an", "a",
                       "The", "But", "And", "Or", "An", "A"};
// three elements; authors maps last name to first
map<string, string> authors = { {"Joyce", "James"},
                                {"Austen", "Jane"},
                                {"Dickens", "Charles"} };
```

As usual, the initializers must be convertible to the type in the container. For set, the element type is the key type.

When we initialize a map, we have to supply both the key and the value. We wrap each key–value pair inside curly braces:

```
{key, value}
```

to indicate that the items together form one element in the map. The key is the first element in each pair, and the value is the second. Thus, authors maps last names to first names, and is initialized with three elements.

Initializing a multimap or multiset

The keys in a map or a set must be unique; there can be only one element with a given key. The multimap and multiset containers have no such restriction;

there can be several elements with the same key. For example, the map we used to count words must have only one element per given word. On the other hand, a dictionary could have several definitions associated with a particular word.

The following example illustrates the differences between the containers with unique keys and those that have multiple keys. First, we'll create a vector of ints named ivec that has 20 elements: two copies of each of the integers from 0 through 9 inclusive. We'll use that vector to initialize a set and a multiset:

```
// define a vector with 20 elements, holding two copies of each number from 0 to 9
vector<int> ivec;
for (vector<int>::size_type i = 0; i != 10; ++i) {
    ivec.push_back(i);
    ivec.push_back(i);   // duplicate copies of each number
}
// iset holds unique elements from ivec; miset holds all 20 elements
set<int> iset(ivec.cbegin(), ivec.cend());
multiset<int> miset(ivec.cbegin(), ivec.cend());
cout << ivec.size() << endl;     // prints 20
cout << iset.size() << endl;     // prints 10
cout << miset.size() << endl;    // prints 20
```

Even though we initialized iset from the entire ivec container, iset has only ten elements: one for each distinct element in ivec. On the other hand, miset has 20 elements, the same as the number of elements in ivec.

EXERCISES SECTION 11.2.1

Exercise 11.5: Explain the difference between a map and a set. When might you use one or the other?

Exercise 11.6: Explain the difference between a set and a list. When might you use one or the other?

Exercise 11.7: Define a map for which the key is the family's last name and the value is a vector of the children's names. Write code to add new families and to add new children to an existing family.

Exercise 11.8: Write a program that stores the excluded words in a vector instead of in a set. What are the advantages to using a set?

 ## 11.2.2 Requirements on Key Type

The associative containers place constraints on the type that is used as a key. We'll cover the requirements for keys in the unordered containers in § 11.4 (p. 445). For the ordered containers—map, multimap, set, and multiset—the key type must define a way to compare the elements. By default, the library uses the < operator for the key type to compare the keys. In the set types, the key is the element type;

in the map types, the key is the first type. Thus, the key type for `word_count` in § 11.1 (p. 421) is `string`. Similarly, the key type for `exclude` is `string`.

Callable objects passed to a sort algorithm (§ 10.3.1, p. 386) must meet the same requirements as do the keys in an associative container.

Key Types for Ordered Containers

Just as we can provide our own comparison operation to an algorithm (§ 10.3, p. 385), we can also supply our own operation to use in place of the `<` operator on keys. The specified operation must define a **strict weak ordering** over the key type. We can think of a strict weak ordering as "less than," although our function might use a more complicated procedure. However we define it, the comparison function must have the following properties:

- Two keys cannot both be "less than" each other; if `k1` is "less than" `k2`, then `k2` must never be "less than" `k1`.

- If `k1` is "less than" `k2` and `k2` is "less than" `k3`, then `k1` must be "less than" `k3`.

- If there are two keys, and neither key is "less than" the other, then we'll say that those keys are "equivalent." If `k1` is "equivalent" to `k2` and `k2` is "equivalent" to `k3`, then `k1` must be "equivalent" to `k3`.

If two keys are equivalent (i.e., if neither is "less than" the other), the container treats them as equal. When used as a key to a map, there will be only one element associated with those keys, and either key can be used to access the corresponding value.

In practice, what's important is that a type that defines a `<` operator that "behaves normally" can be used as a key.

Using a Comparison Function for the Key Type

The type of the operation that a container uses to organize its elements is part of the type of that container. To specify our own operation, we must supply the type of that operation when we define the type of an associative container. The operation type is specified following the element type inside the angle brackets that we use to say which type of container we are defining.

Each type inside the angle brackets is just that, a type. We supply a particular comparison operation (that must have the same type as we specified inside the angle brackets) as a constructor argument when we create a container.

For example, we can't directly define a `multiset` of `Sales_data` because `Sales_data` doesn't have a `<` operator. However, we can use the `compareIsbn` function from the exercises in § 10.3.1 (p. 387) to define a `multiset`. That function defines a strict weak ordering based on their ISBNs of two given `Sales_data` objects. The `compareIsbn` function should look something like

```
bool compareIsbn(const Sales_data &lhs, const Sales_data &rhs)
{
    return lhs.isbn() < rhs.isbn();
}
```

To use our own operation, we must define the `multiset` with two types: the key type, `Sales_data`, and the comparison type, which is a function pointer type (§ 6.7, p. 247) that can point to `compareIsbn`. When we define objects of this type, we supply a pointer to the operation we intend to use. In this case, we supply a pointer to `compareIsbn`:

```
//  bookstore can have several transactions with the same ISBN
//  elements in bookstore will be in ISBN order
multiset<Sales_data, decltype(compareIsbn)*>
    bookstore(compareIsbn);
```

Here, we use `decltype` to specify the type of our operation, remembering that when we use `decltype` to form a function pointer, we must add a `*` to indicate that we're using a pointer to the given function type (§ 6.7, p. 250). We initialize `bookstore` from `compareIsbn`, which means that when we add elements to `bookstore`, those elements will be ordered by calling `compareIsbn`. That is, the elements in `bookstore` will be ordered by their ISBN members. We can write `compareIsbn` instead of `&compareIsbn` as the constructor argument because when we use the name of a function, it is automatically converted into a pointer if needed (§ 6.7, p. 248). We could have written `&compareIsbn` with the same effect.

EXERCISES SECTION 11.2.2

Exercise 11.9: Define a `map` that associates words with a `list` of line numbers on which the word might occur.

Exercise 11.10: Could we define a `map` from `vector<int>::iterator` to int? What about from `list<int>::iterator` to int? In each case, if not, why not?

Exercise 11.11: Redefine `bookstore` without using `decltype`.

11.2.3 The `pair` Type

Before we look at the operations on associative containers, we need to know about the library type named **pair**, which is defined in the `utility` header.

A `pair` holds two data members. Like the containers, `pair` is a template from which we generate specific types. We must supply two type names when we create a `pair`. The data members of the `pair` have the corresponding types. There is no requirement that the two types be the same:

```
pair<string, string> anon;       // holds two strings
pair<string, size_t> word_count; // holds a string and an size_t
pair<string, vector<int>> line;  // holds string and vector<int>
```

The default `pair` constructor value initializes (§ 3.3.1, p. 98) the data members. Thus, anon is a `pair` of two empty `string`s, and `line` holds an empty `string` and an empty `vector`. The `size_t` value in `word_count` gets the value 0, and the `string` member is initialized to the empty `string`.

We can also provide initializers for each member:

```
pair<string, string> author{"James", "Joyce"};
```

creates a `pair` named `author`, initialized with the values `"James"` and `"Joyce"`.

Table 11.2: Operations on `pairs`	
`pair<T1, T2> p;`	p is a pair with value initialized (§ 3.3.1, p. 98) members of types T1 and T2, respectively.
`pair<T1, T2> p(v1, v2);`	p is a pair with types T1 and T2; the first and second members are initialized from v1 and v2, respectively.
`pair<T1, T2> p = {v1, v2};`	Equivalent to p(v1, v2).
`make_pair(v1, v2)`	Returns a pair initialized from v1 and v2. The type of the pair is inferred from the types of v1 and v2.
`p.first`	Returns the (public) data member of p named first.
`p.second`	Returns the (public) data member of p named second.
`p1 relop p2`	Relational operators (<, >, <=, >=). Relational operators are defined as dictionary ordering: For example, p1 < p2 is true if p1.first < p2.first or if !(p2.first < p1.first) && p1.second < p2.second. Uses the element's < operator.
`p1 == p2` `p1 != p2`	Two pairs are equal if their first and second members are respectively equal. Uses the element's == operator.

Unlike other library types, the data members of `pair` are `public` (§ 7.2, p. 268). These members are named `first` and `second`, respectively. We access these members using the normal member access notation (§ 1.5.2, p. 23), as, for example, we did in the output statement of our word-counting program on page 421:

```
// print the results
cout << w.first << " occurs " << w.second
     << ((w.second > 1) ? " times" : " time") << endl;
```

Here, w is a reference to an element in a `map`. Elements in a `map` are `pairs`. In this statement we print the `first` member of the element, which is the key, followed by the `second` member, which is the counter. The library defines only a limited number of operations on `pairs`, which are listed in Table 11.2.

A Function to Create `pair` Objects

Imagine we have a function that needs to return a `pair`. Under the new standard we can list initialize the return value (§ 6.3.2, p. 226):

`C++11`

```
pair<string, int>
process(vector<string> &v)
{
    //  process v
    if (!v.empty())
        return {v.back(), v.back().size()}; //  list initialize
    else
        return pair<string, int>(); //  explicitly constructed return value
}
```

If v isn't empty, we return a pair composed of the last string in v and the size
of that string. Otherwise, we explicitly construct and return an empty pair.

Under earlier versions of C++, we couldn't use braced initializers to return a
type like pair. Instead, we might have written both returns to explicitly construct
the return value:

```
if (!v.empty())
    return pair<string, int>(v.back(), v.back().size());
```

Alternatively, we could have used make_pair to generate a new pair of the appropriate type from its two arguments:

```
if (!v.empty())
    return make_pair(v.back(), v.back().size());
```

EXERCISES SECTION 11.2.3

Exercise 11.12: Write a program to read a sequence of strings and ints, storing each
into a pair. Store the pairs in a vector.

Exercise 11.13: There are at least three ways to create the pairs in the program for
the previous exercise. Write three versions of that program, creating the pairs in each
way. Explain which form you think is easiest to write and understand, and why.

Exercise 11.14: Extend the map of children to their family name that you wrote for the
exercises in § 11.2.1 (p. 424) by having the vector store a pair that holds a child's
name and birthday.

11.3   Operations on Associative Containers

In addition to the types listed in Table 9.2 (p. 330), the associative containers define
the types listed in Table 11.3. These types represent the container's key and value
types.

For the set types, the **key_type** and the **value_type** are the same; the values
held in a set are the keys. In a map, the elements are key–value pairs. That is,
each element is a pair object containing a key and a associated value. Because we
cannot change an element's key, the key part of these pairs is const:

Table 11.3: Associative Container Additional Type Aliases	
key_type	Type of the key for this container type
mapped_type	Type associated with each key; **map types only**
value_type	For sets, same as the key_type
	For maps, pair<const key_type, mapped_type>

```
set<string>::value_type v1;        // v1 is a string
set<string>::key_type v2;          // v2 is a string
map<string, int>::value_type v3;   // v3 is a pair<const string, int>
map<string, int>::key_type v4;     // v4 is a string
map<string, int>::mapped_type v5;  // v5 is an int
```

As with the sequential containers (§ 9.2.2, p. 332), we use the scope operator to fetch a type member—for example, map<string, int>::key_type.

Only the map types (unordered_map, unordered_multimap, multimap, and map) define **mapped_type**.

11.3.1 Associative Container Iterators

When we dereference an iterator, we get a reference to a value of the container's value_type. In the case of map, the value_type is a pair in which first holds the const key and second holds the value:

```
// get an iterator to an element in word_count
auto map_it = word_count.begin();

// *map_it is a reference to a pair<const string, size_t> object
cout << map_it->first;           // prints the key for this element
cout << " " << map_it->second;   // prints the value of the element
map_it->first = "new key";       // error: key is const
++map_it->second;                // ok: we can change the value through an iterator
```

 It is essential to remember that the value_type of a map is a pair and that we can change the value but not the key member of that pair.

Iterators for sets Are const

Although the set types define both the iterator and const_iterator types, both types of iterators give us read-only access to the elements in the set. Just as we cannot change the key part of a map element, the keys in a set are also const. We can use a set iterator to read, but not write, an element's value:

```
set<int> iset = {0,1,2,3,4,5,6,7,8,9};
set<int>::iterator set_it = iset.begin();
if (set_it != iset.end()) {
    *set_it = 42;            // error: keys in a set are read-only
    cout << *set_it << endl; // ok: can read the key
}
```

Iterating across an Associative Container

The map and set types provide all the begin and end operations from Table 9.2 (p. 330). As usual, we can use these functions to obtain iterators that we can use to traverse the container. For example, we can rewrite the loop that printed the results in our word-counting program on page 421 as follows:

```
// get an iterator positioned on the first element
auto map_it = word_count.cbegin();
// compare the current iterator to the off-the-end iterator
while (map_it != word_count.cend()) {
    // dereference the iterator to print the element key--value pairs
    cout << map_it->first << " occurs "
         << map_it->second << " times" << endl;
    ++map_it;   // increment the iterator to denote the next element
}
```

The while condition and increment for the iterator in this loop look a lot like the programs we wrote that printed the contents of a vector or a string. We initialize an iterator, map_it, to refer to the first element in word_count. As long as the iterator is not equal to the end value, we print the current element and then increment the iterator. The output statement dereferences map_it to get the members of pair but is otherwise the same as the one in our original program.

The output of this program is in alphabetical order. When we use an iterator to traverse a map, multimap, set, or multiset, the iterators yield elements in ascending key order.

Associative Containers and Algorithms

In general, we do not use the generic algorithms (Chapter 10) with the associative containers. The fact that the keys are const means that we cannot pass associative container iterators to algorithms that write to or reorder container elements. Such algorithms need to write to the elements. The elements in the set types are const, and those in maps are pairs whose first element is const.

Associative containers can be used with the algorithms that read elements. However, many of these algorithms search the sequence. Because elements in an associative container can be found (quickly) by their key, it is almost always a bad idea to use a generic search algorithm. For example, as we'll see in § 11.3.5 (p. 436), the associative containers define a member named find, which directly fetches the element with a given key. We could use the generic find algorithm to look for an element, but that algorithm does a sequential search. It is much faster to use the find member defined by the container than to call the generic version.

In practice, if we do so at all, we use an associative container with the algorithms either as the source sequence or as a destination. For example, we might use the generic copy algorithm to copy the elements from an associative container into another sequence. Similarly, we can call inserter to bind an insert iterator (§ 10.4.1, p. 401) to an associative container. Using inserter, we can use the associative container as a destination for another algorithm.

EXERCISES SECTION 11.3.1

Exercise 11.15: What are the mapped_type, key_type, and value_type of a map from int to vector<int>?

Exercise 11.16: Using a map iterator write an expression that assigns a value to an element.

Exercise 11.17: Assuming c is a multiset of strings and v is a vector of strings, explain the following calls. Indicate whether each call is legal:

```
copy(v.begin(), v.end(), inserter(c, c.end()));
copy(v.begin(), v.end(), back_inserter(c));
copy(c.begin(), c.end(), inserter(v, v.end()));
copy(c.begin(), c.end(), back_inserter(v));
```

Exercise 11.18: Write the type of map_it from the loop on page 430 without using auto or decltype.

Exercise 11.19: Define a variable that you initialize by calling begin() on the multiset named bookstore from § 11.2.2 (p. 425). Write the variable's type without using auto or decltype.

11.3.2 Adding Elements

The insert members (Table 11.4 (overleaf)) add one element or a range of elements. Because map and set (and the corresponding unordered types) contain unique keys, inserting an element that is already present has no effect:

```
vector<int> ivec = {2,4,6,8,2,4,6,8};     // ivec has eight elements
set<int> set2;                             // empty set
set2.insert(ivec.cbegin(), ivec.cend());  // set2 has four elements
set2.insert({1,3,5,7,1,3,5,7});           // set2 now has eight elements
```

The versions of insert that take a pair of iterators or an initializer list work similarly to the corresponding constructors (§ 11.2.1, p. 423)—only the first element with a given key is inserted.

Adding Elements to a map

When we insert into a map, we must remember that the element type is a pair. Often, we don't have a pair object that we want to insert. Instead, we create a pair in the argument list to insert:

```
// four ways to add word to word_count
word_count.insert({word, 1});
word_count.insert(make_pair(word, 1));
word_count.insert(pair<string, size_t>(word, 1));
word_count.insert(map<string, size_t>::value_type(word, 1));
```

As we've seen, under the new standard the easiest way to create a pair is to use brace initialization inside the argument list. Alternatively, we can call make_pair [C++11] or explicitly construct the `pair`. The argument in the last call to `insert`:

```
map<string, size_t>::value_type(s, 1)
```

constructs a new object of the appropriate `pair` type to insert into the `map`.

Table 11.4: Associative Container `insert` Operations	
`c.insert(v)` `c.emplace(args)`	v value_type object; *args* are used to construct an element. For map and set, the element is inserted (or constructed) only if an element with the given key is not already in c. Returns a pair containing an iterator referring to the element with the given key and a bool indicating whether the element was inserted. For multimap and multiset, inserts (or constructs) the given element and returns an iterator to the new element.
`c.insert(b, e)` `c.insert(il)`	b and e are iterators that denote a range of c::value_type values; il is a braced list of such values. Returns void. For map and set, inserts the elements with keys that are not already in c. For multimap and multiset inserts, each element in the range.
`c.insert(p, v)` `c.emplace(p, args)`	Like insert(v) (or emplace(*args*)), but uses iterator p as a hint for where to begin the search for where the new element should be stored. Returns an iterator to the element with the given key.

Testing the Return from `insert`

The value returned by `insert` (or `emplace`) depends on the container type and the parameters. For the containers that have unique keys, the versions of `insert` and `emplace` that add a single element return a `pair` that lets us know whether the insertion happened. The `first` member of the `pair` is an iterator to the element with the given key; the `second` is a `bool` indicating whether that element was inserted, or was already there. If the key is already in the container, then `insert` does nothing, and the `bool` portion of the return value is `false`. If the key isn't present, then the element is inserted and the `bool` is `true`.

As an example, we'll rewrite our word-counting program to use `insert`:

```
// more verbose way to count number of times each word occurs in the input
map<string, size_t> word_count;  // empty map from string to size_t
string word;
while (cin >> word) {
    // inserts an element with key equal to word and value 1;
    // if word is already in word_count, insert does nothing
    auto ret = word_count.insert({word, 1});
    if (!ret.second)              // word was already in word_count
        ++ret.first->second;  // increment the counter
}
```

For each word, we attempt to `insert` it with a value 1. If word is already in the map, then nothing happens. In particular, the counter associated with word is unchanged. If `word` is not already in the `map`, then that `string` is added to the `map` and its counter value is set to 1.

The `if` test examines the `bool` part of the return value. If that value is `false`, then the insertion didn't happen. In this case, `word` was already in `word_count`, so we must increment the value associated with that element.

Unwinding the Syntax

The statement that increments the counter in this version of the word-counting program can be hard to understand. It will be easier to understand that expression by first parenthesizing it to reflect the precedence (§ 4.1.2, p. 136) of the operators:

```
++((ret.first)->second); // equivalent expression
```

Explaining this expression step by step:

> **ret** holds the value returned by `insert`, which is a `pair`.
>
> **ret.first** is the `first` member of that `pair`, which is a map iterator referring to the element with the given key.
>
> **ret.first->** dereferences that iterator to fetch that element. Elements in the `map` are also `pairs`.
>
> **ret.first->second** is the value part of the map element `pair`.
>
> **++ret.first->second** increments that value.

Putting it back together, the increment statement fetches the iterator for the element with the key `word` and increments the counter associated with the key we tried to insert.

For readers using an older compiler or reading code that predates the new standard, declaring and initializing `ret` is also somewhat tricky:

```
pair<map<string, size_t>::iterator, bool> ret =
          word_count.insert(make_pair(word, 1));
```

It should be easy to see that we're defining a `pair` and that the second type of the `pair` is `bool`. The first type of that `pair` is a bit harder to understand. It is the `iterator` type defined by the `map<string, size_t>` type.

Adding Elements to `multiset` or `multimap`

Our word-counting program depends on the fact that a given key can occur only once. That way, there is only one counter associated with any given word. Sometimes, we want to be able to add additional elements with the same key. For example, we might want to map authors to titles of the books they have written. In this case, there might be multiple entries for each author, so we'd use a `multimap` rather than a `map`. Because keys in a `multi` container need not be unique, `insert` on these types always inserts an element:

```
multimap<string, string> authors;
//   adds the first element with the key Barth, John
authors.insert({"Barth, John", "Sot-Weed Factor"});

//   ok: adds the second element with the key Barth, John
authors.insert({"Barth, John", "Lost in the Funhouse"});
```

For the containers that allow multiple keys, the `insert` operation that takes a single element returns an iterator to the new element. There is no need to return a `bool`, because `insert` always adds a new element in these types.

EXERCISES SECTION 11.3.2

Exercise 11.20: Rewrite the word-counting program from § 11.1 (p. 421) to use `insert` instead of subscripting. Which program do you think is easier to write and read? Explain your reasoning.

Exercise 11.21: Assuming `word_count` is a map from `string` to `size_t` and `word` is a `string`, explain the following loop:

```
while (cin >> word)
    ++word_count.insert({word, 0}).first->second;
```

Exercise 11.22: Given a `map<string, vector<int>>`, write the types used as an argument and as the return value for the version of `insert` that inserts one element.

Exercise 11.23: Rewrite the map that stored `vector`s of children's names with a key that is the family last name for the exercises in § 11.2.1 (p. 424) to use a `multimap`.

11.3.3 Erasing Elements

The associative containers define three versions of `erase`, which are described in Table 11.5. As with the sequential containers, we can `erase` one element or a range of elements by passing `erase` an iterator or an iterator pair. These versions of `erase` are similar to the corresponding operations on sequential containers: The indicated element(s) are removed and the function returns `void`.

The associative containers supply an additional `erase` operation that takes a `key_type` argument. This version removes all the elements, if any, with the given key and returns a count of how many elements were removed. We can use this version to remove a specific word from `word_count` before printing the results:

```
//   erase on a key returns the number of elements removed
if (word_count.erase(removal_word))
    cout << "ok: " << removal_word << " removed\n";
else cout << "oops: " << removal_word << " not found!\n";
```

For the containers with unique keys, the return from `erase` is always either zero or one. If the return value is zero, then the element we wanted to erase was not in the container.

For types that allow multiple keys, the number of elements removed could be greater than one:

```
auto cnt = authors.erase("Barth, John");
```

If `authors` is the `multimap` we created in § 11.3.2 (p. 434), then `cnt` will be 2.

Table 11.5: Removing Elements from an Associative Container	
`c.erase(k)`	Removes every element with key k from c. Returns `size_type` indicating the number of elements removed.
`c.erase(p)`	Removes the element denoted by the iterator p from c. p must refer to an actual element in c; it must not be equal to `c.end()`. Returns an iterator to the element after p or `c.end()` if p denotes the last element in c.
`c.erase(b, e)`	Removes the elements in the range denoted by the iterator pair b, e. Returns e.

11.3.4 Subscripting a `map`

The `map` and `unordered_map` containers provide the subscript operator and a corresponding at function (§ 9.3.2, p. 348), which are described in Table 11.6 (overleaf). The `set` types do not support subscripting because there is no "value" associated with a key in a `set`. The elements are themselves keys, so the operation of "fetching the value associated with a key" is meaningless. We cannot subscript a `multimap` or an `unordered_multimap` because there may be more than one value associated with a given key.

Like the other subscript operators we've used, the `map` subscript takes an index (that is, a key) and fetches the value associated with that key. However, unlike other subscript operators, if the key is not already present, *a new element is created and inserted* into the `map` for that key. The associated value is value initialized (§ 3.3.1, p. 98).

For example, when we write

```
map <string, size_t> word_count; // empty map
// insert a value-initialized element with key Anna; then assign 1 to its value
word_count["Anna"] = 1;
```

the following steps take place:

- `word_count` is searched for the element whose key is `Anna`. The element is not found.

- A new key–value pair is inserted into `word_count`. The key is a `const string` holding `Anna`. The value is value initialized, meaning in this case that the value is 0.

- The newly inserted element is fetched and is given the value 1.

Because the subscript operator might insert an element, we may use subscript only on a map that is not `const`.

 Subscripting a map behaves quite differently from subscripting an array or `vector`: Using a key that is not already present *adds* an element with that key to the map.

Table 11.6: Subscript Operation for `map` and `unordered_map`	
`c[k]`	Returns the element with key k; if k is not in c, adds a new, value-initialized element with key k.
`c.at(k)`	Checked access to the element with key k; throws an `out_of_range` exception (§ 5.6, p. 193) if k is not in c.

Using the Value Returned from a Subscript Operation

Another way in which the `map` subscript differs from other subscript operators we've used is its return type. Ordinarily, the type returned by dereferencing an iterator and the type returned by the subscript operator are the same. Not so for maps: when we subscript a map, we get a `mapped_type` object; when we dereference a map iterator, we get a `value_type` object (§ 11.3, p. 428).

In common with other subscripts, the `map` subscript operator returns an lvalue (§ 4.1.1, p. 135). Because the return is an lvalue, we can read or write the element:

```
cout << word_count["Anna"];    // fetch the element indexed by Anna; prints 1
++word_count["Anna"];          // fetch the element and add 1 to it
cout << word_count["Anna"];    // fetch the element and print it; prints 2
```

 Unlike `vector` or `string`, the type returned by the map subscript operator differs from the type obtained by dereferencing a map iterator.

The fact that the subscript operator adds an element if it is not already in the map allows us to write surprisingly succinct programs such as the loop inside our word-counting program (§ 11.1, p. 421). On the other hand, sometimes we only want to know whether an element is present and *do not* want to add the element if it is not. In such cases, we must not use the subscript operator.

11.3.5 Accessing Elements

The associative containers provide various ways to find a given element, which are described in Table 11.7 (p. 438). Which operation to use depends on what problem we are trying to solve. If all we care about is whether a particular element is in the container, it is probably best to use `find`. For the containers that can hold only unique keys, it probably doesn't matter whether we use `find` or `count`. However, for the containers with multiple keys, `count` has to do more work: If the element

Exercise 11.24: What does the following program do?

```
map<int, int> m;
m[0] = 1;
```

Exercise 11.25: Contrast the following program with the one in the previous exercise

```
vector<int> v;
v[0] = 1;
```

Exercise 11.26: What type can be used to subscript a map? What type does the subscript operator return? Give a concrete example—that is, define a map and then write the types that can be used to subscript the map and the type that would be returned from the subscript operator.

is present, it still has to count how many elements have the same key. If we don't need the count, it's best to use find:

```
set<int> iset = {0,1,2,3,4,5,6,7,8,9};
iset.find(1);    // returns an iterator that refers to the element with key == 1
iset.find(11);   // returns the iterator == iset.end()
iset.count(1);   // returns 1
iset.count(11);  // returns 0
```

Using find Instead of Subscript for maps

For the map and unordered_map types, the subscript operator provides the simplest method of retrieving a value. However, as we've just seen, using a subscript has an important side effect: If that key is not already in the map, then subscript inserts an element with that key. Whether this behavior is correct depends on our expectations. Our word-counting programs relied on the fact that using a nonexistent key as a subscript inserts an element with that key and value 0.

Sometimes, we want to know if an element with a given key is present without changing the map. We cannot use the subscript operator to determine whether an element is present, because the subscript operator inserts a new element if the key is not already there. In such cases, we should use find:

```
if (word_count.find("foobar") == word_count.end())
    cout << "foobar is not in the map" << endl;
```

Finding Elements in a multimap or multiset

Finding an element in an associative container that requires unique keys is a simple matter—the element is or is not in the container. For the containers that allow multiple keys, the process is more complicated: There may be many elements with the given key. When a multimap or multiset has multiple elements of a given key, those elements will be adjacent within the container.

Table 11.7: Operations to Find Elements in an Associative Container
lower_bound and upper_bound not valid for the unordered containers. Subscript and at operations only for map and unordered_map that are not const.

c.find(k)	Returns an iterator to the (first) element with key k, or the off-the-end iterator if k is not in the container.
c.count(k)	Returns the number of elements with key k. For the containers with unique keys, the result is always zero or one.
c.lower_bound(k)	Returns an iterator to the first element with key not less than k.
c.upper_bound(k)	Returns an iterator to the first element with key greater than k.
c.equal_range(k)	Returns a pair of iterators denoting the elements with key k. If k is not present, both members are c.end().

For example, given our map from author to titles, we might want to print all the books by a particular author. We can solve this problem in three different ways. The most obvious way uses find and count:

```
string search_item("Alain de Botton"); // author we'll look for
auto entries = authors.count(search_item); // number of elements
auto iter = authors.find(search_item); // first entry for this author
// loop through the number of entries there are for this author
while(entries) {
    cout << iter->second << endl; // print each title
    ++iter;        // advance to the next title
    --entries;     // keep track of how many we've printed
}
```

We start by determining how many entries there are for the author by calling count and getting an iterator to the first element with this key by calling find. The number of iterations of the for loop depends on the number returned from count. In particular, if the count was zero, then the loop is never executed.

 We are guaranteed that iterating across a multimap or multiset returns all the elements with a given key in sequence.

A Different, Iterator-Oriented Solution

Alternatively, we can solve our problem using lower_bound and upper_bound. Each of these operations take a key and returns an iterator. If the key is in the container, the iterator returned from lower_bound will refer to the first instance of that key and the iterator returned by upper_bound will refer just after the last instance of the key. If the element is not in the multimap, then lower_bound and upper_bound will return equal iterators; both will refer to the point at which the key can be inserted without disrupting the order. Thus, calling lower_bound and upper_bound on the same key yields an iterator range (§ 9.2.1, p. 331) that denotes all the elements with that key.

Of course, the iterator returned from these operations might be the off-the-end iterator for the container itself. If the element we're looking for has the largest key in the container, then upper_bound on that key returns the off-the-end iterator. If the key is not present and is larger than any key in the container, then the return from lower_bound will also be the off-the-end iterator.

> The iterator returned from lower_bound may or may not refer to an element with the given key. If the key is not in the container, then lower_bound refers to the first point at which this key can be inserted while preserving the element order within the container.

Using these operations, we can rewrite our program as follows:

```
//  definitions of authors and search_item as above
//  beg and end denote the range of elements for this author
for (auto beg = authors.lower_bound(search_item),
          end = authors.upper_bound(search_item);
     beg != end; ++beg)
    cout << beg->second << endl; //  print each title
```

This program does the same work as the previous one that used count and find but accomplishes its task more directly. The call to lower_bound positions beg so that it refers to the first element matching search_item if there is one. If there is no such element, then beg refers to the first element with a key larger than search_item, which could be the off-the-end iterator. The call to upper_bound sets end to refer to the element just beyond the last element with the given key. These operations say nothing about whether the key is present. The important point is that the return values act like an iterator range (§ 9.2.1, p. 331).

If there is no element for this key, then lower_bound and upper_bound will be equal. Both will refer to the point at which this key can be inserted while maintaining the container order.

Assuming there are elements with this key, beg will refer to the first such element. We can increment beg to traverse the elements with this key. The iterator in end will signal when we've seen all the elements. When beg equals end, we have seen every element with this key.

Because these iterators form a range, we can use a for loop to traverse that range. The loop is executed zero or more times and prints the entries, if any, for the given author. If there are no elements, then beg and end are equal and the loop is never executed. Otherwise, we know that the increment to beg will eventually reach end and that in the process we will print each record associated with this author.

> If lower_bound and upper_bound return the same iterator, then the given key is not in the container.

The equal_range Function

The remaining way to solve this problem is the most direct of the three approaches: Instead of calling upper_bound and lower_bound, we can call equal_range.

This function takes a key and returns a `pair` of iterators. If the key is present, then the first iterator refers to the first instance of the key and the second iterator refers one past the last instance of the key. If no matching element is found, then both the first and second iterators refer to the position where this key can be inserted.

We can use `equal_range` to modify our program once again:

```
//  definitions of authors and search_item as above
//  pos holds iterators that denote the range of elements for this key
for (auto pos = authors.equal_range(search_item);
     pos.first != pos.second; ++pos.first)
    cout << pos.first->second << endl; // print each title
```

This program is essentially identical to the previous one that used `upper_bound` and `lower_bound`. Instead of using local variables, `beg` and `end`, to hold the iterator range, we use the `pair` returned by `equal_range`. The `first` member of that `pair` holds the same iterator as `lower_bound` would have returned and `second` holds the iterator `upper_bound` would have returned. Thus, in this program `pos.first` is equivalent to `beg`, and `pos.second` is equivalent to `end`.

EXERCISES SECTION 11.3.5

Exercise 11.27: What kinds of problems would you use `count` to solve? When might you use `find` instead?

Exercise 11.28: Define and initialize a variable to hold the result of calling `find` on a `map` from `string` to `vector` of `int`.

Exercise 11.29: What do `upper_bound`, `lower_bound`, and `equal_range` return when you pass them a key that is not in the container?

Exercise 11.30: Explain the meaning of the operand `pos.first->second` used in the output expression of the final program in this section.

Exercise 11.31: Write a program that defines a `multimap` of authors and their works. Use `find` to find an element in the `multimap` and `erase` that element. Be sure your program works correctly if the element you look for is not in the `map`.

Exercise 11.32: Using the `multimap` from the previous exercise, write a program to print the list of authors and their works alphabetically.

11.3.6 A Word Transformation Map

We'll close this section with a program to illustrate creating, searching, and iterating across a map. We'll write a program that, given one `string`, transforms it into another. The input to our program is two files. The first file contains rules that we will use to transform the text in the second file. Each rule consists of a word that might be in the input file and a phrase to use in its place. The idea is that whenever the first word appears in the input, we will replace it with the corresponding phrase. The second file contains the text to transform.

If the contents of the word-transformation file are

```
brb be right back
k okay?
y why
r are
u you
pic picture
thk thanks!
18r later
```

and the text we are given to transform is

```
where r u
y dont u send me a pic
k thk 18r
```

then the program should generate the following output:

```
where are you
why dont you send me a picture
okay? thanks! later
```

The Word Transformation Program

Our solution will use three functions. The word_transform function will manage the overall processing. It will take two ifstream arguments: The first will be bound to the word-transformation file and the second to the file of text we're to transform. The buildMap function will read the file of transformation rules and create a map from each word to its transformation. The transform function will take a string and return the transformation if there is one.

We'll start by defining the word_transform function. The important parts are the calls to buildMap and transform:

```cpp
void word_transform(ifstream &map_file, ifstream &input)
{
    auto trans_map = buildMap(map_file); // store the transformations
    string text;                         // hold each line from the input
    while (getline(input, text)) {       // read a line of input
        istringstream stream(text);      // read each word
        string word;
        bool firstword = true;           // controls whether a space is printed
        while (stream >> word) {
            if (firstword)
                firstword = false;
            else
                cout << " ";   // print a space between words
            // transform returns its first argument or its transformation
            cout << transform(word, trans_map); // print the output
        }
        cout << endl;          // done with this line of input
    }
}
```

The function starts by calling buildMap to generate the word-transformation map. We store the result in trans_map. The rest of the function processes the input file. The while loop uses getline to read the input file a line at a time. We read by line so that our output will have line breaks at the same position as in the input file. To get the words from each line, we use a nested while loop that uses an istringstream (§ 8.3, p. 321) to process each word in the current line.

The inner while prints the output using the bool firstword to determine whether to print a space. The call to transform obtains the word to print. The value returned from transform is either the original string in word or its corresponding transformation from trans_map.

Building the Transformation Map

The buildMap function reads its given file and builds the transformation map.

```
map<string, string> buildMap(ifstream &map_file)
{
    map<string, string> trans_map;    // holds the transformations
    string key;      // a word to transform
    string value;    // phrase to use instead
    // read the first word into key and the rest of the line into value
    while (map_file >> key && getline(map_file, value))
        if (value.size() > 1) // check that there is a transformation
            trans_map[key] = value.substr(1);  // skip leading space
        else
            throw runtime_error("no rule for " + key);
    return trans_map;
}
```

Each line in map_file corresponds to a rule. Each rule is a word followed by a phrase, which might contain multiple words. We use >> to read the word that we will transform into key and call getline to read the rest of the line into value. Because getline does not skip leading spaces (§ 3.2.2, p. 87), we need to skip the space between the word and its corresponding rule. Before we store the transformation, we check that we got more than one character. If so, we call substr (§ 9.5.1, p. 361) to skip the space that separated the transformation phrase from its corresponding word and store that substring in trans_map,

Note that we use the subscript operator to add the key–value pairs. Implicitly, we are ignoring what should happen if a word appears more than once in our transformation file. If a word does appear multiple times, our loops will put the last corresponding phrase into trans_map. When the while concludes, trans_map contains the data that we need to transform the input.

Generating a Transformation

The transform function does the actual transformation. Its parameters are references to the string to transform and to the transformation map. If the given string is in the map, transform returns the corresponding transformation. If the given string is not in the map, transform returns its argument:

```
const string &
transform(const string &s, const map<string, string> &m)
{
    //  the actual map work; this part is the heart of the program
    auto map_it = m.find(s);
    //  if this word is in the transformation map
    if (map_it != m.cend())
        return map_it->second;   //  use the replacement word
    else
        return s;                //  otherwise return the original unchanged
}
```

We start by calling `find` to determine whether the given `string` is in the `map`. If it is, then `find` returns an iterator to the corresponding element. Otherwise, `find` returns the off-the-end iterator. If the element is found, we dereference the iterator, obtaining a `pair` that holds the key and value for that element (§ 11.3, p. 428). We return the `second` member, which is the transformation to use in place of `s`.

EXERCISES SECTION 11.3.6

Exercise 11.33: Implement your own version of the word-transformation program.

Exercise 11.34: What would happen if we used the subscript operator instead of `find` in the `transform` function?

Exercise 11.35: In `buildMap`, what effect, if any, would there be from rewriting

```
    trans_map[key] = value.substr(1);
```

as `trans_map.insert({key, value.substr(1)})`?

Exercise 11.36: Our program does no checking on the validity of either input file. In particular, it assumes that the rules in the transformation file are all sensible. What would happen if a line in that file has a key, one space, and then the end of the line? Predict the behavior and then check it against your version of the program.

11.4   The Unordered Containers

The new standard defines four **unordered associative containers**. Rather than using a comparison operation to organize their elements, these containers use a *hash function* and the key type's `==` operator. An unordered container is most useful when we have a key type for which there is no obvious ordering relationship among the elements. These containers are also useful for applications in which the cost of maintaining the elements in order is prohibitive.

   Although hashing gives better average case performance in principle, achieving good results in practice often requires a fair bit of performance testing and tweaking. As a result, it is usually easier (and often yields better performance) to use an ordered container.

Use an unordered container if the key type is inherently unordered or
if performance testing reveals problems that hashing might solve.

Using an Unordered Container

Aside from operations that manage the hashing, the unordered containers provide
the same operations (find, insert, and so on) as the ordered containers. That
means that the operations we've used on map and set apply to unordered_map
and unordered_set as well. Similarly for the unordered versions of the containers that allow multiple keys.

As a result, we can usually use an unordered container in place of the corresponding ordered container, and vice versa. However, because the elements are
not stored in order, the output of a program that uses an unordered container will
(ordinarily) differ from the same program using an ordered container.

For example, we can rewrite our original word-counting program from § 11.1
(p. 421) to use an unordered_map:

```
//  count occurrences, but the words won't be in alphabetical order
unordered_map<string, size_t> word_count;
string word;
while (cin >> word)
    ++word_count[word]; //  fetch and increment the counter for word
for (const auto &w : word_count) //  for each element in the map
    //  print the results
    cout <<  w.first << " occurs " << w.second
         << ((w.second > 1) ? " times" : " time") << endl;
```

The type of word_count is the only difference between this program and our
original. If we run this version on the same input as our original program,

```
containers. occurs 1 time
use occurs 1 time
can occurs 1 time
examples occurs 1 time
. . .
```

we'll obtain the same count for each word in the input. However, the output is
unlikely to be in alphabetical order.

Managing the Buckets

The unordered containers are organized as a collection of buckets, each of which
holds zero or more elements. These containers use a hash function to map elements
to buckets. To access an element, the container first computes the element's hash
code, which tells which bucket to search. The container puts all of its elements with
a given hash value into the same bucket. If the container allows multiple elements
with a given key, all the elements with the same key will be in the same bucket. As
a result, the performance of an unordered container depends on the quality of its
hash function and on the number and size of its buckets.

The hash function must always yield the same result when called with the same argument. Ideally, the hash function also maps each particular value to a unique bucket. However, a hash function is allowed to map elements with differing keys to the same bucket. When a bucket holds several elements, those elements are searched sequentially to find the one we want. Typically, computing an element's hash code and finding its bucket is a fast operation. However, if the bucket has many elements, many comparisons may be needed to find a particular element.

The unordered containers provide a set of functions, listed in Table 11.8, that let us manage the buckets. These members let us inquire about the state of the container and force the container to reorganize itself as needed.

Table 11.8: Unordered Container Management Operations	
Bucket Interface	
`c.bucket_count()`	Number of buckets in use.
`c.max_bucket_count()`	Largest number of buckets this container can hold.
`c.bucket_size(n)`	Number of elements in the nth bucket.
`c.bucket(k)`	Bucket in which elements with key k would be found.
Bucket Iteration	
`local_iterator`	Iterator type that can access elements in a bucket.
`const_local_iterator`	const version of the bucket iterator.
`c.begin(n)`, `c.end(n)`	Iterator to the first, one past the last element in bucket n.
`c.cbegin(n)`, `c.cend(n)`	Returns `const_local_iterator`.
Hash Policy	
`c.load_factor()`	Average number of elements per bucket. Returns `float`.
`c.max_load_factor()`	Average bucket size that c tries to maintain. c adds buckets to keep `load_factor <= max_load_factor`. Returns `float`.
`c.rehash(n)`	Reorganize storage so that `bucket_count >= n` and and `bucket_count > size/max_load_factor`.
`c.reserve(n)`	Reorganize so that c can hold n elements without a `rehash`.

Requirements on Key Type for Unordered Containers

By default, the unordered containers use the `==` operator on the key type to compare elements. They also use an object of type `hash<key_type>` to generate the hash code for each element. The library supplies versions of the **hash** template for the built-in types, including pointers. It also defines `hash` for some of the library types, including `string`s and the smart pointer types that we will describe in Chapter 12. Thus, we can directly define unordered containers whose key is one of the built-in types (including pointer types), or a `string`, or a smart pointer.

However, we cannot directly define an unordered container that uses a our own class types for its key type. Unlike the containers, we cannot use the hash template directly. Instead, we must supply our own version of the `hash` template. We'll see how to do so in § 16.5 (p. 709).

Instead of using the default `hash`, we can use a strategy similar to the one we used to override the default comparison operation on keys for the ordered

containers (§ 11.2.2, p. 425). To use `Sales_data` as the key, we'll need to supply
functions to replace both the `==` operator and to calculate a hash code. We'll start
by defining these functions:

```
size_t hasher(const Sales_data &sd)
{
    return hash<string>()(sd.isbn());
}
bool eqOp(const Sales_data &lhs, const Sales_data &rhs)
{
    return lhs.isbn() == rhs.isbn();
}
```

Our `hasher` function uses an object of the library `hash` of `string` type to generate
a hash code from the ISBN member. Similarly, the `eqOp` funciton compares two
`Sales_data` objects by comparing their ISBNs.

We can use these functions to define an `unordered_multiset` as follows

```
using SD_multiset = unordered_multiset<Sales_data,
                        decltype(hasher)*, decltype(eqOp)*>;
// arguments are the bucket size and pointers to the hash function and equality operator
SD_multiset bookstore(42, hasher, eqOp);
```

To simplify the declaration of `bookstore` we first define a type alias (§ 2.5.1, p. 67)
for an `unordered_multiset` whose hash and equality operations have the same
types as our `hasher` and `eqOp` functions. Using that type, we define `bookstore`
passing pointers to the functions we want `bookstore` to use.

If our class has its own `==` operator we can override just the hash function:

```
// use FooHash to generate the hash code; Foo must have an == operator
unordered_set<Foo, decltype(FooHash)*> fooSet(10, FooHash);
```

EXERCISES SECTION 11.4

Exercise 11.37: What are the advantages of an unordered container as compared to the
ordered version of that container? What are the advantages of the ordered version?

Exercise 11.38: Rewrite the word-counting (§ 11.1, p. 421) and word-transformation
(§ 11.3.6, p. 440) programs to use an `unordered_map`.

CHAPTER SUMMARY

The associative containers support efficient lookup and retrieval of elements by key. The use of a key distinguishes the associative containers from the sequential containers, in which elements are accessed positionally.

There are eight associative containers, each of which

- Is a map or a set. a map stores key–value pairs; a set stores only keys.

- Requires unique keys or not.

- Keeps keys in order or not.

Ordered containers use a comparison function to order the elements by key. By default, the comparison is the < operator on the keys. Unordered containers use the key type's == operator and an object of type hash<key_type> to organize their elements.

Containers with nonunique keys include the word multi in their names; those that use hashing start with the word unordered. A set is an ordered collection in which each key may appear only once; an unordered_multiset is an unordered collection of keys in which the keys can appear multiple times.

The associative containers share many operations with the sequential containers. However, the associative containers define some new operations and redefine the meaning or return types of some operations common to both the sequential and associative containers. The differences in the operations reflect the use of keys in associative containers.

Iterators for the ordered containers access elements in order by key. Elements with the same key are stored adjacent to one another in both the ordered and unordered containers.

DEFINED TERMS

associative array Array whose elements are indexed by key rather than positionally. We say that the array maps a key to its associated value.

associative container Type that holds a collection of objects that supports efficient lookup by key.

hash Special library template that the unordered containers use to manage the position of their elements.

hash function Function that maps values of a given type to integral (size_t) values. Equal values must map to equal integers; unequal values should map to unequal integers where possible.

key_type Type defined by the associative containers that is the type for the keys used to store and retrieve values. For a map, key_type is the type used to index the map. For set, key_type and value_type are the same.

map Associative container type that defines an associative array. Like vector, map is a class template. A map, however, is defined with two types: the type of the key and the type of the associated value. In a map, a given key may appear only once. Each key is associated with a particular value. Dereferencing a map iterator yields a pair that holds a const key and its associated value.

mapped_type Type defined by map types that is the type of the values associated with the keys in the map.

multimap Associative container similar to map except that in a multimap, a given key may appear more than once. multimap does not support subscripting.

multiset Associative container type that holds keys. In a multiset, a given key may appear more than once.

pair Type that holds two public data members named first and second. The pair type is a template type that takes two type parameters that are used as the types of these members.

set Associative container that holds keys. In a set, a given key may appear only once.

strict weak ordering Relationship among the keys used in an associative container. In a strict weak ordering, it is possible to compare any two values and determine which of the two is less than the other. If neither value is less than the other, then the two values are considered equal.

unordered container Associative containers that use hashing rather than a comparison operation on keys to store and access elements. The performance of these containers depends on the quality of the hash function.

unordered_map Container with elements that are key–value pairs, permits only one element per key.

unordered_multimap Container with elements that are key–value pairs, allows multiple elements per key.

unordered_multiset Container that stores keys, allows multiple elements per key.

unordered_set Container that stores keys, permits only one element per key.

value_type Type of the element stored in a container. For set and multiset, value_type and key_type are the same. For map and multimap, this type is a pair whose first member has type const key_type and whose second member has type mapped_type.

* operator Dereference operator. When applied to a map, set, multimap, or multiset iterator * yields a value_type. Note, that for map and multimap, the value_type is a pair.

[ ] operator Subscript operator. Defined only for nonconst obejcts of type map and unordered_map. For the map types, [] takes an index that must be a key_type (or type that can be converted to key_type). Yields a mapped_type value.

CHAPTER **12**

DYNAMIC MEMORY

CONTENTS

The programs we've written so far have used objects that have well-defined lifetimes. Global objects are allocated at program start-up and destroyed when the program ends. Local, automatic objects are created and destroyed when the block in which they are defined is entered and exited. Local `static` objects are allocated before their first use and are destroyed when the program ends.

In addition to supporting automatic and `static` objects, C++ lets us allocate objects dynamically. Dynamically allocated objects have a lifetime that is independent of where they are created; they exist until they are explicitly freed.

Properly freeing dynamic objects turns out to be a surprisingly rich source of bugs. To make using dynamic objects safer, the library defines two smart pointer types that manage dynamically allocated objects. Smart pointers ensure that the objects to which they point are automatically freed when it is appropriate to do so.

Our programs have used only static or stack memory. Static memory is used for local `static` objects (§ 6.1.1, p. 205), for class `static` data members (§ 7.6, p. 300), and for variables defined outside any function. Stack memory is used for nonstatic objects defined inside functions. Objects allocated in static or stack memory are automatically created and destroyed by the compiler. Stack objects exist only while the block in which they are defined is executing; `static` objects are allocated before they are used, and they are destroyed when the program ends.

In addition to static or stack memory, every program also has a pool of memory that it can use. This memory is referred to as the **free store** or **heap**. Programs use the heap for objects that they **dynamically allocate**—that is, for objects that the program allocates at run time. The program controls the lifetime of dynamic objects; our code must explicitly destroy such objects when they are no longer needed.

> ⚠️ **WARNING** Although necessary at times, dynamic memory is notoriously tricky to manage correctly.

12.1 Dynamic Memory and Smart Pointers

In C++, dynamic memory is managed through a pair of operators: **new**, which allocates, and optionally initializes, an object in dynamic memory and returns a pointer to that object; and **delete**, which takes a pointer to a dynamic object, destroys that object, and frees the associated memory.

Dynamic memory is problematic because it is surprisingly hard to ensure that we free memory at the right time. Either we forget to free the memory—in which case we have a memory leak—or we free the memory when there are still pointers referring to that memory—in which case we have a pointer that refers to memory that is no longer valid.

To make using dynamic memory easier (and safer), the new library provides two **smart pointer** types that manage dynamic objects. A smart pointer acts like a regular pointer with the important exception that it automatically deletes the object to which it points. The new library defines two kinds of smart pointers that differ in how they manage their underlying pointers: **shared_ptr**, which allows multiple pointers to refer to the same object, and **unique_ptr**, which "owns" the object to which it points. The library also defines a companion class named **weak_ptr** that is a weak reference to an object managed by a `shared_ptr`. All three are defined in the `memory` header.

12.1.1 The shared_ptr Class

Like `vectors`, smart pointers are templates (§ 3.3, p. 96). Therefore, when we create a smart pointer, we must supply additional information—in this case, the type to which the pointer can point. As with `vector`, we supply that type inside angle brackets that follow the name of the kind of smart pointer we are defining:

```
shared_ptr<string> p1;     // shared_ptr that can point at a string
```

```
shared_ptr<list<int>> p2;  // shared_ptr that can point at a list of ints
```

A default initialized smart pointer holds a null pointer (§ 2.3.2, p. 53). In § 12.1.3 (p. 464), we'll cover additional ways to initialize a smart pointer.

We use a smart pointer in ways that are similar to using a pointer. Dereferencing a smart pointer returns the object to which the pointer points. When we use a smart pointer in a condition, the effect is to test whether the pointer is null:

```
// if p1 is not null, check whether it's the empty string
if (p1 && p1->empty())
    *p1 = "hi";  // if so, dereference p1 to assign a new value to that string
```

Table 12.1 (overleaf) lists operations common to shared_ptr and unique_ptr. Those that are particular to shared_ptr are listed in Table 12.2 (p. 453).

The `make_shared` Function

The safest way to allocate and use dynamic memory is to call a library function named make_shared. This function allocates and initializes an object in dynamic memory and returns a shared_ptr that points to that object. Like the smart pointers, make_shared is defined in the memory header.

When we call make_shared, we must specify the type of object we want to create. We do so in the same way as we use a template class, by following the function name with a type enclosed in angle brackets:

```
// shared_ptr that points to an int with value 42
shared_ptr<int> p3 = make_shared<int>(42);
// p4 points to a string with value 9999999999
shared_ptr<string> p4 = make_shared<string>(10, '9');
// p5 points to an int that is value initialized (§ 3.3.1 (p. 98)) to 0
shared_ptr<int> p5 = make_shared<int>();
```

Like the sequential-container emplace members (§ 9.3.1, p. 345), make_shared uses its arguments to construct an object of the given type. For example, a call to make_shared<string> must pass argument(s) that match one of the string constructors. Calls to make_shared<int> can pass any value we can use to initialize an int. And so on. If we do not pass any arguments, then the object is value initialized (§ 3.3.1, p. 98).

Of course, ordinarily we use auto (§ 2.5.2, p. 68) to make it easier to define an object to hold the result of make_shared:

```
// p6 points to a dynamically allocated, empty vector<string>
auto p6 = make_shared<vector<string>>();
```

Copying and Assigning `shared_ptrs`

When we copy or assign a shared_ptr, each shared_ptr keeps track of how many other shared_ptrs point to the same object:

```
auto p = make_shared<int>(42);  // object to which p points has one user
auto q(p);  // p and q point to the same object
            // object to which p and q point has two users
```

Table 12.1: Operations Common to `shared_ptr` and `unique_ptr`	
`shared_ptr<T> sp` `unique_ptr<T> up`	Null smart pointer that can point to objects of type `T`.
`p`	Use `p` as a condition; `true` if `p` points to an object.
`*p`	Dereference `p` to get the object to which `p` points.
`p->mem`	Synonym for `(*p).mem`.
`p.get()`	Returns the pointer in `p`. Use with caution; the object to which the returned pointer points will disappear when the smart pointer deletes it.
`swap(p, q)` `p.swap(q)`	Swaps the pointers in `p` and `q`.

We can think of a `shared_ptr` as if it has an associated counter, usually referred to as a **reference count**. Whenever we copy a `shared_ptr`, the count is incremented. For example, the counter associated with a `shared_ptr` is incremented when we use it to initialize another `shared_ptr`, when we use it as the right-hand operand of an assignment, or when we pass it to (§ 6.2.1, p. 209) or return it from a function by value (§ 6.3.2, p. 224). The counter is decremented when we assign a new value to the `shared_ptr` and when the `shared_ptr` itself is destroyed, such as when a local `shared_ptr` goes out of scope (§ 6.1.1, p. 204).

Once a `shared_ptr`'s counter goes to zero, the `shared_ptr` automatically frees the object that it manages:

```
auto r = make_shared<int>(42);  // int to which r points has one user
r = q;   // assign to r, making it point to a different address
         // increase the use count for the object to which q points
         // reduce the use count of the object to which r had pointed
         // the object r had pointed to has no users; that object is automatically freed
```

Here we allocate an `int` and store a pointer to that `int` in `r`. Next, we assign a new value to `r`. In this case, `r` is the only `shared_ptr` pointing to the one we previously allocated. That `int` is automatically freed as part of assigning `q` to `r`.

 It is up to the implementation whether to use a counter or another data structure to keep track of how many pointers share state. The key point is that the class keeps track of how many `shared_ptr`s point to the same object and automatically frees that object when appropriate.

`shared_ptr`s Automatically Destroy Their Objects . . .

When the last `shared_ptr` pointing to an object is destroyed, the `shared_ptr` class automatically destroys the object to which that `shared_ptr` points. It does so through another special member function known as a **destructor**. Analogous to its constructors, each class has a destructor. Just as a constructor controls initialization, the destructor controls what happens when objects of that class type are destroyed.

Table 12.2: Operations Specific to `shared_ptr`	
`make_shared<T>` (*args*)	Returns a `shared_ptr` pointing to a dynamically allocated object of type `T`. Uses *args* to initialize that object.
`shared_ptr<T> p(q)`	p is a copy of the `shared_ptr` q; increments the count in q. The pointer in q must be convertible to `T*` (§ 4.11.2, p. 161).
`p = q`	p and q are `shared_ptr`s holding pointers that can be converted to one another. Decrements p's reference count and increments q's count; deletes p's existing memory if p's count goes to 0.
`p.unique()`	Returns `true` if p.`use_count()` is one; `false` otherwise.
`p.use_count()`	Returns the number of objects sharing with p; may be a slow operation, intended primarily for debugging purposes.

Destructors generally free the resources that an object has allocated. For example, the `string` constructors (and other `string` members) allocate memory to hold the characters that compose the `string`. The `string` destructor frees that memory. Similarly, several `vector` operations allocate memory to hold the elements in the `vector`. The destructor for `vector` destroys those elements and frees the memory used for the elements.

The destructor for `shared_ptr` decrements the reference count of the object to which that `shared_ptr` points. If the count goes to zero, the `shared_ptr` destructor destroys the object to which the `shared_ptr` points and frees the memory used by that object.

...and Automatically Free the Associated Memory

The fact that the `shared_ptr` class automatically frees dynamic objects when they are no longer needed makes it fairly easy to use dynamic memory. For example, we might have a function that returns a `shared_ptr` to a dynamically allocated object of a type named `Foo` that can be initialized by an argument of type `T`:

```
// factory returns a shared_ptr pointing to a dynamically allocated object
shared_ptr<Foo> factory(T arg)
{
    // process arg as appropriate
    // shared_ptr will take care of deleting this memory
    return make_shared<Foo>(arg);
}
```

Because `factory` returns a `shared_ptr`, we can be sure that the object allocated by `factory` will be freed when appropriate. For example, the following function stores the `shared_ptr` returned by `factory` in a local variable:

```
void use_factory(T arg)
{
    shared_ptr<Foo> p = factory(arg);
    // use p
} // p goes out of scope; the memory to which p points is automatically freed
```

Because p is local to use_factory, it is destroyed when use_factory ends (§ 6.1.1, p. 204). When p is destroyed, its reference count is decremented and checked. In this case, p is the only object referring to the memory returned by factory. Because p is about to go away, the object to which p points will be destroyed and the memory in which that object resides will be freed.

The memory will not be freed if there is any other shared_ptr pointing to it:

```
shared_ptr<Foo> use_factory(T arg)
{
    shared_ptr<Foo> p = factory(arg);
    // use p
    return p;   // reference count is incremented when we return p
} // p goes out of scope; the memory to which p points is not freed
```

In this version, the return statement in use_factory returns a copy of p to its caller (§ 6.3.2, p. 224). Copying a shared_ptr adds to the reference count of that object. Now when p is destroyed, there will be another user for the memory to which p points. The shared_ptr class ensures that so long as there are any shared_ptrs attached to that memory, the memory itself will not be freed.

Because memory is not freed until the last shared_ptr goes away, it can be important to be sure that shared_ptrs don't stay around after they are no longer needed. The program will execute correctly but may waste memory if you neglect to destroy shared_ptrs that the program does not need. One way that shared_ptrs might stay around after you need them is if you put shared_ptrs in a container and subsequently reorder the container so that you don't need all the elements. You should be sure to erase shared_ptr elements once you no longer need those elements.

> If you put shared_ptrs in a container, and you subsequently need to use some, but not all, of the elements, remember to erase the elements you no longer need.

Classes with Resources That Have Dynamic Lifetime

Programs tend to use dynamic memory for one of three purposes:

1. They don't know how many objects they'll need

2. They don't know the precise type of the objects they need

3. They want to share data between several objects

The container classes are an example of classes that use dynamic memory for the first purpose and we'll see examples of the second in Chapter 15. In this section, we'll define a class that uses dynamic memory in order to let several objects share the same underlying data.

So far, the classes we've used allocate resources that exist only as long as the corresponding objects. For example, each vector "owns" its own elements. When we copy a vector, the elements in the original vector and in the copy are separate from one another:

```
vector<string> v1;   // empty vector
{ // new scope
    vector<string> v2 = {"a", "an", "the"};
    v1 = v2; // copies the elements from v2 into v1
} // v2 is destroyed, which destroys the elements in v2
    // v1 has three elements, which are copies of the ones originally in v2
```

The elements allocated by a vector exist only while the vector itself exists. When a vector is destroyed, the elements in the vector are also destroyed.

Some classes allocate resources with a lifetime that is independent of the original object. As an example, assume we want to define a class named Blob that will hold a collection of elements. Unlike the containers, we want Blob objects that are copies of one another to share the same elements. That is, when we copy a Blob, the original and the copy should refer to the same underlying elements.

In general, when two objects share the same underlying data, we can't unilaterally destroy the data when an object of that type goes away:

```
Blob<string> b1;     // empty Blob
{ // new scope
    Blob<string> b2 = {"a", "an", "the"};
    b1 = b2; // b1 and b2 share the same elements
} // b2 is destroyed, but the elements in b2 must not be destroyed
    // b1 points to the elements originally created in b2
```

In this example, b1 and b2 share the same elements. When b2 goes out of scope, those elements must stay around, because b1 is still using them.

One common reason to use dynamic memory is to allow multiple objects to share the same state.

Defining the **StrBlob** Class

Ultimately, we'll implement our Blob class as a template, but we won't learn how to do so until § 16.1.2 (p. 658). For now, we'll define a version of our class that can manage strings. As a result, we'll name this version of our class StrBlob.

The easiest way to implement a new collection type is to use one of the library containers to manage the elements. That way, we can let the library type manage the storage for the elements themselves. In this case, we'll use a vector to hold our elements.

However, we can't store the vector directly in a Blob object. Members of an object are destroyed when the object itself is destroyed. For example, assume that b1 and b2 are two Blobs that share the same vector. If that vector were stored in one of those Blobs—say, b2—then that vector, and therefore its elements, would no longer exist once b2 goes out of scope. To ensure that the elements continue to exist, we'll store the vector in dynamic memory.

To implement the sharing we want, we'll give each StrBlob a shared_ptr to a dynamically allocated vector. That shared_ptr member will keep track of how many StrBlobs share the same vector and will delete the vector when the last StrBlob using that vector is destroyed.

We still need to decide what operations our class will provide. For now, we'll implement a small subset of the vector operations. We'll also change the operations that access elements (e.g., front and back): In our class, these operations will throw an exception if a user attempts to access an element that doesn't exist.

Our class will have a default constructor and a constructor that has a parameter of type initializer_list<string> (§ 6.2.6, p. 220). This constructor will take a braced list of initializers.

```
class StrBlob {
public:
    typedef std::vector<std::string>::size_type size_type;
    StrBlob();
    StrBlob(std::initializer_list<std::string> il);
    size_type size() const { return data->size(); }
    bool empty() const { return data->empty(); }
    // add and remove elements
    void push_back(const std::string &t) {data->push_back(t);}
    void pop_back();
    // element access
    std::string& front();
    std::string& back();
private:
    std::shared_ptr<std::vector<std::string>> data;
    // throws msg if data [i] isn't valid
    void check(size_type i, const std::string &msg) const;
};
```

Inside the class we implemented the size, empty, and push_back members. These members forward their work through the data pointer to the underlying vector. For example, size() on a StrBlob calls data->size(), and so on.

StrBlob Constructors

Each constructor uses its constructor initializer list (§ 7.1.4, p. 265) to initialize its data member to point to a dynamically allocated vector. The default constructor allocates an empty vector:

```
StrBlob::StrBlob(): data(make_shared<vector<string>>()) { }
StrBlob::StrBlob(initializer_list<string> il):
              data(make_shared<vector<string>>(il)) { }
```

The constructor that takes an initializer_list passes its parameter to the corresponding vector constructor (§ 2.2.1, p. 43). That constructor initializes the vector's elements by copying the values in the list.

Element Access Members

The pop_back, front, and back operations access members in the vector. These operations must check that an element exists before attempting to access that element. Because several members need to do the same checking, we've given our class a `private` utility function named `check` that verifies that a given index is in range. In addition to an index, `check` takes a `string` argument that it will pass to the exception handler. The `string` describes what went wrong:

```
void StrBlob::check(size_type i, const string &msg) const
{
    if (i >= data->size())
        throw out_of_range(msg);
}
```

The `pop_back` and element access members first call `check`. If `check` succeeds, these members forward their work to the underlying `vector` operation:

```
string& StrBlob::front()
{
    // if the vector is empty, check will throw
    check(0, "front on empty StrBlob");
    return data->front();
}
string& StrBlob::back()
{
    check(0, "back on empty StrBlob");
    return data->back();
}
void StrBlob::pop_back()
{
    check(0, "pop_back on empty StrBlob");
    data->pop_back();
}
```

The `front` and `back` members should be overloaded on `const` (§ 7.3.2, p. 276). Defining those versions is left as an exercise.

Copying, Assigning, and Destroying `StrBlob`s

Like our `Sales_data` class, `StrBlob` uses the default versions of the operations that copy, assign, and destroy objects of its type (§ 7.1.5, p. 267). By default, these operations copy, assign, and destroy the data members of the class. Our `StrBlob` has only one data member, which is a `shared_ptr`. Therefore, when we copy, assign, or destroy a `StrBlob`, its `shared_ptr` member will be copied, assigned, or destroyed.

As we've seen, copying a `shared_ptr` increments its reference count; assigning one `shared_ptr` to another increments the count of the right-hand operand and decrements the count in the left-hand operand; and destroying a `shared_ptr` decrements the count. If the count in a `shared_ptr` goes to zero, the object to which that `shared_ptr` points is automatically destroyed. Thus, the `vector` allocated by the `StrBlob` constructors will be automatically destroyed when the last `StrBlob` pointing to that `vector` is destroyed.

Exercise 12.1: How many elements do b1 and b2 have at the end of this code?

```
StrBlob b1;
{
    StrBlob b2 = {"a", "an", "the"};
    b1 = b2;
    b2.push_back("about");
}
```

Exercise 12.2: Write your own version of the StrBlob class including the const versions of front and back.

Exercise 12.3: Does this class need const versions of push_back and pop_back? If so, add them. If not, why aren't they needed?

Exercise 12.4: In our check function we didn't check whether i was greater than zero. Why is it okay to omit that check?

Exercise 12.5: We did not make the constructor that takes an initializer_list explicit (§ 7.5.4, p. 296). Discuss the pros and cons of this design choice.

12.1.2 Managing Memory Directly

The language itself defines two operators that allocate and free dynamic memory. The new operator allocates memory, and delete frees memory allocated by new.

For reasons that will become clear as we describe how these operators work, using these operators to manage memory is considerably more error-prone than using a smart pointer. Moreover, classes that do manage their own memory—unlike those that use smart pointers—cannot rely on the default definitions for the members that copy, assign, and destroy class objects (§ 7.1.4, p. 264). As a result, programs that use smart pointers are likely to be easier to write and debug.

WARNING
Until you have read Chapter 13, your classes should allocate dynamic memory *only* if they use smart pointers to manage that memory.

Using new to Dynamically Allocate and Initialize Objects

Objects allocated on the free store are unnamed, so **new** offers no way to name the objects that it allocates. Instead, new returns a pointer to the object it allocates:

```
int *pi = new int;        // pi points to a dynamically allocated,
                          // unnamed, uninitialized int
```

This new expression constructs an object of type int on the free store and returns a pointer to that object.

By default, dynamically allocated objects are default initialized (§ 2.2.1, p. 43), which means that objects of built-in or compound type have undefined value; objects of class type are initialized by their default constructor:

```
string *ps = new string;   // initialized to empty string
int *pi = new int;         // pi points to an uninitialized int
```

We can initialize a dynamically allocated object using direct initialization (§ 3.2.1, p. 84). We can use traditional construction (using parentheses), and under the new standard, we can also use list initialization (with curly braces):

```
int *pi = new int(1024); // object to which pi points has value 1024
string *ps = new string(10, '9');   // *ps is "9999999999"
// vector with ten elements with values from 0 to 9
vector<int> *pv = new vector<int>{0,1,2,3,4,5,6,7,8,9};
```

We can also value initialize (§ 3.3.1, p. 98) a dynamically allocated object by following the type name with a pair of empty parentheses:

```
string *ps1 = new string;    // default initialized to the empty string
string *ps = new string();   // value initialized to the empty string
int *pi1 = new int;          // default initialized; *pi1 is undefined
int *pi2 = new int();        // value initialized to 0; *pi2 is 0
```

For class types (such as string) that define their own constructors (§ 7.1.4, p. 262), requesting value initialization is of no consequence; regardless of form, the object is initialized by the default constructor. In the case of built-in types the difference is significant; a value-initialized object of built-in type has a well-defined value but a default-initialized object does not. Similarly, members of built-in type in classes that rely on the synthesized default constructor will also be uninitialized if those members are not initialized in the class body (§ 7.1.4, p. 263).

> For the same reasons as we usually initialize variables, it is also a good idea to initialize dynamically allocated objects.

When we provide an initializer inside parentheses, we can use auto (§ 2.5.2, p. 68) to deduce the type of the object we want to allocate from that initializer. However, because the compiler uses the initializer's type to deduce the type to allocate, we can use auto only with a single initializer inside parentheses:

```
auto p1 = new auto(obj);   // p points to an object of the type of obj
                           // that object is initialized from obj
auto p2 = new auto{a,b,c}; // error: must use parentheses for the initializer
```

The type of p1 is a pointer to the auto-deduced type of obj. If obj is an int, then p1 is int*; if obj is a string, then p1 is a string*; and so on. The newly allocated object is initialized from the value of obj.

Dynamically Allocated const Objects

It is legal to use new to allocate const objects:

```
// allocate and initialize a const int
const int *pci = new const int(1024);
// allocate a default-initialized const empty string
const string *pcs = new const string;
```

Like any other const, a dynamically allocated const object must be initialized. A const dynamic object of a class type that defines a default constructor (§ 7.1.4, p. 263) may be initialized implicitly. Objects of other types must be explicitly initialized. Because the allocated object is const, the pointer returned by new is a pointer to const (§ 2.4.2, p. 62).

Memory Exhaustion

Although modern machines tend to have huge memory capacity, it is always possible that the free store will be exhausted. Once a program has used all of its available memory, new expressions will fail. By default, if new is unable to allocate the requested storage, it throws an exception of type bad_alloc (§ 5.6, p. 193). We can prevent new from throwing an exception by using a different form of new:

```
// if allocation fails, new returns a null pointer
int *p1 = new int; // if allocation fails, new throws std::bad_alloc
int *p2 = new (nothrow) int; // if allocation fails, new returns a null pointer
```

For reasons we'll explain in § 19.1.2 (p. 824) this form of new is referred to as **placement new**. A placement new expression lets us pass additional arguments to new. In this case, we pass an object named nothrow that is defined by the library. When we pass nothrow to new, we tell new that it must not throw an exception. If this form of new is unable to allocate the requested storage, it will return a null pointer. Both bad_alloc and nothrow are defined in the new header.

Freeing Dynamic Memory

In order to prevent memory exhaustion, we must return dynamically allocated memory to the system once we are finished using it. We return memory through a **delete expression**. A delete expression takes a pointer to the object we want to free:

```
delete p;        // p must point to a dynamically allocated object or be null
```

Like new, a delete expression performs two actions: It destroys the object to which its given pointer points, and it frees the corresponding memory.

Pointer Values and `delete`

The pointer we pass to delete must either point to dynamically allocated memory or be a null pointer (§ 2.3.2, p. 53). Deleting a pointer to memory that was not allocated by new, or deleting the same pointer value more than once, is undefined:

```
int i, *pi1 = &i, *pi2 = nullptr;
double *pd = new double(33), *pd2 = pd;
delete i;     // error: i is not a pointer
delete pi1;   // undefined: pi1 refers to a local
delete pd;    // ok
delete pd2;   // undefined: the memory pointed to by pd2 was already freed
delete pi2;   // ok: it is always ok to delete a null pointer
```

The compiler will generate an error for the `delete` of `i` because it knows that `i` is not a pointer. The errors associated with executing `delete` on `pi1` and `pd2` are more insidious: In general, compilers cannot tell whether a pointer points to a statically or dynamically allocated object. Similarly, the compiler cannot tell whether memory addressed by a pointer has already been freed. Most compilers will accept these `delete` expressions, even though they are in error.

Although the value of a `const` object cannot be modified, the object itself can be destroyed. As with any other dynamic object, a `const` dynamic object is freed by executing `delete` on a pointer that points to that object:

```
const int *pci = new const int(1024);
delete pci;    // ok: deletes a const object
```

Dynamically Allocated Objects Exist until They Are Freed

As we saw in § 12.1.1 (p. 452), memory that is managed through a `shared_ptr` is automatically deleted when the last `shared_ptr` is destroyed. The same is not true for memory we manage using built-in pointers. A dynamic object managed through a built-in pointer exists until it is explicitly deleted.

Functions that return pointers (rather than smart pointers) to dynamic memory put a burden on their callers—the caller must remember to delete the memory:

```
//  factory returns a pointer to a dynamically allocated object
Foo* factory(T arg)
{
    //  process arg as appropriate
    return new Foo(arg);  //  caller is responsible for deleting this memory
}
```

Like our earlier `factory` function (§ 12.1.1, p. 453), this version of `factory` allocates an object but does not `delete` it. Callers of `factory` are responsible for freeing this memory when they no longer need the allocated object. Unfortunately, all too often the caller forgets to do so:

```
void use_factory(T arg)
{
    Foo *p = factory(arg);
    //  use p but do not delete it
}  //  p goes out of scope, but the memory to which p points is not freed!
```

Here, our `use_factory` function calls `factory`, which allocates a new object of type `Foo`. When `use_factory` returns, the local variable `p` is destroyed. That variable is a built-in pointer, not a smart pointer.

Unlike class types, nothing happens when objects of built-in type are destroyed. In particular, when a pointer goes out of scope, nothing happens to the object to which the pointer points. If that pointer points to dynamic memory, that memory is not automatically freed.

> ⚠️ **WARNING** Dynamic memory managed through built-in pointers (rather than smart pointers) exists until it is explicitly freed.

In this example, p was the only pointer to the memory allocated by factory. Once use_factory returns, the program has no way to free that memory. Depending on the logic of our overall program, we should fix this bug by remembering to free the memory inside use_factory:

```
void use_factory(T arg)
{
    Foo *p = factory(arg);
    // use p
    delete p;  // remember to free the memory now that we no longer need it
}
```

or, if other code in our system needs to use the object allocated by use_factory, we should change that function to return a pointer to the memory it allocated:

```
Foo* use_factory(T arg)
{
    Foo *p = factory(arg);
    // use p
    return p;  // caller must delete the memory
}
```

CAUTION: MANAGING DYNAMIC MEMORY IS ERROR-PRONE

There are three common problems with using new and delete to manage dynamic memory:

1. Forgetting to delete memory. Neglecting to delete dynamic memory is known as a "memory leak," because the memory is never returned to the free store. Testing for memory leaks is difficult because they usually cannot be detected until the application is run for a long enough time to actually exhaust memory.

2. Using an object after it has been deleted. This error can sometimes be detected by making the pointer null after the delete.

3. Deleting the same memory twice. This error can happen when two pointers address the same dynamically allocated object. If delete is applied to one of the pointers, then the object's memory is returned to the free store. If we subsequently delete the second pointer, then the free store may be corrupted.

These kinds of errors are considerably easier to make than they are to find and fix.

 Best Practices   You can avoid *all* of these problems by using smart pointers exclusively. The smart pointer will take care of deleting the memory *only* when there are no remaining smart pointers pointing to that memory.

Resetting the Value of a Pointer after a delete ...

When we delete a pointer, that pointer becomes invalid. Although the pointer is invalid, on many machines the pointer continues to hold the address of the (freed) dynamic memory. After the delete, the pointer becomes what is referred to as a

dangling pointer. A dangling pointer is one that refers to memory that once held an object but no longer does so.

Dangling pointers have all the problems of uninitialized pointers (§ 2.3.2, p. 54). We can avoid the problems with dangling pointers by deleting the memory associated with a pointer just before the pointer itself goes out of scope. That way there is no chance to use the pointer after the memory associated with the pointer is freed. If we need to keep the pointer around, we can assign `nullptr` to the pointer after we use `delete`. Doing so makes it clear that the pointer points to no object.

...Provides Only Limited Protection

A fundamental problem with dynamic memory is that there can be several pointers that point to the same memory. Resetting the pointer we use to `delete` that memory lets us check that particular pointer but has no effect on any of the other pointers that still point at the (freed) memory. For example:

```
int *p(new int(42));   // p points to dynamic memory
auto q = p;            // p and q point to the same memory
delete p;       // invalidates both p and q
p = nullptr; // indicates that p is no longer bound to an object
```

Here both p and q point at the same dynamically allocated object. We `delete` that memory and set p to `nullptr`, indicating that the pointer no longer points to an object. However, resetting p has no effect on q, which became invalid when we deleted the memory to which p (and q!) pointed. In real systems, finding all the pointers that point to the same memory is surprisingly difficult.

EXERCISES SECTION 12.1.2

Exercise 12.6: Write a function that returns a dynamically allocated `vector` of ints. Pass that `vector` to another function that reads the standard input to give values to the elements. Pass the `vector` to another function to print the values that were read. Remember to `delete` the `vector` at the appropriate time.

Exercise 12.7: Redo the previous exercise, this time using `shared_ptr`.

Exercise 12.8: Explain what if anything is wrong with the following function.

```
bool b() {
    int* p = new int;
    // ...
    return p;
}
```

Exercise 12.9: Explain what happens in the following code:

```
int *q = new int(42), *r = new int(100);
r = q;
auto q2 = make_shared<int>(42), r2 = make_shared<int>(100);
r2 = q2;
```

12.1.3 Using `shared_ptrs` with `new`

As we've seen, if we do not initialize a smart pointer, it is initialized as a null pointer. As described in Table 12.3, we can also initialize a smart pointer from a pointer returned by `new`:

```
shared_ptr<double> p1;  //  shared_ptr that can point at a double
shared_ptr<int> p2(new int(42));  //  p2 points to an int with value 42
```

The smart pointer constructors that take pointers are `explicit` (§ 7.5.4, p. 296). Hence, we cannot implicitly convert a built-in pointer to a smart pointer; we must use the direct form of initialization (§ 3.2.1, p. 84) to initialize a smart pointer:

```
shared_ptr<int> p1 = new int(1024);  //  error: must use direct initialization
shared_ptr<int> p2(new int(1024));  //  ok: uses direct initialization
```

The initialization of `p1` implicitly asks the compiler to create a `shared_ptr` from the `int *` returned by `new`. Because we can't implicitly convert a pointer to a smart pointer, this initialization is an error. For the same reason, a function that returns a `shared_ptr` cannot implicitly convert a plain pointer in its return statement:

```
shared_ptr<int> clone(int p) {
    return new int(p);  //  error: implicit conversion to shared_ptr<int>
}
```

We must explicitly bind a `shared_ptr` to the pointer we want to return:

```
shared_ptr<int> clone(int p) {
    //  ok: explicitly create a shared_ptr<int> from int *
    return shared_ptr<int>(new int(p));
}
```

By default, a pointer used to initialize a smart pointer must point to dynamic memory because, by default, smart pointers use `delete` to free the associated object. We can bind smart pointers to pointers to other kinds of resources. However, to do so, we must supply our own operation to use in place of `delete`. We'll see how to supply our own deletion code in § 12.1.4 (p. 468).

Don't Mix Ordinary Pointers and Smart Pointers ...

A `shared_ptr` can coordinate destruction only with other `shared_ptrs` that are copies of itself. Indeed, this fact is one of the reasons we recommend using `make_shared` rather than `new`. That way, we bind a `shared_ptr` to the object at the same time that we allocate it. There is no way to inadvertently bind the same memory to more than one independently created `shared_ptr`.

Consider the following function that operates on a `shared_ptr`:

```
//  ptr is created and initialized when process is called
void process(shared_ptr<int> ptr)
{
    //  use ptr
}  //  ptr goes out of scope and is destroyed
```

Table 12.3: Other Ways to Define and Change `shared_ptrs`	
`shared_ptr<T> p(q)`	p manages the object to which the built-in pointer q points; q must point to memory allocated by `new` and must be convertible to `T*`.
`shared_ptr<T> p(u)`	p assumes ownership from the `unique_ptr` u; makes u null.
`shared_ptr<T> p(q, d)`	p assumes ownership for the object to which the built-in pointer q points. q must be convertible to `T*` (§ 4.11.2, p. 161). p will use the callable object d (§ 10.3.2, p. 388) in place of `delete` to free q.
`shared_ptr<T> p(p2, d)`	p is a copy of the `shared_ptr` p2 as described in Table 12.2 except that p uses the callable object d in place of `delete`.

`p.reset()`
`p.reset(q)`
`p.reset(q, d)`
	If p is the only `shared_ptr` pointing at its object, `reset` frees p's existing object. If the optional built-in pointer q is passed, makes p point to q, otherwise makes p null. If d is supplied, will call d to free q otherwise uses `delete` to free q.

The parameter to `process` is passed by value, so the argument to `process` is copied into `ptr`. Copying a `shared_ptr` increments its reference count. Thus, inside `process` the count is at least 2. When `process` completes, the reference count of `ptr` is decremented but cannot go to zero. Therefore, when the local variable `ptr` is destroyed, the memory to which `ptr` points will not be deleted.

The right way to use this function is to pass it a `shared_ptr`:

```
shared_ptr<int> p(new int(42)); // reference count is 1
process(p); // copying p increments its count; in process the reference count is 2
int i = *p; // ok: reference count is 1
```

Although we cannot pass a built-in pointer to `process`, we can pass `process` a (temporary) `shared_ptr` that we explicitly construct from a built-in pointer. However, doing so is likely to be an error:

```
int *x(new int(1024)); // dangerous: x is a plain pointer, not a smart pointer
process(x); // error: cannot convert int* to shared_ptr<int>
process(shared_ptr<int>(x)); // legal, but the memory will be deleted!
int j = *x; // undefined: x is a dangling pointer!
```

In this call, we passed a temporary `shared_ptr` to `process`. That temporary is destroyed when the expression in which the call appears finishes. Destroying the temporary decrements the reference count, which goes to zero. The memory to which the temporary points is freed when the temporary is destroyed.

But x continues to point to that (freed) memory; x is now a dangling pointer. Attempting to use the value of x is undefined.

When we bind a `shared_ptr` to a plain pointer, we give responsibility for that memory to that `shared_ptr`. Once we give `shared_ptr` responsibility for a pointer, we should no longer use a built-in pointer to access the memory to which the `shared_ptr` now points.

> It is dangerous to use a built-in pointer to access an object owned by a
> smart pointer, because we may not know when that object is destroyed.

...and Don't Use `get` to Initialize or Assign Another Smart Pointer

The smart pointer types define a function named `get` (described in Table 12.1
(p. 452)) that returns a built-in pointer to the object that the smart pointer is managing. This function is intended for cases when we need to pass a built-in pointer
to code that can't use a smart pointer. The code that uses the return from `get` must
not `delete` that pointer.

Although the compiler will not complain, it is an error to bind another smart
pointer to the pointer returned by `get`:

```
shared_ptr<int> p(new int(42)); // reference count is 1
int *q = p.get();    // ok: but don't use q in any way that might delete its pointer
{ // new block
// undefined: two independent shared_ptrs point to the same memory
shared_ptr<int>(q);
} // block ends, q is destroyed, and the memory to which q points is freed
int foo = *p; // undefined; the memory to which p points was freed
```

In this case, both p and q point to the same memory. Because they were created
independently from each other, each has a reference count of 1. When the block in
which q was defined ends, q is destroyed. Destroying q frees the memory to which
q points. That makes p into a dangling pointer, meaning that what happens when
we attempt to use p is undefined. Moreover, when p is destroyed, the pointer to
that memory will be `deleted` a second time.

> Use `get` only to pass access to the pointer to code that you know will not
> `delete` the pointer. In particular, never use `get` to initialize or assign
> to another smart pointer.

Other `shared_ptr` Operations

The `shared_ptr` class gives us a few other operations, which are listed in Table 12.2 (p. 453) and Table 12.3 (on the previous page). We can use `reset` to assign
a new pointer to a `shared_ptr`:

```
p = new int(1024);       // error: cannot assign a pointer to a shared_ptr
p.reset(new int(1024));  // ok: p points to a new object
```

Like assignment, `reset` updates the reference counts and, if appropriate, deletes
the object to which p points. The `reset` member is often used together with
`unique` to control changes to the object shared among several `shared_ptrs`. Before changing the underlying object, we check whether we're the only user. If not,
we make a new copy before making the change:

```
if (!p.unique())
    p.reset(new string(*p)); // we aren't alone; allocate a new copy
*p += newVal; // now that we know we're the only pointer, okay to change this object
```

Exercise 12.10: Explain whether the following call to the `process` function defined on page 464 is correct. If not, how would you correct the call?

```
shared_ptr<int> p(new int(42));
process(shared_ptr<int>(p));
```

Exercise 12.11: What would happen if we called `process` as follows?

```
process(shared_ptr<int>(p.get()));
```

Exercise 12.12: Using the declarations of p and sp explain each of the following calls to `process`. If the call is legal, explain what it does. If the call is illegal, explain why:

```
auto p = new int();
auto sp = make_shared<int>();
(a) process(sp);
(b) process(new int());
(c) process(p);
(d) process(shared_ptr<int>(p));
```

Exercise 12.13: What happens if we execute the following code?

```
auto sp = make_shared<int>();
auto p = sp.get();
delete p;
```

12.1.4 Smart Pointers and Exceptions

In § 5.6.2 (p. 196) we noted that programs that use exception handling to continue processing after an exception occurs need to ensure that resources are properly freed if an exception occurs. One easy way to make sure resources are freed is to use smart pointers.

When we use a smart pointer, the smart pointer class ensures that memory is freed when it is no longer needed even if the block is exited prematurely:

```
void f()
{
    shared_ptr<int> sp(new int(42)); // allocate a new object
    // code that throws an exception that is not caught inside f
}   // shared_ptr freed automatically when the function ends
```

When a function is exited, whether through normal processing or due to an exception, all the local objects are destroyed. In this case, sp is a shared_ptr, so destroying sp checks its reference count. Here, sp is the only pointer to the memory it manages; that memory will be freed as part of destroying sp.

In contrast, memory that we manage directly is not automatically freed when an exception occurs. If we use built-in pointers to manage memory and an exception occurs after a new but before the corresponding delete, then that memory won't be freed:

```
void f()
{
    int *ip = new int(42);        // dynamically allocate a new object
    // code that throws an exception that is not caught inside f
    delete ip;                    // free the memory before exiting
}
```

If an exception happens between the new and the delete, and is not caught inside f, then this memory can never be freed. There is no pointer to this memory outside the function f. Thus, there is no way to free this memory.

Smart Pointers and Dumb Classes

Many C++ classes, including all the library classes, define destructors (§ 12.1.1, p. 452) that take care of cleaning up the resources used by that object. However, not all classes are so well behaved. In particular, classes that are designed to be used by both C and C++ generally require the user to specifically free any resources that are used.

Classes that allocate resources—and that do not define destructors to free those resources—can be subject to the same kind of errors that arise when we use dynamic memory. It is easy to forget to release the resource. Similarly, if an exception happens between when the resource is allocated and when it is freed, the program will leak that resource.

We can often use the same kinds of techniques we use to manage dynamic memory to manage classes that do not have well-behaved destructors. For example, imagine we're using a network library that is used by both C and C++. Programs that use this library might contain code such as

```
struct destination;      // represents what we are connecting to
struct connection;       // information needed to use the connection
connection connect(destination*);  // open the connection
void disconnect(connection);       // close the given connection
void f(destination &d /* other parameters */)
{
    // get a connection; must remember to close it when done
    connection c = connect(&d);
    // use the connection
    // if we forget to call disconnect before exiting f, there will be no way to close c
}
```

If connection had a destructor, that destructor would automatically close the connection when f completes. However, connection does not have a destructor. This problem is nearly identical to our previous program that used a shared_ptr to avoid memory leaks. It turns out that we can also use a shared_ptr to ensure that the connection is properly closed.

Using Our Own Deletion Code

By default, shared_ptrs assume that they point to dynamic memory. Hence, by default, when a shared_ptr is destroyed, it executes delete on the pointer it holds. To use a `shared_ptr` to manage a `connection`, we must first define a function to use in place of `delete`. It must be possible to call this **deleter** function with the pointer stored inside the `shared_ptr`. In this case, our deleter must take a single argument of type `connection*`:

```
void end_connection(connection *p) { disconnect(*p); }
```

When we create a `shared_ptr`, we can pass an optional argument that points to a deleter function (§ 6.7, p. 247):

```
void f(destination &d /* other parameters */)
{
    connection c = connect(&d);
    shared_ptr<connection> p(&c, end_connection);
    // use the connection
    // when f exits, even if by an exception, the connection will be properly closed
}
```

When `p` is destroyed, it won't execute `delete` on its stored pointer. Instead, `p` will call `end_connection` on that pointer. In turn, `end_connection` will call `disconnect`, thus ensuring that the connection is closed. If `f` exits normally, then `p` will be destroyed as part of the return. Moreover, `p` will also be destroyed, and the connection will be closed, if an exception occurs.

CAUTION: SMART POINTER PITFALLS

Smart pointers can provide safety and convenience for handling dynamically allocated memory only when they are used properly. To use smart pointers correctly, we must adhere to a set of conventions:

- Don't use the same built-in pointer value to initialize (or `reset`) more than one smart pointer.
- Don't `delete` the pointer returned from `get()`.
- Don't use `get()` to initialize or `reset` another smart pointer.
- If you use a pointer returned by `get()`, remember that the pointer will become invalid when the last corresponding smart pointer goes away.
- If you use a smart pointer to manage a resource other than memory allocated by `new`, remember to pass a deleter (§ 12.1.4, p. 468, and § 12.1.5, p. 471).

EXERCISES SECTION 12.1.4

Exercise 12.14: Write your own version of a function that uses a `shared_ptr` to manage a `connection`.

Exercise 12.15: Rewrite the first exercise to use a lambda (§ 10.3.2, p. 388) in place of the `end_connection` function.

12.1.5 `unique_ptr`

A `unique_ptr` "owns" the object to which it points. Unlike `shared_ptr`, only one `unique_ptr` at a time can point to a given object. The object to which a `unique_ptr` points is destroyed when the `unique_ptr` is destroyed. Table 12.4 lists the operations specific to `unique_ptr`s. The operations common to both were covered in Table 12.1 (p. 452).

Unlike `shared_ptr`, there is no library function comparable to `make_shared` that returns a `unique_ptr`. Instead, when we define a `unique_ptr`, we bind it to a pointer returned by `new`. As with `shared_ptr`s, we must use the direct form of initialization:

```
unique_ptr<double> p1;  //  unique_ptr that can point at a double
unique_ptr<int> p2(new int(42));  //  p2 points to int with value 42
```

Because a `unique_ptr` owns the object to which it points, `unique_ptr` does not support ordinary copy or assignment:

```
unique_ptr<string> p1(new string("Stegosaurus"));
unique_ptr<string> p2(p1);  //  error: no copy for unique_ptr
unique_ptr<string> p3;
p3 = p2;                     //  error: no assign for unique_ptr
```

Table 12.4: `unique_ptr` Operations (See Also Table 12.1 (p. 452))	
`unique_ptr<T> u1` `unique_ptr<T, D> u2`	Null `unique_ptr`s that can point to objects of type `T`. `u1` will use `delete` to free its pointer; `u2` will use a callable object of type `D` to free its pointer.
`unique_ptr<T, D> u(d)`	Null `unique_ptr` that point to objects of type `T` that uses `d`, which must be an object of type `D` in place of `delete`.
`u = nullptr`	Deletes the object to which `u` points; makes `u` null.
`u.release()`	Relinquishes control of the pointer `u` had held; returns the pointer `u` had held and makes `u` null.

`u.reset()`
`u.reset(q)`
`u.reset(nullptr)`
	Deletes the object to which `u` points;
	If the built-in pointer `q` is supplied, makes `u` point to that object. Otherwise makes `u` null.

Although we can't copy or assign a `unique_ptr`, we can transfer ownership from one (nonconst) `unique_ptr` to another by calling `release` or `reset`:

```
//  transfers ownership from p1 (which points to the string Stegosaurus) to p2
unique_ptr<string> p2(p1.release());  //  release makes p1 null
unique_ptr<string> p3(new string("Trex"));
//  transfers ownership from p3 to p2
p2.reset(p3.release());  //  reset deletes the memory to which p2 had pointed
```

The `release` member returns the pointer currently stored in the `unique_ptr` and makes that `unique_ptr` null. Thus, `p2` is initialized from the pointer value that had been stored in `p1` and `p1` becomes null.

The reset member takes an optional pointer and repositions the unique_ptr to point to the given pointer. If the unique_ptr is not null, then the object to which the unique_ptr had pointed is deleted. The call to reset on p2, therefore, frees the memory used by the string initialized from "Stegosaurus", transfers p3's pointer to p2, and makes p3 null.

Calling release breaks the connection between a unique_ptr and the object it had been managing. Often the pointer returned by release is used to initialize or assign another smart pointer. In that case, responsibility for managing the memory is simply transferred from one smart pointer to another. However, if we do not use another smart pointer to hold the pointer returned from release, our program takes over responsibility for freeing that resource:

```
p2.release();  // WRONG: p2 won't free the memory and we've lost the pointer
auto p = p2.release();  // ok, but we must remember to delete(p)
```

Passing and Returning unique_ptrs

There is one exception to the rule that we cannot copy a unique_ptr: We can copy or assign a unique_ptr that is about to be destroyed. The most common example is when we return a unique_ptr from a function:

```
unique_ptr<int> clone(int p) {
    // ok: explicitly create a unique_ptr<int> from int*
    return unique_ptr<int>(new int(p));
}
```

Alternatively, we can also return a copy of a local object:

```
unique_ptr<int> clone(int p) {
    unique_ptr<int> ret(new int (p));
    // ...
    return ret;
}
```

In both cases, the compiler knows that the object being returned is about to be destroyed. In such cases, the compiler does a special kind of "copy" which we'll discuss in § 13.6.2 (p. 534).

BACKWARD COMPATIBILITY: AUTO_PTR

Earlier versions of the library included a class named auto_ptr that had some, but not all, of the properties of unique_ptr. In particular, it was not possible to store an auto_ptr in a container, nor could we return one from a function.

Although auto_ptr is still part of the standard library, programs should use unique_ptr instead.

Passing a Deleter to unique_ptr

Like shared_ptr, by default, unique_ptr uses delete to free the object to which a unique_ptr points. As with shared_ptr, we can override the default deleter in a unique_ptr (§ 12.1.4, p. 468). However, for reasons we'll describe in § 16.1.6 (p. 676), the way unique_ptr manages its deleter is differs from the way shared_ptr does.

Overridding the deleter in a unique_ptr affects the unique_ptr type as well as how we construct (or reset) objects of that type. Similar to overriding the comparison operation of an associative container (§ 11.2.2, p. 425), we must supply the deleter type inside the angle brackets along with the type to which the unique_ptr can point. We supply a callable object of the specified type when we create or reset an object of this type:

```
// p points to an object of type objT and uses an object of type delT to free that object
// it will call an object named fcn of type delT
unique_ptr<objT, delT> p (new objT, fcn);
```

As a somewhat more concrete example, we'll rewrite our connection program to use a unique_ptr in place of a shared_ptr as follows:

```
void f(destination &d /* other needed parameters */)
{
    connection c = connect(&d);   // open the connection
    // when p is destroyed, the connection will be closed
    unique_ptr<connection, decltype(end_connection)*>
        p(&c, end_connection);
    // use the connection
    // when f exits, even if by an exception, the connection will be properly closed
}
```

Here we use decltype (§ 2.5.3, p. 70) to specify the function pointer type. Because decltype(end_connection) returns a function type, we must remember to add a * to indicate that we're using a pointer to that type (§ 6.7, p. 250).

EXERCISES SECTION 12.1.5

Exercise 12.16: Compilers don't always give easy-to-understand error messages if we attempt to copy or assign a unique_ptr. Write a program that contains these errors to see how your compiler diagnoses them.

Exercise 12.17: Which of the following unique_ptr declarations are illegal or likely to result in subsequent program error? Explain what the problem is with each one.

```
int ix = 1024, *pi = &ix, *pi2 = new int(2048);
typedef unique_ptr<int> IntP;
```

(a) IntP p0(ix);   (b) IntP p1(pi);
(c) IntP p2(pi2);   (d) IntP p3(&ix);
(e) IntP p4(new int(2048));   (f) IntP p5(p2.get());

Exercise 12.18: Why doesn't shared_ptr have a release member?

12.1.6 `weak_ptr`

A `weak_ptr` (Table 12.5) is a smart pointer that does not control the lifetime of the object to which it points. Instead, a `weak_ptr` points to an object that is managed by a `shared_ptr`. Binding a `weak_ptr` to a `shared_ptr` does not change the reference count of that `shared_ptr`. Once the last `shared_ptr` pointing to the object goes away, the object itself will be deleted. That object will be deleted even if there are `weak_ptr`s pointing to it—hence the name `weak_ptr`, which captures the idea that a `weak_ptr` shares its object "weakly."

When we create a `weak_ptr`, we initialize it from a `shared_ptr`:

```
auto p = make_shared<int>(42);
weak_ptr<int> wp(p);   // wp weakly shares with p; use count in p is unchanged
```

Here both wp and p point to the same object. Because the sharing is weak, creating wp doesn't change the reference count of p; it is possible that the object to which wp points might be deleted.

Because the object might no longer exist, we cannot use a `weak_ptr` to access its object directly. To access that object, we must call `lock`. The `lock` function checks whether the object to which the `weak_ptr` points still exists. If so, `lock` returns a `shared_ptr` to the shared object. As with any other `shared_ptr`, we are guaranteed that the underlying object to which that `shared_ptr` points continues to exist at least as long as that `shared_ptr` exists. For example:

```
if (shared_ptr<int> np = wp.lock()) { // true if np is not null
    // inside the if, np shares its object with p
}
```

Here we enter the body of the `if` only if the call to `lock` succeeds. Inside the `if`, it is safe to use np to access that object.

Table 12.5: `weak_ptr`s	
`weak_ptr<T> w`	Null `weak_ptr` that can point at objects of type T.
`weak_ptr<T> w(sp)`	`weak_ptr` that points to the same object as the `shared_ptr` sp. T must be convertible to the type to which sp points.
`w = p`	p can be a `shared_ptr` or a `weak_ptr`. After the assignment w shares ownership with p.
`w.reset()`	Makes w null.
`w.use_count()`	The number of `shared_ptr`s that share ownership with w.
`w.expired()`	Returns `true` if `w.use_count()` is zero, `false` otherwise.
`w.lock()`	If `expired` is `true`, returns a null `shared_ptr`; otherwise returns a `shared_ptr` to the object to which w points.

Checked Pointer Class

As an illustration of when a `weak_ptr` is useful, we'll define a companion pointer class for our `StrBlob` class. Our pointer class, which we'll name `StrBlobPtr`, will store a weak_ptr to the data member of the StrBlob from which it was initialized. By using a weak_ptr, we don't affect the lifetime of the vector to which a given StrBlob points. However, we can prevent the user from attempting to access a vector that no longer exists.

StrBlobPtr will have two data members: wptr, which is either null or points to a vector in a StrBlob; and curr, which is the index of the element that this object currently denotes. Like its companion StrBlob class, our pointer class has a check member to verify that it is safe to dereference the StrBlobPtr:

```
// StrBlobPtr throws an exception on attempts to access a nonexistent element
class StrBlobPtr {
public:
    StrBlobPtr(): curr(0) { }
    StrBlobPtr(StrBlob &a, size_t sz = 0):
            wptr(a.data), curr(sz) { }
    std::string& deref() const;
    StrBlobPtr& incr();          // prefix version
private:
    // check returns a shared_ptr to the vector if the check succeeds
    std::shared_ptr<std::vector<std::string>>
        check(std::size_t, const std::string&) const;
    // store a weak_ptr, which means the underlying vector might be destroyed
    std::weak_ptr<std::vector<std::string>> wptr;
    std::size_t curr;            // current position within the array
};
```

The default constructor generates a null StrBlobPtr. Its constructor initializer list (§ 7.1.4, p. 265) explicitly initializes curr to zero and implicitly initializes wptr as a null weak_ptr. The second constructor takes a reference to StrBlob and an optional index value. This constructor initializes wptr to point to the vector in the shared_ptr of the given StrBlob object and initializes curr to the value of sz. We use a default argument (§ 6.5.1, p. 236) to initialize curr to denote the first element by default. As we'll see, the sz parameter will be used by the end member of StrBlob.

It is worth noting that we cannot bind a StrBlobPtr to a const StrBlob object. This restriction follows from the fact that the constructor takes a reference to a nonconst object of type StrBlob.

The check member of StrBlobPtr differs from the one in StrBlob because it must check whether the vector to which it points is still around:

```
std::shared_ptr<std::vector<std::string>>
StrBlobPtr::check(std::size_t i, const std::string &msg) const
{
    auto ret = wptr.lock();    // is the vector still around?
    if (!ret)
        throw std::runtime_error("unbound StrBlobPtr");
    if (i >= ret->size())
        throw std::out_of_range(msg);
    return ret; // otherwise, return a shared_ptr to the vector
}
```

Because a `weak_ptr` does not participate in the reference count of its corresponding `shared_ptr`, the `vector` to which this `StrBlobPtr` points might have been deleted. If the `vector` is gone, `lock` will return a null pointer. In this case, any reference to the `vector` will fail, so we throw an exception. Otherwise, `check` verifies its given index. If that value is okay, `check` returns the `shared_ptr` it obtained from `lock`.

Pointer Operations

We'll learn how to define our own operators in Chapter 14. For now, we've defined functions named `deref` and `incr` to dereference and increment the `StrBlobPtr`, respectively.

The `deref` member calls `check` to verify that it is safe to use the `vector` and that `curr` is in range:

```
std::string& StrBlobPtr::deref() const
{
    auto p = check(curr, "dereference past end");
    return (*p)[curr];   //  (*p) is the vector to which this object points
}
```

If `check` succeeds, `p` is a `shared_ptr` to the `vector` to which this `StrBlobPtr` points. The expression `(*p)[curr]` dereferences that `shared_ptr` to get the `vector` and uses the subscript operator to fetch and return the element at `curr`.

The `incr` member also calls `check`:

```
//  prefix: return a reference to the incremented object
StrBlobPtr& StrBlobPtr::incr()
{
    //  if curr already points past the end of the container, can't increment it
    check(curr, "increment past end of StrBlobPtr");
    ++curr;          //  advance the current state
    return *this;
}
```

Of course, in order to access the `data` member, our pointer class will have to be a `friend` of `StrBlob` (§ 7.3.4, p. 279). We'll also give our `StrBlob` class `begin` and `end` operations that return a `StrBlobPtr` pointing to itself:

```
//  forward declaration needed for friend declaration in StrBlob
class StrBlobPtr;
class StrBlob {
    friend class StrBlobPtr;
    //  other members as in § 12.1.1 (p. 456)
    //  return StrBlobPtr to the first and one past the last elements
    StrBlobPtr begin() { return StrBlobPtr(*this); }
    StrBlobPtr end()
        { auto ret = StrBlobPtr(*this, data->size());
          return ret; }
};
```

Exercise 12.19: Define your own version of `StrBlobPtr` and update your `StrBlob` class with the appropriate `friend` declaration and `begin` and `end` members.

Exercise 12.20: Write a program that reads an input file a line at a time into a `StrBlob` and uses a `StrBlobPtr` to print each element in that `StrBlob`.

Exercise 12.21: We could have written `StrBlobPtr`'s `deref` member as follows:

```
std::string& deref() const
{ return (*check(curr, "dereference past end"))[curr]; }
```

Which version do you think is better and why?

Exercise 12.22: What changes would need to be made to `StrBlobPtr` to create a class that can be used with a `const StrBlob`? Define a class named `ConstStrBlobPtr` that can point to a `const StrBlob`.

12.2 Dynamic Arrays

The `new` and `delete` operators allocate objects one at a time. Some applications, need the ability to allocate storage for many objects at once. For example, `vectors` and `strings` store their elements in contiguous memory and must allocate several elements at once whenever the container has to be reallocated (§ 9.4, p. 355).

To support such usage, the language and library provide two ways to allocate an array of objects at once. The language defines a second kind of `new` expression that allocates and initializes an array of objects. The library includes a template class named `allocator` that lets us separate allocation from initialization. For reasons we'll explain in § 12.2.2 (p. 481), using an `allocator` generally provides better performance and more flexible memory management.

Many, perhaps even most, applications have no direct need for dynamic arrays. When an application needs a varying number of objects, it is almost always easier, faster, and safer to do as we did with `StrBlob`: use a `vector` (or other library container). For reasons we'll explain in § 13.6 (p. 531), the advantages of using a library container are even more pronounced under the new standard. Libraries that support the new standard tend to be dramatically faster than previous releases.

> **Best Practices**
> Most applications should use a library container rather than dynamically allocated arrays. Using a container is easier, less likely to contain memory-management bugs, *and* is likely to give better performance.

As we've seen, classes that use the containers can use the default versions of the operations for copy, assignment, and destruction (§ 7.1.5, p. 267). Classes that allocate dynamic arrays must define their own versions of these operations to manage the associated memory when objects are copied, assigned, and destroyed.

> **WARNING**
> Do not allocate dynamic arrays in code inside classes until you have read Chapter 13.

12.2.1 new and Arrays

We ask new to allocate an array of objects by specifying the number of objects to allocate in a pair of square brackets after a type name. In this case, new allocates the requested number of objects and (assuming the allocation succeeds) returns a pointer to the first one:

```
// call get_size to determine how many ints to allocate
int *pia = new int[get_size()]; // pia points to the first of these ints
```

The size inside the brackets must have integral type but need not be a constant.

We can also allocate an array by using a type alias (§ 2.5.1, p. 67) to represent an array type. In this case, we omit the brackets:

```
typedef int arrT[42];  // arrT names the type array of 42 ints
int *p = new arrT;     // allocates an array of 42 ints; p points to the first one
```

Here, new allocates an array of ints and returns a pointer to the first one. Even though there are no brackets in our code, the compiler executes this expression using new[]. That is, the compiler executes this expression as if we had written

```
int *p = new int[42];
```

Allocating an Array Yields a Pointer to the Element Type

Although it is common to refer to memory allocated by new T[] as a "dynamic array," this usage is somewhat misleading. When we use new to allocate an array, we do not get an object with an array type. Instead, we get a pointer to the element type of the array. Even if we use a type alias to define an array type, new does not allocate an object of array type. In this case, the fact that we're allocating an array is not even visible; there is no [num]. Even so, new returns a pointer to the element type.

Because the allocated memory does not have an array type, we cannot call begin or end (§ 3.5.3, p. 118) on a dynamic array. These functions use the array dimension (which is part of an array's type) to return pointers to the first and one past the last elements, respectively. For the same reasons, we also cannot use a range for to process the elements in a (so-called) dynamic array.

It is important to remember that what we call a dynamic array does not have an array type.

Initializing an Array of Dynamically Allocated Objects

By default, objects allocated by new—whether allocated as a single object or in an array—are default initialized. We can value initialize (§ 3.3.1, p. 98) the elements in an array by following the size with an empty pair of parentheses.

```
int *pia = new int[10];          // block of ten uninitialized ints
int *pia2 = new int[10]();       // block of ten ints value initialized to 0
string *psa = new string[10];    // block of ten empty strings
string *psa2 = new string[10](); // block of ten empty strings
```

C++
11

Under the new standard, we can also provide a braced list of element initializers:

```
//  block of ten ints each initialized from the corresponding initializer
int *pia3 = new int[10]{0,1,2,3,4,5,6,7,8,9};
//  block of ten strings; the first four are initialized from the given initializers
//  remaining elements are value initialized
string *psa3 = new string[10]{"a", "an", "the", string(3,'x')};
```

As when we list initialize an object of built-in array type (§ 3.5.1, p. 114), the initial-izers are used to initialize the first elements in the array. If there are fewer initial-izers than elements, the remaining elements are value initialized. If there are more initializers than the given size, then the new expression fails and no storage is al-located. In this case, new throws an exception of type bad_array_new_length. Like bad_alloc, this type is defined in the new header.

C++
11

Although we can use empty parentheses to value initialize the elements of an array, we cannot supply an element initializer inside the parentheses. The fact that we cannot supply an initial value inside the parentheses means that we cannot use auto to allocate an array (§ 12.1.2, p. 459).

It Is Legal to Dynamically Allocate an Empty Array

We can use an arbitrary expression to determine the number of objects to allocate:

```
size_t n = get_size();  //  get_size returns the number of elements needed
int* p = new int[n];    //  allocate an array to hold the elements
for (int* q = p; q != p + n; ++q)
        /* process the array */ ;
```

An interesting question arises: What happens if get_size returns 0? The answer is that our code works fine. Calling new[n] with n equal to 0 is legal even though we cannot create an array variable of size 0:

```
char arr[0];             //  error: cannot define a zero-length array
char *cp = new char[0];  //  ok: but cp can't be dereferenced
```

When we use new to allocate an array of size zero, new returns a valid, nonzero pointer. That pointer is guaranteed to be distinct from any other pointer returned by new. This pointer acts as the off-the-end pointer (§ 3.5.3, p. 119) for a zero-element array. We can use this pointer in ways that we use an off-the-end iterator. The pointer can be compared as in the loop above. We can add zero to (or subtract zero from) such a pointer and can subtract the pointer from itself, yielding zero. The pointer cannot be dereferenced—after all, it points to no element.

In our hypothetical loop, if get_size returns 0, then n is also 0. The call to new will allocate zero objects. The condition in the for will fail (p is equal to q + n because n is 0). Thus, the loop body is not executed.

Freeing Dynamic Arrays

To free a dynamic array, we use a special form of delete that includes an empty pair of square brackets:

```
delete p;        //   p must point to a dynamically allocated object or be null
delete [] pa;    //   pa must point to a dynamically allocated array or be null
```

The second statement destroys the elements in the array to which pa points and frees the corresponding memory. Elements in an array are destroyed in reverse order. That is, the last element is destroyed first, then the second to last, and so on.

When we delete a pointer to an array, the empty bracket pair is essential: It indicates to the compiler that the pointer addresses the first element of an array of objects. If we omit the brackets when we delete a pointer to an array (or provide them when we delete a pointer to an object), the behavior is undefined.

Recall that when we use a type alias that defines an array type, we can allocate an array without using [] with new. Even so, we must use brackets when we delete a pointer to that array:

```
typedef int arrT[42];    //   arrT names the type array of 42 ints
int *p = new arrT;       //   allocates an array of 42 ints; p points to the first one
delete [] p;             //   brackets are necessary because we allocated an array
```

Despite appearances, p points to the first element of an array of objects, not to a single object of type arrT. Thus, we must use [] when we delete p.

WARNING The compiler is unlikely to warn us if we forget the brackets when we delete a pointer to an array or if we use them when we delete a pointer to an object. Instead, our program is apt to misbehave without warning during execution.

Smart Pointers and Dynamic Arrays

The library provides a version of unique_ptr that can manage arrays allocated by new. To use a unique_ptr to manage a dynamic array, we must include a pair of empty brackets after the object type:

```
//   up points to an array of ten uninitialized ints
unique_ptr<int[]> up(new int[10]);
up.release();    //   automatically uses delete[] to destroy its pointer
```

The brackets in the type specifier (<int[]>) say that up points not to an int but to an array of ints. Because up points to an array, when up destroys the pointer it manages, it will automatically use delete[].

unqiue_ptrs that point to arrays provide slightly different operations than those we used in § 12.1.5 (p. 470). These operations are described in Table 12.6 (overleaf). When a unique_ptr points to an array, we cannot use the dot and arrow member access operators. After all, the unqiue_ptr points to an array, not an object so these operators would be meaningless. On the other hand, when a unqiue_ptr points to an array, we can use the subscript operator to access the elements in the array:

```
for (size_t i = 0; i != 10; ++i)
    up[i] = i;    //   assign a new value to each of the elements
```

Table 12.6: `unique_ptrs` to Arrays
Member access operators (dot and arrow) are not supported for `unique_ptrs` to arrays. Other `unique_ptr` operations unchanged.

`unique_ptr<T[]> u`	u can point to a dynamically allocated array of type `T`.
`unique_ptr<T[]> u(p)`	u points to the dynamically allocated array to which the built-in pointer p points. p must be convertible to `T*` (§ 4.11.2, p. 161).
`u[i]`	Returns the object at position i in the array that u owns. **u must point to an array.**

Unlike `unique_ptr`, `shared_ptrs` provide no direct support for managing a dynamic array. If we want to use a `shared_ptr` to manage a dynamic array, we must provide our own deleter:

```
// to use a shared_ptr we must supply a deleter
shared_ptr<int> sp(new int[10], [](int *p) { delete[] p; });
sp.reset(); // uses the lambda we supplied that uses delete[] to free the array
```

Here we pass a lambda (§ 10.3.2, p. 388) that uses `delete[]` as the deleter.

Had we neglected to supply a deleter, this code would be undefined. By default, `shared_ptr` uses `delete` to destroy the object to which it points. If that object is a dynamic array, using `delete` has the same kinds of problems that arise if we forget to use `[]` when we delete a pointer to a dynamic array (§ 12.2.1, p. 479).

The fact that `shared_ptr` does not directly support managing arrays affects how we access the elements in the array:

```
// shared_ptrs don't have subscript operator and don't support pointer arithmetic
for (size_t i = 0; i != 10; ++i)
    *(sp.get() + i) = i;   // use get to get a built-in pointer
```

There is no subscript operator for `shared_ptrs`, and the smart pointer types do not support pointer arithmetic. As a result, to access the elements in the array, we must use `get` to obtain a built-in pointer, which we can then use in normal ways.

EXERCISES SECTION 12.2.1

Exercise 12.23: Write a program to concatenate two string literals, putting the result in a dynamically allocated array of `char`. Write a program to concatenate two library `strings` that have the same value as the literals used in the first program.

Exercise 12.24: Write a program that reads a string from the standard input into a dynamically allocated character array. Describe how your program handles varying size inputs. Test your program by giving it a string of data that is longer than the array size you've allocated.

Exercise 12.25: Given the following new expression, how would you `delete` pa?

```
int *pa = new int[10];
```

12.2.2   The `allocator` Class

An aspect of new that limits its flexibility is that new combines allocating memory with constructing object(s) in that memory. Similarly, delete combines destruction with deallocation. Combining initialization with allocation is usually what we want when we allocate a single object. In that case, we almost certainly know the value the object should have.

When we allocate a block of memory, we often plan to construct objects in that memory as needed. In this case, we'd like to decouple memory allocation from object construction. Decoupling construction from allocation means that we can allocate memory in large chunks and pay the overhead of constructing the objects only when we actually need to create them.

In general, coupling allocation and construction can be wasteful. For example:

```
string *const p = new string[n]; // construct n empty strings
string s;
string *q = p;                    // q points to the first string
while (cin >> s && q != p + n)
    *q++ = s;                     // assign a new value to *q
const size_t size = q - p;        // remember how many strings we read
// use the array
delete[] p;  // p points to an array; must remember to use delete[]
```

This new expression allocates and initializes n strings. However, we might not need n strings; a smaller number might suffice. As a result, we may have created objects that are never used. Moreover, for those objects we do use, we immediately assign new values over the previously initialized strings. The elements that are used are written twice: first when the elements are default initialized, and subsequently when we assign to them.

More importantly, classes that do not have default constructors cannot be dynamically allocated as an array.

The `allocator` Class

The library **allocator** class, which is defined in the memory header, lets us separate allocation from construction. It provides type-aware allocation of raw, unconstructed, memory. Table 12.7 (overleaf) outlines the operations that allocator supports. In this section, we'll describe the allocator operations. In § 13.5 (p. 524), we'll see an example of how this class is typically used.

Like vector, allocator is a template (§ 3.3, p. 96). To define an allocator we must specify the type of objects that a particular allocator can allocate. When an allocator object allocates memory, it allocates memory that is appropriately sized and aligned to hold objects of the given type:

```
allocator<string> alloc;             // object that can allocate strings
auto const p = alloc.allocate(n);  // allocate n unconstructed strings
```

This call to allocate allocates memory for n strings.

Table 12.7: Standard `allocator` Class and Customized Algorithms	
`allocator<T> a`	Defines an `allocator` object named a that can allocate memory for objects of type T.
`a.allocate(n)`	Allocates raw, unconstructed memory to hold n objects of type T.
`a.deallocate(p, n)`	Deallocates memory that held n objects of type T starting at the address in the T* pointer p; p must be a pointer previously returned by `allocate`, and n must be the size requested when p was created. The user must run `destroy` on any objects that were constructed in this memory before calling `deallocate`.
`a.construct(p, args)`	p must be a pointer to type T that points to raw memory; *args* are passed to a constructor for type T, which is used to construct an object in the memory pointed to by p.
`a.destroy(p)`	Runs the destructor (§ 12.1.1, p. 452) on the object pointed to by the T* pointer p.

`allocators` Allocate Unconstructed Memory

The memory an `allocator` allocates is *unconstructed*. We use this memory by constructing objects in that memory. In the new library the `construct` member takes a pointer and zero or more additional arguments; it constructs an element at the given location. The additional arguments are used to initialize the object being constructed. Like the arguments to `make_shared` (§ 12.1.1, p. 451), these additional arguments must be valid initializers for an object of the type being con-

structed. In particular, if the , object is a class type, these arguments must match a constructor for that class:

```
auto q = p;              //   q will point to one past the last constructed element
alloc.construct(q++);          //   *q is the empty string
alloc.construct(q++, 10, 'c');    //   *q is cccccccccc
alloc.construct(q++, "hi");      //   *q is hi !
```

In earlier versions of the library, `construct` took only two arguments: the pointer at which to construct an object and a value of the element type. As a result, we could only copy an element into unconstructed space, we could not use any other constructor for the element type.

It is an error to use raw memory in which an object has not been constructed:

```
cout << *p << endl;    //   ok: uses the string output operator
cout << *q << endl;    //   disaster: q points to unconstructed memory!
```

⚠️ **WARNING** We must `construct` objects in order to use memory returned by `allocate`. Using unconstructed memory in other ways is undefined.

When we're finished using the objects, we must destroy the elements we constructed, which we do by calling `destroy` on each constructed element. The `destroy` function takes a pointer and runs the destructor (§ 12.1.1, p. 452) on the pointed-to object:

```
while (q != p)
    alloc.destroy(--q);          //  free the strings we actually allocated
```

At the beginning of our loop, q points one past the last constructed element. We decrement q before calling destroy. Thus, on the first call to destroy, q points to the last constructed element. We destroy the first element in the last iteration, after which q will equal p and the loop ends.

⚠️ **WARNING** We may destroy only elements that are actually constructed.

Once the elements have been destroyed, we can either reuse the memory to hold other strings or return the memory to the system. We free the memory by calling deallocate:

```
alloc.deallocate(p, n);
```

The pointer we pass to deallocate cannot be null; it must point to memory allocated by allocate. Moreover, the size argument passed to deallocate must be the same size as used in the call to allocate that obtained the memory to which the pointer points.

Algorithms to Copy and Fill Uninitialized Memory

As a companion to the allocator class, the library also defines two algorithms that can construct objects in uninitialized memory. These functions, described in Table 12.8, are defined in the memory header.

Table 12.8: allocator Algorithms
These functions construct elements in the destination, rather than assigning to them.
`uninitialized_copy(b, e, b2)`   Copies elements from the input range denoted by iterators b and e into unconstructed, raw memory denoted by the iterator b2. The memory denoted by b2 must be large enough to hold a copy of the elements in the input range.
`uninitialized_copy_n(b, n, b2)`   Copies n elements starting from the one denoted by the iterator b into raw memory starting at b2.
`uninitialized_fill(b, e, t)`   Constructs objects in the range of raw memory denoted by iterators b and e as a copy of t.
`uninitialized_fill_n(b, n, t)`   Constructs an unsigned number n objects starting at b. b must denote unconstructed, raw memory large enough to hold the given number of objects.

As an example, assume we have a vector of ints that we want to copy into dynamic memory. We'll allocate memory for twice as many ints as are in the vector. We'll construct the first half of the newly allocated memory by copying elements from the original vector. We'll construct elements in the second half by filling them with a given value:

```
//  allocate twice as many elements as vi holds
auto p = alloc.allocate(vi.size() * 2);
//  construct elements starting at p as copies of elements in vi
auto q = uninitialized_copy(vi.begin(), vi.end(), p);
//  initialize the remaining elements to 42
uninitialized_fill_n(q, vi.size(), 42);
```

Like the `copy` algorithm (§ 10.2.2, p. 382), `uninitialized_copy` takes three iterators. The first two denote an input sequence and the third denotes the destination into which those elements will be copied. The destination iterator passed to `uninitialized_copy` must denote unconstructed memory. Unlike `copy`, `uninitialized_copy` constructs elements in its destination.

Like `copy`, `uninitialized_copy` returns its (incremented) destination iterator. Thus, a call to `uninitialized_copy` returns a pointer positioned one element past the last constructed element. In this example, we store that pointer in `q`, which we pass to `uninitialized_fill_n`. This function, like `fill_n` (§ 10.2.2, p. 380), takes a pointer to a destination, a count, and a value. It will construct the given number of objects from the given value at locations starting at the given destination.

EXERCISES SECTION 12.2.2

Exercise 12.26: Rewrite the program on page 481 using an `allocator`.

12.3   Using the Library: A Text-Query Program

To conclude our discussion of the library, we'll implement a simple text-query program. Our program will let a user search a given file for words that might occur in it. The result of a query will be the number of times the word occurs and a list of lines on which that word appears. If a word occurs more than once on the same line, we'll display that line only once. Lines will be displayed in ascending order—that is, line 7 should be displayed before line 9, and so on.

For example, we might read the file that contains the input for this chapter and look for the word `element`. The first few lines of the output would be

```
element occurs 112 times
    (line 36) A set element contains only a key;
    (line 158) operator creates a new element
    (line 160) Regardless of whether the element
    (line 168) When we fetch an element from a map, we
    (line 214) If the element is not found, find returns
```

followed by the remaining 100 or so lines in which the word `element` occurs.

12.3.1 Design of the Query Program

A good way to start the design of a program is to list the program's operations. Knowing what operations we need can help us see what data structures we'll need. Starting from requirements, the tasks our program must do include the following:

- When it reads the input, the program must remember the line(s) in which each word appears. Hence, the program will need to read the input a line at a time and break up the lines from the input file into its separate words

- When it generates output,

  - The program must be able to fetch the line numbers associated with a given word
  - The line numbers must appear in ascending order with no duplicates
  - The program must be able to print the text appearing in the input file at a given line number.

These requirements can be met quite neatly by using various library facilities:

- We'll use a vector<string> to store a copy of the entire input file. Each line in the input file will be an element in this vector. When we want to print a line, we can fetch the line using its line number as the index.

- We'll use an istringstream (§ 8.3, p. 321) to break each line into words.

- We'll use a set to hold the line numbers on which each word in the input appears. Using a set guarantees that each line will appear only once and that the line numbers will be stored in ascending order.

- We'll use a map to associate each word with the set of line numbers on which the word appears. Using a map will let us fetch the set for any given word.

For reasons we'll explain shortly, our solution will also use shared_ptrs.

Data Structures

Although we could write our program using vector, set, and map directly, it will be more useful if we define a more abstract solution. We'll start by designing a class to hold the input file in a way that makes querying the file easy. This class, which we'll name TextQuery, will hold a vector and a map. The vector will hold the text of the input file; the map will associate each word in that file to the set of line numbers on which that word appears. This class will have a constructor that reads a given input file and an operation to perform the queries.

The work of the query operation is pretty simple: It will look inside its map to see whether the given word is present. The hard part in designing this function is deciding what the query function should return. Once we know that a word was found, we need to know how often it occurred, the line numbers on which it occurred, and the corresponding text for each of those line numbers.

The easiest way to return all those data is to define a second class, which we'll name QueryResult, to hold the results of a query. This class will have a print function to print the results in a QueryResult.

Sharing Data between Classes

Our `QueryResult` class is intended to represent the results of a query. Those results include the `set` of line numbers associated with the given word and the corresponding lines of text from the input file. These data are stored in objects of type `TextQuery`.

Because the data that a `QueryResult` needs are stored in a `TextQuery` object, we have to decide how to access them. We could copy the `set` of line numbers, but that might be an expensive operation. Moreover, we certainly wouldn't want to copy the `vector`, because that would entail copying the entire file in order to print (what will usually be) a small subset of the file.

We could avoid making copies by returning iterators (or pointers) into the `TextQuery` object. However, this approach opens up a pitfall: What happens if the `TextQuery` object is destroyed before a corresponding `QueryResult`? In that case, the `QueryResult` would refer to data in an object that no longer exists.

This last observation about synchronizing the lifetime of a `QueryResult` with the `TextQuery` object whose results it represents suggests a solution to our design problem. Given that these two classes conceptually "share" data, we'll use `shared_ptr`s (§ 12.1.1, p. 450) to reflect that sharing in our data structures.

Using the `TextQuery` Class

When we design a class, it can be helpful to write programs using the class before actually implementing the members. That way, we can see whether the class has the operations we need. For example, the following program uses our proposed `TextQuery` and `QueryResult` classes. This function takes an `ifstream` that points to the file we want to process, and interacts with a user, printing the results for the given words:

```
void runQueries(ifstream &infile)
{
    // infile is an ifstream that is the file we want to query
    TextQuery tq(infile);   // store the file and build the query map
    // iterate with the user: prompt for a word to find and print results
    while (true) {
        cout << "enter word to look for, or q to quit: ";
        string s;
        // stop if we hit end-of-file on the input or if a 'q' is entered
        if (!(cin >> s) || s == "q") break;
        // run the query and print the results
        print(cout, tq.query(s)) << endl;
    }
}
```

We start by initializing a `TextQuery` object named `tq` from a given `ifstream`. The `TextQuery` constructor reads that file into its `vector` and builds the `map` that associates the words in the input with the line numbers on which they appear.

The `while` loop iterates (indefinitely) with the user asking for a word to query and printing the related results. The loop condition tests the literal `true` (§ 2.1.3, p. 41), so it always succeeds. We exit the loop through the `break` (§ 5.5.1, p. 190) after the first `if`. That `if` checks that the read succeeded. If so, it also checks whether the user entered a q to quit. Once we have a word to look for, we ask `tq` to find that word and then call `print` to print the results of the search.

EXERCISES SECTION 12.3.1

Exercise 12.27: The `TextQuery` and `QueryResult` classes use only capabilities that we have already covered. Without looking ahead, write your own versions of these classes.

Exercise 12.28: Write a program to implement text queries without defining classes to manage the data. Your program should take a file and interact with a user to query for words in that file. Use `vector`, `map`, and `set` containers to hold the data for the file and to generate the results for the queries.

Exercise 12.29: We could have written the loop to manage the interaction with the user as a do `while` (§ 5.4.4, p. 189) loop. Rewrite the loop to use a do `while`. Explain which version you prefer and why.

12.3.2 Defining the Query Program Classes

We'll start by defining our `TextQuery` class. The user will create objects of this class by supplying an `istream` from which to read the input file. This class also provides the `query` operation that will take a `string` and return a `QueryResult` representing the lines on which that `string` appears.

The data members of the class have to take into account the intended sharing with `QueryResult` objects. The `QueryResult` class will share the `vector` representing the input file and the `sets` that hold the line numbers associated with each word in the input. Hence, our class has two data members: a `shared_ptr` to a dynamically allocated `vector` that holds the input file, and a `map` from `string` to `shared_ptr<set>`. The `map` associates each word in the file with a dynamically allocated `set` that holds the line numbers on which that word appears.

To make our code a bit easier to read, we'll also define a type member (§ 7.3.1, p. 271) to refer to line numbers, which are indices into a `vector` of `strings`:

```
class QueryResult; // declaration needed for return type in the query function
class TextQuery {
public:
    using line_no = std::vector<std::string>::size_type;
    TextQuery(std::ifstream&);
    QueryResult query(const std::string&) const;
private:
    std::shared_ptr<std::vector<std::string>> file; // input file
    // map of each word to the set of the lines in which that word appears
    std::map<std::string,
            std::shared_ptr<std::set<line_no>>> wm;
};
```

The hardest part about this class is untangling the class names. As usual, for code that will go in a header file, we use `std::` when we use a library name (§ 3.1, p. 83). In this case, the repeated use of `std::` makes the code a bit hard to read at first. For example,

```
std::map<std::string, std::shared_ptr<std::set<line_no>>> wm;
```

is easier to understand when rewritten as

```
map<string, shared_ptr<set<line_no>>> wm;
```

The `TextQuery` Constructor

The `TextQuery` constructor takes an `ifstream`, which it reads a line at a time:

```
// read the input file and build the map of lines to line numbers
TextQuery::TextQuery(ifstream &is): file(new vector<string>)
{
    string text;
    while (getline(is, text)) {        // for each line in the file
        file->push_back(text);         // remember this line of text
        int n = file->size() - 1;      // the current line number
        istringstream line(text);      // separate the line into words
        string word;
        while (line >> word) {         // for each word in that line
            // if word isn't already in wm, subscripting adds a new entry
            auto &lines = wm[word]; // lines is a shared_ptr
            if (!lines) // that pointer is null the first time we see word
                lines.reset(new set<line_no>); // allocate a new set
            lines->insert(n);          // insert this line number
        }
    }
}
```

The constructor initializer allocates a new `vector` to hold the text from the input file. We use `getline` to read the file a line at a time and push each line onto the `vector`. Because `file` is a `shared_ptr`, we use the `->` operator to dereference `file` to fetch the `push_back` member of the `vector` to which `file` points.

Next we use an `istringstream` (§ 8.3, p. 321) to process each word in the line we just read. The inner `while` uses the `istringstream` input operator to read each word from the current line into `word`. Inside the `while`, we use the `map` subscript operator to fetch the `shared_ptr<set>` associated with `word` and bind `lines` to that pointer. Note that `lines` is a reference, so changes made to `lines` will be made to the element in `wm`.

If `word` wasn't in the `map`, the subscript operator adds `word` to `wm` (§ 11.3.4, p. 435). The element associated with `word` is value initialized, which means that `lines` will be a null pointer if the subscript operator added `word` to `wm`. If `lines` is null, we allocate a new `set` and call `reset` to update the `shared_ptr` to which `lines` refers to point to this newly allocated `set`.

Regardless of whether we created a new `set`, we call `insert` to add the current line number. Because `lines` is a reference, the call to `insert` adds an element

to the set in wm. If a given word occurs more than once in the same line, the call
to insert does nothing.

The QueryResult Class

The QueryResult class has three data members: a string that is the word whose
results it represents; a shared_ptr to the vector containing the input file; and
a shared_ptr to the set of line numbers on which this word appears. Its only
member function is a constructor that initializes these three members:

```
class QueryResult {
friend std::ostream& print(std::ostream&, const QueryResult&);
public:
    QueryResult(std::string s,
                std::shared_ptr<std::set<line_no>> p,
                std::shared_ptr<std::vector<std::string>> f):
        sought(s), lines(p), file(f) { }
private:
    std::string sought;  // word this query represents
    std::shared_ptr<std::set<line_no>> lines; // lines it's on
    std::shared_ptr<std::vector<std::string>> file;  // input file
};
```

The constructor's only job is to store its arguments in the corresponding data members, which it does in the constructor initializer list (§ 7.1.4, p. 265).

The query Function

The query function takes a string, which it uses to locate the corresponding set
of line numbers in the map. If the string is found, the query function constructs
a QueryResult from the given string, the TextQuery file member, and the
set that was fetched from wm.

The only question is: What should we return if the given string is not found?
In this case, there is no set to return. We'll solve this problem by defining a local
static object that is a shared_ptr to an empty set of line numbers. When the
word is not found, we'll return a copy of this shared_ptr:

```
QueryResult
TextQuery::query(const string &sought) const
{
    // we'll return a pointer to this set if we don't find sought
    static shared_ptr<set<line_no>> nodata(new set<line_no>);
    // use find and not a subscript to avoid adding words to wm!
    auto loc = wm.find(sought);
    if (loc == wm.end())
        return QueryResult(sought, nodata, file);  // not found
    else
        return QueryResult(sought, loc->second, file);
}
```

Printing the Results

The print function prints its given QueryResult object on its given stream:

```
ostream &print(ostream & os, const QueryResult &qr)
{
    //  if the word was found, print the count and all occurrences
    os << qr.sought << " occurs " << qr.lines->size() << " "
       << make_plural(qr.lines->size(), "time", "s") << endl;
    //  print each line in which the word appeared
    for (auto num : *qr.lines) //  for every element in the set
        //  don't confound the user with text lines starting at 0
        os << "\t(line " << num + 1 << ") "
           << *(qr.file->begin() + num) << endl;
    return os;
}
```

We use the size of the set to which the qr.lines points to report how many matches were found. Because that set is in a shared_ptr, we have to remember to dereference lines. We call make_plural (§ 6.3.2, p. 224) to print time or times, depending on whether that size is equal to 1.

In the for we iterate through the set to which lines points. The body of the for prints the line number, adjusted to use human-friendly counting. The numbers in the set are indices of elements in the vector, which are numbered from zero. However, most users think of the first line as line number 1, so we systematically add 1 to the line numbers to convert to this more common notation.

We use the line number to fetch a line from the vector to which file points. Recall that when we add a number to an iterator, we get the element that many elements further into the vector (§ 3.4.2, p. 111). Thus, file->begin() + num is the numth element after the start of the vector to which file points.

Note that this function correctly handles the case that the word is not found. In this case, the set will be empty. The first output statement will note that the word occurred 0 times. Because *res.lines is empty. the for loop won't be executed.

> ### EXERCISES SECTION 12.3.2
>
> **Exercise 12.30:** Define your own versions of the TextQuery and QueryResult classes and execute the runQueries function from § 12.3.1 (p. 486).
>
> **Exercise 12.31:** What difference(s) would it make if we used a vector instead of a set to hold the line numbers? Which approach is better? Why?
>
> **Exercise 12.32:** Rewrite the TextQuery and QueryResult classes to use a StrBlob instead of a vector<string> to hold the input file.
>
> **Exercise 12.33:** In Chapter 15 we'll extend our query system and will need some additional members in the QueryResult class. Add members named begin and end that return iterators into the set of line numbers returned by a given query, and a member named get_file that returns a shared_ptr to the file in the QueryResult object.

CHAPTER SUMMARY

In C++, memory is allocated through new expressions and freed through delete expressions. The library also defines an allocator class for allocating blocks of dynamic memory.

Programs that allocate dynamic memory are responsible for freeing the memory they allocate. Properly freeing dynamic memory is a rich source of bugs: Either the memory is never freed, or it is freed while there are still pointers referring to the memory. The new library defines smart pointers—shared_ptr, unique_ptr, and weak_ptr—that make managing dynamic memory much safer. A smart pointer automatically frees the memory once there are no other users of that memory. When possible, modern C++ programs ought to use smart pointers.

DEFINED TERMS

allocator Library class that allocates unconstructed memory.

dangling pointer A pointer that refers to memory that once had an object but no longer does. Program errors due to dangling pointers are notoriously difficult to debug.

delete Frees memory allocated by new. delete p frees the object and delete [] p frees the array to which p points. p may be null or point to memory allocated by new.

deleter Function passed to a smart pointer to use in place of delete when destroying the object to which the pointer is bound.

destructor Special member function that cleans up an object when the object goes out of scope or is deleted.

dynamically allocated Object that is allocated on the free store. Objects allocated on the free store exist until they are explicitly deleted or the program terminates.

free store Memory pool available to a program to hold dynamically allocated objects.

heap Synonym for free store.

new Allocates memory from the free store. new T allocates and constructs an object of type T and returns a pointer to that object; if T is an array type, new returns a pointer to the first element in the array. Similarly, new [n] T allocates n objects of type T and returns a pointer to the first element in the array. By default, the allocated object is default initialized. We may also provide optional initializers.

placement new Form of new that takes additional arguments passed in parentheses following the keyword new; for example, new (nothrow) int tells new that it should not throw an exception.

reference count Counter that tracks how many users share a common object. Used by smart pointers to know when it is safe to delete memory to which the pointers point.

shared_ptr Smart pointer that provides shared ownership: The object is deleted when the last shared_ptr pointing to that object is destroyed.

smart pointer Library type that acts like a pointer but can be checked to see whether it is safe to use. The type takes care of deleting memory when appropriate.

unique_ptr Smart pointer that provides single ownership: The object is deleted when the unique_ptr pointing to that object is destroyed. unique_ptrs cannot be directly copied or assigned.

weak_ptr Smart pointer that points to an object managed by a shared_ptr. The shared_ptr does not count weak_ptrs when deciding whether to delete its object.

PART III

TOOLS FOR CLASS AUTHORS

CONTENTS

Classes are the central concept in C++. Chapter 7 began our detailed coverage of how classes are defined. That chapter covered topics fundamental to any use of classes: class scope, data hiding, and constructors. It also introduced various important class features: member functions, the implicit `this` pointer, friends, and `const`, `static`, and `mutable` members. In this part, we'll extend our coverage of classes by looking at copy control, overloaded operators, inheritance, and templates.

As we've seen, in C++ classes define constructors to control what happens when objects of the class type are initialized. Classes also control what happens when objects are copied, assigned, moved, and destroyed. In this respect, C++ differs from other languages, many of which do not give class designers the ability to control these operations. Chapter 13 covers these topics. This chapter also covers two important concepts introduced by the new standard: rvalue references and move operations.

Chapter 14 looks at operator overloading, which allows operands of class types to be used with the built-in operators. Operator overloading is one of the ways whereby C++ lets us create new types that are as intuitive to use as are the built-in types.

Among the operators that a class can overload is the funtion call operator. We can "call" objects of such classes just as if they were

493

functions. We'll also look at new library facilities that make it easy to use different types of callable objects in a uniform way.

This chapter concludes by looking at another special kind of class member function—conversion operators. These operators define implicit conversions from objects of class type. The compiler applies these conversions in the same contexts—and for the same reasons—as it does with conversions among the built-in types.

The last two chapters in this part cover how C++ supports object-oriented and generic programming.

Chapter 15 covers inheritance and dynamic binding. Along with data abstraction, inheritance and dynamic binding are fundamental to object-oriented programming. Inheritance makes it easier for us to define related types and dynamic binding lets us write type-indepenent code that can ignore the differences among types that are related by inheritance.

Chapter 16 covers function and class templates. Templates let us write generic classes and functions that are type-independent. A number of new template-related features were introduced by the new standard: variadic templates, template type aliases, and new ways to control instantiation.

Writing our own object-oriented or generic types requires a fairly good understanding of C++. Fortunately, we can use object-oriented and generic types without understanding the details of how to build them. For example, the standard library uses the facilities we'll study in Chapters 15 and 16 extensively, and we've used the library types and algorithms without needing to know how they are implemented.

Readers, therefore, should understand that Part III covers fairly advanced topics. Writing templates or object-oriented classes requires a good understanding of the basics of C++ and a good grasp of how to define more basic classes.

CHAPTER 13

COPY CONTROL

CONTENTS

As we saw in Chapter 7, each class defines a new type and defines the operations that objects of that type can perform. In that chapter, we also learned that classes can define constructors, which control what happens when objects of the class type are created.

In this chapter we'll learn how classes can control what happens when objects of the class type are copied, assigned, moved, or destroyed. Classes control these actions through special member functions: the copy constructor, move constructor, copy-assignment operator, move-assignment operator, and destructor.

When we define a class, we specify—explicitly or implicitly—what happens when objects of that class type are copied, moved, assigned, and destroyed. A class controls these operations by defining five special member functions: **copy constructor**, **copy-assignment operator**, **move constructor**, **move-assignment operator**, and **destructor**. The copy and move constructors define what happens when an object is initialized from another object of the same type. The copy- and move-assignment operators define what happens when we assign an object of a class type to another object of that same class type. The destructor defines what happens when an object of the type ceases to exist. Collectively, we'll refer to these operations as **copy control**.

If a class does not define all of the copy-control members, the compiler automatically defines the missing operations. As a result, many classes can ignore copy control (§ 7.1.5, p. 267). However, for some classes, relying on the default definitions leads to disaster. Frequently, the hardest part of implementing copy-control operations is recognizing when we need to define them in the first place.

> Copy control is an essential part of defining any C++ class. Programmers new to C++ are often confused by having to define what happens when objects are copied, moved, assigned, or destroyed. This confusion is compounded because if we do not explicitly define these operations, the compiler defines them for us—although the compiler-defined versions might not behave as we intend.

13.1 Copy, Assign, and Destroy

We'll start by covering the most basic operations, which are the copy constructor, copy-assignment operator, and destructor. We'll cover the move operations (which were introduced by the new standard) in § 13.6 (p. 531).

13.1.1 The Copy Constructor

A constructor is the copy constructor if its first parameter is a reference to the class type and any additional parameters have default values:

```
class Foo {
public:
    Foo();              //  default constructor
    Foo(const Foo&);    //  copy constructor
    //  ...
};
```

For reasons we'll explain shortly, the first parameter must be a reference type. That parameter is almost always a reference to const, although we can define the copy constructor to take a reference to nonconst. The copy constructor is used implicitly in several circumstances. Hence, the copy constructor usually should not be explicit (§ 7.5.4, p. 296).

The Synthesized Copy Constructor

When we do not define a copy constructor for a class, the compiler synthesizes one for us. Unlike the synthesized default constructor (§ 7.1.4, p. 262), a copy constructor is synthesized even if we define other constructors.

As we'll see in § 13.1.6 (p. 508), the **synthesized copy constructor** for some classes prevents us from copying objects of that class type. Otherwise, the synthesized copy constructor **memberwise copies** the members of its argument into the object being created (§ 7.1.5, p. 267). The compiler copies each nonstatic member in turn from the given object into the one being created.

The type of each member determines how that member is copied: Members of class type are copied by the copy constructor for that class; members of built-in type are copied directly. Although we cannot directly copy an array (§ 3.5.1, p. 114), the synthesized copy constructor copies members of array type by copying each element. Elements of class type are copied by using the elements' copy constructor.

As an example, the synthesized copy constructor for our `Sales_data` class is equivalent to:

```
class Sales_data {
public:
    //  other members and constructors as before
    //  declaration equivalent to the synthesized copy constructor
    Sales_data(const Sales_data&);
private:
    std::string bookNo;
    int units_sold = 0;
    double revenue = 0.0;
};
//  equivalent to the copy constructor that would be synthesized for Sales_data
Sales_data::Sales_data(const Sales_data &orig):
    bookNo(orig.bookNo),            //  uses the string copy constructor
    units_sold(orig.units_sold),    //  copies orig.units_sold
    revenue(orig.revenue)           //  copies orig.revenue
    {   }                           //  empty body
```

Copy Initialization

We are now in a position to fully understand the differences between direct initialization and copy initialization (§ 3.2.1, p. 84):

```
string dots(10, '.');               //  direct initialization
string s(dots);                     //  direct initialization
string s2 = dots;                   //  copy initialization
string null_book = "9-999-99999-9"; //  copy initialization
string nines = string(100, '9');    //  copy initialization
```

When we use direct initialization, we are asking the compiler to use ordinary function matching (§ 6.4, p. 233) to select the constructor that best matches the arguments we provide. When we use **copy initialization**, we are asking the compiler to copy the right-hand operand into the object being created, converting that operand if necessary (§ 7.5.4, p. 294).

Copy initialization ordinarily uses the copy constructor. However, as we'll see in § 13.6.2 (p. 534), if a class has a move constructor, then copy initialization sometimes uses the move constructor instead of the copy constructor. For now, what's useful to know is when copy initialization happens and that copy initialization requires either the copy constructor or the move constructor.

Copy initialization happens not only when we define variables using an =, but also when we

- Pass an object as an argument to a parameter of nonreference type

- Return an object from a function that has a nonreference return type

- Brace initialize the elements in an array or the members of an aggregate class (§ 7.5.5, p. 298)

Some class types also use copy initialization for the objects they allocate. For example, the library containers copy initialize their elements when we initialize the container, or when we call an `insert` or `push` member (§ 9.3.1, p. 342). By contrast, elements created by an `emplace` member are direct initialized (§ 9.3.1, p. 345).

Parameters and Return Values

During a function call, parameters that have a nonreference type are copy initialized (§ 6.2.1, p. 209). Similarly, when a function has a nonreference return type, the return value is used to copy initialize the result of the call operator at the call site (§ 6.3.2, p. 224).

The fact that the copy constructor is used to initialize nonreference parameters of class type explains why the copy constructor's own parameter must be a reference. If that parameter were not a reference, then the call would never succeed—to call the copy constructor, we'd need to use the copy constructor to copy the argument, but to copy the argument, we'd need to call the copy constructor, and so on indefinitely.

Constraints on Copy Initialization

As we've seen, whether we use copy or direct initialization matters if we use an initializer that requires conversion by an `explicit` constructor (§ 7.5.4, p. 296):

```
vector<int> v1(10);   // ok: direct initialization
vector<int> v2 = 10;  // error: constructor that takes a size is explicit

void f(vector<int>);  // f's parameter is copy initialized
f(10);  // error: can't use an explicit constructor to copy an argument
f(vector<int>(10));   // ok: directly construct a temporary vector from an int
```

Directly initializing v1 is fine, but the seemingly equivalent copy initialization of v2 is an error, because the `vector` constructor that takes a single size parameter is `explicit`. For the same reasons that we cannot copy initialize v2, we cannot implicitly use an `explicit` constructor when we pass an argument or return a value from a function. If we want to use an `explicit` constructor, we must do so explicitly, as in the last line of the example above.

The Compiler Can Bypass the Copy Constructor

During copy initialization, the compiler is permitted (but not obligated) to skip the copy/move constructor and create the object directly. That is, the compiler is permitted to rewrite

```
string null_book = "9-999-99999-9";  // copy initialization
```

into

```
string null_book("9-999-99999-9");  // compiler omits the copy constructor
```

However, even if the compiler omits the call to the copy/move constructor, the copy/move constructor must exist and must be accessible (e.g., not `private`) at that point in the program.

EXERCISES SECTION 13.1.1

Exercise 13.1: What is a copy constructor? When is it used?

Exercise 13.2: Explain why the following declaration is illegal:

```
Sales_data::Sales_data(Sales_data rhs);
```

Exercise 13.3: What happens when we copy a `StrBlob`? What about `StrBlobPtrs`?

Exercise 13.4: Assuming `Point` is a class type with a `public` copy constructor, identify each use of the copy constructor in this program fragment:

```
Point global;
Point foo_bar(Point arg)
{
    Point local = arg, *heap = new Point(global);
    *heap = local;
    Point pa[ 4 ] = { local, *heap };
    return *heap;
}
```

Exercise 13.5: Given the following sketch of a class, write a copy constructor that copies all the members. Your constructor should dynamically allocate a new `string` (§ 12.1.2, p. 458) and copy the object to which `ps` points, rather than copying `ps` itself.

```
class HasPtr {
public:
    HasPtr(const std::string &s = std::string()):
        ps(new std::string(s)), i(0) { }
private:
    std::string *ps;
    int    i;
};
```

13.1.2 The Copy-Assignment Operator

Just as a class controls how objects of that class are initialized, it also controls how
objects of its class are assigned:

```
Sales_data trans, accum;
trans = accum; // uses the Sales_data copy-assignment operator
```

As with the copy constructor, the compiler synthesizes a copy-assignment operator
if the class does not define its own.

Introducing Overloaded Assignment

Before we look at the synthesized assignment operator, we need to know a bit
about **overloaded operators**, which we cover in detail in Chapter 14.

Overloaded operators are functions that have the name `operator` followed
by the symbol for the operator being defined. Hence, the assignment operator is a
function named `operator=`. Like any other function, an operator function has a
return type and a parameter list.

The parameters in an overloaded operator represent the operands of the operator. Some operators, assignment among them, must be defined as member functions. When an operator is a member function, the left-hand operand is bound to
the implicit `this` parameter (§ 7.1.2, p. 257). The right-hand operand in a binary
operator, such as assignment, is passed as an explicit parameter.

The copy-assignment operator takes an argument of the same type as the class:

```
class Foo {
public:
    Foo& operator=(const Foo&); // assignment operator
    // ...
};
```

To be consistent with assignment for the built-in types (§ 4.4, p. 145), assignment
operators usually return a reference to their left-hand operand. It is also worth
noting that the library generally requires that types stored in a container have assignment operators that return a reference to the left-hand operand.

> **Best Practices**   Assignment operators ordinarily should return a reference to their left-
> hand operand.

The Synthesized Copy-Assignment Operator

Just as it does for the copy constructor, the compiler generates a **synthesized copy-
assignment operator** for a class if the class does not define its own. Analogously to
the copy constructor, for some classes the synthesized copy-assignment operator
disallows assignment (§ 13.1.6, p. 508). Otherwise, it assigns each `nonstatic`
member of the right-hand object to the corresponding member of the left-hand
object using the copy-assignment operator for the type of that member. Array
members are assigned by assigning each element of the array. The synthesized
copy-assignment operator returns a reference to its left-hand object.

As an example, the following is equivalent to the synthesized `Sales_data` copy-assignment operator:

```
// equivalent to the synthesized copy-assignment operator
Sales_data&
Sales_data::operator=(const Sales_data &rhs)
{
    bookNo = rhs.bookNo;            // calls the string::operator=
    units_sold = rhs.units_sold;   // uses the built-in int assignment
    revenue = rhs.revenue;         // uses the built-in double assignment
    return *this;                  // return a reference to this object
}
```

> ## EXERCISES SECTION 13.1.2
>
> **Exercise 13.6:** What is a copy-assignment operator? When is this operator used? What does the synthesized copy-assignment operator do? When is it synthesized?
>
> **Exercise 13.7:** What happens when we assign one `StrBlob` to another? What about `StrBlobPtrs`?
>
> **Exercise 13.8:** Write the assignment operator for the `HasPtr` class from exercise 13.5 in § 13.1.1 (p. 499). As with the copy constructor, your assignment operator should copy the object to which `ps` points.

13.1.3 The Destructor

The destructor operates inversely to the constructors: Constructors initialize the `nonstatic` data members of an object and may do other work; destructors do whatever work is needed to free the resources used by an object and destroy the `nonstatic` data members of the object.

The destructor is a member function with the name of the class prefixed by a tilde (~). It has no return value and takes no parameters:

```
class Foo {
public:
    ~Foo();    // destructor
    // ...
};
```

Because it takes no parameters, it cannot be overloaded. There is always only one destructor for a given class.

What a Destructor Does

Just as a constructor has an initialization part and a function body (§ 7.5.1, p. 288), a destructor has a function body and a destruction part. In a constructor, members are initialized before the function body is executed, and members are initialized in the same order as they appear in the class. In a destructor, the function body is executed first and then the members are destroyed. Members are destroyed in reverse order from the order in which they were initialized.

The function body of a destructor does whatever operations the class designer wishes to have executed subsequent to the last use of an object. Typically, the destructor frees resources an object allocated during its lifetime.

In a destructor, there is nothing akin to the constructor initializer list to control how members are destroyed; the destruction part is implicit. What happens when a member is destroyed depends on the type of the member. Members of class type are destroyed by running the member's own destructor. The built-in types do not have destructors, so nothing is done to destroy members of built-in type.

> The implicit destruction of a member of built-in pointer type does *not* delete the object to which that pointer points.

Unlike ordinary pointers, the smart pointers (§ 12.1.1, p. 452) are class types and have destructors. As a result, unlike ordinary pointers, members that are smart pointers are automatically destroyed during the destruction phase.

When a Destructor Is Called

The destructor is used automatically whenever an object of its type is destroyed:

- Variables are destroyed when they go out of scope.

- Members of an object are destroyed when the object of which they are a part is destroyed.

- Elements in a container—whether a library container or an array—are destroyed when the container is destroyed.

- Dynamically allocated objects are destroyed when the delete operator is applied to a pointer to the object (§ 12.1.2, p. 460).

- Temporary objects are destroyed at the end of the full expression in which the temporary was created.

Because destructors are run automatically, our programs can allocate resources and (usually) not worry about when those resources are released.

For example, the following fragment defines four Sales_data objects:

```
{ // new scope
    // p and p2 point to dynamically allocated objects
    Sales_data *p = new Sales_data;      // p is a built-in pointer
    auto p2 = make_shared<Sales_data>(); // p2 is a shared_ptr
    Sales_data item(*p);        // copy constructor copies *p into item
    vector<Sales_data> vec;     // local object
    vec.push_back(*p2);         // copies the object to which p2 points
    delete p;                   // destructor called on the object pointed to by p
} // exit local scope; destructor called on item, p2, and vec
    // destroying p2 decrements its use count; if the count goes to 0, the object is freed
    // destroying vec destroys the elements in vec
```

Each of these objects contains a `string` member, which allocates dynamic memory to contain the characters in its `bookNo` member. However, the only memory our code has to manage directly is the object we directly allocated. Our code directly frees only the dynamically allocated object bound to p.

The other `Sales_data` objects are automatically destroyed when they go out of scope. When the block ends, `vec`, `p2`, and `item` all go out of scope, which means that the `vector`, `shared_ptr`, and `Sales_data` destructors will be run on those objects, respectively. The `vector` destructor will destroy the element we pushed onto `vec`. The `shared_ptr` destructor will decrement the reference count of the object to which `p2` points. In this example, that count will go to zero, so the `shared_ptr` destructor will `delete` the `Sales_data` object that `p2` allocated.

In all cases, the `Sales_data` destructor implicitly destroys the `bookNo` member. Destroying `bookNo` runs the `string` destructor, which frees the memory used to store the ISBN.

The destructor is *not* run when a reference or a pointer to an object goes out of scope.

The Synthesized Destructor

The compiler defines a **synthesized destructor** for any class that does not define its own destructor. As with the copy constructor and the copy-assignment operator, for some classes, the synthesized destructor is defined to disallow objects of the type from being destroyed (§ 13.1.6, p. 508). Otherwise, the synthesized destructor has an empty function body.

For example, the synthesized `Sales_data` destructor is equivalent to:

```
class Sales_data {
public:
    //  no work to do other than destroying the members, which happens automatically
    ~Sales_data() { }
    //  other members as before
};
```

The members are automatically destroyed after the (empty) destructor body is run. In particular, the `string` destructor will be run to free the memory used by the `bookNo` member.

It is important to realize that the destructor body does not directly destroy the members themselves. Members are destroyed as part of the implicit destruction phase that follows the destructor body. A destructor body executes *in addition to* the memberwise destruction that takes place as part of destroying an object.

13.1.4 The Rule of Three/Five

As we've seen, there are three basic operations to control copies of class objects: the copy constructor, copy-assignment operator, and destructor. Moreover, as we'll see in § 13.6 (p. 531), under the new standard, a class can also define a move constructor and move-assignment operator.

Exercise 13.9: What is a destructor? What does the synthesized destructor do? When is a destructor synthesized?

Exercise 13.10: What happens when a `StrBlob` object is destroyed? What about a `StrBlobPtr`?

Exercise 13.11: Add a destructor to your `HasPtr` class from the previous exercises.

Exercise 13.12: How many destructor calls occur in the following code fragment?

```
bool fcn(const Sales_data *trans, Sales_data accum)
{
    Sales_data item1(*trans), item2(accum);
    return item1.isbn() != item2.isbn();
}
```

Exercise 13.13: A good way to understand copy-control members and constructors is to define a simple class with these members in which each member prints its name:

```
struct X {
    X() {std::cout << "X()" << std::endl;}
    X(const X&) {std::cout << "X(const X&)" << std::endl;}
};
```

Add the copy-assignment operator and destructor to X and write a program using X objects in various ways: Pass them as nonreference and reference parameters; dynamically allocate them; put them in containers; and so forth. Study the output until you are certain you understand when and why each copy-control member is used. As you read the output, remember that the compiler can omit calls to the copy constructor.

There is no requirement that we define all of these operations: We can define one or two of them without having to define all of them. However, ordinarily these operations should be thought of as a unit. In general, it is unusual to need one without needing to define them all.

Classes That Need Destructors Need Copy and Assignment

One rule of thumb to use when you decide whether a class needs to define its own versions of the copy-control members is to decide first whether the class needs a destructor. Often, the need for a destructor is more obvious than the need for the copy constructor or assignment operator. If the class needs a destructor, it almost surely needs a copy constructor and copy-assignment operator as well.

The `HasPtr` class that we have used in the exercises is a good example (§ 13.1.1, p. 499). That class allocates dynamic memory in its constructor. The synthesized destructor will not `delete` a data member that is a pointer. Therefore, this class needs to define a destructor to free the memory allocated by its constructor.

What may be less clear—but what our rule of thumb tells us—is that `HasPtr` also needs a copy constructor and copy-assignment operator.

Consider what would happen if we gave `HasPtr` a destructor but used the synthesized versions of the copy constructor and copy-assignment operator:

```
class HasPtr {
public:
    HasPtr(const std::string &s = std::string()):
        ps(new std::string(s)), i(0) { }
    ~HasPtr() { delete ps; }
    // WRONG: HasPtr needs a copy constructor and copy-assignment operator
    // other members as before
};
```

In this version of the class, the memory allocated in the constructor will be freed when a `HasPtr` object is destroyed. Unfortunately, we have introduced a serious bug! This version of the class uses the synthesized versions of copy and assignment. Those functions copy the pointer member, meaning that multiple `HasPtr` objects may be pointing to the same memory:

```
HasPtr f(HasPtr hp)    // HasPtr passed by value, so it is copied
{
    HasPtr ret = hp;  // copies the given HasPtr
    // process ret
    return ret;        // ret and hp are destroyed
}
```

When `f` returns, both `hp` and `ret` are destroyed and the `HasPtr` destructor is run on each of these objects. That destructor will `delete` the pointer member in `ret` and in `hp`. But these objects contain the same pointer value. This code will `delete` that pointer twice, which is an error (§ 12.1.2, p. 462). What happens is undefined.

In addition, the caller of `f` may still be using the object that was passed to `f`:

```
HasPtr p("some values");
f(p);              // when f completes, the memory to which p.ps points is freed
HasPtr q(p);  // now both p and q point to invalid memory!
```

The memory to which p (and q) points is no longer valid. It was returned to the system when `hp` (or `ret`!) was destroyed.

> If a class needs a destructor, it almost surely also needs the copy-assignment operator and a copy constructor.

Classes That Need Copy Need Assignment, and Vice Versa

Although many classes need to define all of (or none of) the copy-control members, some classes have work that needs to be done to copy or assign objects but has no need for the destructor.

As an example, consider a class that gives each object its own, unique serial number. Such a class would need a copy constructor to generate a new, distinct serial number for the object being created. That constructor would copy all the other data members from the given object. This class would also need its own copy-assignment operator to avoid assigning to the serial number of the left-hand object. However, this class would have no need for a destructor.

This example gives rise to a second rule of thumb: If a class needs a copy constructor, it almost surely needs a copy-assignment operator. And vice versa—if the class needs an assignment operator, it almost surely needs a copy constructor as well. Nevertheless, needing either the copy constructor or the copy-assignment operator does not (necessarily) indicate the need for a destructor.

EXERCISES SECTION 13.1.4

Exercise 13.14: Assume that `numbered` is a class with a default constructor that generates a unique serial number for each object, which is stored in a data member named `mysn`. Assuming `numbered` uses the synthesized copy-control members and given the following function:

```
void f (numbered s) { cout << s.mysn << endl; }
```

what output does the following code produce?

```
numbered a, b = a, c = b;
f(a); f(b); f(c);
```

Exercise 13.15: Assume `numbered` has a copy constructor that generates a new serial number. Does that change the output of the calls in the previous exercise? If so, why? What output gets generated?

Exercise 13.16: What if the parameter in `f` were `const numbered&`? Does that change the output? If so, why? What output gets generated?

Exercise 13.17: Write versions of `numbered` and `f` corresponding to the previous three exercises and check whether you correctly predicted the output.

13.1.5 Using = `default`

We can explicitly ask the compiler to generate the synthesized versions of the copy-control members by defining them as = `default` (§ 7.1.4, p. 264):

```
class Sales_data {
public:
    // copy control; use defaults
    Sales_data() = default;
    Sales_data(const Sales_data&) = default;
    Sales_data& operator=(const Sales_data &);
    ~Sales_data() = default;
    // other members as before
};
Sales_data& Sales_data::operator=(const Sales_data&) = default;
```

When we specify = `default` on the declaration of the member inside the class body, the synthesized function is implicitly inline (just as is any other member function defined in the body of the class). If we do not want the syntheized member to be an inline function, we can specify = `default` on the member's definition, as we do in the definition of the copy-assignment operator.

 We can use = `default` only on member functions that have a synthesized version (i.e., the default constructor or a copy-control member).

13.1.6 Preventing Copies

 Most classes should define—either implicitly or explicitly—the default and copy constructors and the copy-assignment operator.

Although most classes should (and generally do) define a copy constructor and a copy-assignment operator, for some classes, there really is no sensible meaning for these operations. In such cases, the class must be defined so as to prevent copies or assignments from being made. For example, the `iostream` classes prevent copying to avoid letting multiple objects write to or read from the same IO buffer. It might seem that we could prevent copies by not defining the copy-control members. However, this strategy doesn't work: If our class doesn't define these operations, the compiler will synthesize them.

Defining a Function as Deleted

Under the new standard, we can prevent copies by defining the copy constructor and copy-assignment operator as **deleted functions**. A deleted function is one that is declared but may not be used in any other way. We indicate that we want to define a function as deleted by following its parameter list with = `delete`:

```
struct NoCopy {
    NoCopy() = default;        // use the synthesized default constructor
    NoCopy(const NoCopy&) = delete;             // no copy
    NoCopy &operator=(const NoCopy&) = delete;  // no assignment
    ~NoCopy() = default;       // use the synthesized destructor
    // other members
};
```

The = `delete` signals to the compiler (and to readers of our code) that we are intentionally *not defining* these members.

Unlike = `default`, = `delete` must appear on the first declaration of a deleted function. This difference follows logically from the meaning of these declarations. A defaulted member affects only what code the compiler generates; hence the = `default` is not needed until the compiler generates code. On the other hand, the compiler needs to know that a function is deleted in order to prohibit operations that attempt to use it.

Also unlike = `default`, we can specify = `delete` on any function (we can use = `default` only on the default constructor or a copy-control member that the compiler can synthesize). Although the primary use of deleted functions is to suppress the copy-control members, deleted functions are sometimes also useful when we want to guide the function-matching process.

The Destructor Should Not be a Deleted Member

It is worth noting that we did not delete the destructor. If the destructor is deleted, then there is no way to destroy objects of that type. The compiler will not let us define variables or create temporaries of a type that has a deleted destructor. Moreover, we cannot define variables or temporaries of a class that has a member whose type has a deleted destructor. If a member has a deleted destructor, then that member cannot be destroyed. If a member can't be destroyed, the object as a whole can't be destroyed.

Although we cannot define variables or members of such types, we can dynamically allocate objects with a deleted destructor. However, we cannot free them:

```
struct NoDtor {
    NoDtor() = default;   // use the synthesized default constructor
    ~NoDtor() = delete;   // we can't destroy objects of type NoDtor
};
NoDtor nd;   // error: NoDtor destructor is deleted
NoDtor *p = new NoDtor();   // ok: but we can't delete p
delete p;   // error: NoDtor destructor is deleted
```

WARNING It is not possible to define an object or delete a pointer to a dynamically allocated object of a type with a deleted destructor.

The Copy-Control Members May Be Synthesized as Deleted

As we've seen, if we do not define the copy-control members, the compiler defines them for us. Similarly, if a class defines no constructors, the compiler synthesizes a default constructor for that class (§ 7.1.4, p. 262). For some classes, the compiler defines these synthesized members as deleted functions:

- The synthesized destructor is defined as deleted if the class has a member whose own destructor is deleted or is inaccessible (e.g., `private`).

- The synthesized copy constructor is defined as deleted if the class has a member whose own copy constructor is deleted or inaccessible. It is also deleted if the class has a member with a deleted or inaccessible destructor.

- The synthesized copy-assignment operator is defined as deleted if a member has a deleted or inaccessible copy-assignment operator, or if the class has a `const` or reference member.

- The synthesized default constructor is defined as deleted if the class has a member with a deleted or inaccessible destructor; or has a reference member that does not have an in-class initializer (§ 2.6.1, p. 73); or has a `const` member whose type does not explicitly define a default constructor and that member does not have an in-class initializer.

In essence, these rules mean that if a class has a data member that cannot be default constructed, copied, assigned, or destroyed, then the corresponding member will be a deleted function.

It may be surprising that a member that has a deleted or inaccessible destructor causes the synthesized default and copy constructors to be defined as deleted. The reason for this rule is that without it, we could create objects that we could not destroy.

It should not be surprising that the compiler will not synthesize a default constructor for a class with a reference member or a `const` member that cannot be default constructed. Nor should it be surprising that a class with a `const` member cannot use the synthesized copy-assignment operator: After all, that operator attempts to assign to every member. It is not possible to assign a new value to a `const` object.

Although we can assign a new value to a reference, doing so changes the value of the object to which the reference refers. If the copy-assignment operator were synthesized for such classes, the left-hand operand would continue to refer to the same object as it did before the assignment. It would not refer to the same object as the right-hand operand. Because this behavior is unlikely to be desired, the synthesized copy-assignment operator is defined as deleted if the class has a reference member.

We'll see in § 13.6.2 (p. 539), § 15.7.2 (p. 624), and § 19.6 (p. 849) that there are other aspects of a class that can cause its copy members to be defined as deleted.

In essence, the copy-control members are synthesized as deleted when it is impossible to copy, assign, or destroy a member of the class.

`private` Copy Control

Prior to the new standard, classes prevented copies by declaring their copy constructor and copy-assignment operator as `private`:

```
class PrivateCopy {
    // no access specifier; following members are private by default; see § 7.2 (p. 268)
    // copy control is private and so is inaccessible to ordinary user code
    PrivateCopy(const PrivateCopy&);
    PrivateCopy &operator=(const PrivateCopy&);
    // other members
public:
    PrivateCopy() = default; // use the synthesized default constructor
    ~PrivateCopy(); // users can define objects of this type but not copy them
};
```

Because the destructor is `public`, users will be able to define `PrivateCopy` objects. However, because the copy constructor and copy-assignment operator are `private`, user code will not be able to copy such objects. However, friends and members of the class can still make copies. To prevent copies by friends and members, we declare these members as `private` but do not define them.

With one exception, which we'll cover in § 15.2.1 (p. 594), it is legal to declare, but not define, a member function (§ 6.1.2, p. 206). An attempt to *use* an undefined member results in a link-time failure. By declaring (but not defining) a private copy constructor, we can forestall any attempt to copy an object of the class type: User code that tries to make a copy will be flagged as an error at compile time; copies made in member functions or friends will result in an error at link time.

> **Best Practices** Classes that want to prevent copying should define their copy constructor and copy-assignment operators using = delete rather than making those members private.

EXERCISES SECTION 13.1.6

Exercise 13.18: Define an Employee class that contains an employee name and a unique employee identifier. Give the class a default constructor and a constructor that takes a string representing the employee's name. Each constructor should generate a unique ID by incrementing a static data member.

Exercise 13.19: Does your Employee class need to define its own versions of the copy-control members? If so, why? If not, why not? Implement whatever copy-control members you think Employee needs.

Exercise 13.20: Explain what happens when we copy, assign, or destroy objects of our TextQuery and QueryResult classes from § 12.3 (p. 484).

Exercise 13.21: Do you think the TextQuery and QueryResult classes need to define their own versions of the copy-control members? If so, why? If not, why not? Implement whichever copy-control operations you think these classes require.

 ## 13.2 Copy Control and Resource Management

Ordinarily, classes that manage resources that do not reside in the class must define the copy-control members. As we saw in § 13.1.4 (p. 504), such classes will need destructors to free the resources allocated by the object. Once a class needs a destructor, it almost surely needs a copy constructor and copy-assignment operator as well.

In order to define these members, we first have to decide what copying an object of our type will mean. In general, we have two choices: We can define the copy operations to make the class behave like a value or like a pointer.

Classes that behave like values have their own state. When we copy a valuelike object, the copy and the original are independent of each other. Changes made to the copy have no effect on the original, and vice versa.

Classes that act like pointers share state. When we copy objects of such classes, the copy and the original use the same underlying data. Changes made to the copy also change the original, and vice versa.

Of the library classes we've used, the library containers and string class have valuelike behavior. Not surprisingly, the shared_ptr class provides pointer-like behavior, as does our StrBlob class (§ 12.1.1, p. 456). The IO types and unique_ptr do not allow copying or assignment, so they provide neither valuelike nor pointerlike behavior.

To illustrate these two approaches, we'll define the copy-control members for the HasPtr class used in the exercises. First, we'll make the class act like a value; then we'll reimplement the class making it behave like a pointer.

Our HasPtr class has two members, an int and a pointer to string. Ordinarily, classes copy members of built-in type (other than pointers) directly; such members are values and hence ordinarily ought to behave like values. What we do when we copy the pointer member determines whether a class like HasPtr has valuelike or pointerlike behavior.

EXERCISES SECTION 13.2

Exercise 13.22: Assume that we want HasPtr to behave like a value. That is, each object should have its own copy of the string to which the objects point. We'll show the definitions of the copy-control members in the next section. However, you already know everything you need to know to implement these members. Write the HasPtr copy constructor and copy-assignment operator before reading on.

13.2.1 Classes That Act Like Values

To provide valuelike behavior, each object has to have its own copy of the resource that the class manages. That means each HasPtr object must have its own copy of the string to which ps points. To implement valuelike behavior HasPtr needs

- A copy constructor that copies the string, not just the pointer

- A destructor to free the string

- A copy-assignment operator to free the object's existing string and copy the string from its right-hand operand

The valuelike version of HasPtr is

```cpp
class HasPtr {
public:
    HasPtr(const std::string &s = std::string()):
        ps(new std::string(s)), i(0) { }
    // each HasPtr has its own copy of the string to which ps points
    HasPtr(const HasPtr &p):
        ps(new std::string(*p.ps)), i(p.i) { }
    HasPtr& operator=(const HasPtr &);
    ~HasPtr() { delete ps; }
private:
    std::string *ps;
    int    i;
};
```

Our class is simple enough that we've defined all but the assignment operator in the class body. The first constructor takes an (optional) `string` argument. That constructor dynamically allocates its own copy of that `string` and stores a pointer to that `string` in `ps`. The copy constructor also allocates its own, separate copy of the `string`. The destructor frees the memory allocated in its constructors by executing `delete` on the pointer member, `ps`.

Valuelike Copy-Assignment Operator

Assignment operators typically combine the actions of the destructor and the copy constructor. Like the destructor, assignment destroys the left-hand operand's resources. Like the copy constructor, assignment copies data from the right-hand operand. However, it is crucially important that these actions be done in a sequence that is correct even if an object is assigned to itself. Moreover, when possible, we should also write our assignment operators so that they will leave the left-hand operand in a sensible state should an exception occur (§ 5.6.2, p. 196).

In this case, we can handle self-assignment—and make our code safe should an exception happen—by first copying the right-hand side. After the copy is made, we'll free the left-hand side and update the pointer to point to the newly allocated `string`:

```
HasPtr& HasPtr::operator=(const HasPtr &rhs)
{
    auto newp = new string(*rhs.ps);   // copy the underlying string
    delete ps;          // free the old memory
    ps = newp;          // copy data from rhs into this object
    i = rhs.i;
    return *this;       // return this object
}
```

In this assignment operator, we quite clearly first do the work of the constructor: The initializer of `newp` is identical to the initializer of `ps` in `HasPtr`'s copy constructor. As in the destructor, we next `delete` the `string` to which `ps` currently points. What remains is to copy the pointer to the newly allocated `string` and the `int` value from `rhs` into this object.

KEY CONCEPT: ASSIGNMENT OPERATORS

There are two points to keep in mind when you write an assignment operator:

- Assignment operators must work correctly if an object is assigned to itself.
- Most assignment operators share work with the destructor and copy constructor.

A good pattern to use when you write an assignment operator is to first copy the right-hand operand into a local temporary. *After* the copy is done, it is safe to destroy the existing members of the left-hand operand. Once the left-hand operand is destroyed, copy the data from the temporary into the members of the left-hand operand.

To illustrate the importance of guarding against self-assignment, consider what would happen if we wrote the assignment operator as

```
//  WRONG way to write an assignment operator!
HasPtr&
HasPtr::operator=(const HasPtr &rhs)
{
    delete ps;   // frees the string to which this object points
    // if rhs and *this are the same object, we're copying from deleted memory!
    ps = new string(*(rhs.ps));
    i = rhs.i;
    return *this;
}
```

If rhs and this object are the same object, deleting ps frees the string to which both *this and rhs point. When we attempt to copy *(rhs.ps) in the new expression, that pointer points to invalid memory. What happens is undefined.

WARNING It is crucially important for assignment operators to work correctly, even when an object is assigned to itself. A good way to do so is to copy the right-hand operand before destroying the left-hand operand.

EXERCISES SECTION 13.2.1

Exercise 13.23: Compare the copy-control members that you wrote for the solutions to the previous section's exercises to the code presented here. Be sure you understand the differences, if any, between your code and ours.

Exercise 13.24: What would happen if the version of HasPtr in this section didn't define a destructor? What if HasPtr didn't define the copy constructor?

Exercise 13.25: Assume we want to define a version of StrBlob that acts like a value. Also assume that we want to continue to use a shared_ptr so that our StrBlobPtr class can still use a weak_ptr to the vector. Your revised class will need a copy constructor and copy-assignment operator but will not need a destructor. Explain what the copy constructor and copy-assignment operators must do. Explain why the class does not need a destructor.

Exercise 13.26: Write your own version of the StrBlob class described in the previous exercise.

13.2.2 Defining Classes That Act Like Pointers

For our HasPtr class to act like a pointer, we need the copy constructor and copy-assignment operator to copy the pointer member, not the string to which that pointer points. Our class will still need its own destructor to free the memory allocated by the constructor that takes a string (§ 13.1.4, p. 504). In this case, though, the destructor cannot unilaterally free its associated string. It can do so only when the last HasPtr pointing to that string goes away.

The easiest way to make a class act like a pointer is to use shared_ptrs to manage the resources in the class. Copying (or assigning) a shared_ptr copies (assigns) the pointer to which the `shared_ptr` points. The `shared_ptr` class itself keeps track of how many users are sharing the pointed-to object. When there are no more users, the `shared_ptr` class takes care of freeing the resource.

However, sometimes we want to manage a resource directly. In such cases, it can be useful to use a **reference count** (§ 12.1.1, p. 452). To show how reference counting works, we'll redefine `HasPtr` to provide pointerlike behavior, but we will do our own reference counting.

Reference Counts

Reference counting works as follows:

- In addition to initializing the object, each constructor (other than the copy constructor) creates a counter. This counter will keep track of how many objects share state with the object we are creating. When we create an object, there is only one such object, so we initialize the counter to 1.

- The copy constructor does not allocate a new counter; instead, it copies the data members of its given object, including the counter. The copy constructor increments this shared counter, indicating that there is another user of that object's state.

- The destructor decrements the counter, indicating that there is one less user of the shared state. If the count goes to zero, the destructor deletes that state.

- The copy-assignment operator increments the right-hand operand's counter and decrements the counter of the left-hand operand. If the counter for the left-hand operand goes to zero, there are no more users. In this case, the copy-assignment operator must destroy the state of the left-hand operand.

The only wrinkle is deciding where to put the reference count. The counter cannot be a direct member of a `HasPtr` object. To see why, consider what happens in the following example:

```
HasPtr p1("Hiya!");
HasPtr p2(p1);   // p1 and p2 point to the same string
HasPtr p3(p1);   // p1, p2, and p3 all point to the same string
```

If the reference count is stored in each object, how can we update it correctly when p3 is created? We could increment the count in p1 and copy that count into p3, but how would we update the counter in p2?

One way to solve this problem is to store the counter in dynamic memory. When we create an object, we'll also allocate a new counter. When we copy or assign an object, we'll copy the pointer to the counter. That way the copy and the original will point to the same counter.

Defining a Reference-Counted Class

Using a reference count, we can write the pointerlike version of `HasPtr` as follows:

```
class HasPtr {
public:
    //  constructor allocates a new string and a new counter, which it sets to 1
    HasPtr(const std::string &s = std::string()):
      ps(new std::string(s)), i(0), use(new std::size_t(1)) {}
    //  copy constructor copies all three data members and increments the counter
    HasPtr(const HasPtr &p):
        ps(p.ps), i(p.i), use(p.use) { ++*use; }
    HasPtr& operator=(const HasPtr&);
    ~HasPtr();
private:
    std::string *ps;
    int     i;
    std::size_t *use;   //  member to keep track of how many objects share *ps
};
```

Here, we've added a new data member named `use` that will keep track of how many objects share the same `string`. The constructor that takes a `string` allocates this counter and initializes it to 1, indicating that there is one user of this object's `string` member.

Pointerlike Copy Members "Fiddle" the Reference Count

When we copy or assign a `HasPtr` object, we want the copy and the original to point to the same `string`. That is, when we copy a `HasPtr`, we'll copy `ps` itself, not the `string` to which `ps` points. When we make a copy, we also increment the counter associated with that `string`.

The copy constructor (which we defined inside the class) copies all three members from its given `HasPtr`. This constructor also increments the `use` member, indicating that there is another user for the `string` to which `ps` and `p.ps` point.

The destructor cannot unconditionally `delete ps`—there might be other objects pointing to that memory. Instead, the destructor decrements the reference count, indicating that one less object shares the `string`. If the counter goes to zero, then the destructor frees the memory to which both `ps` and `use` point:

```
HasPtr::~HasPtr()
{
    if (--*use == 0) {    //  if the reference count goes to 0
        delete ps;        //  delete the string
        delete use;       //  and the counter
    }
}
```

The copy-assignment operator, as usual, does the work common to the copy constructor and to the destructor. That is, the assignment operator must increment the counter of the right-hand operand (i.e., the work of the copy constructor) and decrement the counter of the left-hand operand, deleting the memory used if appropriate (i.e., the work of the destructor).

Also, as usual, the operator must handle self-assignment. We do so by incrementing the count in `rhs` before decrementing the count in the left-hand object.

That way if both objects are the same, the counter will have been incremented before we check to see if `ps` (and `use`) should be deleted:

```
HasPtr& HasPtr::operator=(const HasPtr &rhs)
{
    ++*rhs.use;     // increment the use count of the right-hand operand
    if (--*use == 0) {      // then decrement this object's counter
        delete ps;          // if no other users
        delete use;         // free this object's allocated members
    }
    ps = rhs.ps;            // copy data from rhs into this object
    i = rhs.i;
    use = rhs.use;
    return *this;           // return this object
}
```

EXERCISES SECTION 13.2.2

Exercise 13.27: Define your own reference-counted version of `HasPtr`.

Exercise 13.28: Given the following classes, implement a default constructor and the necessary copy-control members.

```
(a) class TreeNode {            (b) class BinStrTree {
        private:                         private:
            std::string value;              TreeNode *root;
            int        count;           };
            TreeNode   *left;
            TreeNode   *right;
    };
```

13.3 Swap

In addition to defining the copy-control members, classes that manage resources often also define a function named `swap` (§ 9.2.5, p. 339). Defining `swap` is particularly important for classes that we plan to use with algorithms that reorder elements (§ 10.2.3, p. 383). Such algorithms call `swap` whenever they need to exchange two elements.

If a class defines its own `swap`, then the algorithm uses that class-specific version. Otherwise, it uses the `swap` function defined by the library. Although, as usual, we don't know how `swap` is implemented, conceptually it's easy to see that swapping two objects involves a copy and two assignments. For example, code to swap two objects of our valuelike `HasPtr` class (§ 13.2.1, p. 511) might look something like:

```
HasPtr temp = v1;   // make a temporary copy of the value of v1
v1 = v2;            // assign the value of v2 to v1
v2 = temp;          // assign the saved value of v1 to v2
```

This code copies the `string` that was originally in `v1` twice—once when the `HasPtr` copy constructor copies `v1` into `temp` and again when the assignment operator assigns `temp` to `v2`. It also copies the `string` that was originally in `v2` when it assigns `v2` to `v1`. As we've seen, copying a valuelike `HasPtr` allocates a new `string` and copies the `string` to which the `HasPtr` points.

In principle, none of this memory allocation is necessary. Rather than allocating new copies of the `string`, we'd like `swap` to swap the pointers. That is, we'd like swapping two `HasPtr`s to execute as:

```
string *temp = v1.ps;   // make a temporary copy of the pointer in v1.ps
v1.ps = v2.ps;          // assign the pointer in v2.ps to v1.ps
v2.ps = temp;           // assign the saved pointer in v1.ps to v2.ps
```

Writing Our Own `swap` Function

We can override the default behavior of `swap` by defining a version of `swap` that operates on our class. The typical implementation of `swap` is:

```
class HasPtr {
    friend void swap(HasPtr&, HasPtr&);
    // other members as in § 13.2.1 (p. 511)
};
inline
void swap(HasPtr &lhs, HasPtr &rhs)
{
    using std::swap;
    swap(lhs.ps, rhs.ps); // swap the pointers, not the string data
    swap(lhs.i, rhs.i);   // swap the int members
}
```

We start by declaring `swap` as a `friend` to give it access to `HasPtr`'s (`private`) data members. Because `swap` exists to optimize our code, we've defined `swap` as an `inline` function (§ 6.5.2, p. 238). The body of `swap` calls `swap` on each of the data members of the given object. In this case, we first `swap` the pointers and then the `int` members of the objects bound to `rhs` and `lhs`.

> Unlike the copy-control members, `swap` is never necessary. However, defining `swap` can be an important optimization for classes that allocate resources.

`swap` Functions Should Call `swap`, Not `std::swap`

There is one important subtlety in this code: Although it doesn't matter in this particular case, it is essential that `swap` functions call `swap` and not `std::swap`. In the `HasPtr` function, the data members have built-in types. There is no type-specific version of `swap` for the built-in types. In this case, these calls will invoke the library `std::swap`.

However, if a class has a member that has its own type-specific `swap` function, calling `std::swap` would be a mistake. For example, assume we had another class named `Foo` that has a member named `h`, which has type `HasPtr`. If we did not write a Foo version of swap, then the library version of swap would be used. As we've already seen, the library swap makes unnecessary copies of the strings managed by HasPtr.

We can avoid these copies by writing a swap function for Foo. However, if we wrote the Foo version of swap as:

```
void swap(Foo &lhs, Foo &rhs)
{
    // WRONG: this function uses the library version of swap, not the HasPtr version
    std::swap(lhs.h, rhs.h);
    // swap other members of type Foo
}
```

this code would compile and execute. However, there would be no performance difference between this code and simply using the default version of swap. The problem is that we've explicitly requested the library version of swap. However, we don't want the version in std; we want the one defined for HasPtr objects.

The right way to write this swap function is:

```
void swap(Foo &lhs, Foo &rhs)
{
    using std::swap;
    swap(lhs.h, rhs.h);   // uses the HasPtr version of swap
    // swap other members of type Foo
}
```

Each call to swap must be unqualified. That is, each call should be to swap, not std::swap. For reasons we'll explain in § 16.3 (p. 697), if there is a type-specific version of swap, that version will be a better match than the one defined in std. As a result, if there is a type-specific version of swap, calls to swap will match that type-specific version. If there is no type-specific version, then—assuming there is a using declaration for swap in scope—calls to swap will use the version in std.

Very careful readers may wonder why the using declaration inside swap does not hide the declarations for the HasPtr version of swap (§ 6.4.1, p. 234). We'll explain the reasons for why this code works in § 18.2.3 (p. 798).

Using swap in Assignment Operators

Classes that define swap often use swap to define their assignment operator. These operators use a technique known as **copy and swap**. This technique *swaps* the left-hand operand with a *copy* of the right-hand operand:

```
// note rhs is passed by value, which means the HasPtr copy constructor
// copies the string in the right-hand operand into rhs
HasPtr& HasPtr::operator=(HasPtr rhs)
{
    // swap the contents of the left-hand operand with the local variable rhs
    swap(*this, rhs);  // rhs now points to the memory this object had used
    return *this;      // rhs is destroyed, which deletes the pointer in rhs
}
```

In this version of the assignment operator, the parameter is not a reference. Instead, we pass the right-hand operand by value. Thus, `rhs` is a copy of the right-hand operand. Copying a `HasPtr` allocates a new copy of that object's `string`.

In the body of the assignment operator, we call `swap`, which swaps the data members of `rhs` with those in `*this`. This call puts the pointer that had been in the left-hand operand into `rhs`, and puts the pointer that was in `rhs` into `*this`. Thus, after the `swap`, the pointer member in `*this` points to the newly allocated `string` that is a copy of the right-hand operand.

When the assignment operator finishes, `rhs` is destroyed and the `HasPtr` destructor is run. That destructor `deletes` the memory to which `rhs` now points, thus freeing the memory to which the left-hand operand had pointed.

The interesting thing about this technique is that it automatically handles self assignment and is automatically exception safe. By copying the right-hand operand before changing the left-hand operand, it handles self assignment in the same was as we did in our original assignment operator (§ 13.2.1, p. 512). It manages exception safety in the same way as the original definition as well. The only code that might throw is the new expression inside the copy constructor. If an exception occurs, it will happen before we have changed the left-hand operand.

> Assignment operators that use copy and swap are automatically exception safe and correctly handle self-assignment.

EXERCISES SECTION 13.3

Exercise 13.29: Explain why the calls to swap inside swap(HasPtr&, HasPtr&) do not cause a recursion loop.

Exercise 13.30: Write and test a swap function for your valuelike version of HasPtr. Give your swap a print statement that notes when it is executed.

Exercise 13.31: Give your class a < operator and define a vector of HasPtrs. Give that vector some elements and then sort the vector. Note when swap is called.

Exercise 13.32: Would the pointerlike version of HasPtr benefit from defining a swap function? If so, what is the benefit? If not, why not?

13.4 A Copy-Control Example

Although copy control is most often needed for classes that allocate resources, resource management is not the only reason why a class might need to define these members. Some classes have bookkeeping or other actions that the copy-control members must perform.

As an example of a class that needs copy control in order to do some bookkeeping, we'll sketch out two classes that might be used in a mail-handling application. These classes, `Message` and `Folder`, represent, respectively, email (or other kinds of) messages, and directories in which a message might appear. Each Message can appear in multiple Folders. However, there will be only one copy of the contents of any given Message. That way, if the contents of a Message are changed, those changes will appear when we view that Message from any of its Folders.

To keep track of which Messages are in which Folders, each Message will store a set of pointers to the Folders in which it appears, and each Folder will contain a set of pointers to its Messages. Figure 13.1 illustrates this design.

Figure 13.1: Message and Folder Class Design

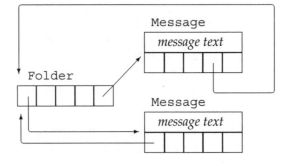

Our Message class will provide save and remove operations to add or remove a Message from a specified Folder. To create a new Message, we will specify the contents of the message but no Folder. To put a Message in a particular Folder, we must call save.

When we copy a Message, the copy and the original will be distinct Messages, but both Messages should appear in the same set of Folders. Thus, copying a Message will copy the contents and the set of Folder pointers. It must also add a pointer to the newly created Message to each of those Folders.

When we destroy a Message, that Message no longer exists. Therefore, destroying a Message must remove pointers to that Message from the Folders that had contained that Message.

When we assign one Message to another, we'll replace the contents of the left-hand Message with those in the right-hand side. We must also update the set of Folders, removing the left-hand Message from its previous Folders and adding that Message to the Folders in which the right-hand Message appears.

Looking at this list of operations, we can see that both the destructor and the copy-assignment operator have to remove this Message from the Folders that point to it. Similarly, both the copy constructor and the copy-assignment operator add a Message to a given list of Folders. We'll define a pair of private utility functions to do these tasks.

The copy-assignment operator often does the same work as is needed in the copy constructor and destructor. In such cases, the common work should be put in private utility functions.

The `Folder` class will need analogous copy control members to add or remove itself from the `Messages` it stores.

We'll leave the design and implementation of the `Folder` class as an exercise. However, we'll assume that the `Folder` class has members named `addMsg` and `remMsg` that do whatever work is need to add or remove this `Message`, respectively, from the set of messages in the given `Folder`.

The `Message` Class

Given this design, we can write our `Message` class as follows:

```
class Message {
    friend class Folder;
public:
    // folders is implicitly initialized to the empty set
    explicit Message(const std::string &str = ""):
        contents(str) { }
    // copy control to manage pointers to this Message
    Message(const Message&);                     // copy constructor
    Message& operator=(const Message&);   // copy assignment
    ~Message();                                   // destructor
    // add/remove this Message from the specified Folder's set of messages
    void save(Folder&);
    void remove(Folder&);
private:
    std::string contents;          // actual message text
    std::set<Folder*> folders;  // Folders that have this Message
    // utility functions used by copy constructor, assignment, and destructor
    // add this Message to the Folders that point to the parameter
    void add_to_Folders(const Message&);
    // remove this Message from every Folder in folders
    void remove_from_Folders();
};
```

The class defines two data members: `contents`, to store the message text, and `folders`, to store pointers to the `Folders` in which this `Message` appears. The constructor that takes a `string` copies the given `string` into `contents` and (implicitly) initializes `folders` to the empty set. Because this constructor has a default argument, it is also the `Message` default constructor (§ 7.5.1, p. 290).

The `save` and `remove` Members

Aside from copy control, the `Message` class has only two `public` members: `save`, which puts the `Message` in the given `Folder`, and `remove`, which takes it out:

```
void Message::save(Folder &f)
{
    folders.insert(&f);  // add the given Folder to our list of Folders
    f.addMsg(this);      // add this Message to f's set of Messages
}
```

```
void Message::remove(Folder &f)
{
    folders.erase(&f);  // take the given Folder out of our list of Folders
    f.remMsg(this);     // remove this Message to f's set of Messages
}
```

To save (or remove) a `Message` requires updating the `folders` member of the `Message`. When we `save` a `Message`, we store a pointer to the given `Folder`; when we `remove` a `Message`, we remove that pointer.

These operations must also update the given `Folder`. Updating a `Folder` is a job that the `Folder` class controls through its `addMsg` and `remMsg` members, which will add or remove a pointer to a given `Message`, respectively.

Copy Control for the `Message` Class

When we copy a `Message`, the copy should appear in the same `Folders` as the original `Message`. As a result, we must traverse the `set` of `Folder` pointers adding a pointer to the new `Message` to each `Folder` that points to the original `Message`. Both the copy constructor and the copy-assignment operator will need to do this work, so we'll define a function to do this common processing:

```
// add this Message to Folders that point to m
void Message::add_to_Folders(const Message &m)
{
    for (auto f : m.folders) // for each Folder that holds m
        f->addMsg(this);     // add a pointer to this Message to that Folder
}
```

Here we call `addMsg` on each `Folder` in `m.folders`. The `addMsg` function will add a pointer to this `Message` to that `Folder`.

The `Message` copy constructor copies the data members of the given object:

```
Message::Message(const Message &m) :
    contents(m.contents), folders(m.folders)
{
    add_to_Folders(m); // add this Message to the Folders that point to m
}
```

and calls `add_to_Folders` to add a pointer to the newly created `Message` to each `Folder` that contains the original `Message`.

The `Message` Destructor

When a `Message` is destroyed, we must remove this `Message` from the `Folders` that point to it. This work is shared with the copy-assignment operator, so we'll define a common function to do it:

```
// remove this Message from the corresponding Folders
void Message::remove_from_Folders()
{
    for (auto f : folders) // for each pointer in folders
        f->remMsg(this);   // remove this Message from that Folder
}
```

The implementation of the `remove_from_Folders` function is similar to that of `add_to_Folders`, except that it uses `remMsg` to remove the current `Message`.

Given the `remove_from_Folders` function, writing the destructor is trivial:

```
Message::~Message()
{
    remove_from_Folders();
}
```

The call to `remove_from_Folders` ensures that no `Folder` has a pointer to the `Message` we are destroying. The compiler automatically invokes the `string` destructor to free `contents` and the `set` destructor to clean up the memory used by those members.

Message Copy-Assignment Operator

In common with most assignment operators, our `Folder` copy-assignment operator must do the work of the copy constructor and the destructor. As usual, it is crucial that we structure our code to execute correctly even if the left- and right-hand operands happen to be the same object.

In this case, we protect against self-assignment by removing pointers to this `Message` from the `folders` of the left-hand operand before inserting pointers in the `folders` in the right-hand operand:

```
Message& Message::operator=(const Message &rhs)
{
    // handle self-assignment by removing pointers before inserting them
    remove_from_Folders();        // update existing Folders
    contents = rhs.contents;      // copy message contents from rhs
    folders = rhs.folders;        // copy Folder pointers from rhs
    add_to_Folders(rhs);          // add this Message to those Folders
    return *this;
}
```

If the left- and right-hand operands are the same object, then they have the same address. Had we called `remove_from_folders` after calling `add_to_folders`, we would have removed this `Message` from all of its corresponding `Folders`.

A swap Function for Message

The library defines versions of swap for both `string` and `set` (§ 9.2.5, p. 339). As a result, our `Message` class will benefit from defining its own version of swap. By defining a `Message`-specific version of swap, we can avoid extraneous copies of the `contents` and `folders` members.

However, our swap function must also manage the `Folder` pointers that point to the swapped `Messages`. After a call such as `swap(m1, m2)`, the `Folders` that had pointed to `m1` must now point to `m2`, and vice versa.

We'll manage the `Folder` pointers by making two passes through each of the `folders` members. The first pass will remove the `Messages` from their respective `Folders`. We'll next call swap to swap the data members. We'll make the second pass through `folders` this time adding pointers to the swapped `Messages`:

```
void swap(Message &lhs, Message &rhs)
{
    using std::swap;   // not strictly needed in this case, but good habit
    // remove pointers to each Message from their (original) respective Folders
    for (auto f: lhs.folders)
        f->remMsg(&lhs);
    for (auto f: rhs.folders)
        f->remMsg(&rhs);
    // swap the contents and Folder pointer sets
    swap(lhs.folders, rhs.folders);   // uses swap(set&, set&)
    swap(lhs.contents, rhs.contents); // swap(string&, string&)
    // add pointers to each Message to their (new) respective Folders
    for (auto f: lhs.folders)
        f->addMsg(&lhs);
    for (auto f: rhs.folders)
        f->addMsg(&rhs);
}
```

EXERCISES SECTION 13.4

Exercise 13.33: Why is the parameter to the save and remove members of Message a Folder&? Why didn't we define that parameter as Folder? Or const Folder&?

Exercise 13.34: Write the Message class as described in this section.

Exercise 13.35: What would happen if Message used the synthesized versions of the copy-control members?

Exercise 13.36: Design and implement the corresponding Folder class. That class should hold a set that points to the Messages in that Folder.

Exercise 13.37: Add members to the Message class to insert or remove a given Folder* into folders. These members are analogous to Folder's addMsg and remMsg operations.

Exercise 13.38: We did not use copy and swap to define the Message assignment operator. Why do you suppose this is so?

13.5 Classes That Manage Dynamic Memory

Some classes need to allocate a varying amount of storage at run time. Such classes often can (and if they can, generally should) use a library container to hold their data. For example, our StrBlob class uses a vector to manage the underlying storage for its elements.

However, this strategy does not work for every class; some classes need to do their own allocation. Such classes generally must define their own copy-control members to manage the memory they allocate.

As an example, we'll implement a simplification of the library `vector` class. Among the simplifications we'll make is that our class will not be a template. Instead, our class will hold `strings`. Thus, we'll call our class `StrVec`.

`StrVec` Class Design

Recall that the `vector` class stores its elements in contiguous storage. To obtain acceptable performance, `vector` preallocates enough storage to hold more elements than are needed (§ 9.4, p. 355). Each `vector` member that adds elements checks whether there is space available for another element. If so, the member constructs an object in the next available spot. If there isn't space left, then the `vector` is reallocated: The `vector` obtains new space, moves the existing elements into that space, frees the old space, and adds the new element.

We'll use a similar strategy in our `StrVec` class. We'll use an `allocator` to obtain raw memory (§ 12.2.2, p. 481). Because the memory an `allocator` allocates is unconstructed, we'll use the `allocator`'s `construct` member to create objects in that space when we need to add an element. Similarly, when we remove an element, we'll use the `destroy` member to destroy the element.

Each `StrVec` will have three pointers into the space it uses for its elements:

- `elements`, which points to the first element in the allocated memory

- `first_free`, which points just after the last actual element

- `cap`, which points just past the end of the allocated memory

Figure 13.2 illustrates the meaning of these pointers.

Figure 13.2: `StrVec` Memory Allocation Strategy

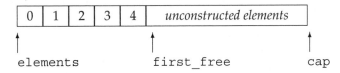

In addition to these pointers, `StrVec` will have a member named `alloc` that is an `allocator<string>`. The `alloc` member will allocate the memory used by a `StrVec`. Our class will also have four utility functions:

- `alloc_n_copy` will allocate space and copy a given range of elements.

- `free` will destroy the constructed elements and deallocate the space.

- `chk_n_alloc` will ensure that there is room to add at least one more element to the `StrVec`. If there isn't room for another element, `chk_n_alloc` will call `reallocate` to get more space.

- `reallocate` will reallocate the `StrVec` when it runs out of space.

Although our focus is on the implementation, we'll also define a few members from `vector`'s interface.

StrVec Class Definition

Having sketched the implementation, we can now define our StrVec class:

```cpp
// simplified implementation of the memory allocation strategy for a vector-like class
class StrVec {
public:
    StrVec(): // the allocator member is default initialized
        elements(nullptr), first_free(nullptr), cap(nullptr) { }
    StrVec(const StrVec&);                    // copy constructor
    StrVec &operator=(const StrVec&);  // copy assignment
    ~StrVec();                                // destructor
    void push_back(const std::string&);   // copy the element
    size_t size() const { return first_free - elements; }
    size_t capacity() const { return cap - elements; }
    std::string *begin() const { return elements; }
    std::string *end() const { return first_free; }
    // ...
private:
    std::allocator<std::string> alloc; // allocates the elements
    // used by the functions that add elements to the StrVec
    void chk_n_alloc()
        { if (size() == capacity()) reallocate(); }
    // utilities used by the copy constructor, assignment operator, and destructor
    std::pair<std::string*, std::string*> alloc_n_copy
        (const std::string*, const std::string*);
    void free();              // destroy the elements and free the space
    void reallocate();        // get more space and copy the existing elements
    std::string *elements;    // pointer to the first element in the array
    std::string *first_free;  // pointer to the first free element in the array
    std::string *cap;         // pointer to one past the end of the array
};
```

The class body defines several of its members:

- The default constructor (implicitly) default initializes alloc and (explicitly) initializes the pointers to nullptr, indicating that there are no elements.

- The size member returns the number of elements actually in use, which is equal to first_free - elements.

- The capacity member returns the number of elements that the StrVec can hold, which is equal to cap - elements.

- The chk_n_alloc causes the StrVec to be reallocated when there is no room to add another element, which happens when cap == first_free.

- The begin and end members return pointers to the first (i.e., elements) and one past the last constructed element (i.e., first_free), respectively.

Using construct

The push_back function calls chk_n_alloc to ensure that there is room for an element. If necessary, chk_n_alloc will call reallocate. When chk_n_alloc returns, push_back knows that there is room for the new element. It asks its allocator member to construct a new last element:

```
void StrVec::push_back(const string& s)
{
    chk_n_alloc();  // ensure that there is room for another element
    // construct a copy of s in the element to which first_free points
    alloc.construct(first_free++, s);
}
```

When we use an allocator to allocate memory, we must remember that the memory is *unconstructed* (§ 12.2.2, p. 482). To use this raw memory we must call construct, which will construct an object in that memory. The first argument to construct must be a pointer to unconstructed space allocated by a call to allocate. The remaining arguments determine which constructor to use to construct the object that will go in that space. In this case, there is only one additional argument. That argument has type string, so this call uses the string copy constructor.

It is worth noting that the call to construct also increments first_free to indicate that a new element has been constructed. It uses the postfix increment (§ 4.5, p. 147), so this call constructs an object in the current value of first_free and increments first_free to point to the next, unconstructed element.

The alloc_n_copy Member

The alloc_n_copy member is called when we copy or assign a StrVec. Our StrVec class, like vector, will have valuelike behavior (§ 13.2.1, p. 511); when we copy or assign a StrVec, we have to allocate independent memory and copy the elements from the original to the new StrVec.

The alloc_n_copy member will allocate enough storage to hold its given range of elements, and will copy those elements into the newly allocated space. This function returns a pair (§ 11.2.3, p. 426) of pointers, pointing to the beginning of the new space and just past the last element it copied:

```
pair<string*, string*>
StrVec::alloc_n_copy(const string *b, const string *e)
{
    // allocate space to hold as many elements as are in the range
    auto data = alloc.allocate(e - b);
    // initialize and return a pair constructed from data and
    // the value returned by uninitialized_copy
    return {data, uninitialized_copy(b, e, data)};
}
```

alloc_n_copy calculates how much space to allocate by subtracting the pointer to the first element from the pointer one past the last. Having allocated memory, the function next has to construct copies of the given elements in that space.

It does the copy in the return statement, which list initializes the return value (§ 6.3.2, p. 226). The first member of the returned pair points to the start of the allocated memory; the second is the value returned from uninitialized_copy

(§ 12.2.2, p. 483). That value will be pointer positioned one element past the last constructed element.

The `free` Member

The `free` member has two responsibilities: It must `destroy` the elements and then deallocate the space that this `StrVec` itself allocated. The `for` loop calls the `allocator` member `destroy` in reverse order, starting with the last constructed element and finishing with the first:

```
void StrVec::free()
{
    // may not pass deallocate a 0 pointer; if elements is 0, there's no work to do
    if (elements) {
        // destroy the old elements in reverse order
        for (auto p = first_free; p != elements; /* empty */)
            alloc.destroy(--p);
        alloc.deallocate(elements, cap - elements);
    }
}
```

The `destroy` function runs the `string` destructor. The `string` destructor frees whatever storage was allocated by the `string`s themselves.

Once the elements have been destroyed, we free the space that this `StrVec` allocated by calling `deallocate`. The pointer we pass to `deallocate` must be one that was previously generated by a call to `allocate`. Therefore, we first check that `elements` is not null before calling `deallocate`.

Copy-Control Members

Given our `alloc_n_copy` and `free` members, the copy-control members of our class are straightforward. The copy constructor calls `alloc_n_copy`:

```
StrVec::StrVec(const StrVec &s)
{
    // call alloc_n_copy to allocate exactly as many elements as in s
    auto newdata = alloc_n_copy(s.begin(), s.end());
    elements = newdata.first;
    first_free = cap = newdata.second;
}
```

and assigns the results from that call to the data members. The return value from `alloc_n_copy` is a `pair` of pointers. The `first` pointer points to the first constructed element and the `second` points just past the last constructed element. Because `alloc_n_copy` allocates space for exactly as many elements as it is given, `cap` also points just past the last constructed element.

The destructor calls `free`:

```
StrVec::~StrVec() { free(); }
```

The copy-assignment operator calls `alloc_n_copy` before freeing its existing elements. By doing so it protects against self-assignment:

```
StrVec &StrVec::operator=(const StrVec &rhs)
{
    // call alloc_n_copy to allocate exactly as many elements as in rhs
    auto data = alloc_n_copy(rhs.begin(), rhs.end());
    free();
    elements = data.first;
    first_free = cap = data.second;
    return *this;
}
```

Like the copy constructor, the copy-assignment operator uses the values returned from `alloc_n_copy` to initialize its pointers.

Moving, Not Copying, Elements during Reallocation

Before we write the `reallocate` member, we should think a bit about what it must do. This function will

- Allocate memory for a new, larger array of `string`s
- Construct the first part of that space to hold the existing elements
- Destroy the elements in the existing memory and deallocate that memory

Looking at this list of steps, we can see that reallocating a `StrVec` entails copying each `string` from the old `StrVec` memory to the new. Although we don't know the details of how `string` is implemented, we do know that `string`s have valuelike behavior. When we copy a `string`, the new `string` and the original `string` are independent from each other. Changes made to the original don't affect the copy, and vice versa.

Because `string`s act like values, we can conclude that each `string` must have its own copy of the characters that make up that `string`. Copying a `string` must allocate memory for those characters, and destroying a `string` must free the memory used by that `string`.

Copying a `string` copies the data because ordinarily after we copy a `string`, there are two users of that `string`. However, when `reallocate` copies the `string`s in a `StrVec`, there will be only one user of these `string`s after the copy. As soon as we copy the elements from the old space to the new, we will immediately destroy the original `string`s.

Copying the data in these `string`s is unnecessary. Our `StrVec`'s performance will be *much* better if we can avoid the overhead of allocating and deallocating the `string`s themselves each time we reallocate.

Move Constructors and `std::move`

We can avoid copying the `string`s by using two facilities introduced by the new library. First, several of the library classes, including `string`, define so-called "move constructors." The details of how the `string` move constructor works—like any other detail about the implementation—are not disclosed. However, we do know that move constructors typically operate by "moving" resources from the given object to the object being constructed. We also know that the library guarantees that the "moved-from" string remains in a valid, destructible state. For string, we can imagine that each string has a pointer to an array of char. Presumably the string move constructor copies the pointer rather than allocating space for and copying the characters themselves.

The second facility we'll use is a library function named **move**, which is defined in the utility header. For now, there are two important points to know about move. First, for reasons we'll explain in § 13.6.1 (p. 532), when reallocate constructs the strings in the new memory it must call move to signal that it wants to use the string move constructor. If it omits the call to move the string the copy constructor will be used. Second, for reasons we'll cover in § 18.2.3 (p. 798), we usually do not provide a using declaration (§ 3.1, p. 82) for move. When we use move, we call std::move, not move.

The reallocate Member

Using this information, we can now write our reallocate member. We'll start by calling allocate to allocate new space. We'll double the capacity of the StrVec each time we reallocate. If the StrVec is empty, we allocate room for one element:

```
void StrVec::reallocate()
{
    // we'll allocate space for twice as many elements as the current size
    auto newcapacity = size() ? 2 * size() : 1;
    // allocate new memory
    auto newdata = alloc.allocate(newcapacity);
    // move the data from the old memory to the new
    auto dest = newdata;    // points to the next free position in the new array
    auto elem = elements;   // points to the next element in the old array
    for (size_t i = 0; i != size(); ++i)
        alloc.construct(dest++, std::move(*elem++));
    free();    // free the old space once we've moved the elements
    // update our data structure to point to the new elements
    elements = newdata;
    first_free = dest;
    cap = elements + newcapacity;
}
```

The for loop iterates through the existing elements and constructs a corresponding element in the new space. We use dest to point to the memory in which to construct the new string, and use elem to point to an element in the original array. We use postfix increment to move the dest (and elem) pointers one element at a time through these two arrays.

The second argument in the call to construct (i.e., the one that determines which constructor to use (§ 12.2.2, p. 482)) is the value returned by move. Calling move returns a result that causes construct to use the string move constructor. Because we're using the move constructor, the memory managed by those strings will not be copied. Instead, each string we construct will take over ownership of the memory from the string to which elem points.

After moving the elements, we call `free` to destroy the old elements and free the memory that this `StrVec` was using before the call to `reallocate`. The strings themselves no longer manage the memory to which they had pointed; responsibility for their data has been moved to the elements in the new `StrVec` memory. We don't know what value the strings in the old `StrVec` memory have, but we are guaranteed that it is safe to run the `string` destructor on these objects.

What remains is to update the pointers to address the newly allocated and initialized array. The `first_free` and `cap` pointers are set to denote one past the last constructed element and one past the end of the allocated space, respectively.

EXERCISES SECTION 13.5

Exercise 13.39: Write your own version of `StrVec`, including versions of `reserve`, `capacity` (§ 9.4, p. 356), and `resize` (§ 9.3.5, p. 352).

Exercise 13.40: Add a constructor that takes an `initializer_list<string>` to your `StrVec` class.

Exercise 13.41: Why did we use postfix increment in the call to `construct` inside `push_back`? What would happen if it used the prefix increment?

Exercise 13.42: Test your `StrVec` class by using it in place of the `vector<string>` in your `TextQuery` and `QueryResult` classes (§ 12.3, p. 484).

Exercise 13.43: Rewrite the `free` member to use `for_each` and a lambda (§ 10.3.2, p. 388) in place of the `for` loop to `destroy` the elements. Which implementation do you prefer, and why?

Exercise 13.44: Write a class named `String` that is a simplified version of the library `string` class. Your class should have at least a default constructor and a constructor that takes a pointer to a C-style string. Use an `allocator` to allocate memory that your `String` class uses.

13.6 Moving Objects

One of the major features in the new standard is the ability to move rather than copy an object. As we saw in § 13.1.1 (p. 497), copies are made in many circumstances. In some of these circumstances, an object is immediately destroyed after it is copied. In those cases, moving, rather than copying, the object can provide a significant performance boost.

As we've just seen, our `StrVec` class is a good example of this kind of superfluous copy. During reallocation, there is no need to copy—rather than move—the elements from the old memory to the new. A second reason to move rather than copy occurs in classes such as the IO or `unique_ptr` classes. These classes have a resource (such as a pointer or an IO buffer) that may not be shared. Hence, objects of these types can't be copied but can be moved.

Under earlier versions of the language, there was no direct way to move an object. We had to make a copy even if there was no need for the copy. If the objects are large, or if the objects themselves require memory allocation (e.g., `string`s), making a needless copy can be expensive. Similarly, in previous versions of the library, classes stored in a container had to be copyable. Under the new standard, we can use containers on types that cannot be copied so long as they can be moved.

> **Note** The library containers, `string`, and `shared_ptr` classes support move as well as copy. The IO and `unique_ptr` classes can be moved but not copied.

13.6.1 Rvalue References

To support move operations, the new standard introduced a new kind of reference, an **rvalue reference**. An rvalue reference is a reference that must be bound to an rvalue. An rvalue reference is obtained by using `&&` rather than `&`. As we'll see, rvalue references have the important property that they may be bound only to an object that is about to be destroyed. As a result, we are free to "move" resources from an rvalue reference to another object.

Recall that lvalue and rvalue are properties of an expression (§ 4.1.1, p. 135). Some expressions yield or require lvalues; others yield or require rvalues. Generally speaking, an lvalue expression refers to an object's identity whereas an rvalue expression refers to an object's value.

Like any reference, an rvalue reference is just another name for an object. As we know, we cannot bind regular references—which we'll refer to as **lvalue references** when we need to distinguish them from rvalue references—to expressions that require a conversion, to literals, or to expressions that return an rvalue (§ 2.3.1, p. 51). Rvalue references have the opposite binding properties: We can bind an rvalue reference to these kinds of expressions, but we cannot directly bind an rvalue reference to an lvalue:

```
int i = 42;
int &r = i;              //  ok: r refers to i
int &&rr = i;            //  error: cannot bind an rvalue reference to an lvalue
int &r2 = i * 42;        //  error: i * 42 is an rvalue
const int &r3 = i * 42;  //  ok: we can bind a reference to const to an rvalue
int &&rr2 = i * 42;      //  ok: bind rr2 to the result of the multiplication
```

Functions that return lvalue references, along with the assignment, subscript, dereference, and prefix increment/decrement operators, are all examples of expressions that return lvalues. We can bind an lvalue reference to the result of any of these expressions.

Functions that return a nonreference type, along with the arithmetic, relational, bitwise, and postfix increment/decrement operators, all yield rvalues. We cannot bind an lvalue reference to these expressions, but we can bind either an lvalue reference to `const` or an rvalue reference to such expressions.

Lvalues Persist; Rvalues Are Ephemeral

Looking at the list of lvalue and rvalue expressions, it should be clear that lvalues and rvalues differ from each other in an important manner: Lvalues have persistent state, whereas rvalues are either literals or temporary objects created in the course of evaluating expressions.

Because rvalue references can only be bound to temporaries, we know that

• The referred-to object is about to be destroyed

• There can be no other users of that object

These facts together mean that code that uses an rvalue reference is free to take over resources from the object to which the reference refers.

 Rvalue references refer to objects that are about to be destroyed. Hence, we can "steal" state from an object bound to an rvalue reference.

Variables Are Lvalues

Although we rarely think about it this way, a variable is an expression with one operand and no operator. Like any other expression, a variable expression has the lvalue/rvalue property. Variable expressions are lvalues. It may be surprising, but as a consequence, we cannot bind an rvalue reference to a variable defined as an rvalue reference type:

```
int &&rr1 = 42;     //  ok: literals are rvalues
int &&rr2 = rr1;    //  error: the expression rr1 is an lvalue!
```

Given our previous observation that rvalues represent ephemeral objects, it should not be surprising that a variable is an lvalue. After all, a variable persists until it goes out of scope.

 A variable is an lvalue; we cannot directly bind an rvalue reference to a variable *even if that variable was defined as an rvalue reference type.*

The Library move Function

Although we cannot directly bind an rvalue reference to an lvalue, we can explicitly cast an lvalue to its corresponding rvalue reference type. We can also obtain an rvalue reference bound to an lvalue by calling a new library function named **move**, which is defined in the `utility` header. The move function uses facilities that we'll describe in § 16.2.6 (p. 690) to return an rvalue reference to its given object.

```
int &&rr3 = std::move(rr1);   // ok
```

Calling move tells the compiler that we have an lvalue that we want to treat as if it were an rvalue. It is essential to realize that the call to move promises that we do not intend to use rr1 again except to assign to it or to destroy it. After a call to move, we cannot make any assumptions about the value of the moved-from object.

Note We can destroy a moved-from object and can assign a new value to it, but we cannot use the value of a moved-from object.

As we've seen, differently from how we use most names from the library, we do not provide a using declaration (§ 3.1, p. 82) for move (§ 13.5, p. 530). We call std::move not move. We'll explain the reasons for this usage in § 18.2.3 (p. 798).

WARNING Code that uses move should use std::move, not move. Doing so avoids potential name collisions.

EXERCISES SECTION 13.6.1

Exercise 13.45: Distinguish between an rvalue reference and an lvalue reference.

Exercise 13.46: Which kind of reference can be bound to the following initializers?

```
int f();
vector<int> vi(100);
int? r1 = f();
int? r2 = vi[0];
int? r3 = r1;
int? r4 = vi[0] * f();
```

Exercise 13.47: Give the copy constructor and copy-assignment operator in your String class from exercise 13.44 in § 13.5 (p. 531) a statement that prints a message each time the function is executed.

Exercise 13.48: Define a vector<String> and call push_back several times on that vector. Run your program and see how often Strings are copied.

 ## 13.6.2 Move Constructor and Move Assignment

Like the string class (and other library classes), our own classes can benefit from being able to be moved as well as copied. To enable move operations for our own types, we define a move constructor and a move-assignment operator. These members are similar to the corresponding copy operations, but they "steal" resources from their given object rather than copy them.

Like the copy constructor, the move constructor has an initial parameter that is a reference to the class type. Differently from the copy constructor, the reference parameter in the move constructor is an rvalue reference. As in the copy constructor, any additional parameters must all have default arguments.

In addition to moving resources, the move constructor must ensure that the moved-from object is left in a state such that destroying that object will be harmless. In particular, once its resources are moved, the original object must no longer point to those moved resources—responsibility for those resources has been assumed by the newly created object.

As an example, we'll define the `StrVec` move constructor to move rather than copy the elements from one `StrVec` to another:

```
StrVec::StrVec(StrVec &&s) noexcept   // move won't throw any exceptions
    // member initializers take over the resources in s
    : elements(s.elements), first_free(s.first_free), cap(s.cap)
{
    // leave s in a state in which it is safe to run the destructor
    s.elements = s.first_free = s.cap = nullptr;
}
```

We'll explain the use of `noexcept` (which signals that our constructor does not throw any exceptions) shortly, but let's first look at what this constructor does.

Unlike the copy constructor, the move constructor does not allocate any new memory; it takes over the memory in the given `StrVec`. Having taken over the memory from its argument, the constructor body sets the pointers in the given object to `nullptr`. After an object is moved from, that object continues to exist. Eventually, the moved-from object will be destroyed, meaning that the destructor will be run on that object. The `StrVec` destructor calls `deallocate` on `first_free`. If we neglected to change `s.first_free`, then destroying the moved-from object would delete the memory we just moved.

Move Operations, Library Containers, and Exceptions

Because a move operation executes by "stealing" resources, it ordinarily does not itself allocate any resources. As a result, move operations ordinarily will not throw any exceptions. When we write a move operation that cannot throw, we should inform the library of that fact. As we'll see, unless the library knows that our move constructor won't throw, it will do extra work to cater to the possibliity that moving an object of our class type might throw.

One way inform the library is to specify `noexcept` on our constructor. We'll cover `noexcept`, which was introduced by the new standard, in more detail in § 18.1.4 (p. 779). For now what's important to know is that `noexcept` is a way for us to promise that a function does not throw any exceptions. We specify `noexcept` on a function after its parameter list. In a constructor, `noexcept` appears between the parameter list and the `:` that begins the constructor initializer list:

```
class StrVec {
public:
    StrVec(StrVec&&) noexcept;      // move constructor
    // other members as before
};
StrVec::StrVec(StrVec &&s) noexcept : /* member initializers */
{ /* constructor body */ }
```

We must specify `noexcept` on both the declaration in the class header and on the definition if that definition appears outside the class.

> *Note* Move constructors and move assignment operators that cannot throw exceptions should be marked as `noexcept`.

Understanding why `noexcept` is needed can help deepen our understanding of how the library interacts with objects of the types we write. We need to indicate that a move operation doesn't throw because of two interrelated facts: First, although move operations usually don't throw exceptions, they are permitted to do so. Second, the library containers provide guarantees as to what they do if an exception happens. As one example, `vector` guarantees that if an exception happens when we call `push_back`, the `vector` itself will be left unchanged.

Now let's think about what happens inside `push_back`. Like the corresponding `StrVec` operation (§ 13.5, p. 527), `push_back` on a `vector` might require that the `vector` be reallocated. When a `vector` is reallocated, it moves the elements from its old space to new memory, just as we did in `reallocate` (§ 13.5, p. 530).

As we've just seen, moving an object generally changes the value of the moved-from object. If reallocation uses a move constructor and that constructor throws an exception after moving some but not all of the elements, there would be a problem. The moved-from elements in the old space would have been changed, and the unconstructed elements in the new space would not yet exist. In this case, `vector` would be unable to meet its requirement that the `vector` is left unchanged.

On the other hand, if `vector` uses the copy constructor and an exception happens, it can easily meet this requirement. In this case, while the elements are being constructed in the new memory, the old elements remain unchanged. If an exception happens, `vector` can free the space it allocated (but could not successfully construct) and return. The original `vector` elements still exist.

To avoid this potential problem, `vector` must use a copy constructor instead of a move constructor during reallocation *unless it knows* that the element type's move constructor cannot throw an exception. If we want objects of our type to be moved rather than copied in circumstances such as `vector` reallocation, we must explicity tell the library that our move constructor is safe to use. We do so by marking the move constructor (and move-assignment operator) `noexcept`.

Move-Assignment Operator

The move-assignment operator does the same work as the destructor and the move constructor. As with the move constructor, if our move-assignment operator won't throw any exceptions, we should make it `noexcept`. Like a copy-assignment operator, a move-assignment operator must guard against self-assignment:

```
StrVec &StrVec::operator=(StrVec &&rhs) noexcept
{
    // direct test for self-assignment
    if (this != &rhs) {
        free();                          // free existing elements
        elements = rhs.elements;    // take over resources from rhs
        first_free = rhs.first_free;
        cap = rhs.cap;
        // leave rhs in a destructible state
        rhs.elements = rhs.first_free = rhs.cap = nullptr;
    }
    return *this;
}
```

In this case we check directly whether the `this` pointer and the address of `rhs` are the same. If they are, the right- and left-hand operands refer to the same object and there is no work to do. Otherwise, we free the memory that the left-hand operand had used, and then take over the memory from the given object. As in the move constructor, we set the pointers in `rhs` to `nullptr`.

It may seem surprising that we bother to check for self-assignment. After all, move assignment requires an rvalue for the right-hand operand. We do the check because that rvalue could be the result of calling `move`. As in any other assignment operator, it is crucial that we not free the left-hand resources before using those (possibly same) resources from the right-hand operand.

A Moved-from Object Must Be Destructible

Moving from an object does not destroy that object: Sometime after the move operation completes, the moved-from object will be destroyed. Therefore, when we write a move operation, we must ensure that the moved-from object is in a state in which the destructor can be run. Our `StrVec` move operations meet this requirement by setting the pointer members of the moved-from object to `nullptr`.

In addition to leaving the moved-from object in a state that is safe to destroy, move operations must guarantee that the object remains valid. In general, a valid object is one that can safely be given a new value or used in other ways that do not depend on its current value. On the other hand, move operations have no requirements as to the value that remains in the moved-from object. As a result, our programs should never depend on the value of a moved-from object.

For example, when we move from a library `string` or container object, we know that the moved-from object remains valid. As a result, we can run operations such as as `empty` or `size` on moved-from objects. However, we don't know what result we'll get. We might expect a moved-from object to be empty, but that is not guaranteed.

Our `StrVec` move operations leave the moved-from object in the same state as a default-initialized object. Therefore, all the operations of `StrVec` will continue to run the same way as they do for any other default-initialized `StrVec`. Other classes, with more complicated internal structure, may behave differently.

> ⚠️ **WARNING** After a move operation, the "moved-from" object must remain a valid, destructible object but users may make no assumptions about its value.

The Synthesized Move Operations

As it does for the copy constructor and copy-assignment operator, the compiler will synthesize the move constructor and move-assignment operator. However, the conditions under which it synthesizes a move operation are quite different from those in which it synthesizes a copy operation.

Recall that if we do not declare our own copy constructor or copy-assignment operator the compiler *always* synthesizes these operations (§ 13.1.1, p. 497 and § 13.1.2, p. 500). The copy operations are defined either to memberwise copy or assign the object or they are defined as deleted functions.

Differently from the copy operations, for some classes the compiler does not synthesize the move operations *at all*. In particular, if a class defines its own copy constructor, copy-assignment operator, or destructor, the move constructor and move-assignment operator are not synthesized. As a result, some classes do not have a move constructor or a move-assignment operator. As we'll see on page 540, when a class doesn't have a move operation, the corresponding copy operation is used in place of move through normal function matching.

The compiler will synthesize a move constructor or a move-assignment operator *only* if the class doesn't define any of its own copy-control members and if every nonstatic data member of the class can be moved. The compiler can move members of built-in type. It can also move members of a class type if the member's class has the corresponding move operation:

```
//   the compiler will synthesize the move operations for X and hasX
struct X {
    int i;          //   built-in types can be moved
    std::string s;  //   string defines its own move operations
};
struct hasX {
    X mem;   //   X has synthesized move operations
};
X x, x2 = std::move(x);        //   uses the synthesized move constructor
hasX hx, hx2 = std::move(hx);  //   uses the synthesized move constructor
```

The compiler synthesizes the move constructor and move assignment only if a class does not define any of its own copy-control members and only if all the data members can be moved constructed and move assigned, respectively.

Unlike the copy operations, a move operation is never implicitly defined as a deleted function. However, if we explicitly ask the compiler to generate a move operation by using = default (§ 7.1.4, p. 264), and the compiler is unable to move all the members, then the move operation will be defined as deleted. With one important exception, the rules for when a synthesized move operation is defined as deleted are analogous to those for the copy operations (§ 13.1.6, p. 508):

- Unlike the copy constructor, the move constructor is defined as deleted if the class has a member that defines its own copy constructor but does not also define a move constructor, or if the class has a member that doesn't define its own copy operations and for which the compiler is unable to synthesize a move constructor. Similarly for move-assignment.

- The move constructor or move-assignment operator is defined as deleted if the class has a member whose own move constructor or move-assignment operator is deleted or inaccessible.

- Like the copy constructor, the move constructor is defined as deleted if the destructor is deleted or inaccessible.

- Like the copy-assignment operator, the move-assignment operator is defined as deleted if the class has a const or reference member.

For example, assuming `Y` is a class that defines its own copy constructor not also define its own move constructor:

```
// assume Y is a class that defines its own copy constructor but not a move constructor
struct hasY {
    hasY() = default;
    hasY(hasY&&) = default;
    Y mem; // hasY will have a deleted move constructor
};
hasY hy, hy2 = std::move(hy); // error: move constructor is deleted
```

The compiler can copy objects of type `Y` but cannot move them. Class `hasY` explicitly requested a move constructor, which the compiler is unable to generate. Hence, `hasY` will get a deleted move constructor. Had `hasY` omitted the declaration of its move constructor, then the compiler would not synthesize the `hasY` move constructor at all. The move operations are not synthesized if they would otherwise be defined as deleted.

There is one final interaction between move operations and the synthesized copy-control members: Whether a class defines its own move operations has an impact on how the copy operations are synthesized. If the class defines either a move constructor and/or a move-assignment operator, then the synthesized copy constructor and copy-assignment operator for that class will be defined as deleted.

Classes that define a move constructor or move-assignment operator must also define their own copy operations. Otherwise, those members are deleted by default.

Rvalues Are Moved, Lvalues Are Copied . . .

When a class has both a move constructor and a copy constructor, the compiler uses ordinary function matching to determine which constructor to use (§ 6.4, p. 233). Similarly for assignment. For example, in our `StrVec` class the copy versions take a reference to `const StrVec`. As a result, they can be used on any type that can be converted to `StrVec`. The move versions take a `StrVec&&` and can be used only when the argument is a (nonconst) rvalue:

```
StrVec v1, v2;
v1 = v2;                    // v2 is an lvalue; copy assignment
StrVec getVec(istream &);   // getVec returns an rvalue
v2 = getVec(cin);           // getVec(cin) is an rvalue; move assignment
```

In the first assignment, we pass `v2` to the assignment operator. The type of `v2` is `StrVec` and the expression, `v2`, is an lvalue. The move version of assignment is not viable (§ 6.6, p. 243), because we cannot implicitly bind an rvalue reference to an lvalue. Hence, this assignment uses the copy-assignment operator.

In the second assignment, we assign from the result of a call to `getVec`. That expression is an rvalue. In this case, both assignment operators are viable—we can bind the result of `getVec` to either operator's parameter. Calling the copy-assignment operator requires a conversion to `const`, whereas `StrVec&&` is an exact match. Hence, the second assignment uses the move-assignment operator.

...But Rvalues Are Copied If There Is No Move Constructor

What if a class has a copy constructor but does not define a move constructor? In this case, the compiler will not synthesize the move constructor, which means the class has a copy constructor but no move constructor. If a class has no move constructor, function matching ensures that objects of that type are copied, even if we attempt to move them by calling `move`:

```
class Foo {
public:
    Foo() = default;
    Foo(const Foo&);    // copy constructor
    // other members, but Foo does not define a move constructor
};
Foo x;
Foo y(x);                    // copy constructor; x is an lvalue
Foo z(std::move(x));    // copy constructor, because there is no move constructor
```

The call to `move(x)` in the initialization of z returns a `Foo&&` bound to x. The copy constructor for `Foo` is viable because we can convert a `Foo&&` to a `const Foo&`. Thus, the initialization of z uses the copy constructor for `Foo`.

It is worth noting that using the copy constructor in place of a move constructor is almost surely safe (and similarly for the assignment operators). Ordinarily, the copy constructor will meet the requirements of the corresponding move constructor: It will copy the given object and leave that original object in a valid state. Indeed, the copy constructor won't even change the value of the original object.

> If a class has a usable copy constructor and no move constructor, objects will be "moved" by the copy constructor. Similarly for the copy-assignment operator and move-assignment.

Copy-and-Swap Assignment Operators and Move

The version of our `HasPtr` class that defined a copy-and-swap assignment operator (§ 13.3, p. 518) is a good illustration of the interaction between function matching and move operations. If we add a move constructor to this class, it will effectively get a move assignment operator as well:

```
class HasPtr {
public:
    // added move constructor
    HasPtr(HasPtr &&p) noexcept : ps(p.ps), i(p.i) {p.ps = 0;}
    // assignment operator is both the move- and copy-assignment operator
    HasPtr& operator=(HasPtr rhs)
                    { swap(*this, rhs); return *this; }
    // other members as in § 13.2.1 (p. 511)
};
```

In this version of the class, we've added a move constructor that takes over the values from its given argument. The constructor body sets the pointer member of the given `HasPtr` to zero to ensure that it is safe to destroy the moved-from object. Nothing this function does can throw an exception so we mark it as `noexcept` (§ 13.6.2, p. 535).

Now let's look at the assignment operator. That operator has a nonreference parameter, which means the parameter is copy initialized (§ 13.1.1, p. 497). Depending on the type of the argument, copy initialization uses either the copy constructor or the move constructor; lvalues are copied and rvalues are moved. As a result, this single assignment operator acts as both the copy-assignment and move-assignment operator.

For example, assuming both `hp` and `hp2` are `HasPtr` objects:

```
hp = hp2;   //  hp2 is an lvalue; copy constructor used to copy hp2
hp = std::move(hp2);  //  move constructor moves hp2
```

In the first assignment, the right-hand operand is an lvalue, so the move constructor is not viable. The copy constructor will be used to initialize `rhs`. The copy constructor will allocate a new `string` and copy the `string` to which `hp2` points.

In the second assignment, we invoke `std::move` to bind an rvalue reference to `hp2`. In this case, both the copy constructor and the move constructor are viable. However, because the argument is an rvalue reference, it is an exact match for the move constructor. The move constructor copies the pointer from `hp2`. It does not allocate any memory.

Regardless of whether the copy or move constructor was used, the body of the assignment operator `swaps` the state of the two operands. Swapping a `HasPtr` exchanges the pointer (and `int`) members of the two objects. After the `swap`, `rhs` will hold a pointer to the `string` that had been owned by the left-hand side. That `string` will be destroyed when `rhs` goes out of scope.

ADVICE: UPDATING THE RULE OF THREE

All five copy-control members should be thought of as a unit: Ordinarily, if a class defines any of these operations, it usually should define them all. As we've seen, some classes *must* define the copy constructor, copy-assignment operator, and destructor to work correctly (§ 13.1.4, p. 504). Such classes typically have a resource that the copy members must copy. Ordinarily, copying a resource entails some amount of overhead. Classes that define the move constructor and move-assignment operator can avoid this overhead in those circumstances where a copy isn't necessary.

Move Operations for the `Message` Class

Classes that define their own copy constructor and copy-assignment operator generally also benefit by defining the move operations. For example, our `Message` and `Folder` classes (§ 13.4, p. 519) should define move operations. By defining move operations, the `Message` class can use the `string` and `set` move operations to avoid the overhead of copying the `contents` and `folders` members.

However, in addition to moving the `folders` member, we must also update each `Folder` that points to the original `Message`. We must remove pointers to the old `Message` and add a pointer to the new one.

Both the move constructor and move-assignment operator need to update the Folder pointers, so we'll start by defining an operation to do this common work:

```
//  move the Folder pointers from m to this Message
void Message::move_Folders(Message *m)
{
    folders = std::move(m->folders); // uses set move assignment
    for (auto f : folders) {  // for each Folder
        f->remMsg(m);        //  remove the old Message from the Folder
        f->addMsg(this);     //  add this Message to that Folder
    }
    m->folders.clear();      //  ensure that destroying m is harmless
}
```

This function begins by moving the folders set. By calling move, we use the set move assignment rather than its copy assignment. Had we omitted the call to move, the code would still work, but the copy is unnecessary. The function then iterates through those Folders, removing the pointer to the original Message and adding a pointer to the new Message.

It is worth noting that inserting an element to a set might throw an exception—adding an element to a container requires memory to be allocated, which means that a bad_alloc exception might be thrown (§ 12.1.2, p. 460). As a result, unlike our HasPtr and StrVec move operations, the Message move constructor and move-assignment operators might throw exceptions. We will not mark them as noexcept (§ 13.6.2, p. 535).

The function ends by calling clear on m.folders. After the move, we know that m.folders is valid but have no idea what its contents are. Because the Message destructor iterates through folders, we want to be certain that the set is empty.

The Message move constructor calls move to move the contents and default initializes its folders member:

```
Message::Message(Message &&m): contents(std::move(m.contents))
{
    move_Folders(&m); //  moves folders and updates the Folder pointers
}
```

In the body of the constructor, we call move_Folders to remove the pointers to m and insert pointers to this Message.

The move-assignment operator does a direct check for self-assignment:

```
Message& Message::operator=(Message &&rhs)
{
    if (this != &rhs) {            //  direct check for self-assignment
        remove_from_Folders();
        contents = std::move(rhs.contents); //  move assignment
        move_Folders(&rhs); //  reset the Folders to point to this Message
    }
    return *this;
}
```

As with any assignment operator, the move-assignment operator must destroy the old state of the left-hand operand. In this case, destroying the left-hand operand requires that we remove pointers to this `Message` from the existing `folders`, which we do in the call to `remove_from_Folders`. Having removed itself from its `Folders`, we call `move` to move the `contents` from `rhs` to `this` object. What remains is to call `move_Messages` to update the `Folder` pointers.

Move Iterators

The `reallocate` member of `StrVec` (§ 13.5, p. 530) used a `for` loop to call `construct` to copy the elements from the old memory to the new. As an alternative to writing that loop, it would be easier if we could call `uninitialized_copy` to construct the newly allocated space. However, `uninitialized_copy` does what it says: It copies the elements. There is no analogous library function to "move" objects into unconstructed memory.

Instead, the new library defines a **move iterator** adaptor (§ 10.4, p. 401). A `C++11` move iterator adapts its given iterator by changing the behavior of the iterator's dereference operator. Ordinarily, an iterator dereference operator returns an lvalue reference to the element. Unlike other iterators, the dereference operator of a move iterator yields an rvalue reference.

We transform an ordinary iterator to a move iterator by calling the library `make_move_iterator` function. This function takes an iterator and returns a move iterator.

All of the original iterator's other operations work as usual. Because these iterators support normal iterator operations, we can pass a pair of move iterators to an algorithm. In particular, we can pass move iterators to `uninitialized_copy`:

```
void StrVec::reallocate()
{
    // allocate space for twice as many elements as the current size
    auto newcapacity = size() ? 2 * size() : 1;
    auto first = alloc.allocate(newcapacity);
    // move the elements
    auto last = uninitialized_copy(make_move_iterator(begin()),
                                   make_move_iterator(end()),
                                   first);
    free();                  // free the old space
    elements = first;        // update the pointers
    first_free = last;
    cap = elements + newcapacity;
}
```

`uninitialized_copy` calls `construct` on each element in the input sequence to "copy" that element into the destination. That algorithm uses the iterator dereference operator to fetch elements from the input sequence. Because we passed move iterators, the dereference operator yields an rvalue reference, which means `construct` will use the move constructor to construct the elements.

It is worth noting that standard library makes no guarantees about which algorithms can be used with move iterators and which cannot. Because moving an object can obliterate the source, you should pass move iterators to algorithms only when you are *confident* that the algorithm does not access an element after it has assigned to that element or passed that element to a user-defined function.

ADVICE: DON'T BE TOO QUICK TO MOVE

Because a moved-from object has indeterminate state, calling `std::move` on an object is a dangerous operation. When we call `move`, we must be absolutely certain that there can be no other users of the moved-from object.

Judiciously used inside class code, `move` can offer significant performance benefits. Casually used in ordinary user code (as opposed to class implementation code), moving an object is more likely to lead to mysterious and hard-to-find bugs than to any improvement in the performance of the application.

Best Practices Outside of class implementation code such as move constructors or move-assignment operators, use `std::move` only when you *are certain* that you need to do a move and that the move is guaranteed to be safe.

EXERCISES SECTION 13.6.2

Exercise 13.49: Add a move constructor and move-assignment operator to your `StrVec`, `String`, and `Message` classes.

Exercise 13.50: Put print statements in the move operations in your `String` class and rerun the program from exercise 13.48 in § 13.6.1 (p. 534) that used a `vector<String>` to see when the copies are avoided.

Exercise 13.51: Although `unique_ptrs` cannot be copied, in § 12.1.5 (p. 471) we wrote a `clone` function that returned a `unique_ptr` by value. Explain why that function is legal and how it works.

Exercise 13.52: Explain in detail what happens in the assignments of the `HasPtr` objects on page 541. In particular, describe step by step what happens to values of `hp`, `hp2`, and of the `rhs` parameter in the `HasPtr` assignment operator.

Exercise 13.53: As a matter of low-level efficiency, the `HasPtr` assignment operator is not ideal. Explain why. Implement a copy-assignment and move-assignment operator for `HasPtr` and compare the operations executed in your new move-assignment operator versus the copy-and-swap version.

Exercise 13.54: What would happen if we defined a `HasPtr` move-assignment operator but did not change the copy-and-swap operator? Write code to test your answer.

 ## 13.6.3 Rvalue References and Member Functions

Member functions other than constructors and assignment can benefit from providing both copy and move versions. Such move-enabled members typically use the same parameter pattern as the copy/move constructor and the assignment operators—one version takes an lvalue reference to `const`, and the second takes an rvalue reference to nonconst.

For example, the library containers that define `push_back` provide two versions: one that has an rvalue reference parameter and the other a `const` lvalue reference. Assuming `X` is the element type, these containers define:

```
void push_back(const X&);  // copy: binds to any kind of X
void push_back(X&&);       // move: binds only to modifiable rvalues of type X
```

We can pass any object that can be converted to type `X` to the first version of `push_back`. This version copies data from its parameter. We can pass only an rvalue that is not `const` to the second version. This version is an exact match (and a better match) for nonconst rvalues and will be run when we pass a modifiable rvalue (§ 13.6.2, p. 539). This version is free to steal resources from its parameter.

Ordinarily, there is no need to define versions of the operation that take a `const X&&` or a (plain) `X&`. Usually, we pass an rvalue reference when we want to "steal" from the argument. In order to do so, the argument must not be `const`. Similarly, copying from an object should not change the object being copied. As a result, there is usually no need to define a version that take a (plain) `X&` parameter.

> Overloaded functions that distinguish between moving and copying a parameter typically have one version that takes a `const T&` and one that takes a `T&&`.

As a more concrete example, we'll give our `StrVec` class a second version of `push_back`:

```
class StrVec {
public:
    void push_back(const std::string&);   // copy the element
    void push_back(std::string&&);         // move the element
    // other members as before
};
// unchanged from the original version in § 13.5 (p. 527)
void StrVec::push_back(const string& s)
{
    chk_n_alloc();  // ensure that there is room for another element
    // construct a copy of s in the element to which first_free points
    alloc.construct(first_free++, s);
}
void StrVec::push_back(string &&s)
{
    chk_n_alloc();  // reallocates the StrVec if necessary
    alloc.construct(first_free++, std::move(s));
}
```

These members are nearly identical. The difference is that the rvalue reference version of `push_back` calls `move` to pass its parameter to `construct`. As we've seen, the `construct` function uses the type of its second and subsequent arguments to determine which constructor to use. Because `move` returns an rvalue reference, the type of the argument to construct is string&&. Therefore, the string move constructor will be used to construct a new last element.

When we call push_back the type of the argument determines whether the new element is copied or moved into the container:

```
StrVec vec;   // empty StrVec
string s = "some string or another";
vec.push_back(s);         // calls push_back(const string&)
vec.push_back("done");  // calls push_back(string&&)
```

These calls differ as to whether the argument is an lvalue (s) or an rvalue (the temporary string created from "done"). The calls are resolved accordingly.

Rvalue and Lvalue Reference Member Functions

Ordinarily, we can call a member function on an object, regardless of whether that object is an lvalue or an rvalue. For example:

```
string s1 = "a value", s2 = "another";
auto n = (s1 + s2).find('a');
```

Here, we called the find member (§ 9.5.3, p. 364) on the string rvalue that results from adding two strings. Sometimes such usage can be surprising:

```
s1 + s2 = "wow!";
```

Here we assign to the rvalue result of concatentating these strings.

Prior to the new standard, there was no way to prevent such usage. In order to maintain backward compatability, the library classes continue to allow assignment to rvalues, However, we might want to prevent such usage in our own classes. In this case, we'd like to force the left-hand operand (i.e., the object to which this points) to be an lvalue.

C++
11

We indicate the lvalue/rvalue property of this in the same way that we define const member functions (§ 7.1.2, p. 258); we place a **reference qualifier** after the parameter list:

```
class Foo {
public:
    Foo &operator=(const Foo&) &;  // may assign only to modifiable lvalues
    // other members of Foo
};
Foo &Foo::operator=(const Foo &rhs) &
{
    // do whatever is needed to assign rhs to this object
    return *this;
}
```

The reference qualifier can be either & or &&, indicating that this may point to an rvalue or lvalue, respectively. Like the const qualifier, a reference qualifier may appear only on a (nonstatic) member function and must appear in both the declaration and definition of the function.

We may run a function qualified by & only on an lvalue and may run a function qualified by && only on an rvalue:

```
Foo &retFoo();   // returns a reference; a call to retFoo is an lvalue
Foo retVal();    // returns by value; a call to retVal is an rvalue
Foo i, j;        // i and j are lvalues
i = j;           // ok: i is an lvalue
retFoo() = j;    // ok: retFoo() returns an lvalue
retVal() = j;    // error: retVal() returns an rvalue
i = retVal();    // ok: we can pass an rvalue as the right-hand operand to assignment
```

A function can be both `const` and reference qualified. In such cases, the reference qualifier must follow the `const` qualifier:

```
class Foo {
public:
    Foo someMem() & const;     // error: const qualifier must come first
    Foo anotherMem() const &;  // ok: const qualifier comes first
};
```

Overloading and Reference Functions

Just as we can overload a member function based on whether it is `const` (§ 7.3.2, p. 276), we can also overload a function based on its reference qualifier. Moreover, we may overload a function by its reference qualifier and by whether it is a `const` member. As an example, we'll give `Foo` a `vector` member and a function named `sorted` that returns a copy of the `Foo` object in which the `vector` is sorted:

```
class Foo {
public:
    Foo sorted() &&;         // may run on modifiable rvalues
    Foo sorted() const &;    // may run on any kind of Foo
    // other members of Foo
private:
    vector<int> data;
};
// this object is an rvalue, so we can sort in place
Foo Foo::sorted() &&
{
    sort(data.begin(), data.end());
    return *this;
}
// this object is either const or it is an lvalue; either way we can't sort in place
Foo Foo::sorted() const & {
    Foo ret(*this);                              // make a copy
    sort(ret.data.begin(), ret.data.end());      // sort the copy
    return ret;                                  // return the copy
}
```

When we run `sorted` on an rvalue, it is safe to sort the `data` member directly. The object is an rvalue, which means it has no other users, so we can change the object itself. When we run `sorted` on a `const` rvalue or on an lvalue, we can't change this object, so we copy `data` before sorting it.

Overload resolution uses the lvalue/rvalue property of the object that calls `sorted` to determine which version is used:

```
retVal().sorted(); //  retVal() is an rvalue, calls Foo::sorted() &&
retFoo().sorted(); //  retFoo() is an lvalue, calls Foo::sorted() const &
```

When we define `const` memeber functions, we can define two versions that differ only in that one is `const` qualified and the other is not. There is no similar default for reference qualified functions. When we define two or more members that have the same name and the same parameter list, we must provide a reference qualifier on all or none of those functions:

```
class Foo {
public:
    Foo sorted() &&;
    Foo sorted() const; // error: must have reference qualifier
    //  Comp is type alias for the function type (see § 6.7 (p. 249))
    //  that can be used to compare int values
    using Comp = bool(const int&, const int&);
    Foo sorted(Comp*);         //  ok: different parameter list
    Foo sorted(Comp*) const;   //  ok: neither version is reference qualified
};
```

Here the declaration of the `const` version of `sorted` that has no parameters is an error. There is a second version of `sorted` that has no parameters and that function has a reference qualifier, so the `const` version of that function must have a reference qualifier as well. On the other hand, the versions of `sorted` that take a pointer to a comparison operation are fine, because neither function has a qualifier.

> If a member function has a reference qualifier, all the versions of that member with the same parameter list must have reference qualifiers.

EXERCISES SECTION 13.6.3

Exercise 13.55: Add an rvalue reference version of push_back to your StrBlob.

Exercise 13.56: What would happen if we defined sorted as:

```
Foo Foo::sorted() const & {
    Foo ret(*this);
    return ret.sorted();
}
```

Exercise 13.57: What if we defined sorted as:

```
Foo Foo::sorted() const & { return Foo(*this).sorted(); }
```

Exercise 13.58: Write versions of class Foo with print statements in their sorted functions to test your answers to the previous two exercises.

CHAPTER SUMMARY

Each class controls what happens when we copy, move, assign, or destroy objects of its type. Special member functions—the copy constructor, move constructor, copy-assignment operator, move-assignment operator, and destructor—define these operations. The move constructor and move-assignment operator take a (usually nonconst) rvalue reference; the copy versions take a (usually const) ordinary lvalue reference.

If a class declares none of these operations, the compiler will define them automatically. If not defined as deleted, these operations memberwise initialize, move, assign, or destroy the object: Taking each nonstatic data member in turn, the synthesized operation does whatever is appropriate to the member's type to move, copy, assign, or destroy that member.

Classes that allocate memory or other resources almost always require that the class define the copy-control members to manage the allocated resource. If a class needs a destructor, then it almost surely needs to define the move and copy constructors and the move- and copy-assignment operators as well.

DEFINED TERMS

copy and swap Technique for writing assignment operators by copying the right-hand operand followed by a call to swap to exchange the copy with the left-hand operand.

copy-assignment operator Version of the assignment operator that takes an object of the same type as its type. Ordinarily, the copy-assignment operator has a parameter that is a reference to const and returns a reference to its object. The compiler synthesizes the copy-assignment operator if the class does not explicitly provide one.

copy constructor Constructor that initializes a new object as a copy of another object of the same type. The copy constructor is applied implicitly to pass objects to or from a function by value. If we do not provide the copy constructor, the compiler synthesizes one for us.

copy control Special members that control what happens when objects of class type are copied, moved, assigned, and destroyed. The compiler synthesizes appropriate definitions for these operations if the class does not otherwise declare them.

copy initialization Form of initialization used when we use = to supply an initializer for a newly created object. Also used when we pass or return an object by value and when we initialize an array or an aggregate class. Copy initialization uses the copy constructor or the move constructor, depending on whether the initializer is an lvalue or an rvalue.

deleted function Function that may not be used. We delete a function by specifying = delete on its declaration. A common use of deleted functions is to tell the compiler not to synthesize the copy and/or move operations for a class.

destructor Special member function that cleans up an object when the object goes out of scope or is deleted. The compiler automatically destroys each data member. Members of class type are destroyed by invoking their destructor; no work is done when destroying members of built-in or compound type. In particular, the object pointed to by a pointer member is not deleted by the destructor.

lvalue reference Reference that can bind to an lvalue.

memberwise copy/assign How the synthesized copy and move constructors and the copy- and move-assignment operators work. Taking each nonstatic data member in turn, the synthesized copy or move constructor initializes each member by copying or moving the corresponding member from the given object; the copy- or move-assignment operators copy-assign or move-assign each member from the right-hand object to the left. Members of built-in or compound type are initialized or assigned directly. Members of class type are initialized or assigned by using the member's corresponding copy/move constructor or copy-/move-assignment operator.

move Library function used to bind an rvalue reference to an lvalue. Calling move implicitly promises that we will not use the moved-from object except to destroy it or assign a new value to it.

move-assignment operator Version of the assignment operator that takes an rvalue reference to its type. Typically, a move-assignment operator moves data from the right-hand operand to the left. After the assignment, it must be safe to run the destructor on the right-hand operand.

move constructor Constructor that takes an rvalue reference to its type. Typically, a move constructor moves data from its parameter into the newly created object. After the move, it must be safe to run the destructor on the given argument.

move iterator Iterator adaptor that generates an iterator that, when dereferenced, yields an rvalue reference.

overloaded operator Function that redefines the meaning of an operator when applied to operand(s) of class type. This chapter showed how to define the assignment operator; Chapter 14 covers overloaded operators in more detail.

reference count Programming technique often used in copy-control members. A reference count keeps track of how many objects share state. Constructors (other than copy/move constructors) set the reference count to 1. Each time a new copy is made the count is incremented. When an object is destroyed, the count is decremented. The assignment operator and the destructor check whether the decremented reference count has gone to zero and, if so, they destroy the object.

reference qualifier Symbol used to indicate that a nonstatic member function can be called on an lvalue or an rvalue. The qualifier, & or &&, follows the parameter list or the const qualifier if there is one. A function qualified by & may be called only on lvalues; a function qualified by && may be called only on rvalues.

rvalue reference Reference to an object that is about to be destroyed.

synthesized assignment operator A version of the copy- or move-assignment operator created (synthesized) by the compiler for classes that do not explicitly define assignment operators. Unless it is defined as deleted, a synthesized assignment operator memberwise assigns (moves) the right-hand operand to the left.

synthesized copy/move constructor A version of the copy or move constructor that is generated by the compiler for classes that do not explicitly define the corresponding constructor. Unless it is defined as deleted, a synthesized copy or move constructor memberwise initializes the new object by copying or moving members from the given object, respectively.

synthesized destructor Version of the destructor created (synthesized) by the compiler for classes that do not explicitly define one. The synthesized destructor has an empty function body.

C H A P T E R **14**
OVERLOADED OPERATIONS
AND CONVERSIONS

CONTENTS

In Chapter 4, we saw that C++ defines a large number of operators and automatic conversions among the built-in types. These facilities allow programmers to write a rich set of mixed-type expressions.

C++ lets us define what the operators mean when applied to objects of class type. It also lets us define conversions for class types. Class-type conversions are used like the built-in conversions to implicitly convert an object of one type to another type when needed.

Operator overloading lets us define the meaning of an operator when applied to operand(s) of a class type. Judicious use of operator overloading can make our programs easier to write and easier to read. As an example, because our original `Sales_item` class type (§ 1.5.1, p. 20) defined the input, output, and addition operators, we can print the sum of two `Sales_items` as

```
cout << item1 + item2;   // print the sum of two Sales_items
```

In contrast, because our `Sales_data` class (§ 7.1, p. 254) does not yet have overloaded operators, code to print their sum is more verbose and, hence, less clear:

```
print(cout, add(data1, data2));   // print the sum of two Sales_datas
```

14.1 Basic Concepts

Overloaded operators are functions with special names: the keyword `operator` followed by the symbol for the operator being defined. Like any other function, an overloaded operator has a return type, a parameter list, and a body.

An overloaded operator function has the same number of parameters as the operator has operands. A unary operator has one parameter; a binary operator has two. In a binary operator, the left-hand operand is passed to the first parameter and the right-hand operand to the second. Except for the overloaded function-call operator, `operator()`, an overloaded operator may not have default arguments (§ 6.5.1, p. 236).

If an operator function is a member function, the first (left-hand) operand is bound to the implicit `this` pointer (§ 7.1.2, p. 257). Because the first operand is implicitly bound to `this`, a member operator function has one less (explicit) parameter than the operator has operands.

> **Note** When an overloaded operator is a member function, `this` is bound to the left-hand operand. Member operator functions have one less (explicit) parameter than the number of operands.

An operator function must either be a member of a class or have at least one parameter of class type:

```
// error: cannot redefine the built-in operator for ints
int operator+(int, int);
```

This restriction means that we cannot change the meaning of an operator when applied to operands of built-in type.

We can overload most, but not all, of the operators. Table 14.1 shows whether or not an operator may be overloaded. We'll cover overloading `new` and `delete` in § 19.1.1 (p. 820).

We can overload only existing operators and cannot invent new operator symbols. For example, we cannot define `operator**` to provide exponentiation.

Four symbols (`+`, `-`, `*`, and `&`) serve as both unary and binary operators. Either or both of these operators can be overloaded. The number of parameters determines which operator is being defined.

An overloaded operator has the same precedence and associativity (§ 4.1.2, p. 136) as the corresponding built-in operator. Regardless of the operand types

```
x == y + z;
```

is always equivalent to `x == (y + z)`.

Table 14.1: Operators					
Operators That May Be Overloaded					
+	-	*	/	%	^
&	|	~	!	,	=
<	>	<=	>=	++	--
<<	>>	==	!=	&&	||
+=	-=	/=	%=	^=	&=
|=	*=	<<=	>>=	[]	()
->	->*	new	new []	delete	delete []
Operators That Cannot Be Overloaded					
::	.*	.	?:		

Calling an Overloaded Operator Function Directly

Ordinarily, we "call" an overloaded operator function indirectly by using the operator on arguments of the appropriate type. However, we can also call an overloaded operator function directly in the same way that we call an ordinary function. We name the function and pass an appropriate number of arguments of the appropriate type:

```
// equivalent calls to a nonmember operator function
data1 + data2;              // normal expression
operator+(data1, data2);   // equivalent function call
```

These calls are equivalent: Both call the nonmember function `operator+`, passing `data1` as the first argument and `data2` as the second.

We call a member operator function explicitly in the same way that we call any other member function. We name an object (or pointer) on which to run the function and use the dot (or arrow) operator to fetch the function we wish to call:

```
data1 += data2;             // expression-based "call"
data1.operator+=(data2);    // equivalent call to a member operator function
```

Each of these statements calls the member function `operator+=`, binding `this` to the address of `data1` and passing `data2` as an argument.

Some Operators Shouldn't Be Overloaded

Recall that a few operators guarantee the order in which operands are evaluated. Because using an overloaded operator is really a function call, these guarantees do not apply to overloaded operators. In particular, the operand-evaluation guarantees of the logical AND, logical OR (§ 4.3, p. 141), and comma (§ 4.10, p. 157) operators are not preserved. Moreover, overloaded versions of && or || operators do not preserve short-circuit evaluation properties of the built-in operators. Both operands are always evaluated.

Because the overloaded versions of these operators do not preserve order of evaluation and/or short-circuit evaluation, it is usually a bad idea to overload them. Users are likely to be surprised when the evaluation guarantees they are accustomed to are not honored for code that happens to use an overloaded version of one of these operators.

Another reason not to overload comma, which also applies to the address-of operator, is that unlike most operators, the language defines what the comma and address-of operators mean when applied to objects of class type. Because these operators have built-in meaning, they ordinarily should not be overloaded. Users of the class will be surprised if these operators behave differently from their normal meanings.

Ordinarily, the comma, address-of, logical AND, and logical OR operators should *not* be overloaded.

Use Definitions That Are Consistent with the Built-in Meaning

When you design a class, you should always think first about what operations the class will provide. Only after you know what operations are needed should you think about whether to define each operation as an ordinary function or as an overloaded operator. Those operations with a logical mapping to an operator are good candidates for defining as overloaded operators:

- If the class does IO, define the shift operators to be consistent with how IO is done for the built-in types.

- If the class has an operation to test for equality, define operator==. If the class has operator==, it should usually have operator!= as well.

- If the class has a single, natural ordering operation, define operator<. If the class has operator<, it should probably have all of the relational operators.

- The return type of an overloaded operator usually should be compatible with the return from the built-in version of the operator: The logical and relational operators should return bool, the arithmetic operators should return a value of the class type, and assignment and compound assignment should return a reference to the left-hand operand.

Assignment and Compound Assignment Operators

Assignment operators should behave analogously to the synthesized operators: After an assignment, the values in the left-hand and right-hand operands should have the same value, and the operator should return a reference to its left-hand operand. Overloaded assignment should generalize the built-in meaning of assignment, not circumvent it.

CAUTION: USE OPERATOR OVERLOADING JUDICIOUSLY

Each operator has an associated meaning from its use on the built-in types. Binary +, for example, is strongly identified with addition. Mapping binary + to an analogous operation for a class type can provide a convenient notational shorthand. For example, the library `string` type, following a convention common to many programming languages, uses + to represent concatenation—"adding" one `string` to the other.

Operator overloading is most useful when there is a logical mapping of a built-in operator to an operation on our type. Using overloaded operators rather than inventing named operations can make our programs more natural and intuitive. Overuse or outright abuse of operator overloading can make our classes incomprehensible.

Obvious abuses of operator overloading rarely happen in practice. As an example, no responsible programmer would define `operator+` to perform subtraction. More common, but still inadvisable, are uses that contort an operator's "normal" meaning to force a fit to a given type. Operators should be used only for operations that are likely to be unambiguous to users. An operator has an ambiguous meaning if it plausibly has more than one interpretation.

If a class has an arithmetic (§ 4.2, p. 139) or bitwise (§ 4.8, p. 152) operator, then it is usually a good idea to provide the corresponding compound-assignment operator as well. Needless to say, the += operator should be defined to behave the same way the built-in operators do: it should behave as + followed by =.

Choosing Member or Nonmember Implementation

When we define an overloaded operator, we must decide whether to make the operator a class member or an ordinary nonmember function. In some cases, there is no choice—some operators are required to be members; in other cases, we may not be able to define the operator appropriately if it is a member.

The following guidelines can be of help in deciding whether to make an operator a member or an ordinary nonmember function:

- The assignment (=), subscript ([ ]), call (( )), and member access arrow (->) operators *must* be defined as members.

- The compound-assignment operators ordinarily *ought* to be members. However, unlike assignment, they are not required to be members.

- Operators that change the state of their object or that are closely tied to their given type—such as increment, decrement, and dereference—usually should be members.

- Symmetric operators—those that might convert either operand, such as the arithmetic, equality, relational, and bitwise operators—usually should be defined as ordinary nonmember functions.

Programmers expect to be able to use symmetric operators in expressions with mixed types. For example, we can add an int and a double. The addition is symmetric because we can use either type as the left-hand or the right-hand operand.

If we want to provide similar mixed-type expressions involving class objects, then the operator must be defined as a nonmember function.

When we define an operator as a member function, then the left-hand operand must be an object of the class of which that operator is a member. For example:

```
string s = "world";
string t = s + "!";   // ok: we can add a const char* to a string
string u = "hi" + s;  // would be an error if + were a member of string
```

If `operator+` were a member of the `string` class, the first addition would be equivalent to `s.operator+("!")`. Likewise, `"hi" + s` would be equivalent to `"hi".operator+(s)`. However, the type of `"hi"` is `const char*`, and that is a built-in type; it does not even have member functions.

Because `string` defines + as an ordinary nonmember function, `"hi" + s` is equivalent to `operator+("hi", s)`. As with any function call, either of the arguments can be converted to the type of the parameter. The only requirements are that at least one of the operands has a class type, and that both operands can be converted (unambiguously) to `string`.

EXERCISES SECTION 14.1

Exercise 14.1: In what ways does an overloaded operator differ from a built-in operator? In what ways are overloaded operators the same as the built-in operators?

Exercise 14.2: Write declarations for the overloaded input, output, addition, and compound-assignment operators for `Sales_data`.

Exercise 14.3: Both `string` and `vector` define an overloaded == that can be used to compare objects of those types. Assuming `svec1` and `svec2` are `vector`s that hold `string`s, identify which version of == is applied in each of the following expressions:

    (a) `"cobble" == "stone"`   (b) `svec1[0] == svec2[0]`
    (c) `svec1 == svec2`   (d) `"svec1[0] == "stone"`

Exercise 14.4: Explain how to decide whether the following should be class members:

    (a) `%`   (b) `%=`   (c) `++`   (d) `->`   (e) `<<`   (f) `&&`   (g) `==`   (h) `()`

Exercise 14.5: In exercise 7.40 from § 7.5.1 (p. 291) you wrote a sketch of one of the following classes. Decide what, if any, overloaded operators your class should provide.

    (a) `Book`   (b) `Date`   (c) `Employee`
    (d) `Vehicle` (e) `Object` (f) `Tree`

14.2 Input and Output Operators

As we've seen, the IO library uses `>>` and `<<` for input and output, respectively. The IO library itself defines versions of these operators to read and write the built-in types. Classes that support IO ordinarily define versions of these operators for objects of the class type.

14.2.1 Overloading the Output Operator <<

Ordinarily, the first parameter of an output operator is a reference to a nonconst
ostream object. The ostream is nonconst because writing to the stream changes
its state. The parameter is a reference because we cannot copy an ostream object.

The second parameter ordinarily should be a reference to const of the class
type we want to print. The parameter is a reference to avoid copying the argument.
It can be const because (ordinarily) printing an object does not change that object.

To be consistent with other output operators, operator<< normally returns
its ostream parameter.

The Sales_data Output Operator

As an example, we'll write the Sales_data output operator:

```
ostream &operator<<(ostream &os, const Sales_data &item)
{
    os << item.isbn() << " " << item.units_sold << " "
       << item.revenue << " " << item.avg_price();
    return os;
}
```

Except for its name, this function is identical to our earlier print function (§ 7.1.3,
p. 261). Printing a Sales_data entails printing its three data elements and the
computed average sales price. Each element is separated by a space. After printing
the values, the operator returns a reference to the ostream it just wrote.

Output Operators Usually Do Minimal Formatting

The output operators for the built-in types do little if any formatting. In particular,
they do not print newlines. Users expect class output operators to behave similarly. If the operator does print a newline, then users would be unable to print
descriptive text along with the object on the same line. An output operator that
does minimal formatting lets users control the details of their output.

> **Best Practices**
> Generally, output operators should print the contents of the object,
> with minimal formatting. They should not print a newline.

IO Operators Must Be Nonmember Functions

Input and output operators that conform to the conventions of the iostream library must be ordinary nonmember functions. These operators cannot be members of our own class. If they were, then the left-hand operand would have to be
an object of our class type:

```
Sales_data data;
data << cout; // if operator<< is a member of Sales_data
```

If these operators are members of any class, they would have to be members of
istream or ostream. However, those classes are part of the standard library,
and we cannot add members to a class in the library.

Thus, if we want to define the IO operators for our types, we must define them as nonmember functions. Of course, IO operators usually need to read or write the nonpublic data members. As a consequence, IO operators usually must be declared as friends (§ 7.2.1, p. 269).

EXERCISES SECTION 14.2.1

Exercise 14.6: Define an output operator for your `Sales_data` class.

Exercise 14.7: Define an output operator for you `String` class you wrote for the exercises in § 13.5 (p. 531).

Exercise 14.8: Define an output operator for the class you chose in exercise 7.40 from § 7.5.1 (p. 291).

 ## 14.2.2 Overloading the Input Operator >>

Ordinarily the first parameter of an input operator is a reference to the stream from which it is to read, and the second parameter is a reference to the (nonconst) object into which to read. The operator usually returns a reference to its given stream. The second parameter must be nonconst because the purpose of an input operator is to read data into this object.

The `Sales_data` Input Operator

As an example, we'll write the `Sales_data` input operator:

```
istream &operator>>(istream &is, Sales_data &item)
{
    double price;   // no need to initialize; we'll read into price before we use it
    is >> item.bookNo >> item.units_sold >> price;
    if (is)            // check that the inputs succeeded
        item.revenue = item.units_sold * price;
    else
        item = Sales_data(); // input failed: give the object the default state
    return is;
}
```

Except for the `if` statement, this definition is similar to our earlier `read` function (§ 7.1.3, p. 261). The `if` checks whether the reads were successful. If an IO error occurs, the operator resets its given object to the empty `Sales_data`. That way, the object is guaranteed to be in a consistent state.

> **Note:** Input operators must deal with the possibility that the input might fail; output operators generally don't bother.

Errors during Input

The kinds of errors that might happen in an input operator include the following:

- A read operation might fail because the stream contains data of an incorrect type. For example, after reading bookNo, the input operator assumes that the next two items will be numeric data. If nonnumeric data is input, that read and any subsequent use of the stream will fail.

- Any of the reads could hit end-of-file or some other error on the input stream.

Rather than checking each read, we check once after reading all the data and before using those data:

```
if (is)          //  check that the inputs succeeded
    item.revenue = item.units_sold * price;
else
    item = Sales_data(); //  input failed: give the object the default state
```

If any of the read operations fails, price will have an undefined value. Therefore, before using price, we check that the input stream is still valid. If it is, we do the calculation and store the result in revenue. If there was an error, we do not worry about which input failed. Instead, we reset the entire object to the empty Sales_data by assigning a new, default-initialized Sales_data object to item. After this assignment, item will have an empty string for its bookNo member, and its revenue and units_sold members will be zero.

Putting the object into a valid state is especially important if the object might have been partially changed before the error occurred. For example, in this input operator, we might encounter an error after successfully reading a new bookNo. An error after reading bookNo would mean that the units_sold and revenue members of the old object were unchanged. The effect would be to associate a different bookNo with those data.

By leaving the object in a valid state, we (somewhat) protect a user that ignores the possibility of an input error. The object will be in a usable state—its members are all defined. Similarly, the object won't generate misleading results—its data are internally consistent.

Best Practices   Input operators should decide what, if anything, to do about error recovery.

Indicating Errors

Some input operators need to do additional data verification. For example, our input operator might check that the bookNo we read is in an appropriate format. In such cases, the input operator might need to set the stream's condition state to indicate failure (§ 8.1.2, p. 312), even though technically speaking the actual IO was successful. Usually an input operator should set only the failbit. Setting eofbit would imply that the file was exhausted, and setting badbit would indicate that the stream was corrupted. These errors are best left to the IO library itself to indicate.

Exercise 14.9: Define an input operator for your `Sales_data` class.

Exercise 14.10: Describe the behavior of the `Sales_data` input operator if given the following input:

    (a) `0-201-99999-9 10 24.95`   (b) `10 24.95 0-210-99999-9`

Exercise 14.11: What, if anything, is wrong with the following `Sales_data` input operator? What would happen if we gave this operator the data in the previous exercise?

```
istream& operator>>(istream& in, Sales_data& s)
{
    double price;
    in >> s.bookNo >> s.units_sold >> price;
    s.revenue = s.units_sold * price;
    return in;
}
```

Exercise 14.12: Define an input operator for the class you used in exercise 7.40 from § 7.5.1 (p. 291). Be sure the operator handles input errors.

14.3 Arithmetic and Relational Operators

Ordinarily, we define the arithmetic and relational operators as nonmember functions in order to allow conversions for either the left- or right-hand operand (§ 14.1, p. 555). These operators shouldn't need to change the state of either operand, so the parameters are ordinarily references to `const`.

An arithmetic operator usually generates a new value that is the result of a computation on its two operands. That value is distinct from either operand and is calculated in a local variable. The operation returns a copy of this local as its result. Classes that define an arithmetic operator generally define the corresponding compound assignment operator as well. When a class has both operators, it is usually more efficient to define the arithmetic operator to use compound assignment:

```
//   assumes that both objects refer to the same book
Sales_data
operator+(const Sales_data &lhs, const Sales_data &rhs)
{
    Sales_data sum = lhs;   // copy data members from lhs into sum
    sum += rhs;             // add rhs into sum
    return sum;
}
```

This definition is essentially identical to our original `add` function (§ 7.1.3, p. 261). We copy `lhs` into the local variable `sum`. We then use the `Sales_data` compound-assignment operator (which we'll define on page 564) to add the values from `rhs` into `sum`. We end the function by returning a copy of `sum`.

Classes that define both an arithmetic operator and the related compound assignment ordinarily ought to implement the arithmetic operator by using the compound assignment.

EXERCISES SECTION 14.3

Exercise 14.13: Which other arithmetic operators (Table 4.1 (p. 139)), if any, do you think Sales_data ought to support? Define any you think the class should include.

Exercise 14.14: Why do you think it is more efficient to define operator+ to call operator+= rather than the other way around?

Exercise 14.15: Should the class you chose for exercise 7.40 from § 7.5.1 (p. 291) define any of the arithmetic operators? If so, implement them. If not, explain why not.

14.3.1 Equality Operators

Ordinarily, classes in C++ define the equality operator to test whether two objects are equivalent. That is, they usually compare every data member and treat two objects as equal if and only if all the corresponding members are equal. In line with this design philosophy, our Sales_data equality operator should compare the bookNo as well as the sales figures:

```
bool operator==(const Sales_data &lhs, const Sales_data &rhs)
{
    return lhs.isbn() == rhs.isbn() &&
           lhs.units_sold == rhs.units_sold &&
           lhs.revenue == rhs.revenue;
}
bool operator!=(const Sales_data &lhs, const Sales_data &rhs)
{
    return !(lhs == rhs);
}
```

The definition of these functions is trivial. More important are the design principles that these functions embody:

- If a class has an operation to determine whether two objects are equal, it should define that function as operator== rather than as a named function: Users will expect to be able to compare objects using ==; providing == means they won't need to learn and remember a new name for the operation; and it is easier to use the library containers and algorithms with classes that define the == operator.

- If a class defines operator==, that operator ordinarily should determine whether the given objects contain equivalent data.

- Ordinarily, the equality operator should be transitive, meaning that if a == b and b == c are both true, then a == c should also be true.

- If a class defines operator==, it should also define operator!=. Users will expect that if they can use == then they can also use !=, and vice versa.

- One of the equality or inequality operators should delegate the work to the other. That is, one of these operators should do the real work to compare objects. The other should call the one that does the real work.

> **Best Practices** Classes for which there is a logical meaning for equality normally should define operator==. Classes that define == make it easier for users to use the class with the library algorithms.

EXERCISES SECTION 14.3.1

Exercise 14.16: Define equality and inequality operators for your StrBlob (§ 12.1.1, p. 456), StrBlobPtr (§ 12.1.6, p. 474), StrVec (§ 13.5, p. 526), and String (§ 13.5, p. 531) classes.

Exercise 14.17: Should the class you chose for exercise 7.40 from § 7.5.1 (p. 291) define the equality operators? If so, implement them. If not, explain why not.

14.3.2   Relational Operators

Classes for which the equality operator is defined also often (but not always) have relational operators. In particular, because the associative containers and some of the algorithms use the less-than operator, it can be useful to define an operator<.

Ordinarily the relational operators should

1. Define an ordering relation that is consistent with the requirements for use as a key to an associative container (§ 11.2.2, p. 424); and

2. Define a relation that is consistent with == if the class has both operators. In particular, if two objects are !=, then one object should be < the other.

Although we might think our Sales_data class should support the relational operators, it turns out that it probably should not do so. The reasons are subtle and are worth understanding.

We might think that we'd define < similarly to compareIsbn (§ 11.2.2, p. 425). That function compared Sales_data objects by comparing their ISBNs. Although compareIsbn provides an ordering relation that meets requirment 1, that function yields results that are inconsistent with our definition of ==. As a result, it does not meet requirement 2.

The Sales_data == operator treats two transactions with the same ISBN as unequal if they have different revenue or units_sold members. If we defined the < operator to compare only the ISBN member, then two objects with the same ISBN but different units_sold or revenue would compare as unequal, but neither object would be less than the other. Ordinarily, if we have two objects, neither of which is less than the other, then we expect that those objects are equal.

We might think that we should, therefore, define operator< to compare each data element in turn. We could define operator< to compare objects with equal isbns by looking next at the units_sold and then at the revenue members.

However, there is nothing essential about this ordering. Depending on how we plan to use the class, we might want to define the order based first on either revenue or units_sold. We might want those objects with fewer units_sold to be "less than" those with more. Or we might want to consider those with smaller revenue "less than" those with more.

For Sales_data, there is no single logical definition of <. Thus, it is better for this class not to define < at all.

Best Practices

If a single logical definition for < exists, classes usually should define the < operator. However, if the class also has ==, define < only if the definitions of < and == yield consistent results.

EXERCISES SECTION 14.3.2

Exercise 14.18: Define relational operators for your StrBlob, StrBlobPtr, StrVec, and String classes.

Exercise 14.19: Should the class you chose for exercise 7.40 from § 7.5.1 (p. 291) define the relational operators? If so, implement them. If not, explain why not.

14.4 Assignment Operators

In addition to the copy- and move-assignment operators that assign one object of the class type to another object of the same type (§ 13.1.2, p. 500, and § 13.6.2, p. 536), a class can define additional assignment operators that allow other types as the right-hand operand.

As one example, in addition to the copy- and move-assignment operators, the library vector class defines a third assignment operator that takes a braced list of elements (§ 9.2.5, p. 337). We can use this operator as follows:

```
vector<string> v;
v = {"a", "an", "the"};
```

We can add this operator to our StrVec class (§ 13.5, p. 526) as well:

```
class StrVec {
public:
    StrVec &operator=(std::initializer_list<std::string>);
    // other members as in § 13.5 (p. 526)
};
```

To be consistent with assignment for the built-in types (and with the copy- and move-assignment operators we already defined), our new assignment operator will return a reference to its left-hand operand:

```
StrVec &StrVec::operator=(initializer_list<string> il)
{
    // alloc_n_copy allocates space and copies elements from the given range
    auto data = alloc_n_copy(il.begin(), il.end());
    free();     // destroy the elements in this object and free the space
    elements = data.first; // update data members to point to the new space
    first_free = cap = data.second;
    return *this;
}
```

As with the copy- and move-assignment operators, other overloaded assignment operators have to free the existing elements and create new ones. Unlike the copy- and move-assignment operators, this operator does not need to check for self-assignment. The parameter is an `initializer_list<string>` (§ 6.2.6, p. 220), which means that `il` cannot be the same object as the one denoted by `this`.

Assignment operators can be overloaded. Assignment operators, regardless of parameter type, must be defined as member functions.

Compound-Assignment Operators

Compound assignment operators are not required to be members. However, we prefer to define all assignments, including compound assignments, in the class. For consistency with the built-in compound assignment, these operators should return a reference to their left-hand operand. For example, here is the definition of the `Sales_data` compound-assignment operator:

```
// member binary operator: left-hand operand is bound to the implicit this pointer
// assumes that both objects refer to the same book
Sales_data& Sales_data::operator+=(const Sales_data &rhs)
{
    units_sold += rhs.units_sold;
    revenue += rhs.revenue;
    return *this;
}
```

Assignment operators must, and ordinarily compound-assignment operators should, be defined as members. These operators should return a reference to the left-hand operand.

14.5 Subscript Operator

Classes that represent containers from which elements can be retrieved by position often define the subscript operator, `operator[]`.

EXERCISES SECTION 14.4

Exercise 14.20: Define the addition and compound-assignment operators for your Sales_data class.

Exercise 14.21: Write the Sales_data operators so that + does the actual addition and += calls +. Discuss the disadvantages of this approach compared to the way these operators were defined in § 14.3 (p. 560) and § 14.4 (p. 564).

Exercise 14.22: Define a version of the assignment operator that can assign a string representing an ISBN to a Sales_data.

Exercise 14.23: Define an initializer_list assignment operator for your version of the StrVec class.

Exercise 14.24: Decide whether the class you used in exercise 7.40 from § 7.5.1 (p. 291) needs a copy- and move-assignment operator. If so, define those operators.

Exercise 14.25: Implement any other assignment operators your class should define. Explain which types should be used as operands and why.

 The subscript operator must be a member function.

To be compatible with the ordinary meaning of subscript, the subscript operator usually returns a reference to the element that is fetched. By returning a reference, subscript can be used on either side of an assignment. Consequently, it is also usually a good idea to define both const and nonconst versions of this operator. When applied to a const object, subscript should return a reference to const so that it is not possible to assign to the returned object.

 If a class has a subscript operator, it usually should define two versions: one that returns a plain reference and the other that is a const member and returns a reference to const.

As an example, we'll define subscript for StrVec (§ 13.5, p. 526):

```
class StrVec {
public:
    std::string& operator[](std::size_t n)
        { return elements[n]; }
    const std::string& operator[](std::size_t n) const
        { return elements[n]; }
    // other members as in § 13.5 (p. 526)
private:
    std::string *elements;    // pointer to the first element in the array
};
```

We can use these operators similarly to how we subscript a vector or array. Because subscript returns a reference to an element, if the StrVec is nonconst, we can assign to that element; if we subscript a const object, we can't:

```
// assume svec is a StrVec
const StrVec cvec = svec; // copy elements from svec into cvec
// if svec has any elements, run the string empty function on the first one
if (svec.size() && svec[0].empty())  {
    svec[0] = "zero"; // ok: subscript returns a reference to a string
    cvec[0] = "Zip";  // error: subscripting cvec returns a reference to const
}
```

EXERCISES SECTION 14.5

Exercise 14.26: Define subscript operators for your `StrVec`, `String`, `StrBlob`, and `StrBlobPtr` classes.

14.6   Increment and Decrement Operators

The increment (++) and decrement (--) operators are most often implemented for iterator classes. These operators let the class move between the elements of a sequence. There is no language requirement that these operators be members of the class. However, because these operators change the state of the object on which they operate, our preference is to make them members.

For the built-in types, there are both prefix and postfix versions of the increment and decrement operators. Not surprisingly, we can define both the prefix and postfix instances of these operators for our own classes as well. We'll look at the prefix versions first and then implement the postfix ones.

Best Practices Classes that define increment or decrement operators should define both the prefix and postfix versions. These operators usually should be defined as members.

Defining Prefix Increment/Decrement Operators

To illustrate the increment and decrement operators, we'll define these operators for our `StrBlobPtr` class (§ 12.1.6, p. 474):

```
class StrBlobPtr {
public:
    // increment and decrement
    StrBlobPtr& operator++();            // prefix operators
    StrBlobPtr& operator--();
    // other members as before
};
```

Best Practices To be consistent with the built-in operators, the prefix operators should return a reference to the incremented or decremented object.

The increment and decrement operators work similarly to each other—they call check to verify that the StrBlobPtr is still valid. If so, check also verifies that its given index is valid. If check doesn't throw an exception, these operators return a reference to this object.

In the case of increment, we pass the current value of curr to check. So long as that value is less than the size of the underlying vector, check will return. If curr is already at the end of the vector, check will throw:

```
//  prefix: return a reference to the incremented/decremented object
StrBlobPtr& StrBlobPtr::operator++()
{
    //  if curr already points past the end of the container, can't increment it
    check(curr, "increment past end of StrBlobPtr");
    ++curr;         //  advance the current state
    return *this;
}

StrBlobPtr& StrBlobPtr::operator--()
{
    //  if curr is zero, decrementing it will yield an invalid subscript
    --curr;         //  move the current state back one element
    check(-1, "decrement past begin of StrBlobPtr");
    return *this;
}
```

The decrement operator decrements curr before calling check. That way, if curr (which is an unsigned number) is already zero, the value that we pass to check will be a large positive value representing an invalid subscript (§ 2.1.2, p. 36).

Differentiating Prefix and Postfix Operators

There is one problem with defining both the prefix and postfix operators: Normal overloading cannot distinguish between these operators. The prefix and postfix versions use the same symbol, meaning that the overloaded versions of these operators have the same name. They also have the same number and type of operands.

To solve this problem, the postfix versions take an extra (unused) parameter of type int. When we use a postfix operator, the compiler supplies 0 as the argument for this parameter. Although the postfix function can use this extra parameter, it usually should not. That parameter is not needed for the work normally performed by a postfix operator. Its sole purpose is to distinguish a postfix function from the prefix version.

We can now add the postfix operators to StrBlobPtr:

```
class StrBlobPtr {
public:
    //  increment and decrement
    StrBlobPtr operator++(int);      //  postfix operators
    StrBlobPtr operator--(int);
    //  other members as before
};
```

To be consistent with the built-in operators, the postfix operators should return the old (unincremented or undecremented) value. That value is returned as a value, not a reference.

The postfix versions have to remember the current state of the object before incrementing the object:

```
//  postfix: increment/decrement the object but return the unchanged value
StrBlobPtr StrBlobPtr::operator++(int)
{
    //  no check needed here; the call to prefix increment will do the check
    StrBlobPtr ret = *this;     //  save the current value
    ++*this;        //  advance one element; prefix ++ checks the increment
    return ret;    //  return the saved state
}
StrBlobPtr StrBlobPtr::operator--(int)
{
    //  no check needed here; the call to prefix decrement will do the check
    StrBlobPtr ret = *this;    //  save the current value
    --*this;        //  move backward one element; prefix -- checks the decrement
    return ret;    //  return the saved state
}
```

Each of our operators calls its own prefix version to do the actual work. For example, the postfix increment operator executes

```
++*this
```

This expression calls the prefix increment operator. That operator checks that the increment is safe and either throws an exception or increments `curr`. Assuming `check` doesn't throw an exception, the postfix functions return the stored copy in `ret`. Thus, after the return, the object itself has been advanced, but the value returned reflects the original, unincremented value.

 The `int` parameter is not used, so we do not give it a name.

Calling the Postfix Operators Explicitly

As we saw on page 553, we can explicitly call an overloaded operator as an alternative to using it as an operator in an expression. If we want to call the postfix version using a function call, then we must pass a value for the integer argument:

```
StrBlobPtr p(a1);  //  p points to the vector inside a1
p.operator++(0);   //  call postfix operator++
p.operator++();    //  call prefix operator++
```

The value passed usually is ignored but is necessary in order to tell the compiler to use the postfix version.

Exercise 14.27: Add increment and decrement operators to your `StrBlobPtr` class.

Exercise 14.28: Define addition and subtraction for `StrBlobPtr` so that these operators implement pointer arithmetic (§ 3.5.3, p. 119).

Exercise 14.29: We did not define a `const` version of the increment and decrement operators. Why not?

14.7 Member Access Operators

The dereference (`*`) and arrow (`->`) operators are often used in classes that represent iterators and in smart pointer classes (§ 12.1, p. 450). We can logically add these operators to our `StrBlobPtr` class as well:

```
class StrBlobPtr {
public:
    std::string& operator*() const
    { auto p = check(curr, "dereference past end");
      return (*p)[curr];   //  (*p) is the vector to which this object points
    }
    std::string* operator->() const
    { //  delegate the real work to the dereference operator
      return & this->operator*();
    }
    //  other members as before
};
```

The dereference operator checks that `curr` is still in range and, if so, returns a reference to the element denoted by `curr`. The arrow operator avoids doing any work of its own by calling the dereference operator and returning the address of the element returned by that operator.

Operator arrow must be a member. The dereference operator is not required to be a member but usually should be a member as well.

It is worth noting that we've defined these operators as `const` members. Unlike the increment and decrment operators, fetching an element doesn't change the state of a `StrBlobPtr`. Also note that these operators return a reference or pointer to nonconst `string`. They do so because we know that a `StrBlobPtr` can only be bound to a nonconst `StrBlob` (§ 12.1.6, p. 474).

We can use these operators the same way that we've used the corresponding operations on pointers or `vector` iterators:

```
StrBlob a1 = {"hi", "bye", "now"};
StrBlobPtr p(a1);              // p points to the vector inside a1
*p = "okay";                  // assigns to the first element in a1
cout << p->size() << endl;    // prints 4, the size of the first element in a1
cout << (*p).size() << endl; // equivalent to p->size()
```

Constraints on the Return from Operator Arrow

As with most of the other operators (although it would be a bad idea to do so), we can define operator* to do whatever processing we like. That is, we can define operator* to return a fixed value, say, 42, or print the contents of the object to which it is applied, or whatever. The same is not true for overloaded arrow. The arrow operator never loses its fundamental meaning of member access. When we overload arrow, we change the object from which arrow fetches the specified member. We cannot change the fact that arrow fetches a member.

When we write point->mem, point must be a pointer to a class object or it must be an object of a class with an overloaded operator->. Depending on the type of point, writing point->mem is equivalent to

```
(*point).mem;           // point is a built-in pointer type
point.operator()->mem;  // point is an object of class type
```

Otherwise the code is in error. That is, point->mem executes as follows:

1. If point is a pointer, then the built-in arrow operator is applied, which means this expression is a synonym for (*point).mem. The pointer is dereferenced and the indicated member is fetched from the resulting object. If the type pointed to by point does not have a member named mem, then the code is in error.

2. If point is an object of a class that defines operator->, then the result of point.operator->() is used to fetch mem. If that result is a pointer, then step 1 is executed on that pointer. If the result is an object that itself has an overloaded operator->(), then this step is repeated on that object. This process continues until either a pointer to an object with the indicated member is returned or some other value is returned, in which case the code is in error.

> The overloaded arrow operator *must* return either a pointer to a class type or an object of a class type that defines its own operator arrow.

EXERCISES SECTION 14.7

Exercise 14.30: Add dereference and arrow operators to your StrBlobPtr class and to the ConstStrBlobPtr class that you defined in exercise 12.22 from § 12.1.6 (p. 476). Note that the operators in constStrBlobPtr must return const references because the data member in constStrBlobPtr points to a const vector.

Exercise 14.31: Our StrBlobPtr class does not define the copy constructor, assignment operator, or a destructor. Why is that okay?

Exercise 14.32: Define a class that holds a pointer to a StrBlobPtr. Define the overloaded arrow operator for that class.

14.8   Function-Call Operator

Classes that overload the call operator allow objects of its type to be used as if they were a function. Because such classes can also store state, they can be more flexible than ordinary functions.

As a simple example, the following `struct`, named `absInt`, has a call operator that returns the absolute value of its argument:

```
struct absInt {
    int operator()(int val) const {
        return val < 0 ? -val : val;
    }
};
```

This class defines a single operation: the function-call operator. That operator takes an argument of type `int` and returns the argument's absolute value.

We use the call operator by applying an argument list to an `absInt` object in a way that looks like a function call:

```
int i = -42;
absInt absObj;       // object that has a function-call operator
int ui = absObj(i); // passes i to absObj.operator()
```

Even though `absObj` is an object, not a function, we can "call" this object. Calling an object runs its overloaded call operator. In this case, that operator takes an `int` value and returns its absolute value.

 The function-call operator must be a member function. A class may define multiple versions of the call operator, each of which must differ as to the number or types of their parameters.

Objects of classes that define the call operator are referred to as **function objects**. Such objects "act like functions" because we can call them.

Function-Object Classes with State

Like any other class, a function-object class can have additional members aside from `operator()`. Function-object classes often contain data members that are used to customize the operations in the call operator.

As an example, we'll define a class that prints a `string` argument. By default, our class will write to `cout` and will print a space following each `string`. We'll also let users of our class provide a different stream on which to write and provide a different separator. We can define this class as follows:

```
class PrintString {
public:
    PrintString(ostream &o = cout, char c = ' '):
        os(o), sep(c) { }
    void operator()(const string &s) const { os << s << sep; }
private:
    ostream &os;     // stream on which to write
    char sep;        // character to print after each output
};
```

Our class has a constructor that takes a reference to an output stream and a character to use as the separator. It uses `cout` and a space as default arguments (§ 6.5.1, p. 236) for these parameters. The body of the function-call operator uses these members when it prints the given `string`.

When we define `PrintString` objects, we can use the defaults or supply our own values for the separator or output stream:

```
PrintString printer;          //  uses the defaults; prints to cout
printer(s);                   //  prints s followed by a space on cout
PrintString errors(cerr, '\n');
errors(s);                    //  prints s followed by a newline on cerr
```

Function objects are most often used as arguments to the generic algorithms. For example, we can use the library `for_each` algorithm (§ 10.3.2, p. 391) and our `PrintString` class to print the contents of a container:

```
for_each(vs.begin(), vs.end(), PrintString(cerr, '\n'));
```

The third argument to `for_each` is a temporary object of type `PrintString` that we initialize from `cerr` and a newline character. The call to `for_each` will print each element in `vs` to `cerr` followed by a newline.

EXERCISES SECTION 14.8

Exercise 14.33: How many operands may an overloaded function-call operator take?

Exercise 14.34: Define a function-object class to perform an if-then-else operation: The call operator for this class should take three parameters. It should test its first parameter and if that test succeeds, it should return its second parameter; otherwise, it should return its third parameter.

Exercise 14.35: Write a class like `PrintString` that reads a line of input from an `istream` and returns a `string` representing what was read. If the read fails, return the empty `string`.

Exercise 14.36: Use the class from the previous exercise to read the standard input, storing each line as an element in a `vector`.

Exercise 14.37: Write a class that tests whether two values are equal. Use that object and the library algorithms to write a program to replace all instances of a given value in a sequence.

14.8.1 Lambdas Are Function Objects

In the previous section, we used a `PrintString` object as an argument in a call to `for_each`. This usage is similar to the programs we wrote in § 10.3.2 (p. 388) that used lambda expressions. When we write a lambda, the compiler translates that expression into an unnamed object of an unnamed class (§ 10.3.3, p. 392). The classes generated from a lambda contain an overloaded function-call operator. For example, the lambda that we passed as the last argument to `stable_sort`:

```
//  sort words by size, but maintain alphabetical order for words of the same size
stable_sort(words.begin(), words.end(),
              [](const string &a, const string &b)
                { return a.size() < b.size();});
```

acts like an unnamed object of a class that would look something like

```
class ShorterString {
public:
    bool operator()(const string &s1, const string &s2) const
    { return s1.size() < s2.size(); }
};
```

The generated class has a single member, which is a function-call operator that takes two `strings` and compares their lengths. The parameter list and function body are the same as the lambda. As we saw in § 10.3.3 (p. 395), by default, lambdas may not change their captured variables. As a result, by default, the function-call operator in a class generated from a lambda is a `const` member function. If the lambda is declared as `mutable`, then the call operator is not `const`.

We can rewrite the call to `stable_sort` to use this class instead of the lambda expression:

```
stable_sort(words.begin(), words.end(), ShorterString());
```

The third argument is a newly constructed `ShorterString` object. The code in `stable_sort` will "call" this object each time it compares two `strings`. When the object is called, it will execute the body of its call operator, returning `true` if the first `string`'s size is less than the second's.

Classes Representing Lambdas with Captures

As we've seen, when a lambda captures a variable by reference, it is up to the program to ensure that the variable to which the reference refers exists when the lambda is executed (§ 10.3.3, p. 393). Therefore, the compiler is permitted to use the reference directly without storing that reference as a data member in the generated class.

In contrast, variables that are captured by value are copied into the lambda (§ 10.3.3, p. 392). As a result, classes generated from lambdas that capture variables by value have data members corresponding to each such variable. These classes also have a constructor to initialize these data members from the value of the captured variables. As an example, in § 10.3.2 (p. 390), the lambda that we used to find the first `string` whose length was greater than or equal to a given bound:

```
//  get an iterator to the first element whose size() is >= sz
auto wc = find_if(words.begin(), words.end(),
                    [sz](const string &a)
```

would generate a class that looks something like

```
class SizeComp {
    SizeComp(size_t n): sz(n) { }  // parameter for each captured variable
    // call operator with the same return type, parameters, and body as the lambda
    bool operator()(const string &s) const
        { return s.size() >= sz; }
private:
    size_t sz;   // a data member for each variable captured by value
};
```

Unlike our `ShorterString` class, this class has a data member and a constructor
to initialize that member. This synthesized class does not have a default constructor; to use this class, we must pass an argument:

```
// get an iterator to the first element whose size() is >= sz
auto wc = find_if(words.begin(), words.end(), SizeComp(sz));
```

Classes generated from a lambda expression have a deleted default constructor,
deleted assignment operators, and a default destructor. Whether the class has a
defaulted or deleted copy/move constructor depends in the usual ways on the
types of the captured data members (§ 13.1.6, p. 508, and § 13.6.2, p. 537).

EXERCISES SECTION 14.8.1

Exercise 14.38: Write a class that tests whether the length of a given `string` matches
a given bound. Use that object to write a program to report how many words in an
input file are of sizes 1 through 10 inclusive.

Exercise 14.39: Revise the previous program to report the count of words that are sizes
1 through 9 and 10 or more.

Exercise 14.40: Rewrite the `biggies` function from § 10.3.2 (p. 391) to use function-
object classes in place of lambdas.

Exercise 14.41: Why do you suppose the new standard added lambdas? Explain
when you would use a lambda and when you would write a class instead.

14.8.2 Library-Defined Function Objects

The standard library defines a set of classes that represent the arithmetic, relational,
and logical operators. Each class defines a call operator that applies the named
operation. For example, the `plus` class has a function-call operator that applies +
to a pair of operands; the `modulus` class defines a call operator that applies the
binary % operator; the `equal_to` class applies ==; and so on.

These classes are templates to which we supply a single type. That type specifies the parameter type for the call operator. For example, `plus<string>` applies
the `string` addition operator to `string` objects; for `plus<int>` the operands are
`int`s; `plus<Sales_data>` applies + to `Sales_data`s; and so on:

```
plus<int> intAdd;         // function object that can add two int values
negate<int>  intNegate;   // function object that can negate an int value
// uses intAdd::operator(int, int) to add 10 and 20
int sum = intAdd(10, 20);                // equivalent to sum = 30
sum = intNegate(intAdd(10, 20));    // equivalent to sum = 30
// uses intNegate::operator(int) to generate -10 as the second parameter
// to intAdd::operator(int, int)
sum = intAdd(10, intNegate(10));    // sum = 0
```

These types, listed in Table 14.2, are defined in the `functional` header.

Table 14.2: Library Function Objects		
Arithmetic	*Relational*	*Logical*
plus<Type>	equal_to<Type>	logical_and<Type>
minus<Type>	not_equal_to<Type>	logical_or<Type>
multiplies<Type>	greater<Type>	logical_not<Type>
divides<Type>	greater_equal<Type>	
modulus<Type>	less<Type>	
negate<Type>	less_equal<Type>	

Using a Library Function Object with the Algorithms

The function-object classes that represent operators are often used to override the
default operator used by an algorithm. As we've seen, by default, the sorting algorithms use `operator<`, which ordinarily sorts the sequence into ascending order.
To sort into descending order, we can pass an object of type `greater`. That class
generates a call operator that invokes the greater-than operator of the underlying
element type. For example, if `svec` is a `vector<string>`,

```
// passes a temporary function object that applies the < operator to two strings
sort(svec.begin(), svec.end(), greater<string>());
```

sorts the `vector` in descending order. The third argument is an unnamed object of
type `greater<string>`. When `sort` compares elements, rather than applying
the `<` operator for the element type, it will call the given `greater` function object.
That object applies `>` to the `string` elements.

One important aspect of these library function objects is that the library guarantees that they will work for pointers. Recall that comparing two unrelated pointers
is undefined (§ 3.5.3, p. 120). However, we might want to `sort` a `vector` of pointers based on their addresses in memory. Although it would be undefined for us to
do so directly, we can do so through one of the library function objects:

```
vector<string *> nameTable;  // vector of pointers
// error: the pointers in nameTable are unrelated, so < is undefined
sort(nameTable.begin(), nameTable.end(),
     [](string *a, string *b) { return a < b; });
// ok: library guarantees that less on pointer types is well defined
sort(nameTable.begin(), nameTable.end(), less<string*>());
```

It is also worth noting that the associative containers use less<key_type> to order their elements. As a result, we can define a set of pointers or use a pointer as the key in a map without specifying less directly.

Exercise 14.42: Using library function objects and adaptors, define an expression to

(a) Count the number of values that are greater than 1024
(b) Find the first string that is not equal to pooh
(c) Multiply all values by 2

Exercise 14.43: Using library function objects, determine whether a given int value is divisible by any element in a container of ints.

14.8.3 Callable Objects and `function`

C++ has several kinds of callable objects: functions and pointers to functions, lambdas (§ 10.3.2, p. 388), objects created by bind (§ 10.3.4, p. 397), and classes that overload the function-call operator.

Like any other object, a callable object has a type. For example, each lambda has its own unique (unnamed) class type. Function and function-pointer types vary by their return type and argument types, and so on.

However, two callable objects with different types may share the same **call signature**. The call signature specifies the type returned by a call to the object and the argument type(s) that must be passed in the call. A call signature corresponds to a function type. For example:

```
int(int, int)
```

is a function type that takes two ints and returns an int.

Different Types Can Have the Same Call Signature

Sometimes we want to treat several callable objects that share a call signature as if they had the same type. For example, consider the following different types of callable objects:

```
//  ordinary function
int add(int i, int j) { return i + j; }
//  lambda, which generates an unnamed function-object class
auto mod = [](int i, int j) { return i % j; };
//  function-object class
struct div {
    int operator()(int denominator, int divisor) {
        return denominator / divisor;
    }
};
```

Each of these callables applies an arithmetic operation to its parameters. Even though each has a distinct type, they all share the same call signature:

```
int(int, int)
```

We might want to use these callables to build a simple desk calculator. To do so, we'd want to define a **function table** to store "pointers" to these callables. When the program needs to execute a particular operation, it will look in the table to find which function to call.

In C++, function tables are easy to implement using a map. In this case, we'll use a string corresponding to an operator symbol as the key; the value will be the function that implements that operator. When we want to evaluate a given operator, we'll index the map with that operator and call the resulting element.

If all our functions were freestanding functions, and assuming we were handling only binary operators for type int, we could define the map as

```
//  maps an operator to a pointer to a function taking two ints and returning an int
map<string, int(*)(int,int)> binops;
```

We could put a pointer to add into binops as follows:

```
//  ok: add is a pointer to function of the appropriate type
binops.insert({"+", add}); //  {"+", add} is a pair § 11.2.3 (p. 426)
```

However, we can't store mod or div in binops:

```
binops.insert({"%",  mod}); //  error: mod is not a pointer to function
```

The problem is that mod is a lambda, and each lambda has its own class type. That type does not match the type of the values stored in binops.

The Library function Type

We can solve this problem using a new library type named **function** that is defined in the functional header; Table 14.3 (p. 579) lists the operations defined by function. $\boxed{\substack{\text{C++} \\ \text{11}}}$

function is a template. As with other templates we've used, we must specify additional information when we create a function type. In this case, that information is the call signature of the objects that this particular function type can represent. As with other templates, we specify the type inside angle brackets:

```
function<int(int, int)>
```

Here we've declared a function type that can represent callable objects that return an int result and have two int parameters. We can use that type to represent any of our desk calculator types:

```
function<int(int, int)> f1 = add;     // function pointer
function<int(int, int)> f2 = div();   // object of a function-object class
function<int(int, int)> f3 = [](int i, int j) // lambda
                                 { return i * j; };
cout << f1(4,2) << endl; // prints 6
cout << f2(4,2) << endl; // prints 2
cout << f3(4,2) << endl; // prints 8
```

We can now redefine our `map` using this `function` type:

```
//   table of callable objects corresponding to each binary operator
//   all the callables must take two ints and return an int
//   an element can be a function pointer, function object, or lambda
map<string, function<int(int, int)>> binops;
```

We can add each of our callable objects, be they function pointers, lambdas, or function objects, to this `map`:

```
map<string, function<int(int, int)>> binops = {
    {"+", add},                       //  function pointer
    {"-", std::minus<int>()},         //  library function object
    {"/",  div()},                    //  user-defined function object
    {"*", [](int i, int j) { return i * j; }}, //  unnamed lambda
    {"%", mod} };                     //  named lambda object
```

Our `map` has five elements. Although the underlying callable objects all have different types from one another, we can store each of these distinct types in the common `function<int(int, int)>` type.

As usual, when we index a `map`, we get a reference to the associated value. When we index `binops`, we get a reference to an object of type `function`. The `function` type overloads the call operator. That call operator takes its own arguments and passes them along to its stored callable object:

```
binops["+"](10, 5); //  calls add(10, 5)
binops["-"](10, 5); //  uses the call operator of the minus<int> object
binops["/"](10, 5); //  uses the call operator of the div object
binops["*"](10, 5); //  calls the lambda function object
binops["%"](10, 5); //  calls the lambda function object
```

Here we call each of the operations stored in `binops`. In the first call, the element we get back holds a function pointer that points to our `add` function. Calling `binops["+"](10, 5)` uses that pointer to call `add`, passing it the values 10 and 5. In the next call, `binops["-"]`, returns a `function` that stores an object of type `std::minus<int>`. We call that object's call operator, and so on.

Overloaded Functions and `function`

We cannot (directly) store the name of an overloaded function in an object of type `function`:

```
int add(int i, int j) { return i + j; }
Sales_data add(const Sales_data&, const Sales_data&);
map<string, function<int(int, int)>> binops;
binops.insert( {"+", add} ); // error: which add?
```

One way to resolve the ambiguity is to store a function pointer (§ 6.7, p. 247) instead of the name of the function:

```
int (*fp)(int,int) = add; //  pointer to the version of add that takes two ints
binops.insert( {"+", fp} ); //  ok: fp points to the right version of add
```

Table 14.3: Operations on `function`	
`function<T> f;`	`f` is a null `function` object that can store callable objects with a call signature that is equivalent to the function type `T` (i.e., `T` is *retType* (*args*)).
`function<T> f(nullptr);`	Explicitly construct a null `function`.
`function<T> f(obj);`	Stores a copy of the callable object `obj` in `f`.
`f`	Use `f` as a condition; `true` if `f` holds a callable object; `false` otherwise.
`f` (*args*)	Calls the object in `f` passing *args*.
Types defined as members of `function<T>`	
`result_type`	The type returned by this `function` type's callable object.

`argument_type`
`first_argument_type`
`second_argument_type`
	Types defined when `T` has exactly one or two arguments. If `T` has one argument, `argument_type` is a synonym for that type. If `T` has two arguments, `first_argument_type` and `second_argument_type` are synonyms for those argument types.

Alternatively, we can use a lambda to disambiguate:

```
// ok: use a lambda to disambiguate which version of add we want to use
binops.insert( {"+", [](int a, int b) {return add(a, b);} } );
```

The call inside the lambda body passes two `int`s. That call can match only the version of `add` that takes two `int`s, and so that is the function that is called when the lambda is executed.

> The `function` class in the new library is not related to classes named `unary_function` and `binary_function` that were part of earlier versions of the library. These classes have been deprecated by the more general `bind` function (§ 10.3.4, p. 401).

EXERCISES SECTION 14.8.3

Exercise 14.44: Write your own version of a simple desk calculator that can handle binary operations.

14.9 Overloading, Conversions, and Operators

In § 7.5.4 (p. 294) we saw that a nonexplicit constructor that can be called with one argument defines an implicit conversion. Such constructors convert an object from the argument's type *to* the class type. We can also define conversions *from* the class type. We define a conversion from a class type by defining a conversion operator. Converting constructors and conversion operators define **class-type conversions**. Such conversions are also referred to as **user-defined conversions**.

14.9.1 Conversion Operators

A **conversion operator** is a special kind of member function that converts a value of a class type to a value of some other type. A conversion function typically has the general form

```
operator type() const;
```

where *type* represents a type. Conversion operators can be defined for any type (other than `void`) that can be a function return type (§ 6.1, p. 204). Conversions to an array or a function type are not permitted. Conversions to pointer types—both data and function pointers—and to reference types are allowed.

Conversion operators have no explicitly stated return type and no parameters, and they must be defined as member functions. Conversion operations ordinarily should not change the object they are converting. As a result, conversion operators usually should be defined as `const` members.

> A conversion function must be a member function, may not specify a return type, and must have an empty parameter list. The function usually should be `const`.

Defining a Class with a Conversion Operator

As an example, we'll define a small class that represents an integer in the range of 0 to 255:

```
class SmallInt {
public:
    SmallInt(int i = 0): val(i)
    {
        if (i < 0 || i > 255)
            throw std::out_of_range("Bad SmallInt value");
    }
    operator int() const { return val; }
private:
    std::size_t val;
};
```

Our `SmallInt` class defines conversions *to* and *from* its type. The constructor converts values of arithmetic type to a `SmallInt`. The conversion operator converts `SmallInt` objects to `int`:

```
SmallInt si;
si = 4;   // implicitly converts 4 to SmallInt then calls SmallInt::operator=
si + 3;   // implicitly converts si to int followed by integer addition
```

Although the compiler will apply only one user-defined conversion at a time (§ 4.11.2, p. 162), an implicit user-defined conversion can be preceded or followed by a standard (built-in) conversion (§ 4.11.1, p. 159). As a result, we can pass any arithmetic type to the `SmallInt` constructor. Similarly, we can use the converion operator to convert a `SmallInt` to an `int` and then convert the resulting `int` value to another arithmetic type:

```
//  the double argument is converted to int using the built-in conversion
SmallInt si = 3.14;  //  calls the SmallInt(int) constructor
//  the SmallInt conversion operator converts si to int;
si + 3.14;  //  that int is converted to double using the built-in conversion
```

Because conversion operators are implicitly applied, there is no way to pass arguments to these functions. Hence, conversion operators may not be defined to take parameters. Although a conversion function does not specify a return type, each conversion function must return a value of its corresponding type:

```
class SmallInt;
operator int(SmallInt&);                   //  error: nonmember
class SmallInt {
public:
    int operator int() const;              //  error: return type
    operator int(int = 0) const;           //  error: parameter list
    operator int*() const { return 42; }   //  error: 42 is not a pointer
};
```

CAUTION: AVOID OVERUSE OF CONVERSION FUNCTIONS

As with using overloaded operators, judicious use of conversion operators can greatly simplify the job of a class designer and make using a class easier. However, some conversions can be misleading. Conversion operators are misleading when there is no obvious single mapping between the class type and the conversion type.

For example, consider a class that represents a `Date`. We might think it would be a good idea to provide a conversion from `Date` to `int`. However, what value should the conversion function return? The function might return a decimal representation of the year, month, and day. For example, July 30, 1989 might be represented as the `int` value 19800730. Alternatively, the conversion operator might return an `int` representing the number of days that have elapsed since some epoch point, such as January 1, 1970. Both these conversions have the desirable property that later dates correspond to larger integers, and so either might be useful.

The problem is that there is no single one-to-one mapping between an object of type `Date` and a value of type `int`. In such cases, it is better not to define the conversion operator. Instead, the class ought to define one or more ordinary members to extract the information in these various forms.

Conversion Operators Can Yield Suprising Results

In practice, classes rarely provide conversion operators. Too often users are more likely to be surprised if a conversion happens automatically than to be helped by the existence of the conversion. However, there is one important exception to this rule of thumb: It is not uncommon for classes to define conversions to `bool`.

Under earlier versions of the standard, classes that wanted to define a conversion to `bool` faced a problem: Because `bool` is an arithmetic type, a class-type object that is converted to `bool` can be used in any context where an arithmetic type is expected. Such conversions can happen in surprising ways. In particular, if `istream` had a conversion to `bool`, the following code would compile:

```
int i = 42;
cin << i;  //  this code would be legal if the conversion to bool were not explicit!
```

This program attempts to use the output operator on an input stream. There is no `<<` defined for `istream`, so the code is almost surely in error. However, this code could use the `bool` conversion operator to convert `cin` to `bool`. The resulting `bool` value would then be promoted to `int` and used as the left-hand operand to the built-in version of the left-shift operator. The promoted `bool` value (either 1 or 0) would be shifted left 42 positions.

`explicit` Conversion Operators

C++
11 To prevent such problems, the new standard introduced **`explicit` conversion operators**:

```
class SmallInt {
public:
    //  the compiler won't automatically apply this conversion
    explicit operator int() const { return val; }
    //  other members as before
};
```

As with an `explicit` constructor (§ 7.5.4, p. 296), the compiler won't (generally) use an `explicit` conversion operator for implicit conversions:

```
SmallInt si = 3;   //  ok: the SmallInt constructor is not explicit
si + 3; //  error: implicit is conversion required, but operator int is explicit
static_cast<int>(si) + 3; //  ok: explicitly request the conversion
```

If the conversion operator is `explicit`, we can still do the conversion. However, with one exception, we must do so explicitly through a cast.

The exception is that the compiler will apply an `explicit` conversion to an expression used as a condition. That is, an `explicit` conversion will be used implicitly to convert an expression used as

- The condition of an `if`, `while`, or `do` statement

- The condition expression in a `for` statement header

- An operand to the logical NOT (`!`), OR (`||`), or AND (`&&`) operators

- The condition expression in a conditional (`? :`) operator

Conversion to `bool`

In earlier versions of the library, the IO types defined a conversion to `void*`. They did so to avoid the kinds of problems illustrated above. Under the new standard, the IO library instead defines an `explicit` conversion to `bool`.

Whenever we use a stream object in a condition, we use the `operator bool` that is defined for the IO types. For example,

```
while (std::cin >> value)
```

The condition in the `while` executes the input operator, which reads into `value` and returns `cin`. To evaluate the condition, `cin` is implicitly converted by the `istream operator bool` conversion function. That function returns `true` if the condition state of `cin` is `good` (§ 8.1.2, p. 312), and `false` otherwise.

> **Best Practices** Conversion to `bool` is usually intended for use in conditions. As a result, `operator bool` ordinarily should be defined as `explicit`.

EXERCISES SECTION 14.9.1

Exercise 14.45: Write conversion operators to convert a `Sales_data` to `string` and to `double`. What values do you think these operators should return?

Exercise 14.46: Explain whether defining these `Sales_data` conversion operators is a good idea and whether they should be `explicit`.

Exercise 14.47: Explain the difference between these two conversion operators:

```
struct Integral {
    operator const int();
    operator int() const;
};
```

Exercise 14.48: Determine whether the class you used in exercise 7.40 from § 7.5.1 (p. 291) should have a conversion to `bool`. If so, explain why, and explain whether the operator should be `explicit`. If not, explain why not.

Exercise 14.49: Regardless of whether it is a good idea to do so, define a conversion to `bool` for the class from the previous exercise.

14.9.2 Avoiding Ambiguous Conversions

If a class has one or more conversions, it is important to ensure that there is only one way to convert from the class type to the target type. If there is more than one way to perform a conversion, it will be hard to write unambiguous code.

There are two ways that multiple conversion paths can occur. The first happens when two classes provide mutual conversions. For example, mutual conversions exist when a class `A` defines a converting constructor that takes an object of class `B` and `B` itself defines a conversion operator to type `A`.

The second way to generate multiple conversion paths is to define multiple conversions from or to types that are themselves related by conversions. The most obvious instance is the built-in arithmetic types. A given class ordinarily ought to define at most one conversion to or from an arithmetic type.

 Ordinarily, it is a bad idea to define classes with mutual conversions or to define conversions to or from two arithmetic types.

Argument Matching and Mutual Conversions

In the following example, we've defined two ways to obtain an A from a B: either by using B's conversion operator or by using the A constructor that takes a B:

```
//  usually a bad idea to have mutual conversions between two class types
struct B;
struct A {
    A() = default;
    A(const B&);            //  converts a B to an A
    //  other members
};
struct B {
    operator A() const; //  also converts a B to an A
    //  other members
};
A f(const A&);
B b;
A a = f(b); //  error ambiguous: f(B::operator A())
            //              or f(A::A(const B&))
```

Because there are two ways to obtain an A from a B, the compiler doesn't know which conversion to run; the call to f is ambiguous. This call can use the A constructor that takes a B, or it can use the B conversion operator that converts a B to an A. Because these two functions are equally good, the call is in error.

If we want to make this call, we have to explicitly call the conversion operator or the constructor:

```
A a1 = f(b.operator A()); //  ok: use B's conversion operator
A a2 = f(A(b));           //  ok: use A's constructor
```

Note that we can't resolve the ambiguity by using a cast—the cast itself would have the same ambiguity.

Ambiguities and Multiple Conversions to Built-in Types

Ambiguities also occur when a class defines multiple conversions to (or from) types that are themselves related by conversions. The easiest case to illustrate—and one that is particularly problematic—is when a class defines constructors from or conversions to more than one arithmetic type.

For example, the following class has converting constructors from two different arithmetic types, and conversion operators to two different arithmetic types:

```
struct A {
    A(int = 0);      //  usually a bad idea to have two
    A(double);       //  conversions from arithmetic types

    operator int() const;      //  usually a bad idea to have two
    operator double() const;  //  conversions to arithmetic types
    //  other members
};
void f2(long double);
A a;
f2(a);  //  error ambiguous: f(A::operator int())
        //               or f(A::operator double())

long lg;
A a2(lg);  //  error ambiguous: A::A(int) or A::A(double)
```

In the call to f2, neither conversion is an exact match to long double. However, either conversion can be used, followed by a standard conversion to get to long double. Hence, neither conversion is better than the other; the call is ambiguous.

We encounter the same problem when we try to initialize a2 from a long. Neither constructor is an exact match for long. Each would require that the argument be converted before using the constructor:

- Standard long to double conversion followed by A(double)

- Standard long to int conversion followed by A(int)

These conversion sequences are indistinguishable, so the call is ambiguous.

The call to f2, and the initialization of a2, are ambiguous because the standard conversions that were needed had the same rank (§ 6.6.1, p. 245). When a user-defined conversion is used, the rank of the standard conversion, if any, is used to select the best match:

```
short s = 42;
//  promoting short to int is better than converting short to double
A a3(s);    //  uses A::A(int)
```

In this case, promoting a short to an int is preferred to converting the short to a double. Hence a3 is constructed using the A::A(int) constructor, which is run on the (promoted) value of s.

> When two user-defined conversions are used, the rank of the standard conversion, if any, *preceding* or *following* the conversion function is used to select the best match.

Overloaded Functions and Converting Constructors

Choosing among multiple conversions is further complicated when we call an overloaded function. If two or more conversions provide a viable match, then the conversions are considered equally good.

As one example, ambiguity problems can arise when overloaded functions take parameters that differ by class types that define the same converting constructors:

> ### CAUTION: CONVERSIONS AND OPERATORS
>
> Correctly designing the overloaded operators, conversion constructors, and conversion functions for a class requires some care. In particular, ambiguities are easy to generate if a class defines both conversion operators and overloaded operators. A few rules of thumb can be helpful:
>
> - Don't define mutually converting classes—if class Foo has a constructor that takes an object of class Bar, do not give Bar a conversion operator to type Foo.
>
> - Avoid conversions to the built-in arithmetic types. In particular, if you do define a conversion to an arithmetic type, then
>
>   - Do not define overloaded versions of the operators that take arithmetic types. If users need to use these operators, the conversion operation will convert objects of your type, and then the built-in operators can be used.
>
>   - Do not define a conversion to more than one arithmetic type. Let the standard conversions provide conversions to the other arithmetic types.
>
> The easiest rule of all: With the exception of an `explicit` conversion to `bool`, avoid defining conversion functions and limit nonexplicit constructors to those that are "obviously right."

```
struct C {
    C(int);
    //  other members
};
struct D {
    D(int);
    //  other members
};
void manip(const C&);
void manip(const D&);
manip(10);  //  error ambiguous: manip(C(10)) or manip(D(10))
```

Here both C and D have constructors that take an `int`. Either constructor can be used to match a version of `manip`. Hence, the call is ambiguous: It could mean convert the `int` to C and call the first version of `manip`, or it could mean convert the `int` to D and call the second version.

The caller can disambiguate by explicitly constructing the correct type:

```
manip(C(10));  //  ok: calls manip(const C&)
```

WARNING   Needing to use a constructor or a cast to convert an argument in a call to an overloaded function frequently is a sign of bad design.

Overloaded Functions and User-Defined Conversion

In a call to an overloaded function, if two (or more) user-defined conversions provide a viable match, the conversions are considered equally good. The rank of any standard conversions that might or might not be required is not considered. Whether a built-in conversion is also needed is considered only if the overload set can be matched *using the same conversion function*.

For example, our call to manip would be ambiguous even if one of the classes defined a constructor that required a standard conversion for the argument:

```
struct E {
    E(double);
    //  other members
};
void manip2(const C&);
void manip2(const E&);
//  error ambiguous: two different user-defined conversions could be used
manip2(10); //  manip2(C(10) or manip2(E(double(10)))
```

In this case, C has a conversion from int and E has a conversion from double. For the call manip2(10), both manip2 functions are viable:

- manip2(const C&) is viable because C has a converting constructor that takes an int. That constructor is an exact match for the argument.

- manip2(const E&) is viable because E has a converting constructor that takes a double and we can use a standard conversion to convert the int argument in order to use that converting constructor.

Because calls to the overloaded functions require *different* user-defined conversions from one another, this call is ambiguous. In particular, even though one of the calls requires a standard conversion and the other is an exact match, the compiler will still flag this call as an error.

> In a call to an overloaded function, the rank of an additional standard conversion (if any) matters only if the viable functions require the same user-defined conversion. If different user-defined conversions are needed, then the call is ambiguous.

14.9.3 Function Matching and Overloaded Operators

Overloaded operators are overloaded functions. Normal function matching (§ 6.4, p. 233) is used to determine which operator—built-in or overloaded—to apply to a given expression. However, when an operator function is used in an expression, the set of candidate functions is broader than when we call a function using the call operator. If a has a class type, the expression a *sym* b might be

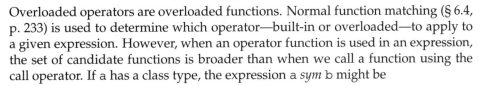

```
a.operatorsym(b); //  a has operatorsym as a member function
operatorsym(a, b);//  operatorsym is an ordinary function
```

Unlike ordinary function calls, we cannot use the form of the call to distinquish whether we're calling a nonmember or a member function.

EXERCISES SECTION 14.9.2

Exercise 14.50: Show the possible class-type conversion sequences for the initializations of ex1 and ex2. Explain whether the initializations are legal or not.

```
struct LongDouble {
    LongDouble(double = 0.0);
    operator double();
    operator float();
};
LongDouble ldObj;
int ex1 = ldObj;
float ex2 = ldObj;
```

Exercise 14.51: Show the conversion sequences (if any) needed to call each version of calc and explain why the best viable function is selected.

```
void calc(int);
void calc(LongDouble);
double dval;
calc(dval); // which calc?
```

When we use an overloaded operator with an operand of class type, the candidate functions include ordinary nonmember versions of that operator, as well as the built-in versions of the operator. Moreover, if the left-hand operand has class type, the overloaded versions of the operator, if any, defined by that class are also included.

When we call a named function, member and nonmember functions with the same name do *not* overload one another. There is no overloading because the syntax we use to call a named function distinguishes between member and nonmember functions. When a call is through an object of a class type (or through a reference or pointer to such an object), then only the member functions of that class are considered. When we use an overloaded operator in an expression, there is nothing to indicate whether we're using a member or nonmember function. Therefore, both member and nonmember versions must be considered.

 The set of candidate functions for an operator used in an expression can contain both nonmember and member functions.

As an example, we'll define an addition operator for our SmallInt class:

```
class SmallInt {
    friend
    SmallInt operator+(const SmallInt&, const SmallInt&);
public:
    SmallInt(int = 0);                        // conversion from int
    operator int() const { return val; } // conversion to int
private:
    std::size_t val;
};
```

We can use this class to add two SmallInts, but we will run into ambiguity problems if we attempt to perform mixed-mode arithmetic:

```
SmallInt s1, s2;
SmallInt s3 = s1 + s2;   //  uses overloaded operator+
int i = s3 + 0;          //  error: ambiguous
```

The first addition uses the overloaded version of + that takes two SmallInt values. The second addition is ambiguous, because we can convert 0 to a SmallInt and use the SmallInt version of +, or convert s3 to int and use the built-in addition operator on ints.

WARNING Providing both conversion functions to an arithmetic type and overloaded operators for the same class type may lead to ambiguities between the overloaded operators and the built-in operators.

EXERCISES SECTION 14.9.3

Exercise 14.52: Which operator+, if any, is selected for each of the addition expressions? List the candidate functions, the viable functions, and the type conversions on the arguments for each viable function:

```
struct LongDouble {
        //  member operator+ for illustration purposes; + is usually a nonmember
        LongDouble operator+(const SmallInt&);
        //  other members as in § 14.9.2 (p. 587)
};
LongDouble operator+(LongDouble&, double);
SmallInt si;
LongDouble ld;
ld = si + ld;
ld = ld + si;
```

Exercise 14.53: Given the definition of SmallInt on page 588, determine whether the following addition expression is legal. If so, what addition operator is used? If not, how might you change the code to make it legal?

```
SmallInt s1;
double d = s1 + 3.14;
```

CHAPTER SUMMARY

An overloaded operator must either be a member of a class or have at least one operand of class type. Overloaded operators have the same number of operands, associativity, and precedence as the corresponding operator when applied to the built-in types. When an operator is defined as a member, its implicit this pointer is bound to the first operand. The assignment, subscript, function-call, and arrow operators must be class members.

Objects of classes that overload the function-call operator, operator(), are known as "function objects." Such objects are often used in combination with the standard algorithms. Lambda expressions are succinct ways to define simple function-object classes.

A class can define conversions to or from its type that are used automatically. Nonexplicit constructors that can be called with a single argument define conversions from the parameter type to the class type; nonexplicit conversion operators define conversions from the class type to other types.

DEFINED TERMS

call signature Represents the interface of a callable object. A call signature includes the return type and a comma-separated list of argument types enclosed in parentheses.

class-type conversion Conversions to or from class types are defined by constructors and conversion operators, respectively. Nonexplicit constructors that take a single argument define a conversion from the argument type to the class type. Conversion operators define conversions from the class type to the specified type.

conversion operator A member function that defines a conversions from the class type to another type. A conversion operator must be a member of the class from which it converts and is usually a const member. These operators have no return type and take no parameters. They return a value convertible to the type of the conversion operator. That is, operator int returns an int, operator string returns a string, and so on.

explicit conversion operator Conversion

operator preceeded by the explicit keyword. Such operators are used for implicit conversions only in conditions.

function object Object of a class that defines an overloaded call operator. Function objects can be used where functions are normally expected.

function table Container, often a map or a vector, that holds values that can be called.

function template Library template that can represent any callable type.

overloaded operator Function that redefines the meaning of one of the built-in operators. Overloaded operator functions have the name operator followed by the symbol being defined. Overloaded operators must have at least one operand of class type. Overloaded operators have the same precedence, associativity and number of operands as their built-in counterparts.

user-defined conversion A synonym for class-type conversion.

C H A P T E R **15**
O B J E C T - O R I E N T E D
P R O G R A M M I N G

CONTENTS

Object-oriented programming is based on three fundamental concepts: data abstraction, which we covered in Chapter 7, and inheritance and dynamic binding, which we'll cover in this chapter.

Inheritance and dynamic binding affect how we write our programs in two ways: They make it easier to define new classes that are similar, but not identical, to other classes, and they make it easier for us to write programs that can ignore the details of how those similar types differ.

Many applications include concepts that are related to but slightly different from one another. For example, our bookstore might offer different pricing strategies for different books. Some books might be sold only at a given price. Others might be sold subject to a discount. We might give a discount to purchasers who buy a specified number of copies of the book. Or we might give a discount for only the first few copies purchased but charge full price for any bought beyond a given limit, and so on. Object-oriented programming (OOP) is a good match to this kind of application.

15.1 OOP: An Overview

The key ideas in **object-oriented programming** are data abstraction, inheritance, and dynamic binding. Using data abstraction, we can define classes that separate interface from implementation (Chapter 7). Through inheritance, we can define classes that model the relationships among similar types. Through dynamic binding, we can use objects of these types while ignoring the details of how they differ.

Inheritance

Classes related by **inheritance** form a hierarchy. Typically there is a **base class** at the root of the hierarchy, from which the other classes inherit, directly or indirectly. These inheriting classes are known as **derived classes**. The base class defines those members that are common to the types in the hierarchy. Each derived class defines those members that are specific to the derived class itself.

To model our different kinds of pricing strategies, we'll define a class named Quote, which will be the base class of our hierarchy. A Quote object will represent undiscounted books. From Quote we will inherit a second class, named Bulk_quote, to represent books that can be sold with a quantity discount.

These classes will have the following two member functions:

- isbn(), which will return the ISBN. This operation does not depend on the specifics of the inherited class(es); it will be defined only in class Quote.

- net_price(size_t), which will return the price for purchasing a specified number of copies of a book. This operation is type specific; both Quote and Bulk_quote will define their own version of this function.

In C++, a base class distinguishes functions that are type dependent from those that it expects its derived classes to inherit without change. The base class defines as **virtual** those functions it expects its derived classes to define for themselves. Using this knowledge, we can start to write our Quote class:

```
class Quote {
public:
    std::string isbn() const;
    virtual double net_price(std::size_t n) const;
};
```

A derived class must specify the class(es) from which it intends to inherit. It does so in a **class derivation list**, which is a colon followed by a comma-separated list of base classes each of which may have an optional access specifier:

```
class Bulk_quote : public Quote { // Bulk_quote inherits from Quote
public:
    double net_price(std::size_t) const override;
};
```

Because `Bulk_quote` uses `public` in its derivation list, we can use objects of type `Bulk_quote` *as if* they were `Quote` objects.

A derived class must include in its own class body a declaration of all the virtual functions it intends to define for itself. A derived class may include the `virtual` keyword on these functions but is not required to do so. For reasons we'll explain in § 15.3 (p. 606), the new standard lets a derived class explicitly note that it intends a member function to **override** a virtual that it inherits. It does so by specifying `override` after its parameter list.

Dynamic Binding

Through **dynamic binding**, we can use the same code to process objects of either type `Quote` or `Bulk_quote` interchangeably. For example, the following function prints the total price for purchasing the given number of copies of a given book:

```
// calculate and print the price for the given number of copies, applying any discounts
double print_total(ostream &os,
                   const Quote &item, size_t n)
{
    // depending on the type of the object bound to the item parameter
    // calls either Quote::net_price or Bulk_quote::net_price
    double ret = item.net_price(n);
    os << "ISBN: " << item.isbn() // calls Quote::isbn
       << " # sold: " << n << " total due: " << ret << endl;
     return ret;
}
```

This function is pretty simple—it prints the results of calling `isbn` and `net_price` on its parameter and returns the value calculated by the call to `net_price`.

Nevertheless, there are two interesting things about this function: For reasons we'll explain in § 15.2.3 (p. 601), because the `item` parameter is a reference to `Quote`, we can call this function on either a `Quote` object or a `Bulk_quote` object. And, for reasons we'll explain in § 15.2.1 (p. 594), because `net_price` is a virtual function, and because `print_total` calls `net_price` through a reference, the version of `net_price` that is run will depend on the type of the object that we pass to `print_total`:

```
// basic has type Quote; bulk has type Bulk_quote
print_total(cout, basic, 20); // calls Quote version of net_price
print_total(cout, bulk, 20);  // calls Bulk_quote version of net_price
```

The first call passes a `Quote` object to `print_total`. When `print_total` calls `net_price`, the `Quote` version will be run. In the next call, the argument is a

Bulk_quote, so the Bulk_quote version of net_price (which applies a discount) will be run. Because the decision as to which version to run depends on the type of the argument, that decision can't be made until run time. Therefore, dynamic binding is sometimes known as **run-time binding**.

> In C++, dynamic binding happens when a virtual function is called through a reference (or a pointer) to a base class.

15.2 Defining Base and Derived Classes

In many, but not all, ways base and derived classes are defined like other classes we have already seen. In this section, we'll cover the basic features used to define classes related by inheritance.

15.2.1 Defining a Base Class

We'll start by completing the definition of our Quote class:

```
class Quote {
public:
    Quote() = default;  // = default see § 7.1.4 (p. 264)
    Quote(const std::string &book, double sales_price):
                    bookNo(book), price(sales_price) { }
    std::string isbn() const { return bookNo; }
    //  returns the total sales price for the specified number of items
    //  derived classes will override and apply different discount algorithms
    virtual double net_price(std::size_t n) const
                { return n * price; }
    virtual ~Quote() = default; // dynamic binding for the destructor
private:
    std::string bookNo;  //  ISBN number of this item
protected:
    double price = 0.0; //  normal, undiscounted price
};
```

The new parts in this class are the use of virtual on the net_price function and the destructor, and the protected access specifier. We'll explain virtual destructors in § 15.7.1 (p. 622), but for now it is worth noting that classes used as the root of an inheritance hierarchy almost always define a virtual destructor.

> Base classes ordinarily should define a virtual destructor. Virtual destructors are needed even if they do no work.

Member Functions and Inheritance

Derived classes inherit the members of their base class. However, a derived class needs to be able to provide its own definition for operations, such as net_price, that are type dependent. In such cases, the derived class needs to **override** the definition it inherits from the base class, by providing its own definition.

In C++, a base class must distinguish the functions it expects its derived classes to override from those that it expects its derived classes to inherit without change. The base class defines as `virtual` those functions it expects its derived classes to override. When we call a virtual function *through a pointer or reference*, the call will be dynamically bound. Depending on the type of the object to which the reference or pointer is bound, the version in the base class or in one of its derived classes will be executed.

A base class specifies that a member function should be dynamically bound by preceding its declaration with the keyword `virtual`. Any nonstatic member function (§ 7.6, p. 300), other than a constructor, may be virtual. The `virtual` keyword appears only on the declaration inside the class and may not be used on a function definition that appears outside the class body. A function that is declared as `virtual` in the base class is implicitly `virtual` in the derived classes as well. We'll have more to say about virtual functions in § 15.3 (p. 603).

Member functions that are not declared as `virtual` are resolved at compile time, not run time. For the `isbn` member, this is exactly the behavior we want. The `isbn` function does not depend on the details of a derived type. It behaves identically when run on a `Quote` or `Bulk_quote` object. There will be only one version of the `isbn` function in our inheritance hierarchy. Thus, there is no question as to which function to run when we call `isbn()`.

Access Control and Inheritance

A derived class inherits the members defined in its base class. However, the member functions in a derived class may not necessarily access the members that are inherited from the base class. Like any other code that uses the base class, a derived class may access the `public` members of its base class but may not access the `private` members. However, sometimes a base class has members that it wants to let its derived classes use while still prohibiting access to those same members by other users. We specify such members after a **protected** access specifier.

Our `Quote` class expects its derived classes to define their own `net_price` function. To do so, those classes need access to the `price` member. As a result, `Quote` defines that member as `protected`. Derived classes are expected to access `bookNo` in the same way as ordinary users—by calling the `isbn` function. Hence, the `bookNo` member is `private` and is inaccessible to classes that inherit from `Quote`. We'll have more to say about `protected` members in § 15.5 (p. 611).

EXERCISES SECTION 15.2.1

Exercise 15.1: What is a virtual member?

Exercise 15.2: How does the `protected` access specifier differ from `private`?

Exercise 15.3: Define your own versions of the `Quote` class and the `print_total` function.

15.2.2 Defining a Derived Class

A derived class must specify from which class(es) it inherits. It does so in its **class
derivation list**, which is a colon followed by a comma-separated list of names of
previously defined classes. Each base class name may be preceded by an optional
access specifier, which is one of `public`, `protected`, or `private`.

A derived class must declare each inherited member function it intends to override. Therefore, our `Bulk_quote` class must include a `net_price` member:

```
class Bulk_quote : public Quote { // Bulk_quote inherits from Quote
    Bulk_quote() = default;
    Bulk_quote(const std::string&, double, std::size_t, double);
    // overrides the base version in order to implement the bulk purchase discount policy
    double net_price(std::size_t) const override;
private:
    std::size_t min_qty = 0; // minimum purchase for the discount to apply
    double discount = 0.0;   // fractional discount to apply
};
```

Our `Bulk_quote` class inherits the `isbn` function and the `bookNo` and `price`
data members of its `Quote` base class. It defines its own version of `net_price`
and has two additional data members, `min_qty` and `discount`. These members specify the minimum quantity and the discount to apply once that number of
copies are purchased.

We'll have more to say about the access specifier used in a derivation list in
§ 15.5 (p. 612). For now, what's useful to know is that the access specifier determines whether users of a derived class are allowed to know that the derived class
inherits from its base class.

When the derivation is `public`, the `public` members of the base class become
part of the interface of the derived class as well. In addition, we can bind an object
of a publicly derived type to a pointer or reference to the base type. Because we
used `public` in the derivation list, the interface to `Bulk_quote` implicitly contains the `isbn` function, and we may use a `Bulk_quote` object where a pointer or
reference to `Quote` is expected.

Most classes inherit directly from only one base class. This form of inheritance,
known as "single inheritance," forms the topic of this chapter. § 18.3 (p. 802) will
cover classes that have derivation lists with more than one base class.

Virtual Functions in the Derived Class

Derived classes frequently, but not always, override the virtual functions that they
inherit. If a derived class does not override a virtual from its base, then, like any
other member, the derived class inherits the version defined in its base class.

A derived class may include the `virtual` keyword on the functions it overrides, but it is not required to do so. For reasons we'll explain in § 15.3 (p. 606), the
new standard lets a derived class explicitly note that it intends a member function
to override a virtual that it inherits. It does so by specifying `override` after the
parameter list, or after the `const` or reference qualifier(s) if the member is a `const`
(§ 7.1.2, p. 258) or reference (§ 13.6.3, p. 546) function.

Derived-Class Objects and the Derived-to-Base Conversion

A derived object contains multiple parts: a subobject containing the (nonstatic) members defined in the derived class itself, plus subobjects corresponding to each base class from which the derived class inherits. Thus, a `Bulk_quote` object will contain four data elements: the `bookNo` and `price` data members that it inherits from `Quote`, and the `min_qty` and `discount` members, which are defined by `Bulk_quote`.

Although the standard does not specify how derived objects are laid out in memory, we can think of a `Bulk_quote` object as consisting of two parts as represented in Figure 15.1.

Figure 15.1: Conceptual Structure of a `Bulk_quote` Object

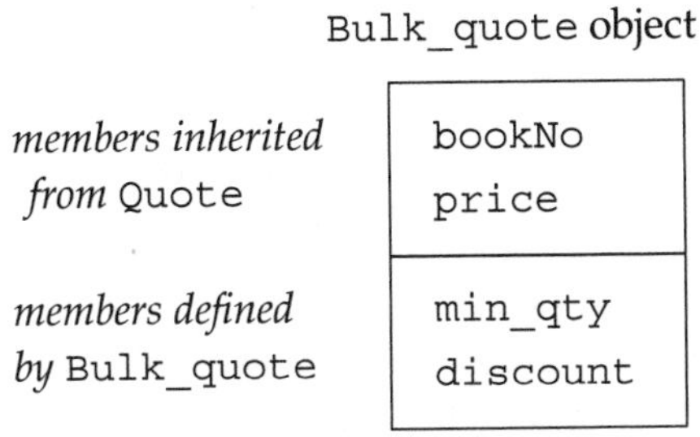

Bulk_quote object

members inherited *from* Quote	bookNo price
members defined *by* Bulk_quote	min_qty discount

The base and derived parts of an object are not guaranteed to be stored contiguously. Figure 15.1 is a conceptual, not physical, representation of how classes work.

Because a derived object contains subparts corresponding to its base class(es), we can use an object of a derived type *as if* it were an object of its base type(s). In particular, we can bind a base-class reference or pointer to the base-class part of a derived object.

```
Quote item;          //  object of base type
Bulk_quote bulk;     //  object of derived type
Quote *p = &item;    //  p points to a Quote object
p = &bulk;           //  p points to the Quote part of bulk
Quote &r = bulk;     //  r bound to the Quote part of bulk
```

This conversion is often referred to as the **derived-to-base** conversion. As with any other conversion, the compiler will apply the derived-to-base conversion implicitly (§ 4.11, p. 159).

The fact that the derived-to-base conversion is implicit means that we can use an object of derived type or a reference to a derived type when a reference to the base type is required. Similarly, we can use a pointer to a derived type where a pointer to the base type is required.

> *Note* The fact that a derived object contains subobjects for its base classes is key to how inheritance works.

Derived-Class Constructors

Although a derived object contains members that it inherits from its base, it cannot
directly initialize those members. Like any other code that creates an object of the
base-class type, a derived class must use a base-class constructor to initialize its
base-class part.

 Each class controls how its members are initialized.

The base-class part of an object is initialized, along with the data members of
the derived class, during the initialization phase of the constructor (§ 7.5.1, p. 288).
Analogously to how we initialize a member, a derived-class constructor uses its
constructor initializer list to pass arguments to a base-class constructor. For example, the Bulk_quote constructor with four parameters:

```
Bulk_quote(const std::string& book, double p,
           std::size_t qty, double disc) :
           Quote(book, p), min_qty(qty), discount(disc) { }
    // as before
};
```

passes its first two parameters (representing the ISBN and price) to the Quote constructor. That Quote constructor initializes the Bulk_quote's base-class part (i.e.,
the bookNo and price members). When the (empty) Quote constructor body
completes, the base-class part of the object being constructed will have been initialized. Next the direct members, min_qty and discount, are initialized. Finally,
the (empty) function body of the Bulk_quote constructor is run.

As with a data member, unless we say otherwise, the base part of a derived
object is default initialized. To use a different base-class constructor, we provide
a constructor initializer using the name of the base class, followed (as usual) by a
parenthesized list of arguments. Those arguments are used to select which base-
class constructor to use to initialize the base-class part of the derived object.

Note The base class is initialized first, and then the members of the derived
class are initialized in the order in which they are declared in the class.

Using Members of the Base Class from the Derived Class

A derived class may access the public and protected members of its base class:

```
//  if the specified number of items are purchased, use the discounted price
double Bulk_quote::net_price(size_t cnt) const
{
    if (cnt >= min_qty)
        return cnt * (1 - discount) * price;
    else
        return cnt * price;
}
```

This function generates a discounted price: If the given quantity is more than min_qty, we apply the discount (which was stored as a fraction) to the price.

We'll have more to say about scope in § 15.6 (p. 617), but for now it's worth knowing that the scope of a derived class is nested inside the scope of its base class. As a result, there is no distinction between how a member of the derived class uses members defined in its own class (e.g., min_qty and discount) and how it uses members defined in its base (e.g., price).

KEY CONCEPT: RESPECTING THE BASE-CLASS INTERFACE

It is essential to understand that each class defines its own interface. Interactions with an object of a class-type should use the interface of that class, even if that object is the base-class part of a derived object.

As a result, derived-class constructors may not directly initialize the members of its base class. The constructor body of a derived constructor can assign values to its public or protected base-class members. Although it *can* assign to those members, it generally *should not* do so. Like any other user of the base class, a derived class should respect the interface of its base class by using a constructor to initialize its inherited members.

Inheritance and `static` Members

If a base class defines a static member (§ 7.6, p. 300), there is only one such member defined for the entire hierarchy. Regardless of the number of classes derived from a base class, there exists a single instance of each static member.

```
class Base {
public:
    static void statmem();
};
class Derived : public Base {
    void f(const Derived&);
};
```

static members obey normal access control. If the member is private in the base class, then derived classes have no access to it. Assuming the member is accessible, we can use a static member through either the base or derived:

```
void Derived::f(const Derived &derived_obj)
{
    Base::statmem();      // ok: Base defines statmem
    Derived::statmem();   // ok: Derived inherits statmem
    //  ok: derived objects can be used to access static from base
    derived_obj.statmem(); //  accessed through a Derived object
    statmem();             //  accessed through this object
}
```

Declarations of Derived Classes

A derived class is declared like any other class (§ 7.3.3, p. 278). The declaration contains the class name but does not include its derivation list:

```
class Bulk_quote : public Quote;  // error: derivation list can't appear here
class Bulk_quote;                 // ok: right way to declare a derived class
```

The purpose of a declaration is to make known that a name exists and what kind of entity it denotes, for example, a class, function, or variable. The derivation list, and all other details of the definition, must appear together in the class body.

Classes Used as a Base Class

A class must be defined, not just declared, before we can use it as a base class:

```
class Quote;  // declared but not defined
// error: Quote must be defined
class Bulk_quote : public Quote { ... };
```

The reason for this restriction should be easy to see: Each derived class contains, and may use, the members it inherits from its base class. To use those members, the derived class must know what they are. One implication of this rule is that it is impossible to derive a class from itself.

A base class can itself be a derived class:

```
class Base { /* ... */ };
class D1: public Base { /* ... */ };
class D2: public D1 { /* ... */ };
```

In this hierarchy, Base is a **direct base** to D1 and an **indirect base** to D2. A direct base class is named in the derivation list. An indirect base is one that a derived class inherits through its direct base class.

Each class inherits all the members of its direct base class. The most derived class inherits the members of its direct base. The members in the direct base include those it inherits from its base class, and so on up the inheritance chain. Effectively, the most derived object contains a subobject for its direct base and for each of its indirect bases.

Preventing Inheritance

Sometimes we define a class that we don't want others to inherit from. Or we might define a class for which we don't want to think about whether it is appropriate as a base class. Under the new standard, we can prevent a class from being used as a base by following the class name with final:

```
class NoDerived final { /* */ }; // NoDerived can't be a base class
class Base { /* */ };
// Last is final; we cannot inherit from Last
class Last final : Base { /* */ }; // Last can't be a base class
class Bad : NoDerived { /* */ };    // error: NoDerived is final
class Bad2 : Last { /* */ };        // error: Last is final
```

15.2.3 Conversions and Inheritance

 Understanding conversions between base and derived classes is essential to understanding how object-oriented programming works in C++.

WARNING

Ordinarily, we can bind a reference or a pointer only to an object that has the same type as the corresponding reference or pointer (§ 2.3.1, p. 51, and § 2.3.2, p. 52) or to a type that involves an acceptable `const` conversion (§ 4.11.2, p. 162). Classes related by inheritance are an important exception: We can bind a pointer or reference to a base-class type to an object of a type derived from that base class. For example, we can use a `Quote&` to refer to a `Bulk_quote` object, and we can assign the address of a `Bulk_quote` object to a `Quote*`.

The fact that we can bind a reference (or pointer) to a base-class type to a derived object has a crucially important implication: When we use a reference (or pointer) to a base-class type, we don't know the actual type of the object to which the pointer or reference is bound. That object can be an object of the base class or it can be an object of a derived class.

Note Like built-in pointers, the smart pointer classes (§ 12.1, p. 450) support the derived-to-base conversion—we can store a pointer to a derived object in a smart pointer to the base type.

Static Type and Dynamic Type

When we use types related by inheritance, we often need to distinguish between the **static type** of a variable or other expression and the **dynamic type** of the object that expression represents. The static type of an expression is always known at compile time—it is the type with which a variable is declared or that an expression yields. The dynamic type is the type of the object in memory that the variable or expression represents. The dynamic type may not be known until run time.

For example, when `print_total` calls `net_price` (§ 15.1, p. 593):

```
double ret = item.net_price(n);
```

we know that the static type of `item` is `Quote&`. The dynamic type depends on the type of the argument to which `item` is bound. That type cannot be known until a call is executed at run time. If we pass a `Bulk_quote` object to `print_total`, then the static type of `item` will differ from its dynamic type. As we've seen, the static type of `item` is `Quote&`, but in this case the dynamic type is `Bulk_quote`.

The dynamic type of an expression that is neither a reference nor a pointer is always the same as that expression's static type. For example, a variable of type `Quote` is always a `Quote` object; there is nothing we can do that will change the type of the object to which that variable corresponds.

> It is crucial to understand that the static type of a pointer or reference to a base class may differ from its dynamic type.

There Is No Implicit Conversion from Base to Derived ...

The conversion from derived to base exists because every derived object contains a base-class part to which a pointer or reference of the base-class type can be bound. There is no similar guarantee for base-class objects. A base-class object can exist either as an independent object or as part of a derived object. A base object that is not part of a derived object has only the members defined by the base class; it doesn't have the members defined by the derived class.

Because a base object might or might not be part of a derived object, there is no automatic conversion from the base class to its derived class(s):

```
Quote base;
Bulk_quote* bulkP = &base;   // error: can't convert base to derived
Bulk_quote& bulkRef = base;  // error: can't convert base to derived
```

If these assignments were legal, we might attempt to use `bulkP` or `bulkRef` to use members that do not exist in `base`.

What is sometimes a bit surprising is that we cannot convert from base to derived even when a base pointer or reference is bound to a derived object:

```
Bulk_quote bulk;
Quote *itemP = &bulk;        // ok: dynamic type is Bulk_quote
Bulk_quote *bulkP = itemP;   // error: can't convert base to derived
```

The compiler has no way to know (at compile time) that a specific conversion will be safe at run time. The compiler looks only at the static types of the pointer or reference to determine whether a conversion is legal. If the base class has one or more virtual functions, we can use a `dynamic_cast` (which we'll cover in § 19.2.1 (p. 825)) to request a conversion that is checked at run time. Alternatively, in those cases when we *know* that the conversion from base to derived is safe, we can use a `static_cast` (§ 4.11.3, p. 162) to override the compiler.

... and No Conversion between Objects

The automatic derived-to-base conversion applies only for conversions to a reference or pointer type. There is no such conversion from a derived-class type to the base-class type. Nevertheless, it is often possible to convert an object of a derived class to its base-class type. However, such conversions may not behave as we might want.

Remember that when we initialize or assign an object of a class type, we are actually calling a function. When we initialize, we're calling a constructor (§ 13.1.1, p. 496, and § 13.6.2, p. 534); when we assign, we're calling an assignment operator (§ 13.1.2, p. 500, and § 13.6.2, p. 536). These members normally have a parameter that is a reference to the const version of the class type.

Because these members take references, the derived-to-base conversion lets us pass a derived object to a base-class copy/move operation. These operations are not virtual. When we pass a derived object to a base-class constructor, the constructor that is run is defined in the base class. That constructor knows *only* about the members of the base class itself. Similarly, if we assign a derived object to a base object, the assignment operator that is run is the one defined in the base class. That operator also knows *only* about the members of the base class itself.

For example, our bookstore classes use the synthesized versions of copy and assignment (§ 13.1.1, p. 497, and § 13.1.2, p. 500). We'll have more to say about copy control and inheritance in § 15.7.2 (p. 623), but for now what's useful to know is that the synthesized versions memberwise copy or assign the data members of the class the same way as for any other class:

```
Bulk_quote bulk;      // object of derived type
Quote item(bulk);     // uses the Quote::Quote(const Quote&) constructor
item = bulk;          // calls Quote::operator=(const Quote&)
```

When `item` is constructed, the `Quote` copy constructor is run. That constructor knows only about the `bookNo` and `price` members. It copies those members from the `Quote` part of `bulk` and *ignores* the members that are part of the `Bulk_quote` portion of `bulk`. Similarly for the assignment of `bulk` to `item`; only the `Quote` part of `bulk` is assigned to `item`.

Because the `Bulk_quote` part is ignored, we say that the `Bulk_quote` portion of `bulk` is **sliced down**.

> ⚠️ **WARNING** When we initialize or assign an object of a base type from an object of a derived type, only the base-class part of the derived object is copied, moved, or assigned. The derived part of the object is ignored.

15.3 Virtual Functions

As we've seen, in C++ dynamic binding happens when a virtual member function is called through a reference or a pointer to a base-class type (§ 15.1, p. 593). Because we don't know which version of a function is called until run time, virtual functions must *always* be defined. Ordinarily, if we do not use a function, we don't

Exercise 15.8: Define static type and dynamic type.

Exercise 15.9: When is it possible for an expression's static type to differ from its dynamic type? Give three examples in which the static and dynamic type differ.

Exercise 15.10: Recalling the discussion from § 8.1 (p. 311), explain how the program on page 317 that passed an `ifstream` to the `Sales_data` read function works.

KEY CONCEPT: CONVERSIONS AMONG TYPES RELATED BY INHERITANCE

There are three things that are important to understand about conversions among classes related by inheritance:

- The conversion from derived to base applies only to pointer or reference types.

- There is no implicit conversion from the base-class type to the derived type.

- Like any member, the derived-to-base conversion may be inaccessible due to access controls. We'll cover accessibility in § 15.5 (p. 613).

Although the automatic conversion applies only to pointers and references, most classes in an inheritance hierarchy (implicitly or explicitly) define the copy-control members (Chapter 13). As a result, we can often copy, move, or assign an object of derived type to a base-type object. However, copying, moving, or assigning a derived-type object to a base-type object copies, moves, or assigns *only* the members in the base-class part of the object.

---

need to supply a definition for that function (§ 6.1.2, p. 206). However, we must define every virtual function, regardless of whether it is used, because the compiler has no way to determine whether a virtual function is used.

Calls to Virtual Functions *May Be* Resolved at Run Time

When a virtual function is called through a reference or pointer, the compiler generates code to *decide at run time* which function to call. The function that is called is the one that corresponds to the dynamic type of the object bound to that pointer or reference.

As an example, consider our `print_total` function from § 15.1 (p. 593). That function calls `net_price` on its parameter named `item`, which has type `Quote&`. Because `item` is a reference, and because `net_price` is virtual, the version of `net_price` that is called depends at run time on the actual (dynamic) type of the argument bound to `item`:

```
Quote base("0-201-82470-1", 50);
print_total(cout, base, 10);    // calls Quote::net_price
Bulk_quote derived("0-201-82470-1", 50, 5, .19);
print_total(cout, derived, 10); // calls Bulk_quote::net_price
```

In the first call, `item` is bound to an object of type `Quote`. As a result, when `print_total` calls `net_price`, the version defined by `Quote` is run. In the second call, `item` is bound to a `Bulk_quote` object. In this call, `print_total` calls the `Bulk_quote` version of `net_price`.

It is crucial to understand that dynamic binding happens only when a virtual function is called through a pointer or a reference.

```
base = derived;          // copies the Quote part of derived into base
base.net_price(20);      // calls Quote::net_price
```

When we call a virtual function on an expression that has a plain—nonreference and nonpointer—type, that call is bound at compile time. For example, when we call `net_price` on `base`, there is no question as to which version of `net_price` to run. We can change the value (i.e., the contents) of the object that `base` represents, but there is no way to change the type of that object. Hence, this call is resolved, at compile time, to the `Quote` version of `net_price`.

KEY CONCEPT: POLYMORPHISM IN C++

The key idea behind OOP is polymorphism. Polymorphism is derived from a Greek word meaning "many forms." We speak of types related by inheritance as polymorphic types, because we can use the "many forms" of these types while ignoring the differences among them. The fact that the static and dynamic types of references and pointers can differ is the cornerstone of how C++ supports polymorphism.

When we call a function defined in a base class through a reference or pointer to the base class, we do not know the type of the object on which that member is executed. The object can be a base-class object or an object of a derived class. If the function is virtual, then the decision as to which function to run is delayed until run time. The version of the virtual function that is run is the one defined by the type of the object to which the reference is bound or to which the pointer points.

On the other hand, calls to nonvirtual functions are bound at compile time. Similarly, calls to any function (virtual or not) on an object are also bound at compile time. The type of an object is fixed and unvarying—there is nothing we can do to make the dynamic type of an object differ from its static type. Therefore, calls made on an object are bound at compile time to the version defined by the type of the object.

 Virtuals are resolved at run time *only* if the call is made through a reference or pointer. Only in these cases is it possible for an object's dynamic type to differ from its static type.

Virtual Functions in a Derived Class

When a derived class overrides a virtual function, it may, but is not required to, repeat the `virtual` keyword. Once a function is declared as `virtual`, it remains `virtual` in all the derived classes.

A derived-class function that overrides an inherited virtual function must have exactly the same parameter type(s) as the base-class function that it overrides.

With one exception, the return type of a virtual in the derived class also must match the return type of the function from the base class. The exception applies to virtuals that return a reference (or pointer) to types that are themselves related by inheritance. That is, if D is derived from B, then a base class virtual can return a B* and the version in the derived can return a D*. However, such return types require that the derived-to-base conversion from D to B is accessible. § 15.5 (p. 613) covers how to determine whether a base class is accessible. We'll see an example of this kind of virtual function in § 15.8.1 (p. 633).

> A function that is virtual in a base class is implicitly virtual in its derived classes. When a derived class overrides a virtual, the parameters in the base and derived classes must match exactly.

The final and override Specifiers

As we'll see in § 15.6 (p. 620), it is legal for a derived class to define a function with the same name as a virtual in its base class but with a different parameter list. The compiler considers such a function to be independent from the base-class function. In such cases, the derived version does not override the version in the base class. In practice, such declarations often are a mistake—the class author intended to override a virtual from the base class but made a mistake in specifying the parameter list.

Finding such bugs can be surprisingly hard. Under the new standard we can specify override on a virtual function in a derived class. Doing so makes our intention clear and (more importantly) enlists the compiler in finding such problems for us. The compiler will reject a program if a function marked override does not override an existing virtual function:

```
struct B {
    virtual void f1(int) const;
    virtual void f2();
    void f3();
};
struct D1 : B {
    void f1(int) const override;  //  ok: f1 matches f1 in the base
    void f2(int) override;        //  error: B has no f2(int) function
    void f3() override;           //  error: f3 not virtual
    void f4() override;           //  error: B doesn't have a function named f4
};
```

In D1, the override specifier on f1 is fine; both the base and derived versions of f1 are const members that take an int and return void. The version of f1 in D1 properly overrides the virtual that it inherits from B.

The declaration of f2 in D1 does not match the declaration of f2 in B—the version defined in B takes no arguments and the one defined in D1 takes an int. Because the declarations don't match, f2 in D1 doesn't override f2 from B; it is a new function that happens to have the same name. Because we said we intended this declaration to be an override and it isn't, the compiler will generate an error.

Because only a virtual function can be overridden, the compiler will also reject f3 in D1. That function is not virtual in B, so there is no function to override.

Similarly f4 is in error because B doesn't even have a function named f4.

We can also designate a function as final. Any attempt to override a function that has been defined as final will be flagged as an error:

```
struct D2 : B {
    //  inherits f2() and f3() from B and overrides f1(int)
    void f1(int) const final; //  subsequent classes can't override f1(int)
};
struct D3 : D2 {
    void f2();              //  ok: overrides f2 inherited from the indirect base, B
    void f1(int) const;   //  error: D2 declared f2 as final
};
```

final and override specifiers appear after the parameter list (including any const or reference qualifiers) and after a trailing return (§ 6.3.3, p. 229).

Virtual Functions and Default Arguments

Like any other function, a virtual function can have default arguments (§ 6.5.1, p. 236). If a call uses a default argument, the value that is used is the one defined by the static type through which the function is called.

That is, when a call is made through a reference or pointer to base, the default argument(s) will be those defined in the base class. The base-class arguments will be used even when the derived version of the function is run. In this case, the derived function will be passed the default arguments defined for the base-class version of the function. If the derived function relies on being passed different arguments, the program will not execute as expected.

Virtual functions that have default arguments should use the same argument values in the base and derived classes.

Circumventing the Virtual Mechanism

In some cases, we want to prevent dynamic binding of a call to a virtual function; we want to force the call to use a particular version of that virtual. We can use the scope operator to do so. For example, this code:

```
//  calls the version from the base class regardless of the dynamic type of baseP
double undiscounted = baseP->Quote::net_price(42);
```

calls the Quote version of net_price regardless of the type of the object to which baseP actually points. This call will be resolved at compile time.

Ordinarily, only code inside member functions (or friends) should need to use the scope operator to circumvent the virtual mechanism.

Why might we wish to circumvent the virtual mechanism? The most common reason is when a derived-class virtual function calls the version from the base class. In such cases, the base-class version might do work common to all types in the hierarchy. The versions defined in the derived classes would do whatever additional work is particular to their own type.

WARNING If a derived virtual function that intended to call its base-class version omits the scope operator, the call will be resolved at run time as a call to the derived version itself, resulting in an infinite recursion.

EXERCISES SECTION 15.3

Exercise 15.11: Add a virtual debug function to your Quote class hierarchy that displays the data members of the respective classes.

Exercise 15.12: Is it ever useful to declare a member function as both override and final? Why or why not?

Exercise 15.13: Given the following classes, explain each print function:

```
class base {
public:
    string name() { return basename; }
    virtual void print(ostream &os) { os << basename; }
private:
    string basename;
};
class derived : public base {
public:
    void print(ostream &os) { print(os); os << " " << i; }
private:
    int i;
};
```

If there is a problem in this code, how would you fix it?

Exercise 15.14: Given the classes from the previous exercise and the following objects, determine which function is called at run time:

```
base bobj;      base *bp1 = &bobj;    base &br1 = bobj;
derived dobj;   base *bp2 = &dobj;    base &br2 = dobj;
(a) bobj.print();   (b) dobj.print();    (c) bp1->name();
(d) bp2->name();    (e) br1.print();     (f) br2.print();
```

15.4 Abstract Base Classes

Imagine that we want to extend our bookstore classes to support several discount strategies. In addition to a bulk discount, we might offer a discount for purchases up to a certain quantity and then charge the full price thereafter. Or we might offer a discount for purchases above a certain limit but not for purchases up to that limit.

Each of these discount strategies is the same in that it requires a quantity and a discount amount. We might support these differing strategies by defining a new class named Disc_quote to store the quantity and the discount amount. Classes, such as Bulk_item, that represent a specific discount strategy will inherit from

`Disc_quote`. Each of the derived classes will implement its discount strategy by defining its own version of `net_price`.

Before we can define our `Disc_Quote` class, we have to decide what to do about `net_price`. Our `Disc_quote` class doesn't correspond to any particular discount strategy; there is no meaning to ascribe to `net_price` for this class.

We could define `Disc_quote` without its own version of `net_price`. In this case, `Disc_quote` would inherit `net_price` from `Quote`.

However, this design would make it possible for our users to write nonsensical code. A user could create an object of type `Disc_quote` by supplying a quantity and a discount rate. Passing that `Disc_quote` object to a function such as `print_total` would use the `Quote` version of `net_price`. The calculated price would not include the discount that was supplied when the object was created. That state of affairs makes no sense.

Pure Virtual Functions

Thinking about the question in this detail reveals that our problem is not just that we don't know how to define `net_price`. In practice, we'd like to prevent users from creating `Disc_quote` objects at all. This class represents the general concept of a discounted book, not a concrete discount strategy.

We can enforce this design intent—and make it clear that there is no meaning for `net_price`—by defining `net_price` as a **pure virtual** function. Unlike ordinary virtuals, a pure virtual function does not have to be defined. We specify that a virtual function is a pure virtual by writing `= 0` in place of a function body (i.e., just before the semicolon that ends the declaration). The `= 0` may appear only on the declaration of a virtual function in the class body:

```
//   class to hold the discount rate and quantity
//   derived classes will implement pricing strategies using these data
class Disc_quote : public Quote {
public:
    Disc_quote() = default;
    Disc_quote(const std::string& book, double price,
               std::size_t qty, double disc):
                   Quote(book, price),
                   quantity(qty), discount(disc) { }
    double net_price(std::size_t) const = 0;
protected:
    std::size_t quantity = 0; //  purchase size for the discount to apply
    double discount = 0.0;    //  fractional discount to apply
};
```

Like our earlier `Bulk_item` class, `Disc_quote` defines a default constructor and a constructor that takes four parameters. Although we cannot define objects of this type directly, constructors in classes derived from `Disc_quote` will use the `Disc_quote` constructors to construct the `Disc_quote` part of their objects. The constructor that has four parameters passes its first two to the `Quote` constructor and directly initializes its own members, `discount` and `quantity`. The default constructor default initializes those members.

It is worth noting that we can provide a definition for a pure virtual. However, the function body must be defined outside the class. That is, we cannot provide a function body inside the class for a function that is = 0.

Classes with Pure Virtuals Are Abstract Base Classes

A class containing (or inheriting without overridding) a pure virtual function is an **abstract base class**. An abstract base class defines an interface for subsequent classes to override. We cannot (directly) create objects of a type that is an abstract base class. Because `Disc_quote` defines `net_price` as a pure virtual, we cannot define objects of type `Disc_quote`. We can define objects of classes that inherit from `Disc_quote`, so long as those classes override `net_price`:

```
//  Disc_quote declares pure virtual functions, which Bulk_quote will override
Disc_quote discounted;   //  error: can't define a Disc_quote object
Bulk_quote bulk;         //  ok: Bulk_quote has no pure virtual functions
```

Classes that inherit from `Disc_quote` must define `net_price` or those classes will be abstract as well.

 We may not create objects of a type that is an abstract base class.

A Derived Class Constructor Initializes Its Direct Base Class Only

Now we can reimplement `Bulk_quote` to inherit from `Disc_quote` rather than inheriting directly from `Quote`:

```
//  the discount kicks in when a specified number of copies of the same book are sold
//  the discount is expressed as a fraction to use to reduce the normal price
class Bulk_quote : public Disc_quote {
public:
    Bulk_quote() = default;
    Bulk_quote(const std::string& book, double price,
            std::size_t qty, double disc):
        Disc_quote(book, price, qty, disc) { }
    //  overrides the base version to implement the bulk purchase discount policy
    double net_price(std::size_t) const override;
};
```

This version of `Bulk_quote` has a direct base class, `Disc_quote`, and an indirect base class, `Quote`. Each `Bulk_quote` object has three subobjects: an (empty) `Bulk_quote` part, a `Disc_quote` subobject, and a `Quote` subobject.

As we've seen, each class controls the initialization of objects of its type. Therefore, even though `Bulk_quote` has no data members of its own, it provides the same four-argument constructor as in our original class. Our new constructor passes its arguments to the `Disc_quote` constructor. That constructor in turn runs the `Quote` constructor. The `Quote` constructor initializes the `bookNo` and `price` members of `bulk`. When the `Quote` constructor ends, the `Disc_quote` constructor runs and initializes the `quantity` and `discount` members. At this point, the `Bulk_quote` constructor resumes. That constructor has no further initializations or any other work to do.

KEY CONCEPT: REFACTORING

Adding `Disc_quote` to the `Quote` hierarchy is an example of *refactoring*. Refactoring involves redesigning a class hierarchy to move operations and/or data from one class to another. Refactoring is common in object-oriented applications.

It is noteworthy that even though we changed the inheritance hierarchy, code that uses `Bulk_quote` or `Quote` would not need to change. However, when classes are refactored (or changed in any other way) we must recompile any code that uses those classes.

EXERCISES SECTION 15.4

Exercise 15.15: Define your own versions of `Disc_quote` and `Bulk_quote`.

Exercise 15.16: Rewrite the class representing a limited discount strategy, which you wrote for the exercises in § 15.2.2 (p. 601), to inherit from `Disc_quote`.

Exercise 15.17: Try to define an object of type `Disc_quote` and see what errors you get from the compiler.

15.5 Access Control and Inheritance

Just as each class controls the initialization of its own members (§ 15.2.2, p. 598), each class also controls whether its members are **accessible** to a derived class.

`protected` Members

As we've seen, a class uses `protected` for those members that it is willing to share with its derived classes but wants to protect from general access. The `protected` specifier can be thought of as a blend of `private` and `public`:

- Like `private`, `protected` members are inaccessible to users of the class.

- Like `public`, `protected` members are accessible to members and friends of classes derived from this class.

In addition, `protected` has another important property:

- A derived class member or friend may access the `protected` members of the base class *only* through a derived object. The derived class has no special access to the `protected` members of base-class objects.

To understand this last rule, consider the following example:

```
class Base {
protected:
    int prot_mem;       // protected member
};
class Sneaky : public Base {
    friend void clobber(Sneaky&);   // can access Sneaky::prot_mem
    friend void clobber(Base&);     // can't access Base::prot_mem
    int j;                          // j is private by default
};
// ok: clobber can access the private and protected members in Sneaky objects
void clobber(Sneaky &s) { s.j = s.prot_mem = 0; }

// error: clobber can't access the protected members in Base
void clobber(Base &b) { b.prot_mem = 0; }
```

If derived classes (and friends) could access protected members in a base-class object, then our second version of `clobber` (that takes a `Base&`) would be legal. That function is not a friend of `Base`, yet it would be allowed to change an object of type `Base`; we could circumvent the protection provided by `protected` for any class simply by defining a new class along the lines of `Sneaky`.

To prevent such usage, members and friends of a derived class can access the `protected` members *only* in base-class objects that are embedded inside a derived type object; they have no special access to ordinary objects of the base type.

public, private, and protected Inheritance

Access to a member that a class inherits is controlled by a combination of the access specifier for that member in the base class, and the access specifier in the derivation list of the derived class. As an example, consider the following hierarchy:

```
class Base {
public:
    void pub_mem();     // public member
protected:
    int prot_mem;       // protected member
private:
    char priv_mem;      // private member
};
struct Pub_Derv : public Base {
    // ok: derived classes can access protected members
    int f() { return prot_mem; }
    // error: private members are inaccessible to derived classes
    char g() { return priv_mem; }
};
struct Priv_Derv : private Base {
    // private derivation doesn't affect access in the derived class
    int f1() const { return prot_mem; }
};
```

The derivation access specifier has no effect on whether members (and friends) of a derived class may access the members of its own direct base class. Access to the members of a base class is controlled by the access specifiers in the base class itself. Both `Pub_Derv` and `Priv_Derv` may access the `protected` member `prot_mem`. Neither may access the `private` member `priv_mem`.

The purpose of the derivation access specifier is to control the access that *users* of the derived class—including other classes derived from the derived class—have to the members inherited from `Base`:

```
Pub_Derv d1;    // members inherited from Base are public
Priv_Derv d2;   // members inherited from Base are private
d1.pub_mem();   // ok: pub_mem is public in the derived class
d2.pub_mem();   // error: pub_mem is private in the derived class
```

Both `Pub_Derv` and `Priv_Derv` inherit the `pub_mem` function. When the inheritance is `public`, members retain their access specification. Thus, `d1` can call `pub_mem`. In `Priv_Derv`, the members of `Base` are `private`; users of that class may not call `pub_mem`.

The derivation access specifier used by a derived class also controls access from classes that inherit from that derived class:

```
struct Derived_from_Public : public Pub_Derv {
    // ok: Base::prot_mem remains protected in Pub_Derv
    int use_base() { return prot_mem; }
};
struct Derived_from_Private : public Priv_Derv {
    // error: Base::prot_mem is private in Priv_Derv
    int use_base() { return prot_mem; }
};
```

Classes derived from `Pub_Derv` may access `prot_mem` from `Base` because that member remains a `protected` member in `Pub_Derv`. In contrast, classes derived from `Priv_Derv` have no such access. To them, all the members that `Priv_Derv` inherited from `Base` are `private`.

Had we defined another class, say, `Prot_Derv`, that used `protected` inheritance, the `public` members of `Base` would be `protected` members in that class. Users of `Prot_Derv` would have no access to `pub_mem`, but the members and friends of `Prot_Derv` could access that inherited member.

Accessibility of Derived-to-Base Conversion

Whether the derived-to-base conversion (§ 15.2.2, p. 597) is accessible depends on which code is trying to use the conversion and may depend on the access specifier used in the derived class' derivation. Assuming `D` inherits from `B`:

- User code may use the derived-to-base conversion *only* if `D` inherits publicly from `B`. User code may not use the conversion if `D` inherits from `B` using either `protected` or `private`.

- Member functions and friends of `D` can use the conversion to `B` regardless of how `D` inherits from `B`. The derived-to-base conversion to a direct base class is always accessible to members and friends of a derived class.

- Member functions and friends of classes derived from D may use the derived-to-base conversion if D inherits from B using either `public` or `protected`. Such code may not use the conversion if D inherits privately from B.

> For any given point in your code, if a `public` member of the base class would be accessible, then the derived-to-base conversion is also accessible, and not otherwise.

KEY CONCEPT: CLASS DESIGN AND PROTECTED MEMBERS

In the absence of inheritance, we can think of a class as having two different kinds of users: ordinary users and implementors. Ordinary users write code that uses objects of the class type; such code can access only the `public` (interface) members of the class. Implementors write the code contained in the members and friends of the class. The members and friends of the class can access both the `public` and `private` (implementation) sections.

Under inheritance, there is a third kind of user, namely, derived classes. A base class makes `protected` those parts of its implementation that it is willing to let its derived classes use. The `protected` members remain inaccessible to ordinary user code; `private` members remain inaccessible to derived classes and their friends.

Like any other class, a class that is used as a base class makes its interface members `public`. A class that is used as a base class may divide its implementation into those members that are accessible to derived classes and those that remain accessible only to the base class and its friends. An implementation member should be `protected` if it provides an operation or data that a derived class will need to use in its own implementation. Otherwise, implementation members should be `private`.

Friendship and Inheritance

Just as friendship is not transitive (§ 7.3.4, p. 279), friendship is also not inherited. Friends of the base have no special access to members of its derived classes, and friends of a derived class have no special access to the base class:

```
class Base {
    // added friend declaration; other members as before
    friend class Pal; // Pal has no access to classes derived from Base
};
class Pal {
public:
    int f(Base b) { return b.prot_mem; } // ok: Pal is a friend of Base
    int f2(Sneaky s) { return s.j; } // error: Pal not friend of Sneaky
    // access to a base class is controlled by the base class, even inside a derived object
    int f3(Sneaky s) { return s.prot_mem; } // ok: Pal is a friend
};
```

The fact that `f3` is legal may seem surprising, but it follows directly from the notion that each class controls access to its own members. `Pal` is a friend of `Base`, so

`Pal` can access the members of `Base` objects. That access includes access to `Base` objects that are embedded in an object of a type derived from `Base`.

When a class makes another class a friend, it is only that class to which friendship is granted. The base classes of, and classes derived from, the friend have no special access to the befriending class:

```
//  D2 has no access to protected or private members in Base
class D2 : public Pal {
public:
    int mem(Base b)
        { return b.prot_mem; }  //  error: friendship doesn't inherit
};
```

> *Note* Friendship is not inherited; each class controls access to its members.

Exempting Individual Members

Sometimes we need to change the access level of a name that a derived class inherits. We can do so by providing a `using` declaration (§ 3.1, p. 82):

```
class Base {
public:
    std::size_t size() const { return n; }
protected:
    std::size_t n;
};
class Derived : private Base {    //  note: private inheritance
public:
    //  maintain access levels for members related to the size of the object
    using Base::size;
protected:
    using Base::n;
};
```

Because `Derived` uses `private` inheritance, the inherited members, `size` and `n`, are (by default) `private` members of `Derived`. The `using` declarations adjust the accessibility of these members. Users of `Derived` can access the `size` member, and classes subsequently derived from `Derived` can access `n`.

A `using` declaration inside a class can name any accessible (e.g., not `private`) member of a direct or indirect base class. Access to a name specified in a `using` declaration depends on the access specifier preceding the `using` declaration. That is, if a `using` declaration appears in a `private` part of the class, that name is accessible to members and friends only. If the declaration is in a `public` section, the name is available to all users of the class. If the declaration is in a `protected` section, the name is accessible to the members, friends, and derived classes.

> *Note* A derived class may provide a `using` declaration only for names it is permitted to access.

Default Inheritance Protection Levels

In § 7.2 (p. 268) we saw that classes defined with the `struct` and `class` keywords have different default access specifiers. Similarly, the default derivation specifier depends on which keyword is used to define a derived class. By default, a derived class defined with the `class` keyword has `private` inheritance; a derived class defined with `struct` has `public` inheritance:

```
class Base { /* ... */ };
struct D1 : Base { /* ... */ };   //  public inheritance by default
class D2 : Base { /* ... */ };    //  private inheritance by default
```

It is a common misconception to think that there are deeper differences between classes defined using the `struct` keyword and those defined using `class`. The only differences are the default access specifier for members and the default derivation access specifier. There are no other distinctions.

Best Practices

> A privately derived class should specify `private` explicitly rather than rely on the default. Being explicit makes it clear that private inheritance is intended and not an oversight.

EXERCISES SECTION 15.5

Exercise 15.18: Given the classes from page 612 and page 613, and assuming each object has the type specified in the comments, determine which of these assignments are legal. Explain why those that are illegal aren't allowed:

```
Base *p = &d1;   //  d1 has type Pub_Derv
p = &d2;         //  d2 has type Priv_Derv
p = &d3;         //  d3 has type Prot_Derv
p = &dd1;        //  dd1 has type Derived_from_Public
p = &dd2;        //  dd2 has type Derived_from_Private
p = &dd3;        //  dd3 has type Derived_from_Protected
```

Exercise 15.19: Assume that each of the classes from page 612 and page 613 has a member function of the form:

```
void memfcn(Base &b) { b = *this; }
```

For each class, determine whether this function would be legal.

Exercise 15.20: Write code to test your answers to the previous two exercises.

Exercise 15.21: Choose one of the following general abstractions containing a family of types (or choose one of your own). Organize the types into an inheritance hierarchy:

    (a) Graphical file formats (such as gif, tiff, jpeg, bmp)
    (b) Geometric primitives (such as box, circle, sphere, cone)
    (c) C++ language types (such as class, function, member function)

Exercise 15.22: For the class you chose in the previous exercise, identify some of the likely virtual functions as well as `public` and `protected` members.

15.6   Class Scope under Inheritance

Each class defines its own scope (§ 7.4, p. 282) within which its members are defined. Under inheritance, the scope of a derived class is nested (§ 2.2.4, p. 48) inside the scope of its base classes. If a name is unresolved within the scope of the derived class, the enclosing base-class scopes are searched for a definition of that name.

The fact that the scope of a derived class nests inside the scope of its base classes can be surprising. After all, the base and derived classes are defined in separate parts of our program's text. However, it is this hierarchical nesting of class scopes that allows the members of a derived class to use members of its base class as if those members were part of the derived class. For example, when we write

```
Bulk_quote bulk;
cout << bulk.isbn();
```

the use of the name isbn is resolved as follows:

- Because we called isbn on an object of type Bulk_quote, the search starts in the Bulk_quote class. The name isbn is not found in that class.

- Because Bulk_quote is derived from Disc_quote, the Disc_quote class is searched next. The name is still not found.

- Because Disc_quote is derived from Quote, the Quote class is searched next. The name isbn is found in that class; the use of isbn is resolved to the isbn in Quote.

Name Lookup Happens at Compile Time

The static type (§ 15.2.3, p. 601) of an object, reference, or pointer determines which members of that object are visible. Even when the static and dynamic types might differ (as can happen when a reference or pointer to a base class is used), the static type determines what members can be used. As an example, we might add a member to the Disc_quote class that returns a pair (§ 11.2.3, p. 426) holding the minimum (or maximum) quantity and the discounted price:

```
class Disc_quote : public Quote {
public:
    std::pair<size_t, double> discount_policy() const
        { return {quantity, discount}; }
    // other members as before
};
```

We can use discount_policy only through an object, pointer, or reference of type Disc_quote or of a class derived from Disc_quote:

```
Bulk_quote bulk;
Bulk_quote *bulkP = &bulk;  // static and dynamic types are the same
Quote *itemP = &bulk;        // static and dynamic types differ
bulkP->discount_policy();    // ok: bulkP has type Bulk_quote*
itemP->discount_policy();    // error: itemP has type Quote*
```

Even though `bulk` has a member named `discount_policy`, that member is not visible through `itemP`. The type of `itemP` is a pointer to `Quote`, which means that the search for `discount_policy` starts in class `Quote`. The `Quote` class has no member named `discount_policy`, so we cannot call that member on an object, reference, or pointer of type `Quote`.

Name Collisions and Inheritance

Like any other scope, a derived class can reuse a name defined in one of its direct or indirect base classes. As usual, names defined in an inner scope (e.g., a derived class) hide uses of that name in the outer scope (e.g., a base class) (§ 2.2.4, p. 48):

```
struct Base {
    Base(): mem(0) { }
protected:
    int mem;
};
struct Derived : Base {
    Derived(int i): mem(i) { } //  initializes Derived::mem to i
                               //  Base::mem is default initialized
    int get_mem() { return mem; }  //  returns Derived::mem
protected:
    int mem;    //  hides mem in the base
};
```

The reference to `mem` inside `get_mem` is resolved to the name inside `Derived`. Were we to write

```
Derived d(42);
cout << d.get_mem() << endl;        //  prints 42
```

then the output would be `42`.

> A derived-class member with the same name as a member of the base class hides direct use of the base-class member.

Using the Scope Operator to Use Hidden Members

We can use a hidden base-class member by using the scope operator:

```
struct Derived : Base {
    int get_base_mem() { return Base::mem; }
    // ...
};
```

The scope operator overrides the normal lookup and directs the compiler to look for `mem` starting in the scope of class `Base`. If we ran the code above with this version of `Derived`, the result of `d.get_mem()` would be `0`.

> **Best Practices**
> Aside from overriding inherited virtual functions, a derived class usually should not reuse names defined in its base class.

KEY CONCEPT: NAME LOOKUP AND INHERITANCE

Understanding how function calls are resolved is crucial to understanding inheritance in C++. Given the call p->mem() (or obj.mem()), the following four steps happen:

- First determine the static type of p (or obj). Because we're calling a member, that type must be a class type.

- Look for mem in the class that corresponds to the static type of p (or obj). If mem is not found, look in the direct base class and continue up the chain of classes until mem is found or the last class is searched. If mem is not found in the class or its enclosing base classes, then the call will not compile.

- Once mem is found, do normal type checking (§ 6.1, p. 203) to see if this call is legal given the definition that was found.

- Assuming the call is legal, the compiler generates code, which varies depending on whether the call is virtual or not:

   - If mem is virtual and the call is made through a reference or pointer, then the compiler generates code to determine at run time which version to run based on the dynamic type of the object.

   - Otherwise, if the function is nonvirtual, or if the call is on an object (not a reference or pointer), the compiler generates a normal function call.

As Usual, Name Lookup Happens before Type Checking

As we've seen, functions declared in an inner scope do not overload functions declared in an outer scope (§ 6.4.1, p. 234). As a result, functions defined in a derived class do *not* overload members defined in its base class(es). As in any other scope, if a member in a derived class (i.e., in an inner scope) has the same name as a base-class member (i.e., a name defined in an outer scope), then the derived member hides the base-class member within the scope of the derived class. The base member is hidden even if the functions have different parameter lists:

```
struct Base {
    int memfcn();
};
struct Derived : Base {
    int memfcn(int);    //  hides memfcn in the base
};
Derived d; Base b;
b.memfcn();          //  calls Base::memfcn
d.memfcn(10);        //  calls Derived::memfcn
d.memfcn();          //  error: memfcn with no arguments is hidden
d.Base::memfcn();    //  ok: calls Base::memfcn
```

The declaration of memfcn in Derived hides the declaration of memfcn in Base. Not surprisingly, the first call through b, which is a Base object, calls the version in the base class. Similarly, the second call (through d) calls the one from Derived. What can be surprising is that the third call, d.memfcn(), is illegal.

To resolve this call, the compiler looks for the name `memfcn` in `Derived`. That class defines a member named `memfcn` and the search stops. Once the name is found, the compiler looks no further. The version of `memfcn` in `Derived` expects an `int` argument. This call provides no such argument; it is in error.

Virtual Functions and Scope

We can now understand why virtual functions must have the same parameter list in the base and derived classes (§ 15.3, p. 605). If the base and derived members took arguments that differed from one another, there would be no way to call the derived version through a reference or pointer to the base class. For example:

```
class Base {
public:
    virtual int fcn();
};
class D1 : public Base {
public:
    //  hides fcn in the base; this fcn is not virtual
    //  D1 inherits the definition of Base::fcn()
    int fcn(int);       // parameter list differs from fcn in Base
    virtual void f2(); // new virtual function that does not exist in Base
};
class D2 : public D1 {
public:
    int fcn(int); // nonvirtual function hides D1::fcn(int)
    int fcn();    // overrides virtual fcn from Base
    void f2();    // overrides virtual f2 from D1
};
```

The `fcn` function in `D1` does not override the virtual `fcn` from `Base` because they have different parameter lists. Instead, it *hides* `fcn` from the base. Effectively, `D1` has two functions named `fcn`: `D1` inherits a virtual named `fcn` from `Base` and defines its own, nonvirtual member named `fcn` that takes an `int` parameter.

Calling a Hidden Virtual through the Base Class

Given the classes above, let's look at several different ways to call these functions:

```
Base bobj;  D1 d1obj; D2 d2obj;
Base *bp1 = &bobj, *bp2 = &d1obj, *bp3 = &d2obj;
bp1->fcn(); // virtual call, will call Base::fcn at run time
bp2->fcn(); // virtual call, will call Base::fcn at run time
bp3->fcn(); // virtual call, will call D2::fcn at run time

D1 *d1p = &d1obj; D2 *d2p = &d2obj;
bp2->f2(); // error: Base has no member named f2
d1p->f2(); // virtual call, will call D1::f2() at run time
d2p->f2(); // virtual call, will call D2::f2() at run time
```

The first three calls are all made through pointers to the base class. Because `fcn` is virtual, the compiler generates code to decide at run time which version to call.

That decision will be based on the actual type of the object to which the pointer is bound. In the case of `bp2`, the underlying object is a `D1`. That class did not override the `fcn` function that takes no arguments. Thus, the call through `bp2` is resolved (at run time) to the version defined in `Base`.

The next three calls are made through pointers with differing types. Each pointer points to one of the types in this hierarchy. The first call is illegal because there is no `f2()` in class `Base`. The fact that the pointer happens to point to a derived object is irrelevant.

For completeness, let's look at calls to the nonvirtual function `fcn(int)`:

```
Base *p1 = &d2obj; D1 *p2 = &d2obj; D2 *p3 =   &d2obj;
p1->fcn(42);   //  error: Base has no version of fcn that takes an int
p2->fcn(42);   //  statically bound, calls D1::fcn(int)
p3->fcn(42);   //  statically bound, calls D2::fcn(int)
```

In each call the pointer happens to point to an object of type `D2`. However, the dynamic type doesn't matter when we call a nonvirtual function. The version that is called depends only on the static type of the pointer.

Overriding Overloaded Functions

As with any other function, a member function (virtual or otherwise) can be overloaded. A derived class can override zero or more instances of the overloaded functions it inherits. If a derived class wants to make all the overloaded versions available through its type, then it must override all of them or none of them.

Sometimes a class needs to override some, but not all, of the functions in an overloaded set. It would be tedious in such cases to have to override every base-class version in order to override the ones that the class needs to specialize.

Instead of overriding every base-class version that it inherits, a derived class can provide a `using` declaration (§ 15.5, p. 615) for the overloaded member. A `using` declaration specifies only a name; it may not specify a parameter list. Thus, a `using` declaration for a base-class member function adds all the overloaded instances of that function to the scope of the derived class. Having brought all the names into its scope, the derived class needs to define only those functions that truly depend on its type. It can use the inherited definitions for the others.

The normal rules for a `using` declaration inside a class apply to names of overloaded functions (§ 15.5, p. 615); every overloaded instance of the function in the base class must be accessible to the derived class. The access to the overloaded versions that are not otherwise redefined by the derived class will be the access in effect at the point of the `using` declaration.

EXERCISES SECTION 15.6

Exercise 15.23: Assuming class `D1` on page 620 had intended to override its inherited `fcn` function, how would you fix that class? Assuming you fixed the class so that `fcn` matched the definition in `Base`, how would the calls in that section be resolved?

15.7 Constructors and Copy Control

Like any other class, a class in an inheritance hierarchy controls what happens when objects of its type are created, copied, moved, assigned, or destroyed. As for any other class, if a class (base or derived) does not itself define one of the copy-control operations, the compiler will synthesize that operation. Also, as usual, the synthesized version of any of these members might be a deleted function.

 ## 15.7.1 Virtual Destructors

The primary direct impact that inheritance has on copy control for a base class is that a base class generally should define a virtual destructor (§ 15.2.1, p. 594). The destructor needs to be virtual to allow objects in the inheritance hierarchy to be dynamically allocated.

Recall that the destructor is run when we delete a pointer to a dynamically allocated object (§ 13.1.3, p. 502). If that pointer points to a type in an inheritance hierarchy, it is possible that the static type of the pointer might differ from the dynamic type of the object being destroyed (§ 15.2.2, p. 597). For example, if we delete a pointer of type Quote*, that pointer might point at a Bulk_quote object. If the pointer points at a Bulk_quote, the compiler has to know it should run the Bulk_quote destructor. As with any other function, we arrange to run the proper destructor by defining the destructor as virtual in the base class:

```
class Quote {
public:
    // virtual destructor needed if a base pointer pointing to a derived object is deleted
    virtual ~Quote() = default; // dynamic binding for the destructor
};
```

Like any other virtual, the virtual nature of the destructor is inherited. Thus, classes derived from Quote have virtual destructors, whether they use the synthe-sized destructor or define their own version. So long as the base class destructor is virtual, when we delete a pointer to base, the correct destructor will be run:

```
Quote *itemP = new Quote;   // same static and dynamic type
delete itemP;               // destructor for Quote called
itemP = new Bulk_quote;     // static and dynamic types differ
delete itemP;               // destructor for Bulk_quote called
```

> ⚠️ **WARNING** Executing delete on a pointer to base that points to a derived object has undefined behavior if the base's destructor is not virtual.

Destructors for base classes are an important exception to the rule of thumb that if a class needs a destructor, it also needs copy and assignment (§ 13.1.4, p. 504). A base class almost always needs a destructor, so that it can make the destructor virtual. If a base class has an empty destructor in order to make it virtual, then the fact that the class has a destructor does not indicate that the assignment operator or copy constructor is also needed.

Virtual Destructors Turn Off Synthesized Move

The fact that a base class needs a virtual destructor has an important indirect impact on the definition of base and derived classes: If a class defines a destructor—even if it uses = `default` to use the synthesized version—the compiler will not synthesize a move operation for that class (§ 13.6.2, p. 537).

EXERCISES SECTION 15.7.1

Exercise 15.24: What kinds of classes need a virtual destructor? What operations must a virtual destructor perform?

15.7.2 Synthesized Copy Control and Inheritance

The synthesized copy-control members in a base or a derived class execute like any other synthesized constructor, assignment operator, or destructor: They memberwise initialize, assign, or destroy the members of the class itself. In addition, these synthesized members initialize, assign, or destroy the direct base part of an object by using the corresponding operation from the base class. For example,

- The synthesized `Bulk_quote` default constructor runs the `Disc_Quote` default constructor, which in turn runs the `Quote` default constructor.

- The `Quote` default constructor default initializes the `bookNo` member to the empty string and uses the in-class initializer to initialize `price` to zero.

- When the `Quote` constructor finishes, the `Disc_Quote` constructor continues, which uses the in-class initializers to initialize `qty` and `discount`.

- When the `Disc_quote` constructor finishes, the `Bulk_quote` constructor continues but has no other work to do.

Similarly, the synthesized `Bulk_quote` copy constructor uses the (synthesized) `Disc_quote` copy constructor, which uses the (synthesized) `Quote` copy constructor. The `Quote` copy constructor copies the `bookNo` and `price` members; and the `Disc_Quote` copy constructor copies the `qty` and `discount` members.

It is worth noting that it doesn't matter whether the base-class member is itself synthesized (as is the case in our `Quote` hierarchy) or has a an user-provided definition. All that matters is that the corresponding member is accessible (§ 15.5, p. 611) and that it is not a deleted function.

Each of our `Quote` classes use the synthesized destructor. The derived classes do so implicitly, whereas the `Quote` class does so explicitly by defining its (virtual) destructor as = `default`. The synthesized destructor is (as usual) empty and its implicit destruction part destroys the members of the class (§ 13.1.3, p. 501). In addition to destroying its own members, the destruction phase of a destructor in a derived class also destroys its direct base. That destructor in turn invokes the destructor for its own direct base, if any. And, so on up to the root of the hierarchy.

As we've seen, `Quote` does not have synthesized move operations because it defines a destructor. The (synthesized) copy operations will be used whenever we move a `Quote` object (§ 13.6.2, p. 540). As we're about to see, the fact that `Quote` does not have move operations means that its derived classes don't either.

Base Classes and Deleted Copy Control in the Derived

The synthesized default constructor, or any of the copy-control members of either a base or a derived class, may be defined as deleted for the same reasons as in any other class (§ 13.1.6, p. 508, and § 13.6.2, p. 537). In addition, the way in which a base class is defined can cause a derived-class member to be defined as deleted:

- If the default constructor, copy constructor, copy-assignment operator, or destructor in the base class is deleted or inaccessible (§ 15.5, p. 612), then the corresponding member in the derived class is defined as deleted, because the compiler can't use the base-class member to construct, assign, or destroy the base-class part of the object.

- If the base class has an inaccessible or deleted destructor, then the synthesized default and copy constructors in the derived classes are defined as deleted, because there is no way to destroy the base part of the derived object.

- As usual, the compiler will not synthesize a deleted move operation. If we use = `default` to request a move operation, it will be a deleted function in the derived if the corresponding operation in the base is deleted or inaccessible, because the base class part cannot be moved. The move constructor will also be deleted if the base class destructor is deleted or inaccessible.

As an example, this base class, B,

```
class B {
public:
    B();
    B(const B&) = delete;
    // other members, not including a move constructor
};
class D : public B {
    // no constructors
};
D d;       // ok: D's synthesized default constructor uses B's default constructor
D d2(d);   // error: D's synthesized copy constructor is deleted
D d3(std::move(d));  // error: implicitly uses D's deleted copy constructor
```

has an accessible default constructor and an explicitly deleted copy constructor. Because the copy constructor is defined, the compiler will not synthesize a move constructor for class B (§ 13.6.2, p. 537). As a result, we can neither move nor copy objects of type B. If a class derived from B wanted to allow its objects to be copied or moved, that derived class would have to define its own versions of these constructors. Of course, that class would have to decide how to copy or move the members in it base-class part. In practice, if a base class does not have a default, copy, or move constructor, then its derived classes usually don't either.

Move Operations and Inheritance

As we've seen, most base classes define a virtual destructor. As a result, by default, base classes generally do not get synthesized move operations. Moreover, by default, classes derived from a base class that doesn't have move operations don't get synthesized move operations either.

Because lack of a move operation in a base class suppresses synthesized move for its derived classes, base classes ordinarily should define the move operations if it is sensible to do so. Our Quote class can use the synthesized versions. However, Quote must define these members explicitly. Once it defines its move operations, it must also explicitly define the copy versions as well (§ 13.6.2, p. 539):

```
class Quote {
public:
    Quote() = default;                    // memberwise default initialize
    Quote(const Quote&) = default;  // memberwise copy
    Quote(Quote&&) = default;        // memberwise copy
    Quote& operator=(const Quote&) = default; // copy assign
    Quote& operator=(Quote&&) = default;       // move assign
    virtual ~Quote() = default;
    // other members as before
};
```

Now, Quote objects will be memberwise copied, moved, assigned, and destroyed. Moreover, classes derived from Quote will automatically obtain synthesized move operations as well, unless they have members that otherwise preclude move.

> **EXERCISES SECTION 15.7.2**
>
> **Exercise 15.25:** Why did we define a default constructor for Disc_quote? What effect, if any, would removing that constructor have on the behavior of Bulk_quote?

15.7.3 Derived-Class Copy-Control Members

As we saw in § 15.2.2 (p. 598), the initialization phase of a derived-class constructor initializes the base-class part(s) of a derived object as well as initializing its own members. As a result, the copy and move constructors for a derived class must copy/move the members of its base part as well as the members in the derived. Similarly, a derived-class assignment operator must assign the members in the base part of the derived object.

Unlike the constructors and assignment operators, the destructor is responsible only for destroying the resources allocated by the derived class. Recall that the members of an object are implicitly destroyed (§ 13.1.3, p. 502). Similarly, the base-class part of a derived object is destroyed automatically.

> **WARNING** When a derived class defines a copy or move operation, that operation is responsible for copying or moving the entire object, including base-class members.

Defining a Derived Copy or Move Constructor

When we define a copy or move constructor (§ 13.1.1, p. 496, and § 13.6.2, p. 534) for a derived class, we ordinarily use the corresponding base-class constructor to initialize the base part of the object:

```
class Base { /* ... */ };
class D: public Base {
public:
    //  by default, the base class default constructor initializes the base part of an object
    //  to use the copy or move constructor, we must explicitly call that
    //  constructor in the constructor initializer list
    D(const D& d): Base(d)           //  copy the base members
                    /* initializers for members of D */ { /* ... */ }
    D(D&& d): Base(std::move(d))  //  move the base members
                    /* initializers for members of D */ { /* ... */ }
};
```

The initializer `Base(d)` passes a `D` object to a base-class constructor. Although in principle, `Base` could have a constructor that has a parameter of type `D`, in practice, that is very unlikely. Instead, `Base(d)` will (ordinarily) match the `Base` copy constructor. The `D` object, `d`, will be bound to the `Base&` parameter in that constructor. The `Base` copy constructor will copy the base part of `d` into the object that is being created. Had the initializer for the base class been omitted,

```
//  probably incorrect definition of the D copy constructor
//  base-class part is default initialized, not copied
D(const D& d) /* member initializers, but no base-class initializer */
    { /* ... */ }
```

the `Base` default constructor would be used to initialize the base part of a `D` object. Assuming `D`'s constructor copies the derived members from `d`, this newly constructed object would be oddly configured: Its `Base` members would hold default values, while its `D` members would be copies of the data from another object.

> **WARNING** By default, the base-class default constructor initializes the base-class part of a derived object. If we want copy (or move) the base-class part, we must explicitly use the copy (or move) constructor for the base class in the derived's constructor initializer list.

Derived-Class Assignment Operator

Like the copy and move constructors, a derived-class assignment operator (§ 13.1.2, p. 500, and § 13.6.2, p. 536), must assign its base part explicitly:

```
// Base::operator=(const Base&) is not invoked automatically
D &D::operator=(const D &rhs)
{
    Base::operator=(rhs);  //  assigns the base part
    //  assign the members in the derived class, as usual,
    //  handling self-assignment and freeing existing resources as appropriate
    return *this;
}
```

This operator starts by explicitly calling the base-class assignment operator to assign the members of the base part of the derived object. The base-class operator will (presumably) correctly handle self-assignment and, if appropriate, will free the old value in the base part of the left-hand operand and assign the new values from `rhs`. Once that operator finishes, we continue doing whatever is needed to assign the members in the derived class.

It is worth noting that a derived constructor or assignment operator can use its corresponding base class operation regardless of whether the base defined its own version of that operator or uses the synthesized version. For example, the call to `Base::operator=` executes the copy-assignment operator in class `Base`. It is immaterial whether that operator is defined explicitly by the `Base` class or is synthesized by the compiler.

Derived-Class Destructor

Recall that the data members of an object are implicitly destroyed after the destructor body completes (§ 13.1.3, p. 502). Similarly, the base-class parts of an object are also implicitly destroyed. As a result, unlike the constructors and assignment operators, a derived destructor is responsible only for destroying the resources allocated by the derived class:

```
class D: public Base {
public:
    // Base::~Base invoked automatically
    ~D() { /*  do what it takes to clean up derived members  */ }
};
```

Objects are destroyed in the opposite order from which they are constructed: The derived destructor is run first, and then the base-class destructors are invoked, back up through the inheritance hierarchy.

Calls to Virtuals in Constructors and Destructors

As we've seen, the base-class part of a derived object is constructed first. While the base-class constructor is executing, the derived part of the object is uninitialized. Similarly, derived objects are destroyed in reverse order, so that when a base class destructor runs, the derived part has already been destroyed. As a result, while these base-class members are executing, the object is incomplete.

To accommodate this incompleteness, the compiler treats the object as if its type changes during construction or destruction. That is, while an object is being constructed it is treated as if it has the same class as the constructor; calls to virtual functions will be bound as if the object has the same type as the constructor itself. Similarly, for destructors. This binding applies to virtuals called directly or that are called indirectly from a function that the constructor (or destructor) calls.

To understand this behavior, consider what would happen if the derived-class version of a virtual was called from a base-class constructor. This virtual probably accesses members of the derived object. After all, if the virtual didn't need to use members of the derived object, the derived class probably could use the version in its base class. However, those members are uninitialized while a base constructor is running. If such access were allowed, the program would probably crash.

> If a constructor or destructor calls a virtual, the version that is run is the one corresponding to the type of the constructor or destructor itself.

EXERCISES SECTION 15.7.3

Exercise 15.26: Define the `Quote` and `Bulk_quote` copy-control members to do the same job as the synthesized versions. Give them and the other constructors print statements that identify which function is running. Write programs using these classes and predict what objects will be created and destroyed. Compare your predictions with the output and continue experimenting until your predictions are reliably correct.

15.7.4 Inherited Constructors

Under the new standard, a derived class can reuse the constructors defined by its direct base class. Although, as we'll see, such constructors are not inherited in the normal sense of that term, it is nonetheless common to refer to such constructors as "inherited." For the same reasons that a class may initialize only its direct base class, a class may inherit constructors only from its direct base. A class cannot inherit the default, copy, and move constructors. If the derived class does not directly define these constructors, the compiler synthesizes them as usual.

A derived class inherits its base-class constructors by providing a `using` declaration that names its (direct) base class. As an example, we can redefine our `Bulk_quote` class (§ 15.4, p. 610) to inherit its constructors from `Disc_quote`:

```
class Bulk_quote : public Disc_quote {
public:
    using Disc_quote::Disc_quote; // inherit Disc_quote's constructors
    double net_price(std::size_t) const;
};
```

Ordinarily, a `using` declaration only makes a name visible in the current scope. When applied to a constructor, a `using` declaration causes the compiler to generate code. The compiler generates a derived constructor corresponding to each constructor in the base. That is, for each constructor in the base class, the compiler generates a constructor in the derived class that has the same parameter list.

These compiler-generated constructors have the form

derived (*parms*) : *base* (*args*) { }

where *derived* is the name of the derived class, *base* is the name of the base class, *parms* is the parameter list of the constructor, and *args* pass the parameters from the derived constructor to the base constructor. In our `Bulk_quote` class, the inherited constructor would be equivalent to

```
Bulk_quote(const std::string& book, double price,
        std::size_t qty, double disc):
    Disc_quote(book, price, qty, disc) { }
```

If the derived class has any data members of its own, those members are default initialized (§ 7.1.4, p. 266).

Characteristics of an Inherited Constructor

Unlike `using` declarations for ordinary members, a constructor `using` declaration does not change the access level of the inherited constructor(s). For example, regardless of where the `using` declaration appears, a `private` constructor in the base is a `private` constructor in the derived; similarly for `protected` and `public` constructors.

Moreover, a `using` declaration can't specify `explicit` or `constexpr`. If a constructor in the base is `explicit` (§ 7.5.4, p. 296) or `constexpr` (§ 7.5.6, p. 299), the inherited constructor has the same property.

If a base-class constructor has default arguments (§ 6.5.1, p. 236), those arguments are not inherited. Instead, the derived class gets multiple inherited constructors in which each parameter with a default argument is successively omitted. For example, if the base has a constructor with two parameters, the second of which has a default, the derived class will obtain two constructors: one with both parameters (and no default argument) and a second constructor with a single parameter corresponding to the left-most, non-defaulted parameter in the base class.

If a base class has several constructors, then with two exceptions, the derived class inherits each of the constructors from its base class. The first exception is that a derived class can inherit some constructors and define its own versions of other constructors. If the derived class defines a constructor with the same parameters as a constructor in the base, then that constructor is not inherited. The one defined in the derived class is used in place of the inherited constructor.

The second exception is that the default, copy, and move constructors are not inherited. These constructors are synthesized using the normal rules. An inherited constructor is not treated as a user-defined constructor. Therefore, a class that contains only inherited constructors will have a synthesized default constructor.

Exercise 15.27: Redefine your `Bulk_quote` class to inherit its constructors.

15.8 Containers and Inheritance

When we use a container to store objects from an inheritance hierarchy, we generally must store those objects indirectly. We cannot put objects of types related by inheritance directly into a container, because there is no way to define a container that holds elements of differing types.

As an example, assume we want to define a `vector` to hold several books that a customer wants to buy. It should be easy to see that we can't use a `vector` that holds `Bulk_quote` objects. We can't convert `Quote` objects to `Bulk_quote` (§ 15.2.3, p. 602), so we wouldn't be able to put `Quote` objects into that `vector`.

It may be somewhat less obvious that we also can't use a `vector` that holds objects of type `Quote`. In this case, we can put `Bulk_quote` objects into the container. However, those objects would no longer be `Bulk_quote` objects:

```
vector<Quote> basket;
basket.push_back(Quote("0-201-82470-1", 50));
//   ok, but copies only the Quote part of the object into basket
basket.push_back(Bulk_quote("0-201-54848-8", 50, 10, .25));
//   calls version defined by Quote, prints 750, i.e., 15 * $50
cout << basket.back().net_price(15) << endl;
```

The elements in `basket` are `Quote` objects. When we add a `Bulk_quote` object to the `vector` its derived part is ignored (§ 15.2.3, p. 603).

> ⚠️ **WARNING**   Because derived objects are "sliced down" when assigned to a base-type object, containers and types related by inheritance do not mix well.

Put (Smart) Pointers, Not Objects, in Containers

When we need a container that holds objects related by inheritance, we typically define the container to hold pointers (preferably smart pointers (§ 12.1, p. 450)) to the base class. As usual, the dynamic type of the object to which those pointers point might be the base-class type or a type derived from that base:

```
vector<shared_ptr<Quote>> basket;
basket.push_back(make_shared<Quote>("0-201-82470-1", 50));
basket.push_back(
    make_shared<Bulk_quote>("0-201-54848-8", 50, 10, .25));
//   calls the version defined by Quote; prints 562.5, i.e., 15 * $50 less the discount
cout << basket.back()->net_price(15) << endl;
```

Because `basket` holds `shared_ptr`s, we must dereference the value returned by `basket.back()` to get the object on which to run `net_price`. We do so by using `->` in the call to `net_price`. As usual, the version of `net_price` that is called depends on the dynamic type of the object to which that pointer points.

It is worth noting that we defined `basket` as `shared_ptr<Quote>`, yet in the second `push_back` we passed a `shared_ptr` to a `Bulk_quote` object. Just as we can convert an ordinary pointer to a derived type to a pointer to an base-class type (§ 15.2.2, p. 597), we can also convert a smart pointer to a derived type to a smart pointer to an base-class type. Thus, `make_shared<Bulk_quote>` returns a `shared_ptr<Bulk_quote>` object, which is converted to `shared_ptr<Quote>` when we call `push_back`. As a result, despite appearances, all of the elements of `basket` have the same type.

EXERCISES SECTION 15.8

Exercise 15.28: Define a `vector` to hold `Quote` objects but put `Bulk_quote` objects into that `vector`. Compute the total `net_price` of all the elements in the `vector`.

Exercise 15.29: Repeat your program, but this time store `shared_ptrs` to objects of type `Quote`. Explain any discrepancy in the sum generated by the this version and the previous program. If there is no discrepancy, explain why there isn't one.

15.8.1 Writing a `Basket` Class

One of the ironies of object-oriented programming in C++ is that we cannot use objects directly to support it. Instead, we must use pointers and references. Because pointers impose complexity on our programs, we often define auxiliary classes to help manage that complexity. We'll start by defining a class to represent a basket:

```
class Basket {
public:
    // Basket uses synthesized default constructor and copy-control members
    void add_item(const std::shared_ptr<Quote> &sale)
        { items.insert(sale); }
    // prints the total price for each book and the overall total for all items in the basket
    double total_receipt(std::ostream&) const;
private:
    // function to compare shared_ptrs needed by the multiset member
    static bool compare(const std::shared_ptr<Quote> &lhs,
                        const std::shared_ptr<Quote> &rhs)
    { return lhs->isbn() < rhs->isbn(); }
    // multiset to hold multiple quotes, ordered by the compare member
    std::multiset<std::shared_ptr<Quote>, decltype(compare)*>
                items{compare};
};
```

Our class uses a `multiset` (§ 11.2.1, p. 423) to hold the transactions, so that we can store multiple transactions for the same book, and so that all the transactions for a given book will be kept together (§ 11.2.2, p. 424).

The elements in our `multiset` are `shared_ptrs` and there is no less-than operator for `shared_ptr`. As a result, we must provide our own comparison operation to order the elements (§ 11.2.2, p. 425). Here, we define a `private static` member, named `compare`, that compares the `isbns` of the objects to which the `shared_ptrs` point. We initialize our `multiset` to use this comparison function through an in-class initializer (§ 7.3.1, p. 274):

```
// multiset to hold multiple quotes, ordered by the compare member
std::multiset<std::shared_ptr<Quote>, decltype(compare)*>
            items{compare};
```

This declaration can be hard to read, but reading from left to right, we see that we are defining a `multiset` of `shared_ptrs` to `Quote` objects. The `multiset` will use a function with the same type as our `compare` member to order the elements. The `multiset` member is named `items`, and we're initializing `items` to use our `compare` function.

Defining the Members of `Basket`

The `Basket` class defines only two operations. We defined the `add_item` member inside the class. That member takes a `shared_ptr` to a dynamically allocated `Quote` and puts that `shared_ptr` into the `multiset`. The second member, `total_receipt`, prints an itemized bill for the contents of the basket and returns the price for all the items in the basket:

```
double Basket::total_receipt(ostream &os) const
{
    double sum = 0.0;      // holds the running total

    // iter refers to the first element in a batch of elements with the same ISBN
    // upper_bound returns an iterator to the element just past the end of that batch
    for (auto iter = items.cbegin();
            iter != items.cend();
            iter = items.upper_bound(*iter)) {
        // we know there's at least one element with this key in the Basket
        // print the line item for this book
        sum += print_total(os, **iter, items.count(*iter));
    }
    os << "Total Sale: " << sum << endl; // print the final overall total
    return sum;
}
```

Our `for` loop starts by defining and initializing `iter` to refer to the first element in the `multiset`. The condition checks whether `iter` is equal to `items.cend()`. If so, we've processed all the purchases and we drop out of the `for`. Otherwise, we process the next book.

The interesting bit is the "increment" expression in the `for`. Rather than the usual loop that reads each element, we advance `iter` to refer to the next key. We skip over all the elements that match the current key by calling `upper_bound` (§ 11.3.5, p. 438). The call to `upper_bound` returns the iterator that refers to the element just past the last one with the same key as in `iter`. The iterator we get back denotes either the end of the set or the next book.

Inside the `for` loop, we call `print_total` (§ 15.1, p. 593) to print the details for each book in the basket:

```
sum += print_total(os, **iter, items.count(*iter));
```

The arguments to `print_total` are an `ostream` on which to write, a `Quote` object to process, and a count. When we dereference `iter`, we get a `shared_ptr` that points to the object we want to print. To get that object, we must dereference that `shared_ptr`. Thus, `**iter` is a `Quote` object (or an object of a type derived from `Quote`). We use the `multiset count` member (§ 11.3.5, p. 436) to determine how many elements in the `multiset` have the same key (i.e., the same ISBN).

As we've seen, `print_total` makes a virtual call to `net_price`, so the resulting price depends on the dynamic type of `**iter`. The `print_total` function prints the total for the given book and returns the total price that it calculated. We add that result into `sum`, which we print after we complete the `for` loop.

Hiding the Pointers

Users of `Basket` still have to deal with dynamic memory, because `add_item` takes a `shared_ptr`. As a result, users have to write code such as

```
Basket bsk;
bsk.add_item(make_shared<Quote>("123", 45));
bsk.add_item(make_shared<Bulk_quote>("345", 45, 3, .15));
```

Our next step will be to redefine `add_item` so that it takes a `Quote` object instead of a `shared_ptr`. This new version of `add_item` will handle the memory allocation so that our users no longer need to do so. We'll define two versions, one that will copy its given object and the other that will move from it (§ 13.6.3, p. 544):

```
void add_item(const Quote& sale);  //  copy the given object
void add_item(Quote&& sale);       //  move the given object
```

The only problem is that `add_item` doesn't know what type to allocate. When it does its memory allocation, `add_item` will copy (or move) its `sale` parameter. Somewhere there will be a `new` expression such as:

```
new Quote(sale)
```

Unfortunately, this expression won't do the right thing: `new` allocates an object of the type we request. This expression allocates an object of type `Quote` and copies the `Quote` portion of `sale`. However, `sale` might refer to a `Bulk_quote` object, in which case, that object will be sliced down.

Simulating Virtual Copy

We'll solve this problem by giving our `Quote` classes a virtual member that allocates a copy of itself.

```
class Quote {
public:
    //  virtual function to return a dynamically allocated copy of itself
    //  these members use reference qualifiers; see § 13.6.3 (p. 546)
    virtual Quote* clone() const & {return new Quote(*this);}
    virtual Quote* clone() &&
                            {return new Quote(std::move(*this));}
    //  other members as before
};
```

```
class Bulk_quote : public Quote {
    Bulk_quote* clone() const & {return new Bulk_quote(*this);}
    Bulk_quote* clone() &&
                    {return new Bulk_quote(std::move(*this));}
    //  other members as before
};
```

Because we have a copy and a move version of add_item, we defined lvalue and
rvalue versions of clone (§ 13.6.3, p. 546). Each clone function allocates a new
object of its own type. The const lvalue reference member copies itself into that
newly allocated object; the rvalue reference member moves its own data.

   Using clone, it is easy to write our new versions of add_item:

```
class Basket {
public:
    void add_item(const Quote& sale)   //  copy the given object
        { items.insert(std::shared_ptr<Quote>(sale.clone())); }
    void add_item(Quote&& sale)         //  move the given object
        { items.insert(
            std::shared_ptr<Quote>(std::move(sale).clone())); }
    //  other members as before
};
```

Like add_item itself, clone is overloaded based on whether it is called on an
lvalue or an rvalue. Thus, the first version of add_item calls the const lvalue
version of clone, and the second version calls the rvalue reference version. Note
that in the rvalue version, although the type of sale is an rvalue reference type,
sale (like any other variable) is an lvalue (§ 13.6.1, p. 533). Therefore, we call
move to bind an rvalue reference to sale.

   Our clone function is also virtual. Whether the Quote or Bulk_quote function is run, depends (as usual) on the dynamic type of sale. Regardless of whether
we copy or move the data, clone returns a pointer to a newly allocated object, of
its own type. We bind a shared_ptr to that object and call insert to add this
newly allocated object to items. Note that because shared_ptr supports the
derived-to-base conversion (§ 15.2.2, p. 597), we can bind a shared_ptr<Quote
to a Bulk_quote*.

EXERCISES SECTION 15.8.1

Exercise 15.30: Write your own version of the Basket class and use it to compute
prices for the same transactions as you used in the previous exercises.

15.9   Text Queries Revisited

As a final example of inheritance, we'll extend our text-query application from
§ 12.3 (p. 484). The classes we wrote in that section let us look for occurrences of a

given word in a file. We'd like to extend the system to support more complicated queries. In our examples, we'll run queries against the following simple story:

```
Alice Emma has long flowing red hair.
Her Daddy says when the wind blows
through her hair, it looks almost alive,
like a fiery bird in flight.
A beautiful fiery bird, he tells her,
magical but untamed.
"Daddy, shush, there is no such thing,"
she tells him, at the same time wanting
him to tell her more.
Shyly, she asks, "I mean, Daddy, is there?"
```

Our system should support the following queries:

- Word queries find all the lines that match a given `string`:

  ```
  Executing Query for: Daddy
  Daddy occurs 3 times
  (line 2) Her Daddy says when the wind blows
  (line 7) "Daddy, shush, there is no such thing,"
  (line 10) Shyly, she asks, "I mean, Daddy, is there?"
  ```

- Not queries, using the ~ operator, yield lines that don't match the query:

  ```
  Executing Query for: ~(Alice)
  ~(Alice) occurs 9 times
  (line 2) Her Daddy says when the wind blows
  (line 3) through her hair, it looks almost alive,
  (line 4) like a fiery bird in flight.
    . . .
  ```

- Or queries, using the | operator, return lines matching either of two queries:

  ```
  Executing Query for: (hair | Alice)
  (hair | Alice) occurs 2 times
  (line 1) Alice Emma has long flowing red hair.
  (line 3) through her hair, it looks almost alive,
  ```

- And queries, using the & operator, return lines matching both queries:

  ```
  Executing query for: (hair & Alice)
  (hair & Alice) occurs 1 time
  (line 1) Alice Emma has long flowing red hair.
  ```

Moreover, we want to be able to combine these operations, as in

```
fiery & bird | wind
```

We'll use normal C++ precedence rules (§ 4.1.2, p. 136) to evaluate compound expressions such as this example. Thus, this query will match a line in which both `fiery` and `bird` appear or one in which `wind` appears:

```
Executing Query for: ((fiery & bird) | wind)
((fiery & bird) | wind) occurs 3 times
(line 2) Her Daddy says when the wind blows
(line 4) like a fiery bird in flight.
(line 5) A beautiful fiery bird, he tells her,
```

Our output will print the query, using parentheses to indicate the way in which the query was interpreted. As with our original implementation, our system will display lines in ascending order and will not display the same line more than once.

15.9.1 An Object-Oriented Solution

We might think that we should use the `TextQuery` class from § 12.3.2 (p. 487) to represent our word query and derive our other queries from that class.

However, this design would be flawed. To see why, consider a Not query. A Word query looks for a particular word. In order for a Not query to be a kind of Word query, we would have to be able to identify the word for which the Not query was searching. In general, there is no such word. Instead, a Not query has a query (a Word query or any other kind of query) whose value it negates. Similarly, an And query and an Or query have two queries whose results it combines.

This observation suggests that we model our different kinds of queries as independent classes that share a common base class:

```
WordQuery // Daddy
NotQuery  // ~Alice
OrQuery   // hair | Alice
AndQuery  // hair & Alice
```

These classes will have only two operations:

- `eval`, which takes a `TextQuery` object and returns a `QueryResult`. The `eval` function will use the given `TextQuery` object to find the query's the matching lines.

- `rep`, which returns the `string` representation of the underlying query. This function will be used by `eval` to create a `QueryResult` representing the match and by the output operator to print the query expressions.

Abstract Base Class

As we've seen, our four query types are not related to one another by inheritance; they are conceptually siblings. Each class shares the same interface, which suggests that we'll need to define an abstract base class (§ 15.4, p. 610) to represent that interface. We'll name our abstract base class `Query_base`, indicating that its role is to serve as the root of our query hierarchy.

Our `Query_base` class will define `eval` and `rep` as pure virtual functions (§ 15.4, p. 610). Each of our classes that represents a particular kind of query must override these functions. We'll derive `WordQuery` and `NotQuery` directly from

---

KEY CONCEPT: INHERITANCE VERSUS COMPOSITION

The design of inheritance hierarchies is a complicated topic in its own right and well beyond the scope of this language Primer. However, there is one important design guide that is so fundamental that every programmer should be familiar with it.

When we define a class as publicly inherited from another, the derived class should reflect an "Is A" relationship to the base class. In well-designed class hierarchies, objects of a publicly derived class can be used wherever an object of the base class is expected.

Another common relationship among types is a "Has A" relationship. Types related by a "Has A" relationship imply membership.

In our bookstore example, our base class represents the concept of a quote for a book sold at a stipulated price. Our `Bulk_quote` "is a" kind of quote, but one with a different pricing strategy. Our bookstore classes "have a" price and an ISBN.

`Query_base`. The `AndQuery` and `OrQuery` classes share one property that the other classes in our system do not: Each has two operands. To model this property, we'll define another abstract base class, named `BinaryQuery`, to represent queries with two operands. The `AndQuery` and `OrQuery` classes will inherit from `BinaryQuery`, which in turn will inherit from `Query_base`. These decisions give us the class design represented in Figure 15.2.

Figure 15.2: `Query_base` Inheritance Hierarchy

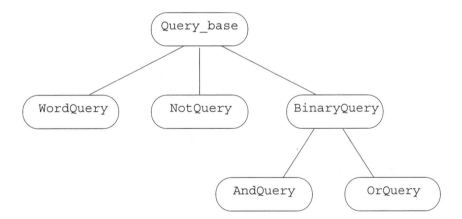

Hiding a Hierarchy in an Interface Class

Our program will deal with evaluating queries, not with building them. However, we need to be able to create queries in order to run our program. The simplest way to do so is to write C++ expressions to create the queries. For example, we'd like to generate the compound query previously described by writing code such as

```
Query q = Query("fiery") & Query("bird") | Query("wind");
```

This problem description implicitly suggests that user-level code won't use the inherited classes directly. Instead, we'll define an interface class named Query, which will hide the hierarchy. The Query class will store a pointer to Query_base. That pointer will be bound to an object of a type derived from Query_base. The Query class will provide the same operations as the Query_base classes: eval to evaluate the associated query, and rep to generate a string version of the query. It will also define an overloaded output operator to display the associated query.

Users will create and manipulate Query_base objects only indirectly through operations on Query objects. We'll define three overloaded operators on Query objects, along with a Query constructor that takes a string. Each of these functions will dynamically allocate a new object of a type derived from Query_base:

- The & operator will generate a Query bound to a new AndQuery.

- The | operator will generate a Query bound to a new OrQuery.

- The ~ operator will generate a Query bound to a new NotQuery.

- The Query constructor that takes a string will generate a new WordQuery.

Figure 15.3: Objects Created by Query Expressions

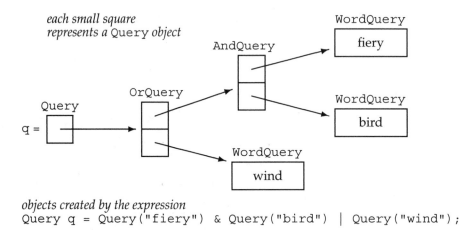

objects created by the expression
Query q = Query("fiery") & Query("bird") | Query("wind");

Understanding How These Classes Work

It is important to realize that much of the work in this application consists of building objects to represent the user's query. For example, an expression such as the one above generates the collection of interrelated objects illustrated in Figure 15.3.

Once the tree of objects is built up, evaluating (or generating the representation of) a query is basically a process (managed for us by the compiler) of following these links, asking each object to evaluate (or display) itself. For example, if we call eval on q (i.e., on the root of the tree), that call asks the OrQuery to which q points to eval itself. Evaluating this OrQuery calls eval on its two operands— on the AndQuery and the WordQuery that looks for the word wind. Evaluating the AndQuery evaluates its two WordQuerys, generating the results for the words fiery and bird, respectively.

When new to object-oriented programming, it is often the case that the hardest part in understanding a program is understanding the design. Once you are thoroughly comfortable with the design, the implementation flows naturally. As an aid to understanding this design, we've summarized the classes used in this example in Table 15.1 (overleaf).

EXERCISES SECTION 15.9.1

Exercise 15.31: Given that s1, s2, s3, and s4 are all strings, determine what objects are created in the following expressions:

```
(a) Query(s1) | Query(s2) & ~ Query(s3);
(b) Query(s1) |. (Query(s2) & ~ Query(s3));
(c) (Query(s1) & (Query(s2)) | (Query(s3) & Query(s4)));
```

15.9.2 The Query_base and Query Classes

We'll start our implementation by defining the Query_base class:

```cpp
// abstract class acts as a base class for concrete query types; all members are private
class Query_base {
    friend class Query;
protected:
    using line_no = TextQuery::line_no; // used in the eval functions
    virtual ~Query_base() = default;
private:
    // eval returns the QueryResult that matches this Query
    virtual QueryResult eval(const TextQuery&) const = 0;
    // rep is a string representation of the query
    virtual std::string rep() const = 0;
};
```

Both eval and rep are pure virtual functions, which makes Query_base an abstract base class (§ 15.4, p. 610). Because we don't intend users, or the derived classes, to use Query_base directly, Query_base has no public members. All use of Query_base will be through Query objects. We grant friendship to the Query class, because members of Query will call the virtuals in Query_base.

The protected member, line_no, will be used inside the eval functions. Similarly, the destructor is protected because it is used (implicitly) by the destructors in the derived classes.

Table 15.1: Recap: Query Program Design	
Query Program Interface Classes and Operations	
TextQuery	Class that reads a given file and builds a lookup map. This class has a query operation that takes a string argument and returns a QueryResult representing the lines on which that string appears (§ 12.3.2, p. 487).
QueryResult	Class that holds the results of a query operation (§ 12.3.2, p. 489).
Query	Interface class that points to an object of a type derived from Query_base.
Query q(s)	Binds the Query q to a new WordQuery holding the string s.
q1 & q2	Returns a Query bound to a new AndQuery object holding q1 and q2.
q1 | q2	Returns a Query bound to a new OrQuery object holding q1 and q2.
~q	Returns a Query bound to a new NotQuery object holding q.
Query Program Implementation Classes	
Query_base	Abstract base class for the query classes.
WordQuery	Class derived from Query_base that looks for a given word.
NotQuery	Class derived from Query_base that represents the set of lines in which its Query operand does not appear.
BinaryQuery	Abstract base class derived from Query_base that represents queries with two Query operands.
OrQuery	Class derived from BinaryQuery that returns the union of the line numbers in which its two operands appear.
AndQuery	Class derived from BinaryQuery that returns the intersection of the line numbers in which its two operands appear.

The Query Class

The Query class provides the interface to (and hides) the Query_base inheritance hierarchy. Each Query object will hold a shared_ptr to a corresponding Query_base object. Because Query is the only interface to the Query_base classes, Query must define its own versions of eval and rep.

The Query constructor that takes a string will create a new WordQuery and bind its shared_ptr member to that newly created object. The &, |, and ~ operators will create AndQuery, OrQuery, and NotQuery objects, respectively. These operators will return a Query object bound to its newly generated object. To support these operators, Query needs a constructor that takes a shared_ptr to a Query_base and stores its given pointer. We'll make this constructor private because we don't intend general user code to define Query_base objects. Because this constructor is private, we'll need to make the operators friends.

Given the preceding design, the Query class itself is simple:

```
// interface class to manage the Query_base inheritance hierarchy
class Query {
    // these operators need access to the shared_ptr constructor
    friend Query operator~(const Query &);
    friend Query operator|(const Query&, const Query&);
    friend Query operator&(const Query&, const Query&);
```

```
public:
    Query(const std::string&);  // builds a new WordQuery
    // interface functions: call the corresponding Query_base operations
    QueryResult eval(const TextQuery &t) const
                            { return q->eval(t); }
    std::string rep() const { return q->rep(); }
private:
    Query(std::shared_ptr<Query_base> query): q(query) { }
    std::shared_ptr<Query_base> q;
};
```

We start by naming as friends the operators that create Query objects. These operators need to be friends in order to use the private constructor.

In the public interface for Query, we declare, but cannot yet define, the constructor that takes a string. That constructor creates a WordQuery object, so we cannot define this constructor until we have defined the WordQuery class.

The other two public members represent the interface for Query_base. In each case, the Query operation uses its Query_base pointer to call the respective (virtual) Query_base operation. The actual version that is called is determined at run time and will depend on the type of the object to which q points.

The Query Output Operator

The output operator is a good example of how our overall query system works:

```
std::ostream &
operator<<(std::ostream &os, const Query &query)
{
    // Query::rep makes a virtual call through its Query_base pointer to rep()
    return os << query.rep();
}
```

When we print a Query, the output operator calls the (public) rep member of class Query. That function makes a virtual call through its pointer member to the rep member of the object to which this Query points. That is, when we write

```
Query andq = Query(sought1) & Query(sought2);
cout << andq << endl;
```

the output operator calls Query::rep on andq. Query::rep in turn makes a virtual call through its Query_base pointer to the Query_base version of rep. Because andq points to an AndQuery object, that call will run AndQuery::rep.

> ### EXERCISES SECTION 15.9.2
>
> **Exercise 15.32:** What happens when an object of type Query is copied, moved, assigned, and destroyed?
>
> **Exercise 15.33:** What about objects of type Query_base?

15.9.3   The Derived Classes

The most interesting part of the classes derived from `Query_base` is how they are represented. The `WordQuery` class is most straightforward. Its job is to hold the search word.

The other classes operate on one or two operands. A `NotQuery` has a single operand, and `AndQuery` and `OrQuery` have two operands. In each of these classes, the operand(s) can be an object of any of the concrete classes derived from `Query_base`: A `NotQuery` can be applied to a `WordQuery`, an `AndQuery`, an `OrQuery`, or another `NotQuery`. To allow this flexibility, the operands must be stored as pointers to `Query_base`. That way we can bind the pointer to whichever concrete class we need.

However, rather than storing a `Query_base` pointer, our classes will themselves use a `Query` object. Just as user code is simplified by using the interface class, we can simplify our own class code by using the same class.

Now that we know the design for these classes, we can implement them.

The `WordQuery` Class

A `WordQuery` looks for a given `string`. It is the only operation that actually performs a query on the given `TextQuery` object:

```
class WordQuery: public Query_base {
    friend class Query; // Query uses the WordQuery constructor
    WordQuery(const std::string &s): query_word(s) { }

    // concrete class: WordQuery defines all inherited pure virtual functions
    QueryResult eval(const TextQuery &t) const
                        { return t.query(query_word); }
    std::string rep() const { return query_word; }
    std::string query_word;     // word for which to search
};
```

Like `Query_base`, `WordQuery` has no `public` members; `WordQuery` must make `Query` a friend in order to allow `Query` to access the `WordQuery` constructor.

Each of the concrete query classes must define the inherited pure virtual functions, `eval` and `rep`. We defined both operations inside the `WordQuery` class body: `eval` calls the `query` member of its given `TextQuery` parameter, which does the actual search in the file; `rep` returns the `string` that this `WordQuery` represents (i.e., `query_word`).

Having defined the `WordQuery` class, we can now define the `Query` constructor that takes a `string`:

```
inline
Query::Query(const std::string &s): q(new WordQuery(s)) { }
```

This constructor allocates a `WordQuery` and initializes its pointer member to point to that newly allocated object.

The `NotQuery` Class and the ~ Operator

The ~ operator generates a `NotQuery`, which holds a `Query`, which it negates:

```
class NotQuery: public Query_base {
    friend Query operator~(const Query &);
    NotQuery(const Query &q): query(q) { }
    // concrete class: NotQuery defines all inherited pure virtual functions
    std::string rep() const {return "~(" + query.rep() + ")";}
    QueryResult eval(const TextQuery&) const;
    Query query;
};
inline Query operator~(const Query &operand)
{
    return std::shared_ptr<Query_base>(new NotQuery(operand));
}
```

Because the members of NotQuery are all private, we start by making the ~ operator a friend. To rep a NotQuery, we concatenate the ~ symbol to the representation of the underlying Query. We parenthesize the output to ensure that precedence is clear to the reader.

It is worth noting that the call to rep in NotQuery's own rep member ultimately makes a virtual call to rep: query.rep() is a nonvirtual call to the rep member of the Query class. Query::rep in turn calls q->rep(), which is a virtual call through its Query_base pointer.

The ~ operator dynamically allocates a new NotQuery object. The return (implicitly) uses the Query constructor that takes a shared_ptr<Query_base>. That is, the return statement is equivalent to

```
// allocate a new NotQuery object
// bind the resulting NotQuery pointer to a shared_ptr<Query_base
shared_ptr<Query_base> tmp(new NotQuery(expr));
return Query(tmp); // use the Query constructor that takes a shared_ptr
```

The eval member is complicated enough that we will implement it outside the class body. We'll define the eval functions in § 15.9.4 (p. 647).

The BinaryQuery Class

The BinaryQuery class is an abstract base class that holds the data needed by the query types that operate on two operands:

```
class BinaryQuery: public Query_base {
protected:
    BinaryQuery(const Query &l, const Query &r, std::string s):
            lhs(l), rhs(r), opSym(s) { }
    // abstract class: BinaryQuery doesn't define eval
    std::string rep() const { return "(" + lhs.rep() + " "
                                          + opSym + " "
                                          + rhs.rep() + ")"; }
    Query lhs, rhs;    // right- and left-hand operands
    std::string opSym; // name of the operator
};
```

The data in a `BinaryQuery` are the two `Query` operands and the corresponding operator symbol. The constructor takes the two operands and the operator symbol, each of which it stores in the corresponding data members.

To `rep` a `BinaryOperator`, we generate the parenthesized expression consisting of the representation of the left-hand operand, followed by the operator, followed by the representation of the right-hand operand. As when we displayed a `NotQuery`, the calls to `rep` ultimately make virtual calls to the `rep` function of the `Query_base` objects to which `lhs` and `rhs` point.

The `BinaryQuery` class does not define the `eval` function and so inherits a pure virtual. Thus, `BinaryQuery` is also an abstract base class, and we cannot create objects of `BinaryQuery` type.

The `AndQuery` and `OrQuery` Classes and Associated Operators

The `AndQuery` and `OrQuery` classes, and their corresponding operators, are quite similar to one another:

```
class AndQuery: public BinaryQuery {
    friend Query operator&(const Query&, const Query&);
    AndQuery(const Query &left, const Query &right):
                        BinaryQuery(left, right, "&") { }
    // concrete class: AndQuery inherits rep and defines the remaining pure virtual
    QueryResult eval(const TextQuery&) const;
};
inline Query operator&(const Query &lhs, const Query &rhs)
{
    return std::shared_ptr<Query_base>(new AndQuery(lhs, rhs));
}

class OrQuery: public BinaryQuery {
    friend Query operator|(const Query&, const Query&);
    OrQuery(const Query &left, const Query &right):
                BinaryQuery(left, right, "|") { }
    QueryResult eval(const TextQuery&) const;
};
inline Query operator|(const Query &lhs, const Query &rhs)
{
    return std::shared_ptr<Query_base>(new OrQuery(lhs, rhs));
}
```

These classes make the respective operator a friend and define a constructor to create their `BinaryQuery` base part with the appropriate operator. They inherit the `BinaryQuery` definition of `rep`, but each overrides the `eval` function.

Like the ~ operator, the & and | operators return a `shared_ptr` bound to a newly allocated object of the corresponding type. That `shared_ptr` gets converted to `Query` as part of the return statement in each of these operators.

EXERCISES SECTION 15.9.3

Exercise 15.34: For the expression built in Figure 15.3 (p. 638):

(a) List the constructors executed in processing that expression.
(b) List the calls to `rep` that are made from `cout << q`.
(c) List the calls to `eval` made from `q.eval()`.

Exercise 15.35: Implement the `Query` and `Query_base` classes, including a definition of `rep` but omitting the definition of `eval`.

Exercise 15.36: Put print statements in the constructors and `rep` members and run your code to check your answers to `(a)` and `(b)` from the first exercise.

Exercise 15.37: What changes would your classes need if the derived classes had members of type `shared_ptr<Query_base>` rather than of type `Query`?

Exercise 15.38: Are the following declarations legal? If not, why not? If so, explain what the declarations mean.

```
BinaryQuery a = Query("fiery") & Query("bird");
AndQuery b = Query("fiery") & Query("bird");
OrQuery c = Query("fiery") & Query("bird");
```

15.9.4 The `eval` Functions

The `eval` functions are the heart of our query system. Each of these functions calls `eval` on its operand(s) and then applies its own logic: The `OrQuery` `eval` operation returns the union of the results of its two operands; `AndQuery` returns the intersection. The `NotQuery` is more complicated: It must return the line numbers that are not in its operand's set.

To support the processing in the `eval` functions, we need to use the version of `QueryResult` that defines the members we added in the exercises to § 12.3.2 (p. 490). We'll assume that `QueryResult` has `begin` and `end` members that will let us iterate through the `set` of line numbers that the `QueryResult` holds. We'll also assume that `QueryResult` has a member named `get_file` that returns a `shared_ptr` to the underlying file on which the query was executed.

 Our `Query` classes use members defined for `QueryResult` in the exercises to § 12.3.2 (p. 490).

OrQuery::eval

An `OrQuery` represents the union of the results for its two operands, which we obtain by calling `eval` on each of its operands. Because these operands are `Query` objects, calling `eval` is a call to `Query::eval`, which in turn makes a virtual call to `eval` on the underlying `Query_base` object. Each of these calls yields a `QueryResult` representing the line numbers in which its operand appears. We'll combine those line numbers into a new `set`:

```
//  returns the union of its operands' result sets
QueryResult
OrQuery::eval(const TextQuery& text) const
{
    //  virtual calls through the Query members, lhs and rhs
    //  the calls to eval return the QueryResult for each operand
    auto right = rhs.eval(text), left = lhs.eval(text);
    //  copy the line numbers from the left-hand operand into the result set
    auto ret_lines =
        make_shared<set<line_no>>(left.begin(), left.end());
    //  insert lines from the right-hand operand
    ret_lines->insert(right.begin(), right.end());
    //  return the new QueryResult representing the union of lhs and rhs
    return QueryResult(rep(), ret_lines, left.get_file());
}
```

We initialize `ret_lines` using the `set` constructor that takes a pair of iterators.
The `begin` and `end` members of a `QueryResult` return iterators into that object's set of line numbers. So, `ret_lines` is created by copying the elements
from `left`'s set. We next call `insert` on `ret_lines` to insert the elements from
`right`. After this call, `ret_lines` contains the line numbers that appear in either
`left` or `right`.

The `eval` function ends by building and returning a `QueryResult` representing the combined match. The `QueryResult` constructor (§ 12.3.2, p. 489)
takes three arguments: a `string` representing the query, a `shared_ptr` to the
set of matching line numbers, and a `shared_ptr` to the `vector` that represents
the input file. We call `rep` to generate the `string` and `get_file` to obtain the
`shared_ptr` to the file. Because both `left` and `right` refer to the same file, it
doesn't matter which of these we use for `get_file`.

AndQuery::eval

The `AndQuery` version of `eval` is similar to the `OrQuery` version, except that it
calls a library algorithm to find the lines in common to both queries:

```
//  returns the intersection of its operands' result sets
QueryResult
AndQuery::eval(const TextQuery& text) const
{
    //  virtual calls through the Query operands to get result sets for the operands
    auto left = lhs.eval(text), right = rhs.eval(text);
    //  set to hold the intersection of left and right
    auto ret_lines = make_shared<set<line_no>>();
    //  writes the intersection of two ranges to a destination iterator
    //  destination iterator in this call adds elements to ret
    set_intersection(left.begin(), left.end(),
                     right.begin(), right.end(),
                     inserter(*ret_lines, ret_lines->begin()));
    return QueryResult(rep(), ret_lines, left.get_file());
}
```

Here we use the library `set_intersection` algorithm, which is described in Appendix A.2.8 (p. 880), to merge these two `set`s.

The `set_intersection` algorithm takes five iterators. It uses the first four to denote two input sequences (§ 10.5.2, p. 413). Its last argument denotes a destination. The algorithm writes the elements that appear in both input sequences into the destination.

In this call we pass an insert iterator (§ 10.4.1, p. 401) as the destination. When `set_intersection` writes to this iterator, the effect will be to insert a new element into `ret_lines`.

Like the `OrQuery` `eval` function, this one ends by building and returning a `QueryResult` representing the combined match.

NotQuery::eval

`NotQuery` finds each line of the text within which the operand is not found:

```
//  returns the lines not in its operand's result set
QueryResult
NotQuery::eval(const TextQuery& text) const
{
    //  virtual call to eval through the Query operand
    auto result = query.eval(text);
    //  start out with an empty result set
    auto ret_lines = make_shared<set<line_no>>();
    //  we have to iterate through the lines on which our operand appears
    auto beg = result.begin(), end = result.end();
    //  for each line in the input file, if that line is not in result,
    //  add that line number to ret_lines
    auto sz = result.get_file()->size();
    for (size_t n = 0; n != sz; ++n) {
        //  if we haven't processed all the lines in result
        //  check whether this line is present
        if (beg == end || *beg != n)
            ret_lines->insert(n);   //  if not in result, add this line
        else if (beg != end)
            ++beg; //  otherwise get the next line number in result if there is one
    }
    return QueryResult(rep(), ret_lines, result.get_file());
}
```

As in the other `eval` functions, we start by calling `eval` on this object's operand. That call returns the `QueryResult` containing the line numbers on which the operand appears, but we want the line numbers on which the operand does not appear. That is, we want every line in the file that is not already in `result`.

We generate that `set` by iterating through sequential integers up to the size of the input file. We'll put each number that is not in `result` into `ret_lines`. We position `beg` and `end` to denote the first and one past the last elements in `result`. That object is a `set`, so when we iterate through it, we'll obtain the line numbers in ascending order.

The loop body checks whether the current number is in `result`. If not, we add that number to `ret_lines`. If the number is in `result`, we increment `beg`, which is our iterator into `result`.

Once we've processed all the line numbers, we return a `QueryResult` containing `ret_lines`, along with the results of running `rep` and `get_file` as in the previous `eval` functions.

EXERCISES SECTION 15.9.4

Exercise 15.39: Implement the `Query` and `Query_base` classes. Test your application by evaluating and printing a query such as the one in Figure 15.3 (p. 638).

Exercise 15.40: In the `OrQuery` `eval` function what would happen if its `rhs` member returned an empty set? What if its `lhs` member did so? What if both `rhs` and `lhs` returned empty sets?

Exercise 15.41: Reimplement your classes to use built-in pointers to `Query_base` rather than `shared_ptrs`. Remember that your classes will no longer be able to use the synthesized copy-control members.

Exercise 15.42: Design and implement one of the following enhancements:

(a) Print words only once per sentence rather than once per line.

(b) Introduce a history system in which the user can refer to a previous query by number, possibly adding to it or combining it with another.

(c) Allow the user to limit the results so that only matches in a given range of lines are displayed.

CHAPTER SUMMARY

Inheritance lets us write new classes that share behavior with their base class(es) but override or add to that behavior as needed. Dynamic binding lets us ignore type differences by choosing, at run time, which version of a function to run based on an object's dynamic type. The combination of inheritance and dynamic binding lets us write type-independent, programs that have type-specific behavior.

In C++, dynamic binding applies *only* to functions declared as `virtual` and called through a reference or pointer.

A derived-class object contains a subobject corresponding to each of its base classes. Because every derived object contains a base part, we can convert a reference or pointer to a derived-class type to a reference or pointer to an accessible base class.

Inherited objects are constructed, copied, moved, and assigned by constructing, copying, moving, and assigning the base part(s) of the object before handling the derived part. Destructors execute in the opposite order; the derived type is destroyed first, followed by destructors for the base-class subobjects. Base classes usually should define a virtual destructor even if the class otherwise has no need for a destructor. The destructor must be virtual if a pointer to a base is ever deleted when it actually addresses a derived-class object.

A derived class specifies a protection level for each of its base class(es). Members of a `public` base are part of the interface of the derived class; members of a `private` base are inaccessible; members of a `protected` base are accessible to classes that derive from the derived class but not to users of the derived class.

DEFINED TERMS

abstract base class Class that has one or more pure virtual functions. We cannot create objects of an abstract base-class type.

accessible Base class member that can be used through a derived object. Accessibility depends on the access specifier used in derivation list of the derived class and the access level of the member in the base class. For example, a `public` member of a class that is inherited via `public` inheritance is accessible to users of the derived class. A `public` base class member is inaccessible if the inheritance is `private`.

base class Class from which other classes inherit. The members of the base class become members of the derived class.

class derivation list List of base classes, each of which may have an optional access level, from which a derived class inher-

its. If no access specifier is provided, the inheritance is `public` if the derived class is defined with the `struct` keyword, and is `private` if the class is defined with the `class` keyword.

derived class Class that inherits from another class. A derived class can override the virtuals of its base and can define new members. A derived-class scope is nested in the scope of its base class(es); members of the derived class can use members of the base class directly.

derived-to-base conversion Implicit conversion of a derived object to a reference to a base class, or of a pointer to a derived object to a pointer to the base type.

direct base class Base class from which a derived class inherits directly. Direct base classes are specified in the derivation list of the derived class. A direct base class may itself be a derived class.

dynamic binding Delaying until run time the selection of which function to run. In C++, dynamic binding refers to the run-time choice of which virtual function to run based on the underlying type of the object to which a reference or pointer is bound.

dynamic type Type of an object at run time. The dynamic type of an object to which a reference refers or to which a pointer points may differ from the static type of the reference or pointer. A pointer or reference to a base-class type can refer to an to object of derived type. In such cases the static type is reference (or pointer) to base, but the dynamic type is reference (or pointer) to derived.

indirect base class Base class that does not appear in the derivation list of a derived class. A class from which the direct base class inherits, directly or indirectly, is an indirect base class to the derived class.

inheritance Programming technique for defining a new class (known as a derived class) in terms of an existing class (known as the base class). The derived class inherits the members of the base class.

object-oriented programming Method of writing programs using data abstraction, inheritance, and dynamic binding.

override Virtual function defined in a derived class that has the same parameter list as a virtual in a base class overrides the base-class definition.

polymorphism As used in object-oriented programming, refers to the ability to obtain type-specific behavior based on the dynamic type of a reference or pointer.

private inheritance In `private` inheritance, the `public` and `protected` members of the base class are `private` members of the derived.

protected access specifier Members defined after the `protected` keyword may be accessed by the members and friends of a derived class. However, these members are only accessible through derived objects. `protected` members are not accessible to ordinary users of the class.

protected inheritance In `protected` inheritance, the `protected` and `public` members of the base class are `protected` members of the derived class.

public inheritance The `public` interface of the base class is part of the `public` interface of the derived class.

pure virtual Virtual function declared in the class header using `= 0` just before the semicolon. A pure virtual function need not be (but may be) defined. Classes with pure virtuals are abstract classes. If a derived class does not define its own version of an inherited pure virtual, then the derived class is abstract as well.

refactoring Redesigning programs to collect related parts into a single abstraction, replacing the original code with uses of the new abstraction. Typically, classes are refactored to move data or function members to the highest common point in the hierarchy to avoid code duplication.

run-time binding See dynamic binding.

sliced down What happens when an object of derived type is used to initialize or assign an object of the base type. The derived portion of the object is "sliced down," leaving only the base portion, which is assigned to the base.

static type Type with which a variable is defined or that an expression yields. Static type is known at compile time.

virtual function Member function that defines type-specific behavior. Calls to a virtual made through a reference or pointer are resolved at run time, based on the type of the object to which the reference or pointer is bound.

CHAPTER 16

TEMPLATES AND GENERIC PROGRAMMING

Both object-oriented programming (OOP) and generic programming deal with types that are not known at the time the program is written. The distinction between the two is that OOP deals with types that are not known until run time, whereas in generic programming the types become known during compilation.

The containers, iterators, and algorithms described in Part II are all examples of generic programming. When we write a generic program, we write the code in a way that is independent of any particular type. When we use a generic program, we supply the type(s) or value(s) on which that instance of the program will operate.

For example, the library provides a single, generic definition of each container, such as `vector`. We can use that generic definition to define many different types of `vectors`, each of which differs from the others as to the type of elements the `vector` contains.

Templates are the foundation of generic programming. We can use and have used templates without understanding how they are defined. In this chapter we'll see how to define our own templates.

Templates are the foundation for generic programming in C++. A template is a blueprint or formula for creating classes or functions. When we use a generic type, such as `vector`, or a generic function, such as `find`, we supply the information needed to transform that blueprint into a specific class or function. That transformation happens during compilation. In Chapter 3 and Part II we learned how to use templates. In this chapter we'll learn how to define them.

16.1 Defining a Template

Imagine that we want to write a function to compare two values and indicate whether the first is less than, equal to, or greater than the second. In practice, we'd want to define several such functions, each of which will compare values of a given type. Our first attempt might be to define several overloaded functions:

```
//  returns 0 if the values are equal, -1 if v1 is smaller, 1 if v2 is smaller
int compare(const string &v1, const string &v2)
{
    if (v1 < v2) return -1;
    if (v2 < v1) return 1;
    return 0;
}
int compare(const double &v1, const double &v2)
{
    if (v1 < v2) return -1;
    if (v2 < v1) return 1;
    return 0;
}
```

These functions are nearly identical: The only difference between them is the type of their parameters. The function body is the same in each function.

Having to repeat the body of the function for each type that we compare is tedious and error-prone. More importantly, we need to know when we write the program all the types that we might ever want to `compare`. This strategy cannot work if we want to be able to use the function on types that our users might supply.

16.1.1 Function Templates

Rather than defining a new function for each type, we can define a **function template**. A function template is a formula from which we can generate type-specific versions of that function. The template version of `compare` looks like

```
template <typename T>
int compare(const T &v1, const T &v2)
{
    if (v1 < v2) return -1;
    if (v2 < v1) return 1;
    return 0;
}
```

A template definition starts with the keyword `template` followed by a **template parameter list**, which is a comma-separated list of one or more **template parameters** bracketed by the less-than (<) and greater-than (>) tokens.

> **Note** In a template definition, the template parameter list cannot be empty.

The template parameter list acts much like a function parameter list. A function parameter list defines local variable(s) of a specified type but does not say how to initialize them. At run time, arguments are supplied that initialize the parameters.

Analogously, template parameters represent types or values used in the definition of a class or function. When we use a template, we specify—either implicitly or explicitly—**template argument(s)** to bind to the template parameter(s).

Our `compare` function declares one type parameter named `T`. Inside `compare`, we use the name `T` to refer to a type. Which *actual type* `T` represents is determined at compile time based on how `compare` is used.

Instantiating a Function Template

When we call a function template, the compiler (ordinarily) uses the arguments of the call to deduce the template argument(s) for us. That is, when we call `compare`, the compiler uses the type of the arguments to determine what type to bind to the template parameter `T`. For example, in this call

```
cout << compare(1, 0) << endl;        // T is int
```

the arguments have type `int`. The compiler will deduce `int` as the template argument and will bind that argument to the template parameter `T`.

The compiler uses the deduced template parameter(s) to **instantiate** a specific version of the function for us. When the compiler instantiates a template, it creates a new "instance" of the template using the actual template argument(s) in place of the corresponding template parameter(s). For example, given the calls

```
// instantiates int compare(const int&, const int&)
cout << compare(1, 0) << endl;        // T is int
// instantiates int compare(const vector<int>&, const vector<int>&)
vector<int> vec1{1, 2, 3}, vec2{4, 5, 6};
cout << compare(vec1, vec2) << endl; // T is vector<int>
```

the compiler will instantiate two different versions of `compare`. For the first call, the compiler will write and compile a version of `compare` with `T` replaced by `int`:

```
int compare(const int &v1, const int &v2)
{
    if (v1 < v2) return -1;
    if (v2 < v1) return 1;
    return 0;
}
```

For the second call, it will generate a version of `compare` with `T` replaced by `vector<int>`. These compiler-generated functions are generally referred to as an **instantiation** of the template.

Template Type Parameters

Our `compare` function has one template **type parameter**. In general, we can use a type parameter as a type specifier in the same way that we use a built-in or class type specifier. In particular, a type parameter can be used to name the return type or a function parameter type, and for variable declarations or casts inside the function body:

```
// ok: same type used for the return type and parameter
template <typename T> T foo(T* p)
{
    T tmp = *p; //  tmp will have the type to which p points
    // ...
    return tmp;
}
```

Each type parameter must be preceded by the keyword `class` or `typename`:

```
// error: must precede U with either typename or class
template <typename T, U> T calc(const T&, const U&);
```

These keywords have the same meaning and can be used interchangeably inside a template parameter list. A template parameter list can use both keywords:

```
// ok: no distinction between typename and class in a template parameter list
template <typename T, class U> calc (const T&, const U&);
```

It may seem more intuitive to use the keyword `typename` rather than `class` to designate a template type parameter. After all, we can use built-in (nonclass) types as a template type argument. Moreover, `typename` more clearly indicates that the name that follows is a type name. However, `typename` was added to C++ after templates were already in widespread use; some programmers continue to use `class` exclusively.

Nontype Template Parameters

In addition to defining type parameters, we can define templates that take **nontype parameters**. A nontype parameter represents a value rather than a type. Nontype parameters are specified by using a specific type name instead of the `class` or `typename` keyword.

When the template is instantiated, nontype parameters are replaced with a value supplied by the user or deduced by the compiler. These values must be constant expressions (§ 2.4.4, p. 65), which allows the compiler to instantiate the templates during compile time.

As an example, we can write a version of `compare` that will handle string literals. Such literals are arrays of `const char`. Because we cannot copy an array, we'll define our parameters as references to an array (§ 6.2.4, p. 217). Because we'd like to be able to compare literals of different lengths, we'll give our template two nontype parameters. The first template parameter will represent the size of the first array, and the second parameter will represent the size of the second array:

```
template<unsigned N, unsigned M>
int compare(const char (&p1)[N], const char (&p2)[M])
{
    return strcmp(p1, p2);
}
```

When we call this version of compare:

```
compare("hi", "mom")
```

the compiler will use the size of the literals to instantiate a version of the template with the sizes substituted for N and M. Remembering that the compiler inserts a null terminator at the end of a string literal (§ 2.1.3, p. 39), the compiler will instantiate

```
int compare(const char (&p1)[3], const char (&p2)[4])
```

A nontype parameter may be an integral type, or a pointer or (lvalue) reference to an object or to a function type. An argument bound to a nontype integral parameter must be a constant expression. Arguments bound to a pointer or reference nontype parameter must have static lifetime (Chapter 12, p. 450). We may not use an ordinary (nonstatic) local object or a dynamic object as a template argument for reference or pointer nontype template parameters. A pointer parameter can also be instantiated by nullptr or a zero-valued constant expression.

A template nontype parameter is a constant value inside the template definition. A nontype parameter can be used when constant expressions are required, for example, to specify the size of an array.

> *Note* Template arguments used for nontype template parameters must be constant expressions.

inline and constexpr Function Templates

A function template can be declared inline or constexpr in the same ways as nontemplate functions. The inline or constexpr specifier follows the template parameter list and precedes the return type:

```
//  ok: inline specifier follows the template parameter list
template <typename T> inline T min(const T&, const T&);
//  error: incorrect placement of the inline specifier
inline template <typename T> T min(const T&, const T&);
```

Writing Type-Independent Code

Simple though it is, our initial compare function illustrates two important principles for writing generic code:

- The function parameters in the template are references to const.

- The tests in the body use only < comparisons.

By making the function parameters references to const, we ensure that our function can be used on types that cannot be copied. Most types—including the built-in types and, except for unique_ptr and the IO types, all the library types we've used—do allow copying. However, there can be class types that do not allow copying. By making our parameters references to const, we ensure that such types can be used with our compare function. Moreover, if compare is called with large objects, then this design will also make the function run faster.

You might think it would be more natural for the comparisons to be done using both the < and > operators:

```
// expected comparison
if (v1 < v2) return -1;
if (v1 > v2) return 1;
return 0;
```

However, by writing the code using only the < operator, we reduce the requirements on types that can be used with our compare function. Those types must support <, but they need not also support >.

In fact, if we were truly concerned about type independence and portability, we probably should have defined our function using the less (§ 14.8.2, p. 575):

```
// version of compare that will be correct even if used on pointers; see § 14.8.2 (p. 575)
template <typename T> int compare(const T &v1, const T &v2)
{
    if (less<T>()(v1, v2)) return -1;
    if (less<T>()(v2, v1)) return 1;
    return 0;
}
```

The problem with our original version is that if a user calls it with two pointers and those pointers do not point to the same array, then our code is undefined.

Best Practices   Template programs should try to minimize the number of requirements placed on the argument types.

Template Compilation

When the compiler sees the definition of a template, it does not generate code. It generates code only when we instantiate a specific instance of the template. The fact that code is generated only when we use a template (and not when we define it) affects how we organize our source code and when errors are detected.

Ordinarily, when we call a function, the compiler needs to see only a declaration for the function. Similarly, when we use objects of class type, the class definition must be available, but the definitions of the member functions need not be present. As a result, we put class definitions and function declarations in header files and definitions of ordinary and class-member functions in source files.

Templates are different: To generate an instantiation, the compiler needs to have the code that defines a function template or class template member function. As a result, unlike nontemplate code, headers for templates typically include definitions as well as declarations

Definitions of function templates and member functions of class templates are ordinarily put into header files.

KEY CONCEPT: TEMPLATES AND HEADERS

Templates contain two kinds of names:

- Those that do not depend on a template parameter
- Those that do depend on a template parameter

It is up to the provider of a template to ensure that all names that do not depend on a template parameter are visible when the template is used. Moreover, the template provider must ensure that the definition of the template, including the definitions of the members of a class template, are visible when the template is instantiated.

It is up to *users* of a template to ensure that declarations for all functions, types, and operators associated with the types used to instantiate the template are visible.

Both of these requirements are easily satisfied by well-structured programs that make appropriate use of headers. Authors of templates should provide a header that contains the template definition along with declarations for all the names used in the class template or in the definitions of its members. Users of the template must include the header for the template and for any types used to instantiate that template.

Compilation Errors Are Mostly Reported during Instantiation

The fact that code is not generated until a template is instantiated affects when we learn about compilation errors in the code inside the template. In general, there are three stages during which the compiler might flag an error.

The first stage is when we compile the template itself. The compiler generally can't find many errors at this stage. The compiler can detect syntax errors—such as forgetting a semicolon or misspelling a variable name—but not much else.

The second error-detection time is when the compiler sees a use of the template. At this stage, there is still not much the compiler can check. For a call to a function template, the compiler typically will check that the number of the arguments is appropriate. It can also detect whether two arguments that are supposed to have the same type do so. For a class template, the compiler can check that the right number of template arguments are provided but not much more.

The third time when errors are detected is during instantiation. It is only then that type-related errors can be found. Depending on how the compiler manages instantiation, these errors may be reported at link time.

When we write a template, the code may not be overtly type specific, but template code usually makes some assumptions about the types that will be used. For example, the code inside our original `compare` function:

```
if (v1 < v2) return -1;   // requires < on objects of type T
if (v2 < v1) return 1;    // requires < on objects of type T
return 0;                 // returns int; not dependent on T
```

assumes that the argument type has a < operator. When the compiler processes the body of this template, it cannot verify whether the conditions in the if statements are legal. If the arguments passed to compare have a < operation, then the code is fine, but not otherwise. For example,

```
Sales_data data1, data2;
cout << compare(data1, data2) << endl; // error: no < on Sales_data
```

This call instantiates a version of compare with T replaced by Sales_data. The if conditions attempt to use < on Sales_data objects, but there is no such operator. This instantiation generates a version of the function that will not compile. However, errors such as this one cannot be detected until the compiler instantiates the definition of compare on type Sales_data.

 WARNING It is up to the caller to guarantee that the arguments passed to the template support any operations that template uses, and that those operations behave correctly in the context in which the template uses them.

EXERCISES SECTION 16.1.1

Exercise 16.1: Define instantiation.

Exercise 16.2: Write and test your own versions of the compare functions.

Exercise 16.3: Call your compare function on two Sales_data objects to see how your compiler handles errors during instantiation.

Exercise 16.4: Write a template that acts like the library find algorithm. The function will need two template type parameters, one to represent the function's iterator parameters and the other for the type of the value. Use your function to find a given value in a vector<int> and in a list<string>.

Exercise 16.5: Write a template version of the print function from § 6.2.4 (p. 217) that takes a reference to an array and can handle arrays of any size and any element type.

Exercise 16.6: How do you think the library begin and end functions that take an array argument work? Define your own versions of these functions.

Exercise 16.7: Write a constexpr template that returns the size of a given array.

Exercise 16.8: In the "Key Concept" box on page 108, we noted that as a matter of habit C++ programmers prefer using ! = to using <. Explain the rationale for this habit.

 ## 16.1.2 Class Templates

A **class template** is a blueprint for generating classes. Class templates differ from function templates in that the compiler cannot deduce the template parameter type(s) for a class template. Instead, as we've seen many times, to use a class template we must supply additional information inside angle brackets following the template's name (§ 3.3, p. 97). That extra information is the list of template arguments to use in place of the template parameters.

Defining a Class Template

As an example, we'll implement a template version of StrBlob (§ 12.1.1, p. 456). We'll name our template Blob to indicate that it is no longer specific to strings. Like StrBlob, our template will provide shared (and checked) access to the elements it holds. Unlike that class, our template can be used on elements of pretty much any type. As with the library containers, our users will have to specify the element type when they use a Blob.

Like function templates, class templates begin with the keyword template followed by a template parameter list. In the definition of the class template (and its members), we use the template parameters as stand-ins for types or values that will be supplied when the template is used:

```
template <typename T> class Blob {
public:
    typedef T value_type;
    typedef typename std::vector<T>::size_type size_type;
    // constructors
    Blob();
    Blob(std::initializer_list<T> il);
    // number of elements in the Blob
    size_type size() const { return data->size(); }
    bool empty() const { return data->empty(); }
    // add and remove elements
    void push_back(const T &t) {data->push_back(t);}
    // move version; see § 13.6.3 (p. 548)
    void push_back(T &&t) { data->push_back(std::move(t)); }
    void pop_back();
    // element access
    T& back();
    T& operator[](size_type i);  // defined in § 14.5 (p. 566)
private:
    std::shared_ptr<std::vector<T>> data;
    // throws msg if data[i] isn't valid
    void check(size_type i, const std::string &msg) const;
};
```

Our Blob template has one template type parameter, named T. We use the type parameter anywhere we refer to the element type that the Blob holds. For example, we define the return type of the operations that provide access to the elements in the Blob as T&. When a user instantiates a Blob, these uses of T will be replaced by the specified template argument type.

With the exception of the template parameter list, and the use of T instead of string, this class is the same as the version we defined in § 12.1.1 (p. 456) and updated in § 12.1.6 (p. 475) and in Chapters 13 and 14.

Instantiating a Class Template

As we've seen many times, when we use a class template, we must supply extra information. We can now see that that extra information is a list of **explicit template arguments** that are bound to the template's parameters. The compiler uses these template arguments to instantiate a specific class from the template.

For example, to define a type from our `Blob` template, we must provide the element type:

```
Blob<int> ia;                    // empty Blob<int>
Blob<int> ia2 = {0,1,2,3,4}; //  Blob<int> with five elements
```

Both `ia` and `ia2` use the same type-specific version of `Blob` (i.e., `Blob<int>`). From these definitions, the compiler will instantiate a class that is equivalent to

```
template <> class Blob<int> {
    typedef typename std::vector<int>::size_type size_type;
    Blob();
    Blob(std::initializer_list<int> il);
    // ...
    int& operator[](size_type i);
private:
    std::shared_ptr<std::vector<int>> data;
    void check(size_type i, const std::string &msg) const;
};
```

When the compiler instantiates a class from our `Blob` template, it rewrites the `Blob` template, replacing each instance of the template parameter `T` by the given template argument, which in this case is `int`.

The compiler generates a different class for each element type we specify:

```
//  these definitions instantiate two distinct Blob types
Blob<string> names;  // Blob that holds strings
Blob<double> prices;// different element type
```

These definitions would trigger instantiations of two distinct classes: The definition of `names` creates a `Blob` class in which each occurrence of `T` is replaced by `string`. The definition of `prices` generates a `Blob` with `T` replaced by `double`.

 Each instantiation of a class template constitutes an independent class. The type `Blob<string>` has no relationship to, or any special access to, the members of any other `Blob` type.

References to a Template Type in the Scope of the Template

In order to read template class code, it can be helpful to remember that the name of a class template is not the name of a type (§ 3.3, p. 97). A class template is used to instantiate a type, and an instantiated type always includes template argument(s).

What can be confusing is that code in a class template generally doesn't use the name of an actual type (or value) as a template argument. Instead, we often use the template's own parameter(s) as the template argument(s). For example, our data member uses two templates, `vector` and `shared_ptr`. Whenever we use a template, we must supply template arguments. In this case, the template argument we supply is the same type that is used to instantiate the `Blob`. Therefore, the definition of `data`

```
std::shared_ptr<std::vector<T>> data;
```

uses `Blob`'s type parameter to say that `data` is the instantiation of `shared_ptr` that points to the instantiation of `vector` that holds objects of type `T`. When we instantiate a particular kind of `Blob`, such as `Blob<string>`, then `data` will be

```
shared_ptr<vector<string>>
```

If we instantiate `Blob<int>`, then `data` will be `shared_ptr<vector<int>>`, and so on.

Member Functions of Class Templates

As with any class, we can define the member functions of a class template either inside or outside of the class body. As with any other class, members defined inside the class body are implicitly inline.

A class template member function is itself an ordinary function. However, each instantiation of the class template has its own version of each member. As a result, a member function of a class template has the same template parameters as the class itself. Therefore, a member function defined outside the class template body starts with the keyword `template` followed by the class' template parameter list.

As usual, when we define a member outside its class, we must say to which class the member belongs. Also as usual, the name of a class generated from a template includes its template arguments. When we define a member, the template argument(s) are the same as the template parameter(s). That is, for a given member function of `StrBlob` that was defined as

```
ret-type StrBlob::member-name (parm-list)
```

the corresponding `Blob` member will look like

```
template <typename T>
ret-type Blob<T>::member-name (parm-list)
```

The check and Element Access Members

We'll start by defining the `check` member, which verifies a given index:

```
template <typename T>
void Blob<T>::check(size_type i, const std::string &msg) const
{
    if (i >= data->size())
        throw std::out_of_range(msg);
}
```

Aside from the differences in the class name and the use of the template parameter list, this function is identical to the original `StrBlob` member.

The subscript operator and `back` function use the template parameter to specify the return type but are otherwise unchanged:

```
template <typename T>
T& Blob<T>::back()
{
    check(0, "back on empty Blob");
    return data->back();
}
template <typename T>
T& Blob<T>::operator[](size_type i)
{
    // if i is too big, check will throw, preventing access to a nonexistent element
    check(i, "subscript out of range");
    return (*data)[i];
}
```

In our original StrBlob class these operators returned string&. The template versions will return a reference to whatever type is used to instantiate Blob.

The pop_back function is nearly identical to our original StrBlob member:

```
template <typename T> void Blob<T>::pop_back()
{
    check(0, "pop_back on empty Blob");
    data->pop_back();
}
```

The subscript operator and back members are overloaded on const. We leave the definition of these members, and of the front members, as an exercise.

Blob Constructors

As with any other member defined outside a class template, a constructor starts by declaring the template parameters for the class template of which it is a member:

```
template <typename T>
Blob<T>::Blob(): data(std::make_shared<std::vector<T>>()) { }
```

Here we are defining the member named Blob in the scope of Blob<T>. Like our StrBlob default constructor (§ 12.1.1, p. 456), this constructor allocates an empty vector and stores the pointer to that vector in data. As we've seen, we use the class' own type parameter as the template argument of the vector we allocate.

Similarly, the constructor that takes an initializer_list uses its type parameter T as the element type for its initializer_list parameter:

```
template <typename T>
Blob<T>::Blob(std::initializer_list<T> il):
                data(std::make_shared<std::vector<T>>(il)) { }
```

Like the default constructor, this constructor allocates a new vector. In this case, we initialize that vector from the parameter, il.

To use this constructor, we must pass an initializer_list in which the elements are compatible with the element type of the Blob:

```
Blob<string> articles = {"a", "an", "the"};
```

The parameter in this constructor has type initializer_list<string>. Each string literal in the list is implicitly converted to string.

Instantiation of Class-Template Member Functions

By default, a member function of a class template is instantiated *only* if the program uses that member function. For example, this code

```
//  instantiates Blob<int> and the initializer_list<int> constructor
Blob<int> squares = {0,1,2,3,4,5,6,7,8,9};
//  instantiates Blob<int>::size() const
for (size_t i = 0; i != squares.size(); ++i)
    squares[i] = i*i;  //  instantiates Blob<int>::operator[](size_t)
```

instantiates the Blob<int> class and three of its member functions: operator[], size, and the initializer_list<int> constructor.

If a member function isn't used, it is not instantiated. The fact that members are instantiated only if we use them lets us instantiate a class with a type that may not meet the requirements for some of the template's operations (§ 9.2, p. 329).

> By default, a member of an instantiated class template is instantiated only if the member is used.

Simplifying Use of a Template Class Name inside Class Code

There is one exception to the rule that we must supply template arguments when we use a class template type. Inside the scope of the class template itself, we may use the name of the template without arguments:

```
//  BlobPtr throws an exception on attempts to access a nonexistent element
template <typename T> class BlobPtr
public:
    BlobPtr(): curr(0) { }
    BlobPtr(Blob<T> &a, size_t sz = 0):
            wptr(a.data), curr(sz) { }
    T& operator*() const
    { auto p = check(curr, "dereference past end");
      return (*p)[curr];   //  (*p) is the vector to which this object points
    }
    //  increment and decrement
    BlobPtr& operator++();              //  prefix operators
    BlobPtr& operator--();
private:
    //  check returns a shared_ptr to the vector if the check succeeds
    std::shared_ptr<std::vector<T>>
        check(std::size_t, const std::string&) const;
    //  store a weak_ptr, which means the underlying vector might be destroyed
    std::weak_ptr<std::vector<T>> wptr;
    std::size_t curr;       //  current position within the array
};
```

Careful readers will have noted that the prefix increment and decrement members of BlobPtr return BlobPtr&, not BlobPtr<T>&. When we are inside the scope of a class template, the compiler treats references to the template itself as if we had supplied template arguments matching the template's own parameters. That is, it is as if we had written:

```
BlobPtr<T>& operator++();
BlobPtr<T>& operator--();
```

Using a Class Template Name outside the Class Template Body

When we define members outside the body of a class template, we must remember that we are not in the scope of the class until the class name is seen (§ 7.4, p. 282):

```
//  postfix: increment/decrement the object but return the unchanged value
template <typename T>
BlobPtr<T> BlobPtr<T>::operator++(int)
{
    //  no check needed here; the call to prefix increment will do the check
    BlobPtr ret = *this;    //  save the current value
    ++*this;        //  advance one element; prefix ++ checks the increment
    return ret;  //  return the saved state
}
```

Because the return type appears outside the scope of the class, we must specify that the return type returns a `BlobPtr` instantiated with the same type as the class. Inside the function body, we are in the scope of the class so do not need to repeat the template argument when we define `ret`. When we do not supply template arguments, the compiler assumes that we are using the same type as the member's instantiation. Hence, the definition of `ret` is as if we had written:

```
BlobPtr<T> ret = *this;
```

Inside the scope of a class template, we may refer to the template without specifying template argument(s).

Class Templates and Friends

When a class contains a friend declaration (§ 7.2.1, p. 269), the class and the friend can independently be templates or not. A class template that has a nontemplate friend grants that friend access to all the instantiations of the template. When the friend is itself a template, the class granting friendship controls whether friendship includes all instantiations of the template or only specific instantiation(s).

One-to-One Friendship

The most common form of friendship from a class template to another template (class or function) establishes friendship between corresponding instantiations of the class and its friend. For example, our `Blob` class should declare the `BlobPtr` class and a template version of the `Blob` equality operator (originally defined for `StrBlob` in the exercises in § 14.3.1 (p. 562)) as friends.

In order to refer to a specific instantiation of a template (class or function) we must first declare the template itself. A template declaration includes the template's template parameter list:

```
// forward declarations needed for friend declarations in Blob
template <typename> class BlobPtr;
template <typename> class Blob; // needed for parameters in operator==
template <typename T>
    bool operator==(const Blob<T>&, const Blob<T>&);
template <typename T> class Blob {
    // each instantiation of Blob grants access to the version of
    // BlobPtr and the equality operator instantiated with the same type
    friend class BlobPtr<T>;
    friend bool operator==<T>
            (const Blob<T>&, const Blob<T>&);
    // other members as in § 12.1.1 (p. 456)
};
```

We start by declaring that Blob, BlobPtr, and operator== are templates. These declarations are needed for the parameter declaration in the operator== function and the friend declarations in Blob.

The friend declarations use Blob's template parameter as their own template argument. Thus, the friendship is restricted to those instantiations of BlobPtr and the equality operator that are instantiated with the same type:

```
Blob<char> ca; // BlobPtr<char> and operator==<char> are friends
Blob<int> ia;  // BlobPtr<int> and operator==<int> are friends
```

The members of BlobPtr<char> may access the nonpublic parts of ca (or any other Blob<char> object), but ca has no special access to ia (or any other Blob<int>) or to any other instantiation of Blob.

General and Specific Template Friendship

A class can also make every instantiation of another template its friend, or it may limit friendship to a specific instantiation:

```
// forward declaration necessary to befriend a specific instantiation of a template
template <typename T> class Pal;
class C {  // C is an ordinary, nontemplate class
    friend class Pal<C>;  // Pal instantiated with class C is a friend to C
    // all instances of Pal2 are friends to C;
    // no forward declaration required when we befriend all instantiations
    template <typename T> friend class Pal2;
};
template <typename T> class C2 { // C2 is itself a class template
    // each instantiation of C2 has the same instance of Pal as a friend
    friend class Pal<T>;  // a template declaration for Pal must be in scope
    // all instances of Pal2 are friends of each instance of C2, prior declaration needed
    template <typename X> friend class Pal2;
    // Pal3 is a nontemplate class that is a friend of every instance of C2
    friend class Pal3;    // prior declaration for Pal3 not needed
};
```

To allow all instantiations as friends, the friend declaration must use template parameter(s) that differ from those used by the class itself.

Befriending the Template's Own Type Parameter

Under the new standard, we can make a template type parameter a friend:

```
template <typename Type> class Bar {
friend Type;  // grants access to the type used to instantiate Bar
    // ...
};
```

Here we say that whatever type is used to instantiate `Bar` is a friend. Thus, for some type named `Foo`, `Foo` would be a friend of `Bar<Foo>`, `Sales_data` a friend of `Bar<Sales_data>`, and so on.

It is worth noting that even though a friend ordinarily must be a class or a function, it is okay for `Bar` to be instantiated with a built-in type. Such friendship is allowed so that we can instantiate classes such as `Bar` with built-in types.

Template Type Aliases

An instantiation of a class template defines a class type, and as with any other class type, we can define a `typedef` (§ 2.5.1, p. 67) that refers to that instantiated class:

```
typedef Blob<string> StrBlob;
```

This `typedef` will let us run the code we wrote in § 12.1.1 (p. 456) using our template version of `Blob` instantiated with `string`. Because a template is not a type, we cannot define a `typedef` that refers to a template. That is, there is no way to define a `typedef` that refers to `Blob<T>`.

However, the new standard lets us define a type alias for a class template:

```
template<typename T> using twin = pair<T, T>;
twin<string> authors;  // authors is a pair<string, string>
```

Here we've defined `twin` as a synonym for `pairs` in which the members have the same type. Users of `twin` need to specify that type only once.

A template type alias is a synonym for a family of classes:

```
twin<int> win_loss;    // win_loss is a pair<int, int>
twin<double> area;     // area is a pair<double, double>
```

Just as we do when we use a class template, when we use `twin`, we specify which particular kind of `twin` we want.

When we define a template type alias, we can fix one or more of the template parameters:

```
template <typename T> using partNo = pair<T, unsigned>;
partNo<string> books;   // books is a pair<string, unsigned>
partNo<Vehicle> cars;   // cars is a pair<Vehicle, unsigned>
partNo<Student> kids;   // kids is a pair<Student, unsigned>
```

Here we've defined `partNo` as a synonym for the family of types that are `pairs` in which the second member is an `unsigned`. Users of `partNo` specify a type for the `first` member of the `pair` but have no choice about `second`.

`static` Members of Class Templates

Like any other class, a class template can declare `static` members (§ 7.6, p. 300):

```
template <typename T> class Foo {
public:
    static std::size_t count() { return ctr; }
    //  other interface members
private:
    static std::size_t ctr;
    //  other implementation members
};
```

Here `Foo` is a class template that has a `public static` member function named `count` and a `private static` data member named `ctr`. Each instantiation of `Foo` has its own instance of the `static` members. That is, for any given type X, there is one `Foo<X>::ctr` and one `Foo<X>::count` member. All objects of type `Foo<X>` share the same `ctr` object and `count` function. For example,

```
//  instantiates static members Foo<string>::ctr and Foo<string>::count
Foo<string> fs;
//  all three objects share the same Foo<int>::ctr and Foo<int>::count members
Foo<int> fi, fi2, fi3;
```

As with any other `static` data member, there must be exactly one definition of each `static` data member of a template class. However, there is a distinct object for each instantiation of a class template. As a result, we define a `static` data member as a template similarly to how we define the member functions of that template:

```
template <typename T>
size_t Foo<T>::ctr = 0; //  define and initialize ctr
```

As with any other member of a class template, we start by defining the template parameter list, followed by the type of the member we are defining and the member's name. As usual, a member's name includes the member's class name, which for a class generated from a template includes its template arguments. Thus, when `Foo` is instantiated for a particular template argument type, a separate `ctr` will be instantiated for that class type and initialized to 0.

As with static members of nontemplate classes, we can access a `static` member of a class template through an object of the class type or by using the scope operator to access the member directly. Of course, to use a `static` member through the class, we must refer to a specific instantiation:

```
Foo<int> fi;                       //  instantiates Foo<int> class
                                   //  and the static data member ctr
auto ct = Foo<int>::count();       //  instantiates Foo<int>::count
ct = fi.count();                   //  uses Foo<int>::count
ct = Foo::count();                 //  error: which template instantiation?
```

Like any other member function, a `static` member function is instantiated only if it is used in a program.

Exercise 16.9: What is a function template? What is a class template?

Exercise 16.10: What happens when a class template is instantiated?

Exercise 16.11: The following definition of `List` is incorrect. How would you fix it?

```
template <typename elemType> class ListItem;
template <typename elemType> class List {
public:
    List<elemType>();
    List<elemType>(const List<elemType> &);
    List<elemType>& operator=(const List<elemType> &);
    ~List();
    void insert(ListItem *ptr, elemType value);
private:
    ListItem *front, *end;
};
```

Exercise 16.12: Write your own version of the `Blob` and `BlobPtr` templates. including the various `const` members that were not shown in the text.

Exercise 16.13: Explain which kind of friendship you chose for the equality and relational operators for `BlobPtr`.

Exercise 16.14: Write a `Screen` class template that uses nontype parameters to define the height and width of the `Screen`.

Exercise 16.15: Implement input and output operators for your `Screen` template. Which, if any, friends are necessary in class `Screen` to make the input and output operators work? Explain why each friend declaration, if any, was needed.

Exercise 16.16: Rewrite the `StrVec` class (§ 13.5, p. 526) as a template named `Vec`.

16.1.3 Template Parameters

Like the names of function parameters, a template parameter name has no intrinsic meaning. We ordinarily name type parameters `T`, but we can use any name:

```
template <typename Foo> Foo calc(const Foo& a, const Foo& b)
{
    Foo tmp = a;  // tmp has the same type as the parameters and return type
    // ...
    return tmp;   // return type and parameters have the same type
}
```

Template Parameters and Scope

Template parameters follow normal scoping rules. The name of a template parameter can be used after it has been declared and until the end of the template declaration or definition. As with any other name, a template parameter hides any declaration of that name in an outer scope. Unlike most other contexts, however, a name used as a template parameter may not be reused within the template:

```
typedef double A;
template <typename A, typename B> void f(A a, B b)
{
    A tmp = a; // tmp has same type as the template parameter A, not double
    double B;  // error: redeclares template parameter B
}
```

Normal name hiding says that the typedef of A is hidden by the type parameter named A. Thus, tmp is not a double; it has whatever type gets bound to the template parameter A when calc is used. Because we cannot reuse names of template parameters, the declaration of the variable named B is an error.

Because a parameter name cannot be reused, the name of a template parameter can appear only once with in a given template parameter list:

```
// error: illegal reuse of template parameter name V
template <typename V, typename V> // ...
```

Template Declarations

A template declaration must include the template parameters :

```
// declares but does not define compare and Blob
template <typename T> int compare(const T&, const T&);
template <typename T> class Blob;
```

As with function parameters, the names of a template parameter need not be the same across the declaration(s) and the definition of the same template:

```
// all three uses of calc refer to the same function template
template <typename T> T calc(const T&, const T&);  // declaration
template <typename U> U calc(const U&, const U&);  // declaration
// definition of the template
template <typename Type>
Type calc(const Type& a, const Type& b) { /* ... */ }
```

Of course, every declaration and the definition of a given template must have the same number and kind (i.e., type or nontype) of parameters.

Best
Practices

For reasons we'll explain in § 16.3 (p. 698), declarations for all the templates needed by a given file usually should appear together at the beginning of a file before any code that uses those names.

Using Class Members That Are Types

Recall that we use the scope operator (::) to access both static members and type members (§ 7.4, p. 282, and § 7.6, p. 301). In ordinary (nontemplate) code, the compiler has access to the class defintion. As a result, it knows whether a name accessed through the scope operator is a type or a static member. For example, when we write `string::size_type`, the compiler has the definition of `string` and can see that `size_type` is a type.

Assuming `T` is a template type parameter, When the compiler sees code such as `T::mem` it won't know until instantiation time whether `mem` is a type or a `static` data member. However, in order to process the template, the compiler must know whether a name represents a type. For example, assuming `T` is the name of a type parameter, when the compiler sees a statement of the following form:

```
T::size_type * p;
```

it needs to know whether we're defining a variable named `p` or are multiplying a `static` data member named `size_type` by a variable named `p`.

By default, the language assumes that a name accessed through the scope operator is not a type. As a result, if we want to use a type member of a template type parameter, we must explicitly tell the compiler that the name is a type. We do so by using the keyword `typename`:

```
template <typename T>
typename T::value_type top(const T& c)
{
    if (!c.empty())
        return c.back();
    else
        return typename T::value_type();
}
```

Our `top` function expects a container as its argument and uses `typename` to specify its return type and to generate a value initialized element (§ 7.5.3, p. 293) to return if `c` has no elements.

> When we want to inform the compiler that a name represents a type, we must use the keyword `typename`, not `class`.

Default Template Arguments

Just as we can supply default arguments to function parameters (§ 6.5.1, p. 236), we can also supply **default template arguments**. Under the new standard, we can supply default arguments for both function and class templates. Earlier versions of the language, allowed default arguments only with class templates.

As an example, we'll rewrite `compare` to use the library `less` function-object template (§ 14.8.2, p. 574) by default:

```
// compare has a default template argument, less<T>
// and a default function argument, F()
template <typename T, typename F = less<T>>
int compare(const T &v1, const T &v2, F f = F())
{
    if (f(v1, v2)) return -1;
    if (f(v2, v1)) return 1;
    return 0;
}
```

Here we've given our template a second type parameter, named F, that represents the type of a callable object (§ 10.3.2, p. 388) and defined a new function parameter, f, that will be bound to a callable object.

We've also provided defaults for this template parameter and its corresponding function parameter. The default template argument specifies that compare will use the library less function-object class, instantiated with the same type parameter as compare. The default function argument says that f will be a default-initialized object of type F.

When users call this version of compare, they may supply their own comparison operation but are not required to do so:

```
bool i = compare(0, 42); // uses less; i is -1
// result depends on the isbns in item1 and item2
Sales_data item1(cin), item2(cin);
bool j = compare(item1, item2, compareIsbn);
```

The first call uses the default function argument, which is a default-initialized object of type less<T>. In this call, T is int so that object has type less<int>. This instantiation of compare will use less<int> to do its comparisons.

In the second call, we pass compareIsbn (§ 11.2.2, p. 425) and two objects of type Sales_data. When compare is called with three arguments, the type of the third argument must be a callable object that returns a type that is convertible to bool and takes arguments of a type compatible with the types of the first two arguments. As usual, the types of the template parameters are deduced from their corresponding function arguments. In this call, the type of T is deduced as Sales_data and F is deduced as the type of compareIsbn.

As with function default arguments, a template parameter may have a default argument only if all of the parameters to its right also have default arguments.

Template Default Arguments and Class Templates

Whenever we use a class template, we must always follow the template's name with brackets. The brackets indicate that a class must be instantiated from a template. In particular, if a class template provides default arguments for all of its template parameters, and we want to use those defaults, we must put an empty bracket pair following the template's name:

```
template <class T = int> class Numbers {    // by default T is int
public:
    Numbers(T v = 0): val(v) { }
    // various operations on numbers
private:
    T val;
};
Numbers<long double> lots_of_precision;
Numbers<> average_precision; // empty <> says we want the default type
```

Here we instantiate two versions of Numbers: average_precision instantiates Numbers with T replaced by int; lots_of_precision instantiates Numbers with T replaced by long double.

Exercise 16.17: What, if any, are the differences between a type parameter that is declared as a typename and one that is declared as a class? When must typename be
used?

Exercise 16.18: Explain each of the following function template declarations and identify whether any are illegal. Correct each error that you find.

(a) `template <typename T, U, typename V> void f1(T, U, V);`

(b) `template <typename T> T f2(int &T);`

(c) `inline template <typename T> T foo(T, unsigned int*);`

(d) `template <typename T> f4(T, T);`

(e) `typedef char Ctype;`
   `    template <typename Ctype> Ctype f5(Ctype a);`

Exercise 16.19: Write a function that takes a reference to a container and prints the
elements in that container. Use the container's size_type and size members to
control the loop that prints the elements.

Exercise 16.20: Rewrite the function from the previous exercise to use iterators returned from begin and end to control the loop.

16.1.4 Member Templates

A class—either an ordinary class or a class template—may have a member function that is itself a template. Such members are referred to as **member templates**.
Member templates may not be virtual.

Member Templates of Ordianary (Nontemplate) Classes

As an example of an ordinary class that has a member template, we'll define a class
that is similar to the default deleter type used by unique_ptr (§ 12.1.5, p. 471).
Like the default deleter, our class will have an overloaded function-call operator
(§ 14.8, p. 571) that will take a pointer and execute delete on the given pointer.
Unlike the default deleter, our class will also print a message whenever the deleter
is executed. Because we want to use our deleter with any type, we'll make the call
operator a template:

```
//  function-object class that calls delete on a given pointer
class DebugDelete {
public:
    DebugDelete(std::ostream &s = std::cerr): os(s) { }
    //  as with any function template, the type of T is deduced by the compiler
    template <typename T> void operator()(T *p) const
        { os << "deleting unique_ptr" << std::endl; delete p; }
private:
    std::ostream &os;
};
```

Like any other template, a member template starts with its own template parameter list. Each DebugDelete object has an ostream member on which to write, and a member function that is itself a template. We can use this class as a replacement for delete:

```
double* p = new double;
DebugDelete d;      //  an object that can act like a delete expression
d(p); //  calls DebugDelete::operator()(double*),which deletes p
int* ip = new int;
//  calls operator()(int*) on a temporary DebugDelete object
DebugDelete()(ip);
```

Because calling a DebugDelete object deletes its given pointer, we can also use DebugDelete as the deleter of a unique_ptr. To override the deleter of a unique_ptr, we supply the type of the deleter inside brackets and supply an object of the deleter type to the constructor (§ 12.1.5, p. 471):

```
//  destroying the the object to which p points
//  instantiates DebugDelete::operator()<int>(int *)
unique_ptr<int, DebugDelete> p(new int, DebugDelete());
//  destroying the the object to which sp points
//  instantiates DebugDelete::operator()<string>(string*)
unique_ptr<string, DebugDelete> sp(new string, DebugDelete());
```

Here, we've said that p's deleter will have type DebugDelete, and we have supplied an unnamed object of that type in p's constructor.

The unique_ptr destructor calls the DebugDelete's call operator. Thus, whenever unique_ptr's destructor is instantiated, DebugDelete's call operator will also be instantiated: Thus, the definitions above will instantiate:

```
//  sample instantiations for member templates of DebugDelete
void DebugDelete::operator()(int *p) const { delete p; }
void DebugDelete::operator()(string *p) const { delete p; }
```

Member Templates of Class Templates

We can also define a member template of a class template. In this case, both the class and the member have their own, independent, template parameters.

As an example, we'll give our Blob class a constructor that will take two iterators denoting a range of elements to copy. Because we'd like to support iterators into varying kinds of sequences, we'll make this constructor a template:

```
template <typename T> class Blob {
    template <typename It> Blob(It b, It e);
    // ...
};
```

This constructor has its own template type parameter, It, which it uses for the type of its two function parameters.

Unlike ordinary function members of class templates, member templates *are* function templates. When we define a member template outside the body of a class template, we must provide the template parameter list for the class template and for the function template. The parameter list for the class template comes first, followed by the member's own template parameter list:

```
template <typename T>      // type parameter for the class
template <typename It>     // type parameter for the constructor
    Blob<T>::Blob(It b, It e):
                data(std::make_shared<std::vector<T>>(b, e)) { }
```

Here we are defining a member of a class template that has one template type parameter, which we have named T. The member itself is a function template that has a type parameter named It.

Instantiation and Member Templates

To instantiate a member template of a class template, we must supply arguments for the template parameters for both the class and the function templates. As usual, argument(s) for the class template parameter(s) are determined by the type of the object through which we call the member template. Also as usual, the compiler typically deduces template argument(s) for the member template's own parameter(s) from the arguments passed in the call (§ 16.1.1, p. 653):

```
int ia[] = {0,1,2,3,4,5,6,7,8,9};
vector<long> vi = {0,1,2,3,4,5,6,7,8,9};
list<const char*> w = {"now", "is", "the", "time"};
// instantiates the Blob<int> class
// and the Blob<int> constructor that has two int * parameters
Blob<int> a1(begin(ia), end(ia));
// instantiates the Blob<int> constructor that has
// two vector<long>::iterator parameters
Blob<int> a2(vi.begin(), vi.end());
// instantiates the Blob<string> class and the Blob<string>
// constructor that has two (list<const char*>::iterator parameters
Blob<string> a3(w.begin(), w.end());
```

When we define a1, we explicitly specify that the compiler should instantiate a version of Blob with the template parameter bound to int. The type parameter for the constructor's own parameters will be deduced from the type of begin(ia) and end(ia). That type is int*. Thus, the definition of a1 instantiates:

```
Blob<int>::Blob(int*, int*);
```

The definition of a2 uses the already instantiated Blob<int> class, and instantiates the constructor with It replaced by vector<short>::iterator. The definition of a3 (explicitly) instantiates the Blob with its template parameter bound to string and (implicitly) instantiates the member template constructor of that class with its parameter bound to list<const char*>.

EXERCISES SECTION 16.1.4

Exercise 16.21: Write your own version of `DebugDelete`.

Exercise 16.22: Revise your `TextQuery` programs from § 12.3 (p. 484) so that the `shared_ptr` members use a `DebugDelete` as their deleter (§ 12.1.4, p. 468).

Exercise 16.23: Predict when the call operator will be executed in your main query program. If your expectations and what happens differ, be sure you understand why.

Exercise 16.24: Add a constructor that takes two iterators to your `Blob` template.

16.1.5 Controlling Instantiations

The fact that instantiations are generated when a template is used (§ 16.1.1, p. 656) means that the same instantiation may appear in multiple object files. When two or more separately compiled source files use the same template with the same template arguments, there is an instantiation of that template in each of those files.

In large systems, the overhead of instantiating the same template in multiple files can become significant. Under the new standard, we can avoid this overhead through an **explicit instantiation**. An explicit instantiation has the form

```
extern template declaration;  // instantiation declaration
template declaration;         // instantiation definition
```

where *declaration* is a class or function declaration in which all the template parameters are replaced by the template arguments. For example,

```
// instantion declaration and definition
extern template class Blob<string>;            // declaration
template int compare(const int&, const int&);  // definition
```

When the compiler sees an `extern` template declaration, it will not generate code for that instantiation in that file. Declaring an instantiation as `extern` is a promise that there will be a nonextern use of that instantiation elsewhere in the program. There may be several `extern` declarations for a given instantiation but there must be exactly one definition for that instantiation.

Because the compiler automatically instantiates a template when we use it, the `extern` declaration must appear before any code that uses that instantiation:

```
// Application.cc
// these template types must be instantiated elsewhere in the program
extern template class Blob<string>;
extern template int compare(const int&, const int&);
Blob<string> sa1, sa2; // instantiation will appear elsewhere
// Blob<int> and its initializer_list constructor instantiated in this file
Blob<int> a1 = {0,1,2,3,4,5,6,7,8,9};
Blob<int> a2(a1);  // copy constructor instantiated in this file
int i = compare(a1[0], a2[0]); // instantiation will appear elsewhere
```

The file `Application.o` will contain instantiations for `Blob<int>`, along with the `initializer_list` and copy constructors for that class. The `compare<int>` function and `Blob<string>` class will not be instantiated in that file. There must be definitions of these templates in some other file in the program:

```
// templateBuild.cc
// instantiation file must provide a (nonextern) definition for every
// type and function that other files declare as extern
template int compare(const int&, const int&);
template class Blob<string>; // instantiates all members of the class template
```

When the compiler sees an instantiation definition (as opposed to a declaration), it generates code. Thus, the file `templateBuild.o` will contain the definitions for `compare` instantiated with `int` and for the `Blob<string>` class. When we build the application, we must link `templateBuild.o` with the `Application.o` files.

 WARNING There must be an explicit instantiation definition somewhere in the program for every instantiation declaration.

Instantiation Definitions Instantiate All Members

An instantiation definition for a class template instantiates *all* the members of that template including inline member functions. When the compiler sees an instantiation definition it cannot know which member functions the program uses. Hence, unlike the way it handles ordinary class template instantiations, the compiler instantiates *all* the members of that class. Even if we do not use a member, that member will be instantiated. Consequently, we can use explicit instantiation only for types that can be used with all the members of that template.

Note An instantiation definition can be used only for types that can be used with every member function of a class template.

 ## 16.1.6 Efficiency and Flexibility

The library smart pointer types (§ 12.1, p. 450) offer a good illustration of design choices faced by designers of templates.

The obvious difference between `shared_ptr` and `unique_ptr` is the strategy they use in managing the pointer they hold—one class gives us shared ownership; the other owns the pointer that it holds. This difference is essential to what these classes do.

These classes also differ in how they let users override their default deleter. We can easily override the deleter of a `shared_ptr` by passing a callable object when we create or `reset` the pointer. In contrast, the type of the deleter is part of the type of a `unique_ptr` object. Users must supply that type as an explicit template argument when they define a `unique_ptr`. As a result, it is more complicated for users of `unique_ptr` to provide their own deleter.

EXERCISES SECTION 16.1.5

Exercise 16.25: Explain the meaning of these declarations:

```
extern template class vector<string>;
template class vector<Sales_data>;
```

Exercise 16.26: Assuming NoDefault is a class that does not have a default constructor, can we explicitly instantiate vector<NoDefault>? If not, why not?

Exercise 16.27: For each labeled statement explain what, if any, instantiations happen.
If a template is instantiated, explain why; if not, explain why not.

```
template <typename T> class Stack { };
void f1(Stack<char>);                      // (a)
class Exercise {
    Stack<double> &rsd;                    // (b)
    Stack<int>    si;                      // (c)
};
int main() {
    Stack<char> *sc;                       // (d)
    f1(*sc);                               // (e)
    int iObj = sizeof(Stack< string >);  // (f)
}
```

The difference in how the deleter is handled is incidental to the functionality
of these classes. However, as we'll see, this difference in implementation strategy
may have important performance impacts.

Binding the Deleter at Run Time

Although we don't know how the library types are implemented, we can infer that
shared_ptr must access its deleter indirectly. That is the deleter must be stored
as a pointer or as a class (such as function (§ 14.8.3, p. 577)) that encapsulates a
pointer.

We can be certain that shared_ptr does not hold the deleter as a direct member, because the type of the deleter isn't known until run time. Indeed, we can
change the type of the deleter in a given shared_ptr during that shared_ptr's
lifetime. We can construct a shared_ptr using a deleter of one type, and subsequently use reset to give that same shared_ptr a different type of deleter. In
general, we cannot have a member whose type changes at run time. Hence, the
deleter must be stored indirectly.

To think about how the deleter must work, let's assume that shared_ptr
stores the pointer it manages in a member named p, and that the deleter is accessed through a member named del. The shared_ptr destructor must include
a statement such as

```
//  value of del known only at run time; call through a pointer
del ? del(p) : delete p; //  del(p) requires run-time jump to del's location
```

Because the deleter is stored indirectly, the call `del(p)` requires a run-time jump to the location stored in `del` to execute the code to which `del` points.

Binding the Deleter at Compile Time

Now, let's think about how `unique_ptr` might work. In this class, the type of the deleter is part of the type of the `unique_ptr`. That is, `unique_ptr` has two template parameters, one that represents the pointer that the `unique_ptr` manages and the other that represents the type of the deleter. Because the type of the deleter is part of the type of a `unique_ptr`, the type of the deleter member is known at compile time. The deleter can be stored directly in each `unique_ptr` object.

The `unique_ptr` destructor operates similarly to its `shared_ptr` counterpart in that it calls a user-supplied deleter or executes `delete` on its stored pointer:

```
//  del bound at compile time; direct call to the deleter is instantiated
del(p);     //  no run-time overhead
```

The type of `del` is either the default deleter type or a user-supplied type. It doesn't matter; either way the code that will be executed is known at compile time. Indeed, if the deleter is something like our `DebugDelete` class (§ 16.1.4, p. 672) this call might even be inlined at compile time.

By binding the deleter at compile time, `unique_ptr` avoids the run-time cost of an indirect call to its deleter. By binding the deleter at run time, `shared_ptr` makes it easier for users to override the deleter.

> **EXERCISES SECTION 16.1.6**
>
> **Exercise 16.28:** Write your own versions of `shared_ptr` and `unique_ptr`.
>
> **Exercise 16.29:** Revise your `Blob` class to use your version of `shared_ptr` rather than the library version.
>
> **Exercise 16.30:** Rerun some of your programs to verify your `shared_ptr` and revised `Blob` classes. (Note: Implementing the `weak_ptr` type is beyond the scope of this Primer, so you will not be able to use the `BlobPtr` class with your revised `Blob`.)
>
> **Exercise 16.31:** Explain how the compiler might inline the call to the deleter if we used `DebugDelete` with `unique_ptr`.

16.2 Template Argument Deduction

We've seen that, by default, the compiler uses the arguments in a call to determine the template parameters for a function template. The process of determining the template arguments from the function arguments is known as **template argument deduction**. During template argument deduction, the compiler uses types of the arguments in the call to find the template arguments that generate a version of the function that best matches the given call.

16.2.1 Conversions and Template Type Parameters

As with a nontemplate function, the arguments we pass in a call to a function template are used to initialize that function's parameters. Function parameters whose type uses a template type parameter have special initialization rules. Only a very limited number of conversions are automatically applied to such arguments. Rather than converting the arguments, the compiler generates a new instantiation.

As usual, top-level `const`s (§ 2.4.3, p. 63) in either the parameter or the argument are ignored. The only other conversions performed in a call to a function template are

- `const` conversions: A function parameter that is a reference (or pointer) to a `const` can be passed a reference (or pointer) to a nonconst object (§ 4.11.2, p. 162).

- Array- or function-to-pointer conversions: If the function parameter is not a reference type, then the normal pointer conversion will be applied to arguments of array or function type. An array argument will be converted to a pointer to its first element. Similarly, a function argument will be converted to a pointer to the function's type (§ 4.11.2, p. 161).

Other conversions, such as the arithmetic conversions (§ 4.11.1, p. 159), derived-to-base (§ 15.2.2, p. 597), and user-defined conversions (§ 7.5.4, p. 294, and § 14.9, p. 579), are not performed.

As examples, consider calls to the functions `fobj` and `fref`. The `fobj` function copies its parameters, whereas `fref`'s parameters are references:

```
template <typename T> T fobj(T, T); // arguments are copied
template <typename T> T fref(const T&, const T&); // references
string s1("a value");
const string s2("another value");
fobj(s1, s2); // calls fobj(string, string); const is ignored
fref(s1, s2); // calls fref(const string&, const string&)
             // uses premissible conversion to const on s1
int a[10], b[42];
fobj(a, b); // calls f(int*, int*)
fref(a, b); // error: array types don't match
```

In the first pair of calls, we pass a `string` and a `const string`. Even though these types do not match exactly, both calls are legal. In the call to `fobj`, the arguments are copied, so whether the original object is `const` doesn't matter. In the call to `fref`, the parameter type is a reference to `const`. Conversion to `const` for a reference parameter is a permitted conversion, so this call is legal.

In the next pair of calls, we pass array arguments in which the arrays are different sizes and hence have different types. In the call to `fobj`, the fact that the array types differ doesn't matter. Both arrays are converted to pointers. The template parameter type in `fobj` is `int*`. The call to `fref`, however, is illegal. When the parameter is a reference, the arrays are not converted to pointers (§ 6.2.4, p. 217). The types of a and b don't match, so the call is in error.

Function Parameters That Use the Same Template Parameter Type

A template type parameter can be used as the type of more than one function parameter. Because there are limited conversions, the arguments to such parameters must have essentially the same type. If the deduced types do not match, then the call is an error. For example, our compare function (§ 16.1.1, p. 652) takes two const T& parameters. Its arguments must have essentially the same type:

```
long lng;
compare(lng, 1024);  // error: cannot instantiate compare(long, int)
```

This call is in error because the arguments to compare don't have the same type. The template argument deduced from the first argument is long; the one for the second is int. These types don't match, so template argument deduction fails.

If we want to allow normal conversions on the arguments, we can define the function with two type parameters:

```
//   argument types can differ but must be compatible
template <typename A, typename B>
int flexibleCompare(const A& v1, const B& v2)
{
    if (v1 < v2) return -1;
    if (v2 < v1) return 1;
    return 0;
}
```

Now the user may supply arguments of different types:

```
long lng;
flexibleCompare(lng, 1024);  // ok: calls flexibleCompare(long, int)
```

Of course, a < operator must exist that can compare values of those types.

Normal Conversions Apply for Ordinary Arguments

A function template can have parameters that are defined using ordinary types—that is, types that do not involve a template type parameter. Such arguments have no special processing; they are converted as usual to the corresponding type of the parameter (§ 6.1, p. 203). For example, consider the following template:

```
template <typename T> ostream &print(ostream &os, const T &obj)
{
    return os << obj;
}
```

The first function parameter has a known type, ostream&. The second parameter, obj, has a template parameter type. Because the type of os is fixed, normal conversions are applied to arguments passed to os when print is called:

```
print(cout, 42);  // instantiates print(ostream&, int)
ofstream f("output");
print(f, 10);     // uses print(ostream&, int); converts f to ostream&
```

In the first call, the type of the first argument exactly matches the type of the first parameter. This call will cause a version of `print` that takes an `ostream&` and an `int` to be instantiated. In the second call, the first argument is an `ofstream` and there is a conversion from `ofstream` to `ostream&` (§ 8.2.1, p. 317). Because the type of this parameter does not depend on a template parameter, the compiler will implicitly convert `f` to `ostream&`.

 Normal conversions are applied to arguments whose type is not a template parameter.

16.2.2 Function-Template Explicit Arguments

In some situations, it is not possible for the compiler to deduce the types of the template arguments. In others, we want to allow the user to control the template instantiation. Both cases arise most often when a function return type differs from any of those used in the parameter list.

Specifying an Explicit Template Argument

As an example in which we want to let the user specify which type to use, we'll define a function template named sum that takes arguments of two different types. We'd like to let the user specify the type of the result. That way the user can choose whatever precision is appropriate.

We can let the user control the type of the return by defining a third template parameter to represent the return type:

```
// T1 cannot be deduced: it doesn't appear in the function parameter list
template <typename T1, typename T2, typename T3>
T1 sum(T2, T3);
```

In this case, there is no argument whose type can be used to deduce the type of T1. The caller must provide an **explicit template argument** for this parameter on each call to sum.

We supply an explicit template argument to a call the same way that we define an instance of a class template. Explicit template arguments are specified inside angle brackets after the function name and before the argument list:

```
// T1 is explicitly specified; T2 and T3 are inferred from the argument types
auto val3 = sum<long long>(i, lng); // long long sum(int, long)
```

This call explicitly specifies the type for T1. The compiler will deduce the types for T2 and T3 from the types of i and lng.

Explicit template argument(s) are matched to corresponding template parameter(s) from left to right; the first template argument is matched to the first template parameter, the second argument to the second parameter, and so on. An explicit template argument may be omitted only for the trailing (right-most) parameters, and then only if these can be deduced from the function parameters. If our sum function had been written as

```
// poor design: users must explicitly specify all three template parameters
template <typename T1, typename T2, typename T3>
T3 alternative_sum(T2, T1);
```

then we would always have to specify arguments for all three parameters:

```
// error: can't infer initial template parameters
auto val3 = alternative_sum<long long>(i, lng);
// ok: all three parameters are explicitly specified
auto val2  = alternative_sum<long long, int, long>(i, lng);
```

Normal Conversions Apply for Explicitly Specified Arguments

For the same reasons that normal conversions are permitted for parameters that are defined using ordinary types (§ 16.2.1, p. 680), normal conversions also apply for arguments whose template type parameter is explicitly specified:

```
long lng;
compare(lng, 1024);        //  error: template parameters don't match
compare<long>(lng, 1024);  //  ok: instantiates compare(long, long)
compare<int>(lng, 1024);   //  ok: instantiates compare(int, int)
```

As we've seen, the first call is in error because the arguments to compare must have the same type. If we explicitly specify the template parameter type, normal conversions apply. Thus, the call to compare<long> is equivalent to calling a function taking two const long& parameters. The int parameter is automatically converted to long. In the second call, T is explicitly specified as int, so lng is converted to int.

16.2.3 Trailing Return Types and Type Transformation

Using an explicit template argument to represent a template function's return type works well when we want to let the user determine the return type. In other cases, requiring an explicit template argument imposes a burden on the user with no compensating advantage. For example, we might want to write a function that takes a pair of iterators denoting a sequence and returns a reference to an element in the sequence:

```
template <typename It>
??? &fcn(It beg, It end)
{
    // process the range
    return *beg;   // return a reference to an element from the range
}
```

We don't know the exact type we want to return, but we do know that we want that type to be a reference to the element type of the sequence we're processing:

```
vector<int> vi = {1,2,3,4,5};
Blob<string> ca = { "hi", "bye" };
auto &i = fcn(vi.begin(), vi.end()); // fcn should return int&
auto &s = fcn(ca.begin(), ca.end()); // fcn should return string&
```

Here, we know that our function will return `*beg`, and we know that we can use `decltype(*beg)` to obtain the type of that expression. However, beg doesn't exist until the parameter list has been seen. To define this function, we must use a trailing return type (§ 6.3.3, p. 229). Because a trailing return appears after the parameter list, it can use the function's parameters:

```
//  a trailing return lets us declare the return type after the parameter list is seen
template <typename It>
auto fcn(It beg, It end) -> decltype(*beg)
{
    //  process the range
    return *beg;    //  return a reference to an element from the range
}
```

Here we've told the compiler that `fcn`'s return type is the same as the type returned by dereferencing its `beg` parameter. The dereference operator returns an lvalue (§ 4.1.1, p. 136), so the type deduced by `decltype` is a reference to the type of the element that beg denotes. Thus, if `fcn` is called on a sequence of `strings`, the return type will be `string&`. If the sequence is `int`, the return will be `int&`.

The Type Transformation Library Template Classes

Sometimes we do not have direct access to the type that we need. For example, we might want to write a function similar to `fcn` that returns an element by value (§ 6.3.2, p. 224), rather than a reference to an element.

The problem we face in writing this function is that we know almost nothing about the types we're passed. In this function, the only operations we know we can use are iterator operations, and there are no iterator operations that yield elements (as opposed to references to elements).

To obtain the element type, we can use a library **type transformation** template. These templates are defined in the `type_traits` header. In general the classes in `type_traits` are used for so-called template metaprogramming, a topic that is beyond the scope of this Primer. However, the type transformation templates are useful in ordinary programming as well. These templates are described in Table 16.1 and we'll see how they are implemented in § 16.5 (p. 710).

In this case, we can use `remove_reference` to obtain the element type. The `remove_reference` template has one template type parameter and a (public) type member named `type`. If we instantiate `remove_reference` with a reference type, then `type` will be the referred-to type. For example, if we instantiate `remove_reference<int&>`, the `type` member will be `int`. Similarly, if we instantiate `remove_reference<string&>`, `type` will be `string`, and so on. More generally, given that `beg` is an iterator:

```
remove_reference<decltype(*beg)>::type
```

will be the type of the element to which beg refers: `decltype(*beg)` returns the reference type of the element type. `remove_reference::type` strips off the reference, leaving the element type itself.

Using `remove_reference` and a trailing return with `decltype`, we can write our function to return a copy of an element's value:

```
//   must use typename to use a type member of a template parameter; see § 16.1.3 (p. 670)
template <typename It>
auto fcn2(It beg, It end) ->
                    ference<decltype(*beg)>::type
```

'turn a copy of an element from the range

class that depends on a template parameter. As
e in the declaration of the return type to tell the
type (§ 16.1.3, p. 670).

rd Type Transformation Templates		
	f is	Then *Mod*<T>::type is
	or X&&	X
	ierwise	T
	const X, or function	T
	.nerwise	const T
	X&	T
	X&&	X&
	otherwise	T&
add_rvalue_reference	X& or X&&	T
	otherwise	T&&
remove_pointer	X*	X
	otherwise	T
add_pointer	X& or X&&	X*
	otherwise	T*
make_signed	unsigned X	X
	otherwise	T
make_unsigned	signed type	unsigned T
	otherwise	T
remove_extent	X[n]	X
	otherwise	T
remove_all_extents	X[n1][n2] ...	X
	otherwise	T

Each of the type transformation templates described in Table 16.1 works similarly to remove_reference. Each template has a public member named type that represents a type. That type may be related to the template's own template type parameter in a way that is indicated by the template's name. If it is not possible (or not necessary) to transform the template's parameter, the type member is the template parameter type itself. For example, if T is a pointer type, then remove_pointer<T>::type is the type to which T points. If T isn't a pointer, then no transformation is needed. In this case, type is the same type as T.

16.2.4 Function Pointers and Argument Deduction

When we initialize or assign a function pointer (§ 6.7, p. 247) from a function template, the compiler uses the type of the pointer to deduce the template argument(s).

As an example, assume we have a function pointer that points to a function returning an int that takes two parameters, each of which is a reference to a const int. We can use that pointer to point to an instantiation of compare:

```
template <typename T> int compare(const T&, const T&);
// pf1 points to the instantiation int compare(const int&, const int&)
int (*pf1)(const int&, const int&) = compare;
```

The type of the parameters in pf1 determines the type of the template argument for T. The template argument for T is int. The pointer pf1 points to the instantiation of compare with T bound to int. It is an error if the template arguments cannot be determined from the function pointer type:

```
// overloaded versions of func; each takes a different function pointer type
void func(int(*)(const string&, const string&));
void func(int(*)(const int&, const int&));
func(compare);  // error: which instantiation of compare?
```

The problem is that by looking at the type of func's parameter, it is not possible to determine a unique type for the template argument. The call to func could instantiate the version of compare that takes ints or the version that takes strings. Because it is not possible to identify a unique instantiation for the argument to func, this call won't compile.

We can disambiguate the call to func by using explicit template arguments:

```
// ok: explicitly specify which version of compare to instantiate
func(compare<int>);  // passing compare(const int&, const int&)
```

This expression calls the version of func that takes a function pointer with two const int& parameters.

When the address of a function-template instantiation is taken, the context must be such that it allows a unique type or value to be determined for each template parameter.

16.2.5 Template Argument Deduction and References

In order to understand type deduction from a call to a function such as

```
template <typename T> void f(T &p);
```

in which the function's parameter p is a reference to a template type parameter T, it is important to keep in mind two points: Normal reference binding rules apply; and consts are low level, not top level.

Type Deduction from Lvalue Reference Function Parameters

When a function parameter is an ordinary (lvalue) reference to a template type parameter (i.e., that has the form T&), the binding rules say that we can pass only an lvalue (e.g., a variable or an expression that returns a reference type). That argument might or might not have a const type. If the argument is const, then T will be deduced as a const type:

```
template <typename T> void f1(T&);    // argument must be an lvalue
// calls to f1 use the referred-to type of the argument as the template parameter type
f1(i);    // i is an int; template parameter T is int
f1(ci);   // ci is a const int; template parameter T is const int
f1(5);    // error: argument to a & parameter must be an lvalue
```

If a function parameter has type const T&, normal binding rules say that we can pass any kind of argument—an object (const or otherwise), a temporary, or a literal value. When the function parameter is itself const, the type deduced for T will not be a const type. The const is already part of the *function* parameter type; therefore, it does not also become part of the *template* parameter type:

```
template <typename T> void f2(const T&); // can take an rvalue
// parameter in f2 is const &; const in the argument is irrelevant
// in each of these three calls, f2's function parameter is inferred as const int&
f2(i);  // i is an int; template parameter T is int
f2(ci); // ci is a const int, but template parameter T is int
f2(5);  // a const & parameter can be bound to an rvalue; T is int
```

Type Deduction from Rvalue Reference Function Parameters

When a function parameter is an rvalue reference (§ 13.6.1, p. 532) (i.e., has the form T&&), normal binding rules say that we can pass an rvalue to this parameter. When we do so, type deduction behaves similarly to deduction for an ordinary lvalue reference function parameter. The deduced type for T is the type of the rvalue:

```
template <typename T> void f3(T&&);
f3(42); // argument is an rvalue of type int; template parameter T is int
```

Reference Collapsing and Rvalue Reference Parameters

Assuming `i` is an `int` object, we might think that a call such as `f3(i)` would be illegal. After all, `i` is an lvalue, and normally we cannot bind an rvalue reference to an lvalue. However, the language defines two exceptions to normal binding rules that allow this kind of usage. These exceptions are the foundation for how library facilities such as `move` operate.

The first exception affects how type deduction is done for rvalue reference parameters. When we pass an lvalue (e.g., `i`) to a function parameter that is an rvalue reference to a template type parameter (e.g, `T&&`), the compiler deduces the template type parameter as the argument's lvalue reference type. So, when we call `f3(i)`, the compiler deduces the type of `T` as `int&`, not `int`.

Deducing `T` as `int&` would seem to mean that `f3`'s function parameter would be an rvalue reference to the type `int&`. Ordinarily, we cannot (directly) define a reference to a reference (§ 2.3.1, p. 51). However, it is possible to do so indirectly through a type alias (§ 2.5.1, p. 67) or through a template type parameter.

In such contexts, we see the second exception to the normal binding rules: If we indirectly create a reference to a reference, then those references "collapse." In all but one case, the references collapse to form an ordinary lvalue reference type. The new standard, expanded the collapsing rules to include rvalue references. References collapse to form an rvalue reference only in the specific case of an rvalue reference to an rvalue reference. That is, for a given type `X`:

*   `X& &`, `X& &&`, and `X&& &` all collapse to type `X&`

*   The type `X&& &&` collapses to `X&&`

> **Note** Reference collapsing applies only when a reference to a reference is created indirectly, such as in a type alias or a template parameter.

The combination of the reference collapsing rule and the special rule for type deduction for rvalue reference parameters means that we can call `f3` on an lvalue. When we pass an lvalue to `f3`'s (rvalue reference) function parameter, the compiler will deduce `T` as an lvalue reference type:

```
f3(i);   // argument is an lvalue; template parameter T is int&
f3(ci);  // argument is an lvalue; template parameter T is const int&
```

When a *template* parameter `T` is deduced as a reference type, the collapsing rule says that the *function* parameter `T&&` collapses to an lvalue reference type. For example, the resulting instantiation for `f3(i)` would be something like

```
// invalid code, for illustration purposes only
void f3<int&>(int& &&);  // when T is int&, function parameter is int& &&
```

The function parameter in `f3` is `T&&` and `T` is `int&`, so `T&&` is `int& &&`, which collapses to `int&`. Thus, even though the form of the function parameter in `f3` is an rvalue reference (i.e., `T&&`), this call instantiates `f3` with an lvalue reference type (i.e., `int&`):

```
void f3<int&>(int&);  // when T is int&, function parameter collapses to int&
```

There are two important consequences from these rules:

- A function parameter that is an rvalue reference to a template type parameter (e.g., T&&) can be bound to an lvalue; and

- If the argument is an lvalue, then the deduced template argument type will be an lvalue reference type and the function parameter will be instantiated as an (ordinary) lvalue reference parameter (T&)

It is also worth noting that by implication, we can pass any type of argument to a T&& function parameter. A parameter of such a type can (obviously) be used with rvalues, and as we've just seen, can be used by lvalues as well.

> An argument of any type can be passed to a function parameter that is an rvalue reference to a template parameter type (i.e., T&&). When an lvalue is passed to such a parameter, the function parameter is instantiated as an ordinary, lvalue reference (T&).

Writing Template Functions with Rvalue Reference Parameters

The fact that the template parameter can be deduced to a reference type can have surprising impacts on the code inside the template:

```
template <typename T> void f3(T&& val)
{
    T t = val;   //  copy or binding a reference?
    t = fcn(t);  //  does the assignment change only t or val and t?
    if (val == t) { /* ... */ } //  always true if T is a reference type
}
```

When we call f3 on an rvalue, such as the literal 42, T is int. In this case, the local variable t has type int and is initialized by copying the value of the parameter val. When we assign to t, the parameter val remains unchanged.

On the other hand, when we call f3 on the lvalue i, then T is int&. When we define and initialize the local variable t, that variable has type int&. The initialization of t binds t to val. When we assign to t, we change val at the same time. In this instantiation of f3, the if test will always yield true.

It is surprisingly hard to write code that is correct when the types involved might be plain (nonreference) types or reference types (although the type transformation classes such as remove_reference can help (§ 16.2.3, p. 684)).

In practice, rvalue reference parameters are used in one of two contexts: Either the template is forwarding its arguments, or the template is overloaded. We'll look at forwarding in § 16.2.7 (p. 692) and at template overloading in § 16.3 (p. 694).

For now, it's worth noting that function templates that use rvalue references often use overloading in the same way as we saw in § 13.6.3 (p. 544):

```
template <typename T> void f(T&&);       //  binds to nonconst rvalues
template <typename T> void f(const T&);  //  lvalues and const rvalues
```

As with nontemplate functions, the first version will bind to modifiable rvalues and the second to lvalues or to const rvalues.

Exercise 16.42: Determine the type of T and of val in each of the following calls:

```
template <typename T> void g(T&& val);
int i = 0; const int ci = i;
(a) g(i);          (b) g(ci);          (c) g(i * ci);
```

Exercise 16.43: Using the function defined in the previous exercise, what would the template parameter of g be if we called g(i = ci)?

Exercise 16.44: Using the same three calls as in the first exercise, determine the types for T if g's function parameter is declared as T (not T&&). What if g's function parameter is const T&?

Exercise 16.45: Given the following template, explain what happens if we call g on a literal value such as 42. What if we call g on a variable of type int?

```
template <typename T> void g(T&& val) { vector<T> v; }
```

16.2.6 Understanding `std::move`

The library move function (§ 13.6.1, p. 533) is a good illustration of a template that uses rvalue references. Fortunately, we can use move without understanding the template mechanisms that it uses. However, looking at how move works can help cement our general understanding, and use, of templates.

In § 13.6.2 (p. 534) we noted that although we cannot directly bind an rvalue reference to an lvalue, we can use move to obtain an rvalue reference bound to an lvalue. Because move can take arguments of essentially any type, it should not be surprising that move is a function template.

How `std::move` Is Defined

The standard defines move as follows:

```
//  for the use of typename in the return type and the cast see § 16.1.3 (p. 670)
//  remove_reference is covered in § 16.2.3 (p. 684)
template <typename T>
typename remove_reference<T>::type&& move(T&& t)
{
    // static_cast covered in § 4.11.3 (p. 163)
    return static_cast<typename remove_reference<T>::type&&>(t);
}
```

This code is short but subtle. First, move's function parameter, T&&, is an rvalue reference to a template parameter type. Through reference collapsing, this parameter can match arguments of any type. In particular, we can pass either an lvalue or an rvalue to move:

```
string s1("hi!"), s2;
s2 = std::move(string("bye!"));  // ok: moving from an rvalue
s2 = std::move(s1);   // ok: but after the assigment s1 has indeterminate value
```

How `std::move` Works

In the first assignment, the argument to `move` is the rvalue result of the `string` constructor, `string("bye")`. As we've seen, when we pass an rvalue to an rvalue reference function parameter, the type deduced from that argument is the referred-to type (§ 16.2.5, p. 687). Thus, in `std::move(string("bye!"))`:

- The deduced type of `T` is `string`.

- Therefore, `remove_reference` is instantiated with `string`.

- The `type` member of `remove_reference<string>` is `string`.

- The return type of `move` is `string&&`.

- `move`'s function parameter, `t`, has type `string&&`.

Accordingly, this call instantiates `move<string>`, which is the function

```
string&& move(string &&t)
```

The body of this function returns `static_cast<string&&>(t)`. The type of `t` is already `string&&`, so the cast does nothing. Therefore, the result of this call is the rvalue reference it was given.

Now consider the second assignment, which calls `std::move(s1)`. In this call, the argument to `move` is an lvalue. This time:

- The deduced type of `T` is `string&` (reference to `string`, not plain `string`).

- Therefore, `remove_reference` is instantiated with `string&`.

- The `type` member of `remove_reference<string&>` is `string`,

- The return type of `move` is still `string&&`.

- `move`'s function parameter, `t`, instantiates as `string& &&`, which collapses to `string&`.

Thus, this call instantiates `move<string&>`, which is

```
string&& move(string &t)
```

and which is exactly what we're after—we want to bind an rvalue reference to an lvalue. The body of this instantiation returns `static_cast<string&&>(t)`. In this case, the type of `t` is `string&`, which the cast converts to `string&&`.

`static_cast` from an Lvalue to an Rvalue Reference Is Permitted

Ordinarily, a `static_cast` can perform only otherwise legitimate conversions (§ 4.11.3, p. 163). However, there is again a special dispensation for rvalue references: Even though we cannot implicitly convert an lvalue to an rvalue reference, we can *explicitly* cast an lvalue to an rvalue reference using `static_cast`.

Binding an rvalue reference to an lvalue gives code that operates on the rvalue reference permission to clobber the lvalue. There are times, such as in our `StrVec` `reallocate` function in § 13.6.1 (p. 533), when we know it is safe to clobber an lvalue. By *letting* us do the cast, the language allows this usage. By *forcing* us to use a cast, the language tries to prevent us from doing so accidentally.

Finally, although we can write such casts directly, it is much easier to use the library move function. Moreover, using `std::move` consistently makes it easy to find the places in our code that might potentially clobber lvalues.

 ## 16.2.7 Forwarding

Some functions need to forward one or more of their arguments with their types *unchanged* to another, forwarded-to, function. In such cases, we need to preserve everything about the forwarded arguments, including whether or not the argument type is `const`, and whether the argument is an lvalue or an rvalue.

As an example, we'll write a function that takes a callable expression and two additional arguments. Our function will call the given callable with the other two arguments in reverse order. The following is a first cut at our flip function:

```
//  template that takes a callable and two parameters
//  and calls the given callable with the parameters "flipped"
//  flip1 is an incomplete implementation: top-level const and references are lost
template <typename F, typename T1, typename T2>
void flip1(F f, T1 t1, T2 t2)
{
    f(t2, t1);
}
```

This template works fine until we want to use it to call a function that has a reference parameter:

```
void f(int v1, int &v2)    //  note v2 is a reference
{
    cout << v1 << " " << ++v2 << endl;
}
```

Here `f` changes the value of the argument bound to `v2`. However, if we call `f` through `flip1`, the changes made by `f` do not affect the original argument:

```
f(42, i);             //  f changes its argument i
flip1(f, j, 42);      //  f called through flip1 leaves j unchanged
```

The problem is that `j` is passed to the `t1` parameter in `flip1`. That parameter has is a plain, nonreference type, `int`, not an `int&`. That is, the instantiation of this call to `flip1` is

```
void flip1(void(*fcn)(int, int&), int t1, int t2);
```

The value of j is copied into t1. The reference parameter in f is bound to t1, not to j.

Defining Function Parameters That Retain Type Information

To pass a reference through our flip function, we need to rewrite our function so that its parameters preserve the "lvalueness" of its given arguments. Thinking ahead a bit, we can imagine that we'd also like to preserve the constness of the arguments as well.

We can preserve all the type information in an argument by defining its corresponding function parameter as an rvalue reference to a template type parameter. Using a reference parameter (either lvalue or rvalue) lets us preserve constness, because the const in a reference type is low-level. Through reference collapsing (§ 16.2.5, p. 688), if we define the function parameters as T1&& and T2&&, we can preserve the lvalue/rvalue property of flip's arguments (§ 16.2.5, p. 687):

```
template <typename F, typename T1, typename T2>
void flip2(F f, T1 &&t1, T2 &&t2)
{
    f(t2, t1);
}
```

As in our earlier call, if we call flip2(f, j, 42), the lvalue j is passed to the parameter t1. However, in flip2, the type deduced for T1 is int&, which means that the type of t1 collapses to int&. The reference t1 is bound to j. When flip2 calls f, the reference parameter v2 in f is bound to t1, which in turn is bound to j. When f increments v2, it is changing the value of j.

> **Note**
> A function parameter that is an rvalue reference to a template type parameter (i.e., T&&) preserves the constness and lvalue/rvalue property of its corresponding argument.

This version of flip2 solves one half of our problem. Our flip2 function works fine for functions that take lvalue references but cannot be used to call a function that has an rvalue reference parameter. For example:

```
void g(int &&i, int& j)
{
    cout << i << " " << j << endl;
}
```

If we try to call g through flip2, we will be passing the parameter t2 to g's rvalue reference parameter. Even if we pass an rvalue to flip2:

```
flip2(g, i, 42); // error: can't initialize int&& from an lvalue
```

what is passed to g will be the parameter named t2 inside flip2. A function parameter, like any other variable, is an lvalue expression (§ 13.6.1, p. 533). As a result, the call to g in flip2 passes an lvalue to g's rvalue reference parameter.

Using `std::forward` to Preserve Type Information in a Call

We can use a new library facility named `forward` to pass `flip2`'s parameters in a way that preserves the types of the original arguments. Like `move`, `forward` is defined in the `utility` header. Unlike `move`, `forward` must be called with an explicit template argument (§ 16.2.2, p. 682). `forward` returns an rvalue reference to that explicit argument type. That is, the return type of `forward<T>` is `T&&`.

Ordinarily, we use `forward` to pass a function parameter that is defined as an rvalue reference to a template type parameter. Through reference collapsing on its return type, `forward` preserves the lvalue/rvalue nature of its given argument:

```
template <typename Type> intermediary(Type &&arg)
{
    finalFcn(std::forward<Type>(arg));
    // ...
}
```

Here we use `Type`—which is deduced from `arg`—as `forward`'s explicit template argument type. Because `arg` is an rvalue reference to a template type parameter, `Type` will represent all the type information in the argument passed to `arg`. If that argument was an rvalue, then `Type` is an ordinary (nonreference) type and `forward<Type>` will return `Type&&`. If the argument was an lvalue, then—through reference collapsing—`Type` itself is an lvalue reference type. In this case, the return type is an rvalue reference to an lvalue reference type. Again through reference collapsing—this time on the return type—`forward<Type>` will return an lvalue reference type.

> **Note**
> When used with a function parameter that is an rvalue reference to template type parameter (`T&&`), `forward` preserves all the details about an argument's type.

Using `forward`, we'll rewrite our flip function once more:

```
template <typename F, typename T1, typename T2>
void flip(F f, T1 &&t1, T2 &&t2)
{
    f(std::forward<T2>(t2), std::forward<T1>(t1));
}
```

If we call `flip(g, i, 42)`, `i` will be passed to `g` as an `int&` and `42` will be passed as an `int&&`.

> **Note**
> As with `std::move`, it's a good idea not to provide a `using` declaration for `std::forward`. § 18.2.3 (p. 798) will explain why.

16.3 Overloading and Templates

Function templates can be overloaded by other templates or by ordinary, nontemplate functions. As usual, functions with the same name must differ either as to the number or the type(s) of their parameters.

EXERCISES SECTION 16.2.7

Exercise 16.47: Write your own version of the flip function and test it by calling functions that have lvalue and rvalue reference parameters.

Function matching (§ 6.4, p. 233) is affected by the presence of function templates in the following ways:

- The candidate functions for a call include any function-template instantiation for which template argument deduction (§ 16.2, p. 678) succeeds.

- The candidate function templates are always viable, because template argument deduction will have eliminated any templates that are not viable.

- As usual, the viable functions (template and nontemplate) are ranked by the conversions, if any, needed to make the call. Of course, the conversions used to call a function template are quite limited (§ 16.2.1, p. 679).

- Also as usual, if exactly one function provides a better match than any of the others, that function is selected. However, if there are several functions that provide an equally good match, then:

  - If there is only one nontemplate function in the set of equally good matches, the nontemplate function is called.

  - If there are no nontemplate functions in the set, but there are multiple function templates, and one of these templates is more specialized than any of the others, the more specialized function template is called.

  - Otherwise, the call is ambiguous.

WARNING

Correctly defining a set of overloaded function templates requires a good understanding of the relationship among types and of the restricted conversions applied to arguments in template functions.

Writing Overloaded Templates

As an example, we'll build a set of functions that might be useful during debugging. We'll name our debugging functions debug_rep, each of which will return a string representation of a given object. We'll start by writing the most general version of this function as a template that takes a reference to a const object:

```
// print any type we don't otherwise handle
template <typename T> string debug_rep(const T &t)
{
    ostringstream ret;  // see § 8.3 (p. 321)
    ret << t;  // uses T's output operator to print a representation of t
    return ret.str();  // return a copy of the string to which ret is bound
}
```

This function can be used to generate a `string` corresponding to an object of any type that has an output operator.

Next, we'll define a version of `debug_rep` to print pointers:

```
//  print pointers as their pointer value, followed by the object to which the pointer points
//  NB: this function will not work properly with char*; see § 16.3 (p. 698)
template <typename T> string debug_rep(T *p)
{
    ostringstream ret;
    ret << "pointer: " << p;          //  print the pointer's own value
    if (p)
        ret << " " << debug_rep(*p);  //  print the value to which p points
    else
        ret << " null pointer";       //  or indicate that the p is null
    return ret.str(); //  return a copy of the string to which ret is bound
}
```

This version generates a `string` that contains the pointer's own value and calls `debug_rep` to print the object to which that pointer points. Note that this function can't be used to print character pointers, because the IO library defines a version of the `<<` for `char*` values. That version of `<<` assumes the pointer denotes a null-terminated character array, and prints the contents of the array, not its address. We'll see in § 16.3 (p. 698) how to handle character pointers.

We might use these functions as follows:

```
string s("hi");
cout << debug_rep(s) << endl;
```

For this call, only the first version of `debug_rep` is viable. The second version of `debug_rep` requires a pointer parameter, and in this call we passed a nonpointer object. There is no way to instantiate a function template that expects a pointer type from a nonpointer argument, so argument deduction fails. Because there is only one viable function, that is the one that is called.

If we call `debug_rep` with a pointer:

```
cout << debug_rep(&s) << endl;
```

both functions generate viable instantiations:

- `debug_rep(const string*&)`, which is the instantiation of the first version of `debug_rep` with `T` bound to `string*`

- `debug_rep(string*)`, which is the instantiation of the second version of `debug_rep` with `T` bound to `string`

The instantiation of the second version of `debug_rep` is an exact match for this call. The instantiation of the first version requires a conversion of the plain pointer to a pointer to `const`. Normal function matching says we should prefer the second template, and indeed that is the one that is run.

Multiple Viable Templates

As another example, consider the following call:

```
const string *sp = &s;
cout << debug_rep(sp) << endl;
```

Here both templates are viable and both provide an exact match:

- `debug_rep(const string*&)`, the instantiation of the first version of the template with T bound to `const string*`

- `debug_rep(const string*)`, the instantiation of the second version of the template with T bound to `const string`

In this case, normal function matching can't distinguish between these two calls. We might expect this call to be ambiguous. However, due to the special rule for overloaded function templates, this call resolves to `debug_rep(T*)`, which is the more specialized template.

The reason for this rule is that without it, there would be no way to call the pointer version of `debug_rep` on a pointer to `const`. The problem is that the template `debug_rep(const T&)` can be called on essentially any type, including pointer types. That template is more general than `debug_rep(T*)`, which can be called only on pointer types. Without this rule, calls that passed pointers to `const` would always be ambiguous.

 When there are several overloaded templates that provide an equally good match for a call, the most specialized version is preferred.

Nontemplate and Template Overloads

For our next example, we'll define an ordinary nontemplate version of `debug_rep` to print `string`s inside double quotes:

```
// print strings inside double quotes
string debug_rep(const string &s)
{
    return '"' + s + '"';
}
```

Now, when we call `debug_rep` on a `string`,

```
string s("hi");
cout << debug_rep(s) << endl;
```

there are two equally good viable functions:

- `debug_rep<string>(const string&)`, the first template with T bound to `string`

- `debug_rep(const string&)`, the ordinary, nontemplate function

In this case, both functions have the same parameter list, so obviously, each function provides an equally good match for this call. However, the nontemplate version is selected. For the same reasons that the most specialized of equally good function templates is preferred, a nontemplate function is preferred over equally good match(es) to a function template.

 When a nontemplate function provides an equally good match for a call as a function template, the nontemplate version is preferred.

Overloaded Templates and Conversions

There's one case we haven't covered so far: pointers to C-style character strings and string literals. Now that we have a version of debug_rep that takes a string, we might expect that a call that passes character strings would match that version. However, consider this call:

```
cout << debug_rep("hi world!") << endl; // calls debug_rep(T*)
```

Here all three of the debug_rep functions are viable:

- debug_rep(const T&), with T bound to char[10]

- debug_rep(T*), with T bound to const char

- debug_rep(const string&), which requires a conversion from const char* to string

Both templates provide an exact match to the argument—the second template requires a (permissible) conversion from array to pointer, and that conversion is considered as an exact match for function-matching purposes (§ 6.6.1, p. 245). The nontemplate version is viable but requires a user-defined conversion. That function is less good than an exact match, leaving the two templates as the possible functions to call. As before, the T* version is more specialized and is the one that will be selected.

If we want to handle character pointers as strings, we can define two more nontemplate overloads:

```
// convert the character pointers to string and call the string version of debug_rep
string debug_rep(char *p)
{
    return debug_rep(string(p));
}
string debug_rep(const char *p)
{
    return debug_rep(string(p));
}
```

Missing Declarations Can Cause the Program to Misbehave

It is worth noting that for the char* versions of debug_rep to work correctly, a declaration for debug_rep(const string&) must be in scope when these functions are defined. If not, the wrong version of debug_rep will be called:

```
template <typename T> string debug_rep(const T &t);
template <typename T> string debug_rep(T *p);
//  the following declaration must be in scope
//  for the definition of debug_rep(char*) to do the right thing
string debug_rep(const string &);

string debug_rep(char *p)
{
    //  if the declaration for the version that takes a const string& is not in scope
    //  the return will call debug_rep(const T&) with T instantiated to string
    return debug_rep(string(p));
}
```

Ordinarily, if we use a function that we forgot to declare, our code won't compile. Not so with functions that overload a template function. If the compiler can instantiate the call from the template, then the missing declaration won't matter. In this example, if we forget to declare the version of debug_rep that takes a string, the compiler will *silently* instantiate the template version that takes a const T&.

> Declare every function in an overload set before you define any of the functions. That way you don't have to worry whether the compiler will instantiate a call before it sees the function you intended to call.

EXERCISES SECTION 16.3

Exercise 16.48: Write your own versions of the debug_rep functions.

Exercise 16.49: Explain what happens in each of the following calls:

```
template <typename T> void f(T);
template <typename T> void f(const T*);
template <typename T> void g(T);
template <typename T> void g(T*);
int i = 42, *p = &i;
const int ci = 0, *p2 = &ci;
g(42);    g(p);    g(ci);    g(p2);
f(42);    f(p);    f(ci);    f(p2);
```

Exercise 16.50: Define the functions from the previous exercise so that they print an identifying message. Run the code from that exercise. If the calls behave differently from what you expected, make sure you understand why.

16.4 Variadic Templates

A **variadic template** is a template function or class that can take a varying number of parameters. The varying parameters are known as a **parameter pack**. There are two kinds of parameter packs: A **template parameter pack** represents zero or more template parameters, and a **function parameter pack** represents zero or more function parameters.

We use an ellipsis to indicate that a template or function parameter represents a pack. In a template parameter list, `class...` or `typename...` indicates that the following parameter represents a list of zero or more types; the name of a type followed by an ellipsis represents a list of zero or more nontype parameters of the given type. In the function parameter list, a parameter whose type is a template parameter pack is a function parameter pack. For example:

```
//  Args is a template parameter pack; rest is a function parameter pack
//  Args represents zero or more template type parameters
//  rest represents zero or more function parameters
template <typename T, typename... Args>
void foo(const T &t, const Args& ... rest);
```

declares that `foo` is a variadic function that has one type parameter named `T` and a template parameter pack named `Args`. That pack represents zero or more additional type parameters. The function parameter list of `foo` has one parameter, whose type is a `const &` to whatever type `T` has, and a function parameter pack named `rest`. That pack represents zero or more function parameters.

As usual, the compiler deduces the template parameter types from the function's arguments. For a variadic template, the compiler also deduces the number of parameters in the pack. For example, given these calls:

```
int i = 0;  double d = 3.14; string s = "how now brown cow";
foo(i, s, 42, d);        //  three parameters in the pack
foo(s, 42, "hi");        //  two parameters in the pack
foo(d, s);               //  one parameter in the pack
foo("hi");               //  empty pack
```

the compiler will instantiate four different instances of `foo`:

```
void foo(const int&, const string&, const int&, const double&);
void foo(const string&, const int&, const char[3]&);
void foo(const double&, const string&);
void foo(const char[3]&);
```

In each case, the type of `T` is deduced from the type of the first argument. The remaining arguments (if any) provide the number of, and types for, the additional arguments to the function.

The `sizeof...` Operator

When we need to know how many elements there are in a pack, we can use the `sizeof...` operator. Like `sizeof` (§ 4.9, p. 156), `sizeof...` returns a constant expression (§ 2.4.4, p. 65) and does not evaluate its argument:

```
template<typename ... Args> void g(Args ... args) {
    cout << sizeof...(Args) << endl;   // number of type parameters
    cout << sizeof...(args) << endl;   // number of function parameters
}
```

Exercise 16.51: Determine what `sizeof...(Args)` and `sizeof...(rest)` return for each call to `foo` in this section.

Exercise 16.52: Write a program to check your answer to the previous question.

16.4.1 Writing a Variadic Function Template

In § 6.2.6 (p. 220) we saw that we can use an `initializer_list` to define a function that can take a varying number of arguments. However, the arguments must have the same type (or types that are convertible to a common type). Variadic functions are used when we know neither the number nor the types of the arguments we want to process. As an example, we'll define a function like our earlier `error_msg` function, only this time we'll allow the argument types to vary as well. We'll start by defining a variadic function named `print` that will print the contents of a given list of arguments on a given stream.

Variadic functions are often recursive (§ 6.3.2, p. 227). The first call processes the first argument in the pack and calls itself on the remaining arguments. Our `print` function will execute this way—each call will print its second argument on the stream denoted by its first argument. To stop the recursion, we'll also need to define a nonvariadic `print` function that will take a stream and an object:

```
//  function to end the recursion and print the last element
//  this function must be declared before the variadic version of print is defined
template<typename T>
ostream &print(ostream &os, const T &t)
{
    return os << t;   //  no separator after the last element in the pack
}
//  this version of print will be called for all but the last element in the pack
template <typename T, typename... Args>
ostream &print(ostream &os, const T &t, const Args&... rest)
{
    os << t << ", ";              //  print the first argument
    return print(os, rest...);   //  recursive call; print the other arguments
}
```

The first version of `print` stops the recursion and prints the last argument in the initial call to `print`. The second, variadic, version prints the argument bound to `t` and calls itself to print the remaining values in the function parameter pack.

The key part is the call to `print` inside the variadic function:

```
return print(os, rest...);  //  recursive call; print the other arguments
```

The variadic version of our `print` function takes three parameters: an `ostream&`, a `const T&`, and a parameter pack. Yet this call passes only two arguments. What happens is that the first argument in `rest` gets bound to `t`. The remaining arguments in `rest` form the parameter pack for the next call to `print`. Thus, on each call, the first argument in the pack is removed from the pack and becomes the argument bound to t. That is, given:

```
print(cout, i, s, 42);   // two parameters in the pack
```

the recursion will execute as follows:

Call	t	rest...
`print(cout, i, s, 42)`	`i`	`s, 42`
`print(cout, s, 42)`	`s`	`42`
`print(cout, 42)` *calls the nonvariadic version of* `print`		

The first two calls can match only the variadic version of `print` because the nonvariadic version isn't viable. These calls pass four and three arguments, respectively, and the nonvariadic `print` takes only two arguments.

For the last call in the recursion, `print(cout, 42)`, both versions of `print` are viable. This call passes exactly two arguments, and the type of the first argument is `ostream&`. Thus, the nonvariadic version of `print` is viable.

The variadic version is also viable. Unlike an ordinary argument, a parameter pack can be empty. Hence, the variadic version of `print` can be instantiated with only two parameters: one for the `ostream&` parameter and the other for the `const T&` parameter.

Both functions provide an equally good match for the call. However, a nonvariadic template is more specialized than a variadic template, so the nonvariadic version is chosen for this call (§ 16.3, p. 695).

> **WARNING** A declaration for the nonvariadic version of `print` must be in scope when the variadic version is defined. Otherwise, the variadic function will recurse indefinitely.

EXERCISES SECTION 16.4.1

Exercise 16.53: Write your own version of the `print` functions and test them by printing one, two, and five arguments, each of which should have different types.

Exercise 16.54: What happens if we call `print` on a type that doesn't have an `<<` operator?

Exercise 16.55: Explain how the variadic version of `print` would execute if we declared the nonvariadic version of `print` after the definition of the variadic version.

 ## 16.4.2 Pack Expansion

Aside from taking its size, the only other thing we can do with a parameter pack is to **expand** it. When we expand a pack, we also provide a **pattern** to be used on each expanded element. Expanding a pack separates the pack into its constituent elements, applying the pattern to each element as it does so. We trigger an expansion by putting an ellipsis (. . .) to the right of the pattern.

For example, our `print` function contains two expansions:

```
template <typename T, typename... Args>
ostream &
print(ostream &os, const T &t, const Args&... rest)// expand Args
{
    os << t << ", ";
    return print(os, rest...);                        // expand rest
}
```

The first expansion expands the template parameter pack and generates the function parameter list for `print`. The second expansion appears in the call to `print`. That pattern generates the argument list for the call to `print`.

The expansion of `Args` applies the pattern `const Args&` to each element in the template parameter pack `Args`. The expansion of this pattern is a comma-separated list of zero or more parameter types, each of which will have the form `const type&`. For example:

```
print(cout, i, s, 42);   // two parameters in the pack
```

The types of the last two arguments along with the pattern determine the types of the trailing parameters. This call is instantiated as

```
ostream&
print(ostream&, const int&, const string&, const int&);
```

The second expansion happens in the (recursive) call to `print`. In this case, the pattern is the name of the function parameter pack (i.e., `rest`). This pattern expands to a comma-separated list of the elements in the pack. Thus, this call is equivalent to

```
print(os, s, 42);
```

Understanding Pack Expansions

The expansion of the function parameter pack in `print` just expanded the pack into its constituent parts. More complicated patterns are also possible when we expand a function parameter pack. For example, we might write a second variadic function that calls `debug_rep` (§ 16.3, p. 695) on each of its arguments and then calls `print` to print the resulting `string`s:

```
// call debug_rep on each argument in the call to print
template <typename... Args>
ostream &errorMsg(ostream &os, const Args&... rest)
{
    // print(os, debug_rep(a1), debug_rep(a2), ..., debug_rep(an)
    return print(os, debug_rep(rest)...);
}
```

The call to `print` uses the pattern `debug_rep(rest)`. That pattern says that we want to call `debug_rep` on each element in the function parameter pack `rest`. The resulting expanded pack will be a comma-separated list of calls to `debug_rep`. That is, a call such as

```
errorMsg(cerr, fcnName, code.num(), otherData, "other", item);
```

will execute as if we had written

```
print(cerr, debug_rep(fcnName), debug_rep(code.num()),
            debug_rep(otherData), debug_rep("otherData"),
            debug_rep(item));
```

In contrast, the following pattern would fail to compile:

```
//  passes the pack to debug_rep; print(os, debug_rep(a1, a2, ..., an))
print(os, debug_rep(rest...));  //  error: no matching function to call
```

The problem here is that we expanded `rest` in the call to `debug_rep`. This call would execute as if we had written

```
print(cerr, debug_rep(fcnName, code.num(),
                    otherData, "otherData", item));
```

In this expansion, we attempted to call `debug_rep` with a list of five arguments. There is no version of `debug_rep` that matches this call. The `debug_rep` function is not variadic and there is no version of `debug_rep` that has five parameters.

> The pattern in an expansion applies separately to each element in the pack.

EXERCISES SECTION 16.4.2

Exercise 16.56: Write and test a variadic version of `errorMsg`.

Exercise 16.57: Compare your variadic version of `errorMsg` to the `error_msg` function in § 6.2.6 (p. 220). What are the advantages and disadvantages of each approach?

16.4.3 Forwarding Parameter Packs

Under the new standard, we can use variadic templates together with `forward` to write functions that pass their arguments unchanged to some other function. To illustrate such functions, we'll add an `emplace_back` member to our `StrVec` class (§ 13.5, p. 526). The `emplace_back` member of the library containers is a variadic member template (§ 16.1.4, p. 673) that uses its arguments to construct an element directly in space managed by the container.

Our version of `emplace_back` for `StrVec` will also have to be variadic, because `string` has a number of constructors that differ in terms of their parameters.

Because we'd like to be able to use the `string` move constructor, we'll also need to preserve all the type information about the arguments passed to `emplace_back`.

As we've seen, preserving type information is a two-step process. First, to preserve type information in the arguments, we must define `emplace_back`'s function parameters as rvalue references to a template type parameter (§ 16.2.7, p. 693):

```
class StrVec {
public:
    template <class... Args> void emplace_back(Args&&...);
    // remaining members as in § 13.5 (p. 526)
};
```

The pattern in the expansion of the template parameter pack, `&&`, means that each function parameter will be an rvalue reference to its corresponding argument.

Second, we must use `forward` to preserve the arguments' original types when `emplace_back` passes those arguments to `construct` (§ 16.2.7, p. 694):

```
template <class... Args>
inline
void StrVec::emplace_back(Args&&... args)
{
    chk_n_alloc();  // reallocates the StrVec if necessary
    alloc.construct(first_free++, std::forward<Args>(args)...);
}
```

The body of `emplace_back` calls `chk_n_alloc` (§ 13.5, p. 526) to ensure that there is enough room for an element and calls `construct` to create an element in the `first_free` spot. The expansion in the call to `construct`:

```
std::forward<Args>(args)...
```

expands both the template parameter pack, `Args`, and the function parameter pack, `args`. This pattern generates elements with the form

$$\text{std::forward}<T_i>(t_i)$$

where T_i represents the type of the ith element in the template parameter pack and t_i represents the ith element in the function parameter pack. For example, assuming `svec` is a `StrVec`, if we call

```
svec.emplace_back(10, 'c');  // adds cccccccccc as a new last element
```

the pattern in the call to `construct` will expand to

```
std::forward<int>(10), std::forward<char>(c)
```

By using `forward` in this call, we guarantee that if `emplace_back` is called with an rvalue, then `construct` will also get an rvalue. For example, in this call:

```
svec.emplace_back(s1 + s2);  // uses the move constructor
```

the argument to `emplace_back` is an rvalue, which is passed to `construct` as

```
std::forward<string>(string("the end"))
```

The result type from `forward<string>` is `string&&`, so `construct` will be called with an rvalue reference. The `construct` function will, in turn, forward this argument to the `string` move constructor to build this element.

Variadic functions often forward their parameters to other functions. Such functions typically have a form similar to our `emplace_back` function:

```
//   fun has zero or more parameters each of which is
//   an rvalue reference to a template parameter type
template<typename... Args>
void fun(Args&&... args)   // expands Args as a list of rvalue references
{
    // the argument to work expands both Args and args
    work(std::forward<Args>(args)...);
}
```

Here we want to forward all of `fun`'s arguments to another function named `work` that presumably does the real work of the function. Like our call to `construct` inside `emplace_back`, the expansion in the call to `work` expands both the template parameter pack and the function parameter pack.

Because the parameters to `fun` are rvalue references, we can pass arguments of any type to `fun`; because we use `std::forward` to pass those arguments, all type information about those arguments will be preserved in the call to `work`.

EXERCISES SECTION 16.4.3

Exercise 16.58: Write the `emplace_back` function for your `StrVec` class and for the `Vec` class that you wrote for the exercises in § 16.1.2 (p. 668).

Exercise 16.59: Assuming `s` is a `string`, explain `svec.emplace_back(s)`.

Exercise 16.60: Explain how `make_shared` (§ 12.1.1, p. 451) works.

Exercise 16.61: Define your own version of `make_shared`.

16.5 Template Specializations

It is not always possible to write a single template that is best suited for every possible template argument with which the template might be instantiated. In some cases, the general template definition is simply wrong for a type: The general definition might not compile or might do the wrong thing. At other times, we may be able to take advantage of some specific knowledge to write more efficient code than would be instantiated from the template. When we can't (or don't want to) use the template version, we can define a specialized version of the class or function template.

Our `compare` function is a good example of a function template for which the general definition is not appropriate for a particular type, namely, character pointers. We'd like `compare` to compare character pointers by calling `strcmp` rather than by comparing the pointer values. Indeed, we have already overloaded the `compare` function to handle character string literals (§ 16.1.1, p. 654):

```
// first version; can compare any two types
template <typename T> int compare(const T&, const T&);
// second version to handle string literals
template<size_t N, size_t M>
int compare(const char (&)[N], const char (&)[M]);
```

However, the version of compare that has two nontype template parameters will be called only when we pass a string literal or an array. If we call compare with character pointers, the first version of the template will be called:

```
const char *p1 = "hi", *p2 = "mom";
compare(p1, p2);        // calls the first template
compare("hi", "mom");   // calls the template with two nontype parameters
```

There is no way to convert a pointer to a reference to an array, so the second version of compare is not viable when we pass p1 and p2 as arguments.

To handle character pointers (as opposed to arrays), we can define a **template specialization** of the first version of compare. A specialization is a separate definition of the template in which one or more template parameters are specified to have particular types.

Defining a Function Template Specialization

When we specialize a function template, we must supply arguments for every template parameter in the original template. To indicate that we are specializing a template, we use the keyword template followed by an empty pair of angle brackets (< >). The empty brackets indicate that arguments will be supplied for all the template parameters of the original template:

```
// special version of compare to handle pointers to character arrays
template <>
int compare(const char* const &p1, const char* const &p2)
{
    return strcmp(p1, p2);
}
```

The hard part in understanding this specialization is the function parameter types. When we define a specialization, the function parameter type(s) must match the corresponding types in a previously declared template. Here we are specializing:

```
template <typename T> int compare(const T&, const T&);
```

in which the function parameters are references to a const type. As with type aliases, the interaction between template parameter types, pointers, and const can be surprising (§ 2.5.1, p. 68).

We want to define a specialization of this function with T as const char*. Our function requires a reference to the const version of this type. The const version of a pointer type is a constant pointer as distinct from a pointer to const (§ 2.4.2, p. 63). The type we need to use in our specialization is const char* const &, which is a reference to a const pointer to const char.

Function Overloading versus Template Specializations

When we define a function template specialization, we are essentially taking over the job of the compiler. That is, we are supplying the definition to use for a specific instantiation of the original template. It is important to realize that a specialization is an instantiation; it is not an overloaded instance of the function name.

> *Note* Specializations instantiate a template; they do not overload it. As a result, specializations do not affect function matching.

Whether we define a particular function as a specialization or as an independent, nontemplate function can impact function matching. For example, we have defined two versions of our `compare` function template, one that takes references to array parameters and the other that takes `const T&`. The fact that we also have a specialization for character pointers has no impact on function matching. When we call `compare` on a string literal:

```
compare("hi", "mom")
```

both function templates are viable and provide an equally good (i.e., exact) match to the call. However, the version with character array parameters is more specialized (§ 16.3, p. 695) and is chosen for this call.

Had we defined the version of `compare` that takes character pointers as a plain nontemplate function (rather than as a specialization of the template), this call would resolve differently. In this case, there would be three viable functions: the two templates and the nontemplate character-pointer version. All three are also equally good matches for this call. As we've seen, when a nontemplate provides an equally good match as a function template, the nontemplate is selected (§ 16.3, p. 695)

KEY CONCEPT: ORDINARY SCOPE RULES APPLY TO SPECIALIZATIONS

In order to specialize a template, a declaration for the original template must be in scope. Moreover, a declaration for a specialization must be in scope before any code uses that instantiation of the template.

With ordinary classes and functions, missing declarations are (usually) easy to find—the compiler won't be able to process our code. However, if a specialization declaration is missing, the compiler will usually generate code using the original template. Because the compiler can often instantiate the original template when a specialization is missing, errors in declaration order between a template and its specializations are easy to make but hard to find.

It is an error for a program to use a specialization and an instantiation of the original template with the same set of template arguments. However, it is an error that the compiler is unlikely to detect.

> **Best Practices** Templates and their specializations should be declared in the same header file. Declarations for all the templates with a given name should appear first, followed by any specializations of those templates.

Class Template Specializations

In addition to specializing function templates, we can also specialize class templates. As an example, we'll define a specialization of the library hash template that we can use to store Sales_data objects in an unordered container. By default, the unordered containers use hash<key_type> (§ 11.4, p. 444) to organize their elements. To use this default with our own data type, we must define a specialization of the hash template. A specialized hash class must define

- An overloaded call operator (§ 14.8, p. 571) that returns a size_t and takes an object of the container's key type

- Two type members, result_type and argument_type, which are the return and argument types, respectively, of the call operator

- The default constructor and a copy-assignment operator (which can be implicitly defined (§ 13.1.2, p. 500))

The only complication in defining this hash specialization is that when we specialize a template, we must do so in the same namespace in which the original template is defined. We'll have more to say about namespaces in § 18.2 (p. 785). For now, what we need to know is that we can add members to a namespace. To do so, we must first open the namespace:

```
// open the std namespace so we can specialize std::hash
namespace std {
}  // close the std namespace; note: no semicolon after the close curly
```

Any definitions that appear between the open and close curlies will be part of the std namespace.

The following defines a specialization of hash for Sales_data:

```
// open the std namespace so we can specialize std::hash
namespace std {
template <>                      // we're defining a specialization with
struct hash<Sales_data>  // the template parameter of Sales_data
{
    // the type used to hash an unordered container must define these types
    typedef size_t result_type;
    typedef Sales_data argument_type; // by default, this type needs ==
    size_t operator()(const Sales_data& s) const;
    // our class uses synthesized copy control and default constructor
};
size_t
hash<Sales_data>::operator()(const Sales_data& s) const
{
    return hash<string>()(s.bookNo) ^
           hash<unsigned>()(s.units_sold) ^
           hash<double>()(s.revenue);
}
}  // close the std namespace; note: no semicolon after the close curly
```

Our hash<Sales_data> definition starts with template<>, which indicates that we are defining a fully specialized template. The template we're specializing is named hash and the specialized version is hash<Sales_data>. The members of the class follow directly from the requirements for specializing hash.

As with any other class, we can define the members of a specialization inside the class or out of it, as we did here. The overloaded call operator must define a hashing function over the values of the given type. This function is required to return the same result every time it is called for a given value. A good hash function will (almost always) yield different results for objects that are not equal.

Here, we delegate the complexity of defining a good hash function to the library. The library defines specializations of the hash class for the built-in types and for many of the library types. We use an (unnamed) hash<string> object to generate a hash code for bookNo, an object of type hash<unsigned> to generate a hash from units_sold, and an object of type hash<double> to generate a hash from revenue. We exclusive OR (§ 4.8, p. 154) these results to form an overall hash code for the given Sales_data object.

It is worth noting that we defined our hash function to hash all three data members so that our hash function will be compatible with our definition of operator== for Sales_data (§ 14.3.1, p. 561). By default, the unordered containers use the specialization of hash that corresponds to the key_type along with the equality operator on the key type.

Assuming our specialization is in scope, it will be used automatically when we use Sales_data as a key to one of these containers:

```
// uses hash<Sales_data> and Sales_data operator== from § 14.3.1 (p. 561)
unordered_multiset<Sales_data> SDset;
```

Because hash<Sales_data> uses the private members of Sales_data, we must make this class a friend of Sales_data:

```
template <class T> class std::hash;   // needed for the friend declaration
class Sales_data {
friend class std::hash<Sales_data>;
    // other members as before
};
```

Here we say that the specific instantiation of hash<Sales_data> is a friend. Because that instantiation is defined in the std namespace, we must remember to that this hash type is defined in the std namespace. Hence, our friend declaration refers to std::hash.

To enable users of Sales_data to use the specialization of hash, we should define this specialization in the Sales_data header.

Class-Template Partial Specializations

Differently from function templates, a class template specialization does not have to supply an argument for every template parameter. We can specify some, but not all, of the template parameters or some, but not all, aspects of the parameters.

A class template **partial specialization** is itself a template. Users must supply arguments for those template parameters that are not fixed by the specialization.

We can partially specialize only a class template. We cannot partially specialize a function template.

In § 16.2.3 (p. 684) we introduced the library `remove_reference` type. That template works through a series of specializations:

```
// original, most general template
template <class T> struct remove_reference {
    typedef T type;
};
// partial specializations that will be used for lvalue and rvalue references
template <class T> struct remove_reference<T&>   // lvalue references
    { typedef T type; };
template <class T> struct remove_reference<T&&> // rvalue references
    { typedef T type; };
```

The first template defines the most general version. It can be instantiated with any type; it uses its template argument as the type for its member named `type`. The next two classes are partial specializations of this original template.

Because a partial specialization is a template, we start, as usual, by defining the template parameters. Like any other specialization, a partial specialization has the same name as the template it specializes. The specialization's template parameter list includes an entry for each template parameter whose type is not completely fixed by this partial specialization. After the class name, we specify arguments for the template parameters we are specializing. These arguments are listed inside angle brackets following the template name. The arguments correspond positionally to the parameters in the original template.

The template parameter list of a partial specialization is a subset of, or a specialization of, the parameter list of the original template. In this case, the specializations have the same number of parameters as the original template. However, the parameter's type in the specializations differ from the original template. The specializations will be used for lvalue and rvalue reference types, respectively:

```
int i;
// decltype(42) is int, uses the original template
remove_reference<decltype(42)>::type a;
// decltype(i) is int&, uses first (T&) partial specialization
remove_reference<decltype(i)>::type b;
// decltype(std::move(i)) is int&&, uses second (i.e., T&&) partial specialization
remove_reference<decltype(std::move(i))>::type c;
```

All three variables, a, b, and c, have type `int`.

Specializing Members but Not the Class

Rather than specializing the whole template, we can specialize just specific member function(s). For example, if `Foo` is a template class with a member `Bar`, we can specialize just that member:

```
template <typename T> struct Foo {
    Foo(const T &t = T()): mem(t) { }
    void Bar() { /* ... */ }
    T mem;
    //  other members of Foo
};
template<>                    //  we're specializing a template
void Foo<int>::Bar()  //  we're specializing the Bar member of Foo<int>
{
        //  do whatever specialized processing that applies to ints
}
```

Here we are specializing just one member of the Foo<int> class. The other members of Foo<int> will be supplied by the Foo template:

```
Foo<string> fs;   //  instantiates Foo<string>::Foo()
fs.Bar();         //  instantiates Foo<string>::Bar()

Foo<int> fi;      //  instantiates Foo<int>::Foo()
fi.Bar();         //  uses our specialization of Foo<int>::Bar()
```

When we use Foo with any type other than int, members are instantiated as usual. When we use Foo with int, members other than Bar are instantiated as usual. If we use the Bar member of Foo<int>, then we get our specialized definition.

EXERCISES SECTION 16.5

Exercise 16.62: Define your own version of hash<Sales_data> and define an unordered_multiset of Sales_data objects. Put several transactions into the container and print its contents.

Exercise 16.63: Define a function template to count the number of occurrences of a given value in a vector. Test your program by passing it a vector of doubles, a vector of ints, and a vector of strings.

Exercise 16.64: Write a specialized version of the template from the previous exercise to handle vector<const char*> and a program that uses this specialization.

Exercise 16.65: In § 16.3 (p. 698) we defined overloaded two versions of debug_rep one had a const char* and the other a char* parameter. Rewrite these functions as specializations.

Exercise 16.66: What are the advantages and disadvantages of overloading these debug_rep functions as compared to defining specializations?

Exercise 16.67: Would defining these specializations affect function matching for debug_rep? If so, how? If not, why not?

CHAPTER SUMMARY

Templates are a distinctive feature of C++ and are fundamental to the library. A template is a blueprint that the compiler uses to generate specific class types or functions. This process is called instantiation. We write the template once, and the compiler instantiates the template for the type(s) or value(s) with which we use the template.

We can define both function templates and class templates. The library algorithms are function templates and the library containers are class templates.

An explicit template argument lets us fix the type or value of one or more template parameters. Normal conversions are applied to parameters that have an explicit template argument.

A template specialization is a user-provided instantiation of a template that binds one or more template parameters to specified types or values. Specializations are useful when there are types that we cannot use (or do not want to use) with the template definition.

A major part of the latest release of the C++ standard is variadic templates. A variadic template can take a varying number and types of parameters. Variadic templates let us write functions, such as the container `emplace` members and the library `make_shared` function, that pass arguments to an object's constructor.

DEFINED TERMS

class template Definition from which specific classes can be instantiated. Class templates are defined using the `template` keyword followed by a comma-separated list of one or more template parameters enclosed in < and > brackets, followed by a class definition.

default template arguments A type or a value that a template uses if the user does not supply a corresponding template argument.

explicit instantiation A declaration that supplies explicit arguments for all the template parameters. Used to guide the instantiation process. If the declaration is `extern`, the template will not be instantiated; otherwise, the template is instantiated with the specified arguments. There must be a `nonextern` explicit instantiation somewhere in the program for every `extern` template declaration.

explicit template argument Template argument supplied by the user in a call to a function or when defining a template class type. Explicit template arguments are supplied inside angle brackets immediately following the template's name.

function parameter pack Parameter pack that represents zero or more function parameters.

function template Definition from which specific functions can be instantiated. A function template is defined using the `template` keyword followed by a comma-separated list of one or more template parameters enclosed in < and > brackets, followed by a function definition.

instantiate Compiler process whereby the actual template argument(s) are used to generate a specific instance of the template in which the parameter(s) are replaced by the corresponding argument(s). Functions are instantiated automatically based on the arguments used in a call. We must supply explicit template arguments whenever we use a class template.

instantiation Class or function generated by the compiler from a template.

member template Member function that is a template. A member template may not be virtual.

nontype parameter A template parameter that represents a value. Template arguments for nontype template parameters must be constant expressions.

pack expansion Process by which a parameter pack is replaced by the corresponding list of its elements.

parameter pack Template or function parameter that represents zero or more parameters.

partial specialization Version of a class template in which some some but not all of the template parameters are specified or in which one or more parameters are not completely specified.

pattern Defines the form of each element in an expanded parameter pack.

template argument Type or value used to instantiate a template parameter.

template argument deduction Process by which the compiler determines which function template to instantiate. The compiler examines the types of the arguments that were specified using a template parameter. It automatically instantiates a version of the function with those types or values bound to the template parameters.

template parameter Name specifed in the template parameter list that may be used inside the definition of a template. Template parameters can be type or nontype parameters. To use a class template, we must supply explicit arguments for each template parameter. The compiler uses those types or

values to instantiate a version of the class in which uses of the parameter(s) are replaced by the actual argument(s). When a function template is used, the compiler deduces the template arguments from the arguments in the call and instantiates a specific function using the deduced template arguments.

template parameter list List of parameters, separated by commas, to be used in the definition or declaration of a template. Each parameter may be a type or nontype parameter.

template parameter pack Parameter pack that represents zero or more template parameters.

template specialization Redefinition of a class template, a member of a class template, or a function template, in which some (or all) of the template parameters are specified. A template specialization may not appear until after the base template that it specializes has been declared. A template specialization must appear before any use of the template with the specialized arguments. Each template parameter in a function template must be completely specialized.

type parameter Name used in a template parameter list to represent a type. Type parameters are specified following the keyword `typename` or `class`.

type transformation Class templates defined by the library that transform their given template type parameter to a related type.

variadic template Template that takes a varying number of template arguments. A template parameter pack is specified using an elipsis (e.g., `class...`, `typename...`, or *type-name...*).

PART IV

ADVANCED TOPICS

CONTENTS

Part IV covers additional features that, although useful in the right context, are not needed by every C++ programmer. These features divide into two clusters: those that are useful for large-scale problems and those that are applicable to specialized problems rather than general ones. Features for specialized problems occur both in the language, the topic of Chapter 19, and in the library, Chapter 17.

In Chapter 17 we cover four special-purpose library facilities: the `bitset` class and three new library facilities: `tuples`, regular expressions, and random numbers. We'll also look at some of the less commonly used parts of the IO library.

Chapter 18 covers exception handling, namespaces, and multiple inheritance. These features tend to be most useful in the context of large-scale problems.

Even programs simple enough to be written by a single author can benefit from exception handling, which is why we introduced the basics of exception handling in Chapter 5. However, the need to deal with run-time errors tends to be more important and harder to manage in problems that require large programming teams. In Chapter 18 we review some additional useful exception-handling facilities. We also look in more detail at how exceptions are handled, and show how we can define and use our own exception classes. This section will also cover improvements from the new standard regarding specifying that a particular function will not throw.

Large-scale applications often use code from multiple independent vendors. Combining independently developed libraries would be difficult (if not impossible) if vendors had to put the names they define into a single namespace. Independently developed libraries would almost inevitably use names in common with one another; a name defined in one library would conflict with the use of that name in another library. To avoid name collisions, we can define names inside a `namespace`.

Whenever we use a name from the standard library, we are using a name defined in the namespace named `std`. Chapter 18 shows how we can define our own namespaces.

Chapter 18 closes by looking at an important but infrequently used language feature: multiple inheritance. Multiple inheritance is most useful for fairly complicated inheritance hierarchies.

Chapter 19 covers several specialized tools and techniques that are applicable to particular kinds of problems. Among the features covered in this chapter are how to redefine how memory allocation works; C++ support for run-time type identification (RTTI), which let us determine the actual type of an expression at run time; and how we can define and use pointers to class members. Pointers to class members differ from pointers to ordinary data or functions. Ordinary pointers only vary based on the type of the object or function. Pointers to members must also reflect the class to which the member belongs. We'll also look at three additional aggregate types: unions, nested classes, and local classes. The chapter closes by looking briefly at a collection of features that are inherently nonportable: the `volatile` qualifier, bit-fields, and linkage directives.

C H A P T E R 17
S P E C I A L I Z E D L I B R A R Y
F A C I L I T I E S

CONTENTS

The latest standard greatly increased the size and scope of the library. Indeed, the portion of the standard devoted to the library more than doubled between the first release in 1998 and the 2011 standard. As a result, covering every C++ library class is well beyond the scope of this Primer. However, there are four library facilities that, although more specialized than other library facilities we've covered, are general enough to warrant discussion in an introductory book: `tuples`, `bitsets`, random-number generation, and regular expressions. In addition, we will also cover some additional, special-purpose parts of the IO library.

The library constitutes nearly two-thirds of the text of the new standard. Although we cannot cover every library facility in depth, there remain a few library facilities that are likely to be of use in many applications: tuples, bitsets, regular expressions, and random numbers. We'll also look at some additional IO library capabilities: format control, unformatted IO, and random access.

17.1 The tuple Type

A **tuple** is a template that is similar to a pair (§ 11.2.3, p. 426). Each pair type has different types for its members, but every pair always has exactly two members. A tuple also has members whose types vary from one tuple type to another, but a tuple can have any number of members. Each distinct tuple type has a fixed number of members, but the number of members in one tuple type can differ from the number of members in another.

A tuple is most useful when we want to combine some data into a single object but do not want to bother to define a data structure to represent those data. Table 17.1 lists the operations that tuples support. The tuple type, along with its companion types and functions, are defined in the tuple header.

> *Note* A tuple can be thought of as a "quick and dirty" data structure.

17.1.1 Defining and Initializing tuples

When we define a tuple, we name the type(s) of each of its members:

```
tuple<size_t, size_t, size_t> threeD;   // all three members set to 0
tuple<string, vector<double>, int, list<int>>
    someVal("constants", {3.14, 2.718}, 42, {0,1,2,3,4,5});
```

When we create a tuple object, we can use the default tuple constructor, which value initializes (§ 3.3.1, p. 98) each member, or we can supply an initializer for each member as we do in the initialization of someVal. This tuple constructor is explicit (§ 7.5.4, p. 296), so we must use the direct initialization syntax:

```
tuple<size_t, size_t, size_t> threeD = {1,2,3};   // error
tuple<size_t, size_t, size_t> threeD{1,2,3};      // ok
```

Alternatively, similar to the make_pair function (§ 11.2.3, p. 428), the library defines a make_tuple function that generates a tuple object:

```
// tuple that represents a bookstore transaction: ISBN, count, price per book
auto item = make_tuple("0-999-78345-X", 3, 20.00);
```

Like make_pair, the make_tuple function uses the types of the supplied initializers to infer the type of the tuple. In this case, item is a tuple whose type is tuple<const char*, int, double>.

Table 17.1: Operations on `tuples`

`tuple<T1, T2, ..., Tn> t;`

 t is a `tuple` with as many members as there are types T1 ... Tn. The members are value initialized (§ 3.3.1, p. 98).

`tuple<T1, T2, ..., Tn> t(v1, v2, ..., vn);`

 t is a `tuple` with types T1 ... Tn in which each member is initialized from the corresponding initializer, v_i. This constructor is `explicit` (§ 7.5.4, p. 296).

`make_tuple(v1, v2, ..., vn)`

 Returns a `tuple` initialized from the given initializers. The type of the `tuple` is inferred from the types of the initializers.

`t1 == t2`
`t1 != t2`
 Two `tuples` are equal if they have the same number of members and if each pair of members are equal. Uses each member's underlying `==` operator. Once a member is found to be unequal, subsequent members are not tested.

`t1` *relop* `t2` Relational operations on `tuples` using dictionary ordering (§ 9.2.7, p. 340). The `tuples` must have the same number of members. Members of t1 are compared with the corresponding members from t2 using the `<` operator

`get<i>(t)` Returns a reference to the ith data member of t; if t is an lvalue, the result is an lvalue reference; otherwise, it is an rvalue reference. All members of a `tuple` are `public`.

`tuple_size<`*tupleType*`>::value`

 A class template that can be instantiated by a tuple type and has a `public constexpr static` data member named `value` of type `size_t` that is number of members in the specified `tuple` type.

`tuple_element<i,` *tupleType*`>::type`

 A class template that can be instantiated by an integral constant and a tuple type and has a `public` member named `type` that is the type of the specified members in the specified `tuple` type.

Accessing the Members of a `tuple`

A `pair` always has two members, which makes it possible for the library to give these members names (i.e., `first` and `second`). No such naming convention is possible for `tuple` because there is no limit on the number of members a `tuple` type can have. As a result, the members are unnamed. Instead, we access the members of a `tuple` through a library function template named **get**. To use `get` we must specify an explicit template argument (§ 16.2.2, p. 682), which is the position of the member we want to access. We pass a `tuple` object to `get`, which returns a reference to the specified member:

```
auto book = get<0>(item);      // returns the first member of item
auto cnt = get<1>(item);       // returns the second member of item
auto price = get<2>(item)/cnt; // returns the last member of item
get<2>(item) *= 0.8;           // apply 20% discount
```

The value inside the brackets must be an integral constant expression (§ 2.4.4, p. 65). As usual, we count from 0, meaning that `get<0>` is the first member.

If we have a `tuple` whose precise type details we don't know, we can use two auxilliary class templates to find the number and types of the `tuple`'s members:

```
typedef decltype(item) trans; // trans is the type of item
// returns the number of members in object's of type trans
size_t sz = tuple_size<trans>::value;   // returns 3
// cnt has the same type as the second member in item
tuple_element<1, trans>::type cnt = get<1>(item); // cnt is an int
```

To use `tuple_size` or `tuple_element`, we need to know the type of a `tuple` object. As usual, the easiest way to determine an object's type is to use `decltype` (§ 2.5.3, p. 70). Here, we use `decltype` to define a type alias for the type of `item`, which we use to instantiate both templates.

`tuple_size` has a `public static` data member named `value` that is the number or members in the specified `tuple`. The `tuple_element` template takes an index as well as a tuple type. `tuple_element` has a `public` type member named `type` that is the type of the specified member of the specified `tuple` type. Like `get`, `tuple_element` uses indices starting at 0.

Relational and Equality Operators

The `tuple` relational and equality operators behave similarly to the corresponding operations on containers (§ 9.2.7, p. 340). These operators execute pairwise on the members of the left-hand and right-hand `tuples`. We can compare two `tuples` only if they have the same number of members. Moreover, to use the equality or inequality operators, it must be legal to compare each pair of members using the `==` operator; to use the relational operators, it must be legal to use `<`. For example:

```
tuple<string, string> duo("1", "2");
tuple<size_t, size_t> twoD(1, 2);
bool b = (duo == twoD); // error: can't compare a size_t and a string

tuple<size_t, size_t, size_t> threeD(1, 2, 3);
b = (twoD < threeD);      // error: differing number of members

tuple<size_t, size_t> origin(0, 0);
b = (origin < twoD);       // ok: b is true
```

 Because `tuple` defines the `<` and `==` operators, we can pass sequences of `tuples` to the algorithms and can use a `tuple` as key type in an ordered container.

EXERCISES SECTION 17.1.1

Exercise 17.1: Define a `tuple` that holds three `int` values and initialize the members to `10`, `20`, and `30`.

Exercise 17.2: Define a `tuple` that holds a `string`, a `vector<string>`, and a `pair<string, int>`.

Exercise 17.3: Rewrite the `TextQuery` programs from § 12.3 (p. 484) to use a `tuple` instead of the `QueryResult` class. Explain which design you think is better and why.

17.1.2   Using a `tuple` to Return Multiple Values

A common use of `tuple` is to return multiple values from a function. For example, our bookstore might be one of several stores in a chain. Each store would have a transaction file that holds data on each book that the store recently sold. We might want to look at the sales for a given book in all the stores.

We'll assume that we have a file of transactions for each store. Each of these per-store transaction files will contain all the transactions for each book grouped together. We'll further assume that some other function reads these transaction files, builds a `vector<Sales_data>` for each store, and puts those `vectors` in a vector of vectors:

```
//  each element in files holds the transactions for a particular store
vector<vector<Sales_data>> files;
```

We'll write a function that will search `files` looking for the stores that sold a given book. For each store that has a matching transaction, we'll create a `tuple` to hold the index of that store and two iterators. The index will be the position of the matching store in `files`. The iterators will mark the first and one past the last record for the given book in that store's `vector<Sales_data>`.

A Function That Returns a `tuple`

We'll start by writing the function to find a given book. This function's arguments are the `vector` of vectors just described, and a `string` that represents the book's ISBN. Our function will return a `vector` of `tuples` that will have an entry for each store with at least one sale for the given book:

```
//  matches has three members: an index of a store and iterators into that store's vector
typedef tuple<vector<Sales_data>::size_type,
              vector<Sales_data>::const_iterator,
              vector<Sales_data>::const_iterator> matches;
//  files holds the transactions for every store
//  findBook returns a vector with an entry for each store that sold the given book
vector<matches>
findBook(const vector<vector<Sales_data>> &files,
         const string &book)
{
    vector<matches> ret;   //  initially empty
    //  for each store find the range of matching books, if any
    for (auto it = files.cbegin(); it != files.cend(); ++it) {
        //  find the range of Sales_data that have the same ISBN
        auto found = equal_range(it->cbegin(), it->cend(),
                                 book, compareIsbn);
        if (found.first != found.second)   //  this store had sales
            //  remember the index of this store and the matching range
            ret.push_back(make_tuple(it - files.cbegin(),
                                     found.first, found.second));
    }
    return ret; //  empty if no matches found
}
```

The `for` loop iterates through the elements in `files`. Those elements are themselves `vector`s. Inside the `for` we call a library algorithm named `equal_range`, which operates like the associative container member of the same name (§ 11.3.5, p. 439). The first two arguments to `equal_range` are iterators denoting an input sequence (§ 10.1, p. 376). The third argument is a value. By default, `equal_range` uses the `<` operator to compare elements. Because `Sales_data` does not have a `<` operator, we pass a pointer to the `compareIsbn` function (§ 11.2.2, p. 425).

The `equal_range` algorithm returns a `pair` of iterators that denote a range of elements. If `book` is not found, then the iterators will be equal, indicating that the range is empty. Otherwise, the `first` member of the returned `pair` will denote the first matching transaction and `second` will be one past the last.

Using a `tuple` Returned by a Function

Once we have built our `vector` of stores with matching transactions, we need to process these transactions. In this program, we'll report the total sales results for each store that has a matching sale:

```
void reportResults(istream &in, ostream &os,
                   const vector<vector<Sales_data>> &files)
{
    string s;    // book to look for
    while (in >> s) {
        auto trans = findBook(files, s);   // stores that sold this book
        if (trans.empty()) {
            cout << s << " not found in any stores" << endl;
            continue;   // get the next book to look for
        }
        for (const auto &store : trans)    // for every store with a sale
            // get<n> returns the specified member from the tuple in store
            os << "store " << get<0>(store) << " sales: "
               << accumulate(get<1>(store), get<2>(store),
                             Sales_data(s))
               << endl;
    }
}
```

The `while` loop repeatedly reads the `istream` named `in` to get the next book to process. We call `findBook` to see if `s` is present, and assign the results to `trans`. We use `auto` to simplify writing the type of `trans`, which is a `vector` of `tuples`.

If `trans` is empty, there were no sales for `s`. In this case, we print a message and return to the `while` to get the next book to look for.

The `for` loop binds `store` to each element in `trans`. Because we don't intend to change the elements in `trans`, we declare `store` as a reference to `const`. We use `get` to print the relevant data: `get<0>` is the index of the corresponding store, `get<1>` is the iterator denoting the first transaction, and `get<2>` is the iterator one past the last.

Because `Sales_data` defines the addition operator (§ 14.3, p. 560), we can use the library `accumulate` algorithm (§ 10.2.1, p. 379) to sum the transactions. We pass a `Sales_data` object initialized by the `Sales_data` constructor that takes a `string` (§ 7.1.4, p. 264) as the starting point for the summation. That constructor initializes the bookNo member from the given `string` and the units_sold and revenue members to zero.

17.2 The bitset Type

In § 4.8 (p. 152) we covered the built-in operators that treat an integral operand as a collection of bits. The standard library defines the **bitset** class to make it easier to use bit operations and possible to deal with collections of bits that are larger than the longest integral type. The bitset class is defined in the bitset header.

17.2.1 Defining and Initializing bitsets

Table 17.2 (overleaf) lists the constructors for bitset. The bitset class is a class template that, like the array class, has a fixed size (§ 9.2.4, p. 336). When we define a bitset, we say how many bits the bitset will contain:

```
bitset<32> bitvec(1U); //  32 bits; low-order bit is 1, remaining bits are 0
```

The size must be a constant expression (§ 2.4.4, p. 65). This statement defines bitvec as a bitset that holds 32 bits. Just as with the elements of a vector, the bits in a bitset are not named. Instead, we refer to them positionally. The bits are numbered starting at 0. Thus, bitvec has bits numbered 0 through 31. The bits starting at 0 are referred to as the **low-order** bits, and those ending at 31 are referred to as **high-order** bits.

Initializing a bitset from an unsigned Value

When we use an integral value as an initializer for a bitset, that value is converted to unsigned long long and is treated as a bit pattern. The bits in the bitset are a copy of that pattern. If the size of the bitset is greater than the number of bits in an unsigned long long, then the remaining high-order bits

---

Table 17.2: Ways to Initialize a `bitset`	
`bitset<n> b;`	b has n bits; each bit is 0. This constructor is a `constexpr` (§ 7.5.6, p. 299).
`bitset<n> b(u);`	b is a copy of the n low-order bits of `unsigned long long` value u. If n is greater than the size of an `unsigned long long`, the high-order bits beyond those in the `unsigned long long` are set to zero. This constructor is a `constexpr` (§ 7.5.6, p. 299).
`bitset<n> b(s, pos, m, zero, one);`	b is a copy of the m characters from the `string` s starting at position pos. s may contain only the characters zero and one; if s contains any other character, throws `invalid_argument`. The characters are stored in b as zeor and one, respectively. pos defaults to 0, m defaults to `string::npos`, zero defaults to `'0'`, and one defaults to `'1'`.
`bitset<n> b(cp, pos, m, zero, one);`	Same as the previous constructor, but copies from the character array to which cp points. If m is not supplied, then cp must point to a C-style string. If m is supplied, there must be at least m characters that are zero or one starting at cp.
The constructors that take a `string` or character pointer are `explicit` (§ 7.5.4, p. 296). The ability to specify alternate characters for 0 and 1 was added in the new standard.	

are set to zero. If the size of the `bitset` is less than that number of bits, then only the low-order bits from the given value are used; the high-order bits beyond the size of the `bitset` object are discarded:

```
// bitvec1 is smaller than the initializer; high-order bits from the initializer are discarded
bitset<13> bitvec1(0xbeef);   // bits are 1111011101111
// bitvec2 is larger than the initializer; high-order bits in bitvec2 are set to zero
bitset<20> bitvec2(0xbeef);   // bits are 00001011111011101111
// on machines with 64-bit long long 0ULL is 64 bits of 0, so ~0ULL is 64 ones
bitset<128> bitvec3(~0ULL);   // bits 0...63 are one; 63...127 are zero
```

Initializing a `bitset` from a `string`

We can initialize a `bitset` from either a `string` or a pointer to an element in a character array. In either case, the characters represent the bit pattern directly. As usual, when we use strings to represent numbers, the characters with the lowest indices in the string correspond to the high-order bits, and vice versa:

```
bitset<32> bitvec4("1100");   // bits 2 and 3 are 1, all others are 0
```

If the `string` contains fewer characters than the size of the `bitset`, the high-order bits are set to zero.

The indexing conventions of `strings` and `bitsets` are inversely related: The character in the `string` with the highest subscript (the rightmost character) is used to initialize the low-order bit in the `bitset` (the bit with subscript 0). When you initialize a `bitset` from a `string`, it is essential to remember this difference.

We need not use the entire string as the initial value for the bitset. Instead, we can use a substring as the initializer:

```
string str("1111111000000011001101");
bitset<32> bitvec5(str, 5, 4); // four bits starting at str[5], 1100
bitset<32> bitvec6(str, str.size()-4); // use last four characters
```

Here bitvec5 is initialized by the substring in str starting at str[5] and continuing for four positions. As usual, the right-most character of the substring represents the lowest-order bit. Thus, bitvec5 is initialized with bit positions 3 through 0 set to 1100 and the remaining bits set to 0. The initializer for bitvec6 passes a string and a starting point, so bitvec6 is initialized from the characters in str starting four from the end of str. The remainder of the bits in bitvec6 are initialized to zero. We can view these initializations as

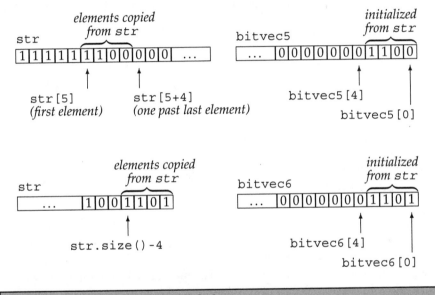

17.2.2 Operations on bitsets

The bitset operations (Table 17.3 (overleaf)) define various ways to test or set one or more bits. The bitset class also supports the bitwise operators that we covered in § 4.8 (p. 152). The operators have the same meaning when applied to bitset objects as the built-in operators have when applied to unsigned operands.

Table 17.3: `bitset` Operations	
`b.any()`	Is any bit in b on?
`b.all()`	Are all the bits in b on?
`b.none()`	Are no bits in b on?
`b.count()`	Number of bits in b that are on.
`b.size()`	A `constexpr` function (§ 2.4.4, p. 65) that returns the number of bits in b.
`b.test(pos)`	Returns `true` if bit at position pos is on, `false` otherwise.
`b.set(pos, v)` `b.set()`	Sets the bit at position pos to the `bool` value v. v defaults to `true`. If no arguments, turns on all the bits in b.
`b.reset(pos)` `b.reset()`	Turns off the bit at position pos or turns off all the bits in b.
`b.flip(pos)` `b.flip()`	Changes the state of the bit at position pos or of every bit in b.
`b[pos]`	Gives access to the bit in b at position pos; if b is const, then `b[pos]` returns a `bool` value `true` if the bit is on, `false` otherwise.
`b.to_ulong()` `b.to_ullong()`	Returns an unsigned `long` or an unsigned `long long` with the same bits as in b. Throws `overflow_error` if the bit pattern in b won't fit in the indicated result type.
`b.to_string(zero, one)`	
	Returns a `string` representing the bit pattern in b. zero and one default to `'0'` and `'1'` and are used to represent the bits 0 and 1 in b.
`os << b`	Prints the bits in b as the characters 1 or 0 to the stream os.
`is >> b`	Reads characters from is into b. Reading stops when the next character is not a 1 or 0 or when `b.size()` bits have been read.

Several operations—count, size, all, any, and none—take no arguments and return information about the state of the entire `bitset`. Others—set, reset, and flip—change the state of the `bitset`. The members that change the `bitset` are overloaded. In each case, the version that takes no arguments applies the given operation to the entire set; the versions that take a position apply the operation to the given bit:

```
bitset<32> bitvec(1U);  //  32 bits; low-order bit is 1, remaining bits are 0
bool is_set = bitvec.any();       //  true, one bit is set
bool is_not_set = bitvec.none();  //  false, one bit is set
bool all_set = bitvec.all();      //  false, only one bit is set
size_t onBits = bitvec.count();   //  returns 1
size_t sz = bitvec.size();        //  returns 32
bitvec.flip();      //  reverses the value of all the bits in bitvec
bitvec.reset();     //  sets all the bits to 0
bitvec.set();       //  sets all the bits to 1
```

The any operation returns `true` if one or more bits of the `bitset` object are turned on—that is, are equal to 1. Conversely, none returns `true` if all the bits are zero. The new standard introduced the all operation, which returns `true` if all the bits are on. The count and size operations return a `size_t` (§ 3.5.2, p. 116) equal to the number of bits that are set, or the total number of bits in the object, respectively. The `size` function is a `constexpr` and so can be used where a constant expression is required (§ 2.4.4, p. 65).

The `flip`, `set`, `reset`, and `test` members let us read or write the bit at a given position:

```
bitvec.flip(0);      // reverses the value of the first bit
bitvec.set(bitvec.size() - 1);   // turns on the last bit
bitvec.set(0, 0);   // turns off the first bit
bitvec.reset(i);   // turns off the ith bit
bitvec.test(0);      // returns false because the first bit is off
```

The subscript operator is overloaded on `const`. The `const` version returns a `bool` value `true` if the bit at the given index is on, `false` otherwise. The nonconst version returns a special type defined by `bitset` that lets us manipulate the bit value at the given index position:

```
bitvec[0] = 0;              // turn off the bit at position 0
bitvec[31] = bitvec[0];    // set the last bit to the same value as the first bit
bitvec[0].flip();          // flip the value of the bit at position 0
~bitvec[0];                 // equivalent operation; flips the bit at position 0
bool b = bitvec[0];        // convert the value of bitvec[0] to bool
```

Retrieving the Value of a `bitset`

The `to_ulong` and `to_ullong` operations return a value that holds the same bit pattern as the `bitset` object. We can use these operations only if the size of the `bitset` is less than or equal to the corresponding size, unsigned `long` for `to_ulong` and unsigned `long long` for `to_ullong`:

```
unsigned long ulong = bitvec3.to_ulong();
cout << "ulong = " << ulong << endl;
```

 These operations throw an `overflow_error` exception (§ 5.6, p. 193) if the value in the `bitset` does not fit in the specified type.

`bitset` IO Operators

The input operator reads characters from the input stream into a temporary object of type `string`. It reads until it has read as many characters as the size of the corresponding `bitset`, or it encounters a character other than 1 or 0, or it encounters end-of-file or an input error. The `bitset` is then initialized from that temporary `string` (§ 17.2.1, p. 724). If fewer characters are read than the size of the `bitset`, the high-order bits are, as usual, set to 0.

The output operator prints the bit pattern in a `bitset` object:

```
bitset<16> bits;
cin >> bits;   // read up to 16 1 or 0 characters from cin
cout << "bits: " << bits << endl; // print what we just read
```

Using `bitset`s

To illustrate using `bitset`s, we'll reimplement the grading code from § 4.8 (p. 154) that used an `unsigned long` to represent the pass/fail quiz results for 30 students:

```
bool status;
//  version using bitwise operators
unsigned long quizA = 0;       //  this value is used as a collection of bits
quizA |= 1UL << 27;            //  indicate student number 27 passed
status = quizA & (1UL << 27);  //  check how student number 27 did
quizA &= ~(1UL << 27);         //  student number 27 failed

//  equivalent actions using the bitset library
bitset<30> quizB;         //  allocate one bit per student; all bits initialized to 0
quizB.set(27);            //  indicate student number 27 passed
status = quizB[27];       //  check how student number 27 did
quizB.reset(27);          //  student number 27 failed
```

EXERCISES SECTION 17.2.2

Exercise 17.10: Using the sequence 1, 2, 3, 5, 8, 13, 21, initialize a `bitset` that has a 1 bit in each position corresponding to a number in this sequence. Default initialize another `bitset` and write a small program to turn on each of the appropriate bits.

Exercise 17.11: Define a data structure that contains an integral object to track responses to a true/false quiz containing 10 questions. What changes, if any, would you need to make in your data structure if the quiz had 100 questions?

Exercise 17.12: Using the data structure from the previous question, write a function that takes a question number and a value to indicate a true/false answer and updates the quiz results accordingly.

Exercise 17.13: Write an integral object that contains the correct answers for the true/false quiz. Use it to generate grades on the quiz for the data structure from the previous two exercises.

17.3 Regular Expressions

A **regular expression** is a way of describing a sequence of characters. Regular expressions are a stunningly powerful computational device. However, describing the languages used to define regular expressions is well beyond the scope of this Primer. Instead, we'll focus on how to use the C++ regular-expression library (RE library), which is part of the new library. The RE library, which is defined in the `regex` header, involves several components, listed in Table 17.4.

C++ 11

If you are not already familiar with using regular expressions, you might want to skim this section to get an idea of the kinds of things regular expressions can do.

Table 17.4: Regular Expression Library Components	
regex	Class that represents a regular expression
regex_match	Matches a sequence of characters against a regular expression
regex_search	Finds the first subsequence that matches the regular expression
regex_replace	Replaces a regular expression using a given format
sregex_iterator	Iterator adaptor that calls regex_search to iterate through the matches in a string
smatch	Container class that holds the results of searching a string
ssub_match	Results for a matched subexpression in a string

The **regex** class represents a regular expression. Aside from initialization and assignment, regex has few operations. The operations on regex are listed in Table 17.6 (p. 731).

The functions **regex_match** and **regex_search** determine whether a given character sequence matches a given regex. The regex_match function returns true if the entire input sequence matches the expression; regex_search returns true if there is a substring in the input sequence that matches. There is also a regex_replace function that we'll describe in § 17.3.4 (p. 741).

The arguments to the regex functions are described in Table 17.5 (overleaf). These functions return a bool and are overloaded: One version takes an additional argument of type **smatch**. If present, these functions store additional information about a successful match in the given smatch object.

17.3.1 Using the Regular Expression Library

As a fairly simple example, we'll look for words that violate a well-known spelling rule of thumb, "*i* before *e* except after *c*":

```
// find the characters ei that follow a character other than c
string pattern("[^c]ei");
// we want the whole word in which our pattern appears
pattern = "[[:alpha:]]*" + pattern + "[[:alpha:]]*";
regex r(pattern); // construct a regex to find pattern
smatch results;    // define an object to hold the results of a search
// define a string that has text that does and doesn't match pattern
string test_str = "receipt freind theif receive";
// use r to find a match to pattern in test_str
if (regex_search(test_str, results, r)) // if there is a match
    cout << results.str() << endl;      // print the matching word
```

We start by defining a string to hold the regular expression we want to find. The regular expression [^c] says we want any character that is not a 'c', and [^c]ei says we want any such letter that is followed by the letters ei. This pattern describes strings containing exactly three characters. We want the entire word that contains this pattern. To match the word, we need a regular expression that will match the letters that come before and after our three-letter pattern.

Table 17.5: Arguments to `regex_search` and `regex_match`
Note: These operations return `bool` indicating whether a match was found.
(*seq*, m, r, mft)   Look for the regular expression in the `regex` object r in the character (*seq*, r, mft)   sequence *seq*. *seq* can be a `string`, a pair of iterators denoting a range, or a pointer to a null-terminated character array. m is a *match* object, which is used to hold details about the match. m and *seq* must have compatible types (see § 17.3.1 (p. 733)). mft is an optional `regex_constants::match_flag_type` value. These values, listed in Table 17.13 (p. 744), affect the match process.

That regular expression consists of zero or more letters followed by our original three-letter pattern followed by zero or more additional characters. By default, the regular-expression language used by `regex` objects is ECMAScript. In ECMAScript, the pattern `[[:alpha:]]` matches any alphabetic character, and the symbols + and * signify that we want "one or more" or "zero or more" matches, respectively. Thus, `[[:alpha:]]*` will match zero or more characters.

Having stored our regular expression in `pattern`, we use it to initialize a `regex` object named `r`. We next define a `string` that we'll use to test our regular expression. We initialize `test_str` with words that match our pattern (e.g., "freind" and "theif") and words (e.g., "receipt" and "receive") that don't. We also define an `smatch` object named `results`, which we will pass to `regex_search`. If a match is found, `results` will hold the details about where the match occurred.

Next we call `regex_search`. If `regex_search` finds a match, it returns `true`. We use the `str` member of `results` to print the part of `test_str` that matched our pattern. The `regex_search` function stops looking as soon as it finds a matching substring in the input sequence. Thus, the output will be

```
freind
```

§ 17.3.2 (p. 734) will show how to find all the matches in the input.

Specifying Options for a `regex` Object

When we define a `regex` or call `assign` on a `regex` to give it a new value, we can specify one or more flags that affect how the `regex` operates. These flags control the processing done by that object. The last six flags listed in Table 17.6 indicate the language in which the regular expression is written. Exactly one of the flags that specify a language must be set. By default, the `ECMAScript` flag is set, which causes the `regex` to use the ECMA-262 specification, which is the regular expression language that many Web browsers use.

The other three flags let us specify language-independent aspects of the regular-expression processing. For example, we can indicate that we want the regular expression to be matched in a case-independent manner.

As one example, we can use the `icase` flag to find file names that have a particular file extension. Most operating systems recognize extensions in a case-independent manner—we can store a C++ program in a file that ends in `.cc`, or

	Table 17.6: `regex` (and `wregex`) Operations
`regex r(re)` `regex r(re, f)`	*re* represents a regular expression and can be a `string`, a pair of iterators denoting a range of characters, a pointer to a null-terminated character array, a character pointer and a count, or a braced list of characters. `f` are flags that specify how the object will execute. `f` is set from the values listed below. If `f` is not specified, it defaults to `ECMAScript`.
`r1 = re`	Replace the regular expression in `r1` with *re*. *re* represents a regular expression and can be another `regex`, a `string`, a pointer to a null-terminated character array, or a braced list of characters.
`r1.assign(re, f)`	Same effect as using the assignment operator (=). *re* and optional flag `f` same as corresponding arguments to `regex` constructors.
`r.mark_count()`	Number of subexpressions (which we'll cover in § 17.3.3 (p. 738)) in `r`.
`r.flags()`	Returns the flags set for `r`.

*Note: Constructors and assignment operations may throw exceptions of type **`regex_error`**.*

Flags Specified When a `regex` Is Defined
Defined in `regex` and `regex_constants::syntax_option_type`

`icase`	Ignore case during the match
`nosubs`	Don't store subexpression matches
`optimize`	Favor speed of execution over speed of construction
`ECMAScript`	Use grammar as specified by ECMA-262
`basic`	Use POSIX basic regular-expression grammar
`extended`	Use POSIX extended regular-expression grammar
`awk`	Use grammar from the POSIX version of the *awk* language
`grep`	Use grammar from the POSIX version of `grep`
`egrep`	Use grammar from the POSIX version of `egrep`

`.Cc`, or `.cC`, or `.CC`. We'll write a regular expression to recognize any of these along with other common file extensions as follows:

```
//  one or more alphanumeric characters followed by a '.' followed by "cpp" or "cxx" or "cc"
regex r("[[:alnum:]]+\\.(cpp|cxx|cc)$", regex::icase);
smatch results;
string filename;
while (cin >> filename)
    if (regex_search(filename, results, r))
        cout << results.str() << endl;  // print the current match
```

This expression will match a string of one or more letters or digits followed by a period and followed by one of three file extensions. The regular expression will match the file extensions regardless of case.

Just as there are special characters in C++ (§ 2.1.3, p. 39), regular-expression languages typically also have special characters. For example, the dot (`.`) character usually matches any character. As we do in C++, we can escape the special nature of a character by preceding it with a backslash. Because the backslash is also a special character in C++, we must use a second backslash inside a string literal to indicate to C++ that we want a backslash. Hence, we must write `\\.` to represent a regular expression that will match a period.

Errors in Specifying or Using a Regular Expression

We can think of a regular expression as itself a "program" in a simple programming language. That language is not interpreted by the C++ compiler. Instead, a regular expression is "compiled" at run time when a `regex` object is initialized with or assigned a new pattern. As with any programming language, it is possible that the regular expressions we write can have errors.

 It is important to realize that the syntactic correctness of a regular expression is evaluated at run time.

If we make a mistake in writing a regular expression, then at *run time* the library will throw an exception (§ 5.6, p. 193) of type **regex_error**. Like the standard exception types, `regex_error` has a `what` operation that describes the error that occurred (§ 5.6.2, p. 195). A `regex_error` also has a member named `code` that returns a numeric code corresponding to the type of error that was encountered. The values `code` returns are implementation defined. The standard errors that the RE library can throw are listed in Table 17.7.

For example, we might inadvertently omit a bracket in a pattern:

```
try {
    //  error: missing close bracket after alnum; the constructor will throw
    regex r("[[:alnum:]+\\.(cpp|cxx|cc)$", regex::icase);
} catch (regex_error e)
    { cout << e.what() << "\ncode: " << e.code() << endl; }
```

When run on our system, this program generates

```
regex_error(error_brack):
The expression contained mismatched [ and ].
code: 4
```

Table 17.7: Regular Expression Error Conditions	
Defined in `regex` and in `regex_constants::error_type`	
`error_collate`	Invalid collating element request
`error_ctype`	Invalid character class
`error_escape`	Invalid escape character or trailing escape
`error_backref`	Invalid back reference
`error_brack`	Mismatched bracket ([or])
`error_paren`	Mismatched parentheses ((or))
`error_brace`	Mismatched brace ({ or })
`error_badbrace`	Invalid range inside a { }
`error_range`	Invalid character range (e.g., [z-a])
`error_space`	Insufficient memory to handle this regular expression
`error_badrepeat`	A repetition character (*, ?, +, or {) was not preceded by a valid regular expression
`error_complexity`	The requested match is too complex
`error_stack`	Insufficient memory to evaluate a match

Our compiler defines the code member to return the position of the error as listed in Table 17.7, counting, as usual, from zero.

ADVICE: AVOID CREATING UNNECESSARY REGULAR EXPRESSIONS

As we've seen, the "program" that a regular expression represents is compiled at run time, not at compile time. Compiling a regular expression can be a surprisingly slow operation, especially if you're using the extended regular-expression grammar or are using complicated expressions. As a result, constructing a regex object and assigning a new regular expression to an existing regex can be time-consuming. To minimize this overhead, you should try to avoid creating more regex objects than needed. In particular, if you use a regular expression in a loop, you should create it outside the loop rather than recompiling it on each iteration.

Regular Expression Classes and the Input Sequence Type

We can search any of several types of input sequence. The input can be ordinary char data or wchar_t data and those characters can be stored in a library string or in an array of char (or the wide character versions, wstring or array of wchar_t). The RE library defines separate types that correspond to these differing types of input sequences.

For example, the regex class holds regular expressions of type char. The library also defines a wregex class that holds type wchar_t and has all the same operations as regex. The only difference is that the initializers of a wregex must use wchar_t instead of char.

The match and iterator types (which we will cover in the following sections) are more specific. These types differ not only by the character type, but also by whether the sequence is in a library string or an array: smatch represents string input sequences; cmatch, character array sequences; wsmatch, wide string (wstring) input; and wcmatch, arrays of wide characters.

Table 17.8: Regular Expression Library Classes	
If Input Sequence Has Type	**Use Regular Expression Classes**
string	regex, smatch, ssub_match, and sregex_iterator
const char*	regex, cmatch, csub_match, and cregex_iterator
wstring	wregex, wsmatch, wssub_match, and wsregex_iterator
const wchar_t*	wregex, wcmatch, wcsub_match, and wcregex_iterator

The important point is that the RE library types we use must match the type of the input sequence. Table 17.8 indicates which types correspond to which kinds of input sequences. For example:

```
regex r("[[:alnum:]]+\\.(cpp|cxx|cc)$", regex::icase);
smatch results;  // will match a string input sequence, but not char*
if (regex_search("myfile.cc", results, r)) // error: char* input
    cout << results.str() << endl;
```

The (C++) compiler will reject this code because the type of the match argument and the type of the input sequence do not match. If we want to search a character array, then we must use a cmatch object:

```
cmatch results;   // will match character array input sequences
if (regex_search("myfile.cc", results, r))
    cout << results.str() << endl;   // print the current match
```

In general, our programs will use string input sequences and the corresponding string versions of the RE library components.

17.3.2   The Match and Regex Iterator Types

The program on page 729 that found violations of the "*i* before *e* except after *c*" grammar rule printed only the first match in its input sequence. We can get all the matches by using an **sregex_iterator**. The regex iterators are iterator adaptors (§ 9.6, p. 368) that are bound to an input sequence and a regex object. As described in Table 17.8 (on the previous page), there are specific regex iterator types that correspond to each of the different types of input sequences. The iterator operations are described in Table 17.9 (p. 736).

When we bind an sregex_iterator to a string and a regex object, the iterator is automatically positioned on the first match in the given string. That is, the sregex_iterator constructor calls regex_search on the given string and regex. When we dereference the iterator, we get an smatch object corresponding to the results from the most recent search. When we increment the iterator, it calls regex_search to find the next match in the input string.

Using an **sregex_iterator**

As an example, we'll extend our program to find all the violations of the "*i* before *e* except after *c*" grammar rule in a file of text. We'll assume that the string named file holds the entire contents of the input file that we want to search. This version of the program will use the same pattern as our original one, but will use a sregex_iterator to do the search:

```
//  find the characters ei that follow a character other than c
string pattern("[^c]ei");
//  we want the whole word in which our pattern appears
pattern = "[[:alpha:]]*" + pattern + "[[:alpha:]]*";
regex r(pattern, regex::icase); //  we'll ignore case in doing the match
//  it will repeatedly call regex_search to find all matches in file
for (sregex_iterator it(file.begin(), file.end(), r), end_it;
        it != end_it; ++it)
        cout << it->str() << endl; //  matched word
```

The for loop iterates through each match to r inside file. The initializer in the for defines it and end_it. When we define it, the sregex_iterator constructor calls regex_search to position it on the first match in file. The empty sregex_iterator, end_it, acts as the off-the-end iterator. The increment in the for "advances" the iterator by calling regex_search. When we dereference the iterator, we get an smatch object representing the current match. We call the str member of the match to print the matching word.

We can think of this loop as jumping from match to match as illustrated in Figure 17.1.

Figure 17.1: Using an **sregex_iterator**

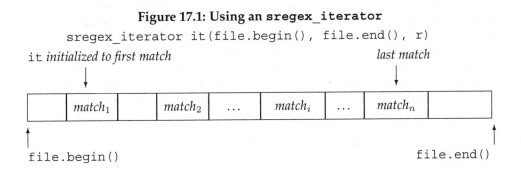

```
sregex_iterator it(file.begin(), file.end(), r)
```

it *initialized to first match*   *last match*

file.begin()   file.end()

Using the Match Data

If we run this loop on test_str from our original program, the output would be

```
freind
theif
```

However, finding just the words that match our expression is not so useful. If we ran the program on a larger input sequence—for example, on the text of this chapter—we'd want to see the context within which the word occurs, such as

```
hey read or write according to the type
        >>> being <<<
handled. The input operators ignore whi
```

In addition to letting us print the part of the input string that was matched, the match classes give us more detailed information about the match. The operations on these types are listed in Table 17.10 (p. 737) and Table 17.11 (p. 741).

Table 17.9: `sregex_iterator` Operations
These operations also apply to `cregex_iterator`,   **`wsregex_iterator`, and `wcregex_iterator`**

`sregex_iterator it(b, e, r);`	`it` is an `sregx_iterator` that iterates through the `string` denoted by iterators b and e. Calls `regex_search(b, e, r)` to position `it` on the first match in the input.
`sregex_iterator end;`	Off-the-end iterator for `sregex_iterator`.
`*it` `it->`	Returns a reference to the `smatch` object or a pointer to the `smatch` object from the most recent call to `regex_search`.
`++it` `it++`	Calls `regex_search` on the input sequence starting just after the current match. The prefix version returns a reference to the incremented iterator; postfix returns the old value.
`it1 == it2` `it1 != it2`	Two `sregex_iterator`s are equal if they are both the off-the-end iterator. Two non-end iterators are equal if they are constructed from the same input sequence and `regex` object.

We'll have more to say about the `smatch` and **`ssub_match`** types in the next section. For now, what we need to know is that these types let us see the context of a match. The match types have members named `prefix` and `suffix`, which return a `ssub_match` object representing the part of the input sequence ahead of and after the current match, respectively. A `ssub_match` object has members named `str` and `length`, which return the matched `string` and size of that `string`, respectively. We can use these operations to rewrite the loop of our grammar program:

```
//   same for loop header as before
for (sregex_iterator it(file.begin(), file.end(), r), end_it;
        it != end_it; ++it) {
    auto pos = it->prefix().length();     //   size of the prefix
    pos = pos > 40 ? pos - 40 : 0;        //   we want up to 40 characters
    cout << it->prefix().str().substr(pos)     //   last part of the prefix
        << "\n\t\t>>> " << it->str() << " <<<\n" //   matched word
        << it->suffix().str().substr(0, 40) //   first part of the suffix
        << endl;
}
```

The loop itself operates the same way as our previous program. What's changed is the processing inside the `for`, which is illustrated in Figure 17.2.

We call `prefix`, which returns an `ssub_match` object that represents the part of `file` ahead of the current match. We call `length` on that `ssub_match` to find out how many characters are in the part of `file` ahead of the match. Next we adjust `pos` to be the index of the character 40 from the end of the prefix. If the prefix has fewer than 40 characters, we set `pos` to 0, which means we'll print the entire prefix. We use `substr` (§ 9.5.1, p. 361) to print from the given position to the end of the prefix.

Figure 17.2: The smatch Object Representing a Particular Match

it->str()

when it *refers to the ith* smatch *object*

it->prefix().str()	*xxxeixxx*	it->suffix().str()

Having printed the characters that precede the match, we next print the match itself with some additional formatting so that the matched word will stand out in the output. After printing the matched portion, we print (up to) the first 40 characters in the part of file that comes after this match.

Table 17.10: smatch Operations	
These operations also apply to the cmatch, wsmatch, wcmatch and the corresponding csub_match, wssub_match, and wcsub_match types.	
m.ready()	true if m has been set by a call to regex_search or regex_match; false otherwise. Operations on m are undefined if ready returns false.
m.size()	Zero if the match failed; otherwise, one plus the number of subexpressions in the most recently matched regular expression.
m.empty()	true if m.size() is zero.
m.prefix()	An ssub_match representing the sequence before the match.
m.suffix()	An ssub_match representing the part after the end of the match.
m.format(...)	See Table 17.12 (p. 742).

In the operations that take an index, n defaults to zero and must be less than m.size(). The first submatch (the one with index 0) represents the overall match.

m.length(n)	Size of the nth matched subexpression.
m.position(n)	Distance of the nth subexpression from the start of the sequence.
m.str(n)	The matched string for the nth subexpression.
m[n]	ssub_match object corresponding to the nth subexpression.
m.begin(), m.end() m.cbegin(), m.cend()	Iterators across the sub_match elements in m. As usual, cbegin and cend return const_iterators.

EXERCISES SECTION 17.3.2

Exercise 17.17: Update your program so that it finds all the words in an input sequence that violiate the "ei" grammar rule.

Exercise 17.18: Revise your program to ignore words that contain "ei" but are not misspellings, such as "albeit" and "neighbor."

17.3.3 Using Subexpressions

A pattern in a regular expression often contains one or more **subexpressions**. A subexpression is a part of the pattern that itself has meaning. Regular-expression grammars typically use parentheses to denote subexpressions.

As an example, the pattern that we used to match C++ files (§ 17.3.1, p. 730) used parentheses to group the possible file extensions. Whenever we group alternatives using parentheses, we are also declaring that those alternatives form a subexpression. We can rewrite that expression so that it gives us access to the file name, which is the part of the pattern that precedes the period, as follows:

```
//   r has two subexpressions: the first is the part of the file name before the period
//   the second is the file extension
regex r("([[:alnum:]]+)\\.(cpp|cxx|cc)$", regex::icase);
```

Our pattern now has two parenthesized subexpressions:

- `([[:alnum:]]+)`, which is a sequence of one or more characters

- `(cpp| cxx| cc)`, which is the file extension

We can also rewrite the program from § 17.3.1 (p. 730) to print just the file name by changing the output statement:

```
if (regex_search(filename, results, r))
    cout << results.str(1) << endl;   // print the first subexpression
```

As in our original program, we call `regex_search` to look for our pattern `r` in the `string` named `filename`, and we pass the `smatch` object `results` to hold the results of the match. If the call succeeds, then we print the results. However, in this program, we print `str(1)`, which is the match for the first subexpression.

In addition to providing information about the overall match, the match objects provide access to each matched subexpression in the pattern. The submatches are accessed positionally. The first submatch, which is at position 0, represents the match for the entire pattern. Each subexpression appears in order thereafter. Hence, the file name, which is the first subexpression in our pattern, is at position 1, and the file extension is in position 2.

For example, if the file name is `foo.cpp`, then `results.str(0)` will hold `foo.cpp`; `results.str(1)` will be `foo`; and `results.str(2)` will be `cpp`. In this program, we want the part of the name before the period, which is the first subexpression, so we print `results.str(1)`.

Subexpressions for Data Validation

One common use for subexpressions is to validate data that must match a specific format. For example, U.S. phone numbers have ten digits, consisting of an area code and a seven-digit local number. The area code is often, but not always, enclosed in parentheses. The remaining seven digits can be separated by a dash, a dot, or a space; or not separated at all. We might want to allow data with any of these formats and reject numbers in other forms. We'll do a two-step process: First, we'll use a regular expression to find sequences that might be phone numbers and then we'll call a function to complete the validation of the data.

Before we write our phone number pattern, we need to describe a few more aspects of the ECMAScript regular-expression language:

- \{d} represents a single digit and \{d}{n} represents a sequence of *n* digits. (E.g., \{d}{3} matches a sequence of three digits.)

- A collection of characters inside square brackets allows a match to any of those characters. (E.g., [-.] matches a dash, a dot, or a space. Note that a dot has no special meaning inside brackets.)

- A component followed by '?' is optional. (E.g., \{d}{3}[-.]?\{d}{4} matches three digits followed by an optional dash, period, or space, followed by four more digits. This pattern would match 555-0132 or 555.0132 or 555 0132 or 5550132.)

- Like C++, ECMAScript uses a backslash to indicate that a character should represent itself, rather than its special meaning. Because our pattern includes parentheses, which are special characters in ECMAScript, we must represent the parentheses that are part of our pattern as \(or \).

Because backslash is a special character in C++, each place that a \ appears in the pattern, we must use a second backslash to indicate to C++ that we want a backslash. Hence, we write \\{d}{3} to represent the regular expression \{d}{3}.

In order to validate our phone numbers, we'll need access to the components of the pattern. For example, we'll want to verify that if a number uses an opening parenthesis for the area code, it also uses a close parenthesis after the area code. That is, we'd like to reject a number such as (908.555.1800.

To get at the components of the match, we need to define our regular expression using subexpressions. Each subexpression is marked by a pair of parentheses:

```
//  our overall expression has seven subexpressions: ( ddd ) separator ddd separator dddd
//  subexpressions 1, 3, 4, and 6 are optional; 2, 5, and 7 hold the number
"(\\()?(\\d{3})(\\))?([-. ])?(\\d{3})([-. ]?)(\\d{4})";
```

Because our pattern uses parentheses, and because we must escape backslashes, this pattern can be hard to read (and write!). The easiest way to read it is to pick off each (parenthesized) subexpression:

1. (\\()? an optional open parenthesis for the area code

2. (\\d{3}) the area code

3. (\\))? an optional close parenthesis for the area code

4. ([-.])? an optional separator after the area code

5. (\\d{3}) the next three digits of the number

6. ([-.])? another optional separator

7. (\\d{4}) the final four digits of the number

The following code uses this pattern to read a file and find data that match our overall phone pattern. It will call a function named `valid` to check whether the number has a valid format:

```
string phone =
    "(\\()?(\\d{3})(\\))?([-. ])?(\\d{3})([-. ]?)(\\d{4})";
regex r(phone);   // a regex to find our pattern
smatch m;
string s;
// read each record from the input file
while (getline(cin, s)) {
    // for each matching phone number
    for (sregex_iterator it(s.begin(), s.end(), r), end_it;
            it != end_it; ++it)
        // check whether the number's formatting is valid
        if (valid(*it))
            cout << "valid: " << it->str() << endl;
        else
            cout << "not valid: " << it->str() << endl;
}
```

Using the Submatch Operations

We'll use submatch operations, which are outlined in Table 17.11, to write the `valid` function. It is important to keep in mind that our `pattern` has seven subexpressions. As a result, each `smatch` object will contain eight `ssub_match` elements. The element at `[0]` represents the overall match; the elements `[1]` ... `[7]` represent each of the corresponding subexpressions.

When we call `valid`, we know that we have an overall match, but we do not know which of our optional subexpressions were part of that match. The `matched` member of the `ssub_match` corresponding to a particular subexpression is `true` if that subexpression is part of the overall match.

In a valid phone number, the area code is either fully parenthesized or not parenthesized at all. Therefore, the work `valid` does depends on whether the number starts with a parenthesis or not:

```
bool valid(const smatch& m)
{
    // if there is an open parenthesis before the area code
    if(m[1].matched)
        // the area code must be followed by a close parenthesis
        // and followed immediately by the rest of the number or a space
        return m[3].matched
            && (m[4].matched == 0 || m[4].str() == " ");
    else
        // then there can't be a close after the area code
        // the delimiters between the other two components must match
        return !m[3].matched
            && m[4].str() == m[6].str();
}
```

Table 17.11: Submatch Operations	
Note: These operations apply to **ssub_match, csub_match, wssub_match, wcsub_match**	
matched	A `public bool` data member that indicates whether this `ssub_match` was matched.
first second	`public` data members that are iterators to the start and one past the end of the matching sequence. If there was no match, then `first` and `second` are equal.
length()	The size of this match. Returns 0 if `matched` is `false`.
str()	Returns a `string` containing the matched portion of the input. Returns the empty `string` if `matched` is `false`.
s = ssub	Convert the `ssub_match` object `ssub` to the `string` s. Equivalent to s = `ssub.str()`. The conversion operator is not `explicit` (§ 14.9.1, p. 581).

We start by checking whether the first subexpression (i.e., the open parenthesis) matched. That subexpression is in m[1]. If it matched, then the number starts with an open parenthesis. In this case, the overall number is valid if the subexpression following the area code also matched (meaning that there was a close parenthesis after the area code). Moreover, if the number is correctly parenthesized, then the next character must be a space or the first digit in the next part of the number.

If m[1] didn't match (i.e., there was no open parenthesis), the subexpression following the area code must also be empty. If it's empty, then the number is valid if the remaining separators are equal and not otherwise.

EXERCISES SECTION 17.3.3

Exercise 17.19: Why is it okay to call m[4].str() without first checking whether m[4] was matched?

Exercise 17.20: Write your own version of the program to validate phone numbers.

Exercise 17.21: Rewrite your phone number program from § 8.3.2 (p. 323) to use the valid function defined in this section.

Exercise 17.22: Rewrite your phone program so that it allows any number of white-space characters to separate the three parts of a phone number.

Exercise 17.23: Write a regular expression to find zip codes. A zip code can have five or nine digits. The first five digits can be separated from the remaining four by a dash.

17.3.4 Using `regex_replace`

Regular expressions are often used when we need not only to find a given sequence but also to replace that sequence with another one. For example, we might want to translate U.S. phone numbers into the form "ddd.ddd.dddd," where the area code and next three digits are separated by a dot.

When we want to find and replace a regular expression in the input sequence, we call **regex_replace**. Like the search functions, regex_replace, which is described in Table 17.12, takes an input character sequence and a regex object. We must also pass a string that describes the output we want.

We compose a replacement string by including the characters we want, intermixed with subexpressions from the matched substring. In this case, we want to use the second, fifth, and seventh subexpressions in our replacement string. We'll ignore the first, third, fourth, and sixth, because these were used in the original formatting of the number but are not part of our replacement format. We refer to a particular subexpression by using a $ symbol followed by the index number for a subexpression:

```
string fmt = "$2.$5.$7"; // reformat numbers to ddd.ddd.dddd
```

We can use our regular-expression pattern and the replacement string as follows:

```
regex r(phone);   // a regex to find our pattern
string number = "(908) 555-1800";
cout << regex_replace(number, r, fmt) << endl;
```

The output from this program is

908.555.1800

Table 17.12: Regular Expression Replace Operations	
m.format(dest, *fmt*, mft) m.format(*fmt*, mft)	Produces formatted output using the format string *fmt*, the match in m, and the optional match_flag_type flags in mft. The first version writes to the output iterator dest (§ 10.5.1, p. 410) and takes *fmt* that is either a string or a pair of pointers denoting a range in a character array. The second version returns a string that holds the output and takes *fmt* that is a string or a pointer to a null-terminated character array. mft defaults to format_default.
regex_replace (dest, *seq*, r, *fmt*, mft) regex_replace (*seq*, r, *fmt*, mft)	Iterates through *seq*, using regex_search to find successive matches to regex r. Uses the format string *fmt* and optional match_flag_type flags in mft to produce its output. The first version writes to the output iterator dest, and takes a pair of iterators to denote *seq*. The second returns a string that holds the output and *seq* can be either a string or a pointer to a null-terminated character array. In all cases, *fmt* can be either a string or a pointer to a null-terminated character array, and mft defaults to match_default.

Replacing Only Part of the Input Sequence

A more interesting use of our regular-expression processing would be to replace phone numbers that are embedded in a larger file. For example, we might have a file of names and phone number that had data like this:

```
    morgan (201) 555-2368 862-555-0123
    drew (973)555.0130
    lee (609) 555-0132 2015550175 800.555-0000
```

that we want to transform to data like this:

```
    morgan 201.555.2368 862.555.0123
    drew 973.555.0130
    lee 609.555.0132 201.555.0175 800.555.0000
```

We can generate this transformation with the following program:

```
int main()
{
    string phone =
        "(\\()?(\\d{3})(\\))?([-. ])?(\\d{3})([-. ])?(\\d{4})";
    regex r(phone);   // a regex to find our pattern
    smatch m;
    string s;
    string fmt = "$2.$5.$7"; //  reformat numbers to ddd.ddd.dddd
    //  read each record from the input file
    while (getline(cin, s))
        cout << regex_replace(s, r, fmt) << endl;
    return 0;
}
```

We read each record into s and hand that record to regex_replace. This function finds and transforms *all* the matches in its input sequence.

Flags to Control Matches and Formatting

Just as the library defines flags to direct how to process a regular expression, the library also defines flags that we can use to control the match process or the formatting done during a replacement. These values are listed in Table 17.13 (overleaf). These flags can be passed to the regex_search or regex_match functions or to the format members of class smatch.

The match and format flags have type match_flag_type. These values are defined in a namespace named regex_constants. Like placeholders, which we used with bind (§ 10.3.4, p. 399), regex_constants is a namespace defined inside the std namespace. To use a name from regex_constants, we must qualify that name with the names of both namespaces:

```
using std::regex_constants::format_no_copy;
```

This declaration says that when our code uses format_no_copy, we want the object of that name from the namespace std::regex_constants. We can instead provide the alternative form of using that we will cover in § 18.2.2 (p. 792):

```
using namespace std::regex_constants;
```

Table 17.13: Match Flags	
Defined in `regex_constants::match_flag_type`	
`match_default`	Equivalent to `format_default`
`match_not_bol`	Don't treat the first character as the beginning of the line
`match_not_eol`	Don't treat the last character as the end of the line
`match_not_bow`	Don't treat the first character as the beginning of a word
`match_not_eow`	Don't treat the last character as the end of a word
`match_any`	If there is more than one match, any match can be returned
`match_not_null`	Don't match an empty sequence
`match_continuous`	The match must begin with the first character in the input
`match_prev_avail`	The input sequence has characters before the first
`format_default`	Replacement string uses the ECMAScript rules
`format_sed`	Replacement string uses the rules from POSIX `sed`
`format_no_copy`	Don't output the unmatched parts of the input
`format_first_only`	Replace only the first occurrence

Using Format Flags

By default, `regex_replace` outputs its entire input sequence. The parts that don't match the regular expression are output without change; the parts that do match are formatted as indicated by the given format string. We can change this default behavior by specifying `format_no_copy` in the call to `regex_replace`:

```
// generate just the phone numbers: use a new format string
string fmt2 = "$2.$5.$7 "; // put space after the last number as a separator
// tell regex_replace to copy only the text that it replaces
cout << regex_replace(s, r, fmt2, format_no_copy) << endl;
```

Given the same input, this version of the program generates

```
201.555.2368 862.555.0123
973.555.0130
609.555.0132 201.555.0175 800.555.0000
```

EXERCISES SECTION 17.3.4

Exercise 17.24: Write your own version of the program to reformat phone numbers.

Exercise 17.25: Rewrite your phone program so that it writes only the first phone number for each person.

Exercise 17.26: Rewrite your phone program so that it writes only the second and subsequent phone numbers for people with more than one phone number.

Exercise 17.27: Write a program that reformats a nine-digit zip code as `ddddd-dddd`.

17.4 Random Numbers

Programs often need a source of random numbers. Prior to the new standard, both C and C++ relied on a simple C library function named `rand`. That function produces pseudorandom integers that are uniformly distributed in the range from 0 to a system-dependent maximum value that is at least 32767.

The `rand` function has several problems: Many, if not most, programs need random numbers in a different range from the one produced by `rand`. Some applications require random floating-point numbers. Some programs need numbers that reflect a nonuniform distribution. Programmers often introduce nonrandomness when they try to transform the range, type, or distribution of the numbers generated by `rand`.

The random-number library, defined in the `random` header, solves these problems through a set of cooperating classes: **random-number engines** and **random-number distribution classes**. These clases are described in Table 17.14. An engine generates a sequence of `unsigned` random numbers. A distribution uses an engine to generate random numbers of a specified type, in a given range, distributed according to a particular probability distribution.

> **Best Practices** C++ programs should not use the library `rand` function. Instead, they should use the `default_random_engine` along with an appropriate distribution object.

Table 17.14: Random Number Library Components	
Engine	Types that generate a sequence of random `unsigned` integers
Distribution	Types that use an engine to return numbers according to a particular probability distribution

17.4.1 Random-Number Engines and Distribution

The random-number engines are function-object classes (§ 14.8, p. 571) that define a call operator that takes no arguments and returns a random `unsigned` number. We can generate raw random numbers by calling an object of a random-number engine type:

```
default_random_engine e;  // generates random unsigned integers
for (size_t i = 0; i < 10; ++i)
    // e() "calls" the object to produce the next random number
    cout << e() << " ";
```

On our system, this program generates:

```
16807 282475249 1622650073 984943658 1144108930 470211272 ...
```

Here, we defined an object named e that has type **default_random_engine**. Inside the `for`, we call the object e to obtain the next random number.

The library defines several random-number engines that differ in terms of their performance and quality of randomness. Each compiler designates one of these engines as the `default_random_engine` type. This type is intended to be the engine with the most generally useful properties. Table 17.15 lists the engine operations and the engine types defined by the standard are listed in § A.3.2 (p. 884).

For most purposes, the output of an engine is not directly usable, which is why we described them earlier as raw random numbers. The problem is that the numbers usually span a range that differs from the one we need. *Correctly* transforming the range of a random number is surprisingly hard.

Distribution Types and Engines

To get a number in a specified range, we use an object of a distribution type:

```
// uniformly distributed from 0 to 9 inclusive
uniform_int_distribution<unsigned> u(0,9);
default_random_engine e;    // generates unsigned random integers
for (size_t i = 0; i < 10; ++i)
    // u uses e as a source of numbers
    // each call returns a uniformly distributed value in the specified range
    cout << u(e) << " ";
```

This code produces output such as

```
0 1 7 4 5 2 0 6 6 9
```

Here we define u as a `uniform_int_distribution<unsigned>`. That type generates uniformly distributed `unsigned` values. When we define an object of this type, we can supply the minimum and maximum values we want. In this program, `u(0,9)` says that we want numbers to be in the range 0 to 9 *inclusive*. The random number distributions use inclusive ranges so that we can obtain every possible value of the given integral type.

Like the engine types, the distribution types are also function-object classes. The distribution types define a call operator that takes a random-number engine as its argument. The distribution object uses its engine argument to produce random numbers that the distribution object maps to the specified distribution.

Note that we pass the engine object itself, `u(e)`. Had we written the call as `u(e())`, we would have tried to pass the next value generated by e to u, which would have been a compile-time error. We pass the engine, not the next result of the engine, because some distributions may need to call the engine more than once.

> When we refer to a **random-number generator**, we mean the combination of a distribution object with an engine.

Comparing Random Engines and the `rand` Function

For readers familiar with the C library `rand` function, it is worth noting that the output of calling a `default_random_engine` object is similar to the output of `rand`. Engines deliver `unsigned` integers in a system-defined range. The range for rand is 0 to RAND_MAX. The range for an engine type is returned by calling the min and max members on an object of that type:

```
cout << "min: " << e.min() << " max: " << e.max() << endl;
```

On our system this program produces the following output:

```
min: 1 max: 2147483646
```

Table 17.15: Random Number Engine Operations	
`Engine e;`	Default constructor; uses the default seed for the engine type
`Engine e(s);`	Uses the integral value s as the seed
`e.seed(s)`	Reset the state of the engine using the seed s
`e.min()` `e.max()`	The smallest and largest numbers this generator will generate
`Engine::result_type`	The unsigned integral type this engine generates
`e.discard(u)`	Advance the engine by u steps; u has type `unsigned long long`

Engines Generate a Sequence of Numbers

Random number generators have one property that often confuses new users: Even though the numbers that are generated appear to be random, a given generator returns the same sequence of numbers each time it is run. The fact that the sequence is unchanging is very helpful during testing. On the other hand, programs that use random-number generators have to take this fact into account.

As one example, assume we need a function that will generate a vector of 100 random integers uniformly distributed in the range from 0 to 9. We might think we'd write this function as follows:

```
// almost surely the wrong way to generate a vector of random integers
// output from this function will be the same 100 numbers on every call!
vector<unsigned> bad_randVec()
{
    default_random_engine e;
    uniform_int_distribution<unsigned> u(0,9);
    vector<unsigned> ret;
    for (size_t i = 0; i < 100; ++i)
        ret.push_back(u(e));
    return ret;
}
```

However, this function will return the same vector every time it is called:

```
vector<unsigned> v1(bad_randVec());
vector<unsigned> v2(bad_randVec());
// will print equal
cout << ((v1 == v2) ? "equal" : "not equal") << endl;
```

This code will print `equal` because the `vectors` `v1` and `v2` have the same values.

The right way to write our function is to make the engine and associated distribution objects `static` (§ 6.1.1, p. 205):

```
//  returns a vector of 100 uniformly distributed random numbers
vector<unsigned> good_randVec()
{
    //  because engines and distributions retain state, they usually should be
    //  defined as static so that new numbers are generated on each call
    static default_random_engine e;
    static uniform_int_distribution<unsigned> u(0,9);
    vector<unsigned> ret;
    for (size_t i = 0; i < 100; ++i)
        ret.push_back(u(e));
    return ret;
}
```

Because `e` and `u` are `static`, they will hold their state across calls to the function. The first call will use the first 100 random numbers from the sequence `u(e)` generates, the second call will get the next 100, and so on.

WARNING

A given random-number generator always produces the same sequence of numbers. A function with a local random-number generator should make that generator (both the engine and distribution objects) `static`. Otherwise, the function will generate the identical sequence on each call.

Seeding a Generator

The fact that a generator returns the same sequence of numbers is helpful during debugging. However, once our program is tested, we often want to cause each run of the program to generate different random results. We do so by providing a **seed**. A seed is a value that an engine can use to cause it to start generating numbers at a new point in its sequence.

We can seed an engine in one of two ways: We can provide the seed when we create an engine object, or we can call the engine's `seed` member:

```
default_random_engine e1;                     //  uses the default seed
default_random_engine e2(2147483646);         //  use the given seed value
//  e3 and e4 will generate the same sequence because they use the same seed
default_random_engine e3;                     //  uses the default seed value
e3.seed(32767);                               //  call seed to set a new seed value
default_random_engine e4(32767);              //  set the seed value to 32767
for (size_t i = 0; i != 100; ++i) {
    if (e1() == e2())
        cout << "unseeded match at iteration: " << i << endl;
    if (e3() != e4())
        cout << "seeded differs at iteration: " << i << endl;
}
```

Here we define four engines. The first two, `e1` and `e2`, have different seeds and *should* generate different sequences. The second two, e3 and e4, have the same seed value. These two objects *will* generate the same sequence.

Picking a good seed, like most things about generating good random numbers, is surprisingly hard. Perhaps the most common approach is to call the system time function. This function, defined in the ctime header, returns the number of seconds since a given epoch. The time function takes a single parameter that is a pointer to a structure into which to write the time. If that pointer is null, the function just returns the time:

```
default_random_engine e1(time(0));    // a somewhat random seed
```

Because time returns time as the number of seconds, this seed is useful only for applications that generate the seed at second-level, or longer, intervals.

WARNING Using time as a seed usually doesn't work if the program is run repeatedly as part of an automated process; it might wind up with the same seed several times.

EXERCISES SECTION 17.4.1

Exercise 17.28: Write a function that generates and returns a uniformly distributed random unsigned int each time it is called.

Exercise 17.29: Allow the user to supply a seed as an optional argument to the function you wrote in the previous exercise.

Exercise 17.30: Revise your function again this time to take a minimum and maximum value for the numbers that the function should return.

17.4.2 Other Kinds of Distributions

The engines produce unsigned numbers, and each number in the engine's range has the same likelihood of being generated. Applications often need numbers of different types or distributions. The library handles both these needs by defining different distributions that, when used with an engine, produce the desired results. Table 17.16 (overleaf) lists the operations supported by the distribution types.

Generating Random Real Numbers

Programs often need a source of random floating-point values. In particular, programs frequently need random numbers between zero and one.

The most common, *but incorrect*, way to obtain a random floating-point from rand is to divide the result of rand() by RAND_MAX, which is a system-defined upper limit that is the largest random number that rand can return. This technique is incorrect because random integers usually have less precision than floating-point numbers, in which case there are some floating-point values that will never be produced as output.

With the new library facilities, we can easily obtain a floating-point random number. We define an object of type `uniform_real_distribution` and let the library handle mapping random integers to random floating-point numbers. As we did for `uniform_int_distribution`, we specify the minimum and maximum values when we define the object:

```
default_random_engine e;   // generates unsigned random integers
// uniformly distributed from 0 to 1 inclusive
uniform_real_distribution<double> u(0,1);
for (size_t i = 0; i < 10; ++i)
    cout << u(e) << " ";
```

This code is nearly identical to the previous program that generated `unsigned` values. However, because we used a different distribution type, this version generates different results:

```
0.131538 0.45865 0.218959 0.678865 0.934693 0.519416 ...
```

Table 17.16: Distribution Operations	
`Dist d;`	Default constructor; makes d ready to use. Other constructors depend on the type of *Dist*; see § A.3 (p. 882). The distribution constructors are `explicit` (§ 7.5.4, p. 296).
`d(e)`	Successive calls with the same e produce a sequence of random numbers according to the distribution type of d; e is a random-number engine object.
`d.min()` `d.max()`	Return the smallest and largest numbers `d(e)` will generate.
`d.reset()`	Reestablish the state of d so that subsequent uses of d don't depend on values d has already generated.

Using the Distribution's Default Result Type

With one exception, which we'll cover in § 17.4.2 (p. 752), the distribution types are templates that have a single template type parameter that represents the type of the numbers that the distribution generates. These types always generate either a floating-point type or an integral type.

Each distribution template has a default template argument (§ 16.1.3, p. 670). The distribution types that generate floating-point values generate `double` by default. Distributions that generate integral results use `int` as their default. Because the distribution types have only one template parameter, when we want to use the default we must remember to follow the template's name with empty angle brackets to signify that we want the default (§ 16.1.3, p. 671):

```
// empty <> signify we want to use the default result type
uniform_real_distribution<> u(0,1); // generates double by default
```

Generating Numbers That Are Not Uniformly Distributed

In addition to correctly generating numbers in a specified range, another advantage of the new library is that we can obtain numbers that are nonuniformly distributed. Indeed, the library defines 20 distribution types! These types are listed in § A.3 (p. 882).

As an example, we'll generate a series of normally distributed values and plot the resulting distribution. Because `normal_distribution` generates floating-point numbers, our program will use the `lround` function from the `cmath` header to round each result to its nearest integer. We'll generate 200 numbers centered around a mean of 4 with a standard deviation of 1.5. Because we're using a normal distribution, we can expect all but about 1 percent of the generated numbers to be in the range from 0 to 8, inclusive. Our program will count how many values appear that map to the integers in this range:

```
default_random_engine e;              // generates random integers
normal_distribution<> n(4,1.5);      // mean 4, standard deviation 1.5
vector<unsigned> vals(9);             // nine elements each 0
for (size_t i = 0; i != 200; ++i) {
    unsigned v = lround(n(e));       // round to the nearest integer
    if (v < vals.size())             // if this result is in range
        ++vals[v];                   // count how often each number appears
}
for (size_t j = 0; j != vals.size(); ++j)
    cout << j << ": " << string(vals[j], '*') << endl;
```

We start by defining our random generator objects and a `vector` named `vals`. We'll use `vals` to count how often each number in the range 0...9 occurs. Unlike most of our programs that use `vector`, we allocate `vals` at its desired size. By doing so, we start out with each element initialized to 0.

Inside the `for` loop, we call `lround(n(e))` to round the value returned by `n(e)` to the nearest integer. Having obtained the integer that corresponds to our floating-point random number, we use that number to index our `vector` of counters. Because `n(e)` can produce a number outside the range 0 to 9, we check that the number we got is in range before using it to index `vals`. If the number is in range, we increment the associated counter.

When the loop completes, we print the contents of `vals`, which will generate output such as

```
0: ***
1: *******
2: *******************
3: *******************************************
4: *****************************************************************
5: ********************************************
6: **********************
7: *******
8: *
```

Here we print a `string` with as many asterisks as the count of the times the current value was returned by our random-number generator. Note that this figure is not perfectly symmetrical. If it were, that symmetry should give us reason to suspect the quality of our random-number generator.

The `bernoulli_distribution` Class

We noted that there was one distribution that does not take a template parameter. That distribution is the `bernoulli_distribution`, which is an ordinary class, not a template. This distribution always returns a `bool` value. It returns `true` with a given probability. By default that probability is .5.

As an example of this kind of distribution, we might have a program that plays a game with a user. To play the game, one of the players—either the user or the program—has to go first. We could use a `uniform_int_distribution` object with a range of 0 to 1 to select the first player. Alternatively, we can use a Bernoulli distribution to make this choice. Assuming that we have a function named `play` that plays the game, we might have a loop such as the following to interact with the user:

```
string resp;
default_random_engine e;   // e has state, so it must be outside the loop!
bernoulli_distribution b;  // 50/50 odds by default
do {
    bool first = b(e);     // if true, the program will go first
    cout << (first ? "We go first"
                   : "You get to go first") << endl;
    // play the game passing the indicator of who goes first
    cout << ((play(first)) ? "sorry, you lost"
                           : "congrats, you won") << endl;
    cout << "play again? Enter 'yes' or 'no'" << endl;
} while (cin >> resp && resp[0] == 'y');
```

We use a do while (§ 5.4.4, p. 189) to repeatedly prompt the user to play.

WARNING

> Because engines return the same sequence of numbers (§ 17.4.1, p. 747), it is essential that we declare engines outside of loops. Otherwise, we'd create a new engine on each iteration and generate the same values on each iteration. Similarly, distributions may retain state and should also be defined outside loops.

One reason to use a `bernoulli_distribution` in this program is that doing so lets us give the program a better chance of going first:

```
bernoulli_distribution b(.55); // give the house a slight edge
```

If we use this definition for b, then the program has 55/45 odds of going first.

17.5 The IO Library Revisited

In Chapter 8 we introduced the basic architecture and most commonly used parts of the IO library. In this section we'll look at three of the more specialized features that the IO library supports: format control, unformatted IO, and random access.

EXERCISES SECTION 17.4.2

Exercise 17.31: What would happen if we defined b and e inside the do loop of the game-playing program from this section?

Exercise 17.32: What would happen if we defined resp inside the loop?

Exercise 17.33: Write a version of the word transformation program from § 11.3.6 (p. 440) that allows multiple transformations for a given word and randomly selects which transformation to apply.

17.5.1 Formatted Input and Output

In addition to its condition state (§ 8.1.2, p. 312), each iostream object also maintains a format state that controls the details of how IO is formatted. The format state controls aspects of formatting such as the notational base for integral values, the precision of floating-point values, the width of an output element, and so on.

The library defines a set of **manipulators** (§ 1.2, p. 7), listed in Tables 17.17 (p. 757) and 17.18 (p. 760), that modify the format state of a stream. A manipulator is a function or object that affects the state of a stream and can be used as an operand to an input or output operator. Like the input and output operators, a manipulator returns the stream object to which it is applied, so we can combine manipulators and data in a single statement.

Our programs have already used one manipulator, endl, which we "write" to an output stream as if it were a value. But endl isn't an ordinary value; instead, it performs an operation: It writes a newline and flushes the buffer.

Many Manipulators Change the Format State

Manipulators are used for two broad categories of output control: controlling the presentation of numeric values and controlling the amount and placement of padding. Most of the manipulators that change the format state provide set/unset pairs; one manipulator sets the format state to a new value and the other unsets it, restoring the normal default formatting.

WARNING

> Manipulators that change the format state of the stream usually leave the format state changed for all subsequent IO.

The fact that a manipulator makes a persistent change to the format state can be useful when we have a set of IO operations that want to use the same formatting. Indeed, some programs take advantage of this aspect of manipulators to reset the behavior of one or more formatting rules for all its input or output. In such cases, the fact that a manipulator changes the stream is a desirable property.

However, many programs (and, more importantly, programmers) expect the state of the stream to match the normal library defaults. In these cases, leaving the state of the stream in a nonstandard state can lead to errors. As a result, it is usually best to undo whatever state changes are made as soon as those changes are no longer needed.

Controlling the Format of Boolean Values

One example of a manipulator that changes the formatting state of its object is the
`boolalpha` manipulator. By default, `bool` values print as 1 or 0. A `true` value is
written as the integer 1 and a `false` value as 0. We can override this formatting
by applying the `boolalpha` manipulator to the stream:

```
cout << "default bool values: " << true << " " << false
     << "\nalpha bool values: " << boolalpha
     << true << " " << false << endl;
```

When executed, this program generates the following:

```
default bool values: 1 0
alpha bool values: true false
```

Once we "write" `boolalpha` on `cout`, we've changed how `cout` will print `bool`
values from this point on. Subsequent operations that print `bool`s will print them
as either `true` or `false`.

To undo the format state change to `cout`, we apply `noboolalpha`:

```
bool bool_val = get_status();
cout << boolalpha      // sets the internal state of cout
     << bool_val
     << noboolalpha;   // resets the internal state to default formatting
```

Here we change the format of `bool` values only to print the value of `bool_val`.
Once that value is printed, we immediately reset the stream back to its initial state.

Specifying the Base for Integral Values

By default, integral values are written and read in decimal notation. We can change
the notational base to octal or hexadecimal or back to decimal by using the manipulators `hex`, `oct`, and `dec`:

```
cout << "default: " << 20 << " " << 1024 << endl;
cout << "octal: " << oct << 20 << " " << 1024 << endl;
cout << "hex: " << hex << 20 << " " << 1024 << endl;
cout << "decimal: " << dec << 20 << " " << 1024 << endl;
```

When compiled and executed, this program generates the following output:

```
default: 20 1024
octal: 24 2000
hex: 14 400
decimal: 20 1024
```

Notice that like `boolalpha`, these manipulators change the format state. They
affect the immediately following output and all subsequent integral output until
the format is reset by invoking another manipulator.

The `hex`, `oct`, and `dec` manipulators affect only integral operands; the
representation of floating-point values is unaffected.

Indicating Base on the Output

By default, when we print numbers, there is no visual cue as to what notational base was used. Is 20, for example, really 20, or an octal representation of 16? When we print numbers in decimal mode, the number is printed as we expect. If we need to print octal or hexadecimal values, it is likely that we should also use the `showbase` manipulator. The `showbase` manipulator causes the output stream to use the same conventions as used for specifying the base of an integral constant:

- A leading 0x indicates hexadecimal.

- A leading 0 indicates octal.

- The absence of either indicates decimal.

Here we've revised the previous program to use `showbase`:

```
cout << showbase;     // show the base when printing integral values
cout << "default: " << 20 << " " << 1024 << endl;
cout << "in octal: " << oct  << 20 << " " << 1024 << endl;
cout << "in hex: " << hex  << 20 << " " << 1024 << endl;
cout << "in decimal: " << dec << 20 << " " << 1024 << endl;
cout << noshowbase;   // reset the state of the stream
```

The revised output makes it clear what the underlying value really is:

```
default: 20 1024
in octal: 024 02000
in hex: 0x14 0x400
in decimal: 20 1024
```

The `noshowbase` manipulator resets `cout` so that it no longer displays the notational base of integral values.

By default, hexadecimal values are printed in lowercase with a lowercase x. We can display the X and the hex digits a–f as uppercase by applying the `uppercase` manipulator:

```
cout << uppercase << showbase << hex
     << "printed in hexadecimal: " << 20 << " " << 1024
     << nouppercase << noshowbase << dec << endl;
```

This statement generates the following output:

```
printed in hexadecimal: 0X14 0X400
```

We apply the `nouppercase`, `noshowbase`, and `dec` manipulators to return the stream to its original state.

Controlling the Format of Floating-Point Values

We can control three aspects of floating-point output:

- How many digits of precision are printed

- Whether the number is printed in hexadecimal, fixed decimal, or scientific notation

- Whether a decimal point is printed for floating-point values that are whole numbers

By default, floating-point values are printed using six digits of precision; the decimal point is omitted if the value has no fractional part; and they are printed in either fixed decimal or scientific notation depending on the value of the number. The library chooses a format that enhances readability of the number. Very large and very small values are printed using scientific notation. Other values are printed in fixed decimal.

Specifying How Much Precision to Print

By default, precision controls the total number of digits that are printed. When printed, floating-point values are rounded, not truncated, to the current precision. Thus, if the current precision is four, then 3.14159 becomes 3.142; if the precision is three, then it is printed as 3.14.

We can change the precision by calling the precision member of an IO object or by using the setprecision manipulator. The precision member is overloaded (§ 6.4, p. 230). One version takes an int value and sets the precision to that new value. It returns the *previous* precision value. The other version takes no arguments and returns the current precision value. The setprecision manipulator takes an argument, which it uses to set the precision.

The setprecision manipulators and other manipulators that take arguments are defined in the iomanip header.

The following program illustrates the different ways we can control the precision used to print floating-point values:

```
// cout.precision reports the current precision value
cout << "Precision: " << cout.precision()
     << ", Value: "   << sqrt(2.0) << endl;
// cout.precision(12) asks that 12 digits of precision be printed
cout.precision(12);
cout << "Precision: " << cout.precision()
     << ", Value: "   << sqrt(2.0) << endl;
// alternative way to set precision using the setprecision manipulator
cout << setprecision(3);
cout << "Precision: " << cout.precision()
     << ", Value: "   << sqrt(2.0) << endl;
```

When compiled and executed, the program generates the following output:

```
Precision: 6, Value: 1.41421
Precision: 12, Value: 1.41421356237
Precision: 3, Value: 1.41
```

Table 17.17: Manipulators Defined in `iostream`	
boolalpha	Display `true` and `false` as strings
* noboolalpha	Display `true` and `false` as 0, 1
showbase	Generate prefix indicating the numeric base of integral values
* noshowbase	Do not generate notational base prefix
showpoint	Always display a decimal point for floating-point values
* noshowpoint	Display a decimal point only if the value has a fractional part
showpos	Display + in nonnegative numbers
* noshowpos	Do not display + in nonnegative numbers
uppercase	Print `0X` in hexadecimal, `E` in scientific
* nouppercase	Print `0x` in hexadecimal, `e` in scientific
* dec	Display integral values in decimal numeric base
hex	Display integral values in hexadecimal numeric base
oct	Display integral values in octal numeric base
left	Add fill characters to the right of the value
right	Add fill characters to the left of the value
internal	Add fill characters between the sign and the value
fixed	Display floating-point values in decimal notation
scientific	Display floating-point values in scientific notation
hexfloat	Display floating-point values in hex (new to C++ 11)
defaultfloat	Reset the floating-point format to decimal (new to C++ 11)
unitbuf	Flush buffers after every output operation
* nounitbuf	Restore normal buffer flushing
* skipws	Skip whitespace with input operators
noskipws	Do not skip whitespace with input operators
flush	Flush the `ostream` buffer
ends	Insert null, then flush the `ostream` buffer
endl	Insert newline, then flush the `ostream` buffer

* indicates the default stream state

This program calls the library `sqrt` function, which is found in the `cmath` header. The `sqrt` function is overloaded and can be called on either a `float`, `double`, or `long double` argument. It returns the square root of its argument.

Specifying the Notation of Floating-Point Numbers

Best Practices

> Unless you need to control the presentation of a floating-point number (e.g., to print data in columns or to print data that represents money or a percentage), it is usually best to let the library choose the notation.

We can force a stream to use scientific, fixed, or hexadecimal notation by using the appropriate manipulator. The `scientific` manipulator changes the stream to use scientific notation. The `fixed` manipulator changes the stream to use fixed decimal.

Under the new library, we can also force floating-point values to use hexadecimal format by using `hexfloat`. The new library provides another manipulator, named `defaultfloat`. This manipulator returns the stream to its default state in

C++
11

which it chooses a notation based on the value being printed.

These manipulators also change the default meaning of the precision for the stream. After executing scientific, fixed, or hexfloat, the precision value controls the number of digits after the decimal point. By default, precision specifies the total number of digits—both before and after the decimal point. Using fixed or scientific lets us print numbers lined up in columns, with the decimal point in a fixed position relative to the fractional part being printed:

```
cout << "default format: " << 100 * sqrt(2.0) << '\n'
     << "scientific: " << scientific << 100 * sqrt(2.0) << '\n'
     << "fixed decimal: " << fixed << 100 * sqrt(2.0) << '\n'
     << "hexadecimal: " << hexfloat << 100 * sqrt(2.0) << '\n'
     << "use defaults: " << defaultfloat << 100 * sqrt(2.0)
     << "\n\n";
```

produces the following output:

```
default format: 141.421
scientific: 1.414214e+002
fixed decimal: 141.421356
hexadecimal: 0x1.1ad7bcp+7
use defaults: 141.421
```

By default, the hexadecimal digits and the e used in scientific notation are printed in lowercase. We can use the uppercase manipulator to show those values in uppercase.

Printing the Decimal Point

By default, when the fractional part of a floating-point value is 0, the decimal point is not displayed. The showpoint manipulator forces the decimal point to be printed:

```
cout << 10.0 << endl;            // prints 10
cout << showpoint << 10.0        // prints 10.0000
     << noshowpoint << endl;     // revert to default format for the decimal point
```

The noshowpoint manipulator reinstates the default behavior. The next output expression will have the default behavior, which is to suppress the decimal point if the floating-point value has a 0 fractional part.

Padding the Output

When we print data in columns, we often need fairly fine control over how the data are formatted. The library provides several manipulators to help us accomplish the control we might need:

- setw to specify the minimum space for the *next* numeric or string value.
- left to left-justify the output.
- right to right-justify the output. Output is right-justified by default.

- internal controls placement of the sign on negative values. internal left-justifies the sign and right-justifies the value, padding any intervening space with blanks.

- setfill lets us specify an alternative character to use to pad the output. By default, the value is a space.

> **Note**
> setw, like endl, does not change the internal state of the output stream. It determines the size of only the *next* output.

The following program illustrates these manipulators:

```
int i = -16;
double d = 3.14159;
//  pad the first column to use a minimum of 12 positions in the output
cout << "i: " << setw(12) << i << "next col" << '\n'
     << "d: " << setw(12) << d << "next col" << '\n';
//  pad the first column and left-justify all columns
cout << left
     << "i: " << setw(12) << i << "next col" << '\n'
     << "d: " << setw(12) << d << "next col" << '\n'
     << right;                 //  restore normal justification
//  pad the first column and right-justify all columns
cout << right
     << "i: " << setw(12) << i << "next col" << '\n'
     << "d: " << setw(12) << d << "next col" << '\n';
//  pad the first column but put the padding internal to the field
cout << internal
     << "i: " << setw(12) << i << "next col" << '\n'
     << "d: " << setw(12) << d << "next col" << '\n';
//  pad the first column, using # as the pad character
cout << setfill('#')
     << "i: " << setw(12) << i << "next col" << '\n'
     << "d: " << setw(12) << d << "next col" << '\n'
     << setfill(' ');    //  restore the normal pad character
```

When executed, this program generates

```
i:          -16next col
d:      3.14159next col
i: -16          next col
d: 3.14159      next col
i:          -16next col
d:      3.14159next col
i: -          16next col
d:      3.14159next col
i: -#########16next col
d: #####3.14159next col
```

Table 17.18: Manipulators Defined in `iomanip`	
`setfill(ch)`	Fill whitespace with `ch`
`setprecision(n)`	Set floating-point precision to `n`
`setw(w)`	Read or write value to `w` characters
`setbase(b)`	Output integers in base `b`

Controlling Input Formatting

By default, the input operators ignore whitespace (blank, tab, newline, formfeed, and carriage return). The following loop

```
char ch;
while (cin >> ch)
    cout << ch;
```

given the input sequence

```
a b    c
d
```

executes four times to read the characters a through d, skipping the intervening blanks, possible tabs, and newline characters. The output from this program is

```
abcd
```

The `noskipws` manipulator causes the input operator to read, rather than skip, whitespace. To return to the default behavior, we apply the `skipws` manipulator:

```
cin >> noskipws;   // set cin so that it reads whitespace
while (cin >> ch)
    cout << ch;
cin >> skipws;     // reset cin to the default state so that it discards whitespace
```

Given the same input as before, this loop makes seven iterations, reading whitespace as well as the characters in the input. This loop generates

```
a b    c
d
```

EXERCISES SECTION 17.5.1

Exercise 17.34: Write a program that illustrates the use of each manipulator in Tables 17.17 (p. 757) and 17.18.

Exercise 17.35: Write a version of the program from page 758, that printed the square root of 2 but this time print hexadecimal digits in uppercase.

Exercise 17.36: Modify the program from the previous exercise to print the various floating-point values so that they line up in a column.

17.5.2 Unformatted Input/Output Operations

So far, our programs have used only **formatted IO** operations. The input and output operators (<< and >>) format the data they read or write according to the type being handled. The input operators ignore whitespace; the output operators apply padding, precision, and so on.

The library also provides a set of low-level operations that support **unformatted IO**. These operations let us deal with a stream as a sequence of uninterpreted bytes.

Single-Byte Operations

Several of the unformatted operations deal with a stream one byte at a time. These operations, which are described in Table 17.19, read rather than ignore whitespace. For example, we can use the unformatted IO operations `get` and `put` to read and write the characters one at a time:

```
char ch;
while (cin.get(ch))
        cout.put(ch);
```

This program preserves the whitespace in the input. Its output is identical to the input. It executes the same way as the previous program that used `noskipws`.

Table 17.19: Single-Byte Low-Level IO Operations	
`is.get(ch)`	Put the next byte from the istream is in character ch. Returns is.
`os.put(ch)`	Put the character ch onto the ostream os. Returns os.
`is.get()`	Returns next byte from is as an int.
`is.putback(ch)`	Put the character ch back on is; returns is.
`is.unget()`	Move is back one byte; returns is.
`is.peek()`	Return the next byte as an int but doesn't remove it.

Putting Back onto an Input Stream

Sometimes we need to read a character in order to know that we aren't ready for it. In such cases, we'd like to put the character back onto the stream. The library gives us three ways to do so, each of which has subtle differences from the others:

- `peek` returns a copy of the next character on the input stream but does not change the stream. The value returned by `peek` stays on the stream.

- `unget` backs up the input stream so that whatever value was last returned is still on the stream. We can call `unget` even if we do not know what value was last taken from the stream.

- `putback` is a more specialized version of `unget`: It returns the last value read from the stream but takes an argument that must be the same as the one that was last read.

In general, we are guaranteed to be able to put back at most one value before the next read. That is, we are not guaranteed to be able to call `putback` or `unget` successively without an intervening read operation.

`int` Return Values from Input Operations

The `peek` function and the version of `get` that takes no argument return a character from the input stream as an `int`. This fact can be surprising; it might seem more natural to have these functions return a `char`.

The reason that these functions return an `int` is to allow them to return an end-of-file marker. A given character set is allowed to use every value in the `char` range to represent an actual character. Thus, there is no extra value in that range to use to represent end-of-file.

The functions that return `int` convert the character they return to `unsigned char` and then promote that value to `int`. As a result, even if the character set has characters that map to negative values, the `int` returned from these operations will be a positive value (§ 2.1.2, p. 35). The library uses a negative value to represent end-of-file, which is thus guaranteed to be distinct from any legitimate character value. Rather than requiring us to know the actual value returned, the `iostream` header defines a `const` named `EOF` that we can use to test if the value returned from `get` is end-of-file. It is essential that we use an `int` to hold the return from these functions:

```
int ch;      //  use an int, not a char to hold the return from get ()
//   loop to read and write all the data in the input
while ((ch = cin.get()) != EOF)
        cout.put(ch);
```

This program operates identically to the one on page 761, the only difference being the version of `get` that is used to read the input.

Multi-Byte Operations

Some unformatted IO operations deal with chunks of data at a time. These operations can be important if speed is an issue, but like other low-level operations, they are error-prone. In particular, these operations require us to allocate and manage the character arrays (§ 12.2, p. 476) used to store and retrieve data. The multi-byte operations are listed in Table 17.20.

The `get` and `getline` functions take the same parameters, and their actions are similar but not identical. In each case, `sink` is a `char` array into which the data are placed. The functions read until one of the following conditions occurs:

- `size - 1` characters are read
- End-of-file is encountered
- The delimiter character is encountered

The difference between these functions is the treatment of the delimiter: `get` leaves the delimiter as the next character of the `istream`, whereas `getline` reads and discards the delimiter. In either case, the delimiter is *not* stored in `sink`.

Table 17.20: Multi-Byte Low-Level IO Operations

`is.get(sink, size, delim)`
    Reads up to `size` bytes from `is` and stores them in the character array beginning at the address pointed to by `sink`. Reads until encountering the `delim` character or until it has read `size` bytes or encounters end-of-file. If `delim` is present, it is left on the input stream and not read into `sink`.

`is.getline(sink, size, delim)`
    Same behavior as the three-argument version of `get` but reads and discards `delim`.

`is.read(sink, size)`
    Reads up to `size` bytes into the character array `sink`. Returns `is`.

`is.gcount()`
    Returns number of bytes read from the stream `is` by the last call to an unformatted read operation.

`os.write(source, size)`
    Writes `size` bytes from the character array `source` to `os`. Returns `os`.

`is.ignore(size, delim)`
    Reads and ignores at most `size` characters up to and including `delim`. Unlike the other unformatted functions, `ignore` has default arguments: `size` defaults to 1 and `delim` to end-of-file.

It is a common error to intend to remove the delimiter from the stream but to forget to do so.

Determining How Many Characters Were Read

Several of the read operations read an unknown number of bytes from the input. We can call `gcount` to determine how many characters the last unformatted input operation read. It is essential to call `gcount` before any intervening unformatted input operation. In particular, the single-character operations that put characters back on the stream are also unformatted input operations. If `peek`, `unget`, or `putback` are called before calling `gcount`, then the return value will be 0.

17.5.3 Random Access to a Stream

The various stream types generally support random access to the data in their associated stream. We can reposition the stream so that it skips around, reading first the last line, then the first, and so on. The library provides a pair of functions to *seek* to a given location and to *tell* the current location in the associated stream.

Random IO is an inherently system-dependent. To understand how to use these features, you must consult your system's documentation.

    Although these seek and tell functions are defined for all the stream types, whether they do anything useful depends on the device to which the stream is bound. On most systems, the streams bound to `cin`, `cout`, `cerr`, and `clog` do

---

CAUTION: LOW-LEVEL ROUTINES ARE ERROR-PRONE

In general, we advocate using the higher-level abstractions provided by the library. The IO operations that return `int` are a good example of why.

It is a common programming error to assign the return, from `get` or `peek` to a `char` rather than an `int`. Doing so is an error, but an error the compiler will not detect. Instead, what happens depends on the machine and on the input data. For example, on a machine in which `char`s are implemented as `unsigned char`s, this loop will run forever:

```
char ch;      //  using a char here invites disaster!
//  the return from cin.get is converted to char and then compared to an int
while ((ch = cin.get()) != EOF)
        cout.put(ch);
```

The problem is that when `get` returns `EOF`, that value will be converted to an `unsigned char` value. That converted value is no longer equal to the `int` value of `EOF`, and the loop will continue forever. Such errors are likely to be caught in testing.

On machines for which `char`s are implemented as `signed char`s, we can't say with confidence what the behavior of the loop might be. What happens when an out-of-bounds value is assigned to a `signed` value is up to the compiler. On many machines, this loop will appear to work, unless a character in the input matches the EOF value. Although such characters are unlikely in ordinary data, presumably low-level IO is necessary only when we read binary values that do not map directly to ordinary characters and numeric values. For example, on our machine, if the input contains a character whose value is `'\377'`, then the loop terminates prematurely. `'\377'` is the value on our machine to which -1 converts when used as a `signed char`. If the input has this value, then it will be treated as the (premature) end-of-file indicator.

Such bugs do not happen when we read and write typed values. If you can use the more type-safe, higher-level operations supported by the library, do so.

EXERCISES SECTION 17.5.2

Exercise 17.37: Use the unformatted version of `getline` to read a file a line at a time. Test your program by giving it a file that contains empty lines as well as lines that are longer than the character array that you pass to `getline`.

Exercise 17.38: Extend your program from the previous exercise to print each word you read onto its own line.

---

not support random access—after all, what would it mean to jump back ten places when we're writing directly to `cout`? We can call the seek and tell functions, but these functions will fail at run time, leaving the stream in an invalid state.

WARNING

Because the `istream` and `ostream` types usually do not support random access, the remainder of this section should be considered as applicable to only the `fstream` and `sstream` types.

Seek and Tell Functions

To support random access, the IO types maintain a marker that determines where the next read or write will happen. They also provide two functions: One repositions the marker by *seek*ing to a given position; the second *tell*s us the current position of the marker. The library actually defines two pairs of *seek* and *tell* functions, which are described in Table 17.21. One pair is used by input streams, the other by output streams. The input and output versions are distinguished by a suffix that is either a g or a p. The g versions indicate that we are "getting" (reading) data, and the p functions indicate that we are "putting" (writing) data.

Table 17.21: Seek and Tell Functions	
`tellg()` `tellp()`	Return the current position of the marker in an input stream (`tellg`) or an output stream (`tellp`).
`seekg(pos)` `seekp(pos)`	Reposition the marker in an input or output stream to the given absolute address in the stream. pos is usually a value returned by a previous call to the corresponding `tellg` or `tellp` function.
`seekp(off, from)` `seekg(off, from)`	Reposition the marker for an input or output stream integral number `off` characters ahead or behind `from`. `from` can be one of • beg, seek relative to the beginning of the stream • cur, seek relative to the current position of the stream • end, seek relative to the end of the stream

Logically enough, we can use only the g versions on an `istream` and on the types `ifstream` and `istringstream` that inherit from `istream` (§ 8.1, p. 311). We can use only the p versions on an `ostream` and on the types that inherit from it, `ofstream` and `ostringstream`. An `iostream`, `fstream`, or `stringstream` can both read and write the associated stream; we can use either the g or p versions on objects of these types.

There Is Only One Marker

The fact that the library distinguishes between the "putting" and "getting" versions of the seek and tell functions can be misleading. Even though the library makes this distinction, it maintains only a single marker in a stream—there is *not* a distinct read marker and write marker.

When we're dealing with an input-only or output-only stream, the distinction isn't even apparent. We can use only the g or only the p versions on such streams. If we attempt to call `tellp` on an `ifstream`, the compiler will complain. Similarly, it will not let us call `seekg` on an `ostringstream`.

The `fstream` and `stringstream` types can read and write the same stream. In these types there is a single buffer that holds data to be read and written and a single marker denoting the current position in the buffer. The library maps both the g and p positions to this single marker.

> Because there is only a single marker, we *must* do a seek to reposition the marker whenever we switch between reading and writing.

Repositioning the Marker

There are two versions of the seek functions: One moves to an "absolute" address within the file; the other moves to a byte offset from a given position:

```
// set the marker to a fixed position
seekg(new_position);    // set the read marker to the given pos_type location
seekp(new_position);    // set the write marker to the given pos_type location

// offset some distance ahead of or behind the given starting point
seekg(offset, from);    // set the read marker offset distance from from
seekp(offset, from);    // offset has type off_type
```

The possible values for `from` are listed in Table 17.21 (on the previous page).

The arguments, `new_position` and `offset`, have machine-dependent types named `pos_type` and `off_type`, respectively. These types are defined in both `istream` and `ostream`. `pos_type` represents a file position and `off_type` represents an offset from that position. A value of type `off_type` can be positive or negative; we can `seek` forward or backward in the file.

Accessing the Marker

The `tellg` or `tellp` functions return a `pos_type` value denoting the current position of the stream. The tell functions are usually used to remember a location so that we can subsequently seek back to it:

```
// remember the current write position in mark
ostringstream writeStr;    // output stringstream
ostringstream::pos_type mark = writeStr.tellp();
// ...
if (cancelEntry)
        // return to the remembered position
        writeStr.seekp(mark);
```

Reading and Writing to the Same File

Let's look at a programming example. Assume we are given a file to read. We are to write a newline at the end of the file that contains the relative position at which each line begins. For example, given the following file,

```
abcd
efg
hi
j
```

the program should produce the following modified file:

```
abcd
efg
hi
j
5 9 12 14
```

Note that our program need not write the offset for the first line—it always occurs at position 0. Also note that the offset counts must include the invisible newline character that ends each line. Finally, note that the last number in the output is the offset for the line on which our output begins. By including this offset in our output, we can distinguish our output from the file's original contents. We can read the last number in the resulting file and seek to the corresponding offset to get to the beginning of our output.

Our program will read the file a line at a time. For each line, we'll increment a counter, adding the size of the line we just read. That counter is the offset at which the next line starts:

```
int main()
{
    //  open for input and output and preposition file pointers to end-of-file
    //  file mode argument see § 8.4 (p. 319)
    fstream inOut("copyOut",
                     fstream::ate | fstream::in | fstream::out);
    if (!inOut) {
        cerr << "Unable to open file!" << endl;
        return EXIT_FAILURE;  //  EXIT_FAILURE see § 6.3.2 (p. 227)
    }
    //  inOut is opened in ate mode, so it starts out positioned at the end
    auto end_mark = inOut.tellg();//  remember original end-of-file position
    inOut.seekg(0, fstream::beg);  //  reposition to the start of the file
    size_t cnt = 0;                //  accumulator for the byte count
    string line;                   //  hold each line of input
    //  while we haven't hit an error and are still reading the original data
    while (inOut && inOut.tellg() != end_mark
            && getline(inOut, line)) {  //  and can get another line of input
        cnt += line.size() + 1;         //  add 1 to account for the newline
        auto mark = inOut.tellg();      //  remember the read position
        inOut.seekp(0, fstream::end);   //  set the write marker to the end
        inOut << cnt;                   //  write the accumulated length
        //  print a separator if this is not the last line
        if (mark != end_mark) inOut << " ";
        inOut.seekg(mark);              //  restore the read position
    }
    inOut.seekp(0, fstream::end);       //  seek to the end
    inOut << "\n";                      //  write a newline at end-of-file
    return 0;
}
```

Our program opens its fstream using the in, out, and ate modes (§ 8.4, p. 319). The first two modes indicate that we intend to read and write the same file. Specifying `ate` positions the read and write markers at the end of the file. As usual, we check that the open succeeded, and exit if it did not (§ 6.3.2, p. 227).

Because our program writes to its input file, we can't use end-of-file to signal when it's time to stop reading. Instead, our loop must end when it reaches the point at which the original input ended. As a result, we must first remember the original end-of-file position. Because we opened the file in `ate` mode, `inOut` is already positioned at the end. We store the current (i.e., the original end) position in `end_mark`. Having remembered the end position, we reposition the read marker at the beginning of the file by seeking to the position 0 bytes from the beginning of the file.

The `while` loop has a three-part condition: We first check that the stream is valid; if so, we check whether we've exhausted our original input by comparing the current read position (returned by `tellg`) with the position we remembered in `end_mark`. Finally, assuming that both tests succeeded, we call `getline` to read the next line of input. If `getline` succeeds, we perform the body of the loop.

The loop body starts by remembering the current position in `mark`. We save that position in order to return to it after writing the next relative offset. The call to `seekp` repositions the write marker to the end of the file. We write the counter value and then `seekg` back to the position we remembered in `mark`. Having restored the marker, we're ready to repeat the condition in the `while`.

Each iteration of the loop writes the offset of the next line. Therefore, the last iteration of the loop takes care of writing the offset of the last line. However, we still need to write a newline at the end of the file. As with the other writes, we call `seekp` to position the file at the end before writing the newline.

EXERCISES SECTION 17.5.3

Exercise 17.39: Write your own version of the `seek` program presented in this section.

CHAPTER SUMMARY

This chapter covered additional IO operations and four library types: `tuple`, `bitset`, regular expressions, and random numbers.

A `tuple` is a template that allows us to bundle together members of disparate types into a single object. Each `tuple` contains a specified number of members, but the library imposes no limit on the number of members we can define for a given `tuple` type.

A `bitset` lets us define collections of bits of a specified size. The size of a `bitset` is not constrained to match any of the integral types, and can even exceed them. In addition to supporting the normal bitwise operators (§ 4.8, p. 152), `bitset` defines a number of named operations that let us manipulate the state of particular bits in the `bitset`.

The regular-expression library provides a collection of classes and functions: The `regex` class manages regular expressions written in one of several common regular-expression languages. The match classes hold information about a specific match. These classes are used by the `regex_search` and `regex_match` functions. These functions take a `regex` object and a character sequence and detect whether the regular expression in that `regex` matches the given character sequence. The `regex` iterator types are iterator adaptors that use `regex_search` to iterate through an input sequence and return each matching subsequence. There is also a `regex_replace` function that lets us replace the matched part of a given input sequence with a specified alternative.

The random-number library is a collection of random-number engines and distribution classes. A random-number engine returns a sequence of uniformly distributed integral values. The library defines several engines that have different performance characteristics. The `default_random_engine` is defined as the engine that should be suitable for most casual uses. The library also defines 20 distribution types. These distribution types use an engine to deliver random numbers of a specified type in a given range that are distributed according to a specified probability distribution.

DEFINED TERMS

bitset Standard library class that holds a collection of bits of a size that is known at compile time, and provides operations to test and set the bits in the collection.

cmatch Container of `csub_match` objects that provides information about the match to a `regex` on `const char*` input sequences. The first element in the container describes the overall match results. The subsequent elements describe the results for the subexpressions.

cregex_iterator Like `sregex_iterator`

except that it iterates over an array of `char`.

csub_match Type that holds the results of a regular expression match to a `const char*`. Can represent the entire match or a subexpression.

default random engine Type alias for the random number engine intended for normal use.

formatted IO IO operations that use the types of the objects being read or written to define the actions of the operations. Formatted input operations perform whatever transformations are appropriate to the type being read, such as converting ASCII numeric strings to the indicated arithmetic type and (by default) ignoring whitespace. Formatted output routines convert types to printable character representations, pad the output, and may perform other, type-specific transformations.

get Template function that returns the specified member for a given tuple. For example, `get<0>(t)` returns the first element from the `tuple t`.

high-order Bits in a `bitset` with the largest indices.

low-order Bits in a `bitset` with the lowest indices.

manipulator A function-like object that "manipulates" a stream. Manipulators can be used as the right-hand operand to the overloaded IO operators, `<<` and `>>`. Most manipulators change the internal state of the object. Such manipulators often come in pairs—one to change the state and the other to return the stream to its default state.

random-number distribution Standard library type that transforms the output of a random-number engine according to its named distribution. For example, `uniform_int_distribution<T>` generates uniformly distributed integers of type `T`, `normal_distribution<T>` generates normally distributed numbers, and so on.

random-number engine Library type that generates random unsigned numbers. Engines are intended to be used only as inputs to random-number distributions.

random-number generator Combination of a random-number engine type and a distribution type.

regex Class that manages a regular expression.

regex_error Exception type thrown to indicate a syntactic error in a regular expression.

regex_match Function that determines whether the entire input sequence matches the given `regex` object.

regex_replace Function that uses a `regex` object to replace matching subexpressions in an input sequence using a given format.

regex_search Function that uses a `regex` object to find a matching subsequence of a given input sequence.

regular expression A way of describing a sequence of characters.

seed Value supplied to a random-number engine that causes it to move to a new point in the sequence of number that it generates.

smatch Container of `ssub_match` objects that provides information about the match to a `regex` on `string` input sequences. The first element in the container describes the overall match results. The subsequent elements describe the results for the subexpressions.

sregex_iterator Iterator that iterates over a `string` using a given `regex` object to find matches in the given `string`. The constructor positions the iterator on the first match by calling `regex_search`. Incrementing the iterator calls `regex_search` starting just after the current match in the given `string`. Dereferencing the iterator returns an `smatch` object describing the current match.

ssub_match Type that holds results of a regular expression match to a `string`. Can represent the entire match or a subexpression.

subexpression Parenthesized component of a regular expression pattern.

tuple Template that generates types that hold unnamed members of specified types. There is no fixed limit on the number of members a `tuple` can be defined to have.

unformatted IO Operations that treat the stream as an undifferentiated byte stream. Unformatted operations place more of the burden for managing the IO on the user.

CHAPTER 18

TOOLS FOR LARGE PROGRAMS

CONTENTS

C++ is used on problems small enough to be solved by a single programmer after a few hours' work and on problems requiring enormous systems consisting of tens of millions of lines of code developed and modified by hundreds of programmers over many years. The facilities that we covered in the earlier parts of this book are equally useful across this range of programming problems.

The language includes some features that are most useful on systems that are more complicated than those that a small team can manage. These features—exception handling, namespaces, and multiple inheritance—are the topic of this chapter.

Large-scale programming places greater demands on programming languages than do the needs of systems that can be developed by small teams of programmers. Among the needs that distinguish large-scale applications are

- The ability to handle errors across independently developed subsystems

- The ability to use libraries developed more or less independently

- The ability to model more complicated application concepts

This chapter looks at three features in C++ that are aimed at these needs: exception handling, namespaces, and multiple inheritance.

18.1 Exception Handling

Exception handling allows independently developed parts of a program to communicate about and handle problems that arise at run time. Exceptions let us separate problem detection from problem resolution. One part of the program can detect a problem and can pass the job of resolving that problem to another part of the program. The detecting part need not know anything about the handling part, and vice versa.

In § 5.6 (p. 193) we introduced the basic concepts and mechanics of using exceptions. In this section we'll expand our coverage of these basics. Effective use of exception handling requires understanding what happens when an exception is thrown, what happens when it is caught, and the meaning of the objects that communicate what went wrong.

18.1.1 Throwing an Exception

In C++, an exception is **raised** by **throwing** an expression. The type of the thrown expression, together with the current call chain, determines which **handler** will deal with the exception. The selected handler is the one nearest in the call chain that matches the type of the thrown object. The type and contents of that object allow the throwing part of the program to inform the handling part about what went wrong.

When a `throw` is executed, the statement(s) following the `throw` are not executed. Instead, control is transferred from the `throw` to the matching `catch`. That `catch` might be local to the same function or might be in a function that directly or indirectly called the function in which the exception occurred. The fact that control passes from one location to another has two important implications:

- Functions along the call chain may be prematurely exited.

- When a handler is entered, objects created along the call chain will have been destroyed.

Because the statements following a `throw` are not executed, a `throw` is like a `return`: It is usually part of a conditional statement or is the last (or only) statement in a function.

Stack Unwinding

When an exception is thrown, execution of the current function is suspended and the search for a matching catch clause begins. If the throw appears inside a **try block**, the catch clauses associated with that try are examined. If a matching catch is found, the exception is handled by that catch. Otherwise, if the try was itself nested inside another try, the search continues through the catch clauses of the enclosing trys. If no matching catch is found, the current function is exited, and the search continues in the calling function.

If the call to the function that threw is in a try block, then the catch clauses associated with that try are examined. If a matching catch is found, the exception is handled. Otherwise, if that try was nested, the catch clauses of the enclosing trys are searched. If no catch is found, the calling function is also exited. The search continues in the function that called the just exited one, and so on.

This process, known as **stack unwinding**, continues up the chain of nested function calls until a catch clause for the exception is found, or the main function itself is exited without having found a matching catch.

Assuming a matching catch is found, that catch is entered, and the program continues by executing the code inside that catch. When the catch completes, execution continues at the point immediately after the last catch clause associated with that try block.

If no matching catch is found, the program is exited. Exceptions are intended for events that prevent the program from continuing normally. Therefore, once an exception is raised, it cannot remain unhandled. If no matching catch is found, the program calls the library **terminate** function. As its name implies, terminate stops execution of the program.

> An exception that is not caught terminates the program.

Objects Are Automatically Destroyed during Stack Unwinding

During stack unwinding, blocks in the call chain may be exited prematurely. In general, these blocks will have created local objects. Ordinarily, local objects are destroyed when the block in which they are created is exited. Stack unwinding is no exception. When a block is exited during stack unwinding, the compiler guarantees that objects created in that block are properly destroyed. If a local object is of class type, the destructor for that object is called automatically. As usual, the compiler does no work to destroy objects of built-in type.

If an exception occurs in a constructor, then the object under construction might be only partially constructed. Some of its members might have been initialized, but others might not have been initialized before the exception occurred. Even if the object is only partially constructed, we are guaranteed that the constructed members will be properly destroyed.

Similarly, an exception might occur during initialization of the elements of an array or a library container type. Again, we are guaranteed that the elements (if any) that were constructed before the exception occurred will be destroyed.

Destructors and Exceptions

The fact that destructors are run—but code inside a function that frees a resource may be bypassed—affects how we structure our programs. As we saw in § 12.1.4 (p. 467), if a block allocates a resource, and an exception occurs before the code that frees that resource, the code to free the resource will not be executed. On the other hand, resources allocated by an object of class type generally will be freed by their destructor. By using classes to control resource allocation, we ensure that resources are properly freed, whether a function ends normally or via an exception.

The fact that destructors are run during stack unwinding affects how we write destructors. During stack unwinding, an exception has been raised but is not yet handled. If a new exception is thrown during stack unwinding and not caught in the function that threw it, `terminate` is called. Because destructors may be invoked during stack unwinding, they should never throw exceptions that the destructor itself does not handle. That is, if a destructor does an operation that might throw, it should wrap that operation in a `try` block and handle it locally to the destructor.

In practice, because destructors free resources, it is unlikely that they will throw exceptions. All of the standard library types guarantee that their destructors will not raise an exception.

WARNING

During stack unwinding, destructors are run on local objects of class type. Because destructors are run automatically, they should not throw. If, during stack unwinding, a destructor throws an exception that it does not also catch, the program will be terminated.

The Exception Object

The compiler uses the thrown expression to copy initialize (§ 13.1.1, p. 497) a special object known as the **exception object**. As a result, the expression in a `throw` must have a complete type (§ 7.3.3, p. 278). Moreover, if the expression has class type, that class must have an accessible destructor and an accessible copy or move constructor. If the expression has an array or function type, the expression is converted to its corresponding pointer type.

The exception object resides in space, managed by the compiler, that is guaranteed to be accessible to whatever `catch` is invoked. The exception object is destroyed after the exception is completely handled.

As we've seen, when an exception is thrown, blocks along the call chain are exited until a matching handler is found. When a block is exited, the memory used by the local objects in that block is freed. As a result, it is almost certainly an error to throw a pointer to a local object. It is an error for the same reasons that it is an error to return a pointer to a local object (§ 6.3.2, p. 225) from a function. If the pointer points to an object in a block that is exited before the `catch`, then that local object will have been destroyed before the `catch`.

When we throw an expression, the static, compile-time type (§ 15.2.3, p. 601) of that expression determines the type of the exception object. This point is essential to keep in mind, because many applications throw expressions whose type comes from an inheritance hierarchy. If a `throw` expression dereferences a pointer to a base-class type, and that pointer points to a derived-type object, then the thrown object is sliced down (§ 15.2.3, p. 603); only the base-class part is thrown.

 WARNING Throwing a pointer requires that the object to which the pointer points exist wherever the corresponding handler resides.

EXERCISES SECTION 18.1.1

Exercise 18.1: What is the type of the exception object in the following `throw`s?

  (a) `range_error r("error");` (b) `exception *p = &r;`
      `throw r;`   `throw *p;`

What would happen if the `throw` in (b) were written as `throw p`?

Exercise 18.2: Explain what happens if an exception occurs at the indicated point:

```
void exercise(int *b, int *e)
{
    vector<int> v(b, e);
    int *p = new int[v.size()];
    ifstream in("ints");
    // exception occurs here
}
```

Exercise 18.3: There are two ways to make the previous code work correctly if an exception is thrown. Describe them and implement them.

18.1.2 Catching an Exception

The **exception declaration** in a **catch clause** looks like a function parameter list with exactly one parameter. As in a parameter list, we can omit the name of the catch parameter if the `catch` has no need to access the thrown expression.

The type of the declaration determines what kinds of exceptions the handler can catch. The type must be a complete type (§ 7.3.3, p. 278). The type can be an lvalue reference but may not be an rvalue reference (§ 13.6.1, p. 532).

When a `catch` is entered, the parameter in its exception declaration is initialized by the exception object. As with function parameters, if the `catch` parameter has a nonreference type, then the parameter in the `catch` is a copy of the exception object; changes made to the parameter inside the `catch` are made to a local copy, not to the exception object itself. If the parameter has a reference type, then like any reference parameter, the `catch` parameter is just another name for the exception object. Changes made to the parameter are made to the exception object.

Also like a function parameter, a `catch` parameter that has a base-class type can be initialized by an exception object that has a type derived from the parameter type. If the `catch` parameter has a nonreference type, then the exception object will be sliced down (§ 15.2.3, p. 603), just as it would be if such an object were passed to an ordinary function by value. On the other hand, if the parameter is a reference to a base-class type, then the parameter is bound to the exception object in the usual way.

Again, as with a function parameter, the static type of the exception declaration determines the actions that the catch may perform. If the catch parameter has a base-class type, then the catch cannot use any members that are unique to the derived type.

> Ordinarily, a catch that takes an exception of a type related by inheritance ought to define its parameter as a reference.

Finding a Matching Handler

During the search for a matching catch, the catch that is found is not necessarily the one that matches the exception best. Instead, the selected catch is the *first* one that matches the exception at all. As a consequence, in a list of catch clauses, the most specialized catch must appear first.

Because catch clauses are matched in the order in which they appear, programs that use exceptions from an inheritance hierarchy must order their catch clauses so that handlers for a derived type occur before a catch for its base type.

The rules for when an exception matches a catch exception declaration are much more restrictive than the rules used for matching arguments with parameter types. Most conversions are not allowed—the types of the exception and the catch declaration must match exactly with only a few possible differences:

- Conversions from nonconst to const are allowed. That is, a throw of a nonconst object can match a catch specified to take a reference to const.

- Conversions from derived type to base type are allowed.

- An array is converted to a pointer to the type of the array; a function is converted to the appropriate pointer to function type.

No other conversions are allowed to match a catch. In particular, neither the standard arithmetic conversions nor conversions defined for class types are permitted.

> Multiple catch clauses with types related by inheritance must be ordered from most derived type to least derived.

Rethrow

Sometimes a single catch cannot completely handle an exception. After some corrective actions, a catch may decide that the exception must be handled by a function further up the call chain. A catch passes its exception out to another catch by **rethrowing** the exception. A rethrow is a throw that is not followed by an expression:

```
throw;
```

An empty `throw` can appear only in a `catch` or in a function called (directly or indirectly) from a `catch`. If an empty `throw` is encountered when a handler is not active, `terminate` is called.

A rethrow does not specify an expression; the (current) exception object is passed up the chain.

In general, a `catch` might change the contents of its parameter. If, after changing its parameter, the `catch` rethrows the exception, then those changes will be propagated only if the `catch`'s exception declaration is a reference:

```
catch (my_error &eObj) {        // specifier is a reference type
    eObj.status = errCodes::severeErr; //  modifies the exception object
    throw; //  the status member of the exception object is severeErr
} catch (other_error eObj) { //  specifier is a nonreference type
    eObj.status = errCodes::badErr;      //  modifies the local copy only
    throw; //  the status member of the exception object is unchanged
}
```

The Catch-All Handler

Sometimes we want to catch any exception that might occur, regardless of type. Catching every possible exception can be a problem: Sometimes we don't know what types might be thrown. Even when we do know all the types, it may be tedious to provide a specific `catch` clause for every possible exception. To catch all exceptions, we use an ellipsis for the exception declaration. Such handlers, sometimes known as **catch-all** handlers, have the form `catch(...)`. A catch-all clause matches any type of exception.

A `catch(...)` is often used in combination with a rethrow expression. The `catch` does whatever local work can be done and then rethrows the exception:

```
void manip() {
    try {
        // actions that cause an exception to be thrown
    }
    catch (...) {
        // work to partially handle the exception
        throw;
    }
}
```

A `catch(...)` clause can be used by itself or as one of several `catch` clauses.

 If a `catch(...)` is used in combination with other `catch` clauses, it must be last. Any `catch` that follows a catch-all can never be matched.

18.1.3 Function `try` Blocks and Constructors

In general, exceptions can occur at any point in the program's execution. In particular, an exception might occur while processing a constructor initializer. Constructor initializers execute before the constructor body is entered. A `catch` inside

Exercise 18.4: Looking ahead to the inheritance hierarchy in Figure 18.1 (p. 783), explain what's wrong with the following `try` block. Correct it.

```
try {
        // use of the C++ standard library
} catch(exception) {
        // ...
} catch(const runtime_error &re) {
        // ...
} catch(overflow_error eobj) { /* ... */ }
```

Exercise 18.5: Modify the following `main` function to catch any of the exception types shown in Figure 18.1 (p. 783):

```
int main() {
        // use of the C++ standard library
}
```

The handlers should print the error message associated with the exception before calling `abort` (defined in the header `cstdlib`) to terminate `main`.

Exercise 18.6: Given the following exception types and `catch` clauses, write a `throw` expression that creates an exception object that can be caught by each `catch` clause:

```
(a) class exceptionType { };
    catch(exceptionType *pet) { }
(b) catch(...) { }
(c) typedef int EXCPTYPE;
    catch(EXCPTYPE) { }
```

the constructor body can't handle an exception thrown by a constructor initializer because a `try` block inside the constructor body would not yet be in effect when the exception is thrown.

To handle an exception from a constructor initializer, we must write the constructor as a **function `try` block**. A function `try` block lets us associate a group of `catch` clauses with the initialization phase of a constructor (or the destruction phase of a destructor) as well as with the constructor's (or destructor's) function body. As an example, we might wrap the `Blob` constructors (§ 16.1.2, p. 662) in a function `try` block:

```
template <typename T>
Blob<T>::Blob(std::initializer_list<T> il) try :
            data(std::make_shared<std::vector<T>>(il)) {
        /* empty body */
} catch(const std::bad_alloc &e) { handle_out_of_memory(e); }
```

Notice that the keyword `try` appears before the colon that begins the constructor initializer list and before the curly brace that forms the (in this case empty) constructor function body. The `catch` associated with this `try` can be used to handle exceptions thrown either from within the member initialization list or from within the constructor body.

It is worth noting that an exception can happen while initializing the constructor's parameters. Such exceptions are *not* part of the function `try` block. The function `try` block handles only exceptions that occur once the constructor begins executing. As with any other function call, if an exception occurs during parameter initialization, that exception is part of the calling expression and is handled in the caller's context.

 The only way for a constructor to handle an exception from a constructor initializer is to write the constructor as a function `try` block.

Exercise 18.7: Define your `Blob` and `BlobPtr` classes from Chapter 16 to use function `try` blocks for their constructors.

18.1.4 The `noexcept` Exception Specification

It can be helpful both to users and to the compiler to know that a function will not throw any exceptions. Knowing that a function will not throw simplifies the task of writing code that calls that function. Moreover, if the compiler knows that no exceptions will be thrown, it can (sometimes) perform optimizations that must be suppressed if code might throw.

Under the new standard, a function can specify that it does not throw exceptions by providing a **noexcept specification**. The keyword noexcept following the function parameter list indicates that the function won't throw: `C++ 11`

```
void recoup(int) noexcept;   //  won't throw
void alloc(int);             //  might throw
```

These declarations say that `recoup` will not throw any exceptions and that `alloc` might. We say that `recoup` has a **nonthrowing specification**.

The noexcept specifier must appear on all of the declarations and the corresponding definition of a function or on none of them. The specifier precedes a trailing return (§ 6.3.3, p. 229). We may also specify noexcept on the declaration and definition of a function pointer. It may not appear in a `typedef` or type alias. In a member function the noexcept specifier follows any const or reference qualifiers, and it precedes `final`, `override`, or = 0 on a virtual function.

Violating the Exception Specification

It is important to understand that the compiler does not check the noexcept specification at compile time. In fact, the compiler is not permitted to reject a function with a noexcept specifier merely because it contains a throw or calls a function that might throw (however, kind compilers will warn about such usages):

```
//  this function will compile, even though it clearly violates its exception specification
void f() noexcept         //  promises not to throw any exception
{
    throw exception();    //  violates the exception specification
}
```

As a result, it is possible that a function that claims it will not throw will in fact throw. If a `noexcept` function does throw, `terminate` is called, thereby enforcing the promise not to throw at run time. It is unspecified whether the stack is unwound. As a result, `noexcept` should be used in two cases: if we are confident that the function won't throw, and/or if we don't know what we'd do to handle the error anyway.

Specifying that a function won't throw effectively promises the *callers* of the nonthrowing function that they will never need to deal with exceptions. Either the function won't throw, or the whole program will terminate; the caller escapes responsibility either way.

 The compiler in general cannot, and does not, verify exception specifications at compile time.

WARNING

BACKWARD COMPATIBILITY: EXCEPTION SPECIFICATIONS

Earlier versions of C++ had a more elaborate scheme of exception specifications that allowed us to specify the types of exceptions that a function might throw. A function can specify the keyword `throw` followed by a parenthesized list of types that the function might throw. The `throw` specifier appeared in the same place as the `noexcept` specifier does in the current language.

This approach was never widely used and has been deprecated in the current standard. Although these more elaborate specifiers have been deprecated, there is one use of the old scheme that is in widespread use. A function that is designated by `throw()` promises not to throw any exceptions:

```
void recoup(int) noexcept;  //  recoup doesn't throw
void recoup(int) throw();   //  equivalent declaration
```

These declarations of `recoup` are equivalent. Both say that `recoup` won't throw.

Arguments to the `noexcept` Specification

The `noexcept` specifier takes an optional argument that must be convertible to `bool`: If the argument is `true`, then the function won't throw; if the argument is `false`, then the function might throw:

```
void recoup(int) noexcept(true);   //  recoup won't throw
void alloc(int) noexcept(false);   //  alloc can throw
```

The `noexcept` Operator

Arguments to the `noexcept` specifier are often composed using the **noexcept operator**. The `noexcept` operator is a unary operator that returns a `bool` rvalue constant expression that indicates whether a given expression might throw. Like `sizeof` (§ 4.9, p. 156), `noexcept` does not evaluate its operand.

For example, this expression yields `true`:

```
noexcept(recoup(i)) // true if calling recoup can't throw, false otherwise
```

because we declared `recoup` with a `noexcept` specifier. More generally,

```
noexcept(e)
```

is `true` if all the functions called by `e` have nonthrowing specifications and `e` itself does not contain a `throw`. Otherwise, `noexcept(e)` returns `false`.

We can use the `noexcept` operator to form an exception specifier as follows:

```
void f() noexcept(noexcept(g())); // f has same exception specifier as g
```

If the function `g` promises not to throw, then `f` also is nonthrowing. If `g` has no exception specifier, or has an exception specifier that allows exceptions, then `f` also might throw.

> noexcept has two meanings: It is an exception specifier when it follows a function's parameter list, and it is an operator that is often used as the bool argument to a noexcept exception specifier.

Exception Specifications and Pointers, Virtuals, and Copy Control

Although the `noexcept` specifier is not part of a function's type, whether a function has an exception specification affects the use of that function.

A pointer to function and the function to which that pointer points must have compatible specifications. That is, if we declare a pointer that has a nonthrowing exception specification, we can use that pointer only to point to similarly qualified functions. A pointer that specifies (explicitly or implicitly) that it might throw can point to any function, even if that function includes a promise not to throw:

```
// both recoup and pf1 promise not to throw
void (*pf1)(int) noexcept = recoup;
// ok: recoup won't throw; it doesn't matter that pf2 might
void (*pf2)(int) = recoup;
pf1 = alloc; // error: alloc might throw but pf1 said it wouldn't
pf2 = alloc; // ok: both pf2 and alloc might throw
```

If a virtual function includes a promise not to throw, the inherited virtuals must also promise not to throw. On the other hand, if the base allows exceptions, it is okay for the derived functions to be more restrictive and promise not to throw:

```
class Base {
public:
    virtual double f1(double) noexcept;  // doesn't throw
    virtual int f2() noexcept(false);    // can throw
    virtual void f3();                   // can throw
};
```

```
class Derived : public Base {
public:
    double f1(double);        //  error: Base::f1 promises not to throw
    int f2() noexcept(false); //  ok: same specification as Base::f2
    void f3() noexcept;       //  ok: Derived f3 is more restrictive
};
```

When the compiler synthesizes the copy-control members, it generates an exception specification for the synthesized member. If all the corresponding operation for all the members and base classes promise not to throw, then the synthesized member is noexcept. If any function invoked by the synthesized member can throw, then the synthesized member is noexcept(false). Moreover, if we do not provide an exception specification for a destructor that we do define, the compiler synthesizes one for us. The compiler generates the same specification as it would have generated had it synthesized the destructor for that class.

EXERCISES SECTION 18.1.4

Exercise 18.8: Review the classes you've written and add appropriate exception specifications to their constructors and destructors. If you think one of your destructors might throw, change the code so that it cannot throw.

18.1.5 Exception Class Hierarchies

The standard-library exception classes (§ 5.6.3, p. 197) form the inheritance hierarchy (Chapter 15) as shown in Figure 18.1.

The only operations that the exception types define are the copy constructor, copy-assignment operator, a virtual destructor, and a virtual member named what. The what function returns a const char* that points to a null-terminated character array, and is guaranteed not to throw any exceptions.

The exception, bad_cast, and bad_alloc classes also define a default constructor. The runtime_error and logic_error classes do not have a default constructor but do have constructors that take a C-style character string or a library string argument. Those arguments are intended to give additional information about the error. In these classes, what returns the message used to initialize the exception object. Because what is virtual, if we catch a reference to the base-type, a call to the what function will execute the version appropriate to the dynamic type of the exception object.

Exception Classes for a Bookstore Application

Applications often extend the exception hierarchy by defining classes derived from exception (or from one of the library classes derived from exception). These application-specific classes represent exceptional conditions specific to the application domain.

Figure 18.1: Standard exception Class Hierarchy

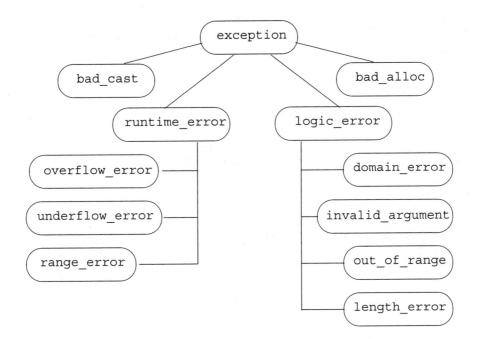

If we were building a real bookstore application, our classes would have been much more complicated than the ones presented in this Primer. One such complexity would be how these classes handled exceptions. In fact, we probably would have defined our own hierarchy of exceptions to represent application-specific problems. Our design might include classes such as

```cpp
// hypothetical exception classes for a bookstore application
class out_of_stock: public std::runtime_error {
public:
    explicit out_of_stock(const std::string &s):
                        std::runtime_error(s) { }
};
class isbn_mismatch: public std::logic_error {
public:
    explicit isbn_mismatch(const std::string &s):
                        std::logic_error(s) { }
    isbn_mismatch(const std::string &s,
        const std::string &lhs, const std::string &rhs):
        std::logic_error(s), left(lhs), right(rhs) { }
    const std::string left, right;
};
```

Our application-specific exception types inherit them from the standard exception classes. As with any hierarchy, we can think of the exception classes as being organized into layers. As the hierarchy becomes deeper, each layer becomes a more specific exception. For example, the first and most general layer of the hierarchy is represented by class exception. All we know when we catch an object of type exception is that something has gone wrong.

The second layer specializes exception into two broad categories: run-time or logic errors. Run-time errors represent things that can be detected only when the program is executing. Logic errors are, in principle, errors that we could have detected in our application.

Our bookstore exception classes further refine these categories. The class named out_of_stock represents something, particular to our application, that can go wrong at run time. It would be used to signal that an order cannot be fulfilled. The class isbn_mismatch represents a more particular form of logic_error. In principle, a program could prevent and handle this error by comparing the results of isbn() on the objects.

Using Our Own Exception Types

We use our own exception classes in the same way that we use one of the standard library classes. One part of the program throws an object of one of these types, and another part catches and handles the indicated problem. As an example, we might define the compound addition operator for our Sales_data class to throw an error of type isbn_mismatch if it detected that the ISBNs didn't match:

```
//  throws an exception if both objects do not refer to the same book
Sales_data&
Sales_data::operator+=(const Sales_data& rhs)
{
    if (isbn() != rhs.isbn())
        throw isbn_mismatch("wrong isbns", isbn(), rhs.isbn());
    units_sold += rhs.units_sold;
    revenue += rhs.revenue;
    return *this;
}
```

Code that uses the compound addition operator (or ordinary addition operator, which itself uses the compound addition operator) can detect this error, write an appropriate error message, and continue:

```
//  use the hypothetical bookstore exceptions
Sales_data item1, item2, sum;
while (cin >> item1 >> item2) {   //  read two transactions
    try {
        sum = item1 + item2;      //  calculate their sum
        //  use sum
    } catch (const isbn_mismatch &e) {
      cerr << e.what() << ": left isbn(" << e.left
           << ") right isbn(" << e.right << ")" << endl;
    }
}
```

Exercise 18.9: Define the bookstore exception classes described in this section and rewrite your `Sales_data` compound assigment operator to throw an exception.

Exercise 18.10: Write a program that uses the `Sales_data` addition operator on objects that have differing ISBNs. Write two versions of the program: one that handles the exception and one that does not. Compare the behavior of the programs so that you become familiar with what happens when an uncaught exception occurs.

Exercise 18.11: Why is it important that the `what` function doesn't throw?

18.2 Namespaces

Large programs tend to use independently developed libraries. Such libraries also tend to define a large number of global names, such as classes, functions, and templates. When an application uses libraries from many different vendors, it is almost inevitable that some of these names will clash. Libraries that put names into the global namespace are said to cause **namespace pollution**.

Traditionally, programmers avoided namespace pollution by using very long names for the global entities they defined. Those names often contained a prefix indicating which library defined the name:

```
class cplusplus_primer_Query { ... };
string cplusplus_primer_make_plural(size_t, string&);
```

This solution is far from ideal: It can be cumbersome for programmers to write and read programs that use such long names.

Namespaces provide a much more controlled mechanism for preventing name collisions. Namespaces partition the global namespace. A namespace is a scope. By defining a library's names inside a namespace, library authors (and users) can avoid the limitations inherent in global names.

18.2.1 Namespace Definitions

A namespace definition begins with the keyword `namespace` followed by the namespace name. Following the namespace name is a sequence of declarations and definitions delimited by curly braces. Any declaration that can appear at global scope can be put into a namespace: classes, variables (with their initializations), functions (with their definitions), templates, and other namespaces:

```
namespace cplusplus_primer {
    class Sales_data { /* ... */};
    Sales_data operator+(const Sales_data&,
                         const Sales_data&);
    class Query { /* ... */ };
    class Query_base { /* ... */};
} // like blocks, namespaces do not end with a semicolon
```

This code defines a namespace named `cplusplus_primer` with four members: three classes and an overloaded + operator.

As with any name, a namespace name must be unique within the scope in which the namespace is defined. Namespaces may be defined at global scope or inside another namespace. They may not be defined inside a function or a class.

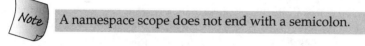 A namespace scope does not end with a semicolon.

Each Namespace Is a Scope

As is the case for any scope, each name in a namespace must refer to a unique entity within that namespace. Because different namespaces introduce different scopes, different namespaces may have members with the same name.

Names defined in a namespace may be accessed directly by other members of the namespace, including scopes nested within those members. Code outside the namespace must indicate the namespace in which the name is defined:

```
cplusplus_primer::Query q =
                cplusplus_primer::Query("hello");
```

If another namespace (say, `AddisonWesley`) also provides a `Query` class and we want to use that class instead of the one defined in `cplusplus_primer`, we can do so by modifying our code as follows:

```
AddisonWesley::Query q = AddisonWesley::Query("hello");
```

Namespaces Can Be Discontiguous

As we saw in § 16.5 (p. 709), unlike other scopes, a namespace can be defined in several parts. Writing a namespace definition:

```
namespace nsp {
// declarations
}
```

either defines a new namespace named `nsp` or adds to an existing one. If the name `nsp` does not refer to a previously defined namespace, then a new namespace with that name is created. Otherwise, this definition opens an existing namespace and adds declarations to that already existing namespace.

The fact that namespace definitions can be discontiguous lets us compose a namespace from separate interface and implementation files. Thus, a namespace can be organized in the same way that we manage our own class and function definitions:

- Namespace members that define classes, and declarations for the functions and objects that are part of the class interface, can be put into header files. These headers can be included by files that use those namespace members.

- The definitions of namespace members can be put in separate source files.

Organizing our namespaces this way also satisfies the requirement that various entities—non-inline functions, static data members, variables, and so forth—may be defined only once in a program. This requirement applies equally to names defined in a namespace. By separating the interface and implementation, we can ensure that the functions and other names we need are defined only once, but the same declaration will be seen whenever the entity is used.

> **Best Practices** Namespaces that define multiple, unrelated types should use separate files to represent each type (or each collection of related types) that the namespace defines.

Defining the Primer Namespace

Using this strategy for separating interface and implementation, we might define the cplusplus_primer library in several separate files. The declarations for Sales_data and its related functions would be placed in Sales_data.h, those for the Query classes of Chapter 15 in Query.h, and so on. The corresponding implementation files would be in files such as Sales_data.cc and Query.cc:

```
// ---- Sales_data.h ----
// #includes should appear before opening the namespace
#include <string>
namespace cplusplus_primer {
    class Sales_data { /* ... */};
    Sales_data operator+(const Sales_data&,
                         const Sales_data&);
    // declarations for the remaining functions in the Sales_data interface
}
// ---- Sales_data.cc ----
// be sure any #includes appear before opening the namespace
#include "Sales_data.h"

namespace cplusplus_primer {
// definitions for Sales_data members and overloaded operators
}
```

A program using our library would include whichever headers it needed. The names in those headers are defined inside the cplusplus_primer namespace:

```
// ---- user.cc ----
// names in the Sales_data.h header are in the cplusplus_primer namespace
#include "Sales_data.h"

int main()
{
    using cplusplus_primer::Sales_data;
    Sales_data trans1, trans2;
    // ...
    return 0;
}
```

This program organization gives the developers and the users of our library the needed modularity. Each class is still organized into its own interface and implementation files. A user of one class need not compile names related to the others. We can hide the implementations from our users, while allowing the files `Sales_data.cc` and `user.cc` to be compiled and linked into one program without causing any compile-time or link-time errors. Developers of the library can work independently on the implementation of each type.

It is worth noting that ordinarily, we do not put a `#include` inside the namespace. If we did, we would be attempting to define all the names in that header as members of the enclosing namespace. For example, if our `Sales_data.h` file opened the `cplusplus_primer` before including the `string` header our program would be in error. It would be attempting to define the `std` namespace nested inside `cplusplus_primer`.

Defining Namespace Members

Assuming the appropriate declarations are in scope, code inside a namespace may use the short form for names defined in the same (or in an enclosing) namespace:

```
#include "Sales_data.h"
namespace cplusplus_primer {    // reopen cplusplus_primer
// members defined inside the namespace may use unqualified names
std::istream&
operator>>(std::istream& in, Sales_data& s) { /* ... */}
}
```

It is also possible to define a namespace member outside its namespace definition. The namespace declaration of the name must be in scope, and the definition must specify the namespace to which the name belongs:

```
// namespace members defined outside the namespace must use qualified names
cplusplus_primer::Sales_data
cplusplus_primer::operator+(const Sales_data& lhs,
                            const Sales_data& rhs)
{
    Sales_data ret(lhs);
    // ...
}
```

As with class members defined outside a class, once the fully qualified name is seen, we are in the scope of the namespace. Inside the `cplusplus_primer` namespace, we can use other namespace member names without qualification. Thus, even though `Sales_data` is a member of the `cplusplus_primer` namespace, we can use its unqualified name to define the parameters in this function.

Although a namespace member can be defined outside its namespace, such definitions must appear in an enclosing namespace. That is, we can define the `Sales_data operator+` inside the `cplusplus_primer` namespace or at global scope. We cannot define this operator in an unrelated namespace.

Template Specializations

Template specializations must be defined in the same namespace that contains the original template (§ 16.5, p. 709). As with any other namespace name, so long as

we have declared the specialization inside the namespace, we can define it outside
the namespace:

```
//  we must declare the specialization as a member of std
namespace std {
    template <> struct hash<Sales_data>;
}
//  having added the declaration for the specialization to std
//  we can define the specialization outside the std namespace
template <> struct std::hash<Sales_data>
{
    size_t operator()(const Sales_data& s) const
    { return hash<string>()(s.bookNo)  ^
            hash<unsigned>()(s.units_sold)  ^
            hash<double>()(s.revenue); }
    //  other members as before
};
```

The Global Namespace

Names defined at global scope (i.e., names declared outside any class, function,
or namespace) are defined inside the **global namespace**. The global namespace is
implicitly declared and exists in every program. Each file that defines entities at
global scope (implicitly) adds those names to the global namespace.

The scope operator can be used to refer to members of the global namespace.
Because the global namespace is implicit, it does not have a name; the notation

```
::member_name
```

refers to a member of the global namespace.

Nested Namespaces

A nested namespace is a namespace defined inside another namespace:

```
namespace cplusplus_primer {
    //  first nested namespace: defines the Query portion of the library
    namespace QueryLib {
        class Query { /* ... */ };
        Query operator&(const Query&, const Query&);
        // ...
    }
    //  second nested namespace: defines the Sales_data portion of the library
    namespace Bookstore {
        class Quote { /* ... */ };
        class Disc_quote : public Quote { /* ... */ };
        // ...
    }
}
```

The `cplusplus_primer` namespace now contains two nested namespaces: the
namespaces named `QueryLib` and `Bookstore`.

A nested namespace is a nested scope—its scope is nested within the namespace that contains it. Nested namespace names follow the normal rules: Names declared in an inner namespace hide declarations of the same name in an outer namespace. Names defined inside a nested namespace are local to that inner namespace. Code in the outer parts of the enclosing namespace may refer to a name in a nested namespace only through its qualified name: For example, the name of the class declared in the nested namespace `QueryLib` is

```
cplusplus_primer::QueryLib::Query
```

Inline Namespaces

The new standard introduced a new kind of nested namespace, an **inline namespace**. Unlike ordinary nested namespaces, names in an inline namespace can be used as if they were direct members of the enclosing namespace. That is, we need not qualify names from an inline namespace by their namespace name. We can access them using only the name of the enclosing namespace.

An inline namespace is defined by preceding the keyword `namespace` with the keyword `inline`:

```
inline namespace FifthEd {
    // namespace for the code from the Primer Fifth Edition
}
namespace FifthEd { // implicitly inline
    class Query_base { /* ... */};
    // other Query-related declarations
}
```

The keyword must appear on the first definition of the namespace. If the namespace is later reopened, the keyword `inline` need not be, but may be, repeated.

Inline namespaces are often used when code changes from one release of an application to the next. For example, we can put all the code from the current edition of the Primer into an inline namespace. Code for previous versions would be in non-inlined namespaces:

```
namespace FourthEd {
    class Item_base { /* ... */};
    class Query_base { /* ... */};
    // other code from the Fourth Edition
}
```

The overall `cplusplus_primer` namespace would include the definitions of both namespaces. For example, assuming that each namespace was defined in a header with the corresponding name, we'd define `cplusplus_primer` as follows:

```
namespace cplusplus_primer {
#include "FifthEd.h"
#include "FourthEd.h"
}
```

Because FifthEd is inline, code that refers to cplusplus_primer:: will get the version from that namespace. If we want the earlier edition code, we can access it as we would any other nested namespace, by using the names of all the enclosing namespaces: for example, cplusplus_primer::FourthEd::Query_base.

Unnamed Namespaces

An **unnamed namespace** is the keyword namespace followed immediately by a block of declarations delimited by curly braces. Variables defined in an un-named namespace have static lifetime: They are created before their first use and destroyed when the program ends.

An unnamed namespace may be discontiguous within a given file but does not span files. Each file has its own unnamed namespace. If two files contain unnamed namespaces, those namespaces are unrelated. Both unnamed namespaces can de-fine the same name; those definitions would refer to different entities. If a header defines an unnamed namespace, the names in that namespace define different en-tities local to each file that includes the header.

 Unlike other namespaces, an unnamed namespace is local to a particu-lar file and never spans multiple files.

Names defined in an unnamed namespace are used directly; after all, there is no namespace name with which to qualify them. It is not possible to use the scope operator to refer to members of unnamed namespaces.

Names defined in an unnamed namespace are in the same scope as the scope at which the namespace is defined. If an unnamed namespace is defined at the outermost scope in the file, then names in the unnamed namespace must differ from names defined at global scope:

```
int i;    // global declaration for i
namespace {
    int i;
}
// ambiguous: defined globally and in an unnested, unnamed namespace
i = 10;
```

In all other ways, the members of an unnamed namespace are normal program entities. An unnamed namespace, like any other namespace, may be nested inside another namespace. If the unnamed namespace is nested, then names in it are accessed in the normal way, using the enclosing namespace name(s):

```
namespace local {
    namespace {
        int i;
    }
}
// ok: i defined in a nested unnamed namespace is distinct from global i
local::i = 42;
```

UNNAMED NAMESPACES REPLACE FILE STATICS

Prior to the introduction of namespaces, programs declared names as `static` to make them local to a file. The use of *file statics* is inherited from C. In C, a global entity declared `static` is invisible outside the file in which it is declared.

 WARNING The use of file `static` declarations is deprecated by the C++ standard. File statics should be avoided and unnamed namespaces used instead.

EXERCISES SECTION 18.2.1

Exercise 18.12: Organize the programs you have written to answer the questions in each chapter into their own namespaces. That is, namespace `chapter15` would contain code for the `Query` programs and `chapter10` would contain the `TextQuery` code. Using this structure, compile the `Query` code examples.

Exercise 18.13: When might you use an unnamed namespace?

Exercise 18.14: Suppose we have the following declaration of the `operator*` that is a member of the nested namespace `mathLib::MatrixLib`:

```
namespace mathLib {
    namespace MatrixLib {
        class matrix {  /* ... */  };
        matrix operator*
                (const matrix &, const matrix &);
        // ...
    }
}
```

How would you declare this operator in global scope?

18.2.2 Using Namespace Members

Referring to namespace members as `namespace_name::member_name` is admittedly cumbersome, especially if the namespace name is long. Fortunately, there are ways to make it easier to use namespace members. Our programs have used one of these ways, `using` declarations (§ 3.1, p. 82). The others, namespace aliases and `using` directives, will be described in this section.

Namespace Aliases

A **namespace alias** can be used to associate a shorter synonym with a namespace name. For example, a long namespace name such as

```
namespace cplusplus_primer      { /* ... */ };
```

can be associated with a shorter synonym as follows:

```
namespace primer = cplusplus_primer;
```

A namespace alias declaration begins with the keyword `namespace`, followed by the alias name, followed by the = sign, followed by the original namespace name and a semicolon. It is an error if the original namespace name has not already been defined as a namespace.

A namespace alias can also refer to a nested namespace:

```
namespace Qlib = cplusplus_primer::QueryLib;
Qlib::Query q;
```

 Note   A namespace can have many synonyms, or aliases. All the aliases and the original namespace name can be used interchangeably.

`using` Declarations: A Recap

A **`using` declaration** introduces only one namespace member at a time. It allows us to be very specific regarding which names are used in our programs.

Names introduced in a `using` declaration obey normal scope rules: They are visible from the point of the `using` declaration to the end of the scope in which the declaration appears. Entities with the same name defined in an outer scope are hidden. The unqualified name may be used only within the scope in which it is declared and in scopes nested within that scope. Once the scope ends, the fully qualified name must be used.

A `using` declaration can appear in global, local, namespace, or class scope. In class scope, such declarations may only refer to a base class member (§ 15.5, p. 615).

`using` Directives

A **`using` directive**, like a `using` declaration, allows us to use the unqualified form of a namespace name. Unlike a `using` declaration, we retain no control over which names are made visible—they all are.

A `using` directive begins with the keyword `using`, followed by the keyword `namespace`, followed by a namespace name. It is an error if the name is not a previously defined namespace name. A `using` directive may appear in global, local, or namespace scope. It may not appear in a class scope.

These directives make all the names from a specific namespace visible without qualification. The short form names can be used from the point of the `using` directive to the end of the scope in which the `using` directive appears.

⚠️ **WARNING**   Providing a `using` directive for namespaces, such as `std`, that our application does not control reintroduces all the name collision problems inherent in using multiple libraries.

`using` Directives and Scope

The scope of names introduced by a `using` directive is more complicated than the scope of names in `using` declarations. As we've seen, a `using` declaration puts the name in the same scope as that of the `using` declaration itself. It is as if the `using` declaration declares a local alias for the namespace member.

A using directive does not declare local aliases. Rather, it has the effect of lifting the namespace members into the nearest scope that contains both the name-space itself and the using directive.

This difference in scope between a using declaration and a using directive stems directly from how these two facilities work. In the case of a using declara-tion, we are simply making name directly accessible in the local scope. In contrast, a using directive makes the entire contents of a namespace available In general, a namespace might include definitions that cannot appear in a local scope. As a consequence, a using directive is treated as if it appeared in the nearest enclosing namespace scope.

In the simplest case, assume we have a namespace A and a function f, both defined at global scope. If f has a using directive for A, then in f it will be as if the names in A appeared in the global scope prior to the definition of f:

```
//   namespace A and function f are defined at global scope
namespace A {
    int i, j;
}
void f()
{
    using namespace A;      //   injects the names from A into the global scope
    cout << i * j << endl; //   uses i and j from namespace A
    //   ...
}
```

using Directives Example

Let's look at an example:

```
namespace blip {
    int i = 16, j = 15, k = 23;
    //   other declarations
}
int j = 0;   //   ok: j inside blip is hidden inside a namespace
void manip()
{
    //   using directive; the names in blip are "added" to the global scope
    using namespace blip; //   clash between ::j and blip::j
                          //   detected only if j is used
    ++i;              //   sets blip::i to 17
    ++j;              //   error ambiguous: global j or blip::j?
    ++::j;            //   ok: sets global j to 1
    ++blip::j;        //   ok: sets blip::j to 16
    int k = 97; //   local k hides blip::k
    ++k;              //   sets local k to 98
}
```

The using directive in manip makes all the names in blip directly accessible; code inside manip can refer to the names of these members, using their short form.

The members of `blip` appear as if they were defined in the scope in which both `blip` and `manip` are defined. Assuming `manip` is defined at global scope, then the members of `blip` appear as if they were declared in global scope.

When a namespace is injected into an enclosing scope, it is possible for names in the namespace to conflict with other names defined in that (enclosing) scope. For example, inside `manip`, the `blip` member `j` conflicts with the global object named `j`. Such conflicts are permitted, but to use the name, we must explicitly indicate which version is wanted. Any unqualified use of `j` within `manip` is ambiguous.

To use a name such as `j`, we must use the scope operator to indicate which name is wanted. We would write `::j` to obtain the variable defined in global scope. To use the `j` defined in `blip`, we must use its qualified name, `blip::j`.

Because the names are in different scopes, local declarations within `manip` may hide some of the namespace member names. The local variable `k` hides the namespace member `blip::k`. Referring to `k` within `manip` is not ambiguous; it refers to the local variable `k`.

Headers and `using` Declarations or Directives

A header that has a `using` directive or declaration at its top-level scope injects names into every file that includes the header. Ordinarily, headers should define only the names that are part of its interface, not names used in its own implementation. As a result, header files should not contain `using` directives or `using` declarations except inside functions or namespaces (§ 3.1, p. 83).

CAUTION: AVOID `using` DIRECTIVES

`using` directives, which inject all the names from a namespace, are deceptively simple to use: With only a single statement, all the member names of a namespace are suddenly visible. Although this approach may seem simple, it can introduce its own problems. If an application uses many libraries, and if the names within these libraries are made visible with `using` directives, then we are back to square one, and the global namespace pollution problem reappears.

Moreover, it is possible that a working program will fail to compile when a new version of the library is introduced. This problem can arise if a new version introduces a name that conflicts with a name that the application is using.

Another problem is that ambiguity errors caused by `using` directives are detected only at the point of use. This late detection means that conflicts can arise long after introducing a particular library. If the program begins using a new part of the library, previously undetected collisions may arise.

Rather than relying on a `using` directive, it is better to use a `using` declaration for each namespace name used in the program. Doing so reduces the number of names injected into the namespace. Ambiguity errors caused by `using` declarations are detected at the point of declaration, not use, and so are easier to find and fix.

 One place where `using` directives are useful is in the implementation files of the namespace itself.

Exercise 18.15: Explain the differences between using declarations and directives.

Exercise 18.16: Explain the following code assuming using declarations for all the members of namespace Exercise are located at the location labeled *position 1*. What if they appear at *position 2* instead? Now answer the same question but replace the using declarations with a using directive for namespace Exercise.

```
namespace Exercise {
    int ivar = 0;
    double dvar = 0;
    const int limit = 1000;
}
int ivar = 0;
// position 1
void manip() {
    // position 2
    double dvar = 3.1416;
    int iobj = limit + 1;
    ++ivar;
    ++::ivar;
}
```

Exercise 18.17: Write code to test your answers to the previous question.

18.2.3 Classes, Namespaces, and Scope

Name lookup for names used inside a namespace follows the normal lookup rules: The search looks outward through the enclosing scopes. An enclosing scope might be one or more nested namespaces, ending in the all-encompassing global namespace. Only names that have been declared before the point of use that are in blocks that are still open are considered:

```
namespace A {
    int i;
    namespace B {
        int i;          // hides A::i within B
        int j;
        int f1()
        {
            int j;      // j is local to f1 and hides A::B::j
            return i;   // returns B::i
        }
    }   // namespace B is closed and names in it are no longer visible
    int f2() {
        return j;       // error: j is not defined
    }
    int j = i;          // initialized from A::i
}
```

When a class is wrapped in a namespace, the normal lookup still happens: When a name is used by a member function, look for that name in the member first, then within the class (including base classes), then look in the enclosing scopes, one or more of which might be a namespace:

```
namespace A {
    int i;
    int k;
    class C1 {
    public:
        C1(): i(0), j(0) { }    //  ok: initializes C1::i and C1::j
        int f1() { return k; } //  returns A::k
        int f2() { return h; }  //  error: h is not defined
        int f3();
    private:
        int i;                          //  hides A::i within C1
        int j;
    };
    int h = i;                        //  initialized from A::i
}
//  member f3 is defined outside class C1 and outside namespace A
int A::C1::f3() { return h; }    //  ok: returns A::h
```

With the exception of member function definitions that appear inside the class body (§ 7.4.1, p. 283), scopes are always searched upward; names must be declared before they can be used. Hence, the `return` in `f2` will not compile. It attempts to reference the name `h` from namespace `A`, but `h` has not yet been defined. Had that name been defined in `A` before the definition of `C1`, the use of `h` would be legal. Similarly, the use of `h` inside `f3` is okay, because `f3` is defined after `A::h`.

The order in which scopes are examined to find a name can be inferred from the qualified name of a function. The qualified name indicates, in reverse order, the scopes that are searched.

The qualifiers `A::C1::f3` indicate the reverse order in which the class scopes and namespace scopes are to be searched. The first scope searched is that of the function `f3`. Then the class scope of its enclosing class `C1` is searched. The scope of the namespace `A` is searched last before the scope containing the definition of `f3` is examined.

Argument-Dependent Lookup and Parameters of Class Type

Consider the following simple program:

```
std::string s;
std::cin >> s;
```

As we know, this call is equivalent to (§ 14.1, p. 553):

```
operator>>(std::cin, s);
```

This `operator>>` function is defined by the `string` library, which in turn is defined in the `std` namespace. Yet we can we call `operator>>` without an `std::` qualifier and without a `using` declaration.

We can directly access the output operator because there is an important exception to the rule that names defined in a namespace are hidden. When we pass an object of a class type to a function, the compiler searches the namespace in which the argument's class is defined *in addition* to the normal scope lookup. This exception also applies for calls that pass pointers or references to a class type.

In this example, when the compiler sees the "call" to `operator>>`, it looks for a matching function in the current scope, including the scopes enclosing the output statement. In addition, because the `>>` expression has parameters of class type, the compiler also looks in the namespace(s) in which the types of `cin` and `s` are defined. Thus, for this call, the compiler looks in the `std` namespace, which defines the `istream` and `string` types. When it searches `std`, the compiler finds the `string` output operator function.

This exception in the lookup rules allows nonmember functions that are conceptually part of the interface to a class to be used without requiring a separate `using` declaration. In the absence of this exception to the lookup rules, either we would have to provide an appropriate `using` declaration for the output operator:

```
using std::operator>>;              // needed to allow cin >> s
```

or we would have to use the function-call notation in order to include the namespace qualifer:

```
std::operator>>(std::cin, s);   // ok: explicitly use std::>>
```

There would be no way to use operator syntax. Either of these declarations is awkward and would make simple uses of the IO library more complicated.

Lookup and `std::move` and `std::forward`

Many, perhaps even most, C++ programmers never have to think about argument-dependent lookup. Ordinarily, if an application defines a name that is also defined in the library, one of two things is true: Either normal overloading determines (correctly) whether a particular call is intended for the application version or the one from the library, or the application never intends to use the library function.

Now consider the library `move` and `forward` functions. Both of these functions are template functions, and the library defines versions of them that have a single rvalue reference function parameter. As we've seen, in a function template, an rvalue reference parameter can match any type (§ 16.2.6, p. 690). If our application defines a function named `move` that takes a single parameter, then—no matter what type the parameter has—the application's version of `move` will collide with the library version. Similarly for `forward`.

As a result, name collisions with `move` (and `forward`) are more likely than collisions with other library functions. In addition, because `move` and `forward` do very specialized type manipulations, the chances that an application specifically wants to override the behavior of these functions are pretty small.

The fact that collisions are more likely—and are less likely to be intentional—explains why we suggest always using the fully qualified versions of these names (§ 12.1.5, p. 470). So long as we write `std::move` rather than `move`, we know that we will get the version from the standard library.

Friend Declarations and Argument-Dependent Lookup

Recall that when a class declares a friend, the friend declaration does not make the friend visible (§ 7.2.1, p. 270). However, an otherwise undeclared class or function that is first named in a friend declaration is assumed to be a member of the closest enclosing namespace. The combination of this rule and argument-dependent lookup can lead to surprises:

```
namespace A {
    class C {
        //  two friends; neither is declared apart from a friend declaration
        //  these functions implicitly are members of namespace A
        friend void f2();        //  won't be found, unless otherwise declared
        friend void f(const C&); //  found by argument-dependent lookup
    };
}
```

Here, both `f` and `f2` are members of namespace `A`. Through argument-dependent lookup, we can call `f` even if there is no additional declaration for `f`:

```
int main()
{
    A::C cobj;
    f(cobj);   //  ok: finds A::f through the friend declaration in A::C
    f2();      //  error: A::f2 not declared
}
```

Because `f` takes an argument of a class type, and `f` is implicitly declared in the same namespace as `C`, `f` is found when called. Because `f2` has no parameter, it will not be found.

EXERCISES SECTION 18.2.3

Exercise 18.18: Given the following typical definition of swap § 13.3 (p. 517), determine which version of swap is used if mem1 is a `string`. What if mem1 is an `int`? Explain how name lookup works in both cases.

```
void swap(T v1, T v2)
{
    using std::swap;
    swap(v1.mem1, v2.mem1);
    //  swap remaining members of type T
}
```

Exercise 18.19: What if the call to swap was `std::swap(v1.mem1, v2.mem1)`?

18.2.4 Overloading and Namespaces

Namespaces have two impacts on function matching (§ 6.4, p. 233). One of these should be obvious: A using declaration or directive can add functions to the candidate set. The other is much more subtle.

Argument-Dependent Lookup and Overloading

As we saw in the previous section, name lookup for functions that have class-type arguments includes the namespace in which each argument's class is defined. This rule also impacts how we determine the candidate set. Each namespace that defines a class used as an argument (and those that define its base classes) is searched for candidate functions. Any functions in those namespaces that have the same name as the called function are added to the candidate set. These functions are added *even though they otherwise are not visible at the point of the call*:

```
namespace NS {
    class Quote { /* ... */ };
    void display(const Quote&) { /* ... */ }
}
// Bulk_item's base class is declared in namespace NS
class Bulk_item : public NS::Quote { /* ... */ };
int main() {
    Bulk_item book1;
    display(book1);
    return 0;
}
```

The argument we passed to display has class type Bulk_item. The candidate functions for the call to display are not only the functions with declarations that are in scope where display is called, but also the functions in the namespace where Bulk_item and its base class, Quote, are declared. The function display(const Quote&) declared in namespace NS is added to the set of candidate functions.

Overloading and using Declarations

To understand the interaction between using declarations and overloading, it is important to remember that a using declaration declares a name, not a specific function (§ 15.6, p. 621):

```
using NS::print(int);    // error: cannot specify a parameter list
using NS::print;         // ok: using declarations specify names only
```

When we write a using declaration for a function, all the versions of that function are brought into the current scope.

A using declaration incorporates all versions to ensure that the interface of the namespace is not violated. The author of a library provided different functions for a reason. Allowing users to selectively ignore some but not all of the functions from a set of overloaded functions could lead to surprising program behavior.

The functions introduced by a using declaration overload any other declarations of the functions with the same name already present in the scope where the using declaration appears. If the using declaration appears in a local scope, these names hide existing declarations for that name in the outer scope. If the using declaration introduces a function in a scope that already has a function of the same name with the same parameter list, then the using declaration is in error. Otherwise, the using declaration defines additional overloaded instances of the given name. The effect is to increase the set of candidate functions.

Overloading and using Directives

A using directive lifts the namespace members into the enclosing scope. If a namespace function has the same name as a function declared in the scope at which the namespace is placed, then the namespace member is added to the overload set:

```
namespace libs_R_us {
    extern void print(int);
    extern void print(double);
}
//   ordinary declaration
void print(const std::string &);
//   this using directive adds names to the candidate set for calls to print:
using namespace libs_R_us;
//   the candidates for calls to print at this point in the program are:
//      print(int) from libs_R_us
//      print(double) from libs_R_us
//      print(const std::string &) declared explicitly
void fooBar(int ival)
{
    print("Value: ");  //  calls global print(const string &)
    print(ival);       //  calls libs_R_us::print(int)
}
```

Differently from how using declarations work, it is not an error if a using directive introduces a function that has the same parameters as an existing function. As with other conflicts generated by using directives, there is no problem unless we try to call the function without specifying whether we want the one from the namespace or from the current scope.

Overloading across Multiple using Directives

If many using directives are present, then the names from each namespace become part of the candidate set:

```
namespace AW {
    int print(int);
}
namespace Primer {
    double print(double);
}
```

```
//  using directives create an overload set of functions from different namespaces
using namespace AW;
using namespace Primer;

long double print(long double);

int main() {
    print(1);    // calls AW::print(int)
    print(3.1);  // calls Primer::print(double)
    return 0;
}
```

The overload set for the function `print` in global scope contains the functions `print(int)`, `print(double)`, and `print(long double)`. These functions are all part of the overload set considered for the function calls in `main`, even though these functions were originally declared in different namespace scopes.

EXERCISES SECTION 18.2.4

Exercise 18.20: In the following code, determine which function, if any, matches the call to `compute`. List the candidate and viable functions. What type conversions, if any, are applied to the argument to match the parameter in each viable function?

```
namespace primerLib {
    void compute();
    void compute(const void *);
}
using primerLib::compute;
void compute(int);
void compute(double, double = 3.4);
void compute(char*, char* = 0);

void f()
{
    compute(0);
}
```

What would happen if the `using` declaration were located in `main` before the call to `compute`? Answer the same questions as before.

18.3 Multiple and Virtual Inheritance

Multiple inheritance is the ability to derive a class from more than one direct base class (§ 15.2.2, p. 600). A multiply derived class inherits the properties of all its parents. Although simple in concept, the details of intertwining multiple base classes can present tricky design-level and implementation-level problems.

To explore multiple inheritance, we'll use a pedagogical example of a zoo animal hierarchy. Our zoo animals exist at different levels of abstraction. There are the individual animals, distinguished by their names, such as Ling-ling, Mowgli, and Balou. Each animal belongs to a species; Ling-Ling, for example, is a giant panda. Species, in turn, are members of families. A giant panda is a member of the bear family. Each family, in turn, is a member of the animal kingdom—in this case, the more limited kingdom of a particular zoo.

We'll define an abstract `ZooAnimal` class to hold information that is common to all the zoo animals and provides the most general interface. The `Bear` class will contain information that is unique to the `Bear` family, and so on.

In addition to the `ZooAnimal` classes, our application will contain auxiliary classes that encapsulate various abstractions such as endangered animals. In our implementation of a `Panda` class, for example, a `Panda` is multiply derived from `Bear` and `Endangered`.

18.3.1 Multiple Inheritance

The derivation list in a derived class can contain more than one base class:

```
class Bear : public ZooAnimal {
class Panda : public Bear, public Endangered { /* ... */ };
```

Each base class has an optional access specifier (§ 15.5, p. 612). As usual, if the access specifier is omitted, the specifier defaults to `private` if the `class` keyword is used and to `public` if `struct` is used (§ 15.5, p. 616).

As with single inheritance, the derivation list may include only classes that have been defined and that were not defined as `final` (§ 15.2.2, p. 600). There is no language-imposed limit on the number of base classes from which a class can be derived. A base class may appear only once in a given derivation list.

Multiply Derived Classes Inherit State from Each Base Class

Under multiple inheritance, an object of a derived class contains a subobject for each of its base classes (§ 15.2.2, p. 597). For example, as illustrated in Figure 18.2, a `Panda` object has a `Bear` part (which itself contains a `ZooAnimal` part), an `Endangered` class part, and the `nonstatic` data members, if any, declared within the `Panda` class.

Figure 18.2: Conceptual Structure of a `Panda` Object

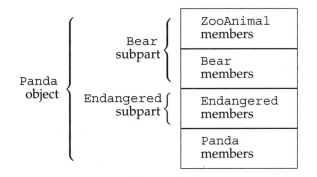

Derived Constructors Initialize All Base Classes

Constructing an object of derived type constructs and initializes all its base subobjects. As is the case for inheriting from a single base class (§ 15.2.2, p. 598), a
derived type's constructor initializer may initialize only its direct base classes:

```
//  explicitly initialize both base classes
Panda::Panda(std::string name, bool onExhibit)
      : Bear(name, onExhibit, "Panda"),
        Endangered(Endangered::critical) { }
//  implicitly uses the Bear default constructor to initialize the Bear subobject
Panda::Panda()
      : Endangered(Endangered::critical) { }
```

The constructor initializer list may pass arguments to each of the direct base classes.
The order in which base classes are constructed depends on the order in which they
appear in the class derivation list. The order in which they appear in the constructor initializer list is irrelevant. A `Panda` object is initialized as follows:

- `ZooAnimal`, the ultimate base class up the hierarchy from `Panda`'s first direct base class, `Bear`, is initialized first.

- `Bear`, the first direct base class, is initialized next.

- `Endangered`, the second direct base, is initialized next.

- `Panda`, the most derived part, is initialized last.

Inherited Constructors and Multiple Inheritance

Under the new standard, a derived class can inherit its constructors from one or
more of its base classes (§ 15.7.4, p. 628). It is an error to inherit the same constructor (i.e., one with the same parameter list) from more than one base class:

```
struct Base1 {
    Base1() = default;
    Base1(const std::string&);
    Base1(std::shared_ptr<int>);
};
struct Base2 {
    Base2() = default;
    Base2(const std::string&);
    Base2(int);
};
//  error: D1 attempts to inherit D1::D1 (const string&) from both base classes
struct D1: public Base1, public Base2 {
    using Base1::Base1;  //  inherit constructors from Base1
    using Base2::Base2;  //  inherit constructors from Base2
};
```

A class that inherits the same constructor from more than one base class must
define its own version of that constructor:

```
struct D2: public Base1, public Base2 {
    using Base1::Base1;  // inherit constructors from Base1
    using Base2::Base2;  // inherit constructors from Base2
    // D2 must define its own constructor that takes a string
    D2(const string &s): Base1(s), Base2(s) { }
    D2() = default;  // needed once D2 defines its own constructor
};
```

Destructors and Multiple Inheritance

As usual, the destructor in a derived class is responsible for cleaning up resources allocated by that class only—the members and all the base class(es) of the derived class are automatically destroyed. The synthesized destructor has an empty function body.

Destructors are always invoked in the reverse order from which the constructors are run. In our example, the order in which the destructors are called is ~Panda, ~Endangered, ~Bear, ~ZooAnimal.

Copy and Move Operations for Multiply Derived Classes

As is the case for single inheritance, classes with multiple bases that define their own copy/move constructors and assignment operators must copy, move, or assign the whole object (§ 15.7.2, p. 623). The base parts of a multiply derived class are automatically copied, moved, or assigned only if the derived class uses the synthesized versions of these members. In the synthesized copy-control members, each base class is implicitly constructed, assigned, or destroyed, using the corresponding member from that base class.

For example, assuming that Panda uses the synthesized members, then the initialization of ling_ling:

```
Panda ying_yang("ying_yang");
Panda ling_ling = ying_yang;     // uses the copy constructor
```

will invoke the Bear copy constructor, which in turn runs the ZooAnimal copy constructor before executing the Bear copy constructor. Once the Bear portion of ling_ling is constructed, the Endangered copy constructor is run to create that part of the object. Finally, the Panda copy constructor is run. Similarly, for the synthesized move constructor.

The synthesized copy-assignment operator behaves similarly to the copy constructor. It assigns the Bear (and through Bear, the ZooAnimal) parts of the object first. Next, it assigns the Endangered part, and finally the Panda part. Move assignment behaves similarly.

18.3.2 Conversions and Multiple Base Classes

Under single inheritance, a pointer or a reference to a derived class can be converted automatically to a pointer or a reference to an accessible base class (§ 15.2.2, p. 597, and § 15.5, p. 613). The same holds true with multiple inheritance. A pointer or reference to any of an object's (accessible) base classes can be used to point or

---

EXERCISES SECTION 18.3.1

Exercise 18.21: Explain the following declarations. Identify any that are in error and explain why they are incorrect:

```
(a) class CADVehicle : public CAD, Vehicle { ... };
(b) class DblList: public List, public List { ... };
(c) class iostream: public istream, public ostream { ... };
```

Exercise 18.22: Given the following class hierarchy, in which each class defines a default constructor:

```
class A { ... };
class B : public A { ... };
class C : public B { ... };
class X { ... };
class Y { ... };
class Z : public X, public Y { ... };
class MI : public C, public Z { ... };
```

what is the order of constructor execution for the following definition?

```
MI mi;
```

---

refer to a derived object. For example, a pointer or reference to `ZooAnimal`, `Bear`, or `Endangered` can be bound to a `Panda` object:

```
//   operations that take references to base classes of type Panda
void print(const Bear&);
void highlight(const Endangered&);
ostream& operator<<(ostream&, const ZooAnimal&);

Panda ying_yang("ying_yang");

print(ying_yang);      // passes Panda to a reference to Bear
highlight(ying_yang);  // passes Panda to a reference to Endangered
cout << ying_yang << endl; // passes Panda to a reference to ZooAnimal
```

The compiler makes no attempt to distinguish between base classes in terms of a derived-class conversion. Converting to each base class is equally good. For example, if there was an overloaded version of `print`:

```
void print(const Bear&);
void print(const Endangered&);
```

an unqualified call to `print` with a `Panda` object would be a compile-time error:

```
Panda ying_yang("ying_yang");
print(ying_yang);                    // error: ambiguous
```

Lookup Based on Type of Pointer or Reference

As with single inheritance, the static type of the object, pointer, or reference determines which members we can use (§ 15.6, p. 617). If we use a `ZooAnimal` pointer, only the operations defined in that class are usable. The `Bear`-specific, `Panda`-specific, and `Endangered` portions of the `Panda` interface are invisible. Similarly, a `Bear` pointer or reference knows only about the `Bear` and `ZooAnimal` members; an `Endangered` pointer or reference is limited to the `Endangered` members.

As an example, consider the following calls, which assume that our classes define the virtual functions listed in Table 18.1:

```
Bear *pb = new Panda("ying_yang");
pb->print();        //  ok: Panda::print()
pb->cuddle();       //  error: not part of the Bear interface
pb->highlight();    //  error: not part of the Bear interface
delete pb;          //  ok: Panda::~Panda()
```

When a `Panda` is used via an `Endangered` pointer or reference, the `Panda`-specific and `Bear` portions of the `Panda` interface are invisible:

```
Endangered *pe = new Panda("ying_yang");
pe->print();        //  ok: Panda::print()
pe->toes();         //  error: not part of the Endangered interface
pe->cuddle();       //  error: not part of the Endangered interface
pe->highlight();    //  ok: Panda::highlight()
delete pe;          //  ok: Panda::~Panda()
```

Table 18.1: Virtual Functions in the `ZooAnimal`/`Endangered` Classes

Function	Class Defining Own Version
print	ZooAnimal::ZooAnimal
	Bear::Bear
	Endangered::Endangered
	Panda::Panda
highlight	Endangered::Endangered
	Panda::Panda
toes	Bear::Bear
	Panda::Panda
cuddle	Panda::Panda
destructor	ZooAnimal::ZooAnimal
	Endangered::Endangered

18.3.3 Class Scope under Multiple Inheritance

Under single inheritance, the scope of a derived class is nested within the scope of its direct and indirect base classes (§ 15.6, p. 617). Lookup happens by searching up the inheritance hierarchy until the given name is found. Names defined in a derived class hide uses of that name inside a base.

Under multiple inheritance, this same lookup happens *simultaneously* among all the direct base classes. If a name is found through more than one base class, then use of that name is ambiguous.

EXERCISES SECTION 18.3.2

Exercise 18.23: Using the hierarchy in exercise 18.22 along with class D defined below, and assuming each class defines a default constructor, which, if any, of the following conversions are not permitted?

```
class D : public X, public C { ... };
D *pd = new D;
```

(a) X *px = pd;   (b) A *pa = pd;
(c) B *pb = pd;   (d) C *pc = pd;

Exercise 18.24: On page 807 we presented a series of calls made through a Bear pointer that pointed to a Panda object. Explain each call assuming we used a ZooAnimal pointer pointing to a Panda object instead.

Exercise 18.25: Assume we have two base classes, Base1 and Base2, each of which defines a virtual member named print and a virtual destructor. From these base classes we derive the following classes, each of which redefines the print function:

```
class D1 : public Base1 { /* ... */ };
class D2 : public Base2 { /* ... */ };
class MI : public D1, public D2 { /* ... */ };
```

Using the following pointers, determine which function is used in each call:

```
Base1 *pb1 = new MI;
Base2 *pb2 = new MI;
D1 *pd1 = new MI;
D2 *pd2 = new MI;
```

(a) pb1->print();   (b) pd1->print();   (c) pd2->print();
(d) delete pb2;   (e) delete pd1;   (f) delete pd2;

In our example, if we use a name through a Panda object, pointer, or reference, both the Endangered and the Bear/ZooAnimal subtrees are examined in parallel. If the name is found in more than one subtree, then the use of the name is ambiguous. It is perfectly legal for a class to inherit multiple members with the same name. However, if we want to use that name, we must specify which version we want to use.

> **WARNING** When a class has multiple base classes, it is possible for that derived class to inherit a member with the same name from two or more of its base classes. Unqualified uses of that name are ambiguous.

For example, if both ZooAnimal and Endangered define a member named max_weight, and Panda does not define that member, this call is an error:

```
double d = ying_yang.max_weight();
```

The derivation of Panda, which results in Panda having two members named max_weight, is perfectly legal. The derivation generates a *potential* ambiguity. That ambiguity is avoided if no Panda object ever calls max_weight. The error would also be avoided if each call to `max_weight` specifically indicated which version to run—`ZooAnimal::max_weight` or `Endangered::max_weight`. An error results only if there is an ambiguous attempt to use the member.

The ambiguity of the two inherited `max_weight` members is reasonably obvious. It might be more surprising to learn that an error would be generated even if the two inherited functions had different parameter lists. Similarly, it would be an error even if the `max_weight` function were `private` in one class and `public` or `protected` in the other. Finally, if `max_weight` were defined in `Bear` and not in `ZooAnimal`, the call would still be in error.

As always, name lookup happens before type checking (§ 6.4.1, p. 234). When the compiler finds `max_weight` in two different scopes, it generates an error noting that the call is ambiguous.

The best way to avoid potential ambiguities is to define a version of the function in the derived class that resolves the ambiguity. For example, we should give our `Panda` class a `max_weight` function that resolves the ambiguity:

```
double Panda::max_weight() const
{
    return std::max(ZooAnimal::max_weight(),
                    Endangered::max_weight());
}
```

EXERCISES SECTION 18.3.3

Exercise 18.26: Given the hierarchy in the box on page 810, why is the following call to `print` an error? Revise `MI` to allow this call to `print` to compile and execute correctly.

```
MI mi;
mi.print(42);
```

Exercise 18.27: Given the class hierarchy in the box on page 810 and assuming we add a function named `foo` to `MI` as follows:

```
int ival;
double dval;
void MI::foo(double cval)
{
    int dval;
    // exercise questions occur here
}
```

(a) List all the names visible from within `MI::foo`.
(b) Are any names visible from more than one base class?
(c) Assign to the local instance of `dval` the sum of the `dval` member of `Base1` and the `dval` member of `Derived`.
(d) Assign the value of the last element in `MI::dvec` to `Base2::fval`.
(e) Assign `cval` from `Base1` to the first character in `sval` from `Derived`.

CODE FOR EXERCISES TO SECTION 18.3.3

```
struct Base1 {
    void print(int) const;       // public by default
protected:
    int    ival;
    double dval;
    char   cval;
private:
    int    *id;
};
struct Base2 {
    void print(double) const;            // public by default
protected:
    double  fval;
private:
    double  dval;
};
struct Derived : public Base1 {
    void print(std::string) const;    // public by default
protected:
    std::string sval;
    double      dval;
};
struct MI : public Derived, public Base2 {
    void print(std::vector<double>); // public by default
protected:
    int                  *ival;
    std::vector<double>  dvec;
};
```

18.3.4 Virtual Inheritance

Although the derivation list of a class may not include the same base class more than once, a class can inherit from the same base class more than once. It might inherit the same base indirectly from two of its own direct base classes, or it might inherit a particular class directly and indirectly through another of its base classes.

As an example, the IO library istream and ostream classes each inherit from a common abstract base class named basic_ios. That class holds the stream's buffer and manages the stream's condition state. The class iostream, which can both read and write to a stream, inherits directly from both istream and ostream. Because both types inherit from basic_ios, iostream inherits that base class twice, once through istream and once through ostream.

By default, a derived object contains a separate subpart corresponding to each class in its derivation chain. If the same base class appears more than once in the derivation, then the derived object will have more than one subobject of that type.

This default doesn't work for a class such as iostream. An iostream object wants to use the same buffer for both reading and writing, and it wants its condition state to reflect both input and output operations. If an `iostream` object has two copies of its `basic_ios` class, this sharing isn't possible.

In C++ we solve this kind of problem by using **virtual inheritance**. Virtual inheritance lets a class specify that it is willing to share its base class. The shared base-class subobject is called a **virtual base class**. Regardless of how often the same virtual base appears in an inheritance hierarchy, the derived object contains only one, shared subobject for that virtual base class.

A Different `Panda` Class

In the past, there was some debate as to whether panda belongs to the raccoon or the bear family. To reflect this debate, we can change `Panda` to inherit from both `Bear` and `Raccoon`. To avoid giving `Panda` two `ZooAnimal` base parts, we'll define `Bear` and `Raccoon` to inherit virtually from `ZooAnimal`. Figure 18.3 illustrates our new hierarchy.

Looking at our new hierarchy, we'll notice a nonintuitive aspect of virtual inheritance. The virtual derivation has to be made before the need for it appears. For example, in our classes, the need for virtual inheritance arises only when we define `Panda`. However, if `Bear` and `Raccoon` had not specified `virtual` on their derivation from `ZooAnimal`, the designer of the `Panda` class would be out of luck.

In practice, the requirement that an intermediate base class specify its inheritance as virtual rarely causes any problems. Ordinarily, a class hierarchy that uses virtual inheritance is designed at one time either by one individual or by a single project design group. It is exceedingly rare for a class to be developed independently that needs a virtual base in one of its base classes and in which the developer of the new base class cannot change the existing hierarchy.

> *Note* Virtual derivation affects the classes that subsequently derive from a class with a virtual base; it doesn't affect the derived class itself.

Figure 18.3: Virtual Inheritance `Panda` Hierarchy

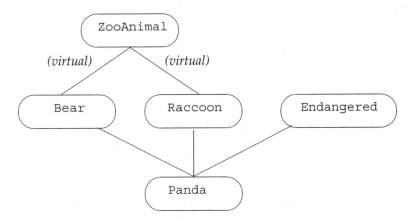

Using a Virtual Base Class

We specify that a base class is virtual by including the keyword `virtual` in the derivation list:

```
// the order of the keywords public and virtual is not significant
class Raccoon : public virtual ZooAnimal { /* ... */ };
class Bear : virtual public ZooAnimal { /* ... */ };
```

Here we've made `ZooAnimal` a virtual base class of both `Bear` and `Raccoon`.

The `virtual` specifier states a willingness to share a single instance of the named base class within a subsequently derived class. There are no special constraints on a class used as a virtual base class.

We do nothing special to inherit from a class that has a virtual base:

```
class Panda : public Bear,
              public Raccoon, public Endangered {
};
```

Here `Panda` inherits `ZooAnimal` through both its `Raccoon` and `Bear` base classes. However, because those classes inherited virtually from `ZooAnimal`, `Panda` has only one `ZooAnimal` base subpart.

Normal Conversions to Base Are Supported

An object of a derived class can be manipulated (as usual) through a pointer or a reference to an accessible base-class type regardless of whether the base class is virtual. For example, all of the following `Panda` base-class conversions are legal:

```
void dance(const Bear&);
void rummage(const Raccoon&);
ostream& operator<<(ostream&, const ZooAnimal&);
Panda ying_yang;
dance(ying_yang);     // ok: passes Panda object as a Bear
rummage(ying_yang);  // ok: passes Panda object as a Raccoon
cout << ying_yang;   // ok: passes Panda object as a ZooAnimal
```

Visibility of Virtual Base-Class Members

Because there is only one shared subobject corresponding to each shared virtual base, members in that base can be accessed directly and unambiguously. Moreover, if a member from the virtual base is overridden along only one derivation path, then that overridden member can still be accessed directly. If the member is overridden by more than one base, then the derived class generally must define its own version as well.

For example, assume class B defines a member named x; class D1 inherits virtually from B as does class D2; and class D inherits from D1 and D2. From the scope of D, x is visible through both of its base classes. If we use x through a D object, there are three possibilities:

- If x is not defined in either D1 or D2 it will be resolved as a member in B; there is no ambiguity. A D object contains only one instance of x.

- If x is a member of B and also a member in one, but not both, of D1 and D2, there is again no ambiguity—the version in the derived class is given precedence over the shared virtual base class, B.

- If x is defined in both D1 and D2, then direct access to that member is ambiguous.

As in a nonvirtual multiple inheritance hierarchy, ambiguities of this sort are best resolved by the derived class providing its own instance of that member.

EXERCISES SECTION 18.3.4

Exercise 18.28: Given the following class hierarchy, which inherited members can be accessed without qualification from within the VMI class? Which require qualification? Explain your reasoning.

```
struct Base {
    void bar(int);   // public by default
protected:
    int ival;
};
struct Derived1 : virtual public Base {
    void bar(char);   // public by default
    void foo(char);
protected:
    char cval;
};
struct Derived2 : virtual public Base {
    void foo(int);    // public by default
protected:
    int  ival;
    char cval;
};
class VMI : public Derived1, public Derived2 { };
```

18.3.5 Constructors and Virtual Inheritance

In a virtual derivation, the virtual base is initialized by the *most derived constructor*. In our example, when we create a Panda object, the Panda constructor alone controls how the ZooAnimal base class is initialized.

To understand this rule, consider what would happen if normal initialization rules applied. In that case, a virtual base class might be initialized more than once. It would be initialized along each inheritance path that contains that virtual base. In our ZooAnimal example, if normal initialization rules applied, both Bear and Raccoon would initialize the ZooAnimal part of a Panda object.

Of course, each class in the hierarchy might at some point be the "most derived" object. As long as we can create independent objects of a type derived from a virtual base, the constructors in that class must initialize its virtual base. For example, in our hierarchy, when a `Bear` (or a `Raccoon`) object is created, there is no further derived type involved. In this case, the `Bear` (or `Raccoon`) constructors directly initialize their `ZooAnimal` base as usual:

```
Bear::Bear(std::string name, bool onExhibit):
          ZooAnimal(name, onExhibit, "Bear") { }
Raccoon::Raccoon(std::string name, bool onExhibit)
        : ZooAnimal(name, onExhibit, "Raccoon") { }
```

When a `Panda` is created, it is the most derived type and controls initialization of the shared `ZooAnimal` base. Even though `ZooAnimal` is not a direct base of `Panda`, the `Panda` constructor initializes `ZooAnimal`:

```
Panda::Panda(std::string name, bool onExhibit)
      : ZooAnimal(name, onExhibit, "Panda"),
        Bear(name, onExhibit),
        Raccoon(name, onExhibit),
        Endangered(Endangered::critical),
        sleeping_flag(false)   { }
```

How a Virtually Inherited Object Is Constructed

The construction order for an object with a virtual base is slightly modified from the normal order: The virtual base subparts of the object are initialized first, using initializers provided in the constructor for the most derived class. Once the virtual base subparts of the object are constructed, the direct base subparts are constructed in the order in which they appear in the derivation list.

For example, when a `Panda` object is created:

- The (virtual base class) `ZooAnimal` part is constructed first, using the initializers specified in the `Panda` constructor initializer list.

- The `Bear` part is constructed next.

- The `Raccoon` part is constructed next.

- The third direct base, `Endangered`, is constructed next.

- Finally, the `Panda` part is constructed.

If the `Panda` constructor does not explicitly initialize the `ZooAnimal` base class, then the `ZooAnimal` default constructor is used. If `ZooAnimal` doesn't have a default constructor, then the code is in error.

 Virtual base classes are always constructed prior to nonvirtual base classes regardless of where they appear in the inheritance hierarchy.

Constructor and Destructor Order

A class can have more than one virtual base class. In that case, the virtual subobjects are constructed in left-to-right order as they appear in the derivation list. For example, in the following whimsical `TeddyBear` derivation, there are two virtual base classes: `ToyAnimal`, a direct virtual base, and `ZooAnimal`, which is a virtual base class of `Bear`:

```
class Character { /* ... */ };
class BookCharacter : public Character { /* ... */ };
class ToyAnimal { /* ... */ };
class TeddyBear : public BookCharacter,
                  public Bear, public virtual ToyAnimal
                  { /* ... */ };
```

The direct base classes are examined in declaration order to determine whether there are any virtual base classes. If so, the virtual bases are constructed first, followed by the nonvirtual base-class constructors in declaration order. Thus, to create a `TeddyBear`, the constructors are invoked in the following order:

```
ZooAnimal();          // Bear's virtual base class
ToyAnimal();          // direct virtual base class
Character();          // indirect base class of first nonvirtual base class
BookCharacter();      // first direct nonvirtual base class
Bear();               // second direct nonvirtual base class
TeddyBear();          // most derived class
```

The same order is used in the synthesized copy and move constructors, and members are assigned in this order in the synthesized assignment operators. As usual, an object is destroyed in reverse order from which it was constructed. The `TeddyBear` part will be destroyed first and the `ZooAnimal` part last.

EXERCISES SECTION 18.3.5

Exercise 18.29: Given the following class hierarchy:

```
class Class { ... };
class Base : public Class { ... };
class D1 : virtual public Base { ... };
class D2 : virtual public Base { ... };
class MI : public D1, public D2 { ... };
class Final : public MI, public Class { ... };
```

(a) In what order are constructors and destructors run on a `Final` object?
(b) A `Final` object has how many `Base` parts? How many `Class` parts?
(c) Which of the following assignments is a compile-time error?

```
Base *pb;     Class *pc;     MI *pmi;     D2 *pd2;
(a) pb = new Class;     (b) pc = new Final;
(c) pmi = pb;           (d) pd2 = pmi;
```

Exercise 18.30: Define a default constructor, a copy constructor, and a constructor that has an `int` parameter in `Base`. Define the same three constructors in each derived class. Each constructor should use its argument to initialize its `Base` part.

CHAPTER SUMMARY

C++ is used to solve a wide range of problems—from those solvable in a few hours' time to those that take years of development by large teams. Some features in C++ are most applicable in the context of large-scale problems: exception handling, namespaces, and multiple or virtual inheritance.

Exception handling lets us separate the error-detection part of the program from the error-handling part. When an exception is thrown, the current executing function is suspended and a search is started to find the nearest matching `catch` clause. Local variables defined inside functions that are exited while searching for a `catch` clause are destroyed as part of handling the exception.

Namespaces are a mechanism for managing large, complicated applications built from code produced by independent suppliers. A namespace is a scope in which objects, types, functions, templates, and other namespaces may be defined. The standard library is defined inside the namespace named `std`.

Conceptually, multiple inheritance is a simple notion: A derived class may inherit from more than one direct base class. The derived object consists of the derived part and a base part contributed by each of its base classes. Although conceptually simple, the details can be more complicated. In particular, inheriting from multiple base classes introduces new possibilities for name collisions and resulting ambiguous references to names from the base part of an object.

When a class inherits directly from more than one base class, it is possible that those classes may themselves share another base class. In such cases, the intermediate classes can opt to make their inheritance virtual, which states a willingness to share their virtual base class with other classes in the hierarchy that inherit virtually from that same base class. In this way there is only one copy of the shared virtual base in a subsequently derived class.

DEFINED TERMS

catch-all A `catch` clause in which the exception declaration is (...). A catch-all clause catches an exception of any type. It is typically used to catch an exception that is detected locally in order to do local cleanup. The exception is then rethrown to another part of the program to deal with the underlying cause of the problem.

catch clause Part of the program that handles an exception. A `catch` clause consists of the keyword `catch` followed by an exception declaration and a block of statements. The code inside a `catch` does whatever is necessary to handle an exception of the type defined in its exception declaration.

constructor order Under nonvirtual inheritance, base classes are constructed in the order in which they are named in the class derivation list. Under virtual inheritance, the virtual base class(es) are constructed before any other bases. They are constructed in the order in which they appear in the derivation list of the derived type. Only the most derived type may initialize a virtual base; constructor initializers for that base that appear in the intermediate base classes are ignored.

exception declaration `catch` clause declaration that specifies the type of exception that the `catch` can handle. The declaration acts like a parameter list, whose single parameter is initialized by the exception object. If the exception specifier is a non-reference type, then the exception object is copied to the `catch`.

exception handling Language-level support for managing run-time anomalies. One independently developed section of code can detect and "raise" an exception that another independently developed part of the program can "handle." The error-detecting part of the program throws an exception; the error-handling part handles the exception in a `catch` clause of a `try` block.

exception object Object used to communicate between the `throw` and `catch` sides of an exception. The object is created at the point of the `throw` and is a copy of the thrown expression. The exception object exists until the last handler for the exception completes. The type of the object is the static type of the thrown expression.

file static Name local to a file that is declared with the `static` keyword. In C and pre-Standard versions of C++, file statics were used to declare objects that could be used in a single file only. File statics are deprecated in C++, having been superseded by the use of unnamed namespaces.

function try block Used to catch exceptions from a constructor initializer. The keyword `try` appears before the colon that starts the constructor initializer list (or before the open curly of the constructor body if the initizlier list is empty) and closes with one or more `catch` clauses that appear after the close curly of the constructor body.

global namespace The (implicit) namespace in each program that holds all global definitions.

handler Synonym for a `catch` clause.

inline namespace Members of a namespace designated as `inline` can be used as if they were members of an enclosing namespace.

multiple inheritance Class with more than one direct base class. The derived class inherits the members of all its base classes. A separate access specifier may be provided for each base class.

namespace Mechanism for gathering all the names defined by a library or other collection of programs into a single scope. Unlike other scopes in C++, a namespace scope may be defined in several parts. The namepsace may be opened and closed and reopened again in disparate parts of the program.

namespace alias Mechanism for defining a synonym for a given namespace:

```
namespace N1 = N;
```

defines `N1` as another name for the namespace named `N`. A namespace can have multiple aliases; the namespace name or any of its aliases may be used interchangeably.

namespace pollution Occurs when all the names of classes and functions are placed in the global namespace. Large programs that use code written by multiple independent parties often encounter collisions among names if these names are global.

noexcept operator Operator that returns a `bool` indicating whether a given expression might throw an exception. The expression is unevaluated. The result is a constant expression. Its value is `true` if the expression does not contain a `throw` and calls only functions designated as nonthrowing; otherwise the result is `false`.

noexcept specification Keyword used to indicate whether a function throws. When `noexcept` follows a function's parameter list, it may be optionally followed by a parenthesized constant expression that must be convertible to `bool`. If the expression is omitted, or if it is `true`, the function throws no exceptions. An expression that is `false` or a function that has no exception specification may throw any exception.

nonthrowing specification An exception specification that promises that a function won't throw. If a nonthrowing functions does throw, `terminate` is called. Nonthrowing specifiers are `noexcept` without an argument or with an argument that evaluates as `true` and `throw()`.

raise Often used as a synonym for throw. C++ programmers speak of "throwing" or "raising" an exception interchangably.

rethrow A `throw` that does not specify an expression. A rethrow is valid only from inside a `catch` clause, or in a function called directly or indirectly from a `catch`. Its effect is to rethrow the exception object that it received.

stack unwinding The process whereby the functions are exited in the search for a `catch`. Local objects constructed before the exception are destroyed before entering the corresponding `catch`.

terminate Library function that is called if an exception is not caught or if an exception occurs while a handler is in process. `terminate` ends the program.

throw e Expression that interrupts the current execution path. Each `throw` transfers control to the nearest enclosing `catch` clause that can handle the type of exception that is thrown. The expression `e` is copied into the exception object.

try block Block of statements enclosed by the keyword `try` and one or more `catch` clauses. If the code inside the `try` block raises an exception and one of the `catch` clauses matches the type of the exception, then the exception is handled by that `catch`. Otherwise, the exception is passed out of the `try` to a `catch` further up the call chain.

unnamed namespace Namespace that is defined without a name. Names defined in an unnamed namespace may be accessed directly without use of the scope operator. Each file has its own unique unnamed namespace. Names in an unnamed namespace are not visible outside that file.

using declaration Mechanism to inject a single name from a namespace into the current scope:

```
using std::cout;
```

makes the name `cout` from the namespace `std` available in the current scope. The name `cout` can subseuquently be used without the `std::` qualifier.

using directive Declaration of the form

```
using NS;
```

makes *all* the names in the namespace named `NS` available in the nearest scope containing both the `using` directive and the namespace itself.

virtual base class Base class that specifies `virtual` in its own derivation list. A virtual base part occurs only once in a derived object even if the same class appears as a virtual base more than once in the hierarchy. In nonvirtual inheritance a constructor may initialize only its direct base class(es). When a class is inherited virtually, that class is initialized by the most derived class, which therefore should include an initializer for all of its virtual parent(s).

virtual inheritance Form of multiple inheritance in which derived classes share a single copy of a base that is included in the hierarchy more than once.

:: operator Scope operator. Used to access names from a namespace or a class.

C H A P T E R **19**
SPECIALIZED TOOLS AND TECHNIQUES

CONTENTS

The first three parts of this book discussed apects of C++ that most C++ programmers are likely to use at some point. In addition, C++ defines some features that are more specialized. Many programmers will never (or only rarely) need to use the features presented in this chapter.

C++ is intended for use in a wide variety of applications. As a result, it contains features that are particular to some applications and that need never be used by others. In this chapter we look at some of the less-commonly used features in the language.

19.1 Controlling Memory Allocation

Some applications have specialized memory allocation needs that cannot be met by the standard memory management facilities. Such applications need to take over the details of how memory is allocated, for example, by arranging for new to put objects into particular kinds of memory. To do so, they can overload the new and delete operators to control memory allocation.

19.1.1 Overloading `new` and `delete`

Although we say that we can "overload new and delete," overloading these operators is quite different from the way we overload other operators. In order to understand how we overload these operators, we first need to know a bit more about how new and delete expressions work.

When we use a new expression:

```
// new expressions
string *sp = new string("a value"); // allocate and initialize a string
string *arr = new string[10];   // allocate ten default initialized strings
```

three steps actually happen. First, the expression calls a library function named **operator new** (or **operator new[]**). This function allocates raw, untyped memory large enough to hold an object (or an array of objects) of the specified type. Next, the compiler runs the appropriate constructor to construct the object(s) from the specified initializers. Finally, a pointer to the newly allocated and constructed object is returned.

When we use a delete expression to delete a dynamically allocated object:

```
delete sp;        // destroy *sp and free the memory to which sp points
delete [] arr;    // destroy the elements in the array and free the memory
```

two steps happen. First, the appropriate destructor is run on the object to which sp points or on the elements in the array to which arr points. Next, the compiler frees the memory by calling a library function named **operator delete** or **operator delete[]**, respectively.

Applications that want to take control of memory allocation define their own versions of the operator new and operator delete functions. Even though the library contains definitions for these functions, we can define our own versions of them and the compiler won't complain about duplicate definitions. Instead, the compiler will use our version in place of the one defined by the library.

WARNING

When we define the global `operator new` and `operator delete` functions, we take over responsibility for all dynamic memory allocation. These functions *must* be correct: They form a vital part of all processing in the program.

Applications can define `operator new` and `operator delete` functions in the global scope and/or as member functions. When the compiler sees a `new` or `delete` expression, it looks for the corresponding `operator` function to call. If the object being allocated (deallocated) has class type, the compiler first looks in the scope of the class, including any base classes. If the class has a member `operator new` or `operator delete`, that function is used by the `new` or `delete` expression. Otherwise, the compiler looks for a matching function in the global scope. If the compiler finds a user-defined version, it uses that function to execute the `new` or `delete` expression. Otherwise, the standard library version is used.

We can use the scope operator to force a `new` or `delete` expression to bypass a class-specific function and use the one from the global scope. For example, `::new` will look only in the global scope for a matching `operator new` function. Similarly for `::delete`.

The `operator new` and `operator delete` Interface

The library defines eight overloaded versions of `operator new` and `delete` functions. The first four support the versions of `new` that can throw a `bad_alloc` exception. The next four support nonthrowing versions of new:

```
// these versions might throw an exception
void *operator new(size_t);              // allocate an object
void *operator new[](size_t);            // allocate an array
void *operator delete(void*) noexcept;   // free an object
void *operator delete[](void*) noexcept; // free an array

// versions that promise not to throw; see § 12.1.2 (p. 460)
void *operator new(size_t, nothrow_t&) noexcept;
void *operator new[](size_t, nothrow_t&) noexcept;
void *operator delete(void*, nothrow_t&) noexcept;
void *operator delete[](void*, nothrow_t&) noexcept;
```

The type `nothrow_t` is a `struct` defined in the new header. This type has no members. The new header also defines a `const` object named `nothrow`, which users can pass to signal they want the nonthrowing version of new (§ 12.1.2, p. 460). Like destructors, an `operator delete` must not throw an exception (§ 18.1.1, p. 774). When we overload these operators, we must specify that they will not throw, which we do through the `noexcept` exception specifier (§ 18.1.4, p. 779).

An application can define its own version of any of these functions. If it does so, it must define these functions in the global scope or as members of a class. When defined as members of a class, these operator functions are implicitly static (§ 7.6, p. 302). There is no need to declare them `static` explicitly, although it is legal to do so. The member new and `delete` functions must be static because they are used either before the object is constructed (`operator new`) or after it has been destroyed (`operator delete`). There are, therefore, no member data for these functions to manipulate.

An `operator new` or `operator new[]` function must have a return type of `void*` and its first parameter must have type `size_t`. That parameter may not have a default argument. The `operator new` function is used when we allocate an object; `operator new[]` is called when we allocate an array. When the compiler calls `operator new`, it initializes the `size_t` parameter with the number of bytes required to hold an object of the specified type; when it calls `operator new[]`, it passes the number of bytes required to store an array of the given number of elements.

When we define our own `operator new` function, we can define additional parameters. A new expression that uses such functions must use the placement form of new (§ 12.1.2, p. 460) to pass arguments to these additional parameters. Although generally we may define our version of `operator new` to have whatever parameters are needed, we may not define a function with the following form:

```
void *operator new(size_t, void*); // this version may not be redefined
```

This specific form is reserved for use by the library and may not be redefined.

An `operator delete` or `operator delete[]` function must have a `void` return type and a first parameter of type `void*`. Executing a `delete` expression calls the appropriate `operator` function and initializes its `void*` parameter with a pointer to the memory to free.

When `operator delete` or `operator delete[]` is defined as a class member, the function may have a second parameter of type `size_t`. If present, the additional parameter is initialized with the size in bytes of the object addressed by the first parameter. The `size_t` parameter is used when we delete objects that are part of an inheritance hierarchy. If the base class has a virtual destructor (§ 15.7.1, p. 622), then the size passed to `operator delete` will vary depending on the dynamic type of the object to which the deleted pointer points. Moreover, the version of the `operator delete` function that is run will be the one from the dynamic type of the object.

TERMINOLOGY: NEW EXPRESSION VERSUS OPERATOR NEW FUNCTION

The library functions `operator new` and `operator delete` are misleadingly named. Unlike other operator functions, such as `operator=`, these functions do not overload the new or delete expressions. In fact, we cannot redefine the behavior of the new and delete expressions.

A new expression always executes by calling an `operator new` function to obtain memory and then constructing an object in that memory. A delete expression always executes by destroying an object and then calling an `operator delete` function to free the memory used by the object.

By providing our own definitions of the `operator new` and `operator delete` functions, we can change how memory is allocated. However, we cannot change this basic meaning of the new and delete operators.

The `malloc` and `free` Functions

If you define your own global `operator new` and `operator delete`, those functions must allocate and deallocate memory somehow. Even if you define these functions in order to use a specialized memory allocator, it can still be useful for testing purposes to be able to allocate memory similarly to how the implementation normally does so.

To this end, we can use functions named **malloc** and **free** that C++ inherits from C. These functions, are defined in `cstdlib`.

The `malloc` function takes a `size_t` that says how many bytes to allocate. It returns a pointer to the memory that it allocated, or 0 if it was unable to allocate the memory. The `free` function takes a `void*` that is a copy of a pointer that was returned from `malloc` and returns the associated memory to the system. Calling `free(0)` has no effect.

A simple way to write `operator new` and `operator delete` is as follows:

```
void *operator new(size_t size) {
    if (void *mem = malloc(size))
        return mem;
    else
        throw bad_alloc();
}
void operator delete(void *mem) noexcept { free(mem); }
```

and similarly for the other versions of `operator new` and `operator delete`.

EXERCISES SECTION 19.1.1

Exercise 19.1: Write your own `operator new(size_t)` function using `malloc` and use `free` to write the `operator delete(void*)` function.

Exercise 19.2: By default, the `allocator` class uses `operator new` to obtain storage and `operator delete` to free it. Recompile and rerun your `StrVec` programs (§ 13.5, p. 526) using your versions of the functions from the previous exercise.

19.1.2 Placement new Expressions

Although the `operator new` and `operator delete` functions are intended to be used by `new` expressions, they are ordinary functions in the library. As a result, ordinary code can call these functions directly.

In earlier versions of the language—before the `allocator` (§ 12.2.2, p. 481) class was part of the library—applications that wanted to separate allocation from initialization did so by calling `operator new` and `operator delete`. These functions behave analogously to the `allocate` and `deallocate` members of `allocator`. Like those members, `operator new` and `operator delete` functions allocate and deallocate memory but do not construct or destroy objects.

Differently from an `allocator`, there is no `construct` function we can call to construct objects in memory allocated by `operator new`. Instead, we use the **placement new** form of new (§ 12.1.2, p. 460) to construct an object. As we've seen, this form of new provides extra information to the allocation function. We can use placement `new` to pass an address, in which case the placement `new` expression has the form

```
new (place_address) type
new (place_address) type (initializers)
new (place_address) type [size]
new (place_address) type [size] { braced initializer list }
```

where *place_address* must be a pointer and the *initializers* provide (a possibly empty) comma-separated list of initializers to use to construct the newly allocated object.

When called with an address and no other arguments, placement `new` uses `operator new(size_t, void*)` to "allocate" its memory. This is the version of `operator new` that we are not allowed to redefine (§ 19.1.1, p. 822). This function does *not* allocate any memory; it simply returns its pointer argument. The overall new expression then finishes its work by initializing an object at the given address. In effect, placement `new` allows us to construct an object at a specific, preallocated memory address.

 When passed a single argument that is a pointer, a placement `new` expression constructs an object but does not allocate memory.

Although in many ways using placement new is analogous to the `construct` member of an `allocator`, there is one important difference. The pointer that we pass to `construct` must point to space allocated by the same `allocator` object. The pointer that we pass to placement `new` need not point to memory allocated by `operator new`. Indeed, as we'll see in § 19.6 (p. 851), the pointer passed to a placement `new` expression need not even refer to dynamic memory.

Explicit Destructor Invocation

Just as placement `new` is analogous to using `allocate`, an explicit call to a destructor is analogous to calling `destroy`. We call a destructor the same way we call any other member function on an object or through a pointer or reference to an object:

```
string *sp = new string("a value"); // allocate and initialize a string
sp->~string();
```

Here we invoke a destructor directly. The arrow operator dereferences the pointer `sp` to obtain the object to which `sp` points. We then call the destructor, which is the name of the type preceded by a tilde (~).

Like calling `destroy`, calling a destructor cleans up the given object but does not free the space in which that object resides. We can reuse the space if desired.

Note Calling a destructor destroys an object but does not free the memory.

19.2 Run-Time Type Identification

Run-time type identification (RTTI) is provided through two operators:

- The `typeid` operator, which returns the type of a given expression

- The `dynamic_cast` operator, which safely converts a pointer or reference to a base type into a pointer or reference to a derived type

When applied to pointers or references to types that have virtual functions, these operators use the dynamic type (§ 15.2.3, p. 601) of the object to which the pointer or reference is bound.

These operators are useful when we have a derived operation that we want to perform through a pointer or reference to a base-class object and it is not possible to make that operation a virtual function. Ordinarily, we should use virtual functions if we can. When the operation is virtual, the compiler automatically selects the right function according to the dynamic type of the object.

However, it is not always possible to define a virtual. If we cannot use a virtual, we can use one of the RTTI operators. On the other hand, using these operators is more error-prone than using virtual member functions: The programmer must *know* to which type the object should be cast and must check that the cast was performed successfully.

 RTTI should be used with caution. When possible, it is better to define a
WARNING virtual function rather than to take over managing the types directly.

19.2.1 The `dynamic_cast` Operator

A **dynamic_cast** has the following form:

```
dynamic_cast<type*>(e)
dynamic_cast<type&>(e)
dynamic_cast<type&&>(e)
```

where *type* must be a class type and (ordinarily) names a class that has virtual functions. In the first case, e must be a valid pointer (§ 2.3.2, p. 52); in the second, e must be an lvalue; and in the third, e must not be an lvalue.

In all cases, the type of e must be either a class type that is publicly derived from the target *type*, a `public` base class of the target *type*, or the same as the target *type*. If e has one of these types, then the cast will succeed. Otherwise, the cast fails. If a `dynamic_cast` to a pointer type fails, the result is 0. If a `dynamic_cast` to a reference type fails, the operator throws an exception of type `bad_cast`.

Pointer-Type `dynamic_casts`

As a simple example, assume that `Base` is a class with at least one virtual function and that class `Derived` is publicly derived from `Base`. If we have a pointer to `Base` named bp, we can cast it, at run time, to a pointer to `Derived` as follows:

```
if (Derived *dp = dynamic_cast<Derived*>(bp))
{
    // use the Derived object to which dp points
} else {   // bp points at a Base object
    // use the Base object to which bp points
}
```

If bp points to a Derived object, then the cast will initialize dp to point to the Derived object to which bp points. In this case, it is safe for the code inside the if to use Derived operations. Otherwise, the result of the cast is 0. If dp is 0, the condition in the if fails. In this case, the else clause does processing appropriate to Base instead.

We can do a dynamic_cast on a null pointer; the result is a null pointer of the requested type.

It is worth noting that we defined dp inside the condition. By defining the variable in a condition, we do the cast and corresponding check as a single operation. Moreover, the pointer dp is not accessible outside the if. If the cast fails, then the unbound pointer is not available for use in subsequent code where we might forget to check whether the cast succeeded.

Performing a dynamic_cast in a condition ensures that the cast and test of its result are done in a single expression.

Reference-Type dynamic_casts

A dynamic_cast to a reference type differs from a dynamic_cast to a pointer type in how it signals that an error occurred. Because there is no such thing as a null reference, it is not possible to use the same error-reporting strategy for references that is used for pointers. When a cast to a reference type fails, the cast throws a std::bad_cast exception, which is defined in the typeinfo library header.

We can rewrite the previous example to use references as follows:

```
void f(const Base &b)
{
    try {
        const Derived &d = dynamic_cast<const Derived&>(b);
        // use the Derived object to which b referred
    } catch (bad_cast) {
        // handle the fact that the cast failed
    }
}
```

19.2.2 The typeid Operator

The second operator provided for RTTI is the **typeid operator**. The typeid operator allows a program to ask of an expression: What type is your object?

Exercise 19.3: Given the following class hierarchy in which each class defines a public default constructor and virtual destructor:

```
class A { /* ... */ };
class B : public A { /* ... */ };
class C : public B { /* ... */ };
class D : public B, public A { /* ... */ };
```

which, if any, of the following dynamic_casts fail?

```
(a) A *pa = new C;
    B *pb = dynamic_cast< B* >(pa);
(b) B *pb = new B;
    C *pc = dynamic_cast< C* >(pb);
(c) A *pa = new D;
    B *pb = dynamic_cast< B* >(pa);
```

Exercise 19.4: Using the classes defined in the first exercise, rewrite the following code to convert the expression *pa to the type C&:

```
if (C *pc = dynamic_cast< C* >(pa)) {
    // use C's members
} else {
    // use A's members
}
```

Exercise 19.5: When should you use a dynamic_cast instead of a virtual function?

A typeid expression has the form typeid(e) where e is any expression or a type name. The result of a typeid operation is a reference to a const object of a library type named type_info, or a type publicly derived from type_info. § 19.2.4 (p. 831) covers this type in more detail. The type_info class is defined in the typeinfo header.

The typeid operator can be used with expressions of any type. As usual, top-level const (§ 2.4.3, p. 63) is ignored, and if the expression is a reference, typeid returns the type to which the reference refers. When applied to an array or function, however, the standard conversion to pointer (§ 4.11.2, p. 161) is not done. That is, if we take typeid(a) and a is an array, the result describes an array type, not a pointer type.

When the operand is not of class type or is a class without virtual functions, then the typeid operator indicates the static type of the operand. When the operand is an lvalue of a class type that defines at least one virtual function, then the type is evaluated at run time.

Using the typeid Operator

Ordinarily, we use typeid to compare the types of two expressions or to compare the type of an expression to a specified type:

```
Derived *dp = new Derived;
Base *bp = dp;    //  both pointers point to a Derived object
//  compare the type of two objects at run time
if (typeid(*bp) == typeid(*dp)) {
    //  bp and dp point to objects of the same type
}
//  test whether the run-time type is a specific type
if (typeid(*bp) == typeid(Derived)) {
    //  bp actually points to a Derived
}
```

In the first `if`, we compare the dynamic types of the objects to which bp and dp point. If both point to the same type, then the condition succeeds. Similarly, the second `if` succeeds if bp currently points to a `Derived` object.

Note that the operands to the `typeid` are objects—we used `*bp`, not bp:

```
//  test always fails: the type of bp is pointer to Base
if (typeid(bp) == typeid(Derived)) {
    //  code never executed
}
```

This condition compares the type `Base*` to type `Derived`. Although the pointer *points* at an object of class type that has virtual functions, the pointer *itself* is not a class-type object. The type `Base*` can be, and is, evaluated at compile time. That type is unequal to `Derived`, so the condition will always fail *regardless of the type of the object to which* bp *points*.

WARNING
> The `typeid` of a pointer (as opposed to the object to which the pointer points) returns the static, compile-time type of the pointer.

Whether `typeid` requires a run-time check determines whether the expression is evaluated. The compiler evaluates the expression only if the type has virtual functions. If the type has no virtuals, then `typeid` returns the static type of the expression; the compiler knows the static type without evaluating the expression.

If the dynamic type of the expression might differ from the static type, then the expression must be evaluated (at run time) to determine the resulting type. The distinction matters when we evaluate `typeid(*p)`. If p is a pointer to a type that does not have virtual functions, then p does not need to be a valid pointer. Otherwise, `*p` is evaluated at run time, in which case p must be a valid pointer. If p is a null pointer, then `typeid(*p)` throws a `bad_typeid` exception.

19.2.3 Using RTTI

As an example of when RTTI might be useful, consider a class hierarchy for which we'd like to implement the equality operator (§ 14.3.1, p. 561). Two objects are equal if they have the same type and same value for a given set of their data members. Each derived type may add its own data, which we will want to include when we test for equality.

Exercise 19.6: Write an expression to dynamically cast a pointer to a `Query_base` to a pointer to an `AndQuery` (§ 15.9.1, p. 636). Test the cast by using objects of `AndQuery` and of another query type. Print a statement indicating whether the cast works and be sure that the output matches your expectations.

Exercise 19.7: Write the same cast, but cast a `Query_base` object to a reference to `AndQuery`. Repeat the test to ensure that your cast works correctly.

Exercise 19.8: Write a `typeid` expression to see whether two `Query_base` pointers point to the same type. Now check whether that type is an `AndQuery`.

We might think we could solve this problem by defining a set of virtual functions that would perform the equality test at each level in the hierarchy. Given those virtuals, we would define a single equality operator that operates on references to the base type. That operator could delegate its work to a virtual `equal` operation that would do the real work.

Unfortunately, this strategy doesn't quite work. Virtual functions must have the same parameter type(s) in both the base and derived classes (§ 15.3, p. 605). If we wanted to define a virtual `equal` function, that function must have a parameter that is a reference to the base class. If the parameter is a reference to base, the `equal` function could use only members from the base class. `equal` would have no way to compare members that are in the derived class but not in the base.

We can write our equality operation by realizing that the equality operator ought to return `false` if we attempt to compare objects of differing type. For example, if we try to compare a object of the base-class type with an object of a derived type, the `==` operator should return `false`.

Given this observation, we can now see that we can use RTTI to solve our problem. We'll define an equality operator whose parameters are references to the base-class type. The equality operator will use `typeid` to verify that the operands have the same type. If the operands differ, the `==` will return `false`. Otherwise, it will call a virtual `equal` function. Each class will define `equal` to compare the data elements of its own type. These operators will take a `Base&` parameter but will cast the operand to its own type before doing the comparison.

The Class Hierarchy

To make the concept a bit more concrete, we'll define the following classes:

```
class Base {
    friend bool operator==(const Base&, const Base&);
public:
    //  interface members for Base
protected:
    virtual bool equal(const Base&) const;
    //  data and other implementation members of Base
};
```

```
class Derived: public Base {
public:
    //  other interface members for Derived
protected:
    bool equal(const Base&) const;
    //  data and other implementation members of Derived
};
```

A Type-Sensitive Equality Operator

Next let's look at how we might define the overall equality operator:

```
bool operator==(const Base &lhs, const Base &rhs)
{
    //  returns false if typeids are different; otherwise makes a virtual call to equal
    return typeid(lhs) == typeid(rhs) && lhs.equal(rhs);
}
```

This operator returns `false` if the operands are different types. If they are the
same type, then it delegates the real work of comparing the operands to the (virtual) `equal` function. If the operands are `Base` objects, then `Base::equal` will
be called. If they are `Derived` objects, `Derived::equal` is called.

The Virtual `equal` Functions

Each class in the hierarchy must define its own version of `equal`. All of the functions in the derived classes will start the same way: They'll cast their argument to
the type of the class itself:

```
bool Derived::equal(const Base &rhs) const
{
    //  we know the types are equal, so the cast won't throw
    auto r = dynamic_cast<const Derived&>(rhs);
    //  do the work to compare two Derived objects and return the result
}
```

The cast should always succeed—after all, the function is called from the equality
operator only after testing that the two operands are the same type. However,
the cast is necessary so that the function can access the derived members of the
right-hand operand.

The Base-Class `equal` Function

This operation is a bit simpler than the others:

```
bool Base::equal(const Base &rhs) const
{
    //  do whatever is required to compare to Base objects
}
```

There is no need to cast the parameter before using it. Both `*this` and the parameter are `Base` objects, so all the operations available for this object are also defined
for the parameter type.

19.2.4 The `type_info` Class

The exact definition of the **`type_info`** class varies by compiler. However, the standard guarantees that the class will be defined in the `typeinfo` header and that the class will provide at least the operations listed in Table 19.1.

The class also provides a `public` virtual destructor, because it is intended to serve as a base class. When a compiler wants to provide additional type information, it normally does so in a class derived from `type_info`.

	Table 19.1: Operations on `type_info`
`t1 == t2`	Returns `true` if the `type_info` objects `t1` and `t2` refer to the same type, `false` otherwise.
`t1 != t2`	Returns `true` if the `type_info` objects `t1` and `t2` refer to different types, `false` otherwise.
`t.name()`	Returns a C-style character string that is a printable version of the type name. Type names are generated in a system-dependent way.
`t1.before(t2)`	Returns a `bool` that indicates whether `t1` comes before `t2`. The ordering imposed by `before` is compiler dependent.

There is no `type_info` default constructor, and the copy and move constructors and the assignment operators are all defined as deleted (§ 13.1.6, p. 507). Therefore, we cannot define, copy, or assign objects of type `type_info`. The only way to create a `type_info` object is through the `typeid` operator.

The `name` member function returns a C-style character string for the name of the type represented by the `type_info` object. The value used for a given type depends on the compiler and in particular is not required to match the type names as used in a program. The only guarantee we have about the return from `name` is that it returns a unique string for each type. For example:

```
int arr[10];
Derived d;
Base *p = &d;
cout << typeid(42).name() << ", "
     << typeid(arr).name() << ", "
     << typeid(Sales_data).name() << ", "
     << typeid(std::string).name() << ", "
     << typeid(p).name() << ", "
     << typeid(*p).name() << endl;
```

This program, when executed on our machine, generates the following output:

```
i, A10_i, 10Sales_data, Ss, P4Base, 7Derived
```

The `type_info` class varies by compiler. Some compilers provide additional member functions that provide additional information about types used in a program. You should consult the reference manual for your compiler to understand the exact `type_info` support provided.

Exercise 19.9: Write a program similar to the last one in this section to print the names your compiler uses for common type names. If your compiler gives output similar to ours, write a function that will translate those strings to more human-friendly form.

Exercise 19.10: Given the following class hierarchy in which each class defines a public default constructor and virtual destructor, which type name do the following statements print?

```
class A { /* ... */ };
class B : public A { /* ... */ };
class C : public B { /* ... */ };

(a) A *pa = new C;
    cout << typeid(pa).name() << endl;
(b) C cobj;
    A& ra = cobj;
    cout << typeid(&ra).name() << endl;
(c) B *px = new B;
    A& ra = *px;
    cout << typeid(ra).name() << endl;
```

19.3 Enumerations

Enumerations let us group together sets of integral constants. Like classes, each enumeration defines a new type. Enumerations are literal types (§ 7.5.6, p. 299).

C++ has two kinds of enumerations: scoped and unscoped. The new standard introduced **scoped enumerations**. We define a scoped enumeration using the keywords enum class (or, equivalently, enum struct), followed by the enumeration name and a comma-separated list of **enumerators** enclosed in curly braces. A semicolon follows the close curly:

```
enum class open_modes {input, output, append};
```

Here we defined an enumeration type named open_modes that has three enumerators: input, output, and append.

We define an **unscoped enumeration** by omitting the class (or struct) keyword. The enumeration name is optional in an unscoped enum:

```
enum color {red, yellow, green};        // unscoped enumeration
// unnamed, unscoped enum
enum {floatPrec = 6, doublePrec = 10, double_doublePrec = 10};
```

If the enum is unnamed, we may define objects of that type only as part of the enum definition. As with a class definition, we can provide a comma-separated list of declarators between the close curly and the semicolon that ends the enum definition (§ 2.6.1, p. 73).

Enumerators

The names of the enumerators in a scoped enumeration follow normal scoping rules and are inaccessible outside the scope of the enumeration. The enumerator names in an unscoped enumeration are placed into the same scope as the enumeration itself:

```
enum color {red, yellow, green};       // unscoped enumeration
enum stoplight {red, yellow, green};   // error: redefines enumerators
enum class peppers {red, yellow, green}; // ok: enumerators are hidden

color eyes = green; // ok: enumerators are in scope for an unscoped enumeration
peppers p = green;   // error: enumerators from peppers are not in scope
                     //        color::green is in scope but has the wrong type
color hair = color::red;    // ok: we can explicitly access the enumerators
peppers p2 = peppers::red;  // ok: using red from peppers
```

By default, enumerator values start at 0 and each enumerator has a value 1 greater than the preceding one. However, we can also supply initializers for one or more enumerators:

```
enum class intTypes {
    charTyp = 8, shortTyp = 16, intTyp = 16,
    longTyp = 32, long_longTyp = 64
};
```

As we see with the enumerators for intTyp and shortTyp, an enumerator value need not be unique. When we omit an initializer, the enumerator has a value 1 greater than the preceding enumerator.

Enumerators are const and, if initialized, their initializers must be constant expressions (§ 2.4.4, p. 65). Consequently, each enumerator is itself a constant expression. Because the enumerators are constant expressions, we can use them where a constant expression is required. For example, we can define constexpr variables of enumeration type:

```
constexpr intTypes charbits = intTypes::charTyp;
```

Similarly, we can use an enum as the expression in a switch statement and use the value of its enumerators as the case labels (§ 5.3.2, p. 178). For the same reason, we can also use an enumeration type as a nontype template parameter (§ 16.1.1, p. 654). and can initialize class static data members of enumeration type inside the class definition (§ 7.6, p. 302).

Like Classes, Enumerations Define New Types

So long as the enum is named, we can define and initialize objects of that type. An enum object may be initialized or assigned only by one of its enumerators or by another object of the same enum type:

```
open_modes om = 2;        // error: 2 is not of type open_modes
om = open_modes::input;   // ok: input is an enumerator of open_modes
```

Objects or enumerators of an unscoped enumeration type are automatically converted to an integral type. As a result, they can be used where an integral value is required:

```
int i = color::red;    // ok: unscoped enumerator implicitly converted to int
int j = peppers::red;  // error: scoped enumerations are not implicitly converted
```

Specifying the Size of an enum

Although each enum defines a unique type, it is represented by one of the built-in integral types. Under the new standard, we may specify that type by following the enum name with a colon and the name of the type we want to use:

```
enum intValues : unsigned long long {
    charTyp = 255, shortTyp = 65535, intTyp = 65535,
    longTyp = 4294967295UL,
    long_longTyp = 18446744073709551615ULL
};
```

If we do not specify the underlying type, then by default scoped enums have int as the underlying type. There is no default for unscoped enums; all we know is that the underlying type is large enough to hold the enumerator values. When the underlying type is specified (including implicitly specified for a scoped enum), it is an error for an enumerator to have a value that is too large to fit in that type.

Being able to specify the underlying type of an enum lets us control the type used across different implementations. We can be confident that our program compiled under one implementation will generate the same code when we compile it on another.

Forward Declarations for Enumerations

Under the new standard, we can forward declare an enum. An enum forward declaration must specify (implicitly or explicitly) the underlying size of the enum:

```
// forward declaration of unscoped enum named intValues
enum intValues : unsigned long long; // unscoped, must specify a type
enum class open_modes;   // scoped enums can use int by default
```

Because there is no default size for an unscoped enum, every declaration must include the size of that enum. We can declare a scoped enum without specifying a size, in which case the size is implicitly defined as int.

As with any declaration, all the declarations and the definition of a given enum must match one another. In the case of enums, this requirement means that the size of the enum must be the same across all declarations and the enum definition. Moreover, we cannot declare a name as an unscoped enum in one context and redeclare it as a scoped enum later:

```
// error: declarations and definition must agree whether the enum is scoped or unscoped
enum class intValues;
enum intValues;   // error: intValues previously declared as scoped enum
enum intValues : long; // error: intValues previously declared as int
```

Parameter Matching and Enumerations

Because an object of enum type may be initialized only by another object of that enum type or by one of its enumerators (§ 19.3, p. 833), an integral value that happens to have the same value as an enumerator cannot be used to call a function expecting an enum argument:

```
//  unscoped enumeration; the underlying type is machine dependent
enum Tokens {INLINE = 128, VIRTUAL = 129};
void ff(Tokens);
void ff(int);
int main() {
    Tokens curTok = INLINE;
    ff(128);     //  exactly matches ff(int)
    ff(INLINE);  //  exactly matches ff(Tokens)
    ff(curTok);  //  exactly matches ff(Tokens)
    return 0;
}
```

Although we cannot pass an integral value to an enum parameter, we can pass an object or enumerator of an unscoped enumeration to a parameter of integral type. When we do so, the enum value promotes to int or to a larger integral type. The actual promotion type depends on the underlying type of the enumeration:

```
void newf(unsigned char);
void newf(int);
unsigned char uc = VIRTUAL;
newf(VIRTUAL);   //  calls newf(int)
newf(uc);        //  calls newf(unsigned char)
```

The enum Tokens has only two enumerators, the larger of which has the value 129. That value can be represented by the type unsigned char, and many compilers will use unsigned char as the underlying type for Tokens. Regardless of its underlying type, objects and the enumerators of Tokens are promoted to int. Enumerators and values of an enum type are not promoted to unsigned char, even if the values of the enumerators would fit.

19.4 Pointer to Class Member

A **pointer to member** is a pointer that can point to a nonstatic member of a class. Normally a pointer points to an object, but a pointer to member identifies a member of a class, not an object of that class. static class members are not part of any object, so no special syntax is needed to point to a static member. Pointers to static members are ordinary pointers.

The type of a pointer to member embodies both the type of a class and the type of a member of that class. We initialize such pointers to point to a specific member of a class without identifying an object to which that member belongs. When we use a pointer to member, we supply the object whose member we wish to use.

To explain pointers to members, we'll use a version of the `Screen` class from §7.3.1 (p. 271):

```
class Screen {
public:
    typedef std::string::size_type pos;
    char get_cursor() const { return contents[cursor]; }
    char get() const;
    char get(pos ht, pos wd) const;
private:
    std::string contents;
    pos cursor;
    pos height, width;
};
```

19.4.1 Pointers to Data Members

As with any pointer, we declare a pointer to member using a `*` to indicate that the name we're declaring is a pointer. Unlike ordinary pointers, a pointer to member also incorporates the class that contains the member. Hence, we must precede the `*` with *classname*`::` to indicate that the pointer we are defining can point to a member of *classname*. For example:

```
// pdata can point to a string member of a const (or nonconst) Screen object
const string Screen::*pdata;
```

declares that `pdata` is a "pointer to a member of class `Screen` that has type `const string`." The data members in a `const` object are themselves `const`. By making our pointer a pointer to `const string` member, we say that we can use `pdata` to point to a member of any `Screen` object, `const` or not. In exchange we can use `pdata` to read, but not write to, the member to which it points.

When we initialize (or assign to) a pointer to member, we say to which member it points. For example, we can make `pdata` point to the `contents` member of an unspecified `Screen` object as follows:

```
pdata = &Screen::contents;
```

Here, we apply the address-of operator not to an object in memory but to a member of the class `Screen`.

Of course, under the new standard, the easiest way to declare a pointer to member is to use `auto` or `decltype`:

```
auto pdata = &Screen::contents;
```

Using a Pointer to Data Member

It is essential to understand that when we initialize or assign a pointer to member, that pointer does not yet point to any data. It identifies a specific member but not the object that contains that member. We supply the object when we dereference the pointer to member.

Analogous to the member access operators, . and ->, there are two pointer-to-member access operators, .* and ->*, that let us supply an object and dereference the pointer to fetch a member of that object:

```
Screen myScreen, *pScreen = &myScreen;
// .* dereferences pdata to fetch the contents member from the object myScreen
auto s = myScreen.*pdata;
// ->* dereferences pdata to fetch contents from the object to which pScreen points
s = pScreen->*pdata;
```

Conceptually, these operators perform two actions: They dereference the pointer to member to get the member that we want; then, like the member access operators, they fetch that member from an object (.*) or through a pointer (->*).

A Function Returning a Pointer to Data Member

Normal access controls apply to pointers to members. For example, the contents member of Screen is private. As a result, the use of pdata above must have been inside a member or friend of class Screen or it would be an error.

Because data members are typically private, we normally can't get a pointer to data member directly. Instead, if a class like Screen wanted to allow access to its contents member, it would define a function to return a pointer to that member:

```
class Screen {
public:
    // data is a static member that returns a pointer to member
    static const std::string Screen::*data()
        { return &Screen::contents; }
    // other members as before
};
```

Here we've added a static member to class Screen that returns a pointer to the contents member of a Screen. The return type of this function is the same type as our original pdata pointer. Reading the return type from right to left, we see that data returns a pointer to a member of class Screen that is a string that is const. The body of the function applies the address-of operator to the contents member, so the function returns a pointer to the contents member of Screen.

When we call data, we get a pointer to member:

```
// data() returns a pointer to the contents member of class Screen
const string Screen::*pdata = Screen::data();
```

As before, pdata points to a member of class Screen but not to actual data. To use pdata, we must bind it to an object of type Screen

```
// fetch the contents of the object named myScreen
auto s = myScreen.*pdata;
```

19.4.2 Pointers to Member Functions

We can also define a pointer that can point to a member function of a class. As with pointers to data members, the easiest way to form a pointer to member function is to use `auto` to deduce the type for us:

```
// pmf is a pointer that can point to a Screen member function that is const
// that returns a char and takes no arguments
auto pmf = &Screen::get_cursor;
```

Like a pointer to data member, a pointer to a function member is declared using *classname*`::*`. Like any other function pointer (§ 6.7, p. 247), a pointer to member function specifies the return type and parameter list of the type of function to which this pointer can point. If the member function is a `const` member (§ 7.1.2, p. 258) or a reference member (§ 13.6.3, p. 546), we must include the `const` or reference qualifier as well.

As with normal function pointers, if the member is overloaded, we must distinguish which function we want by declaring the type explicitly (§ 6.7, p. 248). For example, we can declare a pointer to the two-parameter version of `get` as

```
char (Screen::*pmf2)(Screen::pos, Screen::pos) const;
pmf2 = &Screen::get;
```

The parentheses around `Screen::*` in this declaration are essential due to precedence. Without the parentheses, the compiler treats the following as an (invalid) function declaration:

```
// error: nonmember function p cannot have a const qualifier
char Screen::*p(Screen::pos, Screen::pos) const;
```

This declaration tries to define an ordinary function named p that returns a pointer to a member of class `Screen` that has type `char`. Because it declares an ordinary function, the declaration can't be followed by a `const` qualifier.

Unlike ordinary function pointers, there is no automatic conversion between a member function and a pointer to that member:

```
// pmf points to a Screen member that takes no arguments and returns char
pmf = &Screen::get;  // must explicitly use the address-of operator
pmf = Screen::get;   // error: no conversion to pointer for member functions
```

Using a Pointer to Member Function

As when we use a pointer to a data member, we use the `.*` or `->*` operators to call a member function through a pointer to member:

```
Screen myScreen, *pScreen = &myScreen;
// call the function to which pmf points on the object to which pScreen points
char c1 = (pScreen->*pmf)();
// passes the arguments 0, 0 to the two-parameter version of get on the object myScreen
char c2 = (myScreen.*pmf2)(0, 0);
```

The calls `(myScreen->*pmf)()` and `(pScreen.*pmf2)(0,0)` require the parentheses because the precedence of the call operator is higher than the precedence of the pointer to member operators.

Without the parentheses,

```
myScreen.*pmf()
```

would be interpreted to mean

```
myScreen.*(pmf())
```

This code says to call the function named `pmf` and use its return value as the operand of the pointer-to-member operator (`.*`). However, `pmf` is not a function, so this code is in error.

> Because of the relative precedence of the call operator, declarations of pointers to member functions and calls through such pointers must use parentheses: `(C::*p)(parms)` and `(obj.*p)(args)`.

Using Type Aliases for Member Pointers

Type aliases or `typedef`s (§ 2.5.1, p. 67) make pointers to members considerably easier to read. For example, the following type alias defines `Action` as an alternative name for the type of the two-parameter version of `get`:

```
// Action is a type that can point to a member function of Screen
// that returns a char and takes two pos arguments
using Action =
char (Screen::*)(Screen::pos, Screen::pos) const;
```

`Action` is another name for the type "pointer to a `const` member function of class `Screen` taking two parameters of type `pos` and returning `char`." Using this alias, we can simplify the definition of a pointer to `get` as follows:

```
Action get = &Screen::get; // get points to the get member of Screen
```

As with any other function pointer, we can use a pointer-to-member function type as the return type or as a parameter type in a function. Like any other parameter, a pointer-to-member parameter can have a default argument:

```
// action takes a reference to a Screen and a pointer to a Screen member function
Screen& action(Screen&, Action = &Screen::get);
```

`action` is a function taking two parameters, which are a reference to a `Screen` object and a pointer to a member function of class `Screen` that takes two `pos` parameters and returns a `char`. We can call `action` by passing it either a pointer or the address of an appropriate member function in `Screen`:

```
Screen myScreen;
//  equivalent calls:
action(myScreen);          //  uses the default argument
action(myScreen, get);  //  uses the variable get that we previously defined
action(myScreen, &Screen::get);    //  passes the address explicitly
```

> Type aliases make code that uses pointers to members much easier to read and write.

Pointer-to-Member Function Tables

One common use for function pointers and for pointers to member functions is to store them in a function table (§ 14.8.3, p. 577). For a class that has several members of the same type, such a table can be used to select one from the set of these members. Let's assume that our `Screen` class is extended to contain several member functions, each of which moves the cursor in a particular direction:

```
class Screen {
public:
    //  other interface and implementation members as before
    Screen& home();       //  cursor movement functions
    Screen& forward();
    Screen& back();
    Screen& up();
    Screen& down();
};
```

Each of these new functions takes no parameters and returns a reference to the `Screen` on which it was invoked.

We might want to define a `move` function that can call any one of these functions and perform the indicated action. To support this new function, we'll add a `static` member to `Screen` that will be an array of pointers to the cursor movement functions:

```
class Screen {
public:
    //  other interface and implementation members as before
    //  Action is a pointer that can be assigned any of the cursor movement members
    using Action = Screen& (Screen::*)();
    //  specify which direction to move; enum see § 19.3 (p. 832)
    enum Directions { HOME, FORWARD, BACK, UP, DOWN };
    Screen& move(Directions);
private:
    static Action Menu[];       //  function table
};
```

The array named `Menu` will hold pointers to each of the cursor movement functions. Those functions will be stored at the offsets corresponding to the enumerators in `Directions`. The `move` function takes an enumerator and calls the appropriate function:

```
Screen& Screen::move(Directions cm)
{
    // run the element indexed by cm on this object
    return (this->*Menu[cm])(); // Menu[cm] points to a member function
}
```

The call inside `move` is evaluated as follows: The `Menu` element indexed by `cm` is fetched. That element is a pointer to a member function of the `Screen` class. We call the member function to which that element points on behalf of the object to which `this` points.

When we call `move`, we pass it an enumerator that indicates which direction to move the cursor:

```
Screen myScreen;
myScreen.move(Screen::HOME); // invokes myScreen.home
myScreen.move(Screen::DOWN); // invokes myScreen.down
```

What's left is to define and initialize the table itself:

```
Screen::Action Screen::Menu[] = { &Screen::home,
                                  &Screen::forward,
                                  &Screen::back,
                                  &Screen::up,
                                  &Screen::down,
                                };
```

EXERCISES SECTION 19.4.2

Exercise 19.14: Is the following code legal? If so, what does it do? If not, why?

```
auto pmf = &Screen::get_cursor;
pmf = &Screen::get;
```

Exercise 19.15: What is the difference between an ordinary function pointer and a pointer to a member function?

Exercise 19.16: Write a type alias that is a synonym for a pointer that can point to the `avg_price` member of `Sales_data`.

Exercise 19.17: Define a type alias for each distinct `Screen` member function type.

19.4.3 Using Member Functions as Callable Objects

As we've seen, to make a call through a pointer to member function, we must use the `.*` or `->*` operators to bind the pointer to a specific object. As a result, unlike ordinary function pointers, a pointer to member is *not* a callable object; these pointers do not support the function-call operator (§ 10.3.2, p. 388).

Because a pointer to member is not a callable object, we cannot directly pass a pointer to a member function to an algorithm. As an example, if we wanted to find the first empty `string` in a `vector` of `strings`, the obvious call won't work:

```
auto fp = &string::empty;   // fp points to the string empty function
// error: must use .* or ->* to call a pointer to member
find_if(svec.begin(), svec.end(), fp);
```

The `find_if` algorithm expects a callable object, but we've supplied `fp`, which is a pointer to a member function. This call won't compile, because the code inside `find_if` executes a statement something like

```
// check whether the given predicate applied to the current element yields true
if (fp(*it))    // error: must use ->* to call through a pointer to member
```

which attempts to call the object it was passed.

Using `function` to Generate a Callable

One way to obtain a callable from a pointer to member function is by using the library `function` template (§ 14.8.3, p. 577):

```
function<bool (const string&)> fcn = &string::empty;
find_if(svec.begin(), svec.end(), fcn);
```

Here we tell `function` that `empty` is a function that can be called with a `string` and returns a `bool`. Ordinarily, the object on which a member function executes is passed to the implicit `this` parameter. When we want to use `function` to generate a callable for a member function, we have to "translate" the code to make that implicit parameter explicit.

When a `function` object holds a pointer to a member function, the `function` class knows that it must use the appropriate pointer-to-member operator to make the call. That is, we can imagine that `find_if` will have code something like

```
// assuming it is the iterator inside find_if, so *it is an object in the given range
if (fcn(*it))    // assuming fcn is the name of the callable inside find_if
```

which `function` will execute using the proper pointer-to-member operator. In essence, the `function` class will transform this call into something like

```
// assuming it is the iterator inside find_if, so *it is an object in the given range
if (((*it).*p)())  // assuming p is the pointer to member function inside fcn
```

When we define a `function` object, we must specify the function type that is the signature of the callable objects that object can represent. When the callable is a member function, the signature's first parameter must represent the (normally implicit) object on which the member will be run. The signature we give to `function` must specify whether the object will be passed as a pointer or a reference.

When we defined `fcn`, we knew that we wanted to call `find_if` on a sequence of `string` objects. Hence, we asked `function` to generate a callable that took `string` objects. Had our `vector` held pointers to `string`, we would have told `function` to expect a pointer:

```
vector<string*> pvec;
function<bool (const string*)> fp = &string::empty;
// fp takes a pointer to string and uses the ->* to call empty
find_if(pvec.begin(), pvec.end(), fp);
```

Using `mem_fn` to Generate a Callable

To use `function`, we must supply the call signature of the member we want to call. We can, instead, let the compiler deduce the member's type by using another library facility, **`mem_fn`**, which, like `function`, is defined in the `functional` header. Like `function`, `mem_fn` generates a callable object from a pointer to member. Unlike `function`, `mem_fn` will deduce the type of the callable from the type of the pointer to member:

```
find_if(svec.begin(), svec.end(), mem_fn(&string::empty));
```

Here we used `mem_fn(&string::empty)` to generate a callable object that takes a `string` argument and returns a `bool`.

The callable generated by `mem_fn` can be called on either an object or a pointer:

```
auto f = mem_fn(&string::empty); // f takes a string or a string*
f(*svec.begin()); // ok: passes a string object; f uses . * to call empty
f(&svec[0]);      // ok: passes a pointer to string; f uses . -> to call empty
```

Effectively, we can think of `mem_fn` *as if* it generates a callable with an overloaded function call operator—one that takes a `string*` and the other a `string&`.

Using `bind` to Generate a Callable

For completeness, we can also use `bind` (§ 10.3.4, p. 397) to generate a callable from a member function:

```
// bind each string in the range to the implicit first argument to empty
auto it = find_if(svec.begin(), svec.end(),
                  bind(&string::empty, _1));
```

As with `function`, when we use `bind`, we must make explicit the member function's normally implicit parameter that represents the object on which the member function will operate. Like `mem_fn`, the first argument to the callable generated by `bind` can be either a pointer or a reference to a `string`:

```
auto f =  bind(&string::empty, _1);
f(*svec.begin()); // ok: argument is a string f will use . * to call empty
f(&svec[0]); //  ok: argument is a pointer to string f will use . -> to call empty
```

19.5 Nested Classes

A class can be defined within another class. Such a class is a **nested class**, also referred to as a **nested type**. Nested classes are most often used to define implementation classes, such as the `QueryResult` class we used in our text query example (§ 12.3, p. 484).

EXERCISES SECTION 19.4.3

Exercise 19.18: Write a function that uses `count_if` to count how many empty `strings` there are in a given `vector`.

Exercise 19.19: Write a function that takes a `vector<Sales_data>` and finds the first element whose average price is greater than some given amount.

Nested classes are independent classes and are largely unrelated to their enclosing class. In particular, objects of the enclosing and nested classes are independent from each other. An object of the nested type does not have members defined by the enclosing class. Similarly, an object of the enclosing class does not have members defined by the nested class.

The name of a nested class is visible within its enclosing class scope but not outside the class. Like any other nested name, the name of a nested class will not collide with the use of that name in another scope.

A nested class can have the same kinds of members as a nonnested class. Just like any other class, a nested class controls access to its own members using access specifiers. The enclosing class has no special access to the members of a nested class, and the nested class has no special access to members of its enclosing class.

A nested class defines a type member in its enclosing class. As with any other member, the enclosing class determines access to this type. A nested class defined in the `public` part of the enclosing class defines a type that may be used anywhere. A nested class defined in the `protected` section defines a type that is accessible only by the enclosing class, its friends, and its derived classes. A `private` nested class defines a type that is accessible only to the members and friends of the enclosing class.

Declaring a Nested Class

The `TextQuery` class from § 12.3.2 (p. 487) defined a companion class named `QueryResult`. The `QueryResult` class is tightly coupled to our `TextQuery` class. It would make little sense to use `QueryResult` for any other purpose than to represent the results of a `query` operation on a `TextQuery` object. To reflect this tight coupling, we'll make `QueryResult` a member of `TextQuery`.

```
class TextQuery {
public:
    class QueryResult;   // nested class to be defined later
    // other members as in § 12.3.2 (p. 487)
};
```

We need to make only one change to our original `TextQuery` class—we declare our intention to define `QueryResult` as a nested class. Because `QueryResult` is a type member (§ 7.4.1, p. 284), we must declare `QueryResult` before we use it. In particular, we must declare `QueryResult` before we use it as the return type for the `query` member. The remaining members of our original class are unchanged.

Defining a Nested Class outside of the Enclosing Class

Inside `TextQuery` we declared `QueryResult` but did not define it. As with member functions, nested classes must be declared inside the class but can be defined either inside or outside the class.

When we define a nested class outside its enclosing class, we must qualify the name of the nested class by the name of its enclosing class:

```
// we're defining the QueryResult class that is a member of class TextQuery
class TextQuery::QueryResult {
    // in class scope, we don't have to qualify the name of the QueryResult parameters
    friend std::ostream&
            print(std::ostream&, const QueryResult&);
public:
    // no need to define QueryResult::line_no; a nested class can use a member
    // of its enclosing class without needing to qualify the member's name
    QueryResult(std::string,
                std::shared_ptr<std::set<line_no>>,
                std::shared_ptr<std::vector<std::string>>);
    // other members as in § 12.3.2 (p. 487)
};
```

The only change we made compared to our original class is that we no longer define a `line_no` member in `QueryResult`. The members of `QueryResult` can access that name directly from `TextQuery`, so there is no need to define it again.

WARNING   Until the actual definition of a nested class that is defined outside the class body is seen, that class is an incomplete type (§ 7.3.3, p. 278).

Defining the Members of a Nested Class

In this version, we did not define the `QueryResult` constructor inside the class body. To define the constructor, we must indicate that `QueryResult` is nested within the scope of `TextQuery`. We do so by qualifying the nested class name with the name of its enclosing class:

```
// defining the member named QueryResult for the class named QueryResult
// that is nested inside the class TextQuery
TextQuery::QueryResult::QueryResult(string s,
                shared_ptr<set<line_no>> p,
                shared_ptr<vector<string>> f):
        sought(s), lines(p), file(f) { }
```

Reading the name of the function from right to left, we see that we are defining the constructor for class `QueryResult`, which is nested in the scope of class `TextQuery`. The code itself just stores the given arguments in the data members and has no further work to do.

Nested-Class `static` Member Definitions

If `QueryResult` had declared a `static` member, its definition would appear outside the scope of the `TextQuery`. For example, assuming `QueryResult` had a `static` member, its definition would look something like

```
//  defines an int static member of QueryResult
//  which is a class nested inside TextQuery
int TextQuery::QueryResult::static_mem = 1024;
```

Name Lookup in Nested Class Scope

Normal rules apply for name lookup (§ 7.4.1, p. 283) inside a nested class. Of course, because a nested class is a nested scope, the nested class has additional enclosing class scopes to search. This nesting of scopes explains why we didn't define `line_no` inside the nested version of `QueryResult`. Our original `QueryResult` class defined this member so that its own members could avoid having to write `TextQuery::line_no`. Having nested the definition of our results class inside `TextQuery`, we no longer need this `typedef`. The nested `QueryResult` class can access `line_no` without specifying that `line_no` is defined in `TextQuery`.

As we've seen, a nested class is a type member of its enclosing class. Members of the enclosing class can use the name of a nested class the same way it can use any other type member. Because `QueryResult` is nested inside `TextQuery`, the query member of `TextQuery` can refer to the name `QueryResult` directly:

```
//  return type must indicate that QueryResult is now a nested class
TextQuery::QueryResult
TextQuery::query(const string &sought) const
{
    //  we'll return a pointer to this set if we don't find sought
    static shared_ptr<set<line_no>> nodata(new set<line_no>);
    //  use find and not a subscript to avoid adding words to wm!
    auto loc = wm.find(sought);
    if (loc == wm.end())
        return QueryResult(sought, nodata, file);  //  not found
    else
        return QueryResult(sought, loc->second, file);
}
```

As usual, the return type is not yet in the scope of the class (§ 7.4, p. 282), so we start by noting that our function returns a `TextQuery::QueryResult` value. However, inside the body of the function, we can refer to `QueryResult` directly, as we do in the `return` statements.

The Nested and Enclosing Classes Are Independent

Although a nested class is defined in the scope of its enclosing class, it is important to understand that there is no connection between the objects of an enclosing class and objects of its nested classe(s). A nested-type object contains only the members defined inside the nested type. Similarly, an object of the enclosing class has only those members that are defined by the enclosing class. It does not contain the data members of any nested classes.

More concretely, the second `return` statement in `TextQuery::query`

```
return QueryResult(sought, loc->second, file);
```

uses data members of the `TextQuery` object on which `query` was run to initialize a `QueryResult` object. We have to use these members to construct the `QueryResult` object we return because a `QueryResult` object does not contain the members of its enclosing class.

EXERCISES SECTION 19.5

Exercise 19.20: Nest your `QueryResult` class inside `TextQuery` and rerun the programs you wrote to use `TextQuery` in § 12.3.2 (p. 490).

19.6   union: A Space-Saving Class

A **union** is a special kind of class. A `union` may have multiple data members, but at any point in time, only one of the members may have a value. When a value is assigned to one member of the `union`, all other members become undefined. The amount of storage allocated for a `union` is at least as much as is needed to contain its largest data member. Like any class, a `union` defines a new type.

Some, but not all, class features apply equally to unions. A `union` cannot have a member that is a reference, but it can have members of most other types, including, under the new standard, class types that have constructors or destructors. A `union` can specify protection labels to make members `public`, `private`, or `protected`. By default, like `struct`s, members of a `union` are `public`.

A `union` may define member functions, including constructors and destructors. However, a `union` may not inherit from another class, nor may a `union` be used as a base class. As a result, a `union` may not have virtual functions.

Defining a union

`union`s offer a convenient way to represent a set of mutually exclusive values of different types. As an example, we might have a process that handles different kinds of numeric or character data. That process might define a `union` to hold these values:

```
//  objects of type Token have a single member, which could be of any of the listed types
union Token {
//  members are public by default
    char    cval;
    int     ival;
    double dval;
};
```

A union is defined starting with the keyword `union`, followed by an (optional) name for the union and a set of member declarations enclosed in curly braces. This code defines a union named `Token` that can hold a value that is either a `char`, an `int`, or a `double`.

Using a union Type

The name of a union is a type name. Like the built-in types, by default unions are uninitialized. We can explicitly initialize a union in the same way that we can explicitly initialize aggregate classes (§ 7.5.5, p. 298) by enclosing the initializer in a pair of curly braces:

```
Token first_token = {'a'}; //  initializes the cval member
Token last_token;          //  uninitialized Token object
Token *pt = new Token;     //  pointer to an uninitialized Token object
```

If an initializer is present, it is used to initialize the first member. Hence, the initialization of first_token gives a value to its cval member.

The members of an object of union type are accessed using the normal member access operators:

```
last_token.cval = 'z';
pt->ival = 42;
```

Assigning a value to a data member of a union object makes the other data members undefined. As a result, when we use a union, we must always know what type of value is currently stored in the union. Depending on the types of the members, retrieving or assigning to the value stored in the union through the wrong data member can lead to a crash or other incorrect program behavior.

Anonymous unions

An **anonymous union** is an unnamed union that does not include any declarations between the close curly that ends its body and the semicolon that ends the union definition (§ 2.6.1, p. 73). When we define an anonymous union the compiler automatically creates an unnamed object of the newly defined union type:

```
union {                   //  anonymous union
    char   cval;
    int    ival;
    double dval;
};  //  defines an unnamed object, whose members we can access directly
cval = 'c';  //  assigns a new value to the unnamed, anonymous union object
ival = 42;   //  that object now holds the value 42
```

The members of an anonymous union are directly accessible in the scope where the anonymous union is defined.

An anonymous union cannot have private or protected members, nor can an anonymous union define member functions.

unions with Members of Class Type

Under earlier versions of C++, unions could not have members of a class type that defined its own constructors or copy-control members. Under the new standard, this restriction is lifted. However, unions with members that define their

own constructors and/or copy-control members are n̶
unions that have members of built-in type.

When a union has members of built-in type, we can us̶
to change the value that the union holds. Not so for unions th̶
nontrivial class types. When we switch the union's value to and̶
of class type, we must construct or destroy that member, respectiv̶
switch the union to a member of class type, we must run a construc̶
member's type; when we switch from that member, we must run its destr̶

When a union has members of built-in type, the compiler will synthesi̶
memberwise versions of the default constructor or copy-control members. T̶
same is not true for unions that have members of a class type that defines its
own default constructor or one or more of the copy-control members. If a union
member's type defines one of these members, the compiler synthesizes the corresponding member of the union as deleted (§ 13.1.6, p. 508).

For example, the string class defines all five copy-control members and the
default constructor. If a union contains a string and does not define its own
default constructor or one of the copy-control members, then the compiler will
synthesize that missing member as deleted. If a class has a union member that has
a deleted copy-control member, then that corresponding copy-control operation(s)
of the class itself will be deleted as well.

Using a Class to Manage union Members

Because of the complexities involved in constructing and destroying members of
class type, unions with class-type members ordinarily are embedded inside another class. That way the class can manage the state transitions to and from the
member of class type. As an example, we'll add a string member to our union.
We'll define our union as an anonymous union and make it a member of a class
named Token. The Token class will manage the union's members.

To keep track of what type of value the union holds, we usually define a separate object known as a **discriminant**. A discriminant lets us discriminate among
the values that the union can hold. In order to keep the union and its discriminant in sync, we'll make the discriminant a member of Token as well. Our class
will define a member of an enumeration type (§ 19.3, p. 832) to keep track of the
state of its union member.

The only functions our class will define are the default constructor, the copy-
control members, and a set of assignment operators that can assign a value of one
of our union's types to the union member:

```
class Token {
public:
    // copy control needed because our class has a union with a string member
    // defining the move constructor and move-assignment operator is left as an exercise
    Token(): tok(INT), ival{0} { }
    Token(const Token &t): tok(t.tok) { copyUnion(t); }
    Token &operator=(const Token&);
    // if the union holds a string, we must destroy it; see § 19.1.2 (p. 824)
    ~Token() { if (tok == STR) sval.~string(); }
```

ering members of the union
`:string&);`

`tok; //` *discriminant*
`//` *anonymous union*

nnamed member of this unnamed `union` type
the `union` member as appropriate
`n&);`

nscoped enumeration (§ 19.3, p. 832) that we use as the type for the member named tok. We defined tok following the close curly and before the semicolon that ends the definition of the enum, which defines tok to have this unnamed enum type (§ 2.6.1, p. 73).

We'll use tok as our discriminant. When the union holds an int value, tok will have the value INT; if the union has a string, tok will be STR; and so on.

The default constructor initializes the discriminant and the union member to hold an int value of 0.

Because our union has a member with a destructor, we must define our own destructor to (conditionally) destroy the string member. Unlike ordinary members of a class type, class members that are part of a union are not automatically destroyed. The destructor has no way to know which type the union holds, so it cannot know which member to destroy.

Our destructor checks whether the object being destroyed holds a string. If so, the destructor explicitly calls the string destructor (§ 19.1.2, p. 824) to free the memory used by that string. The destructor has no work to do if the union holds a member of any of the built-in types.

Managing the Discriminant and Destroying the `string`

The assignment operators will set tok and assign the corresponding member of the union. Like the destructor, these members must conditionally destroy the string before assigning a new value to the union:

```
Token &Token::operator=(int i)
{
    if (tok == STR) sval.~string();   //  if we have a string, free it
    ival = i;                         //  assign to the appropriate member
    tok = INT;                        //  update the discriminant
    return *this;
}
```

If the current value in the union is a string, we must destroy that string before assigning a new value to the union. We do so by calling the string destructor.

Once we've cleaned up the `string` member, we assign the given value to the member that corresponds to the parameter type of the operator. In this case, our parameter is an `int`, so we assign to `ival`. We update the discriminant and return.

The `double` and `char` assignment operators behave identically to the `int` version and are left as an exercise. The `string` version differs from the others because it must manage the transition to and from the `string` type:

```
Token &Token::operator=(const std::string &s)
{
    if (tok == STR)  // if we already hold a string, just do an assignment
        sval = s;
    else
        new(&sval) string(s);  // otherwise construct a string
    tok = STR;                 // update the discriminant
    return *this;
}
```

In this case, if the `union` already holds a `string`, we can use the normal `string` assignment operator to give a new value to that `string`. Otherwise, there is no existing `string` object on which to invoke the `string` assignment operator. Instead, we must construct a `string` in the memory that holds the `union`. We do so using placement `new` (§ 19.1.2, p. 824) to construct a `string` at the location in which `sval` resides. We initialize that `string` as a copy of our `string` parameter. We next update the discriminant and return.

Managing Union Members That Require Copy Control

Like the type-specific assignment operators, the copy constructor and assignment operators have to test the discriminant to know how to copy the given value. To do this common work, we'll define a member named copyUnion.

When we call copyUnion from the copy constructor, the `union` member will have been default-initialized, meaning that the first member of the `union` will have been initialized. Because our `string` is not the first member, we know that the `union` member doesn't hold a `string`. In the assignment operator, it is possible that the `union` already holds a `string`. We'll handle that case directly in the assignment operator. That way copyUnion can assume that if its parameter holds a `string`, copyUnion must construct its own `string`:

```
void Token::copyUnion(const Token &t)
{
    switch (t.tok) {
        case Token::INT: ival = t.ival; break;
        case Token::CHAR: cval = t.cval; break;
        case Token::DBL: dval = t.dval; break;
        // to copy a string, construct it using placement new; see (§ 19.1.2 (p. 824))
        case Token::STR: new(&sval) string(t.sval); break;
    }
}
```

This function uses a `switch` statement (§ 5.3.2, p. 178) to test the discriminant. For the built-in types, we assign the value to the corresponding member; if the member we are copying is a string, we construct it.

The assignment operator must handle three possibilities for its string member: Both the left-hand and right-hand operands might be a string; neither operand might be a string; or one but not both operands might be a string:

```
Token &Token::operator=(const Token &t)
{
    // if this object holds a string and t doesn't, we have to free the old string
    if (tok == STR && t.tok != STR) sval.~string();
    if (tok == STR && t.tok == STR)
        sval = t.sval;   // no need to construct a new string
    else
        copyUnion(t);    // will construct a string if t.tok is STR
    tok = t.tok;
    return *this;
}
```

If the union in the left-hand operand holds a string, but the union in the right-hand does not, then we have to first free the old string before assigning a new value to the union member. If both unions hold a string, we can use the normal string assignment operator to do the copy. Otherwise, we call copyUnion to do the assignment. Inside copyUnion, if the right-hand operand is a string, we'll construct a new string in the union member of the left-hand operand. If neither operand is a string, then ordinary assignment will suffice.

EXERCISES SECTION 19.6

Exercise 19.21: Write your own version of the Token class.

Exercise 19.22: Add a member of type Sales_data to your Token class.

Exercise 19.23: Add a move constructor and move assignment to Token.

Exercise 19.24: Explain what happens if we assign a Token object to itself.

Exercise 19.25: Write assignment operators that take values of each type in the union.

19.7 Local Classes

A class can be defined inside a function body. Such a class is called a **local class**. A local class defines a type that is visible only in the scope in which it is defined. Unlike nested classes, the members of a local class are severely restricted.

All members, including functions, of a local class must be completely defined inside the class body. As a result, local classes are much less useful than nested classes.

In practice, the requirement that members be fully defined within the class limits the complexity of the member functions of a local class. Functions in local classes are rarely more than a few lines of code. Beyond that, the code becomes difficult for the reader to understand.

Similarly, a local class is not permitted to declare static data members, there being no way to define them.

Local Classes May Not Use Variables from the Function's Scope

The names from the enclosing scope that a local class can access are limited. A local class can access only type names, static variables (§ 6.1.1, p. 205), and enumerators defined within the enclosing local scopes. A local class may not use the ordinary local variables of the function in which the class is defined:

```
int a, val;
void foo(int val)
{
    static int si;
    enum Loc { a = 1024, b };
    //  Bar is local to foo
    struct Bar {
        Loc locVal; //  ok: uses a local type name
        int barVal;
        void fooBar(Loc l = a)    //  ok: default argument is Loc::a
        {
            barVal = val;      //  error: val is local to foo
            barVal = ::val;    //  ok: uses a global object
            barVal = si;       //  ok: uses a static local object
            locVal = b;        //  ok: uses an enumerator
        }
    };
    //  ...
}
```

Normal Protection Rules Apply to Local Classes

The enclosing function has no special access privileges to the private members of the local class. Of course, the local class could make the enclosing function a friend. More typically, a local class defines its members as public. The portion of a program that can access a local class is very limited. A local class is already encapsulated within the scope of the function. Further encapsulation through information hiding is often overkill.

Name Lookup within a Local Class

Name lookup within the body of a local class happens in the same manner as for other classes. Names used in the declarations of the members of the class must be in scope before the use of the name. Names used in the definition of a member can appear anywhere in the class. If a name is not found as a class member, then the search continues in the enclosing scope and then out to the scope enclosing the function itself.

Nested Local Classes

It is possible to nest a class inside a local class. In this case, the nested class definition can appear outside the local-class body. However, the nested class must be defined in the same scope as that in which the local class is defined.

```
void foo()
{
    class Bar {
    public:
        // ...
        class Nested;       // declares class Nested
    };
    // definition of Nested
    class Bar::Nested {
        // ...
    };
}
```

As usual, when we define a member outside a class, we must indicate the scope of the name. Hence, we defined `Bar::Nested`, which says that `Nested` is a class defined in the scope of `Bar`.

A class nested in a local class is itself a local class, with all the attendant restrictions. All members of the nested class must be defined inside the body of the nested class itself.

19.8 Inherently Nonportable Features

To support low-level programming, C++ defines some features that are inherently **nonportable**. A nonportable feature is one that is machine specific. Programs that use nonportable features often require reprogramming when they are moved from one machine to another. The fact that the sizes of the arithmetic types vary across machines (§ 2.1.1, p. 32) is one such nonportable feature that we have already used.

In this section we'll cover two additional nonportable features that C++ inherits from C: bit-fields and the `volatile` qualifier. We'll also cover linkage directives, which is a nonportable feature that C++ adds to those that it inherits from C.

19.8.1 Bit-fields

A class can define a (`nonstatic`) data member as a **bit-field**. A bit-field holds a specified number of bits. Bit-fields are normally used when a program needs to pass binary data to another program or to a hardware device.

 The memory layout of a bit-field is machine dependent.

A bit-field must have integral or enumeration type (§ 19.3, p. 832). Ordinarily, we use an unsigned type to hold a bit-field, because the behavior of a signed bit-field is implementation defined. We indicate that a member is a bit-field by following the member name with a colon and a constant expression specifying the number of bits:

```
typedef unsigned int Bit;
class File {
    Bit mode: 2;        //  mode has 2 bits
    Bit modified: 1;    //  modified has 1 bit
    Bit prot_owner: 3;  //  prot_owner has 3 bits
    Bit prot_group: 3;  //  prot_group has 3 bits
    Bit prot_world: 3;  //  prot_world has 3 bits
    //  operations and data members of File
public:
    //  file modes specified as octal literals; see § 2.1.3 (p. 38)
    enum modes { READ = 01, WRITE = 02, EXECUTE = 03 };
    File &open(modes);
    void close();
    void write();
    bool isRead() const;
    void setWrite();
};
```

The mode bit-field has two bits, modified only one, and the other members each have three bits. Bit-fields defined in consecutive order within the class body are, if possible, packed within adjacent bits of the same integer, thereby providing for storage compaction. For example, in the preceding declaration, the five bit-fields will (probably) be stored in a single unsigned int. Whether and how the bits are packed into the integer is machine dependent.

The address-of operator (&) cannot be applied to a bit-field, so there can be no pointers referring to class bit-fields.

WARNING

> Ordinarily it is best to make a bit-field an unsigned type. The behavior of bit-fields stored in a signed type is implementation defined.

Using Bit-fields

A bit-field is accessed in much the same way as the other data members of a class:

```
void File::write()
{
    modified = 1;
    // ...
}
void File::close()
{
    if (modified)
        // ... save contents
}
```

Bit-fields with more than one bit are usually manipulated using the built-in bitwise
operators (§ 4.8, p. 152):

```
File &File::open(File::modes m)
{
    mode |= READ;        // set the READ bit by default
    // other processing
    if (m & WRITE) // if opening READ and WRITE
    // processing to open the file in read/write mode
    return *this;
}
```

Classes that define bit-field members also usually define a set of inline member
functions to test and set the value of the bit-field:

```
inline bool File::isRead() const { return mode & READ; }
inline void File::setWrite() { mode |= WRITE; }
```

19.8.2 `volatile` Qualifier

WARNING

The precise meaning of `volatile` is inherently machine dependent
and can be understood only by reading the compiler documentation.
Programs that use `volatile` usually must be changed when they are
moved to new machines or compilers.

Programs that deal directly with hardware often have data elements whose
value is controlled by processes outside the direct control of the program itself.
For example, a program might contain a variable updated by the system clock. An
object should be declared **volatile** when its value might be changed in ways
outside the control or detection of the program. The `volatile` keyword is a directive to the compiler that it should not perform optimizations on such objects.

The `volatile` qualifier is used in much the same way as the `const` qualifier.
It is an additional modifier to a type:

```
volatile int display_register; //  int value that might change
volatile Task *curr_task;      //  curr_task points to a volatile object
volatile int iax[max_size];    //  each element in iax is volatile
volatile Screen bitmapBuf;     //  each member of bitmapBuf is volatile
```

There is no interaction between the `const` and `volatile` type qualifiers. A type
can be both `const` and `volatile`, in which case it has the properties of both.

In the same way that a class may define `const` member functions, it can also
define member functions as `volatile`. Only `volatile` member functions may
be called on `volatile` objects.

§ 2.4.2 (p. 62) described the interactions between the `const` qualifier and pointers. The same interactions exist between the `volatile` qualifier and pointers. We
can declare pointers that are `volatile`, pointers to `volatile` objects, and pointers that are `volatile` that point to `volatile` objects:

```
volatile int v;        //  v is a volatile int
int *volatile vip;     //  vip is a volatile pointer to int
volatile int *ivp;     //  ivp is a pointer to volatile int
//  vivp is a volatile pointer to volatile int
volatile int *volatile vivp;

int *ip = &v;    //  error: must use a pointer to volatile
*ivp = &v;       //  ok: ivp is a pointer to volatile
vivp = &v;       //  ok: vivp is a volatile pointer to volatile
```

As with const, we may assign the address of a volatile object (or copy a pointer to a volatile type) only to a pointer to volatile. We may use a volatile object to initialize a reference only if the reference is volatile.

Synthesized Copy Does Not Apply to volatile Objects

One important difference between the treatment of const and volatile is that the synthesized copy/move and assignment operators cannot be used to initialize or assign from a volatile object. The synthesized members take parameters that are references to (nonvolatile) const, and we cannot bind a nonvolatile reference to a volatile object.

If a class wants to allow volatile objects to be copied, moved, or assigned, it must define its own versions of the copy or move operation. As one example, we might write the parameters as const volatile references, in which case we can copy or assign from any kind of Foo:

```
class Foo {
public:
    Foo(const volatile Foo&);    //  copy from a volatile object
    //  assign from a volatile object to a nonvolatile object
    Foo& operator=(volatile const Foo&);
    //  assign from a volatile object to a volatile object
    Foo& operator=(volatile const Foo&) volatile;
    //  remainder of class Foo
};
```

Although we can define copy and assignment for volatile objects, a deeper question is whether it makes any sense to copy a volatile object. The answer to that question depends intimately on the reason for using volatile in any particular program.

19.8.3 Linkage Directives: extern "C"

C++ programs sometimes need to call functions written in another programming language. Most often, that other language is C. Like any name, the name of a function written in another language must be declared. As with any function, that declaration must specify the return type and parameter list. The compiler checks calls to functions written in another language in the same way that it handles ordinary C++ functions. However, the compiler typically must generate different code to call functions written in other languages. C++ uses **linkage directives** to indicate the language used for any non-C++ function.

 Mixing C++ with code written in any other language, including C, requires access to a compiler for that language that is compatible with your C++ compiler.

Declaring a Non-C++ Function

A linkage directive can have one of two forms: single or compound. Linkage directives may not appear inside a class or function definition. The same linkage directive must appear on every declaration of a function.

As an example, the following declarations shows how some of the C functions in the `cstring` header might be declared:

```
//  illustrative linkage directives that might appear in the C++ header <cstring>
//  single-statement linkage directive
extern "C" size_t strlen(const char *);
//  compound-statement linkage directive
extern "C" {
    int strcmp(const char*, const char*);
    char *strcat(char*, const char*);
}
```

The first form of a linkage directive consists of the `extern` keyword followed by a string literal, followed by an "ordinary" function declaration.

The string literal indicates the language in which the function is written. A compiler is required to support linkage directives for C. A compiler may provide linkage specifications for other languages, for example, `extern "Ada"`, `extern "FORTRAN"`, and so on.

Linkage Directives and Headers

We can give the same linkage to several functions at once by enclosing their declarations inside curly braces following the linkage directive. These braces serve to group the declarations to which the linkage directive applies. The braces are otherwise ignored, and the names of functions declared within the braces are visible as if the functions were declared outside the braces.

The multiple-declaration form can be applied to an entire header file. For example, the C++ `cstring` header might look like

```
//  compound-statement linkage directive
extern "C" {
#include <string.h>        //  C functions that manipulate C-style strings
}
```

When a `#include` directive is enclosed in the braces of a compound-linkage directive, all ordinary function declarations in the header file are assumed to be functions written in the language of the linkage directive. Linkage directives can be nested, so if a header contains a function with its own linkage directive, the linkage of that function is unaffected.

> The functions that C++ inherits from the C library are permitted to be defined as C functions but are not required to be C functions—it's up to each C++ implementation to decide whether to implement the C library functions in C or C++.

Pointers to `extern "C"` Functions

The language in which a function is written is part of its type. Hence, every declaration of a function defined with a linkage directive must use the same linkage directive. Moreover, pointers to functions written in other languages must be declared with the same linkage directive as the function itself:

```
// pf points to a C function that returns void and takes an int
extern "C" void (*pf) (int);
```

When `pf` is used to call a function, the function call is compiled assuming that the call is to a C function.

A pointer to a C function does not have the same type as a pointer to a C++ function. A pointer to a C function cannot be initialized or be assigned to point to a C++ function (and vice versa). As with any other type mismatch, it is an error to try to assign two pointers with different linkage directives:

```
void (*pf1) (int);                     // points to a C++ function
extern "C" void (*pf2) (int);    // points to a C function
pf1 = pf2; // error: pf1 and pf2 have different types
```

> **WARNING** Some C++ compilers may accept the preceding assignment as a language extension, even though, strictly speaking, it is illegal.

Linkage Directives Apply to the Entire Declaration

When we use a linkage directive, it applies to the function and any function pointers used as the return type or as a parameter type:

```
// f1 is a C function; its parameter is a pointer to a C function
extern "C" void f1(void(*) (int));
```

This declaration says that `f1` is a C function that doesn't return a value. It has one parameter, which is a pointer to a function that returns nothing and takes a single `int` parameter. The linkage directive applies to the function pointer as well as to `f1`. When we call `f1`, we must pass it the name of a C function or a pointer to a C function.

Because a linkage directive applies to all the functions in a declaration, we must use a type alias (§ 2.5.1, p. 67) if we wish to pass a pointer to a C function to a C++ function:

```
//  FC is a pointer to a C function
extern "C" typedef void FC(int);
//  f2 is a C++ function with a parameter that is a pointer to a C function
void f2(FC *);
```

Exporting Our C++ Functions to Other Languages

By using the linkage directive on a function definition, we can make a C++ function available to a program written in another language:

```
//  the calc function can be called from C programs
extern "C" double calc(double dparm) { /* ... */ }
```

When the compiler generates code for this function, it will generate code appropriate to the indicated language.

It is worth noting that the parameter and return types in functions that are shared across languages are often constrained. For example, we can almost surely not write a function that passes objects of a (nontrivial) C++ class to a C program. The C program won't know about the constructors, destructors, or other class-specific operations.

PREPROCESSOR SUPPORT FOR LINKING TO C

To allow the same source file to be compiled under either C or C++, the preprocessor defines __cplusplus (two underscores) when we compile C++. Using this variable, we can conditionally include code when we are compiling C++:

```
#ifdef __cplusplus
//  ok: we're compiling C++
extern "C"
#endif
int strcmp(const char*, const char*);
```

Overloaded Functions and Linkage Directives

The interaction between linkage directives and function overloading depends on the target language. If the language supports overloaded functions, then it is likely that a compiler that implements linkage directives for that language would also support overloading of these functions from C++.

The C language does not support function overloading, so it should not be a surprise that a C linkage directive can be specified for only one function in a set of overloaded functions:

```
//  error: two extern "C" functions with the same name
extern "C" void print(const char*);
extern "C" void print(int);
```

If one function among a set of overloaded functions is a C function, the other functions must all be C++ functions:

```
class SmallInt { /* ... */ };
class BigNum { /* ... */ };
//   the C function can be called from C and C++ programs
//   the C++ functions overload that function and are callable from C++
extern "C" double calc(double);
extern SmallInt calc(const SmallInt&);
extern BigNum calc(const BigNum&);
```

The C version of `calc` can be called from C programs and from C++ programs. The additional functions are C++ functions with class parameters that can be called only from C++ programs. The order of the declarations is not significant.

EXERCISES SECTION 19.8.3

Exercise 19.26: Explain these declarations and indicate whether they are legal:

```
extern "C" int compute(int *, int);
extern "C" double compute(double *, double);
```

CHAPTER SUMMARY

C++ provides several specialized facilities that are tailored to particular kinds of problems.

Some applications need to take control of how memory is allocated. They can do so by defining their own versions—either class specific or global—of the library `operator new` and `operator delete` functions. If the application defines its own versions of these functions, `new` and `delete` expressions will use the application-defined version.

Some programs need to directly interrogate the dynamic type of an object at run time. Run-time type identification (RTTI) provides language-level support for this kind of programming. RTTI applies only to classes that define virtual functions; type information for types that do not define virtual functions is available but reflects the static type.

When we define a pointer to a class member, the pointer type also encapsulates the type of the class containing the member to which the pointer points. A pointer to member may be bound to any member of the class that has the appropriate type. When we dereference a pointer to member, we must supply an object from which to fetch the member.

C++ defines several additional aggregate types:

- Nested classes, which are classes defined in the scope of another class. Such classes are often defined as implementation classes of their enclosing class.

- `unions` are a special kind of class that may define several data members, but at any point in time, only one member may have a value. `unions` are most often nested inside another class type.

- Local classes, which are defined inside a function. All members of a local class must be defined in the class body. There are no `static` data members of a local class.

C++ also supports several inherently nonportable features, including bit-fields and `volatile`, which make it easier to interface to hardware, and linkage directives, which make it easier to interface to programs written in other languages.

DEFINED TERMS

anonymous union Unnamed union that is not used to define an object. Members of an anonymous union become members of the surrounding scope. These unions may not have member functions and may not have private or protected members.

bit-field Class member with a integral type that specifies the number of bits to allocate to the member. Bit-fields defined in consecutive order in the class are, if possible, compacted into a common integral value.

discriminant Programming technique that uses an object to determine which actual type is held in a union at any given time.

dynamic_cast Operator that performs a checked cast from a base type to a derived type. When the base type has at least one virtual function, the operator checks the dynamic type of the object to which the reference or pointer is bound. If the object type is the same as the type of the cast (or a type derived from that type), then the cast is done. Otherwise, a zero pointer is returned for a pointer cast, or an exception is thrown for a cast to a reference type.

enumeration Type that groups a set of named integral constants.

enumerator Member of an enumeration. Enumerators are `const` and may be used where integral constant expressions are required.

free Low-level memory deallocation function defined in `cstdlib`. `free` may be used *only* to free memory allocated by `malloc`.

linkage directive Mechanism used to allow functions written in a different language to be called from a C++ program. All compilers must support calling C and C++ functions. It is compiler dependent whether any other languages are supported.

local class Class defined inside a function. A local class is visible only inside the function in which it is defined. All members of the class must be defined inside the class body. There can be no `static` members of a local class. Local class members may not access the nonstatic variables defined in the enclosing function. They may use type names, `static` variables, or enumerators defined in the enclosing function.

malloc Low-level memory allocation function defined in `cstdlib`. Memory allocated by `malloc` must be freed by `free`.

mem_fn Library class template that generates a callable object from a given pointer to member function.

nested class Class defined inside another class. A nested class is defined inside its enclosing scope: Nested-class names must be unique within the class scope in which they are defined but can be reused in scopes outside the enclosing class. Access to the nested class outside the enclosing class requires use of the scope operator to specify the scope(s) in which the class is nested.

nested type Synonym for nested class.

nonportable Features that are inherently machine specific and may require change when a program is ported to another machine or compiler.

operator delete Library function that frees untyped, unconstructed memory allocated by `operator new`. The library `operator delete[]` frees memory used to hold an array that was allocated by `operator new[]`.

operator new Library function that allocates untyped, unconstructed memory of a given size. The library function `operator new[]` allocates raw memory for arrays. These library functions provide a more primitive allocation mechanism than the library `allocator` class. Modern C++ programs should use the `allocator` classes rather than these library functions.

placement new expression Form of `new` that constructs its object in specified memory. It does no allocation; instead, it takes an argument that specifies where the object should be constructed. It is a lower-level analog of the behavior provided by the `construct` member of the `allocator` class.

pointer to member Pointer that encapsulates the class type as well as the member type to which the pointer points. The definition of a pointer to member must specify the class name as well as the type of the member(s) to which the pointer may point:

```
T C::*pmem = &C::member;
```

This statement defines `pmem` as a pointer that can point to members of the class named `C` that have type `T` and initializes `pmem` to point to the member in `C` named `member`. To use the pointer, we must supply an object or pointer to type `C`:

```
classobj.*pmem;
classptr->*pmem;
```

fetches `member` from the object `classobj` of the object pointed to by `classptr`.

run-time type identification Language and library facilities that allow the dynamic type of a reference or pointer to be obtained at run time. The RTTI operators, `typeid` and `dynamic_cast`, provide the dynamic type only for references or pointers to class types with virtual functions. When applied to other types, the type returned is the static type of the reference or pointer.

scoped enumeration New-style enumeration in which the enumerator are not accessible directly in the surrounding scope.

typeid operator Unary operator that returns a reference to an object of the library type named `type_info` that describes the type of the given expression. When the expression is an object of a type that has virtual functions, then the dynamic type of the expression is returned; such expressions are evaluated at run time. If the type is a reference, pointer, or other type that does not define virtual functions, then the type returned is the static type of the reference, pointer, or object; such expressions are not evaluated.

type_info Library type returned by the `typeid` operator. The `type_info` class is inherently machine dependent, but must provide a small set of operations, including a `name` function that returns a character string representing the type's name. `type_info` objects may not be copied, moved, or assigned.

union Classlike aggregate type that may define multiple data members, only one of which can have a value at any one point. Unions may have member functions, including constructors and destructors. A union may not serve as a base class. Under the new standard, unions can have members that are class types that define their own copy-control members. Such unions obtain deleted copy control if they do not themselves define the corresponding copy-control functions.

unscoped enumeration Enumeration in which the enumerators are accessible in the surrounding scope.

volatile Type qualifier that signifies to the compiler that a variable might be changed outside the direct control of the program. It is a signal to the compiler that it may not perform certain optimizations.

APPENDIX A

THE LIBRARY

This Appendix contains additional details about the algorithms and random number parts of the library. We also provide a list of all the names we used from the standard library along with the name of the header that defines that name.

In Chapter 10 we used some of the more common algorithms and described the architecture that underlies the algorithms. In this Appendix, we list all the algorithms, organized by the kinds of operations they perform.

In § 17.4 (p. 745) we described the architecture of the random number library and used several of the library's distribution types. The library defines a number or random number engines and 20 different distributions. In this Appendix, we list all the engines and distributions.

A.1 Library Names and Headers

Our programs mostly did not show the actual #include directives needed to compile the program. As a convenience to readers, Table A.1 lists the library names our programs used and the header in which they may be found.

Table A.1: Standard Library Names and Headers

Name	Header
abort	`<cstdlib>`
accumulate	`<numeric>`
allocator	`<memory>`
array	`<array>`
auto_ptr	`<memory>`
back_inserter	`<iterator>`
bad_alloc	`<new>`
bad_array_new_length	`<new>`
bad_cast	`<typeinfo>`
begin	`<iterator>`
bernoulli_distribution	`<random>`
bind	`<functional>`
bitset	`<bitset>`
boolalpha	`<iostream>`
cerr	`<iostream>`
cin	`<iostream>`
cmatch	`<regex>`
copy	`<algorithm>`
count	`<algorithm>`
count_if	`<algorithm>`
cout	`<iostream>`
cref	`<functional>`
csub_match	`<regex>`
dec	`<iostream>`
default_float_engine	`<iostream>`
default_random_engine	`<random>`
deque	`<deque>`
domain_error	`<stdexcept>`
end	`<iterator>`
endl	`<iostream>`
ends	`<iostream>`
equal_range	`<algorithm>`
exception	`<exception>`
fill	`<algorithm>`
fill_n	`<algorithm>`
find	`<algorithm>`
find_end	`<algorithm>`
find_first_of	`<algorithm>`

Table A.1: Standard Library Names and Headers (continued)

Name	Header
find_if	<algorithm>
fixed	<iostream>
flush	<iostream>
for_each	<algorithm>
forward	<utility>
forward_list	<forward_list>
free	cstdlib
front_inserter	<iterator>
fstream	<fstream>
function	<functional>
get	<tuple>
getline	<string>
greater	<functional>
hash	<functional>
hex	<iostream>
hexfloat	<iostream>
ifstream	<fstream>
initializer_list	<initializer_list>
inserter	<iterator>
internal	<iostream>
ios_base	<ios_base>
isalpha	<cctype>
islower	<cctype>
isprint	<cctype>
ispunct	<cctype>
isspace	<cctype>
istream	<iostream>
istream_iterator	<iterator>
istringstream	<sstream>
isupper	<cctype>
left	<iostream>
less	<functional>
less_equal	<functional>
list	<list>
logic_error	<stdexcept>
lower_bound	<algorithm>
lround	<cmath>
make_move_iterator	<iterator>
make_pair	<utility>
make_shared	<memory>
make_tuple	<tuple>
malloc	cstdlib
map	<map>

Table A.1: Standard Library Names and Headers (continued)

Name	Header
max	`<algorithm>`
max_element	`<algorithm>`
mem_fn	`<functional>`
min	`<algorithm>`
move	`<utility>`
multimap	`<map>`
multiset	`<set>`
negate	`<functional>`
noboolalpha	`<iostream>`
normal_distribution	`<random>`
noshowbase	`<iostream>`
noshowpoint	`<iostream>`
noskipws	`<iostream>`
not1	`<functional>`
nothrow	`<new>`
nothrow_t	`<new>`
nounitbuf	`<iostream>`
nouppercase	`<iostream>`
nth_element	`<algorithm>`
oct	`<iostream>`
ofstream	`<fstream>`
ostream	`<iostream>`
ostream_iterator	`<iterator>`
ostringstream	`<sstream>`
out_of_range	`<stdexcept>`
pair	`<utility>`
partial_sort	`<algorithm>`
placeholders	`<functional>`
placeholders::_1	`<functional>`
plus	`<functional>`
priority_queue	`<queue>`
ptrdiff_t	`<cstddef>`
queue	`<queue>`
rand	`<random>`
random_device	`<random>`
range_error	`<stdexcept>`
ref	`<functional>`
regex	`<regex>`
regex_constants	`<regex>`
regex_error	`<regex>`
regex_match	`<regex>`
regex_replace	`<regex>`
regex_search	`<regex>`

Table A.1: Standard Library Names and Headers (continued)

Name	Header
remove_pointer	`<type_traits>`
remove_reference	`<type_traits>`
replace	`<algorithm>`
replace_copy	`<algorithm>`
reverse_iterator	`<iterator>`
right	`<iostream>`
runtime_error	`<stdexcept>`
scientific	`<iostream>`
set	`<set>`
set_difference	`<algorithm>`
set_intersection	`<algorithm>`
set_union	`<algorithm>`
setfill	`<iomanip>`
setprecision	`<iomanip>`
setw	`<iomanip>`
shared_ptr	`<memory>`
showbase	`<iostream>`
showpoint	`<iostream>`
size_t	`<cstddef>`
skipws	`<iostream>`
smatch	`<regex>`
sort	`<algorithm>`
sqrt	`<cmath>`
sregex_iterator	`<regex>`
ssub_match	`<regex>`
stable_sort	`<algorithm>`
stack	`<stack>`
stoi	`<string>`
strcmp	`<cstring>`
strcpy	`<cstring>`
string	`<string>`
stringstream	`<sstream>`
strlen	`<cstring>`
strncpy	`<cstring>`
strtod	`<string>`
swap	`<utility>`
terminate	`<exception>`
time	`<ctime>`
tolower	`<cctype>`
toupper	`<cctype>`
transform	`<algorithm>`
tuple	`<tuple>`
tuple_element	`<tuple>`

Table A.1: Standard Library Names and Headers (continued)

Name	Header
tuple_size	<tuple>
type_info	<typeinfo>
unexpected	<exception>
uniform_int_distribution	<random>
uniform_real_distribution	<random>
uninitialized_copy	<memory>
uninitialized_fill	<memory>
unique	<algorithm>
unique_copy	<algorithm>
unique_ptr	<memory>
unitbuf	<iostream>
unordered_map	<unordered_map>
unordered_multimap	<unordered_map>
unordered_multiset	<unordered_set>
unordered_set	<unordered_set>
upper_bound	<algorithm>
uppercase	<iostream>
vector	<vector>
weak_ptr	<memory>

A.2   A Brief Tour of the Algorithms

The library defines more than 100 algorithms. Learning to use these algorithms effectively requires understanding their structure rather than memorizing the details of each algorithm. Accordingly, in Chapter 10 we concentrated on describing and understanding that architecture. In this section we'll briefly describe every algorithm. In the following descriptions,

- beg and end are iterators that denote a range of elements (§ 9.2.1, p. 331). Almost all of the algorithms operate on a sequence denoted by beg and end.

- beg2 is an iterator denoting the beginning of a second input sequence. If present, end2 denotes the end of the second sequence. When there is no end2, the sequence denoted by beg2 is assumed to be as large as the input sequence denoted by beg and end. The types of beg and beg2 need not match. However, it must be possible to apply the specified operation or given callable object to elements in the two sequences.

- dest is an iterator denoting a destination. The destination sequence must be able to hold as many elements as necessary given the input sequence.

- unaryPred and binaryPred are unary and binary predicates (§ 10.3.1, p. 386) that return a type that can be used as a condition and take one and two arguments, respectively, that are elements in the input range.

- comp is a binary predicate that meets the ordering requirements for key in an associative container (§ 11.2.2, p. 425).

- unaryOp and binaryOp are callable objects (§ 10.3.2, p. 388) that can be called with one and two arguments from the input range, respectively.

A.2.1 Algorithms to Find an Object

These algorithms search an input range for a specific value or sequence of values.

Each algorithm provides two overloaded versions. The first version uses equality (==) operator of the underlying type to compare elements; the second version compares elements using the user-supplied unaryPred or binaryPred.

Simple Find Algorithms

These algorithms look for specific values and require *input iterators*.

```
find(beg, end, val)
find_if(beg, end, unaryPred)
find_if_not(beg, end, unaryPred)
count(beg, end, val)
count_if(beg, end, unaryPred)
```
find returns an iterator to the first element in the input range equal to val. find_if returns an iterator to the first element for which unaryPred succeeds; find_if_not returns an iterator to the first element for which unaryPred is false. All three return end if no such element exists.
count returns a count of how many times val occurs; count_if counts elements for which unaryPred succeeds.

```
all_of(beg, end, unaryPred)
any_of(beg, end, unaryPred)
none_of(beg, end, unaryPred)
```
Returns a bool indicating whether the unaryPred succeeded for all of the elements, any element, or no element respectively. If the sequence is empty, any_of returns false; all_of and none_of return true.

Algorithms to Find One of Many Values

These algorithms require *forward iterators*. They look for a repeated elements in the input sequence.

```
adjacent_find(beg, end)
adjacent_find(beg, end, binaryPred)
```
Returns an iterator to the first adjacent pair of duplicate elements. Returns end if there are no adjacent duplicate elements.

```
search_n(beg, end, count, val)
search_n(beg, end, count, val, binaryPred)
```
Returns an iterator to the beginning of a subsequence of count equal elements. Returns end if no such subsequence exists.

Algorithms to Find Subsequences

With the exception of `find_first_of`, these algorithms require two pairs of *forward iterators*. `find_first_of` uses *input iterators* to denote its first sequence and *forward iterators* for its second. These algorithms search for subsequences rather than for a single element.

```
search(beg1, end1, beg2, end2)
search(beg1, end1, beg2, end2, binaryPred)
```
Returns an iterator to the first position in the input range at which the second range occurs as a subsequence. Returns `end1` if the subsequence is not found.

```
find_first_of(beg1, end1, beg2, end2)
find_first_of(beg1, end1, beg2, end2, binaryPred)
```
Returns an iterator to the first occurrence in the first range of any element from the second range. Returns `end1` if no match is found.

```
find_end(beg1, end1, beg2, end2)
find_end(beg1, end1, beg2, end2, binaryPred)
```
Like `search`, but returns an iterator to the last position in the input range at which the second range occurs as a subsequence. Returns `end1` if the second subsequence is empty or is not found.

A.2.2   Other Read-Only Algorithms

These algorithms require *input iterators* for their first two arguments.

The `equal` and `mismatch` algorithms also take an additional *input iterator* that denotes the start of a second range. They also provide two overloaded versions. The first version uses equality (`==`) operator of the underlying type to compare elements; the second version compares elements using the user-supplied `unaryPred` or `binaryPred`.

```
for_each(beg, end, unaryOp)
```
Applies the callable object (§ 10.3.2, p. 388) `unaryOp` to each element in its input range. The return value from `unaryOp` (if any) is ignored. If the iterators allow writing to elements through the dereference operator, then `unaryOp` may modify the elements.

```
mismatch(beg1, end1, beg2)
mismatch(beg1, end1, beg2, binaryPred)
```
Compares the elements in two sequences. Returns a `pair` (§ 11.2.3, p. 426) of iterators denoting the first elements in each sequence that do not match. If all the elements match, then the `pair` returned is `end1`, and an iterator into `beg2` offset by the size of the first sequence.

```
equal(beg1, end1, beg2)
equal(beg1, end1, beg2, binaryPred)
```
Determines whether two sequences are equal. Returns `true` if each element in the input range equals the corresponding element in the sequence that begins at `beg2`.

A.2.3 Binary Search Algorithms

These algorithms require *forward iterators* but are optimized so that they execute much more quickly if they are called with *random-access iterators*. Technically speaking, regardless of the iterator type, these algorithms execute a logarithmic number of comparisons. However, when used with forward iterators, they must make a linear number of iterator operations to move among the elements in the sequence.

These algorithms require that the elements in the input sequence are already in order. These algorithms behave similarly to the associative container members of the same name (§ 11.3.5, p. 438). The equal_range, lower_bound, and upper_bound algorithms return iterators that refer to positions in the sequence at which the given element can be inserted while still preserving the sequence's ordering. If the element is larger than any other in the sequence, then the iterator that is returned might be the off-the-end iterator.

Each algorithm provides two versions: The first uses the element type's less-than operator (<) to test elements; the second uses the given comparison operation. In the following algorithms, "x is less than y" means x < y or that comp(x, y) succeeds.

```
lower_bound(beg, end, val)
lower_bound(beg, end, val, comp)
```
Returns an iterator denoting the first element such that val is not less than that element, or end if no such element exists.

```
upper_bound(beg, end, val)
upper_bound(beg, end, val, comp)
```
Returns an iterator denoting the first element such that is val is less than that element, or end if no such element exists.

```
equal_range(beg, end, val)
equal_range(beg, end, val, comp)
```
Returns a pair (§ 11.2.3, p. 426) in which the first member is the iterator that would be returned by lower_bound, and second is the iterator upper_bound would return.

```
binary_search(beg, end, val)
binary_search(beg, end, val, comp)
```
Returns a bool indicating whether the sequence contains an element that is equal to val. Two values x and y are considered equal if x is not less than y and y is not less than x.

A.2.4 Algorithms That Write Container Elements

Many algorithms write new values to the elements in the given sequence. These algorithms can be distinguished from one another both by the kinds of iterators they use to denote their input sequence and by whether they write elements in the input range or write to a given destination.

Algorithms That Write but Do Not Read Elements

These algorithms require an *output iterator* that denotes a destination. The _n versions take a second argument that specifies a count and write the given number of elements to the destination.

```
fill(beg, end, val)
fill_n(dest, cnt, val)
generate(beg, end, Gen)
generate_n(dest, cnt, Gen)
```
Assigns a new value to each element in the input sequence. `fill` assigns the value `val`; `generate` executes the generator object `Gen()`. A generator is a callable object (§ 10.3.2, p. 388) that is expected to produce a different return value each time it is called. `fill` and `generate` return `void`. The _n versions return an iterator that refers to the position immediately following the last element written to the output sequence.

Write Algorithms with Input Iterators

Each of these algorithms reads an input sequence and writes to an output sequence. They require `dest` to be an *output iterator*, and the iterators denoting the input range must be *input iterators*.

```
copy(beg, end, dest)
copy_if(beg, end, dest, unaryPred)
copy_n(beg, n, dest)
```
Copies from the input range to the sequence denoted by `dest`. `copy` copies all elements, `copy_if` copies those for which `unaryPred` succeeds, and `copy_n` copies the first n elements. The input sequence must have at least n elements.

```
move(beg, end, dest)
```
Calls `std::move` (§ 13.6.1, p. 533) on each element in the input sequence to move that element to the sequence beginning at iterator `dest`.

```
transform(beg, end, dest, unaryOp)
transform(beg, end, beg2, dest, binaryOp)
```
Calls the given operation and writes the result of that operation to `dest`. The first version applies a unary operation to each element in the input range. The second applies a binary operation to elements from the two input sequences.

```
replace_copy(beg, end, dest, old_val, new_val)
replace_copy_if(beg, end, dest, unaryPred, new_val)
```
Copies each element to `dest`, replacing the specified elements with `new_val`. The first version replaces those elements that are `==` `old_val`. The second version replaces those elements for which `unaryPred` succeeds.

```
merge(beg1, end1, beg2, end2, dest)
merge(beg1, end1, beg2, end2, dest, comp)
```
Both input sequences must be sorted. Writes a merged sequence to `dest`. The first version compares elements using the < operator; the second version uses the given comparison operation.

Write Algorithms with Forward Iterators

These algorithms require *forward iterators* because they write to elements in their
input sequence. The iterators must give write access to the elements.

```
iter_swap(iter1, iter2)
swap_ranges(beg1, end1, beg2)
```
Swaps the element denoted by `iter1` with the one denoted by `iter2`; or swaps
all of the elements in the input range with those in the second sequence beginning
at `beg2`. The ranges must not overlap. `iter_swap` returns `void`; `swap_ranges`
returns `beg2` incremented to denote the element just after the last one swapped.

```
replace(beg, end, old_val, new_val)
replace_if(beg, end, unaryPred, new_val)
```
Replaces each matching element with `new_val`. The first version uses `==` to compare elements with `old_val`; the second version replaces those elements for which
`unaryPred` succeeds.

Write Algorithms with Bidirectional Iterators

These algorithms require the ability to go backward in the sequence, so they require *bidirectional iterators*.

```
copy_backward(beg, end, dest)
move_backward(beg, end, dest)
```
Copies or moves elements from the input range to the given destination. Unlike
other algorithms, `dest` is the off-the-end iterator for the output sequence (i.e., the
destination sequence will end immediately *before* `dest`). The last element in the
input range is copied or moved to the last element in the destination, then the
second-to-last element is copied/moved, and so on. Elements in the destination
have the same order as those in the input range. If the range is empty, the return
value is `dest`; otherwise, the return denotes the element that was copied or moved
from `*beg`.

```
inplace_merge(beg, mid, end)
inplace_merge(beg, mid, end, comp)
```
Merges two sorted subsequences from the same sequence into a single, ordered
sequence. The subsequences from `beg` to `mid` and from `mid` to `end` are merged
and written back into the original sequence. The first version uses `<` to compare
elements; the second version uses a given comparison operation. Returns `void`.

A.2.5 Partitioning and Sorting Algorithms

The sorting and partitioning algorithms provide various strategies for ordering the
elements of a sequence.

Each of the sorting and partitioning algorithms provides stable and unstable
versions (§ 10.3.1, p. 387). A stable algorithm maintains the relative order of equal
elements. The stable algorithms do more work and so may run more slowly and
use more memory than the unstable counterparts.

Partitioning Algorithms

A partition divides elements in the input range into two groups. The first group consists of those elements that satisfy the specified predicate; the second, those that do not. For example, we can partition elements in a sequence based on whether the elements are odd, or on whether a word begins with a capital letter, and so forth. These algorithms require *bidirectional iterators*.

`is_partitioned(beg, end, unaryPred)`
Returns true if all the elements for which unaryPred succeeds precede those for which unaryPred is false. Also returns true if the sequence is empty.

`partition_copy(beg, end, dest1, dest2, unaryPred)`
Copies elements for which unaryPred succeeds to dest1 and copies those for which unaryPred fails to dest2. Returns a pair (§ 11.2.3, p. 426) of iterators. The first member denotes the end of the elements copied to dest1, and the second denotes the end of the elements copied to dest2. The input sequence may not overlap either of the destination sequences.

`partition_point(beg, end, unaryPred)`
The input sequence must be partitioned by unaryPred. Returns an iterator one past the subrange for which unaryPred succeeds. If the returned iterator is not end, then unaryPred must be false for the returned iterator and for all elements that follow that point.

`stable_partition(beg, end, unaryPred)`
`partition(beg, end, unaryPred)`
Uses unaryPred to partition the input sequence. Elements for which unaryPred succeeds are put at the beginning of the sequence; those for which the predicate is false are at the end. Returns an iterator just past the last element for which unaryPred succeeds, or beg if there are no such elements.

Sorting Algorithms

These algorithms require *random-access iterators*. Each of the sorting algorithms provides two overloaded versions. One version uses the element's operator < to compare elements; the other takes an extra parameter that specifies an ordering relation (§ 11.2.2, p. 425). partial_sort_copy returns an iterator into the destination; the other sorting algorithms return void.

The partial_sort and nth_element algorithms do only part of the job of sorting the sequence. They are often used to solve problems that might otherwise be handled by sorting the entire sequence. Because these algorithms do less work, they typically are faster than sorting the entire input range.

`sort(beg, end)`
`stable_sort(beg, end)`
`sort(beg, end, comp)`
`stable_sort(beg, end, comp)`
Sorts the entire range.

```
is_sorted(beg, end)
is_sorted(beg, end, comp)
is_sorted_until(beg, end)
is_sorted_until(beg, end, comp)
```
`is_sorted` returns a `bool` indicating whether the entire input sequence is sorted. `is_sorted_until` finds the longest initial sorted subsequence in the input and returns an iterator just after the last element of that subsequence.

```
partial_sort(beg, mid, end)
partial_sort(beg, mid, end, comp)
```
Sorts a number of elements equal to `mid` − `beg`. That is, if `mid` − `beg` is equal to 42, then this function puts the lowest-valued elements in sorted order in the first 42 positions in the sequence. After `partial_sort` completes, the elements in the range from `beg` up to but not including `mid` are sorted. No element in the sorted range is larger than any element in the range after `mid`. The order among the unsorted elements is unspecified.

```
partial_sort_copy(beg, end, destBeg, destEnd)
partial_sort_copy(beg, end, destBeg, destEnd, comp)
```
Sorts elements from the input range and puts as much of the sorted sequence as fits into the sequence denoted by the iterators `destBeg` and `destEnd`. If the destination range is the same size or has more elements than the input range, then the entire input range is sorted and stored starting at `destBeg`. If the destination size is smaller, then only as many sorted elements as will fit are copied.

   Returns an iterator into the destination that refers just past the last element that was sorted. The returned iterator will be `destEnd` if that destination sequence is smaller than or equal in size to the input range.

```
nth_element(beg, nth, end)
nth_element(beg, nth, end, comp)
```
The argument `nth` must be an iterator positioned on an element in the input sequence. After `nth_element`, the element denoted by that iterator has the value that would be there if the entire sequence were sorted. The elements in the sequence are partitioned around `nth`: Those before `nth` are all smaller than or equal to the value denoted by `nth`, and the ones after it are greater than or equal to it.

A.2.6 General Reordering Operations

Several algorithms reorder the elements of the input sequence. The first two, `remove` and `unique`, reorder the sequence so that the elements in the first part of the sequence meet some criteria. They return an iterator marking the end of this subsequence. Others, such as `reverse`, `rotate`, and `random_shuffle`, rearrange the entire sequence.

   The base versions of these algorithms operate "in place"; they rearrange the elements in the input sequence itself. Three of the reordering algorithms offer "copying" versions. These `_copy` versions perform the same reordering but write the reordered elements to a specified destination sequence rather than changing the input sequence. These algorithms require *output iterator* for the destination.

Reordering Algorithms Using Forward Iterators

These algorithms reorder the input sequence. They require that the iterators be at least *forward iterators*.

```
remove(beg, end, val)
remove_if(beg, end, unaryPred)
remove_copy(beg, end, dest, val)
remove_copy_if(beg, end, dest, unaryPred)
```
"Removes" elements from the sequence by overwriting them with elements that are to be kept. The removed elements are those that are == val or for which unaryPred succeeds. Returns an iterator just past the last element that was not removed.

```
unique(beg, end)
unique(beg, end, binaryPred)
unique_copy(beg, end, dest)
unique_copy_if(beg, end, dest, binaryPred)
```
Reorders the sequence so that adjacent duplicate elements are "removed" by overwriting them. Returns an iterator just past the last unique element. The first version uses == to determine whether two elements are the same; the second version uses the predicate to test adjacent elements.

```
rotate(beg, mid, end)
rotate_copy(beg, mid, end, dest)
```
Rotates the elements around the element denoted by mid. The element at mid becomes the first element; elements from mid + 1 up to but not including end come next, followed by the range from beg up to but not including mid. Returns an iterator denoting the element that was originally at beg.

Reordering Algorithms Using Bidirectional Iterators

Because these algorithms process the input sequence backward, they require *bidirectional iterators*.

```
reverse(beg, end)
reverse_copy(beg, end, dest)
```
Reverses the elements in the sequence. reverse returns void; reverse_copy returns an iterator just past the element copied to the destination.

Reordering Algorithms Using Random-Access Iterators

Because these algorithms rearrange the elements in a random order, they require *random-access iterators*.

```
random_shuffle(beg, end)
random_shuffle(beg, end, rand)
shuffle(beg, end, Uniform_rand)
```
Shuffles the elements in the input sequence. The second version takes a callable that must take a positive integer value and produce a uniformly distributed random integer in the exclusive range from 0 to the given value. The third argument

to `shuffle` must meet the requirements of a uniform random number generator (§ 17.4, p. 745). All three versions return `void`.

A.2.7   Permutation Algorithms

The permutation algorithms generate lexicographical permutations of a sequence. These algorithms reorder a permutation to produce the (lexicographically) next or previous permutation of the given sequence. They return a `bool` that indicates whether there was a next or previous permutation.

To understand what is meant by next or previous permutaion, consider the following sequence of three characters: `abc`. There are six possible permutations on this sequence: `abc`, `acb`, `bac`, `bca`, `cab`, and `cba`. These permutations are listed in lexicographical order based on the less-than operator. That is, `abc` is the first permutation because its first element is less than or equal to the first element in every other permutation, and its second element is smaller than any permutation sharing the same first element. Similarly, `acb` is the next permutation because it begins with `a`, which is smaller than the first element in any remaining permutation. Permutations that begin with `b` come before those that begin with `c`.

For any given permutation, we can say which permutation comes before it and which after it, assuming a particular ordering between individual elements. Given the permutation `bca`, we can say that its previous permutation is `bac` and that its next permutation is `cab`. There is no previous permutation of the sequence `abc`, nor is there a next permutation of `cba`.

These algorithms assume that the elements in the sequence are unique. That is, the algorithms assume that no two elements in the sequence have the same value.

To produce the permutation, the sequence must be processed both forward and backward, thus requiring *bidirectional iterators*.

`is_permutation(beg1, end1, beg2)`
`is_permutation(beg1, end1, beg2, binaryPred)`
Returns `true` if there is a permutation of the second sequence with the same number of elements as are in the first sequence and for which the elements in the permutation and in the input sequence are equal. The first version compares elements using `==`; the second uses the given `binaryPred`.

`next_permutation(beg, end)`
`next_permutation(beg, end, comp)`
If the sequence is already in its last permutation, then `next_permutation` reorders the sequence to be the lowest permutation and returns `false`. Otherwise, it transforms the input sequence into the lexicographically next ordered sequence, and returns `true`. The first version uses the element's `<` operator to compare elements; the second version uses the given comparison operation.

`prev_permutation(beg, end)`
`prev_permutation(beg, end, comp)`
Like `next_permutation`, but transforms the sequence to form the previous permutation. If this is the smallest permutation, then it reorders the sequence to be the largest permutation and returns `false`.

A.2.8 Set Algorithms for Sorted Sequences

The set algorithms implement general set operations on a sequence that is in sorted order. These algorithms are distinct from the library `set` container and should not be confused with operations on `set`s. Instead, these algorithms provide setlike behavior on an ordinary sequential container (`vector`, `list`, etc.) or other sequence, such as an input stream.

These algorithms process elements sequentially, requiring *input iterators*. With the exception of `includes`, they also take an *output iterator* denoting a destination. These algorithms return their `dest` iterator incremented to denote the element just after the last one that was written to `dest`.

Each algorithm is overloaded. The first version uses the `<` operator for the element type. The second uses a given comparison operation.

```
includes(beg, end, beg2, end2)
includes(beg, end, beg2, end2, comp)
```
Returns `true` if every element in the second sequence is contained in the input sequence. Returns `false` otherwise.

```
set_union(beg, end, beg2, end2, dest)
set_union(beg, end, beg2, end2, dest, comp)
```
Creates a sorted sequence of the elements that are in either sequence. Elements that are in both sequences occur in the output sequence only once. Stores the sequence in `dest`.

```
set_intersection(beg, end, beg2, end2, dest)
set_intersection(beg, end, beg2, end2, dest, comp)
```
Creates a sorted sequence of elements present in both sequences. Stores the sequence in `dest`.

```
set_difference(beg, end, beg2, end2, dest)
set_difference(beg, end, beg2, end2, dest, comp)
```
Creates a sorted sequence of elements present in the first sequence but not in the second.

```
set_symmetric_difference(beg, end, beg2, end2, dest)
set_symmetric_difference(beg, end, beg2, end2, dest, comp)
```
Creates a sorted sequence of elements present in either sequence but not in both.

A.2.9 Minimum and Maximum Values

These algorithms use either the `<` operator for the element type or the given comparison operation. The algorithms in the first group operate on values rather than sequences. The algorithms in the second set take a sequence that is denoted by *input iterators*.

```
min(val1, val2)
min(val1, val2, comp)
min(init_list)
min(init_list, comp)
```

```
max(val1, val2)
max(val1, val2, comp)
max(init_list)
max(init_list, comp)
```
Returns the minimum/maximum of `val1` and `val2` or the minimum/maximum value in the `initializer_list`. The arguments must have exactly the same type as each other. Arguments and the return type are both references to `const`, meaning that objects are not copied.

```
minmax(val1, val2)
minmax(val1, val2, comp)
minmax(init_list)
minmax(init_list, comp)
```
Returns a `pair` (§ 11.2.3, p. 426) where the `first` member is the smaller of the supplied values and the `second` is the larger. The `initializer_list` version returns a `pair` in which the `first` member is the smallest value in the list and the `second` member is the largest.

```
min_element(beg, end)
min_element(beg, end, comp)
max_element(beg, end)
max_element(beg, end, comp)
minmax_element(beg, end)
minmax_element(beg, end, comp)
```
`min_element` and `max_element` return iterators referring to the smallest and largest element in the input sequence, respectively. `minmax_element` returns a `pair` whose `first` member is the smallest element and whose `second` member is the largest.

Lexicographical Comparison

This algorithm compares two sequences based on the first unequal pair of elements. Uses either the `<` operator for the element type or the given comparison operation. Both sequences are denoted by *input iterators*.

```
lexicographical_compare(beg1, end1, beg2, end2)
lexicographical_compare(beg1, end1, beg2, end2, comp)
```
Returns `true` if the first sequence is lexicographically less than the second. Otherwise, returns `false`. If one sequence is shorter than the other and all its elements match the corresponding elements in the longer sequence, then the shorter sequence is lexicographically smaller. If the sequences are the same size and the corresponding elements match, then neither is lexicographically less than the other.

A.2.10 Numeric Algorithms

The numeric algorithms are defined in the `numeric` header. These algorithms require *input iterators*; if the algorithm writes output, it uses an *output iterator* for the destination.

```
accumulate(beg, end, init)
accumulate(beg, end, init, binaryOp)
```
Returns the sum of all the values in the input range. The summation starts with the initial value specified by `init`. The return type is the same type as the type of `init`. The first version applies the + operator for the element type; the second version applies the specified binary operation.

```
inner_product(beg1, end1, beg2, init)
inner_product(beg1, end1, beg2, init, binOp1, binOp2)
```
Returns the sum of the elements generated as the product of two sequences. The two sequences are processed in tandem, and the elements from each sequence are multiplied. The product of that multiplication is summed. The initial value of the sum is specified by `init`. The type of `init` determines the return type.

The first version uses the element's multiplication (*) and addition (+) operators. The second version applies the specified binary operations, using the first operation in place of addition and the second in place of multiplication.

```
partial_sum(beg, end, dest)
partial_sum(beg, end, dest, binaryOp)
```
Writes a new sequence to `dest` in which the value of each new element represents the sum of all the previous elements up to and including its position within the input range. The first version uses the + operator for the element type; the second version applies the specified binary operation. Returns the `dest` iterator incremented to refer just past the last element written.

```
adjacent_difference(beg, end, dest)
adjacent_difference(beg, end, dest, binaryOp)
```
Writes a new sequence to `dest` in which the value of each new element other than the first represents the difference between the current and previous elements. The first version uses the element type's - operation; the second version applies the specified binary operation.

```
iota(beg, end, val)
```
Assigns `val` to the first element and increments `val`. Assigns the incremented value to the next element, and again increments `val`, and assigns the incremented value to the next element in the sequence. Continues incrementing `val` and assigning its new value to successive elements in the input sequence.

A.3 Random Numbers

The library defines a collection of random number engine classes and adaptors that use differing mathematical approaches to generating pseudorandom numbers. The library also defines a collection of distribution templates that provide numbers according to various probability distributions. Both the engines and the distributions have names that correspond to their mathematical properties.

The specifics of how these classes generate numbers is well beyond the scope of this Primer. In this section, we'll list the engine and distribution types, but the reader will need to consult other resources to learn how to use these types.

A.3.1 Random Number Distributions

With the exception of the `bernouilli_distribution`, which always generates type `bool`, the distribution types are templates. Each of these templates takes a single type parameter that names the result type that the distribution will generate.

The distribution classes differ from other class templates we've used in that the distribution types place restrictions on the types we can specify for the template type. Some distribution templates can be used to generate only floating-point numbers; others can be used to generate only integers.

In the following descriptions, we indicate whether a distribution generates floating-point numbers by specifying the type as *template_name*<`RealT`>. For these templates, we can use `float`, `double`, or `long double` in place of `RealT`. Similarly, `IntT` requires one of the built-in integral types, not including `bool` or any of the `char` types. The types that can be used in place of `IntT` are `short`, `int`, `long`, `long long`, `unsigned short`, `unsigned int`, `unsigned long`, or `unsigned long long`.

The distribution templates define a default template type parameter (§ 17.4.2, p. 750). The default for the integral distributions is `int`; the default for the classes that generate floating-point numbers is `double`.

The constructors for each distribution has parameters that are specific to the kind of distribution. Some of these parameters specify the range of the distribution. These ranges are always *inclusive*, unlike iterator ranges.

Uniform Distributions

```
uniform_int_distribution<IntT> u(m, n);
uniform_real_distribution<RealT> u(x, y);
```
Generates values of the specified type in the given inclusive range. m (or x) is the smallest number that can be returned; n (or y) is the largest. m defaults to 0; n defaults to the maximum value that can be represented in an object of type `IntT`. x defaults to 0.0 and y defaults to 1.0.

Bernoulli Distributions

```
bernoulli_distribution b(p);
```
Yields `true` with given probability p; p defaults to 0.5.

```
binomial_distribution<IntT> b(t, p);
```
Distribution computed for a sample size that is the integral value t, with probability p; t defaults to 1 and p defaults to 0.5.

```
geometric_distribution<IntT> g(p);
```
Per-trial probability of success p; p defaults to 0.5.

```
negative_binomial_distribution<IntT> nb(k, p);
```
Integral value k trials with probability of success p; k defaults to 1 and p to 0.5.

Poisson Distributions

```
poisson_distribution<IntT> p(x);
```
Distribution around `double` mean x.

```
exponential_distribution<RealT> e(lam);
```
Floating-point valued lambda lam; lam defaults to 1.0.

```
gamma_distribution<RealT> g(a, b);
```
With alpha (shape) a and beta (scale) b; both default to 1.0.

```
weibull_distribution<RealT> w(a, b);
```
With shape a and scale b; both default to 1.0.

```
extreme_value_distribution<RealT> e(a, b);
```
a defaults to 0.0 and b defaults to 1.0.

Normal Distributions

```
normal_distribution<RealT> n(m, s);
```
Mean m and standard deviation s; m defaults to 0.0, s to 1.0.

```
lognormal_distribution<RealT> ln(m, s);
```
Mean m and standard deviation s; m defaults to 0.0, s to 1.0.

```
chi_squared_distribution<RealT> c(x);
```
x degrees of freedom; defaults to 1.0.

```
cauchy_distribution<RealT> c(a, b);
```
Location a and scale b default to 0.0 and 1.0, respectively.

```
fisher_f_distribution<RealT> f(m, n);
```
m and n degrees of freedom; both default to 1.

```
student_t_distribution<RealT> s(n);
```
n degrees of freedom; n defaults to 1.

Sampling Distributions

```
discrete_distribution<IntT> d(i, j);
discrete_distribution<IntT> d{il};
```
i and j are input iterators to a sequence of weights; il is a braced list of weights. The weights must be convertible to double.

```
piecewise_constant_distribution<RealT> pc(b, e, w);
```
b, e, and w are input iterators.

```
piecewise_linear_distribution<RealT> pl(b, e, w);
```
b, e, and w are input iterators.

A.3.2   Random Number Engines

The library defines three classes that implement different algorithms for generating random numbers. The library also defines three adaptors that modify the sequences produced by a given engine. The engine and engine adaptor classes are templates. Unlike the parameters to the distributions, the parameters to these engines are complex and require detailed understanding of the math used by the particular engine. We list the engines here so that the reader is aware of their existence, but describing how to generate these types is beyond the scope of this Primer.

The library also defines several types that are built from the engines or adaptors. The `default_random_engine` type is a type alias for one of the engine types parameterized by variables designed to yield good performance for casual use. The library also defines several classes that are fully specialized versions of an engine or adaptor. The engines and the specializations defined by the library are:

`default_random_engine`
Type alias for one of the other engines intended to be used for most purposes.

`linear_congruential_engine`
`minstd_rand0` Has a multiplier of 16807, a modulus of 2147483647, and an increment of 0.
`minstd_rand` Has a multiplier of 48271, a modulus of 2147483647, and an increment of 0.

`mersenne_twister_engine`
`mt19937` 32-bit unsigned Mersenne twister generator.
`mt19937_64` 64-bit unsigned Mersenne twister generator.

`subtract_with_carry_engine`
`ranlux24_base` 32-bit unsigned subtract with carry generator.
`ranlux48_base` 64-bit unsigned subtract with carry generator.

`discard_block_engine`
Engine adaptor that discards results from its underlying engine. Parameterized by the underlying engine to use the block size, and size of the used blocks.
`ranlux24` Uses the `ranlux24_base` engine with a block size of 223 and a used block size of 23.
`ranlux48` Uses the `ranlux48_base` engine with a block size of 389 and a used block size of 11.

`independent_bits_engine`
Engine adaptor that generates numbers with a specified number of bits. Parameterized by the underlying engine to use, the number of bits to generate in its results, and an unsigned integral type to use to hold the generated bits. The number of bits specified must be less than the number of digits that the specified unsigned type can hold.

`shuffle_order_engine`
Engine adaptor that returns the same numbers as its underlying engine but delivers them in a different sequence. Parameterized by the underlying engine to use and the number of elements to shuffle.
`knuth_b` Uses the `minstd_rand0` engine with a table size of 256.

Index

Bold face numbers refer to the page on which the term was first defined.
Numbers in *italic* refer to the "Defined Terms" section in which the term is defined.

What's new in C++11

```
= default, 265, 506
= delete, 507
allocator, construct forwards to any
        constructor, 482
array container, 327
auto, 68
```
 for type abbreviation, 88, 129
 not with dynamic array, 478
 with dynamic object, 459
`begin` function, 118
`bind` function, 397
`bitset` enhancements, 726
`constexpr`
 constructor, 299
 function, 239
 variable, 66
container
 `cbegin` and `cend`, 109, 334
 `emplace` members, 345
 `insert` return type, 344
 nonmember `swap`, 339
 of container, 97, 329
 `shrink_to_fit`, 357
`decltype`, 70
 function return type, 250
delegating constructor, 291
deleted copy-control, 624
division rounding, 141
`end` function, 118
enumeration
 controlling representation, 834
 forward declaration, 834
 scoped, 832
`explicit` conversion operator, 582
explicit instantiation, 675
`final` class, 600

format control for floating-point, 757
`forward` function, 694
`forward_list` container, 327
`function` interface to callable objects, 577
in-class initializer, 73, 274
inherited constructor, 628, 804
`initializer_list`, 220
inline namespace, 790
lambda expression, 388
list initialization
 = (assignment), 145
 container, 336, 423
 dynamic array, 478
 dynamic object, 459
 `pair`, 431
 return value, 226, 427
 variable, 43
 `vector`, 98
`long long`, 33
`mem_fn` function, 843
`move` function, 533
move avoids copies, 529
move constructor, 534
move iterator, 543
move-enabled `this` pointer, 546
`noexcept`
 exception specification, 535, 779
 operator, 780
`nullptr`, 54
random-number library, 745
`range for` statement, 91, 187
 not with dynamic array, 477
regular expression-library, 728
rvalue reference, 532
 cast from lvalue, 691
 reference collapsing, 688
`sizeof` data member, 157
`sizeof`... operator, 700

Symbols

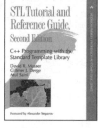

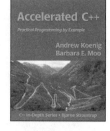

informIT.com
THE TRUSTED TECHNOLOGY LEARNING SOURCE

PEARSON

InformIT is a brand of Pearson and the online presence for the world's leading technology publishers. It's your source for reliable and qualified content and knowledge, providing access to the top brands, authors, and contributors from the tech community.

Addison-Wesley · Cisco Press · EXAM/**CRAM** · **IBM** Press. · que · PRENTICE HALL · S**A**MS · Safari Books Online

LearnIT at InformIT

Looking for a book, eBook, or training video on a new technology? Seeking timely and relevant information and tutorials? Looking for expert opinions, advice, and tips? **InformIT has the solution.**

- Learn about new releases and special promotions by subscribing to a wide variety of newsletters. Visit **informit.com/newsletters**.

- Access FREE podcasts from experts at **informit.com/podcasts**.

- Read the latest author articles and sample chapters at **informit.com/articles**.

- Access thousands of books and videos in the Safari Books Online digital library at **safari.informit.com**.

- Get tips from expert blogs at **informit.com/blogs**.

Visit **informit.com/learn** to discover all the ways you can access the hottest technology content.

Are You Part of the **IT** Crowd?

Connect with Pearson authors and editors via RSS feeds, Facebook, Twitter, YouTube, and more! Visit **informit.com/socialconnect**.

Your purchase of **C++ Primer, Fifth Edition** includes access to a free online edition for 45 days through the **Safari Books Online** subscription service. Nearly every Addison-Wesley Professional book is available online through **Safari Books Online**, along with thousands of books and videos from publishers such as Cisco Press, Exam Cram, IBM Press, O'Reilly Media, Prentice Hall, Que, Sams, and VMware Press.

Safari Books Online is a digital library providing searchable, on-demand access to thousands of technology, digital media, and professional development books and videos from leading publishers. With one monthly or yearly subscription price, you get unlimited access to learning tools and information on topics including mobile app and software development, tips and tricks on using your favorite gadgets, networking, project management, graphic design, and much more.